T0371762

"If there is any doubt that the field of thinking and reasoning is central to current psychological science, this Handbook should dispel those doubts. I can't imagine a young scholar in cognitive science who wouldn't find something of interest in this set of up-to-date empirical and theoretical chapters."

—**Keith E. Stanovich**, *University of Toronto, author of The Rationality Quotient*

"This book offers authoritative overviews of every major topic in reasoning research, written by leading scholars from around the world. Its 35 chapters capture the field's history as well as its exciting cutting-edge developments, making this Handbook a valuable resource for years to come."

—**Norbert Schwarz**, *University of Southern California*

"The Routledge International Handbook of Thinking and Reasoning brings together an impressive collection of highly esteemed experts and represents a comprehensive review of the psychology of thought. While it may appeal most to academics working in the field, it also represents a useful resource for anyone interested in the characteristics of the human mind and the underlying cognitive processes that constitute our reasoning."

—**Gordon Pennycook**, *Banting Postdoctoral Fellow, Yale University*

THE ROUTLEDGE INTERNATIONAL HANDBOOK OF THINKING AND REASONING

The Routledge International Handbook of Thinking and Reasoning is an authoritative reference work providing a well-balanced overview of current scholarship spanning the full breadth of the rapidly developing and expanding field of thinking and reasoning. It contains 35 chapters by leading international researchers, covering foundational issues as well as state-of-the-art developments, both in relation to empirical evidence and theoretical analyses.

Topics covered range across all sub-areas of thinking and reasoning, including deduction, induction, abduction, judgment, decision making, argumentation, problem solving, expertise, creativity and rationality. The contributors engage with cutting-edge debates and pressing conceptual issues such as the status of dual-process theories of thinking, the role of unconscious, intuitive, emotional and metacognitive processes in thinking and the importance of probabilistic conceptualisations of thinking and reasoning. In addition, authors examine the importance of neuroscientific findings in informing theoretical developments, as well as the situated nature of thinking and reasoning across a range of real-world contexts such as mathematics, medicine and science.

The Handbook provides a clear sense of the way in which contemporary ideas are challenging traditional viewpoints in what is now referred to as the "new paradigm psychology of reasoning". This paradigm-shifting research is paving the way toward a far richer and more encompassing understanding of the nature of thinking and reasoning, where important new questions drive a forward-looking research agenda. It is essential reading for both established researchers in the field of thinking and reasoning as well as advanced students wishing to learn more about both the historical foundations and the very latest developments in this rapidly growing area.

Linden J. Ball is Professor of Cognitive Psychology and Dean of Psychology at the University of Central Lancashire. He is Editor-in-Chief of *Journal of Cognitive Psychology*, Associate Editor of *Thinking & Reasoning* and Editor of Routledge's *Current Issues in Thinking & Reasoning* book series.

Valerie A. Thompson is Professor of Cognitive Psychology at the University of Saskatchewan. She is Past President of the Canadian Society of Brain, Behaviour, and Cognitive Science, and is currently Editor-in-Chief of *Thinking & Reasoning*.

THE ROUTLEDGE INTERNATIONAL HANDBOOK SERIES

THE ROUTLEDGE INTERNATIONAL HANDBOOK OF CONSUMER PSYCHOLOGY
Edited by Cathrine V. Jansson-Boyd, Magdalena J. Zawisza

THE ROUTLEDGE INTERNATIONAL HANDBOOK OF SANDPLAY THERAPY
Edited by Barbara A. Turner

THE ROUTLEDGE INTERNATIONAL HANDBOOK OF SEXUAL ADDICTION
Edited by Thaddeus Birchard and Joanna Benfield

THE ROUTLEDGE INTERNATIONAL HANDBOOK OF FORENSIC PSYCHOLOGY IN SECURE SETTINGS
Edited by Jane L. Ireland, Carol A. Ireland, Martin Fisher, Neil Gredecki

THE ROUTLEDGE INTERNATIONAL HANDBOOK OF CRITICAL POSITIVE PSYCHOLOGY
Edited by Nicholas J. L. Brown, Tim Lomas, Francisco Jose Eiroa-Orosa

THE ROUTLEDGE INTERNATIONAL HANDBOOK OF SELF-CONTROL IN HEALTH AND WELL-BEING
Edited by Denise de Ridder, Marieke Adriaanse, Kentaro Fujita

THE ROUTLEDGE INTERNATIONAL HANDBOOK OF PSYCHOSOCIAL EPIDEMIOLOGY
Edited by Mika Kivimaki, David G. Batty, Ichiro Kawachi, Andrew Steptoe

THE ROUTLEDGE INTERNATIONAL HANDBOOK OF HUMAN AGGRESSION: CURRENT ISSUES AND PERSPECTIVES
Edited by Jane L. Ireland, Philip Birch, Carol A. Ireland

THE ROUTLEDGE INTERNATIONAL HANDBOOK OF JUNGIAN FILM STUDIES
Edited by Luke Hockley

THE ROUTLEDGE INTERNATIONAL HANDBOOK OF THINKING AND REASONING

Edited by Linden J. Ball and Valerie A. Thompson

ROUTLEDGE
Routledge
Taylor & Francis Group
LONDON AND NEW YORK

First published 2018 by Routledge

2 Park Square, Milton Park, Abingdon, Oxfordshire OX14 4RN
52 Vanderbilt Avenue, New York, NY 10017

Routledge is an imprint of the Taylor & Francis Group, an informa business

First issued in paperback 2019

British Library Cataloguing-in-Publication Data
A catalogue record for this book is available from the British Library

Library of Congress Cataloging-in-Publication Data
A catalog record for this book has been requested

ISBN: 978-1-138-84930-3 (hbk)
ISBN: 978-0-367-22630-5 (pbk)

Typeset in Bembo
by Apex CoVantage, LLC

We would like to dedicate this Handbook to our academic advisors, who mentored and inspired us:

Linden to Jonathan St. B. T. Evans, who helped to set me off down the fascinating path of thinking and reasoning research and who was always an exemplar of what it means to be an exceptional cognitive scientist.

Valerie to the memory of Allan Paivio, who was a model of experimental rigour, theoretical precision, and integrity in and out of the laboratory. I constantly aspire to meet the stellar standard he set.

CONTENTS

CONTRIBUTORS

Rakefet Ackerman
Faculty of Industrial Engineering and Management
Technion – Israel Institute of Technology
Haifa, Israel

Linden J. Ball
School of Psychology
University of Central Lancashire
Preston, UK

Tilmann Betsch
Department of Psychology
University of Erfurt
Erfurt, Germany

Isabelle Blanchette
Département de Psychologie
Université du Québec à Trois-Rivières
Trois-Rivières, Québec, Canada

Jean-François Bonnefon
Center for Research in Management
Université Toulouse 1 Capitole
Toulouse, France

Alexander P. Burgoyne
Department of Psychology
Michigan State University
East Lansing, Michigan, USA

Ruth M. J. Byrne
School of Psychology and Institute of Neuroscience
Trinity College Dublin
University of Dublin
Dublin, Ireland

Guillermo Campitelli
School of Arts and Humanities
Edith Cowan University
Joondalup, Western Australia, Australia

Serge Caparos
Psychology, Literature, Language, and History
Université de Nîmes
Nîmes, France

Nick Chater
Behavioural Science Group
Warwick Business School
University of Warwick
Coventry, UK

Peter J. Collins
Department of Psychological Sciences
Birkbeck, University of London
London, UK

Pat Croskerry
Department of Emergency Medicine
Dalhousie University
Halifax Infirmary
Halifax, Nova Scotia, Canada

Nicole Cruz
Department of Psychological Sciences
Birkbeck, University of London
London, UK

Wim De Neys
Laboratory for the Psychology of Child Development and Education Sorbonne
Paris Descartes University
Paris, France

Shira Elqayam
School of Applied Social Sciences
De Montfort University
Leicester, UK

Jonathan St. B. T. Evans
School of Psychology
University of Plymouth
Plymouth, UK

Aidan Feeney
School of Psychology
Queen's University Belfast
Belfast, UK

Dedre Gentner
Department of Psychology
Northwestern University
Evanston, Illinois, USA

Bart Geurts
Department of Philosophy
Radboud University
Nijmegen, The Netherlands

Kenneth J. Gilhooly
Psychology Department
University of Hertfordshire
Hatfield, UK

Vinod Goel
Department of Psychology
York University
Toronto, Ontario, Canada

Geoffrey P. Goodwin
Department of Psychology
University of Pennsylvania
Philadelphia, Pennsylvania, USA

Michael E. Gorman
Department of Science, Technology and Society
University of Virginia
Charlottesville, Virginia, USA

Sebastian Hafenbrädl
IESE Business School
University of Navarra
Barcelona, Spain [Current Address]
and
School of Management
Yale University
New Haven, Connecticut, USA

and
Faculty of Business and Economics
University of Lausanne
Lausanne, Switzerland

Ulrike Hahn
Department of Psychological Sciences
Birkbeck, University of London
London, UK

David Z. Hambrick
Department of Psychology
Michigan State University
East Lansing, Michigan, USA

Rebecca K. Helm
School of Law
University of Exeter
Exeter, UK [Current Affiliation]
and
Department of Human Development
Cornell University
Ithaca, New York, USA

Denis J. Hilton
Laboratoire Cognition, Langage, Langues, Ergonomie
Université de Toulouse Le Mirail
Toulouse, France

Ulrich Hoffrage
Faculty of Business and Economics
University of Lausanne
Lausanne, Switzerland

Philip N. Johnson-Laird
Psychology Department
Princeton University
Princeton, New Jersey, USA
and
Department of Psychology
New York University
New York, New York, USA

Sangeet S. Khemlani
Navy Center for Applied Research in Artificial Intelligence
Naval Research Laboratory
Washington, District of Columbia, USA

Barbara Koslowski
Department of Human Development
Cornell University
Ithaca, New York, USA

Brooke N. Macnamara
Department of Psychological Sciences
Case Western Reserve University
Cleveland, Ohio, USA

Francisco Maravilla
Department of Psychology
Northwestern University
Evanston, Illinois, USA

Julian N. Marewski
Faculty of Business and Economics
University of Lausanne
Lausanne, Switzerland

Henry Markovits
Département de Psychologie
Université du Québec à Montréal
Montréal, Québec, Canada

Michael J. McCormick
Department of Psychology
Auburn University
Auburn, Alabama, USA

Hugo Mercier
Centre National de la Recherche Scientifique
Institut des Sciences Cognitives Marc Jeannerod—UMR5304
Bron, France

Kevin C. Moore
Department of Mathematics & Science Education
University of Georgia
Athens, Georgia, USA

Ben R. Newell
School of Psychology
University of New South Wales
Sydney, Australia

Mike Oaksford
Department of Psychological Sciences
Birkbeck, University of London
London, UK

David E. Over
Department of Psychology
Durham University
Durham, UK

Tim Rakow
Department of Psychology
Institute of Psychiatry, Psychology and Neuroscience
King's College London
London, UK

Valerie F. Reyna
Human Neuroscience Institute
Cornell University
Ithaca, New York, USA

Pablina Roth
Institut für Sport und Sportwissenschaft
University of Heidelberg
Heidelberg, Germany

Mark A. Runco
American Institute of Behavioral Research and Technology
Leucadia, California, USA
and
University of Georgia
Athens, Georgia, USA

Jan Maarten Schraagen
Netherlands Organisation for Applied Scientific Research TNO
University of Twente
Soesterberg/Enschede, The Netherlands

Christin Schulze
Center for Adaptive Rationality Max Planck Institute for Human Development
Berlin, Germany

Peter Sedlmeier
Institut für Psychologie
Technische Universität Chemnitz
Chemnitz, Germany

William J. Skylark
Department of Psychology
University of Cambridge
Cambridge, UK

Keith Stenning
School of Informatics
University of Edinburgh
Edinburgh, UK

Valerie A. Thompson
Department of Psychology
University of Saskatchewan
Saskatoon, Saskatchewan, Canada

Maggie E. Toplak
LaMarsh Centre for Child and Youth Research
Department of Psychology
York University
Toronto, Ontario, Canada

Sascha Topolinski
Department of Psychology
Social and Economic Cognition
University of Cologne
Cologne, Germany

Bastien Trémolière
Département de Psychologie
Université du Québec à Trois-Rivières
Trois-Rivières, Québec, Canada

Alexandra Varga
Titu Maiorescu University
Bucharest, Romania

Randall Waechter
School of Medicine
School of Veterinary Medicine
Windward Islands Research and Education Foundation
St. George's University
Grenada, West Indies

Keith Weber
Graduate School of Education
Rutgers University
New Brunswick, New Jersey, USA

Robert W. Weisberg
Department of Psychology
Temple University
Philadelphia, Pennsylvania, USA

Hiroshi Yama
School of Literature and Human Sciences
Osaka City University
Osaka, Japan

PREFACE

What is the goal of a handbook? Clearly one goal must be to cover a wide overview of a discipline. It should be thorough and authoritative and provide both researchers and students with a well-balanced synopsis of contemporary scholarship across the full breadth of an area of enquiry. To this end, our Handbook surveys the current state of the art in the rapidly developing and expanding field of thinking and reasoning research, in relation to both empirical evidence and theoretical analyses.

Having said that, we also believe that it is insufficient for a handbook merely to provide an overview of the current state of affairs and the history leading up to it. We also wanted our Handbook to capture the incredible momentum that is apparent in the field of thinking and reasoning research at the moment. As such, we sought to provide the reader with a strong sense of where the field is going by addressing the new questions that researchers are attempting to answer – and with which tools: what do researchers perceive to be profitable avenues for future research? What are the latest conceptual challenges? Thus, our second goal was to cover emerging trends and cutting-edge debates and to position these in relation to established findings and theories so as to give a clear impression of the way in which new ideas are challenging traditional viewpoints and charting new territory.

Within this context, a discerning reader might note that many of our chapter titles are similar to those that appeared in the first *Handbook of Thinking and Reasoning* that was edited by Keith Holyoak and Robert Morrison back in 2005 and published by Cambridge University Press. Indeed, had there been a handbook put together even 20 years ago, chapters on the topics of deduction, induction, problem solving and decision making would certainly have been included, as they are staples in our field. Many of the same themes that permeate the present volume have permeated the field for over 20 years, including debates about the nature of rationality and the standards by which it should be evaluated. Less clear from a surface glance, however, is that the *content* of the current chapters would be novel to readers of an earlier generation, with the new emphasis on probability (versus deductive logic), multimodal and multidisciplinary approaches to theorising and the application of mathematical modelling and neuroimaging techniques. Researchers today also rely extensively on eye-movement tracking, mouse tracking, reaction-time data, confidence measures and data that derive from other process-tracing methods. The use of multiple, converging evidence in understanding reasoning phenomena represents possibly one of the largest single transformations of our field as we move away from established approaches in which the primary (and usually only) measurement of interest has been a single outcome measure: the answer. Thus, instead of having to infer backwards from the answer to the processes that produced the answer, we now have access to a variety of techniques to examine those processes as they unfold over the time-course of thinking and reasoning.

We have also emphasised situated reasoning in our Handbook, with several chapters explicitly dedicated to studying reasoning in context. These chapters include, but are not limited to, approaches emphasising the role of fast-and-frugal heuristics and naturalistic decision-making strategies in everyday reasoning, but also extend to chapters discussing informal inference, reasoning by argumentation, conversational inference, expert reasoning, abductive reasoning, analogical reasoning and cultural and emotional influences on reasoning. As our field has grown more sophisticated in its theoretical and empirical approaches, we are very glad to see researchers expanding their vision to move from the laboratory to the real world.

In addition, we have included a large number of chapters that address emerging issues and paradigms in reasoning research, again with an emphasis on both informal as well as formal reasoning. This emphasis is in keeping with the larger movement of the field away from formalisms (or at least a single formalism) towards capturing reasoning that is nonmonotonic and probabilistic, and that is guided by emotion and is culturally situated. The role of intuition in thinking is another pervasive theme in the current volume. Again, the origins of this work are historical in nature, dating back to the original work on judgment, decision making and problem solving by the likes of Daniel Kahneman, Amos Tversky, Herbert Simon and Janet Metcalfe, but it is clear that intuition now plays a pervasive role in many different applications, ranging from creativity and innovation to medical practice and metacognition. There appears to be a growing recognition that thinking and reasoning, as is the case with most other cognitive activities, requires at least as much attention to the vast cognitive underground of implicit processes as to more explicit ones. Given that both thinking and reasoning are traditionally defined with reference to consciousness, this represents a significant shift in the way that we think about thinking.

Note that, rather than trying to assemble the chapters into themes, we have organised them alphabetically by author. The reason for this is that we were more or less defeated in our attempts at other organisational structures given that many chapters could legitimately be classified in multiple categories. In this respect our final observation on the state of thinking and reasoning research is that the issues common to various areas of inquiry seem nowadays to be far greater than the issues that separate these areas. Consider, for a moment, what differentiates the field of problem solving from the field of reasoning, other than the paradigms being used to investigate them. Both involve a combination of implicit and explicit processes and require the reasoner to have a goal and a plan to carry out that goal; both require the transformation of a representation from one state to another; and both may rely on stored knowledge, insight, logical reasoning, probabilistic reasoning and the like. One runs into similar difficulties when trying to separate the topics of reasoning and decision making, or when trying to carve up the various subtypes of reasoning. The interconnectedness of theories, explanatory constructs and conceptual issues makes it difficult to sort things into silos. In our view, an important step forward for the future of our discipline is to continue to work our way out of the silos towards a more integrated view of the processes that contribute to thinking and reasoning, broadly defined.

We were very fortunate in this endeavour to have had cooperation and contributions from such a wide range of authors. Many are established experts in their fields and others are midcareer researchers with a reputation for excellent work, whilst a few are "rising stars" who are still at an early career stage but who are nevertheless already being recognised for producing outstanding research. It has been a genuine pleasure to interact with such an exceptional group of authors, and the quality of the current Handbook is, of course, entirely due to the high-quality, accessible chapters that they have produced. We are also grateful to our authors for serving as each other's peer reviewers so as to enable further enhancements to the research presented in this volume. We also thank four external reviewers – Jamie Campbell, Niall Galbraith, Ed Stupple and Dries Trippas – who graciously gave up their time to provide additional expert reviews of certain chapters. Finally, we thank Ceri Griffiths, our wonderful editor at Routledge, who was instrumental in initiating this Handbook and who has provided us with considerable support and encouragement throughout the whole project. We are now happy to bring this endeavour to its fruition and very much hope that you will enjoy the experience of reading these chapters as much as we did.

Valerie A. Thompson
University of Saskatchewan
Saskatoon, Canada

Linden J. Ball
University of Central Lancashire
Preston, UK
April 2017

1

META-REASONING

Shedding metacognitive light on reasoning research

Rakefet Ackerman and Valerie A. Thompson

In this chapter, we argue that understanding the processes that underlie reasoning, problem solving, and decision-making[1] can be informed by understanding the metacognitive processes that monitor and control them. Our goal is to show that a metacognitive analysis applies to a wide range of reasoning tasks and theoretical perspectives, including Dual Process Theories, Mental Models Theory (Johnson-Laird & Byrne, 1991), Fast and Frugal Heuristics (e.g., Gigerenzer, Todd, & the ABC Group, 1999), probabilistic models of reasoning (Oaksford & Chater, 2007), and a wide variety of problem-solving paradigms. We hope that the range of examples that we provide will allow the reader to usefully extend these principles even further, to theories of analogy, induction, causal inference, and so on.

Metacognition is often defined as "thinking about thinking", which implies a reflective, introspective set of processes by which we evaluate and alter our approach to the world. In contrast, most theorists conceive of metacognitive processes as those that are responsible for monitoring and controlling our ongoing cognitive processes (Nelson & Narens, 1990). They are thought to be running in the background and monitoring the success of ongoing cognitive processes (such as reading, remembering, reasoning) in much the same way as a thermostat monitors the temperature of the air. Like the thermostat, which can send a signal to the furnace to start or terminate functioning, metacognitive processes are assumed to have an analogous control function over the initiation or cessation of mental effort.

From the point of view of reasoning research, understanding these processes is important because there is compelling evidence from other domains (e.g., memorisation by Metcalfe & Finn, 2011 and reading comprehension by Thiede, Anderson, & Therriault, 2003) that these monitoring processes are the input to control processes, which then allocate attentional and working memory resources. By extension, therefore, we would expect analogous control processes in reasoning, problem-solving, and decision-making tasks. Equally important is the evidence that the processes that monitor performance are often based on aspects of said performance that may be irrelevant to achieving good outcomes. Thus, control processes may misdirect or prematurely terminate processing based on poorly calibrated input cues. We argue that understanding the factors that inform these monitoring processes is necessary to understanding the outcome of any reasoning endeavor and for improving reasoners' allocation of resources.

Metacognition and reasoning theories

Implicit to most reasoning theories is the inclusion of a metacognitive component, namely the assumption that reasoners terminate their work on a problem either because they don't know the answer or they are satisfied with the solution (see Evans, 2006 for a discussion of satisficing). This, of course, then raises the question of when and on what basis reasoners become satisfied with their answer or decide that they don't know the answer, which is the goal of the current chapter. Stanovich (2009) was more explicit than most theorists in his argument regarding the need to separate reasoning per se from monitoring and control processes; the latter, he argued, form part of the "reflective mind", which represents individual dispositions to engage analytic thinking. Our analysis, whilst in the same spirit, aims to offer a detailed theoretical framework of the metacognitive mechanisms that continuously monitor and control ongoing cognitive processes.

An initial framework for understanding monitoring and control processes was developed in the context of dual process theories (Thompson, 2009; Thompson, Prowse Turner, & Pennycook, 2011). This family of theories assumes that reasoning and decision-making are mediated by two qualitatively different sets of processes: autonomous Type 1 processes and working-memory demanding Type 2 processes (Evans, this volume; see Evans & Stanovich, 2013 for a review). The dual process explanation for many of the classic heuristics and biases derives from the fact that the former processes are faster and form a default response based on heuristic cues such as availability, representativeness, belief, and so on; more deliberate, effortful, time consuming, and working memory demanding Type 2 processes may or may not be engaged to find an alternative solution (Kahneman, 2011). A crucial issue for this view is to explain when and why these more effortful processes are or are not engaged.

Thompson (2009) argued that this was essentially a metacognitive question and provided an analysis that was grounded in the rich metacognitive literature (for a similar view, see Fletcher & Carruthers, 2012). According to her framework, Type 1 processes have two outputs: the cognitive output derived from Type 1 processes and the metacognitive output in the form of a Feeling of Rightness (FOR) that accompanies that answer. In this view, the FOR is a monitoring process that mediates the probability of Type 2 engagement: low FORs are a signal that the answer needs further analysis, whereas a strong FOR is a signal that this is not needed (Thompson et al., 2011; Thompson, Evans, & Campbell, 2013; Thompson & Johnson, 2014).

However, there have been challenges to the processing assumptions of dual process theories, which might lead some researchers to think that the metacognitive analysis proposed above has limited scope. One such challenge is to the serial processing assumption implied by the default-interventionist architecture described above (Evans, 2007). For example, De Neys (2014) and others (Sloman, 2002) argue that belief-based and logical processes are engaged simultaneously. When they produce conflicting outputs, analytic processes may or may not be engaged to resolve the conflict (De Neys & Bonnefon, 2013). However, regardless of whether one assumes sequential or parallel processes, one must still be able to explain how the conflict is detected and under what circumstances analytic processes are engaged to resolve it; this is an essentially metacognitive question.

A second challenge concerns the distinction between Type 1 and Type 2 processes (Kruglanski & Gigerenzer, 2011), with many theorists arguing that there is only a single type of process that exists on a continuum of speed and complexity (Osman, 2004). We argue that regardless of whether one assumes that Type 1 and Type 2 processes are qualitatively different, the fact that some answers are produced more quickly than others (Evans & Curtis Holmes, 2005; Finucane, Alhakami, Slovic, & Johnson, 2000; Markovits, Brunet, Thompson, & Brisson, 2013) means that there is potential for a reasoner to change their initial answer via deliberate analysis. It does not matter whether one assumes that the fast and the slow answer are delivered by qualitatively different processes – the fact that the initial answer may be changed invites the question of when and under what circumstances the answer is changed or kept. It also invites an explanation for the length of time the reasoner spends deliberating as well as the variables that determine how satisfied she is with the final answer. Again, these are fundamentally metacognitive questions.

A case in point is the well-known Mental Models theory (Johnson-Laird & Byrne, 2002; Johnson-Laird, Goodwin, & Khemlani, this volume). This is a theory of how people represent information in a problem space, and how those representations afford inferences about that information. A key assumption of the theory is that people often form an incomplete representation of the problem space, which can be, but which is not always, fleshed out. For example, consider the following pair of premises:

Some of the artists are beekeepers.
All of the chemists are artists.

What follows?

According to Mental Model theory, reasoners construct a model that integrates the premise information and then draw a conclusion from it. For example, the following notation describes a mental representation of the premises that support the conclusion that all of the beekeepers are chemists:

chemist	artist	beekeeper
chemist	artist	beekeeper
chemist	artist	

There is, however, another way to represent the premises that undermines that conclusion:

		beekeeper
chemist	artist	beekeeper
chemist	artist	beekeeper
chemist	artist	

Consequently, the conclusions that reasoners draw are determined, at least in part, by whether they are content with their initial answer or whether they search for an alternative. Thus, monitoring and control processes are key for understanding why and when reasoners are content with their initial representations, and the conditions that lead them to expend the necessary effort to supplement it.

Similarly, several theories of reasoning posit that the search for counter-examples to a putative conclusion plays a crucial role in reasoning outcomes (e.g., Cummins, Lubart, Alksnis, & Rist, 1991; Markovits, 1986; Thompson, 2000); again, the goal is to understand when and why reasoners initiate or fail to initiate such a search. Across a wide spectrum of tasks and paradigms, therefore, a complete understanding of the processes that operate therein requires us to

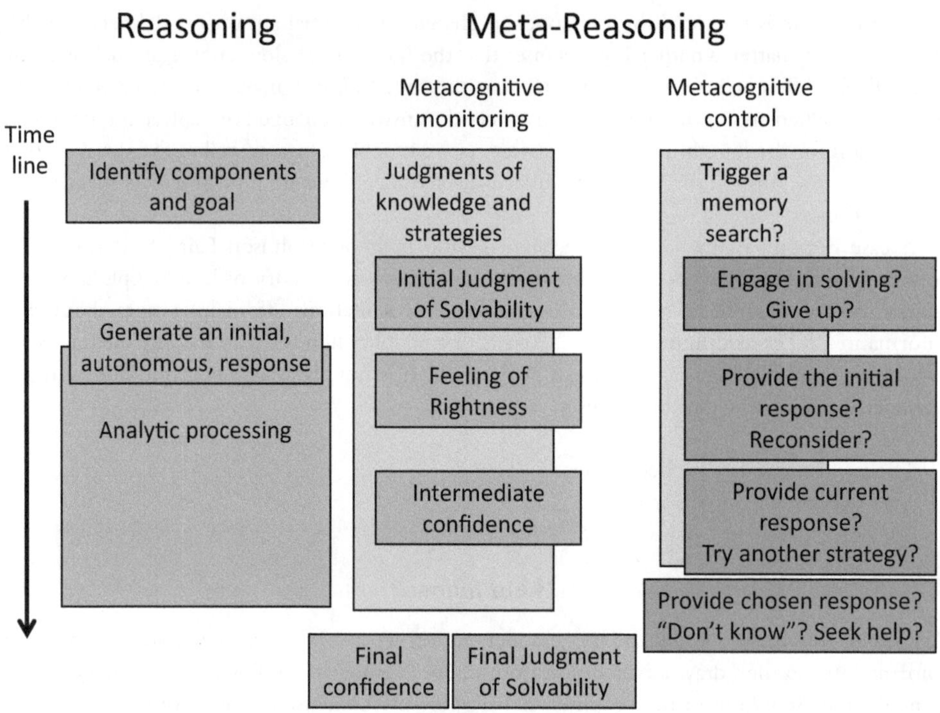

Figure 1.1 Main reasoning and Meta-Reasoning components presented on a schematic time line

understand when an initial response is deemed adequate and when further reasoning is undertaken. In sum, we argue that no theory of reasoning is complete without understanding the metacognitive processes by which reasoning processes are engaged, formulated, and terminated.

The Meta-Reasoning framework

Historically, metacognitive research has been carried out in the context of memory research, and has mostly focussed on the processes that monitor and control learning and retrieval from memory (see Bjork, Dunlosky, & Kornell, 2013, for a review). Typical tasks in Meta-Memory studies involve memorising paired associates (e.g., king–sofa) and answering general knowledge questions based on semantic (e.g., In what year did a man walk on the Moon for the first time?) or episodic memory (e.g., What did the woman in a blue shirt hold in her hand?). Monitoring of memorising is measured by Judgments of Learning (JOLs), which reflect the learners' estimate of the probability they will recall the item in a subsequent test. The typical control decision studied with this task is allocation of study time. Study time is measured from the pair's presentation till the decision to move on to the next pair. In question answering, the relevant monitoring process is confidence – self-assessment of the chance of each provided answer to be correct. Answering time is measured from question presentation till the decision to move on to the next question. Empirical evidence establishes the causal link between the monitoring and control decisions (Metcalfe & Finn, 2008; Thiede et al., 2003). Triangulating response time, the relevant monitoring type, and actual success in the task allows delving into the processes that underlie effort regulation (e.g., Ackerman & Leiser, 2014; Undorf & Erdfelder, 2015; Weber & Brewer, 2006).

Many studies have demonstrated that metacognitive monitoring of all types is sensitive to heuristic cues (Koriat, 1997). For instance, retrieval fluency – the ease with which an answer is retrieved – creates a subjective sense of confidence, even when actual performance may be either unrelated or inversely related to it (e.g., Benjamin, Bjork, Schwartz, 1998; Rhodes & Castel, 2008). In addition to relying on heuristic cues that may be misleading, people also underweight factors that consistently affect performance. We know, for example, that repeated rehearsal enhances learning; however, a more effective strategy is repeated testing. In addition, instructions may guide learners to use effective strategies (e.g., imagining words and the relation between them). In all these cases, the pronounced benefit in performance is underestimated in learners' JOLs and confidence judgments (e.g., Karpicke & Roediger, 2008; Koriat, Sheffer, & Ma'ayan, 2002; Rabinowitz, Ackerman, Craik, & Hinchley, 1982). Similarly, people underestimate the impact of forgetting on their ability to recall information, predicting similar recall performance for a test to be taken immediately after studying and one that would take place after a week of retention (Koriat, Bjork, Sheffer, & Bar, 2004).

Recently, we proposed a Meta-Reasoning framework (Ackerman & Thompson, 2015), which extends the metacognitive conceptualization to the domain of reasoning (see Figure 1.1, 2017). In particular, we outlined several ways in which Meta-Reasoning processes share features with their Meta-Memory counterparts. For example, the monitoring of reasoning processes relies on some of the same heuristic cues shared with memory processes. Specifically, reasoners have been found to rely on answer fluency; that is, the ease with which a solution comes to mind, and the familiarity of the material being reasoned about (e.g., Markovits, 2015; Thompson et al., 2011; Thompson, Prowse Turner et al., 2013). FORs are weakened by variables such as the presence of conflicting answers (Thompson & Johnson, 2014) and by the presence of unfamiliar terms in the problems (Markovits et al., 2015). The JOS, in contrast, was postulated to occur before solving begins and to reflect an estimate of the probability of successfully finding a solution; it is most relevant to situations where an immediate answer to a problem does not come to mind. Much less is known about JOS than about FOR. The initial indication is that they are prone, like other monitoring processes, to relying on heuristic cues (Ackerman & Beller, in press; Topolinski, 2014). We speculate that the initial Judgment of Solvability is related to the decision to attempt solving at the first place, as well as to the length of time that the respondent persists with solving attempts, once the process is initiated.

Terminating analytic thinking

In addition to initiating analytic thinking, a second important control process concerns the decision to terminate thinking about a problem. There are at least two bases for disengaging with a problem: (a) the current state of affairs is considered satisfactory so that no more resources needed to be invested, and (b) there is no reasonable chance of finding the correct solution, so that any further time devoted to the task would be wasted. Here, the reasoner could either guess or give up (e.g., "I don't know" response); alternatively, they may generate a response consistent with their incomplete processing, presumably with low confidence, or default to a heuristic answer (e.g., beliefs) if one was available (Quayle & Ball, 2000). Our discussion below reflects the fact that the former has been studied much more than the latter (see Ackerman, 2014). We consider two monitoring types as underlying termination decisions: FOR and intermediate confidence, which differ in terms of when they occur (see Figure 1.2): FOR is used to monitor an initial answer, while intermediate confidence keeps track of reasoning progress and feeds the decision to terminate it. In a dual process framework, the FOR monitors Type 1 processes and intermediate confidence monitors Type 2 processes. Final confidence reflects the assessment of the chance of the chosen solution to be correct.

FOR. A strong FOR is a sign that further analysis is not needed (Thompson et al., 2011; Thompson, Evans, & Campbell, 2013). Evidence for this assertion is obtained using the two-response paradigm developed by Thompson et al. (2011): reasoners provide an initial intuitive answer to a problem, often under time pressure, followed by an answer without time pressure. The amount of time spent rethinking the answer, as well as the probability that the reasoner changes the initial answer, varies with the strength of the FOR for the initial answer. This relationship has now been observed in a large number of reasoning tasks, ranging from simple to complex.

Moreover, because the FOR is cue-based, the depth of subsequent analysis may not be related to item difficulty. For example, answers that come to mind fluently may do so because they are based on a heuristic process, which produces a strong sense of confidence in incorrect answers (Thompson et al., 2011; Thompson & Johnson, 2014). Similarly, familiarity is a strong cue to confidence, but is not necessarily diagnostic of problem difficulty (Markovits et al., 2015; Shynkaruk & Thompson, 2006). In other cases, FOR may rightly signal problem difficulty, as when the problem cues conflicting answers (De Neys, Cromheeke, & Osman, 2011; Thompson et al., 2011). The point is that analytic processing is engaged in response to a monitoring process that may or may not reliably track problem difficulty.

Whereas the preceding work was undertaken in a Dual Process context, here we demonstrate the utility of extending a metacognitive analysis to two types of "fast and frugal" decision strategies (e.g., Gigerenzer, Todd, & the ABC Research Group). The first one comes from a theory of syllogistic reasoning developed by Chater and Oaksford (1999). Syllogistic reasoning is a type of logical reasoning in which reasoners are asked to generate (or evaluate) conclusions from two quantified premises, as the "beekeeper" problem above illustrates. Chater and Oaksford proposed that rather than using logical rules or mental models to solve these problems, people rely on simple heuristics based on information gain. The primary heuristic used to generate conclusions to problems such as the "beekeeper" problem is called the "min" heuristic, which mandates reasoners to choose the quantifier of the conclusion to be the same as the least informative premise. In the beekeeper example, above, reasoners would look at the two quantifiers (all and some) and choose "some" because is it the least informative. Thus, they would conclude that "some beekeepers are chemists". In their meta-analysis of past data and in a new experiment designed to test this theory, Chater and Oaksford (1999) demonstrated that reasoners did just that.

Whilst Chater and Oaksford (1999) demonstrated the importance of ***min*** for conclusion generation, Thompson and colleagues demonstrated that the ***min*** principle also played a role in how reasoners evaluate their confidence in a conclusion (Thompson et al., 2011). Using the two-response paradigm described above, reasoners were asked to evaluate conclusions that were either consistent or inconsistent with the ***min*** rule. They found that ***min*** conclusions were processed more fluently (i.e., more quickly) than their non-***min*** counterparts and consequently gave rise to stronger FORs. The difference in FORs also had the expected down-stream effect on analytic thinking: problems with ***min*** conclusions were subject to less re-analysis and fewer answer changes than their non-min counterparts. In other words, using a fast-and-frugal strategy such as ***min*** may give rise to confidently held responses that were less likely to be re-considered, regardless of whether they were, in fact, logically valid.

Another potential extension of the FOR to fast and frugal heuristics is in experiments that focus on information search. Many termination decisions are posited to be non-compensatory, in that processing is supposed to be terminated whenever a satisfactory answer is found (see Bröder & Newell, 2008; Hilbig, 2010, for reviews). An example is the "take-the-best" heuristic for choosing amongst a set of alternatives (e.g., deciding which car to buy, which university to attend, which of several brands of consumer goods to buy). This heuristic operates in two steps. The first step operates on the recognition principle, which states that if one of the options is recognised and the others are not, then choose that one and search no further. If more than one alternative is recognised, or if recognition does not discriminate amongst alternatives, the second step is to search for discriminative evidence. The search is assumed to compare each alternative along a single feature, beginning with the feature that has the highest validity, and to continue, one feature at a time until one finds a feature that discriminates amongst alternatives. As an example, let us assume that you are in the grocery store to buy yoghurt. If there is only one brand that you recognise, you would choose that one. If, on the other hand, you recognise more than one, you would compare the brands according to the most important criteria, which, for the sake of argument, might be flavour: you want strawberry. If there are several different strawberry yoghurts, you would then compare them on the next most important cues, possibly calorie count. You proceed in such a fashion until one brand stands out from the others. Importantly, your search is assumed to stop when you reach this point and it is assumed that you would not need to compare the alternatives on another dimension, such as price.

Evidence suggests, however, that people do not stop looking for information, even when they have enough information to make a decision (see Bröder & Newell, 2008; Hilbig, 2010 for reviews). In the example above, you might have recognised only one of the products, but nonetheless investigated price and calorie count for several options (e.g., Newell & Shanks, 2003). This is true even when participants have to pay for each additional bit of information and the information obtained is not helpful to making the decision (Newell, Weston, & Shanks, 2003). Why would people continue to pay for objectively useless information? Bröder and Newell (2008) suggested that people need to feel well informed before making a decision. A metacognitive reframing of this explanation is that people aspire to a certain level of confidence before a decision is reached. That is, they may have reached an initial decision, but the FOR associated with that decision is below their desired level of confidence, so they continue their search. This, of course, raises the question about what signals a strong or weak FOR in the paradigms used to investigate the "take-the-best" heuristic. It also suggests that people are reluctant to commit to a decision until a threshold of confidence has been reached, such that they continue to gather information until that threshold is reached, as is the case for memorising under the Meta-Memory framework (Nelson & Narens, 1990). Interestingly, the findings described above suggest that confidence varies as a function of the *quantity* of information available, parallel to the accessibility heuristic cue in Meta-Memory research (Koriat, 1995). Another cue recently suggested in the Meta-Memory literature that seems to be relevant here is consistency (Koriat, 2012). Thus, a further question is whether the *consistency* of the gathered information also matters, in terms of both predicting the extent of the search for additional information and the confidence in which the final choice is made.

Intermediate and final confidence. At a first glance, confidence when answering a knowledge question should be similar to confidence regarding a reasoning challenge. However, there are signs that this is not always the case. For instance, Rozenblit and Keil (2002) examined the extent to which people acknowledge their understanding of the way mechanical instruments work (e.g., bicycle, sewing machine). This is important, for example for people to decide whether to look for professional help or additional information or use their own reasoning for solving a case of failure (e.g., breakdown of their bicycle gear). They found that people consistently suffer from an illusion of explanatory depth – they think that they understand quite well how these instruments work as long as they think about them at a high level. Not until they are faced with the challenge of writing down a detailed explanation and/or reading an explanation written by an expert, do they realise their ignorance. This illusion is a reasoning bias, which resembles the overconfidence effect observed in many other domains (Dunning, Johnson, Ehrlinger, & Kruger, 2003; Metcalfe, 1998). However, the illusion varies across domains. Rozenblit and Keil (2002) compared the illusion of explanatory depth across various types of knowledge (e.g., capital cities) and procedures (e.g., bake chocolate chip cookies from scratch), and found that the illusion is particularly severe regarding understanding how mechanical instruments and natural phenomena (e.g., how tides occur) work.

To complicate matters somewhat, evidence is beginning to show that the target level of confidence reasoners set is not constant, as is the case for text learning, but decreases as more effort is invested. Ackerman (2014) gave participants compound remote associate problems, in which the goal is to find one word that is associated with three others (e.g., "apple" completes the triad formed by pine, crab, and sauce) (see Bowden & Jung-Beeman, 2003). Intermediate confidence ratings (see Figure 1.2) were collected every 15 seconds. She found that, for any given solution attempt, confidence increased from the initial to the final judgment. However, the confidence level at which participants gave their final solutions decreased over time: when problems were solved quickly, participants tended to respond with solutions that they were highly confident in. When problems took longer to solve, participants appeared to compromise on their confidence criterion, and were willing to provide solutions with less confidence. See Figure 1.2, Panel A.

In one condition, participants were also provided the option to say that they "don't know". This option allowed Ackerman (2014) to examine a less-well-studied termination decision, namely the one in which people essentially "give up". Even when the option to give up was made legitimate, allowing participants to provide only those solutions in which they were highly confident, they nonetheless continued to provide solutions with low confidence after a lengthy solution attempt. See Figure 1.2, Panel B. Taken together, these findings suggest that people's aspirational level of confidence decreases over time, which Ackerman referred to as the Diminishing Criterion Model.

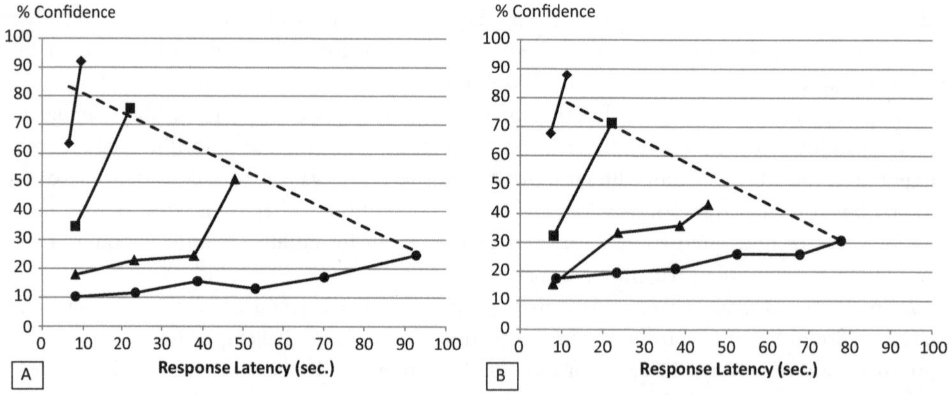

Figure 1.2 Intermediate and final confidence ratings provided along solving of compound remote associate problems. For this figure, the problems each participant solved were divided into four response latency quartiles. Each line represents the means of a quartile across participants. The dashed lines represent the regression lines for final confidence predicted by response latency. Panel A presents data without the option to answer "I don't know" and Panel B presents data with this option. The figures were adapted from Ackerman (2014), Figure 5b and Figure 6b, respectively.

In sum, collecting metacognitive judgments in reasoning tasks allows us to understand variables that determine control decisions to initiate analytic thinking (or not), to continue investing effort (or not), when to terminate effort, and how to convey the outcome (e.g., a concrete answer vs. a "don't know" response, or the detail level of the explanation one can provide).

Knowledge activation

Clearly, successful reasoning is facilitated by the retrieval and application of relevant background knowledge (Butler & Winne, 1995). This knowledge falls into several categories. First, there is knowledge of the specific concepts being reasoned about, like category relatedness in an inference task (e.g., "all canaries are birds"). Second, structured knowledge facilitates retrieval of relevant associations, such as analogies from different domains (e.g., Duncker's radiation problem in which participants must make the analogy for how treating a tumor is like attacking a fortress from several directions; see Holyoak, 1990). Third, one may access knowledge about the procedures needed to solve the problem (e.g., the set of steps required for solving a cubic equation). Finally, adequate proficiency is required for performing each step (e.g., calculating X^2 or sin(X)).

At a first glance, it seems that having a lot of knowledge associated with a reasoning task is an advantage, because additional knowledge allows more solution alternatives and strategies to be considered, which should increase the probability of solving (see Chi, Glaser, & Farr, 1988; Ericsson & J. Smith, 1991; Thibodeau & Boroditsky, 2013). However, in addition to retrieving relevant knowledge, one needs to be able to ignore or suppress *irrelevant* information (Passolunghi & Siegel, 2001). In particular, background knowledge may appear to be relevant, based on surface level cues, but can be quite misleading. Thus, it may not facilitate a solution, but actually hinder it (e.g., Storm & Hickman, 2015; Wiley, 1998). For example, in logical reasoning tasks, reasoners are often instructed to put aside their beliefs and reason only about the logical structure of the argument. Instead, however, reasoners often judge the validity of the conclusion according to whether or not they believe it to be true (see Thompson, Newstead, & Morley, 2011, for a review; Ball & Thompson, this volume).

Clearly, therefore, accurate monitoring of retrieved knowledge is required for effective reasoning (see Figure 1.1). As with the other forms of monitoring that we have discussed, the evidence shows that monitoring our knowledge is not always accurate. On the one hand, a robust finding is that people who are more knowledgeable in a domain are also better at assessing their knowledge than those who are less knowledgeable (Dunning et al., 2003; Kleitman & Moscrop, 2010). On the other hand, a recent study demonstrated that monitoring of reasoning may also be biased by the subjective feeling of having a lot of knowledge related to a task, even if it is not relevant. Ackerman and Beller (in press) asked participants to solve compound remote associates, as described previously, except that half of the problems were unsolvable (i.e., three words without a shared association). Participants quickly provided an initial Judgment of Solvability (2 seconds) about whether or not the triad was solvable. In addition, their procedure included also a final Judgment of Solvability, which was not included in the original Meta-Reasoning framework (Ackerman & Thompson, 2015). This judgment was collected when the respondents gave up the problem ("don't know"). It reflects the assessed chance that the problem is solvable despite the participant's failure to solve it (see Figure 1.1).

Ackerman and Beller (in press) examined accessibility as a heuristic cue for both Judgments of Solvability. Accessibility is defined as the amount, rather than the correctness or relevance, of information that comes to mind while performing a cognitive task. It was found to underlie Feeling of Knowing while answering knowledge questions (Koriat, 1995; Koriat & Levy-Sadot, 2001). Similarly, in the remote associates task, both Judgments of Solvability (initial and final) were led astray so to be higher for the high accessibility triads than for low accessibility ones, even though the accessible knowledge was not useful for solving the problems. Thus, having a lot of related knowledge may lead people to predict a high probability of success in the task, even when this knowledge does not predict actual success rates. These findings may generalise to the "take the best" heuristic discussed above, because it appears in both cases that monitoring processes are biased by the volume of available information.

Others have also observed that reasoning monitoring may be influenced by irrelevant information. Josephs, Silvera, and Giesler (1996) gave their participants either a large (200) or a small (25) number of anagrams as a practice set. Importantly, they emphasised that the size of the practice set was arbitrary and the participants could ask for more practice problems as needed. The participants were free to practice as much as they wanted and to decide when they were ready to take the test. Thus, the participants were encouraged to monitor their skill level in solving anagrams, and take a control decision to stop practicing. When the anagrams were all of a similar level of difficulty, the participants were good at identifying when they were ready to take the test. However, when the problems were of mixed difficulty levels, the participants used the number of practice problems in the given practice package (200 or 25) as a cue that guided their decision when to take the solving test. When the practice set was large (200), the participants continued practicing longer than when it was small (25), despite the package size being random and unrelated to their actual solving skill. In sum, knowing when the information one has available is relevant or misleading is important to achieving good reasoning outcomes. To date, we have barely begun to understand how this monitoring is achieved.

Strategy selection

In addition to the types of online monitoring and control strategy described above, there is a rich educational literature on other aspects of metacognition that fall under the umbrella of Self-Regulated Learning (SRL). Strategy selection for learning and problem solving is a central topic in this literature (e.g., Edwards, Weinstein, Goetz, & Alexander, 2014; Schneider & Artelt, 2010). It has been consistently observed that posing questions like "how", "why", and "in which circumstances" to students encourages reflection, promotes deliberate engagement in strategy choice, and yields improved performance (e.g., Mevarech, Terkieltaub, Vinberger, & Nevet, 2010; see Zimmerman, 2000, for a review).

Less work has been done to understand how reasoners select a strategy. Most research in this domain has focussed on the costs of carrying out each potential strategy, with the ultimate goal to choose the least demanding strategy that might work (e.g., Beilock & deCaro, 2007). However, we know very little about metacognitive monitoring and control processes involved in strategy search and selection (see Figure 1.1). An early exception to this general statement is a study conducted by Reder and Ritter (1992), who demonstrated that monitoring based on misleading information may then mislead strategy selection. They presented participants with arithmetic problems (e.g., 23 + 27), some of which were repeated several times. They then presented problems that shared surface, but not functional features with the previous problems (i.e., 23 × 27) and asked participants to rapidly decide whether they needed to calculate the answer or could remember the answer from their previous encounters. They found that familiarity was a misleading cue for this decision: numbers which appeared familiar from the previous trials misled participants into thinking that they could retrieve the answer without calculation.

Recent evidence suggests that the decision to adopt one strategy or another may be a substantial component of effortful, deliberate thinking. Empirical support for this idea comes from several studies which compared reasoning with and without time pressure (e.g., Bröder & Newell,

2008; Rieskamp & Hoffrage, 2008). For instance, Markovits, Brunet, Thompson, and Brisson (2013) used a conditional inference task, in which people are asked to make inferences about statements of the form "if *p*, then *q*", and assessed whether reasoners evaluated inferences on the basis of the probability that it was true, or by using counter-examples. As an illustration, one might accept the following argument because it has a high probability of being true: "If an animal is a dog, then it has four legs; this animal is a dog, therefore it has four legs" or reject it on the basis that not every dog has four legs (i.e., there are counter-examples to the conclusion). When put under time pressure, reasoners relied on the probabilistic strategy; when given the opportunity to solve the problems in free time, they switched and used the counter-example strategy. In contrast, those who first solved the problems under free time used the counter-example strategy even when put under time pressure. Thus, it is not merely a lack of capacity that drove reasoners to use the probabilistic strategy, but, instead, that time pressure disrupted their ability to choose the preferred strategy.

In our view, choosing the appropriate strategy is essentially a metacognitive process (see also Bröder & Newell, 2008). The metacognitive monitoring involved in strategy selection requires assessing relevant background knowledge and skills and predicting in advance which strategy would be most effective; the metacognitive control process is the choice of the strategy. As is the case for the other types of monitoring we have discussed, it seems reasonable to speculate that the assessment of strategy effectiveness is based on heuristic cues. It follows, therefore, that the quality of strategy selection will depend on the reliability of the cues that inform these monitoring processes, as is the case for the other processes we have discussed.

Cognitive ability

The positive relationship between measures of general cognitive ability and reasoning is clear and well established (Sonnleitner, Keller, Martin, & Brunner, 2013; Stanovich & West, 2000). A central factor underlying this association is working memory capacity (Colom, Rebollo, Palacios, Juan-Espinosa, & Kyllonen, 2004). Working memory determines whether one has the capacity to solve a problem. It also affects people's choice of a solution strategy (Beilock & DeCaro, 2007). In contrast, we know little about the relationship between cognitive ability and the metacognitive processes involved in reasoning.

What we do know is that there is a personal confidence trait which is generally reliable (see Stankov, Kleitman, & Jackson, 2014, for a review). That is, averaged across tasks, a person's confidence judgments show high internal consistency; confidence judgments tend to be consistent across different cognitive tests and they are positively associated with the person's average performance. In addition, the tendency to be under- or overconfident is also consistent across tasks. Another measure of monitoring accuracy, called resolution, the extent to which confidence judgments discriminate between correct and wrong responses, is also correlated with performance measures (Jackson & Kleitman, 2014). Particularly relevant for this section is the finding that these metacognitive measures at the individual level are positively associated with measures of general cognitive ability (Jackson & Kleitman, 2014; Kleitman & Moscrop, 2010), meaning that the confidence judgments of high ability reasoners show better resolution. Similarly, from learning studies, we know that overconfidence tends to get higher with lower performance (Dunning et al., 2003; Dunlosky & Rawson, 2012). This is also the case in reasoning (Stankov & Lee, 2014).

Recently, theorists (e.g., Fletcher & Carruthers, 2012; Stanovich, 2009) have suggested that an important component in reasoning performance is the ability to be reflective – that is, the disposition to monitor the adequacy of one's intermediate reactions before settling on a final response. This is in line with the conceptualization of metacognition as a deliberate reflective process mentioned above. Indeed, Thompson and Johnson (2014) found that high-capacity reasoners (relative to their low-capacity peers) showed more sensitivity to features of the problem (response conflict) that were signs of problem difficulty, adjusting their rethinking time and the probability of changing answers accordingly.

Conclusion

In this chapter, we have presented evidence to support the conclusion that metacognitive monitoring and control processes are central elements of every aspect of reasoning: initiating and terminating thinking, strategy selection, knowledge monitoring, and individual differences. Also, despite the origins of metacognitive reasoning theory in a dual process framework, we have shown how a metacognitive analysis extends beyond those borders to apply in a wide range of theoretical views, including mental model theory, probabilistic reasoning approaches, and fast-and-frugal decision-making. In sum, an adequate understanding of performance on a broad spectrum of reasoning tasks requires a concomitant understanding of the metacognitive processes involved.

Note

1 These are all referred to collectively under the umbrella term "reasoning".

References

Ackerman, R. (2014). The Diminishing Criterion Model for metacognitive regulation of time investment. *Journal of Experimental Psychology: General, 143*(3), 1349–1368.

Ackerman, R., & Beller, Y. (in press). Shared and distinct cue utilization for metacognitive judgments during reasoning and memorization. *Thinking & Reasoning.*

Ackerman, R., & Leiser, D. (2014). The effect of concrete supplements on metacognitive regulation during learning and open-book test taking. *British Journal of Educational Psychology, 84*(2), 329–348.

Ackerman, R., & Thompson, V. A. (2017). Meta-reasoning: Monitoring and control of thinking and reasoning. *Trends in Cognitive Sciences, 21*, 607–617.

Ackerman, R., & Thompson, V. (2015). Meta-reasoning: What can we learn from meta-memory. In A. Feeney & V. Thompson (Eds.), *Reasoning as memory* (pp. 164–178). Hove, UK: Psychology Press.

Ackerman, R., & Zalmanov, H. (2012). The persistence of the fluency – confidence association in problem solving. *Psychonomic Bulletin & Review, 19*(6), 1187–1192.

Alter, A. L., Oppenheimer, D. M., Epley, N., & Eyre, R. N. (2007). Overcoming intuition: Metacognitive difficulty activates analytic reasoning. *Journal of Experimental Psychology: General, 136*(4), 569–576.

Beilock, S. L., & DeCaro, M. S. (2007). From poor performance to success under stress: Working memory, strategy selection, and mathematical problem solving under pressure. *Journal of Experimental Psychology: Learning, Memory, and Cognition, 33*(6), 983–998.

Benjamin, A. S., Bjork, R. A., & Schwartz, B. L. (1998). The mismeasure of memory: When retrieval fluency is misleading as a metamnemonic index. *Journal of Experimental Psychology: General, 127*(1), 55–68.

Bjork, R. A., Dunlosky, J., & Kornell, N. (2013). Self-regulated learning: Beliefs, techniques, and illusions. *Annual Review of Psychology, 64*, 417–444.

Bowden, E. M., & Jung-Beeman, M. (2003). Normative data for 144 compound remote associate problems. *Behavior Research Methods, 35*(4), 634–639.

Bröder, A., & Newell, B. R. (2008). Challenging some common beliefs: Empirical work within the adaptive toolbox metaphor. *Judgment and Decision Making, 3*(3), 205–214.

Butler, D. L., & Winne, P. H. (1995). Feedback and self-regulated learning: A theoretical synthesis. *Review of Educational Research, 65*(3), 245–281.

Chater, N., & Oaksford, M. (1999). The probability heuristics model of syllogistic reasoning. *Cognitive Psychology, 38*, 191–258.

Chi, M. T. H., Glaser, R., & Farr, M. J. (1988). *The nature of expertise*. Hillsdale, NJ: Lawrence Erlbaum.
Colom, R., Rebollo, I., Palacios, A., Juan-Espinosa, M., & Kyllonen, P. C. (2004). Working memory is (almost) perfectly predicted by *g*. *Intelligence, 32*(3), 277–296.
Cummins, D. D., Lubart, T., Alksnis, O., & Rist, R. (1991). Conditional reasoning and causation. *Memory & Cognition, 19*(3), 274–282.
De Neys, W. (2014). Conflict detection, dual processes, and logical intuitions: Some clarifications. *Thinking & Reasoning, 20*(2), 169–187.
De Neys, W., & Bonnefon, J. F. (2013). The 'whys' and 'whens' of individual differences in thinking biases. *Trends in Cognitive Sciences, 17*(4), 172–178.
De Neys, W., Cromheeke, S., & Osman, M. (2011). Biased but in doubt: Conflict and decision confidence. *PLoS One, 6*, e15954. doi:10.1371/journal.pone.0015954.
Dunlosky, J., & Rawson, K. A. (2012). Overconfidence produces underachievement: Inaccurate self evaluations undermine students' learning and retention. *Learning and Instruction, 22*(4), 271–280.
Dunning, D., Johnson, K., Ehrlinger, J., & Kruger, J. (2003). Why people fail to recognize their own incompetence. *Current Directions in Psychological Science, 12*, 83–87.
Edwards, A. J., Weinstein, C. E., Goetz, E. T., & Alexander, P. A. (2014). *Learning and study strategies: Issues in assessment, instruction, and evaluation*. London: Academic Press.
Ericsson, K. A., & Smith, J. (1991). *Toward a general theory of expertise: Prospects and limits*. Cambridge: Cambridge University Press.
Evans, J. St. B. T. (2006). The heuristic-analytic theory of reasoning: Extension and evaluation. *Psychonomic Bulletin & Review, 13*(3), 378–395.
Evans, J. St. B. T. (2007). On the resolution of conflict in dual process theories of reasoning. *Thinking & Reasoning, 13*(4), 321–339.
Evans, J. St. B. T., & Curtis-Holmes, J. (2005). Rapid responding increases belief bias: Evidence for the dual-process theory of reasoning. *Thinking & Reasoning, 11*(4), 382–389.
Evans, J. St. B. T., & Stanovich, K. E. (2013). Dual-process theories of higher cognition advancing the debate. *Perspectives on Psychological Science, 8*(3), 223–241.
Finucane, M. L., Alhakami, A., Slovic, P., & Johnson, S. M. (2000). The affect heuristic in judgments of risks and benefits. *Journal of Behavioral Decision Making, 13*, 1–17.
Fletcher, L., & Carruthers, P. (2012). Metacognition and reasoning. *Philosophical Transactions of the Royal Society of London. Series B, Biological Sciences, 367*, 1366–1378.
Funke, J. (2010). Complex problem solving: a case for complex cognition? *Cognitive Processing, 11*(2), 133–142.
Gigerenzer, G., Todd, P., & ABC Research Group (1999). *Simple heuristics that make us smart*. New York: Oxford University Press.
Gilovich, T., Griffin, D., & Kahneman, D. (2002). *Heuristics and biases: The psychology of intuitive judgment*. Cambridge: Cambridge University Press.
Hilbig, B. E. (2010). Reconsidering "evidence" for fast-and-frugal heuristics. *Psychonomic Bulletin & Review, 17*(6), 923–930.
Holyoak, K. J. (1990). Problem solving. *Thinking: An Invitation to Cognitive Science, 3*, 117–146.
Jackson, S. A., & Kleitman, S. (2014). Individual differences in decision-making and confidence: capturing decision tendencies in a fictitious medical test. *Metacognition and Learning, 9*(1), 25–49.
Johnson-Laird, P. N., & Byrne, R. M. (1991). *Deduction*. Mahwah, NJ: Lawrence Erlbaum Associates.
Johnson-Laird, P. N., & Byrne, R. M. (2002). Conditionals: A theory of meaning, pragmatics, and inference. *Psychological Review, 109*(4), 646.
Josephs, R. A., Silvera, D. H., & Giesler, R. B. (1996). The learning curve as a metacognitive tool. *Journal of Experimental Psychology. Learning, Memory, and Cognition, 22*(2), 510–524.
Kahneman, D. (2011). *Thinking, fast and slow*. New York: Farrar, Straus and Giroux.
Karpicke, J. D., & Roediger, H. L. (2008). The critical importance of retrieval for learning. *Science, 319*, 966–968.
Kleitman, S., & Moscrop, T. (2010). Self-confidence and academic achievements in primary-school children: Their relationships and links to parental bonds, intelligence, age, and gender. In A. Efklides & P. Misailidi (Ed.), *Trends and prospects in metacognition research* (pp. 293–326) New York: Springer.
Koriat, A. (1995). Dissociating knowing and the feeling of knowing: Further evidence for the accessibility model. *Journal of Experimental Psychology: General; Journal of Experimental Psychology: General, 124*(3), 311–333.

Koriat, A. (1997). Monitoring one's own knowledge during study: A cue-utilization approach to judgments of learning. *Journal of Experimental Psychology: General, 126*, 349–370.
Koriat, A. (2012). The self-consistency model of subjective confidence. *Psychological Review, 119*(1), 80–113.
Koriat, A., Bjork, R. A., Sheffer, L., & Bar, S. K. (2004). Predicting one's own forgetting: The role of experience-based and theory-based processes. *Journal of Experimental Psychology: General, 133*(4), 643–656.
Koriat, A., & Levy-Sadot, R. (2001). The combined contributions of the cue-familiarity and accessibility heuristics to feelings of knowing. *Journal of Experimental Psychology: Learning, Memory, and Cognition, 27*(1), 34–53.
Koriat, A., Sheffer, L., & Ma'ayan, H. (2002). Comparing objective and subjective learning curves: Judgments of learning exhibit increased underconfidence with practice. *Journal of Experimental Psychology-General, 131*(2), 147–162.
Kruglanski, A. W., & Gigerenzer, G. (2011). Intuitive and deliberate judgments are based on common principles. *Psychological Review, 118*(1), 97.
Markovits, H. (1986). Familiarity effects in conditional reasoning. *Journal of Educational Psychology, 78*(6), 492.
Markovits, H., Brunet, M. L., Thompson, V., & Brisson, J. (2013). Direct evidence for a dual process model of deductive inference. *Journal of Experimental Psychology: Learning, Memory, and Cognition, 39*(4), 1213.
Markovits, H., Thompson, V. A., & Brisson, J. (2015). Metacognition and abstract reasoning. *Memory & Cognition, 43*(4), 681–693.
Metcalfe, J. (1998). Cognitive optimism: Self-deception or memory-based processing heuristics? *Personality and Social Psychology Review, 2*(2), 100–110. Retrieved from FTXT – OSL
Metcalfe, J., & Finn, B. (2008). Evidence that judgments of learning are causally related to study choice. *Psychonomic Bulletin & Review, 15*(1), 174–179.
Metcalfe, J., & Finn, B. (2011). People's hypercorrection of high-confidence errors: Did they know it all along? *Journal of Experimental Psychology: Learning, Memory, and Cognition, 37*(2), 437–448.
Mevarech, Z. R., Terkieltaub, S., Vinberger, T., & Nevet, V. (2010). The effects of meta-cognitive instruction on third and sixth graders solving word problems. *ZDM, 42*(2), 195–203.
Meyer, A., Frederick, S., Burnham, T. C., Guevara Pinto, J. D., Boyer, T. W., Ball, L. J., . . . Schuldt, J. P. (2015). Disfluent fonts don't help people solve math problems. *Journal of Experimental Psychology: General, 144*(2), e16.
Nelson, T. O., & Narens, L. (1990). Meta-Memory: A theoretical framework and new findings. In G. Bower (Ed.), *The psychology of learning and motivation: Advances in research and theory* (Vol. 26, pp. 125–173). San Diego, CA: Academic Press.
Newell, B. R., & Bröder, A. (2008). Cognitive processes, models and metaphors in decision research. *Judgment and Decision Making, 3*(3), 195–204.
Newell, B. R., & Shanks, D. R. (2003). Take the best or look at the rest? Factors influencing "one-reason" decision making. *Journal of Experimental Psychology: Learning, Memory, and Cognition, 29*(1), 53.
Newell, B. R., Weston, N. J., & Shanks, D. R. (2003). Empirical tests of a fast-and-frugal heuristic: Not everyone "takes-the-best". *Organizational Behavior and Human Decision Processes, 91*(1), 82–96.
Oaksford, M., & Chater, N. (2007). *Bayesian rationality: The probabilistic approach to human reasoning*. Oxford University Press.
Osman, M. (2004). An evaluation of dual-process theories of reasoning. *Psychonomic Bulletin & Review, 11*(6), 988–1010.
Passolunghi, M. C., & Siegel, L. S. (2001). Short-term memory, working memory, and inhibitory control in children with difficulties in arithmetic problem solving. *Journal of Experimental Child Psychology, 80*(1), 44–57.
Prowse Turner, J. A., & Thompson, V. A. (2009). The role of training, alternative models, and logical necessity in determining confidence in syllogistic reasoning. *Thinking & Reasoning, 15*, 69–100.
Quayle, J. D., & Ball, L. J. (2000). Working memory, metacognitive uncertainty, and belief bias in syllogistic reasoning. *Quarterly Journal of Experimental Psychology, 53A*, 1202–1223.
Rabinowitz, J. C., Ackerman, B. P., Craik, F. I. M., & Hinchley, J. L. (1982). Aging and Meta-Memory: The roles of relatedness and imagery. *Journal of Gerontology, 37*(6), 688–695.
Reder, L. M., & Ritter, F. E. (1992). What determines initial feeling of knowing? Familiarity with question terms, not with the answer. *Journal of Experimental Psychology: Learning, Memory, and Cognition, 18*(3), 435–451.
Rhodes, M. G., & Castel, A. D. (2008). Memory predictions are influenced by perceptual information: Evidence for metacognitive illusions. *Journal of Experimental Psychology: General, 137*(4), 615–625.
Rieskamp, J., & Hoffrage, U. (2008). Inferences under time pressure: How opportunity costs affect strategy selection. *Acta Psychologica, 127*(2), 258–276.

Rozenblit, L., & Keil, F. (2002). The misunderstood limits of folk science: An illusion of explanatory depth. *Cognitive Science, 26*, 521–562.
Schneider, W., & Artelt, C. (2010). Metacognition and mathematics education. *ZDM, 42*(2), 149–161.
Shynkaruk, J. M., & Thompson, V. A. (2006). Confidence and accuracy in deductive reasoning. *Memory & Cognition, 34*, 619–632.
Sloman, S. A. (2002). Two systems of reasoning. In T. Gilovich, D. Griffin, & D. Kahneman (Eds.), *Heuristics and biases: The psychology of intuitive judgment* (pp. 379–398). Cambridge, UK: Cambridge University Press.
Sonnleitner, P., Keller, U., Martin, R., & Brunner, M. (2013). Students' complex problem-solving abilities: Their structure and relations to reasoning ability and educational success. *Intelligence, 41*(5), 289–305.
Stankov, L., Kleitman, S., & Jackson, S. A. (2014). Measures of the trait of confidence. In G. J. Boyle, D. H. Saklofske, & G. Matthews (Eds.), *Measures of personality and social psychological constructs* (pp. 158–189). London: Academic Press.
Stankov, L., & Lee, J. (2014). Overconfidence across world regions. *Journal of Cross-Cultural Psychology, 45*(5), 821–837.
Stanovich, K. E. (1999). *Who is rational? Studies of individual differences in reasoning.* Hove, UK: Psychology Press.
Stanovich, K. E. (2009). Distinguishing the reflective, algorithmic, and autonomous minds: Is it time for a tri-process theory? In J. Evans & K. Frankish (Eds.), *In two minds: Dual processes and beyond* (pp. 55–88). Oxford, UK: Oxford University Press.
Stanovich, K. E., & West, R. F. (2000). Individual difference in reasoning: Implication for the rationality debate. *Behavioural and Brain Science, 23*, 645–665.
Storm, B. C., & Hickman, M. L. (2015). Mental fixation and metacognitive predictions of insight in creative problem solving. *The Quarterly Journal of Experimental Psychology, 68*(4), 802–813.
Sungkhasettee, V. W., Friedman, M. C., & Castel, A. D. (2011). Memory and Meta-Memory for inverted words: Illusions of competency and desirable difficulties. *Psychonomic Bulletin & Review, 18*, 973–978.
Thibodeau, P. H., & Boroditsky, L. (2013). Natural language metaphors covertly influence reasoning. *PLoS One, 8*(1), e52961.
Thiede, K. W., Anderson, M. C. M., & Therriault, D. (2003). Accuracy of metacognitive monitoring affects learning of texts. *Journal of Educational Psychology, 95*(1), 66–73.
Thompson, V. A. (2000). The task-specific nature of domain-general reasoning. *Cognition, 76*, 209–268.
Thompson, V. A. (2009). Dual-process theories: A metacognitive perspective. In J. Evans & K. Frankish (Eds.), *In two minds: Dual processes and beyond* (pp. 171–195). Oxford, UK: Oxford University Press.
Thompson, V. A., Evans, J. St. B. T., & Campbell, J. I. (2013). Matching bias on the selection task: It's fast and feels good. *Thinking & Reasoning, 19*(3–4), 431–452.
Thompson, V. A., & Johnson, S. C. (2014). Conflict, metacognition, and analytic thinking. *Thinking & Reasoning, 20*(2), 215–244.
Thompson, V. A., Newstead, S. E., & Morley, N. J. (2011). Methodological and theoretical issues in belief bias. In K. I. Manktelow, D. E. Over, & S. Elqayam (Eds.), *The Science of Reason: A Festschrift for Jonathan St. B. T. Evans* (pp. 309-338). Hove, UK: Psychology Press.
Thompson, V. A., Prowse Turner, J. A., & Pennycook, G. (2011). Intuition, reason, and metacognition. *Cognitive Psychology, 63*(3), 107–140.
Thompson, V. A., Prowse Turner, J. A., Pennycook, G., Ball, L. J., Brack, H., Ophir, Y., & Ackerman, R. (2013). The role of answer fluency and perceptual fluency as metacognitive cues for initiating analytic thinking. *Cognition, 128*(2), 237–251.
Topolinski, S. (2014). Intuition: Introducing affect into cognition. In A. Feeney & V. Thompson (Eds.), *Reasoning as memory* (pp. 146–163). Hove, UK: Psychology Press.
Topolinski, S., & Reber, R. (2010). Immediate truth-Temporal contiguity between a cognitive problem and its solution determines experienced veracity of the solution. *Cognition, 114*(1), 117–122.
Undorf, M., & Erdfelder, E. (2015). The relatedness effect on judgments of learning: A closer look at the contribution of processing fluency. *Memory & Cognition, 43*(4), 647–658.
Vernon, D., & Usher, M. (2003). Dynamics of metacognitive judgments: Pre-and postretrieval mechanisms. *Journal of Experimental Psychology: Learning, Memory, and Cognition, 29*(3), 339–346.
Weber, N., & Brewer, N. (2006). Positive versus negative face recognition decisions: Confidence, accuracy, and response latency. *Applied Cognitive Psychology, 20*(1), 17–31.
Wiley, J. (1998). Expertise as mental set: The effects of domain knowledge in creative problem solving. *Memory & Cognition, 26*(4), 716–730.
Zimmerman, B. J. (2000). Self-efficacy: An essential motive to learn. *Contemporary Educational Psychology, 25*(1), 82–91.

2

BELIEF BIAS AND REASONING

Linden J. Ball and Valerie A. Thompson

> "*We want the facts to fit the preconceptions. When they don't, it is easier to ignore the facts than to change the preconceptions*".
>
> Jessamyn West, 1902–1984

Belief effects in reasoning are some of the most robust, replicable and widely investigated phenomena that can be measured in a wide range of paradigms. Believable conclusions are deemed more acceptable than unbelievable ones regardless of their logical validity (Evans, Barston, & Pollard, 1983), regardless of the strength of the presented arguments (Stanovich & West, 1997), and regardless of whether tasks involve formal or informal reasoning (Thompson & Evans, 2012). In this chapter, we will use the accepted term for this phenomena, namely *belief bias*, but we will also discuss later the appropriateness of this label.

As a field, we have been examining belief bias scientifically for around nine decades (Wilkins, 1929), without reaching a consensus on how best to explain it. In this chapter, we will provide a brief overview of the paradigms used to investigate belief bias and the historical foundations of the scientific inquiries into its underpinnings. We will then trace the evolution of modern theories of belief bias and demonstrate how the adoption of novel methodologies has provided us with new conceptual challenges. Subsequent sections will discuss the present state of dual-process theories of belief bias, since they are currently the source of much controversy. Finally, we will discuss how the so-called new paradigm psychology of reasoning (e.g., Elqayam & Over, 2013; Manktelow, Over, & Elqayam, 2011; Oaksford & Chater, 2013), with its emphasis on Bayesian approaches to reasoning, may alter the way in which we understand belief bias. We will wrap up with a few words on the many different ways that belief bias may pervade our thinking, and offer suggestions for future avenues of investigation.

Basic tasks and fundamental questions

Belief bias has traditionally been studied using *categorical syllogisms*. These are deductive arguments that involve two premises and a conclusion, each of which features a standard logical quantifier (i.e., *all*, *no*, *some* or *some ... are not*). A logically valid conclusion describes the relationship between the premise terms in a way that is necessarily true. This means that a conclusion that is merely consistent with the premises but which is not necessitated by them is invalid. In studies of belief bias using categorical syllogisms, participants are typically asked to evaluate the validity of a conclusion that is presented as part of the argument. As an alternative to this ***conclusion-evaluation*** paradigm, some studies have used a ***conclusion-generation*** paradigm, where participants are asked to produce a conclusion that follows logically from given premises. The present chapter focuses primarily on findings and theories that derive from the dominant conclusion-evaluation paradigm, although it is important to acknowledge that an integrative account of belief bias should generalise across different task formats.

In a standard conclusion-evaluation paradigm, participants are presented with a series of syllogisms in which the validity and believability of conclusions are manipulated. As Table 2.1 shows, the systematic crossing of conclusion validity and conclusion believability produces problems in which validity and believability are either in opposition (*conflict* items) or problems in which validity and believability are congruent (*no-conflict* items). Although many recent belief-bias studies aggregate data and simply compare people's responses to conflict items versus no-conflict items, this aggregation conceals item-specific effects that may be theoretically important. In this chapter we highlight such problem-specific findings when they shed light on theoretical debates.

In the next section we examine key findings that derive from pioneering belief-bias studies and the important theoretical insights that these findings have engendered. For the present, however, we note that the most fundamental question to ask in relation to the standard conclusion-evaluation paradigm is whether people bother to reason at all when they are confronted with belief-laden conclusions, or whether they just give an answer that is consistent with their beliefs. There is certainly evidence that in some cases people largely ignore the premises or other information they are provided with and generate responses principally based on beliefs. On the other hand, there is also evidence suggesting that people do make a motivated attempt at reasoning.

Several sources of evidence indicate that people at least attend to the premises of an argument. In one of the most influential papers on belief bias, Jonathan Evans and colleagues collected verbal "think aloud" protocols from people while they were performing a syllogistic reasoning task (Evans et al., 1983). In some cases, people largely attempted to rationalise the presented conclusion based on whether or not they believed it. In other cases however, it was clear

Table 2.1 Examples of the four permutations of belief-oriented syllogisms that arise from the systematic crossing of a presented conclusion's logical status and believability status (items adapted from De Neys & Franssens, 2009)

Believability status	*Logical status*	
	Valid	*Invalid*
Believable	***Valid–Believable*** All birds have wings All crows are birds Therefore, All crows have wings	***Invalid–Believable*** All flowers need water All roses need water Therefore, All roses are flowers
Unbelievable	***Valid–Unbelievable*** All mammals can walk All whales are mammals Therefore, All whales can walk	***Invalid–Unbelievable*** All meat products can be eaten All apples can be eaten Therefore, All apples are meat products

that reasoners were attempting to draw a link between the premises and the conclusion, typically trying first to integrate the premise information prior to evaluating the conclusion based upon such integration. In these instances, the degree of belief bias was lessened.

There are also three other forms of evidence that converge on the view that people often do consider the premises of presented arguments. First, at least two studies have demonstrated that the believability of the premises themselves influences reasoners' assessment of validity, which would not be expected if people just focussed on conclusion believability. For example, Thompson (1996) found that reasoners were sensitive to the *soundness* of the argument, which is the extent to which it is both valid and based on true premises. Cherubini, Garnham, Oakhill, and Morley (1998) similarly found that belief bias was suppressed when the premises were empirically false, again consistent with the notion that soundness plays a role in argument evaluation. Both of these findings suggest that reasoners not only encode the premise information but that the quality of that information informs their judgments.

Second, studies using eye-tracking and other methods to examine people's moment-to-moment attention to the components of belief-oriented syllogisms clearly indicate that people not only process the presented conclusions but also premise information (e.g., Ball, Phillips, Wade, & Quayle, 2006; Stupple & Ball, 2008). Aspects of this inspection-time evidence (e.g., Stupple, Ball, Evans, & Kamal-Smith, 2011) are also consistent with Evans et al.'s (1993) think-aloud data in that individuals who spend longer processing premise information are less susceptible to the biasing effects of conclusion believability.

Third, there is solid evidence showing that premises that are difficult to represent and process produce more belief bias, again suggesting that people are attempting to reason about the arguments they are provided with. For example, a well-known property of syllogistic reasoning is the *figural* effect, which refers to the order in which information is presented. Figures that are easy to integrate (e.g., Some A are B; No B are C; Therefore, Some A are not C) produce less belief bias than difficult-to-integrate figures (e.g., Some B are A; No C are B; Therefore, Some A are not C; Stupple & Ball, 2008). Andrews (2010) found that measures that disrupt a reasoner's ability to integrate premise information increased reliance on conclusion believability in transitive inference problems (i.e., Chris is taller than Tim; Tim is taller than Joe; Therefore, Chris is taller than Joe). Roberts and Sykes (2003) reported similar findings in spatial reasoning problems. Finally, Andrews and Mihelic (2014) showed that reasoners who were good at identifying sets of premises that could not be integrated were better at discriminating valid from invalid conclusions, but did not necessarily show less belief bias.

In sum, it is clear that at least some reasoners make an attempt at reasoning from the premises to the conclusion, and that such reasoners show either reduced degrees of belief bias or better overall reasoning. This, however, still leaves a number of questions unanswered, including the critical one: *why* is there a belief bias? Given that people are attempting to reason, how do they end up preferring conclusions that are belief-consistent and rejecting those that are belief-inconsistent? In the next section, we begin by overviewing a number of early attempts at explaining belief bias in reasoning. These explanations have underpinned the development of more modern accounts, which we consider later in the section.

Pioneering findings and historical perspectives

We have already mentioned Evans et al.'s (1983) seminal study of belief bias, which marked a turning point in the study of the phenomenon because of the rigour of the experimental controls that were implemented and the clarity of the resulting observations. This study revealed three key findings concerning people's responses to syllogisms in which conclusion validity and conclusion believability are systematically manipulated. First, believable conclusions are more readily endorsed than unbelievable ones, which is the standard, belief-bias effect. Second, valid conclusions are more readily endorsed than invalid ones, which indicates that as well as being biased by their beliefs, participants simultaneously show some capacity to reason logically. Third, there is an interaction between logic and belief such that the effect of believability (i.e., belief bias) is stronger on invalid problems than on valid problems (Table 2.2 presents the archetypal data from Evans et al., 1983). An alternative way to view this interaction is that the effect of validity is stronger for unbelievable conclusions than for believable conclusions. As will be seen, these two different ways of conceptualising the interaction effect have influenced the formulation of different theoretical accounts of belief bias.

Numerous studies have corroborated the robustness and reliability of these three effects, although devising an encompassing explanatory account of them has proved challenging. In a single chapter it not possible to review all the theories of belief bias that have been developed since the early 1980s. Such a review would also not be particularly profitable because some theories have been short-lived, having succumbed to rapid falsification. Instead, we aim in this section to provide a brief overview of foundational theories that had some longevity and that held some sway over more contemporary theorising, which we examine later.

One early explanation of belief-bias effects was advanced by Evans et al. (1983) and was referred to as the *selective-scrutiny model*. According to this model, when a conclusion is believable people are inclined to accept it uncritically without further scrutiny (explaining the basic belief-bias effect), whereas when a conclusion is unbelievable they are more likely to engage in a rigorous logical analysis of the problem. The more diligent scrutiny that is directed at syllogisms with unbelievable conclusions allows reasoners to discriminate between valid and invalid conclusions, such that the effect of validity is larger for unbelievable conclusions than for believable ones, thereby explaining the logic-by-belief interaction.

Another early model of belief bias is the ***mental models theory***, which was advanced by Oakhill and Johnson-Laird (1985) and Oakhill, Johnson-Laird, & Garnham (1989). This theory embodied the key insight of the selective scrutiny model by likewise proposing that people engage in the increased analysis of problems with unbelievable conclusions as part of a motivated effort to refute these unconvincing conclusions. According to the mental models account, people first establish an integrated representation of the premises of a presented argument (i.e., an ***initial mental model***). A conclusion that is supported by this initial model will simply be accepted if it is believable, but if a conclusion is unbelievable it will be tested more rigorously against alternative and potentially falsifying models of the premises. The logic-by-belief interaction can thereby be explained in terms of believable conclusions typically being endorsed, whereas unbelievable

Table 2.2 Percentage of conclusions accepted as a function of their logical status and their believability status, aggregated across three experiments reported by Evans et al. (1983). These data are taken from Evans, Newstead, and Byrne (1993).

Believability status	*Logical status*		
	Valid	*Invalid*	*Mean*
Believable	89	71	80
Unbelievable	56	10	33
Mean	72	40	

conclusions may either be endorsed or rejected, dependent on the outcome of the search for counterexamples to establish their validity or invalidity.

During the 1990s the mental models theory was the dominant explanatory account of belief bias and it initially attracted good empirical support (e.g., Newstead, Pollard, Evans, & Allen, 1992; Santamaria, Garcia-Madruga, & Carretero, 1996). For example, Newstead et al. (1992) manipulated the complexity of syllogistic problems (i.e., the number of alternative models afforded by the premises), and found that the mental models theory explained how problem complexity interacted with a conclusion's believability and validity. Subsequent findings by Torrens, Thompson, and Cramer (1999), however, whilst broadly supportive of the mental models theory, also presented some challenges by showing that it was only a subset of reasoners who tended to engage in the motivated search for counterexample models of premises. Torrens et al.'s observations also aligned well with other emergent research showing that most people do not normally try to identify counterexamples in syllogistic reasoning, but instead base their decisions on the first model that comes to mind (e.g., Evans, Handley, Harper, & Johnson-Laird, 1999; Newstead, Handley, & Buck, 1999). Another important finding at this time was that when syllogisms with ***belief-neutral*** conclusions are introduced into the standard belief-bias paradigm, these tend to be endorsed at equivalent rates to believable ones (e.g., Evans, Handley, & Harper, 2001). This suggests that unbelievable conclusions somehow serve to counteract people's default tendency to accept the conclusion that is provided (cf. Evans & Feeney, 2004).

The observations that people tend to construct only single models of premises and that unbelievable conclusions may serve to *debias* reasoning were influential in prompting a radical re-evaluation of the mental models theory of belief bias at the turn of the new millennium. Indeed, two independently conducted studies (Evans et al., 2001; Klauer, Musch, & Naumer, 2000) drew very similar conclusions about the nature of belief bias. First, these researchers proposed that a general *response bias* is operating, which leads to the overarching default acceptance of believable (and neutral) conclusions and the rejection of unbelievable conclusions, irrespective of other factors such as an argument's logic. This explains why belief bias arises with both valid and invalid inferences, thereby accounting for the main effect of belief. Second, it was proposed that a process of *motivated reasoning* – driven by a conclusion's believability or unbelievability – gives rise to a further chain of events that can explain the logic-by-belief interaction, whereby logic has a greater impact when conclusions are unbelievable compared to when they are believable.

More specifically, according to Evans et al.'s (2001) *selective processing model*, if an attempt at motivated reasoning occurs, then this involves an effort to construct just a ***single*** model of the premises. This construction process is, however, biased by the believability of presented conclusions, so that for a believable conclusion an attempt is made to construct a single model that *supports* the conclusion, whereas for an unbelievable conclusion an attempt is made to construct a single model that *refutes* the conclusion. These latter assumptions provide a clear rationale for the emergence of a logic-by-belief interaction. When conclusions are valid, despite unbelievable content motivating a search for a counterexample model, such a model cannot be found, thus limiting the influence of belief bias. When conclusions are invalid, however, models exist that both support ***and*** refute such conclusions, thus leading to high levels of erroneous acceptance of invalid–believable items and high levels of correct rejection of invalid–unbelievable items.

Methodological developments and attendant theoretical advances

There is much to recommend the view espoused by Evans et al. (2001) and Klauer et al. (2000) that belief-bias effects have a dual source, reflecting the operation of both: (1) an overarching response bias that favours believable conclusions in general; and (2) a bias that arises as a consequence of motivated reasoning that accounts for the logic-by-belief interaction. Since the response-bias component should operate more quickly than the motivated-reasoning component, this model readily predicts the findings reported by Evans and Curtis-Holmes (2005), who used a speeded-response paradigm whereby participants had to make rapid decisions regarding the validity of presented conclusions. The increase in belief-bias that was observed can be explained in terms of the response-bias component gaining dominance because of the speeded-response requirement. In contrast, the disappearance of the logic-by-belief interaction can be accounted for because there was insufficient time available for participants to engage in motivated reasoning.

Despite the explanatory success of Evans et al.'s (2001) selective processing model, it is noteworthy that when it was proposed its primary focus was on accounting for conclusion-endorsement data (i.e., whether or not participants accept presented conclusions). This narrow theoretical focus on explaining variation in a single dependent variable was, in fact, the norm for all of the historical models of belief bias that we have summarised so far. This observation foregrounds a very important issue, which is whether these models can also explain other behavioural measures. What, for example, about response times, which can be acquired either using standard chronometric methods (i.e., by timing the latency from problem presentation to a decision being registered) or through the use of novel methodologies such as eye-movement tracking?

Interestingly, when studies started to emerge that measured people's response times to belief-oriented syllogisms, the established theories succumbed to immediate conceptual difficulties. In the first such study, Thompson, Striemer, Reikoff, Gunter, and Campbell (2003) showed that people reason for the longest time when responding to *believable* conclusions, a finding that was successfully replicated using inspection-time measures such as those deriving from the application of eye-tracking and mouse-tracking methodologies (e.g., Ball et al., 2006; Stupple & Ball, 2008; see also Ball, 2011, 2013a; Thompson, Morley, & Newstead, 2011a). Recall, however, that according to the mental models theory it should be ***unbelievable*** conclusions that trigger more diligent analysis aimed at testing conclusion validity, such that these syllogisms should be the ones that are processed more slowly rather than those with believable conclusions. The evidence therefore appears to undermine a key tenet of the mental models theory of belief bias. Likewise, the selective processing model seemingly predicts that both believable and unbelievable conclusions will be subjected to similar processing effort. This is because participants should be equally likely to engage in the motivated search for a single model of the premises when confronted with either a believable or an unbelievable conclusion – albeit a confirming model in the former case and a disconfirming model in the latter case.

Aspects of the response-time data are even more curious, however, since they additionally reveal the existence of a reliable but unpredicted logic-by-belief interaction. For example, Thompson et al. (2003) showed that believable conclusions take longer to process than unbelievable ones for invalid problems, but not for valid problems. Ball et al. (2006) likewise found that invalid–believable syllogisms take significantly longer to process than other items, but they also demonstrated a similar (but weaker) increase in processing times for valid–unbelievable items, where again logic and belief are in conflict. In attempting to reconcile these findings with the selective processing model, Stupple et al. (2011) suggested that the particularly long latencies observed for invalid–believable items may well reflect the performance of a subset of individuals who are better able to understand the logic of these problems, but whose reasoning necessitates time-consuming processing. Some support for these proposals derives from an earlier study of individual differences in belief bias reported by Sá, West, and Stanovich (1999), who showed that high cognitive ability, dispositions toward active and open-minded thinking, and skills in cognitive decontextualization are all associated with the avoidance of responding to syllogistic conclusions on the basis of prior beliefs. As Stupple et al. (2011) note, such a sub-group of "logical" participants would fall outside the explanatory reach of the selective processing model as formulated by Evans et al. (2001), which is essentially designed to capture the behaviour of the *average* reasoner, who demonstrates a combination of logicality and bias when responding to belief-oriented problems.

Stupple et al. (2011) provided evidence in support of their proposals in an inspection-time study, which identified three distinct subsets of reasoners: (1) a *low-logic* group showing high levels of belief bias and very fast response times, seemingly indicative of them succumbing to a dominant response bias; (2) a *medium-logic* group showing moderate belief bias and slower response times, consistent with enhanced motivated reasoning, albeit selectively biased by conclusion believability as per the assumptions of the selective processing model; and (3) a *high-logic* group showing low belief bias, where such unbiased responses were also associated with increased processing times, especially for invalid–believable conclusions. These findings indicate that people of varying logical ability have rather different endorsement rate and response-time profiles, with perhaps the profile for the middle-ability group appearing to align best with the assumptions of the selective processing model. A further, intriguing aspect of Stupple et al.'s (2011) study, however, was evidence showing that whilst the response-time difference for conflict versus no-conflict problems was particularly marked for high-ability reasoners it was nevertheless still reliably present (albeit diminished) for low-ability reasoners. This finding indicates that even in low-logic individuals – who are evaluating conclusions primarily on the basis of a response bias – there is still significant evidence for them having "sensitivity" to logic/belief conflicts (i.e., that the logic of the conclusion and its belief status are in opposition). We explore this issue further in subsequent sections.

Recently, another methodological development – this time in relation to the optimal way to analyse belief-bias data (e.g., Dube, Rotello, & Heit, 2010) – has again challenged established theories that envisage two component sources underpinning belief-bias effects, that is, a response-bias component and a motivated-reasoning component. Dube et al. argued that the specific characteristics of conclusion-endorsement data in the belief-bias paradigm necessitate analysis using the methods of Signal Detection Theory, or SDT (e.g., Macmillan & Creelman, 2005). They claimed, moreover, that when an SDT analysis is applied to the data it reveals that all belief-bias effects, including the apparent logic-by-belief interaction, can be explained in terms of a pure response bias, without any need to postulate the existence of a motivated-reasoning component.

It turns out, however, that Dube et al.'s (2010) conclusions depend on some complex and controversial technical arguments that have been disputed on both empirical and theoretical grounds (see Klauer & Kellen, 2011; Trippas, Handley, & Verde, 2013; Trippas, Handley, & Verde, 2014a). Indeed, a key outcome from recent studies that have used the SDT approach to analyse belief-bias data is that under certain conditions and with certain participants (i.e., those of higher ability or a more analytic cognitive style) there is evidence for the existence of *both* a response-bias component and a motivated-reasoning component to belief-bias, with accuracy being higher for unbelievable conclusions than for believable conclusions (e.g., Trippas et al., 2013). This motivated-reasoning component seems, therefore, to be akin to that predicted by the selective processing model of belief bias, whereby reasoners undertake a search for counterexample models that can falsify *unbelievable* conclusions, leading to the correct rejection of invalid–unbelievable arguments and the correct acceptance of valid–unbelievable arguments (as reflected in the standard logic-by-belief interaction observed in traditional analyses).

A recent study reported by Trippas, Verde, and Handley (2014b) appears to present decisive evidence in support of these latter conclusions. Trippas et al. used a two-alternative, forced-choice procedure in which participants were presented simultaneously with two syllogisms and were asked to choose which conclusion was valid. An ingenious aspect of this paradigm was that in some trials the believability of the two presented conclusions was equated (i.e., the competing conclusions were either both believable or were both unbelievable), which ensured that the response-bias component of belief-bias was removed from a participant's decision-making process. This enabled the researchers to isolate any effects arising from motivated reasoning in relation to the presented items, where accuracy should be higher in the unbelievable-conclusion condition than in the believable-conclusion condition.

In their first experiment using this paradigm, Trippas et al. (2014b) found that there was no overall effect of conclusion believability, which is inconsistent with a motivated-reasoning component to belief bias. In their subsequent experiments, however, Trippas et al. introduced some important procedural changes into their two-alternative, forced-choice paradigm so as to create more standardised task formats. In addition, they also took into account the cognitive ability of participants as well as their analytic thinking dispositions (i.e., the propensity to engage in motivated reasoning). Evidence from these follow-on experiments revealed that the more cognitively able and more analytic reasoners showed the motivated-reasoning effect, performing better on unbelievable than believable syllogisms, whilst the less cognitively able and less analytic reasoners showed patterns consistent with a response bias. These findings resonate with aspects of Stupple et al.'s (2011) data discussed above, which showed that reasoners' endorsement-rate patterns and response-time profiles are mediated by individual differences in logical ability. Current research (Trippas, Pennycook, Verde, & Handley, 2015) suggests that analytic thinking dispositions may be the more important predictor of motivated reasoning than cognitive ability.

The discerning reader may have picked up on an apparent contradiction between the response-time data reported above, indicating that the better reasoners take *longer* on invalid–believable problems than on any other type, whereas Trippas et al. (2014b) noted that their high-ability reasoners performed *worse* on believable than unbelievable problems. One way to reconcile these data is to point to differences in the reasoning tasks used (i.e., the forced-choice procedure used by Trippas et al. is unusual) and in how ability was determined (i.e., using performance on the reasoning task to categorise reasoners versus using an independent assessment of cognitive ability). For example, the use of the forced-choice paradigm may well have placed additional processing demands on the reasoner, which may have changed the way that they approached the task.

Alternatively, assuming the data paint a valid picture, we clearly require an explanation for why it takes good reasoners longer to reason about believable than unbelievable problems, whilst achieving a poorer outcome. Taken at face value, the data suggest that achieving correct answers for invalid–believable problems is both more difficult and more time consuming than getting the correct answers for valid–unbelievable ones. A speculative hypothesis is as follows: to get the correct answer to invalid–believable problems, the reasoner likely must find an alternative representation of the problem that is inconsistent with the conclusion that was provided, which may be both time-consuming and error-prone. Instead, to find the correct answer for valid–unbelievable problems, the reasoner does not need to find an alternative representation of the premises, because any model (including the first) constructed of the premises will be consistent with the conclusion and thus be grounds to accept it. This process may be less time consuming and less error-prone. As such, the signature that we have interpreted as motivated reasoning (better performance on unbelievable than believable problems) may be, instead, simply a difference in the type of reasoning required to achieve correct performance on the two types of problems.

To summarise, in this section and the preceding one we have reviewed a variety of theories that have arisen over the years to explain belief-bias effects in reasoning. The dominant view that has persisted through the application of different chronometric methodologies (e.g., eye-tracking and response-time measures) and different data-analysis approaches (i.e., the use of the SDT model) is that belief bias has two components, as is captured very effectively by the selective processing model (e.g., Evans et al., 2001; Klauer et al. 2000; see also Trippas et al., 2014b). First, there is a basic response-bias component, which is the overarching tendency to accept believable conclusions as valid, irrespective of their actual validity. Second, beliefs may also influence the so-called *quality* of reasoning via a motivated-reasoning component, with people (especially those who are more cognitively able or more analytically inclined) subjecting unbelievable conclusions to more diligent analysis, which leads to greater accuracy. Alternatively, as suggested above, the pattern that has been ascribed to motivated reasoning may reflect differences in problem difficulty between believable and unbelievable problems, a possibility that is ripe for future investigation.

Dual-process theories as a conceptual framework for understanding belief-bias effects

In concluding the previous section, we noted that the selective processing model (e.g., Evans et al., 2001; Klauer et al. 2000) appears to provide a good explanatory fit for much of the available evidence relating to belief-bias effects in reasoning. This model is a form of *dual-process theory*, of which a large variety have been proposed in the reasoning literature (e.g., Evans, 2007, 2008; Evans & Over, 1996; Kahneman, 2011; Sloman, 1996; Stanovich, 1999, 2011; Stanovich & West, 2000). Dual-process theories afford a useful and elegant conceptual framework for explaining many phenomena in reasoning, judgment and decision making (see Evans, this volume). In this section, we will examine Evans and Stanovich's (2013a, 2013b) version of dual-process theory (henceforth DPT), since this arguably represents the most up-to-date and fully articulated account of dual processes in reasoning that also facilitates further understanding of belief-bias phenomena.

Evans and Stanovich's (2013a, 2013b) DPT framework proposes that reasoning depends on the operation of two qualitatively different types of processes: type 1 processes have two key, defining features, which are that they are relatively undemanding of working memory (WM) resources and are autonomous, running to completion whenever a relevant cue triggers them. They also tend to be fast, high capacity, non-conscious and capable of running in parallel, but these are merely examples of correlated features rather than defining or necessary features. Type 2 processes, in contrast, are defined in terms of requiring WM resources and being focused on cognitive decoupling and mental simulation, which are critical for hypothetical thinking. Type 2 processes also tend to be slow, capacity limited, conscious and serial, but again, these are merely correlated features rather than defining features.

According to this DPT framework, belief bias arises because Type 1 processes quickly deliver an answer based on beliefs; this default answer may or may not be intervened upon and analysed by the slower Type 2 processes that are necessary to determine whether the conclusion is logically valid (see Evans, this volume, for further discussion of the *default–interventionist* assumptions that underpin DPT). Again, we note that speed is not the defining quality of either Type 1 or Type 2 processes, but nonetheless, the DPT explanation for many phenomena, including belief bias, rests on this relative asymmetry of processing speed. Moreover, there is evidence to support this asymmetry, at least in the domain of complex, syllogistic reasoning. In particular, when reasoners are forced to reason under a deadline, they are more likely to give belief-based responses than when allowed to reason in free time (Evans & Curtis Holmes, 2005), and they are also less accurate (Shynkaruk & Thompson, 2006; Thompson & Johnson, 2014). This evidence is consistent with the assumption that beliefs lead to a fast, default response, producing the response-bias component of belief bias, and that additional time is needed to intervene on these default responses and assess logical validity (i.e., through a process of motivated reasoning). Evidence favouring this DPT explanation of belief bias comes from a variety of sources, of which three will be briefly reviewed here: (1) studies using dual-task methodologies; (2) studies using brain-imaging techniques; and (3) studies of individual differences in reasoning.

Studies using a dual-task paradigm involve participants attempting belief-oriented syllogisms whilst simultaneously operating under a secondary WM load (e.g., maintaining information that needs to be recalled once each reasoning task is completed). The assumption in this paradigm is that because Type 2 processing is dependent on WM resources, then any evidence of a WM load disrupting reasoning performance would support the view that Type 2 processing is involved in responding to the presented syllogisms (see Trémolière, De Neys, & Bonnefon, this volume). De Neys (2006) reported a study using this paradigm in which participants who varied in WM capacity tackled belief-oriented syllogisms under a WM load. The results supported the DPT in that the load hampered reasoning for items where logic and belief conflicted, but not for items where the conclusion's belief status cued the correct response (no-conflict problems). Additionally, although the participants with higher WM capacities performed better on the conflict items than those with lower WM capacities, all reasoners showed similar disruptive effects of load on reasoning.

In relation to neural-imaging research, this has again provided much evidence that is consistent with the DPT view of belief-bias effects, with studies supporting the existence of a qualitative distinction between belief-based and reasoning-based responses (e.g., De Neys, Vartanian, & Goel, 2008; Goel & Dolan, 2003; Houdé et al., 2000; Prado & Noveck, 2007; Tsujii & Watanabee, 2009). For example, brain-imaging studies have shown that logic/belief conflicts are detected by the brain and that reasoning-based responses are associated with the activation of different brain areas than is the case when belief-based responses are made. In particular, conflict detection is correlated with activation of the anterior cingulate cortex, whilst the override of belief-based responding with reasoning is correlated with the activation of the regions of the right prefrontal cortex known to be associated with executive control and the inhibition of prepotent but erroneous responses.

Interestingly, De Neys and Franssens (2009) have presented compelling evidence that belief bias arises from participants' failure to *complete* the inhibition process rather than from a failure to recognise the need to inhibit inappropriate beliefs in the first place. This evidence points strongly to the conclusion that most people are, in fact, highly sensitive to logic/belief conflicts and that they strive to inhibit the influence of prior beliefs, albeit often unsuccessfully (see also De Neys, 2014; Luo et al., 2013; Luo, Tang, Zhang, & Stupple, 2014). This view also appears to generalise beyond the belief-bias paradigm to other reasoning tasks where conflict exists between a Type 1 default response and a Type 2 analytic response (e.g., Bonner & Newell, 2010; Mevel, Poirel, Rossi, Cassotti, Simon, Houdé, & De Neys, 2015; Sanfey, Rilling, Aronson, Nystrom, & Cohen, 2003; Stupple, Ball, & Ellis, 2013; Villejoubert, 2009).

When it comes to individual differences research, Stanovich and colleagues (e.g., Stanovich, 1999; Stanovich & West, 2008; Toplak, West, & Stanovich, 2011) have provided substantial evidence for the role of *two* key individual-difference variables in the susceptibility to belief bias and a large variety of other reasoning biases (see also the evidence from Trippas et al., 2014b, discussed in the previous section). These two variables are general intelligence (e.g., IQ or other measures of cognitive capacity) and the disposition towards analytic thinking. That is, reasoners of higher general intelligence who therefore have higher WM capacities (e.g., Conway, Kane, & Engle, 2003) perform better on syllogisms where belief and logic conflict than do individuals of lower general intelligence. This is consistent with the DPT assumption that WM capacity is needed to overturn a Type 1 default response based on belief and substitute it with one based on logic via a Type 2 motivated-reasoning process. In addition, people who are more disposed to engage in analytic thinking also do better on logic/belief conflict problems than those who are less inclined. Interestingly, and consistent with the predictions of DPT, similar relationships are not observed on problems where the belief and logic do not conflict (Pennycook, Fugelsang, & Koehler, 2015) – that is, where an answer based on beliefs will deliver the logically correct response.

One important caveat when interpreting individual differences in belief bias is that the observed relationships with cognitive ability and analytic thinking dispositions, although robust, are modest at best. Thus, there will be occasions when Type 2 thinking is engaged but where it still results in an incorrect answer. Interestingly, this is just as likely to be true of high-capacity as low-capacity reasoners (Thompson & Johnson, 2014). In other words, engaging Type 2 thinking is not a magic bullet that delivers only correct responses (see also Evans, 2007; Stanovich, 2012). One reason for this (as already discussed above) is that beliefs may guide subsequent Type 2 analysis of the problem to either confirm believable or disconfirm unbelievable conclusions, which on occasion can lead to logical errors. This is the case, for example, with invalid–believable items, where a confirming model of the premises can be found, which thereby supports the endorsement of a conclusion that is, in fact, invalid. It is also possible that Type 2 processes are engaged but reasoners lack the knowledge or "mindware" that is necessary to solve the problem (Stanovich, 2012).

Thompson and colleagues (Shynkaruk & Thompson, 2006; Thompson, Prowse Turner, & Pennycook, 2011b) have provided direct evidence for this latter conclusion using a novel *two response paradigm*. Although originally developed to study the origins of confidence in reasoning, this paradigm has also produced valuable insights into Type 1 and Type 2 processes in reasoning. In this paradigm, reasoners are instructed to provide two responses: the first is to be an intuitive, fast response (sometimes given under time pressure), while the second is a slower, considered response with no time limit. In some, but not all reasoning tasks, there is a slight increase in correct responses over time, despite a substantial period of rethinking. Indeed, reasoners are almost as likely to change a wrong answer to a right one as vice versa, which is consistent with the conclusion that Type 2 processes may be engaged but do not lead to correct conclusions. Further, these researchers have observed that most of the time, the second answer is the same as the first, again despite a period of rethinking. These data suggest that many Type 2 processes may not be engaged in logical analysis but instead are applied to justify or rationalise the initial conclusion (see Evans, this volume).

We conclude this section on the DPT framework by noting that despite the fact that Type 2 processes do not always produce logical answers, there is nonetheless a large body of evidence that supports the assumption that *beliefs* are Type 1 processes that form *default* answers. This evidence also aligns directly with claims reviewed in previous sections for the existence of a response-bias component to belief-bias effects. In addition, there is good evidence that the *likelihood* of Type 2 processes being successfully engaged to overturn an original answer varies according to individual differences in a reasoner's cognitive capacity and cognitive motivation. This evidence is consistent with the assumption that Type 2 processes are needed for successful, logical responding as well as the evidence reviewed in earlier sections for a motivated-reasoning component to belief-bias phenomena. It also comes as little surprise that adding a WM load to reasoning or imposing time constraints appears to increases people's reliance on beliefs since there is a reduced opportunity for Type 2, motivated-reasoning processes to intervene in order to attempt to overturn Type 1 default responses. In all of these respects, the broad-based DPT framework appears to embody very effectively the core assumptions of the selective processing model (e.g., Evans et al., 2001; Klauer et al. 2000), including its emphasis on the default–interventionist operation of response-bias followed by motivated reasoning.

The case for Type 1 logic and Type 2 beliefs

Despite the coherent picture in support of a DPT explanation of belief bias that has been provided by the evidence discussed so far, recent findings have directly challenged the DPT view that the initial operation of autonomous, fast beliefs is followed by slower, WM-dependent, analytic reasoning that has the potential to deliver a normative response. In this section we examine the emerging evidence that appears to undermine the key default–interventionist tenets of the DPT explanation of belief bias. To simplify the discussion, we follow Newman, Gibb, and Thompson (2017) and use the term *belief-based* to describe responses that are consistent with prior beliefs and the term *rule-based* to describe responses that are consistent with the application of rules of logic, whilst acknowledging that these are not necessarily qualities of the cognitive processes that give rise to these response outputs.

As Newman et al. (2017) explain, given the default–interventionist DPT assumption that rule-based processes take longer than belief-based processes, then the former should not be able to interfere with the latter. That is, the belief-based response should always be completed *before* a rule-based response has been initiated. However, across a number of reasoning tasks, including belief-oriented syllogisms, there is substantial evidence that reasoners are highly sensitive to the conflict between the belief-based and rule-based information that is presented to them (see De Neys, 2012, 2014). For example, people demonstrate increased response times when evaluating logic/belief conflict problems compared to no-conflict problems (De Neys & Glumicic, 2008), even when responding to the problems relatively quickly (Stupple et al., 2011). People also show heightened autonomic arousal to logic/belief conflict items, as determined by galvanic skin conductance measures (De Neys, Moyens, & Vansteenwegen, 2010) and reduced confidence in their responses (De Neys, Cromheeke, & Osman, 2011; Thompson et al., 2011b).

Not only do reasoners appear to be sensitive to conflicts between belief-based and rule-based information, but it also seems that rule-based processes can directly *interfere* with belief-based judgments, which, again, should be impossible if belief-based processes are faster than rule-based ones. In typical belief-bias studies, reasoners are instructed to respond based on the rules of logic at the outset of the task. A very different methodology, however, is to instruct participants at the end of each reasoning problem whether to base their response either on their own beliefs or on the rules of logic. When evaluating belief-oriented syllogisms under this type of instruction it has been found that participants are slower at making *belief-based* responses when a conclusion conflicts with a problem's logical validity than when it does not (Handley, Newstead, & Trippas, 2011; Handley & Trippas, 2015; Howarth, Handley, & Walsh, 2016). This intriguing finding suggests that rule-based processes produce outputs fast enough to interfere with belief-based ones, thereby pointing to the existence of *Type 1 logic* – or what De Neys (e.g., 2012, 2014) refers to as *logical intuitions* (see Morsanyi & Handley, 2012, for the first evidence of people's intuitive detection of logicality in syllogistic reasoning and Trippas, Handley, Verde, & Morsanyi, 2016, for recent corroboration; for similar findings in research using other reasoning tasks, see Pennycook, Fugelsang, & Koehler, 2012; Pennycook, Trippas, Handley, & Thompson, 2014).

The observation that the logical status of a presented conclusion can interfere with its belief-based assessment seems inconsistent with the assumption that rule-based processes are slow relative to belief-based ones. As Newman et al. (2017) point out, however, one potential limitation of these findings relating to apparent Type 1 logic is that the reasoning problems used in these studies have tended to be very simple ones such that any rule-based processing would be expected to be straightforward. For example, Handley et al. (2011) mainly examined belief and logic effects with conditional syllogisms involving ***modus ponens*** inferences ("If p then q; p, therefore q"), which are well within the deductive capability of the majority of reasoners. Thus, the processes required to make these inferences could be straightforward enough to be computed autonomously, with the observed interference effect perhaps being restricted to logic/belief conflict items involving such simple logical rules. That said, Handley et al.'s (2011) study also featured an experiment using more complex reasoning items that produced the same pattern of results, so there is at least some evidence to counter the notion that rapid sensitivity to logical validity arises only with simple deductive arguments.

A second limitation of the research demonstrating apparent Type 1 logic that is also noted by Newman et al. (2017) is that the reasoners being studied were typically not put under any time pressure. This allows for the possibility that the observed conflicts were between rule-based responses and belief-based responses that were both generated relatively slowly and were of a Type 2 nature. In support of this proposal is evidence that belief-based processing can indeed be slow and of a Type 2 form. For example, participants have been observed to rely on slow, effortful belief-based processing when they apply a strategy involving counterexample search during conditional reasoning (De Neys, Schaeken, & d'Ydewalle, 2005; Markovits, Forgues, & Brunet, 2012; Verschueren, Schaeken, & d'Ydewalle, 2005). In addition, Thompson and colleagues have observed in many tasks that when participants are given a chance to rethink an initial, intuitive answer, they frequently change a rule-based logical response to a belief-based one, again demonstrating that a period of relatively slow deliberation can result in the application of Type 2 beliefs (e.g., Shynkaruk & Thompson, 2006; Thompson et al., 2011b). Thus, it appears that although belief-based responses *can* be generated quickly and easily via Type 1 processes, there are also circumstances in which reasoners will engage in slow and deliberate belief-based processing of a Type 2 kind.

Newman et al. (2017) proposed that three criteria should be met to demonstrate conclusively that Type 1 rule-based processes have occurred quickly. First, responses must be made under time pressure to eliminate any opportunity for Type 2 rule-based processing. Second, responses need to reflect the properties of rule-based responding. Third, the tasks studied should *not* be limited to simple inferences such as modus ponens. All three criteria were met in the experiments they report. These utilised the two-response paradigm (Thompson et al., 2011b), whereby initial responses under logical-reasoning instructions occurred under a very short response-time deadline, whereas subsequent responses gave participants time to rethink and alter their decisions. Newman et al. hypothesised that if people's capacity for fast, rule-based processes extends beyond simple inferences, then initial responses should be sensitive to the manipulation of logical information. This prediction gained convincing support across the series of studies they report. Related work by Bago and De Neys (2017) also sought to derive evidence for Type 1 logic using the two-response paradigm and procedures to eradicate initial Type 2 processing, including setting challenging response deadlines and establishing high, concurrent WM loads. Bago and De Neys' findings supported Newman et al.'s observations that correct, logical responses can arise as the very first, immediate answer, although it should be noted that because their belief-oriented syllogisms were very simple ones they failed to meet one of Newman et al.'s key criteria, which is that problems need to be of at least moderate difficulty.

Other recent research, however, which has been reported by Trippas, Thompson, and Handley (2017), lends further convincing support to the view that fast, rule-based processes of a

Type 1 variety can arise in a belief-bias paradigm even with reasoning problems of intermediate complexity. They used moderate-complexity items (i.e., single-model categorical syllogisms and *modus tollens* inferences: "if p then q; not q, therefore not p") and showed that the validity of conclusions interfered with evaluations of conclusion believability to the same extent that the believability of conclusions interfered with evaluations of conclusion validity. For the simplest reasoning problems (i.e., modus ponens inferences) they corroborated Handley et al.'s (2011) previous findings that conclusion validity interfered more with judgments of conclusion believability than the converse. However, with complex reasoning problems (i.e., multiple-model categorical syllogisms) the interference pattern flipped, with conclusion believability interfering more with judgments of conclusion validity than vice versa. Trippas et al. (2017) view these findings as supporting a parallel-processing model in which multiple problem features – including belief-content and logical structure – are processed *simultaneously*. In the case where both problem features can be assessed in a relatively simple way, then they can cause mutual interference, but in cases where either a belief-based or a logic-based response requires more complex processing, then an interference asymmetry can arise.

When the evidence reviewed in this section is considered holistically, then the emerging picture is a fascinating one in which both rule-based *and* belief-based processes appear to be able to operate either according to a fast Type 1 route or a slow Type 2 route. Such evidence can either be viewed as a profound challenge to the fundamental assumptions of the traditional DPT account of belief bias – and reasoning in general – especially in relation to the theory's key default–interventionist tenet, or alternatively as the building blocks for shaping the next generation of DPT views. In the following section we adopt the latter approach and offer some suggestions for how the findings outlined above might be integrated with the basic assumptions of the DPT account.

Advancing an understanding of Type 1 and Type 2 processes

In this penultimate section we attempt to reconcile the apparently contradictory findings arising from: (1) foundational studies of belief bias, which support a DPT view in which belief-based processing produces a fast, default response that may then be subjected to slower, rule-based processing; and (2) recent studies of belief bias, which show that rule-based processing can be fast and that belief-based processes can be slow. What seems to be pivotal to this reconciliation is the recognition that although Type 1 and Type 2 processes are *qualitatively different* in terms of what triggers them and how much they draw on WM capacity, they do not necessarily differ in terms of the answer that they can produce (cf. Evans & Stanovich, 2013a). That is, we need to assume – as indeed the recent evidence appears to show convincingly – that answers based on belief or on logic can arise from *either* Type 1 *or* Type 2 processes.

More specifically, we propose that Type 1 processes produce answers autonomously in response to *triggering conditions* in the environment, which may, for example, relate to the belief content of presented problems or to the structural form of these problems, including features that correlate with logical validity (e.g., see Chater & Oaksford, 1999; Klauer & Singmann, 2013). These Type 1 processes tend to be fast, they can operate in parallel and they draw very little upon WM capacity. Type 2 processes, on the other hand, require WM capacity, they rely on serial processing and they tend to be slower. They can be triggered autonomously, as arises when a reasoner has a low "Feeling of Rightness" in their Type 1 response (Thompson et al., 2011b, 2013; see also Ackerman & Thompson, this volume), or they can be initiated deliberately, at the command of the reasoner. Although both Type 1 and Type 2 processes may be cued autonomously, these processes differ fundamentally in that the former run to completion once triggered, meaning they are an obligatory aspect of the problem representation, whereas the latter can be continued, discontinued or altered at the behest of the reasoner (Thompson, 2013).

As we have seen, moreover, there is evidence that many, if not all inferences rely, at least in part, on Type 1 processes. On this analysis, there are two Type 1 outputs that are typically generated in response to a belief-oriented reasoning task, one based on beliefs and one based on structural features that may directly or indirectly reflect logical validity. A corollary to this is the assumption that Type 1 processes are *default* such that they do all of the heavy cognitive lifting, with Type 2 processes then being activated as needed. For example, Type 2 processes may be used to resolve a conflict between competing Type 1 outputs (e.g., for believable but invalid conclusions; De Neys, 2012, 2014), or they may become engaged in response to a low Feeling of Rightness regarding an initial intuitively based solution (e.g., Thompson et al., 2011b, 2013). In addition, Type 2 processing may be further augmented because of a reasoner's inherent disposition to engage in actively open-minded thinking (e.g., Trippas et al., 2015).

These aforementioned ways in which Type 2 processing can move beyond initial Type 1 outputs clearly have much in common with notions stemming from traditional default–interventionist views in which belief-bias arises form a combination of Type 1 response bias and Type 2 motivated reasoning. Also in line with default–interventionist assumptions are findings confirming that the potential to initiate Type 2 processing is severely hampered by factors such as the absence of available time or the lack of WM resources (e.g., as arises with a concurrent WM load; De Neys, 2006; Gilhooly, Logie, Wetherick, & Wynn, 1993). Especially convincing data to support the proposal that Type 2 processing is WM-dependent derive from a study reported by Evans, Handley, Neilens, and Over (2010), which examined the role of cognitive capacity and Type 2 thinking in overcoming belief-based responding. In their study, Evans et al. asked participants to make conditional inferences either under strict deductive instructions (i.e., to assume the truth of the premises and draw only necessary inferences) or under pragmatic instructions (i.e., as a test of how people reason in real life). They observed belief bias in both tasks, but this disappeared for high-capacity reasoners in the strict-instructions group. In other words, the default response when reasoning pragmatically appears to be belief-based, but when people are instructed to reason logically, this tendency can be suppressed by those with high WM capacity. These findings therefore strongly support the role of Type 2 thinking in overcoming beliefs.

Notwithstanding the evidence that effective Type 2 thinking is WM-dependent, the picture is complicated somewhat by recent, equally compelling evidence that WM capacity can affect Type 1 thinking. For example, Thompson and Johnson (2014) used the two-response procedure in which reasoners first provide fast, intuitive answers before having an opportunity to revise their responses. As expected, final performance on these problems correlated with cognitive capacity. Unexpectedly, the correlation was also observed for the fast, intuitive answers, suggesting that at least part of the relationship between cognitive capacity and reasoning may arise because high-capacity reasoners produce *different* Type 1 responses than low-capacity reasoners.

Overall, then, our proposal is that there may be both Type 1 and Type 2 routes to the *same* answer, whether this is a logical response or a belief-based response. In the former case, fast heuristics (Chater & Oaksford, 1999) or logical intuitions (De Neys, 2012, 2014) can deliver an equivalent Type 1, logical output as can slow, WM-dependent, Type 2 reasoning. In the case of a belief-based response, this may arise from either a fast, Type 1 judgment or from the slow analysis of belief content (e.g., from deliberate Type 2 thinking assessing the likelihood of counterexamples; see De Neys et al., 2005; Markovits et al., 2012; Verschueren et al., 2005).

We can also see throughout the discussion of recent belief-bias findings how *problem complexity* is very likely to be a factor central to a full understanding of the interplay between Type 1 and Type 2 processes in generating responses under either belief or logic instructions (e.g., Handley et al., 2011; Howarth et al., 2016; Trippas et al., 2017). Indeed, it may be the case that a traditional default–interventionist theory that involves a mix of Type 1 and Type 2 processing is well placed to capture belief-bias findings that arise with more complex reasoning problems of the type that were studied in many of the pioneering experiments up to a decade or so ago (cf. Trippas et al., 2017). In contrast, belief-bias effects that are seen with the easier problems that have featured in more recent studies may rely more (or perhaps even solely) on Type 1 processing (again see Trippas et al., 2017).

Future directions in the study of belief bias

We have shown throughout this chapter that beliefs have pervasive effects on reasoning, with these effects typically being viewed as giving rise to "biases", that is, systematic errors in our deductive capability. This negative view of belief effects in reasoning derives from the traditional "old paradigm" perspective on deduction, which assesses people's assumption-based reasoning, in which they must always evaluate the *form* of logical arguments and assume that their premises are true (see Evans, 2016). The belief-bias effects that we have discussed clearly demonstrate that it is difficult for most people to reason in this way.

The old paradigm view seems to be justified in remonstrating with reasoners about the *response-bias* element of belief bias, which is the overarching tendency for people to accept believable and reject unbelievable conclusions. We have also noted, however, that there appears to be a second, important aspect to the data arising in belief-bias studies, whereby *unbelievable* conclusions appear to motivate deeper, analytic reasoning that can often lead to the rejection of invalid–unbelievable conclusions and the acceptance of valid–unbelievable ones. One caveat to this conclusion was outlined earlier, in that it is not clear whether this pattern represents motivated reasoning or differences in problem difficulty. A second caveat is that it may be only those of high cognitive ability or with strong dispositions toward actively open-minded thinking who are capable of this kind of reasoning. Regardless, the potential for this latter process to be beneficial in real-world, practical contexts is readily apparent. For example, in everyday, informal argumentation, where people may be trying to persuade us to accept conclusions that run contrary to our own beliefs, it would be very sensible to scrutinise their arguments more assiduously. To date there has been only limited research on belief-bias effects in informal reasoning (e.g., Mercier & Sperber, 2011; Stanovich & West, 1997; Thompson & Evans, 2012), and this clearly represents an area that is ripe for further investigation.

A further direction for future research is to determine psychological interventions to enhance people's reasoning with belief-oriented materials. This so-called *Meliorist* agenda (e.g., Stanovich & West, 2000) is fundamentally concerned with improving people's everyday reasoning and explores the potential benefits for reasoning that can derive from a whole host of manipulations, including ones relating to instructions and training. Only a few studies have explored such manipulations, including research that has used instructions stressing the importance of logical analysis, which showed some early promise in reducing belief-bias (Newstead et al., 1992), although there was a subsequent failure to replicate these instructional effects (Evans, Newstead, Allen, & Pollard, 1994). Greater success has been identified in studies investigating the provision of feedback on performance (Ball, 2013b) and the use of fantasy contents (Markovits, Venet, Janveau-Brennan, Malfait, Pion, & Vadeboncoeur, 1996), although more effort is clearly needed to replicate these apparent reasoning enhancements and understand their underlying basis.

Another instructional manipulation that has been shown to alleviate the impact of belief bias – specifically in a scientific-reasoning task – is to ask people to change perspectives from their own to another's (Beatty & Thompson, 2012). The researchers propose that the positive effects of perspective change may be interpreted from a "new paradigm" Bayesian viewpoint given that their task asked participants to revise their prior beliefs in light of newly presented evidence. Beatty and Thompson suggest that people may be unwilling to modify their own belief systems based on presented arguments, but may be more willing to accept that belief updating is appropriate for a "hypothetical other". In this way beliefs would have more weight when evaluating arguments from one's own perspective than from another's perspective. Further tests of this Bayesian account of belief-bias would require participants to rate their degree of belief in a conclusion both before and after the presentation of new evidence. Under this new-paradigm view, an unwillingness to change beliefs in response to reliable evidence would constitute a belief bias. In contrast, an unwillingness to change one's beliefs in response to unreliable evidence would be viewed as entirely reasonable.

These latter suggestions neatly foreground new-paradigm considerations in the study of belief-bias effects as well as the view that most people are rational enough to make fairly good decisions most of the time, at least in the sense that they achieve their everyday goals. Moreover, it seems likely that people achieve this reasoning more effectively by belief-based processes than by abstract logical deductions. Furthermore, on this view, people should make decisions by using *all* of their relevant knowledge and beliefs. From this Bayesian perspective it can be argued that reasoners will be rightly reluctant to set aside their beliefs, which are based on many years of learning and experience, so as instead to privilege an experimenter's artificially presented arguments (cf. Evans & Over, 1996). Considering belief-bias effects in reasoning through a new-paradigm lens is certain to open up many profitable avenues of investigation based around novel tasks and manipulations. We look forward to the new findings and conceptual insights that such research will engender to further extend our understanding of belief-bias effects in reasoning.

Acknowledgement

We are very grateful to Dries Trippas for helpful feedback on a previous version of this chapter.

References

Andrews, G. (2010). Belief-based and analytic processing in transitive inference depends on premise integration difficulty. *Memory & Cognition, 38*, 928–940.

Andrews, G., & Mihelic, M. (2014). Belief-based and analytic processing in transitive inference: Further evidence for the importance of premise integration. *Journal of Cognitive Psychology, 26*, 588–596.

Bago, B., & De Neys, W. (2017). Fast logic? Examining the time course assumption of dual process theory. *Cognition, 158*, 90–109.

Ball, L. J. (2011). The dynamics of reasoning: Chronometric analysis and dual-process theories. In K. I. Manktelow, D. E. Over, & S. Elqayam (Eds.), *The science of reason: A Festschrift for Jonathan St. B. T. Evans* (pp. 283–307). Hove, UK: Psychology Press.

Ball, L. J. (2013a). Eye-tracking and reasoning: What your eyes tell about your inferences. In W. De Neys & M. Osman (Eds.), *New approaches in reasoning research* (pp. 51–69). Hove, UK: Psychology Press.

Ball, L. J. (2013b). Microgenetic evidence for the beneficial effects of feedback and practice on belief bias. *Journal of Cognitive Psychology, 25*, 183–191.

Ball, L. J., Phillips, P., Wade, C. N., & Quayle, J. D. (2006). Effects of belief and logic on syllogistic reasoning: Eye-movement evidence for selective processing models. *Experimental Psychology, 53*, 77–86.

Beatty, E. L., & Thompson, V. A. (2012). Effects of perspective and belief on analytic reasoning in a scientific reasoning task. *Thinking & Reasoning*, *18*, 441–460.

Bonner, C., & Newell, B. R. (2010). In conflict with ourselves? An investigation of heuristic and analytic processes in decision making. *Memory & Cognition*, *38*, 186–196.

Chater, N., & Oaksford, M. (1999). The probability heuristics model of syllogistic reasoning. *Cognitive Psychology*, *38*, 191–258.

Cherubini, P., Garnham, A., Oakhill, J., & Morley, E. (1998). Can any ostrich fly? Some new data on belief bias in syllogistic reasoning. *Cognition*, *69*, 179–218.

Conway, A. R., Kane, M. J., & Engle, R. W. (2003). Working memory capacity and its relation to general intelligence. *Trends in Cognitive Sciences*, 7, 547–552.

De Neys, W. (2006). Dual processing in reasoning: Two systems but one reasoner. *Psychological Science*, *17*, 428–433.

De Neys, W. (2012). Bias and conflict: A case for logical intuitions. *Perspectives on Psychological Science*, 7, 28–38.

De Neys, W. (2014). Conflict detection, dual processes, and logical intuitions: Some clarifications. *Thinking & Reasoning*, *20*, 169–187.

De Neys, W., Cromheeke, S., & Osman, M. (2011). Biased but in doubt: Conflict and decision confidence. *PLoS ONE*, *6*, e15954.

De Neys, W., & Franssens, S. (2009). Belief inhibition during thinking: Not always winning but at least taking part. *Cognition*, *113*, 45–61.

De Neys, W., & Glumicic, T. (2008). Conflict monitoring in dual process theories of reasoning. *Cognition*, *106*, 1248–1299.

De Neys, W., Moyens, E., & Vansteenwegen, D. (2010). Feeling we're biased: Autonomic arousal and reasoning conflict. *Cognitive, Affective, & Behavioral Neuroscience*, *10*, 208–216.

De Neys, W., Schaeken, W., & d'Ydewalle, G. (2005). Working memory and everyday conditional reasoning: Retrieval and inhibition of stored counterexamples. *Thinking & Reasoning*, *11*, 349–381.

De Neys, W., Vartanian, O., & Goel, V. (2008). Smarter than we think: When our brains detect that we are biased. *Psychological Science*, *19*, 483–489.

Dube, C., Rotello, C. M., & Heit, E. (2010). Assessing the belief bias effect with ROCs: It's a response bias effect. *Psychological Review*, *117*, 831–863.

Elqayam, S., & Over, D. E. (2013). New paradigm psychology of reasoning: An introduction to the special issue edited by Elqayam, Bonnefon, and Over. *Thinking & Reasoning*, *19*, 249–265.

Evans, J. St. B. T. (2007). *Hypothetical thinking: Dual processes in reasoning and judgement*. Hove, UK: Psychology Press.

Evans, J. St. B. T. (2008). Dual-processing accounts of reasoning, judgment and social cognition. *Annual Review of Psychology*, *59*, 255–278.

Evans, J. St. B. T. (2016). Belief bias in deductive reasoning. In R. F. Pohl (Ed.), *Cognitive illusions: Intriguing phenomena in judgment, thinking and memory* (pp. 165–181). Abingdon, UK: Routledge.

Evans, J. St. B. T., Barston, J. L., & Pollard, P. (1983). On the conflict between logic and belief in syllogistic reasoning. *Memory & Cognition*, *11*, 295–306.

Evans, J. St. B. T., & Curtis-Holmes, J. (2005). Rapid responding increases belief bias: Evidence for the dual process theory of reasoning. *Thinking & Reasoning*, *11*, 382–389.

Evans, J. St. B. T., & Feeney, A. (2004). The role of prior belief in reasoning. In J. P. Leighton & R. J. Sternberg (Eds.), *The nature of reasoning* (pp. 78–102). Cambridge, UK: Cambridge University Press.

Evans, J. St. B. T., Handley, S. J., & Harper, C. (2001). Necessity, possibility and belief: A study of syllogistic reasoning. *Quarterly Journal of Experimental Psychology*, *54*, 935–958.

Evans, J. St. B. T., Handley, S. J., Harper, C. N., & Johnson-Laird, P. N. (1999). Reasoning about necessity and possibility: A test of the mental model theory of deduction. *Journal of Experimental Psychology: Learning, Memory, & Cognition*, *25*, 1495–1513.

Evans, J. St. B. T., Handley, S. J., Neilens, H., & Over, D. (2010). The influence of cognitive ability and instructional set on causal conditional inference. *Quarterly Journal of Experimental Psychology*, *63*, 892–909.

Evans, J. St. B. T., Newstead, S. E., Allen, J. L., & Pollard, P. (1994). Debiasing by instruction: The case of belief bias. *European Journal of Cognitive Psychology*, *6*, 263–285.

Evans, J. St. B. T., Newstead, S. E., & Byrne, R. M. J. (1993). *Human reasoning: The psychology of deduction*. Hove, UK: Erlbaum.

Evans, J. St. B. T., & Over, D. E. (1996). *Rationality and reasoning*. Hove, UK: Psychology Press.

Evans, J. St. B. T., & Stanovich, K. E. (2013a). Dual-process theories of higher cognition: Advancing the debate. *Perspectives on Psychological Science*, *8*, 223–241.

Evans, J. St. B. T., & Stanovich, K. E. (2013b). Theory and metatheory in the study of dual processing: Reply to comments. *Perspectives on Psychological Science, 8*, 263–271.

Gilhooly, K. J., Logie, R. H., Wetherick, N. E., & Wynn, V. (1993). Working memory and strategies in syllogistic-reasoning tasks. *Memory & Cognition, 21*, 115–124.

Goel, V., & Dolan, R. J. (2003). Explaining modulation of reasoning by belief. *Cognition, 87*, B11–B22.

Handley, S. J., Newstead, S. E., & Trippas, D. (2011). Logic, beliefs, and instruction: A test of the default interventionist account of belief bias. *Journal of Experimental Psychology: Learning, Memory, & Cognition, 37*, 28–43.

Handley, S. J., & Trippas, D. (2015). Dual processes and the interplay between knowledge and structure: A new parallel processing model. *Psychology of Learning and Motivation, 62*, 33–58.

Houdé, O., Zago, L., Mellet, E., Moutier, S., Pineau, A., Mazoyer, B., & Tzourio-Mazoyer, N. (2000). Shifting from the perceptual brain to the logical brain: The neural impact of cognitive inhibition training. *Journal of Cognitive Neuroscience, 12*, 721–728.

Howarth, S., Handley, S. J., & Walsh, C. (2016). The logic-bias effect: The role of effortful processing in the resolution of belief–logic conflict. *Memory & Cognition, 44*, 330–349.

Kahneman, D. (2011). *Thinking, fast and slow*. New York, NY: Farrar, Straus and Giroux.

Klauer, K. C., & Kellen, D. (2011). Assessing the belief bias effect with ROCs: Reply to Dube, Rotello, and Heit (2010). *Psychological Review, 118*, 155–164.

Klauer, K. C., Musch, J., & Naumer, B. (2000). On belief bias in syllogistic reasoning. *Psychological Review, 107, 852*–884.

Klauer, K. C., & Singmann, H. (2013). Does logic feel good? Testing for intuitive detection of logicality in syllogistic reasoning. *Journal of Experimental Psychology: Learning, Memory, & Cognition, 39*, 1265–1273.

Luo, J., Liu, X., Stupple, E. J., Zhang, E., Xiao, X., Jia, L., Yang, Q., Li, H., & Zhang, Q. (2013). Cognitive control in belief-laden reasoning during conclusion processing: An ERP study. *International Journal of Psychology, 48*, 224–231.

Luo, J., Tang, X., Zhang, E., & Stupple, E. J. (2014). The neural correlates of belief-bias inhibition: The impact of logic training. *Biological Psychology, 103*, 276–282.

Macmillan, N. A., & Creelman, C. D. (2005). *Detection theory: A user's guide* (2nd ed.). Mahwah, NJ: Erlbaum.

Manktelow, K. I., Over, D. E., & Elqayam, S. (2011). Paradigm shift: Jonathan Evans and the science of reason. In K. I. Manktelow, D. E. Over, & S. Elqayam (Eds.), *The science of reason: A Festschrift for Jonathan St. B. T Evans* (pp. 1–16). Hove, UK: Psychology Press.

Markovits, H., Forgues, H. L., & Brunet, M.-L. (2012). More evidence for a dual-process model of conditional reasoning. *Memory & Cognition, 40*, 736–747.

Markovits, H., Venet, M., Janveau-Brennan, G., Malfait, N., Pion, N., & Vadeboncoeur, I. (1996). Reasoning in young children: Fantasy and information retrieval. *Child Development, 67*, 2857–2872.

Mercier, H., & Sperber, D. (2011). Why do humans reason? Arguments for an argumentative theory. *Behavioral & Brain Sciences, 34*, 57–74.

Mevel, K., Poirel, N., Rossi, S., Cassotti, M., Simon, G., Houdé, O., & De Neys, W. (2015). Bias detection: Response confidence evidence for conflict sensitivity in the ratio bias task. *Journal of Cognitive Psychology, 27*, 227–237.

Morsanyi, K., & Handley, S. J. (2012). Logic feels so good – I like it! Evidence for intuitive detection of logicality in syllogistic reasoning. *Journal of Experimental Psychology: Learning, Memory, & Cognition, 38*, 596–616.

Newman, I. R., Gibb, M., & Thompson, V. A. (2017). Rule-based reasoning is fast and belief-based reasoning can be slow: Challenging current explanations of belief-bias and base-rate neglect. *Journal of Experimental Psychology: Learning, Memory, & Cognition, 43*, 1154–1170.

Newstead, S. E., Handley, S. J., & Buck, E. (1999). Falsifying mental models: Testing the predictions of theories of syllogistic reasoning. *Memory & Cognition, 27*, 344–354.

Newstead, S. E., Pollard, P., Evans, J. St. B. T., & Allen, J. L. (1992). The source of belief bias effects in syllogistic reasoning. *Cognition, 45*, 257–284.

Oakhill, J., & Johnson-Laird, P. N. (1985). The effect of belief on the spontaneous production of syllogistic conclusions. *Quarterly Journal of Experimental Psychology, 37A*, 553–570.

Oakhill, J., Johnson-Laird, P. N., & Garnham, A. (1989). Believability and syllogistic reasoning. *Cognition, 31*, 117–140.

Oaksford, M., & Chater, N. (2013). Dynamic inference and everyday conditional reasoning in the new paradigm. *Thinking & Reasoning, 19*, 346–379.

Pennycook, G., Fugelsang, J. A., & Koehler, D. J. (2012). Are we good at detecting conflict during reasoning? *Cognition, 124*, 101–106.
Pennycook, G., Fugelsang, J. A., & Koehler, D. J. (2015). What makes us think? A three-stage dual-process model of analytic engagement. *Cognitive Psychology, 80*, 34–72.
Pennycook, G., Trippas, D., Handley, S. J., & Thompson, V. A. (2014). Base rates: Both neglected and intuitive. *Journal of Experimental Psychology: Learning, Memory, and Cognition, 40*, 544–554.
Prado, J., & Noveck, I. A. (2007). Overcoming perceptual features in logical reasoning: A parametric fMRI study. *Journal of Cognitive Neuroscience, 19*, 642–657.
Roberts, M. J., & Sykes, E. D. A (2003). Belief bias and relational reasoning. *Quarterly Journal of Experimental Psychology, 56A*, 131–154.
Sá, W. C., West, R. F., & Stanovich, K. E. (1999). The domain specificity and generality of belief bias: Searching for a generalizable critical thinking skill. *Journal of Educational Psychology, 91*, 497–510.
Sanfey, A. G., Rilling, J. K., Aronson, J. A., Nystrom, L. E., & Cohen, J. D. (2003). The neural basis of economic decision making in the ultimatum game. *Science, 300*, 1755–1758.
Santamaria, C., Garcia-Madruga, J. A., & Carretero, M. (1996). Beyond belief bias: Reasoning from conceptual structures by mental models manipulation. *Memory & Cognition, 24*, 250–261.
Shynkaruk, J. M., & Thompson, V. A. (2006). Confidence and accuracy in deductive reasoning. *Memory & Cognition, 34*, 619–632.
Sloman, S. A. (1996). The empirical case for two systems of reasoning. *Psychological Bulletin, 119*, 3–22.
Stanovich, K. E. (1999). Who is rational? *Studies of individual differences in reasoning.* Mahwah, NJ: Erlbaum.
Stanovich, K. E. (2011). *Rationality and the reflective mind.* New York, NY: Oxford University Press.
Stanovich, K. E. (2012). On the distinction between rationality and intelligence: Implications for understanding individual differences in reasoning. In K. J. Holyoak, & R. G. Morrison (Eds.), *The Oxford handbook of thinking and reasoning* (pp. 343–365). Oxford, UK: Oxford University Press.
Stanovich, K. E., & West, R. F. (1997). Reasoning independently of prior belief and individual differences in actively open-minded thinking. *Journal of Educational Psychology, 89*, 342.
Stanovich, K. E., & West, R. F. (2000). Individual differences in reasoning: Implications for the rationality debate. *Behavioral & Brain Sciences, 23*, 645–726.
Stanovich, K. E., & West, R. F. (2008). On the relative independence of thinking biases and cognitive ability. *Journal of Personality & Social Psychology, 94*, 672–695.
Stupple, E. J. N., & Ball, L. J. (2008). Belief–logic conflict resolution in syllogistic reasoning: Inspection-time evidence for a parallel process model. *Thinking & Reasoning, 14*, 168–189.
Stupple, E. J. N., Ball, L. J., Evans, J. St. B. T., & Kamal-Smith, E. (2011). When logic and belief collide: Individual differences in reasoning times support a selective processing model. *Journal of Cognitive Psychology, 23*, 931–941.
Stupple, E. J., Ball, L. J., & Ellis, D. (2013). Matching bias in syllogistic reasoning: Evidence for a dual-process account from response times and confidence ratings. *Thinking & Reasoning, 19*, 54–77.
Thompson, V. A. (1996). Reasoning from false premises: The role of soundness in making logical deductions. *Canadian Journal of Experimental Psychology, 50*, 315–319.
Thompson, V. A. (2013). Why it matters: The implications of autonomous processes for dual process theories – Commentary on Evans & Stanovich (2013). *Perspectives on Psychological Science, 8*, 253–256.
Thompson, V. A., & Evans, J. St. B. T. (2012). Belief bias in informal reasoning. *Thinking & Reasoning, 18*, 278–310.
Thompson, V. A., & Johnson, S. C. (2014). Conflict, metacognition, and analytic thinking. *Thinking & Reasoning, 20*, 215–244.
Thompson, V. A., Morley, N. J., & Newstead, S. E. (2011a). Methodological and theoretical issues in belief-bias: Implications for dual process theories. In K. I. Manktelow, D. E. Over, & S. Elqayam (Eds.), *The science of reason: A Festschrift for Jonathan St. B. T Evans* (pp. 309–338). Hove, UK: Psychology Press.
Thompson, V. A., Prowse Turner, J. A., & Pennycook, G. (2011b). Intuition, reason, and metacognition. *Cognitive Psychology, 63*, 107–140.
Thompson, V. A., Prowse Turner, J. A., Pennycook, G., Ball, L. J., Brack, H., Ophir, Y., & Ackerman, R. (2013). The role of answer fluency and perceptual fluency as metacognitive cues for initiating analytic thinking. *Cognition, 128*, 237–251.
Thompson, V. A., Striemer, C. L., Reikoff, R., Gunter, R. W., & Campbell, J. D. (2003). Syllogistic reasoning time: Disconfirmation disconfirmed. *Psychonomic Bulletin & Review, 10*, 184–189.

Toplak, M. E., West, R. F., & Stanovich, K. E. (2011). The cognitive reflection test as a predictor of performance on heuristics-and-biases tasks. *Memory & Cognition, 39*, 1275–1289.

Torrens, D., Thompson, V. A., & Cramer, K. M. (1999). Individual differences and the belief bias effect: Mental models, logical necessity, and abstract reasoning. *Thinking & Reasoning, 5*, 1–28.

Trippas, D., Handley, S. J., & Verde, M. F. (2013). The SDT model of belief bias: Complexity, time, and cognitive ability mediate the effects of believability. *Journal of Experimental Psychology. Learning, Memory, & Cognition, 39*, 1393–1402.

Trippas, D., Handley, S. J., & Verde, M. F. (2014a). Fluency and belief bias in deductive reasoning: New indices for old effects. *Frontiers in Psychology, 5*, No. 631.

Trippas, D., Handley, S. J., Verde, M. F., & Morsanyi, K. (2016). Logic brightens my day: Evidence for implicit sensitivity to logical validity. *Journal of Experimental Psychology: Learning, Memory, & Cognition, 42*, 1448–1457.

Trippas, D., Pennycook, G., Verde, M. F., & Handley, S. J. (2015). Better but still biased: Analytic cognitive style and belief bias. *Thinking & Reasoning, 21*, 431–445.

Trippas, D., Thompson, V. A., & Handley, S. J. (2017). When fast logic meets slow belief: Evidence for a parallel-processing model of belief bias. Memory & Cognition, *45,* 539–552.

Trippas, D., Verde, M. F., & Handley, S. J. (2014b). Using forced choice to test belief bias in syllogistic reasoning. *Cognition, 133*, 586–600.

Tsujii, T., & Watanabee, S. (2009). Neural correlates of dual-task effect on belief-bias syllogistic reasoning: A near-infrared spectroscopy study. *Brain Research, 1287*, 118–125.

Verschueren, N., Schaeken, W., & d'Ydewalle, G. (2005). A dual-process specification of causal conditional reasoning. *Thinking & Reasoning, 11*, 239–278.

Villejoubert, G. (2009). Are representativeness judgments automatic and rapid ? The effect of time pressure on the conjunction fallacy. In N. Taatgen, & H. van Rijn (Eds.), *Proceedings of the thirty-first annual conference of the cognitive science society* (pp. 2980–2985). Austin, TX: Cognitive Science Society.

Wilkins, M. C. (1929). The effect of changed material on ability to do formal syllogistic reasoning. *Archives of Psychology, 102*, No. 83.

3
INTUITIVE THINKING

Tilmann Betsch and Pablina Roth

Approaching the concept of intuition is a risky endeavor. Traps lurk everywhere and one is prone to be sniped at for disseminating misconceptions about intuitive thinking. Psychologists widely agree that intuition is a phenomenon of paramount importance characterized by distinct properties. Unfortunately, they also disagree about what those properties are. For example, the Take-The-Best heuristic (Gigerenzer & Goldstein, 1999; see also Hoffrage, Hafenbrädl, & Marewski, this volume) is a lexicographic rule of decision making that simply compares arguments or outcomes on the most important dimension while ignoring all the others. The option with the best value on this single dimension is chosen. Some researchers view this heuristic as an example of intuitive thinking (Gigerenzer, 2007). Others conceive such rules as shortcuts to deliberation (T. Betsch, 2008; Frederick, 2002) and show that children have difficulty learning these simple rules (Mata, von Helversen, & Rieskamp, 2011).

We do not see much merit in debating definitions. Instead, in this chapter we wish to illustrate the diversity of theoretical approaches and accompanying proposed processes subsumed under the concept of intuitive thought. This diversity emanates to a considerable extent from the selection of research paradigms and tasks. Specific task environments provide habitats for certain processes to reveal their power and, at the same time, obstruct the flourishing of others. Research habits may occasionally yield voodoo-correlations (Fiedler, 2011) but, at the same time, have important virtues. Tailoring tasks for processes allows us to gain insight into their functioning and power. It is our motivation to convince the reader that intuitive thinking is driven by a multitude of processes with strikingly diverse properties. We begin our illustration of diversity with an attribute list reflecting the well-known two-faculty view of the human mind that underlies most assumptions about intuitive thinking. In the second section, we show that sorting processes into faculties does not remedy the problem that intuitive processes sometimes differ strikingly from each other. We discuss two processes in more detail in the third section and argue that the diversity of processes should be acknowledged on a theoretical level. In the fourth section, we consider some topics much discussed in the literature, such as neural correlates of intuition, the accuracy of intuitive thought, and the role of learning and emotions. We close with a remark on the nature of intuition.

Attribute lists and a two-faculty view

Psychologists often come up with attribute lists to describe the concept of intuition (Winerman, 2005). Typically, these lists are presented as semantic differentials so that intuition is delimited from its alleged opposite, which is given different labels such as reflection, deliberation, or analysis. Attribute lists describing intuition and its counterpart vary strikingly with respect to the number of attributes, content, and precision. Although some attributes are jointly agreed upon by different scholars, the various lists hosted in the literature make no reference to one another and contain contradictory features (e.g., fallible vs. non-fallible; cf. Abernathy & Hamm, 1995 for an early review). To illustrate this problem, Table 3.1 presents an attribute list compiled from three contributions (Evans & Stanovich, 2013; Plessner, Betsch, & Betsch, 2008; special issue on intuition in *Psychological Inquiry*, Vol. 21, No. 4, 2010). The list is far from comprehensive and could have easily been extended if we considered a larger sample of papers. The content of Table 3.1 strongly reflects a phenomenological orientation. The sheer number of features results in a challenge to construct validity. Attribute lists seem to "replace mystery with mystery" (Hammond, 2010, p. 327) and make us "wonder whether the term [intuition] has any meaning at all" (Epstein, 2008, p. 23). Notwithstanding the diversity, attribute lists share the conceptual idea of contrasting intuition with a reflective opponent. This confrontation with intuition and its opponent is familiar to all of us. Sometimes insights, judgments, and decisions suddenly pop into our awareness, and we have no idea how it happened. Other times, we engage in effortful deliberation until we eventually solve a problem and make estimations or decisions under seemingly full conscious control.

Defining intuition in contrast to other types of thinking implies at least three specific assumptions about the faculties in our mind: (1) There is a determinable number of faculties, namely two (and not three, four, or an infinite number); (2) these faculties are discrete entities; and (3) the faculties are alternative ways of thinking. The two-faculty view is not necessarily justified by pure induction. It assimilates with a preconception that is deeply rooted in cultural traditions. The Kantian distinction between *a priori* knowledge and rational justification, the Freudian battle between the conscious and the unconscious, the layperson's affection for the close and cozy gut reaction that is so often believed to outperform the calculating mind – all of these conceptions still resonate in the psychological two-faculty approach to intuitive and non-intuitive thinking. However, it was not until the late 1970s that the two-faculty view began to proliferate in the literature (e.g., Schneider & Shiffrin, 1977; Shiffrin & Schneider, 1977). In subsequent decades, it became prominent and spread widely across various subfields of our discipline, from social psychology (Chaiken & Trope, 1999) to developmental psychology (Stanovich, West, & Toplak, 2011) to judgment and decision making (Evans, 2008; Gilovich, Griffin, & Kahneman, 2002; Kahneman, 2011) to personality psychology (C. Betsch, 2008; Epstein, Pacini, Denes-Raj, & Heier, 1996) and various areas of practical application (Furley, Schweizer, & Bertrams, 2015; Myers, 2010; Sadler-Smith, 2008; Sinclair, 2010).

Similarly to the diversity of intuitive processes, dual-process theories present a heterogeneous picture. There are various levels on which dual-process theories can be arranged according to specific criteria (Evans, 2008; Evans & Stanovich, 2013) – for example, in regard to terminology (e.g., minds, characters, brains, systems, modes), the degree of interplay between both faculties (e.g., independence, reciprocity, or default-interventionism), and classes of attributes associated with both faculties (e.g., role of consciousness, interpersonal difference, age of evolution). As an answer to the wide array of assumptions, Evans and Stanovich (2013, p. 225) provided a conceptual clean sweep. They separated ***defining*** features from correlates. Assuming that there are two qualitatively distinct processes, they define the (intuitive) Type 1 process as ***autonomous*** – that

Table 3.1 Attributes aligned with intuition in contrast to reasoning

Intuition		*Reasoning*	
fast	1, 2, 3, 4, 7, 9, 10	slow	1, 3, 4, 7, 10
parallel	1, 4, 10	serial	1, 4, 10
automatic	1, 3, 4, 5, 7, 9, 10	controlled, deliberative	1, 3, 4, 5, 7, 10
effortless	1, 4, 6, 10	effortful	1, 4, 6, 10
associative	1, 3, 4, 7, 10	rule-governed	1, 3, 4, 5, 7, 10
slow-learning	1, 3, 4	flexible	1, 3, 4
emotional/affective	1, 2, 3, 4	neutral	1, 3, 4
non-analytic	2	analytic	3, 5, 10
pattern recognition	2		
arises from symbolic rules	2		
non-symbolic	2		
functional reasoning	2		
lazy thinking	2		
unavoidable	2		
infallible	2		
fallible	2		
feeling of certainty, confidence	2, 5		
based on experience	2, 3, 7	logical learning	3
preconscious, non-conscious	3, 5, 6, 9	conscious	3, 5, 6
concrete	3	abstract	3, 7
holistic	3, 10		
hedonic principle	3	reality principle	3
outcome oriented	3	process oriented	3
crudely differentiated	3	highly differentiated	3
crudely integrated	3	highly integrated	3
experienced passively	3	experienced actively	3
self-evidently valid	3	requires justification	3
tacit	5		
reactive	5	proactive	5
implicit	5	explicit	5
approximate	5	precise	5
no need for working memory	7, 10	need for working memory	7, 10
autonomous	7	cognitive decoupling	7
		consequential decision making	7
based on small samples	8, 9		
efficient	9		

Key: 1 = Kahneman (2002), 2 = Abernathy & Hamm (1995), 3 = Epstein (2008), 4 = Myers (2010), 5 = Hogarth (2001), 6 = Sinclair (2010), 7 = Evans & Stanovich (2013), 8 = Fiedler & Kareev (2008), 9 = Ambady (2010), 10 = T. Betsch (2008)

is, it can function automatically without cognitive control. Moreover, it does ***not require working memory*** to operate. The (reflective) Type 2 process, in contrast, ***requires working memory***. It is capable of performing ***decoupling operations***, such as hypothetical thinking and actively separating representations. The authors claim that all the other labels and attributes carry with them "some semantic baggage" (p. 227) and are not necessary to define the two types of processes (see also Evans, this volume).

The diversity of intuitive processes

In this section we show that Type 1 processes have unique properties. Nonetheless, they can be assigned to the same type as Type 2 processes (see also Stanovich, 2004). It is far beyond the scope of this chapter to come up with a detailed description of all the processes, rules, and heuristics that are declared intuitive. In contrast to theoretically grounded systematizations of process characteristics of intuition (e.g., Glöckner & Witteman, 2009, 2010), we simply consider two aspects that relate to informational input. A broad classification suffices to achieve three goals. First, we seek to illustrate the diversity of processes that are subsumed by the term *intuition*. Second, we aim to show that this diversity evokes incoherent conceptions of intuition reflecting pronounced different assumptions regarding the capabilities of the human mind. Third, we wish to allude to the design of experimental paradigms and accompanied task selection as one cause for this diversity. Pre-conceptions of intuition drive the selection of task environments and research paradigms. For instance, the assumption that intuition tends to rest on one reason may direct the researcher's attention to situations in which samples of information are small due to, for instance, high costs of information access. In contrast, if one assumes that the power of intuition stems from its holistic character, which allows the integration of many pieces of information, one may focus on situations in which the given sample of information is large and costs to access information are low. For example, several heuristics described in the literature are assumed to exploit peripheral cues, proxies, or even irrelevant information. Not surprisingly, evidence of such heuristics is often sought in tasks in which relevant information is difficult to access. As a means to cluster the diverse intuitive processes, we consider two aspects of the stimulus environment in which the operation of a particular process is studied – information *quantity* and *quality*.

Quality refers to the state of information. We distinguish between *surrogate* and *primary* information. Primary information is commonly described in the literature as normatively relevant, central, on-target, and analytic. Ideally, validity is known and weights in the decision or judgment process can be determined. Primary pieces of information in a persuasion task, for example, are the given arguments that differ in terms of the strength to which they affect attitude change (Petty & Cacioppo, 1986). In decision tasks, described or experienced outcomes of the options differ in terms of value, while their weight is a function of the probability of their occurrence (e.g., Edwards, 1954) or goal-importance (e.g., von Winterfeld & Edwards, 1986). In probabilistic inference tasks, the cues (e.g., advice givers) differ with regard to their stated or learned validity, i.e. the probability that they predict an outcome (e.g., Bröder, 2003). In judgments of frequency of occurrence, primary information stems from on-target observations of the number of times that a particular stimulus (e.g., a name) is encountered during an encoding episode (e.g., Hasher & Zacks, 1984).

Surrogates are pieces of information that are usually described as non-analytic, off-target, remote, or peripheral. Their validity is volatile, unknown, or opaque to the actor at the time of judgment or decision making. In certain situations, surrogates are normatively invalid and lead to systematic biases in judgment and decisions. For example, the physical attractiveness of a communicator is an often considered surrogate in persuasion research (e.g., Chaiken, 1979). In risk assessment, individuals may neglect stated probabilities and instead use their affective reactions towards a threatening outcome to judge risk (Loewenstein, Weber, Hsee, & Welch, 2001; Slovic, Finucane, Peters, & McGregor, 2002). Advice takers may neglect validities of the advice and rely on their personal relation to the advice giver (Betsch, Lang, Lehmann, & Axmann, 2014). When judging frequency of a category, individuals can base their estimates on availability – the ease with which instances can be brought to mind (Tversky & Kahneman, 1973).

Note that quality of the stimulus input does *not* refer to performance. Surrogates can yield a high level of decision accuracy in some situations but not in others. Relying on recognition in emergency situations, for example, can yield decisions of high quality if the learned behavioral routines apply to the current situation (e.g., Klein, 1999). If the world has changed, however, so that learned behavioral rules have become obsolete, recognition-based decisions can lead to severely mal-adaptive behavior (Betsch et al., 2001). Relying on primary information can also decrease decision accuracy, for example, if the individual attempts to apply a complex analytic rule under situational constraints (e.g., Payne, Bettman, & Johnson, 1988). "Thinking too much" can decrease decision accuracy (Wilson & Schooler, 1991), for instance if extensive consideration of information causes dilution effects in integration (e.g., Anderson, 1971).

Quantity, or the size of the sample of information, can be a function of the environment, the process, or both. Some processes are capable of handling multiple pieces of information but can also process small samples. In decision research, evidence accumulation models (e.g., Busemeyer & Townsend, 1993, Lee & Cummins, 2004) and connectionist models (e.g., Glöckner & Betsch, 2008b; Simon & Holyoak, 2002) assume that a single process (or all-purpose rule) integrates information and selects a choice candidate. The process is normally assumed to operate automatically or intuitively (e.g., Betsch & Glöckner, 2010; Busemeyer & Townsend, 1993). Information input can vary in size dependent on the situation. In contrast, multiple strategy models (e.g., Beach & Mitchell, 1978; Gigerenzer, Todd, & the ABC Research Group, 1999; Payne, Bettman, & Johnson, 1993) propose that individuals have a toolbox of strategies, some utilizing large and others small samples of information (see Söllner & Bröder, 2016, for a critical empirical test between these two types of models). Especially under the umbrella of multiple strategy models, researchers impose constraints to the access of large samples in order to provide existence proofs of small-sample strategies.

Figure 3.1 shows four clusters of processes associated with intuition resulting from a cross tabulation of quality and quantity. The following sections describe exemplars of each cluster in more detail. All examples satisfy the defining criteria put forward by Evans and Stanovich (2013). They are described, for instance, as essentially effortless in terms of working memory load. They can function autonomously without cognitive control, although some strategies require repetition before they become automatic (cf. Kruglanski & Gigerenzer, 2011). Note again that it was not our decision whether a particular process was considered intuitive. We simply followed the authors and their suggestions regarding what represents an intuitive process.

Small samples of primary information

It is the backbone tenet of the bounded rationality approach (Simon, 1955) that individuals can cope with task complexity by applying low-effort strategies that minimize the size of the sample of information (Beach & Mitchell, 1978; Gigerenzer et al., 1999; Kahneman et al., 1982; Payne et al., 1993; Shah & Oppenheimer, 2008). In the most extreme case, low-effort strategies rely on just one reason. We already mentioned the lexicographic strategies (e.g., Fishburn, 1974) such as the Take-the-Best heuristic (Gigerenzer & Goldstein, 1999). A user of a lexicographic strategy inspects attributes or cues in the order of their importance (validity) until one is identified that differentiates between options. If the most important attribute differentiates, information search is stopped and a choice is made. For example, a consumer who is interested only in minimizing monetary costs could make a decision very quickly among dozens of detergents by choosing the least expensive product. In a similar vein, Fiedler and Kareev (2008, p. 150) state that "judgments and decisions are intuitive to the extent that they rest on small samples". Ambady's notion

– Withdrawal of conscious focus to access remote associations (Sinclair, 2010) – Representational change (Öllinger, Jones, Faber, & Knoblich, 2013) by chunk decomposition and constraint relaxation (Knoblich, Ohlsson, Haider, & Rhenius, 1999) – Information intrusion in multiple-cue decision making (Betsch et al., 2014; Söllner, Bröder, Glöckner, & Betsch, 2014) QUANTITY	Large sample of information – Spatial perception (Cheng, Shettleworth, Huttenlocher, & Rieser, 2007) – Categorization of motion (Troje, 2002) – Detection of irony (Gibbs & Colston, 2007) – Automatic information integration in decision making (Glöckner & Betsch, 2008a) – Frequency storage (Hasher & Zacks, 1979; Sedlmeier & Betsch, 2002) – Implicit attitude formation (Betsch et al., 2001) QUALITY
Surrogate information – Availability heuristic (Tversky & Kahneman, 1973) – Fluency heuristic (Schooler & Hertwig, 2005) – Representativeness heuristic (Tversky & Kahneman, 1982) – Feeling of rightness (Thompson, Prowse Turner, & Pennycook, 2011) – Affect heuristic (Finucane, Alhakami, Slovic & Johnson, 2000) – Judgments by attractiveness (Chaiken, 1979; Petty & Cacioppo, 1986) – Recognition heuristic (Goldstein & Gigerenzer, 2002)	Primary information – One reason decision making: e.g., lexicographic strategy (Fishburn, 1974), Take-the-Best heuristic (Gigerenzer & Goldstein, 1999) – Small sample strategies (Fiedler & Kareev, 2008) – Thin slice judgments (Ambady, 2010) – Peak-and-End heuristic (Kahneman, Fredrickson, Schreiber, & Redelmeier, 1993) Small sample of information

Figure 3.1 Examples of intuitive processes clustered by quantity and quality of information input

of thin slice judgments also aligns with this view (Ambady, 2010). Individuals are able to form (quite accurate) impressions about other people from brief observations ("thin slices") of their behavior. Kahneman and colleagues (Kahneman et al., 1993) have put forward a small-sample strategy for forming summary evaluations. According to the peak-and-end heuristic, evaluative judgments of past experiences reflect the average of the peak and the end of a sequence of values. Strategies relying on small samples may have to be learned (Mata et al., 2011) and solidified into a routine before they can be performed without conscious control (Gigerenzer, 2007; Kruglanski & Gigerenzer, 2011).

These examples of heuristics, rules, and strategies are usually studied in environments that provide primary information. Information can be presented to the participant by description such as monetary pay-offs of options in an information board (e.g., "Mouselab", Payne et al., 1988). In other paradigms, individuals make their decisions or judgments (e.g., assessment of discomfort during a medical exam) after having made pertinent experiences on their own (e.g., pain during a colonoscopy, Redelmeier & Kahneman, 1996). Fostering the use of small samples can be achieved by several means – for example, when one is required to complete memory-based rather than on-line tasks (Hastie & Park, 1986). In memory-based tasks, decreases in sample size are simply caused by a decrease in accessibility because, at the time of judgment, not all of the prior experiences can be explicitly remembered. As for a medical exam, Redelmeier and Kahneman (1996) argue that probably only the worst and the final, painful moments are remembered. These peaks and end experiences provide the input for the eponymous heuristic. In decision research, the information board is a widely applied tool to track information search and choice. For this purpose, the information contained in an option-by-attribute matrix is hidden. The individual must sequentially open cells in the matrix by using the computer mouse. An opened cell may close when another is inspected. Thus, sampling information is costly because it consumes time and memory resources. Manipulations, such as time pressure or monetary payments for information acquisition, impose additional constrains. Not surprisingly, adult decision makers adapt to such constraints by reducing the size of sampled information (see Glöckner & Betsch, 2008a,b, for discussions).

Small samples of surrogate information

Individuals can also apply small-sample strategies that rely on surrogates. They must do so if they lack access to primary information. At the foremost, research from the heuristics-and-biases program identified intuition as an omnivore when it comes to information intake. Representativeness (Tversky & Kahneman, 1982), feeling of rightness (Thompson et al., 2011), attractiveness of an information source (Petty & Cacioppo, 1986), affective reactions evoked by the issue under consideration (Finucane et al., 2000) – individuals exploit a plethora of non-analytic, off-target, remote, peripheral pieces of information when thinking intuitively. A famous example for a surrogate-strategy is the availability heuristic. It relies on a process feeling that is, how difficult it is to retrieve certain instances from memory or identify objects in a perceptual task. Tversky and Kahneman (1973) defined the availability heuristic as an intuitive device to estimate frequency or probability based on the ease with which instances come to mind. In a similar vein, the fluency heuristic (Schooler & Hertwig, 2005) uses the speed with which the event category itself is recognized or retrieved from memory (cf. also Jacoby & Dallas, 1981). Although proponents of the mutual approach stress differences (Hertwig, Herzog, Schooler, & Reimer, 2008), they spotlight a recursive capability of the human mind to use a by-product of thought as informational input.

Another important process is recognition, which is widely considered to be a key process of intuitive thought. With reference to chess experts, Herbert Simon stated: "the situation has provided a cue; this cue has given the expert access to information stored in memory, and the information provides the answer. Intuition is nothing more and nothing less than recognition" (Simon, 1992). In a similar vein, Klein (1999) proposes that most expert decisions are recognition-based. Goldstein and Gigerenzer (2002) put forward the recognition heuristic for probabilistic inference (see Hoffrage et al., this volume). Assume you ask a child in America: which city has the larger population, Detroit or Düsseldorf? One can consider good methods with which to infer city size, for example, whether the city is a state capital, has a professional soccer team in the premier league, and so on. American children, however, might know something about Detroit but may have never heard of Düsseldorf. This ignorance can turn out to be advantage. They could use recognition as a proxy for inferring city size and decide that Detroit is larger than Düsseldorf, which is actually true. For German children, it is likely the other way round. If they recognize Düsseldorf but not Detroit and judge size by recognition, their judgment would be incorrect. Thus, depending on the environment, recognition can be a valid or invalid cue for judgment criteria. Obviously, the prevalence of the recognition-based intuitions depends on the task. If the individual recognizes all or none of the eligible candidates, intuition cannot rely on the process of recognition. Hence, existence proofs for recognition-based judgments and decisions often stem from studies in which candidates differ only with regard to recognition (e.g., one city is recognized, whereas the other is not).

Large samples of primary information

Whereas simple heuristics are prominent in the judgment-and-decision-making literature, they are comparatively rare in other areas of cognition. Perception, categorization, speech comprehension – individuals regularly perform these and other fundamental cognitive tasks very quickly and without noticeable effort. The underlying operations can handle a vast amount of primary information without cognitive control and, hence, are widely considered to be autonomous or automatic.

Cheng and colleagues (2007) reviewed a large body of literature on the integration of spatial cues. The evidence on this topic is uncontroversial. Spatial perception/categorization is regularly based on multiple cues of different modalities (e.g., visual, audio, haptic). Individuals are capable of performing weighted integration procedures "in a near optimal fashion" (Cheng et al., 2007, p. 625) and without effortful and deliberative calculation (cf. also Hillis, Ernst, Banks, & Landy, 2002).

A fascinating example stems from the categorization of biological motion. Troje (2002) presented participants with point-light displays of walking figures. A variety of structural and dynamic cues were found to systematically direct categorization, among them arm swing amplitude and velocity, walking speed, lateral sway of upper body, and elbow-body distance. Viewers were intuitively capable of accurately identifying a walking pattern as male or female. Most notably, accuracy in gender classification drops to chance level when cues are eliminated – that is, when the information sample becomes smaller (e.g., Kozlowski & Cutting, 1977). Troje concludes that judgments are not a matter of a single feature but rather a "complex process with a holistic character" (Troje, 2002, p. 373) that corresponds to a weighted linear integration rule.

The literature on speech comprehension converges with the notion that individuals routinely integrate multiple pieces of information. For instance, adult recipients simultaneously utilize prosodic cues, mimic, gesture, and prior knowledge about the communicator to understand irony (see Gibbs & Colston, 2007, for overviews). This can happen in less than 600 to 800 milliseconds (e.g., Schwoebel, Dews, Winner, & Srinivas, 2000). Interestingly, *increasing* the amount of information (e.g., by providing contextual cues) can result in a *faster* detection of irony (Amenta & Balconi, 2008).

Human and non-human animals are remarkably good at registering the relative frequency of events (Sedlmeier & Betsch, 2002). Frequency encoding and storage is an implicit and automated process that neither requires motivation nor consumes cognitive resources in a noticeable fashion. Similar skills were observed in attitude formation. Individuals are capable of implicitly aggregating the values associated with successive encounters with an attitude object (Betsch, Hoffmann, Hoffrage, & Plessner, 2003; Betsch et al., 2001).

Evidence for intuitions based on large samples of primary information can also be found in the domain of judgment and decision making. Glöckner and Betsch (2008a) presented adult participants with two versions of an information board in a probabilistic choice task. The hidden presentation format was similar to the standard Mouselab (Payne et al., 1988), in which participants must uncover information (values, probabilities) by clicking on cells in the matrix with the computer mouse. In the open format, all information was displayed simultaneously and could be inspected by the individuals at once. This manipulation had a tremendous effect. With the classic version, individuals tended to employ simple strategies that reduced the effort of predecisional information search. Their decisions were informed by small samples of information. With the open board, however, the overwhelming majority of participants used all available information and employed weighted-additive-like integration procedures in an astoundingly narrow time frame. The authors propose a component approach for explaining decision making (Betsch & Glöckner, 2010; Glöckner & Betsch, 2008b). Accordingly, intuitive and deliberative processes interplay. The intuitive processes consider encoded information in a parallel fashion and function automatically and rapidly. They are formally described by a parallel-constraint satisfaction (PCS) rule that identifies a promising option by changing activations of nodes in a connectionist network that represents the decision problem at stake. Deliberate processes are necessary to control the formation of the network by active information search, determining and changing relations between information, suppressing irrelevant information, and subjecting the identified option to intentional processes of implementation (for example, performing motor operations to select an option via mouse-click on a computer screen). According to such a component approach, intuitive processes are always involved in decision making as a default to integrate information and detect a solution (cf. the default-interventionist view by Evans, 2008; Evans, this volume). As such, even decisions that are commonly considered to be "deliberate" (because the individual actively seeks information and becomes consciously aware of a final preference) involve intuitive processes.

In research on large sample processing, the paradigms and experimental settings vary strongly. Nevertheless, most of them share a common feature: information acquisition is largely unconstrained and encoding is easy. For example, Glöckner and Betsch (2008a) presented their participants with an open information board, relieving them of the need to sequentially open cells in the matrix and remember the contents. In multi-modality research on spatial categorization and speech comprehension, participants can perceive and encode simultaneously via different perceptual channels.

Large samples of surrogate information

In problem solving, the pieces of primary information provided are not sufficient to come up with a solution. The sample space must be enlarged. To this end, one must "go beyond the information given" (Bruner, 1957). Perceived stimuli activate prior knowledge (e.g., schemata), which in turn enables decision makers to associate meaning with the stimuli. Creative thinking and problem solving exploit the potentials of spreading activation in an associative network – a process genuinely non-intentional, autonomous, and capable of accessing remote knowledge (Gilhooly, Ball, & Macchi, 2015; see also Gilhooly, this volume; Runco, this volume). Additionally, the absence of cognitive control and conscious focus of attention appear to promote the access of new information as well as the combination of disparate, initially surrogate information in a new, original way (Sinclair, 2010). During this process, large samples of information are accessed to pave the way for an unexpected solution to appear. Several mechanisms can cause such "aha" experiences (Öllinger et al., 2013) as chunk decomposition and constraint relaxation (Knoblich et al., 1999). These mechanisms yield a change in representation, assign new meaning to elements of the problem, and open paths to new solutions. Intuitive problem solving is promoted by a good mood – a factor known to reduce the bottom-up scrutinization of stimuli (Bless & Fiedler, 1995; Bolte, Goschke, & Kuhl, 2003).

Some authors differentiate intuition from insight ("aha" experiences). For instance, Sadler-Smith (2010) stresses that insight is objective, clear, and easy to articulate, whereas intuitions are subjective, fuzzy, and difficult to articulate (for related views see Hogarth, 2010; Topolinski & Reber, 2010; see also Topolinski, this volume). Despite these phenomenological differences on the output level, the underlying processes of spreading activation, creating meaning, and figuring out a solution under constraints of other pieces of information still fit into the category of Type 1 processes. In the section above, we described the PCS rule. PCS processes are assumed to function autonomously and without cognitive control – even in situations in which the individual deliberatively searches information and explicitly intends to make a decision. According to a component view, conscious decisions (as insights) involve intuitive processes capable of handling large samples of information.

Intrusion effects in decision making provide an additional example evidencing this capability. Unfortunately, in this case, the power of intuitive processing can lead to biases. In intrusion paradigms, the individual is provided with primary information together with surrogate information that is normatively irrelevant. The consideration of the surrogates manifests itself in dilution effects or even decreased decision accuracy. Betsch and colleagues (2014) presented children and adults with choice tasks in which several probabilistic cues (advice givers) made outcome predictions. Prior to the choice tasks, one advice giver was announced as a personal friend (the "lure" information). In one condition, the information board was closed and predictions had to be sequentially opened, thus increasing the time needed to make a decision. In this condition, the lure had no effect on choices, neither in children nor in adults. In an open-board condition, in which decisions could be made very quickly (so that the intrusion of irrelevant information was more difficult to control), participants of all age groups were influenced by the lure. Specifically, if the lure was associated with the low-validity cue, the relative impact of the other cues (with higher validities) on decisions decreased. Söllner and colleagues (2014) trained participants to use a simple take-the-best (TTB) strategy when making probabilistic inference decisions in an information board paradigm. Although TTB led to optimal results in this decision environment, individuals were not able to ignore TTB-irrelevant information. If predictions of low validity cues opened "for free" on the computer screen, individuals altered their choices and showed varying confidence judgments contingent on the quality of the "irrelevant" information.

Research on insight and intrusion effects jointly indicates that intuitive thinking can make full use of the richness of memory and the stimulus environment. It can be profitable for the individual to extend information search and breach the boundaries of initial samples of primary information. Surrogates may provide trajectories to new combinations of information resulting in creative solutions. If invalid surrogates mingle with primary information, however, implicit aggregation can yield biases in judgment and decision making. The individual may control for such biases by attempting to inhibit the influence of surrogate information. However, control requires Type 2 processing, which consumes cognitive resources.

Acknowledging differences between intuitive processes

In Figure 3.1 we illustrated the diversity of processes considered to be intuitive by various theoretical approaches in psychology. Although they all conform to the definition of Type 1 processes, they appear to have different properties evidenced by the quantity and quality of information they use. This position, however, is controversial. Kruglanski (2013; see also Kruglanski & Gigerenzer, 2011) proposed a uni-model rather than a dual-model of thought. Accordingly, he does not consider Type 1 and Type 2 to be qualitatively distinct processes; consequently, his model denies differences between intuitive and rational processes. The uni-model conceptualizes all processes as rule-based. Within this framework, intuitive processes only differ with regard to the amount of deliberate activity involved in their operation, which can be projected on a continuum of cognitive effort and speed. Thus, according to the uni-model, intuitive thought reflects rules that have become automatic and, as a result, can be performed quickly and without conscious awareness.

We have doubts regarding the appropriateness of this approach because the model's assumptions neglect important facets of intuition. Consider, for example, the recognition heuristic. Goldstein and Gigerenzer (1999, 2002) view the recognition heuristic as an example *par excellence* of simple heuristics that rely on just one piece of information. Although recognition is an automatic process that is virtually unconstrained by working memory, it exploits the entire richness of our knowledge. To illustrate this point, consider how the process of recognition is modelled in memory research. Hintzman (1988) put forward MINERVA 2, a multiple trace model that accounts for a wide range of memory judgments including recognition. The model assumes that experience of each event creates a new trace in memory that can be formally described as a vector of features. If a judgment requires retrieval (such as recognition), a probe vector representing the stimulus is simultaneously compared with a huge sample of trace vectors in memory. The judgment criterion is a function of the degree of overlap between probe and aggregated trace vectors. According to the multiple trace approach, recognition reflects large samples of information accessed in parallel in long-term memory.

On the surface, the recognition heuristic can be described in rule-like terms such as, for instance, the Take-The-Best heuristic (cf. Gigerenzer, 2007, pp. 8 and 149). Nevertheless, their underlying processes are strikingly different (see also Thompson, 2013). Recognition is an innate process capability (see below). In contrast, lexicographic strategies comprise rules of search. Search, in turn, rests on executive functioning (e.g., focusing attention, inhibition) and planning – processes that require maturation and learning. These process capabilities are not fully developed until the age of 10 (Betsch, Lehmann, Lindow, Lang, & Schoemann, 2016; Mata et al., 2011). Recognition occurs autonomously and involuntarily. We cannot prevent ourselves from recognizing a stimulus. Lexicographic strategies require focus of attention and controlled inhibition of information that should not be considered by the rule. If decisions are made quickly or additional information becomes salient, automatic processes of integration cause an intrusion of irrelevant information into the decision process and so debauch the functioning of the strategy (Betsch et al., 2014; Söllner et al., 2014). Recognition rests on parallel processing of a huge amount of information. Otherwise, it could not be performed so quickly. Lexicographic strategies involve serial search processes, which are slow and consume memory resources. They capitalize on information neglect to speed up the process. The multiplicity of processes must be mirrored on the theoretical level. Treating all such processes alike (e.g., as rule-based) veils their emergent properties and alleviates precision in explanation and prediction.

Debates

Are there two brains?

The two faculty approach may suggest the assumption that intuitive and non-intuitive processes are located in different regions of the brain. Stanovich (2004), for example, described the (intuitive) System 1 as the "old mind" that evolved early. In contrast, the (reflective) System 2, the "new mind", evolved late in phylogenesis and continues to do so in human ontogenesis.

Accordingly, one might suspect that older regions of the brain, such as the limbic system, would operate by intuitive processes, whereas phylogenetically younger areas, such as the prefrontal cortex, would be responsible for reflective processing.

Empirical evidence from neuroimaging studies, however, clearly shows that intuitive judgment and decision making involves neural activation that is widespread across different areas of the human brain (e.g., Volz & von Cramon, 2008). Results do not indicate a common neural network for intuitive processing. Therefore, Evans and Stanovich (2013) decided to replace the term "system" with "type" in order to avoid misleading connotations. Kahneman put it nicely: "and of course [. . .] the two systems do not really exist in the brain or anywhere else" (Kahneman, 2011, p. 415). Nevertheless, intuitive processes may be accompanied by different *activation patterns* compared to those associated with reflective processing. Again, consider the case of understanding irony, which often happens very quickly. Wang and colleagues (2006) compared accuracy and speed in the identification of irony in average and clinical patients. In the latter, parallel activation of brain regions was impaired. Whereas average participants showed simultaneous activation of different brain regions and were quick to understand irony, clinical patients had to engage in time-consuming deliberative thought to grasp the ironic intention behind the message.

The role of learning

"There is almost universal agreement that [. . .] intuition is shaped by learning" (Hogarth, 2010, p. 343). What do we have to learn before we can form intuitions? Not every kind of knowledge is the product of the individual's own learning history. Seven-month-old infants are capable of inferring linguistic rules from speech (Marcus, Vijayan, Rao, & Vishton, 1999). Conditioning not only reflects contiguity and reinforcement schedules but is also determined by stimulus categories. For example, nausea is easily conditioned to the taste of food but not audiovisual stimuli (preparedness effect, Seligman, 1970). Accordingly, some knowledge structures appear to be innate, providing a phylogenetically acquired database for further learning and intuition.

Similarly, several processes underlying intuition do not require learning, such as recognition. Fortunately, individuals are endowed with this process capability from birth. For instance, three-day-old infants are able to recognize their mother's voice (DeCasper & Fifer, 1980). We cannot and need not further train the recognition process because of its automaticity and austerity of deliberate surveillance. Nevertheless, recognition capitalizes on learned knowledge. In routine behavior, we rely on a consolidated and rich source of knowledge that reflects intensive experience.

Gary Klein compiled numerous ethograms on what he called recognition-primed decisions in experts. One episode describes behavioral choices of a rescue team leader:

> The first decision facing Lieutenant M. is to diagnose the problem. As he ran to the man, even before listening to his wife, he made his diagnosis. He can see from the amount of blood that the man has cut open an artery, and from the dishcloths held against the man's arm he can tell which artery. Next comes the decision of how to treat the wound. In fact, there is nothing to deliberate over. As quickly as possible, Lieutenant M. applies firm pressure.
>
> (Klein, 1999, p. 3)

Obviously, Lieutenant M.'s decision capitalized on knowledge he has acquired during extensive training.

However, there are also processes that require learning and experience in order to function without effort and cognitive control. Betsch and colleagues (Betsch & Lang, 2013; Betsch et al., 2014, 2016) studied probabilistic inference decisions in children with an information board in which predictions of outcomes have to be actively inspected by opening doors in a cue-by-option matrix. The children's task was to find treasures in houses (options). They chose a house based on predictions of three animals that differed with regard to the probability that they correctly predicted whether or not a house contained a treasure. The probability structure was non-compensatory; that is, it invited the application of simple lexicographic strategies. Specifically, it was sufficient to inspect only the prediction of the animal with the highest predictive validity and follow this prediction to maximize the amount of treasures in a series of decision trials. Prior to decision making, children learned the validities of the animals by experience. Results from a series of experiments reliably showed that a substantial proportion of nine-year-olds used probabilities as decision weights in their choices. However, probability weighting did not transfer to information search. Although children effectively limited the number of inspected predictions under varying context factors (increase in probability dispersion, instructions to limit search), they were unable to employ a simple lexicographic strategy (Betsch et al., 2016). None of the children systematically focused on the predictions of the best cue. The likelihood that a certain prediction was considered was completely random. Mata and colleagues (2011) report a similar reluctance to apply simple strategies in even older children (10- to 11-year-olds) – a phenomenon that these authors nicely described as "when easy comes hard". This difference between children and adults shows that some intuitive processes require maturation and learning until they can be implemented effectively.

There are numerous studies on the use of such small-sample strategies that use primary information (e.g., Beach & Mitchell, 1978; Payne et al., 1988, 1993; Newell & Shanks, 2003). After being acquainted with the information presentation format, adults can apply search strategies in information boards in a quite routinized fashion (Bröder & Schiffer, 2006; Rieskamp & Otto, 2006). Note, however, that information in this paradigm is given and not retrieved from memory. Thus, there are good reasons to assume that the application of intuitive strategies can also deal with new information, even in domains in which the individuals lack expertise.

The role of feelings

Intuition is often regarded to be wedded with feelings (e.g., T. Betsch, 2008; Epstein, 2008; Gilovich et al., 2002; Slovic et al., 2002; see also Topolinski, this volume). Heuristics exploit feelings of risk, preference, liking, knowing, familiarity, fluency, and others as judgmental proxies. Feelings arise involuntarily and break into consciousness (Wundt, 1907; Zajonc, 1968, 1980). They may serve as communication devices within the organism (e.g., Simon, 1967). As an output of implicit processes, they can be used as a basis for a wide range of intuitive judgments and decisions. However, are all of these feelings real? Presumably, evidence from self-report is of dubious validity. Intuitive processes are opaque and cannot be accessed by introspection. Lacking facts to communicate, individuals may be tempted to describe their internal reactions in terms of feelings; surely it is possible to describe all sorts of experiences in this specific way. The distinction between emotional (e.g., risks as a negative affect) and non-emotional feelings (e.g., the feeling of knowing, Hart, 1965), renders the construct even more fuzzy. Especially if cognition and affect converge in meaning and behavioral inclinations, it is a purely semantic game to distinguish feelings from cognitions.

If feelings play a genuine role in intuition, we must precisely define their emergent properties and support those with empirical level. Affective reactions, for example, manifest themselves in physiological changes. Accordingly, intuitions that use affective reactions towards a stimulus as a basis for judgment (e.g., affect as information, Schwarz & Clore, 1983; affect heuristic, Slovic et al., 2002) should be accompanied by changes in peripheral physiological reactions such as heart rate and galvanic skin response. To determine whether it is truly affect on which the individual relies, changes in the physiological pattern should covary with judgments and decisions. In evaluating the risk-as-feelings hypothesis, Loewenstein and colleagues (2001) collected empirical evidence for this notion based on a comprehensive review of psychological, physiological, and neuropsychological studies. For instance, when the connections between the prefrontal cortices and the limbic system are impaired (e.g., due to permanent tissue injury by stroke), patients lack access to the affective input during decision making. Lacking access to such "somatic markers" (Damasio, 1994) increases risk taking compared to non-clinical controls (Bechara, Damasio, Tranel, & Damasio, 1997; but see Loewenstein et al., 2001, p. 273, for a critical discussion). Schwarz and Clore (1983) applied a misattribution paradigm from emotion research and showed that the availability heuristic was not applied when the feeling of ease or difficulty could be attributed to an external source.

These examples show that feelings can play an emergent role in intuition. It is important to note that feelings are not necessarily always involved in intuitive judgments and decisions. For example, heuristics using small samples of central information do not make the assumption that feelings must be involved.

Good and bad intuitions

Some individuals trust intuition more than deliberation. Others mistrust intuition and prefer to think carefully before they make a decision (C. Betsch, 2008; Betsch & Kunz, 2008). Are intuitions good or bad? Granting empirical evidence, the answer is straightforward: it depends! Sometimes intuitions produce serious shortcomings compared to normative standards (Nisbett & Ross, 1980; Kahneman et al., 1982). In other situations, shortcut heuristics can even outperform formal rules (Gigerenzer et al., 1999; see also Hoffrage et al., this volume). Dijksterhuis (2004) postulated that unconscious thought leads to better decisions in complex tasks. In contrast, conscious thinking should increase performance in simple tasks consisting of small samples of information (for critical discussions and counter-evidence, cf. Acker, 2008; Payne, Samper, Bettman, & Luce, 2008).

A more fine-grained approach assumes that specific heuristics are tailored to specific environmental structures (Gigerenzer et al., 1999) or cognitive niches (Marewski & Schooler, 2011). For instance, Goldstein and Gigerenzer (2002) propose that the recognition heuristic has evolved for and is primarily used in situations in which recognition is correlated with the judgment criterion. Consequently, intuition will drop in accuracy or may even lead to mal-adaptive performance if there is a mismatch between the process and situation.

The output quality resulting from any thinking process is also contingent upon the quality of the information input. Fiedler demonstrated that even an ideal calculating device (a computer) can produce biases similar to those observed in humans when the stimulus matrix is noisy (Fiedler, 1996) or the sample itself is biased due to proximity, salience, or attentional focus (Fiedler, 2000; Fiedler, Brinkmann, Betsch, & Wild, 2000). At worst, the information itself is false. For instance, in judging other people, our intuitions can reflect personal schemata regarding the target's group membership. Such stereotypes sometimes contain a kernel of truth but can also reflect mere prejudice. For example, it may be true that Germans lack a sense of humor but it is definitely wrong to assume that their favorite dish is sauerkraut (in fact, it is pizza).

Changes in the world are responsible for a substantial portion of errors in intuitive decisions. For example, experts' intuitions exploit consolidated prior experience. If the contingency structure in the environment changes, the knowledge base is no longer representative for the task. Under such conditions, inertia effects are likely to occur, yielding maladaptive outcomes (Betsch & Haberstroh, 2005, for an overview). Interestingly, such routine effects can even occur counter to the intention to quit a maladaptive course of action. This is likely to happen when situational factors such as time pressure foster intuitive thinking in decision making (Betsch, Haberstroh, Molter, & Glöckner, 2004).

The nature of intuition

The nature of intuitive thoughts is subject to persistent dispute among psychologists and researchers in other disciplines. The various views on intuition strongly reflect the beholder's background and lead to the sense that one is studying a mysterious creature. Expertise researchers emphasize learning and recognition; proponents of the bounded rationality approach equate intuition with shortcut heuristics; and neural networkers claim the very opposite: that intuition builds on holistic processes unbound by capacity constraints. Some scholars see affect as a constitutive feature of intuition; others as an epi-phenomenon. Some of the proposed processes utilize primary information; others use surrogate information. Some handle large samples very quickly; others rely on just one piece of information. All these features associated with intuition may simply reflect different facets of the potentials of the human mind. While illuminating these diverse facets, it should have become evident that it is impossible to come up with a satisfying integrative conceptualization of the nature of intuition. It is not helpful to add another list of attributes to the literature. Eclectic attempts exist often enough. Though pretending to be integrative, they yield conceptual dilution and confusion. Clear-cut definitions, and they do exist in the literature, are possible only if one systematically ignores findings outside one's own research camp. Neither of the two alternatives is acceptable from an epistemological point of view.

In conclusion, we make the case for taking the plethora of findings on intuitive thought seriously. Skimming results from various domains of cognitive research, such as perception, categorization, speech comprehension, judgment, decision making, and problem solving, we must acknowledge the virtuosity with which our minds can handle a variety of tasks without apparent effort and conscious control.

In this chapter we showed that individuals can apply different processes when thinking intuitively. We suggest that researchers should focus on the *sublevel of core processes of intuition* rather than ruminating about categorizations on the superordinate level. With core processes, we do not refer to heuristics or strategies. The latter are compounds of the former. Recognition is surely one of these core processes and a mighty one at that. Others, such as implicit aggregation (forming representations of key variables such as frequency and value) and an all-purpose device for integrating stimuli (in spatial perception, speech, decision making), probably add to this list. We believe that the number of core processes is limited because they are not domain specific, do not have to be learned, and apply to diverse environments. Through lifetime learning, they may be combined with strategies that help obtain mastery in specific situations. Learning can eventually result in strategy routines that can be performed automatically just as in the case of the core processes right from birth. Becoming curious about the fascinating process diversity may encourage us to zoom deeper into the cosmos of intuitive thinking. Hopefully, this approach will evoke new questions and a striving for future research designs capable of tracing the interaction of different processes. With a more fine-grained view, we might overcome the futile debate regarding what intuition really is.

References

Abernathy, C. M., & Hamm, R. M. (1995). ***Surgical intuition: What it is and how to get it.*** Philadelphia: Hanley & Belfus.

Acker, F. (2008). New findings on unconscious versus conscious thought in decision making: Additional empirical data and meta-analysis. ***Judgment and Decision Making***, *3*, 292–303.

Ambady, N. (2010). The perils of pondering: Intuition and thin slice judgments. ***Psychological Inquiry***, *21*, 271–278.

Amenta, S., & Balconi, M. (2008). Understanding irony: An ERP analysis on the elaboration of acoustic ironic statements. *Neuropsychological Trends*, *3*, 7–27.

Anderson, N. H. (1971). Integration theory and attitude change. *Psychological Review*, *78*, 171–206.

Beach, L. R., & Mitchell, T. R. (1978). A contingency model for the selection of decision strategies. *Academy Management Review*, *3*, 439–449.

Bechara, A., Damasio, H., Tranel, D., & Damasio, A. R. (1997). Deciding advantageously before knowing the advantageous strategy. *Science*, *275*, 1293–1295.

Betsch, C. (2008). Chronic preferences for intuition and deliberation in decision making: Lessons learned about intuition from an individual differences approach. In H. Plessner, C. Betsch, & T. Betsch (Eds.), ***Intuition in judgment and decision making*** (pp. 231–248). Mahwah, NJ: Lawrence Erlbaum Associates.

Betsch, C., & Kunz, J. J. (2008). Individual strategy preferences and decisional fit. ***Journal of Behavioral Decision Making***, *21*, 532–555.

Betsch, T. (2008). The nature of intuition and its neglect in research on judgment and decision making. In H. Plessner, C. Betsch, & T. Betsch (Eds.), ***Intuition in judgment and decision making*** (pp. 3–22). New York, NY: Lawrence Erlbaum Associates.

Betsch, T., & Glöckner, A. (2010). Intuition in judgment and decision making: Extensive thinking without effort. ***Psychological Inquiry***, *21*, 279–294.

Betsch, T., & Haberstroh, S. (Eds.). (2005). ***The routines of decision making.*** Mahwah, NJ: Lawrence Erlbaum Associates.

Betsch, T., Haberstroh, S., Molter, B., & Glöckner, A. (2004). Oops, I did it again – relapse errors in routinized decision making. ***Organizational Behavior and Human Decision Processes***, *93*, 62–74.

Betsch, T., Hoffmann, K., Hoffrage, U., & Plessner, H. (2003). Intuition beyond recognition: When less familiar events are liked more. ***Experimental Psychology***, *50*, 49–54.

Betsch, T., & Lang, A. (2013). Utilization of probabilistic cues in the presence of irrelevant information: A comparison of risky choice in children and adults. ***Journal of Experimental Child Psychology***, *115*, 108–125.

Betsch, T., Lang, A., Lehmann, A., & Axmann, J. M. (2014). Utilizing probabilities as decision weights in closed and open information boards: A comparison of children and adults. *Acta Psychologica*, *153*, 74–86.

Betsch, T., Lehmann, A., Lindow, S., Lang, A., & Schoemann, M. (2016). Lost in search: (Mal-) Adaptation to probabilistic decision environments in children and adults. ***Developmental Psychology***, *52*, 311–325.

Betsch, T., Plessner, H., Schwieren, C., & Gütig, R. (2001). I like it but I don't know why: A value-account approach to implicit attitude formation. ***Personality and Social Psychology Bulletin***, *27*, 242–253.

Bless, H., & Fiedler, K. (1995). Affective states and the influence of activated general knowledge. ***Personality and Social Psychology Bulletin***, *21*, 766–778.

Bolte, A., Goschke, T., & Kuhl, J. (2003). Emotion and intuition: Effects of positive and negative mood on implicit judgments of semantic coherence. ***Psychological Science***, *14*, 416–421.

Bröder, A. (2003). Decision making with the "adaptive toolbox": Influence of environmental structure, intelligence, and working memory load. ***Journal of Experimental Psychology: Learning, Memory, & Cognition***, *29*, 611–625.

Bröder, A., & Schiffer, S. (2006). Adaptive flexibility and maladaptive routines in selecting fast and frugal decision strategies. ***Journal of Experimental Psychology: Learning, Memory, and Cognition***, *32*, 904–918.

Bruner, J. S. (1957). Going beyond the information given. ***Contemporary Approaches to Cognition***, *1*, 119–160.

Busemeyer, J. R., & Townsend, J. T. (1993). Decision field theory: A dynamic-cognitive approach to decision making in an uncertain environment. *Psychological Review*, *100*, 432–459.

Chaiken, S. (1979). Communicator physical attractiveness and persuasion. ***Journal of Personality and Social Psychology***, *37*, 1387–1397.

Chaiken, S., & Trope, Y. (1999). *Dual-process theories in social psychology*. New York: Guilford Press.

Cheng, K., Shettleworth, S. J., Huttenlocher, J., & Rieser, J. J. (2007). Bayesian integration of spatial information. *Psychological Bulletin*, *133*, 625–637.

Damasio, A. R. (1994). *Descartes' Error: **Emotion, reason, and the human brain.*** New York: Putnam Publishing.
DeCasper, A. J., & Fifer, W. P. (1980). Of human bonding: Newborns prefer their mothers' voices. *Science, 208*, 1174–1176.
Dijksterhuis, A. (2004). Think different: The merits of unconscious though in preference development and decision making. *Journal of Personality and Social Psychology, 87*, 586–598.
Edwards, W. (1954). The theory of decision making. *Psychological Bulletin, 51*, 380–417.
Epstein, S. (2008). Intuition from the perspective of cognitive-experiential self-theory. In H. Plessner, C. Betsch, T. Betsch, H. Plessner, C. Betsch, & T. Betsch (Eds.), ***Intuition in judgment and decision making*** (pp. 23–37). Mahwah, NJ: Lawrence Erlbaum Associates.
Epstein, S., Pacini, R., Denes-Raj, V., & Heier, H. (1996). Individual differences in intuitive experiential and analytical rational thinking styles. *Journal of Personality and Social Psychology, 71*, 390–405.
Evans, J. St. B. T. (2008). Dual-processing accounts of reasoning, judgment, and social cognition. *Annual Review of Psychology, 59*, 255–278.
Evans, J. St. B. T., & Stanovich, K. E. (2013). Dual-process theories of higher cognition: Advancing the debate. *Perspectives on Psychological Science, 8*, 223–241.
Fiedler, K. (1996). Explaining and simulating judgment biases as an aggregation phenomenon in probabilistic, multiple-cue environments. *Psychological Review, 103*, 193–214.
Fiedler, K. (2000). Beware of samples! A cognitive-ecological sampling approach to judgment biases. *Psychological Review, 107*, 659–676.
Fiedler, K. (2011). Voodoo correlations are everywhere – Not only in neuroscience. *Perspectives On Psychological Science, 6*, 163–171.
Fiedler, K., Brinkmann, B., Betsch, T., & Wild, B. (2000). A sampling approach to biases in conditional probability judgments: Beyond base rate neglect and statistical format. *Journal of Experimental Psychology: General, 129*, 399–418.
Fiedler, K., & Kareev, Y. (2008). Implications and ramifications of a sample-size approach to intuition. In H. Plessner, C. Betsch, & T. Betsch (Eds.), ***Intuition in judgment and decision making*** (pp. 149–172). Mahwah, NJ: Lawrence Erlbaum Associates.
Finucane, M. L., Alhakami, A., Slovic, P., & Johnson, S. M. (2000). The affect heuristic in judgments of risks and benefits. *Journal of Behavioral Decision Making, 13*, 1–17.
Fishburn, P. C. (1974). Lexicographic orders, utilities, and decision rules: A survey. *Management Science, 20*, 1442–1472.
Frederick, S. (2002). Automated choice heuristics. In T. Gilovich, D. Griffin, & D. Kahneman (Eds.), *Heuristics & biases: The psychology of intuitive judgment* (pp. 548–558). New York: Cambridge University Press.
Furley, P., Schweizer, G., & Bertrams, A. (2015). The two modes of an athlete: dual-process theories in the field of sport. *International Review of Sport and Exercise Psychology, 8*, 1–19.
Gibbs, R. W., & Colston, H. L. (Eds.). (2007). ***Irony in language and thought: A cognitive science reader.*** Hillsdale, NJ: Lawrence Erlbaum Associates.
Gigerenzer, G. (2007). ***Gut feelings: The intelligence of the unconscious.*** New York: Viking Press.
Gigerenzer, G., & Goldstein, D. G. (1999). Betting on one good reason: The take the best heuristic. In G. Gigerenzer, P. M. Todd, & the ABC Research Group (Eds.), *Simple heuristics that make us smart* (pp. 75–95). Oxford: Oxford University Press.
Gigerenzer, G., Todd, P. M., & the ABC Research Group. (1999). *Simple heuristics that make us smart.* Oxford: Oxford University Press.
Gilhooly, K. J., Ball, L. J., & Macchi, L. (2015). Insight and creative thinking processes: Routine and special. *Thinking & Reasoning, 21*, 1–4.
Gilovich, T., Griffin, D., & Kahneman, D. (Eds.). (2002) *Heuristics and biases: The psychology of intuitive judgment.* Cambridge: Cambridge University Press.
Glöckner, A., & Betsch, T. (2008a). Multiple-reason decision making based on automatic processing. *Journal of Experimental Psychology: Learning, Memory and Cognition, 34*, 1055–1075.
Glöckner, A., & Betsch, T. (2008b). Modeling option and strategy choices with connectionist networks: Towards an integrative model of automatic and deliberate decision making. *Judgment and Decision Making, 3*, 215–228.
Glöckner, A., & Witteman, C. L. M. (Eds.). (2009) ***Foundations of tracing intuition: Challenges and methods.*** London: Psychology Press.
Glöckner, A., & Witteman, C. L. M. (2010). Beyond dual-process models: A categorization of processes underlying intuitive judgment and decision making. *Thinking & Reasoning, 16*, 1–25.

Goldstein, D. G., & Gigerenzer, G. (1999). The recognition heuristic: How ignorance makes us smart. In G. Gigerenzer, P. M. Todd, & the ABC Research Group (Eds.), *Simple heuristics that make us smart* (pp. 37–58). New York: Oxford University Press.

Goldstein, D. G., & Gigerenzer, G. (2002). Models of ecological rationality: The recognition heuristic. *Psychological Review, 109*, 75–90.

Hammond, K. R. (2010). Intuition, no! . . . Quasirationality, yes! *Psychological Inquiry, 21*, 327–337.

Hart, J. T. (1965). Memory and the feeling-of-knowing experience. *Journal of Educational Psychology, 56*, 208–216.

Hasher, L., & Zacks, R. T. (1979). Automatic and effortful processes in memory. *Journal of Experimental Psychology: General, 108*, 356–388.

Hasher, L, & Zacks, R.T. (1984). Automatic processing of fundamental information: The case of frequency of occurrence. *American Psychologist, 12*, 1372–1388.

Hastie, R., & Park, B. (1986). The relationship between memory and judgment depends on whether the judgment task is memory-based or on-line. *Psychological Review, 93*, 258–268.

Hertwig, R., Herzog, S. M., Schooler, L. J., & Reimer, T. (2008). Fluency heuristic: A model of how the mind exploits a by-product of information retrieval. *Journal of Experimental Psychology: Learning, Memory, and Cognition, 34*, 1191–1206.

Hillis, J. M., Ernst, M. O., Banks, M. S., & Landy, M. S. (2002). Combining sensory information: Mandatory fusion within, but not between, senses. *Science, 298*, 1627–1630.

Hintzman, D. L. (1988). Judgments of frequency and recognition memory in a multiple-trace memory model. *Psycholgoical Review, 95*, 528–551.

Hogarth, R. M. (2001). *Educating intuition.* Chicago: University of Chicago Press.

Hogarth, R. M. (2010). Intuition: A challenge for psychological research on decision making. *Psychological Inquiry, 21*, 338–353.

Jacoby, L. L., & Dallas, M. (1981). On the relationship between autobiographical memory and perceptual learning. *Journal of Experimental Psychology: General, 110*, 306–340.

Kahneman, D. (2002). *Maps of bounded rationality: A perspective on intuitive judgment and choice.* Princeton: manuscript of the Nobel price lecture.

Kahneman, D. (2011). *Thinking, fast and slow.* New York, NY: Farrar, Straus and Giroux.

Kahneman, D., Fredrickson, B. L., Schreiber, C. A., & Redelmeier, D. A. (1993). When more pain is preferred to less: Adding a better end. *Psychological Science, 4*, 401–405.

Kahneman, D., Slovic, P., & Tversky, A. (1982). *Judgment under uncertainty: Heuristics and biases.* Cambridge: Cambridge University Press.

Klein, G. (1999). *Sources of power. How people make decisions.* Cambridge, MA: MIT Press.

Knoblich, G., Ohlsson, S., Haider, H., & Rhenius, D. (1999). Constraint relaxation and chunk decomposition in insight problem solving. *Journal of Experimental Psychology: Learning, Memory, and Cognition, 25*, 1534–1555.

Kozlowski, L. T., & Cutting, J. E. (1977). Recognizing the sex of a walker from a dynamic point-light display. *Perception & Psychophysics, 21*, 575–580.

Kruglanski, A. W. (2013). Only one? The default interventionist perspective as a unimodel – Commentary on Evans & Stanovich. *Perspectives on Psychological Science, 8*, 242–247.

Kruglanski, A. W., & Gigerenzer, G. (2011). Intuitive and deliberate judgments are based on common principles. *Psychological Review, 118*, 97–109.

Lee, M. D., & Cummins, T. R. (2004). Evidence accumulation in decision making: Unifying the 'take the best' and the 'rational' models. *Psychonomic Bulletin & Review, 11*, 343–352.

Loewenstein, G. F., Weber, E. U., Hsee, C. K., & Welch, N. (2001). Risk as feelings. *Psychological Bulletin, 127*, 267–286.

Marcus, G. F., Vijayan, S., Rao, S. B., & Vishton, P. M. (1999). Rule learning by seven-month-old infants. *Science, 283*, 77–80.

Marewski, J. N., & Schooler, L. J. (2011). Cognitive niches: An ecological model of strategy selection. *Psychological Review, 118*, 393–437.

Mata, R., von Helversen, B., & Rieskamp, J. (2011). When easy comes hard: The development of adaptive strategy selection. *Child Development, 82*, 687–700.

Myers, D. G. (2010). Intuition's powers and perils. *Psychological Inquiry, 21*, 371–377.

Newell, B. R., & Shanks, D. R. (2003). Take the best or look at the rest? Factors influencing "one-reason" decision making. *Journal of Experimental Psychology: Learning, Memory and Cognition, 29*, 53–65.

Nisbett, R. E., & Ross, L. (1980). ***Human inference and shortcoming of social judgment.*** Englewood-Cliffs, NJ: Prentice-Hall.
Öllinger, M., Jones, G., Faber, A. H., & Knoblich, G. (2013). Cognitive mechanisms of insight: The role of heuristics and representational change in solving the eight-coin problem. *Journal of Experimental Psychology: Learning, Memory, and Cognition, 39,* 931–939.
Payne, J. W., Bettman, J. R., & Johnson, E. J. (1988). Adaptive strategy selection in decision making. *Journal of Experimental Psychology: Learning, Memory and Cognition, 14,* 534–552.
Payne, J. W., Bettman, J. R., & Johnson, E. J. (1993). *The adaptive decision maker.* Cambridge: Cambridge University Press.
Payne, J. W., Samper, A., Bettman, J. R., & Luce, M. F. (2008). Boundary conditions on unconscious thought in complex decision making. *Psychological Science, 19,* 1118–1123.
Petty, R., & Cacioppo, J. (1986). *Communication and persuasion: Central and peripheral routes to attitude change.* New York: Springer.
Plessner, H., Betsch, C., & Betsch, T. (Eds.). (2008) ***Intuition in judgment and decision making.*** New York: Lawrence Erlbaum Associates.
Redelmeier, D. A., & Kahneman, D. (1996). Patient's memories of painful medical treatments: Real-time and retrospective evaluations of two minimally invasive procedures. *Paine, 66,* 3–8.
Rieskamp, J., & Otto, P. E. (2006). SSL: A theory of how people learn to select strategies. *Journal of Experimental Psychology: General, 135,* 207–236.
Sadler-Smith, E. (2008). ***Inside intuition.*** New York: Routledge/Taylor & Francis Group.
Sadler-Smith, E. (2010). ***The intuitive mind: Profiting from the power of your sixth sense.*** Chichester, UK: Wiley.
Schneider, W., & Shiffrin, R. M. (1977). Controlled and automatic human information processing: I. Detection, Search, and Attention. *Psychological Review, 84,* 1–65.
Schooler, L. J., & Hertwig, R. (2005). How forgetting aids heuristic inference. *Psychological Review, 112,* 610–628.
Schwarz, N., & Clore, G. L. (1983). Mood, misattribution, and judgments of well-being: Informative and directive functions of affective states. *Journal of Personality and Social Psychology, 45,* 513–523.
Schwoebel, J., Dews, S., Winner, E., & Srinivas, K. (2000). Obligatory processing of the literal meaning of ironic utterances: Further evidence. *Metaphor and Symbol, 15,* 47–61.
Sedlmeier, P., & Betsch, T. (2002). *Etc.: Frequency processing and cognition.* Oxford: Oxford University Press.
Seligman, M. E. (1970). On the generality of the laws of learning. *Psychological Review,* 77, 406–418.
Shah, A. K., & Oppenheimer, D. M. (2008). Heuristics made easy: An effort-reduction framework. *Psychological Bulletin, 134,* 207–222.
Shiffrin, R. M., & Schneider, W. (1977). Controlled and automatic human information processing: II. Perceptual learning, automatic attending, and general theory. *Psychological Review, 84,* 127–190.
Simon, D., & Holyoak, K. J. (2002). Structural dynamics of cognition: From consistency theories to constraint satisfaction. *Personality and Social Psychology Review, 6,* 283–294.
Simon, H. A. (1955). A behavioral model of rational choice. *Quarterly Journal of Economics, 69,* 99–118.
Simon, H. A. (1967). Motivational and emotional controls of cognition. *Psychological Review, 74,* 29–39.
Simon, H. A. (1992). What is an "explanation" of behavior? *Psychological Science, 3,* 150–161.
Sinclair, M. (2010). Misconceptions about intuition. *Psychological Inquiry, 21,* 378–386.
Slovic, P., Finucane, M., Peters, E., & McGregor, D. G. (2002). The affect heuristic. In T. Gilovich, D. Griffin, & D. Kahneman (Eds.), *Heuristics and biases: The psychology of intuitive judgment* (pp. 397–420). Cambridge, UK: Cambridge University Press.
Söllner, A., & Bröder, A. (2016). Toolbox or adjustable spanner? A critical comparison of two metaphors for adaptive decision making. *Journal of Experimental Psychology: Learning, Memory, And Cognition, 42,* 215–237.
Söllner, A., Bröder, A., Glöckner, A., & Betsch, T. (2014). Single-process versus multiple-strategy models of decision making: Evidence from an information intrusion paradigm. *Acta Psychologica, 146, 84–96.* (Open Access: www.sciencedirect.com/science/article/pii/S0001691813002692).
Stanovich, K. E. (2004). *The robot's rebellion: Finding meaning in the age of Darwin.* Chicago: University of Chicago Press.
Stanovich, K. E., West, R. F., & Toplak, M. E. (2011). The complexity of developmental predictions from dual process models. *Developmental Review, 31,* 103–118.
Thompson, V. A. (2013). Why it matters: The implications of autonomous processes for dual process theories. *Perspectives in Psychological Sciences, 8,* 253–256.

Thompson, V. A., Prowse Turner, J. A., & Pennycook, G. (2011). Intuition, reason, and metacognition. *Cognitive Psychology*, *63*, 107–140.
Topolinski, S., & Reber, R. (2010). Gaining insight into the "Aha"- experience. Current *Directions in Psychological Science*, *19*, 402–405.
Troje, N. F. (2002). Decomposing biological motion: A framework for analysis and synthesis of human gait patterns. *Journal of Vision*, *2*, 371–387.
Tversky, A., & Kahneman, D. (1973). Availability: A heuristic for judging frequency and probability. *Cognitive Psychology*, *5*, 207–232.
Tversky, A., & Kahneman, D. (1982). Judgment of and by representativeness. In D. Kahneman, P. Slovic, & A. Tversky (Eds), *Judgment under uncertainty: Heuristics and biases* (pp. 84–98). Cambridge: Cambridge University Press.
Volz, K. G., & von Cramon, D. Y. (2008). Can neuroscience tell a story about intuition? In H. Plessner, C. Betsch, & T. Betsch (Eds.), *Intuition in judgment and decision making* (pp. 71–87). Mahwah, NJ: Lawrence Erlbaum Associates.
Von Winterfeld, D., & Edwards, W. (1986). *Decision analysis and behavioral research*. Cambridge: Cambridge University Press.
Wang, A. T., Lee, S. S., Sigman, M., & Dapretto, M. (2006). Neural basis of irony comprehension in children with autism: The role of prosody and context. *Brain*, *12*, 932–943.
Wilson, T. D., & Schooler, J. W. (1991). Thinking too much: Introspection can reduce the quality of preferences and decisions. *Journal of Personality and Social Psychology*, *60*, 181–192.
Winerman, L. (2005). Intuition (special issue). *APA Monitor on Psychology*, *36*(3), 50–64.
Wundt, W. (1907). *Outlines of psychology*. Leipzig: Wilhelm Engelmann.
Zajonc, R. B. (1968). Attitudinal effects of mere exposure. *Journal of Personality and Social Psychology*, *9*, 1–27.
Zajonc, R. B. (1980). Feeling and thinking: Preferences need no inferences. *American Psychologist*, *35*, 151–175.

4
EMOTION AND REASONING

Isabelle Blanchette, Serge Caparos, and Bastien Trémolière

Much of the work reported in this chapter was supported by a Discovery grant awarded to the first author by the Natural Sciences and Engineering Research Council of Canada (NSERC) as well as grants of the Social Sciences and Humanities Research Council (SSHRC) of Canada.

Emotion and reasoning

Humans are not robots. Robots methodically and dispassionately process information and produce logical inferences based on this information. Their computing capacities may also be quite impressive, seemingly unlimited. In contrast, human beings feel emotions. These emotions are associated with subjective affective states, changes in physiological arousal, and expressive behaviours. Humans also have limited computational capacities. Both of these human features have an important impact on reasoning. There is a widespread intuition that emotions may have a negative effect on reasoning. What research has started to reveal in recent years is that this effect is not arbitrary or erratic. While most of these effects are indeed negative, some are positive. Importantly, there are systematic ways in which emotion affects reasoning; multiple robust effects have now been confirmed by numerous empirical investigations (e.g., Blanchette & Richards, 2004). In this chapter we present some of these effects of emotion on reasoning as well as some possible mechanisms that may underlie these effects. In the first section of the chapter, we provide an overview of important findings on the effect of emotion on deductive reasoning (specifically on people's ability to use logic), and on the balance between analytic and heuristic processing (i.e., on people's tendency to use deliberative reflective thinking versus reflexive thinking, shortcuts, and simplifications). In the second section, we present potential cognitive and physiological mechanisms that could underlie these effects, and this includes limited computational capacity. In the last section, we present data from studies that illustrate the important interactions between emotion and reasoning outside the laboratory.

1. Emotion and reasoning: empirical effects

Research on the link between emotion and reasoning has asked two important questions: (1) does emotion impair people's ability to use logic in deductive reasoning? And (2) does emotion increase people's tendency to use heuristics (shortcuts, simplifications, that often lead to biases) when reasoning, as opposed to more analytical processing? The first question has been tested using deductive reasoning tasks, the second using both inductive and deductive reasoning paradigms. Below, we present some of the results in the literature that provide answers to these questions.

(a) Influence of emotions on logicality in deductive reasoning

A number of studies have used deductive reasoning tasks to test whether emotions affect people's logicality, the ability to provide conclusions in line with the prescription of normative, propositional logic. Consider the following example:

(1) a. There are old people who are retired;
    b. No retired person is an astronaut.
    c. Therefore, there are old people who are not astronauts.

In syllogistic reasoning, participants are asked to determine whether a conclusion (1c) follows logically from premises (1a and 1b). According to normative logic, the validity of an inference depends on the structure of the problem, not on its content (in the above example, the conclusion logically follows from the two premises). When studying the impact of emotion, one can compare semantic problem contents that are negative, positive, or neutral, while keeping the logical structure unchanged. One should be able to assess the logical validity of a conclusion regardless of its emotional valence. For example, an emotional problem reads:

(2) a. There are victims who are ugly;
    b. No ugly person is raped.
    c. Therefore, there are victims who are not raped.

Following the rationale that content is irrelevant and that determining the logical validity of inferences depends on structure, people should reason similarly about problems (1) and (2), which share the same logical structure. The validity of the conclusion in principle remains constant whether the semantic content includes emotionally neutral elements (astronauts, old people) or emotionally negative elements (victims, raped).

Yet, results from a number of studies show that negative emotional contents are associated with decreased logicality (Blanchette & Leese, 2011; Blanchette & Richards, 2004; Blanchette, 2006). For instance, Blanchette and Richards (2004) studied the impact of emotionally negative contents on logicality using conditional reasoning. Participants had to determine the logical validity of conclusions from conditional syllogisms of the form 'if P then Q; P, therefore Q'. When the problems included semantic contents that were intrinsically emotional (e.g., words such as 'death', 'suffering', or 'disease'), participants showed a decrease in logicality, compared to neutral contents (e.g., problems including words such as 'car', 'vehicle', or 'transport'; Blanchette & Richards, 2004, Study 1; see also Blanchette & Leese, 2011). A similar effect had been shown in an early study, where participants were less likely to provide normatively correct answers when reasoning about categorical syllogisms presenting controversial contents, likely to arouse emotion, compared to more neutral topics (Lefford, 1946). These findings suggest that beyond the referential value of the reasoning contents (e.g., the word 'car' refers to a vehicle which has four wheels and can be used to move more efficiently), the affective value of the contents influences reasoning.

While these studies suggest that affective value has an impact on reasoning, the fact that different semantic contents are presented to manipulate emotion does not allow for unambiguous conclusions. Studies manipulating emotion while keeping semantics constant allow for stronger causal conclusions concerning the impact of the affective value, independently from semantics. In one study, the emotional valence of the reasoning contents was manipulated experimentally before participants performed the reasoning task (Blanchette & Richards, 2004, Study 2). This was done using an evaluative conditioning procedure: intrinsically neutral semantic contents were combined with images of either neutral or negative valence. By counterbalancing the associations, semantically identical contents thus became either emotionally negative (by association with negative images) or remained emotionally neutral (by association with neutral images). Despite the fact that the reasoning problems were exactly the same in terms of structure and semantic content, participants were less logical with contents conditioned to become emotionally negative, compared to contents conditioned to remain neutral. This confirms that affect has an impact on reasoning independently of semantics.

Another approach to test the impact of emotions on logicality has been to manipulate participants' mood. For instance, in one study positive or negative moods were induced using videos presented prior to a reasoning task. Participants were asked to reason about conditional rules enouncing what people should or should not do (Oaksford, Morris, Grainger, & Williams, 1996). In such a deontic reasoning situation, a normatively correct strategy is to falsify – that is, to try to find situations where the rule may have been broken, rather than to look for situations where the rule is confirmed. Compared to a neutral control condition, participants in the positive and negative mood conditions were less likely to falsify, and tended to adopt a confirmatory strategy, consistent with the idea that emotion decreases normatively correct reasoning. Similar effects of mood have been observed in other studies with different types of reasoning tasks (Melton, 1995; Palfai & Salovey, 1993), using other mood inductions (Jung, Wranke, Hamburger, & Knauff, 2014) as well as with clinical populations (Kemp, Chua, McKenna, & David, 1997). These results on emotional state, as well as the results of studies examining emotional contents, support the widespread intuition that emotion generally has a deleterious effect on cognitive performance. Stress has been shown to have an analogous effect, not only on reasoning, but also on other cognitive processes such as vigilance, attention, and memory (e.g., Lieberman et al., 2005).

While a large set of results shows that emotions have a negative impact on logicality, some recent results suggest that, in some cases, this negative impact decreases or is even reversed into a positive one (Blanchette & Campbell, 2012; Gangemi, Mancini, & Johnson-Laird, 2006). One factor that has been put forward to account for this reversal is relevance: relevance would act as a moderator of the effect of emotions. A relevant emotional response has been described as one which is consistent with emotions previously experienced during a personally significant event or, more technically, an emotional response that is not orthogonal to the semantic contents processed in the cognitive task (Blanchette & Caparos, 2013). In the context of reasoning, relevance is high when there is good agreement between three elements: (1) the semantic content being reasoned about, (2) the current emotional state, and (3) the personal concerns and emotional history of the individual (i.e., the familiarity and personal significance of the semantic contents) (Caparos & Blanchette, 2015, 2016). For instance, when victims of sexual abuse reason about topics semantically related to sexual abuse, the processing of these contents evokes an emotional response related to highly significant events in personal history and personal concerns. This contrasts with the situation where an emotional state is evoked, for example, by watching an emotion-inducing video unrelated to the semantic contents of the reasoning task. In the latter case the emotional response is orthogonal, or irrelevant to personal concerns, prior experience, or the semantic contents of the reasoning task.

The postulated link between relevance, emotions, and reasoning has been tested directly by Blanchette, Gavigan, and Johnston (2014). Their study comprised several phases. In the first phase, the emotional state of the participants was manipulated using pictures and short films containing either emotional negative contents (e.g., a video showing a person with a severe case of anorexia) or neutral contents (e.g., a video showing a cooking recipe). In a second phase, participants solved deductive reasoning problems. The semantic contents of the problems could be either semantically related to the video clips (e.g., 'If you eat enough, then you feel good') or unrelated (e.g., 'If you are ready, then you can leave'). The results showed that when the semantic contents of the problems did not match the content of the pictures/video previously watched, participants gave less logical responses to emotional than to neutral problems. However, this difference disappeared when the contents of the problems matched those of the pictures/video. These results are consistent with the hypothesis that the effect of emotions on reasoning is moderated by the relevance of the contents in light of the previous experience. A few other results in the literature suggest a moderating effect of relevance. For instance, in one study war veterans reasoned more logically on emotional contents related to war than on neutral contents (Blanchette & Campbell, 2012). Also, participants suffering from different psychological disorders can reason more logically on emotional contents related to their condition than on non-emotional contents (Gangemi et al., 2006). We explore such studies of emotional reasoning in different populations in more detail in the final part of this chapter.

Not all studies have reported an improvement in logical reasoning as a result of relevant emotions. For instance, Jung, Wranke, Hamburger, and Knauff (2014) observed no moderation by relevance in a conditional reasoning task (on the form of 'if P then Q') which included exam- or spider-related contents. Participants with exam or spider phobia did not show an improvement for self-relevant emotional contents. Thus, there are contradictory findings in the literature on this topic.

In sum, numerous findings show that emotion affects logicality in deductive reasoning. When an affective state is induced, when participants reason about emotional contents unrelated to previous personal experiences (proximal or distal), or when contents acquire emotional value through evaluative conditioning, emotion has a deleterious effect on logicality. This deleterious effect seems to be moderated and can even be reversed when relevance is high. However, the boundaries and details of when emotions improve and deplete analytic processing remain to be fully determined.

(b) Influence of emotions on heuristic-based versus analytical reasoning

A few studies have looked at whether emotions alter the balance between heuristic (System 1) and analytic (System 2) processing in reasoning (see Kahneman, 2011, for a review of dual system approaches, and also see Evans, this volume, for a review of dual-process theories that capitalizes on the distinction between heuristic and analytic processes in reasoning). In one study, Eliades, Mansell, and Blanchette (2013) observed that participants made more use of anecdotal (stereotypical) information (heuristic; System 1) and less use of statistical information (algorithmic; System 2) when the content of the reasoning problems was emotional, compared to when it was neutral. The researchers used a base rate task, in which participants are presented with a situation where an individual (e.g., George) is drawn at random from a group of 1,000 individuals. Participants are given statistical information regarding prior probabilities (e.g., in this group 95% of individuals are lawyers and 5% are engineers). They are also given anecdotal (stereotypical) information (e.g., George has few friends, he is not interested in politics, and he likes math puzzles). By manipulating the congruency between the two types of information, it is possible to quantify the relative influence of anecdotal and statistical information on participants' reasoning. Eliades and collaborators compared problems with neutral content (e.g., George is an engineer) to problems with emotional content (e.g., George is a paedophile). Results showed that participants were influenced by anecdotal information to a greater extent when the problems included emotional contents, compared to neutral contents.

In another study, Eliades, Mansell, Stewart, and Blanchette (2012) used a belief-bias paradigm with categorical syllogisms (of the type: 'no A is a B; some Bs are Cs; therefore, some As are not Cs'. Here the conclusion is logically invalid; the conclusion 'some Cs are not As' on the other hand would have been logically valid). The conclusions of the syllogisms were manipulated in terms of both their logical validity (valid or invalid) and their believability (believable or unbelievable). The influence of heuristic processing can be indexed by comparing performance on problems where the believability and validity of the conclusion are congruent (i.e., problems with believable/valid or unbelievable/invalid conclusions) to performance on problems where believability and validity are incongruent (i.e., problems with unbelievable/valid or believable/invalid conclusions). The stronger the effect of congruence is, the more participants are biased by their beliefs. In the study by Eliades and colleagues (Experiment 2; 2012), the problems could be emotionally negative (linked to sexual abuse; e.g., 'no women are traumatised...') or emotionally neutral (e.g., 'no men are animals...'). The results showed that the influence of believability was stronger with emotional than with neutral contents, suggesting greater heuristic processing in the former case. It has recently been shown that this increased belief bias for emotional contents is particularly pronounced in individuals genetically predisposed to greater emotional reactivity (individuals carrying a specific genotype of the 5-HTTLPR gene, related to serotonin; see Stollstorff, Bean, Anderson, Devaney, & Vaidya, 2013).

In sum, the above studies show that emotions promote a form of reasoning which is less analytical and more heuristic-based. Similar effects have been observed in the social cognition literature. For instance, in persuasive communication, individuals in a positive mood tend to be influenced by the superficial features of a message rather than the strength of arguments (Mackie & Worth, 1989; Worth & Mackie, 1987). They also tend to rely on heuristics (such as the ease of retrieval heuristic) more than participants in a neutral mood, who are more likely to systematically process the contents (Ruder & Bless, 2003). Quraishi and Oaksford (2014) examined this in the context of informal reasoning and showed that participants in both positive and negative moods were less able to identify weak slippery slope arguments. This is a type of argument where it is proposed that a specific small change will inevitably lead to a significant and unwanted negative ulterior change, without a logical demonstration (e.g., if abortion is legalized, people will eventually be allowed to kill newborn babies; see also Collins & Hahn, this volume, for additional information about slippery slope fallacies). Though there are distinctions between effects of specific moods (see Edwards & Weary, 1993; Gold, 2002; Semmler & Brewer, 2002; Sinclair, 1988; Tiedens & Linton, 2001), an increase in heuristic processing as a result of emotional mood states has been a general finding observed under different conditions. This increase in heuristic processing could account for the fact the emotion is generally associated with decreased logicality.

Interestingly, emotions do not always increase heuristic processing and reduce analytical reasoning; some results are once again consistent with the idea that relevance moderates the effect of emotions on reasoning (see Section 1a). In one study, individuals concerned by the 2005 terrorist attacks in London (i.e., individuals in the vicinity of where the attacks took place) reported more intense levels of emotions regarding these attacks compared to individuals less personally concerned by the attacks (i.e., individuals in Manchester or in Canada). Yet the individuals more personally involved were more analytical and less affected by their beliefs when reasoning about terrorism-related contents compared to those less involved (Blanchette, Richards, Melnyk, & Lavda, 2007). The difference was not observed with neutral contents, suggesting a specific effect of relevant emotional contents. Such positive effect of emotion on reasoning has also been seen in laboratory-based tasks comparing emotional and neutral contents. Goel and Vartanian (2011) observed that while participants exhibited the classic belief bias on neutral control problems, this effect was less present on problems featuring negative contents. The negative contents used in that study featured violation of important social norms with political or moral dimensions (e.g., 'some raping of women is not unjustified'). The researchers suggest these contents were likely to 'engage internalised emotions' (p. 123), which could be interpreted as relevant, according to our definition. Specifically, participants were less likely to endorse the believable but invalid conclusion when it was negative, suggesting that they allocated extra attention to these problems. The authors interpreted their results according to the Affect Infusion Model (Forgas, 1995), which stipulates that negative emotions foster a more vigilant and systematic information processing style, probably because of the negative consequences associated with endorsing negative invalid conclusions. We would suggest that this effect may be restricted to cases where emotions are relevant, related to personally meaningful topics. In those cases, the intrinsic motivation for the task could result in an enhancement in analytical reasoning and a decrease in heuristic processing.

2. Mechanisms underlying effects of emotion on reasoning

While the systematic impact of emotion on reasoning has been well documented, the mechanisms underlying its effects remain largely unknown. Potential mechanisms could relate to one of the three dimensions of emotional responses. Emotion is typically described as including a cognitive dimension (either in the appraisals/evaluations that lead to the emotion, or the conscious, subjective element of the emotional response), an arousal dimension (that includes changes in autonomous nervous system activity related to arousal), and a behavioural dimension (in the form of facial expressions of emotion or action tendencies). In the reasoning literature, the focus has been on the cognitive dimension and less on the physiological and behavioural dimensions. In this section, we review some recent research that has identified promising candidate mechanisms related to each of these dimensions.

(a) Cognitive mechanisms

Emotions might represent an additional source of information to be processed and, as a result, might cause the diversion of a portion of the available cognitive resources away from the inference making process. In other words, emotions could be thought of as a form of cognitive load. Consistent with this idea, several results have shown that states of stress or anxiety have a negative impact on the availability of cognitive resources (e.g., Channon & Baker, 1994; Darke, 1988; Derakshan & Eysenck, 1998; Kensinger & Corkin, 2003; Lieberman et al., 2005).

In a series of recent experiments, a timing paradigm was used to examine the potential role of cognitive load, and to differentiate it from a possible effect of arousal. Time production is sensitive to cognitive load and arousal in opposite ways; increased cognitive load lengthens time productions (makes them longer) while increased arousal shortens them. Participants had to produce specific time intervals while reasoning about emotional or neutral contents (Viau-Quesnel, Savary & Blanchette, submitted). The results showed that time productions were longer when participants reasoned about syllogisms featuring emotional contents, compared to neutral contents. This result directly supports the cognitive load account, explaining the reduced logicality observed with emotional contents as resulting from the unavailability of limited cognitive resources for the inferential process.

Additional studies are currently being conducted to investigate the cognitive load account using the dual-process framework (Caparos & Blanchette, in preparation; Trémolière, Gagnon, & Blanchette, 2016). If emotions are associated with increased cognitive load, effects from emotion manipulations should be more prominent on difficult problems that require the mobilization of a greater portion of available cognitive resources. For instance, effects should be greater on problems that present a conflict between heuristic-based and analytic-based answers. Furthermore, emotions should little impair performance when people are forced to answer quickly (System 1 processing), but they should impair performance when people are given the possibility to answer at their own pace (System 2 processing).

The cognitive load hypothesis can readily account for the effect of emotion on the balance between heuristic-based and analytical reasoning (see Section 1b). If emotions deplete available cognitive resources, this will affect analytical reasoning to a greater extent since the latter requires the involvement of cognitive resources (De Neys, 2006). In contrast, heuristic-based reasoning should be little affected given that it is mostly automatic and requires few cognitive resources. A depletion of cognitive resources resulting from emotion processing should thus lead to an increase in the relative influence of heuristic reasoning over analytical reasoning, which would result in decreased logicality.

The increased cognitive load associated with emotion might be underpinned by the activation of semantic concepts and/or mental imagery. Specifically, emotions might activate task-irrelevant semantic concepts and mental images in autobiographical or semantic memory. When irrelevant for the reasoning task, these activated concepts would have to be inhibited and this inhibition process would monopolize cognitive resources. Some results obtained in the previously mentioned study by Blanchette et al. (2014) support this hypothesis. Participants took longer when they reasoned about emotional contents than neutral contents, consistent with the possibility that emotional stimuli drew attention and activated concepts or images that required additional processing resources. This finding was obtained when emotional contents were irrelevant (that is, when emotional contents did not appeal to a previous emotional experience; see Section 1). Interestingly, when participants reasoned about relevant emotional contents, their response times were not longer for emotional contents than neutral contents (Blanchette et al., 2014). It is thus possible that when reasoning about relevant contents, the concepts or mental representations activated by emotional stimuli overlap with the representations necessary for the resolution of the reasoning problem. Hence activating relevant associated emotional contents may improve, or at least not hinder, participants' performance on the task. This hypothesis could account for the finding that when participants reason about personally relevant emotional contents, the negative effect of emotions may be reduced, or even reversed.

Another potential cognitive account of the moderating effect of relevant emotions on reasoning involves motivation and engagement (Mercier & Sperber, 2011). When emotions are associated with personally relevant topics, this may be associated with an increase in motivation and engagement with the task. This is in line with the explanation of reduced belief bias for politically incorrect negative contents, proposed by Goel and Vartanian (2011). More generally, this concurs with several theories about the nature of emotions (LeDoux, 2012; Mulligan & Scherer, 2012; Panksepp, 1998). According to these theories, one major function of emotions is to indicate whether a situation is congruent with the goals, beliefs, and identity of the individual. Emotions related to personal experiences, because they indicate high relevance for the individual, could increase attentional focus and engagement with the task.

This hypothesis about the effect of relevant emotions on task engagement is also consistent with recent utility theories. These theories suggest that when utility of problem content and of problem solving is high, reasoning performance should be increased or facilitated. Any event, action or situation which increases the prospect of an agent reaching his/her goals has a high utility (Bonnefon, 2009; Von Neumann & Morgenstern, 1945). Utility is intrinsically linked to relevance. In that sense, experience-related (relevant) emotional contents would be associated with higher utility and promote an increase in motivation and engagement to solve a problem, translating in increased resource allocation (Oaksford & Chater, 2009). Relevant emotional contents may be associated with higher utility due to the fact that they signal information is related to central personal concerns.

(b) Neurophysiological mechanisms

Another angle from which the effect of emotions on reasoning may be examined relates to their physiological dimension. Few studies have examined the role of emotion-related physiological arousal in reasoning. One exception is a series of studies by Blanchette and Leese (2011). Results of these studies showed that emotional stimuli that evoked stronger arousal responses, as measured by increases in skin conductance, were more likely to be associated with logical errors in the reasoning task. The same was true of participants who showed stronger arousal responses in reaction to emotional stimuli, as they were more likely to show a difference in reasoning about emotional and neutral stimuli. These results are consistent with work on 'affective reactivity' showing more errors in language production, including logical and semantic (in)coherences when participants discuss negative emotional topics (Burbridge, Larsen, & Barch, 2005). This affective reactivity effect seems to be particularly linked with indices of sympathetic arousal, including increased heart rate (HR) and heart rate variability (HRV) (Cohen & Docherty, 2004; Docherty, Rhinewine, Nienow, & Cohen, 2001).

In addition to skin conductance, pupil dilation has also been used to examine the role of sympathetic arousal in emotional reasoning. In one study, Prehn and van der Meer (2014) presented their participants with an analogical reasoning task. They manipulated both the conceptual relation (e.g., boat and port) and the emotional relation (e.g., tumor and brain) between concepts. Participants were instructed to indicate whether two word pairs held the same relation. Pupil size was recorded as they performed the task and compared as a function of the conceptual and emotional similarity between stimuli. The results showed that pupil dilation was highest when both conceptual and emotional relations were similar across pairs. Pupil size was also greater when only one of the relational dimensions was similar (either conceptual or emotional) as compared to when word pairs where both conceptually and emotionally dissimilar. These results highlight the fact that the interaction between emotion and reasoning can be traced precisely using indices of sympathetic nervous system arousal.

The precise mechanisms through which peripheral arousal responses, such as those indexed by skin conductance and pupil dilation, may be related to central reasoning processes remain to be elucidated. One possibility is that arousal may be useful generically, in the reasoning process, to detect conflict or index situations where additional resources are required for reasoning. For instance, when people implicitly or explicitly perceive a discrepancy between their intuition and another response that may be more logical, they might experience an increase in physiological arousal. Additionally, when meta-cognitive processes suggest the problem is difficult, this may lead to an arousal response that implicitly indicates to the reasoner that cognitive resources need to be invested to reason successfully. This is in line with the work on logical intuition (De Neys, 2012). Logical intuitions reflect people's sensitivity to the conflict between analytic and heuristic responses, despite the fact that they provide the heuristic answer. At least under some circumstances, changes in arousal are observed on problems presenting a conflict between heuristic and analytic responses, even when participants provide the heuristic response. The arousal response may in some cases trigger greater involvement of analytic processing, or the involvement of executive function to arbitrate between the two possible responses. When similar arousal responses are induced by the emotional stimuli processed in the reasoning problems, or elicited by the emotional state of the reasoner, it may interfere with this process and reduce the possibility that arousal responses are used to orient analytical reasoning. In the case of relevant emotional topics, however, strong arousal responses evoked by personally relevant topics may be associated with a motivation to invest more cognitive resources in the reasoning process. Assuredly the role and consequences of arousal responses may be multiple and will need to be further investigated as a function of specific contexts.

Studying the brain bases of emotional reasoning will provide further information on how peripheral arousal responses may be involved in reasoning. Nicolle and Goel (2014) explain the important role of the ventromedial prefrontal cortex both for heuristic processes and for emotional reasoning. Peripheral arousal is centrally represented in the brain, and skin conductance responses in particular have been shown to be related to activation in the ventromedial prefrontal cortex (Critchley, Elliott, Mathias, & Dolan, 2000). It is possible, for example, that arousal responses evoked by the emotional nature of the stimuli included in a reasoning task, especially when irrelevant, are related to an increased activation of the ventromedial prefrontal cortex. The increased activation of this area is also likely to increase reliance on heuristic processing, leading to less logical responses on the reasoning task. This is one example providing a possible pathway to explain the link between bodily changes and central abstract cognitive processing.

(c) Mechanisms related to expressive behaviours

While few studies have examined the neurophysiological correlates of emotional reasoning, even fewer have examined the third dimension of emotional responses: expressive behaviours. These behaviours importantly feature facial expressions, but also include changes in voice prosody, posture, and action tendencies. Effects involving the behavioural dimension of emotions may be linked with embodied cognition, which generally shows that the physical features of conceptually represented stimuli have an important impact on cognitive operations (Niedenthal & Maringer, 2009). Congruent with this general idea, there is some work in the emotion-cognition literature showing links between body movements and affective processing. For instance, induced approach tendencies or induced positive facial expressions are associated with more positive judgments of ambiguous stimuli while avoidance behaviours (participants moving away from a target) or negative facial expressions induce more negative judgements (Chen & Bargh, 1999; Davis, Senghas, Brandt, & Ochsner, 2010; Onal-Hartmann, Pauli, Ocklenburg, & Güntürkün, 2012; Strack, Martin, & Stepper, 1988).

Analogous effects of expressive behaviour are starting to be investigated in reasoning. Some of our results suggest that induced negative facial expressions (asking participants to frown while they encode a reasoning problem) increase the deleterious effect of negative contents on reasoning (Blanchette & Amato, 2013). This may result from an increase in the emotional intensity of the stimuli when emotional expressions are induced. This is generally consistent with the facial feedback hypothesis (Davis et al., 2010), which suggests that individuals reflectively use information provided by their own emotional responses, including facial expressions, as a source of information. In the context of reasoning, negative facial expressions may indicate greater emotional intensity of the stimuli, which may augment the effect of emotion on reasoning. This represents one way in which changes in the body can affect central cognitive operations.

3. Emotional reasoning outside the laboratory

One of the criticisms that has sometimes been voiced about reasoning research is that it lacks ecological validity. Because reasoning research often takes place in the laboratory, using abstract, decontextualized logical problems, it is thought to be divorced from real life, where reasoning is set in a complex context and has tangible consequences by influencing our judgments and decisions. On the topic of emotion and reasoning, however, there are a number of studies featuring ecological or clinical investigations, though reasoning is often not the primary object of study. Many researchers and thinkers have examined the link between reasoning and psychological disorders, from schizophrenia to depression. The role of reasoning is particularly prominent in cognitive models of psychopathology. For many scholars, irrational inferences are associated with psychological disorder (see Berenbaum & Boden, 2014, for their work on beliefs, emotion, and psychopathology; see also Bögels & Mansell, 2004); and psychological disorder is seen as prominently featuring aberrant emotions (Gangemi, Mancini, & Johnson-Laird, 2014). Following that rationale, logic would be intimately related to psychological health.

The possibility that the effects of emotions on reasoning are linked with psychological disorder has been examined empirically. For instance, it was found that depressed participants (not using anti-depressant medication) were less likely to endorse positively valenced conclusions to syllogisms than were control participants (Gangemi, Mancini, & Johnson-Laird, 2014). A similar pattern was observed in a study involving reasoning by anxious participants (who were susceptible to panic attacks) on problems which featured anxiety-provoking conclusions: anxious participants were more likely to endorse anxiety-provoking conclusions than were control participants. Despite this emotion-congruent bias, in these two studies, both depressed and anxious participants reasoned generally more logically compared to control participants. While control participants showed the classic belief bias effect, depressed and anxious participants showed less belief bias on problems with contents related to their illness. They only exhibited belief bias when reasoning on other, less personally relevant topics. These results may represent another example of a beneficial effect of relevance and suggest that 'faulty' reasoning is not necessarily at the root of affective disorders.

However, there is also evidence that some reasoning biases may contribute to the development or at least the maintenance of certain disorders. For instance, experiments conducted by Engelhard and colleagues (Engelhard, Macklin, McNally, van den Hout, & Arntz, 2001), presented Vietnam War veterans with short stories that included information about objective danger (e.g., losing control of the wheels and stalling in the wrong place in high density traffic) and information about subjective emotional responses (e.g., upsetting thoughts about Vietnam). The researchers compared responses of veterans with and without post-traumatic stress disorder (PTSD). While both groups inferred danger from objective information, veterans with PTSD also inferred danger from subjective emotional responses in the absence of actual objective danger. That is, veterans with PTSD inferred that danger must be present based on the presence of signs of anxiety or intrusions. This suggests that certain emotional reasoning 'errors' may also be present in psychopathology, and these are likely candidates for intervention.

Even excluding clinical research, questions on emotion and reasoning have led researchers to venture out of the laboratory to investigate more ecologically valid situations. It is impossible to induce strong emotions experimentally, in laboratory setting (for obvious ethical reasons). To examine the impact of more intense emotions, researchers have had to investigate 'real-life' situations, studying the reasoning of populations who have experienced intense emotional events. Research on emotion and reasoning has included, to date, war veterans, individuals closely concerned by terrorist attacks, victims of sexual abuse, victims of car accidents, individuals suffering from different psychopathologies, and survivors of the Rwandan genocide.

One of the first studies interested in exposure to highly emotional events (Blanchette et al., 2007) examined heuristic-based versus analytical reasoning in individuals closely affected by a terrorist attack, namely Londoners tested just a few days after the 2005 London bombings (as described above). Another study (Blanchette & Campbell, 2012) examined deductive reasoning in war veterans, with or without PTSD, using categorical syllogisms with neutral, generally emotional, or war-related contents. Other recent studies (Blanchette, Lindsay, & Davies, 2014; Caparos & Blanchette, 2016) have examined deductive reasoning in victims of sexual abuse and car accidents, using problems with neutral, generally emotional, and trauma-specific contents (sexual abuse or car accident). One of the major contributions of these studies has been to show that when participants reasoned about emotional contents that were related to an emotional (potentially traumatic) event that they had previously experienced, they were more analytical and more logical than when they reasoned about generally emotional, personally irrelevant material.

In a current study (publications in preparation), 150 survivors of the Rwandan genocide have been tested on both deductive reasoning (using linear and conditional syllogisms) and inductive reasoning (using a base-rate task) with genocide-related and neutral contents. This is one of very few studies investigating the link between emotion and reasoning in a non-Western sample. Preliminary results suggest a positive link between participants' ability to be analytical (i.e., use System 2) with genocide-related contents, participants' optimism towards the society they live in, and their attitudes towards reconciliation. The more participants were able to reason analytically about contents related to the genocide (i.e., the less they were influenced by anecdotal information and beliefs), the more open they were towards reconciliation. This and the other studies reviewed in this section show that outside the laboratory, individuals' reasoning about personally relevant emotional contents might have important consequences for both individual and societal well-being.

4. Conclusions

Un-emotional robots, programmed to reason logically, would reason similarly on problems featuring highly emotional topics (e.g., thinking of another robot that has been deprogrammed) and neutral problems. They would also provide the same responses whether they have just experienced a horrible situation (e.g., having seen a robot being deprogrammed) or not. Human beings' ability to feel emotions affects reasoning in important ways. Interestingly, however, research is illustrating that this effect is relatively systematic and predictable (and therefore eventually potentially programmable). In this chapter, we have tried to provide an overview of the work that has documented the important impact of emotion on reasoning. Results show that incidental emotional states and incidental emotional value generally reduce the propensity for analytic processing and lead to decreased logicality in deductive reasoning. Some work, however, shows an important moderating role for relevance, in that the negative impact of emotion on analytic reasoning may be reduced, or even reversed, when participants reason about personally meaningful emotional experiences. This may be related to utility, motivation, or to the fact that the emotional concepts activated in these circumstances are not orthogonal to those activated to solve the reasoning task.

Research on emotion and reasoning illustrates the rich interplay between laboratory and non-laboratory studies, as well as the important contribution of reasoning research to understanding complex real-life situations. Emotions are typically evoked in high-stakes situations, which are also situations in which reasoning may be particularly consequential, and where we crucially need to rely on efficient adaptive cognitive operations. Some of the research conducted outside the laboratory shows the potential importance of reasoning and emotion under such circumstances, for instance in the aftermath of difficult traumatic situations or in the context of psychological disorders. Studying these situations and the ways in which reasoning is deployed as well as its consequences is proving to be fruitful, not only to provide a more ecologically valid perspective on reasoning, but also because it generates hypotheses concerning basic mechanisms that would not otherwise have been considered. These can, in turn, be tested experimentally under controlled laboratory conditions. This dual approach will be helpful to understand the psychological processes involving emotion and reasoning that are likely to be crucial in determining individual and collective well-being.

References

Berenbaum, H., & Boden, M. T. (2014). Emotions, beliefs, and psychopathology. In I. Blanchette (Ed.), *Emotion and reasoning* (pp. 65–83). Hove, UK: Psychology Press.

Blanchette, I. (2006). The effect of emotion on interpretation and logic in a conditional reasoning task. *Memory & Cognition, 34*(5), 1112–1125.

Blanchette, I., & Amato, J.-N. (2013). Emotion and reasoning in the body. In *Emotion and reasoning* (pp. 119–133). Hove, UK: Psychology Press.

Blanchette, I., & Campbell, M. (2012). Reasoning about highly emotional topics: Syllogistic reasoning in a group of war veterans. *Journal of Cognitive Psychology, 24*(2), 157–164. doi:10.1080/20445911.2011.603693

Blanchette, I., & Caparos, S. (2013). When emotions improve reasoning: The possible roles of relevance and utility. *Thinking & Reasoning, 19*(3–4), 399–413.

Blanchette, I., Gavigan, S., & Johnston, K. (2014). Does emotion help or hinder reasoning? The moderating role of relevance. *Journal of Experimental Psychology: Applied, 143*, 1049–1064.

Blanchette, I., & Leese, J. (2011). Physiological arousal and logicality: The effect of emotion on conditional reasoning. *Experimental Psychology, 58*(3), 235–246. doi:10.1027/1618-3169/a000090

Blanchette, I., Lindsay, P., & Davies, S. (2014). Intense emotional experiences and logicality: An exploration of deductive reasoning in victims of sexual abuse. *Psychological Record, 64,* 859–867. doi: 10.1007/s40732-014-0073-4.

Blanchette, I., & Richards, A. (2004). Reasoning about emotional and neutral materials is logic affected by emotion? *Psychological Science, 15*(11), 745–752. doi:10.1111/j.0956-7976.2004.00751.x

Blanchette, I., Richards, A., Melnyk, L., & Lavda, A. (2007). Reasoning about emotional contents following shocking terrorist attacks: A tale of three cities. *Journal of Experimental Psychology: Applied, 13*(1), 47–56. doi:10.1037/1076-1898x.13.1.47

Bögels, S. M., & Mansell, W. (2004). Attention processes in the maintenance and treatment of social phobia: hypervigilance, avoidance and self-focused attention. *Clinical Psychology Review, 24*(7), 827–856.

Bonnefon, J.-F. (2009). A theory of utility conditionals: Paralogical reasoning from decision-theoretic leakage. *Psychological Review, 116*(4), 888–907. doi:10.1037/a0017186

Burbridge, J. A., Larsen, R. J., & Barch, D. M. (2005). Affective reactivity in language: The role of psychophysiological arousal. *Emotion, 5*(2), 145–153.

Caparos, S., & Blanchette, I. (2014). *Emotions affect reasoning via System 2.* Poster presented at the 55th Annual Meeting of the Psychonomic Society, Long Beach, CA.

Caparos, S., & Blanchette, I. (2015). Affect et pensée logique: comment les émotions influencent notre raisonnement. *Revue Québecoise de Psychologie, 36*, 57–70.

Caparos, S., & Blanchette, I. (2016). Independent effects of relevance and arousal on deductive reasoning. *Cognition & Emotion*, 31, 1012–1022.

Caparos, S., & Blanchette, I. (in preparation). Emotions affect reasoning via System 2.

Channon, S., & Baker, J. (1994). Reasoning strategies in depression: Effects of depressed mood on a syllogism task. *Personality and Individual Differences, 17*(5), 707–711.
Chen, M., & Bargh, J. A. (1999). Consequences of automatic evaluation: Immediate behavioral predispositions to approach or avoid the stimulus. *Personality and Social Psychology Bulletin, 25*(2), 215–224. doi:10.1177/0146167299025002007
Cohen, A. S., & Docherty, N. M. (2004). Affective reactivity of speech and emotional experience in patients with schizophrenia. *Schizophrenia Research, 69*(1), 7–14.
Critchley, H. D., Elliott, R., Mathias, C. J., & Dolan, R. J. (2000). Neural activity relating to feneration and representation of Galvanic skin conductance responses: A functional magnetic resonance imaging study. *Journal of Neuroscience, 20*(8), 3033–3040.
Darke, S. (1988). Anxiety and working memory capacity. *Cognition & Emotion, 2*(2), 145–154. doi:10.1080/02699938808408071
Davis, J. I., Senghas, A., Brandt, F., & Ochsner, K. N. (2010). The effects of BOTOX injections on emotional experience. *Emotion, 10*, 433–440.
De Neys, W. (2006). Dual processing in reasoning: two systems but one reasoner. *Psychological Science, 17*(5), 428–433. doi:10.1111/j.1467–9280.2006.01723.x
De Neys, W. (2012). Bias and conflict: A case for logical intuitions. *Perspectives on Psychological Science, 7*(1), 28–38. doi:10.1177/1745691611429354
Derakshan, N., & Eysenck, M. W. (1998). Working memory capacity in high trait-anxious and repressor groups. *Cognition and Emotion, 12*(5), 697–713.
Docherty, N. M., Rhinewine, J. P., Nienow, T. M., & Cohen, A. S. (2001). Affective reactivity of language symptoms, startle responding, and inhibition in schizophrenia. *Journal of Abnormal Psychology, 110*(1), 194–198.
Edwards, J. A., & Weary, G. (1993). Depression and the impression-formation continuum: Piecemeal processing despite the availability of category information. *Journal of Personality and Social Psychology, 64*(4), 636–645.
Eliades, M., Mansell, W., & Blanchette, I. (2013). The effect of emotion on statistical reasoning: Findings from a base rates task. *Journal of Cognitive Psychology, 25*(3), 277–282. doi:10.1080/20445911.2012.761632
Eliades, M., Mansell, W., Stewart, A. J., & Blanchette, I. (2012). An investigation of belief-bias and logicality in reasoning with emotional contents. *Thinking & Reasoning, 18*(4), 461–479. doi:10.1080/13546783.2012.713317
Engelhard, I. M., Macklin, L., McNally, R. J., van den Hout, M. A., & Arntz, A. (2001). Emotion- and intrusion-based reasoning in Vietnam veterans with and without chronic posttraumatic stress disorder. *Behaviour Research and Therapy, 39*(11), 1339–1348.
Forgas, J. P. (1995). Mood and judgment: The affect infusion model (AIM). *Psychological Bulletin, 117*, 39–66.
Gangemi, A., Mancini, F., & Johnson-Laird, P. N. (2006). *Reasoning in obsessive compulsive disorder*. Paper presented at the British Psychological Society Annual Cognitive Psychology Section Conference, Lancaster University, Lancaster, UK.
Gangemi, A., Mancini, F., & Johnson-Laird, P. N. (2014). Emotion, reasoning, and psychopathology. In I. Blanchette (Ed.), *Emotion and reasoning* (pp. 44–83). Hove, UK: Psychology Press.
Goel, V., & Vartanian, O. (2011). Negative emotions can attenuate the influence of beliefs on logical reasoning. *Cognition & Emotion, 25*(1), 121–131.
Gold, R. S. (2002). The effects of mood states on the AIDS-related judgements of gay men. *International Journal of STD & AIDS, 13*(7), 475–481.
Jung, N., Wranke, C., Hamburger, K., & Knauff, M. (2014). How emotions affect logical reasoning: Evidence from experiments with mood-manipulated participants, spider phobics, and people with exam anxiety. *Frontiers in Psychology, 5*, 570. doi:10.3389/fpsyg.2014.00570
Kahneman, D. (2011). *Thinking, fast and slow*. New York, NY: Farrar, Straus and Giroux.
Kemp, R., Chua, S., McKenna, P., & David, A. (1997). Reasoning and delusions. *The British Journal of Psychiatry, 170*(5), 398–411.
Kensinger, E. A., & Corkin, S. (2003). Effect of negative emotional content on working memory and long-term memory. *Emotion, 3*(4), 378–393.
LeDoux, J. (2012). Rethinking the emotional brain. *Neuron, 73*(4), 653–676. doi:10.1016/j.neuron.2012.02.004
Lefford, A. (1946). The influence of emotional subject matter on logical reasoning. *Journal of General Psychology, 34*, 127–151.

Lieberman, H. R., Bathalon, G. P., Falco, C. M., Morgan, C. A. I. I. I., Niro, P. J., & Tharion, W. J. (2005). The fog of war: Decrements in cognitive performance and mood associated with combat-like stress. *Aviation, Space, and Environmental Medicine*, *76*(7), 7–14.
Mackie, D. M., & Worth, L. T. (1989). Processing deficits and the mediation of positive affect in persuasion. *Journal of Personality and Social Psychology*, *57 (1)*, 27–40.
Melton, R. J. (1995). The role of positive affect in syllogism performance. *Personality & Social Psychology Bulletin*, *21*, 788–794.
Mercier, H., & Sperber, D. (2011). Why do humans reason? Arguments for an argumentative theory. *The Behavioral and Brain Sciences*, *34*(2), 57–74; discussion 74–111. doi:10.1017/S0140525X10000968
Mulligan, K., & Scherer, K. R. (2012). Toward a working definition of emotion. *Emotion Review*, *4*(4), 345–357. doi:10.1177/1754073912445818
Nicolle, A., & Goel, V. (2014). What is the role of the ventromedial prefrontal cortex in emotional influences on reason? In I. Blanchette (Ed.), *Emotion and reasoning* (pp. 154–173). Hove, UK: Psychology Press.
Niedenthal, P. M., & Maringer, M. (2009). Embodied emotion considered. *Emotion Review*, *1*(2), 122–128. doi:10.1177/1754073908100437
Oaksford, M., & Chater, N. (2009). Précis of Bayesian rationality: The probabilistic approach to human reasoning. *The Behavioral and Brain Sciences*, *32*(1), 69–84; discussion 85–120. doi:10.1017/S0140525X09000284
Oaksford, M., Morris, F., Grainger, B., & Williams, J. M. G. (1996). Mood, reasoning, and central executive processes. *Journal of Experimental Psychology: Learning, Memory, and Cognition*, *22*(2), 476–492. doi:10.1037/0278-7393.22.2.476
Onal-Hartmann, C., Pauli, P., Ocklenburg, S., & Güntürkün, O. (2012). The motor side of emotions: investigating the relationship between hemispheres, motor reactions and emotional stimuli. *Psychological Research*, *76*(3), 311–316.
Palfai, T. P., & Salovey, P. (1993). The influence of depressed and elated mood on deductive and inductive reasoning. *Imagination, Cognition and Personality*, *13*(1), 57–71.
Panksepp, J. (1998). *Affective neuroscience*. New York: Oxford University Press.
Prehn, K., & van der Meer, E. (2014). Pupil size reflects cognition emotion interactions in analogical reasoning. In I. Blanchette (Ed.), *Emotion reasoning* (pp. 134–153). Hove, UK: Psychology Press.
Quraishi, S., & Oaksford, M. (2014, February 26). Emotion as an argumentative strategy: How induced mood affects the evaluation of neutral and inflammatory slippery slope arguments. In I. Blanchette (Ed.), *Emotion and reasoning* (pp. 95–118). Hove, UK: Psychology Press.
Ruder, M., & Bless, H. (2003). Mood and the reliance on the ease of retrieval heuristic. *Journal of Personality and Social Psychology*, *85*, 20–32.
Semmler, C., & Brewer, N. (2002). Effects of mood and emotion on juror processing and judgments. *Behavioral Sciences & the Law*, *20*(4), 423–436.
Sinclair, R. C. (1988). Mood, categorization breadth, and performance appraisal: The effects of order of information acquisition and affective state on halo, accuracy, information retrieval, and evaluations. *Organizational Behavior and Human Decision Processes*, *42*(1), 22–46.
Stollstorff, M., Bean, S. E., Anderson, L. M., Devaney, J. M., & Vaidya, C. J. (2013). Rationality and emotionality: Serotonin transporter genotype influences reasoning bias. *Social Cognitive and Affective Neuroscience*, *8*(4), 404–409. doi:10.1093/scan/nss011
Strack, F., Martin, L. L., & Stepper, S. (1988). Inhibiting and facilitating conditions of the human smile: A nonobtrusive test of the facial feedback hypothesis. *Journal of Personality and Social Psychology*, *54*, 768–777.
Tiedens, L. Z., & Linton, S. (2001). Judgments under emotional certainty and uncertainty: The effects of specific emotions on information processing. *Journal of Personality and Social Psychology*, *81*(6), 973–988.
Trémolière, B., Gagnon, M.-È., & Blanchette, I. (2016). Cognitive load mediates the effect of emotion on analytical thinking. *Experimental Psychology*, *63*, 343–350.
Viau-Quesnel, C., Savary, M., & Blanchette, I. (under review). Reasoning and concurrent timing: A study of the mechanisms underlying the effect of emotions on reasoning.
Von Neumann, J., & Morgenstern, O. (1945). *Theory of games and economic behavior*. Princeton, NJ: Princeton University Press.
Worth, L. T., & Mackie, D. M. (1987). Cognitive mediation of positive affect in persuasion. *Social Cognition*, *5*(1), 76–94.

5
COUNTERFACTUAL REASONING AND IMAGINATION

Ruth M. J. Byrne

Counterfactual thinking

Suppose you usually take your vacation in the same place most years, but this year for a change you go somewhere new. It turns out badly, the weather is awful, the accommodation is unpleasant, the food is expensive, and you have a miserable time. You might find it tempting to think, 'If only I'd gone to my usual favorite spot. . .'. When things go wrong, people tend to imagine how they could have turned out differently. They create a counterfactual alternative to reality in their 'if only. . .' thoughts by mentally 'undoing' some of the things that they believe contributed to the outcome. For example, most people focus on something exceptional – such as the choice of a new vacation location – and mentally change it back to normal (Kahneman & Tversky, 1982a). The discovery of this 'exceptionality effect' in counterfactual thinking over 30 years ago marked the start of an enduring and extensive examination of how people create counterfactual alternatives to reality.

In Kahneman and Tversky's (1982a) original demonstration, participants read about Mr. Jones, who left the office at his usual time but drove home by an unusual route, and was killed by a truck that crashed into his car at an intersection. Most people imagined that things could have turned out differently if he had gone home by his usual route. Other participants were told instead that the accident happened when Mr. Jones was driving home by his usual route but had left the office earlier than usual, and they imagined that things could have turned out differently if he had left at his usual time. The result shows that people change whatever event they believe to be exceptional, regardless of its content. It also shows that people do not tend to change a normal event to be exceptional. The tendency has been found to have widespread practical consequences, for example, people wish to punish a robber more harshly for injuring a victim who was shopping in a store she didn't usually shop in, compared to when the victim was shopping in a store she usually shopped in (e.g., Macrae, Milne, & Griffiths, 1993).

One striking implication of the discovery, pointed out by Kahneman and Tversky (1982a) at the time, is that people do not seem to create counterfactuals guided by beliefs about the likelihood of events. The most improbable event in the story about Mr. Jones's car accident is that two vehicles were in exactly the same place at exactly the same time. Yet no-one imagines an alternative to this highly unlikely event. This disregard for probability is echoed in everyday spontaneous counterfactuals. For example, tourists who survived the 2004 tsunami in Southeast

Asia spontaneously imagined how things could have turned out differently by thinking about how they or their loved ones could have been killed or injured in various ways; they did not mentally change the most improbable event – that they happened to be on vacation at the very time and in the very place of a very rare natural disaster (e.g., Teigen & Jensen, 2011). Rather than beliefs about likelihood and the calculation of probabilities, people appear to rely on a mental simulation of the situation – a process that Kahneman and Tversky (1982a) suggested was based on a 'simulation heuristic'.

Around the same time as Kahneman and Tversky's seminal work, an intriguing observation was made about the way in which people understand and reason about counterfactual conditionals (Fillenbaum, 1974). Suppose a colleague says to you, 'If John had caught the plane, he would have arrived on time'. What will you later remember of the meaning of what your colleague said? In an ingenious experiment, participants were given various sentences to read, including categorical assertions such as 'He didn't get a raise', and ordinary conditionals such as 'If he ate the fish, he got sick'. They were also given counterfactuals, such as 'If he had caught the plane, he would have arrived on time'. At the end of the experiment, they were given a surprise memory test. They were shown a set of sentences and had to say whether or not each sentence was one they had read earlier. The set of sentences contained some of the sentences they had been given earlier and some new ones. Strikingly, participants misremembered the counterfactual conditionals. They often mistakenly thought they had been given assertions such as 'He did not catch the plane' and 'He did not arrive on time' (Fillenbaum, 1974). One implication of the discovery is that people seem to understand counterfactuals not only by simulating what is mentioned in the conjecture – he caught the plane and he arrived on time – but also by simulating the presupposed facts – he didn't catch the plane and he didn't arrive on time (e.g., Byrne & Tasso, 1999).

Following these parallel discoveries in the 1970s and 1980s, subsequent research on counterfactual thinking has revealed much about the nature and function of mental simulations of alternatives to reality. Research on counterfactual imagination and counterfactual reasoning has to a large extent proceeded separately in the intervening years. In this chapter I assess first the current state of research on the counterfactual imagination, and then of research on counterfactual reasoning. In the final section, I consider recent advances in explaining how the mind gives rise to both sorts of counterfactual thoughts.

Counterfactual imagination

Counterfactuals can be alluring. Research on the social, emotional, and moral processes associated with the counterfactual imagination shows that in some cases people appear to be completely enthralled by an imagined alternative, such as a vivid sense of having been almost hit by a truck after a near-miss experience, or an intense feeling that success was nearly within one's grasp in a soccer match before the other team snatched it away. People can seem to become veritably transported into an alternative to reality (e.g., Markman & McMullen, 2003; Markman, McMullen, & Elizaga, 2008). The simulation of an alternative can be so powerful that it can even be mistaken for a remembered event. In an elegant experiment, participants selected an action from a pair; for instance, they chose to clap their hands or snap their fingers. Later they were asked to recall the action they had performed, or else they were asked to imagine they had performed the other action. Subsequently, they tended to mistakenly remember that they had actually performed the action that they had merely counterfactually imagined, far more than actions they had not imagined (e.g., Gerlach, Dornblaser, & Schacter, 2014). And older adults do so more than younger ones. Actions contained in a counterfactual conjecture are understood by creating such a vivid mental simulation that they may even activate the same sensory motor processes in the brain as required for real actions (e.g., De Vega & Urrutia, 2011).

Such simulations of counterfactual alternatives to reality are pervasive. Of course, individuals differ in their tendency to create them. People who engage in daydreaming and fantasy, and those with a strong belief in free will, tend to be most inclined to do so (e.g., Bacon, Walsh, & Martin, 2013; Alquist, Ainsworth, Baumeister, Daly, & Stillman, 2015). Nonetheless, most people create counterfactuals after bad events, such as accidents or deaths or failures of various sorts (e.g., Sanna & Turley, 1996; Roese, 1997). Even good events can trigger counterfactuals – for example, near misses or especially lucky wins. Most people imagine alternatives to reality about how things could have turned out better rather than worse and they readily imagine how bad events in their own past could have had a good outcome (e.g., Rim & Summerville, 2014; De Brigard, Addis, Ford, Schacter, & Giovanello, 2013). Here too there are individual differences, reflecting differences in personality characteristics such as self-esteem and other factors such as mood (e.g., Rye, Cahoon, Ali, & Daftary, 2008).

The creation of counterfactuals

Of considerable interest has been what sorts of counterfactual alternatives to reality people construct. Most people tend to create 'additive' counterfactuals that add something extra to an event, such as 'If only I'd studied harder for the exam', rather than 'subtractive' counterfactuals that delete something about the event, such as 'if only I hadn't run out of time' (e.g., Epstude & Roese, 2008; Kahneman & Tversky, 1982a). Research on the sorts of counterfactual alternatives to reality that people create has led to the fascinating and somewhat prosaic discovery that most of us tend to imagine the very same sorts of things.

Counterfactuals and plausibility Just as most people tend to zoom in on exceptional events and mentally change them to be normal in their 'if only . . .' thoughts, most people tend to change controllable events rather than uncontrollable ones, actions rather than inactions, the first event in a causal sequence of events, and the last event in a temporal sequence of causally independent events (e.g., for a review see Byrne, 2016). Remarkably, some aspects of reality seem to be more 'mutable' than others when people create a counterfactual.

For example, most people create counterfactuals that change an event within their own control. Suppose Steven is delayed on the way home by several events, some within his control and some not, such as a traffic jam, collecting his asthma medicine, stopping for a beer at a bar. He arrives home too late to save his dying wife. Most people believe that he will think things could have turned out differently if only he had not stopped at the bar, the event within his control (e.g., Girotto, Legrenzi, & Rizzo, 1991; see also Davis et al., 1995). Another example is that most people create counterfactuals that change actions rather than inactions. Suppose Paul has shares in Company A, then thinks about switching to Company B and decides to do so. He finds out he lost €1000. Joe has shares in Company B, then thinks about switching to Company A but decides to stay where he is. He also finds out he lost €1000. Most people judge that Paul, the person who acted, will feel worse and think 'if only' most (e.g., Byrne & McEleney, 2000; Kahneman & Tversky, 1982b; see also Ritov & Baron, 1990). Most people create counterfactuals that change the first cause in a causal sequence of event. Suppose Mary is delayed on her way to a sale. She had to wait while people crossed a pedestrian crossing, which then caused her to be held up in a subsequent traffic jam, which then caused her to be in a queue at the petrol station. Most people judge that things could have been different if Mary had not had to wait at the pedestrian crossing (e.g., Wells, Taylor, & Turtle, 1987; see also Segura, Fernandez-Berrocal, & Byrne, 2002). A final example is that most people create counterfactuals that change the most recent event in a temporal sequence of causally independent events. Suppose two people take part in a game in which they toss a coin and if they toss the same face coin they will both win €1000. Alicia goes first and tosses heads, Laura goes second and tosses tails, and so they both lose. Most people judge that things could have been different if Laura had tossed heads (e.g., Byrne, Segura Culhane, Tasso, & Berrocal, 2000; Miller & Gunasegaram, 1990).

The similarities in the counterfactual alternatives to reality that most people create are so notable that they have been referred to as 'fault-lines' in the mental representation of reality, 'junctures' or 'joints' in the perceived reality that most people zoom in on when they think 'if only . . .' (Kahneman & Tversky, 1982a). Young children between the ages of six and eight years begin to create counterfactuals that zoom in on these 'fault-lines' (e.g., Meehan & Byrne, 2005; Guttentag & Ferrell, 2004). Even in different cultures, people tend to focus on them (e.g., Gilovich, Wang, Regan, & Nishina, 2003). Notably, however, individuals who have sustained injuries to the prefrontal cortex do *not* tend to zoom in on the same fault-lines (e.g., Hooker et al., 2000; McNamara et al., 2003). A long-standing explanation of the cognitive processes that lead people to focus on the same sorts of fault-lines has been that people create simulations of alternative possibilities.

Counterfactuals and possibility. People tend to focus on the same sorts of events in their imagined alternatives to reality because 'joints' in their mental representation of reality provide readily available alternative possibilities (e.g., Kahneman & Tversky, 1982a). For example, in another version of the coin toss game, participants believed that Alicia and Laura were taking part in a game show. Alicia went first and tossed heads, but then there was a technical hitch in the game show and the game had to be restarted. This time Alicia tossed tails and Laura tossed heads. In this version participants imagined things could have been different if Alicia had tossed heads, as often as they imagined if Laura had tossed tails. They explicitly represent the alternative possibilities in their mental representation of the events, and the pre-hitch choice provides a ready-made counterfactual alternative (e.g., Byrne et al., 2000; Walsh & Byrne, 2004). The temporal order tendency to focus on the most recent event can be reversed by an available alternative.

Likewise, in the story about Paul who switched shares from Company A to Company B, people think about the current facts – Paul has shares in Company B – but they also think about the previous, now counterfactual, situation – Paul had shares in Company A. The explicit representation of the different previous possibility provides a ready-made counterfactual alternative, if only Paul had stayed in Company A, and so people tend to create this counterfactual. In contrast, for Joe who stayed with shares in Company B, people think about the current facts – Joe has shares in Company B – but since the previous situation was the same as the current one, it does not provide a ready-made counterfactual alternative (e.g., Byrne & McEleney, 2000). People tend to imagine an alternative to the action rather than the inaction because their mental representation of the action explicitly contains information about the way things were before the action, as well as information about the ways things are after the action. Moreover, the action effect can be reversed when other alternative possibilities are made salient. For example, participants were told about two soccer coaches. Steenland is the coach of the Blue-Black team who decides to field three new players, and Straathof is the coach of the E.D.O. team who decides not to change his team. Both teams lose their current match 3–0, and most people judged that the coach who fielded the three new players would feel most regret. But other participants were told that both teams had lost their prior game 4–0; these participants judged that the coach who decided *not* to change his team would feel most regret. The previous failure ensures that a reason to act is mentally represented as a salient alternative possibility (e.g., Zeelenberg, Van den Bos, Van Dijk, & Pieters, 2002). Similarly, people create counterfactuals that focus on inaction when they take a long-term perspective on events – for example, they regret missed educational opportunities or not spending enough time with their family (e.g., Gilovich & Medvec, 1995; Morrison & Roese, 2011).

Another example is the tendency to focus on controllable events. In one experiment, participants read about Anna, who had to chose between two envelopes that contained an easy or a difficult sum and then try to solve the sum within a given time of 30 seconds. When Anna chose an envelope that turned out to contain the difficult sum and then failed to solve it, participants tended to say, 'If only she had chosen the other envelope'. They mentally undid the controllable decision. But when participants acted as players in the game, and were presented with the envelopes to choose from, and then tried and failed to solve the difficult sum, they focused on uncontrollable constraints of the situation, such as 'If only I had had more time' or 'If only I had had a paper and pencil' (e.g., Girotto, Ferrante, Pighin, & Gonzalez, 2007). Observers of the game also created counterfactuals about the events outside the player's control (e.g., Pighin, Byrne, Ferrante, Gonzalez, & Girotto, 2011). People explicitly represent the choice of the envelope when they read about the game, but they also represent performance factors of the game when they experience them as a result of acting in the game or witnessing it. These examples support the idea that people create counterfactuals by simulating alternative possibilities (see also Dixon & Byrne, 2011).

Counterfactuals and probability An alternative idea is that people mentally undo 'fault-lines' such as exceptions or the most recent event because these 'joints' correspond to events that are most likely to change the outcome (e.g., Spellman, 1999; Petrocelli, Percy, Sherman & Tormala, 2011). The probability of a counterfactual on this view is its conditional probability. A counterfactual such as 'If Sam had chosen door 2 then he would have won' is judged to be of more impact when it has a high conditional probability, that is, when Sam nearly chose door 2, and when he would have been able to answer the questions that he would have been asked if he had chosen door 2 (e.g., Petrocelli et al., 2011). One puzzling observation for the idea that people rely on probabilities to assess counterfactuals is the tendency to change the most recent event in an independent sequence of events. In the coin toss game, the probability of a good outcome is 50–50 before either Alicia or Laura plays, and it remains 50–50 after Alicia plays, but after Laura plays it changes to either 1 or 0. On a probability view, people update their probability estimates after each play and so they view the second play as having a greater causal role because it determines the probability of the outcome most (e.g., Spellman, 1997). As a result, they tend to imagine 'If only Laura had tossed heads'. But people do not create this counterfactual when the context provides an alternative to the first event. In the technical hitch version, Alicia goes first and tosses heads, but after the technical hitch she tosses tails, and Laura tosses heads; participants imagined things could have been different if Alicia had tossed heads, as often as they imagined if Laura had tossed tails (e.g., Byrne, et al., 2000). They did not tend to change the most recent event. In another version, Alicia went first and tossed heads, and after the technical hitch, she tossed heads and Laura tossed tails, and participants imagined things could have been different if Laura had tossed heads. They tended to change the most recent event. The difficulty for the probability view is that the technical hitch does not alter the probabilities: they remain the same for the story in which Alicia had tossed heads before the hitch, and the story in which she had tossed tails before the hitch (see also Walsh & Byrne, 2004).

Another challenge for the idea that people create counterfactuals based on probabilities concerns counterfactuals and causal sequences. Consider one view about a counterfactual's probability, that it is determined by the causal facts as captured by Bayesian nets of conditional probability information about the dependence of events on their immediate causes (e.g., Sloman & Lagnado, 2005; see also Pearl, 2013). In a crucial experiment, participants were told about simple devices that consist of four components, A, B, C, and D; in which A and B jointly cause C (neither alone is sufficient to cause C), and C causes D; or in which A or B cause C (either alone is sufficient to cause C), and C causes D. Their task was to make judgments about counterfactuals such as 'If C hadn't operated, would A have operated?' (Rips, 2010). On one probability view, the counterfactual requires an intervention to change the setting for C so that it is not operating, and to minimally prune the causal model to remove links into C. The values of all the other variables remain as they are, and hence if C hadn't operated, A would still have operated (e.g., Sloman & Lagnado, 2005). But in the experiment, people gave different answers for the two devices. They judged that A would not have operated for the device in which A separately caused C – perhaps they believed that when C is not operating, neither A nor B could be operating. In contrast, they judged A would have operated for the device in which A and B both caused C – perhaps they believed that when C is not operating, A might be operating but B might not (e.g., Rips, 2010). Hence, the results show that people do not assume that an intervention on C changes only the most recent event in a causal sequence of events. In fact, most people create counterfactuals that change the first cause in a causal sequence, as described earlier in the story about Mary who was delayed on her way to a sale (e.g., Wells et al., 1987; see also Segura et al., 2002).

In summary, the similarities in the counterfactual alternatives to reality that most people imagine are remarkable. They appear to implicate the mental representation of available possibilities as central to the cognitive processes that create imagined alternatives to reality (e.g., Byrne 2017). Equally fascinating has been the discovery that the creation of counterfactuals serves crucial cognitive, emotional, and moral functions.

The functions of counterfactuals

Counterfactuals affect the way people understand the past and prepare for the future, and they amplify the ascription of moral judgments and the experience of emotions.

Counterfactuals and preparations for the future The creation of counterfactuals can enable people to prepare for the future, ensuring that people learn from mistakes and prevent bad outcomes in the future (e.g., Epstude & Roese, 2008). Importantly, counterfactuals affect intentions to improve, for example to stop smoking (e.g., Page & Colby, 2003). When people create a counterfactual alternative about the past, they are primed to read an intention about the future based on it (e.g., Smallman & McCulloch, 2012). In one experiment, most of the participants who played a card game spontaneously created counterfactuals about how things could have turned out better, but notably, those who thought they would play again created the most counterfactuals (e.g., Markman, Gavanski, Sherman, & McMullen, 1993). Moreover, participants who create counterfactuals about how things could have turned out better, rather than worse, form intentions that are useful in bringing about a better outcome next time (e.g., Markman et al., 2008; Roese, 1997). Interestingly, counterfactuals activate the same brain areas, not only as episodic recollections of past experiences, but also as thinking about intentions (e.g., Schacter, Benoit, De Brigard, & Szpunar, 2015; Van Hoeck, Ma, Ampe, Baetens, Vandekerckhove, & Van Overwalle, 2013). Such preparatory counterfactuals about sub-goals have been useful in artificial intelligence systems to help in solving problems (e.g., Ginsberg, 1986). And people who have sustained injuries to the prefrontal cortex rarely spontaneously mention counterfactual alternatives when they talk about a bad event from their past, unlike healthy adults who tend to mention several ways things could have turned out differently (e.g., Gomez-Beldarrain, Garcia-Monco, Astigarraga, Gonzalez, & Grafman, 2005; see also Hooker et al., 2000). Unfortunately, the impairment in counterfactual thinking may underlie their failure to learn from mistakes as well as their insensitivity to the consequences of decisions (e.g., McNamara et al., 2003).

Counterfactuals and explanations of the past Some counterfactuals help people prepare for the future, whereas others explain the past (e.g., Ferrante, Girotto, Stragà, & Walsh, 2013).

Counterfactuals often provide justifying and excusatory explanations of past events, for example by denying that the actor had control of the outcome: 'if I had had more time . . .' (e.g., Markman & Tetlock, 2000; McCrea, 2008). Perhaps unsurprisingly, they are common in accident safety reports and also in political discourse (e.g., Catellani & Covelli, 2013; Morris & Moore, 2000).

Counterfactuals can explain the past by identifying relations such as causes and effects (e.g., Spellman & Mandel, 1999). A causal relation, e.g., 'Switching on the ignition causes the engine to start' appears to implicitly evoke a contrast between reality and a counterfactual alternative, e.g., 'If the ignition had not been switched on, then the engine would not have started' (see Nickerson, 2015). People judge that an action caused an outcome more often when they can imagine that the outcome would not have happened if the action had not happened, compared to when they can imagine the outcome would have happened even if the action had not (e.g., McCloy & Byrne, 2002). Overall, they tend to create more causal thoughts than counterfactual ones (e.g., McEleney & Byrne, 2006). And their causal thoughts often identify a strong cause of an outcome, such a drunk driver who swerved into the middle of the road and caused a car accident, whereas their counterfactual thoughts often identify the enabling conditions that could have prevented the outcome, e.g., the accident would not have happened if the actor had left his office earlier (e.g., Mandel & Lehman, 1996; Frosch & Byrne, 2012). Counterfactuals also help explain the past by identifying other sorts of relations, such as the relation between reasons and actions (e.g., Walsh & Byrne, 2007; see also Juhos, Quelhas, & Byrne, 2015).

Counterfactuals and moral judgments People have strong moral intuitions about some situations, and their judgments can be influenced by both emotion and reason (e.g., Bucciarelli, Khemlani, & Johnson-Laird, 2008; Greene, Nystrom, Engell, Darley, & Cohen, 2004; Gubbins & Byrne, 2014). Counterfactuals are often used to work out the culpability of individuals. For example, participants listened to legal arguments that contained counterfactuals, such as a suggestion that the outcome of an assault would have been different if the victim had behaved differently. They blamed the victim more, and the attacker less, compared to participants who listened to counterfactuals that suggested the outcome would have been the same even if the victim had behaved differently (e.g., Branscombe, Owen Garstka, & Coleman, 1996; see also Parkinson & Byrne, 2017). Counterfactuals also affect people's own moral behavior, which is influenced not only by their thoughts about good things they did, but also when they think about bad things they could have done but did not do (e.g., Effron, Miller, & Monin, 2012).

The violation of social norms influences blame ascriptions (e.g., Malle, Monroe, & Guglielmo, 2014). For example, participants who read about Steven who arrived home too late to save his dying wife because he was delayed by some events outside his control, such as a traffic jam, and some within his control, such as stopping for a beer at a bar, tended to create a counterfactual that changed the event within his control: 'if only he had not stopped at the bar' (e.g., Girotto et al., 1991). But those who read that he arrived home too late because he was delayed by various events including some within his control that fit with moral norms, such as stopping to visit his elderly parents, did *not* tend to create a counterfactual that changed the event within his control (e.g., McCloy & Byrne, 2000).

And just as causal judgments often identify strong causes, judgments about blame often focus on the strong cause of an outcome. For example, people tended to blame a drunk driver for a car accident in which a young boy was injured when a neighbor drove him home, but their counterfactual thoughts identified enabling conditions that violated moral norms and that could have prevented the outcome, e.g., the young boy would not have been injured if his father had not dallied on his way to collect him from school (e.g., N'gbala & Branscombe, 1995; see also Migliore, Curcio, Mancini, & Cappa, 2014).

Counterfactuals and emotions The creation of a counterfactual 'if only . . .' thought can amplify emotions such as regret and guilt, or relief and sympathy (e.g., Kahneman & Miller, 1986). As a result counterfactuals can affect well-being, for example in recovery following traumatic events (e.g., Davis et al., 1995; El Leithy, Brown, & Robbins, 2006). Counterfactuals amplify emotions such as regret (e.g., Davison & Feeney, 2008; Gilovich & Medvec, 1995). Regret is associated with depression and anxiety (e.g., Markman & Miller, 2006). The sorts of counterfactuals that people create can even pinpoint specific emotions. For example, guilt is amplified when people create a counterfactual that changes an action, whereas shame is amplified when they create a counterfactual that changes a personality characteristic (e.g., Niedenthal, Tangney, & Gavanski, 1994).

In summary, people readily create counterfactual alternatives to reality. There are remarkable regularities in the sorts of changes most people make to reality when they create a counterfactual. The imagination of counterfactual alternatives seems to be guided by available alternative possibilities. People create counterfactuals for many reasons. They help people prepare for the future by forming intentions and explain the past by identifying important relations such as causes and their effects. They also underlie judgments about moral matters such as blame and fault, and they amplify the experience of emotions such as guilt and regret. Research on counterfactual imagination has flourished in the years since Kahneman and Tversky's seminal work on a simulation heuristic in the 1980s. In parallel, research on counterfactual reasoning has also proliferated, to which we now turn.

Counterfactual reasoning

People can reason well from counterfactual conditionals, and their comprehension of them appears to result in a detailed and explicit representation of their meaning. But the cognitive processes that underlie the comprehension of counterfactuals have remained a puzzle. A counterfactual such as 'If John had caught the plane, he would have arrived on time' conveys the presupposition that its 'if' part is false – he did not catch the plane – and that its 'then' part is false – he did not arrive on time. Consequently, the truth or falsity of a counterfactual cannot be calculated based on the truth or falsity of its components since its components are false, both the 'if' part and the 'then' part (e.g., Nickerson, 2015). Yet people readily distinguish between plausible and implausible counterfactuals. In fact, when people imagine how episodes from their past could have been different, the counterfactual alternatives that they consider to be likely activate the same core brain network as their episodic recollections, whereas the counterfactual alternatives that they consider to be unlikely require more imaginative work (e.g., De Brigard et al., 2013). A significant step in the logical analyses of counterfactuals was the idea that their meaning depends on their truth in a possible world, a world that is just the same as this one except that the counterfactual conjecture is true in it (e.g., Stalnaker, 1968; Lewis, 1973). But it is difficult to establish for any given counterfactual the possible world that is as close as possible to this one (e.g., Williamson, 2007). And people do not have the cognitive capacity to consider a potentially infinite set of possible worlds (e.g., Byrne, 2005). How, then, do they establish their truth and plausibility?

Conjectures and presuppositions

Several observations provide important clues about how people understand and reason about counterfactual conditionals. One observation is that their judgments of what counterfactuals mean often refer to the opposite of what was mentioned. One clue is that participants judge that someone who utters a counterfactual such as 'If John had caught the plane, he would have arrived on time' meant to imply that he didn't catch the plane, and that he didn't arrive on time (Thompson & Byrne, 2002). Another clue is that when people read a short story that contains a counterfactual, such as 'If he had caught the plane, he would have arrived on time', they are 'primed' to read a subsequent conjunction, such as 'He didn't catch the plane and he didn't arrive on time', more quickly than when they are primed by an ordinary indicative conditional, such as 'If he caught the plane, he arrived on time'. The result suggests that from the outset their understanding of the counterfactual activates this additional information. And the counterfactual also primes them to read the conjunction, 'He caught the plane and he arrived on time', just as quickly as when they are primed by the ordinary conditional (e.g., Santamaria, Espino, & Byrne, 2005). The result suggests that counterfactuals prime people to think about not only the conjecture, 'He caught the plane and he arrived on time', but also the presupposed facts, 'He didn't catch the plane and he didn't arrive on time'.

A third clue is the counterfactual inference effect: people make more inferences from counterfactual conditionals than from ordinary conditionals. When participants are given a counterfactual as well as some further information, such as 'He didn't catch the plane', they readily make the *denial of the antecedent* inference, 'He didn't arrive on time'. When they are told 'He didn't arrive on time', they readily make the modus tollens inference 'He didn't catch the plane' (Byrne & Tasso, 1999). They make these two inferences much more often from a counterfactual than an ordinary conditional. Their inferential performance suggests they have ready access to the information 'He didn't catch the plane and he didn't arrive on time'. Nonetheless, when they are given the information that in fact 'He caught the plane', they readily make the modus ponens inference 'He arrived on time', and when they are told 'He arrived on time', they readily make the *affirmation of the consequent* inference 'He caught the plane'. They make these two inferences just as often from a counterfactual as from an ordinary conditional. Thus, their inferential performance also suggests they have ready access to the information, 'He caught the plane and he arrived on time'. The inferences they make are also influenced by their linguistic form and their content (e.g., Egan, Garcia-Madruga, & Byrne, 2009; Moreno-Rios, Garcia-Madruga, & Byrne, 2008; Frosch & Byrne, 2012; Quelhas & Byrne, 2003; Egan & Byrne, 2012). Any account of the cognitive processes underlying understanding and reasoning about counterfactuals must be able to account for these core observations.

Counterfactual conditionals and possibilities One view is that people understand and reason from counterfactuals by mentally simulating multiple possibilities (e.g., Byrne, 2005). They construct 'iconic' mental models that capture structural aspects of the elements envisaged (e.g., Johnson-Laird & Byrne, 2002). For the ordinary conditional, 'if he caught the plane he arrived on time', they think at the outset about just one possibility corresponding to the way the world would be if the assertion were true (Johnson-Laird & Byrne, 2002):

Caught plane and arrived on time
...

Their mental representations are guided by a principle of parsimony, because of the limitations of human working memory, and so they simulate few possibilities. They can make a 'mental note' that there may be other possibilities which they have not yet thought about (captured by the three dots in the diagram) and so their understanding of the conditional is not merely a conjunction (e.g., Johnson-Laird & Byrne, 2002; Johnson-Laird, Khemlani, & Goodwin, 2015). They can 'flesh out' their models to include alternative true possibilities if necessary. Their mental representations are guided by a principle of truth and so they do not simulate the false possibilities ruled out by the conditional, such as, 'He caught the plane and he did not arrive on time'. (e.g., Espino, Santamaria, & Byrne, 2009; Johnson-Laird & Byrne, 2002). There are many different interpretations that they may come to for a conditional (e.g., Johnson-Laird & Byrne, 2002).

In contrast, when people understand a counterfactual conditional, such as, 'If he had caught the plane he would have arrived on time', they think from the outset about dual possibilities, and they keep track of their epistemic status as a conjecture or the presupposed facts:

Counterfactual conjecture:	Caught plane and arrived on time
Presupposed facts:	Did not catch plane and did not arrive on time

This dual-meaning view of counterfactuals, that participants mentally simulate both reality and an alternative to it to understand a counterfactual, readily explains the core observations described earlier. People have ready access in their mental models to a simulation of the presupposed facts, in which he did not catch the plane and did not arrive on time, as well as a simulation of the conjecture in which he caught the plane and he arrived on time (e.g., Byrne, 2017). Hence, they misremember the counterfactual and believe they were told the presupposed facts, they believe someone uttering a counterfactual meant to imply this possibility, they are primed to read the presupposed facts very readily, and they make inferences about this possibility more often from a counterfactual than from an ordinary conditional.

Moreover, brain imaging results show greater activation for counterfactuals in areas of the brain associated with increased mental imagery compared to ordinary conditionals (e.g., Kulakova, Aichhorn, Schurz, Kronbichler, & Perner, 2013). And if people understand a counterfactual by considering both the conjecture and the presupposed facts, they must resolve the conflict between what they know about the real world and what they conjecture as a counterfactual alternative to it. Indeed, counterfactuals activate areas of the medial prefrontal cortex related to conflict detection (e.g., Van Hoeck et al., 2013). The attempt to resolve the conflict between the real world and the counterfactual alternative can lead to an initial brief disruption in the comprehension of a counterfactual (e.g., Ferguson & Sanford, 2008). The initial disruption is rapidly resolved, and when the counterfactual context supports an immediate simulation of the counterfactual conjecture 'as if' it actually happened, no disruption by real world knowledge occurs (e.g., Nieuwland & Martin, 2012).

Counterfactual conditionals and probabilities

On the alternative view that people understand a counterfactual such as 'If he had caught the plane, he would have arrived on time' by thinking about its probability, the knowledge that he did not catch the plane and he did not arrive on time is a prerequisite for asserting such a counterfactual. People understand the counterfactual by setting aside their knowledge of the actual world, adding the 'if' part, 'He caught the plane' to their beliefs and calculating the probability of the 'then' part, 'he would have arrived on time' (e.g., Evans, 2007). For an ordinary conditional, they think about true antecedents only – the situation in which he caught the plane. They do not think about their belief in the negated 'if' clause – situations in which he did not catch the plane, or whether or not the 'then' clause follows in such situations (e.g., Handley, Evans, & Thompson, 2006). They compare the situation 'He caught the plane and he arrived on time' to the situation 'He caught the plane and he did *not* arrive on time', so that they can compare their belief in the probability of each situation. And according to a principle of singularity, they think about only one model (e.g., Evans & Over, 2004). The probability of a counterfactual is its conditional probability – for instance, the probability that he would have arrived on time given that he had caught the plane: *probability (B | A)* (Over, Hadjichristidis, Evans, Handley, & Sloman, 2007). Only one model is constructed to combine numerical values that represent the strength of belief in the counterfactual consequent, 'he would have arrived on time', given the counterfactual antecedent, 'he had caught the plane', and strengths of belief in each of the implied facts – that he did not arrive on time, and that he did not catch the plane (e.g., Evans, Over, & Handley, 2005, p. 1049). Proponents of this view suggest, 'We do not believe there is a fundamental difference in the mental representation of indicatives and counterfactuals' (Evans, 2007, p. 74).

The view that participants think only about one situation is problematic in explaining the core observations described earlier. One possible solution is to suggest that people make inferences such as modus tollens from a counterfactual by accessing their knowledge of the facts, rather than their mental representation of the counterfactual. A problem for this suggestion is that it does not explain how people reason about counterfactuals for which they do not know the facts. Moreover, the idea that they compare the situation 'He caught the plane and he arrived on time' with the situation, 'He caught the plane and he did *not* arrive on time' predicts that they should have ready access to the situation 'He caught the plane and he did not arrive on time'. Yet experiments show that this situation is not primed by a counterfactual (e.g., Santamaria et al., 2005), and in fact it is not primed by an ordinary conditional either (e.g., Espino et al., 2009).

In summary, people readily understand and reason about counterfactual conditionals. They appear to consider both the counterfactual conjecture mentioned in the conditional and the presupposed facts, the opposite of what is mentioned. The idea that people mentally simulate dual possibilities accounts for observations such as the counterfactual inference effect, that is, the tendency to make more inferences from a counterfactual than from an ordinary conditional, even for content for which participants have no prior beliefs. Research on counterfactual reasoning has flourished in the years since Fillenbaum's innovative work on memory for counterfactuals. Recent developments have brought about something of a rapprochement between the otherwise parallel research into counterfactual imagination and counterfactual reasoning to which we now turn.

Counterfactual imagination and reasoning

In recent years neuropsychological research on counterfactual impairments and neuroscience research on the role of counterfactual emotions in decision making has brought research on counterfactual imagination and counterfactual reasoning into closer alignment. In this final section, I sketch two recent developments that contribute to explaining how the mind gives rise to both sorts of counterfactual thoughts.

One advance is that an important link has been established between the creation of counterfactual alternatives that lead to the experience of counterfactual emotions such as regret on the one hand, and counterfactual reasoning about choices and decisions on the other. For example, people often experience regret when something bad happens as a result of their choices, such as a long delay at the airport as a result of the choice of a budget airline, and when they do so, they are more inclined to say they will decide to switch to a different provider in future (e.g., Zeelenberg & Pieters, 2007; see also Epstude & Roese, 2008). Counterfactual alternatives and the experience of regret affects decision-making even in children as young as seven years. Some children experience regret when they find out that the box they chose contained two stickers and the box they did not choose contained five stickers. The next time they make a choice, they tend to switch to the other box (e.g., O'Connor, McCormack & Feeney, 2014; see also Weisberg & Beck, 2010; Guttentag & Ferrell, 2008).

Conversely, impairments in the creation of counterfactuals affect decision making. Increased activation occurs in various brain regions, including the medial orbitofrontal cortex, when adults experience regret after they compare the outcome of a gamble with an alternative, now counterfactual outcome. Individuals with injuries to these areas do not report experiencing regret after they compare the outcome of their gamble with an alternative. Importantly, they do not seem to anticipate regret and avoid similar bad outcomes on subsequent gambles (e.g., Coricelli, Critchley, Joffily, O'Doherty, Sirigu, & Dolan, 2005; Camille, Coricelli, Sallet, Pradat-Diehl, Duhamel, & Sirigu, 2004; see also Gillan, Morein-Zamir, Kaser, Fineberg, Sule, Sahakian, Cardinal, & Robbins, 2014).

A second advance is the discovery that the creation of counterfactuals, such as 'If Anne had not moved the chocolate, where would it be?' is crucial to other sorts of reasoning, such as reasoning about other people's beliefs (e.g., Riggs, Peterson, Robinson, & Mitchell, 1998). For example, suppose Sally and Anne are in the kitchen. Sally puts some chocolate in the cupboard and leaves. Anne moves the chocolate to the fridge. Then Sally returns. Where will Sally look for the chocolate? Three-year-old children tend to make mistakes in false-belief reasoning and they say Sally will look in the fridge. In contrast, four- and five-year-olds tend to say she will look in the cupboard (e.g., Wimmer & Perner, 1983). The older children appreciate that other people's mental states – beliefs, desires, and knowledge – may differ from their own. False-belief reasoning may depend on counterfactual reasoning. Counterfactual reasoning develops earlier than false-belief reasoning and the two are correlated even when factors such as age and verbal intelligence are controlled (e.g., Guajardo, Parker, & Turley-Ames, 2009; Perner, Sprung, & Steinkogler, 2004; Rasga, Quelhas, & Byrne 2016). Counterfactual and false-belief inferences activate similar brain areas (e.g., Van Hoeck, Begtas, Steen, Kestemont, Vandekerckhove, & Overwalle, 2014), and children with autism spectrum disorders have difficulties with both (e.g., Grant, Riggs, & Boucher, 2004; Rasga, Quelhas & Byrne, 2017). Counterfactual and false-belief reasoning both require the development of working memory to simulate several possibilities, and representational flexibility to simulate different perspectives on a single situation (e.g., Beck, Carroll, Brunsden, & Gryg, 2011; Drayton, Turley-Ames, & Guajardo, 2011).

Conclusions

Counterfactuals provide an important bridge between reasoning and imagination (e.g., Byrne, 2005; 2007). The same core cognitive processes may support the creation of counterfactual alternatives and reasoning with counterfactuals. The creation of counterfactual alternatives relies on cognitive processes that simulate reality, modify the simulation in systematic ways to create a counterfactual alternative, and switch attention from one simulation to the other. Reasoning with counterfactuals requires the simulation of alternative possibilities and the consideration of counterexamples to conclusions. Hence reasoning and imagination may depend on the same sorts of underlying computational processes.

Acknowledgments

I would like to thank Valerie Thompson, Linden Ball, and David Over for helpful comments on an earlier version of this chapter.

References

Alquist, J. L., Ainsworth, S. E., Baumeister, R. F., Daly, M., & Stillman, T. F. (2015). The making of might-have-beens: Effects of free will belief on counterfactual thinking. *Personality and Social Psychology Bulletin, 41*(2), 268–283.

Bacon, A. M., Walsh, C. R., & Martin, L. (2013). Fantasy proneness and counterfactual thinking. *Personality and Individual Differences, 54*(4), 469–473.

Beck, S. R., Carroll, D. J., Brunsdon, V. E. A., & Gryg, C. K. (2011). Supporting children's counterfactual thinking with alternative modes of responding. *Journal of Experimental Child Psychology, 108*, 190–202.
Branscombe, N. R., Owen, S., Garstka, T. A., & Coleman, J. (1996). Rape and accident counterfactuals: Who might have done otherwise and would it have changed the outcome? *Journal of Applied Social Psychology, 26*(12), 1042–1067.
Bucciarelli, M., Khemlani, S., & Johnson-Laird, P. N. (2008). The psychology of moral reasoning. *Judgment and Decision Making, 3*(2), 121–139.
Byrne, R. M. J. (2005). *The rational imagination: How people create alternatives to reality*. Cambridge, MA: MIT Press.
Byrne, R. M. J., (2007). Precis of the rational imagination: How people create alternatives to reality. *Behavioral and Brain Sciences, 30*, 439–453.
Byrne, R. M. J. (2016). Counterfactual thought. *Annual Review of Psychology, 67*, 135–157.
Byrne, R. M. J. (2017). Counterfactual thinking: From logic to morality. *Current Directions in Psychological Science, 26*, 314–322.
Byrne, R. M. J., & Johnson-Laird, P. N. (2009). 'If' and the problems of conditional reasoning. *Trends in Cognitive Sciences, 13*, 282–287.
Byrne, R. M. J., & McEleney, A. (2000). Counterfactual thinking about actions and failures to act. *Journal of Experimental Psychology: Learning, Memory, and Cognition, 26*, 1318–1331.
Byrne, R. M. J., Segura, S., Culhane, R., Tasso, A., & Berrocal, P. (2000) The temporality effect in counterfactual thinking about what might have been. *Memory & Cognition, 28*, 264–281.
Byrne, R. M. J., & Tasso, A. (1999) Deductive reasoning with factual, possible, and counterfactual conditionals. *Memory & Cognition, 27*(4), 726–740.
Camille, N., Coricelli, G., Sallet, J., Pradat-Diehl, P., Duhamel, J. R., & Sirigu, A. (2004). The involvement of the orbitofrontal cortex in the experience of regret. *Science, 304*(5674), 1167–1170.
Catellani, P., & Covelli, V. (2013). The strategic use of counterfactual communication in politics. *Journal of Language and Social Psychology, 32*(4), 480–489.
Coricelli, G., Critchley, H. D., Joffily, M., O'Doherty, J. P., Sirigu, A., & Dolan, R. J. (2005). Regret and its avoidance: A neuroimaging study of choice behavior. *Nature Neuroscience, 8*(9), 1255–1262.
Davis, C. G., Lehman, D. R., Wortman, C. B., Silver, R. C., & Thompson, S. C. (1995). The undoing of traumatic life events. *Personality and Social Psychology Bulletin, 21*, 109–124.
Davison, I. M., & Feeney, A. (2008). Regret as autobiographical memory. *Cognitive Psychology, 57*(4), 385–403.
De Brigard, F., Addis, D. R., Ford, J. H., Schacter, D. L., & Giovanello, K. S. (2013). Remembering what could have happened: Neural correlates of episodic counterfactual thinking. *Neuropsychologia, 51*(12), 2401–2414.
De Brigard, F., Szpunar, K. K., & Schacter, D. L. (2013). Coming to grips with the past effect of repeated simulation on the perceived plausibility of episodic counterfactual thoughts. *Psychological Science, 24*(7), 1329–1334.
De Vega, M., & Urrutia, M. (2011). Counterfactual sentences activate embodied meaning: An action sentence compatibility effect study. *Journal of Cognitive Psychology, 23*, 962–973.
Dixon, J., & Byrne, R. M. J. (2011). 'If only' counterfactual thoughts about exceptional actions. *Memory & Cognition, 39*(7), 1317–1331.
Drayton, S., Turley-Ames, K. J., & Guajardo, N. R. (2011). Counterfactual thinking and false belief: The role of executive function. *Journal of Experimental Child Psychology, 108*(3), 532–548.
Effron, D. A., Miller, D. T., & Monin, B. (2012). Inventing racist roads not taken: The licensing effect of immoral counterfactual behaviors. *Journal of Personality and Social Psychology, 103*(6), 916.
Egan, S., & Byrne, R. M. J. (2012). Inferences from counterfactual threats and promises. *Experimental Psychology, 59*(4), 227–235.
Egan, S., Garcia-Madruga, J., & Byrne, R. M. J. (2009). Indicative and counterfactual 'only if' conditionals. *Acta Psychologica*. 132, (3), 240–249.
El Leithy, S., Brown, G. P., & Robbins, I. (2006). Counterfactual thinking and posttraumatic stress reactions. *Journal of Abnormal Psychology, 115*(3), 629.
Epstude, K., & Roese, N. J. (2008). The functional theory of counterfactual thinking. *Personality and Social Psychology Review, 12*(2), 168–192.
Espino, O., & Byrne, R. M. J. (2013). The compatibility heuristic in non-categorical hypothetical reasoning: Inferences between conditionals and disjunctions. *Cognitive Psychology, 67*(3), 98–129.

Espino, O., Santamaria, C., & Byrne, R. M. J. (2009). People think about what is true for conditionals, not what is false: Only true possibilities prime the comprehension of 'if'. *Quarterly Journal of Experimental Psychology, 62*, 1072–1078.

Evans, J. St. B. T. (2007). *Hypothetical thinking: Dual processes in reasoning and judgement.* Hove, UK: Psychology Press.

Evans, J. St. B. T., & Over, D. E. (2004). *If.* Oxford, UK: Oxford University Press.

Evans, J. St. B. T., Over, D. E., & Handley, S. J. (2005). Suppositions, extensionality, and conditionals: A critique of the mental model theory of Johnson-Laird and Byrne (2002). *Psychological Review, 112,* 1040–1052.

Ferguson, H., & Sanford, A. (2008). Anomalies in real and counterfactual worlds: An eye-movement investigation. *Journal of Memory and Language* 58, 609–626.

Ferrante, D., Girotto, V., Stragà, M., & Walsh, C. (2013). Improving the past and the future: A temporal asymmetry in hypothetical thinking. *Journal of Experimental Psychology: General, 142*(1), 23–27.

Fillenbaum, S. (1974). Information amplified: Memory for counterfactual conditionals. *Journal of Experimental Psychology, 102,* 44–49.

Frosch, C., & Byrne, R. M. J. (2012). Causal conditionals and counterfactuals. *Acta Psychologica, 14*, 54–66.

Gerlach, K. D., Dornblaser, D. W., & Schacter, D. L. (2014). Adaptive constructive processes and memory accuracy: Consequences of counterfactual simulations in young and older adults. *Memory, 22*(1), 145–162.

Gillan, C. M., Morein-Zamir, S., Kaser, M., Fineberg, N. A., Sule, A., Sahakian, B. J., Cardinal, R. N., & Robbins, T. W. (2014). Counterfactual processing of economic action-outcome alternatives in obsessive-compulsive disorder. *Biological Psychiatry, 75*(8), 639–646.

Gilovich, T., & Medvec, V. H. (1995). The experience of regret: What, when, and why. *Psychological Review, 102*, 379–395.

Gilovich, T., Wang, R. F., Regan, D., & Nishina, S. (2003). Regrets of action and inaction across cultures. *Journal of Cross-Cultural Psychology, 34*, 61–71.

Ginsberg, M. L. (1986). Counterfactuals. *Artificial Intelligence, 30*(1), 35–79.

Girotto, V., Ferrante, D., Pighin, S., & Gonzalez, M. (2007). Postdecisional counterfactual thinking by actors and readers. *Psychological Science, 18*, 510–515.

Girotto, V., Legrenzi, P., & Rizzo, A. (1991). Event controllability in counterfactual thinking. *Acta Psychologica, 78*, 111–133.

Gomez-Beldarrain, M., Garcia-Monco, J. C., Astigarraga, E., Gonzalez, A., & Grafman, J. (2005). Only spontaneous counterfactual thinking is impaired in patients with prefrontal cortex lesions. *Cognitive Brain Research, 24*(3), 723–726.

Grant, C. M., Riggs, K. J., & Boucher, J. (2004). Counterfactual and mental state reasoning in children with autism. *Journal of Autism and Developmental Disorders, 34*(2), 177–188.

Greene, J. D., Nystrom, L. E., Engell, A. D., Darley, J. M., & Cohen, J. D. (2004). The neural bases of cognitive conflict and control in moral judgment. *Neuron, 44*, 389–400.

Guajardo, N. R., Parker, J., & Turley-Ames, K. (2009). Associations among false belief understanding, counterfactual reasoning, and executive function. *British Journal of Developmental Psychology, 27*(3), 681–702.

Gubbins, E., & Byrne, R. M. (2014). Dual processes of emotion and reason in judgments about moral dilemmas. *Thinking & Reasoning, 20*(2), 245–268.

Guttentag, R., & Ferrell, J. (2008). Children's understanding of anticipatory regret and disappointment. *Cognition and Emotion, 22*(5) 815–832.

Guttentag, R. E., & Ferrell, J. (2004). Reality compared with its alternatives: Age differences in judgments of regret and relief. *Developmental Psychology, 40,* 764–775.

Handley, S. J., Evans, J. St. B. T., & Thompson, V. A. (2006). The negated conditional: A litmus test for the suppositional conditional? *Journal of Experimental Psychology: Learning, Memory, & Cognition, 32,* 559–569.

Hooker, C., Roese, N. J., & Park, S. (2000). Impoverished counterfactual thinking is associated with schizophrenia. *Psychiatry, 63*(4), 326–335.

Johnson-Laird, P. N., & Byrne, R. M. J. (2002). Conditionals: A theory of meaning, pragmatics, and inference. *Psychological Review, 109*, 646–678.

Johnson-Laird, P. N., Khemlani, S. S., & Goodwin, G. P. (2015). Logic, probability, and human reasoning. *Trends in Cognitive Sciences, 19*(4), 201–214.

Juhos, C., Quelhas, A. C., & Byrne, R. M. J. (2015). Reasoning about intentions: Counterexamples to reasons for actions. *Journal of Experimental Psychology: Learning, Memory & Cognition, 41*(1), 55–76.

Kahneman, D., & Miller, D. T. (1986). Norm theory: Comparing reality to its alternatives. *Psychological Review, 93*(2), 136–153.

Kahneman, D., & Tversky, A. (1982a). The simulation heuristic. In D. Kahneman, P. Slovic, & A. Tversky (Eds.), *Judgment under uncertainty: Heuristics and biases* (pp. 201–208). New York: Cambridge University Press.
Kahneman, D., & Tversky, A. (1982b). The psychology of preferences. *Scientific American, 246*(1), 160–173.
Kulakova, E., Aichhorn, M., Schurz, M., Kronbichler, M., & Perner, J. (2013). Processing counterfactual and hypothetical conditionals: An fMRI investigation. *NeuroImage, 72*, 265–271.
Lewis, D. (1973). *Counterfactuals*. Oxford, UK: John Wiley & Sons.
Macrae, C. N., Milne, A. B., & Griffiths, R. J. (1993). Counterfactual thinking and the perception of criminal behaviour. *British Journal of Psychology, 84*(2), 221–226.
Malle, B. F., Monroe, A. E., & Guglielmo, S. (2014). A theory of blame. *Psychological Inquiry, 25*(2), 147–186.
Mandel, D. R., & Lehman, D. R. (1996). Counterfactual thinking and ascriptions of cause and preventability. *Journal of Personality and Social Psychology, 71*(3), 450–463.
Markman, K. D., Gavanski, I., Sherman, S. J., & McMullen, M. N. (1993.) The mental simulation of better and worse possible worlds. *Journal of Experimental Social Psychology, 29*(1), 87–109.
Markman, K. D., & McMullen, M. N. (2003). A reflection and evaluation model of comparative thinking. *Personality and Social Psychology Review*, 7(3), 244–267.
Markman, K. D., McMullen, M. N., & Elizaga, R. A. (2008). Counterfactual thinking, persistence, and performance: A test of the reflection and evaluation model. *Journal of Experimental Social Psychology, 44*(2), 421–428.
Markman, K., & Miller, A. (2006). Depression, control, and counterfactual thinking: Functional for whom? *Journal of Social and Clinical Psychology, 25*, 210–227.
Markman, K. D., & Tetlock, P. E. (2000). I couldn't have known: Accountability, foreseeability, and counterfactual denials of responsibility. *British Journal of Social Psychology, 39*, 313–325.
McCloy, R., & Byrne, R. M. J. (2000). Counterfactual thinking about controllable actions. *Memory & Cognition, 28*, 1071–1078.
McCloy, R., & Byrne, R. M. J. (2002). Semifactual "even if" thinking. *Thinking & Reasoning, 8*, 41–67.
McCrea, S. M. (2008). Self-handicapping, excuse making, and counterfactual thinking: Consequences for self-esteem and future motivation. *Journal of Personality and Social Psychology, 95*, 274–292.
McEleney, A., & Byrne, R. M. J. (2006). Spontaneous causal and counterfactual thoughts. *Thinking and Reasoning, 12*, 235–255.
McNamara, P., Durso, R., Brown, A., & Lynch, A. (2003). Counterfactual cognitive deficit in persons with Parkinson's disease. *Journal of Neurology, Neurosurgery & Psychiatry, 74*(8), 1065–1070.
Meehan, J. E., & Byrne, R. M. J. (2005). Children's counterfactual thinking: The temporal order effect. In B. G. Bara, L. Barsalou, & M. Bucciarelli (Eds.), *Proceedings of the 27th annual conference of the cognitive science society* (pp. 1467–1473). Mahwah, NJ: Lawrence Erlbaum Associates.
Migliore, S., Curcio, G., Mancini, F., & Cappa, S. F. (2014). Counterfactual thinking in moral judgment: An experimental study. *Frontiers in Psychology, 5*, Article 51.
Miller, D.T., & Gunasegaram, S. (1990). Temporal order and the perceived mutability of events: Implications for blame assignment. *Journal of Personality and Social Psychology, 59*(6), 1111.
Moreno-Rios, S., Garcia-Madruga, J., & Byrne, R. M. J. (2008). Semifactual 'even if' reasoning, *Acta Psychologica, 128*, 197–209.
Morris, M. N., & Moore, P. C. (2000). The lessons we (don't) learn: Counterfactual thinking and organizational accountability after a close call. *Administrative Science Quarterly, 45*, 737–765.
Morrison, M., & Roese, N. J. (2011). Regrets of the typical American: Findings from a nationally representative sample. *Social Psychological & Personality Science, 2*, 576–583.
N'gbala, A., & Branscombe, N. R. (1995). Mental simulation and causal attribution: when simulating an event does not affect fault assignment. *Journal of Experimental Social Psychology, 31*, 139–162.
Nickerson, R. (2015). *Conditional reasoning*. Oxford: Oxford University Press.
Niedenthal, P. M., Tangney, J. P., & Gavanski, I. (1994). "If only I weren't" versus "if only I hadn't": Distinguishing shame and guilt in counterfactual thinking. *Journal of Personality and Social Psychology, 67*(4), 585–595.
Nieuwland, M. S., & Martin, A. E. (2012). If the real world were irrelevant, so to speak: The role of propositional truth-value in counterfactual sentence comprehension. *Cognition, 122*(1), 102–109.
O'Connor, E., McCormack, T., & Feeney, A. (2014). Do children who experience regret make better decisions? A developmental study of the behavioral consequences of regret. *Child Development, 85*(5), 1995–2010.

Over, D. E., Hadjichristidis, C., Evans, J. ST. B. T., Handley, S. J., & Sloman, S. A. (2007). The probability of causal conditionals, *Cognitive Psychology*, *54*, 62–97.

Page, C. M., & Colby, P. M. (2003). If only I hadn't smoked: The impact of counterfactual thinking on a smoking-related behavior. *Psychology & Marketing*, *20*(11), 955–976.

Parkinson, M. & Byrne, R. M. J. (2017). Counterfactual and semifactual thoughts in moral judgments about failed attempts to harm. In press.

Pearl, J. (2013). Structural counterfactuals. *Cognitive Science*, *37*(7), 1382–1382.

Perner, J., Sprung, M., & Steinkogler, B. (2004). Counterfactual conditionals and false belief: A developmental dissociation. *Cognitive Development*, *19*(2), 179–201.

Petrocelli, J.V., Percy, E. J., Sherman, S. J., & Tormala, Z. L. (2011). Counterfactual potency. *Journal of Personality and Social Psychology*, *100*(1), 30.

Pighin, S., Byrne, R. M. J., Ferrante, D., Gonzalez, M., & Girotto, V. (2011). Counterfactual thoughts about experienced, observed, and narrated events. *Thinking and Reasoning*, *17*(2), 197–211.

Quelhas, A. C., & Byrne, R. M. J. (2003). Reasoning with deontic and counterfactual conditionals. *Thinking and Reasoning*, *9*(1), 43–65.

Rasga, C., Quelhas, A. C., & Byrne, R. M. (2016). Children's reasoning about other's intentions: False-belief and counterfactual conditional inferences. *Cognitive Development*, *40*, 46–59.

Rasga, C., Quelhas, A.C., & Byrne, R .M. J. (2017). How children with autism reason about other's intentions: False belief and counterfactual inferences. *Journal of Autism and Developmental Disorders*, *47*, 1806–1817.

Riggs, K. J., Peterson, D. M., Robinson, E. J., & Mitchell, P. (1998). Are errors in false belief tasks symptomatic of a broader difficulty with counterfactuality? *Cognitive Development*, *13*(1), 73–90.

Rim, S., & Summerville, A. (2014). How far to the road not taken? The effect of psychological distance on counterfactual direction. *Personality and Social Psychology Bulletin*, *40*(3), 391–401.

Rips, L. J. (2010). Two causal theories of counterfactual conditionals. *Cognitive Science*, *34*(2), 175–221.

Ritov, I., & Baron, J. (1990). Reluctance to vaccinate: Omission bias and ambiguity. *Journal of Behavioral Decision Making*, *3*, 263–277.

Roese, N. J. (1997). Counterfactual thinking. *Psychological Bulletin*, *121*(1), 133.

Rye, M. S., Cahoon, M. B., Ali, R. S., & Daftary, T. (2008). Development and validation of the counterfactual thinking for negative events scale. *Journal of Personality Assessment*, *90*(3), 261–269.

Sanna, L. J., & Turley, K. J. (1996). Antecedents to spontaneous counterfactual thinking: effects of expectancy violation and outcome valence. *Personality and Social Psychology Bulletin*, *22*(9), 906–919.

Santamaria, C., Espino, O., & Byrne, R. M. J. (2005). Counterfactual and semifactual conditionals prime alternative possibilities. *Journal of Experimental Psychology: Learning, Memory, and Cognition*, *31*, 1149–1154.

Schacter, D. L., Benoit, R. G., De Brigard, F., & Szpunar, K. K. (2015). Episodic future thinking and episodic counterfactual thinking: Intersections between memory and decisions. *Neurobiology of Learning and Memory*, *117*, 14–21.

Segura, S., Fernandez-Berrocal, P., & Byrne, R. M. J. (2002). Temporal and causal order effects in counterfactual thinking. *Quarterly Journal of Experimental Psychology*, *55*, 1295–1305.

Sloman, S. A., & Lagnado, D. A. (2005). Do we "do"? *Cognitive Science*, *29*, 5–39.

Smallman, R., & McCulloch, K. C. (2012). Learning from yesterday's mistakes to fix tomorrow's problems: When functional counterfactual thinking and psychological distance collide. *European Journal of Social Psychology*, *42*(3), 383–390.

Spellman, B. A. (1997). Crediting causality. *Journal of Experimental Psychology: General, 126*, 323–348.

Spellman, B. A., & Mandel, D. R. (1999). When possibility informs reality: Counterfactual thinking as a cue to causality. *Current Directions in Psychological Science*, *8*(4), 120–123.

Stalnaker, R. C. (1968). A theory of conditionals. In N. Rescher (Ed.), *Studies in logical theory* (pp. 98–112). Oxford: Basil Blackwell.

Teigen, K. H., & Jensen, T. K. (2011). Unlucky victims or lucky survivors? Spontaneous counterfactual thinking by families exposed to the tsunami disaster. *European Psychologist*, *16*(1), 48–57.

Thompson, V., & Byrne, R. M. J. (2002). Reasoning counterfactually: making inferences about things that didn't happen. *Journal of Experimental Psychology: Learning, Memory & Cognition*, *28*, 1154–1170.

Van Hoeck, N., Begtas, E., Steen, J., Kestemont, J., Vandekerckhove, M., & Van Overwalle, F. (2014). False belief and counterfactual reasoning in a social environment. *NeuroImage*, *90*, 315–325.

Van Hoeck, N., Ma, N., Ampe, L., Baetens, K., Vandekerckhove, K., & Van Overwalle, F. (2013). Counterfactual thinking: An fMRI study on changing the past for a better future. *Social Cognitive and Affective Neuroscience*, *8*, 556–564.

Walsh, C. R., & Byrne, R. M. J. (2004). Counterfactual thinking: The temporal order effect. *Memory & Cognition, 32*, 369–378.
Walsh, C. R., & Byrne, R. M. J. (2007). How people think "if only . . . " about reasons for actions. *Thinking & Reasoning, 13*(4), 461–483.
Weisberg, D. P., & Beck, S. R. (2010). Children's thinking about their own and others' regret and relief. *Journal of Experimental Child Psychology, 106*(2), 184–191.
Wells, G. L., Taylor, B. R., & Turtle, J. W. (1987). The undoing of scenarios. *Journal of Personality and Social Psychology, 53*(3), 421–430.
Williamson, T. (2007). Philosophical knowledge and knowledge of counterfactuals. *Grazer Philosophische Studien, 74*(1), 89–124.
Wimmer, H., & Perner, J. (1983). Beliefs about beliefs: Representation and constraining function of wrong beliefs in young children's understanding of deception. *Cognition, 13*(1), 103–128.
Zeelenberg, M., & Pieters, R. (2007). A theory of regret regulation 1.0. *Journal of Consumer Psychology, 17*(1), 3–18.
Zeelenberg, M., Van den Bos, K., Van Dijk, E., & Pieters, R. (2002). The inaction effect in the psychology of regret. *Journal of Personality and Social Psychology, 82*(3), 314–327.

6
FALLACIES OF ARGUMENTATION

Peter J. Collins and Ulrike Hahn

Introduction

The British Parliament recently debated legislation to permit IVF techniques allowing three-parent babies in order to prevent inherited mitochondrial diseases. Opponents objected that the legislation 'marked the start of a "slippery slope" towards designer babies and eugenics' (Knapton, 2015) and that it 'put the UK out in front of a race to the bottom' in human dignity (Rush, 2015). This slippery slope argument is one of a family of arguments – the informal fallacies – that have traditionally been viewed as persuasive but improper (see, for example, Hamblin, 1970; Toulmin, Rieke, & Janik, 1979; Walton, 2008).

Informal fallacies – and accusations of fallaciousness – abound in public reasoning. Take the putatively false analogy in debates about national debt between state and family finances (Krugman, 2012) or celebrity endorsements providing dubious arguments from authority (Walton, Reed, & Macagno, 2008). Are these bad arguments, and if so, why? Are they persuasive? These questions about human rationality parallel those in neighbouring fields, such as judgment and decision-making. Persuasive but bad arguments are to reasoning what biases are to judgment and decision-making, if normative standards for argument quality can be found.

Fallacies are widely debated but lack a consensus definition, list, or taxonomy, hence are best understood by example. Table 6.1 lists representative fallacies, with examples and explanations.

How one defines fallacies depends on which norms one accepts for arguments. Historically, fallacies struck researchers as arguments that, to some, seem valid – thus persuasive – though they are in fact logically invalid (Hamblin, 1970). This definition presupposes formal logic as a standard for arguments (van Eemeren & Grootendorst, 1995). Certain fallacies follow from this view: in our table, 'formal' fallacies follow from classical propositional and predicate logic, syllogistics, and standard modal extensions.

However, it becomes immediately apparent from the traditional catalogue of fallacies that classical logic does not suffice. Circular arguments (e.g., 'God exists, because God exists') are deductively valid: if the premise 'God exists' is true, the conclusion that therefore 'God exists' is necessarily true also. Nevertheless, circular arguments (or 'begging the question') are paradigmatically fallacious (on circular arguments, see Hahn, 2011).

Furthermore, classical logic is insufficient, because most real-world arguments involve uncertainty, almost by their very nature. In everyday life, people argue where disagreement exists;

Table 6.1 Representative fallacies from the literature, adapted from Curtis (2015)

Category	*Type*	*Name*	***Example/Explanation***
Formal	Propositional	Denial of Antecedent	If p then q; not p; therefore not q.
		Affirmation of Consequent	If p then q; q; therefore p.
		Improper Transposition	If p then q; therefore if not p then not q.
		Denying Conjunct	Not both p and q; not p; therefore not q.
		Commutation of Conditional	If p then q; therefore if q then p.
	Syllogistic	Illicit Process – Major	All X are Y; no Z are X; therefore no Z are Y.
		Illicit Process – Minor	All X are Y; All Y are Z; therefore all Z are X.
		Exclusive Premises	No X are Y; no Z are X; therefore no Z are X.
		Undistributed Middle	All X are Y; all Z are Y; therefore all Z are X.
		Negative Premises, Affirmative Conclusion	No X are Y; some Z are not X; therefore some Z are X.
		Affirmative Premises, Negative Conclusion	All X are Y; some Z are X; therefore some Z are not X.
		Four Term	No X are Y; all Z are X; therefore no Z are A.
	Quantification	Quantifier Shift	For every X there is a cause Y; therefore there is some cause Y which is the cause of every X.
	Modality	Modal Scope	Necessarily, if p then q; therefore, if p, then necessarily q.
Informal	Causal	***Ad consequentiam***	Appeal to consequences; belief accepted/rejected in virtue of good/bad consequences
		Common Cause	X believed to cause Y, when both caused by Z
		Cum hoc, ergo propter hoc	X and Y co-occur; therefore X causes Y
		Post hoc, ergo propter hoc	X precedes Y; therefore X causes Y
		Regression Fallacy	Regression to mean mistaken for causation
		Slippery Slope	Inoffensive move W leads, by steps X, Y etc, to unacceptable situation Z
	Diversion	Irrelevant Conclusion	Ignoratio elenchi; conclusion irrelevant to issue at hand
		Straw Man	Argues against a caricature of an opponent's argument
	Emotion	*Ad baculum*	Threatens force if conclusion not accepted
		Ad misericordiam	Argues for conclusion using irrelevant appeal to pity
	Language	Ambiguity	Structural or lexical (equivocation); cogency depends on ambiguous meanings
		Analogy	Argument hinges on likeness of A and B; likeness is weak or spurious

(*Continued*)

Table 6.1 (Continued)

Category	*Type*	*Name*	***Example/Explanation***
		Complex Question	Abusive presupposition: when did you stop beating your wife?
		Composition	The parts of X have property Y; therefore X, as a whole, has property Y.
		Division	X has, as a whole, property Y; therefore all parts of X have Y.
		Vagueness	Hinges on vagueness of argument's terms
	Source	***Ad hominem***	Attacks the source, not content, of argument
		Ad populum	Hinges on vagueness of argument's terms
		*Ad **verecundiam***	Cites popularity of argument, not content
	Other	Accident	Hasty generalization from unrepresentative (e.g., too small) sample
		Ad ignorantiam	Argument from ignorance; conclusion is true, because we don't know it to be false
		Question Begging	Petitio Principii; premise assumes conclusion

disagreement is least likely where states of affairs are true or false by necessity. It would be highly unsatisfactory to label everyday argumentation 'fallacious' simply because it typically involves non-deductive inference. Instead, standards seem desirable that allow a distinction between seemingly reasonable arguments and seemingly misguided ones.

Informal argument thus needs a different standard from classical logic. Various potential standards have been proposed. Given further that non-classical logic is an area subject to continual development (see, e.g., Prakken & Vreeswijk, 2002, for an overview), potential standards may continue to evolve. At present, however, non-classical logics have prompted very limited amounts of psychological research (for exceptions, see, e.g., Stenning & Lambalgen, 2008). This chapter consequently focuses on the most prominent approaches to fallacies of argumentation: procedural rules, argument schemes, and probability theory.

In the remainder of this chapter, we first survey norms for informal, real-world arguments, before discussing recent empirical work on people's responses to putative fallacies. We draw parallels with the psychology of judgment and decision-making, and social psychology.

Logical pragmatics and procedural norms

Traditionally, researchers have discussed arguments in terms of formal logic – more specifically, in terms of logical semantics: 'relationships between sets of true or false propositions' (Walton, 2008:1). Toulmin (1958) initiated an alternative program, which Walton (2008) calls logical pragmatics, that focuses on the use of arguments in reasoned dialogue. Toulmin (1958) exchanged formal logic for the following argument components, presented here as in Toulmin et al. (1979). In arguments, people make a claim, taking a stand about something or asking their audience to agree to something. They base their claim on grounds, presenting factual data for their claim. They link claim and grounds, often implicitly, through a warrant, drawing on general principles to justify the link between grounds and claim. They can buttress that warrant through backing, explaining why it holds. They can indicate the strength of a claim through modal qualifiers, calibrating the claim to their certainty with words and phrases like 'certainly', 'possibly', and 'so it seems'. Lastly, they can hedge against possible refutations, adding caveats like 'other things being equal'. During debate, arguers make these moves and audiences question them. To illustrate, witness the following example, adapted from Toulmin et al. (1979).

> *Claim*: the epidemic was caused by a bacterial infection carried between wards on food-service equipment.
> *Grounds*: our tests ruled out everything else, and we located a defect in the canteen washing equipment.
> *Warrant:* defective washing equipment is the sort of thing that could account for epidemics of this proportion.
> *Backing*: this is based on the scientific experience of waterborne bacteria and their control.
> *Modal qualification*: presumably the food-service equipment was the source of the epidemic.
> *Rebuttal*: within the limits of our bacteriological test procedures.

The example is typical of everyday informal argument in that it involves ampliative inference – the claim necessarily goes beyond the actual data – and is thus inherently uncertain. This puts such arguments beyond the scope of classical logic. Toulmin's framework addresses two key properties of arguments: audience relativity – that is, the same argument form can seem weak to some audiences, strong to others (Perelman & Olbrechts-Tyteca, 1969; Toulmin, 1958; Toulmin et al., 1979); and content relativity – that is, the same argument form can seem weak in some contexts, strong in others (Toulmin et al., 1979). Toulmin and colleagues (Toulmin, 1958; Toulmin et al., 1979) doubted absolute truth or validity, preferring an analogy with court cases: validity is established relative to certain legal proceedings, affirmed by judge and jury. The contents and contexts of arguments invoke particular criteria for truth; validity is established by the argument's participants.

Audience and content relativity seem equally relevant to putative fallacies (see, e.g., Hahn & Oaksford, 2012; Hahn & Oaksford, 2006a, 2006b; Hahn & Oaksford, 2007; Hahn & Oaksford, 2012; Walton, 2008). In general, fallacies, on Toulmin's view, largely result (intentionally or accidentally) from faulty warrants – unwarranted assumptions about the link between claim and grounds – or from ambiguity in an argument's terms (Toulmin et al., 1979). For example, Toulmin et al. argue that a fallacious argument from authority occurs below, because the warrant is untenable:

> *Claim*: we can be certain there are no 'spots' on the sun.
> *Grounds*: Aristotle assures us that the stuff of which the heavenly bodies are made is not subject to change.
> *Warrant*: whatever Aristotle asserted about the nature of material things can be accepted as true without reservation and cannot be refuted by observation.
> (Adapted from Toulmin et al., 1979:171)

This is not the only source of fallacies, but faulty warrants are a common source.[1]

However, Toulmin's framework remains insufficient for full characterization of when and why particular arguments should be viewed as weak or strong. Toulmin's framework describes argument structures more subtly than the traditional labels 'premise' and 'conclusion'. However, Toulmin offers no general way to establish an argument's strength. In particular, it remains unclear what makes a warrant tenable. In Toulmin's framework, the problem of strength is, in effect, simply pushed back. The same holds for the other components: for example, does the backing really support the warrant, or the warrant the grounds, or the grounds the claim? Without a principled way to address these questions, Toulmin's framework is ultimately restricted to assessing arguments merely through whether there *is* backing, or a warrant, and so on, but not the extent to which the conclusion is ultimately justified (see also Hahn, Bluhm, & Zenker, 2017).

Similar problems plague attempts to elucidate argument quality, and with it fallacies, via procedural rules of dialogue. Researchers have sought a more concrete pragmatic account of argument by identifying procedural rules, most prominently in the theory known as pragma-dialectics (e.g., van Eemeren & Grootendorst, 1984, 1992, 1995, 2004). Pragma-dialectics begins with the observation that arguments occur in dialectical contexts: individual arguments are put forward by parties in argumentative exchange. There are rules governing such exchanges, these rules being relevant to argument evaluation.

According to pragma-dialectics, there are different types of dialogues, which are defined by different goals. Table 6.2 outlines the principal types of dialogue.

Fallacies can result from mistaking the type of dialogue or switching between types. For instance, in a quarrel (or eristic dialogue) the goal is to attack and defeat an opponent, hence personal attacks are legitimate. But in a persuasion dialogue, the goal is persuasion or resolution of an issue, hence personal attacks are largely illegitimate (Walton, 2008). The emphasis on rational debate makes persuasion dialogues less lenient, and most fallacies, consequently, are seen in this type of dialogue (Walton, 2008; Van Eemeren & Grootendorst, 1995).

Table 6.2 Dialogue types, adapted from Walton (2008:8)

Type of dialogue	*Initial situation*	*Participant's goal*	*Goal of dialogue*
Persuasion	Conflict of opinions	Persuade other party	Resolve/clarify issue
Inquiry	Need for proof	Find, verify evidence	Prove (disprove) hypothesis
Negotiation	Conflict of interests	Get what you most want	Reasonable settlement for both
Information-seeking	Need information	Acquire/give new information	Exchange information
Deliberation	Dilemma/practical choice	Coordinate goals and actions	Decide best available action
Eristic	Personal conflict	Verbally hit out at opponent	Reveal deeper basis of conflict

All dialogues, however, comprise stages, and different argumentative moves are licensed at different stages. Van Eemeren and Grootendorst (e.g., 1984, 1992, 1995, 2004) distinguish four stages: confrontation, opening, argumentation, and conclusion. In the confrontation stage, a difference of opinion arises between participants. In the opening stage, the participants identify themselves, laying out their initial positions. In the argumentation stage, the participants begin the discussion: the arguer asserts and defends a position against audience questioning. In the conclusion stage, the participants reach their final positions: they agree, disagree, or fall somewhere in between. The final component is the procedural rules. Van Eemeren and Grootendorst (e.g., 1984, 1992, 1995, 2004) identify 10 rules. When these rules are violated, fallacies are taken to result. Table 6.3 lists the rules and corresponding fallacies, as presented in van Eemeren and Grootendorst (1995).

As this table shows, pragma-dialectics offers more detail than Toulmin's theory (Toulmin, 1958; Toulmin et al., 1979), providing a set of principles that seems to explain both good arguments and a fair number of fallacies. However, the account has its limitations.

First and foremost, there remain limitations concerning argument strength. As we have seen, fallacies are relative to audiences: some audiences will perceive an argument as fallacious; others, as strong (Hahn & Oaksford, 2012; Hahn & Oaksford, 2006a, 2006b; Perelman & Olbrechts-Tyteca, 1969; Toulmin, 1958; Toulmin et al., 1979). This may, of course, reflect an 'error' by one audience. However, some scope for rational disagreement seems likely to remain. Procedural rules allow audience relativity to the extent that whether an argument is acceptable depends, in part, on whether aspects of it are challenged; here, different audiences may be more or less accepting. However, it is unclear whether this is enough, as can be seen from a more fundamental limitation of procedural rules: fallacies are relative to content. With some contents an argument form seems fallacious, while with others it seems strong. Hahn and Oaksford (2012) illustrate this point with the following arguments from ignorance.

(1) Ghosts exist, because nobody has proven that they don't.
(2) The drug is safe, because clinical trials have found no evidence of side effects.
(3) The book is in the library, because the catalogue does not say that it is on loan.

Pre-theoretically these arguments differ in strength: (1) seems fallacious; (2) and (3) seem non-fallacious, though defeasible: their conclusions can be overturned by further information.

Table 6.3 Pragma-dialectic procedural rules and corresponding fallacies, as presented in van Eemeren & Grootendorst (1995)

Rule	*Definition & associated fallacies*
Freedom rule (confrontation stage)	Parties must not prevent each other from advancing standpoints or from casting doubt on standpoints. *Ad baculum, ad misericoridam, ad hominem*
Burden of proof rule (opening stage)	A party that advances a standpoint is obliged to defend it if asked by the other party to do so. *Shifting burden of proof, e.g., ad verecundiam, ad ignorantiam*
Standpoint rule (all stages)	A party's attack on a standpoint must relate to the standpoint that has indeed been advanced by the other party. *Straw man*
Relevance rule (argumentation stage)	A party may defend a standpoint only by advancing argumentation relating to that standpoint. *Ignoratio elenchi, ad populum, ad verecundium, emotive*
Unexpressed premise rule (argumentation stage)	A party may not deny premise that he or she has left implicit or falsely present something as a premise that has been left unexpressed by the other party. *Denying reasonable unexpressed premises or unfairly attributing unreasonable unexpressed premises*
Starting point rule (argumentation stage)	A party may not falsely present a premise as an accepted starting point nor deny a premise representing an accepted starting point. *Evading burden of proof, invoked in explaining, e.g., many questions, petitio principii*
Argument scheme rule (argumentation stage)	A party may not regard a standpoint as conclusively defended if the defense does not take place by means of an appropriate argumentation scheme that is correctly applied. *Ad verecundium, ad populam, hasty generalization, false analogy, ad consequentiam, causal fallacies, slippery slope*
Validity rule (argumentation stage)	A party may use in its argumentation only arguments that are logically valid or capable of being made logically valid by making explicit one or more unexpressed premises. *Formal fallacies*
Closure rule (closing stage)	A failed defense of a standpoint must result in the party that put forward the standpoint retracting it and a conclusive defense of the standpoint must result in the other party retracting its doubt about the standpoint. *Ad ignoratiam*
Usage rule (all stages)	A party must not use formulations that are insufficiently clear or confusingly ambiguous and a party must interpret the other party's formulations as carefully and accurately as possible. *Ambiguity, equivocation, amphiboly*

To explain the fallaciousness of (1), pragma-dialectics must invoke procedural rules: either the burden of proof rule or the closure rule. But this account does not explain why (1) is weak but (2) and (3) are not (Hahn & Oaksford, 2012). We cannot simply say that a given procedural rule is violated in one context but respected in another, because even when these arguments are presented without context they differ in strength (Hahn & Oaksford, 2012). Although pragma-dialectics can also draw on types of dialogue, we could easily insert (1), (2), and (3) into a persuasion dialogue (critical discussion), and the differences in strength would still obtain (Hahn & Hornikx, 2015).

The crucial ingredient seems to be content: it is the content of arguments one through three that makes them differ in strength, not how they are brought to the discussion. Pointing to the burden of proof to distinguish these examples reverses cause and effect: as an argument, (1) may be fallacious because it fails to meet a burden of proof. However, the very reason it so fails is that the argument is intrinsically weak. In short, the argument's weakness is a function of its content, and that is explanatorily prior to what roles it can assume in a given argumentative exchange (see also Hahn & Oaksford, 2007).

Finally, it remains unclear what the normative basis of these procedural rules is meant to be (see also Corner & Hahn, 2012). The pragma-dialectical framework appeals to 'reasonable critics', but it remains unexplained why reasonable critics should endorse these rules.

Content and argumentation schemes

We have seen that procedural rules alone cannot fully capture argument strength, hence the fallacies. Another way to capture content is argumentation schemes: part descriptive, part normative representations of the structure of common argument types (Walton et al., 2008), focusing on everyday, defeasible arguments. Argument schemes comprise a set of argumentative moves and corresponding critical questions. While the argumentative moves are descriptive, deriving from commonplace arguments, the critical questions are supposedly normative, providing criteria for the audience to evaluate the strength of an argument (Walton et al., 2008). Of the different inventories of argument schemes (e.g., Garssen, 1997; Hastings, 1962; Kienpointner, 1992; Perelman & Olbrechts-Tyteca, 1969; Schellens, 1985), the most extensive is the set of 60 schemes offered by Walton et al. (2008). Consider the slippery slope argument, for which Walton et al. (2008:339) give the following scheme:

> *First Step Premise*: A_0 is up for consideration as a proposal that seems initially like something that should be brought about.
> *Recursive Premise*: bringing up A_0 would plausibly lead (in the given circumstances, as far as we know) to A_1, which would in turn plausibly lead to A_2, and so forth through the sequence $A_2 \ldots A_{n.}$
> *Bad Outcome Premise*: A_n is a horrible (disastrous, bad) outcome.
> *Conclusion*: A_0 should not be brought about.

Walton et al. (2008) suggest the following critical questions: (1) What intervening propositions in the sequence linking up A_0 with A_n are actually given? (2) What other steps are required to fill in the sequence of events, to make it plausible? (3) What are the weakest links in the sequence, where specific critical questions should be asked on whether one event will really lead to another? Let us reconsider the argument about three-parent babies from the opening paragraph, and elaborate it as an illustration.

First Step Premise: IVF procedures are being proposed to allow three-parent babies, to prevent mitochondrial diseases.

Recursive Premise: introducing these procedures would lead people to accept changes to the DNA in the nucleus, thus designer babies and, ultimately, eugenics.

Bad Outcome Premise: eugenics would be an affront to human decency.

Conclusion: these IVF procedures should not be introduced.

To evaluate this argument, we apply Walton et al.'s (2008) critical questions. (1) The argument above presents no evidence for intermediate stages on the slippery slope. (2) We could add many possible intervening steps. For instance, public opinion might be profoundly changed by acceptance of these procedures, creating demand for further liberalization. This might then be reflected in legal changes, allowing procedures on the DNA in the nucleus. Further steps would need to demonstrate that such legal changes would allow designer babies and eugenics. (3) The argument, as presented here, contains many weak links. Perhaps the weakest is the initial link between IVF procedures and changes to DNA in the nucleus. These critical questions do not exhaust analysis. We might ask: what is meant by the terms 'designer babies' and 'eugenics', both being somewhat loaded terms; what criteria are there for violations of human decency; and do they make human decency an appropriate metric for laws? Walton et al.'s (2008) argument scheme provides a starting point, but does not deliver a complete treatment.

Because argument schemes treat argument content, they can also treat content relativity: content systematically influences argument strength. A scheme-based approach also has some capacity to deal with audience relativity. On a procedural understanding of critical questions, some audiences may choose to pose critical questions; others might not.

However, one may question whether 'critical questions' really satisfactorily capture all normative issues in the first place. Critical questions never seem exhaustive. For example, 'Is a source an expert?' might be answered by appeal to a university degree, but one can then ask whether this degree is in fact genuine and so on (see Hahn & Hornikx, 2015; Walton et al., 2008). It is impossible to foresee all possible scenarios and summarize them in appropriate critical questions. Many critical questions thus simply push back the question of the strength of the empirical evidence – whether a correlation truly exists, or how strong the evidence is for a hypothesis. They thus seem to rely on external criteria for assessing strength. Most fundamentally, however, it is unclear what the normative basis for any of these critical questions actually is. Many seem intuitively appealing, but intuition can be misleading (for specific examples in the context of the appeal to popular opinion, for example, see Hahn & Hornikx, 2015).

In fact, both procedural rules and argument schemes mix description and prescription. This gives both theories a strong practical focus. But their prescriptions lack external justification. Why should we accept them? To clarify, compare these theories with formal logic. Formal logic can be construed as a system of mathematical symbols that can be manipulated algebraically; its rules can be given mathematical proofs (Arthur, 2011). These rules guarantee consistency, or coherence: no such guarantee exists for procedural rules or schemes. Like logic, however, probabilistic norms, which we consider next, guarantee consistency.

Probabilistic norms

When people argue – that is, enter persuasion dialogue or critical discussion – they are reasoning under uncertainty, for which the natural calculus is probability theory (Korb & Nicholson, 2011; Pearl, 1988). Like formal logic, and unlike procedural rules and argument schemes, the rules of probability theory are justified mathematically: consistent probabilistic reasoning must follow the axioms of probability; conversely, following the axioms of probability guarantees probabilistic consistency (see, e.g., Hajek, 2008). A burgeoning literature applies a type of probabilistic reasoning, namely Bayesian inference, to argumentation.

Why Bayesian norms?

Applying Bayesian inference to argumentation is the goal of the research program that has been referred to as Bayesian Argumentation (see Hahn & Oaksford, 2006b, 2007, 2012). From a Bayesian perspective, probabilities are subjective degrees of belief (see, e.g., Bolstad, 2007; Korb & Nicholson, 2011). Central to Bayesianism is the use of Bayes' rule as an update rule for belief revision. The inferential goal is to calculate the probability of a conclusion in light of evidence, that is, the posterior probability, $P(C \mid E)$. Calculating the posterior probability involves three key terms: the prior degree of belief in a conclusion, $P(C)$; the likelihood, or how likely the evidence would be if the claim were true, $P(E \mid C)$; and the probability of the evidence, $P(E)$. The Bayesian reasoner first weights the likelihood by the prior probability, then normalizes that value to between 0 and 1 by dividing by the probability of the evidence. Thus:

$$P(C|E) = \frac{P(E|C)P(C)}{P(E)} \qquad \text{Equation 1}$$

The probability of the evidence can also be expanded, by the law of total probability, to include all the ways in which the evidence can be true: when the conclusion is true and when the conclusion is false. Thus:

$$P(C|E) = \frac{P(E|C)P(C)}{\left(P(E|C)P(C)\right) + (P(E \mid \neg C)P(\neg C)} \qquad \text{Equation 2}$$

The ratio of the probabilities associated with these two ways the evidence could be true (that is, given either the truth or the falsity of the hypothesis) also provides a simple measure of how informative the given evidence is about a conclusion. This measure, the likelihood ratio, is the ratio of how likely the evidence is given that the conclusion is true and how likely the evidence is given that the conclusion is false. Thus:

$$\frac{P(E \mid C)}{P(E \mid \neg C)} \qquad \text{Equation 3}$$

These equations capture crucial aspects of arguments: firstly, the equations capture content relativity. As Hahn and Oaksford argue (2012), the constituent probabilities are determined by the content of an argument, varying systematically with that content. Secondly, the equations capture audience relativity in two senses. The subjective probabilities are assigned by the audience, including the crucial prior, which represents the audience's previous beliefs. Thus Bayesian reasoners will arrive at new beliefs based on subjective assessment of the evidence and its fit with their prior beliefs. While these equations neatly account for relativity, they also impose an absolute standard: the demand for probabilistic coherence means that not 'anything goes' (see also, Hahn & Oaksford, 2012).

Argumentation theory has historically been hostile towards the use of probabilities. For example, Walton et al. (2008:187) object, 'It is difficult to assign numbers to [causal generalizations that represent "every day knowledge"] with statistical precision, and it is misleading to then calculate outcomes based on Bayesian assumptions used to model the logical reasoning'.

However, they seem not to take into account that the numbers, in Bayesian statistics, are subjective probabilities. While they take a specific value, this does not have to represent any precise value in the world. Bayesian statistics, in general, uses subjective probabilities to remarkably good effect in a wide variety of fields (see, e.g., Bolstad, 2007; Korb & Nicholson, 2011). But if we are hesitant to assign seemingly precise numbers, we can reject point estimates and adopt distributions or use a coarser scale (see, e.g., Howson & Urbach, 1993; Hahn & Oaksford, 2006b). Recently, there have been more fundamental critiques of Bayesian approaches to cognitive modeling; however, we cannot deal with all these criticisms here (for references and discussion, see Hahn, 2014). It suffices to note the following. Bayesian inference is justified as a normative model because it is demonstrably optimal under given conditions, it avoids Dutch book arguments, and it minimizes the inaccuracy of beliefs (Hahn, 2014; Rosenkrantz, 1992). Given that 'fallacy' is an intrinsically evaluative, normative term, it is impossible to see how fallacy research could be conducted without reference to a normative standard.

Concerning the fallacies, which had largely resisted a unified treatment, probabilistic accounts are useful also in that they draw together a remarkable range of fallacies, from the formal to the statistical. Bayesian accounts consider both how people should optimally reason, and how people actually reason.

For traditional informal fallacies, there are Bayesian accounts of circular arguments (Hahn, 2011; Hahn & Oaksford, 2012), arguments from ignorance (Corner & Hahn, 2009; Hahn, Harris, & Corner, 2009; Hahn & Oaksford, 2007, 2012; Harris, Corner, & Hahn, 2009; Oaksford & Hahn, 2004; Hahn, Oaksford, & Bayindir, 2005), slippery slope arguments (Corner et al., 2011), ***ad hominem*** arguments (Harris, Hsu, & Madsen, 2012; Oaksford & Hahn, 2012; Bhatia & Oaksford, 2015), the appeal to popular opinion (Hahn & Oaksford, 2006b; Hahn & Hornikx, 2015), and appeals to pity or threat (Hahn & Oaksford, 2006a). For many of these, there also exists experimental work examining how far people's judgments of argument strength match Bayesian prescriptions. As we will see, this work suggests that these judgments are, indeed, broadly Bayesian.

This body of research naturally incorporates Oaksford and Chater's earlier work on formal fallacies of logical reasoning (e.g., Oaksford & Chater, 1994; Chater & Oaksford, 1999), which themselves appear in everyday argumentation (Godden & Walton, 2004). This work includes fallacies of conditional inference such as denial of the antecedent (if *p* then *q*; not *p*; therefore not *q*) and affirmation of the consequent (if *p* then *q*; *q*, therefore *p*) (Oaksford & Chater, 2007; Oaksford, Chater, & Larkin, 2000), as well as systematic 'errors' in syllogistic reasoning (Chater & Oaksford, 1999).

Unsurprisingly, probabilistic accounts have considerable traction for statistical fallacies. A Bayesian account, for instance, may argue that the conjunction fallacy may be justified on some interpretations of the task (Bovens & Hartmann, 2003; though see Jarvstad & Hahn, 2011, for a mismatch between these prescriptions and the descriptive data). A Bayesian account, therefore, links work on informal argumentation to work on the psychology of judgment, where Bayesian inference has long provided the normative standard (Newell, Lagnado, & Shanks, 2015).

Finally, the probabilistic approach extends naturally from arguments about facts to arguments about actions through the framework of decision theory. This further links work on informal argumentation to the psychology of decision-making.

We next illustrate these points with specific case studies.

Slippery slope arguments and decision-making

In slippery slope argumentation, the protagonist argues against a proposition by citing future consequences: accepting the proposition is supposedly the first in a chain of events leading to an unacceptable event. Slippery slopes have received extensive treatment from argumentation schemes (e.g., Walton et al., 2008) that gives limited guidance for judging whether a slippery slope is fallacious. Slippery slopes receive rather different treatment in Bayesian Argumentation (e.g., Hahn & Oaksford, 2007; Corner, Hahn, & Oaksford, 2011). Here, they feature as decision problems under uncertainty, and are given both a normative and a descriptive account.

Bayesian Argumentation assumes that rational decision-makers, faced with slippery slopes, will seek to maximize subjective expected utility (SEU). The SEU of an outcome x is given by the following equation: SEU = P(x)U(x). Bayesians view slippery slopes as utility conditionals: arguments of the form 'if p then q' whose strength depends on the (dis-)utility of antecedent and consequent and the conditional probability P(q | p) (see, e.g, Bonnefon, 2012). The most relevant utility conditional here is the conditional warning (see Evans, Neilens, Handley, & Over, 2008). Take the example 'If you go camping this weekend, it will rain'. This warning should be convincing if the conditional probability and disutility of rain are high enough. In conditional warnings, the conditional probability reflects knowledge about the world; but in slippery slopes the conditional probability reflects an implied mechanism linking antecedent and consequent (Corner et al., 2011). For Sorites-type slippery slope arguments, which trade on the fuzziness of category boundaries, this mechanism is categorization: more specifically, reappraisal of category boundaries. New category exemplars added near the category boundary extend that boundary in subsequent classification, as decades of categorization research attests (for references, see Corner et al., 2011).

Consider the example about procedures on mitochondria, expressed here as a conditional: 'if we grant that these procedures on mitochondria are acceptable, then we will end up granting that designer babies and eugenics are acceptable'. Classifying procedures on mitochondria as acceptable will extend the boundary of the category 'acceptable things', making the categorization of other items close to that boundary more probable in future. But a crucial question is how much more probable. This will be governed by the similarity of those other items to the newly established category member. In other words, what is the conditional probability P(q | p)? In the example, this will rest on the similarity between the procedures on mitochondria and those for designer babies or eugenics. The second critical question is this: what is the (dis-)utility of designer babies and eugenics?

Corner et al. (2011) tested both conditional probability through category-boundary reappraisal and the impact of utility in a series of experiments. They predicted, and found, that category-boundary reappraisal and utility would influence participants' judgments of argument strength. Their first experiment tested the principle that utility and probability influence argument strength. Participants read slippery slope arguments that varied in two key ways: the disutility of the consequences (e.g., euthanasia leading to increases in medical murder [high] versus the psychological effects on other patients [low]) and the probability (e.g., whether or not euthanasia would be tightly controlled). Participants were sensitive to both probability and utility across a range of topics, using this information in a broadly normative way. Corner et al.'s (2011) remaining experiments examined a probability manipulation based on category-boundary reappraisals. These experiments linked performance on a classification task with perceptions of an argument strength. Similarity predicted classification, which in turn predicted the strength of slippery slope arguments.

Corner et al.'s (2011) Bayesian account of the slippery slope argument has several benefits over procedural rules and argumentation schemes. Bayesian statistics and decision theory provide a normative framework that captures both content and audience relativity. These norms successfully predict participants' performance. This Bayesian account of argumentation sits cheek by jowl with more general psychological theories: though a probabilistic account, the probabilities were implemented indirectly through category-boundary reappraisal, a general psychological phenomenon. Thus, the account integrates argumentation with more general psychology, rather than treating argumentation in comparative isolation as in procedural rules and argumentation schemes.

Arguments from ignorance

Various other supposed fallacies have been given a Bayesian treatment. One such is the argument from ignorance (*argumentum ad ignorantiam*). Textbook examples include arguments such as 'ghosts exist because nobody has proven they don't', which does indeed seem weak. This argument takes the following form (Walton, 1996):

If A were true (false) it would be known (proved, presumed) to be true (false).
A is not known (proved, presumed) to be true (false).
Therefore, A is presumably false (true).

Closer inspection reveals various subtypes of arguments from ignorance. Some entail a shift in the burden of proof, as in the reasoning of McCarthyism: 'there is nothing in the files to disprove his communist connections' (Kahane, 1992), from which we are meant to conclude 'Therefore he has communist connections' (on types of arguments from ignorance, see, e.g., Walton, 1996, and Hahn & Oaksford, 2006b). Some entail epistemic closure. These arguments assume that all true relevant facts are represented in some knowledge database; anything not represented there is false (Walton, 1996; Oaksford & Hahn, 2004). An example is a train timetable, which should list all the stops that a train makes: a passenger on the Cardiff-to-London train will assume that, if Oxford is not listed as a stop, the train will not stop in Oxford. Lastly, some arguments from ignorance invoke negative evidence: for example, we might set out to test a hypothesis, derive positive predictions, and test them in a hypothesis; if the experiment does not provide evidence for the predictions, then we conclude that the hypothesis is false (Oaksford & Hahn, 2004).

The latter two examples show that one can easily imagine non-fallacious forms at least for these two types of argument from ignorance. A full train timetable *should* list all stops on a train journey, so we can reasonably assume that if a place is not listed the train will not stop there (Oaksford & Hahn, 2004). In such cases, an epistemic closure argument is reasonable. Epistemic closure, though, is a matter of degree. For example, someone searching a library catalogue may conclude that a given book will be on the shelf because the catalogue lists the book as available (Hahn, Bayindir, & Oaksford, 2005). But other relevant facts are whether the book has been returned but not yet re-shelved, or whether it is being read in the library, or whether it will be taken out before the person gets to the library. Similarly, if a thorough clinical trial yields no evidence that a drug has toxic effects, we can reasonably conclude that the drug does not have toxic effects (Oaksford & Hahn, 2004). In such cases, a negative evidence argument is reasonable, but again, it also varies with the probabilistic features of those drug safety trials: if the trial is extensive and has included many participants, we will be more convinced than if the sample was small. Both types of argument from ignorance thus lend themselves to a probabilistic treatment.

Oaksford and Hahn (2004) provided a Bayesian treatment of the argument for ignorance. We follow Oaksford and Hahn (2004) in using drug testing as an example. Let T stand for a drug being toxic and e stand for an experiment in which a toxic effect is observed. The negative evidence argument depends, for its strength, on the conditional probability that a drug is not toxic given that no toxic effects were observed, $P(\neg T \mid \neg e)$. This is the negative test validity (NTV). To evaluate the negative argument, we compare the NTV to the corresponding positive evidence argument: the conditional probability that a drug is toxic given that toxic effects were observed,

$P(T \mid e)$. This is the positive test validity (PTV). We can calculate the relevant conditional probabilities with the following versions of Bayes' Theorem.

$$NTV = P(\neg T \mid \neg e) = \frac{P(\neg T)P(\neg e \mid \neg T)}{P(\neg e)} \qquad \text{Equation 4}$$

Note here that the term $P(\neg e \mid \neg T)$ is the specificity of a test: in other words, the probability of a negative result given non-toxicity. The strength of the NTV is given by calculating the product of the test specificity and the prior probability of non-toxicity, and dividing (normalizing) by the probability of a negative test result.

PTV, by contrast, is simply $P(T \mid e)$, calculated again via Bayes' rule.

As Oaksford and Hahn show, several general intuitions about arguments from ignorance can be captured by this formalization. Firstly, in general, PTV will be higher than NTV when the base rate of toxicity is low and the sensitivity is high. Under these conditions, then, the positive evidence argument will be stronger than the negative evidence argument (argument from ignorance) (Oaksford & Hahn, 2004). Secondly, as long as the specificity of a test is high enough, then the PTV will be higher than NTV across a wide range of sensitivities, even when the prior probability of toxicity, $P(e)$, is low (Oaksford & Hahn, 2004; Hahn & Oaksford, 2007).

Oaksford and Hahn (2004) tested participants' judgments of argument strength for fictitious dialogues, examining the extent to which participants' judgments matched three qualitative aspects of this Bayesian formalization: (1) Positive evidence will tend to be stronger. (2) Prior belief matters. (3) The more evidence, the stronger the argument.

These predictions are supported by experimental data, which argues for the view that people are sensitive to degrees of strength in arguments from ignorance, from the fallacious to the strong. Oaksford and Hahn (2004) tested these predictions using materials such as the following:

Barbara: Are you taking digesterole for it?
Adam: Yes, why?
Barbara: Good, because I strongly believe that it does not have side effects.
Adam: It does not have any side effects.
Barbara: How do you know?
Adam: Because I know of an experiment where they failed to find any.

In all dialogues, one character presented a prior belief and the other presented an argument. The dialogues manipulated the topic, the strength of prior belief, the polarity (e.g., there are/are not side effects), and the strength of evidence (e.g., 1 or 50 experiments). In a repeated-measures format, participants judged the posterior belief of one character (equivalent to Barbara above). Positive arguments were significantly stronger than negative ones, though these were significantly above zero. Stronger prior beliefs increased the strength of posterior belief, as did the stronger evidence.

Hahn, Oaksford, and Bayindir (2005) replicated these findings with new scenarios and a non-numerical way of expressing degrees of evidence, and extended the method to include arguments from ignorance that rely on epistemic closure.

The epistemic closure version of the argument from ignorance involves a double negation, from which a positive is inferred. Hahn et al. (2005) and Hahn and Oaksford (2007) detail how this argument can be captured by considering three possibilities: evidence for the claim, evidence against it, and no evidence at all. Hahn et al. (2005) devised real-world examples of the epistemic closure form that varied the degree of epistemic closure the domain affords (these arguments were about whether a book was on a library shelf, given that it was listed as such in the catalogue; whether a train stopped somewhere, given what was said in the timetable; and whether a medical procedure had been carried out, given what was in the medical notes). They then contrasted positive evidence versions of these arguments with the two types of argument from ignorance just discussed. Participants' ratings of the strength of these arguments were broadly consistent with the Bayesian predictions, and were sensitive to the degree of epistemic closure, showing both that arguments from ignorance can be reasonable and that they vary intuitively in strength in ways predicted by the Bayesian formalization.

Corner and Hahn (2009) introduced source reliability as a factor in a study exploring whether people assess scientific and non-scientific arguments in different ways. In one of their tasks, they presented participants with arguments from ignorance about scientific and non-scientific topics, and gave information about amount of evidence and the reliability of the source. They asked participants to rate the argument and strength and the reliability of the source. They found significant main effects of evidence (the stronger, the better) and reliability (the higher, the better), and significant interactions between the two: the arguments rated best were those with strong evidence and reliable sources. Science and non-science arguments differed also, with non-science arguments being considered weaker, but this difference appeared to be due to perceived source reliability.

Harris, Hahn, and Corner (2013), finally, extended this treatment of arguments from ignorance to a further type that corresponds to the familiar phenomenon of 'damning with faint praise'. They presented participants with a fictional scenario of a student applying for a mathematics degree who was given an underwhelming reference: 'James is polite and punctual'. The implication here is a lack of recommendation. The reference acts as an argument from ignorance: the conclusion follows because of what is not said (i.e., that James possesses appropriate mathematical abilities). Harris et al. (2013) showed, however, that this conclusion is moderated by beliefs about the source. The argument (reference) was only considered persuasive when its source was expert (James' maths teacher), not when it was inexpert (James' personal tutor).

The Bayesian approach is not, of course, the only approach to the argument from ignorance. A different approach is taken by van Eemeren, Garssen, and Meuffels (2009). Van Eemeren et al. (2009) studied the argument for ignorance as part of a large experimental study into the pragma-dialectical procedural rules. Their general approach was to test whether people are sensitive to violations of procedural rules by having them rate the reasonableness of arguments with and without violations. Pragma-dialectics holds that arguments from ignorance occur at the concluding stage of a discussion. At this stage, arguments can go awry in the following ways (van Eemeren et al., 2009:195). The protagonist (proponent) can refuse to retract a standpoint that has not been successfully defended, or can conclude that a standpoint that has been successfully defended is therefore true. The antagonist (opponent) can refuse to retract criticism of a standpoint that has been successfully defended, or can conclude that a standpoint is true because the opposite has not been successfully defended. This last case is, on van Eemeren et al.'s account, the argument from ignorance. They showed participants arguments from ignorance such as the following (van Eemeren et al., 2009:197):

> Thijs and Lieke's dog is sleeping the whole time in his basket. Thijs and Lieke are wondering what is wrong. Thijs claims that their dog is ill. Lieke is not so sure. The discussion concludes as follows:
>
> *Lieke:* After all your explanations and arguments I'm still not convinced.
> *Thijs:* Well, what else can I say?
> *Lieke:* That proves that I'm right. The dog's not ill.

Participants also saw control arguments in which the final move was reasonable alongside filler arguments, which were other fallacious arguments. Participants considered arguments from ignorance to be significantly worse than reasonable controls. Participants were also asked to explain their judgments for a subset of the arguments. Of these cases, some 51% gave answers showing clear insight into the argument from ignorance, consisting of answers such as 'Not being able to be convinced does not mean that it is not so' (van Eemeren et al., 2009:200).

Although van Eemeren et al. (2009) use these and similar data to argue for procedural rules, the data do not contradict the Bayesian approach. Indeed, the Bayesian and pragma-dialectic experiments both suggest that participants are sensitive to the quality of arguments from ignorance. However, as Bhatia and Oaksford (2015) argue, pragma-dialectic rules seem to function analogously to (classical) logical validity: just as an argument is either logically valid or invalid, a procedural rule is either obeyed or disobeyed. But van Eemeren et al.'s (2009) experiments, like those that test Bayesian predictions, yield graded reasonableness judgments. Such judgments seem more compatible with a graded view of argument strength, such as in Bayesian Argumentation.

Source fallacies

As we have seen, a Bayesian account links the slippery slope argument with the psychology of decision-making. Bayesian accounts of arguments from sources parallel work in social psychology and formal epistemology. Prominent social psychology theories suggest that source information is typically handled in a peripheral and qualitatively inferior fashion (e.g., Eagly & Chaiken, 1993; Petty & Cacioppo, 1984; Petty, Cacioppo, & Goldman, 1981). Work in formal epistemology suggests a rather more profound and subtle role for source information (e.g., Bovens & Hartmann, 2003). We will discuss two argument forms here: the *ad hominem* argument and the argument from expertise (*argumentum ad verecundiam*).

Harris, Hsu, and Madsen (2012) explored the *argumentum ad Hitlerum*, which argues against an action (belief) because Hitler acted (believed) the same way. For example, one might argue against vegetarianism by noting that Hitler was vegetarian. Harris et al. (2012) used arguments across a range of topics of the following form (321):

A: Have you heard about the new transport policy being considered?
B: Yes, why?
A: I have no idea if it's a good idea or not.
B: It's definitely not.
A: Why?
B: Because Hitler implemented the same policy when he was in power.

Harris et al. treated these arguments as Bayesian inference. The key terms in the inference were as follows: the posterior probability is the probability that that policy (action) is good given that Hitler implemented it; the likelihood, the probability that Hitler implemented an action given that it was good; and the prior, the prior probability that the policy is good. In the first experiment, participants provided judgments of the likelihood and of the posterior, the prior being fixed in the dialogues. The Bayesian model accounted for participants' judgments, they found that the Bayesian model accounted for 89% of the variance in participants' judgments across topics. Subsequent experiments replicated this high level of fit with (fictional) objective values and when the likelihood was systematically manipulated. Participants, then, conformed well to normative prescriptions for *ad hominem* arguments.

This Bayesian account contrasts starkly with the account proposed in pragma-dialectics. The contrasting accounts have been tested comparatively in a recent study by Bhatia and Oaksford (2015). Pragma-dialectics explains arguments from authority by referring to procedural rules and stages of discourse. Thus, ***ad hominem*** arguments are fallacious when they violate the Freedom Rule: 'parties must not prevent each other from advancing standpoints or from casting doubt on standpoints' (van Eemeren & Grootendorst, 1995). The Freedom Rule applies at the Confrontation Stage, when the difference of opinion first arises. But when ***ad hominem*** arguments occur at later stages, they are, on the pragma-dialectic view, perfectly legitimate. Recent experimental tests suggest that people *are* sensitive to violations of the Freedom Rule (van Eemeren, Garssen, & Meuffels, 2012). Bhatia and Oaksford (2015), however, show graded acceptability of ***ad hominem*** arguments even where there is no information about the argumentation stage.

Harris et al. (in press) investigated a different source argument, the argument from expert opinion (also known, in the context of the fallacies, as ***argumentum ad verecundiam***). They explored a Bayesian model of appeals to expert opinion, and found support for the model. The model takes as its point of departure the argumentation scheme for the appeal to expert opinion (Walton et al., 2008:218). According to Walton et al., a good appeal to expert opinion will answer the following critical questions:

Expertise Question:	How credible is the source, *S*, as an expert source?
Field Question:	Is S an expert in the field that *H* [a factual claim] is in?
Opinion Question:	What did *S* assert that implies *H*?
Trustworthiness Question:	Is *S* personally reliable as a source?
Consistency Question:	Is *H* consistent with what other expert sources assert?
Backup Evidence Question:	Is *S*'s assertion based on evidence?

Harris et al. (in press) use a simplified version of the Bayesian model developed in Hahn, Oaksford, and Harris (2012), which represents the critical questions as nodes in a Bayesian belief network.[2] Harris et al. (in press) then tested the Bayesian model in the following experiments. The experiments used dialogues between a proponent and recipient about the positive or negative effects of a fictional medicine. These arguments appealed to experts who were either trustworthy (the proponent's friend) or untrustworthy (the proponent's enemy). The experts were also high or low expertise, and were unsupported, supported, or contradicted by other experts. Arguments were rated as stronger when they were supported by other experts, when the sources had high expertise, and when the sources were trustworthy, although trustworthiness had no effect when other experts disagreed. Overall, the Bayesian model had a reasonable fit with the data, explaining 89% of the variance across conditions, and there was little systematic difference between the model and data. A second experiment replicated these results but removed free parameters by having participants estimate the prior probability of the conclusion. In this more rigorous test, there was again a good fit, accounting for 94% of the variance, and no systematic mismatch.

When we take the data gathered in Bayesian Argumentation together, we can see that there is a reasonably good fit between Bayesian norms and participants' behavior. In other words, Bayesian accounts specify the conditions under which these informal arguments can be considered strong or weak (fallacious). Participants show broadly rational Bayesian behavior, at least at a qualitative level.

Conclusions

We have discussed fallacies and informal argumentation from the point of view of the most prominent current theories of informal argumentation, arguing that while all of the approaches have their advantages, procedural rules and argumentation schemes ultimately lack an account of argument strength. Probability theory – specifically Bayesian inference – provides a normatively justified account of argument. Bayesian Argumentation has begun to apply these norms to experimentation, and to use them as a measure of participants' rationality. Experiments thus far suggest a reasonably good fit between Bayesian norms and participants' judgments.

Adopting a probabilistic framework amounts to a substantial theoretical advance with respect to argument quality, and enables a whole new program of experimental research that simply was not possible a few decades ago. Through a common language of probabilities and utilities, this program brings continuity with neighbouring fields in the study of human rationality (Bonnefon, 2013), including judgment, decision-making, formal epistemology, and social psychology. Nevertheless, continuity does not imply uniformity (Bonnefon, 2013). The psychology of argumentation has its own challenges, which make it a discipline every bit as rich as its longer-established neighbours.

Notes

1 Other fallacies can result from ambiguities in the use of terms (see, for discussion, Toulmin et al., 1979:179). Take, for example, the fallacy of equivocation. Curtis (2015) offers the following example of an alleged fallacy of equivocation: 'it is fair to conclude from medicine that the humanity of the life growing in a mother's womb is undeniable and, in itself, a powerful reason for treating the unborn with respect'. On Curtis' (2015) analysis, the argument trades on the ambiguity of 'humanity'. There are at least two relevant senses of 'humanity': being a member of the human species; being characteristic of humans, as, for example, is the human heart. For the humanity of a foetus to be indisputable, the latter 'characteristic of humans' sense seems to apply. But for the argument to have moral force, the 'member of the human species' sense would have to apply.

2 Bayesian belief networks consist of nodes and connecting arcs. Nodes represent variables; arcs represent dependencies between variables. They may be used both for representation and for the simplification of complex Bayesian analyses. See Harris et al. (in press) or Korb and Nicholson (2011) for discussion.

References

Arthur, R. T. W. (2011). *Natural deduction: An introduction to logic with real arguments, a little history, and some humour*. Peterborough, Ontario: Broadview.

Bhatia, J. S., & Oaksford, M. (2015). Belief change, relevance, and procedural rules in argumentation: Discounting testimony with the argument ad hominem and a Bayesian congruent prior model. *Journal of Experimental Psychology: Learning, Memory and Cognition, 41*(5), 1548–1559.

Bolstad, W. M. (2007). *Introduction to Bayesian statistics* (2nd ed.). Hoboken, NJ: Wiley.

Bonnefon, J.-F. (2012). Utility conditionals as consequential arguments: A random sampling experiment. *Thinking & Reasoning, 18*, 379–393.

Bonnefon, J-F. (2013). New ambitions for a new paradigm: Putting the psychology of reasoning at the service of humanity. *Thinking & Reasoning, 19*(3), 381–398.

Bovens, L., & Hartmann, S. (2002). Bayesian networks and the problem of unreliable instruments. *Philosophy of Science, 69*(1), 29–72.

Bovens, L., & Hartmann, S. (2003). *Bayesian epistemology* (OUP Catalogue). Oxford: Oxford University Press.

Chater, N., & Oaksford, M. (1999). The probability heuristics model of syllogistic reasoning. *Cognitive Psychology, 38*(2), 191–258.

Coady, C. A. J. (1992). *Testimony: A philosophical study*. Oxford: Oxford University Press.

Corner, A., & Hahn, U. (2009). Evaluating science arguments: evidence, uncertainty, and argument strength. *Journal of Experimental Psychology: Applied, 15*(3), 199–212.

Corner, A., & Hahn, U. (2012). Normative theories of argumentation: are some norms better than others? *Synthese, 190*(16), 3579–3610. http://doi.org/10.1007/s11229-012-0211-y

Corner, A., Hahn, U., & Oaksford, M. (2011). The psychological mechanism of the slippery slope argument. *Journal of Memory and Language, 64*(2), 133–152.

Curtis, G. N. (2015). *Taxonomy of logical fallacies*. Retrieved from www.fallacyfiles.org/taxonomy.html
Curtis, G. N. (2015). *The fallacy of equivocation*. Retrieved from www.fallacyfiles.org/equivoqu.html
Eagly, A. H., & Chaiken, S. (1993). *The psychology of attitudes*. Belmont, CA: Thompson/Wadsworth.
Evans, J. St. B. T., Neilens, H., Handley, S. J., & Over, D. E. (2008). When can we say "if"? *Cognition, 108*(1), 100–116.
Garssen, B. J. (1997). *Argumentatieschema's in pragma-dialectisch perspectief: Een theoretisch en empirisch onderzoek*. Amsterdam: IFOTT.
Godden, D., & Walton, D. (2004). Denying the antecedent as a legitimate argumentative strategy: A dialectical model. *Informal Logic: Reasoning and Argumentaion Theory in Practice, 24*, 219–243.
Grice, H. (1975). Logic and conversation. In D. Davidson & G. Harman (Eds.), *The logic of grammar* (pp. 64–75). Encino, CA: Dickenson.
Hahn, U. (2011). The problem of circularity in evidence, argument, and explanation. *Perspectives on Psychological Science, 6*(2), 172–182.
Hahn, U. (2014). The Bayesian boom: Good thing or bad? *Cognitive Science, 5*, 765.
Hahn, U., Bluhm, R., & Zenker, F. (2017). Causal argument. In M. Waldmann (Ed.), *The Oxford handbook of causal cognition* (pp. 475–493). Oxford, UK: Oxford University Press.
Hahn, U., Harris, A. J. L., & Corner, A. (2009). Argument content and argument source: An exploration. *Informal Logic, 29*(4), 337–367.
Hahn, U., & Hornikx, J. (2015). A normative framework for argument quality: Argumentation schemes with a Bayesian foundation. *Synthese, 193,* 1833–1873.
Hahn, U., & Oaksford, M. (2004). A Bayesian approach to the argument from ignorance. *Canadian Journal of Experimental Psychology, 58*(2), 75–85.
Hahn, U., & Oaksford, M. (2006a). A Bayesian approach to informal reasoning fallacies. *Synthese, 152*, 207–223.
Hahn, U., & Oaksford, M. (2006b). Why a normative theory of argument strength and why might one want it to be Bayesian? *Informal Logic, 26*, 1–24.
Hahn, U., & Oaksford, M. (2007). The rationality of informal argumentation: A Bayesian approach to reasoning fallacies. *Psychological Review, 114*(3), 704–732.
Hahn, U., & Oaksford, M. (2008). Inference from absence in language and thought. In N. Chater & M. Oaksford (Eds.), *The probabilistic mind: Prospects for Bayesian cognitive science* (pp. 3–31). Oxford: Oxford University Press.
Hahn, U., & Oaksford, M. (2012). Rational argument. In K. J. Holyoak & R. G. Morrison (Eds.), *The Oxford handbook of thinking and reasoning* (pp. 277–298). Oxford: Oxford University Press.
Hahn, U., Oaksford, M., & Bayindir, H. (2005). How convinced should we be by negative evidence. In B. Bara, L. Barsalou, & M. Bucciarelli (Eds.), *Proceedings of the 27th Annual Conference of the Cognitive Science Society* (pp. 887–892). New York: Cognitive Science Society.
Hahn, U., Oaksford, M., & Harris, A. J. L. (2012). Testimony and argument: A Bayespian perspective. In F. Zenker (Ed.), *Bayesian argumentation* (pp. 15–38). Dordrecht: Springer.
Hajek, A. (2008). Dutch book arguments. In P. Anand, P. Pattanik, & C. Puppe (Eds.), *The handbook of rational and social choice* (pp. 173–196). Oxford: Oxford University Press.
Hamblin, C. L. (1970). *Fallacies*. London: Methuen.
Harris, A. J., Corner, A., & Hahn, U. (2013). James is polite and punctual (and useless): A Bayesian formalisation of faint praise. *Thinking & Reasoning, 19,* 414-429.
Harris, A. J. L., Hahn, U., Madsen, J. K., & Hsu, A. S. (in press). The appeal to expert opinion: Quantitative support for a Bayesian network approach. *Cognitive Science.*
Harris, A. J. L., Hsu, A. S., & Madsen, J. K. (2012). Because Hitler did it! Quantitative tests of Bayesian argumentation using ad hominem. *Thinking & Reasoning, 18*(3), 311–343.
Hastings, A. C. (1962). A reformulation of the modes of reasoning in argumentation. Unpublished dissertation. Evanston, IL: Northwestern University.
Howson, C., & Urbach, P. (1993). *Scientific reasoning: The Bayesian approach*. Chicago/La Salle, IL: Open Court.
Jarvstad, A., & Hahn, U. (2011). Source reliability and the conjunction fallacy. *Cognitive Science, 35*(4), 682–711.
Kahane, H. (1992). *Logic and contemporary rhetoric*. Belmont, CA: Wadsworth.
Kienpointner, M. (1992). *Alltagslogik: Struktur und Funktion von Argumentationsmustern*. Stuttgart-Bad Cannstatt: Friedrich Fromman.

Knapton, S. (2015, February 24). *Three-parent babies: House of Lords approves law despite fears children could be born sterile*. Retrieved February 25, 2015, from www.telegraph.co.uk/news/science/science-news/11432058/Three-parent-babies-House-of-Lords-approves-law-despite-fears-children-could-be-sterile.html

Korb, K. B., & Nicholson, A. E. (2011). *Bayesian artificial intelligence* (2nd ed.). Boca Raton, FL: CRC Press.

Krugman, P. (2012, January 1). Nobody understands debt. *The New York Times*. Retrieved from www.nytimes.com/2012/01/02/opinion/krugman-nobody-understands-debt.html

Leitgeb, H., & Pettigrew, R. (2010a). An objective justification of Bayesianism I: Measuring inaccuracy. *Philosophy of Science*, 77(2), 201–235.

Leitgeb, H., & Pettigrew, R. (2010b). An objective justification of Bayesianism II: The consequences of minimizing inaccuracy*. *Philosophy of Science*, 77, 236–272.

Lewis, D. (1980). A subjectivist's guide to objective chance. In R. Jeffrey (Ed.), *Studies in inductive logic and probability, Volume 2*. Berkeley, CA: University of California Press.

Newell, B. R., Lagnado, D. A., & Shanks, D. R. (2015). *Straight choices: The psychology of decision making* (2nd ed.). Hove: Psychology Press.

Oaksford, M., & Chater, N. (1994). A rational analysis of the selection task as optimal data selection. *Psychological Review, 101*, 608–631.

Oaksford, M., & Chater, N. (2007). *Bayesian rationality: The probabilistic approach to human reasoning*. Oxford: Oxford University Press.

Oaksford, M., Chater, N., & Larkin, J. (2000). Probabilities and polarity biases in conditional inference. *Journal of Experimental Psychology: Learning, Memory, and Cognition, 26*(4), 883–899.

Oaksford, M., & Hahn, U. (2004). A Bayesian approach to the argument from ignorance. *Canadian Journal of Experimental Psychology, 58*, 75–85.

Oaksford, M., & Hahn, U. (2012). Why are we convinced by the ad hominem argument? Source reliability or pragma-dialectictics? In F. Zenker (Ed.), *Bayesian Argumentation* (pp. 39–58). Dordrecht: Springer.

Olsson, E. J. (2005). *Against coherence: Truth, probability, and justification*. Oxford: Oxford University Press.

Pearl, J. (1988). *Probabilistic reasoning in intelligent systems*. San Mateo, CA: Morgan Kaufman.

Perelman, C., & Olbrechts-Tyteca, L. (1969). *The new rhetoric: A treatise on argumentation* (J. Wilkinson & P. Weaver, Trans.). Notre Dame: University of Notre Dame Press.

Petty, R. E., & Cacioppo, J. T. (1984). Source factors and the elaboration likelihood model of Persuasion. *Advances in Consumer Research, 11*, 668–672.

Petty, R. E., Cacioppo, J. T., & Goldman, R. (1981). Personal involvement as a determinant of argument-based persuasion. *Journal of Personality and Social Psychology, 41*(5), 847–855.

Pornpitakpan, C. (2004). The persuasiveness of source credibility: A critical review of five decades' evidence. *Journal of Applied Social Psychology, 34*(2), 243–281.

Prakken, H., & Vreeswijk (2002). Logics for defeasible argumentation. In D. Gabbay and F. Guenther (Eds.), *Handbook of philosophical logic* (2nd ed., Vol. 4, pp. 219–318). Dordrecth: Kluwer Academic Publishers.

Rosenkrantz, R. (1992). The justification of induction. *Philosophy of Science, 15*, 527–539.

Rush, J. (2015). *Three-parent babies: Britain is breaching EU law and has "violated human dignity", MEPs warn*. Retrieved February 27, 2015, from www.independent.co.uk/news/science/britain-is-breaching-eu-law-and-has-violated-human-dignity-by-allowing-creation-of-threeparent-babies-meps-war-10067017.html

Schellens, P. J. (1985). *Redelijke argumenten: Een onderzoek naar normen voor kritische lezers*. Dordrecht: Foris Press.

Sperber, D., & Wilson, D. (1995). *Relevance: Communication and cognition* (2nd ed.). Oxford: Blackwell.

Stenning, K., & van Lambalgen, M. (2008). *Human reasoning and cognitive science*. Cambridge, MA: MIT Press.

Toulmin, S. (1958). *The uses of argument*. Cambridge: Cambridge University Press.

Toulmin, S., Rieke, R., & Janik, A. (1979). *An introduction to reasoning*. New York: Macmillan.

van Eemeren, F. H., Garssen, B., & Meuffels, B. (2009). *Fallacies and judgments of reasonableness*. Dordrecht: Springer.

van Eemeren, F. H., Garssen, B., & Meuffels, B. (2012). The disguised abusive ad hominem empirically investigated: Strategic maneuvering with direct personal attacks. *Thinking & Reasoning, 18*(3), 344–364. http://doi.org/10.1080/13546783.2012.678666

van Eemeren, F. H., & Grootendorst, R. (1984). *Speech acts in argumentative discussions: A theoretical model for the analysis of discussions directed toward solving conflicts of opinion*. Dordrecht: Floris Press.

van Eemeren, F. H., & Grootendorst, R. (1992). *Argumentation, communication, and fallacies: A pragma-dialectical perspective*. Hillsdale, NJ: Lawrence Erlbaum Associates.

van Eemeren, F. H., & Grootendorst, R. (1995). The pragma-dialectical approach to fallacies. In H. V. Hansen & R. C. Pinto (Eds.), *Fallacies: Classical and contemporary readings*. Philadelphia: Pennsylvania State University Press.

van Eemeren, F. H., & Grootendorst, R. (2004). *A systematic theory of argumentation: The pragma-dialectical approach*. Cambridge: Cambridge University Press.

Walton, D. (1996). *Arguments from ignorance*. Philadelphia, PA: Pennsylvania State University Press.

Walton, D. (2008). *Informal logic: A pragmatic approach* (2nd ed.). Cambridge: Cambridge University Press.

Walton, D., Reed, C., & Macagno, F. (2008). *Argumentation schemes*. Cambridge: Cambridge University Press.

7
MEDICAL DECISION MAKING

Pat Croskerry

Introduction

Decision making is a critical aspect of medicine. The two most important decisions to make about patients concern their diagnosis and how to manage their illness. Unless the first is accurate, the second is likely to be ineffective. In the majority of cases, decisions about the patient's diagnosis are sound and the management effective. However, multiple factors may influence decisions around a patient's diagnosis, and error is inevitable. There is considerable variation in diagnostic failure rates across the various disciplines within medicine, but the overall rate is put at 10–15% (Berner & Graber, 2008) with a significant associated mortality. It is estimated that 40,000–80,000 patients die annually from *preventable* diagnostic failure in US hospitals (Leape, Berwick & Bates, 2002), but this may well be underestimating the problem as autopsy studies in intensive care units alone have estimated the annual rate at 40,000 (Winters et al., 2012). The vastness of the problem has attracted the interest of the US National Academies of Sciences, Engineering and Medicine, which recently published an extensive report covering its major aspects (National Academies of Science, Engineering and Medicine, 2015). While some diagnostic failure is due to system issues (patient follow-up failures, lost reports, laboratory error and many others), much of it is due to problems with human reasoning and decision making. Early workers in this field noted: 'a physician's judgment is human judgment and susceptible to human limitations' (Detmer, Fryback & Gassner, 1978, p. 682), and more recent expert opinion has attributed the root cause of diagnostic failure to 'misplaced dependence on the clinical judgments of expert physicians' (Weed & Weed, 2014, p. 13). When James Reason, author of the classic *Human Error* (Reason, 2000), was asked, 'How is it that so many errors are made in medicine, I mean, it's not rocket science, is it?', he replied 'No, it isn't, it's more complicated' (Croskerry, 2012). Some degree of the complexity is illustrated in the following real case (Croskerry, 2008).

Anatomy of a case

It is Christmas Day in the Emergency Department of a general hospital. As the day has worn on, all 15 beds have filled up with fairly sick patients and the emergency staff is struggling to keep up. In a smaller cottage hospital about 30 miles away, an ambulance has just arrived with a patient in her 60s who was found in her nightdress on her floor by neighbours. She was breathing but unresponsive, with a slowed heart rate (bradycardia) and a weak pulse. The paramedics were told she had a history of heart disease and diabetes. At the hospital, a general practitioner, concerned she might go into heart block, applied an external pacemaker and then called the cardiologist at a general hospital requesting permission to transfer the patient for further care. The cardiologist accepted the patient and informed the emergency department to immediately notify him on her arrival.

At the general hospital, the patient was taken immediately to the cardiac room and the cardiologist was paged. Routine bloodwork and an electrocardiogram were done and she was connected to a heart monitor which showed a paced rhythm. The cardiologist arrived quickly and proceeded to replace the external pacemaker with an intravenous one, which he expected to be more effective. Shortly after her arrival, the emergency physician came into the cardiac room to help with the patient but was informed by the cardiologist that he would manage her care. The patient's initial bloodwork did not look encouraging. There were significant abnormalities as well as signs of kidney failure and she still had not regained consciousness. The cardiologist believed the patient had a very guarded prognosis, and proceeded with an admission plan to his coronary care unit (CCU) but was informed that it was full. Instead, he arranged for her to be transferred to a nearby tertiary care centre CCU.

It is now 3 p.m. and the emergency physician has reached the end of his shift. The oncoming physician has arrived and is concerned by how busy the department is. He noted that his colleague appeared fatigued and in low spirits. The off-going physician transferred the care of six sick patients and then mentions the patient in the cardiac room. He says that she has been managed by the cardiologist who told him her prognosis was poor, but that she will be transferred to the tertiary care hospital imminently, so the oncoming physician will not need to get involved in her case. He does comment, incidentally, on the domineering behaviour of the cardiologist who is well known to the emergency department.

The oncoming physician set about reviewing the patients transferred to him. Shortly after, he is informed that the CCU bed at the tertiary hospital has been taken and it will be necessary to keep the patient for several more hours. Given her 'cardiac' diagnosis, he decided to assess her first and went to the cardiac room. The nurses there appeared disengaged from the patient. Their demeanor was consistent with the grave prognosis that she had been given. It was clearly conveyed to him that future effort would probably be futile. She was covered with a sheet and it almost appeared that she might have already died. She was motionless, did not appear to be conscious and was not arousable. Her bedside monitor displayed a low blood pressure and a paced cardiac rhythm. He proceeded to examine her chest and noticed immediately that her skin was very cool. When he enquired about her temperature, he was told it hadn't been taken as the patient had arrived directly to cardiology, by-passing the usual triage process. The departmental protocol for all patients was to have a set of vital signs (blood pressure, pulse, temperature and respiratory rate) completed at triage on admission. The nurse could not now measure the patient's temperature on a regular thermometer but, using a deep rectal device, recorded it at 31.4°C, which is more than 5 degrees below normal (37°C) and into the moderate hypothermia range. Cardiac arrhythmias typically appear at around 32°C, and anything less than 32°C is frequently fatal. When the emergency physician looked back at the cardiogram the paramedics had obtained at the scene, he saw characteristic Osborn J waves associated with a slowed heart rate – pathognomonic for hypothermia. Immediate resuscitative efforts were now commenced and the patient's temperature slowly began to rise. After three hours, she was awake and talking. She was transferred to the tertiary care CCU in a stable state. She spent three weeks in the hospital before being discharged back to independent living in her own home.

The emergency physician later checked back through the medical record into events before the patient had first been found. Apparently, she had been seen by her family physician several days earlier. She was diagnosed with a urinary tract infection (UTI) and prescribed an antibiotic. On the day before the event, she was taken by her daughter to the local hospital for 'weak spells'. Her blood sugar was found to be low and she was advised to take oral sugar to keep her levels up. The UTI antibiotic is known to interact with the diabetic medication the patient was prescribed and may have produced a significant lowering of her blood sugar which might have led to her collapse. She lived in a trailer home and presumably spent a significant period of time on the cold floor before she was found.

This case gives some idea of the range and complexity of decisions that are made in medicine. The sequence of errors, and their classification, is summarised in Table 7.1. Some, but not all, of the multiple decision failures in her care are listed. The chain of error begins at her first visit to her general practitioner who diagnoses a UTI and prescribes an antibiotic without cautioning her against the possibility it might augment the hypoglycemic action of the medication she is taking

Table 7.1 Sequence of events and decision failures in management of the clinical case

Event	*Nature of error*	*Source of error*
Visit to general practitioner for urinary tract infection and prescription for antibiotic	Decision failure Medication error Failure to inform patient of medication interaction	Error of omission Knowledge deficit Memory Cognitive lassitude
First visit to cottage hospital for weak spells	Decision failure	Poor judgment Unpacking principle
Paramedics fail to record vital signs at scene	Breach of protocol	Error of omission
Paramedics assume patient has cardiac condition	Decision failure	Anchoring Search satisficing Premature closure
Second visit to Cottage hospital. Physician applies external pacemaker and makes referral to cardiologist at general hospital	Decision failure	Search satisficing Diagnosis momentum
Patient bypasses admission procedure at general hospital and doesn't have temperature recorded	Breach of protocol	Cognitive overload
Emergency physician allows cardiologist to take over care of patient	Breach of protocol	Cognitive overload Negative affective state Authority gradient Fatigue
Cardiologist fails to recognise source of patient's bradycardia	Decision failure	Overconfidence Diagnosis momentum *Déformation professionelle* Knowledge deficit
Nurses fail to get involved in patient's care and accept poor prognosis	Decision failure	Affective bias Knowledge deficit Bandwagon effect Groupthink Authority gradient

for her diabetes and significantly lower her blood sugar. This may have been due to a knowledge deficit, memory lapse or other possibilities at the time the patient was seen. At the first visit to the cottage hospital, her lowered blood sugar is recorded and correctly attributed to the medication interaction, but the advice to simply increase her sugar intake is inappropriate. She should at least have been admitted overnight for blood sugar monitoring as her level might have dropped dangerously further during sleep. This appears to be simply poor decision making, but again we do not know enough about resources and prevailing conditions at the time she was seen.

While some systemic issues are clearly contributory (inadequate resources, overcrowding, lack of beds) some obvious cognitive biases explain a number of significant events in the subsequent management of the patient. It is often difficult to attribute cause to various breaches of protocol, but to breach protocol whether actively or by default is a decision failure, except in extenuating circumstances. Protocols and check-lists are in place to protect against such memory failures and protect against other lapses. The first breach, when the paramedics fail to record her temperature at the scene, is a significant one in that had she been known to be hypothermic at that point she would have been taken directly to the tertiary care hospital and probably spared the intravenous pacemaker. However, one can imagine that finding an unresponsive patient, rural-based paramedics may have had more on their minds than following protocol. It may have been a simple knowledge deficit to have failed to recognise a connection between bradycardia and body temperature, although this should have been covered in their basic training. Nevertheless, recognising the possibility of imminent cardiac arrest, they considered that the most expedient action was to get to the nearest medical facility.

The second breach occurs at the cottage hospital. Assuming the problem to be cardiac in origin, staff fail to check the patient's vital signs. The physician immediately attaches an external pacemaker and arranges for her transfer to a cardiologist at the general hospital.

The third breach occurs at the general hospital, and is perhaps more understandable. As soon as the patient arrived in the cardiac room, she would have been connected to a monitor that would have displayed blood pressure and heart rate, as well as some other variables, but not temperature in this case. Again, both nurses and cardiologist anchored to the obvious and directed their efforts towards improving the output from her heart by inserting an intravenous pacemaker. The cardiologist's failure to recognise other possible causes of her bradycardia may be attributed to ***anchoring*** (the tendency to lock onto salient features at the outset and fail to adjust later), ***search satisficing*** (an amalgam of satisfy and sufficient: being satisfied that a search can be called off once something 'sufficient' is found) and other cognitive biases including ***déformation professionelle*** (the tendency to look at things through the lens of one's specialised training). Common things being common, it is a lot easier for a cardiologist to see a slowed heart as an intrinsic failure of the heart rather than the manifestation of an uncommon systemic problem such as hypothermia. The acquiescence of the nurses in accepting the poor prognosis and failing to do more for the patient reflects an authority gradient effect – probably fearful rather than respectful of a senior physician. The cardiologist was known for having a difficult temperament and definitely did not enjoy a reputation as a team player.

This is not an exceptional or rare case. Similar scenarios are played out in medical settings around the world every day. Although the outcome in the present case was favourable, diagnostic failure due to flawed decision making is a big problem. Generally, diagnostic failure is attributed to the system or the individual, or some combination of the two. Among the many factors that contribute to diagnostic failure in the individual clinician, cognitive and affective biases loom large (Croskerry, 2003). Extensive lists of cognitive biases have been published: https://en.wikipedia.org/wiki/List_of_cognitive_biases

Table 7.2 Major influences on clinical decision making

Influence	*Details*
Individual characteristics of decision maker	Type of training, extent and depth of knowledge, rationality, intellectual ability, experience, expertise, age, gender, personality, demeanour, affective disposition and others
Disease characteristics	Common or rare, representativeness of presentation, specificity of signs and symptoms, nature of onset (abrupt, slow, gradual), course of disease (slow, rapid), presentation time (hour of day, day of week, time of year) and others
Ambient conditions	Nature of local work environment, local culture, morale, supportive qualities of staff and management, ergonomic design of workplace, noise levels, temperature, humidity, air quality and others
Resources	Nature of medical setting where patient presents, staff support, equipment, bed availability, access to clinical decision support, laboratory support, diagnostic imaging, consultation staff availability and others
Team characteristics	Does the team work well together? Is it cohesive, supportive? Do members communicate clearly and effectively?
Patient	Is patient conscious, alert, coherent, cooperative? Is their behaviour appropriate? Can they communicate effectively? Are they able to clearly describe symptoms and signs of illness? Are family members present who can assist?

Medical complexity

A major challenge for decision making in medicine is the sheer complexity of the topic. The principal influences on decision making are described further in Table 7.2.

There are presently in the order of 12,000 known diagnoses that physicians need to be aware of, many of which they will be expected to recognize and treat. Unfortunately, each unique diagnosis does not have a unique way of presenting itself. For example, there are multiple ways in which the abdomen can become diseased but only a limited number of ways the diseased abdomen can provide clues to its variable ills. Abdominal pain may signal a wide variety of unrelated disorders: appendicitis, colon cancer, a rupturing blood vessel, kidney stone and many others. The patient may not even be competent or conscious to offer a description of their signs and symptoms. Further, some illnesses may manifest themselves in organ systems seemingly unrelated to the affected organ; for instance, both pneumonia and migraine may present with abdominal pain.

An important concept at the outset in the decision making that surrounds the process of diagnosis is the degree of manifestness of the disease or illness. Highly manifest diseases are those that present with well-differentiated signs and symptoms. If these are relatively exclusive to a particular disease, they are referred to as pathognomonic, for example the characteristic pathognomic rash of shingles (herpes zoster). In such cases, decision making around the diagnostic

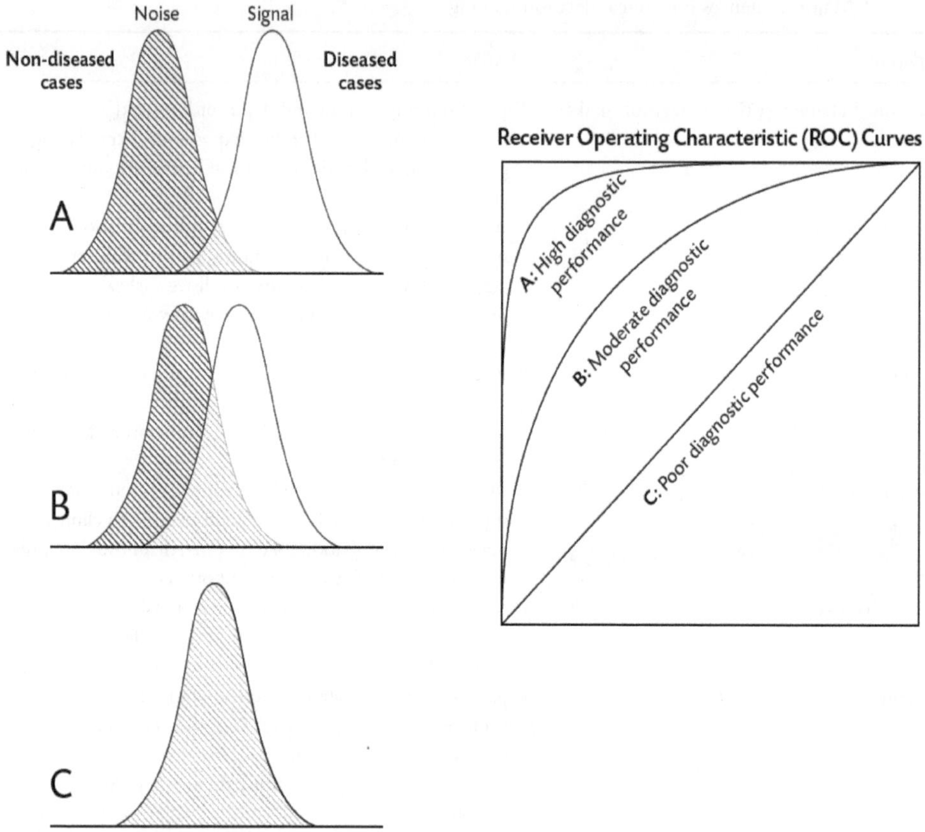

Figure 7.1 The relation of signal-to-noise ratio (S/R) and calibration of medical decision making (adapted from Croskerry et al., 2014)

possibilities is straightforward as the signal is easily distinguished from noise (Figure 7.1). In contrast, if an elderly patient presents with symptoms of weakness and dizziness, the underlying disease process is considerably less manifest and the diagnostic possibilities are many. In one study of diagnostic accuracy in emergency department patients, the misdiagnosis rate for patients across the board was estimated at about 10%, whereas for those with non-specific symptoms and signs it was above 50% (Nickel et al., 2011). Thus, representative diseases are more likely to be diagnosed accurately than atypical ones.

In condition A, the symptoms and signs of the disease being diagnosed are virtually all characteristic ones, with almost no overlap of noise and signal, and the expected diagnostic performance is high. In condition B, some overlap is occurring and the likelihood of a diagnostic error increases. In condition C, the S/R is low, with complete overlap of noise and signal, and the diagnostic performance is correspondingly low, with the receiver operating characteristic (ROC) curve at a chance level.

Given the non-specificity of many symptoms and signs of illness, it is essential at the outset for physicians to gather information to help refine the problem at hand. A variety of tools are available to facilitate the decision making process and help differentiate the diagnosis: assessment of the presenting complaint, past medical history, physical examination of the patient, measurements of the blood and urine, various imaging techniques (X-rays, ultrasound, computerized tomography [CT], magnetic resonance imaging [MRI] and others), as well as a variety of specialists to consult in the various specialties and subspecialties. An important skill of the well-calibrated medical decision maker lies in knowing how to access these various resources appropriately.

Also, an essential determinant of good decision making is currency of knowledge. What may have been an accepted standard of practice a year ago may not now be the case. Good decision making requires being up to date in a rapidly changing and evolving field. There has been a burgeoning and somewhat overwhelming abundance of medical information over the past 40 years. The number of journal articles published on health care topics annually quadrupled between 1970 and 2010 (Smith, Saudners, Stuckhardt & McGinnis, 2012). Further, it is estimated that in order for a primary care physician to remain up to date requires over 600 hours of reading journal articles each month, or about 20 hours each day of the week (Alper et al., 2004)!

Reliability of medical data

A good foundation of knowledge is required in order to make reliable decisions about anything. A major problem in medical decision making is the quality of the information that the physician uses in the final decision making process; good decision making absolutely depends upon the veracity of the data that is used. Physicians depend upon accurate data from sources such as the laboratory, which has a known error rate of less than 1% to 10% (Lippi et al., 2009). Diagnostic imaging, often a significant component of a physician's decision making, has an estimated baseline error rate of about 4% (Bruno, Walker & Abujudeh, 2015). Another issue, of even greater proportions, is that despite the ever increasing insistence on evidence-based decision making, it has become clear that what physicians see as evidence has likely been corrupted by a variety of factors (Seshia, Makhinson, Phillips & Young, 2014; Seshia, Makhinson & Young, 2014, 2015) (Figure 7.2). Seshia and his colleagues describe an amalgam of problems that threaten the integrity of evidence in health care, referred to as 'cognitive biases plus' (cognitive bias, conflicts of interest, ethical violations and reasoning fallacies). Thus, the concern is not just with the accuracy of the individuals' decision making but also with all the other sources of information that the physician uses. One cannot make accurate decisions based on fallacious data. For many clinical decisions in medicine, the physician is the final arbiter through which much of this corrupted evidence flows.

Science and art

Medicine indeed is not like rocket science. It does not necessarily follow science, mathematics, rationality, logic and predictable rules. It has always allowed itself a degree of latitude by claiming to be both an art and a science. In *How Doctors Think*, Montgomery (2006) noted that if illness followed scientific rules, the difficulty that physicians have with their thinking and decision making would have been solved long ago. Instead, they have to deal with 'mushy but unavoidable ineffabilities', processes that take place at the dynamic interface with their patients and their respective thoughts, feelings, reasoning and decision making. These ineffabilities, these phenomena that are difficult to express or describe, are the non-scientific aspects of medicine, historically referred to as its art moiety. Even in current treatments of medical decision making they continue to be recognised as such. The cardiologist John Brush (2015), in *The Science of the Art of Medicine*, deftly draws the two together. Part of the problem has been that medical judgment and decision making has been included in its art aspect. Great clinicians, such as William Osler (1849–1919), were seen as having sound judgment and acumen that accrued from experience,

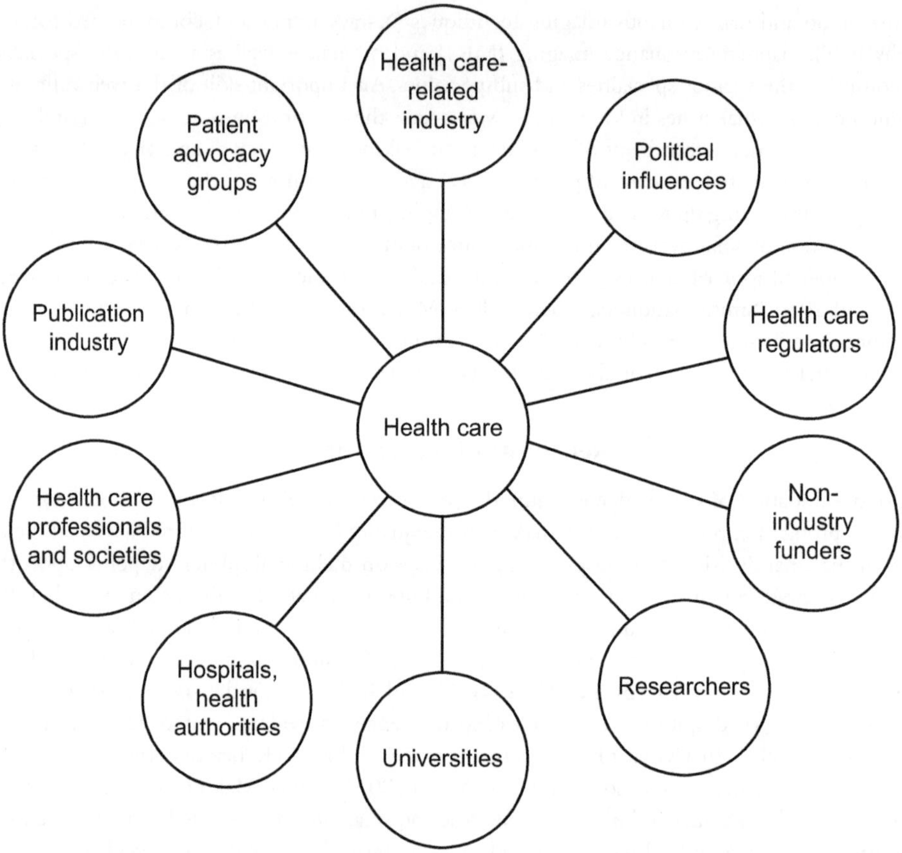

Figure 7.2 Major organizations (includes individuals who belong to or work in them) that influence the quality of evidence informing person-centered health care (reproduced with permission from Seshia et al., 2014)

and a general pessimism has prevailed as to whether or not the road to achieving such acumen could be shortened. Before Osler, and to a large extent since, successive generations of physicians learned their clinical decision making skills at the feet of their instructors and mentors. Until the emergence of clinical prediction rules (Meehl, 1954) and evidence-based medicine (EBM), such evidence as there was derived largely from clinical experience and the brutal lessons learned from clinical error. Good decision making absolutely depends upon good information, but this was limited. The EBM movement began to gather serious momentum with the work of David Eddy (1982a, 1982b, 1984), who published a series of 27 papers in *JAMA* in the early 1990s that were a major contribution to the standardisation of EBM practice. First Guyatt and colleagues (1992) and then Sackett's group (1996) later refined the definition of evidence-based medicine as the 'conscientious, explicit and judicious use of current best evidence in making decisions about the care of individual patients' (Sackett, Rosenberg, Gray, Haynes & Richardson, 1996, p. 71).

While the uptake of EBM (and its presumably improved decision making) has been slow to emerge, other major developments in cognitive science occurred relatively quickly. In the early days of the 'cognitive revolution' some were quick to see the application to medicine. Soon after Kahneman and Tversky's (1973) description of the availability heuristic, a medical group at the

University of Wisconsin demonstrated clinical evidence of the availability heuristic along with several other biases in a group of surgeons who were asked to make estimates of mortality rate (Detmer, Fryback & Gassner, 1978). Despite this early uptake, the general body of medicine, and medical educators in particular, have been slow to recognise the impact of bias on medical decision making, with little appetite for exploring what cognitive science has to offer. A major difficulty has been that there is little or no exposure in medical training to the processes that underlie cognition, especially biases and heuristics. The traditional approach towards clinical decision making has been a rational one in which the basics of biostatistics have been taught (Rao, 2007). This is, of course, essential; much of medical decision making requires an understanding of such concepts (specificity, sensitivity, probability theory, likelihood ratios, number needed to treat, etc.) in decision making and disease management. However, medical decision making also involves intuitive processes and there is a pressing need to understand how they work, so much so that some have called for basic training in cognitive psychology in the undergraduate years. Redelmeier and his colleagues (2001) published a series of papers promoting an approach to the cognitive aspects of medical decision making and judgment, advocating for cognitive psychology as one of the basic sciences. Elstein (2009) echoed the sentiment, noting: 'it would be good if physicians were as well acquainted with the relevant principles of cognitive psychology as they are with comparable principles in pathophysiology' (Elstein, 2009, p. 14).

Emergence of dual process theory in medicine

In a paper prescient of dual process theory, Elstein (1976) recognised the distinction between *actuarial* and *clinical* approaches. Following Schneider and Shiffrin's (1977) paper on a dual process approach towards decision making which described two separate forms of processing, automatic and controlled, the dual process model was progressively refined in the cognitive science literature with Evans emphasising the distinction between heuristic and analytic processing in a two-stage theory (Evans, 1984). Publications later began to appear in clinical journals (Dawson, 1993; Croskerry, 2005). In 2009, a schematic model was presented that explicitly described the application of the model in the context of diagnostic decision making (Croskerry, 2009). There has been widespread uptake of the dual process approach over the past five years in medicine and it has entered the texts on decision making (Croskerry, Cosby, Schenkel & Wears, 2008; Brush, 2015; Trowbridge, Rencic & Durning, 2015; Croskerry, 2016). A schematic that is widely used in the medical literature is shown in Figure 7.3.

The model runs from left to right. If the patient's symptoms and signs are immediately recognised on initial presentation to the clinician, a Type 1 (intuitive) response occurs, such as with the shingles rash. It is also the response of paramedics in the example at the beginning of this chapter, who, on finding an elderly woman with a cardiac history unconscious on the floor, assume a cardiac diagnosis and completely miss the life-threatening diagnosis of hypothermia. The diagnosis is missed through anchoring and other biases (Table 7.1) which typically occur in Type 1 processing. The topmost of the four channels of Type 1 processing represents any intuitive response that undergoes no modification, while the others may undergo some degree of calibration through input from Type 2 processes. Conceptually, the multiple channels of Type 1 processing correspond to those described by Stanovich (2011). If the patient presentation is not recognised, Type 2 (analytical) processing will be necessary. Repetitive presentations to Type 2 processing may eventually lead to a (learned) Type 1 response, for instance in the acquisition of a decision skill. An example would be the development of decisions around diagnosing stroke, a cerebrovascular accident. On first exposure a novice clinician would be unlikely to recognise any pattern among the various symptoms and signs: visual changes, confusion, dizziness, headache, balance problems,

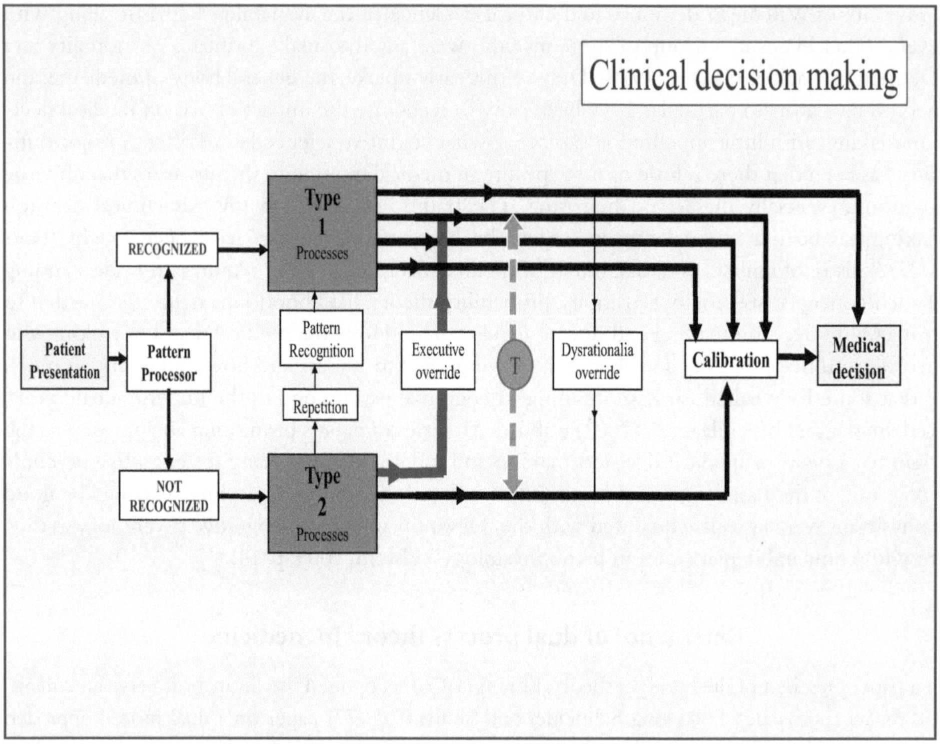

Figure 7.3 Clinical decision making model utilising dual process theory (adapted from Croskerry, 2009)

vomiting, one-sided weakness or numbness and others. The diagnosis, if it is to be made at all, will occur only through slow, analytical Type 2 processing, involving major cognitive effort and deliberation. After numerous clinical experiences with stroke syndromes, in the hands of a neurologist, for example, this complex decision making may be mostly relegated to Type 1 fast decision making. The T box represents a toggle option to move between the two processing systems – some physicians say they get all their ideas through Type 1 but check them out using Type 2 processing. The heavy track going from Type 2 processing to Type 1 (executive override) indicates de-coupling from Type 1 processing, and corresponds to the metacognitive processes of reflection and mindfulness. In contrast, dysrationalia override occurs when, despite knowing the most rational option, intuitive processes prevail.

While it might seem reasonable that any well-calibrated decision maker in medicine would adopt a balance of intuitive and analytical approaches, an undue polarisation has developed between those who have been persuaded by the heuristics and biases part of the cognitive science literature and those who have not. In what has come to be known as the Great Rationality Debate, these two groups are known as Meliorists and Panglossians respectively (Stanovich, 2012). Some parallel can be seen with the actuarial–clinical divide described by Elstein (1976). Actuarial methods were those in which medical decisions were made using formal quantitative techniques, whereas the clinical approach involved 'artful, informal, qualitative, or not explicitly quantitative strategies' (Elstein, 1976, p. 696). This division has parallels with System 1 and System 2 processing in medical decision making. Those in the modern-day actuarial camp have recognised the contribution of cognitive science, its experimental observations, objectivity and, most importantly, the properties and predictive nature of biases and heuristics. They have also recognised that decision making is a capricious process subject to a variety of distorting influences that need to be reckoned with (Croskerry et al., 2014) and for which appropriate strategies derived from past learning experiences, referred to as 'mindware' (Perkins, 2002), need to be developed.

A major thrust of this approach involves the understanding of cognitive biases and their mitigation (Croskerry, Singhal & Mamede, 2013a, 2013b). Those promoting the opposing view have emphasised the value of heuristics and are generally dismissive of the impact of bias on clinical outcomes (McLaughlin, Eva & Norman, 2014). If nothing else, the debate has been illustrative of *myside bias*, which describes the tendency to evaluate evidence, generate evidence and test hypotheses that support their own belief systems (Toplak & Stanovich, 2003) as well as other biases (Croskerry, 2012; Croskerry, 2016). Clinical decision making clearly uses both intuitive and analytic processes, and we need to know as much as possible about the operating characteristics of the two systems in order to develop an optimally calibrated approach (Croskerry et al., 2014).

Medical approaches to cognitive bias mitigation

Since Hippocrates, many lessons and aphorisms from the practice of medicine, both in diagnosis and treatment, have been offered, ostensibly to help decision making in novitiates. Prior to the revelations of flawed human decision making that emerged from cognitive science over the past 40 years, practitioners of medicine appear to have been implicitly aware of at least some of these failings, and specifically of the impact of bias, memory deficits and fallacious reasoning in clinical decision making. A variety of strategies have evolved to reduce or prevent them. Many came in the era that preceded evidence-based medicine, when little effort was made to validate them experimentally. However, they do appear to have stood the test of time. Various strategies and the biases they potentially deal with are listed in Table 7.3.

- **The history and physical exam**: the deliberate process of taking a history from a patient and performing a physical examination were established in modern medicine to gather data in a systematic way so that important information was not missed. This supported the *unpacking principle* (Redelmeier et al., 1995) – the more information gleaned, the greater likelihood of not missing something important. It remains vital to the decision making process, although in times of expediency or cognitive lassitude the process may be less thorough or even ignored.
- **The differential diagnosis**: establishing a differential diagnosis means a consideration of the most likely cause of a patient's disease but also listing competing possibilities. It is especially useful when judging the relative likelihood of a particular disease in patients suffering symptoms that might be common to several diseases. Establishing a differential diagnosis works against *anchoring* onto a particular diagnosis too early in the diagnostic process, thereby avoiding additional traps such as *confirmation bias*, *search satisficing* and perhaps *premature diagnostic closure*. The built-in cognitive forcing function (Croskerry, 2003) of the differential diagnosis is that it forces asking the important question: 'what else could this be?' Electronic applications are now available that provide extensive differential diagnostic checklists as well as flagging diseases that are commonly missed and must not be missed (Ely, Graber & Croskerry, 2011).
- **Checklists**: the use of checklists is long-standing in medicine. Mnemonics are checklists. The simple ABC (**A**irway-**B**reathing-**C**irculation) in resuscitation protocols forces consideration of critical issues that might otherwise be missed, especially under the conditions of increased stress that usually exist in such life-threatening situations. Checklists are also

Table 7.3 Existing strategies in medicine to mitigate cognitive and affective bias

Strategy	*Purpose*	*Potential biases addressed*
History and physical exam	Deliberate and systematic gathering of data	Augenblick or spot diagnoses; Unpacking principle Ascertainment bias Others
Differential diagnosis (DDx)	Forces consideration of diagnostic possibilities other than the obvious or the most likely	Anchoring and adjustment Search satisficing Premature diagnostic closure Availability Representativeness Confirmation bias Others
Clinical prediction rules	Force a scientific, statistical assessment of patient's signs and symptoms, and other data to develop numerical probabilities of the presence/absence of a disease or an outcome	Base rate fallacy Errors of reasoning Many other biases
Evidence-based medicine	Establishes imperative for objective scientific data to support analytic decision making	Many
Checklists	Ensure that important issues have been considered and completed, especially under conditions of complexity, stress and fatigue, but also when routine processes are being followed	Anchoring and adjustment Availability Memory failures Others
Mnemonics	Protect against memory failures and ensure that the full range of possibilities is considered on the DDx. Force thinking outside the obvious possibilities	Availability Anchoring and adjustment Others
Pitfalls	Alert inexperienced clinicians to predictable failures commonly encountered in a particular discipline	Many
Rule out worst case scenario (ROWS)	Ensures that the most serious condition in a particular clinical setting is not missed	Anchoring and adjustment Premature diagnostic closure Others
Until proven otherwise (UPO)	Ensures that a particular diagnosis cannot be made unless other specific diagnoses have been excluded	Many
Caveats	Often discipline-specific warnings to ensure important rules are followed to avoid missing significant conditions	Many
Red flags	Specific signs and symptoms to look out for, often in the context of commonly presenting conditions, to avoid missing serious conditions	Many

highly effective in ensuring that evidence-based aspects of patient safety (bundles) are followed in routine procedures, for example prevention of catheter-related bloodstream infections in the intensive care unit (Pronovost et al., 2006).

- **Evidence-based medicine**: prior to the endorsement of EBM, many clinical practices were sustained in the absence of any proof of efficacy. This allowed mistaken beliefs, idiosyncratic approaches and often harmful practices to continue unchallenged. EBM forces critical appraisal of the evidence with a view towards detecting defects and biases in the methods used to obtain such evidence.
- **Clinical prediction rules**: probabilistic or Bayesian reasoning provides a formal method to avoid some cognitive biases. The emergence of clinical prediction rules provided objective data on which medical decisions could be made; numeric probabilities could be attached to the likelihood of a specific disorder or outcome (Meehl, 1954). Examples are the Wells criteria for deciding about the likelihood of pulmonary embolus and the Ottawa ankle rules to support decisions around the ordering of X-rays for foot or ankle injuries.
- **Mnemonics**: given the complexity that often accompanies medical issues, memory failures have long been recognised as a cause of failed decision making. Unless all the main elements of a problem are considered, any decision will be vulnerable to an error of omission. A major solution has been provided in the use of mnemonics (Bloomfield & Chandler, 1982). They reduce reliance on fallible memory, especially of possibilities that are not coherently connected. A classic example is VINDICATES, a general acronym for differential diagnosis of disease (**V**ascular, **I**nflammatory, **N**eoplastic, **D**egenerative/**D**eficiency, **I**diopathic/**I**ntoxication, **C**ongenital, **A**utoimmune/**A**llergic, **T**raumatic, **E**ndocrine, **S**omething else/p**S**ychological/p**S**ychiatric). Faced with a complex and poorly differentiated problem, physicians can quickly go through the mnemonic to make sure they have considered the varied causes of disease.
- **Caveats**: most disciplines in medicine have identified specific traps and pitfalls that repeatedly occur, especially for the novitiate. They warn the inexperienced or unwary about clinical situations in which predictable decision errors occur. They have emerged over time and are often spread by word of mouth, such as 'Always examine the joint above and below the apparent injury in children'. Similarly, general and specific caveats have been established in many disciplines, such as 'Beware the patient who returns to the Emergency Department', and 'The most commonly missed fracture is the second one'. Caveats may also take the form of forcing functions to address potentially serious decision failures, such as the following:
  - A diagnosis of conversion disorder should not be made unless somatic explanations have been excluded.
  - No neurological diagnosis should be made until the patient's blood sugar is measured.
  - No psychological scales or tests ensure reliable prediction of suicide.
  - Obtain a blood glucose and pulse oximetry (blood oxygen level) on all patients before making a psychiatric diagnosis.
- **Forcing functions**: the heuristic that rules out the worst case scenario (ROWS) is a forcing function to always include the most significant illness that might explain a particular presentation; for instance, always consider pulmonary embolus in any patient with chest symptoms or tachycardia; always consider an injury to a tendon, nerve or artery in any laceration; always consider a scaphoid fracture with wrist sprain. A similar forcing function is the heuristic that a (usually) important condition is present until proven otherwise (UPO). In this case, the physician is obliged to exclude other specific possibilities before accepting a diagnosis, such as an athlete with an on-field head injury has a neck injury UPO; new onset nystagmus in an adult is multiple sclerosis UPO; the agitated, belligerent patient is hypoxic UPO.

- **Red flags**: red flags are another form of forcing function that alerts clinicians to the possibility of a serious illness that may appear in the context of a common presentation. For example, lower back pain is often what it appears to be, a musculoskeletal problem. But occasionally it is the harbinger of something very serious such as a spinal abscess (red flags: fever plus intravenous track marks or a history of drug use), or cauda equina syndrome (red flags: proximal leg weakness, urinary retention, decreased sphincter tone).
- **Reflection and mindfulness:** reflective thinking and mindfulness are now accepted tools in medical education to enhance deeper learning and clinical reasoning (Epstein, 1999). There is evidence that mindfulness reduces susceptibility to certain biases such as implicit bias and prejudicial behavior (Lueke & Gibson, 2015) as well as to other biases (Sibinga & Wu, 2010). Reflection is integral to critical thinking and ultimately to improved decision making. It has been described as a cornerstone of critical thinking and is widely used at the website of the Foundation for Critical Thinking (www.criticalthinking.org). In Figure 7.3, the channel labelled 'Executive override' represents the pathway for reflection and mindfulness.
- **Critical thinking:** the well-calibrated thinker has long been appreciated in medicine, but only recently have the potential benefits of explicit training in critical thinking been considered. Impetus was provided in 2011 by a Harvard Millennium Conference on critical thinking (Huang, Newman & Schwartzstein, 2011). The rationale for critical thinking interventions in medical training is compelling: a large meta-analytic study of international studies of the quantitative impact of interventions found that teaching thinking skills was by far the most effective intervention for improving reasoning and problem solving (Higgins, Hall, Baumfield & Moseley, 2005). The study of pupils in the age range 5–16 years found a strong effect size of 0.62, the equivalent of moving a class from the 50th to the 26th percentile. Medical undergraduates and postgraduates are beyond the age range of the group studied. However, from the limited studies on development of critical skills (Friend & Zubek, 1958; Denney, 1995), there do not appear to be any temporal restrictions on when critical thinking interventions might be made. Thus, among a highly motivated group such as physicians in training, even modest gains in problem solving and reasoning skills might be expected, and would be of significant benefit in reasoning, problem solving and decision making. Importantly, the ability to recognize and deal with bias is considered a hallmark of the critical thinker (West, Toplak & Stanovich, 2008). Critical thinking as a 'meta-competency' has been promoted in medical education (Papp et al., 2014). A critical thinking program has been established at Dalhousie Medical School in Canada (Croskerry, Smith, Petrie, Campbell & Sargeant, 2013), as well as on-line courses in teaching and assessing critical thinking for faculty. Figure 7.4 schematically summarises the integration of critical thinking and several of the other important concepts discussed here in the process of clinical reasoning and decision making in the medical undergraduate program at Dalhousie.

Every major discipline in medicine has now acknowledged the role of cognitive bias in clinical reasoning (Croskerry, 2014). Several of the more common cognitive biases underlie the errors described in Table 7.1. The important question that follows is: how do we fix biases? How does cognitive bias mitigation (CBM) work in medical decision making, and what explicit strategies are there? At the outset, some of the early pessimism that pervaded the cognitive psychology literature around CBM was evident (Croskerry, 2003), but more recently efforts have been made to describe the nature of the problem (Graber et al. 2012; Croskerry, Singhal & Mamede, 2013a; Croskerry, 2014), along with some potential solutions (Croskerry, Singhal & Mamede, 2013b; Lambe, O'Reilly, Kelly, & Curristan 2016). Some domains, such as radiology, have developed specific strategies for CBM (Bruno, Walker & Abujudeh, 2015). In other areas,

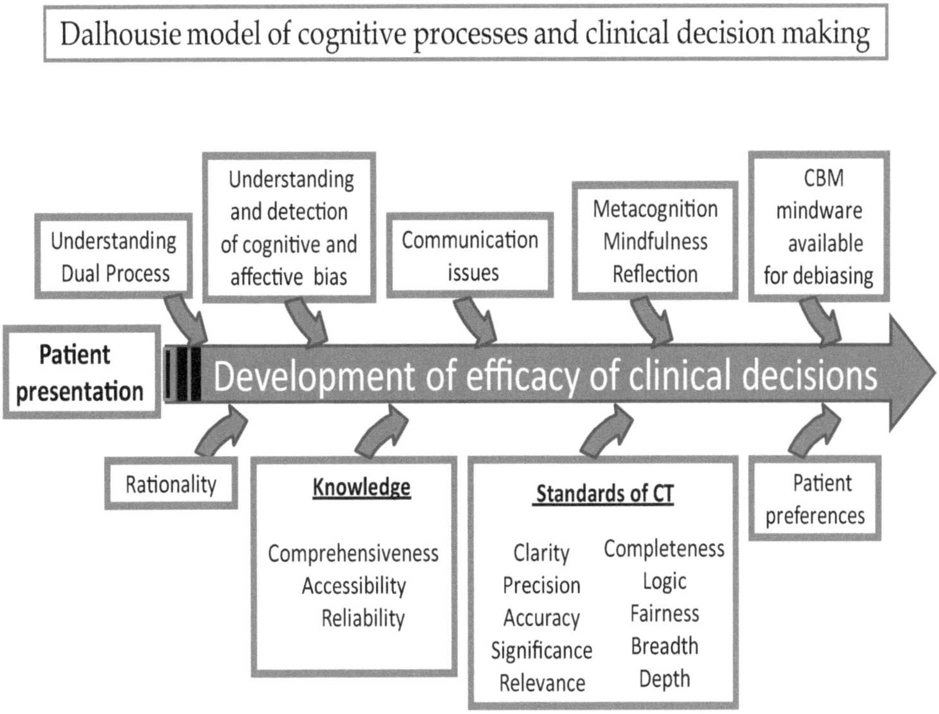

Figure 7.4 Model for development of clinical reasoning and decision making

such as anatomic pathology, software technology has been developed to detect cognitive bias among residents which might enable the development of CBM strategies (Crowley et al., 2012).

Clinical decision support systems

Given the volume of information and complexity of the decision making process in medicine, it is not surprising that efforts have been made to use information technology tools to improve the quality of decision making over the past 40 years. Whereas support was aimed initially at mainly diagnosis and selection of medications, using the electronic medical record (EMR) as a foundation, all areas of clinical decision making may now be technologically assisted using electronic clinical decision support (CDS) systems (Berner, 2009). They contain current compilations of knowledge, including clinical decision rules, clinical guidelines and protocols, to improve diagnostic support in systems that provide differential diagnoses such as DxPlain, Iliad, QMR, Isabel and others. Taxonomies of CDS functions have been developed (Osheroff, 2009). Using computerized physician order entry (CPOE), the accuracy of decisions around medication use can be improved, as well as flagging potential interactions between medications. Once designed, these systems have the advantage of being implemented on a variety of convenient platforms (Internet, personal computer, handheld device, EMR network).

Nevertheless, these CDS tools have not been without their problems (Berner, 2009). Diagnostic programs have so far had fairly limited uptake in clinical practice settings. It takes time to input the data necessary for accurate decisions and workflow may be compromised in the process. Busy physicians may be disinclined to take the time to input data into the system. The timing of the decision made to access decision support may be important; early access to decision support appears to be more beneficial (Kostopoulou et al., 2015). Repetitive pop-ups and alerts can become distracting and fatiguing, especially when they do not appear relevant in the clinical context. Knowledge has to be constantly updated. Differential diagnosis lists may seem a little redundant and not particularly helpful at times. There are, too, issues around physician autonomy; some physicians do not like the idea of a computer doing their thinking for them and, in particular, suggesting various standards of care. There are also concerns that an over-reliance on CDS might lead to erosion of clinical decision making skills though automaticity bias. Despite some obvious limitations, however, there appears to be a general acceptance of the potential benefits of CDS. Further development and refinement will likely result in more widespread uptake.

Additional promise might be held for computer systems that have the capability to effectively answer natural language questions over a wide range of medical problems, and which are presumably less vulnerable to cognitive biases. The IBM Deep QA project provided a demonstration of such artificial intelligence, powering Watson to a victory over experts on the popular television game show of general knowledge *Jeopardy* in February 2011. The ability of IBM Watson Health (www.ibm.comsmarterplanet/us/en/ibmwatson/health/) to store massive amounts of information accurately, to be consistent and available whatever the time of day or night and to generate and test hypotheses and learn from the data is already finding medical application at some medical centers in the United States.

Research issues in medical decision making

Perhaps the first objective in research should be to determine the actual incidence of decision failures in medicine. This has been attempted in a variety of ways (Table 7.4). While many factors

Table 7.4 Estimates of diagnostic error rate in internal medicine using different methodologies (adapted from Graber, 2013)

Research approach	*Method*	*Observation*
Patient surveys		33% of patients relate a diagnostic error that affected themselves, a family member or close friend
Second reviews	Image or sample is reviewed by another clinician	10–30% of breast cancers are missed on mammography; 1–2% of cancers misread on biopsy samples
Standard patients	Clinician is unaware that patient is trained to act as a real patient to simulate a set of symptoms or problems	Internist misdiagnosed 13% of patients presenting with common conditions (chronic obstructive pulmonary disease, rheumatoid arthritis, others)
Look-backs	Specific conditions are retroactively investigated to see if diagnosis could have been made at an earlier stage	30% of subarachnoid hemorrhage misdiagnosed; 39% of dissecting abdominal aortic aneurysm; Delayed diagnosis; 25–50% of women with cervical cancer – last PAP abnormal on re-read
Autopsies		Major unexpected discrepancies that would have changed the management found in 10–20%

contribute to the failure rate, the estimates provide an approximation at about 15%. This will vary depending on the discipline and setting being studied: in the visual specialties (dermatology, radiology, anatomic pathology) it is probably around 1–2%, whereas when the patterns of presentation are less obvious (emergency medicine, family practice, internal medicine), it gets closer to 10–15% (Berner & Graber, 2008).

The experimental study of medical decision making does not lend itself readily to traditional scientific approaches studying the properties of a dependent variable. Any attempt at reductionism and controlling independent variables inevitably strips away parts of the essential process that underlies medical decision making with a resulting loss of external and ecological validity. The problem has been likened to studying the characteristics of cholera toxin in the laboratory. It reveals very little about a cholera epidemic which is 'influenced by independent variables not usually found in a Petri dish (population demographics, group immunity, crowding, local water supply, sanitation, and climate)' (Croskerry et al., 2014, p. 199; Fang & Casadevall, 2011). A recent review of studies of cognitive biases and heuristics in medicine found that of 213 studies reviewed, 164 (77%) were based on hypothetical vignettes (Blumenthal-Barby & Krieger, 2015). Given the complexities and dynamics of medical decision making, it would not be surprising if something got lost in experimental translation. The art of medicine may sometimes get in the way of science.

Some useful advances have been achieved in experimental studies using designs that attempt to preserve as much of the natural environment as possible while manipulating particular heuristics and biases (Schmidt et al., 2014; Mamede et al., 2014; Mamede, Schmidt & Penaforte, 2008). Nevertheless, there remain major ethical and methodological issues in designing experiments on such a dynamic and complex process as medical decision making.

Conclusion

Of all the applied fields of decision making, it would seem that medical decision making would be seen by many as of particular relevance and importance. Yet, it was not until relatively recently that this was explicitly recognized as a critical skill in clinical medicine. Several factors have contributed to this. Historically, medicine has isolated itself, not just from mainstream scientific methods, but in particular from cognitive science. A major issue has been the inherent complexity of decision making processes that may be influenced by multiple variables. The tardiness in recognizing cognitive science as relevant to decision making, and in particular the role of bias in clinical judgments and decision making, has resulted in an unacceptable rate of diagnostic failure.

However, in recent years, some major gains have been made. There is widespread acceptance of dual process theory, which has provided a platform on which a basic understanding of decision making processes can be established. Much further work needs to be done, but it has become clear that this is no longer an option but an ethical imperative (Stark & Fins, 2014).

References

Alper, B., Hand, J. A., Elliott, S. G., Kinkade, S., Hauan, M. J., Onion, D. K., & Sklar, B. M. (2004). How much effort is needed to keep up with the literature relevant for primary care? *Journal of the Medical Library Association, 92*, 429–437.

Berner, E. S. (2009, June). *Clinical decision support systems: State of the art* (AHRQ Publication No. 09-0069-EF). Rockville, MD: Agency for Healthcare Research and Quality.

Berner, E. S., & Graber, M. L.(2008). Overconfidence as a cause of diagnostic error in medicine. *American Journal of Medicine, 121*, S2–S23.
Bloomfield, R. L., & Chandler, E. T. (1982). *Mnemonics, rhetoric and poetics for medics.* Winston-Salem, NC: Harbinger Medical Press.
Blumenthal-Barby, J. S., & Krieger, H. (2015). Cognitive biases and heuristics in medical decision making: A critical review using a systematic search strategy. *Medical Decision Making, 35*, 539–557.
Bruno, M. A., Walker, E. A., & Abujudeh, H. H. (2015, October). Understanding and confronting our mistakes: The epidemiology of error in radiology and strategies for error reduction. *RadioGraphics, 35*(6). doi: http://dx.doi.org/10.1148/rg.2015150023
Brush, J. E. (2015). *The science of the art of medicine.* Retrieved from https://itunes.apple.com/us/book/science-art-medicine/id643948555?mt=13
Croskerry, P. (2003). The importance of cognitive errors in diagnosis and strategies to prevent them. *Academic Medice, 78*, 1–6.
Croskerry, P. (2003). Cognitive forcing strategies in clinical decision making. *Annals of Emergency Medicine, 41*, 110–120.
Croskerry, P. (2005). The theory and practice of clinical decision making. *Canadian Journal of Anesthesiology, 52*, R1–R8.
Croskerry, P. (2008). The cognitive autopsy: Gaining insight into diagnostic failure. In P. Croskerry, K. S. Cosby, S. Schenkel, & R. Wears (Eds.), *Patient safety in emergency medicine* (pp. 302–307). Philadelphia: Lippincott Williams & Wilkins.
Croskerry, P. (2009). A universal model for diagnostic reasoning. *Academic Medicine, 84*(8), 1022–1028. doi: 10.1097/ACM.0b013e3181ace703
Croskerry, P. (2012a). Not rocket science. *Canadian Medical Association Journal, 185*, E130.
Croskerry, P. (2012b). Perspectives on diagnostic failure and patient safety. *Healthcare Quarterly, 15*, 50–56.
Croskerry, P. (2014). Bias: A normal operating characteristic of the diagnosing brain. *Diagnosis, 1*, 23–27.
Croskerry, P. (2016a). Metacognition and cognitive debiasing. In N. Cooper & J. Frain (Eds.), *ABC of clinical reasoning* (ABC Series). Chichester, UK: Wiley-Blackwell.
Croskerry, P. (2016b). Our better angels and black boxes. *EMJ, 33*, 242–244.
Croskerry, P., Cosby, K. S., Schenkel, S., & Wears, R. (Eds.). (2008). *Patient safety in emergency medicine.* Philadelphia: Lippincott Williams & Wilkins.
Croskerry, P., Petrie, D., Reilly, J., & Tait, G. (2014). Deciding about fast and slow decisions. *Academic Medicine, 89*, 197–200.
Croskerry, P., Singhal, G., & Mamede, S. (2013a). Cognitive debiasing 1: Origins of bias and theory of debiasing. *British Medical Journal Quality and Safety, 22*(Suppl. 2), ii58–ii64. doi: 10.1136/bmjqs-2012–001712
Croskerry, P., Singhal, G., & Mamede, S. (2013b). Cognitive debiasing 2: Impediments to and strategies for change. *British Medical Journal Quality and Safety, 22*(Suppl. 2), ii65–ii72. doi: 10.1136/bmjqs-2012–001713
Croskerry, P., Smith, P., Petrie, D., Campbell, S., & Sargeant, J. (2013). *Teaching critical thinking across the curriculum.* Workshop at the Canadian Conference on Medical Education (CCME 2013: The quest for quality improvement: Going for gold through medical education). Quebec City, Quebec, April 20–23.
Crowley, R. S., Legowski, E., Medvedeva, O., Reitmeyer, K., Tseytlin, E., Castine, M., Jukic, D., & Mello-Thoms, C. (2012). Automated detection of heuristics and biases among pathologists in a computer-based system. *Advances in Health Science Education, 18*, 343–363.
Dawson, N. V. (1993). Physician judgment in clinical settings: Methodological influences and cognitive performance. *Clinical Chemistry, 39*, 1468–1480.
Denney, N. W. (1995). Critical thinking during the adult years (Has the developmental function changed over the last four decades?). *Experimental Aging Research, 21*, 191–207.
Detmer, D. E., Fryback, D. G., & Gassner, K. (1978). Heuristics and biases in medical decision making. *Journal of Medical Education, 53*, 682–683.
Eddy, D. M. (1982a). Clinical policies and the quality of clinical practice. *New England Journal of Medicine, 307*, 343–347.
Eddy, D. M. (1982b). Probabilistic reasoning in clinical medicine: Problems and opportunities. In D. Kahneman, P. Slovic, & A. Tversky (Eds.), *Judgment under uncertainty: Heuristics and biases* (pp. 249–267). New York: Cambridge University Press.

Eddy, D. M. (1984). Variations in physician practice: The role of uncertainty. *Health Affairs, 3*, 74–89.

Elstein, A. (1976). Clinical judgment: Psychological research and medical practice interdisciplinary effort may lead to more relevant research and improved clinical decisions. *Science, 194*, 696–700.

Elstein, A. S. (2009). Thinking about diagnostic thinking: A 30-year perspective. *Advances in Health Science Education Theory and Practice, 14*, 7–18.

Ely, J., Graber, M., & Croskerry, P. (2011). Checklists to reduce diagnostic errors. *Academic Medicine, 86*, 307–313. doi: 10.1097/ACM.0b013e31820824cd

Epstein, R. M. (1999). Mindful practice. *Journal of the American Medical Association, 282*, 833–839.

Evans, J. (1984). Heuristic and analytic processes in reasoning. *British Journal of Psychology, 75*, 451–468.

Fang, F. C., & Casadevall, A. (2011). Reductionistic and holistic science. *Infectious Immunology, 79*, 1401–1404.

Friend, C. M., & Zubek, J. P. (1958). The effects of age on critical thinking ability. *Journal of Gerontology, 13*, 407–413.

Graber, M. L. (2013). The incidence of diagnostic error in medicine. *BMJ Quality Safety, 22*, ii21–ii27. doi:10.1136/bmjqs-2012-001615

Graber, M. L., Kissam, S., Payne, V. L., Meyer, A. N., Sorensen, A., Lenfestey, N., Tant, E., Henriksen, K., LaBresh, K., & Singh, H. (2012). Cognitive interventions to reduce diagnostic error: A narrative review. *BMJ Quality Safety, 21*, 535–557.

Guyatt, G., Cairns, J., Churchill, D., Cook, D., Haynes, B., Hirsch, J., Irvine, J., Levine, M., Levine, M., Nishikawa, J., & Sackett, D. (1992). Evidence-based medicine: A new approach to teaching the practice of medicine. *Journal of the American Medical Association, 268*, 2420–2425.

Higgins, S., Hall, E., Baumfield, V., & Moseley, D. (2005). A meta-analysis of the impact of the implementation of thinking skills approaches on pupils. Project Report. EPPI-Centre, Social Science Research Unit, Institute of Education, University of London.

Huang, G. C., Newman, L. R., & Schwartzstein, R. M. (2011). Critical thinking in health professions education: Summary and consensus statements of the Millennium Conference. *Teaching and Learning in Medicine, 26*, 95–102. doi: 10.1080/10401334.2013.857335

Kahneman, D., & Tversky, A. (1973). On the psychology of prediction. *Psychological Review, 80*, 237–251.

Kostopoulou, O., Rosen, A., Round, T., Wright, E., Douiri, A., & Delaney, B. C. (2015). Early diagnostic suggestions improve accuracy of GPs: A randomised controlled trial using computer-simulated patients. *British Journal of General Practice, 65*, e49–e54.

Lambe, K. A., O'Reilly, G., Kelly, B. D., & Curristan, S. (2016, February 12). Dual-process cognitive interventions to enhance diagnostic reasoning: a systematic review. *BMJ Quality Safety*, pii: bmjqs-2015-004417. doi: 10.1136/bmjqs-2015-004417. [Epub ahead of print]

Leape, L. L., Berwick, D. M., & Bates, D. W. (2002). What practices will most improve safety? Evidence-based medicine meets patient safety. *Journal of the American Medical Association, 288*, 501–507.

Lippi, G., Blanckaert, N., Bonini, P., Green, S., Kitchen, S., Palicka, V., Vassault, A.J., Mattiuzzi, C., & Plebani, M. (2009). Causes, consequences, detection, and prevention of identification errors in laboratory diagnostics. *Clinical Chemistry and Laboratory Medicine, 47*, 143–153.

Lueke, A., & Gibson, B. (2015). Mindfulness meditation reduces implicit age and race bias: The role of reduced automaticity of responding. *Social Psychological and Personality Science, 6*, 284–291. doi: 10.1177/1948550614559651

Mamede, S., Schmidt, H. G., & Penaforte, J. C. (2008). Effects of reflective practice on the accuracy of medical diagnoses. *Medical Education, 42*, 468–475.

Mamede, S., van Gog, T., van den Berge, K., van Saase, J. L., & Schmidt, H. G. (2014). Why do doctors make mistakes? A study of the role of salient distracting clinical features. *Academic Medicine, 89*, 114–120.

McLaughlin, T., Eva, K. W., & Norman, G. (2014). Re-examining our bias against heuristics. *Advances in Health Science Education, 19*, 457–464.

Meehl, P. E. (1954). *Clinical versus statistical prediction: A theoretical analysis and a review of the evidence.* Minneapolis: University of Minnesota Press.

Montgomery, K. (2006). *How doctors think: Clinical judgment and the practice of medicine.* New York: Oxford University Press.

National Academies of Sciences, Engineering, and Medicine. (2015). ***Improving diagnosis in health care.*** Washington, DC: The National Academies Press.

Nickel, C. H., Ruedinger, J., Misch, F., Blume, K., Maile, S., & Shulte, S (2011). Copeptin and peroxiredoxin-4 independently predict mortality in patients with nonspecific complaints presenting to the emergency department. *Academic Emergency Medicine, 18*, 851–859. doi: 10.1111/j.1553–2712.2011.01126.x

Osheroff, J. A. (2009). ***Improving medication use and outcomes with clinical decision support: A step-by-step guide.*** Chicago, IL: The Healthcare Information and Management Systems Society.

Papp, K. K., Huang, G. C., Lauzon, C., Laurie, M., Delva, D., Fischer, M., Konopasek, L., Schwartzstein, R.M., & Gusic, M. (2014). Milestones of critical thinking: A developmental model for medicine and nursing. *Academic Medicine, 89*, 715–720.

Perkins, D. N. (2002). Mindware and the metacurriculum. In D. Dickinson (Ed.), ***Creating the future: Perspectives on educational change.*** Baltimore: Johns Hopkins School of Education.

Pronovost, P., Needham, D., Berenholtz, S., Sinopoli, D., Chu, H., Cosgrove, S., Sexton, B., Hyzy, R., Welsh, R., Roth, G., & Bander, J. (2006). An intervention to decrease catheter-related bloodstream infections in the ICU. *New England Journal of Medicine, 355*, 2725–2732. doi: 10.1056/NEJMoa061115

Rao, G. (2007). ***Rational medical decision making: A case based approach.*** New York: McGraw-Hill Medical.

Reason, J. (2000). Human error: Models and management. *BMJ: British Medical Journal, 320,* 768–770.

Redelmeier, D. A., Ferris, L. E., Tu, J. V., Hux, J. E., & Schull, M. J. (2001). Problems for clinical judgement: Introducing cognitive psychology as one more basic science. *Canadian Medical Association Journal, 164*, 358–360.

Redelmeier, D. A., Koehler, D. J., Liberman, V., & Tversky, A. (1995). Probability judgment in medicine: Discounting unspecified possibilities. *Medical Decision Making, 15*, 227–230.

Sackett, D. L., Rosenberg, W. M., Gray, J. A., Haynes, R. B., & Richardson, W. S. (1996). Evidence based medicine: What it is and what it isn't. *British Medical Journal, 312*, 71–72.

Schmidt, H. G., Mamede, S., van den Berge, K., van Gog, T., van Saase, J. L., Rikers, R. M. (2014). Exposure to media information about a disease can cause doctors to misdiagnose similar-looking clinical cases. *Academic Medicine, 89*, 285–291.

Schneider, W., & Shiffrin, R. M. (1977). Controlled and automatic human information processing: 1. Detection, search, and attention. *Psychological Review, 84*, 1–66.

Seshia, S. S., Makhinson, M., Phillips, D. F., & Young, G. B. (2014). Evidence-informed person-centered healthcare (part I): Do "cognitive biases plus" at organizational levels influence quality of evidence? *Journal of Evaluation in Clinical Practice, 20*, 734–747.

Seshia, S. S., Makhinson, M., & Young, G. B. (2014). Evidence-informed person-centred health care (part II): Are 'cognitive biases plus' underlying the EBM paradigm responsible for undermining the quality of evidence? *Journal of Evaluation in Clinical Practice, 20*, 748–758.

Seshia, S. S., Makhinson, M., & Young, G. B. (2015, November 26). "Cognitive biases plus": Covert subverters of healthcare evidence. ***Evidence-Based Medicine*** Online First, 10.1136/ebmed-2015–110302

Sibinga, E. M. S., & Wu, A. W. (2010). Clinician mindfulness and patient safety. *JAMA, 304*, 2532–2533.

Smith, M., Saudners, R., Stuckhardt, L., & McGinnis, J. M. (Eds.). (2012). ***Best care at lower cost: The path to continuously learning health care in America.*** Washington, DC: The National Academies Press (Institute of Medicine).

Stanovich, K. E. (2011). ***Rationality and the reflective mind.*** New York: Oxford University Press.

Stanovich, K. E. (2012). On the distinction between rationality and intelligence: Implications for understanding individual differences in reasoning. In K. Holyoak & R. Morrison (Eds.), ***The Oxford handbook of thinking and reasoning*** (pp. 343–365). New York: Oxford University Press.

Stark, M., & Fins, J. J. (2014). The ethical imperative to think about thinking. Diagnostics, metacognition, and medical professionalism. *Cambridge Quarterly of Healthcare Ethics, 23*, 386–396.

Toplak, M. E., & Stanovich, K. E. (2003). Associations between myside bias on an informal reasoning task and amount of post-secondary education. *Applied Cognitive Psychology, 17*, 851–860.

Trowbridge, R. L., Rencic, J. J., & Durning, S. J. (Eds.). (2015). ***Teaching clinical reasoning.*** (ACP Teaching Medicine Series). Philadelphia: American College of Physicians.

Weed, L. L., & Weed, L. (2014). Diagnosing diagnostic failure. ***Diagnosis,*** *1*, 13–17.

West, R. F., Toplak, M. E., & Stanovich, K. E. (2008). Heuristics and biases as measures of critical thinking: Associations with cognitive ability and thinking dispositions. *Journal of Educational Psychology*, *100*, 930–941.

Winters, B., Custer, J., Galvagno, S. M. Jr., Colantuoni, E., Kapoor, S. G., Lee, H. W., Goode, V., Robinson, K., Nakhasi, A., Pronovost, P., & Newman-Toker, D. (2012). Diagnostic errors in the intensive care unit: A systematic review of autopsy studies. *British Medical Journal Quality and Safety*, *21*, 894–902.

8

THE NEW PARADIGM IN PSYCHOLOGY OF REASONING

Shira Elqayam

Introduction: truth and belief

What do people do when they reason? *Prima facie*, this would seem to be a straightforward question with a straightforward answer. When people reason, they draw (or at least attempt to draw) *logical inferences*. Reasoning, by this approach, is about classical logic. In classical logic,[1] a valid inference is one in which the conclusion necessarily follows from the premises (what is assumed to be given as true): if the premises are true, so is the conclusion. So reasoning helps us determine what is true and what is false. In psychology, the foremost representatives of this approach are Inhelder and Piaget (1958): their theory depicts 'formal operations' – that is, logical thinking – as the pinnacle of human cognitive development. Similarly, in philosophy, Copi's (2013) influential introduction to logic still refers to logic as the way to achieve correct, fully reliable reasoning. Retrospectively dubbed 'logicism' (Evans, 2002; Oaksford & Chater, 1991), 'the deduction paradigm' (Evans, 2002), 'the binary paradigm' (Over, 2009), or simply 'the traditional paradigm' (Elqayam & Over, 2012), this view dominated psychology of reasoning for a long time: that logic at least is the correct norm showing how humans *ought* to reason, and perhaps even a good theory describing how we actually *do* reason.

Doubts in the descriptive adequacy of logic emerged much sooner than doubts in its normative appropriateness. I will discuss this in more detail later, but for now I will just note that when the psychology of reasoning emerged as a modern experimental science in the mid-twentieth century, some of its very first dramatic findings showed that humans do *not* reason logically; in other words, logic was found to be a poor *descriptive* system. In contrast, it took the psychology of reasoning nearly half a century to doubt that humans *ought* to reason logically: that is, to doubt that logic is a good *normative* standard.

Since the early 1990s, doubts in logic as an adequate model of human reasoning culminated in a scientific revolution, simply labelled the 'new paradigm' (Evans, 2012; Manktelow, 2012; Manktelow, Over, & Elqayam, 2011; Over, 2009; see Elqayam & Over, 2013, and other contributions to the special issue of *Thinking & Reasoning*), and sometimes referred to as 'probabilistic', 'Bayesian', or 'decision-theoretic'. The last-named term is the key to understanding what the new paradigm is about: that the same psychological machinery that underlies decision making, underlies reasoning as well – and ought to do so. The new paradigm offers a radically different answer to the question posed at the start of this chapter: what do people do when they reason? The answer is that when people reason, what they do is ***make decisions***. This, in a nutshell, is what the new paradigm is about. The new paradigm approach is that reasoning is not about determining truth and falsity; rather, it is about determining what we believe and to what extent, and what things we consider good for us – in technical terms, probability and utility, respectively. New paradigm scientists also reject classical logic as the rulebook for good inference, replacing it with normative rules for probabilistic thinking.

To get an impression of what the new paradigm is, and how it differs from the traditional paradigm, take a look at two well-known tasks in the psychology of reasoning, depicted in Figure 8.1. I will have more to say about this later, but for now it is enough to note that both of these are *truth table* tasks. Truth tables represent all possible permutations of truth values of a logical operator in combined propositions. For example, Table 8.1 is the truth table for the conjunction (sentence combined with ***and***) 'Linda is a banker and a feminist'. Using T for True and F for False, we can abbreviate the table as shown in Table 8.2.

Reading the table from top to bottom, we say that the truth table for the conjunction has a TFFF pattern. In truth table tasks, participants respond to the rows in the table in various ways depending on the specifics of the task. The classical truth table evaluation task in Figure 8.1 (taken from Johnson-Laird & Tagart, 1969) asks participants to evaluate the truth value of these cases for conditional sentences. In contrast, the new paradigm version (from Over, Hadjichristidis, Evans, Handley, & Sloman, 2007) draws on a *probabilistic truth table task*, in which participants are asked for probability estimates of combinations of everyday events.

At first blush, the difference between the classical truth table evaluation task, and the probabilistic truth table task, might look subtle: in the former, participants are asked to provide a true/false evaluation; in the latter, participants are asked to rate the likelihood of the same true/false evaluation. Nevertheless, from the perspective of the new paradigm, the difference is nothing short of revolutionary. Theories have a story to tell, and here the story changes. Truth and falsity no longer occupy centre stage; they are replaced by *belief* (or, more precisely, degrees of belief), expressed as *probability*. The concept of truth lends itself easily to binary terms (hence the appellation 'binary paradigm' for the traditional paradigm): a statement is either true or false. Belief, on the other hand, comes in many shades of grey. I have a relatively firm belief that if I order a latte in my local coffee shop, the liquid I will get will contain the extract of coffee beans; my belief that if I asked for it to be decaf it will contain relatively little caffeine is somewhat shakier (baristas have made mistakes in the past). I can express my belief in the former as highly probable, say, 99%; and in the latter as reasonably probable, say, 70%. In the new paradigm, probability is often used as a handy stand-in for degrees of belief.

The formal framework that the new paradigm draws on is Bayesianism, the normative framework for belief revision, decision making, and probabilistic thinking (Ramsey, 1990; von Neumann & Morgenstern, 1947; for a recent review see Howson & Urbach, 2006; and see Oaksford & Chater, Chapter 23, this volume). Bayesians see probability as subjective, a reflection of uncertainty or degrees of belief: for example, my uncertainty that the coffee is decaf reflects the strength of my belief (influenced, for example, by how far I know and trust the coffee shop), rather than a count of all the times in the past that the coffee was (or was not) decaf. The new paradigm adopts this approach. Formal decision-theoretic models also take into account *utility*, the positive or negative value we assign to things happening in the world – whatever we want or do not want to happen. In decision making generally, and in the new paradigm specifically, utility is no less important than probability. After all, utility is the bridge to action: if I suspect my coffee might be caffeinated (hence depriving me of sleep, something which I would definitely not want to happen), I will double-check, and if necessary ask to have it replaced.

Traditional paradigm task

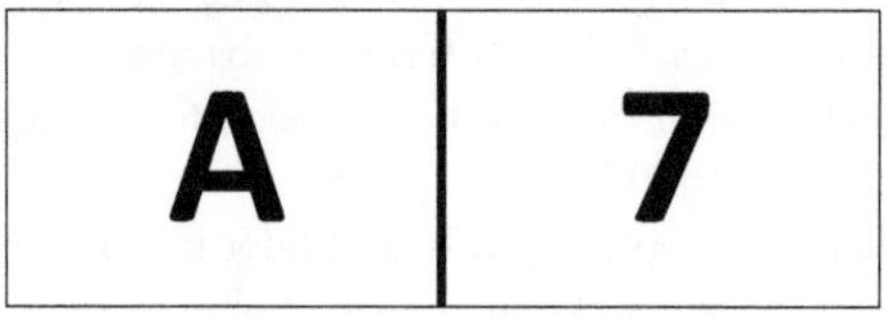

If there is an A on the left, then there is a 7 on the right.

TRUE / FALSE / IRRELEVANT

Johnson-Laird & Tagart, 1969.

New paradigm task

What is the probability that the following events will occur in the UK within the next ten years?

Global warming continues and London gets flooded.	____
Global warming continues and London does not get flooded.	____
Global warming does not continue and London gets flooded.	____
Global warming does not continue and London does not get flooded.	____
	100%

Over et al., 2007

Figure 8.1 Traditional paradigm and new paradigm tasks. Top panel: in Johnson-Laird and Tagart (1969), participants were instructed to classify cases of the truth table (represented by the cards) as true, false, or irrelevant to the conditional rule. Bottom panel: in Over et al. (2007) participants were instructed to provide probability estimates (summing up to 100%) of truth table cases of everyday events.

Table 8.1 The truth table for the conjunction 'Linda is a banker and a feminist'

Suppose that Linda turns out to be . . .	*Then the sentence is . . .*
A banker and a feminist	True
A banker and not a feminist	False
Not a banker and a feminist	False
Not a banker and not a feminist	False

Table 8.2 The truth table for the conjunction using T for True and F for False

Case	*Conjunction truth value*
TT	T
TF	F
FT	F
FF	F

(See Appendix, www.researchgate.net/profile/Shira_Elqayam, for a brief outline of some key Bayesian principles.)

Although there are variants within the new paradigm, the adoption of a decision-theoretic framework means that most new paradigm researchers accept a number of shared research questions and working postulates: we reject classical logic as a good theory (normative or descriptive) of human thinking; and we emphasise the role of probability and utility, the two main parameters of decision making and of Bayesian analysis. One advantage of this is that psychology of reasoning as seen from a new paradigm perspective has an on-going dialogue with the psychology of judgement and decision making and related disciplines, with which it shares a common language and a theoretical toolkit. In addition to probability and utility, the new paradigm also shares with decision making research a strong interest in dual processing, distinguishing between fast, intuitive processes on the one hand, and effortful, resource-guzzling processes on the other hand. (More on this later.)

The rest of this chapter is structured as follows. I start with a brief history of the beginnings of the new paradigm. The two sections following this take up the two decision-theoretic parameters, probability and utility, respectively. I then discuss dual process theories from the perspective of the new paradigm. I conclude with an overview of the larger picture, with a discussion of rationality in the new paradigm, and thoughts about the future of the new paradigm.

Dawn of a new paradigm

In *The Structure of Scientific Revolutions*, Kuhn (1970) developed a view of science as a social activity: a collection of puzzle-solving activities run by community of researchers, where progress is determined not by confirmation or refutation of scientific hypotheses, but by a series of crises and scientific revolutions, a.k.a. *paradigm shifts*. The term 'paradigm' (as Kuhn himself readily owns) is rather slippery, but it helps to think of it as a set of commitments shared by a scientific community: prominent exemplars, methods, aims, and a lexicon of scientific terms. In the lifetime of a paradigm, one of the significant events is that an established paradigm (the technical term is *normal science*) becomes increasingly racked by findings that cannot be accommodated (termed *anomalies*), leading to a crisis state and eventually to a paradigm shift: a scientific revolution leading to a new set of shared commitments. The result is a dramatically changed scientific landscape in which even language no longer has the same meaning, becoming *incommensurable*: a scientific Tower of Babel, as scientists from different paradigms communicate at cross purposes. A new paradigm not only offers better solutions to old puzzles, it also generates new research questions, shaping a new set of scientific puzzles to be solved.

The term 'new paradigm', coined by David Over (2009), strongly hints at a Kuhnian perspective. And indeed the history of the new paradigm reads almost like a *Structure* textbook, complete with normal science, anomalies, crisis states, and incommensurabilities. Here is its story.

In many ways, the traditional or deduction paradigm in psychology of reasoning can be said to have become established – normal science, if you will – with Wason and Johnson-Laird's (1972) volume on the psychology of reasoning. The monograph's subtitle, *Structure and Content*, hints at what was to become the flagship hypothesis of the deduction paradigm: the dichotomy between deduction ('structure'), and the content and context in which it is carried out. This is straight out of classical logic textbook lore: recall that an argument is classically valid, when, if its premises are true, its conclusion is necessarily true. Thus, in the deduction paradigm, participants are typically instructed to assume that the premises are true, a manipulation intended to neutralise the effects of belief.

Nevertheless, the contents of the inference do strongly affect reasoning, in a way that has no place in classical logic. Nowhere did the effect of content and context seem most striking, at least initially, as in the classic – and notoriously difficult – Wason selection task (Wason, 1966; see Evans, 2016; Evans & Over, 2004, Chapter 5, for reviews). In addition to the global meaning in the sense outlined above, the Kuhnian term 'paradigm' has also a local meaning – roughly, an experimental paradigm – and both senses have a role to play in the drama which is the history of the new paradigm (Evans, 2002). The Wason selection task is perhaps the clearest demonstration of this.

There are several versions of the task, but in the usual form of the abstract version, participants are presented with four cards with letters on one side and numbers on the other side. Only one side of each card is seen, for example: N, T, 6, 8 (see the top panel of Figure 8.2 for an illustration). The participants are given a conditional rule that pertains to the cards and can be true or false; for instance, 'If there is an N on one side of the card, then there is a 6 on the other side'. More generally, we can say that the rule has the conditional form *if p then q*, and the cards are *p*, *not-p*, *q*, and *not-q* respectively. Participants are instructed to turn over the cards that are needed to decide whether the rule is true or false – and only those cards.

According to the traditional paradigm, the correct normative solution is to turn over the *p* card (N in our example), and the *not-q* card (8 in our example): N, because if there is anything on the other side except 6 it would prove the rule false; and 8, because it is not a 6, so an N on the other side would similarly prove the rule false. This is not what most participants select, however: most people choose to turn over the *p* card only (N in this case), or the *p* card plus the *q* card (N and 6, respectively). This is one of the most robust findings in the history of psychology of reasoning, if not of cognitive psychology generally.

Striking differences in performance on the task soon emerged, though. By 1972, Wason and Johnson-Laird were able to report two studies with a higher proportion of the classically normative responses *p* and *not-q*: a transportation version (Wason & Shapiro, 1971), in which participants were presented with sentences such as 'Every time I go to Manchester I travel by train'; and a postal rule version (Johnson-Laird, Legrenzi, & Legrenzi, 1972), with conditionals such as 'If a letter is sealed, then it has a 5 penny stamp on it' (familiar to British participants at that time). The facilitated performance on these versions paved the way for the *thematic facilitation*

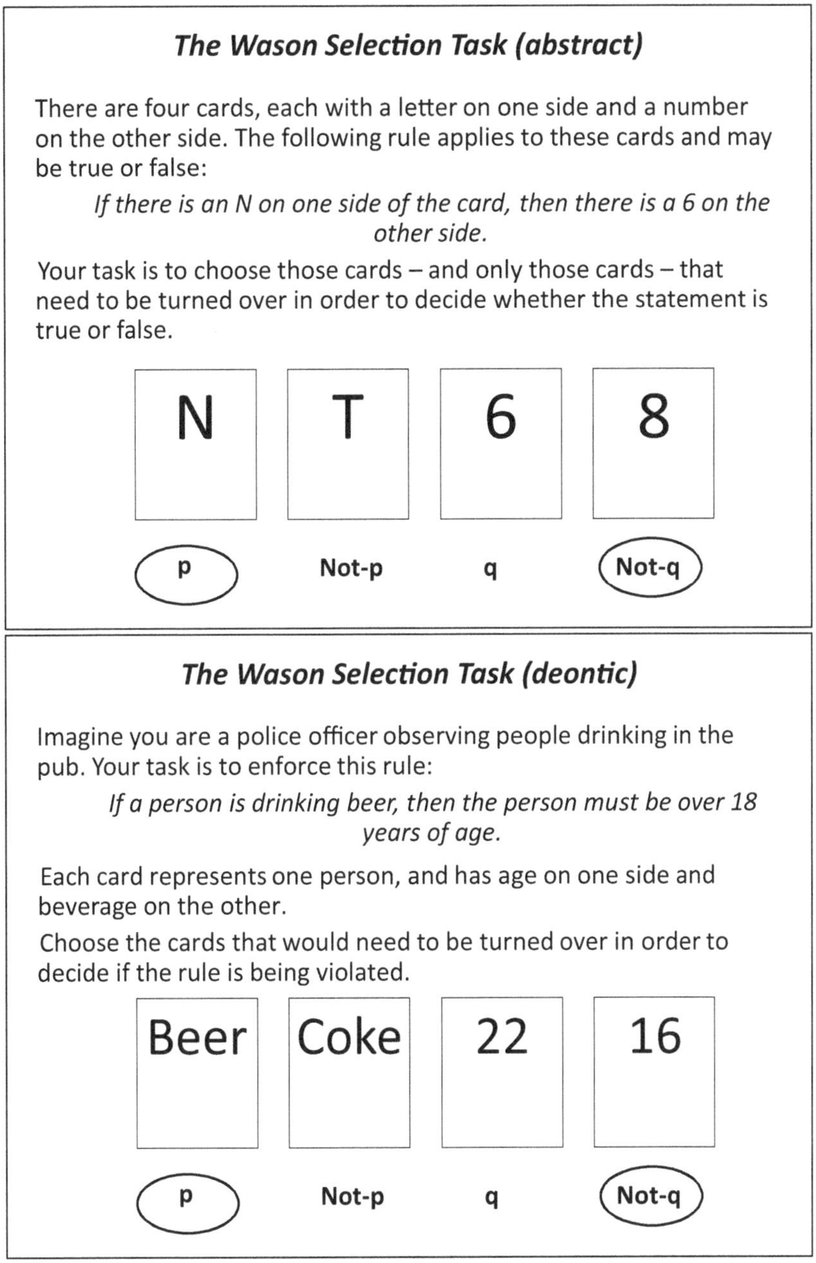
The Wason Selection Task (abstract)
There are four cards, each with a letter on one side and a number on the other side. The following rule applies to these cards and may be true or false:
If there is an N on one side of the card, then there is a 6 on the other side.
Your task is to choose those cards – and only those cards – that need to be turned over in order to decide whether the statement is true or false.
N
T
6
8
p
Not-p
q
Not-q
The Wason Selection Task (deontic)
Imagine you are a police officer observing people drinking in the pub. Your task is to enforce this rule:
If a person is drinking beer, then the person must be over 18 years of age.
Each card represents one person, and has age on one side and beverage on the other.
Choose the cards that would need to be turned over in order to decide if the rule is being violated.
Beer
Coke
22
16
p
Not-p
q
Not-q

Figure 8.2 The Wason selection task. Top panel: abstract version. Bottom panel: deontic version. Circled: the traditionally normative selections, *p* and *not-q*.

hypothesis: with 'sensible' materials, people are better able to exercise 'rational thought' (i.e., comply with the rules of classical logic). This was such a powerfully elegant explanation that it continues to be held as an article of faith to this very day. It is also a quintessentially traditional paradigm hypothesis: there is logic and there is content, and they are (and ought to be) separable.

It was not long, however, before the emergence of Kuhnian *anomalies*: the metaphorical cracks in the walls of the paradigm, with thematic facilitation effects proving erratic and hard to replicate (Griggs & Cox, 1982; Manktelow & Evans, 1979). Griggs and Cox also presented the first reliably facilitating effect with their *drinking age* rule: the conditional was 'If a person is drinking beer, then that person is over 19 years of age', and the cards showed *beer, coke, 22*, and *16*, respectively (see the bottom panel of Figure 8.2). Unlike the standard abstract version, participants were not instructed to discover if the rule was true or false; rather, they were instructed to imagine that they were police officers, and find out if the rule was being *violated*. Selections of the normative *p* and *not-q* cards (beer and 16, in this case) were overwhelming, and this effect, too, has been replicated many times since.

Anomalies in themselves are not enough to trigger a scientific revolution: human tendency to paper over the cracks takes it course. A better paradigm must be available first. Researchers (Cheng & Holyoak, 1985; and later on Cosmides, 1989) soon realised that the facilitated materials no longer drew on the standard type of logic taught in textbooks. As it turns out, all reliable facilitation effects either mentioned or strongly implied the sort of regulations that govern human social life: obligations, permissions. The relevant formal system is *deontic logic* (McNamara, 2014), the type of logic that philosophers use to analyse norms, permissions, and obligations. The drinking age problem and others like it are *deontic* versions of the selection task: the task is to identify violators, rather than verify truth value. Even acknowledging this much went beyond the deduction paradigm, with its acceptance of classical logic as the only normative standard against which to measure human reasoning performance.

Pinpointing precisely when the paradigm started to shift is a matter for debate. (As Jorge Luis Borges once wryly commented, "Every writer creates his own precursors".) However, researchers first explicitly drew on decision theory to explain the selection task in two seminal works from the 1990s: Manktelow and Over (1991) were the first to report[2] *perspective effects*: how differences in the utility (i.e., psychological value) associated with social roles affect card choices in the deontic selection task. The by-now classic example is a mother telling her son: "if you tidy your room, then you may go out to play." From the point of view of the mother, what she desires is for her son to tidy up – in other words, a tidy room bears utility for her (recall that *utility* stands for what is desirable). The son, in contrast, wants to go out to play, and this is where the utility for him lies. Out of several ways in which this rule could be violated, two are of particular interest. The mother will be mainly interested in cases in which the son does not tidy up but nevertheless goes out to play (*not-p* and *q*), whereas the son will be particularly interested in cases in which he tidies up his room but his mother does not allow him to play (*p* and *not-q*). This, then, is the card combination we would expect participants to select when they reason from the mother's and the son's perspective, respectively; and this is indeed what Manktelow and Over found.

If Manktelow and Over were the first to draw on decision theory to explain a reasoning task, Oaksford and Chater's (1994) soon-to-follow classic reanalysis of the selection task was the first to propose an explicitly Bayesian modelling. Bayesianism is the formal, normative system of decision making, based on principles such as utility and subjective probabilities. Oaksford and Chater's idea was that, rather than trying to prove the conditional rule true or false, participants in the selection task were trying to find out if *q* depended on *p*; for this end, they were trying to select the most informative cards. Oaksford and Chater then drew on Bayesian analysis to argue that the *p* card was the most informative, with the *q* card as a runner-up, and the *not-q* and *not-p* card trailing far behind.[3] On this argument, based on Bayesian analysis, participants in the selection task were being perfectly rational. I will have more to say about rationality in the new paradigm later, but for now suffice it to note that in both of these seminal papers, the appeal to utility in particular and decision-theoretic and Bayesian principles generally is a game changer.

It means that the deduction paradigm's hitherto sacrosanct distinction between structure and content was lost forever. A new paradigm was afoot.

Belief, uncertainty, and probability: the suppositional turn

The new paradigm is sometimes referred to as 'probabilistic', and indeed probability is a central issue in any decision-theoretic approach. However, the new paradigm is not just about probability: probability as such is arguably not really a psychological construct. Of course, people can occasionally reason probabilistically – as they can reason according to classical logic – but probability as a formal system is no more psychological than logic is. Probability, however, is a good stand-in for something much closer to home, for a psychologist: belief, or, if you will, degrees of belief, or uncertainty (Elqayam & Evans, 2013; Elqayam & Over, 2012). Psychologists and philosophers often find it useful to express degrees of belief as probabilities, as the latter provide a convenient numerical scale.

A good demonstration of how degrees of belief can usefully be formalised as probabilities in a psychological experiment is the probabilistic truth table task, mentioned briefly earlier in this chapter. If there is a single task that epitomises the new paradigm, it is the probabilistic truth table task, motivated by new paradigm research questions in the first place – whereas the Wason selection task is the brainchild of the traditional deduction paradigm. We start with Over et al.'s (2007) paradigm mentioned in the introduction to this chapter. Imagine that you are a participant in a psychological experiment. You are given a conditional, a sentence of the form 'If *p* then *q*': *if global warming continues, then London will be flooded.* You are asked to rate the probability that the conditional statement given is true (or false), on a scale from 0% to 100%. In a separate task, you are given the task portrayed in the bottom panel of Figure 8.1: to judge the probability that the events in Figure 8.1 would occur in the UK within the next 10 years. The four sentences correspond to the four rows of the truth table for the conditional: TT, TF, FT, FF, respectively (recall that T stands for True and F for False). The advantage of this method is that it taps into participants' own subjective estimates of probabilities – that is, their degrees of belief. Now comes the clever step: the separate estimates of truth table cases can be usefully combined in ways that have theoretical significance. The most important combination is the ratio P(TT)/P(TT+TF), where P denotes probability. It means the probability of the TT case divided by the combined probabilities of the TT and the TF cases (where TT = global warming continues and London gets flooded; and TF = global warming continues and London does *not* get flooded). This ratio is called 'conditional probability', and it stands, in this case, for the probability that London will get flooded, assuming that global warming continues.

For example, suppose you think that the probability that global warming will continue and London will get flooded (TT) is 70%; and that the probability that global warming will continue but London will not get flooded is 20%. The conditional probability will be .7 / (.7 + .2) = .7 / .9 = .78, or 78%. The typical finding is that there is a strong correlation between this conditional probability ratio, computed based on the responses to the separate truth table rows, and the ratings of the probability that the conditional statement ('If global warming continues, then London will be flooded'), which participants rated in the separate task, is true. Thus, the subjective probability that, if global warming continues, London will be flooded equals the subjective probability that London will be flooded, given that global warming continues: the probability of the conditional equals the conditional probability, respectively. This may sound like a no-brainer, but you might be surprised to learn that rivers of ink have been spilled (and no doubt will continue to) over this very equation. Or, if you will, Equation: the relationship is so central to philosophical logic and psychology of reasoning, that it fully merits the capitalisation (Edgington, 1995).

The term often heard in this context is 'Ramsey test' (and see Over & Cruz, Chapter 24, this volume): people evaluate conditionals of the form *'if p then q'*, suggested Ramsey (1931) in a much-quoted footnote, by adding the antecedent (the *p* part of the conditional) hypothetically to their stock of beliefs, and evaluating the consequent (the *q* part of the conditional) in this context. For example, asked to evaluate the global warming conditional, people will hypothetically suppose that global warming continues, and evaluate the strength of belief in London being flooded given this supposition. The Equation (i.e., that the probability of the conditional is the conditional probability) is a direct translation of the Ramsey test. The Ramsey test forms the basis of what has come to be termed in psychology of reasoning *the suppositional conditional* (Evans, Handley, & Over, 2003; Evans & Over, 2004), a psychological version of the Ramsey test: people *suppose* that the antecedent is true, using the uniquely human ability to mentally simulate things that have not happened yet, and evaluate the conditional under this supposition.

The Ramsey test and the suppositional conditional also fit with a well-known psychological effect, going back to the early days of the deduction paradigm – the *defective* truth table[4] (Evans & Over, 2004). Recall that we can represent all possible permutations of a logical term (*operator* is the technical term) in a table. So what is the truth table of the conditional, the *if* operator? As it turns out, more often than not, participants respond with the defective truth table. This means that, in traditional truth table tasks such as the one in the top panel of Figure 8.1, people tend to classify the TT case as True, the TF case as False, but when it comes to the FT and FF cases, they tend to be classified as neither true nor false, or as irrelevant. Table 8.3 shows the defective conditional, using the global warming conditional as an illustration.

In Table 8.3, the # sign means that something is missing – irrelevant, or neither true nor false – technically referred to in philosophical logic as a *truth value gap*. Reading the table top down, we can use the abbreviation TF## to refer to the defective truth table pattern. You can see how this pattern fits with the Ramsey test: because people focus on the antecedent being true, they focus on the TT and TF cases, with no attention left for cases where the antecedent is false – an effect known in the psychology of reasoning as the *if-heuristic* (Evans & Over, 2004).

However, in classical logic, the logic that the traditional paradigm accepts as a standard, the conditional is false when the antecedent is true and the consequent is false, but true in all other cases. The rightmost column in the table above represents this type of conditional, known as the *material conditional*: TFTT, again reading the table top down. Although there are no psychological

Table 8.3 The defective conditional, illustrated using the conditional 'If global warming continues, London will get flooded'

If global warming continues, London will get flooded	*Defective conditional*	*Material conditional*
Global warming continues and London gets flooded (TT)	T	T
Global warming continues and London does not get flooded (TF)	F	F
Global warming does not continue and London gets flooded (FT)	#	T
Global warming does not continue and London does not get flooded (FF)	#	T

theories that accept the material conditional as a full theory of how people reason with conditionals, the one that comes closest is mental model theory (Johnson-Laird, 1983, 2006, and Chapter 19, this volume; Johnson-Laird & Byrne, 1991). The most prominent extant theory within the deduction paradigm, mental model theory sees reasoning as based on representations of possibilities in the world. Events are represented in ***mental models***: a set of logical possibilities, rather like a truth table, which can be combined to produce inference. According to mental model theory, people reason by reading the results off the combined mental models. Due to limitations on working memory, not all such possibilities are initially represented, but the missing possibilities can be added to the mental model, a process known as ***fleshing out***. In the classic mental model treatment of conditionals (Johnson-Laird & Byrne, 2002), the initial, missing representation of conditionals produces the defective truth table (considered by mental model theorists to be erroneous), but the material conditional is characteristic of abstract conditionals once they have been fleshed out.

Whether the material conditional or the defective truth table is how people *ought* to reason is not something that we can test empirically. We can, however, test how people actually reason. Both the Ramsey test and the Equation are constructs of philosophical logic, but both – especially the Ramsey test – are easily translatable to psychological terms, and, just as importantly, lending themselves to be tested experimentally. Over et al. (2007) is a classic example, but the probabilistic truth table task first came to prominence in psychology of reasoning in an abstract version: Evans, Handley, and Over (2003; see also Oberauer & Wilhelm, 2003) presented participants with conditionals such as 'If the card is yellow, then it has a circle printed on it', and a description of the pack of cards to which the conditional refers; for example:

1 yellow circle (TT)
4 yellow diamonds (TF)
16 red circles (FT)
16 red diamonds (FF)

Participants were instructed to evaluate the likelihood of the conditional. The robust finding – replicated many times since (e.g., Fugard, Pfeifer, Mayerhofer, & Kleiter, 2011; Oberauer & Wilhelm, 2003) – is that for the majority of participants, these ratings show a close match to the Equation. In the example above, this is 1 out of 5 cards: one yellow circle (TT) out of a total of five yellow cards (TT+TF). There are several other minor response patterns, but the noteworthy one is the one that hardly ever surfaces: that of the material conditional. With the material conditional, the true cases are yellow circles (TT), red circles (FT), and red diamonds (FF); in other words, the probability of the material conditional being true is 33 out of 37. However, responses conforming to this pattern are vanishingly rare.[5]

This might sound like Scholastic arguments over how many angels can dance on the head of a pin, but there is crucial psychological reality behind the numbers. These are not just different formal logics of the conditional, but entirely different psychological insights as to how the mind works when we reason. With mental model theory, the psychological engine powering reasoning is semantic models representing possibilities in the world. And this is all they represent: there is no place for representing things like a timeline of events, how we feel, or what we think about them. In contrast, the suppositional conditional draws on *epistemic* mental models (Evans, 2006, 2007), which are a product of hypothetical thinking, the ability to imagine events. Epistemic mental models represent more than logical possibilities; they also represent beliefs and attitudes, rather than the bare bones of logical possibilities. Once again we see how the contrast is between truth and belief.

The idea of uncertainty as both a psychological and philosophical construct also provides a better fit with one of the main characteristics of human reasoning – *defeasibility* (Oaksford & Chater, 1991, 2013). Classical logic is ***monotonic***, which means that an inference once drawn cannot be withdrawn, regardless of what extra information is revealed. But human reasoning clearly does not work like this. Consider the following inference, taken from Stevenson and Over (1995)

If John goes fishing, he will have a fish supper
John goes fishing
Therefore, John will have a fish supper

This inference seems innocuous enough; indeed, it has the structure of a ***modus ponens*** inference, a type of inference of the structure *If p then q; p; therefore q*, which participants are generally happy to endorse; and this is what happens here as well. But what happens if we add the following premises?

If John catches a fish he will have a fish supper
John is rarely lucky when he goes fishing

The conclusion that John will have a fish supper now seems rather shaky, and indeed participants tend to reject it (see also Byrne, 1989; Stevenson & Over, 2001). It is, however, still valid according to classical logic, because classical logic is ***monotonic***: valid is valid, regardless of any additional information. Although mental model theory provided an account of defeasibility (Byrne, 1989), it had to treat defeasibility as an error, a logical fallacy. In contrast, defeasibility is central to new paradigm theories, which explain it as a Bayesian function: specifically, as a derivative of *Bayes' theorem* (Howson & Urbach, 2006), the theorem specifying how to revise belief by combining the earlier information (the *base rate*) with the new information (see Appendix on www.researchgate.net/profile/Shira_Elqayam for the formula and further explanation). Bayes' theorem played a major role in Oaksford and Chater's (1994) reanalysis of the selection task, and belief revision and nonmonotonicity continues to be a main topic of interest in the new paradigm (e.g., Harris, Corner, & Hahn, 2013; Oaksford & Chater, 2013, 2014; and see Over & Cruz, Chapter 24, this volume).

Utility and pragmatics

Martin wants to cook an Italian dish. He knows a fine brand of Italian olive oil: if he buys this brand, his recipe will taste better. It seems natural to conclude that Martin *should* buy this brand, and indeed participants readily endorse such inferences (Elqayam, Thompson, Wilkinson, Evans, & Over, 2015), thus in effect creating a new deontic norm: a normative rule to direct behaviour, where none existed before. We find it easy to create these new deontic norms when an action results in a desirable outcome (or when it results in an undesirable outcome, in which case we create deontic rules using negatives such as 'should not'). We also tend to think that people who tell us conditionals with a desirable (or undesirable) outcome want to persuade us to take action that brings about (or forestalls) this outcome (Thompson, Evans, & Handley, 2005); for example, told 'If tuition fees are increased, then there will be a drop in student recruitment', participants infer that the writer thinks that tuition fees should not be increased. Thompson et al. called these types of conditionals ***persuasions*** and ***dissuasions***, respectively. The technical term for the psychological mechanism underlying these effects is *utility* – whatever we desire to happen or to not-happen (see Appendix on www.researchgate.net/profile/Shira_Elqayam for SEU, the normative theory of utility). There is a clear link between utility, decision making, and action – we tend to make decisions when we want something to happen. Thus, utility anchors the new paradigm in the psychology of decision making, and in decision theory, more firmly than ever.

Utility first came on board the new paradigm with the deontic selection task, so it is small wonder that research on utility in the new paradigm focuses a lot on deontic reasoning in general and deontic conditionals specifically. Much of this is on deontic speech acts, such as inducement and advice conditionals: conditional threats and promises, tips and warnings, such as 'If you wash the car this afternoon, you may borrow it tomorrow'. One typical finding shows that conditional promises and tips are rated more useful and persuasive when their benefit outweighs their costs (Evans, Neilens, Handley, & Over, 2008) – for example, when the incentive of borrowing the car is enough to overcome the boredom and hard work of washing it; the opposite is true for conditional threats and warnings. It also takes longer to read explicit threats and promises if their utility mismatches these expectations (Haigh, Ferguson, & Stewart, 2014).

Bonnefon (2009) outlined a useful scheme for classifying *utility conditionals* – conditional sentences that bear utilities. The scheme identifies the actor and recipient of the actions of the antecedent (the *if* part of the conditional) and the consequent (the *then* part of the conditional), and the utility associated with them, all represented in abbreviated format in a *utility grid*. Different utility grid patterns are associated with different types of utility conditionals. For example, in conditional promises of the sort above, the hearer of the conditional washes the car, thus creating positive utility for the speaker but a somewhat negative utility for himself; the speaker allows the hearer to borrow the car afterwards, creating a positive utility for him. Similarly, consequential conditionals (Bonnefon & Hilton, 2004) such as 'If Sophie takes this drug, then she will be entirely cured' are characterised by a utility grid in which a positive (or negative) outcome happens to someone who is neither the speaker nor the hearer; and so on. There is a psychological reality behind these grids: when people are given ambiguous information which is close to a specific grid, they tend to interpret the information so that it conforms to the grid (Bonnefon, Haigh, & Stewart, 2013).

A particularly noteworthy angle of new paradigm interest in utility is the recent surge of research into the role of argumentation in psychology of reasoning (Hahn & Oaksford, 2007; and see also Mercier, Chapter 22, and Collins & Hahn, Chapter 6, this volume). This surge was boosted by Mercier and Sperber's (2011; and see open peer commentary there) thesis that argumentation is the core function of human reasoning: we reason because we want to convince. The term *argumentation* means exactly what it says on the tin: the way speakers produce arguments when they want to convince a hearer. There are types of informal arguments traditionally considered to be *fallacies*, erroneous arguments. Such informal argumentation fallacies include, for example, the appeal to emotion, such as a defence attorney arguing that her client could not have stolen the money because she is such a sweet, frail old lady.

Hahn and Oaksford developed a Bayesian framework to analyse such informal argumentation fallacies. Take, for example, slippery slope arguments (Corner, Hahn, & Oaksford, 2011), such as 'If voluntary euthanasia is legalised, then in the future there will be more cases of "medical murder"'. People find such arguments subjectively stronger and more convincing when the conditional probability of the outcome given the cause (in this case, the probability of medical murder increasing given that voluntary euthanasia is legalised) is higher, and when the negative utility (i.e., bad things happening) associated with the outcome is higher, triggering a wish to avoid it – in this case, the desire to avoid increase in cases of medical murder, a clearly negative outcome.

Dual processing: old and new

Dual process theories in reasoning and decision making (Evans, 2008; Evans & Stanovich, 2013; Kahneman, 2011; and see Evans, Chapter 9, this volume; Rakow & Skylark, Chapter 25, this volume) distinguish between two main types of processes: fast, intuitive processes, drawing much on heuristics, or rules of thumb; and, in contrast, effortful, analytic processes, which allow us to solve new problems that we had never encountered before. These are sometimes labelled type 1 versus type 2, or system 1 versus system 2, respectively. A typical illustration is the well-documented effect of *belief bias* (Evans, Barston, & Pollard, 1983; and see Ball & Thompson, Chapter 2, this volume). Belief bias is the way that what we believe to be true or false influences how we reason – regardless of whether the inference is actually valid or not. Recall that a classically valid argument is one in which, if the premises are true, the conclusion is necessarily true. Accordingly, the traditional deduction paradigm (Evans, 2002) typically uses an instruction set that effectively tells participants to ignore their beliefs, by instructing them to make the assumption that the premises are true, and draw only logically necessary conclusions. However, separating logical inference from believability takes a great deal of effort. Here is an example. Consider the following argument:

Premise A: all roses are flowers
Premise B: all flowers are birds
Conclusion: therefore, all roses are birds

Is this argument logically valid? The first thing that grabs our attention is that premise B is patently false, and so is the conclusion. Recall, however, that premises are what we *assume* to be true. It should not matter if the premises (or the conclusion) are true or false, only that the conclusion necessarily follows – and it does. The argument is valid. Nevertheless, people often fail to grasp this, because the lure of the unbelievable conclusion is so strong. This is what belief bias is about. The term *bias* in the deduction paradigm is used to refer to a systematic but non-logical pattern of behaviour (Evans, 2002). Most theoretical explanations to belief bias focus on the differences between the fast, intuitive processes associated with belief and the effortful processes associated with logic (although cf. Handley, Newstead, & Trippas, 2011): it only takes reading the conclusion to respond based on belief, but for a judgement of validity, the argument structure needs to be considered, and this is generally more difficult.

Belief bias is more than a good illustration of dual processing, however: it is a demonstration of how even familiar theoretical landmarks change when paradigms shift. Kuhn called this 'incommensurability'. Incommensurability means that scientists stop understanding each other: they each mean something different even when they use what seems to be, superficially, the same scientific term. Thus, theoretical terms no longer retain their meaning, so scientists from different paradigms talk somewhat at cross purposes. Communication becomes more difficult (although not impossible). For example, Ptolemy, who thought that the Earth was the centre around which planets revolve, listed the Sun amongst the planets; whereas Copernicus, who first suggested that planets revolve around the Sun, listed the Earth amongst the planets. Now imagine a Ptolemaic astronomer discussing planets with a Copernican one. They cannot even agree what is considered to be a planet and what is not, let alone how a planet is defined. This is incommensurability.

Evans et al. (1983), the paper that shaped the belief bias paradigm, identified logic with type 2 processing and belief with type 1 processing. This was typical of dual processing in the deduction paradigm, which assumed as a matter of course that analytic processing leads to correct, normative thinking – that is, logical thinking. The equation was type 2 processing = normative = logic; and type 1 processing = bias = belief. None of this is the case any more in dual processing research under the umbrella of the new paradigm. Type 2 processing is no longer thought to correspond to logic (Elqayam & Over, 2012; Oaksford & Chater, 2011, 2012) or to any normative standard, for that matter (Evans & Stanovich, 2013). Nor is classical logic considered to be an appropriate normative standard for reasoning (although it might be a good descriptive model; see De Neys, 2012). Belief effects are no longer considered a bias, because probabilistic models of inference take into account degrees of belief (e.g., Evans, Thompson, & Over, 2015). The term 'belief bias' stuck, but it is no longer used in a pejorative sense (Evans, 2002). All in all, the concept of dual processing is as different between the deduction paradigm and the new paradigm as the concept of planet is between the Ptolemaic and Copernican systems respectively.

Research on dual processing in the new paradigm increasingly focuses on exploring boundaries and ramifications. One of the main lines of research is the role of metacognition (e.g., Ackerman & Thompson, 2017; Thompson et al., 2013; Thompson, Prowse Turner, & Pennycook, 2011; Thompson & Johnson, 2014; also see Ackerman & Thompson, Chapter 1, this volume): the mechanisms that underlie the switch from intuitive to effortful processing. By and large, people tend to stick with their initial intuitive response when they have subjective confidence – *feeling of rightness*, or *FOR* – in this response. When the level of FOR is low, they tend to invest more cognitive effort, and to switch their response, although they are as likely to switch from a normatively correct to a normatively erroneous response as the other way around (another nail in the coffin of the type 2 = norm equation). Metacognitive confidence also plays a role in the popular theory of logical intuition (e.g., De Neys, 2012; De Neys & Glumicic, 2008; De Neys, Vartanian, & Goel, 2008; Morsanyi & Handley, 2012) – the idea that people identify when their own responses are wrong (although they do not modify them). The jury is still out on this one, with opponents arguing that what looks like logic is no more than a response to shallow cues (see, for example, Aczel, Szollosi, & Bago, 2016; Klauer & Singmann, 2013).

Another development of the new paradigm is that theorists are becoming increasingly interested in what dual processing implies about cognitive architecture, the structure of the mind. Stanovich (e.g., 1999, 2004) argued for a cognitive map relating type 1 processing to evolutionary pressures coming directly from the genes, whereas type 2 processing is related to evolutionary processes that allow individuals to protect their own personal interests. Evolutionary considerations also characterise Evans's (2010b) two-minds theory, which argues for a cognitive architecture based on the distinction between the old mind – evolutionarily ancient, past-oriented processes; and the new mind – evolutionarily new, future-oriented processes that enable planning and creative problem solving. This architecture very loosely maps into type 1 and type 2 processing, respectively. Each mind comprises multiple systems, although the old mind contains only type 1 systems, whereas the new mind contains both type 1 and type 2 systems: the difference is that type 2 systems always draw on working memory whereas type 1 systems are autonomous (Evans, 2010a). With different systems computing different functions in the old mind and the new mind, the question now arises if all these functions are still essentially 'Bayesian', a question which triggered different answers from different theorists. On the one hand, Oaksford and Chater (2011, 2012) argue that both systems compute the same probabilistic function. This raises a problem, though: if two systems compute the same function, this seems a rather pointless redundancy (Evans, 2010b). Elqayam and Over (2012) propose, therefore, that the two types of process compute different functions. For example, consequential decision making requires hypothetical thinking and hence type 2 processing.

Rationality in the new paradigm

Are humans rational? This question is the basis of what has been termed 'the great rationality debate'. Can human beings be said to think rationally, or are we essentially an irrational lot? To answer this, we first need to understand what rationality actually means, and, no less importantly, what it does not mean. The new paradigm has a specific angle on this question.

Many people, when asked what it means to be rational, will tell you that to be rational is to be logical: rationality and logic are the same. However, we have already seen that humans do not always think logically. Does this mean, then, that people are inherently irrational? The traditional paradigm must answer in the affirmative: people might have a modicum of rationality (read: logicality), but they are also prone to many a logical error and fallacy. The idea to be considered in this context is *logicism* (Evans, 2002; Oaksford & Chater, 1991) – that classical logic provides a good description of how people reason as well as a rational standard for how people *ought* to reason. Oaksford and Chater (1998) pointed out that even though mental model theory explicitly rejected the idea that people have some kind of mental logic in their heads, it was still logicist: all it did was replace one logical method with another (that of truth tables). Thus, theories within the deduction paradigm may differ on the particulars of *how* people reason, what the processes are, but they are still in agreement about *what* is being computed, and what is being computed is classical logic (the technical term is algorithmic- versus computational-level explanations; Marr, 1982). Conversely, although new paradigm theories differ along several dimensions, they (for the most part) share a rejection of classical logic: it is neither a good description of *how* people reason, nor a good normative standard of how people *ought* to reason. Most importantly, logic does not give us a good description of *what* we do when we reason, because when we reason, we make decisions, and logic is at loss to account for this.

To address human rationality within the new paradigm, we must first ask what it means for people to be 'Bayesian' (and see the Appendix on www.researchgate.net/profile/Shira_Elqayam for a brief introduction to Bayesian decision theory). Does it mean that every inference, judgement, and decision we make is consistent with normative Bayesian strictures – that is, that the probability calculus is a good *descriptive* system of how people *actually* think and make decisions? True, human behaviour fits Bayesian models in some notable cases, such as the Wason selection task. Nonetheless, people violate probabilistic normative rules as much as they violate classical logical rules. A good example is belief revision, the way we update our beliefs when new evidence comes in. Bayes' theorem, the normative rule for belief revision, specifies exactly how you should integrate the new information with the previous one (*base rate* is the technical term). But people do not conform to Bayes' theorem when they revise their beliefs. There is plenty of evidence in the decision making literature that people neglect base rates, or at least fail to integrate them sufficiently with new evidence (for reviews, see Barbey & Sloman, 2007; Koehler, 1996).

However, we can ask a more modest question: do people reason by the same principles that they make decisions? Do people make inferences by taking into account their subjective, uncertain beliefs; by estimating how good or bad an outcome is for them; by revising their beliefs? We can say that people do make use of these principles when they reason, although not necessarily (or even usually) in a way that conforms to the strictures of the probability calculus. This theoretical approach has been dubbed 'soft' Bayesianism (Elqayam & Evans, 2013; and cf. Jones & Love, 2011).

We can also ask if Bayesian probability is a good *normative* system, a good rulebook on how we *ought* to reason. This is a moot topic within the new paradigm. Some authors (most notably Oaksford & Chater; see, e.g., 2007) take a 'strict' Bayesian approach, that rationality is impossible without conforming to normative Bayesian rules. If people violate the normative rules of the probability calculus, they can find themselves in a position of making bets that inevitably lead to certain loss (called 'Dutch books'; see Gilio & Over, 2012, for an example). But if people conform to the laws of probability, they are immune to such bets. Nobody likes to lose money! Thus, Dutch book arguments are a good way to convince people that the probability calculus is a useful normative system (Corner & Hahn, 2013; although cf. Elqayam, 2016).

If we need to choose a normative system, then, it would seem that the probability calculus makes a better candidate than classical logic: it is closer to how people actually think (although, admittedly, neither is very close), and there are good reasons to support its pragmatic usefulness as well. But why do we need a normative system at all? Arguably, all the new paradigm is doing is repeat the mistakes made by the traditional paradigm – the same old game, only with the normative system replaced. Elqayam and Evans (2011; Evans & Elqayam, 2011) argued that psychology of reasoning and decision making is unique within cognitive psychology – indeed, within the broader field of cognitive science – to focus so much on issues of right and wrong. If participants fail to spot a light in a vigilance task, we do not bemoan the frailty of human attention; if they forget the middle part of a long list of words, we do not condemn human memory by making comparisons against an impossible standard of total recall. We simply regard it as an addition to our knowledge of how the mind works (Evans, 2014). It is the scientist's role to describe what is, they argued, rather than set the rules for what ought to be. This position is called 'descriptivism', and it is contrasted with 'normativism', the position that people ought to conform to a normative system. By this argument, the position that the probability calculus is the appropriate normative system for psychologists to study is just as normativist as logicism. The change is in the identity of the rulebook, but not in substance.

An offshoot of this view is the idea of ***grounded rationality*** (Elqayam, 2011, 2012, 2015): the theory argues that, far from being the source of bias and error it is traditionally considered to be, the context of reasoning and decision making is crucially important in achieving pragmatic rationality. There is a strong connection here to Simon's (e.g., 1982) idea of ***bounded rationality***, widely accepted within the new paradigm and more generally in the field of higher mental processing. Simon pointed out that people do not have unlimited biological and cognitive resources, and sometimes computing a normative solution is simply not worth the investment of time and effort: if you need a pocket calculator to compute whether the strange noise in a dark alley is a mugger, you will never get away in time. Hence, the pragmatic option is often not to optimise (find the best solution) but to *satisfice*, or find a solution that is just good enough. You might be better off treating all noises in the dark as suspicious and avoiding them. You might not be right all the time, or even most of the time, but the rule of the thumb is ***good enough*** to provide some protection from urban violence. However, cognitive cost and benefit is relative: what people can or cannot profitably compute will depend on how smart they are, how motivated to think hard, what they already know from past experience and training. If you are a trained police officer, you might have better ways to classify which noises are suspicious and which are innocuous. Hence, grounded rationality argues for taking into account contextual, relative constraints as well as universal ones.

Concluding comments

When we think, we make decisions: this is the foundational insight of the new paradigm in psychology of reasoning, variously dubbed 'probabilistic', 'Bayesian', and 'decision theoretic'. Just as we make decisions on a background of uncertainty, so we reason, not with the binary truth and falsity of classical logic, but with the many shades of uncertainty and of degrees of belief. Just as we make decisions based on what we want or do not want, so is our reasoning shaped by utility. And just as we can make quick and intuitive decisions as well as slow and analytic ones, so is reasoning governed by dual processing. It is not for nothing that probability, utility, and dual processing have been hailed as the three pillars of the new paradigm (Bonnefon, 2013).

The history of the new paradigm shows all the hallmarks of a truly Kuhnian scientific revolution: from the increasing anomalies in the then-normal science of the deduction paradigm, through the emergence of new explanations and research questions – complete with incommensurability as old concepts acquired new meanings – to the establishment of a new normal science. Multiple chapters throughout the volume would not have existed had the new paradigm never come into being, including chapters on probability and Bayesian rationality (Oaksford & Chater, Chapter 23) and conditional reasoning (Over & Cruz, Chapter 24), to chapters on argumentation (Mercier, Chapter 22) and informal argument fallacies (Collins & Hahn, Chapter 6). Other chapters are re-shaped by new paradigm ideas, including the chapter on dual process theory (Evans, Chapter 9) and the chapter on metareasoning (Ackerman & Thompson, Chapter 1). The very inclusion of chapters on decision making and on reasoning within the same volume is an editorial decision that owes a lot to the new paradigm. It would not be excessive to argue that, for better or worse, the new paradigm irrevocably changed the face of reasoning research. The new paradigm is (*pace* mental model theorists) the new normal science.

If we count back from the early 1990s, new paradigm research is now in young adulthood. The psychology of reasoning tends to undergo scientific revolutions on a remarkably regular basis (perhaps unavoidable in a discipline where scientists think about thinking): the previous one, that of mental model theory (Johnson-Laird, 1983), is barely into middle age. The next paradigm shift might be just around the corner. Until this happens, we can still ask about the future of the new paradigm. One development is already underway: as the field of reasoning becomes better integrated with decision making, it also becomes increasingly inclusive, branching out to research topics such as argumentation, moral judgement (Bonnefon, 2013; and Trémolière, De Neys, & Bonnefon, Chapter 32, this volume), and even religiosity (Pennycook, Cheyne, Barr, Koehler, & Fugelsang, 2013). Reasoning is no longer the hallowed ivory-tower function it used to be under the deduction paradigm. The downside of this is that the paradigm is also becoming increasingly fragmented. It is not that we lack second-order meta-theories to integrate the field – in fact we have several of these, especially in dual processing and in rationality. There is, of course, considerable overlap, and in recent years the field witnessed third-order (!) attempts to outline the common denominator, such as Evans and Stanovich's (2013) defence of dual process theories, but there is much that still defeats integration attempts. Perhaps this is an inevitable price for a paradigm which is a family of theories rather than one influential theory which dominates the whole paradigm.

Within rationality, the debate goes as strongly as ever, but the focus seems to be shifting. The new focus is increasingly on how viable Bayesianism is as a normative system, and whether a normative system is needed in the first place. There is fragmentation here, too, with mounting challenges to the classic probability theory of strict Bayesianism (Bowers & Davis, 2012; Elqayam & Evans, 2011, 2013; Jones & Love, 2011; and see Hahn, 2014, for a response). The new contextualised, relativist perspective of grounded rationality (Elqayam, 2012) has not gone unchallenged either (Oaksford, 2014). If there is one thing we can be reasonably certain about for the future of the new paradigm, it is that it will remain as stormy as it has been from its inception to present times; and that it will keep challenging us and fascinating us at the same time.

Acknowledgements

I am grateful to Jonathan Evans for critical reading and helpful feedback on several versions of this chapter; and to David Over, Denis Hilton, Linden Ball, and Valerie Thompson for helpful comments on a previous version.

Notes

1 Classical logic is (among other things) binary – it only recognises truth and falsity. I will occasionally refer simply to 'logic' as short for 'classical logic'.
2 The effect was independently discovered by Politzer and Nguyen-Xuan (1992).
3 More precisely, the ***not-q*** card is only informative when the probability of *p* is high, but Oaksford and Chater had a ***rarity assumption***, that participants treat both *p* and *q* as rare events.
4 Philosophers sometimes prefer the term 'de Finetti truth table' as the term 'defective' might sound pejorative.
5 Needless to say, the finding did no go unchallenged by proponents of mental model theory; see, for example, Schroyens (2010).

References

Ackerman, R., & Thompson, V. A. (2017). Meta-reasoning: Monitoring and control of thinking and reasoning. *Trends in Cognitive Sciences, 21*, 607–617.

Aczel, B., Szollosi, A., & Bago, B. (2016). Lax monitoring versus logical intuition: The determinants of confidence in conjunction fallacy. *Thinking & Reasoning, 22*(1), 99–117.

Barbey, A. K., & Sloman, S. A. (2007). Base-rate respect: From ecological rationality to dual processes. *Behavioral and Brain Sciences, 30*, 241–297.

Bonnefon, J. F. (2009). A theory of utility conditionals: Paralogical reasoning from decision-theoretic leakage. *Psychological Review, 116*, 888–907.

Bonnefon, J. F. (2013). New ambitions for a new paradigm: Putting the psychology of reasoning at the service of humanity. *Thinking & Reasoning, 19*, 381–398.

Bonnefon, J. F., Haigh, M., & Stewart, A. J. (2013). Utility templates for the interpretation of conditional statements, *68*, 350–361.

Bonnefon, J. F., & Hilton, D. J. (2004). Consequential conditionals: Invited and suppressed inferences from valued outcomes. *Journal of Experimental Psychology: Learning Memory and Cognition, 30*, 28–37.

Bowers, J. S., & Davis, C. J. (2012). Bayesian just-so stories in psychology and neuroscience. *Psychological Bulletin, 138*, 389–414.

Byrne, R. M. J. (1989). Suppressing valid inferences with conditionals. *Cognition, 31*, 61–83.

Cheng, P. W., & Holyoak, K. J. (1985). Pragmatic reasoning schemas. *Cognitive Psychology*, 17, 391–416.

Copi, I. M. (2013). *Introduction to logic*. Harlow: Pearson Education.

Corner, A., & Hahn, U. (2013). Normative theories of argumentation: Are some norms better than others? *Synthese, 190*, 3579–3610.

Corner, A., Hahn, U., & Oaksford, M. (2011). The psychological mechanism of the slippery slope argument. *Journal of Memory and Language, 64*(2), 133–152.

Cosmides, L. (1989). The logic of social exchange: Has natural selection shaped how humans reason? *Cognition, 31*, 187–276.

De Neys, W. (2012). Bias and conflict: A case for logical intuitions. *Perspectives on Psychological Science*, 7, 28–38.

De Neys, W., & Glumicic, T. (2008). Conflict monitoring in dual process theories of thinking. *Cognition, 106*, 1248–1299.

De Neys, W., Vartanian, O., & Goel, V. (2008). Smarter than we think: When our brains detect that we are biased. *Psychological Science, 19*, 483–489.

Edgington, D. (1995). On conditionals. *Mind, 104*, 235–329.

Elqayam, S. (2011). Grounded rationality: A relativist framework for normative rationality. In K. I. Manktelow, D. E. Over, & S. Elqayam (Eds.) *The Science of Reason: A Festschrift for Jonathan St. B. T. Evans* (pp. 397–420). Hove, UK: Psychology Press.

Elqayam, S. (2012). Grounded rationality: Descriptivism in epistemic context. *Synthese, 189*, 39–49.
Elqayam, S. (2015). Grounded rationality and the new paradigm psychology of reasoning. In L. Maachi, M. Bagassi, & R. Viale (Eds.), *Human rationality: Thinking thanks to constraints*. Cambridge, MA: MIT Press.
Elqayam, S. (2016). Scams and rationality: Dutch book arguments are not all they're cracked up to be. In N. Galbraith, D. E. Over, & E. J. Lucas (Eds.), *The thinking mind: A Festschrift for Ken Manktelow* (pp. 151–165). Hove, UK: Psychology Press.
Elqayam, S. (2017). The new paradigm in psychology of reasoning. In L. J. Ball & V. A. Thompson (Eds.), *International handbook of thinking and reasoning*. London, UK: Routledge.
Elqayam, S., & Evans, J. St. B. T. (2011). Subtracting 'ought' from 'is': Descriptivism versus normativism in the study of human thinking. *Behavioral and Brain Sciences, 34*, 233–248.
Elqayam, S., & Evans, J. St. B. T. (2013). Rationality in the new paradigm: Strict versus soft Bayesian approaches. *Thinking and Reasoning, 19*, 453–470.
Elqayam, S., & Over, D. (2012). Probabilities, beliefs, and dual processing: The paradigm shift in the psychology of reasoning. *Mind and Society, 11*, 27–40.
Elqayam, S., & Over, D. E. (2013). New paradigm psychology of reasoning: An introduction to the special issue edited by Elqayam, Bonnefon, and Over. *Thinking & Reasoning, 19*, 249–265.
Elqayam, S., Thompson, V. A., Wilkinson, M. R., Evans, J. St. B. T., & Over, D. E. (2015). Deontic introduction: A theory of inference from is to ought. *Journal of Experimental Psychology: Learning, Memory, and Cognition, 41*(5), 1516–1532.
Evans, J. St. B. T. (2002). Logic and human reasoning: An assessment of the deduction paradigm. *Psychological Bulletin, 128*, 978–996.
Evans, J. St. B. T. (2006). The heuristic-analytic theory of reasoning: Extension and evaluation. *Psychonomic Bulletin & Review, 13*, 378–395.
Evans, J. St. B. T. (2007). *Hypothetical thinking: Dual processes in reasoning and judgement*. Hove, UK: Psychology Press.
Evans, J. St. B. T. (2008). Dual-processing accounts of reasoning, judgment, and social cognition. *Annual Review of Psychology, 59*, 255–278.
Evans, J. St. B. T. (2010a). *Dual process theories of dedcutive reasoning: Facts and fallacies* (K. J. Holyoak & R. G. Morrison, Eds.). Oxford: Oxford University Press.
Evans, J. St. B. T. (2010b). *Thinking twice: Two minds in one brain*. Oxford: Oxford University Press.
Evans, J. St. B. T. (2012). Questions and challenges for the new psychology of reasoning. *Thinking and Reasoning, 18*, 5–31.
Evans, J. St. B. T. (2014). Rationality and the illusion of choice. *Frontiers in Psychology, 5*, Article 104.
Evans, J. St. B. T. (2016). Whatever happened to the selection task? In N. Galbraith, D. E. Over, & E. J. Lucas (Eds.), *The thinking mind: A Festschrift for Ken Manktelow*. Hove, UK: Psychology Press.
Evans, J. St. B. T., Barston, J. L., & Pollard, P. (1983). On the conflict between logic and belief in syllogistic reasoning. *Memory and Cognition, 11*, 295–306.
Evans, J. St. B. T., & Elqayam, S. (2011). Towards a descriptivist psychology of reasoning and decision making. *Behavioral and Brain Sciences, 34*, 275–290.
Evans, J. St. B. T., Handley, S. H., & Over, D. E. (2003). Conditionals and conditional probability. *Journal of Experimental Psychology: Learning, Memory and Cognition, 29*, 321–355.
Evans, J. St. B. T., Neilens, H., Handley, S. J., & Over, D. E. (2008). When can we say 'if'? *Cognition, 108*, 100–116.
Evans, J. St. B. T., & Over, D. E. (2004). *If*. Oxford: Oxford University Press.
Evans, J. St. B. T., & Stanovich, K. E. (2013). Dual-process theories of higher cognition: *Advancing the Debate, 8*, 223–241.
Evans, J. St. B. T., Thompson, V. A., & Over, D. E. (2015). Uncertain deduction and conditional reasoning. *Frontiers in Psychology, 6*, 398.
Fugard, A. J. B., Pfeifer, N., Mayerhofer, B., & Kleiter, G. (2011). How people interpret conditionals: Shifts towards the conditional event. *Journal of Experimental Psychology. Learning, Memory, and Cognition, 37*, 635–648.
Gilio, A., & Over, D. (2012). The psychology of inferring conditionals from disjunctions: A probabilistic study. *Journal of Mathematical Psychology, 56*, 118–131.
Griggs, R. A., & Cox, J. R. (1982). The elusive thematic materials effect in the Wason selection task. *British Journal of Psychology, 73*, 407–420.
Hahn, U. (2014). The Bayesian boom: Good thing or bad? *Frontiers in Psychology, 5*, Article 765.

Hahn, U., & Oaksford, M. (2007). The rationality of informal argumentation: A Bayesian approach to reasoning fallacies. *Psychological Review, 114*, 704–732.
Haigh, M., Ferguson, H. J., & Stewart, A. J. (2014). An eye-tracking investigation into readers' sensitivity to actual versus expected utility in the comprehension of conditionals. *Quarterly Journal of Experimental Psychology, 67*(1), 166–185.
Handley, S. J., Newstead, S. E., & Trippas, D. (2011). Logic, beliefs, and instruction: A test of the default interventionist account of belief bias. *Journal of Experimental Psychology: Learning, Memory, and Cognition, 37*, 28–43.
Harris, A. J. L., Corner, A., & Hahn, U. (2013). James is polite and punctual (and useless): A Bayesian formalisation of faint praise. *Thinking and Reasoning, 19,* 414–429.
Howson, C., & Urbach, P. (2006). *Scientific reasoning: The Bayesian approach* (3rd ed.). Chicago: Open Court.
Inhelder, B., & Piaget, J. (1958). *The growth of logical thinking.* New York: Basic Books.
Johnson-Laird, P. N. (1983). *Mental models.* Cambridge: Cambridge University Press.
Johnson-Laird, P. N. (2006). *How we reason.* Oxford; New York: Oxford University Press.
Johnson-Laird, P. N., & Byrne, R. M. J. (1991). *Deduction.* Hove & London: Erlbaum.
Johnson-Laird, P. N., & Byrne, R. M. J. (2002). Conditionals: a theory of meaning, pragmatics and inference. *Psychological Review, 109*, 646–678.
Johnson-Laird, P. N., Legrenzi, P., & Legrenzi, M. S. (1972). Reasoning and a sense of reality. *British Journal of Psychology, 63*, 395–400.
Johnson-Laird, P. N., & Tagart, J. (1969). How implication is understood. *American Journal of Psychology, 2*, 367–373.
Jones, M., & Love, B. C. (2011). Bayesian fundamentalism or enlightenment? On the explanatory status and theoretical contributions of Bayesian models of cognition. *Behavioral and Brain Sciences, 34*, 169–188.
Kahneman, D. (2011). *Thinking, fast and slow.* New York, NY: Farrar, Straus and Giroux.
Klauer, K. C., & Singmann, H. (2013). Does logic feel good? Testing for intuitive detection of logicality in syllogistic reasoning. *Journal of Experimental Psychology: Learning Memory and Cognition, 39*, 1265–1273.
Koehler, J. J. (1996). The base rate fallacy reconsidered: Descriptive, normative and methodological challenges. *Behavioral and Brain Sciences, 19*, 1–53.
Kuhn, T. S. (1970). *The structure of scientific revolutions* (2nd ed.). Chicago: University of Chicago Press.
Manktelow, K. I. (2012). *Thinking and reasoning: Psychological perspectives on reason, judgment and decision making.* Hove, UK: Psychology Press.
Manktelow, K. I., & Evans, J. St. B. T. (1979). Facilitation of reasoning by realism: effect or non-effect? *British Journal of Psychology, 70*, 477–488.
Manktelow, K. I., & Over, D. E. (1991). Social roles and utilities in reasoning with deontic conditionals. *Cognition, 39*, 85–105.
Manktelow, K. I., Over, D. E., & Elqayam, S. (2011). *Paradigms shift: Jonathan Evans and the science of reason* (K. I. Manktelow, D. E. Over, & S. Elqayam, Eds.). Hove, UK: Psychology Press.
Marr, D. (1982). *Vision: A computational investigation into the human representation and processing of visual information.* San Francisco: Freeman.
McNamara, P. (2014). Deontic logic. In E. N. Zalta (Ed.), *Stanford encyclopedia of philosophy* (Winter 2014 ed.). Stanford: Stanford University Press. Retrieved from http://plato.stanford.edu/archives/win2014/entries/logic-deontic/
Mercier, H., & Sperber, D. (2011). Why do humans reason? Arguments for an argumentative theory. *The Behavioral and Brain Sciences, 34*, 57–74.
Morsanyi, K., & Handley, S. J. (2012). Logic feels so good-I like it! Evidence for intuitive detection of logicality in syllogistic reasoning. *Journal of Experimental Psychology. Learning, Memory, and Cognition, 38*(3), 596–616.
Oaksford, M. (2014). Normativity, interpretation and Bayesian models. *Frontiers in Psychology, 5*, Article 332.
Oaksford, M., & Chater, N. (1991). Against logicist cognitive science. *Mind & Language, 6*, 1–38.
Oaksford, M., & Chater, N. (1994). A rational analysis of the selection task as optimal data selection. *Psychological Review, 101*, 608–631.
Oaksford, M., & Chater, N. (1998). *Rationality in an uncertain world.* Hove, UK: Psychology Press.
Oaksford, M., & Chater, N. (2007). *Bayesian rationality: The probabilistic approach to human reasoning.* Oxford: Oxford University Press.
Oaksford, M., & Chater, N. (2011). Dual systems and dual processes but a single function. In K. I. Manktelow, D. E. Over, & S. Elqayam (Eds.) *The Science of Reason: A Festschrift for Jonathan St. B. T. Evans* (pp. 339–351). Psychology Press.

Oaksford, M., & Chater, N. (2012). Dual processes, probabilities, and cognitive architecture. *Mind & Society, 11*, 15–26.

Oaksford, M., & Chater, N. (2013). Dynamic inference and everyday conditional reasoning in the new paradigm. *Thinking & Reasoning, 19*, 346–379.

Oaksford, M., & Chater, N. (2014). Probabilistic single function dual process theory and logic programming as approaches to non-monotonicity in human vs. artificial reasoning. *Thinking & Reasoning, 20*, 269–295.

Oberauer, K., & Wilhelm, O. (2003). The meaning(s) of conditionals: Conditional probabilities, mental models and personal utlities. *Journal of Experimental Psychology: Learning, Memory and Cognition, 29*, 680–693.

Over, D. E. (2009). New paradigm psychology of reasoning. *Thinking & Reasoning, 15*, 431–438.

Over, D. E., Hadjichristidis, C., Evans, J. S., Handley, S. J., & Sloman, S. A. (2007). The probability of causal conditionals. *Cognitive Psychology, 54*, 62–97.

Pennycook, G., Cheyne, J. A., Barr, N., Koehler, D. J., & Fugelsang, J. A. (2013). The role of analytic thinking in moral judgements and values. *Thinking & Reasoning, 20*, 188–214.

Politzer, G., & Nguyen-Xuan, A. (1992). Reasoning about conditional promises and warnings: Darwinian algorithms, mental models, relevance judgements or pragmatic schemas? *Quarterly Journal of Experimental Psychology, 44*, 401–412.

Ramsey, F. P. (1931). *The foundations of mathematics and other logical essays*. London: Routledge and Kegan Paul.

Ramsey, F. P. (1990). Truth and probability (original publication 1926). In D. H. Mellor (Ed.), (pp. 52–94). Cambridge, UK: Cambridge University Press.

Schroyens, W. (2010). Mistaking the instance for the rule: A critical analysis of the truth-table evaluation paradigm. *Quarterly Journal of Experimental Psychology, 63*(2), 246–259. https://doi.org/10.1080/17470210902888726

Simon, H. A. (1982). *Models of bounded rationality*. Cambridge, MA: MIT Press.

Stanovich, K. E. (1999). *Who is rational? Studies of individual differences in reasoning*. Mahway, NJ: Lawrence Elrbaum Associates.

Stanovich, K. E. (2004). *The robot's rebellion: Finding meaning in the age of Darwin*. Chicago: Chicago University Press.

Stevenson, R. J., & Over, D. E. (1995). Deduction from uncertain premises. *The Quarterly Journal of Experimental Psychology, 48A*, 613–643.

Stevenson, R. J., & Over, D. E. (2001). Reasoning form uncertain premises: Effects of expertise and conversational context. *Thinking and Reasoning*, 7, 367–390.

Thompson, V. A., Evans, J. St. B. T., & Handley, S. H. (2005). Persuading and dissuading by conditional argument. *Journal of Memory and Language*.

Thompson, V. A., & Johnson, S. C. (2014). Conflict, metacognition, and analytic thinking. *Thinking & Reasoning, 20*, 215–244.

Thompson, V. A., Prowse Turner, J. A., & Pennycook, G. (2011). Intuition, reason, and metacognition. *Cognitive Psychology, 63*, 107–140.

Thompson, V. A., Prowse Turner, J. A., Pennycook, G., Ball, L. J., Brack, H., Ophir, Y., & Ackerman, R. (2013). The role of answer fluency and perceptual fluency as metacognitive cues for initiating analytic thinking. *Cognition, 128*, 237–251.

von Neumann, J., & Morgenstern, O. (1947). *Theory of games and economic behavior* (2nd ed.). Princeton, NJ: Princeton University Press.

Wason, P. C. (1966). Reasoning. In B. M. Foss (Ed.), *New horizons in psychology* (pp. 106–137). Harmandsworth: Penguin.

Wason, P. C., & Johnson-Laird, P. N. (1972). *Psychology of reasoning: Structure and content*. London: Batsford.

Wason, P. C., & Shapiro, D. (1971). Natural and contrived experience in a reasoning problem. *Quarterly Journal of Experimental Psychology, 23*, 63–71.

9
DUAL-PROCESS THEORIES

Jonathan St. B. T. Evans

The idea that there are two kinds of thinking, one fast and intuitive, the other slow and reflective, has multiple origins in philosophy and psychology. It is found in ancient Greek philosophy and in Freudian theory, to name but two examples (Frankish & Evans, 2009, p. 24). So while a number of late 20th-century authors have proposed some form of dual-process theory as an apparently original idea, none can truly be attributed as the original source. However, several authors have proposed dual-process accounts that were original to themselves and their immediate research fields and which had distinctive features. This happened, for example, in the study of attention (Schneider & Shiffrin, 1977), reasoning (Sloman, 1996; Wason & Evans, 1975), learning (Reber, 1993) and social psychology (Chaiken, 1980; Epstein, 1994).

Attempts to describe family resemblances between these various theories, and many others that have developed since in cognitive and social psychology (e.g. Evans, 2008), created a fashion for use of the terms *System 1* and *System 2*, originally coined by Stanovich (1999). Unfortunately, this has led to a 'received' dual process theory (Evans, 2012), a perceived generic theory that incorporates all features associated with Systems 1 and 2 as though they were necessary and defining elements. Such is our human tendency to schematise and simplify that both friends and critics of the approach have tended to talk as though such a generic theory can be tested and evaluated, when in fact no single author has proposed it (Evans & Stanovich, 2013a). While some contemporary authors still use the terms System 1 and 2 (most notably Kahneman, 2011), both Stanovich and I now prefer the terms Type 1 (rapid and autonomous processing) and Type 2 (slow and controlled processing.) This is partly to discourage use of the generic theory but also to recognise that the 'systems' terminology has connotations to which not all authors subscribe. That is not to say, of course, that there is a universally agreed view on exactly what Type 1 and 2 processes are. That is far from the case.

In my view, dual-process theories should be viewed as *family* whose members share some features. Like all families it includes close relatives (e.g. the theories of Stanovich and myself) who share many features, as well as distant cousins (e.g. Stanovich, Sloman) who have a degree of resemblance to each other as well as some significant differences. As this a handbook on thinking and reasoning, I do not discuss the family branches that inhabit fields such as learning, memory, attention and social cognition. Instead, I focus on the particular dual-processing accounts that have been given of phenomena in the psychology of reasoning and decision making. I first describe of some of the main dual-process theories in these fields in chronological order of publication, trying in each case to identify what these theorists propose about the nature of Type 1 and 2 processing. Next I examine similarities and differences between these accounts with particular attention to issues of cognitive architecture at three levels: processes, systems and minds. Then I consider the kinds of evidence that have been proposed to support dual-process accounts of reasoning and decision making. Finally, I examine the debate which these approaches have engendered, including critiques and alternative theoretical accounts.

Origins of the dual-process theory of reasoning

The work of Peter Wason

Peter Wason is generally regarded as the founder of the modern psychology of reasoning. He was a very creative man who is particularly known for his invention of reasoning tasks. The '2 4 6' task (Wason, 1960) and the four-card selection task (Wason, 1966) have engendered dozens of published studies by later authors and continue to be researched to the present day. Although his last journal article was published some 20 years ago, citations of Wason's work in the current literature have continued steadily increasing to the current day (Evans, 2016a). And despite being first author of the earliest paper explicitly to identify the dual-process theory of reasoning (Wason & Evans, 1975), Wason has not received sufficient recognition for his seminal work in this topic. As I have recently discussed, the key ideas for this dual-processing account were already present in his writings about the 2 4 6 and selection tasks (Evans, 2016b).

The 2 4 6 task was originally presented as a test of conceptual thinking and scientific hypothesis testing. Participants were told that the experimenter had in mind a rule which classified triples of three whole numbers, an example of which was 2 4 6. They were to try to discover the rule by generating their own triples. In each case, the experimenter would say either yes, it conforms to the rule, or no, it does not. The example given prompted most participants to generate a quite specific hypothesis, such as ascending with equal intervals. However, the rule itself was very general: *any* ascending sequence. Most participants generated positive examples of their hypothesis which necessarily conformed to the rule: for example, 2 5 7, 10 20 30, 11 12 13 would all receive the answer 'yes'. Given this positive feedback, participants would typically announce that they had discovered the rule, only to be told that they were wrong and should continue testing further triples. Wason proposed that they were demonstrating a verification bias (later known as confirmation bias), which became a very contentious claim (Evans, 2016b).

As all who knew him will attest, Wason was highly influenced by Freudian theory and references to unconscious thinking, fixation, regression and rationalisation figure heavily in his writing about his reasoning tasks. In the case of the 2 4 6 task, he was particularly interested in the tendency of participants to hold on to a hypothesis that has been refuted by reformulating it in different words. For example, having been told that the rule 'ascending by equal intervals' was wrong, one participant then announced that the rule was 'the difference between the first two figures added to the second figure gives the third' and so on. Wason (e.g. 1968) refers to this as fixated and obsessional behaviour. These findings were later related to Wason and Evans's (1975) claim that unconscious thinking may be rationalised by a separate conscious process.

The first reasoning paper to use the term 'dual processes' explicitly was that of Wason and Evans (1975) and involved the selection task (Wason, 1966; Wason & Johnson-Laird, 1972). Again, the basic ideas were present in some of Wason's earlier writing about this task. This resulted from my discovery that 'matching bias' accounted for the selections on the basic task, rather than 'verification bias' as Wason had previously claimed. An example of a typical abstract selection task is shown in Figure 9.1. Most participants would choose just the A card, or the

There are four cards lying on a table. Each has a capital letter on one side and a single-digit number on the other side. The exposed sides are shown below:

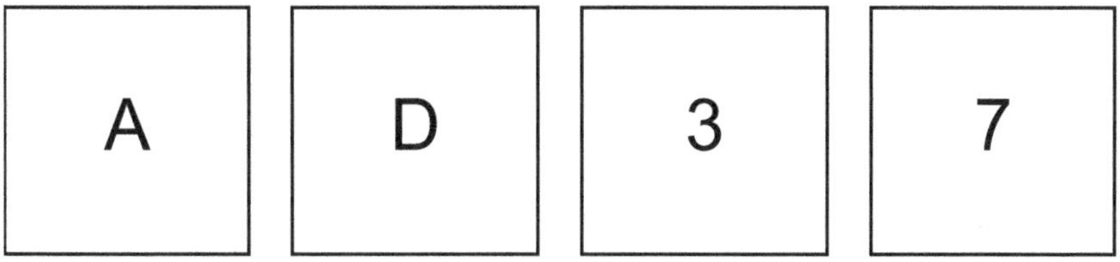

The rule shown below applies to these four cards and may be true or false:

If there is an A on one side of the card, then there is a 3 on the other side of the card.

Your task is to decide those cards, and only those cards, that need to be turned over in order to discover whether the rule is true or false.

Figure 9.1 Example of a standard abstract Wason selection task

A and 3. However, the correct answer, according to Wason, was to choose the A and 7 cards, as only an A paired with a number *other* than a 3 could prove the rule false. This is generally accepted as the right answer, although it has been disputed in the later literature (Oaksford & Chater, 1994). Wason originally believed that participants were trying to make the statement true due to a verification bias. However, Evans and Lynch (1973) showed that when a negation was placed in the second part of the rule (e.g. If there is an A on one side of the card then there is NOT a 3 on the other side of the card), participants mostly continued to choose the A and 3 cards which are now, by Wason's analysis, logically correct (this rule is disproved by an A3 card). My own explanation was that participants chose cards which matched the lexical content of the rule, termed 'matching bias'. Wason accepted immediately that this verification bias account was wrong, but was puzzled by a study of verbal protocols in which participants appeared to exhibit insight when finding the correct choices (Goodwin & Wason, 1972).

In our collaboration (Wason & Evans, 1975) we gave both affirmative and negative forms of the rule and found matching choices on each. However, the verbal explanation offered depended on the rule and choice made. For example, when matching on the standard abstract problems, participants would typically say that they were turning over the A because a 3 on the back would make the rule true. When giving the response to the negative rule, they said they were turning over A because a 3 on the back would make the rule *false*. What was striking was that the same participant would do this on both rules, even if they had the negative rule first. Hence, they first solved the problem with apparent 'insight' and then got the standard one wrong, with apparent verification bias. (These findings were much later replicated in essential respects by Lucas & Ball, 2005.) I think this finding finally clarified ideas that Wason had been developing in previous papers (e.g. Wason, 1969) about unconscious thinking and rationalisation. Our conclusion was that unconscious Type 1 processes were determining selections (by matching bias) and conscious Type 2 processes were serving to rationalise or justify the response made. In our second collaboration, we showed that participants would happily justify each of four putative 'solutions' with which different groups were presented, including the correct choice and three others (Evans & Wason, 1976).

The original heuristic-analytic theory

In the 1980s, I took dual-process theory in a different direction, forgetting (for the time being) all about the original Wason and Evans account with its heavily Freudian overtones. This work has its origin in my studies of cognitive bias and the 'two factor' theory of reasoning (an idea recently re-invented as the 'dual source' theory of reasoning, e.g. Klauer, Beller, & Hutter, 2010). The two-factor theory was that reasoning responses (nothing to do with verbalisations) reflected a combination of logical and non-logical influences, as a descriptive rather than cognitive model. This was described mathematically as a competing choice model (Evans, 1977; it was later greatly improved by Klauer, Stahl, & Erdfelder, 2007) and developed into a dual-process account by Evans, Barston, and Pollard (1983) in their early paper on belief bias. In the latter, it was argued that a tendency to reason logically competed with a belief bias in which believable conclusions to syllogistic arguments were preferred to unbelievable ones.

The original theory Evans (1984, 1989) described the rapid Type 1 processes as *heuristic* and the slower Type 2 processes as *analytic*, terms still commonly employed in the reasoning literature. Consider two examples of cognitive biases already mentioned: matching bias in the selection task, and belief bias in syllogistic reasoning (again modelled with much greater mathematical sophistocation by Klauer & Kellen, 2011). In the theory, these were attributed to the operation of matching and belief heuristics, respectively. It was proposed that heuristic processing occurred first and was succeeded by analytic processing. The prime purpose of the heuristic stage was to deliver rapid and preconscious representations of relevant information. Biases were attributed to failures to represent logically relevant information or representation of irrelevant information. For example, if attention on the selection task is limited to matching cards, no amount of good reasoning will allow the participant to solve the problem.

Parallel dual-process theory

While this heuristic-analytic account is clearly sequential (as is the Wason and Evans theory), some of my early writing is suggestive of parallel processing. For example, my early statistical model of the selection task proposed that with some probability people *either* based their response on logical reasoning *or*, on a cognitive bias. Similarly, my first paper on belief bias (Evans et al., 1983) proposed a *competition* between logic and belief which might be resolved in different ways, even within the same participant. It may seem that such competing responses suggest some kind of parallel dual-process theory, but I showed in a much later paper (Evans, 2007b) that such behavioural data are in fact consistent with two quite different cognitive architectures which I called *parallel-competitive* and *default-interventionist.*

The bulk of dual-process theories in these fields are of the default-interventionist type which I consider in the next section. However, Sloman (1996) proposed two systems of reasoning which operate in parallel and compete to control the response made. He called these two systems *associative* and *rule-based* (for application of a similar distinction in social psychology, see Smith & DeCoster, 2000). According to Sloman (1996, p. 4), the associative system 'encodes and processes statistical regularities of its environment, frequencies and correlations amongst the various features of the world'. Rule-based processing is more what most people normally envisage by the term 'reasoning' allowing arguments to be composed from one or more propositional rules. Rule-based reasoning is also abstract and based on form, whereas associative reasoning accesses semantic networks. There is, of course, a clear resemblance between the idea of associative and Type 1 processes in other dual-process theories and between rule-based and Type 2 processing.

Where Sloman's account is strikingly different from typical dual-process theories, however, is in the proposal of parallel processing. They are two distinct forms of computation that are active simultaneously. Either may be responsible (or both may contribute to) the response observed and telling which can be difficult. One or other system will be better for some kinds of tasks. Sloman suggests that people often become aware of two different answers to the same problem: one intuitive and the other the result of conscious reasoning. However, in apparent contrast, a number of recent studies suggest that conflict between competing cues on reasoning tasks may be detected rapidly and preconsciously by the brain (De Neys, 2014; De Neys & Glumicic, 2008). Sloman's theory has more recently been applied to explain why using base rate information in Bayesian reasoning may be more or less difficult according to the problem format (Barbey & Sloman, 2007).

Default-interventionist dual-process theories

It is generally agreed that Type 1 processes are relatively quick and Type 2 processes relatively slow. This creates a problem in parallel form dual-process theory, in that any conflict detection and resolution would require an output from a fast process to wait until that from a slower one is available. For this reason, perhaps, most theorists prefer the idea that rapid Type 1 processes provide a default intuition which may or may not be intervened upon by subsequent and slower Type 2 processing. Such intervention can result in a change of this default to answer based on reflective reasoning. This is known as default-interventionist (DI) dual-process theory. In earlier work, it was generally assumed that Type 1 processes were responsible for bias and Type 2 for correct responses, although this is now regarded as a dangerous simplification (Evans & Stanovich, 2013a). It has become quite clear in more recent literature both that intuitive processing can deliver normatively correct judgements and reflection can lead to bias under certain circumstances. However, in the deductive reasoning literature as in the statistical inference literature (Gilovich, Griffin, & Kahneman, 2002; Kahneman, Slovic, & Tversky, 1982), particular biases were often attributed to heuristics, for example a matching-heuristic or a belief-heuristic. At the same time, correct solutions are also observed on these tasks, their frequency now known to depend upon a number of factors such as cognitive ability, rationality thinking dispositions, instructions and time available (Evans, 2007a; Stanovich, 2011). The challenge for all DI models is to account for the production of these different answers.

Revised heuristic-analytic theory

I eventually presented a much revised and updated version of the heuristic-analytic theory (Evans, 2006, 2007a) in which the DI structure of the theory was made explicit (see Figure 9.2). It retained the idea from the earlier account that heuristic processing resulted in mental representations (called models in the diagram) which are cued by attentional and pragmatic factors resulting from the presentation of the problem and the context. However, the analytic system always examines this model and at a minimum uses it to form a response in the context of the instructions. For example, matching bias may direct attention to particular cards on the Wason selection task which are represented as relevant, but a decision to choose such cards because they *feel* right is nevertheless analytic. It always requires justification, even though that may be

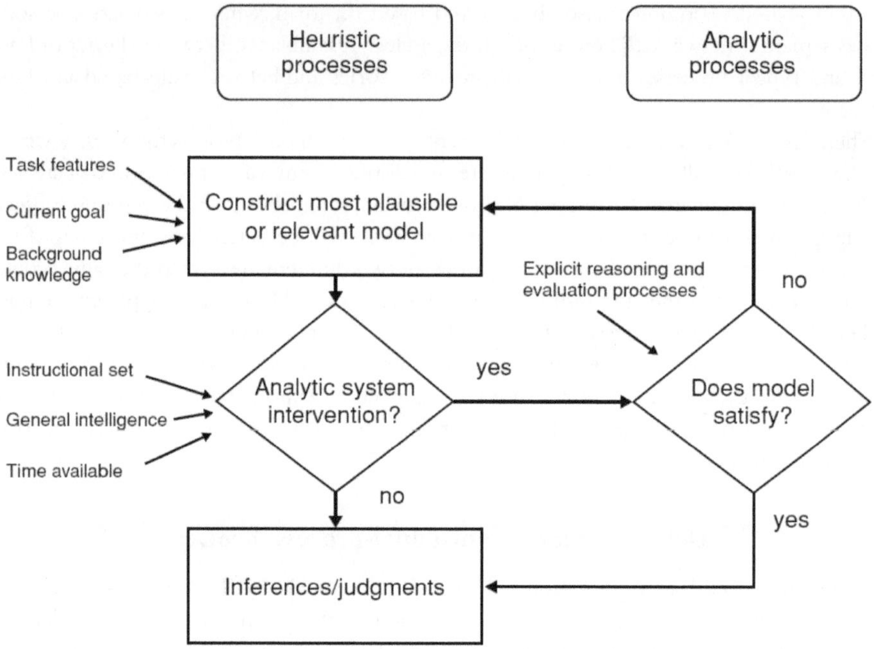

Figure 9.2 The revised heuristic-analytic theory (from Evans, 2006)

regarded as a rationalisation, as studies of verbal protocols support (Lucas & Ball, 2005; Wason & Evans, 1975). Studies of time spent examining cards before selection show that those selected are thought about for several seconds first, allowing time for this process to occur (Ball, Lucas, Miles, & Gale, 2003; Evans, 1996).

The model also allows that the analytic system may not be satisfied with the default response and may intervene to change it. Again taking the selection task as an example, the matching heuristic can lead to examination of a patently irrelevant card, as when the antecedent of the rule is negated:

If there is NOT an A on one side of the card then there is a 3 on the other side of the card

Here the matching card A falsifies the antecedent of the statement and cannot readily be used to justify selection of the card. Participants do choose this logical case more often than on the standard rule (the D card in Figure 9.1) but the overall rate of selection of the false-antecedent card is much lower than for the other three cards. Evans and Ball (2010) showed in a re-analysis of the data of Ball et al. (2003) that when the false-antecedent card matches, it is inspected for longer periods, as with other matching cards. However, frequently participants do *not* end up selecting it. This is an important finding because it shows that the attempted justification sometimes fails and leads to an alternative response: participants are not *just* rationalising. They reason when they see the need but are too easily satisfied. Stanovich (2011) describes this as the 'cognitive miser' principle. I consider his theory in more detail below.

The revised heuristic-analytic theory also incorporated three principles of *hypothetical thinking theory* (Evans, Over, & Handley, 2003). In addition to relevance, these include singularity and satisficing. Specifically, people consider only one model at a time (singularity) and will accept it if it is good enough (satisficing). Hence, if a matching card can be justified either by verification or falsification it will usually be accepted. Most participants lack the insight that falsification alone is the key. The theory and these principles were applied to a wide range of reasoning and decision making tasks by Evans (2007a), who also explicitly attributed biases to both Type 1 and Type 2 processing, in contrast with the early heuristic-analytic theory. The main Type 1 cause of bias is preconscious selection of information (relevance), while the Type 2 bias results from a combination of singularity and satisficing. In essence, we fail to consider alternatives when the default can easily be justified. This is similar, of course, to Stanovich's cognitive miser hypothesis.

Stanovich's dual-process theory

Keith Stanovich embraced the dual-process framework in the 1990s and together with his collaborator Rich West launched a major individual differences research programme, spanning tasks on reasoning, judgement and decision making. This programme continues to the present day, and over this time period Stanovich has made substantial theoretical contributions to dual-process theory and written several books on the subject. Much of his writing concerns rationality, which I will mostly leave aside for the present purposes, but it should be noted that his concern to improve human judgement is a key motivator for this programme.

In his first book on the topic, Stanovich (1999) laid out a description of the empirical programme to that date and also made a number of theoretical proposals about dual processes which he described as belonging to Systems 1 and 2 (see also Stanovich & West, 2000). The essence of the programme was to examine how reasoning and decision making were influenced by individual differences in both cognitive ability and cognitive style. The latter are sensitive to what are now termed *rational thinking dispositions*. Stanovich and West used style measures already in the literature as well as one of their own invention, the *argument evaluation task* or AET (Stanovich & West, 1997). For cognitive ability they mostly used SAT scores, known to correlate highly with IQ, even when self-reported. Other researchers have frequently used measures of individual differences in working-memory capacity, but this too is known to correlate very highly with general intelligence (Colom, Rebollo, Palacios, Juan-Espinosa, & Kyllonen, 2004; Kyllonen & Christal, 1990).

Investigating a wide range of reasoning and decision making tasks, Stanovich and West found in general that normatively correct solutions were highly correlated with cognitive ability. Moreover, when the residual variance unaccounted for by ability was examined, there was a significant relationship with rational thinking dispositions. As in my own earlier work, normative solutions were generally taken to be an indicator of successful Type 2 or System 2 thinking and biases generally attributed to System 1. Stanovich especially took the view that System 1 contextualises problems when abstract reasoning is needed for their solution. He inferred from his findings that rational (normative) performance requires a combination of ability and disposition. It is not sufficient to have the ability; you must also have in the inclination to apply it. Stanovich (2009) later argued that IQ tests are inadequate for this reason, and need to be replaced by tests which also measure thinking dispositions, an RQ (rationality quotient).

A more recent book (Stanovich, 2011) updated both the research programme and the theory of dual-processes and rationality. As in my own recent writing, Stanovich (see also Evans & Stanovich, 2013a) acknowledges that Type 1 processing (System 1 and System 2 terms now abandoned) does not necessarily lead to biases, nor does Type 2 processing necessarily yield normatively correct results. His individual differences model, while not strictly a cognitive model, clearly implies a default-interventionist form of dual-process theory as Stanovich explicitly acknowledges (Evans & Stanovich, 2013a). Stanovich (2011, p. 143) indicates clearly that a heuristic response is the default as it can occur in three different ways:

(a) when a person lacks the 'mindware' to solve a problem; that is, they do not possess the necessary knowledge for rule-based reasoning, they will give the heuristic response
(b) when they fail to see the need to engage Type 2 reasoning, they will also give this response
(c) when they lack the cognitive capacity to solve a problem by reasoning, they will also respond heuristically

The key facility in (c) is what Stanovich describes as 'cognitive decoupling': the ability to abstract the relevant features and disregard the context. The interventional aspect of the theory arises at step (b). People can only solve a problem by reasoning only when they intervene with Type 2 reasoning *and* have the necessary mindware *and* have the necessary cognitive capacity. In Stanovich's research programme, the likelihood of intervention is related to individual differences in rational thinking style. Some people are more disposed than others to apply explicit reasoning, rather than rely on intuition. However, there are other results consistent with his general theory. For example, when people are instructed to reason deductively by assuming the truth of premises and looking for necessary conclusions, they are less influenced by belief than when simply asked to decide what follows from some premises. Consistent with his theory, however, this benefit applies only to those of higher cognitive ability, who have the capacity to apply abstract Type 2 reasoning to the task (Evans, Handley, Neilens, Bacon, & Over, 2010). In this case, participants are motivated to intervene by instructions rather than by personality.

Kahneman's dual-process theory

Kahneman and Tversky famously proposed that a number of heuristics were responsible for biases in statistical judgement from the early 1970s onwards (For collections of papers, see Gilovich et al., 2002; Kahneman et al., 1982). While a dual-process distinction was arguably implicit in earlier writing (e.g. Kahneman & Tversky, 1982), this programme was relatively recently re-interpreted explicitly in terms of dual-process theory by Kahneman and Frederick (2002). Using the System 1 and 2 terminology, Kahneman and Frederick proposed what is clearly a default-interventionist form of the theory as the following quote illustrates:

> In the particular dual-process model we assume, System 1 quickly proposes intuitive answers to judgement problems as they arise, and System 2 monitors the quality of these proposals, which it may endorse, correct or override.
>
> (Kahneman & Frederick, 2002, p. 51)

In a later, engaging and accessible book, Kahneman (2011) applied his dual-process theory to a wide range of phenomena in cognitive and social psychology involving reasoning and judgement. His further comments on the theory itself confirm its DI structure:

> System 1 continuously generates suggestions for System 2: impressions, intuitions, intentions and feelings. If endorsed by System 2, impressions and intuitions turn into beliefs, and impulses turn into voluntary actions. When all goes smoothly, which is most of the time, System 2 adopts the suggestions of System 1 with little or no modification.
>
> (Kahneman, 2011, p. 24)

We can see echoes here of Stanovich's (2011) discussion of the cognitive miser. System 1 provides default answers because most of the time it works well and System 2 is applied sparingly. Not all DI dual-process theories are the same in all details, of course. System 2, in Kahneman's theory, seems to monitor itself as well as System 1 and to have the ultimate say: 'one of the tasks of System 2 is to overcome the impulses of System 1. In other words, System 2 is in charge of self-control' (Kahneman, 2011, p. 26). Kahneman's theory diverges from my own here, as I have suggested that such a conscious control system is an illusion fostered by folk psychology (see Evans, 2010, Chapter 1).

Frederick (2005) devised the Cognitive Reflection Test or CRT, which shows that even people of high intelligence may fail to apply reasoning when an intuitive answer strongly suggests itself. The test has three small questions, an example of which is 'If it takes 5 machines 5 minutes to make 5 widgets, how long would it take 100 machines to make 100 widgets?' Since each machine is taking 5 minutes to make a widget, 100 machines would also need 5 minutes to make 100. However, the intuitive answer – the wildly wrong 100 minutes – is given by many Ivy League students to whom the task was presented. Toplak, West, and Stanovich (2014) showed performance on the CRT is related to both cognitive ability and rational thinking dispositions. They also devised an alternative version, as the original CRT items have become very well-known via teaching and textbook coverage.

Thompson's feeling of rightness (FOR) programme

Explaining when and why intervention occurs is the biggest challenge for DI dual-process theory. The idea in Kahneman's work that the same system both decides whether to intervene and also carries out the analytic reasoning that follows seems very odd. I have argued that the causes of intervention must be preconscious and that System 2 cannot be self-policing in this manner (Evans, 2009). It is really no different a problem from that which has been discussed in the psychology of attention for many years. If we are talking in a crowded room we consciously hear only the person we are speaking to, until our name is mentioned in another conversation. Immediately our attention switches to that other speaker, indicating that some part of our brain was monitoring the unattended conversations. Bur clearly we did not make a conscious decision to switch our attention.

One approach to the problem is to focus on the factors which determine intervention. Stanovich has identified rational thinking disposition as a personality characteristic that makes some individuals more likely to check their intuitions than others. I have both investigated and reviewed (Evans, 2006, 2007a) experimental manipulations such as speeded tasks and working memory loads which reduce Type 2 processing, and logical reasoning instructions which increase it. A novel contribution to this problem, however, was made when Thompson (2009) proposed that we should examine people's metacognitive intuitions. Perhaps they leave the default answer in place when it *feels* right and question it when it feels wrong. Thompson defines this as *feeling of rightness* or FOR for short. She invented a special *two choice paradigm* to investigate her hypothesis (Thompson, Prowse Turner, & Pennycook, 2011). Participants are given a reasoning or judgement problem and asked to give a quick intuitive response without reflection. They then rate their FOR in this initial answer. Subsequently, participants are asked to think about the problem again, taking as much time as they want, with the option to change the answer given initially. The evidence supports these predictions:

1 The lower the initial FOR, the more time people will take rethinking the answer
2 The lower the initial FOR, the more likely people will be to change the initial answer
3 The faster the initial response, the higher the FOR

It is clear from Thompson's work that rethinking an intuitive answer does not necessarily improve it: people may change a right answer to wrong as well as vice versa. Of course, people cannot have a FOR based on whether a response is actually accurate. Some other aspect must influence this, and Thompson and colleagues have suggested it is fluency. Hence, the more quickly the initial answer comes to mind, the more people will be convinced that it must be right. Recently, Thompson, Evans, and Campbell (2013) applied the method to an adapted version of the Wason selection task. As predicted, matching bias is a manifestation of an intuitively compelling answer. Matching responses are made more quickly and with a higher feeling of rightness, even though they often result in an incorrect selection.

Mental model theory

The mental model theory of reasoning was first introduced by Johnson-Laird (1983) and initiated a major programme of work on deductive reasoning. It has not usually been presented as a dual-process theory and researchers in this paradigm have pursued somewhat different theoretical objectives. It is beyond my scope here to discuss this work, which is well covered by Johnson-Laird, Goodwin, and Khemlani in this volume, but I will comment briefly on its relation to dual-process theory. The theory proposes that people form initial mental models of the premises rapidly and effortlessly and that these models suggest an initial conclusion. This conclusion may – or may not – be modified by a subsequent explicit search for alternative models which is both slower and limited by working memory capacity. I agree with Johnson-Laird et al. (this volume) that this framework is fully compatible with a dual-processing distinction in which the initial stage is Type 1 and the optional second stage Type 2. In fact, as one can see, it is specifically compatible with a *default-interventionist* approach. A good and more specific example of this compatibility is the mental models theory of belief bias in syllogistic reasoning (Oakhill, Johnson-Laird, & Garnham, 1989) which essentially proposes that people are more motivated to reason (search for counterexamples) when they disbelieve the conclusion to the argument. This account is very similar to those offered for belief bias in standard default-interventionist dual-process theory (see Evans, 2007a).

Dualities: processes, modes, systems and minds

There is a confusion to be avoided between types and *modes* of thinking. Modes correspond to thinking styles and are in effect two kinds of Type 2 processing (Evans & Stanovich, 2013a). For example, people can by reason of personality apply Type 2 thinking in a slow and careful or quick and careless manner. As a result, the latter will more often accept default intuitions, which can result in biases. Hence, they may make simple mistakes in spite of high intelligence, as demonstrated by the cognitive reflection test (Frederick, 2005). Critics who suggest that Type 1 and 2 processing represent continua may be confusing them with modes.

Talk of two systems (Evans & Over, 1996; Sloman, 2002; Stanovich, 1999) is less fashionable than it was. The problem is that there are, for example, many kinds of Type 1 (autonomous) processes – associative, pragmatic, modular and so on – and they evidently are not executed by a single cognitive or neural system. The inheritors of the two systems idea are theories that propose two or more *minds* within the brain (Evans, 2010; Stanovich, 2004, 2011). For example, my own discussion of an old, intuitive mind contrasted with a new, reflective mind has clear similarities with the two systems discussed by Evans and Over (1996). However, in the newer theory, certain processes with the rapid and autonomous Type 1 characteristics are placed in the *new* rather than the old mind. For example, I suggest that the new mind could not function without the modular cognition supporting language and meta-representation, neither of which are found in other animals. This version of the two minds theory also proposes that each mind has access to distinct implicit and explicit knowledge systems, an idea present in some earlier accounts by other authors (Epstein, 1994; Reber, 1993).

Discussion of the two minds theory is beyond the scope of the present chapter. I will confine the remaining assessment to the proposals that there are two types of cognitive processes in experimental tasks which can account for different forms of responding.

Critiques and debate

Most of the empirical evidence supporting dual processing in reasoning and decision making has been mentioned above, but here is a brief summary. Demonstrations revolve around the idea that Type 2 thinking is generally slower than Type 1 and makes more demands on working memory. Thus we can expect more intuitive or heuristic responding when people are given a short time limit: this has been shown to increase belief bias (Evans & Curtis-Holmes, 2005) and matching bias (Roberts & Newton, 2001), for example. Type 2 reasoning should also be disrupted by concurrent working memory load, and there are again studies that suggest this is the case (De Neys, 2006a, 2006b), as intuitive errors increase under these conditions. In terms of individual differences, there are many studies showing that intuitive responding is associated with lower intelligence or lower rational thinking dispositions (Stanovich, 2011).

There is, however, a significant methodological problem. Both Stanovich and I are agreed that it is a fallacy necessarily to equate Type 1 processing with bias and Type 2 processing with normatively correct solutions (Evans & Stanovich, 2013a). I will call this the *normative fallacy*. The problem, however, is that the bulk of evidence for dual processing is derived from tasks where this equation seems reasonably to hold. For example, belief bias and matching bias seem to arise from reliance on intuitions. In addition, much of the work of Stanovich and West rests on showing that normatively correct solutions are associated with higher intelligence and rational thinking dispositions. The supposition is that on a number of particular tasks studied by reasoning and decision researchers, correct answers normally require extended reasoning (e.g. combining two premises and three terms in syllogistic reasoning) whereas biases arise from some simple heuristic (e.g. agreeing with conclusions that are believable, regardless of the premises).

The normative fallacy may arise when quick and simple processing can give rise to normatively correct answers. In one example, Handley, Newstead and Trippas (2011) challenged the default-interventionist theory of belief bias on the basis of some surprising experimental results. Like Evans et al. (1983) they put logic and belief in conflict but added a new twist. In addition to a group instructed to make logical decisions while ignoring belief, they had another group asked to make judgements based on belief while ignoring logic. They found not only that belief could interfere with logical judgments but that logic could interfere with belief judgments. An important difference between this study and that of Evans et al. (1983), however, is that the latter used relatively complex three-term syllogisms whereas Handley et al. used the very simple modus ponens form. Thus a problem where logic interferes would be 'If you finish your glass it will be full; suppose you finish your drink, will your glass be empty?' The belief-based answer is YES, but MP suggests the answer NO, which interferes with the belief judgment. Handley et al. talk about logical reasoning as if this were a single category with the implication that it involves Type 2 processing. But does it? MP makes minimal demands on working memory capacity, is universally and rapidly endorsed with abstract problem materials and may arguably arise from the language module (Braine & O'Brien, 1991). So it is plausible to argue that MP does not require Type 2 processing and will provide a rapid and automatic cue. Hence, participants are perhaps experiencing a Type1–Type 1 conflict.

A similar issue arises with statistical inferences using extreme base rates, as in a series of studies by De Neys and colleagues (e.g. De Neys & Glumicic, 2008). In this task people are given cues based on stereotypes and statistical information, which may be put into conflict. For example:

> In a study 1000 people are tested. Among the participants there were 4 men and 9996 women. Jo is a randomly chosen participant of this study.
>
> Jo is 23 years old and finishing a degree in engineering. On Friday nights, Jo likes to go out cruising with friends while listening to loud music and drinking beer.
>
> What is more likely?
>
> a. Jo is a man
> b. Jo is a woman

In this case the statistical information suggests that Jo is a woman but the stereotype information suggests that Jo is a man. Verbal protocols showed no evidence of conscious awareness of conflict (in contrast with Sloman's [1996] prediction), but implicit measures showed that conflict was registering. This was later demonstrated using neural imaging (De Neys & Goel, 2011). By making base rates so extreme, De Neys assumed that they would give a normatively correct answer – that is, it should outweigh the stereotype. However, this does not make them the result of Type 2 processing, and again we may be looking a Type1–Type 1 conflict. De Neys has more recently suggested that people have logical intuitions (De Neys, 2012), although it is debatable whether this can apply regardless of the complexity of normative answers on different tasks. Recently, however, Thompson and Johnson (2014) have provided evidence of a different kind that supports the view that logical form may be detected quickly. Using several reasoning tasks with the two-response method developed for testing the influence of FOR, they found that higher ability participants showed as much advantage on the initial quick response as on the slower reflective one. The effect was present on a task involving three-term syllogistic reasoning as well as three other tasks. These findings clearly propose challenges for DI accounts, including Stanovich's theory of individual differences on such tasks.

There have been a number of general attacks on dual-process theories which were discussed recently by Evans and Stanovich (2013a). Criticisms discussed included those by Keren and Schul (2009), Kruglanski and Gigerenzer (2011) and Osman (2004). Evans and Stanovich classified criticisms under five main headings: (a) theories offer multiple and vague definitions of dual processing, (b) proposed clusters of attributes are not reliably aligned, (c) there is a continuum of styles and not discrete types, (d) single-process accounts may be offered for dual-process phenomena and (e) evidence of dual processing is ambiguous and unconvincing. Evans and Stanovich dealt in detail with these criticisms and I do not have space to repeat those arguments here. I should note, however, that Evans and Stanovich made these general points: (1) It is improper to attack a 'received' or generic dual process theory proposed by no individual author, (2) The cluster of attributes associated with two types of processing (e.g. slow versus fast, high capacity versus low capacity, pragmatic versus logical) are not necessarily *defining* features of dual-process theory but simply typical correlates. The normative fallacy discussed above is a good example: Type 1 processing often results in biases but does not do so *by definition*. What defines Type 1 processing, they claim, is automaticity. Evans and Stanovich argue that the defining characteristics of Type 2 processing are cognitive decoupling and engagement of working memory.

Conclusions

The distinction between rapid and intuitive (Type 1) processes and slow and deliberative (Type 2) processes has featured strongly in theoretical accounts of human reasoning for the past 40 years and more recently in accounts of judgement and decision making. The theory stands in parallel to dual-processing accounts in other fields, including social cognition, learning and memory. It is supported by a wide range of experimental and psychometric evidence but has also proved controversial, with a number of critical attacks published. There has been a strong tendency to refer to a single, generic dual-process theory, although more accurately there is really a family of related theories. It is often this generic theory owned by no single author that attracts criticisms.

While narrowing the definition of dual processing offered by Evans and Stanovich (2013a) makes the theory more precise and avoids some of the critiques, it must be admitted that it also makes the theory somewhat harder to test. It would be convenient, for example, if the normative correctness of an answer could be taken as unambiguously diagnostic of Type 2 thinking, but of course it cannot. We often get things right via habit or reliable intuition, as all dual-process authors agree (e.g. Kahneman, 2011). And as anyone who has achieved less than full marks on a mathematics test knows, high-effort reasoning does not always succeed in finding solutions. The absence of a clear and general definition of a Type 1 or 2 *response* does create difficulties for experimenters wishing to test the theories. However, it is perfectly possible to provide well-defined task level models based on dual-processing principles and subject these to empirical tests. Psychologists often refer to theory when they really mean meta-theory (Evans & Stanovich, 2013b). In this sense dual-process theory, like mental model theory (Johnson-Laird et al., this volume) provides a valuable high-level framework within which more specific and testable models can be developed.

As shown here, dual-process accounts of human reasoning have become increasingly popular (as well as controversial) over this time and applied also to many tasks in judgement and decision making. This family of theories has inspired much empirical research and increasingly much theoretical debate and argument. The nature of the (meta-) theory is under continuous review by its proponents, as well as its critics, as new evidence and sometimes difficult findings emerge. It remains to be seen what direction the field will take in future. However, I suspect that an idea that has pervaded much of philosophy and psychology since the time of Aristotle will not easily be dismissed or replaced.

References

Ball, L. J., Lucas, E. J., Miles, J. N. V., & Gale, A. G. (2003). Inspection times and the selection task: What do eye-movements reveal about relevance effects? *Quarterly Journal of Experimental Psychology, 56 A*(6), 1053–1077.

Barbey, A. K., & Sloman, S. A. (2007). Base-rate respect: From ecological validity to dual processes. *Behavioral and Brain Sciences, 30*, 241–297.

Braine, M. D. S., & O'Brien, D. P. (1991). A theory of If: A lexical entry, reasoning program, and pragmatic principles. *Psychological Review, 98*, 182–203.

Chaiken, S. (1980). Heuristic versus systematic information processing and the use of source versus message cues in in persuasion. *Journal of Personality and Social Psychology, 39*, 752–766.

Colom, R., Rebollo, I., Palacios, A., Juan-Espinosa, M., & Kyllonen, P. C. (2004). Working memory is (almost) perfectly predicted by g. *Intelligence, 32*(3), 277–296.

De Neys, W. (2006a). Automatic-heuristic and executive-analytic processing during reasoning: Chronometric and dual-task considerations. *Quarterly Journal of Experimental Psychology, 59*, 1070–1100.

De Neys, W. (2006b). Dual processing in reasoning – Two systems but one reasoner. *Psychological Science, 17*(5), 428–433.

De Neys, W. (2012). Bias and conflict: A case for logical intuitions. *Perspectives on Psychological Science*, 7, 28–38.

De Neys, W. (2014). Conflict detection, dual processes, and logical intuitions: Some clarifications. *Thinking & Reasoning, 20*(2), 169–187. doi: http://dx.doi.org/10.1080/13546783.2013.854725

De Neys, W., & Glumicic, T. (2008). Conflict monitoring in dual process theories of thinking. *Cognition, 106*, 1248–1299.

De Neys, W., & Goel, V. (2011). Heuristics and biases in the brain: Dual neural pathways for decision making. In O. Vartanian, & D. R. Mandel (Eds.) *Neuroscience of decision making* (pp. 125–141). New York: Psychology Press.

Epstein, S. (1994). Integration of the cognitive and psychodynamic unconscious. *American Psychologist, 49*, 709–724.

Evans, J. St. B. T. (1977). Toward a statistical theory of reasoning. *Quarterly Journal of Experimental Psychology, 29*, 297–306.

Evans, J. St. B. T. (1984). Heuristic and analytic processes in reasoning. *British Journal of Psychology, 75*, 451–468.

Evans, J. St. B. T. (1989). *Bias in human reasoning: Causes and consequences.* Brighton: Erlbaum.

Evans, J. St. B. T. (1996). Deciding before you think: Relevance and reasoning in the selection task. *British Journal of Psychology, 87*, 223–240.

Evans, J. St. B. T. (2006). The heuristic-analytic theory of reasoning: Extension and evaluation. *Psychonomic Bulletin and Review, 13*(3), 378–395.

Evans, J. St. B. T. (2007a). *Hypothetical thinking: Dual processes in reasoning and judgement.* Hove, UK: Psychology Press.

Evans, J. St. B. T. (2007b). On the resolution of conflict in dual-process theories of reasoning. *Thinking & Reasoning, 13*, 321–329.

Evans, J. St. B. T. (2008). Dual-processing accounts of reasoning, judgment and social cognition. *Annual Review of Psychology, 59*, 255–278.

Evans, J. St. B. T. (2009). How many dual-process theories do we need: One, two or many? In J. S. B. T. Evans & K. Frankish (Eds.), *In two minds: Dual processes and beyond* (pp. 31–54). Oxford: Oxford University Press.

Evans, J. St. B. T. (2010). *Thinking twice: Two minds in one brain.* Oxford: Oxford University Press.

Evans, J. St. B. T. (2012). Dual-process theories of reasoning: Facts and fallacies. In K. Holyoak & R. G. Morrison (Eds.), *The Oxford handbook of thinking and reasoning* (pp. 115–133). New York: Oxford University Press.

Evans, J. St. B. T. (2016a). A brief history of the Wason selection task. In N. Galbraith (Ed.), *The thinking mind: The use of thinking in everyday life* (pp. 1-14). Hove, UK: Psychology Press.

Evans, J. St. B. T. (2016b). Reasoning, biases and dual processes: The lasting impact of Wason (1960). *Quarterly Journal of Experimental Psychology, 69*, 2076-2092. doi:10.1080/17470218.2014.914547

Evans, J. St. B. T., & Ball, L. J. (2010). Do people reason on the Wason selection task: A new look at the data of Ball et al. (2003). *Quarterly Journal of Experimental Psychology, 63*(3), 434–441.

Evans, J. St. B. T., Barston, J. L., & Pollard, P. (1983). On the conflict between logic and belief in syllogistic reasoning. *Memory & Cognition, 11*, 295–306.

Evans, J. St. B. T., & Curtis-Holmes, J. (2005). Rapid responding increases belief bias: Evidence for the dual-process theory of reasoning. *Thinking & Reasoning, 11*(4), 382–389.

Evans, J. St. B. T., Handley, S., Neilens, H., Bacon, A. M., & Over, D. E. (2010). The influence of cognitive ability and instructional set on causal conditional inference. *Quarterly Journal of Experimental Psychology, 63*(5), 892–909.

Evans, J. St. B. T., & Lynch, J. S. (1973). Matching bias in the selection task. *British Journal of Psychology, 64*, 391–397.

Evans, J. St. B. T., & Over, D. E. (1996). *Rationality and reasoning.* Hove: Psychology Press.

Evans, J. St. B. T., Over, D. E., & Handley, S. J. (2003). A theory of hypothetical thinking. In D. Hardman & L. Maachi (Eds.), *Thinking: Psychological perspectives on reasoning, judgement and decision making* (pp. 3–22). Chichester: Wiley.

Evans, J. St. B. T., & Stanovich, K. E. (2013a). Dual process theories of higher cognition: Advancing the debate. *Perspectives on Psychological Science, 8*, 223–241.

Evans, J. St. B. T., & Stanovich, K. E. (2013b). Theory and metatheory in the study of dual processing: A reply to comments. *Perspectives on Psychological Science, 8*, 263–271.

Evans, J. St. B. T., & Wason, P. C. (1976). Rationalisation in a reasoning task. *British Journal of Psychology, 63*, 205–212.

Frankish, K., & Evans, J. St. B. T. (2009). The duality of mind: An historical perspective. In J. S. B. T. Evans & K. Frankish (Eds.), ***In two minds: Dual processes and beyond*** (pp. 1–30). Oxford: Oxford University Press.

Frederick, S. (2005). Cognitive reflection and decision making. *Journal of Economic Perspectives, 19 (4)*(4), 25–42.

Gilovich, T., Griffin, D., & Kahneman, D. (2002). *Heuristics and biases: The psychology of intuitive judgement.* Cambridge: Cambridge University Press.

Goodwin, R. Q., & Wason, P. C. (1972). Degrees of insight. *British Journal of Psychology, 63*, 205–212.

Handley, S. J., Newstead, S. E., & Trippas, D. (2011). Logic, beliefs, and instruction: A test of the default interventionist account of belief bias. *Journal of Experimental Psychology-Learning Memory and Cognition, 37*(1), 28–43. doi:10.1037/a0021098

Johnson-Laird, P. N. (1983). *Mental models.* Cambridge: Cambridge University Press.

Kahneman, D. (2011). *Thinking, fast and slow.* New York: Farrar, Straus and Giroux.

Kahneman, D., & Frederick, S. (2002). Representativeness revisited: Attribute substitution in intuitive judgement. In T. Gilovich, D. Griffin, & D. Kahneman (Eds.), *Heuristics and biases: The psychology of intuitive judgment* (pp. 49–81). Cambridge: Cambridge University Press.

Kahneman, D., Slovic, P., & Tversky, A. (1982). *Judgment under uncertainty: Heuristics and biases.* Cambridge: Cambridge University Press.

Kahneman, D., & Tversky, A. (1982). On the study of statistical intuition. *Cognition, 12*, 325–326.

Keren, G., & Schul, Y. (2009). Two is not always better than one: A critical evaluation of two-system theories. *Perspectives on Psychological Science, 4*, 533–550.

Klauer, K. C., Beller, S., & Hutter, M. (2010). Conditional reasoning in context: A dual-source model of probabilistic inference. *Journal of Experimental Psychology: Learning Memory and Cognition, 36*(2), 298–323.

Klauer, K. C., & Kellen, D. (2011). Assessing the belief bias effect with ROCs: Reply to Dube, Rotello & Heit (2010). *Psychological Review, 118*(1), 164–173.

Klauer, K. C., Stahl, C., & Erdfelder, E. (2007). The abstract selection task: new data and an almost comprehensive model. *Journal of Experimental Psychology: Learning, Memory and Cognition, 33*(4), 680–703.

Kruglanski, A. W., & Gigerenzer, G. (2011). Intuitive and deliberative judgements are based on common principles. *Psychological Review, 118*(1), 97–109.

Kyllonen, P., & Christal, R. E. (1990). Reasoning ability is (little more than) working memory capacity? *Intelligence, 14*, 389–433.

Lucas, E. J., & Ball, L. J. (2005). Think-aloud protocols and the selection task: Evidence for relevance effects and rationalisation processes. *Thinking and Reasoning, 11*(1), 35–66.

Oakhill, J., Johnson-Laird, P. N., & Garnham, A. (1989). Believability and syllogistic reasoning. *Cognition, 31*, 117–140.

Oaksford, M., & Chater, N. (1994). A rational analysis of the selection task as optimal data selection. *Psychological Review, 101*, 608–631.

Osman, M. (2004). An evaluation of dual-process theories of reasoning. *Psychonomic Bulletin and Review, 11*(6), 988–1010.

Reber, A. S. (1993). *Implicit learning and tacit knowledge.* Oxford: Oxford University Press.

Roberts, M. J., & Newton, E. J. (2001). Inspection times, the change task, and the rapid-response selection task. *Quarterly Journal of Experimental Psychology, 54*(4), 1031–1048.

Schneider, W., & Shiffrin, R. M. (1977). Controlled and automatic human information processing I: Detection, search and attention. *Psychological Review, 84*, 1–66.

Sloman, S. A. (1996). The empirical case for two systems of reasoning. *Psychological Bulletin, 119*, 3–22.

Sloman, S. A. (2002). Two systems of reasoning. In T. Gilovich, D. Griffin, & D. Kahneman (Eds.), *Heuristics and biases: The psychology of intuitive judgment* (pp. 379–398). Cambridge: Cambridge University Press.

Smith, E. R., & DeCoster, J. (2000). Dual-process models in social and cognitive psychology: Conceptual integration and links to underlying memory systems. *Personality and Social Psychology Review, 4*(2), 108–131.

Stanovich, K. E. (1999). *Who is rational? Studies of individual differences in reasoning.* Mahway, NJ: Lawrence Elrbaum Associates.

Stanovich, K. E. (2004). *The robot's rebellion: Finding meaning the age of Darwin.* Chicago: University of Chicago Press.

Stanovich, K. E. (2009). ***What intelligence tests miss. The psychology of rational thought.*** New Haven and London: Yale University Press.
Stanovich, K. E. (2011). ***Rationality and the reflective mind.*** New York: Oxford University Press.
Stanovich, K. E., & West, R. F. (1997). Reasoning independently of prior belief and individual differences in actively open-minded thinking. *Journal of Educational Psychology, 89*(2), 342–357.
Stanovich, K. E., & West, R. F. (2000). Individual differences in reasoning: Implications for the rationality debate. *Behavioral and Brain Sciences, 23*, 645–726.
Thompson, V. A. (2009). Dual-process theories: A metacognitive perspective. In J. S. B. T. Evans & K. Frankish (Eds.), ***In two minds: Dual processes and beyond*** (pp. 171–196). Oxford: Oxford University Press.
Thompson, V. A., Evans, J. St. T., & Campbell, J. I. D. (2013). Matching bias on the selection task: It's fast and feels good. ***Thinking & Reasoning,*** *19*(3–4), 431–452. doi:10.1080/13546783.2013.820220
Thompson, V. A., & Johnson, S. C. (2014). Conflict, metacognition, and analytic thinking. ***Thinking & Reasoning,*** *20*(2), 215–244. doi: http://dx.doi.org/10.1080/13546783.2013.869763
Thompson, V. A., Prowse Turner, J. A., & Pennycook, G. (2011). Intuition, reason, and metacognition. *Cognitive Psychology, 63*(3), 107–140.
Toplak, M. E., West, R. F., & Stanovich, K. E. (2014). Assessing miserly information processing: An expansion of the Cognitive Reflection Test. ***Thinking & Reasoning,*** *20*(2), 147–168.
Wason, P. C. (1960). On the failure to eliminate hypotheses in a conceptual task. *Quarterly Journal of Experimental Psychology*, 12–40.
Wason, P. C. (1966). Reasoning. In B. M. Foss (Ed.), *New horizons in psychology I* (pp. 106–137). Harmandsworth: Penguin.
Wason, P. C. (1968). On the failure to eliminate hypotheses: A second look. In P. C. Wason & P. N. Johnson-Laird (Eds.), ***Thinking and reasoning*** (pp. 165–174). Harmandsworth: Penguin.
Wason, P. C. (1969). Regression in reasoning? *British Journal of Psychology, 60*, 471–480.
Wason, P. C., & Evans, J. St. B. T. (1975). Dual processes in reasoning? ***Cognition,*** *3*, 141–154.
Wason, P. C., & Johnson-Laird, P. N. (1972). ***Psychology of reasoning: Structure and content.*** London: Batsford.

10

FORTY YEARS OF PROGRESS ON CATEGORY-BASED INDUCTIVE REASONING

Aidan Feeney

Inductive reasoning is often described very broadly as a form of thinking that leads to conclusions which are not deductively valid (Chater, Oaksford, Hahn & Heit, 2010), but it has also been defined as thinking which permits us to go from specific observations to general conclusions (see Heit, 2007). In common with many researchers in this area (Kemp & Jern, 2014; Sloman, 2007), I adopt the broad definition here. One problem with such a broad definition is that it makes the category of inductive inferences a very large one. Indeed, it places many of the types of thinking reviewed elsewhere in this book in that category. In order to constrain things somewhat, in this chapter I focus on category-based inductive reasoning, which has been the subject of considerable research over the past 40 years. Because much of our knowledge is organised in the form of categories (Murphy, 2002), many of our inductive inferences are category-based, and as well as illustrating general principles of inductive reasoning, the phenomena of category-based inductive inference very nicely illustrate the way that our categories make our cognition efficient. For example, when we make inductive inferences about individuals, our knowledge about categories may play an important role. So, upon meeting someone who describes themselves as a carpenter, we don't have to ask lots of questions or observe their behaviour very closely to infer that they are likely to work with wood as part of their job. Category membership also allows us to make inferences about properties with which we are unfamiliar. If we are told that a particular carpenter uses a pocket hole jig, we might expect a different carpenter, encountered in an entirely different context, to also have a pocket hole jig in their toolbox. Furthermore, because carpenters use pocket hole jigs, we might expect furniture makers to use them, but we might be surprised if choreographers, electricians or doctors do.

A recent taxonomy of inductive problems focused on objects, categories, properties and the relations amongst them (Kemp & Jern, 2014). Even this very small list of ingredients results in a large set of inductive inferences which includes problems of generalisation, discovery and identification. I focus here on generalisations about properties based on category membership, not because this is necessarily the most important problem, but because it has attracted much attention (Feeney & Heit, 2007; Hayes, Heit & Swendsen, 2010), and attempts to understand this kind of inference have already revealed much about induction and posed important questions which will guide future research.

As we will see, the central questions in this area have concerned the role played in reasoning by our knowledge about categories and the properties that they possess. Category members possess many different kinds of properties. For example, although most readers will be unfamiliar with pocket hole jigs, the context above suggests that they have something to do with carpenters' behaviour. *Suffering from dyspnoea* or *having omentum inside* are other properties with which we might be unfamiliar but which we might guess to be related to carpenters' work environment or to their membership in the categories *animal, mammal* or *human*. Much of the theoretical development in the area of categorical inductive reasoning has been driven by observations about the way in which people's knowledge about categories and their knowledge about the properties of members of those categories interact in order to make particular properties more projectible than others. This work is only somewhat related to discussions in philosophy and psychology of why some properties are projectible and some are not. For example, information that a single member of a tribe possesses skin of a certain colour is better evidence that all members of the tribe share that skin colour than is information that one tribe member is obese evidence that all tribe members are obese (Nisbett, Krantz, Jepson & Kunda, 1983). As Goodman (1983) notes, the sharing of some properties is likely to be governed by laws, whereas sharing other properties is more likely to be accidental. In the recent literature on category-based induction, researchers have been concerned, not so much with the distinction between law-like and accidental generalisations, but with how different types of knowledge about category relations selectively promote the projection of different sets of features.

Having reviewed the basic phenomena of category-based induction and a variety of accounts of those phenomena, I argue that these accounts fall into two types and suggest a way by which they can be reconciled. I then consider how category-based induction may relate to other types of thinking, and more broadly, to other cognitive abilities. Finally, I try to identify a number of areas for future research.

The basic phenomena

Knowledge about categories

The paradigm that is still widely used to study category-based inductive reasoning was devised by Rips (1975). He told participants that on a small island, members of a base category, such as *robins*, had a new type of contagious disease and asked them to estimate what proportion of a number of other target categories also had the disease. Rips found that the typicality of the base category and the similarity between the base and target predicted participants' judgements. Although Rips' paper has turned out to be very influential, very little additional work was carried out with adults (for an exception, see Nisbett, Krantz, Jepson & Kunda, 1983) over the next decade. However, in the intervening years, variants of the category-based paradigm were used to great effect to study children's inductive inferences (e.g. Carey, 1985; Gelman & Markman, 1986). Because the primary goal of this research was to understand children's beliefs about categories or how their categories are organised, it will not be reviewed here.

In a landmark paper, Osherson, Smith, Wilkie, López and Shafir (1990) described 13 separate phenomena of category-based induction, including premise typicality and similarity effects. For example, the premises in argument 1 are judged by most participants to more strongly support the conclusion than do the premises in argument 2.

Hippopotamuses require Vitamin K for the liver to function (1)
Hamsters require Vitamin K for the liver to function

All mammals require Vitamin K for the liver to function
Hippopotamuses require Vitamin K for the liver to function (2)

Rhinoceroses require Vitamin K for the liver to function
All mammals require Vitamin K for the liver to function

This is known as the diversity effect because the premise categories in argument 1 are more diverse than the premise categories in argument 2. Osherson et al. demonstrated the effect with general conclusion categories as in arguments 1 and 2 and with specific conclusions such as *All rabbits require Vitamin K for the liver to function.* The diversity effect has engendered much debate (Lo, Sides, Rozelle & Osherson, 2002; Heit, Hahn & Feeney, 2005) and there have been several studies which have investigated the extent to which children are sensitive to evidential diversity (e.g. Heit & Hahn, 2001; Rhodes & Liebenson, 2015).

If we consider the premise categories in a category-based inductive argument to constitute a sample, then a diverse premise set can be thought of as more representative of the population from which it is drawn than a non-diverse sample. Size is another important characteristic of samples, and better inferences can be based on bigger samples (see Nisbett et al., 1983). Osherson et al. demonstrated monotonicity effects in arguments with specific and general conclusions such that arguments containing more premise categories were rated stronger than arguments with fewer premise categories. Feeney (2007) demonstrated that sensitivity to both diversity and monotonicity principles is associated with cognitive ability.

Osherson et al. described non-monotonicity effects, where more premise categories resulted in lower ratings of argument strength. Such effects occurred when the additional premise category came from outside the lowest-level subordinate category that contained all of the other categories in the argument. For example, argument 4 is judged weaker than argument 3,

Cows secrete uric acid crystals (3)
Peacocks secrete uric acid crystals
All birds secrete uric acid crystals

Cows secrete uric acid crystals (4)
Peacocks secrete uric acid crystals
Rabbits secrete uric acid crystals
All birds secrete uric acid crystals

even though the greater number of premises in argument 4 constitutes a bigger sample. In some respects, non-monotonicity effects are controversial and their normative basis is unclear (see Heit, 1998).

Osherson et al. also described premise-conclusion inclusion effects: arguments whose conclusion category is included in the premise category should be perfectly strong. For example, knowing that all animals have property Y entirely confirms that all birds have property Y. Notably, Sloman (1993; 1998) has shown such arguments to be judged less than perfectly strong, and that the similarity between the categories in the argument rather than the class inclusion relation often determines ratings of inductive strength. This tendency, to judge deductively valid arguments as less than perfectly strong, is sometimes called the inclusion fallacy (Shafir, Smith & Osherson, 1990). Finally, Hampton and Cannon (2004) have described conclusion typicality effects such that given identical premises, participants prefer arguments with more typical conclusion categories.

Property knowledge

All of the phenomena described above were demonstrated using blank properties, with which participants are unfamiliar. This was so the researchers could investigate the effects of people's knowledge about the categories in the argument. Heit and Rubinstein (1994) demonstrated an interaction between the nature of the property in the argument and the nature of the relation between the categories in the argument. For example, anatomical properties (*as it ages, its body contains more salts*) were more likely to be projected between pairs of categories that are anatomically similar (*mouse, bat*), whereas behavioural properties (*never travels directly in the direction of the sun*) were more likely to be projected between pairs of categories that are behaviourally similar (*worm, snake*). Inductive selectivity effects have also been shown in children (see Bright & Feeney, 2014a; Coley, 2012; Kalish & Gelman, 1992). Coley (2012) showed that whether children lived in an urban or rural environment predicted the age at which they began to show sensitivity to the nature of the property in the argument, and there have been a number of analogous demonstrations of effects of experience. For example, Shafto and Coley (2003) compared inductive reasoning about fish in commercial fishermen and students and found that both groups relied on similarity when the property was entirely blank, but the commercial fishermen reasoned on the basis of factors such as shared habitat and food chain membership (ecological relations) when the property was suffering from a particular disease. In a number of cross-cultural studies, Medin and colleagues (López, Atran, Coley, Medin & Smith, 1997; Bailenson, Schum, Atran, Medin & Coley, 2002) have shown that North American undergraduates reason about anatomical properties on the basis of taxonomic relations between the categories in the argument, whereas Itza′ Maya participants from Guatemala reasoned on the basis of their knowledge of ecological relations.

Causal knowledge

A final set of phenomena that we will consider concerns the effects of causal knowledge on inductive reasoning. There are strong claims that causality is at the core of our cognition. Because of the importance of mechanism to an understanding of causality, causal thinking is more than an assessment of probabilistic relations (Sloman & Lagnado, 2015). In addition, because of its directional nature (causes lead to effects but not vice versa), causal thinking is more than mere association. Lassaline (1996) showed that participants were sensitive to causal relations involving the property to be projected when evaluating category-based inductive inferences, and Rehder and Burnett (2005) have demonstrated similar effects. Rehder (2006) pitted similarity against knowledge about causal relations between properties and found that causal knowledge dominated people's judgements of inductive strength.

Other effects of causal knowledge concern relations between the categories in the argument. Medin et al. (2003) constructed arguments from pairs of categories whose relationship to each other provided a causal basis for the transmission of properties from members of one category to members of the other. The relationship was often an ecological one. For example, carrots and rabbits belong to the same food chain. Medin et al. found that arguments such as 5 where the categories appeared in a predictive order were rated stronger than arguments such as 6 where the order was diagnostic.

Carrots have property J6 (5)
Rabbits have property J6

Rabbits have property J6 (6)
Carrots have property J6

This asymmetry effect has been replicated by Bright and Feeney (2014a, 2014b). Medin et al. also demonstrated causal conjunction effects in which arguments such as 7 were judged stronger than arguments such as 8.

Grain has property M4 (7)
Mice and owls have property M4

Grain has property M4 (8)
Owls have property M4

Feeney, Shafto and Dunning (2007) showed that susceptibility to this effect was not associated with cognitive ability whereas susceptibility to the analogous effect based on category membership (see arguments 9 and 10) was.

Andean people have property X12 (9)
Himalayan people and Alpine people have property X12

Andean people have property X12 (10)
Himalayan people have property X12

Feeney et al. (2007) interpreted the selective associations with cognitive ability as suggesting that causal knowledge may be particularly important for inductive reasoning and that even reasoners high in cognitive ability may find it hard to integrate their causal knowledge with the probabilistic structure of the reasoning task.

Summary

The phenomena of category-based inductive reasoning are numerous: reasoners are sensitive to a variety of properties of the premise categories; the interaction between their knowledge about the premises and the property to be projected varies by culture and area of expertise; causal knowledge seems particularly important and its effects have been intensively studied. These are the phenomena which must be explained by any successful theory of category-based reasoning. Of course, because not all of the phenomena emerged at the same time, explanations were proposed to account for the phenomena known at the time that they were proposed. Thus, we will see that theoretical approaches in this area have gradually increased in sophistication as the set of findings to be explained increased in size.

Accounts of category-based induction

Initial accounts

Osherson et al. (1990) suggested that the strength of a category-based inductive argument depends on two factors: the similarity between the categories in the argument, and the degree to which the categories in the premises "cover" the lowest level superordinate category that contains all of the categories in the argument. "Coverage" here is defined in terms of the similarity between the premise categories and members of the superordinate that come to mind. An alternative account was offered by Sloman (1993). Whereas Osherson et al. assume the existence of a hierarchical structure summarising people's knowledge about taxonomic relations, Sloman attempted to account for the extant phenomena using a connectionist model of argument strength in which strength is proportional to the proportion of the features of the conclusion category that are shared with the premise categories. One can think of strength in this model relating to the degree of feature coverage which is achieved by the premises.

Both of these models can account for basic phenomena such as typicality, similarity, diversity and monotonicity. For example, diversity, where premise categories which are less similar to each other result in stronger arguments, is explained in the similarity-coverage model because diverse categories cover the superordinate better than non-diverse categories. On the other hand, according to the feature-based approach, because diverse categories share fewer features than do non-diverse categories, they are also likely to cover the features of the conclusion category better. Although the models do equally well in accounting for some of Osherson et al.'s phenomena, they have different strengths and weaknesses when tested by some of the other phenomena. For example, the feature-based model has difficulties in accounting for non-monotonicity effects (Sloman & Lagnado, 2005), whereas the similarity coverage model explains the effect by positing that the additional premise from outside the lowest level superordinate that contains all of the other categories in the argument necessitates generation of a higher-level superordinate. For example, adding a premise about *bees* to an argument already containing premises about *cod* and *mackerel* and a conclusion about *trout*, necessitates the generation of *animals* as a covering category, which *cod* and *mackerel* do not cover as well as they do the superordinate *fish*. As generation of a superordinate category is likely to be effortful, this account predicts that children might struggle with arguments containing specific conclusions. Developmental work shows that although second graders are sensitive to diversity and monotonicity when the argument contains a superordinate category in the conclusion, they do not show these effects when the conclusion category is specific (Lopez, Gelman, Gutheil & Smith, 1992). That generation of a superordinate category is effortful is also suggested by the results of studies with adults showing lower rates of sensitivity to monotonicity and diversity for arguments with specific conclusions (Feeney, 2007). Both findings support the similarity-coverage model, which holds that for specific arguments, reasoners must generate the lowest level superordinate that contains all of the categories in the argument, and are problematic for the feature-based model, which makes no assumptions about the involvement of categories in reasoning.

Because it assumes a hierarchical category structure, the similarity coverage model predicts that deductively valid arguments such as 11, where the conclusion category is a sub-ordinate of the premise category, should be perfectly strong.

Birds have an ulnar artery (11)
Robins have an ulnar artery

Birds have an ulnar artery (12)
Penguins have an ulnar artery

As we have seen, Sloman (1993, 1998) has demonstrated that the strength of such arguments is judged on the basis of the similarity between their categories. Even though argument 11 and argument 12 are both deductively valid and thus should both be judged perfectly strong, Sloman (1993) found that argument 11 was judged stronger than argument 12, because robins are more similar to birds than are penguins. The existence of such premise-conclusion "inclusion fallacies" is, at first inspection, extremely problematic for the similarity coverage model. However, Calvillo and Revlin (2005) pointed out that such arguments are enthymemes because they are missing a premise. For example, in argument 11 the missing premise is *all robins are birds*. They show that the similarity of the categories in the argument predicts the degree to which people believe the missing premise, which in turn predicts ratings of argument strength. Calvillo and Revlin (2005) argue that similarity (feature overlap) has a much smaller role in the reasoning process than Sloman claims.

Finally, the conclusion typicality effect reported by Hampton and Cannon (2004) appears to be inconsistent with both the feature-based and similarity coverage model. The similarity coverage model predicts no effect of conclusion typicality, and the feature-based model predicts that arguments with typical conclusions should be weaker than those with atypical conclusions. This is because argument strength depends on the proportion of conclusion features covered by features of the premise categories, and people know more about, and therefore have more featural knowledge of, typical categories.

Although the conclusion typicality effect was problematic for the dominant models of inductive reasoning, the problems it created are dwarfed by the problems caused by property effects. Both of these models are very good at accounting for findings from arguments with blank properties, or properties which suggest that taxonomic relations between the categories are relevant, but neither can cope with the property effects that were reviewed above. For example, neither model can cope with the observation that people judge arguments about biological properties to be strong when they contain biologically similar categories, and arguments about behavioural properties are stronger when they concern behaviourally similar categories (for a review, see Shafto, Vitkin & Coley, 2007). As argued by Medin, Goldstone and Gentner (1993), there are many possible similarity relations between a pair of categories, including their biological and behavioural similarity, and the property seems to determine which of these relations participants attend to (Heit & Rubinstein, 1994). Neither the similarity coverage nor the feature-based model contain a mechanism for deciding which of the many relations between the categories in the argument should be used when judging argument strength.

Medin et al. (2003) proposed a relevance framework to explain how people determine which relations between the categories should be used when evaluating an argument. They argued that when people read the premise of an inductive argument (e.g. *magpies have property x*), they associate the blank property with features that come to mind (*coloration* in this example). Furthermore, they compare the premise and conclusion categories to test their initial hypotheses about the nature of the blank property. So, given *magpies* in the premise, *zebras* in the conclusion would appear to confirm the coloration hypothesis, whereas *crows* would disconfirm that hypothesis and suggest another. The relevance framework can account for property effects, as well as for the effects of causal knowledge described by Medin et al. and a variety of other effects. In addition, Feeney, Coley and Crisp (2010) derived and confirmed reading time predictions from the relevance account. These predictions relate to dynamic processes of hypothesis generation and evaluation in the course of evaluating arguments. As none of the other accounts described in this chapter seek to understand the dynamics of inductive reasoning over time, these findings cannot be predicted by those accounts (for very recent work on the dynamics of inductive reasoning, see Hawkins, Hayes & Heit, 2016).

One real strength of the literature on category-based induction is the mathematical precision with which most models have been specified. For many researchers in this area, the relevance framework, although extremely useful for priming experiments, is too loosely specified. Alternative Bayesian and parallel distributed processing (PDP) approaches to inductive reasoning, which are precisely specified and can more easily handle a range of property effects, have received much recent attention.

Structured Bayesian accounts

Structured Bayesian accounts of inductive reasoning (see Tenenbaum, Kemp & Shafto, 2007; Kemp & Tenenbaum, 2009) consist of a set of structures that captures people's knowledge about relations between categories. Each structure specifies knowledge about the relations between categories in a particular domain as well as knowledge about how particular properties depend on those relations. From such a structure one can derive the prior probability that, for example, two categories might share a property. These probabilities are updated using simple Bayesian updating in the light of the evidence in the argument (see also Heit, 1998). In principle, any number of knowledge structures are possible, but Kemp and Tenenbaum (2009) focus on four: taxonomic knowledge captured by a tree structure; causal knowledge captured by directed graphs roughly corresponding to a food web; spatial knowledge captured by multidimensional scaling; and threshold properties (e.g. earnings over £50,000) modelled along a single dimension. In each case the structure is different, as is the mechanism for capturing the spread of properties throughout the structure. Shafto, Kemp, Bonawitz, Coley and Tenenbaum (2008) contrasted people's reasoning about diseases and genes and showed that whereas a Bayesian model using a taxonomic structure to estimate priors captured people's reasoning about genes, the food web structure captured reasoning about diseases. Kemp and Tenenbaum (2009) provide further empirical evidence of the predictive power of the various structures given a variety of property types.

The achievements of the Bayesian approach to category-based induction are impressive, none more so than the success that has been achieved in modelling people's reasoning about different properties. As Kemp and Tenenbaum (2009) point out, there are a variety of approaches which posit the existence of different theories about domains of knowledge (see Carey, 1985; Murphy and Medin, 1985) as well as approaches which focus on just one domain in order to achieve mathematical precision (see Osherson et al., 1990; Sloman, 1993). The remarkable achievement of the Bayesian approach is that it captures a range of domain theories in a precise mathematical form. That said, there have been recent criticisms of the Bayesian approach in cognition more generally (Bowers & Davis, 2012; Marcus & Davis, 2013). For example, Jones and Love (2011) have lamented the unconstrained nature of many Bayesian models which they argue are often uninformed by process-level data and succeed by making a variety of assumptions that are embedded in the machinery used to generate priors. Often these assumptions are not empirically tested and unlikely to be true. For example, Shafto, Kemp, Mansinghka and Tenenbaum (2011) proposed a model of how people learn overlapping systems of categories, assuming, among other things, that each category feature is relevant to just one category and that each category appears in just one system. These assumptions are embodied in the model, allowing it to successfully predict people's learning of category structure, but as Jones and Love point out, the assumptions are arbitrary and other assumptions could have been made. For example, we have multiple categorisation systems for clothes which relate to their colour, manufacture and laundering. Arguably, colour relates to all of these systems, but according to Shafto et al.'s model it can be associated with only one of them.

Jones and Love (2011) also argue that although there are often a number of possible Bayesian models of a particular phenomenon, these possibilities are rarely pitted against each other. Furthermore, like most Bayesian models, Kemp and Tenenbaum's does not explain psychological phenomena at the level of mechanism or process (see Jones & Love, 2011). Thus, this model cannot capture findings that relate to psychological process. For example, reaction time findings such as those described by Feeney et al. (2010) cannot be predicted by this model. However, as the model was intended neither to predict nor to explain such findings, it is not clear that it should be evaluated against them (for recent discussion of the explanatory level at which Bayesian models work, see Peebles & Cooper, 2015; Griffiths, Lieder & Goodman, 2015). Scepticism about Bayesian models of high-level cognition is not new (see Feeney, Handley & Kentridge, 2003), but as we have seen, Kemp and Tenenbaum's (2009) account of category-based induction is laudable for a number of reasons.

The parallel distributed processing approach

Rogers and McClelland (2004) described a PDP account of semantic cognition which grew out of an attempt to account for how conceptual knowledge (a) becomes differentiated across development, and (b) deteriorates in dementia. Drawing on previous work by Rumelhart (1990),

Rogers and McClelland describe a feed forward network comprising nodes which represent the features of items, nodes which represent relations, a layer of hidden nodes and a layer of nodes which allow the network to represent novel conclusions about relations between items and features. The model learns by back propagation, and makes inferences in much the same way that Sloman's (1993) model does.

Rogers and McClelland have not applied their model to most of the phenomena described earlier. Instead, they have focussed on providing an account of how domain theories emerge across development (Carey, 1985). One accomplishment of the model is that it predicts a number of property effects observed in children. Carey (1985) showed that children project properties with greater specificity as they develop, as does Rogers and McClelland's model, and Gelman and Markman (1986) showed that children distinguish between biological (is cold-blooded) and physical (weighs over one tonne) properties when reasoning inductively, as does the model. Interestingly, the model represents different categories as being more or less similar depending on the context created by the feature to be projected.

Although Rogers and McClelland's models are certainly impressive, it is not clear whether they could predict the kinds of property effects observed by Heit and Rubinstein (1994) nor whether they could ever match the precision with which Kemp and Tenenbaum's models distinguish between domain theories. In support of the general approach, Sloutsky and Fisher (2008) attempted to demonstrate that children as young as six can learn to selectively project properties by implicitly learning associations between sets of features and different contexts. However, Hayes and Lim (2013) have shown that the original learning procedure works for only some adults, and that a learning procedure which works with both adults and young children results in awareness of the relations, suggesting that the learning is not implicit.

Another very serious issue is the extent to which PDP models can be said to represent causality. One account of the marked selectivity observed when people project properties is that they reason causally (see Sloman & Lagnado, 2005). Birds have biological properties in common which might explain which two birds will share a biological property, whereas tigers and hawks are hunters and carnivores, which would explain why they might share a biological property. Causal relations are central to the relational structures suggested by Kemp and Tenenbaum. In some cases, as in the directed graphs used to model food chain relations, the structure is explicitly causal, and in others the mechanism that accounts for the spread of properties through the structure is implicitly causal. For example, properties spread through a taxonomic tree via a mechanism that mimics genetic transmission, which is itself amenable to explanation in causal terms. Although Rogers and McClelland argue that their models can account for causal knowledge, they present no simulations to support those arguments.

A recent theme in the literature is how the Bayesian and PDP approaches relate to each other (see Rogers & McClelland, 2008; Griffiths, Chater, Kemp, Perfors & Tenenbaum, 2010). One possibility is that they account for the same phenomena but at different levels (Kemp & Tenenbaum, 2009); Bayesian models work by specifying the computations which reasoners must carry out, whereas connectionist models account for the processing that actually takes place (for an interesting account of the parallels between Bayesian and connectionist approaches in cognitive science, see Jones & Love, 2011). In the next section I will review very recent work which suggests that this cannot be the case.

Reconciling the approaches: a hybrid account of inductive reasoning

Thus far, we have seen that theories of inductive reasoning make entirely different assumptions about how our knowledge of the world is represented. What I will refer to as structured accounts assume that our knowledge of the world is organised in some structured way. Osherson et al. (1990) assume a taxonomic hierarchy and Bayesian modellers assume a variety of structured knowledge representations which correspond to theories about domains (see Murphy & Medin, 1985). On the other hand, associative knowledge develops as a result of co-occurrence, contiguity or similarity (see Kruschke, 1992; McClelland & Rumelhart, 1985; Rescorla & Wagner, 1972), and there have been at least two attempts to model inductive reasoning in associative terms (Sloman, 1993; Rogers & McClelland, 2004). Bright and Feeney (2014b) argued that perhaps both associative and structured knowledge drive reasoning, and suggested that a hybrid account might be required to explain how people generalise on the basis of category membership (see also Calvillo & Revlin, 2005). According to this account, both types of knowledge might drive inductive reasoning, but to different extents under different processing conditions. Specifically, when time and cognitive resources are scarce, they suggested that associative knowledge might be more important. On the other hand, under more favourable processing conditions when time and resources are plentiful, they expected to see a greater role played by structured knowledge.

To test their suggestion, Bright and Feeney developed measures of associative and structured knowledge. They showed that people's estimates of the degree of association between categories did not correlate with judgements about whether particular pairs of categories belonged to the same biological class or to the same food chain. In addition, they showed that whereas the measure of association correlated well with the results of co-occurrence searches via a search engine, the measures of structured knowledge did not correlate well with the co-occurrence search results. Thus, the measures of associative and structured knowledge appear to reflect different aspects of people's knowledge about categories.

In a series of experiments, Bright and Feeney (2014b) asked people to evaluate category-based inductive arguments (Experiments 1 and 2), or to generate a category to which they could generalise properties said to be possessed by members of another category (Experiment 3). The categories in these arguments were chosen so that they were taxonomically related (13), belonged to the same food chain (14) and were likely to vary in their perceived degree of association. The nature of the property was manipulated in all of these experiments, with some arguments involving cells and others involving infections.

Wheat has infection 9TT7 (13)
How likely is it that bamboo has infection 9TT7?

Grass has 45T cells (14)
How likely is it that sheep have 45T cells?

If participants are using structured knowledge of the kind identified by, for example, the structured Bayesian approach (Kemp & Tenenbaum, 2009), then food chain knowledge should be particularly important when reasoning about infections. Taxonomic knowledge, on the other hand, might be important when reasoning about both cells and infections. We might expect taxonomically related categories to share cells, and we might expect them to be susceptible to the same infections (for corroborating evidence, see Shafto, Coley & Baldwin, 2007). In each of the experiments, some participants reasoned under conditions unfavourable to processing (under speeded conditions or under heavy load) while other participants reasoned under favourable conditions (they were forced to delay their response or were subject to a light load).

Associative knowledge better predicted people's ratings of inductive strength when they reasoned under unfavourable conditions, and this was true whether they were reasoning about cells or diseases. Under favourable conditions, the measures of structured knowledge predicted reasoning better than they did under unfavourable conditions. Knowledge of food chain relations was a significant predictor of argument strength when people reasoned about infections, whereas taxonomic knowledge was a significant predictor when people reasoned about both types of property. The results of these experiments suggest that it is possible to dissociate associative from structured knowledge, and demonstrate that each type of knowledge has greatest effect under different processing conditions. Associative knowledge appears to be most easily available to reasoning processes, hence its effects are most visible when processing conditions are unfavourable. Structured knowledge, on the other hand, requires favourable processing conditions in order to have its greatest influence on the reasoning process.

Bright and Feeney's (2014b) results raise the possibility that in order for structured knowledge to influence reasoning, the effects of quickly available associative knowledge must be inhibited. Travers, Rolison, Bright and Feeney (2015) describe a triad task where participants are told that members of a base category (e.g. carrots) possess cells, and must decide whether members of a strongly associated but taxonomically unrelated foil category (rabbits) or members of a weakly associated but taxonomically related target category (bamboo) also possess the property. Performance on these conflict trials is compared to performance on control trials where the foil is not associated with the base category. Travers et al. (2015) have tracked the movement of the mouse cursor whilst participants are completing a computerised version of this task. They find that participants are significantly more likely to select the foil when it is strongly associated with the base, thus suggesting that conflict between associative and structured knowledge impairs category-based inductive reasoning. They also find that on a substantial minority of conflict trials, the cursor moves towards the associated foil before moving towards the taxonomically related target. Such "changes of mind" are almost never seen to operate in the opposite direction. That is, participants who end up choosing the strongly associated foil almost never initially consider selecting the taxonomically related target. These results suggest that associative and structured knowledge may sometimes be in conflict during inductive reasoning and that in order for structured knowledge to inform inference, the effects of associative knowledge must be inhibited.

The findings just described are problematic for any argument that Bayesian and PDP models account for the same phenomena but at different levels of explanation. Instead, they are consistent with the claim that each kind of model captures reasoning under certain circumstances, but that neither on its own will suffice as a general account of inductive reasoning.

Relations to other types of thinking

At the outset of this chapter I defined inductive reasoning as a form of thinking that leads to conclusions that are not deductively valid. Defining something in terms of what it is not can be problematic. Apart from the over-inclusiveness of the definition, there is also a problem if our view of deduction changes, and this is exactly what has happened over the last twenty years (Elqayam, this volume; Oaksford & Chater, this volume; Over & Cruz, this volume). In fact, many of the contributors to this volume regard deductive inferences as being uncertain because of the uncertainty inherent in their premises. Although people can be instructed to assume that the premises are true (see George, 1995; Handley & Trippas, 2015), often they seem to take this uncertainty into account. At first glance, this appears to lead to a situation where we cannot distinguish between inductive and deductive reasoning. However, Evans and Over (2013) argued that it is still possible to distinguish deduction from induction, both logically and functionally. Deductive arguments are "probabilistically valid"; that is, our uncertainty about the conclusion to a deductive argument cannot be greater than our uncertainty about its premises. In inductive arguments, on the other hand, we are always more uncertain about the conclusion than we are about the premises. Furthermore, inductive reasoning is used to add to our set of beliefs about the world, whereas deduction makes explicit what is implied by our already existing beliefs.

Thinking about induction and deduction in this way is to take what Heit (2007) calls the "problem view" of thinking where we define different types of thinking in terms of the problems to which they are applied. Heit (2007) contrasted the problem view with the "process view", where we are concerned with the processes which allow us to make particular kinds of inferences. Some researchers appear to claim that the same processes underlie deduction and induction. Rips (2001a) has referred to this view as "reasoning imperialism". For example, mental model theory (Johnson-Laird, Legrenzi, Girotto, Legrenzi & Caverni, 1999) has been applied to both deduction and induction. Similarly, it has been claimed that a probabilistic approach can be extended to both deductive and inductive thinking (for a clarification of this claim in the light of Rips' argument, see Oaksford & Hahn, 2007). The mental model account of inductive reasoning does not seem particularly strong; although it explains inductive reasoning when we possess information about only a proportion of members of some category, it contains no way of accounting for the similarity relations which we know to be so important to category-based induction.

Rips (2001b) described an experiment where he compared people's reasoning about a set of arguments in which logical validity was placed in conflict with conclusion plausibility. Participants were instructed to reason on the basis of what necessarily (deductive instructions) or plausibly (inductive instructions) followed. He argued that a single process account of reasoning might predict that under different reasoning instructions, people merely adjust their criterion for distinguishing between conclusions that follow from the premises and those that do not. Thus, people might accept only the very strongest arguments under deductive instructions but be prepared to accept weaker arguments under inductive instructions. Instead, Rips found an interaction such that participants tended to distinguish between arguments more on the basis of validity under deductive instructions and on the basis of plausibility under inductive instructions.

Rotello and Heit (2009) used an instructional manipulation in experiments where they manipulated argument length and validity. They found that length had the greatest effect under induction instructions and validity under deductive instructions. Furthermore, they showed that a two-factor signal detection theory model provided a better fit to their data than did a single-factor model. One of the factors in the two-factor model was most heavily weighted when accounting for inferences under deduction instructions and the other when accounting for inferences under inductive instructions. Heit and Rotello (2010) further showed that similarity has a greater effect under induction instructions, and that deduction judgements made under speeded conditions resemble induction judgements. Singmann and Klauer (2011) extended these dissociations to judgements made about conditional arguments under deductive or inductive judgements.

All of these results may be interpreted in the context of dual process theories of reasoning (Evans, 2008, this volume; Kahneman, 2011; Sloman, 1996). Such theories distinguish between Type 1 or intuitive processes, which are autonomous, fast and massively parallel, and Type 2 or analytic processes, which are slower and tied to working memory. Although Rotello and Heit (2009) point out that the factors in their model do not correspond to psychological processes, their results might plausibly be interpreted as consistent with the claim that intuitive processes play a greater role in inductive reasoning whereas analytic processes are more important to deduction. Certainly, they suggest that inductive reasoning is related to deductive reasoning because there is overlap in the processes which enable each kind of reasoning. However, the degree to which each process is involved appears to differ according to the instructions given to participants. Bright and Feeney's (2014b) findings, that the use of structured knowledge for evaluating inductive arguments is affected by response time and secondary task manipulations, appears to rule out an interpretation of these results in which the "intuitive" factor corresponds to background knowledge and the "analytic" factor corresponds to logical structure. Further work will be required to sort out relations between knowledge types and types of process used in reasoning, and careful consideration of what has recently been discovered about how background knowledge drives inductive reasoning may lead to more precise and comprehensive accounts of deduction.

Although there has been considerable recent focus on relations between inductive and deductive reasoning, there are also clear relations between inductive reasoning and other types of thinking, such as analogical reasoning, for example. Holyoak, Lee and Lu (2010) have demonstrated how an account of causal category-based inductive reasoning based on causal models (Rehder, 2006; 2009) may be extended to analogical reasoning. The recently demonstrated effects of conflict between knowledge types (Travers et al., 2015) have parallels in the literature on analogical reasoning where it is known that structure mapping can be impeded by the presence of associatively related distracters (Krawczyk et al., 2008). Thus, although clearly distinct from other types of reasoning, inductive reasoning shares many similarities with both deductive and analogical reasoning, not least the fact that all three types of reasoning may be characterised as involving, to varying extents, sensitivity to both structure and background belief. However, it is important not to lose sight of the unique contribution to a more general understanding of reasoning which has been made by models of category-based inductive reasoning. In particular, our understanding of how best to characterise knowledge stored in memory and its dynamic interaction with reasoning processes has been greatly advanced by the study of such reasoning.

Relations with memory

A distinguishing feature of the recent literature has been exploration of the relationship between inductive reasoning and memory (see Heit, Rotello & Hayes, 2012; Feeney, Hayes & Heit, 2014). This has proceeded along two fronts: testing participants' recognition memory for the items they have reasoned about has provided a methodological tool which has enabled theoretical claims about how the ability to make inductive inferences develops; and the application of models of recognition memory to results of inductive reasoning experiments has permitted theoretical integration across different areas of cognition.

Sloutsky and Fisher (2004) devised the Induction Then Recognition paradigm where participants were shown a picture of a cat said to possess a property, and were asked whether other cats, bears and birds shared the property. Next, participants were given a surprise recognition memory test where they were asked to decide whether a series of old and new animals had appeared in the reasoning part of the study. Results showed that whereas children and adults did equally well on the reasoning task, five-year-old children were significantly better at recognising the items they had reasoned about than were adults. Sloutsky and Fisher interpreted this finding as showing that there are important developmental differences in the way that children and adults make inductive inferences. However, subsequent work (Wilburn & Feeney, 2008; Hayes, McKinnon & Sweller, 2008) has demonstrated that children look at the reasoning stimuli for longer than adults and when inspection time is dramatically curtailed to 250 milliseconds, continue to make inferences at adult rates, but do worse on the recognition memory part of the procedure. Although claims about developmental differences do not appear to be licensed by findings with the paradigm, it has been successfully used to examine adult reasoning with novel stimuli (Fisher & Sloutsky, 2005). Furthermore, by showing that people have better memory for diversity than for monotonicity items, Travers and Feeney (2013) have recently used the paradigm to distinguish between processes involved in sensitivity to diversity and monotonicity in adults.

The second line of work exploring relations between inductive reasoning and recognition memory has involved presenting different participants with the same set of pictures and asking them to make recognition judgements or property inferences (for a review, see Heit et al., 2012). Because recognition memory is expected to be driven by perceptual similarity, whereas a variety of more complex knowledge is hypothesised to play a role in induction (Bright & Feeney, 2014b; Kemp & Tenenbaum, 2009; Medin et al., 2003), we might expect induction judgements to differ from memory judgements and to be more complex to model. However, when the properties in the induction arguments were blank, the single difference observed was that participants were less conservative in their induction judgments than in their recognition judgments (Heit & Hayes, 2011). This finding held up in the face of manipulations of response time and frequency of exposure to the study items (Heit & Hayes, 2011), and was observed in young children (Hayes, Fritz & Heit, 2013). In all cases, the recognition and reasoning data could be modelled using the same exemplar model. Hayes and Heit (2013) manipulated the nature of the properties so that they were blank or related to habitat or reproduction. They observed selectivity effects in inductive reasoning and found that a version of the exemplar model which included separate measures of overall similarity, similarity with respect to habitat and with respect to reproduction, fit the induction data better than any simpler model. A model with a single similarity factor fit the recognition data. The best interpretation of these results are unclear. It could be that the measure of overall similarity reflects degree of association between the stimuli, whereas the more selective similarity measures reflect structured relations. On this reading, the results are broadly consistent with claims made by Bright and Feeney (2014b) that different types of knowledge drive inductive reasoning under different processing conditions. Heit and Hayes (2011) do not interpret their findings in this way. They see the findings as evidence for a deep correspondence, due to the central role played by similarity, between reasoning and recognition memory. Resolving some of these differences of interpretation will require further research.

Future directions and conclusion

Perhaps the liveliest current debates about induction concern how children make inductive inferences. There are long-running debates about the role of categories in children's induction (see Gelman & Davidson, 2013; Deng & Sloutsky, 2013) as well as disagreements about the extent to which children are sensitive to causal structure when making inferences (Bright & Feeney, 2014a; Hayes & Thompson, 2007; Kloos & Sloutsky, 2013). It seems likely that if adults' inductive inferences are driven by associative as well as structured knowledge (Bright & Feeney, 2014b), then so too will children's, although the weighting of these two types of knowledge may turn out to vary at different developmental points.

Questions about the role played by causal knowledge in children's inductive reasoning seem particularly important given the central role played by causality in adult cognition (see Sloman & Lagnado, 2015), and a surprisingly small proportion of the literature concerns the degree to which children's inductive inferences are sensitive to their emerging causal understanding of the world. Walker, Lombrozo, Legare and Gopnik (2014) showed that asking children aged 3–5 to explain the behaviour of a set of objects during a causal learning task increased the frequency with which they projected properties amongst those objects on the basis of causal relations rather than perceptual similarity. As well as suggesting an early role for causal understanding in children's inductive inference, this work stresses the relation between abductive and inductive reasoning, which is also likely to be a theme in future research (see Johnson, Merchant & Keil, 2015).

The vast majority of the work surveyed in this chapter has involved novel or biological categories. Recent work has examined children's beliefs about social categories and the effect of those beliefs on inductive inferences (see Diesendruck & HaLevi, 2006; Kinzler & Dautel, 2012; Smyth, Feeney, Eidson, & Coley, 2017). Because this work demonstrates effects of beliefs about social category essences (e.g. that membership in certain social categories is naturally determined and that category members are homogeneous) on how children reason about those categories, it has implications for arguments about the role of categories in children's reasoning (see Gelman, 2003; Sloutsky, 2003). It also opens up the possibility of further study of the effects of experience on beliefs about categories and inferences drawn from them (Coley, 2012). Different societies have different beliefs about social categories, and members of different social groups within a society have different experiences by virtue of belonging to different categories. These facts lead to the possibility of a variety of naturally occurring experiments, which have the potential to greatly increase our understanding of the role played by inferences about categories in determining people's beliefs about and interactions with a variety of social categories. For example, Leslie, Cimpian, Meyer and Freeland (2015) studied academics' beliefs that members of different STEM categories (e.g. maths, physics, engineering) share fixed innate talent, and found that their beliefs were associated with the extent to which women are represented in those categories. As well as priming a number of intriguing hypotheses about the use of STEM category membership for social inference, Leslie et al.'s findings illustrate how widely held beliefs about social categories might play a central role in important social trends such as gender equality (or lack thereof) in the sciences.

We have seen that there is considerable recent work on the relations between inductive reasoning and recognition memory (Heit et al., 2012). Another exciting avenue for future work will be exploring the role played by semantic memory in inductive reasoning. One possibility is to look directly at relations between brain activation and behaviour. For example, Weber and Osherson (2014) have shown that the overlap in brain activation in response to pictures of category exemplars predicts judgments about inductive arguments involving those categories. Another possibility is to examine how retrieval processes in semantic memory (for a review, see Jeffries, 2013) map onto processes of knowledge retrieval for inductive reasoning. Given the very strong relations between recognition memory and induction, it is possible that, at least for simple, single-premise arguments, there will be very little reasoning left to explain once the effects of retrieval processes in semantic memory have been accounted for.

By focussing here on category-based inductive reasoning, just one out of many of the inductive problems that we solve every day, I hope to have emphasised how rich the literature on category-based induction has become. The simplicity of the category-based paradigm has led to its use by developmentalists to study the structure of children's knowledge, as a proving ground by a variety of modellers and by experimental psychologists interested in studying the processes involved in reasoning. A final, very desirable direction for future research is widening the scope of investigation beyond inferences based on categories. Kemp and Jern's (2014) taxonomy, which provides a basis for this widening of scope, has already led to work on a variety of other inductive problems such as how people reason inductively from observations to conclusions about unobserved objects (Carroll & Kemp, 2015). Nonetheless, even the relatively narrow focus on categories has led to a range of different perspectives on the problem of induction. The very recent literature suggests that reconciliation between these perspectives is possible and that the processes involved in inductive reasoning may have more in common with other reasoning and more general cognitive abilities than anyone might have suspected forty years ago.

References

Bailenson, J. B., Shum, M. S., Atran, S., Medin, D., & Coley, J. D. (2002). A bird's eye view: Biological categorization and reasoning within and across cultures. *Cognition, 84*, 1–53.

Bowers, J. S., & Davis, C. J. (2012). Bayesian just-so stories in psychology and neuroscience. *Psychological Bulletin, 138*, 389–414.

Bright, A. K., & Feeney, A. (2014a). Causal knowledge and the development of inductive reasoning. *Journal of Experimental Child Psychology, 122*, 48–61.

Bright, A. K., & Feeney, A. (2014b). The engine of thought is a hybrid: Roles of associative and structured knowledge in reasoning. *Journal of Experimental Psychology: General, 143*, 2082–2102.

Calvillo, D. P., & Revlin, R. (2005). The role of similarity in deductive categorical inference. *Psychonomic Bulletin and Review, 12*, 938–944.

Carey, S. (1985). *Conceptual change in childhood*. Cambridge, MA: Bradford Books, MIT Press.

Carroll, C. D., & Kemp, C. (2015). Evaluating the inverse reasoning account of object discovery. *Cognition, 139*, 130–153.

Chater, N., Oaksford, M., Heit, E., & Hahn, U. (2010). Inductive logic and empirical psychology. In D. M. Gabbay, S. Hartmann, & J. Woods (Eds.), *Handbook of the history of logic* (Vol. 10, pp. 553–624). Berlin: Springer-Verlag.

Coley, J. D. (2012). Where the wild things are: Informal experience and ecological reasoning. *Child Development, 83*, 992–1006.

Deng, W., & Sloutsky, V. M. (2013) The role of linguistic labels in inductive generalization. *Journal of Experimental Child Psychology, 114*, 432–455.

Diesendruck, G., & HaLevi, H. (2006). The role of language, appearance, and culture in children's social category based induction. *Child Development, 77*, 539–553.

Evans, J. St. B. T. (2008). Dual-processing accounts of reasoning, judgment, and social cognition. *Annual Review of Psychology, 59*, 255–278.

Evans, J. St. B. T., & Over, D. E. (2013). Reasoning to and from belief: Deduction and induction are still distinct. *Thinking and Reasoning, 19*, 267–283.

Feeney, A. (2007). How many processes underlie category-based induction? Effects of conclusion specificity and cognitive ability. *Memory & Cognition, 35*, 1830–1839.

Feeney, A., Coley, J. D., & Crisp, A. K. (2010). The relevance framework for category-based induction: Evidence from garden path arguments. *Journal of Experimental Psychology: Learning, Memory and Cognition, 36*, 906–916.

Feeney, A., Handley, S. J., & Kentridge, R. (2003). Deciding between accounts of the selection task: A reply to Oaksford. *Quarterly Journal of Experimental Psychology, 56*, 1079–1088.

Feeney, A., Hayes, B., & Heit, E. (2014). From tool to theory: What recognition memory reveals about induction reasoning. In A. Feeney & V. A. Thompson (Eds.), *Reasoning as memory* (pp. 110–127). Hove, UK: Psychology Press.

Feeney, A., & Heit, E. (Eds.). (2007). *Inductive reasoning: Experimental, developmental and computational approaches*. Cambridge: Cambridge University Press.

Feeney, A., Shafto, P., & Dunning, D. (2007). Who is susceptible to conjunction fallacies in category-based induction? *Psychonomic Bulletin and Review, 14*, 884–889.

Fisher, A.V., & Sloutsky, V. M. (2005). When induction meets memory: Evidence for gradual transition from similarity-based to category-based induction. *Child Development, 76*, 583–597.

Gelman, S. A. (2003). *The essential child: Origins of essentialism in everyday thought*. New York: Oxford University Press.

Gelman, S. A., & Davidson, N. S. (2013). Conceptual influences on category-based induction. *Cognitive Psychology, 66*, 327–353.

Gelman, S. A., & Markman, E. M. (1986). Categories and induction in young children. *Cognition, 23*, 183–209.

George, C. (1995). The endorsement of the premises: Assumption-based or belief-based reasoning. *British Journal of Psychology, 86*, 93–111.

Goodman, N. (1983). *Faction, fiction and forecast*. Cambridge, MA: Harvard University Press.
Griffiths, T. L., Chater, N., Kemp, C., Perfors, A., & Tenenbaum, J. B. (2010). Probabilistic models of cognition: Exploring representations and inductive biases. *Trends in Cognitive Sciences, 14*, 357–364.
Griffiths, T. L., Lieder, F., & Goodman, N. D. (2015). Rational use of cognitive resources: Levels of analysis between the computational and the algorithmic. *Topics in Cognitive Science*, 7, 217–229.
Hampton, J. A., & Cannon, I. (2004). Category-based induction: An effect of conclusion typicality. *Memory and Cognition, 32*, 235–243.
Handley, S. J., & Trippas, D. (2015). Dual processes and the interplay between knowledge and structure: A new parallel processing model. In B. H. Ross (Ed.) *Psychology of Learning and Motivation, 62*, 33–58.
Hawkins, G., Hayes, B., & Heit, E. (2016). A dynamic model of reasoning and memory. *Journal of Experimental Psychology: General, 145*, 155–180.
Hayes, B., Fritz, K., & Heit, E. (2013). The relationship between memory and inductive reasoning: Does it develop? *Developmental Psychology, 49*, 848–860.
Hayes, B., & Heit, E. (2013). How similar are recognition memory and inductive reasoning? *Memory & Cognition, 41*, 781–795.
Hayes, B., Heit, E., & Swendsen, H. (2010). Inductive reasoning. *Wiley Interdisciplinary Reviews: Cognitive Science, 1*, 278–292.
Hayes, B. K., & Lim, M. (2013). Development, awareness and inductive selectivity. *Journal of Experimental Psychology: Learning, Memory and Cognition, 39*, 821–831.
Hayes, B. K., McKinnon R., Sweller N. (2008). The development of category-based induction: Reexamining conclusions from the induction then recognition (ITR) paradigm. *Developmental Psychology, 44*, 1430–1441.
Hayes, B. K., & Thompson S. P. (2007). Causal relations and feature similarity in children's inductive reasoning. *Journal of Experimental Psychology: General, 136*, 470–484.
Heit, E. (1998). A Bayesian analysis of some forms of inductive reasoning. In M. Oaksford & N. Chater (Eds.), *Rational models of cognition* (pp. 248–274). Oxford: Oxford University Press.
Heit, E. (2007). What is induction and why study it? In A. Feeney & E. Heit (Eds.), *Inductive reasoning: Experimental, developmental and computational approaches* (pp. 1–24). Cambridge: Cambridge University Press.
Heit, E., & Hahn, U. (2001). Diversity-based reasoning in children. *Cognitive Psychology, 47*, 243–273.
Heit, E., Hahn, U., & Feeney, A. (2005). Defending diversity. In W. Ahn, B. C. Goldstone, A. B. Love, & P. Wolff (Eds.), *Categorization inside and outside of the lab: Festscrift in Honor of Douglas L. Medin* (pp. 87–100). Washington, DC: American Psychological Association.
Heit, E., & Hayes, B. (2011). Predicting reasoning from memory. *Journal of Experimental Psychology: General, 140*,76–101.
Heit, E., & Rotello, C. (2010). Relations between inductive reasoning and deductive reasoning. *Journal of Experimental Psychology: Learning, Memory, and Cognition, 36*, 805–812.
Heit, E., Rotello, C., & Hayes, B. (2012). Relations between memory and reasoning. In Ross, B. H. (Ed.), *Psychology of Learning and Motivation, 57*, 57–101.
Heit, E., & Rubinstein, J. (1994). Similarity and property effects in inductive reasoning. *Journal of Experimental Psychology: Learning, Memory, and Cognition, 20*, 411–422.
Holyoak, K. J., Lee, H. S., & Lu, H. J. (2010). Analogical and category-based inference: A theoretical integration with Bayesian causal models. *Journal of Experimental Psychology: General, 139*, 702–727.
Jeffries, E. (2013). The neural basis of semantic cognition: Converging evidence from neuropsychology, neuroimaging and TMS. *Cortex, 49*, 611–625.
Johnson, S. G. B., Merchant, T., & Keil, F. (2015). Argument scope in inductive reasoning: Evidence for an abductive account of induction. In D. C. Noelle, R. Dale, A. S. Warlaumont, J. Yoshimi, T. Matlock, C. D. Jennings, & P. P. Maglio (Eds.), *Proceedings of the 37th annual conference of the Cognitive Science Society*. Austin, TX: Cognitive Science Society.
Johnson-Laird, P. N., Legrenzi, P., Girotto, V., Legrenzi, M., & Caverni, J-P. (1999). Naive probability: A mental model theory of extensional reasoning. *Psychological Review, 106*, 62–88.
Jones, M., & Love, B. C. (2011). Bayesian fundamentalism or enlightenment? On the explanatory status and theoretical contributions of Bayesian models of cognition. *Behavioral and Brain Sciences, 34*, 169–188.
Kahneman, D. (2011). *Thinking fast and slow*. London: Allen Lane.
Kalish, C. W., & Gelman, S. A. (1992). On wooden pillows: Young children's understanding of category implications. *Child Development, 63*, 1536–1557.

Kemp, C., & Jern, A. (2014). A taxonomy of inductive problems. *Psychonomic Bulletin & Review, 21*, 23–46.

Kemp, C., & Tenenbaum, J. B. (2009). Structured statistical models of inductive reasoning. *Psychological Review, 116*, 20–58.

Kinzler, K. D., & Dautel, J. (2012). Children's essentialist reasoning about language and race. *Developmental Science, 15*, 131–138.

Kloos, H., & Sloutsky, V. M. (2013) Blocking a competing cue: Is preschoolers' reasoning guided by causal knowledge. *Developmental Science, 16*, 713–727.

Krawczyk, D. C., Morrison, R. G., Viskontas, I., Holyoak, K. J., Chow, T. W., Mendez, M. F., Miller, B. L., & Knowlton, B. J. (2008). Distraction during relational reasoning: The role of prefrontal cortex in interference control. *Neuropsychologia, 46*, 2020–2032.

Kruschke, J. K. (1992). Alcove – an exemplar-based connectionist model of category learning. *Psychological Review, 99*, 22–44.

Lassaline, M. E. (1996). Structural alignment in induction and similarity. *Journal of Experimental Psychology: Learning, Memory, and Cognition, 22*, 754–770.

Leslie, S. J., Cimpian, A, Meyer, M., & Freeland, E. (2015). Expectations of brilliance underlie women's representation across academic disciplines. *Science, 347*(6219), 262–265.

Lo, Y., Sides, A., Rozelle, J., & Osherson, D. (2002). Evidential diversity and premise probability in young children's inductive judgment. *Cognitive Science, 26*, 181–206.

López, A., Atran, S., Coley, J. D., Medin, D., & Smith, E. E. (1997). The tree of life: Universal and cultural features of folkbiological taxonomies and inductions. *Cognitive Psychology, 32*, 251–295.

Lopez, A., Gelman, S. A., Gutheil, G., & Smith, E. E. (1992). The development of category-based induction. *Child Development, 63*, 1070–1090.

Marcus, G. F., & Davis, E. (2013). How robust are probabilistic models of high-level cognition. *Psychological Science, 24*, 2351–2360.

McClelland, J. L., & Rumelhart, D. E. (1985). Distributed memory and the representation of general and specific information. *Journal of Experimental Psychology: General, 114*, 159–197.

Medin, D., Coley, J. D., Storms, G., & Hayes, B. (2003). A relevance theory of induction. *Psychonomic Bulletin and Review, 10*, 517–532.

Medin, D. L., Goldstone, R. L., & Gentner, D. (1993). Respects for similarity. *Psychological Review, 100*, 254–278.

Murphy, G. L. (2002). *The big book of concepts*. Cambridge, MA: MIT Press.

Murphy, G. L., & Medin, D. L. (1985). The role of theories in conceptual coherence. *Psychological Review, 92*, 289–316.

Nisbett, R. E., Krantz, D. H., Jepson, D., & Kunda, Z. (1983). The use of statistical heuristics in everyday reasoning. *Psychological Review, 90*, 339–363.

Oaksford, M., & Hahn, U. (2007). Induction, deduction and argument strength in human reasoning and argumentation. In A. Feeney & E. Heit (Eds.), *Inductive reasoning: Experimental, developmental and computational approaches* (pp. 269–301). Cambridge: Cambridge University Press.

Osherson, D. N., Smith, E. E., Wilkie, O., López, A., & Shafir, E. (1990). Category-based induction. *Psychological Review, 97*, 185–200.

Peebles, D., & Cooper, R. P. (2015). Thirty years after Marr's vision: Levels of analysis in cognitive science. *Topics in Cognitive Science*, 7, 187–190.

Rehder, B. (2006). When causality and similarity compete in category-based property induction. *Memory & Cognition, 34*, 3–16.

Rehder, B. (2009). Causal-based property generalization. *Cognitive Science, 33*, 301–344.

Rehder, B., & Burnett, R. (2005). Feature inference and the causal structure of categories. *Cognitive Psychology, 50*, 264–314.

Rescorla, R. A., & Wagner, A. R. (1972). A theory of Pavlovian conditioning: Variations in the effectiveness of reinforcement and nonreinforcement. In A. H. Black & W. F. Prokasy (Eds.), *Classical conditioning II: Current research and theory* (pp. 64–99). New York: Appleton-Century-Crofts.

Rhodes, M., & Liebenson, P. (2015). Continuity and change in the development of category-based induction: The test case of diversity-based reasoning. *Cognitive Psychology, 82*, 74–95.

Rips, L. J. (1975). Inductive judgments about natural categories. *Journal of Verbal Learning & Verbal Behavior, 14*, 665–681.

Rips, L. J. (2001a). Two kinds of reasoning. *Psychological Science, 12*, 129–134.

Rips, L. J. (2001b). Reasoning imperialism. In R. Elio (Ed.), *Common sense, reasoning, and rationality* (pp. 215–235). Oxford: Oxford University Press.

Rogers, T. T., & McClelland, J. L. (2004). *Semantic cognition: A parallel distributed processing approach*. Cambridge, MA: MIT Press.
Rogers, T. T., & McClelland, J. L. (2008). A simple model from a powerful framework that spans levels of analysis. *Behavioral and Brain Sciences, 31*, 729–749.
Rotello, C., & Heit, E. (2009). Modeling the effects of argument length and validity on inductive and deductive reasoning. *Journal of Experimental Psychology: Learning, Memory, and Cognition, 35*, 1317–1330.
Rumelhart, D. E. (1990). Brain style computation: Learning and generalization. In S. F. Zornetzer, J. L. Davis, & C. Lau (Eds.), *An introduction to neural and electronic networks* (pp. 405–420). London: Academic Press.
Shafir, E., Smith, E. E., & Osherson, D. N. (1990). Typicality and reasoning fallacies. *Memory & Cognition, 18*, 229–239.
Shafto, P., & Coley, J. D. (2003). Development of categorization and reasoning in the natural world: Novices to experts, naïve similarity to ecological knowledge. *Journal of Experimental Psychology: Learning, Memory & Cognition, 29*, 641–649.
Shafto, P., Coley, J. D., & Baldwin, D. (2007). Effects of time pressure on context-sensitive property induction. *Psychonomic Bulletin & Review, 14*, 890–894.
Shafto, P., Kemp, C., Bonawitz, L. B., Coley, J. D., & Tenenbaum, J. B. (2008). Inductive reasoning about causally transmitted properties. *Cognition, 109*, 175–192.
Shafto, P., Kemp, C., Mansinghka, V. K., & Tenenbaum, J. B. (2011). A probabilistic model of cross-categorization. *Cognition, 120*, 1–25.
Shafto, P., Vitkin, A., & Coley, J. D. (2007). Availability in category-based induction. In A. Feeney & E. Heit (Eds.), *Inductive reasoning: Experimental, developmental and computational approaches*. Cambridge: Cambridge University Press.
Singmann, H., & Klauer, K. C. (2011). Deductive and inductive conditional inferences: Two modes of reasoning. *Thinking & Reasoning, 17*, 247–281.
Sloman, S. A. (1993). Feature-based induction. *Cognitive Psychology, 25*, 231–280.
Sloman, S. A. (1996). The empirical case for two systems of reasoning. *Psychological Bulletin, 119*, 3–22.
Sloman, S. A. (1998). Categorical inference is not a tree: The myth of inheritance hierarchies. *Cognitive Psychology, 35*, 1–33.
Sloman, S. A. (2007). Taxonomising induction. In A. Feeney & E. Heit (Eds.), *Inductive reasoning: Experimental, developmental and computational approaches* (pp. 328–343). Cambridge: Cambridge University Press.
Sloman, S. A., & Lagnado, D. (2005). The problem of induction. In R. Morrison & K. Holyoak (Eds.), *Cambridge handbook of thinking & reasoning* (pp. 95–116). Cambridge: Cambridge University Press.
Sloman, S. A., & Lagnado D. (2015). Causality in thought. *Annual Review of Psychology, 66*, 223–247.
Sloutsky, V. M. (2003) The role of similarity in the development of categorization. *Trends in Cognitive Sciences*, 7, 246–251.
Sloutsky, V. M., & Fisher, A. V. (2004). Induction and categorization in young children: A similarity-based model. *Journal of Experimental Psychology: General, 133*, 166–188.
Sloutsky, V. M., & Fisher, A. V. (2008). Attentional learning and flexible induction: How mundane mechanisms give rise to smart behaviors. *Child Development, 79*, 639–651.
Smyth, K., Feeney, A., Eidson, R. C., & Coley, J. D. (2017). Development of essentialist thinking about religion categories in Northern Ireland (and the United States). *Developmental Psychology, 53*, 475–496.
Tenenbaum, J. B., Kemp, C., & Shafto, P. (2007). Theory-based Bayesian models of category-based induction. In A. Feeney & E. Heit (Eds.), *Inductive reasoning: Experimental, developmental and computational approaches*. Cambridge: Cambridge University Press.
Travers, E., & Feeney, A. (2013) Diverse evidence for dissociable processes in inductive reasoning. In M. Knauff, M. Pauen, N. Sebanz, & I. Wachsmuth (Eds.), *Proceedings of the 35th annual conference of the Cognitive Science Society* (pp. 1474–1479). Austin, TX: Cognitive Science Society.
Travers, E., Rolison, J., Bright, A. K., & Feeney, A. (2015). Relations between associative and structured knowledge in category-based induction. In B. G. Bara, G. Airenti, N. Miyake, & G. Sandini (Eds.), *Proceedings of EuroAsianPacific joint conference on cognitive science*. Austin, TX: Cognitive Science Society.
Walker, C. M., Lombrozo, T., Legare, C., & Gopnik, A. (2014). Explaining prompts children to privilege inductively rich properties. *Cognition, 133*, 343–357.
Weber, M. J., & Osherson, D. (2014). Category-based induction from similarity of neural activation. *Cognitive, Affective & Behavioral Neuroscience, 14*, 24–36.
Wilburn, C., & Feeney, A. (2008). Do development and learning really decrease memory? On similarity and category-based induction in adults and children. *Cognition, 106*, 1451–1464.

11
ANALOGICAL REASONING

Dedre Gentner and Francisco Maravilla

Author note

This research was supported by a grant to the senior author from the Office of Naval Research; award number N00014-16-1-2613.

Introduction

Analogical ability – the ability to recognize and reason about common relational structure across different contexts – is a core mechanism in human cognition and a key contributor to higher-order cognition. This chapter describes the processes that underlie analogical reasoning and reviews findings in the field as well as future directions for analogical research.

Defining analogy

Analogy is a kind of similarity in which the same system of relations holds across different sets of elements. Analogies thus capture parallels across different situations. The elements that belong to the two situations need not be similar, but the relations that hold the systems together must be alike. However, as discussed below, analogical processing is easier if some concrete features are also shared.

Analogical mapping is often used to connect a familiar situation – the *base* or *source* analog – with an unfamiliar or abstract situation – the *target* analog. When such an alignment has been established, the base situation provides a model that can be used to explain and draw predictions concerning the target situation. For example, an analogy used in explaining cell metabolism is "Mitochondria are the furnace (or powerhouse) of the cell." This analogy conveys that mitochondria produce energy for cells, and also highlights the shared relational structure – that both mitochondrial behavior and the behavior of a furnace carry out energy-generating transformations that consume fuel:

- A furnace takes in fuel and generates energy in the form of heat.
- Mitochondria take in fuel (glucose) and generate energy in the form of ATP (adenosine triphosphate, a molecule that the cell can use for energy).

An analogy often invites further reasoning. For example, knowing that burning requires oxygen, one might (correctly) guess that mitochondria might also require oxygen to perform their transformation, and whether CO_2 is produced as a byproduct.

Although analogical reasoning is prominent in explanation and instruction, it is also widely used in informal contexts, and in areas from visual perception to social cognition. For example, analogy is a common method of argumentation in the social and political arena. After the Supreme Court removed a major section of the Voting Rights Act in 2013, Ruth Bader Ginsburg stated,

> Throwing out preclearance when it has worked and is continuing to work to stop discriminatory changes is like throwing away your umbrella in a rainstorm because you are not getting wet.

Analogy is also used in advice and prediction. When the stock market plunged after the World Trade Center attack on September 11, 2001, many writers argued by analogy to the 1929 crash that the market would be higher after a few years. Although analogical thinking seems to come naturally to people, it nonetheless involves an intricate set of underlying processes. We next describe these processes.

Analogical mapping

Mapping is the central process involved in analogical reasoning, and has been the main focus of research in both psychology and computer science (Gentner & Forbus, 2011). Theories of analogy have largely converged on a set of assumptions laid out in Gentner's structure-mapping theory (Gentner, 1983; Gentner & Markman, 1997). According to this theory, the mapping process involves establishing a ***structural alignment*** between two representations based on their common relational structure.

The process of structural alignment is guided by tacit constraints that lead to the extraction of shared systems with maximal structural consistency. One such constraint is ***one-to-one correspondence*** – the requirement that each element of one representation may match with, at most, one element from the other. The second requirement for structural consistency is *parallel connectivity*: if two predicates correspond, their arguments must also correspond, playing like roles.

There is considerable empirical support for structural consistency in analogical processing (Krawczyk, Holyoak, & Hummel, 2005; Markman, 1997; Markman & Gentner, 1993a; Spellman & Holyoak, 1992). For example, Spellman and Holyoak (1992) asked people to draw analogies from a then-current political event (Operation Desert Storm) to a historically salient one (World War II). People differed on the best mapping, but they generally maintained structural consistency within their mappings. Those who matched George Bush with FDR went on to generate the structurally consistent mapping of the United States during Desert Storm to the United States in World War II. Those who matched George Bush with Winston Churchill went on to map the United States during Desert Storm to Britain during World War II. Even when reasoning about then-current events, people maintained internal consistency in the mappings they made, suggesting that this kind of structural consistency is important in the mapping process.

Markman and Gentner (1993a) used pairs like that, as shown in Figure 11.1, to test the claim that the comparison process involves structural alignment. To do this, they devised a ***one-shot mapping task***. With both pictures in front of the participant, the researcher pointed to the woman in A and asked, "What does this go with in the other picture?" Subjects often choose the object match (e.g., the woman in B). A second group was asked to perform the same one-shot mapping

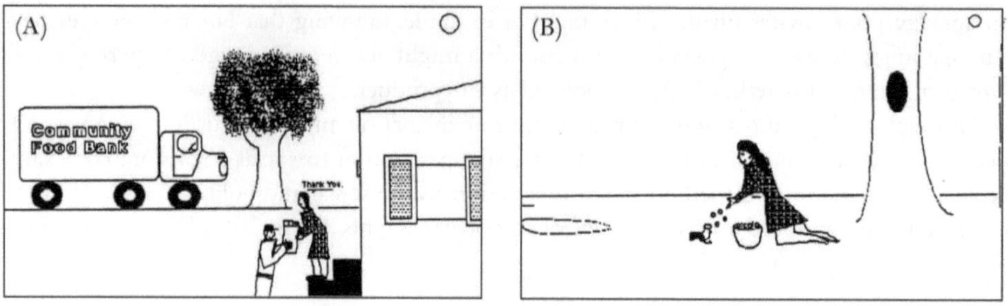

Figure 11.1 Example of a causal analogy (Markman & Gentner, 1993b). Scene (B) has both an object match (the woman) and a relational match (GIVING) with (A), though the role in which each object participates in the relation is different. After comparing the two scenes, people tend to match objects that have the same role (mapping woman in (A) to squirrel in (B)), based on the structural alignment between the scenes.

task, but before doing so they were asked to rate the similarity of each pair. These people were far more likely to choose the squirrel in B – evidence that the process of comparison induced a structural alignment based on common relational structure (man gives food to *woman*/woman gives food to *squirrel*). Further, the higher the similarity rating, the stronger was the tendency to choose the relational match, suggesting that finding a relational alignment induces a sense of similarity.

The pair in Figure 11.1 is an example of a *cross-mapping* – a pair in which there are object similarities that are inconsistent with the best relational alignment (Gentner & Toupin, 1986). Cross-mappings are useful in analogical research, because they allow us to gauge whether a person can arrive at a relational alignment despite the immediate appeal of the object match. For example, early in learning, children often choose an object match over a relational match. Even for adults, overcoming a cross-mapping can be challenging, as discussed below.

Along with structural consistency, analogical mapping is guided by what Gentner (1983) termed the *systematicity principle*. In analogical mapping, people prefer to match large, deeply connected systems, rather than sets of unrelated matches. To put it more precisely, systematicity reflects a preference for common systems that include higher-order constraining relations, such as causal relations (Clement & Gentner, 1991). For example, Gentner, Rattermann, and Forbus (1993) asked people to rate the similarity and soundness of pairs of stories that shared a set of events. (Soundness was described as the extent to which inferences could be made from one story to the other; it was intended as a proxy for relational similarity.) Half the stories also shared higher-order relations that linked those events into a system; the other half did not. As predicted by the systematicity principle, people rated stories with shared higher-order structure (such as causal relations between events) as more sound than those without such structure. Perhaps surprisingly, they also rated these pairs as more similar than pairs without shared higher-order relational structure. We suggest that this desire for systematicity reflects an implicit preference for coherence and inferential power.

Work in cognitive modeling has bolstered these empirical findings. The Structure-Mapping Engine (SME) is a computational model of the structure-mapping process including both alignment and inference projection (Falkenhainer, Forbus, & Gentner, 1989; Forbus, Ferguson, Lovett, & Gentner, 2017; Forbus, Gentner, & Law, 1995). SME operates in a local-to-global fashion. It first finds all possible local matches between representational elements of the two analogs, without regard for structural consistency. Structural consistency is imposed at the next stage, when SME combines the local matches into structurally consistent clusters (called kernels), which are in turn combined into overall mappings. The largest and most deeply connected structures are favored in this consolidation process (following systematicity). Though SME is specifically built on the cognitive principles of structure-mapping, many of its features have been incorporated into other models of analogical reasoning, including ACME (Holyoak & Thagard, 1989), AMBR (Kokinov & Petrov, 2001), CAB (Larkey & Love, 2003), DORA (Doumas, Hummel, & Sandhofer, 2008), and LISA (Hummel & Holyoak, 1997, 2003; see Gentner & Forbus, 2011, for a review).

Inference projection

Analogical inference is important in learning and reasoning, but it poses a challenge for theories of analogy. Between any two nonidentical things there may be countless potential inferences. If we had to consider them all, analogy would be useless. This *selection problem* is dealt with in structure-mapping by requiring that inferences be connected to the common system. Once the representations have been aligned and the common relational structure identified, *candidate inferences* are projected from the base to the target. Candidate inferences are further assertions that belong to the common system and are present in the base but not (yet) in the target. Importantly, these inferences are not guaranteed to be valid in the target; they must be further evaluated, as discussed in the next section.

In a good explanatory analogy, the common system is more elaborated in the base than in the target. Once the two are aligned, candidate inferences from the base serve to complete the relational pattern in the target. For example, in the "Mitochondria are like a furnace" analogy, we might infer that just as oxidation of fuel in a furnace generates undesirable by-products (e.g., soot), so the oxidation of glucose by mitochondria produces undesirable by-products – in this case, free radicals (highly reactive atoms).

To make this clearer, consider a schematic representation of the process of structural alignment and inference projection (Figure 11.2). Once the base and target have been aligned and a common structure has been identified (Figure 11.2A), if there are additional assertions in the base representation connected to this common structure, they will be automatically projected to the target as candidate inferences (Figure 11.2B). Whether or not there are new inferences, the common system that emerges from structural alignment may be retained as an abstraction of the structure shared (Figure 11.2C).

These predictions are supported by psychological studies. For example, when making comparisons, people prefer to make inferences from structurally consistent mappings (Markman, 1997). Further, people project these inferences in a structurally sensitive way, attaching them to the appropriate role in the relational structure of the target domain (Clement & Gentner, 1991; Day & Gentner, 2007; Spellman & Holyoak, 1996).

Evaluation

As mentioned in the previous section, the inferences generated via analogical processing are only *plausible guesses;* discovering whether they are true in the target requires further reasoning. If an analogy produces inferences that are clearly false or untenable in the target, people will generally reject the analogy. One mitigating factor is *adaptability*: inferences that can readily be modified to fit the target are accepted more readily than those that are less so (Keane, 1996). In problem-solving, the adaptability of inferences from one domain to another can influence the

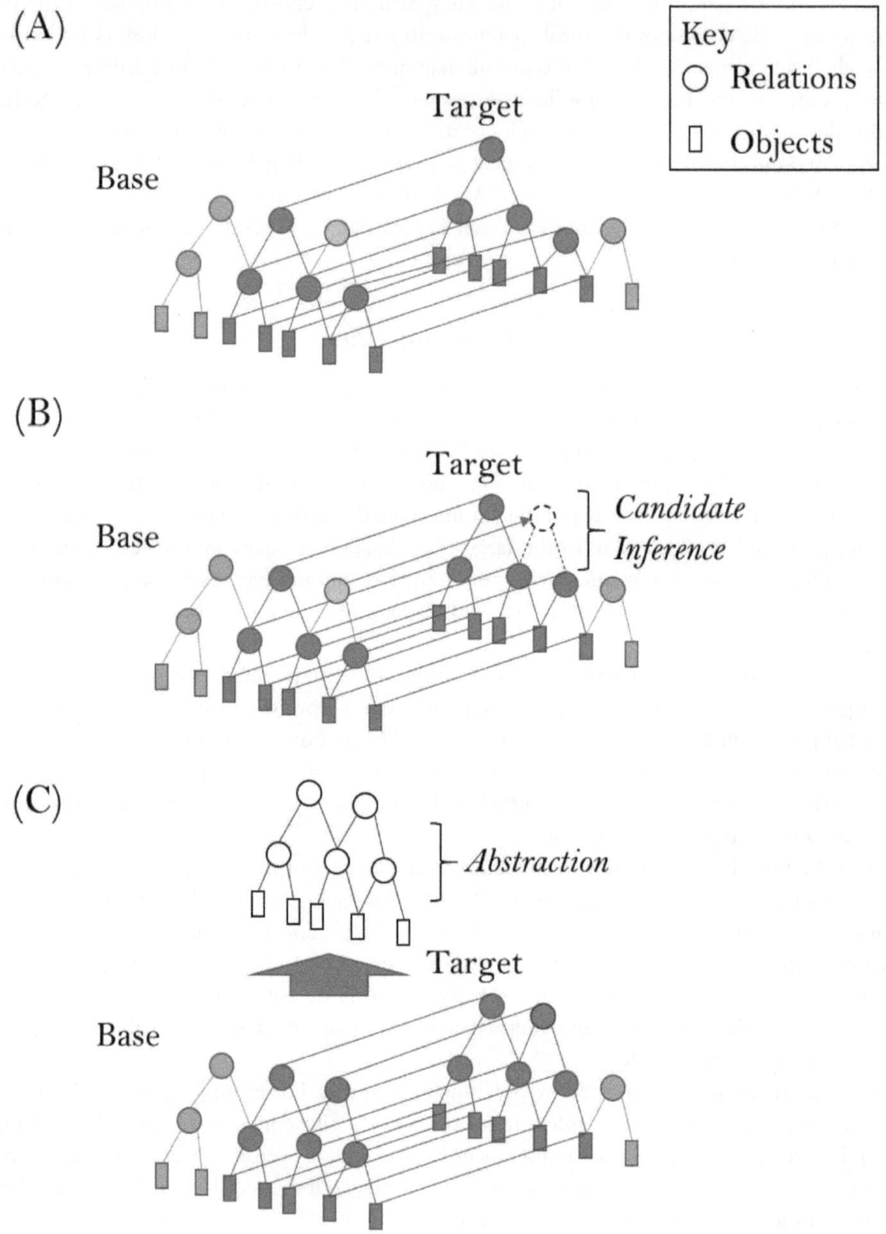

Figure 11.2 Analogy as structure-mapping. (A) Initial alignment of common relational structure. (B) Candidate inferences are generated by exporting structurally-consistent elements from target to base. (C) Abstraction of common structure.

ease with which subjects solve mathematical problems (Novick & Holyoak, 1991). An exception to this generality occurs in scientific inquiry: even if it is not possible to determine the truth of an inference, it may be retained as a prediction, especially if there is good support for the analogy as a whole (Forbus, Gentner, Everett, & Wu, 1997; Nersessian, 1984).

A second factor in the evaluation of inferences, especially in problem-solving contexts, is *goal relevance.* Even if an inference is both structurally consistent and valid, it is likely to be discarded if it is irrelevant to the task at hand (Clement & Gentner, 1991). Goal relevance has been explored as a major factor in analogical reasoning in the theories of Keith Holyoak (1985) and colleagues. They propose that inferences that are relevant to the current goals of the reasoner are more likely to be projected during analogical inference, and are more important in evaluating the analogy. For example, Spellman and Holyoak (1996) showed that when two possible mappings are available for an analogy, people prefer the one that generates candidate inferences most applicable to their current goals.

Another factor often considered in inference evaluation is the analogy's potential for ***knowledge generation*** (Forbus et al., 1997). Analogies that yield unexpected new inferences represent a greater potential gain of knowledge (as long as the inferences are not proven false). Though this strategy is potentially risky – huge leaps are not always warranted – it can prove advantageous. When reasoning about new domains or brainstorming for creative solutions, bold advances are often worth considering.

Analogy and similarity

The structure-mapping framework applies not only to analogy but also to overall similarity (Gentner & Markman, 1997; Goldstone, Medin, & Gentner, 1991; Markman & Gentner, 1993a). Analogy and similarity differ primarily in the overlap of shared relations and objects between base and target. In analogy, only the relational structure is shared, whereas in overall similarity the two representations share both relational structure and object properties.

Importantly, the difference between literal similarity and analogy is not dichotomous – it is a continuum. Examples of shared relational structure may be purely analogical (*anger is like a tea kettle*), literally similar (*my tea kettle is like your tea kettle*), or somewhere in the middle (*a steam engine is like a teakettle*). The continuum from overall similarity to analogy is psychologically important. Generally, it is easier for people to recognize and map overall similarity comparisons than pure analogies. For this reason, overall similarity comparisons often serve as points of entry for children and other novice learners, as discussed below.

Analogical learning

Analogy is a powerful learning mechanism. As discussed above, analogies can project information from one analog to the other. Though the role of inference projection is widely studied and central to the mapping process, it is not the only process that facilitates learning. Analogy can augment and extend knowledge in at least three other ways: *schema abstraction* (generalization), ***difference detection*** (contrast), and ***re-representation.*** The following section discusses these processes and their role in analogical learning.

Schema abstraction

As just discussed, structural alignment highlights commonalities between two analogs. This promotes the abstraction of common relational structure across different exemplars. The common structure may be stored in memory as an abstraction and used again for later exemplars (Gick & Holyoak, 1983; Loewenstein, Thompson, & Gentner, 1999; Markman & Gentner, 1993b; Namy & Gentner, 2002). This may be seen in studies of analogical problem solving. When people compare two analogous cases before solving an analogous test case, they show high transfer of the study solution, relative to studying only one prior case (Gick & Holyoak, 1983) or studying the same two cases without comparing them (Catrambone & Holyoak, 1989; Loewenstein et al., 1999). For example, Loewenstein et al. (1999) gave business school students two cases to study. The cases were analogous to each other, although different in surface content – that is, they both depicted the same negotiation strategy. Half the students were told to compare the two scenarios; the other half read each scenario in succession and gave advice. Then pairs of students engaged in a test negotiation that was analogous to the cases. Those who had explicitly compared the two scenarios were over twice as likely to transfer the negotiation strategy to the new test case than those who had studied the same two scenarios without comparing them. Further, the quality of the relational schema that was abstracted from the two analogs predicted the degree of successful transfer (Gick & Holyoak, 1983; Loewenstein et al., 1999). This is evidence that the common schema generated through analogical comparison is an important mediator of transfer to new situations (Gentner & Kurtz, 2005; Gick & Holyoak, 1983).

Difference detection

In addition to facilitating the abstraction of relational commonalities, the structural alignment process also highlights ***alignable differences*** between analogs (Markman & Gentner, 1993b). These are differences that play the same role in the common system in both analogs. Psychologically, alignable differences tend to be rapidly noticed – there is a kind of pop-out effect. Consider the pairs in Figure 11.3. When asked to indicate whether the exemplars of a pair were *same* or ***different***, people were faster for pair B than pair A, consistent with prior findings that 'different' judgments are faster the more different the pairs are (Goldstone & Medin, 1994; Luce, 1986). However, when asked to state a *specific* difference, the opposite was true – people were faster for pair A than for pair B (Sagi, Gentner & Lovett, 2012).

At first glance, this might seem counterintuitive – one might expect that the sheer number of differences in pair B would hasten finding any single difference, compared to having to find one of the many fewer differences in pair A. Yet on further examination, these findings are explained by considering that the high spatial alignability of pair A facilitates the alignment of shared structure. This alignment in turn leads to pop-out of alignable differences, such as the difference in petal color or shape (Sagi, Gentner, & Lovett, 2012).

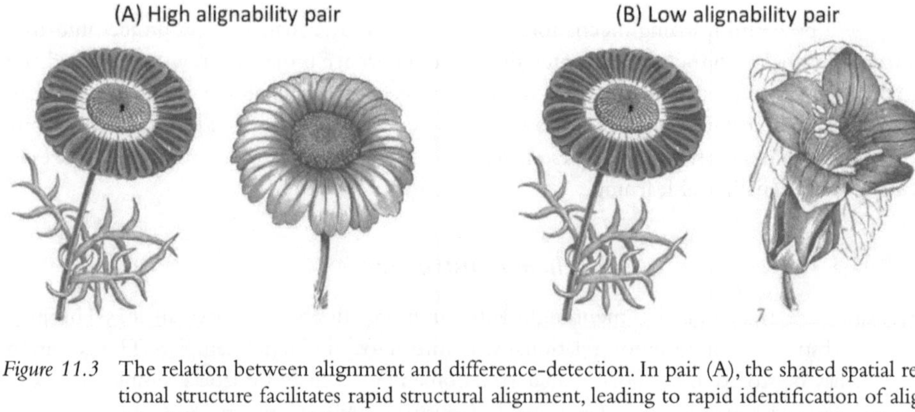

Figure 11.3 The relation between alignment and difference-detection. In pair (A), the shared spatial relational structure facilitates rapid structural alignment, leading to rapid identification of alignable differences (e.g. black versus white petals, or flat versus curved petals). Pair (B) lacks this spatial overlap, resulting in slower identification of specific differences (Sagi, Gentner, & Lovett, 2012).

The advantage of alignable differences is also seen for conceptual comparisons. For example, Gentner and Markman (1994) gave people a set of word pairs and asked them to list a difference for as many pairs as possible in a brief time period. Participants identified differences for many more high-similarity pairs than low-similarity pairs, and this surplus was chiefly made up of alignable differences. For instance, for the high-similar pair *hotel–motel*, people typically listed an alignable difference such as "A hotel is expensive; a motel is cheap". This is an alignable difference (because *expensive* and *cheap* play the same roles in their respective representations). In contrast, for the low-similarity pair *magazine–kitten*, those who listed differences often simply stated a fact about one item and negated it for the other: e.g., "You read a magazine, but you do not read a kitten" (a nonalignable difference).

Thus, alignment processes influence which differences people notice as well as which commonalities they notice. The high salience of alignable differences can be used to facilitate learning and reasoning. For example, in a study in the Chicago Children's Museum, children were shown two model buildings, one with a diagonal brace (conferring stability) and the other with a horizontal piece instead. All children were shown which building was stable and which was wobbly. But only if the two buildings were highly similar – supporting alignment and the pop-out of alignable differences – did children detect this critical difference and transfer it to their own constructions (Gentner et al., 2016).

Re-representation

In analogical mapping, people seek identical relations between the two analogs (Gentner, 1983). Of course, this refers to the conceptual relations, not to the words used to describe the relations. For example, *Attila burned the fort* and *Napoleon torched the castle* convey the same conceptual relation. But even when two potential analogs have nonidentical conceptual relations, they may still be found to be analogous, if processes of re-representation reveal relational identicalities. For example, *Attila burned the fort* and *Napoleon tore down the castle* can be considered analogous if the two relations *burned* and *tore down* are re-represented as *destroyed*. When there is evidence that initially non-identical relations should match, they may be re-represented to fit a consistent mapping (Forbus et al., 1995; Kotovsky & Gentner, 1996; Yan, Forbus, & Gentner, 2003). This flexibility allows for some of the productivity of analogical processing and provides another route by which analogy can lead to abstraction.

Summary

Structural alignment identifies common systems of relations between two analogs. This process potentiates learning and reasoning in several ways: (1) highlighting of common relational systems, often resulting in abstracting and retaining that common structure; (2) projection of candidate inferences from the base to the target; and (3) detection of alignable differences. We now turn to analogical retrieval from memory.

Analogical retrieval

As we have seen, people are quite sophisticated in analogical reasoning when both analogs are present (physically or mentally) during the mapping process. But what makes us think of an analogy in the first place? We now turn to another important case of analogy in action – namely, *analogical retrieval*. This refers to the phenomenon by which, while thinking about a topic or scenario, people are reminded of a similar past experience, which they then align (or attempt to align) with the current situation that sparked this retrieval. It is generally agreed that analogical reminding involves a set of overlapping but distinct processes (Forbus et al., 1995; Gentner et al., 1993; Holyoak & Koh, 1987; Novick, 1988):

- *Retrieval*: given some current topic in working memory, a person may be reminded of a prior analogous situation in long-term memory.
- *Mapping:* once the two cases are present in working memory (in this case, through analogical retrieval), mapping is carried out as already described: by aligning the representations (and if all goes well, noting their commonalities and or alignable differences, and projecting inferences from one analog to the other).
- *Evaluation:* once an analogical mapping has been done, the analogy and its inferences are judged for relevance and validity in the target.

We have already discussed mapping and evaluation. Now we turn to retrieval. The sad conclusion from a large body of research is that analogical retrieval often fails. The classic study was done by Gick and Holyoak (1980, 1983). They gave people a difficult thought problem (Duncker, 1945): how can a surgeon cure an inoperable tumor without using so much radiation that the surrounding flesh will be killed? Only about 10% of the participants came up with the ideal solution, which is to converge on the tumor with several weak beams of radiation. Performance improved if, prior to the tumor problem, participants read an analogous story (in which soldiers converged on a fort from many directions). In that case, about 30% produced convergence solutions. Yet the majority of participants still failed; they did not experience any reminding of the converging-army story, even though they had heard it earlier in the same session. Importantly, they had not forgotten the earlier story: when they were given the hint to "think about that story you heard before," the percentage of correct convergence solutions nearly tripled, to about 80%. This shows that even when a highly useful relational match is present in LTM, we often fail to retrieve it. Failure to access useful analogs is a major cause of failure to transfer in education.

Further research has shown that similarity-based retrieval relies heavily on surface similarities, such as similarities in object features, rather than on common relational structure (Brooks, Norman, & Allen, 1991; Catrambone, 2002; Gentner et al., 1993; Holyoak & Koh, 1987; Ross, 1984, 1987). For example, Gentner, Rattermann, and Forbus (1993) gave participants an initial set of stories to memorize. Participants were later given new stories that varied both in surface and relational similarity from the first set and were asked to indicate any previous stories of which they were reminded. Participants were reminded of many more stories that shared surface similarities than stories that shared common relational structure (including plot structure). Yet when asked to rate the similarity and inferential soundness of pairs of stories, the same participants rated stories that shared relational commonalities, such as plot structure, as more similar. Figure 11.4 shows the surprising dissociation between the kind of similarity that promotes memory and the kind that people consider useful for mapping and inference.

In sum, although we are highly effective at analogical mapping once we have two items co-present in our attention, the weak point in the chain is reminding. Not only do we fail to retrieve good matches, but we often instead retrieve poor matches – matches that share surface features, but not relational structure, with the situation we're reasoning about. On the positive side, retrieval of overall similarity matches is quite good: across studies, people retrieved about 60% of the overall similarity matches, as compared to 10% of the purely relational matches (Gentner et al., 1993). This is important, because overall similarity matches, though mundane,

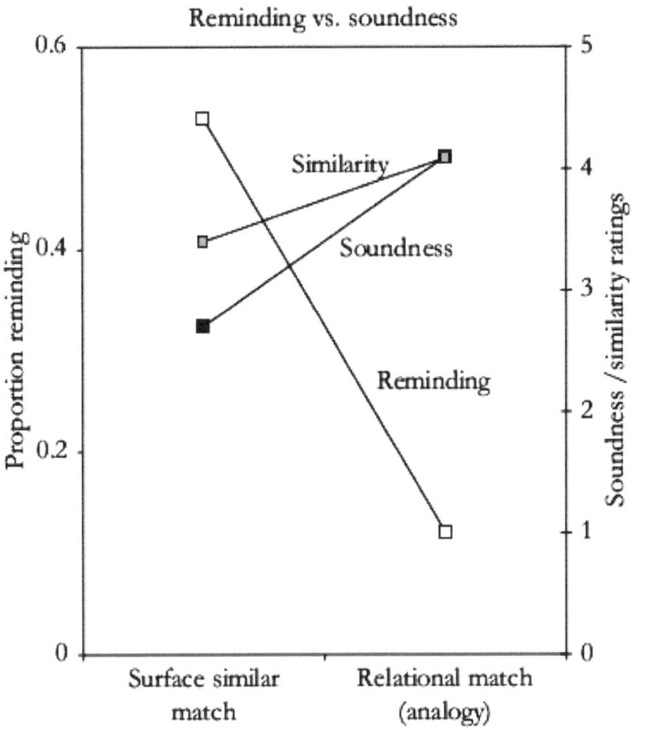

Figure 11.4 Results from Gentner, Rattermann, and Forbus (1993), Experiment 2. Surface-similar matches produce more remindings, even though relational matches were rated higher in both soundness and similarity.

have strong predictive power. If your jammed toaster reminds you of another jammed toaster, it is likely that the same solution will work.

Some researchers have argued that the above studies underestimate the level of relational reminding in real life and that with familiar materials, people would show more relational reminding (Blanchette & Dunbar, 2001). Trench and Minervino (2015) addressed this issue by using an arena in which participants had considerable prior experience – namely, popular films such as *Jurassic Park*. (All participants were tested after this study to ensure familiarity with the films.) The researchers gave people new situations that were analogous to key situations from these films, but which varied in surface similarity. The task was to generate a persuasive analogy that would guide the new character's behavior. This allowed participants to draw on personal experience, while controlling for prior knowledge and the similarity of the prior knowledge items. The results bore out the laboratory results, showing strong effects of surface similarity. When the target was highly surface-similar to a prior film, people retrieved and used that film as an analogy about 70% of the time; however, when the prior film was relationally similar but not surface similar, people retrieved it only 30% of the time.

Although retrieving pure relational analogs from memory is challenging, there are some mitigating factors. First, as people gain expertise in a domain, they become better able to retrieve true relational remindings (Novick, 1988). This effect may be due in part to learning a unifying conceptual vocabulary (Jamrozik & Gentner, 2013). Second, surface similarity is often correlated with relational similarity in real experience. This is the ***kind world*** hypothesis (Gentner,

1989): what looks like a tiger is very likely to *be* a tiger, with the relational characteristics of a tiger, such as 'eats other animals'. Third, when we do retrieve matches that have only surface similarity, and no deeper relational match to what we're thinking about, we can often quickly reject the reminding as irrelevant. For example, in the story-memory task described earlier Gentner, Rattermann, and Forbus (1993) asked people to rate story pairs (consisting of the probe story along with a story from the memory list) after they completed the memory task. The pairs they were given included the surface-similar stories they had been reminded of, as well as pairs that were relationally similar. People rated the surface-similar stories – even the ones they had been reminded of – as poor matches to the probes, and considered relational matches to be highly similar and inferentially sound (whether or not they had retrieved them). In other words, we are not at the mercy of our remindings; people are often able to filter out the poor matches that memory may provide.

Indeed, there is evidence that people can generate good analogies by an iterative process of retrieving, adjusting, and filtering candidate analogs. For example, Clement (1988) gave physicists challenging problems to solve, such as deciding which (if either) would stretch more: a spring with a weight hung on it or another spring with the same weight whose coils are twice the diameter of the first spring. People used a variety of methods to generate and test analogies. For example, some subjects analogized the spring problem to long and short horizontal rods bent by the same weight; the long rod would bend more, so they inferred (correctly) that the larger spring would extend more. This and other productive analogies were not simply retrieved from memory. Clement observed active construction and adaptation processes during the reasoning sessions, which typically required over 20 minutes. The active generation and filtering of analogies also occurs in less formal domains. For example, Blanchette and Dunbar (2000) gave participants the task of generating an analogy to defend a political decision to cut the national deficit. They found that people were able to generate relationally appropriate analogies, often without relying on surface similarity. As Blanchette and Dunbar point out, participants in this task were not obliged to report their first reminding; they had the opportunity to select among possible analogs.

Development of analogical ability

When young children are given an analogy they tend to be influenced strongly by object matches, attending less to relational matches than do adults and older children (Gentner, 1988; Gentner & Rattermann, 1991; Honomichl & Chen, 2006; Mix, 2008; Paik & Mix, 2006; Richland, Morrison, & Holyoak, 2006). The transition in the course of development from a focus on objects to a focus on relations has been termed the ***relational shift*** (Gentner, 1988). In the past 30 years there has been widespread agreement that this shift occurs. Gentner and Rattermann (1991) proposed that the shift is primarily driven by gains in domain knowledge, based on two kinds of evidence: (1) the same kind of relational shift is seen in adults as they learn a new domain (e.g., Chi, Feltovich, & Glaser, 1981); and (2) if young children are given new relational knowledge, they can make rapid gains in analogical performance within a single session (Gentner & Rattermann, 1991; Loewenstein & Gentner, 2005). However, the shift could also be driven by developmental increases in relational processing capacity (Halford, 1993), or executive functioning (e.g., better ability to inhibit a focus on object matches) (Richland et al., 2006; Thibaut, French, & Vezneva, 2010). Of course, these views are not mutually exclusive; it is likely that some combination of these factors explains the relational shift in development.

How do children learn to focus on relational commonalities? One way is by learning and using relational language, which can invite and support the use of relational representations (Gentner & Rattermann, 1991). For example, three-year-old children perform at chance in a challenging spatial analogy task (Figure 11.1); they often mistakenly choose an object match instead of a relational match. However, if the array is described using spatial relational language (*top, middle, bottom*) the children do much better (Loewenstein & Gentner, 2005); further, they retain their ability to do the task even after a few days' delay, with no reinstatement of the language – evidence that the spatial relational language invited a relational representation.

When does analogical mapping fail?

As we have reviewed, analogy can be valuable in learning and reasoning. However, analogical mapping does not always succeed. Three kinds of factors influence the outcome of an analogical mapping: first, factors internal to the mapping process itself; second, individual characteristics of the reasoner; and, third, task and context factors such as cognitive load and processing time.

Factors internal to the mapping. Transparency and systematicity have been found to be important in analogical problem-solving. The *transparency* of the mapping between two analogous situations – that is, the degree of similarity between corresponding objects – is a good predictor of people's ability to notice and apply solutions from one problem to the other. Highly transparent analogies are both readily noticed and easy to align. For example, Gentner and Kurtz (2006) asked adults to judge whether pairs of sentences were analogous. People were faster for highly transparent pairs than for equally analogous (but less surface-similar) matches. High transparency also aids transfer, not only by contributing to memory reminding (as discussed earlier), but also by facilitating the process of aligning the earlier problem with the current problem. Ross (1989) taught people algebra problems and later gave them new problems that followed the same principles. People were better able to map the solution from a prior problem to a current problem when the corresponding objects were highly similar between the two problems: for example, "How many golf balls per golfer" ◊ "How many tennis balls per tennis player." They performed worst in the cross-mapped condition, in which similar objects appeared in different roles across the two problems: for example, "How many golf balls per golfer" ◊ "How many tennis players per tennis ball."

The second internal factor is *systematicity* – the degree to which the common system forms a coherent, interconnected system connected by higher-order constraining relations, such as causality. When relational matches form an interconnected system, people are more likely to preserve a relational match, as amplified just below.

Characteristics of the reasoner. These factors internal to the analogy interact with characteristics of the reasoner, including age and experience. For example, cross-mapped analogies are especially difficult for children (Gentner & Rattermann, 1991; Gentner & Toupin, 1986; Richland et al., 2006), especially in cases where the object matches are rich and distinctive (Gentner & Rattermann, 1991; Paik & Mix, 2006). However, the ability to represent systematic relational structure can compensate for low transparency as learners progress in a domain. For example, Gentner and Toupin (1986) gave six- and nine-year-olds simple stories (illustrated with stuffed animals) and asked the children to reenact them with a new set of characters. The accuracy of retelling varied with the transparency of the stories. Children were nearly perfect in the high-transparency condition (where similar characters occupied corresponding roles), less accurate in the medium-transparency condition (where dissimilar characters had corresponding roles), and least accurate in the cross-mapped condition (where similar characters played different roles). Notably, older (but not younger) children benefited strongly from a manipulation that highlighted systematicity; when nine-year-olds were given a statement that summarized the higher-order structure of the plot, their mapping accuracy remained high across all conditions. This suggests that older children (like adult experts) were able to use the relational constraints provided by the higher-order structure to avoid tempting (but incorrect) object-mappings. These findings are emblematic of general principles of learning and development – the deeper and better-connected the relational knowledge structure, the better we are able to maintain the structure in the face of surface-level competition (Gentner & Toupin, 1986; Markman & Gentner, 1993a).

A final characteristic of the reasoner that affects analogical ability is damage to the cortical systems that support reasoning. Morrison et al. (2004) studied patients suffering from frontal or temporal lobe degeneration, using a one-shot mapping task similar to that used by Markman and Gentner (1993a) (with object matches competing with the relational alignment; see Figure 11.1). Both groups of patients showed deficits in analogical reasoning relative to age-matched controls. However, although both patient groups were impaired in selecting a relation-based match when there was a competing object match, the results suggested that the inability to inhibit the competing object match may have been a larger factor for patients with frontal degeneration. Other studies have also implicated the prefrontal cortex in relational reasoning. Using a task akin to Raven's matrix task (which requires relational alignment), Waltz et al. (1999) found that patients with prefrontal cortical damage showed selective impairment on problems requiring integrating multiple relations, relative to patients with anterior temporal lobe damage and to control subjects.

Task conditions. The third class of factors that can affect analogical processing are task conditions such as time pressure and processing load. For example, Goldstone and Medin (1994) found that when people were forced to terminate an analogy matching task early, they were strongly influenced by local object matches; with more time, they were more likely to choose a relational match. Another factor is cognitive load. Waltz et al. (2000) gave participants a task modeled on Markman and Gentner's (1993a) one-shot mapping task (with cross-mappings, as described earlier). Participants who were given a working memory load – a digit string to hold in memory during the task – performed worse than those who were not. Under memory load, people were more likely to match objects instead of following a relational match than were people who carried out the task with no load.

Analogy in the real world

Our discussion so far has emphasized laboratory studies. We now turn to analogy in real-world contexts. As we will see, many of the phenomena studied in the lab can be seen in the world at large. The history of science offers many examples of analogical thinking. Great pioneering figures such as Kepler and Faraday relied heavily on analogy in arriving at their discoveries (Gentner et al., 1997; Nersessian, 1984; Thagard, 1992), and the same pattern is seen among contemporary scientists (Dunbar, 1997). In pioneering work investigating the day-to-day reasoning of contemporary microbiologists, Dunbar (1993, 1997) found that analogical thinking was a central element in nearly all aspects of scientific reasoning, including hypothesis generation, experimental design, and data interpretation. Interestingly, many of the analogies Dunbar observed were high-transparency, sharing both causal structure and surface features. For example, a scientist investigating the functionality of a gene in one organism (e.g., an oyster) might draw an analogy to a gene in a similar organism (e.g., another kind of oyster), that had a well-understood function (Dunbar, 1997). It seems that scientists at the cutting edge of their field rely mainly on high-transparency analogies, just like college students and young children. This pattern is less surprising if we reflect that (a) high-transparency analogies are readily retrieved from memory; and (b) strong overall similarity matches allow for high confidence that the candidate inferences are likely to be correct. Although great breakthroughs are sometimes made by invoking far analogies that lead to major paradigm shifts (Gentner et al., 1997; Holyoak & Thagard, 1997; Nersessian, 1984; Thagard, 1992), science (like other kinds of human learning) often makes progress by mundane overall similarity.

Analogy is also prevalent in informal situations, such as politics and social judgment. People often make use of previous experience with familiar individuals when judging strangers (Andersen & Chen, 2002) or making sense of new social experiences (Mussweiler & Rüter, 2003). For example, Mussweiler and Rüter (2003) found that people make social judgments faster when they are primed to make analogical comparisons, with no loss of accuracy relative to a control group. People often argue for or against positions by analogy, and it is common to attack elements of an opponent's position by pointing out weakness in an analogy they have used. For instance, during the 2012 presidential election, Mitt Romney criticized President Obama's economic record and claimed that he, Romney, would be "the coach that leads America to its winning season," continuing, "If you have a coach that is zero and 23 million [referring to unemployment numbers], you say it's time to get a new coach." As reported in *New York* magazine (Amira, 2013), President Obama responded in kind by extending the analogy:

> He said he's going to be the coach that leads America to a winning season. The problem is everybody's already seen his economic playbook. We know what's in it. On first down, he hikes taxes by nearly $2,000 on the average family with kids. . . . On second down, he calls an audible and undoes reforms that are there to prevent another financial crisis and bank bailout. . . . And then on third down, he calls for a Hail Mary: ending Medicare as we know it. . . . That's their playbook.

Argument by analogy can be effective in politics. In addition to vividly describing the issue, such analogies may convey a relational structure – such as "Romney's plan doesn't make sense" – through a domain more accessible to some voters, such as sports. Likewise, Blanchette and Dunbar (2001) surveyed a large set of newspaper articles on the issue of Québécois secession, and found that they often used analogies, which tended to be from familiar arenas such as agriculture, family, and sports.

Part of the appeal of President Obama's analogy is its humor; a humorous analogy can bring home a conceptual point. For example, Frank Oppenheimer, the brother of Robert Oppenheimer and a noted physicist in his own right, offered this analogy: "understanding is a lot like sex. It's got a practical purpose, but that's not why people do it normally" (Cole, 1997, p. 5).

Oppenheimer's point – that pursuing understanding is intrinsically and intensely rewarding – is all the more persuasive in its humorous clothing. Loewenstein and Heath (2009) conducted a large-scale survey of jokes and discovered that many of them follow a specific analogical pattern, which they call the ***repetition-break*** sequence.[1] This is a three-part structure that begins with two highly similar episodes – high-transparency matches for which structural alignment is virtually automatic, leading the common schema to emerge. The third episode breaks the structure – it is partly parallel, but differs in some striking way. This incongruity generates a humorous outcome, as in "A doctor, a lawyer, and a psychologist walk into a bar . . ."

The final instance of everyday analogical reasoning that we will discuss concerns the use and adaptation of figurative language. Conventional metaphor systems, extensively studied by George Lakoff and colleagues, serve to connect abstract domains with more concrete domains

(Lakoff & Johnson, 1980). Metaphors like "their relationship has reached a crossroads" and "the last few months of our marriage have been rocky, but we'll reach the other side" belong to a larger metaphorical system, characterized as "a relationship is a journey." Such metaphorical systems may begin as series of literal comparison statements, entering the language over time through repeated structural alignment (Bowdle & Gentner, 2005). Such systematic mappings may affect how people conceptualize policy issues (Thibodeau & Boroditsky, 2011), though the extent of this effect is debated (Steen, Reijnierse, & Burgers, 2014).

Conclusion

Analogical ability – the ability to recognize relational similarity across situations – is a core capacity of higher-order learning and reasoning. We have reviewed research on the cognitive processes that underlie analogical reasoning and support analogical learning and abstraction. We have provided examples of the use of analogical reasoning from politics, scientific investigation, and learning and development.

Over the roughly thirty years that analogy has been the subject of committed research in cognitive science, great strides have been made in understanding and modeling analogical processing. Yet there are still many open questions. We are only beginning to probe the neural underpinnings of analogical processing and to investigate the analogical abilities of other species. As the study of relational reasoning progresses, we will better understand its role in the range of human cognitive experience.

Note

1 The repetition-break structure is also used in many children's stories – for instance, *The Three Little Pigs*. Here the high similarity of the first two episodes invites alignment, allowing the child to see a pattern; this makes the change in the third episode salient.

References

Amira, D. (2013, January 17). An illustrated guide to President Obama's favorite political analogies. *New York Magazine*. Retrieved from http://nymag.com/daily/intelligencer/2013/01/obama-metaphors-analogies-dinner-slurpee-mop.html

Andersen, S. M., & Chen, S. (2002). The relational self: An interpersonal social-cognitive theory. *Psychological Review, 109*(4), 619–645. https://doi.org/10.1037/0033-295X.109.4.619

Blanchette, I., & Dunbar, K. (2000). How analogies are generated: The roles of structural and superficial similarity. *Memory & Cognition, 28*(1), 108–124. https://doi.org/10.3758/BF03211580

Blanchette, I., & Dunbar, K. (2001). Analogy use in naturalistic settings: The influence of audience, emotion, and goals. *Memory & Cognition, 29*(5), 730–735. https://doi.org/10.3758/BF03200475

Blanchette, I., & Dunbar, K. (2002). Representational change and analogy: How analogical inferences alter target representations. *Journal of Experimental Psychology: Learning Memory and Cognition, 28*(4), 672–685.

Bowdle, B. F., & Gentner, D. (2005). The career of metaphor. *Psychological Review, 112*(1), 193–216. https://doi.org/10.1037/0033-295X.112.1.193

Brooks, L. R., Norman, G. R., & Allen, S. W. (1991). Role of specific similarity in a medical diagnostic task. *Journal of Experimental Psychology: General, 120*(3), 278–287. https://doi.org/10.1037/0096-3445.120.3.278

Catrambone, R. (2002). The effects of surface and structural feature matches on the access of story analogs. *Journal of Experimental Psychology: Learning, Memory, and Cognition, 28*(2), 318–334. https://doi.org/10.1037/0278-7393.28.2.318

Catrambone, R., & Holyoak, K. J. (1989). Overcoming contextual limitations on problem-solving transfer. *Journal of Experimental Psychology: Learning, Memory, and Cognition, 15*(6), 1147–1156. https://doi.org/10.1037/0278-7393.15.6.1147

Chi, M. T. H., Feltovich, P. J., & Glaser, R. (1981). Categorization and representation of physics problems by experts and novices. *Cognitive Science, 5*(2), 121–152. https://doi.org/10.1207/s15516709cog0502_2

Clement, C. A., & Gentner, D. (1991). Systematicity as a selection constraint in analogical mapping. *Cognitive Science, 15*(1), 89–132. https://doi.org/10.1207/s15516709cog1501_3

Clement, J. J. (1988). Observed methods for generating analogies in scientific problem solving. *Cognitive Science, 12*(4), 563–586. https://doi.org/10.1207/s15516709cog1204_3

Cole, K. C. (1997). *The universe and the teacup: The mathematics of truth and beauty*. Orlando, FL: Harcourt Books.

Day, S. B., & Gentner, D. (2007). Nonintentional analogical inference in text comprehension. *Memory & Cognition, 35*, 39–49.

Doumas, L., Hummel, J. E., & Sandhofer, C. M. (2008). A theory of the discovery and predication of relational concepts. *Psychological Review, 115*(1), 1–43. https://doi.org/10.1037/0033-295X.115.1.1

Dunbar, K. (1993). Concept discovery in a scientific domain. *Cognitive Science, 17*(3), 397–434. https://doi.org/http://dx.doi.org/

Dunbar, K. (1997). How scientists think: On-line creativity and conceptual change in science. In T. B. Ward, S. M. Smith, & J. Vaid (Eds.), *Creative thought: An investigation of conceptual structures and processes* (pp. 461–493). Washington, DC: American Psychological Association.

Duncker, K. (1945). On problem-solving. *Psychological Monographs, 58*(5), i. https://doi.org/10.1037/h0093599

Falkenhainer, B., Forbus, K. D., & Gentner, D. (1989). The structure-mapping engine: Algorithm and examples. *Artificial Intelligence, 41*(1), 1–63. https://doi.org/10.1016/0004-3702(89)90077-5

Forbus, K. D., Ferguson, R. W., Lovett, A., & Gentner, D. (2017). Extending SME to handle large-scale cognitive modeling. *Cognitive Science, 41*, 1152–1201.

Forbus, K. D., Gentner, D., Everett, J., & Wu, M. (1997). Towards a computational model of evaluating and using analogical inferences. In M. G. Shafto & P. Langley (Eds.), *Proceedings of the nineteenth annual conference of the cognitive science society* (pp. 229–234). Stanford: Stanford University & Psychology Press.

Forbus, K. D., Gentner, D., & Law, K. (1995). MAC/FAC: A model of similarity-based retrieval. *Cognitive Science, 19*(2), 141–205. https://doi.org/10.1207/s15516709cog1902_1

Gentner, D. (1983). Structure-mapping: A theoretical framework for analogy. *Cognitive Science*, 7(2), 155–170. https://doi.org/10.1016/S0364-0213(83)80009-3

Gentner, D. (1988). Metaphor as structure mapping: The relational shift. *Child Development, 59*(1), 47–59. https://doi.org/10.2307/1130388

Gentner, D. (1989). The mechanisms of analogical learning. In S. Vosniadou & A. Ortony (Eds.), *Similarity and analogical reasoning* (pp. 199–241). London: Cambrige University Press.

Gentner, D., Brem, S., Ferguson, R. W., Markman, A. B., Levidow, B. B., Wolff, P., & Forbus, K. D. (1997). Analogical reasoning and conceptual change: A case study of Johannes Kepler. *Journal of the Learning Sciences, 6*(1), 3–40. https://doi.org/10.1207/s15327809jls0601_2

Gentner, D., & Forbus, K. D. (2011). Computational models of analogy. *Wiley Interdisciplinary Reviews: Cognitive Science, 2*(3), 266–276. https://doi.org/10.1002/wcs.105

Gentner, D., & Kurtz, K. J. (2005). Relational categories. In A. Woo-Kyoung, R. L. Goldstone, B. C. Love, A. B. Markman, & P. Wolff (Eds.), *Categorization inside and outside the laboratory: Essays in honor of Douglas L. Medin* (pp. 151–175). Washington, DC: American Psychological Association.

Gentner, D., & Kurtz, K. J. (2006). Relations, objects, and the composition of analogies. *Cognitive Science, 30*(4), 609–642. https://doi.org/10.1207/s15516709cog0000_60

Gentner, D., Levine, S. C., Ping, R., Isaia, A., Dhillon, S., Bradley, C., & Honke, G. (2016). Rapid learning in a children's museum via analogical comparison. *Cognitive Science, 40*(1), 224–240. https://doi.org/10.1111/cogs.12248

Gentner, D., & Markman, A. B. (1994). Structural alignment in comparison: No difference without similarity. *Psychological Science, 5*(3), 152–158. https://doi.org/10.1111/j.1467-9280.1994.tb00652.x

Gentner, D., & Markman, A. B. (1997). Structure mapping in analogy and similarity. *American Psychologist, 52*(1), 45–56. https://doi.org/10.1037/0003-066X.52.1.45

Gentner, D., & Rattermann, M. J. (1991). Language and the career of similarity. In S. A. Gelman & J. P. Byrnes (Eds.), *Perspectives on language and thought: Interrelations in development* (pp. 225–277). London: Cambridge University Press.

Gentner, D., Rattermann, M. J., & Forbus, K. D. (1993). The roles of similarity in transfer: Separating retrievability from inferential soundness. *Cognitive Psychology, 25*(4), 524–575. https://doi.org/10.1006/cogp.1993.1013

Gentner, D., & Toupin, C. (1986). Systematicity and surface similarity in the development of analogy. *Cognitive Science, 10*(3), 277–300. https://doi.org/10.1207/s15516709cog1003_2
Gick, M. L., & Holyoak, K. J. (1980). Analogical problem solving. *Cognitive Psychology, 12*(3), 306–355. https://doi.org/10.1016/0010-0285(80)90013-4
Gick, M. L., & Holyoak, K. J. (1983). Schema induction and analogical transfer. *Cognitive Psychology, 15*(1), 1–38. https://doi.org/10.1016/0010-0285(83)90002-6
Goldstone, R. L., & Medin, D. L. (1994). Time course of comparison. *Journal of Experimental Psychology: Learning, Memory, and Cognition, 20*(1), 29–50. https://doi.org/10.1037/0278-7393.20.1.29
Goldstone, R. L., Medin, D. L., & Gentner, D. (1991). Relational similarity and the nonindependence of features in similarity judgments. *Cognitive Psychology, 23*(2), 222–262. https://doi.org/10.1016/0010-0285(91)90010-L
Halford, G. S. (1993). *Children's understanding: The development of mental models*. New York: Psychology Press.
Holyoak, K. J. (1985). Analogy as the core of cognition. In G. Bower (Ed.), *The psychology of learning and motivation* (Vol. 19, pp. 59–87). New York: Academic Press.
Holyoak, K. J., & Koh, K. (1987). Surface and structural similarity in analogical transfer. *Memory & Cognition, 15*(4), 332–340. https://doi.org/10.3758/BF03197035
Holyoak, K. J., & Thagard, P. (1989). Analogical mapping by constraint satisfaction. *Cognitive Science, 13*(3), 295–355. https://doi.org/10.1207/s15516709cog1303_1
Holyoak, K. J., & Thagard, P. (1997). The analogical mind. *American Psychologist, 52*(1), 35–44. https://doi.org/10.1037/0003-066X.52.1.35
Honomichl, R. D., & Chen, Z. (2006). Learning to align relations: the effects of feedback and self-explanation. *Journal of Cognition and Development*, 7(4), 527–550.
Hummel, J. E., & Holyoak, K. J. (1997). Distributed representations of structure: A theory of analogical access and mapping. *Psychological Review, 104*(3), 427–466. https://doi.org/10.1037/0033-295X.104.3.427
Hummel, J. E., & Holyoak, K. J. (2003). A symbolic-connectionist theory of relational inference and generalization. *Psychological Review, 110*(2), 220–264. https://doi.org/10.1037/0033-295X.110.2.220
Jamrozik, A., & Gentner, D. (2013). Relational labels can improve relational retrieval. In M. Knauff, M. Pauen, N. Sebanz, & I. Wachsmuth (Eds.), *Proceedings of the thirty-fifth annual meeting of the cognitive science society* (pp. 651–656). Austin, TX: Cognitive Science Society.
Keane, M. T. (1996). On adaptation in analogy: Tests of pragmatic importance and adaptability in analogical problem solving. *The Quarterly Journal of Experimental Psychology Section A, 49*(4), 1062–1085. https://doi.org/10.1080/713755671
Kokinov, B., & Petrov, A. (2001). Integrating memory and reasoning in analogy-making: The AMBR model. In D. Gentner, K. J. Holyoak, & B. Kokinov (Eds.), *The analogical mind: Perspectives from cognitive science* (pp. 161–196). Cambridge, MA: MIT Press.
Kotovsky, L., & Gentner, D. (1996). Comparison and categorization in the development of relational similarity. *Child Development, 67*(6), 2797–2822. https://doi.org/10.1111/j.1467-8624.1996.tb01889.x
Krawczyk, D. C., Holyoak, K. J., & Hummel, J. E. (2005). The one-to-one constraint in analogical mapping and inference. *Cognitive Science, 29*(5), 797–806. https://doi.org/10.1207/s15516709cog0000_27
Lakoff, G., & Johnson, M. (1980). The metaphorical structure of the human conceptual system. *Cognitive Science, 4*(2), 195–208. https://doi.org/10.1016/S0364-0213(80)80017-6
Larkey, L. B., & Love, B. C. (2003). CAB: Connectionist analogy builder. *Cognitive Science, 27*(5), 781–794. https://doi.org/10.1016/S0364-0213(03)00066-1
Loewenstein, J., & Gentner, D. (2005). Relational language and the development of relational mapping. *Cognitive Psychology, 50*(4), 315–353. https://doi.org/10.1016/j.cogpsych.2004.09.004
Loewenstein, J., & Heath, C. (2009). The repetition-break plot structure: A cognitive influence on selection in the marketplace of ideas. *Cognitive Science, 33*(1), 1–19. https://doi.org/10.1111/j.1551-6709.2008.01001.x
Loewenstein, J., Thompson, L., & Gentner, D. (1999). Analogical encoding facilitates knowledge transfer in negotiation. *Psychonomic Bulletin & Review, 6*(4), 586–597. https://doi.org/10.3758/BF03212967
Luce, R. D. (1986). *Response times: Their role in inferring elementary mental organization*. New York: Oxford University Press.
Markman, A. B. (1997). Constraints on analogical inference. *Cognitive Science, 21*(4), 373–418. https://doi.org/10.1207/s15516709cog2104_1
Markman, A. B., & Gentner, D. (1993a). Splitting the differences: A structural alignment view of similarity. *Journal of Memory and Language, 32*(4), 517–535. https://doi.org/10.1006/jmla.1993.1027
Markman, A. B., & Gentner, D. (1993b). Structural alignment during similarity comparisons. *Cognitive Psychology, 25*(4), 431–467. https://doi.org/10.1006/cogp.1993.1011

Mix, K. S. (2008). Children's equivalence judgments: Crossmapping effects. *Cognitive Development, 23*(1), 191–203. https://doi.org/10.1016/j.cogdev.2007.03.001

Morrison, R. G., Krawczyk, D. C., Holyoak, K. J., Hummel, J. E., Chow, T. W., Miller, B. L., & Knowlton, B. J. (2004). A neurocomputational model of analogical reasoning and its breakdown in frontotemporal lobar degeneration. *Journal of Cognitive Neuroscience, 16*(2), 260–271. https://doi.org/10.1162/089892904322984553

Mussweiler, T., & Rüter, K. (2003). What friends are for! The use of routine standards in social comparison. *Journal of Personality and Social Psychology, 85*(3), 467–481. https://doi.org/10.1037/0022-3514.85.3.467

Namy, L. L., & Gentner, D. (2002). Making a silk purse out of two sow's ears: Young children's use of comparison in category learning. *Journal of Experimental Psychology: General, 131*(1), 5–15. https://doi.org/10.1037/0096-3445.131.1.5

Nersessian, N. (1984). *Faraday to Einstein: Constructing meaning in scientific theories*. Dordrecht, NL: Kluwer Academic.

Novick, L. R. (1988). Analogical transfer, problem similarity, and expertise. *Journal of Experimental Psychology: Learning, Memory, and Cognition, 14*(3), 510–520. https://doi.org/10.1037/0278-7393.14.3.510

Novick, L. R., & Holyoak, K. J. (1991). Mathematical problem solving by analogy. *Journal of Experimental Psychology: Learning, Memory, and Cognition, 17*(3), 398–415. https://doi.org/10.1037/0278-7393.17.3.398

Paik, J. H., & Mix, K. S. (2006). Preschoolers' use of surface similarity in object comparisons: Taking context into account. *Journal of Experimental Child Psychology, 95*(3), 194–214. https://doi.org/10.1016/j.jecp.2006.06.002

Richland, L. E., Morrison, R. G., & Holyoak, K. J. (2006). Children's development of analogical reasoning: Insights from scene analogy problems. *Journal of Experimental Child Psychology, 94*(3), 249–273. https://doi.org/10.1016/j.jecp.2006.02.002

Ross, B. H. (1984). Remindings and their effects in learning a cognitive skill. *Cognitive Psychology, 16*(3), 371–416. https://doi.org/10.1016/0010-0285(84)90014-8

Ross, B. H. (1987). This is like that: The use of earlier problems and the separation of similarity effects. *Journal of Experimental Psychology: Learning, Memory, and Cognition, 13*(4), 629–639. https://doi.org/10.1037/0278-7393.13.4.629

Ross, B. H. (1989). Distinguishing types of superficial similarities: Different effects on the access and use of earlier problems. *Journal of Experimental Psychology: Learning, Memory, and Cognition, 15*(3), 456–468. https://doi.org/10.1037/0278-7393.15.3.456

Sagi, E., Gentner, D., & Lovett, A. (2012). What difference reveals about similarity. *Cognitive Science, 36*(6), 1019–1050. https://doi.org/10.1111/j.1551-6709.2012.01250.x

Spellman, B. A., & Holyoak, K. J. (1992). If Saddam is Hitler then who is George Bush? Analogical mapping between systems of social roles. *Journal of Personality and Social Psychology, 62*(6), 913–933. https://doi.org/10.1037/0022-3514.62.6.913

Spellman, B. A., & Holyoak, K. J. (1996). Pragmatics in analogical mapping. *Cognitive Psychology, 31*(3), 307–346. https://doi.org/10.1006/cogp.1996.0019

Steen, G., Reijnierse, W. G., & Burgers, C. (2014). When do natural language metaphors influence reasoning? A follow-up study to Thibodeau and Boroditsky (2013). *PLoS ONE, 9*(12), e113536. https://doi.org/10.1371/journal.pone.0113536

Thagard, P. (1992). *Conceptual revolutions*. Princeton, NJ: Princeton University Press.

Thibaut, J.-P., French, R., & Vezneva, M. (2010). The development of analogy making in children: Cognitive load and executive functions. *Journal of Experimental Child Psychology, 106*(1), 1–19. https://doi.org/10.1016/j.jecp.2010.01.001

Thibodeau, P. H., & Boroditsky, L. (2011). Metaphors we think with: The role of metaphor in reasoning. *PLoS ONE, 6*(2), e16782. https://doi.org/10.1371/journal.pone.0016782

Trench, M., & Minervino, R. A. (2015). The role of surface similarity in analogical retrieval: Bridging the gap between the naturalistic and the experimental traditions. *Cognitive Science, 39*(6), 1292–1319. https://doi.org/10.1111/cogs.12201

Waltz, J. A., Knowlton, B. J., Holyoak, K. J., Boone, K. B., Mishkin, F. S., Santos, M. de M., . . . Miller, B. L. (1999). A system for relational reasoning in human prefrontal cortex. *Psychological Science, 10*(2), 119–125. https://doi.org/10.1111/1467-9280.00118

Waltz, J. A., Lau, A., Grewal, S. K., & Holyoak, K. J. (2000). The role of working memory in analogical mapping. *Memory & Cognition, 28*(7), 1205–1212. https://doi.org/10.3758/BF03211821

Yan, J., Forbus, K. D., & Gentner, D. (2003). A theory of rerepresentation in analogical matching. In R. Alterman & D. Kirsh (Eds.), *Proceedings of the twenty-fifth annual meeting of the Cognitive Science Society* (pp. 1265–1270). Mahwah, NJ: Lawrence Erlbaum Associates.

12

INCUBATION, PROBLEM SOLVING AND CREATIVITY

Kenneth J. Gilhooly

Introduction

Some seventy years ago, Karl Duncker (1945) produced a useful definition of a problem situation as one in which a person has a goal but does not know how to reach that goal. Problems come in many guises but can be classified in various ways. One classification is into those in which all the elements of the problem – the starting situation or state, the goal state and the means available for moving from the starting state to the goal, – are well defined as against problems where some or all elements are ill defined (Reitman, 1964; Simon, 1977; Lynch, Ashley, Alevan & Pinkwart, 2006). A chess problem is a prototypical example of a well-defined problem, in which the starting state is given, the goal is well defined (say, checkmate for white in three moves) and the means available are specified by the legal moves in the game. On the other hand, a problem may be very ill-defined, such as that of "improving the quality of life", in which the starting state, the goal state and the means available are not well defined. In ill-defined problems, it seems likely that an initial step is generally to convert the problem into a better-defined one by specifying some of the missing information (Weisberg, 2006, p. 139). In the "improve the quality of life" problem, some of the missing information could be specified by deciding on a particular way of measuring quality of life such as using the World Health Organization Quality of Life (WHO-QOL) questionnaire (WHO-QOL group, 1995) which would help determine the starting state and could be used to assess any effects of interventions as strong or weak.

Problems can be divided another way: into those that can be solved by routine search processes without any need to re-interpret the problem statement and those which require re-interpretation or "re-structuring". An example of a problem that could be solved by routine search is an anagram; by searching possible re-arrangements of the letters "ccpteno", one could find the scrambled word "concept". Some problems, however, do generally require a re-interpretation – for example, "How could a man marry 30 women in one month and break no laws against bigamy?" Here the word "marry" must be re-interpreted as causing others to become married, as against the default interpretation of becoming married. Thus, the man is authorised to conduct marriages. Another example is "How could a man walk over the surface of a deep, mile-wide lake without any floatation devices or aids?" This problem requires the solver to move from a default representation (at least in non-arctic regions) of the water in the lake as being in its liquid state and to represent the water in its solid frozen state. Such problems which require re-structuring or re-interpretation are often labelled "insight" problems.

Some problems, particularly those generally referred to as "creative problems", require the production of new approaches and many possible new solutions before an acceptable solution is found. "New" solutions and approaches are taken as those novel to the solver and may or may not be historically novel (Boden, 2004). Nearly 100 years ago, Ogburn and Thomas (1922) noted that often in technological and scientific developments, two or more thinkers may solve the same problem completely independently of each other within a short time frame. Such events are known as "multiple inventions". The electric battery, the telegraph, the steam engine and hundreds of other cases of multiple inventions have been documented (Johnson, 2014, pp. 58–59). Independent thinkers who solve the same problem can all be said to have been personally creative on reaching the solution, although only the first to solve would have been historically creative.

In the case of creative and insight problem solving, it has frequently been argued that stopping conscious work on such problems for a period of time (known as an "incubation" period) can help in the production of novel solutions. It is suggested that solution ideas might occur spontaneously, while not focussing on the problem ("inspiration"), or alternatively very quickly when the previously unsolved problem is attended to again. In the next section, I discuss the historical origins of the idea of incubation in the psychology of thinking.

Historical background to the "incubation" concept

Graham Wallas (1926, p. 80) developed Poincaré's (1910) analysis of mathematical creation (or *l'invention mathematique*, which could equally have been translated as "mathematical invention") to construct a four-stage model of creative thinking. In this model, Wallas labelled an intermediate stage, in which a problem is put aside and not consciously worked on, as the "Incubation" stage. Poincaré did not use the term "Incubation" in his 1910 paper, although he reported examples from his own experience, such as solutions occurring while he was travelling by bus or at the seaside on holiday but had not consciously thought about the problem for some time. Such accounts fit Wallas's description of incubation periods. In Wallas's analysis, Incubation is proposed as a useful stage that comes after a necessary initial period of conscious work (i.e., Preparation) and occurs before Illumination (or Inspiration). Illumination is the stage in which a promising idea comes to mind, following which there is a stage of conscious work known as Verification, during which the promising idea is consciously developed and tested. This final phase is necessary since there can be false inspirations which do not fulfil their apparent promise when examined and developed in detail. Of Wallas's classic four stages, the Incubation stage is the focus of this chapter.

Useful pointers to the processes involved in creative thinking might be obtained if we could understand why Incubation periods during creative and insight problem solving may be helpful. But first, what evidence is there for the reality of Incubation effects? Personal accounts by acknowledged creative thinkers in the arts and the sciences have often been taken as evidence for the existence of this phenomenon (Poincaré, 1910; Ghiselin, 1952; Csikszentmihalyi, 1996). An example provided by Poincaré (1910) involved solving a mathematical problem through a sudden inspiration while on holiday at the seaside and thinking of other things. Interestingly, Poincaré built incubation opportunities into his normal work schedule, which involved concentrated work on mathematical research between 10 A.M. and 12 noon and between 5 P.M. and 7 P.M. but not outside those times (Toulouse, 1910). He habitually went to bed at 10 P.M. and rose at 7 A.M., so about 11 hours per day were available for waking periods of incubation and about nine hours for possible sleeping incubation. More recently, the English writer and novelist Martin Amis (2012) noted that when he lacks inspiration to solve a plot problem, he walks away and reads something else; when he returns to his desk, he reports, that the problem tends to be fixed. However, since personal accounts of incubation have often been given many years after the supposed events – and this is particularly the case with famous creators in the 19th century and earlier – the reliability of such reports is clearly questionable. Poincaré's own account of his creative work was first publicly reported in a talk ("L'invention mathématique") of 1908, given to the Psychological Society of Paris at the Institut Géneral Psychologique (published in French in 1908 and in English in 1910), and much of it was based on a problem solving episode said to have occurred in 1881, 27 years before. Some support for the 1908/1910 account may be drawn from a report by a psychiatrist, Dr. Eduard Toulouse, who interviewed Poincaré in 1897 about his working processes. Toulouse reported in 1909 that Poincaré had in 1897 given a similar account in 1908. However, even the earlier account of 1897 was still some 16 years after the events described, which must raise questions of reliability. Indeed, other frequently cited personal accounts, given long after the purported events, by Coleridge, Mozart and Kekulé, that appeared to involve incubation and illumination/inspiration, have subsequently been shown to be unequivocally false in the cases of Coleridge and Mozart (Weisberg, 2006, pp. 73–78) and highly dubious in the case of Kekulé (Wotiz & Rudofsky, 1984; see also Miller, 2000, pp. 340–341).

We now turn to a consideration of laboratory studies, which should provide a sounder basis for establishing the existence of incubation effects and analysing their mechanisms than can either introspection or retrospection. Following the pioneering theoretical analyses by Wallas (1926) and Poincaré (1910), a considerable volume of experimental laboratory research on incubation effects has been carried out with both (a) *insight* problems, in which new ways of representing or structuring the task must be found in order to reach a solution; and (b) *divergent* problems, in which there is no single correct solution but rather many novel and useful ideas need to be generated to reach good solutions. The most commonly used divergent task in laboratory studies is the Alternative Uses Task, in which participants are asked to come up with as many uses different from the normal use as they can for one or more familiar objects, such as a brick, a pencil, a tyre or a shoe, in a limited time period (Guilford, 1971; Guilford, Christensen, Merrifield & Wilson, 1978; Gilhooly, Fioratou, Anthony & Wynn, 2007).

Laboratory-based studies of incubation

Early laboratory studies of incubation followed the *Delayed Incubation paradigm*, in which participants in the incubation condition work on the target problem for an experimenter-determined time (preparation time) before being given an *interpolated activity* for a fixed time (incubation period) and then resume the target problem for a fixed post-incubation work period. Performance of the incubation group can then be compared to that of a control group that works without interruption on the target task for a time equal to the sum of the preparation time and the post-incubation working time of the incubation group. A relatively new paradigm (*Immediate Incubation paradigm*) gives participants an interpolated task for a fixed period *immediately* after instructions on the target problem, but *before* any conscious work time has been allowed on the target problem. The immediate incubation period is then followed by continuous work on the target problem for a fixed post-incubation time (Dijksterhuis & Meurs, 2006). We will now review key results from laboratory studies using both delayed and immediate incubation paradigms.

Delayed incubation effects

The earliest empirical studies that attempted to examine incubation appear to be those by Catherine Patrick (1935; 1937;1938). In the first two studies, participants produced poems in response to a painting and sketches in response to a poem respectively. Patrick encouraged thinking aloud and recorded, by means of shorthand, as much as she could of their thinking aloud and problem solving activities. She noted that early mentioned ideas often recurred later and took these recurrences as signs of incubation. However, the 1935 and 1937 studies did not involve ever setting the problem aside, so although intended as studies of incubation, they do not meet the usual requirement of setting the task aside. In the last study in the sequence, Patrick (1938) did compare a group that worked continuously on the task of proposing ways of testing for effects of heredity versus environment, with a second group who took the task away for two weeks. The second group did better, but as there was no control for time spent on the task, it is difficult to be sure that the better performance was due to incubation rather than, say, greater total time on the task.

After what might be seen as the false starts of Patrick's work, there is now considerable evidence from better-controlled laboratory studies for the efficacy of Delayed Incubation; that is, that setting a problem aside after a period of work is beneficial. Dodds, Ward and Smith (2012) provided a narrative review of laboratory studies between 1938 and 1991. Dodds et al. identified 39 experiments on incubation, of which 26 (75%) reported significant benefits. They concluded that a number of variables appeared to affect incubation effectiveness. Thus, longer periods of preparation were generally better than shorter periods. Incubation periods of about 30 minutes seemed best, but effects were still found at longer periods of 3.5 and 24 hours. Incidentally presented clues appeared to be more helpful during incubation than during other periods. No clear effects emerged of problem type or of the nature of the activities during the incubation period.

There was marked variation in the experimental parameters among the studies reviewed by Dodds et al. (2012), which makes it difficult to draw strong cross-experiment conclusions from their narrative review. A meta-analysis which overcame these problems to a large extent was reported by Sio and Ormerod (2009). This analysis of 117 studies found a positive effect of Delayed Incubation, where the overall average effect size was in the low-medium band (mean $d = .29$) over a range of linguistic and visuo-spatial insight and divergent tasks. The effects of incubation were significant for the three types of tasks considered separately but were greatest for divergent tasks and somewhat less for linguistic and visual insight tasks, which were not different from each other. Other possible moderators in addition to task type were examined and it was found that longer preparation periods yielded larger incubation effects (as had been concluded also by Dodds et al., 2012). Highly cognitively demanding tasks in the incubation period produced lower incubation benefits. Linguistic insight problems benefitted more from lower cognitively demanding incubation activities than from rest during incubation.

Overall, from both a narrative and a meta-analytic review, the basic existence of Delayed Incubation effects can now be regarded as well established, particularly in the case of creative problems but also, if to a lesser degree, in visual and linguistic insight tasks.

Immediate incubation effects

Dijksterhuis and Nordgren (2006) reported that better decisions and more creative solutions were generated when Immediate Incubation periods were given after the presentation of both decision problems and divergent tasks as compared to continuous work on these tasks. Nordgren,

Bos and Dijksterhuis (2011) found that Delayed Incubation produced better decisions than Immediate Incubation and both were better than No Incubation. The benefits of immediate incubation for decision making has proven to be controversial and have not always been easy to reproduce. Unsuccessful replication attempts have been reported (e.g., Acker, 2008; Newell, Wong, Cheung & Rakow, 2009; Rey, Goldstein & Perruchet, 2009; Payne, Samper, Bettman & Luce, 2008). On the other hand, a meta-analysis by Strick, Dijksterhuis, Bos, Sjoerdsma and van Baaren (2011), which integrated data from 92 decision studies, found a significant beneficial aggregate effect size of g = .224 for Immediate Incubation in decision tasks. However, as the present chapter focuses on creative thinking and insight problem solving, I will leave the issue of incubation in decision making aside.

Creative problem solving with Immediate Incubation was studied by Dijksterhuis and Meurs (2006) using a divergent task, and their Experiment 3 found that participants produced more creative responses when instructions to list things one can do with a brick were followed immediately by a three-minute distracting task, compared to participants who began reporting uses immediately after the instructions explaining the brick use task. However, the instructions in this study did not require unusual uses, and so it is uncertain whether participants were trying to be creative as against simply fluent. Participants may have been reporting infrequent uses that they knew already, rather than creatively producing uses novel to them. Infrequent responses tend to be rated by judges as creative even though they could reflect memory retrieval rather than on-the-spot generation of subjectively novel responses (Quellmalz, 1985). Gilhooly, Georgiou, Garrison, Reston and Sirota (2012) used more standard Alternative Uses task instructions that emphasised the production of unusual uses and found a stronger positive effect of Immediate Incubation compared to Delayed Incubation, but with both incubation effects beneficial relative to controls in terms of fluency and of response novelty.

Zhong, Dijksterhuis and Galinsky (2008), explored the Immediate Incubation paradigm with the Remote Associates Task (RAT). In this task participants attempt to find an associate common to three given words (e.g., *cottage, blue, mouse.* Answer: *cheese*). Zhong et al. (2008) found that, although Immediate Incubation did not help produce solutions, it did appear to activate solution words to a measurable extent on unsolved trials. This was indicated by faster lexical decisions to target words following unsolved trials with Immediate Incubation as compared to controls.

To sum up this review of empirical studies, from a meta-analysis (Sio & Ormerod, 2009; Strick et al., 2011), a narrative review (Dodds et al., 2012), and recent studies (Gilhooly et al., 2012; Gilhooly, Georgiou & Devery, 2013; Gilhooly, Georgiou, Sirota & Paphiti-Galeano, 2015), there is support for the view that incubation periods, whether they are Delayed or Immediate, are helpful, particularly for creative problems. The question now becomes, not whether incubation effects exist, but how such effects come about. I will now outline the three main theoretical approaches seeking to explain incubation effects. These approaches are labelled "Intermittent Conscious Work", "Fresh Look" and "Unconscious Work".

Theoretical approaches to incubation effects

1 *Intermittent conscious work:* on this view, although incubation periods are intended to be periods without conscious work on the target task, participants might not actually follow instructions and might carry out intermittent conscious work during the incubation period (Seifert, Meyer, Davidson, Patalano & Yaniv, 1995), a process which Olton (1979) labelled "creative worrying". Weisberg (2006, pp. 443–445) argued strongly that in the light of the evidence available to him, this option could not be ruled out. Conscious work on the target task in the intended incubation period, however intermittent or fleeting, would

aid solution when the participant returned to the target problem. On this approach, apparently mysterious incubation effects could be explained as due to nothing more than extra time being surreptitiously spent on the task. This view has the attraction of parsimony and essentially explains away incubation effects as not involving any special processes different those found in normal problem solving without incubation breaks.

Interestingly, Poincaré's nephew, the philosopher Pierre Boutroux, in a memoir written soon after Poincaré's death in 1912, painted a picture of Poincaré as an inveterate "creative worrier". Boutroux wrote of Poincaré:

> He thought in the street as he went to the Sorbonne, while he was attending some scientific meeting or while he was taking one of his habitual grand walks after lunch. He thought in his antechamber or in the hall of meetings at the institute, while he walked with little steps, his physiognomy tense, shaking a bunch of keys. He thought at the dinner table at family get-together, even in the sitting room, interrupting himself; often brusquely in the midst of a conversation.
>
> (Darboux, 1916/1956; Fitzgerald & James, 2007)

For more biographical details of Poincaré, see also Weinstein (2012).

This indication that Poincaré was something of a creative worrier does not, of course, in itself invalidate the notion of unconscious work in creativity as put forward by Poincaré, but intriguingly suggests that Poincaré himself may not have been the best exemplar of his own theory!

2 *"Fresh Look":* this approach (e.g., Woodworth, 1938; Simon, 1966; Smith, 1995; Segal, 2004; see also Dijksterhuis & Meurs, 2006) suggests a major role for automatic reduction in idea strength (activation) during incubation. The hypothesis is that misleading strategies, mistaken assumptions, fixations and related "mental sets" become automatically weaker through forgetting during incubation, permitting a fresh start or "set shifting" when the problem is returned to after incubation. This view is essentially one of passive changes which happen with no active goal-directed work on the problem materials. Segal (2004) proposed a variant of the Fresh Look view in which simply switching attention away from the main task allowed a new start but did not require forgetting. The Fresh Look approach does not predict an effect of Immediate Incubation because in Immediate Incubation there is not sufficient time for sets or fixations to have developed, and so forgetting or weakening in activation of misleading approaches would not occur.

3 *Unconscious work:* this view suggests that incubation effects involve active (although unconscious) processing of the problem materials in contrast to the automatic passive forgetting processes proposed in the Fresh Look approach. The phrase "unconscious work" seems to have first been used in relation to problem solving by Poincaré (1908), in its French equivalent, when he wrote of *le travail de l'inconscient.* Other terms in the literature which refer to the same general idea include "nonconscious idea generation" (Snyder, Mitchell, Ellwood, & Yates, 2004) and "unconscious thought" (Dijsterhuis & Nordgren, 2006), but I will generally use the phrase "unconscious work". If the general idea of unconscious work is accepted, the question immediately arises of what kind of processes could constitute unconscious work. Could unconscious work be essentially the same as conscious work but minus any conscious awareness? Or is unconscious work better conceived of as a different form of processing to that involved in conscious work, such as automatic spreading activation along associative links, rather than as a strategy-governed activity typical of normal

conscious solving processes? In relation to unconscious work, Wallas (1926) proposed the notion of "associative chains", which anticipated the modern idea of spreading activation and were in turn anticipated by Johann Friedrich Herbart in the early 19th century (Claxton, 2005, p. 214). Both Poincaré and Wallas argued that the suddenness of Illumination or Inspiration, together with the feeling of confidence in the sudden insights of the Illumination stage, arose from extended unconscious work during Incubation. As is well known, Wallas's four-stage theory comprised Preparation, Incubation, Illumination and Verification. Often overlooked is a sub-stage of Illumination, labelled Intimation (Wallas, 1926, p. 97). Wallas considered this sub-stage of Intimation both practically and theoretically important. Intimation is a sub-stage in the Illumination period when the solver begins to feel that an insight is about to be experienced. Theoretically, Wallas argued that Intimation reflected the increasing activation of a successful association train, that was about to cross the threshold level of activation required to become conscious. Thus, the existence of an Intimation sub-stage was consistent with the unconscious-work view of Incubation. From a practical point of view, Wallas felt it was important that solvers recognise the Intimation feeling, so that when it was noticed, the solver could stop distracting activities to allow the solution to cross the threshold of consciousness. Wallas was particularly critical of the habit of continuously reading during spare moments as likely to reduce the chances of Intimation being noticed and allowed to come to fruition.

The three suggested mechanisms outlined above are not mutually exclusive (or exhaustive). A Delayed Incubation period could involve all three, with the solver engaging in some intermittent conscious work when attention wanders from the interpolated incubation task, with some beneficial forgetting and some unconscious work also taking place when the person is attending consciously to the interpolated incubation task as instructed. An Immediate Incubation effect would not be consistent with a Fresh Look explanation, since there is not time in the Immediate paradigm to develop sets or misleading directions, but Immediate paradigm effects would be consistent with some intermittent conscious work and/or some unconscious work during the incubation period.

Theoretical approaches to incubation: empirical evidence

In the next section I review research which addresses the possible mechanisms of incubation.

Intermittent work

As a way of checking for possible intermittent conscious work during incubation, performance on the interpolated task during the incubation period could be compared with performance of a control group working on the same interpolated task as a stand-alone task – that is, without the task being done as an incubation task. Poorer performance in the interpolated task by the incubation group would be consistent with a departure of attention from the interpolated task and would be expected on the hypothesis of intermittent conscious work on the target task during the incubation period. This basic methodological check for the presence of intermittent conscious work did not appear to have been carried out in the many studies reviewed by Dodds et al. (2012) and by Sio and Ormerod (2009). Recently, Gilhooly et al. (2012, 2013, 2015) included checks for intermittent conscious work on their target divergent thinking task (Alternative Uses) during the incubation period. In these studies there was no evidence of poorer performance on the incubation period tasks, mental rotations and anagrams, compared to controls who carried out mental rotations and anagrams as stand-alone tasks rather than as interpolated tasks. These studies found beneficial incubation effects but no evidence for intermittent conscious work. As a further check on the intermittent work explanation, Gilhooly et al. (2012) looked at the correlations between performance quality on the interpolated incubation tasks and divergent production measures. The intermittent work hypothesis suggests that these correlations would be negative since, if participants attend fully to the interpolated tasks, they would perform them better but be unable to undertake intermittent work on the divergent task and so do worse on that task. Eight correlations were examined, of which only one was significant and it was positive rather than negative. Again, the intermittent work hypothesis was not supported.

A relevant independent study by Baird et al. (2012) used thought-monitoring methods and reported that the frequency of target-task-related intermittent thoughts during the incubation period was not related to quality of performance on the target task in the post-incubation period. Thus, it appears that any intermittent thoughts about the target task were not effective in facilitating a solution and so do not explain the beneficial effects of incubation. Overall, on the basis of Gilhooly et al. (2012, 2013, 2015) and Baird et al. (2012), it may be concluded that Intermittent Conscious Work can be ruled out as the sole explanation of beneficial incubation effects. Clearly, intermittent conscious work or "creative worrying" *could* play a role in some cases, but incubation effects have still been found even when experimental and statistical controls rule it out and so it can also be concluded that other explanations remain in contention.

Fresh look

Woodworth (1938) suggested that incubation effects could be due to forgetting of misleading sets which would permit a new start when the problem was revisited. This "Fresh Look" hypothesis was directly addressed by Segal (2004) in a study that involved a spatial insight problem in which a square had a parallelogram superimposed on it and the goal was to find the sum of the areas of the two shapes (see Figure 12.1). The problem is greatly facilitated when it is realised that the diagram can be restructured (re-perceived) as two equal right-angled triangles which if slid form a rectangle whose area is easily obtained. Participants received an incubation break or not, and the duration of the break and the cognitive load of the interpolated activity was varied, being either high load (doing crosswords) or low load (reading magazines).

Results indicated significant benefits from an incubation period versus not having a break, but no effects for short versus long break or for the cognitive load of the activity during the incubation period. Segal proposed that the results supported a variant of the Fresh Look view, in which removing attention from the target task was in itself sufficient to weaken misleading sets and that it was not actually important what particular tasks filled the incubation period or how long the incubation period lasted.

Using a different paradigm but still addressing the Fresh Look hypothesis, Smith (1995) suggested that cues at presentation can lead people into mental sets or mental ruts that interfere with developing new approaches that could be alleviated by forgetting. Participants were given misleading cues to word problems. It was found that after a break the chances of solving the problems with the misleading cues were better when the cues could not be remembered. In this study, the longer the break, the better the results that were obtained. These findings are consistent with a role for forgetting misleading sets which permits a fresh start after an incubation period and so are consistent with the Fresh Look view.

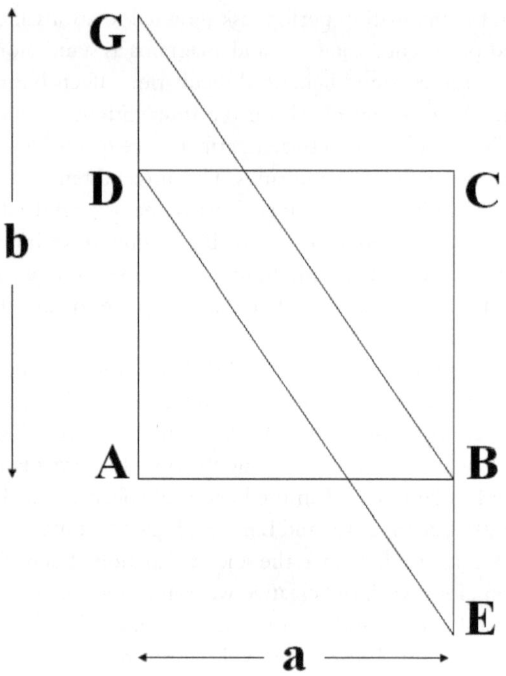

Figure 12.1 Segal insight problem

Given that AB = a and AG = b, find the sum of the area of square ABCD and parallelogram EBGD.

Unconscious work

In contrast to Woodworth (1938), Segal (2004) and Smith (1995), Dijksterhuis and Meurs (2006) proposed that in the Immediate Incubation paradigm, the Fresh Look approach, which is based on forgetting, may be ruled out, because there is no period of initial work during which misleading fixations could be developed. So, if Immediate Incubation was shown to be helpful, the Fresh Look view could be ruled out, at least for that paradigm, and the Unconscious Work hypothesis would remain viable for Immediate Incubation effects and would also still be a candidate explanation for Delayed Incubation. Dijksterhuis and Meurs (2006) found beneficial effects of the Immediate Incubation paradigm on a divergent task in their Experiment 3 and argued that this supported the hypothesis of unconscious work in incubation. However, as already mentioned, the instructions in this study did not fully match those normally used in creative tasks, since participants were not explicitly instructed to produce novel uses, so this study did not unambiguously involve creative thinking as against retrieval of information already available in episodic and semantic memory.

Gilhooly et al. (2012) followed up Dijksterhuis and Meurs (2006) but used explicit instructions for novelty and they found that both delayed and immediate incubation were helpful for the divergent Alternative Uses task. They also found that immediate incubation produced more benefit than did delayed incubation. Gilhooly et al. concluded that their results supported the hypothesis of unconscious work in creative divergent thinking, particularly in the case of Immediate Incubation.

Snyder, Mitchell, Ellwood and Yates (2004) reported results consistent with unconscious work in a study which used the Delayed Incubation paradigm coupled with a surprise return to the target task. Their study found beneficial effects of incubation, even when a return to the target task was not expected, which suggested an automatic continuation of unconscious work when the task was set aside. However, Snyder et al. used a task that required only production of uses for a piece of paper as against generation of novel uses for a piece of paper and so it could be argued their task did not necessarily involve creative thinking as against recall.

Target-interpolated task modality similarity effects

Both Segal (2004) and Dijksterhuis and Meurs (2006) used interpolated tasks during their incubation periods that were different in modality from the target tasks. Segal's target task was spatial (geometric problem) while the interpolated tasks were verbal (reading or crossword puzzles); Dijksterhuis and Meurs's target task was verbal but the interpolated task was spatial (spatial tracking). It is likely that the similarity relationship between target and interpolated tasks could be important, since the competing hypotheses are consistent with different effects of similarity. The unconscious work hypothesis suggests that interpolated tasks similar to the target task should interfere with any unconscious work using the same mental resources and so a high degree of similarity between target tasks and incubation tasks should lead to weaker (or even reversed) incubation effects when compared to effects of dissimilarity between target and interpolated tasks. On the other hand, a Fresh Look forgetting account suggests that interpolated tasks similar to the target task would cause greater interference which would lead to more forgetting and so enhanced incubation effects. Some support for the unconscious work hypothesis was found in a Delayed Incubation experiment by Ellwood, Pallier, Snyder and Gallate (2009), who reported a beneficial effect on number of responses post-incubation in an Idea Generation task that involved a dissimilar interpolated task as opposed to a similar divergent task. However, this study used a "fluency of uses" task rather than a "novel uses" task, so it did not directly address creative solving processes.

Using a Delayed Incubation paradigm, Gilhooly et al. (2013) studied the effects of varying incubation activities (verbal: anagram solving versus spatial: mental rotations) and involved either a clearly verbal divergent task (alternate uses) or a clearly spatial divergent task (mental synthesis). Both target tasks were scored for novelty as well as fluency. Significant simple incubation effects and interactions were found, in that spatial incubation activities facilitated verbal divergent thinking and verbal incubation activity helped spatial divergent thinking but not vice versa. The results thus supported the hypothesis of unconscious work during incubation periods in creative thinking tasks and did not support the hypotheses that incubation effects are due to selective forgetting or attention shifting, as proposed in the Fresh Look view. The Fresh Look selective forgetting account predicted the opposite pattern of facilitation to that obtained, and the purely attention-shifting version of the Fresh Look approach as proposed by Segal (2004) predicted no differential effects of different types of interpolated tasks, again contrary to what was found.

Theoretical discussion

From recent research it seems that the Unconscious Work hypothesis has been well supported, given the effectiveness of Immediate Incubation, in which sets are unlikely to have been developed. In addition, Gilhooly et al. (2012, 2013, 2015) found no support for the idea of intermittent work from studies in which suitable control conditions were included. Unconscious work remains as the best candidate explanation for the effects of Immediate Incubation periods. Gilhooly et al. (2012) found that Delayed Incubation was beneficial, but less so than Immediate Incubation, in a divergent thinking task (Alternative Uses). It could be that in Delayed Incubation, sets build up during the initial period of conscious work and are then reduced by selective forgetting, after which beneficial unconscious work could come into play. In contrast, with Immediate Incubation, there are no sets to be overcome and beneficial unconscious work can start sooner than in the Delayed paradigm, leading to better performance than with Delayed incubation.

The question still remains: of what does unconscious work consist? In particular, is it possible that unconscious work could be just the same as conscious work but, somehow, carried out without conscious awareness? Kounios and Beeman (2015) give, as an illustration of that idea, an imaginary scenario in which you work in an anagram-solving office. After a day at work, systematically searching through possible letter orders, you still have not solved a very long anagram. When you leave for home in the evening, another worker takes over and begins work on the same anagram from where you left off, using the same systematic search methods as you had been using. A few hours later, the colleague phones your home to say the puzzle is solved and gives you the answer. Could this imaginary example be analogous to unconscious work in incubation, leading to Illumination (the phone call)? Poincaré (1910, p. 330) also considered the possibility of what he called a "subliminal self" that worked in just the same way as the conscious self, but without consciousness, and he suggested that such a self might be, not only subliminal, but also a "superior self" since it could find solutions that the conscious mind could not. The main alternative to the notion that unconscious work is basically similar to conscious work is the view that incubation is better thought of as involving automatic spreading activation along associative connections. This view better reflects Poincaré's final position, as he did ultimately reject the idea of a superior, albeit unconscious, subliminal self.

Gilhooly et al. (2012) also discussed the theoretical notion that unconscious work might be a subliminal version of conscious work. They first considered the nature of conscious processing in the Alternative Uses task, which is so often used in studies of incubation in creative thinking. In a think aloud study of a brick uses task Gilhooly et al. (2007) found that participants used strategies such as retrieving the target object's properties ("It's heavy", "It's solid" and so on) and employed the retrieved properties to cue possible uses ("Heavy objects can hold down things like sheets, rugs, tarpaulins and so on, so a heavy brick could do those things too"). It seems implausible that unconscious work could simply duplicate this form of conscious strategy-based processing, but without awareness, since strategy-based processing requires highly activated mental contents as inputs and generates highly activated content as outputs. That is, the processing involved in applying complex strategies uses and produces highly activated contents in working memory, of which we are necessarily aware, given that material is in consciousness if and only if it is above a high activation threshold. It therefore seems theoretically impossible that unconscious processes could duplicate conscious processes in every way while remaining unconscious. This, we suggest, is why unconscious multiplication of even moderately large numbers, such as two-digit numbers, not previously practised, seems impossible. Poincaré made much the same argument, writing: "it never happens that the unconscious work gives us the result of a somewhat long calculation *all made*, where we only have to apply fixed rules" (1910, p. 334).

If the idea can be dismissed that unconscious work or thought is just the same as conscious work but without awareness, of what, then, might unconscious work consist? A number of theorists, such as Poincaré (1910), Campbell (1960) and Simonton (1995), have proposed that unconscious work during incubation periods involves the quasi-random generation of associations to produce novel combinations of ideas, of which some prove valuable. Parallel spreading activation through a semantic network has been suggested as a way to form remote and unusual associations (Jung-Beeman, Bowden, Haberman et al., 2004) without requiring the high activation levels that would give rise to conscious awareness. In a related approach, Seifert et al. (1995) proposed a key role for persisting activation, principally of the unmet goal during incubation periods following unsuccessful conscious work. During incubation, Seifert et al. suggest, incidental cues related to the solution might activate the goal above threshold, causing the solver to realise that an environmental cue indicates a solution.

In Helie and Sun's (2010) Explicit-Implicit Interaction model, incubation periods are seen as allowing activity by unconscious implicit associative processes, which require little attentional capacity, as compared to conscious explicit rule governed and attentionally demanding processes. In terms of Dijksterhuis and Nordgren's (2006) related Unconscious Thought Theory (UTT), unconscious thought, or work, has the following characteristics. It is parallel, bottom-up, inexact and divergent, whereas conscious thought is serial, exact and generally convergent. Thus, there is agreement among a number of theorists that unconscious work, in the form of implicit associative processes, based on parallel spreading activation and similar to Wallas's (1926) concept of "associative trains", can explain many incubation effects.

Concluding comments

Overall, although current researchers routinely acknowledge the pioneering theoretical work of Poincaré (1910) and Wallas (1926), the field has made marked progress in the past century. The benefits of incubation periods in creative thinking have been established in a large number of controlled laboratory studies (Dodds et al., 2012; Sio & Ormerod, 2009), so that the field no longer depends on unreliable, long-delayed introspective and retrospective accounts. Novel paradigms, such as Immediate Incubation, have been developed to add to the long established Delayed Incubation paradigm as a method in the experimenters' tool kit, and this new paradigm has supported the Unconscious Work hypothesis, particularly as against the Fresh Look approach. The tempting idea of Intermittent Work as a parsimonious way of explaining away incubation has not been supported by suitably controlled studies, and, I feel, can now be discounted. Finally, theoretical ideas have been clarified and may soon lead to computer simulations (Helie & Sun, 2010) that could help in developing tests of specific theories of unconscious work and how it meshes with conscious work in the Preparation-Incubation-Illumination cycle.

References

Acker, F. (2008). New findings on unconscious versus conscious thought in decision making: Additional empirical data and meta-analysis. *Judgment and Decision Making, 3*, 292–303.

Amis, M. (2012, June 10). Interview. *Sunday Times Magazine (London).*

Baird, B., Smallwood, J., Mrazek, M. D., Kam, J. W. Y, Franklin, M. S., & Schooler, J. W. (2012). Inspired by distraction: Mind wandering facilitates creative incubation. *Psychological Science, 23*, 1117–1122.

Boden, M. (2004) *Creative mind: Myths and mechanisms* (2nd ed.). London: Routledge.

Campbell, D. T. (1960). Blind variation and selective retention in creative thought as in other knowledge processes. *Psychological Review, 67*, 380–400.

Claxton, G. (2005). *The wayward mind: An intimate history of the unconscious.* London: Abacus.

Csikszentmihalyi, M. (1996). *Creativity: Flow and the psychology of discovery and invention.* New York: HarperCollins.

Darboux, G. (1916/1956). Eloge historique d' Henri Poincaré. In P. Appell (Ed.), *Oeuvres d' Henri Poincaré* (Vol. II). Paris: Gauthiers Villars.

Dijksterhuis, A., & Meurs, T. (2006). Where creativity resides: The generative power of unconscious thought. *Consciousness and Cognition, 15*, 135–146.

Dijksterhuis, A., & Nordgren, L. F. (2006). A theory of unconscious thought. *Perspectives on Psychological Science, 1*, 95–109.

Dodds, R. A., Ward, T. B., & Smith, S. M. (2012). A review of the experimental literature on incubation in problem solving and creativity. In M. A. Runco (Ed.), *Creativity research handbook* (Vol. 3). Cresskill, NJ: Hampton Press.

Duncker, K. (1945). On problem solving. *Psychological Monographs, 58*, 1–113.

Ellwood, S., Pallier, P., Snyder, A., & Gallate, J. (2009). The incubation effect: Hatching a solution? *Creativity Research Journal, 21*, 6–14.

Fitzgerald, M., & James, I. (2007). *The mind of the mathematician*. Baltimore, MD: John Hopkins University Press.

Ghiselin, B. (1952). *The creative process: A symposium*. New York: Mentor.

Gilhooly, K. J., Fioratou, E., Anthony, S. H., & Wynn, V. (2007). Divergent thinking: Strategies and executive involvement in generating novel uses for familiar objects. *British Journal of Psychology, 98*, 611–625.

Gilhooly, K. J., Georgiou, G. J., & Devery, U. (2013). Incubation and creativity: Do something different. *Thinking & Reasoning, 19*, 137–149.

Gilhooly, K. J., Georgiou, G. J., Garrison, J., Reston, J., & Sirota, M. (2012). Don't wait to incubate: Immediate versus delayed incubation in divergent thinking. *Memory & Cognition, 40*, 966–975.

Gilhooly, K. J., Georgiou, G. J., Sirota, M., & Paphiti-Galeano, A. (2015). Incubation and suppression processes in creative problem solving. *Thinking & Reasoning, 21*, 130–146.

Guilford, J. P. (1971). *The nature of human intelligence*. New York, NY: McGraw-Hill.

Guilford, J. P., Christensen, P. R., Merrifield, P. R., & Wilson, R. C. (1978). *Alternate uses: Manual of instructions and interpretations*. Orange, CA: Sheridan Psychological Services.

Helie, S., & Sun, R. (2010). Incubation, insight, and creative problem solving: a unified theory and a connectionist model. *Psychological Review, 117*, 994–1024.

Helie, S., Sun, R., & Xiong, L. (2008). Mixed effects of distractor tasks on incubation. In B. C. Love, K. McRae, & V. M. Sloutsky (Eds.), *Proceedings of the 30th annual meeting of the cognitive science society* (pp. 1251–1256). Austin, TX: Cognitive Science Society.

Johnson, S. (2014). *How we got to now: Six innovations that made the modern world*. London: Penguin Books Ltd.

Jung-Beeman, M., Bowden, E. M., Haberman, J., Frymiare, J. L., Arambel-Liu, S., Greenblatt, R., Reber, P. J., & Kounios, J. (2004). Neural activity when people solve verbal problems with insight. *Public Library of Science – Biology, 2*, 500–510.

Kounios, J., & Beeman, M. (2015). *The eureka factor: Creative insights and the brain*. London. William Heinemann.

Lynch, C., Ashley, K., Aleven, V., & Pinkwart, N. (2006). Defining ill-defined domains: a literature survey. In V. Aleven, K. Ashley, C. Lynch, & N. Pinkwart (Eds.), *Proceedings of the workshop on intelligent tutoring systems for ill-defined domains at the 8th international conference on intelligent tutoring systems* (pp. 1–10). Jhongli (Taiwan): National Central University. Retrieved from www.cs.pitt.edu/~collinl/Papers/ITS06_illdefinedworkshop_LynchEtAl.pdf

Miller, A. I. (2000). *Insights of genius: Imagery and creativity in science and art*. Cambridge, MA: MIT Press.

Newell, B. R., Wong, K. Y., Cheung, J. C. H., & Rakow, T. (2009). Think, blink or sleep on it? The impact of modes of thought on complex decision making. *Quarterly Journal of Experimental Psychology, 62*, 707–732.

Nordgren, L. F., Bos, M. W., & Dijksterhuis, A. (2011). The best of both worlds: Integrating conscious and unconscious thought best solves complex decisions. *Journal of Experimental Social Psychology, 47*, 509–511.

Ogburn, W. F., & Thomas, D. (1922). Are inventions inevitable? A note on social evolution. *Political Science Quarterly, 37*, 83–98.

Olton, R. M. (1979). Experimental studies of incubation: Searching for the elusive. *Journal of Creative Behavior, 13*, 9–22.

Patrick, C. (1935). Creative thought in poets. *Archives of Psychology, 178*, 1–74.

Patrick, C. (1937). Creative thought in artists. *Journal of Psychology, 4*, 35–73.

Patrick, C. (1938). Scientific thought. *Journal of Psychology, 5*, 55–83.

Payne, J., Samper, A., Bettman, J. R., & Luce, M. F. (2008). Boundary conditions on unconscious thought in complex decision making. *Psychological Science, 19*, 1118–1123.

Poincaré, H. (1908). L'invention mathématique. *Enseignement Mathématique, 10*, 357–371.

Poincaré, H. (1910). Mathematical creation. *The Monist, 20*, 321–333.
Quellmalz, E. (1985). Test review of alternate uses. In J.V. Mitchell, Jr. (Ed.), *The ninth mental measurements yearbook* [Electronic version]. Retrieved from Buros Institute's *Test Reviews Online* website: www.unl.edu/buros
Reitman, W. (1964). Heuristic decision procedures, open constraints, and the structure of illdefined problems. In M. W. Shelley & G. L. Bryan (Eds.), *Human judgment and optimality*. New York: Wiley.
Rey, A., Goldstein, R. M., & Perruchet, P. (2009). Does unconscious thought improve complex decision making? *Psychological Research, 73*, 372–379.
Segal, E. (2004). Incubation in insight problem solving. *Creativity Research Journal, 16*, 141–148.
Seifert, C. M., Meyer, D. E., Davidson, N., Patalano, A. L., & Yaniv, I. (1995). Demystification of cognitive insight: Opportunistic assimilation and the prepared-mind perspective. In R. J. Sternberg and J. E. Davidson (Eds.), *The nature of insight*. Cambridge, MA: MIT Press.
Simon, H. A. (1966). Scientific discovery and the psychology of problem solving. In R. Colodny (Ed.), *Mind and cosmos*. Pittsburgh, PA: University of Pittsburgh Press.
Simon, H. A. (1977). The structure of ill-structured problems. In H. A. Simon (Ed.), *Models of discovery* (pp. 304–325). Dordrecht, NL: Springer.
Simonton, D. K. (1995). Foresight in insight? A Darwinian answer. In R. J. Sternberg & J. E. Davidson (Eds.), *The nature of insight*. Cambridge, MA: MIT Press.
Sio, U. N., & Ormerod, T. C. (2009). Does incubation enhance problem solving? A meta-analytic review. *Psychological Bulletin, 135*, 94–120.
Smith, S. M. (1995). Getting into and out of mental ruts: A theory of fixation, incubation, and insight. In R. J. Sternberg & J. E. Davidson (Eds.), *The nature of insight*. Cambridge, MA: MIT Press.
Snyder, A., Mitchell, J., Ellwood, S., Yates, A., & Pallier, G. (2004). Nonconscious idea generation. *Psychological Reports, 94*, 1325–1330.
Strick, M., Dijksterhuis, A., Bos, M. W., Sjoerdsma, A., Van Baaren, R. B., & Nordgren, L. F. (2011). A meta-analysis on unconscious thought effects. *Social Cognition, 29*, 738–762.
Toulouse, E. (1910). *Henri Poincaré*. Paris: Ernest Flammarion Editeur.
Varendonck, J. (1921). *The psychology of daydreams*. New York: Palgrave Macmillan.
Wallas, G. (1926). *The art of thought*. London: Jonathan Cape.
Weinstein, G. (2012). *A biography of Henri Poincaré -2012 Centenary of the death of Poincaré*. Retrieved from www.arxiv.org/pdf/1207.0759.pdf
Weisberg, R. W. (2006). *Creativity: Understanding innovation in problem solving, science, invention, and the arts*. New York: J. Wiley & Sons.
WHOQOL group. (1995). The World Health Organization quality of life assessment (WHOQOL): position paper from the World Health Organization. *Social Science & Medicine, 41*, 1403–1409.
Woodworth, R. (1938). *Experimental psychology*. New York: Holt.
Wotiz, J. H., & Rudofsky, S. (1984). Kekulé's dream: Fact or fiction?. *Chemistry in Britain, 20*, 720–723.
Zhong, C.-B., Dijksterhuis, A., & Galinsky, A. D. (2008). The merits of unconscious thought in creativity. *Psychological Science, 19*, 912–918.

13

INDUCTIVE AND DEDUCTIVE REASONING

Integrating insights from philosophy, psychology, and neuroscience

Vinod Goel and Randall Waechter

Introduction

Reasoning is the process of evaluating given information and reaching conclusions that are not explicitly stated. Here is literature's most celebrated reasoner (Arthur Conan Doyle's Sherlock Holmes) impressing his friend Watson (in "A Scandal in Bohemia"):

> Then he stood before the fire, and looked me over in his singular introspective fashion.
>
> "Wedlock suits you," he remarked. . . . "And in practice again, I observe. You did not tell me that you intended to go into harness."
>
> "Then how do you know?"
>
> "I see it, I deduce it. How do I know that you have been getting yourself very wet lately, and that you have a most clumsy and careless servant girl?"
>
> "It is simplicity itself," said he; "my eyes tell me that on the inside of your left shoe, just where the firelight strikes it, the leather is scored by six almost parallel cuts. Obviously they have been caused by someone who has very carelessly scraped round the edges of the sole in order to remove crusted mud from it. Hence, you see, my double deduction that you had been out in vile weather, and that you had a particularly malignant boot-slicking specimen of the London slavery. As to your practice, if a gentleman walks into my room, smelling of iodoform, with a black mark of nitrate of silver upon his right fore-finger, and a bulge on the side of his top-hat to show where he has secreted his stethoscope, I must be dull indeed if I do not pronounce him to be an active member of the medical profession."
>
> (Doyle, 1892)

More mundane examples include the following: upon being told that George is a bachelor, one automatically infers that George is not married. Or upon learning that Linda will not come to our barbecue if it rains on Saturday, and noting that it is indeed raining on Saturday, we do not set a place for her. While not as impressive as Holmes' conclusions, they emerge in a straightforward way from the provided information, and have a certainty lacking in Holmes' inferences.

Reasoning has long been of interest to philosophers, and more recently psychologists and neuroscientists. Philosophers are interested primarily in the epistemic relationship between premises and conclusions; that is, they want to know the nature of the warrant the premises provide for accepting the conclusion. Psychologists are concerned with the cognitive processes/mechanisms involved in drawing the inference. Neuroscientists are concerned with the neural mechanisms underwriting these processes. In this chapter we briefly discuss the contributions made to our understanding of inductive and deductive reasoning by each of these disciplines. Given its broad scope, the review is by necessity incomplete, but we address and integrate the major issues, note the progress that has been made, and point out shortcomings and dilemmas that need to be addressed to move the field forward.

Philosophical issues

One major area of study for philosophy is the acquisition and justification of knowledge. Reasoning from given information (premises) to conclusions is one important source of knowledge. Therefore, it should not be surprising that the major philosophical issue in the study of reasoning is the nature of the warrant that the premises provide for accepting the conclusion. Based on this relationship, philosophers have sorted arguments into two broad categories: deduction and induction.

Deduction

Consider the following deductive arguments:

(A) All men are mortal; Socrates is a man

\ Socrates is mortal.

(B) All men are short; Socrates is a man

\ Socrates is short.

Deductive arguments can be evaluated for validity and soundness. An argument is valid if the premises provide absolute grounds for accepting the conclusion. Given the truth of the premises in arguments A and B, there can be no doubt about the truth of the conclusion. Validity is, however, independent of the actual truth of the propositions. Arguments A and B are equally valid, even though B contains some questionable premises which may lead to an untrue conclusion. An argument is considered sound when the premises are true and the argument is valid, as in A.

Validity is a function of the logical structure of the argument as opposed to sentence content. Consider the following examples:

(C) Tweety is a robin; no robins are migrants;

\ Tweety is not a migrant.

(D) Oxygen is an element; no elements are molecular;

\ Oxygen is not molecular.

If we give you the premises of these arguments and ask you whether the conclusion is valid, in both cases you will respond in the affirmative. Now we turn around and ask whether you know Tweety the Robin. If you don't, how could you possibly know that he's not a migrant? Similarly, do you know enough chemistry to be certain that oxygen is not molecular? You certainly don't know Tweety the Robin, and you may or may not know enough chemistry to be certain about the status of oxygen. However, this is all beside the point. Your certainty that Tweety is not a migrant and that oxygen is not molecular arises from the logical form of the arguments, which can be written as such:

(E) M has F; nothing with F has G;

\ M does not have G.

It is by virtue of this logical form, not the content of the sentences, that you can be certain the conclusion follows from the premises. You can substitute any content whatsoever into this logical form and the conclusion will still follow from the premises. The fact that validity is a function of logical form (rather than content) has made it possible to develop very sophisticated calculi for deductive inferences, which has turned the philosophical branch of deductive logic into a quasi-mathematical discipline that is heavily rule dependent.

Induction

Arguments where the premises provide only limited grounds for accepting the conclusion are broadly called inductive arguments.[1] The classic form studied is that of enumerative induction. Consider the following example:

(F) Socrates was a dinosaur; the skeletal remains of Socrates reveal four legs;

\ All dinosaurs had four legs.

This is clearly not a valid argument. The premises involve the observation of one (or a few) dinosaurs. Their truth cannot guarantee the truth of the conclusion, which involves all dinosaurs. However, most of us would be prepared to accept the argument in F as plausible or reasonable. The question is: what justifies this inference? Hume (1748/1910) famously considered this problem in the guise of causal inference. He argued that the conclusion is neither a report of direct experience nor a logical consequence of it. It cannot be the former because we have viewed a limited number of dinosaur remains, and it cannot be the latter because an inference from the premises (or our experience) would require an appeal to the Principle of the Uniformity of Nature, where "instances, of which we have had no experience, must resemble those, of which we have had experience, and that the course of nature continues always uniformly the same." (Hume, 1748/1910, section IV). But such a principle cannot, of course, be established by observation or deductive inference. It can be established only by inductive inference, which presupposes the principle, thus leading to a vicious circle. If Hume is correct, this negative argument rules out the possibility of justifying induction. In other words, the epistemological problem of induction is insoluble.

Despite Hume's observation, it is a fact that human beings are almost compelled to draw inferences from limited information, as in argument F. Why? Hume's positive contribution to the problem of induction is an answer to this latter question. He suggests that the experience of constant conjunction results in a "habit of mind" that leads us to anticipate the same conclusion whenever we encounter another instance of the premises (Hume, 1748, section V, part I). For example, having seen several dinosaur skeletons and noting that they all have four legs results in a "habit of mind" leading to the expectation that the next dinosaur skeleton encountered will also have four legs. On this account, the basis of induction is not to be found in some objective feature of the world, as is the case with (rule dependent) calculi for making deductive inferences, but rather in the structure of our minds. That is, he provides a ***psychological solution*** to the problem.

Now consider the following argument:

(G) Socrates was a dinosaur; the skeletal remains of Socrates reveal a broken leg

\ All dinosaurs had a broken leg.

Most of us would not be prepared to accept the conclusion of G. Frankly, it sounds crazy. So, what is the difference between F and G such that we would accept argument F as plausible but consider argument G to be implausible? Interestingly, unlike in the case of deduction, we cannot appeal to logical form to differentiate between the plausibility of F and G because both of them have an identical logical form, namely:

(H) X has the property alpha and X has the property beta

\ Everything with the property alpha has the property beta.

To state the problem in Hume's vocabulary, why does observing the regularity in finding dinosaur bones with four legs (all broken) result in the formation of a "habit of mind" or expectation that all dinosaurs had four legs, but not the expectation that all dinosaurs had broken legs? Even if every skeletal find that reveals four legs also reveals broken legs, why is the mind prepared to generalize the former regularity but not the latter?

This is the New Riddle of Induction articulated by Goodman (1955) with the famous grue example. Consider the following plausible inference:

(I) Emerald x is green;

Emerald y is green;
etc.
\ All emeralds are green.

Goodman introduced the predicate "grue", which applies "to all things examined before [time] *t* just in case they are green but to other things just in case they are blue" and not examined before time *t* (Goodman, 1955, p. 74). This leads to the following inference:

(J) Emerald x is grue;

Emerald y is grue;
etc.
\ All emeralds are grue.

The dilemma is that the very same observations support the incompatible conclusions that all emeralds observed in the future will be green and all future observed emeralds will be grue. How do we select which predicate to project?

Goodman points out that while Hume was correct in appealing to "habits of mind", he failed to notice that the mind is only prepared to generalize or project certain regularities but not others. It is often said that properties that project or generalize in the required manner (like all members of a species having the same number of legs) are law-like, while those that do not project or generalize (like having a broken leg) are a matter of individual accident. But this is not particularly helpful because law-like properties are defined as those that project or generalize.

So far we have stated the problem of induction utilizing the classical form of enumerative induction, where a generalization is drawn from the observation of specific instances, as in examples F through J. Induction can also involve drawing a specific conclusion from specific instances, as in the following example:

(K) Some cats have a broken leg; Socrates is a cat;

\ Socrates has a broken leg.

One particular form of induction, called abduction, is often singled out for special treatment (Thagard & Shelley, 1997). Abduction is a form of fallacious deductive reasoning known as affirming the consequent, as in L. It can sometimes lead to a good inductive inference.

(L) All (some) cats have four legs; Socrates has four legs;

\ Socrates is a cat.

While it is possible to identify different forms of induction, it is not at all clear whether this deepens our understanding of the fundamental issues. Certainly, the core issues discussed above apply across the board.

Psychology of reasoning

While philosophers are interested primarily in the epistemic relationship between premises and conclusions, psychologists are concerned with the cognitive processes/mechanisms involved in drawing inferences. Psychologists have three reasons to be interested in reasoning. The first obvious reason is that humans have the ability to evaluate arguments, so cognitive psychology needs to be able to articulate the mechanisms underlying this ability. The second reason is less obvious but much deeper. Deductive inferences underpin the information processing mechanism (be it physical symbol systems or the language of thought) that cognitive scientists postulate to account for cognitive processes (Fodor, 1975; Newell, 1980a; Pylyshyn, 1984). The third reason is even more compelling: cognitive theories of every phenomenon, be it vision, categorization, or problem solving, assume/require an inductive step at certain key points.

Given that psychologists are interested in cognitive mechanisms underlying logical inferences, rather than the epistemic relationship between premises and conclusions, the philosophical distinction between induction and deduction may or may not be relevant for psychology. It is an empirical question. If it turns out that different cognitive mechanisms are required to account for deductive and inductive inferences, the distinction will need to be retained at the psychological level. If, on the other hand, it turns out that the same cognitive mechanism can account for both deductive and inductive inferences, the distinction will be unnecessary at the psychological level. At the moment, most researchers (but not all) think that different cognitive mechanisms are involved in deductive and inductive reasoning. In fact, researchers studying deduction and induction constitute separate communities and use different tasks and frameworks, as reviewed in the next section. Elqayam and Over (2012) provide an interesting discussion of this issue in the context of probabilistic theories of deductive reasoning (see next section).

Psychology of deduction

Tasks and methods

Psychologists present subjects with logical arguments, such as M through P. In each case, subjects are then asked to exhibit their knowledge of logical relationships by either determining whether the given conclusion follows from the premises or selecting a logical conclusion from several given conclusions.

(M) No lizards are felines; some felines are tigers;

\ No lizards are tigers.

(N) Sally is taller than Mary; Mary is taller than Betty;

\ Sally is taller than Betty

(O) If David presses the brake pedal, the car will stop.

David presses the brake pedal.

\ The car stops.

(P) Scott will choose either a black car or a blue car.

Scott does not choose a blue car.

\ Scott chooses a black car.

The forms most frequently studied by psychologists are categorical syllogisms (example M), three-term transitive relations (example N), conditional (if–then) relations (example O), and disjunctive forms (example P). The categorical syllogism tests knowledge of quantification and negation. Three-term relational arguments test knowledge of transitivity relations, while operators focus on implication (if–then) and disjunction (or).

Findings

The basic finding is that intelligent, educated subjects make numerous mistakes in deductive reasoning. Most psychologists accept that humans are rational beings. Therefore, the enterprise is one of analyzing the pattern of mistakes subjects make and from this analysis drawing conclusions about the nature of the psychological mechanisms underlying human reasoning abilities.

Perhaps the oldest and most robust finding in the psychological literature is the content effect. In the early 20th century Mary Wilkins (1928) reported that subjects reason much more accurately when the logical conclusion of the argument is consistent with their beliefs about the world (arguments 4–6 in Table 13.2 on page 235) than when it is inconsistent with their beliefs (arguments 7–9 in Table 13.2). Subject responses fall between these two extremes when they have no beliefs about the conclusions (arguments 1–3 in Table 13.2). This effect is extremely robust and has been replicated on numerous occasions (e.g., Evans, Barston, & Pollard, 1983; Goel & Dolan, 2003; see also Ball & Thompson, this volume). It is also the source of the deepest puzzle in developing a psychological theory of human deduction. The dilemma it presents is the following: given that deduction is a function of the logical form of the argument (and not the content) as discussed above, how can the content of the argument have such a significant effect on our ability to reason logically?

Other errors related to the content effect include "misidentification of the task", where subjects evaluate the truth of the conclusion rather than the validity of the argument (Evans, Handley, & Harper, 2001), and the supplementation of the given information in the premises with additional information from subjects' knowledge of the world, which leads them to draw an inference that would not follow from the original information (Evans, Newstead, & Byrne, 1993).

Human reasoners make other common errors that are unrelated to the content effect. One such error is the "atmosphere" or "mood effect" (Woodworth & Sells, 1935), wherein subjects prefer a conclusion with an existential quantifier if one of the premises has an existential quantifier, and prefer a conclusion with a negation if one of the premises contains a negation. In another error, subjects will assume the premises are symmetrical. For example, the premise "all A are B" might be treated the same as "all B are A" (compare these to "all apples are fruits" and "all fruits are apples").

Common errors in conditional reasoning include the following: subjects accept *modus ponens* (i.e. affirming the antecedent) as valid around 97% of the time but accept *modus tollens* (i.e. denying the consequent), which is equally valid, only about 65% of the time. They also accept the fallacious forms of denying the antecedent and affirming the consequent as valid about 40% of the time.

The goal of psychological theories of deductive reasoning is to explain these patterns of data.

Theories of deductive reasoning

Psychologists are engaged in the business of articulating the cognitive mechanisms underlying our ability to draw deductive inferences. They do this by examining the pattern of errors generated by subjects as they engage in deductive reasoning. Given that we have a formal theory of deductive inference, and a mechanism eminently suited for carrying out deductive inferences (physical symbol systems/classical computational systems), the most natural starting point for psychological theories of deduction is to assume that the cognitive system utilizes a similar type of mechanism and explain any deviations between expected performance and actual performance as performance errors (Chomsky, 1981), due to short-term memory limitations, attention limitations, misunderstanding the task, and so forth. Two major theories of reasoning, mental logic and mental models, follow this approach.

Mental logic theories (Braine, 1978; Henle, 1962; Rips, 1994) postulate that reasoners have an underlying competence knowledge of the *inferential role* of the closed-form, or logical terms, of the language ('all', 'some', 'none', 'and', etc.). The internal representation of arguments preserves the structural properties of the propositional strings in which the premises are stated. A mechanism of inference is applied to these representations to draw conclusions from premises. Essentially, the claim is that deductive reasoning is a rule-governed process defined over syntactic strings. Performance factors such as short-term memory limitations, attention capacity, and misunderstanding the task can result in substandard performance.

By contrast, mental model theory (Johnson-Laird, 1983; Johnson-Laird & Byrne, 1991; see also Johnson-Laird, Goodwin, & Khemlani, this volume) postulates that reasoners have an underlying competence knowledge of the *meaning* of the closed-form, or logical terms, of the language (e.g. "all", "some", "none", "and", etc.)[2] and use this knowledge to construct and search alternative scenarios.[3] The internal representation of arguments preserves the structural properties of the world (e.g., spatial relations) that the propositional strings are about rather than the structural properties of the propositional strings themselves. The basic claim is that deductive reasoning is a process requiring spatial manipulation and search. Errors are explained by performance factors, such as using background knowledge to flesh out models, terminating search too early, and memory and attentional factors.

A third popular account, dual mechanism theory, makes a distinction between formal, deliberate, rule-based processes and implicit, unschooled, automatic processes (see Evans, this volume). Where we have knowledge about the domain, we are more likely to use the latter processes. Where we have no knowledge about the domain, we must rely upon the former processes. However, dual mechanism theories come in various flavors that differ on the exact nature and properties of these two systems. Theories differentially emphasize explicit and implicit processes (Evans & Over, 1996), conscious and preconscious processes (Stanovich & West, 2000), formal and heuristic processes (Newell & Simon, 1972), and associative and rule-based processes (Goel, 1995; Sloman, 1996). The relationship among these proposals has yet to be clarified. A more recent proposal suggests that the critical distinction between the two systems is the utilization of working memory (Evans & Stanovich, 2013). The formal system utilizes working memory while the heuristic system does not.[4] One obvious shortcoming of dual mechanism theory is that while it postulates two different systems for reasoning, it does not actually provide an account of either, in the sense that mental models and mental logic theories do.

A fourth proposal, currently referred to as the "New Paradigm" (Elqayam & Evans, 2013; Elqayam & Over, 2012; see also Elqayam, this volume) is based upon the study of the conditional inference (if p, then q). Philosophers have long worried about the fact that the formal interpretation of the conditional, as material implication, leads to some paradoxes and does not do justice to its everyday use in natural language (Lewis, 1912). Consider the conditional in example O: if the brakes are pressed, then the car will stop. On the material implication account, either the brakes are not pressed or the car stops. So if we believe that the brakes are pressed, we should conclude with absolute certainty that the car stops. However, some philosophers (Ramsey, 1929/1990; Stalnaker, 1968, 1970), have argued that intuition and actual natural language use of the conditional is not consistent with this interpretation. Oaksford and Chater (2007, 2009) make a similar case in the psychological literature. One influential solution has been to account for intuitions and everyday language use of the conditional by recognizing that contextual factors affect reasoners' judgments. This is the Ramsey test (Ramsey, 1929/1990). It proposes that to determine the truth of a conditional requires the hypothetical addition of the antecedent to our stock of beliefs, making any modifications needed to maintain consistency, and then judging whether the consequent follows (Ramsey, 1929). For example, augmenting the antecedent in the above conditional, with the knowledge that the brakes need servicing, will reduce the probability of concluding that the car will stop. Similarly, knowing that the brakes have been recently serviced will increase the probability of accepting the consequent. This has led to a probabilistic approach that handles conditionals by assigning subjective conditional probabilities (de Finetti, 1937/1964; Stalnaker, 1968, 1970; Oaksford & Chater, 2007; see also Oaksford & Chater, this volume).

Thus, the natural/intuitive interpretation of O is that, given what we know, the conditional probability of a car stopping, given that the brakes are pressed, is high, say, 0.9 [P(stopping | brakes) = 0.9]. However, the probability of it stopping, given the additional knowledge that the brakes require servicing is less, say, 0.6 [P(stopping | brakes, need servicing) = 0.6], and the probability of it stopping given that the brakes have recently been serviced may be, say, 0.96 [P(stopping | brakes, serviced) = 0.96]. Our confidence in the conclusion is a function of the subjective probability assigned, based upon our background/contextual beliefs. Once these probabilities are signed, there is a nicely developed formal mechanism (Bayesian probability theory) for drawing the inference.

The ability of contextual/additional information to affect inference is a feature of induction, but is inconsistent with our understanding of deduction. Oaksford and Chater (2009) argue that such an account is necessary to explain the data. In fact, they claim that *all* logical inference, not just conditionals, is probabilistic. The probabilistic approach does seem to provide better coverage of some data and natural language use of the conditional. It also has the additional benefit of integrating the literature on decision-making and reasoning. However, it comes at a price. One consequence of it is that there is no such thing as deductive reasoning. That is, our competence knowledge (and basic innate intuitions) are captured by probability theory, rather than formal logics. A second consequence is that all reasoning is induction, insofar as it requires drawing upon context and selecting relevant/salient information, and determining the level of salience, to assign conditional probabilities. For example, is knowing that the car above has been recently painted, or the tires rotated, relevant to assigning the conditional probabilities? Once subjective probabilities are assigned, one can apply the probability calculus, but a complete account of deductive inference (which in the "new paradigm" needs to include contextualization) cannot be given until we have a resolution to the riddle of induction.[5]

Psychology of induction

The philosophical analysis of induction provides psychology with two basic empirical questions that need to be answered: (1) Hume's question: what is the cognitive mechanism responsible for forming "habits of mind" from previously observed regularities (i.e., what structures of mind allow us to generalize from past experience to the future)?; and (2) Goodman's question: what are the cognitive structures and mechanisms involved in determining that a particular property is generalizable (or projectable) or not? While there may be no epistemological solutions to the problems of induction, we know that psychological and biological solutions do exist. The psychological problem of induction is one of discovering these solutions. Psychologists have made considerable progress with respect to the first issue, but the second remains elusive.

In fact, much of the research program of the behaviorists, focused on the study of learning, and addressed the issue of how minds make connections between antecedent and consequent events. For example, when a pigeon learns to associate a certain arbitrary action (e.g., the movement of its neck one inch to the right) with the presentation of a food pellet, through repeated occurrences, it is exhibiting Hume's "habit of mind". Much of this research paradigm was concerned with how such associations could be formed and modified and extinguished. This basic mechanism of association was thought to explain all behaviors, from that of the pigeon to language acquisition and problem-solving in humans.

Psychologists eventually concluded that the mechanism of association may have limited application for human behavior (Chomsky, 1959). By the 1960s the behaviorist paradigm gave way to the cognitive paradigm and the association mechanism was replaced with an inference mechanism based upon computational information processing theory (Chomsky, 1981; Miller, Galanter, & Pribram, 1960; Newell & Simon, 1972). The relationship between these two mechanisms is elegantly articulated by Fodor and Pylyshyn (1988).

With respect to the question of how we determine the relevant or projectable properties of events and entities, psychologists are pursuing two central themes: similarity and causation. Below we discuss some of the tasks and methods utilized for this purpose.

Tasks and methods

In contrast to the experimental literature on deductive reasoning, the experimental literature on induction is large and varied. Due to space limitations we will review a small aspect of the literature that explicitly solicits judgments of the strength of the relationship between premises and conclusions in arguments. Directly asking subjects to judge the strength (or plausibility) of the relationship between premises and conclusions in simple enumerative inductive inference is perhaps the most direct way of doing this. For example, given:

(Q) All the swans in Central Park are white;

\ All swans are white

subjects' intuitive judgment of the strength of the conclusion allows researchers to compare different arguments and see what is common across the ones that are judged to be more plausible than others.

A more controlled way of accomplishing the same thing is through direct comparison between arguments. Here subjects are presented with competing arguments that have been selected to vary along certain dimensions (e.g., similarity), and asked to identify which is the most plausible or strongest, as in examples R and S below. Other experimental designs compare more complex argument forms, as in examples X and Y below, used to explore the issue of diversity. Yet others compare across pairs of arguments, as in examples AB, AC, AD, and AE below, which are used to probe the relative importance of similarity and causality of the underlying causal story.

Findings

The findings from this body of research consist of the identification of a number of "principles" which seem to guide subjects in terms of selecting the regularities to generalize or project. These principles can be organized into two broad categories: similarity and causality. We discuss each below.

Similarity

Similarity in properties between the instances in the observation (or premises) and instances in the conclusion increases the confidence in the conclusion. Consider the following examples drawn from Heit (2007):

(R) Dogs have hearts;

\ Wolves have hearts

is judged to be a stronger conclusion than

(S) Dogs have hearts;

\ Bees have hearts

because wolves are much more similar to dogs than bees are to dogs. These types of inferences inherit/exhibit many of the features of human categorization, such as typicality and asymmetry (Sloman & Lagnado, 2005). An illustration of the former is the following example drawn from Sloman (1998):

(T) Robins have sesamoid bones;

\ Sparrows have sesamoid bones.

is judged to be a stronger conclusion than

(U) Ostriches have sesamoid bones;

\ Sparrows have sesamoid bones.

The explanation is that robins are considered more typical or central members of the category of birds than ostriches and suggests that subjects are more willing to project properties from typical or central members of the overall category than from peripheral members of the overall category.

Another related phenomenon is asymmetry in inference (Sloman & Lagnado, 2005), illustrated in the following example:

(V) Robins have 38 chromosomes;

\ Ostriches have 38 chromosomes

is to judged to be a stronger conclusion than

(W) Ostriches have 38 chromosomes;

\ Robins have 38 chromosomes.

The explanation is that we are more prepared to project properties from typical or central members of categories to nontypical members than from nontypical members to typical members. Because robins are more typical or central members of the category of birds than are ostriches, we more readily project properties from robins to ostriches than from ostriches to robins.

However, there is also a diversity effect at work (Sloman & Lagnado, 2005), which seems to undercut the principle of similarity. Subjects tend to judge the following argument

(X) Robins require magnesium to live; Ostriches require magnesium to live;

\ All birds require magnesium to live

as stronger than

(Y) Robins require magnesium to live; Sparrows require magnesium to live;

\ All birds require magnesium to live.

This suggests that instances of a property found in peripheral members of a category strengthens the likelihood of the property being projected to the whole category.

There are also a number of fallacies or counterexamples in this literature. For example, in the inclusion fallacy (Osherson, Smith, Wilkie, López, & Shafir, 1990), many people consider

(Z) Robins have sesamoid bones;

\ Birds have sesamoid bones

to be stronger than

(AA) Robins have sesamoid bones;

\ Ostriches have sesamoid bones.

This is problematic because the first conclusion implies the second. If ostriches belong to the category of birds, even given their peripheral status, there is no reason to suspect that they do not have sesamoid bones.

Causality

An appeal to causality is the other means of differentiating between regularities that humans are prepared to project and those that they are not. The basic idea here is that generalization/projection from one instance to another instance is warranted if the same causal laws or mechanisms underwrite both instances. For example (Heit & Rubinstein, 1994), subjects prefer the inference

(AB) Hawks have a liver with two chambers;

\ Chickens have a liver with two chambers

to the inference

(AC) Hawks have a liver with two chambers;

\ Tigers have a liver with two chambers.

This is consistent with the similarity account. However, subjects also prefer the inference

(AD) Hawks prefer to feed at night;

\ Tigers prefer to feed at night

to the inference

(AE) Hawks prefer to feed at night;

\ Chickens prefer to feed at night

The explanation is that inference strength is not simply a matter of similarity but rather a function of the underlying causal stories that subjects believe or assume. In the former example, subjects are focusing on the biological properties of chickens, hawks, and tigers and concluding that chickens and hawks are more closely related than hawks and tigers in terms of anatomy. In the latter example, subjects are focusing on the fact that hawks and tigers are hunters and carnivores, while chickens are not.

Causal chains can also be used to explain certain asymmetries in inference strengths. For example (Sloman & Lagnado, 2005):

(AF) Gazelles contain retinum;

\ Lions contain retinum

is usually considered stronger than

(AG) Lions contain retinum;

\ Gazelles contain retinum.

The rationale is that lions eat gazelles and the digestive tract may be a possible mechanism for transmitting retinum.

Thus, what we have emerging from this line of research are series of "principles" that presumably constrain the observed regularities that humans are and are not willing to project or generalize.

Theories of induction

Induction is typically viewed as a form of hypothesis generation and testing, where the crucial issue is one of searching a large database and determining which pieces of information are relevant and how they are to be mapped onto the present situation. The determination of relevance and generalization of certain properties, but not others, is guided by a series of principles or constraints such as provided by similarity and causality. The theoretical efforts in this area have been devoted to discovering these principles and incorporating them into models that can explain the varying strength of connections between premises and conclusions.

The similarity-coverage model developed by Osherson et al. (1990) is often considered the most well-known mathematical model of property induction. It predicts the strength of inductive arguments based on the degree to which the premise categories resemble the conclusion category and/or the extent to which the premises account for the smallest superordinate taxonomic category that includes both the premises and the conclusion (e.g., robins use serotonin as a neurotransmitter; blue jays use serotonin as a neurotransmitter; geese use serotonin as a neurotransmitter. Since robins and blue jays have the property, it may be the case that all birds have the property. Geese are birds, so maybe geese have the property too; Osherson et al., 1990). Sloman (1993) proposed a competing model of induction that relies on a normalized measure of feature overlap between the premises and conclusion of an argument. This feature-based model has been adapted using a feed-forward connectionist network (Rogers & McClelland, 2004). However, it has been argued that neither of these feature-based models overcomes the original limitations of the similarity-coverage model: its inability to account for inductive arguments that cannot be expressed as pairwise similarities or taxonomic categories (e.g., X uses heraticulin; Y uses heraticulin; Z uses heraticulin) and its lack of a principled mathematical foundation (see Tenenbaum, Kemp, & Shafto, 2007, for a more detailed discussion).

These models provide interesting and valuable insights. However, it is important to understand what these models do and do not explain. Most importantly, they do not explain the notion of similarity. It is a value that must be inserted into the model. One can, of course, appeal to other models that purport to calculate the similarity between two objects or events (Goldstone, Day, & Son, 2010; Tversky, 1977), but these models leave unexplained why certain properties or features are relevant, and how relevant they are. This information must be provided to the model for it to perform the calculation. This highlights the limitations of the psychological research and elusiveness of the New Riddle of Induction raised by Goodman (1955).

More generally, reviewing the state of our understanding of inductive inference at a psychological level is a humbling experience. First, with regard to similarity, while many psychologists believe that similarity is a useful explanatory concept, philosophers (Goodman, 1955) and some psychologists (Sloman & Rips, 1998) recognize that it largely begs the question. Any two objects can share an infinite number of properties.[6] What matters for purposes of inductive reasoning is the identification of the relevant properties. The appeal to similarity was meant to explain the notion of relevance, but it seems that an independent notion of relevance is required to explain similarity. Also, notions of typicality and asymmetry from the categorization literature require a notion of similarity for their definitions, so to appeal to these properties as features of similarity is less than satisfying.

With respect to causality, there is something intuitively very right about this approach. However, the problem is that causality seems to be a projection of the mind onto the world rather than an objective property of the world. While scientists widely use the concept of causation in their informal discourse, the formal theories do not contain such a notion. This returns us to the circularity that Hume pointed out. The justification of causation requires a principle of uniformity, that itself can only be established via an inductive inference. Therefore, the appeal to causation for an understanding of induction may be less than satisfactory.

Finally, even if we were to sort out the above issues and settle on a number of principles and constraints that guide the selection of projectable predicates, we would still be left with the problem of how to determine which ones to apply in any given case. This is, of course, again, the problem of induction.

Lest we despair, it is worth remembering that there is a solution to the psychological problem of induction. There does exist a mechanism (the human brain) that is capable of making such inferences. We just need to articulate the underlying principles. Perhaps we are misunderstanding or misconceptualizing the structure of the cognitive system. The underlying assumption, in much of the cognitive literature, is that of a general-purpose reasoning system with access to (in principle) all available information (Fodor, 1975; Newell, 1980a). In this context, it is becoming increasingly clear that the problem of projectable predicates (also known as the frame problem in cognitive science) is insoluble. Perhaps what is needed is a reconceptualization of the cognitive architecture in a way that this problem does not arise. One such reconceptualization is offered by the "massive modularity" hypothesis (Cosmides & Tooby, 1994). On this account the mind consists of hundreds, perhaps hundreds of thousands of special-purpose mechanisms that are directly triggered by specific features in the environment. That is, there is a tight causal coupling (i.e., no gap) between input-output pairs. If this is correct, then our ability to respond to wide-ranging stimuli in extremely flexible ways is simply an illusion. While such an account is intuitively implausible, the cognitive architecture of our brains may predispose us to tight causal coupling under the illusion of flexible responding, and this account does sidestep the riddle of induction. There may be other reconceptualizations that are more in keeping with the data and our intuitions that also sidestep the problem.

Cognitive neuroscience of reasoning

In terms of the neuroscience of reasoning, the goal is to identify the neuronal systems and understand how they causally interact to enable us to draw various logical inferences. In the context of our current knowledge of brain functions, and the methodologies for studying them, this means identifying disassociations and interconnections between gross anatomical structures involved in reasoning processes. Popular psychological doctrine would have it that deduction, being analytical, is carried out by the left hemisphere, while induction, being synthetic, is a right-hemisphere process. Unsurprisingly, the actual story emerging from the current research is much more complex and interesting.

Cognitive neuroscience of deduction

Tasks

The cognitive neuroscience of deduction literature has utilized the same tasks as the psychological literature summarized previously.

Findings

Given the formal nature of deductive reasoning and the incorporation of this formal mechanism in the psychological theories of deduction, early researchers expected to find a "reasoning module" for deduction (Goel, Gold, Kapur, & Houle, 1997, 1998). The major question seemed to be whether it would be a linguistic system, as predicted by the mental logic theory, or a visuospatial system, as predicted by mental model theory (Johnson-Laird, 1994).

Over the years, dozens of neuroimaging studies have been undertaken (Acuna, Eliassen, Donoghue, & Sanes, 2002; Canessa et al., 2005; Fangmeier, Knauff, Ruff, & Sloutsky, 2006; Heckers, Zalesak, Weiss, Ditman, & Titone, 2004; Houde et al., 2000; Knauff, Fangmeier, Ruff, & Johnson-Laird, 2003; Knauff, Mulack, Kassubek, Salih, & Greenlee, 2002; Noveck, Goel, & Smith, 2004; Prado & Noveck, 2007; Baggio et al., 2016; Reverberi et al., 2012), and the overall results, if nothing else, at least suggest there is no single reasoning module. These studies have been discussed and the results qualitatively summarized in a review article (Goel, 2007) and more recently in a quantitative meta-study (Prado, Chadha, & Booth, 2011). A summary table from the former article is reproduced as Table 13.1. The results suggest that different brain areas are recruited for logical reasoning depending upon factors such as type of argument (syllogisms, transitive inferences, conditionals, etc.; Prado et al., 2011), presence of negation, the presence of unbelievable sentences, form of the argument (valid, inconsistent, indeterminate), presence or absence of content, emotional valence of content, and the like. In this section we briefly summarize how brain recruitment for deductive reasoning differs based upon three manipulations: the presence or absence of content, conflict, and indeterminacy. The transitive inference examples in Table 13.2 serve to illustrate each of the three issues.

Systems for dealing with familiar and unfamiliar material

To explore this issue, Goel and colleagues carried out a series of studies using syllogisms and transitive inferences and holding logical form constant while systematically manipulating content of arguments (Goel, Buchel, Frith, & Dolan, 2000; Goel & Dolan, 2001, 2003; Goel, Makale, & Grafman, 2004). These studies indicate that two distinct systems are involved in reasoning about unfamiliar and familiar material (arguments 1–3 versus 4–9 in Table 13.2). More specifically, a left lateralized frontal-temporal conceptual/language system (Figure 13.1a) processes familiar, conceptually coherent material, while a bilateral parietal visuospatial system, with some dorsal frontal involvement (Figure 13.1b), processes unfamiliar, nonconceptual, or conceptually incoherent material. Areas of activation common to both familiar and unfamiliar material include the left inferior prefrontal cortex (BA 44), left fusiform gyrus (BA 18), right fusiform gyrus (BA 37), bilateral basal ganglia nuclei (accumbens, caudate nucleus, and putamen), and right cerebellum.

The involvement of the left frontal-temporal system in reasoning about familiar or meaningful content has also been demonstrated in neurological patients with focal unilateral lesions to prefrontal cortex (i.e., parietal lobes intact), using the Wason card selection task (Goel, Shuren,

Table 13.1 Summary of particulars of 19 neuroimaging studies of deductive reasoning and reported regions of activation corresponding most closely to the main effect of reasoning

Studies (Organized by Tasks)	***Scanning Method***	*Stimuli Modality*	*Occipital Lobes*		*Parietal Lobes*		*Temporal Lobes*		***Basal Ganglia***		***Cingulate***		***Frontal Lobes***	
			RH	*LH*	*RH*	*LH*	*RH*	*LH*	*RH*	*LH*	*RH*	*LH*	*RH*	*LH*
Transitivity (Explicit)														
Goel et al. (1998)	PET	visual, linguistic		19				37		yes	24, 32			45, 46
Goel & Dolan (2001)	fMRI	visual, linguistic	17, 18, 19	19	7,40	7, 40			yes	yes			6	6,9
Knauff et al. (2003)	fMRI	auditory, linguistic			7	7	21	21, 38					6	46, 47
Goel et al. (2004)	fMRI	visual, linguistic	18, 19	18,19	7,40	7	21, 22, Hi	21,22, Hi					11, 47	6, 9, 46,11
Fangmeier et al. (2006)	fMRI	visual, nonlinguistic			7	40					32		6	6,9
Transitivity (Implicit)														
Acuna et al. (2002)	fMRI	visual, nonlinguistic			7, 39, 40	39, 40				yes			6, 8, 9, 46	6, 8, 9, 46
Heckers et al. (2004)	fMRI	visual, nonlinguistic			40	40	37, Hi	37, 21		yes	24		PSMA, 6	6,47
Categorical Syllogisms														
Goel et al. (1998)	PET	visual, linguistic						21, 22			24, 32			45, 46, 47
Osherson et al. (1998)	PET	visual, linguistic	18						yes					6
Goel et al. (2000)	fMRI	visual, linguistic	18, 19	18		7	21/22		yes	yes			45	44, 45
Goel & Dolan (2003)	fMRI	visual, linguistic	17, 18	17, 18				21,22, 38	yes				6	6,44
Goel & Dolan (2004)	fMRI	visual, linguistic	18	18, 19	7	37		39	yes	yes			6	6, 44, 45
Conditionals (Simple)														
Noveck et al. (2004)	fMRI	visual, linguistic		19		7		37			32			6,47
Prado & Noveck (2007)	fMRI	visual, linguistic	18	17	39,40	40							6, 45, 46	9,46

(*Continued*)

Table 13.1 (Continued)

Studies (Organized by Tasks)	***Scanning Method***	*Stimuli Modality*	*Occipital Lobes*		*Parietal Lobes*		*Temporal Lobes*		*Basal Ganglia*		***Cingulate***		***Frontal Lobes***	
			RH	*LH*	*RH*	*LH*	*RH*	*LH*	*RH*	*LH*	*RH*	*LH*	*RH*	*LH*
Conditionals (Complex)														
Houde et al. (2000)*	PET	visual, nonlinguistic												
Parsons & Osherson (2001)	PET	visual, linguistic	18	18			21, 37, 39		yes	yes	24	31	10, 44,9	
Canessa et al. (2005)	fMRI	visual, linguistic	19	19	7, 39, 40	7, 39, 40				yes	32	32	6, 8, 9,10, 46	6, 8, 9, 46
Mixed Stimuli														
Goel et al. (1997)	PET	visual, linguistic												
Knauff et al. (2002)	fMRI	auditory, linguistic	19	19	7,40	7, 14	21,22	21, 22			32	32	6,9	6,9

*Brodmann Areas not provided by authors.

Note: Numbers denote Brodmann areas. RH = right hemisphere; LH = left hemisphere; Hi = hippocampus; PSMA = pre-sensory-motor area. Blank cells indicate absence of activation in region. "Stimuli modality" refers to the form and manner of presentation of the stimuli. Cerebellum activations are not noted in the table. Reproduced from Goel (2007).

Table 13.2 Three-term transitive arguments sorted into nine categories

	Determinate arguments		*Indeterminate arguments*
	Valid	*Invalid*	*Invalid*
No meaningful content (content has no effect on the task)	City A is north of City B City B is north of City C City A is north of City C (1)	City A is north of City B City B is north of City C City C is north of City A (2)	City A is north of City B City A is north of City C City B is north of City C (3)
Congruent (content facilitates the task)	London is north of Paris Paris is north of Cairo London is north of Cairo (4)	London is north of Paris Paris is north of Cairo Cairo is north of London (5)	London is north of Paris London is north of Cairo Cairo is north of Paris (6)
Incongruent (content inhibits the task)	London is north of Paris Cairo is north of London Cairo is north of Paris (7)	London is north of Paris Cairo is north of London Paris is north of Cairo (8)	London is north of Paris London is north of Cairo Paris is north of London (9)

Note: Brodmann areas not provided by authors.

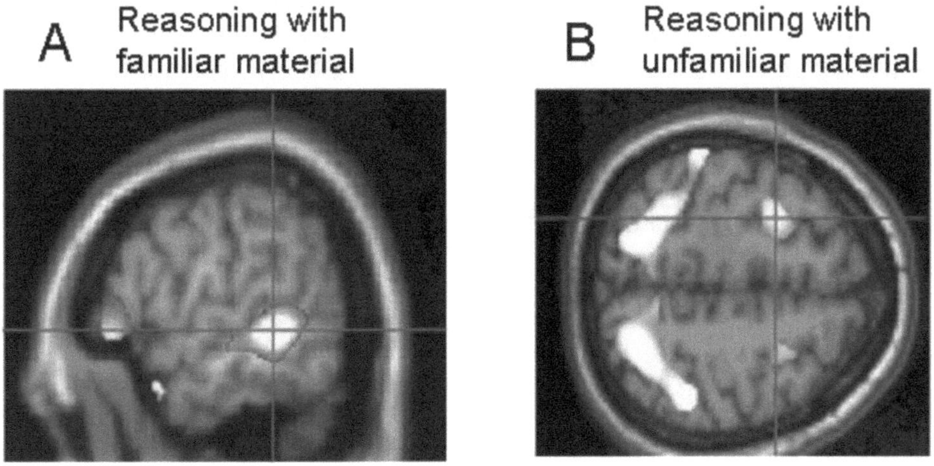

Figure 13.1 (A) Reasoning with syllogisms such as "All apples are fruit; all fruit are nutritious; all apples are nutritious" activates a left hemisphere frontal-temporal system. (B) Reasoning with logically equivalent syllogisms but without believable/familiar content, such as, "All A are B; all B are C; all A are C" activates a bilateral occipital-parietal and dorsal frontal system (Goel et al., 2000).

Sheesley, & Grafman, 2004). These patients performed as well as normal controls on the arbitrary version of the task, but unlike the normal controls they failed to benefit from the presentation of familiar content in a meaningful version of the task. In fact, the latter result was driven by the exceptionally poor performance of patients with left frontal lobe lesions. Patients with lesions to right prefrontal cortex performed as well as normal controls. A recent patient study with frontotemporal dementia patients shows a similar dissociation between the frontal-temporal system and the parietal system using three-term transitive arguments with familiar and unfamiliar content (Vartanian, Goel, Tierney, Huey, & Grafman, 2009).

Systems for dealing with conflict and belief-bias

A robust consequence of the content effect is that subjects reason much more accurately about valid arguments involving believable conclusions and invalid arguments involving unbelievable conclusions (arguments 4–6 in Table 13.2) than valid arguments involving unbelievable conclusions and invalid arguments involving believable conclusions (arguments 7–9 in Table 13.2) (Evans, Barston, & Pollard, 1983; Wilkins, 1928; see also Ball & Thompson, this volume). In the former case (congruent condition), subjects' beliefs facilitate the task while in the latter case (incongruent condition) their beliefs inhibit the logical task. In inhibitory belief trials, the prepotent response is the incorrect response associated with belief-bias. Incorrect responses in such trials indicate that subjects failed to detect the conflict between their beliefs and the logical inference or they detected the conflict but failed to inhibit the prepotent response associated with the belief-bias (De Neys & Bonnefon, 2013). These belief-biased responses activate ventral medial prefrontal cortex (VMPFC) (BA 11, 32), highlighting its role in non-logical, belief-based responses. The correct response indicates that subjects detected the conflict between their beliefs and the logical inference, inhibited the prepotent response associated with the belief-bias, and engaged the formal reasoning mechanism. The detection of this conflict requires engagement of right lateral/dorsal lateral prefrontal cortex (BA 45, 46) (see Figure 13.2) (Goel et al., 2000; Goel & Dolan, 2003; Prado & Noveck, 2007). This conflict detection role of right lateral/dorsolateral prefrontal cortex (rL/DLPFC) is a generalized phenomenon that has been documented in a wide range of paradigms in the cognitive neuroscience literature (Caramazza, Gordon, Zurif, & DeLuca, 1976; Fink et al., 1999; Stavy, Goel, Critchley, & Dolan, 2006).

One very simple demonstration of this system using lesion data was carried out by Caramazza and colleagues (Caramazza et al., 1976) using two-term reasoning problems such as the following: "Mike is taller than George"; who is taller"? They reported that – consistent with imaging data (Goel et al., 2000; Goel & Dolan, 2003) – patients with lesions to the right hemisphere were impaired only when the form of the question was incongruent with the premise (e.g., who is shorter?).

Systems for dealing with certain and uncertain information

Cognitive theories of reasoning do not typically postulate different mechanisms for reasoning with complete and incomplete information (arguments 1, 2, 4, 6, 7, 8 versus 3, 6, 9 in Table 13.2). However, patient and neuroimaging data suggest that different neural systems underwrite these inferences. Goel and colleagues (2007) tested neurological patients with focal unilateral frontal lobe lesions (see Figure 13.3) on a transitive inference task while systematically manipulating completeness of information regarding the status of the conclusion (i.e., determinate and indeterminate trials). The results demonstrated a double dissociation such that patients with left prefrontal cortex (PFC) lesions were selectively impaired in trials with complete information (i.e., determinate trials), while patients with right PFC lesions were selectively impaired in trials with incomplete information (i.e., indeterminate trials). These results have been duplicated and further clarified in a recent imaging study (Goel, Stollstorff, Nakic, Knutson, & Grafman, 2009).

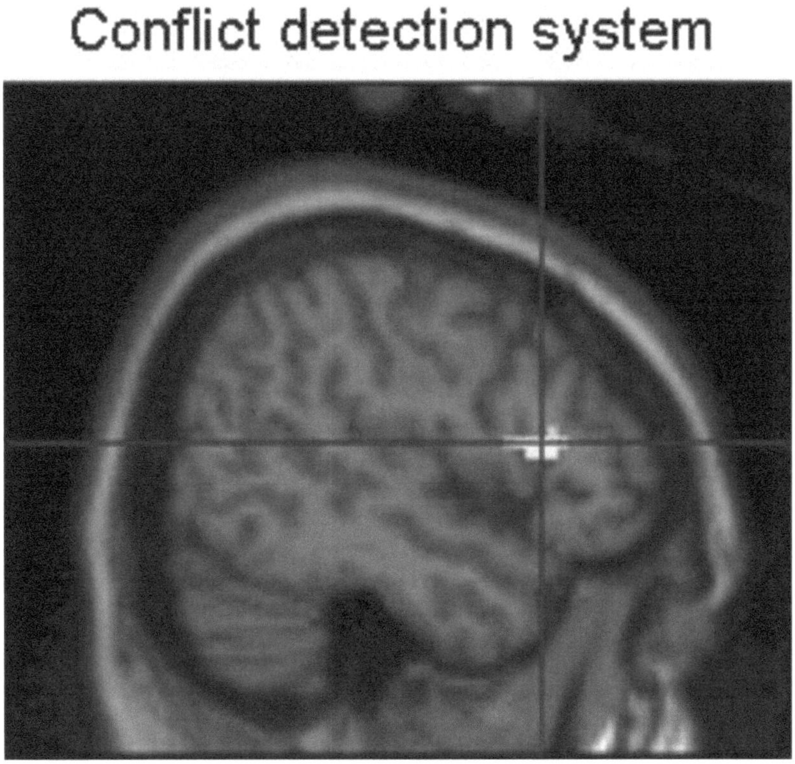

Figure 13.2 When there is a conflict between the validity of an argument and the believability of the conclusion, such as in the argument "All apples are fruit; All fruit are poisonous; All apples are poisonous", the right lateral/dorsolateral PFC is activated (Goel & Dolan, 2003).

Implications for cognitive theories of deductive reasoning

The major cognitive theories of deductive reasoning do not fare well with respect to the neuropsychological data. Mental models theory predicts the involvement of the visuospatial system in logical reasoning while mental logic theory predicts involvement of the language/syntactic system. The cognitive neuroscience data shows that both systems can be engaged depending on the nature of the stimuli. Dual mechanism theory predicts the involvement of two systems, an effortful formal system and an automatic reflex-type system that we share with rats and pigeons (Evans & Over, 1996; Stanovich, 2004), and more recently, a system involving working memory and a system not involving working memory (e.g., Evans & Stanovich, 2013). However, while the cognitive neuroscience data do show the involvement of multiple systems, one which does correspond to the effortful formal system, the other is a very sophisticated conceptual, language-mediated system that we certainly do not share with rats and pigeons (Goel, 2009), nor can it operate in the absence of working memory. Finally, while there have been no cognitive neuroscience experiments to directly test the probabilistic account of deductive reasoning, there are, nevertheless, experiments that introduce uncertainty or indeterminacy into deductive reasoning tasks and show a double dissociation between certain and uncertain inferences, suggesting that the brain is quite capable of engaging in both types of reasoning. So, insofar as the "new

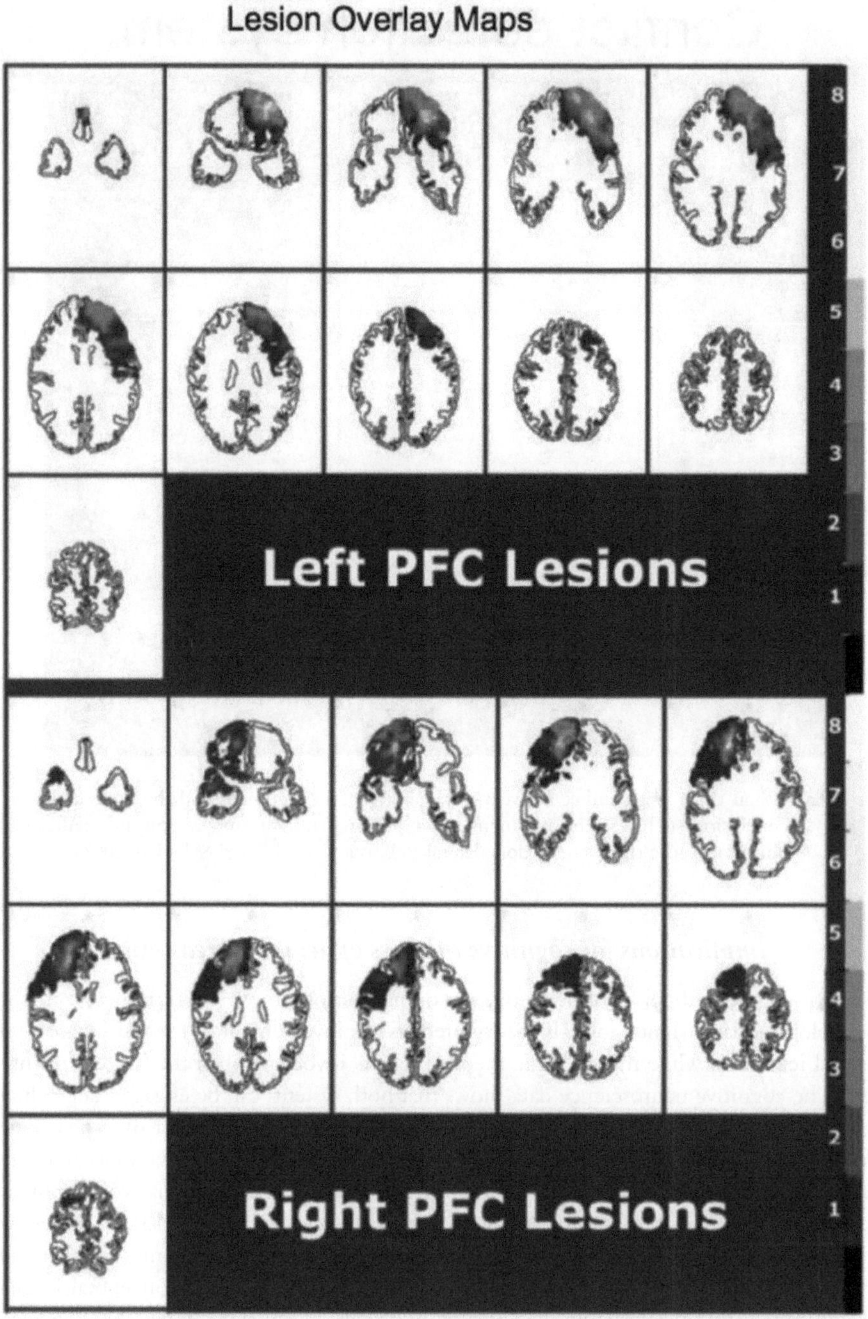

Figure 13.3 Brain areas of damage underlying impairment in determinate reasoning trials (Left PFC Lesions) versus indeterminate reasoning trials (Right PFC Lesions) reproduced from Goel et al. (2007). Lesions to left PFC impair reasoning in determinate trials, such as, "Mary is taller than Natasha; Natasha is taller than Michelle; Mary is taller than Michelle". Lesions to right PFC specifically impair reasoning in indeterminate trials, such as, "Mary is taller than Natasha; Mary is taller than Michelle; Natasha is taller than Michelle".

paradigm" wants to suggest that all deductive inferences contain a degree of uncertainty, this claim would seem to be inconsistent with the neuropsychological data.

More positively, the data tell us that the brain is organized in ways not anticipated by cognitive theory. In particular, there is no unitary system for deductive reasoning in the brain (be it mental model, mental logic, or probability theory). The evidence points to a fractionated system that is dynamically configured in response to certain task and environmental cues. We have reviewed three lines of demarcation above, including systems for heuristic and formal processes, conflict detection/resolution systems, and systems for dealing with certain and uncertain inferences. There are undoubtedly others.

While there is considerable evidence for the existence of these systems, their time course of processing and interaction is largely unknown. One *speculative* account of how processing of arguments might proceed through these systems is presented in Figure 13.4. It draws upon the interplay between Gazzaniga's "left hemisphere interpreter" (Gazzaniga, 2000) and right PFC systems for conflict detection and uncertainty maintenance. The function of this interpreter is to make sense of the environment by completing patterns and filling in the gaps in the available information. We don't think the system is specific to particular types of patterns. It doesn't care whether the pattern is logical, causal, social, or statistical. It simply abhors uncertainty and will complete any pattern, often prematurely, to the detriment of the organism. The roles of the conflict detection and uncertainty maintenance systems are, respectively, to detect conflicts in patterns and actively maintain representations of indeterminate/ambiguous situations and bring them to the attention of the interpreter.

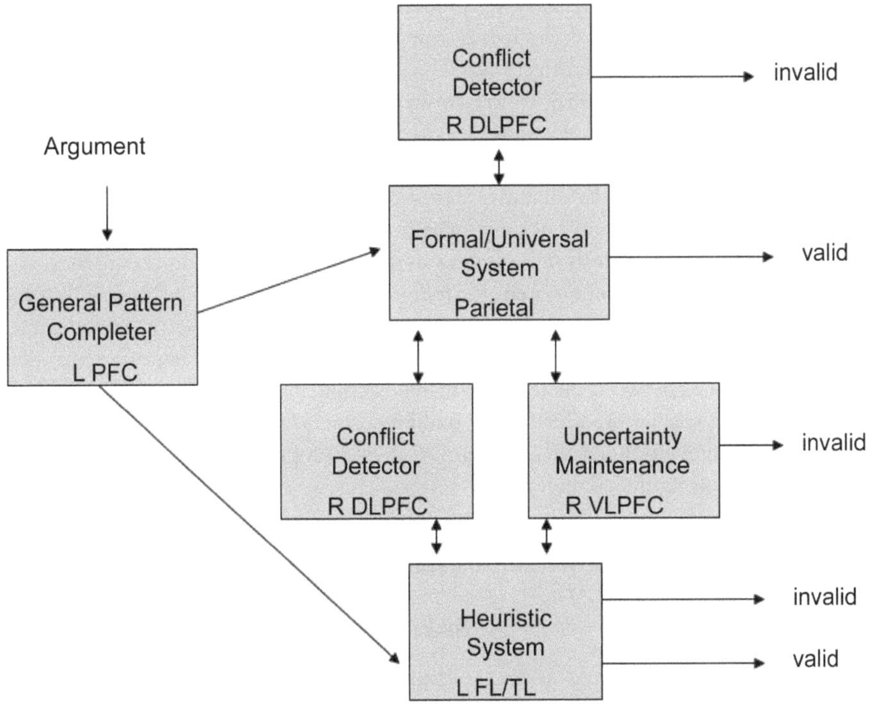

Figure 13.4 Speculative account of the processing of arguments through neural systems (reproduced from Goel, 2009)

Consider again the nine possible types of three-term transitive arguments reproduced in Table 13.2. Arguments 1–3 that subjects can have no beliefs about are relegated to the formal/universal methods processing system. This system is continually monitored by a conflict detector (right dorsal lateral prefrontal cortex) and uncertainty maintenance system (right ventral lateral prefrontal cortex). In the case of argument 2, an inconsistency will be detected between the premises and the conclusion and an "invalid" determination made. In the case of arguments 1 and 3, there is no conflict. Further pattern completion should validate the consistency of argument 1, resulting in a "valid" response. In the case of argument 3, the uncertainty maintenance system will highlight the uncertainty inherent in the premises and inhibit the left hemisphere interpreter from making unwarranted assumptions, eventually allowing an "invalid" response to be generated.

Arguments 4–9, containing propositions that subjects have beliefs about, are initially passed on to the left frontal-temporal system for heuristic processing. However, if a conflict is detected between the believability of the conclusion and the logical response (arguments 7–9), the processing is rerouted to, or at least shared with, the formal pattern matcher in the parietal system. In the formal system these arguments are dealt with in a similar manner as arguments 1–3, except for the following important differences: (1) the conflict detection system has to continually monitor for belief–logic conflict while also monitoring for logical inconsistency; and (2) the fact that subjects have beliefs about the content will also make the task of the uncertainty maintenance system much more difficult. Often it will fail to inhibit the left hemisphere interpreter. Both of these situations place greater demands on the cognitive system, resulting in longer reaction times and lower accuracy scores in these types of trials (Goel & Dolan, 2003).

Arguments 4–6 are passed to the left frontal-temporal heuristic/conceptual system and are largely (though not necessarily exclusively) processed by this system. The believability of the conclusion response is the same as the logical response, facilitating the conflict detection in 5 and pattern completion in 4. Even the "invalid" response in 6 is facilitated, but for the wrong reason. As above, the unbelievability of the conclusion makes it difficult for the uncertainty maintenance system to maintain uncertainty of the conclusion, but in this case failure facilitates the correct response.

The main contribution of the cognitive neuroscience literature to the study of deductive reasoning has been the fractionation of the system and the identification of some of the component parts, such as a conflict detection system, a system sensitive to conceptual content, a system sensitive to formal structure, and a system for maintaining uncertainty. The data do not tell us anything about the internal mechanisms of these systems, or indeed, how the systems interact with each other. Nonetheless, the findings are an important first step because they identify mid-level concepts (i.e., between the level of Turing machine descriptions and phenomenological descriptions) that can be used for theory building. One way to move forward, in terms of understanding the interactions of these systems, is the development of computer programs of deductive reasoning using these concepts.

Cognitive neuroscience of induction

Tasks

The literature examining the neuroscience of induction is sparse. It perhaps begins with the split-brain patient studies (Gazzaniga, 1989; Gazzaniga & Smylie, 1984) involving implicit inference tasks (as described below).

More recently a few studies have focused on differential patterns of brain activation for inductive versus deductive inference (Goel & Dolan, 2004; Goel et al., 1997). These studies involve placing subjects in brain scanners and presenting them with inductive arguments (AH) in one condition and deductive arguments (AI) in another condition and asking them to make judgments of plausibility in the former case and judgments of validity in the latter case. Following are examples of inductive (AH) and deductive (AI) items used in these studies:

(AH) House cats have 32 teeth;

Lions have 32 teeth;

\ All felines have 32 teeth.

(AI) All animals with 32 teeth are cats;

No cats are dogs;

\ No dogs have 32 teeth.

A related study examined deductive versus probabilistic reasoning (Osherson et al., 1998) by presenting similar three-term arguments and instructing participants to decide whether the conclusion was valid or invalid (logic task) or whether it had a greater chance of being true than false (probability task):

(AJ) None of the bakers play chess;

Some of the chess players listen to opera;

\ Some of the opera listeners are not bakers.

Other neuroimaging-based studies have examined inductive reasoning by way of analogical mapping. In one study, participants viewed pictures of colored geometric shapes and determined whether the shapes were analogous (analogy condition) or identical (literal condition) compared to a source picture of shapes (Wharton et al., 2000). Other studies have examined brain activation associated with judgment of analogous word pairs (Green, Fugelsang, Kraemer, Shamosh, & Dunbar, 2006):

(AK) Planet: Sun versus Electron: Nucleus

or verbal analogies (Luo et al., 2003):

(AL) Soldier is to army as drummer is to band

Findings

In one classic experiment, a patient with a split-brain was presented with a picture of a winter scene projected to the right hemisphere and a picture of a chicken claw projected to the left hemisphere. The patient must then select, from an array of other pictures, one picture with each hand, determining which two are related to the projected pictures. The patient's left hand points to a shovel (because the right hemisphere, controlling that hand, has seen a snow-covered winter scene) and the right hand points to a chicken (because the left hemisphere, controlling that hand, has seen the chicken claw). When the patient is asked to explain why his left hand (guided by the right hemisphere) is pointing to the shovel, the left/language hemisphere has no access to the information about the winter scene seen by the right hemisphere. The left hemisphere instead responds by noting that the shovel is required to clean the chicken coop (Gazzaniga, 1989). In a simpler paradigm, again with split brain patients (Gazzaniga & Smylie, 1984), a picture of a pan is shown to one hemisphere, followed by a picture of water. When the pictures are shown to the left hemisphere, the patient can draw the causal inference of "boiling water." When the pictures are shown to the right hemisphere, the patient cannot draw the inference. These findings have been interpreted as an indication of the left hemisphere's ability to effortlessly connect familiar facts together and make sense of the world.

The results of the few neuroimaging studies on evaluating inductive arguments generally indicate activation in large areas including the left frontal and parietal lobes. These regions overlap with the cortical regions involved in deductive reasoning with familiar material. However, evaluation of inductive arguments seems to be distinguished from the evaluation of deductive arguments by the involvement of the medial aspect of the left superior frontal gyrus (BA 8, 9) (Goel & Dolan, 2004; Goel et al., 1997; Osherson et al., 1998).

Similar areas of activation are found in analogical mapping and judgment tasks. Wharton and colleagues (2000) demonstrated enhanced brain activation in the medial frontal cortex (BA 8), the left prefrontal cortex (BA 6, 10, 44, 45, 46, and 47), the anterior insula, and the left inferior parietal cortex (BA 40) when subjects made analogical match judgments. Even when subjects are correctly judging analogous word pairs (example AK), Green and colleagues (2006) report enhanced activation of a left-sided network of parietal-frontal regions, most notably the left superior frontal gyrus (BA 9, 10). Examining analogous concepts (example AL), Luo and colleagues (2003) reported a network of activation in the left and right frontal lobes (BA 45, BA 47, BA 11) and left temporal lobe/hippocampus (BA 22). These areas are generally consistent with the areas of activation reported for other studies that have examined the neuroscience of induction.

Implications for cognitive theories of inductive reasoning

Unlike in the case of deduction, it is unclear how the cognitive neuroscience findings regarding inductive reasoning affect cognitive theories of induction. There are two obvious reasons for this. First, the dataset is sparse and unsystematic. Second, and perhaps more importantly, within our current cognitive framework there can be no non-question-begging theories of inductive reasoning without a solution to Goodman's Riddle of Induction, as discussed above.

Overall, the studies show consistent involvement of the left hemisphere, and more specifically a left prefrontal-temporal system in resolving inductive/analogical arguments. Several investigators have argued that activation in the parietal, temporal, and inferior frontal lobes associated with inductive reasoning reflects the supporting cognitive processes (e.g., working memory, linguistic processing) required to effectively carry out these tasks (Green et al., 2006; Wharton et al., 2000). However, the left superior prefrontal cortex and frontal pole (i.e., BA 8, 9, 10) are consistently activated across these studies and appear to be important cortical regions for inductive reasoning (Goel & Dolan, 2004).

Just as neuroscience evidence is suggesting that deduction may not be a unitary concept, the same may be true for induction. One line of inquiry would be to see if there are dissociations between different forms of inductive inference (instance to population, instance to instance, abduction, etc.). Another line of inquiry would be to look for neural differences between drawing generalizations and selecting "relevant/salient" information. We would be surprised if interesting dissociations are not discovered along these lines.

Conclusion

The study of logic has preoccupied philosophers for at least 2,500 years, psychologists for the past 100 years, and cognitive neuroscientists for the past 20 years. It is important to remember that the three enterprises are focused on different questions and are looking for different types of answers. The goal of this article has been to briefly and selectively review the questions they have asked and the answers they have provided.

Much more progress has been made (by each of the three disciplines) in terms of understanding deduction than induction. This is not surprising. We have a formal theory of deduction but no such theory for induction. Deductive logic has become a sophisticated formal discipline leading to new developments in mathematics and computation (Turing, 1937; Whitehead & Russell, 1927) and anticipating its own limitations (Godel, 1931/1962). The formal theory of deduction has also informed the development of sophisticated psychological theories such as Mental Logic and Mental Models (Braine, 1978; Johnson-Laird, 1994; Rips, 1994), which in turn have guided the cognitive neuroscience work.[7] The cognitive neuroscience data are now questioning the adequacy and pushing the boundaries of the psychological theories. This is all as it should be.

The state of affairs for our understanding of induction is much less clear. Many philosophers (e.g., Goodman, 1955) are resigning themselves to accept that there may be no adequate solution forthcoming to the epistemological problem of induction, be it Hume's (1748) original formulation or Goodman's (1955) New Riddle. However, the problems may be amenable to solutions that appeal to the structure of the mind (i.e., psychological solutions).

Indeed, psychologists (and to some extent neuroscientists) have been able to say something interesting about the mechanisms that may underlie Hume's "habits of mind" in terms of associative and inferential mechanisms (Fodor & Pylyshyn, 1988). However, the New Riddle of Induction – of selecting the relevant or "projectable" predicates – is proving much more challenging. Both the psychological theories and empirical results lack coherence and systematicity. They have been able to provide only minimal guidance to the cognitive neuroscience research on induction. In turn, this research has had a limited impact on illuminating psychological theories of inductive inference.

But despite the lack of substantive progress we do know there is a mechanism capable of engaging in inductive inference (i.e., the human brain). Our lack of success in this regard may result from a misconceptualization of our reasoning abilities. In particular, our belief that we can, in principle, access any piece of knowledge in any given situation may be an illusion. We may not be general-purpose reasoning systems after all (Cosmides & Tooby, 1994; Gigerenzer & Goldstein, 1996). Exploring this line of thought does have some serious consequences (Fodor, 2000), but it may serve to dissolve the New Riddle of Induction.

Notes

1 It is important to separate the use of the term "induction" here from its use in the term "mathematical induction." Mathematical induction, despite the name, is a species of deduction.

2 Whether there is any substantive difference between "knowing the inferential role" and "knowing the meaning" of the closed-form terms, and thus the two theories, is a moot point, debated in the literature.

3 See Newell (1980b) for a discussion of the relationship between search and inference.

4 It is unclear how a cognitive process that requires no working memory can be accommodated within information processing theory.
5 See Elqayam and Over (2012) for a different viewpoint.
6 For example, Mount Everest and my neighbor share the properties of being located more than one mile from the sun, more than two miles from the sun, . . . less than 100,000,000 miles from the sun, less than 100,000,001 miles from the sun, and so on. See also Murphy and Medin (1985).
7 The probabilistic accounts of inference appeal to the formal apparatus of probability theory while dual mechanism theory does not actually commit to any specific mechanisms.

References

Acuna, B. D., Eliassen, J. C., Donoghue, J. P., & Sanes, J. N. (2002). Frontal and parietal lobe activation during transitive inference in humans. *Cerebral Cortex, 12*(12), 1312–1321.

Baggio, G., Cherubini, P., Pischedda, D., Blumenthal, A., Haynes, J.-D., & Reverberi, C., (2016). Multiple neural representations of elementary logical connectives. *NeuroImage, 135*, 300–310. doi:10.1016/j.neuroimage.2016.04.061

Braine, M. D. S. (1978). On the relation between the natural logic of reasoning and standard logic. *Psychological Review, 85*(1), 1–21.

Canessa, N., Gorini, A., Cappa, S. F., Piattelli-Palmarini, M., Danna, M., Fazio, F., et al. (2005). The effect of social content on deductive reasoning: An fMRI study. *Human Brain Mapping, 26*(1), 30–43.

Caramazza, A., Gordon, J., Zurif, E. B., & DeLuca, D. (1976). Right-hemispheric damage and verbal problem solving behavior. *Brain Lang, 3*(1), 41–46.

Chomsky, N. (1959). A Review of B. F. Skinner's verbal behavior. *Language, 35*(1), 26–58.

Chomsky, N. (1981). On cognitive capacity. In N. Block (Ed.), *Readings in philosophy of psychology* (Vol. 2, pp. 305–323). London: Methuen.

Conan Doyle, A. (2011). A scandal in Bohemia. In *The Adventures of Sherlock Holmes*. Retrieved from www.gutenberg.org/ebooks/1661

Cosmides, L., & Tooby, J. (1994). Origins of domain specificity: The evolution of functional organization. In L. Hirschfeld & S. Gelman (Eds.), *Mapping the mind: Domain specificity in cognition and culture*. New York: Cambridge University Press.

de Finetti, B. (1937/1964). Foresight: Its logical laws, its subjective sources. In H. E. Kyburg & H. E. Smokier (Eds.), *Studies in subjective probability* (pp. 55–118). New York: Wiley.

De Neys, W., & Bonnefon, J-F. (2013). The 'whys' and 'whens' of individual differences in thinking biases. *Trends in Cognitive Sciences, 17*(4), 172–178.

Elqayam, S., & Evans, J. St. B. T. (2013). Rationality in the new paradigm: Strict versus soft Bayesian approaches. *Thinking & Reasoning, 19*(3–4), 453–470.

Elqayam, S., & Over, D. (2012). Probabilities, beliefs, and dual processing: The paradigm shift in the psychology of reasoning. *Mind and Society, 11*(1), 27–40.

Evans, J. St. B. T., Barston, J., & Pollard, P. (1983). On the conflict between logic and belief in syllogistic reasoning. *Memory and Cognition, 11*, 295–306.

Evans, J. St. B. T., Handley, S. J., & Harper, C. N. (2001). Necessity, possibility and belief: A study of syllogistic reasoning. *Q J Exp Psychol A, 54*(3), 935–958.

Evans, J. St. B. T., Newstead, S. E., & Byrne, R. M. J. (1993). *Human reasoning: The psychology of deduction*. Hillsdale, NJ: Lawrence Erlbaum Associates.

Evans, J. St. B. T., & Over, D. E. (1996). *Rationality and reasoning*. New York: Psychology Press.

Evans, J. St. B. T., & Stanovich, K. E. (2013). Dual-process theories of higher cognition: Advancing the debate. *Perspectives on Psychological Science, 8*, 223–241.

Fangmeier, T., Knauff, M., Ruff, C. C., & Sloutsky, V. (2006). FMRI evidence for a three-stage model of deductive reasoning. *Journal of Cognitive Neuroscience, 18*(3), 320–334.

Fink, G. R., Marshall, J. C., Halligan, P. W., Frith, C. D., Driver, J., Frackowiak, R. S., et al. (1999). The neural consequences of conflict between intention and the senses. *Brain, 122*(Pt 3), 497–512.

Fodor, J. (2000). *The mind doesn't work that way: The scope and limits of computational psychology*. Cambridge, MA: MIT Press.

Fodor, J. A. (1975). *The language of thought*. Cambridge, MA: Harvard University Press.

Fodor, J. A., & Pylyshyn, Z. W. (1988). Connectionism and cognitive architecture: A critical analysis. *Cognition, 28*, 3–71.

Gazzaniga, M. S. (1989). Organization of the human brain. *Science, 245*(4921), 947–952.
Gazzaniga, M. S. (2000). Cerebral specialization and interhemispheric communication: Does the corpus callosum enable the human condition? *Brain, 123*(Pt 7), 1293–1326.
Gazzaniga, M. S., & Smylie, C. S. (1984). Dissociation of language and cognition: A psychological profile of two disconnected right hemispheres. *Brain, 107*(Pt 1), 145–153.
Gigerenzer, G., & Goldstein, D. G. (1996). Reasoning the fast and frugal way: Models of bounded rationality. *Psychol Rev, 103*(4), 650–669.
Godel, K. (1931/1962). *On formally undecidable propositions of principia mathematica and related systems.* London: Dover.
Goel, V. (1995). *Sketches of thought.* Cambridge, MA: MIT Press.
Goel, V. (2007). Anatomy of deductive reasoning. *Trends in the Cognitive Sciences, 11*(10), 435–441.
Goel, V. (2009). Fractionating the system of deductive reasoning. In E. Pöppel, B. Gulyas & E. Kraft (Eds.), *The neural correlates of thinking.* New York: Springer Science.
Goel, V., Buchel, C., Frith, C., & Dolan, R. J. (2000). Dissociation of mechanisms underlying syllogistic reasoning. *NeuroImage, 12*(5), 504–514.
Goel, V., & Dolan, R. J. (2001). Functional neuroanatomy of three-term relational reasoning. *Neuropsychologia, 39*(9), 901–909.
Goel, V., & Dolan, R. J. (2003). Explaining modulation of reasoning by belief. *Cognition, 87*(1), B11–22.
Goel, V., & Dolan, R. J. (2004). Differential involvement of left prefrontal cortex in inductive and deductive reasoning. *Cognition, 93*(3), B109–121.
Goel, V., Gold, B., Kapur, S., & Houle, S. (1997). The seats of reason: A localization study of deductive & inductive reasoning using PET (O15) blood flow technique. *NeuroReport, 8*(5), 1305–1310.
Goel, V., Gold, B., Kapur, S., & Houle, S. (1998). Neuroanatomical correlates of human reasoning. *Journal of Cognitive Neuroscience, 10*(3), 293–302.
Goel, V., Makale, M., & Grafman, J. (2004). The hippocampal system mediates logical reasoning about familiar spatial environments. *Journal of Cognitive Neuroscience, 16*(4), 654–664.
Goel, V., Shuren, J., Sheesley, L., & Grafman, J. (2004). Asymmetrical involvement of frontal lobes in social reasoning. *Brain, 127*(Pt 4), 783–790.
Goel, V., Stollstorff, M., Nakic, M., Knutson, K., & Grafman, J. (2009). A role for right ventrolateral prefrontal cortex in reasoning about indeterminate relations. *Neuropsychologia, 47*(13), 2790–2797.
Goel, V., Tierney, M., Sheesley, L., Bartolo, A., Vartanian, O., & Grafman, J. (2007). Hemispheric specialization in human prefrontal cortex for resolving certain and uncertain inferences. *Cerebral Cortex, 17*(10), 2245–2250.
Goldstone, R. L., Day, S., & Son, J. Y. (2010). Comparison. In B. M. Glatzeder, V. Goel, & A. v. Müller (Eds.), *Towards a theory of thinking: Building blocks for a conceptual framework* (pp. 103–122). Dordrecht, NL: Springer.
Goodman, N. (1955). *Fact, fiction, and forecast.* Cambridge, MA: Harvard University Press.
Green, A. E., Fugelsang, J. A., Kraemer, D. J. M., Shamosh, N. A., & Dunbar, K. N. (2006). Frontopolar cortex mediates abstract integration in analogy. *Brain Research, 109*, 125–137.
Heckers, S., Zalesak, M., Weiss, A. P., Ditman, T., & Titone, D. (2004). Hippocampal activation during transitive inference in humans. *Hippocampus, 14*(2), 153–162.
Heit, E. (2007). What is induction and why study it? In E. Heit & A. Feeney (Eds.), *Inductive reasoning: Experimental, developmental, and computational approaches* (pp. 1–24). Cambridge, UK: Cambridge University Press.
Heit, E., & Rubinstein, J. (1994). Similarity and property effects in inductive reasoning. *Journal of Experimental Psychology, 20*, 411–422.
Henle, M. (1962). On the relation between logic and thinking. *Psychological Review, 69*(4), 366–378.
Houde, O., Zago, L., Mellet, E., Moutier, S., Pineau, A., Mazoyer, B., et al. (2000). Shifting from the perceptual brain to the logical brain: the neural impact of cognitive inhibition training. *Journal of Cognitive Neuroscience, 12*(5), 721–728.
Hume, D. (1748/1910). An enquiry concerning human understanding. In C. W. Eliot (Ed.), *Harvard classics* (Vol. 37, pp. 287–420). New York: P. F. Collier & Son.
Johnson-Laird, P. N. (1983). *Mental models: Towards a cognitive science of language, inference, and consciousness.* Cambridge, MA: Harvard University Press.
Johnson-Laird, P. N. (1994). Mental models, deductive reasoning, and the brain. In M. S. Gazzaniga (Ed.), *The cognitive neurosciences* (pp. 999–1008). Cambridge, MA: MIT Press.
Johnson-Laird, P. N., & Byrne, R. M. J. (1991). *Deduction.* Hillsdale, NJ: Lawrence Erlbaum Associates.

Knauff, M., Fangmeier, T., Ruff, C. C., & Johnson-Laird, P. N. (2003). Reasoning, models, and images: behavioral measures and cortical activity. *Journal of Cognitive Neuroscience, 15*(4), 559–573.
Knauff, M., Mulack, T., Kassubek, J., Salih, H. R., & Greenlee, M. W. (2002). Spatial imagery in deductive reasoning: a functional MRI study. *Brain Research Cognitive Brain Research, 13*(2), 203–212.
Lewis, C. I. (1912). Implication and the algebra of logic. *Mind, 21*(84), 522–531.
Luo, Q., Perry, C., Peng, D., Jin, Z., Xu, D., Ding, G., et al. (2003). The neural substrate of analogical reasoning: an fMRI study. *Cognitive Brain Research, 17*(3), 527–534.
Miller, G. A., Galanter, E., & Pribram, K. H. (1960). *Plans and the structure of behavior.* New York: Holt, Rinehart and Winston.
Murphy, G. L., & Medin, D. L. (1985). The role of theories in conceptual coherence. *Psychological Review, 92*(3), 289–316.
Newell, A. (1980a). Physical symbol systems. *Cognitive Science, 4*, 135–183.
Newell, A. (1980b). Reasoning, problem solving, and decision processes: The problem space as a fundamental category. In R. S. Nickerson (Ed.), *Attention and Performance VIII.* Hillsdale, NJ: Lawrence Erlbaum.
Newell, A., & Simon, H. A. (1972). *Human problem solving.* Englewood Cliffs, NJ: Prentice-Hall.
Noveck, I. A., Goel, V., & Smith, K. W. (2004). The neural basis of conditional reasoning with arbitrary content. *Cortex, 40*(4–5), 613–622.
Oaksford, M., & Chater, N. (1994). A rational analysis of the selection task as optimal data selection. *Psychological Review, 101*(4), 608–631.
Oaksford, M., & Chater, N. (2001). The probabilistic approach to human reasoning. *Trends in Cognitive Sciences, 5*(8), 349–357.
Oaksford, M., & Chater, N. (2007). *Bayesian rationality: The probabilistic approach to human reasoning.* Oxford: Oxford University Press.
Oaksford, M., & Chater, N. (2009). Précis of Bayesian rationality: The probabilistic approach to human reasoning. *Behavioral and Brain Sciences, 32*, 69–120.
Osherson, D., Perani, D., Cappa, S., Schnur, T., Grassi, F., & Fazio, F. (1998). Distinct brain loci in deductive versus probabilistic reasoning. *Neuropsychologia, 36*(4), 369–376.
Osherson, D. N., Smith, E. E., Wilkie, O., López, A., & Shafir, E. (1990). Category-based induction. *Psychological Review, 97*, 185–200.
Over, D. E. (2009). Book review: New paradigm psychology of reasoning. *Thinking & Reasoning, 15*(4), 431–438.
Parsons, L. M., & Osherson, D. (2001). New evidence for distinct right and left brain systems for deductive versus probabilistic reasoning. *Cerebral Cortex, 11*, 954–965.
Prado, J., Chadha, A., & Booth, J. R. (2011). The brain network for deductive reasoning: a quantitative meta-analysis of 28 neuroimaging studies. *Journal of Cognitive Neuroscience, 23*(11), 3483–3497.
Prado, J., & Noveck, I. A. (2007). Overcoming perceptual features in logical reasoning: a parametric functional magnetic resonance imaging study. *Journal of Cognitive Neuroscience, 19*(4), 642–657.
Pylyshyn, Z. W. (1984). *Computation and cognition: Toward a foundation for cognitive science.* Cambridge, MA: MIT Press.
Ramsey, F. P. (1929/1990). General propositions and causality. In D. H. Mellor (Ed.), *Philosophical papers* (pp. 145–163). Cambridge: Cambridge University Press.
Reverberi, C., Bonatti, L. L., Frackowiak, R. S. J., Paulesu, E., Cherubini, P., & Macaluso, E. (2012). Large scale brain activations predict reasoning profiles. *NeuroImage, 59*, 1752–1764. doi:10.1016/j.neuroimage.2011.08.027
Rips, L. J. (1994). *The psychology of proof: Deductive reasoning in human thinking.* Cambridge, MA: MIT Press.
Rogers, T. T., & McClelland, J. L. (2004). *Semantic cognition: A parallel distributed processing approach.* Cambridge, MA: MIT Press.
Sloman, S. A. (1993). Feature based induction. *Cognitive Psychology, 25*, 231–280.
Sloman, S. A. (1996). The empirical case for two systems of reasoning. *Psychological Bulletin, 119*(1), 3–22.
Sloman, S. A., & Lagnado, D. A. (2005). The problem of induction. In K. J. Holyoak & R. G. Morrison (Eds.), *The Cambridge handbook of thinking and reasoning* (pp. 95–116). Cambridge: Cambridge University Press.
Sloman, S. A., & Rips, L. J. (1998). Similarity as an explanatory construct. *Cognition, 65*, 87–101.
Stalnaker, R. (1968). A theory of conditionals. *Studies in Logical Theory, American Philosophical Quarterly*, Monograph: 2, 98–112.
Stalnaker, R. (1970). Probability and conditionals", *Philosophy of Science*, 37: 64–80.

Stanovich, K. (2004). *The robot's rebellion: Finding meaning in the age of Darwin*. Chicago: University of Chicago Press.
Stanovich, K. E., & West, R. F. (2000). Individual differences in reasoning: Implications for the rationality debate. *Behavioral & Brain Sciences, 22*, 645–665.
Stavy, R., Goel, V., Critchley, H., & Dolan, R. (2006). Intuitive interference in quantitative reasoning. *Brain Research, 1073–1074*, 383–388.
Tenenbaum, J. B., Kemp, C., & Shafto, P. (2007). Theory-based bayesian models of inductive reasoning. In A. Feeney & E. Heit (Eds.), *Inductive reasoning: Experimental, developmental, and computational approaches* (pp. 167–204). Cambridge, UK: Cambridge University Press.
Thagard, P., & Shelley, C. P. (1997). Abductive reasoning: Logic, visual thinking, and coherence. In M.-L. Dalla Chiara et al. (Ed.), *Logic and scientific methods* (pp. 413–427). Dordrecht: Kluwer.
Turing, A. (1937). On computable numbers, with an application to the Entscheidungsproblem. *Proceedings of the London Mathematical Society, 2*(42), 230–265.
Tversky, A. (1977). Features of similarity. *Psychological Review, 84*, 327–352.
Vartanian, O., Goel, V., Tierney, M., Huey, E. D., & Grafman, J. (2009). Frontotemporal dementia selectively impairs transitive reasoning about familiar spatial environments. *Neuropsychology, 23*(5), 619–626.
Wason, P. C. (1960). On the failure to eliminate hypotheses in a conceptual task. *The Qurterly Journal of Experimental Psychology, 12*, 129–140.
Wharton, C. M., Grafman, J., Flitman, S. S., Hansen, E. K., Brauner, J., Marks, A., et al. (2000). Toward neuroanatomical models of analogy: A positron emission tomography study of analogical mapping. *Cognit Psychol, 40*(3), 173–197.
Whitehead, A. N., & Russell, B. (1927). *Principia mathematica* (2nd ed.). Cambridge: Cambridge University Press.
Wilkins, M. C. (1928). The effect of changed material on the ability to do formal syllogistic reasoning. *Archives of Psychology, 16*(102), 5–83.
Woodworth, R. J., & Sells, S. B. (1935). An atmosphere effect in formal syllogistic reasoning. *Journal of Experimental Psychology, 18*, 451–460.

14
SCIENTIFIC THINKING

Michael E. Gorman

In this review, I rely on Dunbar and Fugelsang's (2005) way of organizing approaches to the study of scientific thinking according to their methodological approach:

- *In vitro*, which corresponds to the biological term for laboratory research. I begin with experimental studies of scientific reasoning, which are in vitro in two senses: they involve laboratory tasks that model scientific reasoning, and the typical participants are college students – perhaps an analogy to the tendency biologists have to use a model organism for in vitro studies.
- *Ex vivo*, in which a scientist is taken out of her or his laboratory and investigated using an in vitro task.
- *In vivo* refers to observing and studying scientists in their working environments, for example, laboratories.
- *In silico*, involving computational simulation and modelling of the cognitive processes underlying scientific thinking, including a diversity of approaches and case studies.
- *Sub species historiae*, or detailed historical accounts of scientific and technological problem-solving, such as detailed studies of Faraday's notebooks.
- *In magnetico* research, using techniques like magnetic resonance imaging (MRI) to study brain patterns during problem-solving.

Instead of covering every study – which would take an encyclopaedia, not an essay – I will go more deeply into exemplar projects, so that the methodologies and assumptions are clear.[1] I will place particular emphasis on my own work not because it is better but because I have access to all the details.

In vitro

My experimental work on scientific thinking began when a fellow graduate student directed me to the work of the "Bowling Green Group" (Ryan Tweney, Michael Doherty and Clifford Mynatt) who had just published a book entitled *On Scientific Thinking* (Tweney, Doherty, & Mynatt, 1981), which included excerpts on scientific reasoning from philosophers and scientists and also a précis of some of the work the authors had done themselves. Ryan Tweney was kind enough to invite me to Bowling Green at the same time as Peter Wason, who had a knack for developing simple paper-and-pencil tasks that produced provocative results.

Consider his 2–4–6 task, in which a participant tries to guess a rule known to the experimenter by proposing number triples. The triple 2–4–6 is provided as an example that corresponds to the rule. Wason observed that participants would often try several triples like 6–8–10 and 12–14–16 that followed the pattern suggested by the initial triple and then guess the rule was something like even numbers going up by twos (Wason, 1960). This strategy became identified with a confirmation bias because participants did not try to test their hypothesis by proposing instances that would have tested their boundaries, and therefore most did not discover that the rule was "ascending numbers" (Gorman, 1992).

I saw the implications for the philosopher of science Karl Popper's effort to distinguish science from non-science. Scientific theories not only predict things that should happen but also forbid events that should not. Consider Einstein's special relativity, which specified that no object can go faster than the speed of light. A recent study at CERN seemed to falsify Einstein's theory by discovering that neutrinos could go faster than the speed of light. But the result was due to a measurement error, so special relativity still stands.[2]

The philosopher of science Imre Lakatos took Popper's falsification and turned it into a methodological heuristic, or rule of thumb, that he justified using his reconstruction of in vivo cases of scientific reasoning. Lakatos proposed that scientists should engage in sophisticated methodological falsification, which emphasizes that scientists do not abandon theories and research programs unless there is an alternative. Similarly, Kuhn (1962) argued that normal science prevails until enough anomalous results undermine the existing paradigm, creating a crisis situation that is resolved only when a new paradigm emerges. Scientists should prefer the theory that explains all the evidence accounted for by its rival and also makes novel predictions. Special relativity made the same predictions as the Newtonian paradigm but accounted for anomalies like the perihelion of Mercury and also novel predictions like the increase in the mass of an electron when it neared the speed of light.

Experimental studies can help determine the effectiveness of heuristics under controlled conditions. Tweney and his colleagues (Tweney et al., 1980) replicated Wason's 2–4–6 work and labelled as a confirmation bias participants' tendencies to propose only triples that correspond to their hypothesis. Clearly, looking only for confirmations of a pattern was not consistent with sophisticated methodological falsification. But the participants in these studies had no training in such a heuristic.

I wondered if instructions could induce participants to follow a strategy more akin to Lakatos'. I compared two kinds of instructions in my own study using the 2–4–6 task: ones that encouraged participants to confirm their hypotheses by trying to keep getting triples right and another that encouraged them to disconfirm their hypotheses by trying to get triples wrong. If the student participants in my study could falsify their hypotheses, that was a step towards sophisticated methodological falsification. About half of the 40 students given confirmatory instructions solved the rule; 38 of the 40 given disconfirmatory instructions solved it.

But as Wetherick (1962) pointed out, there is a problem with equating disconfirmation and trying to get triples wrong. A participant could propose a triple that she expected to be wrong, which would be a confirmatory trial. Wason's sample triple (2–4–6) suggested a simple pattern that was a sub-set of the actual rule; in this situation, trying to get triples wrong would reveal that hypotheses like "even numbers" or "numbers go up by 2s" would be wrong (see also Klayman & Ha, 1987). So whether telling participants to try to propose triples that should be wrong was a methodological falsification strategy depended on the hypotheses and alternatives participants were considering.

I felt it was dangerous to generalize too much from a single task. Mynatt, Doherty and Tweney (1978) had paved the way by developing an artificial universe task where participants fired particles at shapes to determine the laws governing this universe. On the most sophisticated version of the universe, no participant was able to discover the relationship despite working assiduously on the task. Attempts to disconfirm did not help on this task, in part because participants could not come up with alternative hypotheses that explained the relationships they were observing. In short, they were unable to follow a methodological falsification heuristic because they were unable to come up with alternate hypotheses.

I could not create an artificial universe because I had no lab or equipment. I had a tea cart I could wheel to whatever room I had managed to reserve for an experiment. So for more complex tasks I turned to a deck of cards and New Eleusis, a game designed to model the search for truth (Gardner, 1977). One person would make up a rule governing which cards fit a rule and others would try playing cards to see if they could guess it. So, for example, one rule I used was cards must alternate odd and even. Any cards that did not follow this pattern were put below the card they failed to follow, for example, an even card following an even card would be put below that card – only an odd card could follow in the sequence. One advantage of Eleusis over the 2–4–6 task was that the former had multiple salient dimensions that could be used in a rule (e.g., number, color, suit).

What I liked about the 2–4–6 and Eleusis tasks is that they modelled the process of deciding what experiment should be tried next in a research program, which meant these tasks were useful for exploring the value of heuristics like methodological falsification. What was missing were all the ecological features of the decision, like how to fund additional experiments and which experiments were most likely to be published.

The advantage to groups is that they had to discuss those decisions: I made each group member responsible for playing a card in turn so that no one would be left out. In the card task, I also had more dimensions to experiment with: rules could involve color, suit, number or any combination of the above.

In the group situation, after I gave participants a couple of warm-up tasks, they tried to discover the key rule: "odd and even cards must alternate", which is not a natural pattern for card players. I compared confirmatory and disconfirmatory instructions with a set of instructions that came from work by Mynatt, Doherty and Tweney, who thought that it made sense to look for evidence confirming a pattern before testing it by disconfirming. All of the groups in the disconfirmatory condition solved the odd-even rule, as opposed to half in the combined instructions and only one in the confirmatory (Gorman & Gorman, 1984).

What I liked about my results is that they passed the intraocular tests: although I did statistics to confirm the significance of the differences among conditions, the statistics were not necessary – anyone could see the pattern of results for themselves. Methodological falsification does not prescribe how an alternate theory ought to emerge. One group in the Eleusis study disconfirmed its initial "cards go up and down by one" hypothesis by playing a 5D after a 2D and noting that the 5D fit the rule. One member of the group inspected the previous cards and noted that all those that were correct had followed an odd-even-odd pattern. The group quickly adopted this hypothesis, tried to disconfirm it and when it held up, proposed it as the rule. In this case, and in others, inspection of prior results was one way to come up with an alternate hypothesis.

What surprised me was that Tweney et al. (1980) did not get a positive effect for instructions to disconfirm by studying negative instances. He and I sat down at Bowling Green State University and showed each other how we did our experiments. The key difference was when participants tried to guess the rule in Tweney's experiments he told them whether they were right.

I, instead, encouraged them to find out for themselves by doing further testing. So in Tweney's experiments, participants could do the equivalent of asking God whether they had discovered a scientific law; in mine, they had to continue to test, and the disconfirmatory strategy had a powerful advantage in this situation.

The role of error in scientific problem-solving

Scientists are continuously aware that a result may be due to a variety of sources of error, which means replication is essential (Nosek, 2012). Therefore, Tweney and I added the possibility of error to these tasks. Kern (1982), one of Tweney's students, led the way when she did an experiment where participants were asked to determine which parts of a planet could support life by dropping probes (called Tribbles after a small creature on *Star Trek*). She compared two possible sources of error: measurement, in which the position of the probe might be reported inaccurately, and system-failure, in which the actual fate of the probe might be reported incorrectly – if it died, it would be reported as having lived, and vice versa. There was no effect for measurement error, but system-failure errors were typically assigned to trials that appeared to disconfirm the participant's hypothesis.

Kern's system-failure error is illustrated by an experiment measuring the mass of the electron as it got close to the speed of light. The result appeared to disconfirm Einstein's Special Relativity. Einstein was unperturbed: "whether there is an unsuspected systematic error or whether the foundations of relativity theory do not correspond with the facts one will be able to decide with certainty only if a great variety of observational material is at hand" (Holton, 1973, 235).

I replicated Kern's result with a study of system-failure on my Eleusis task. I told participants the possibility of error was anywhere from 0 to 20%; they could turn over any cards whose results they thought were errors and therefore should be ignored. The errors would be determined at random. In fact, there were no errors, but the possibility greatly changed strategy. There was now a good reason to try to replicate cards. Groups did this some of the time, but they also focused on replicating simple patterns. On the odd-even rule, there were no significant differences between confirmatory and disconfirmatory groups.

When I used the possible-error design with participants on the 2–4–6 task, I found that most disconfirmatory and control (no strategy instructions) conditions solved the rule without replicating many triples. Instead, most focused on replicating a pattern, thereby both confirming a hypothesis and determining there was no error (Gorman, 1986).

In vitro tasks allow controlled comparisons of types of strategy and tasks that human beings can use to solve problems that simulate specific aspects of scientific reasoning, for example, the presence or absence of possible and actual error. But this research has low ecological validity compared with studies of actual scientists working on problems in their domains.

The role of error in scientific inference

In 1912, R. A. Millikan published a paper in which he announced that he measured the charge on the electron using a procedure where oil drops were suspended in an electrical field, and found that the motion of the oil drops showed they had multiples of the same unitary charge, which he proposed as the charge of the electron. Felix Ehrenhaft, another physicist, had run experiments that showed the electron could have multiple charges, including small fractions of the one Millikan had found.

The historian Gerald Holton (1978) looked at the original notebooks from the experiment and found that Millikan and his technical assistant had actually conducted 140 trials: Millikan labelled 82 errors. These oil drops showed fractional charges, suggesting that Millikan's hypothesis about the unitary nature of the electron's charge may have played a role in which trials were considered errors, though he also used a method that allowed him to manipulate individual drops, whereas Ehrenhaft took the averages of multiple runs and discarded none. Millikan ultimately won the Nobel Prize for this work. Ehrenhaft never abandoned his hypothesis, but other work supported Millikan. This example illustrates the way in which measurement error could serve a role similar to system-failure error in preserving hypotheses. Both types can be eliminated by improving procedures and replicating.

The problem with the psychological literature incorporating actual error is that none of the studies provide the kind of detailed procedures Millikan and other experimentalists had to follow, and how they decided what was precise enough (see Gorman, 1992). Doherty and Tweney (1988) used Kern's task in which participants dropped probes on the surface of a planet to determine habitable and uninhabitable zones. They crossed three levels of measurement error with three levels of system-failure error; these levels were disclosed to the participants. Doherty and Tweney (1988, p. 112) concluded that "[system-failure] error caused a small proportion of subjects to do very poorly, [and] increasing levels of [measurement error] appeared to cause a large number of subjects to perform slightly less well". Unlike actual scientists and engineers, participants had no way to reduce measurement error by improving the performance of the probe.

I followed their work by adding a 20% error to the 2–4–6 task. I used a random number generator to determine the actual errors, which I kept the same across all participants so they would see the same pattern evolve. By chance, the first two triples were errors, which would have been realistic if I were focusing on measurement error: early attempts at a new experiment often contain equipment and procedural errors that have to be ironed out. Only 2 out of 15 participants in the error condition solved the rule, as opposed to 9 in no error and 11 in the possible error conditions. Participants in the error condition solved the rule significantly less often than those in the no and possible error conditions. Not one of the no-error participants replicated a triple; possible error participants had a mean replication rate of .29 and error had a mean replication rate of 3.4 (a significant difference). Participants in the error condition were more likely to follow a confirmatory heuristic than were those in the others. One participant, for example, proposed 24 triples following a "numbers must go up by twos" hypothesis, correctly identified all of the errors and concluded her hypothesis was right – without testing the limits of her rule by proposing triples at variance with it. Other participants who tried to disconfirm were observed to assign errors to the results that did not fit their hypotheses.

To see if the effect was limited to cases where the first two triples were errors, I ran a follow-up where random errors occurred later. The 20% error participants still replicated more often than possible-error participants and were significantly less likely to solve the rule.

In vitro tasks that incorporate error show the critical importance of replication, and how replication takes time that might be devoted to a search for a more general rule.

Increasing the ecological validity of in vitro tasks

Kevin Dunbar criticized tasks like 2–4–6: "rather than inventing an arbitrary task that embodies certain aspects of science it is possible to give subjects a real scientific task to work with" (Dunbar, 1989, p. 427). One strategy for increasing the ecological validity of in vitro experiments is to make them resemble actual scientific tasks. Dunbar created a computerized simulation of a molecular genetics laboratory in which subjects were posed a problem similar to the one for which Monod and Jacob won the Nobel Prize in 1961.[3] Dunbar wanted "to use a task that involves some real scientific concepts and experimentation to address the cognitive components of the scientific discovery process" (Dunbar, 1989, p. 427).

Participants were given elementary training in concepts of molecular genetics, using an interactive computer environment. The core concept they studied was activation, which was the first mechanism Monod and Jacob proposed. Then they were allowed to perform experiments with three controller and three enzyme-producing genes; they could vary the amount of nutrient, remove genes and measure the enzyme output. The mechanism the subjects had to discover was inhibition, replicating in simplified form Monod and Jacob's discovery. But the similarities between Dunbar's molecular genetics problem and the 2–4–6 task outweigh their differences. Participants on both are given instructions which explain their little universe; these instructions, like the starting triple 2–4–6, bias them towards a hypothesis that is different from the one they are trying to find, and they are able to do a wide variety of mini-experiments to discover the rule. There are none of the potential sources of error that occur in actual genetics experiments and no new techniques to be mastered. The key task difference is that Dunbar's students have a small amount of training in the domain-specific knowledge of molecular biology which is related to the task. Other, similar tasks could be created for other domains.

Another advantage of Dunbar's research is that he employed protocol analysis, so he could study the reasoning processes of participants. All Dunbar's participants eventually disconfirmed their initial hypotheses about the role of the activator gene – no matter what genes were present or absent, there was always an output. What is interesting is what they did next: 6 groups re-interpreted activation to mean a search for the gene that facilitated enzyme production, 7 searched diligently for an activator gene and eventually gave up, and 7 set the goal of explaining their surprising results. Five of the 7 groups in this category actually found the inhibitor gene. Dunbar's results support the idea that successful disconfirmation depends on how subjects or scientists represent the task.

Conclusions from experiments using tasks that model aspects of scientific reasoning

The preceding series of experiments shows the advantages and disadvantages of experimental research on scientific thinking that uses tasks that model aspects of scientific reasoning and college students as participants. Controlled comparisons are possible, with sufficient numbers of participants in each to do statistics that will confirm when a difference between conditions had less than a 5% probability of occurring by chance. I preferred the differences that were obvious just from looking at the data and therefore had extremely low probabilities of occurring by chance.

Experiments with tasks like the 2–4–6 rule discovery problem cannot tell us anything about actual scientific practice, but they can help us operationalize and evaluate normative heuristics like methodological falsification under ideal circumstances. If these normative heuristics fail under ideal conditions, they are unlikely to be of much use in actual practice. Tasks like Dunbar's simulation of Monod and Jacob's discovery can potentially be normatively useful for fields like molecular biology.

How did methodological falsification fare? Participants could be trained to look for evidence that could disconfirm their current hypothesis, and could successfully come up with new ones on most of these simple tasks. The exception was Mynatt et al.'s complex artificial universe experiment, which was too complex for college student participants. One aspect of methodological falsification that was not modelled in these experiments was getting a hypothesis from another group. In science, the alternative to an existing paradigm does not have to be generated within a research group – it can come from outside, from a theorist or from another lab. Future research could be directed at this possibility.

Confirmation is not a bias – it is another heuristic that can be very useful in certain situations. Koslowski (2013; see also Koslowski, this volume) includes multiple examples of when it makes sense to prefer confirmatory evidence, including situations where error in the data is possible. Disconfirmation has heuristic value in situations where a scientist thinks she has discovered a reliable pattern but wants to make sure it is not a sub-set of a more general rule or pattern.

Ex vivo

One solution to increasing ecological validity is to bring scientists themselves into the psychology laboratory, in effect taking them out of their in vivo context. Mahoney (1976) compared physicists and psychologists to Protestant ministers on the 2–4–6 task (15 in each group), using the design where participants could get feedback from the experimenter on their guesses about the rule. Physicists and psychologists generated more hypotheses than the ministers, and almost all of the physicists and psychologists returned to a previously disconfirmed hypothesis, whereas less than half of the ministers did. It appears that scientists were both more speculative and tenacious on this task.[4]

Other ex vivo research has compared the performance of expert scientists to novices using word problems and visual problems that are akin to thought experiments (Anzai, 1991; Cheng, 1996). One goal of this literature is to figure out how to bridge the gap between novice and expert by examining how each works. Think-aloud protocols are an essential part of this methodology, so that expert and novice processes can be compared. On a textbook physics problem the novice typically works backward from the unknown solution to the quantities and constraints given in the problem. The expert, in contrast, recognizes the type of problem almost immediately from the givens, which dictate which equations to use (Chi, Feltovich & Glaser, 1981; Larkin, McDermott, Simon & Simon, 1980). These comparisons are typically embodied in computational models of the processes involved (see section "In silico", pg. 258). This kind of work has led to important educational applications that are beyond the scope of this chapter (Carver & Shrager, 2012).

Clement (2009) did a detailed study of one mathematician solving a thought experiment. Einstein, Maxwell and Faraday were a few of the prominent scientists who relied on thought experiments. Clement's goal was to explore Thomas Kuhn's hypothesis that thought experiments were used to reveal conflicts between existing concepts and nature; a thought experiment therefore could serve a disconfirmatory role, creating the kind of anomaly that might trigger a paradigm shift (Clement, 2009).

Clement's problem was for the mathematician to think about what would happen if a spring with a weight stretching it is replaced by a spring made of the same kind of wire, with the same number of coils, but with coils that are twice as wide in diameter. Clement used a think-aloud protocol to track the mathematician's work. He observed that the mathematician used forms of imagistic reasoning, often complemented by motions of the hands as they imagined how the spring would behave. The process Clement observed is an indication of how a new mental model of a process can be created through mental and motor simulation in the course of a thought experiment. Clement concluded that Kuhn identified only one use of thought experiments; they could also be used to confirm existing theories and to generate new theories and explanations.

Ex vivo research has higher ecological validity than in vitro work because the participants are scientists and because it can involve controlled comparisons of scientists and non-scientists or comparisons across different scientific fields. For example, Schraagen (1993) asked design experts and domain experts to design an empirical taste comparison between Coke and Pepsi. The design experts were experimental psychologists, and the domain experts were experimental psychologists who conducted sensory research. Both groups applied the same structured approach to the problem, but the solutions of the domain experts were superior. Schraagen's work reminds us of the importance of comparing different types and aspects of scientific expertise on the same problem or problems.

But none of the studies above focus on tasks generated by scientists in the course of their own research. Therefore, ex vivo research needs to be complemented by studies of actual scientific practice.

In vivo

In vivo work involves observing and interacting with scientists in the wild. Kevin Dunbar studied two cell biology labs, one molecular biology and one that did both cell and molecular biology. He attended their laboratory meetings and analyzed their presentations and discussions over a year (Dunbar, 1997). He supplemented this work with interviews. Dunbar's background in molecular biology helped him understand what was going on in the laboratories.

Unexpected, potentially disconfirmatory findings were dealt with in two ways: (1) a minor adjustment was made in the hypothesis, for example, from "particular sequence A is necessary to bind a protein" to "any sequence that has a base-pair mismatch in this region will be bound by this protein"; or (2) a new hypothesis had to be developed because the evidence was inconsistent with any hypothesis of the type under consideration.

Dunbar observed that over half of the findings were unexpected. Less experienced scientists tended to maintain the current hypothesis by doing adjustments of type 1. More experienced scientists displayed something akin to a falsification bias; not only were they willing to consider a new hypothesis when an unexpected result occurred, they were also suspicious of data that appeared to confirm the hypothesis because of their experience of being proved wrong. Other members of the laboratory often challenged findings and engaged in joint deductive reasoning, resulting in a different conceptualization of the problem. The exception was cases of falsification "bias", where the researcher attributed the result to a measurement or design error; in these cases, no amount of discussion would result in reconceptualization.

Baker and Dunbar (2000) identified two kinds of controls used by scientists. Baseline involves removing or adding a feature to an experiment that is relevant to an experimental condition – for example, testing for the expression of a gene without the condition that the researcher thinks should cause its expression. Known standard is akin to replicating an experiment with a well-known result; this kind of control is a good check on whether there are problems with the experimental set-up (the section on Bell's invention of the telephone below contains a good example). Dunbar found that the baseline controls in the laboratory often produced surprising results because scientists select these controls to expose any hidden causes that might account for the results.

Dunbar emphasized analogical reasoning in his analysis of the laboratories, and noted that most methodological errors were identified by local analogies to another experiment with the same organism which yielded similar results; usually, this local analogy was sufficient to suggest a solution (Dunbar, 2001). When an unexpected finding was replicated, then the analogies became more distant, often involving other organisms and/or research conducted outside the laboratory. When queried later, scientists have no memory of this analogical reasoning process, reinforcing the importance of in vivo studies. The analogies serve as scaffolding for building new models and explanations, and are discarded afterwards.

Scientists in Dunbar's laboratories rarely used distant analogies. One example was using the Hotel California analogy to clarify that a big molecule like LDL could get into a flagellar pocket and never get out; this analogy was explanatory, and did not aid in solving the problem. The participants in Clement's study used local analogies,[5] like imagining what would happen if the coils were replaced by a U-shaped spring of the same length (Clement, 1988).

Nancy Nersessian (2009) and her colleagues (Osbeck, Nersessian, Malone & Newstetter, 2010) became participant-observers in ongoing bio-medical research conducted by several laboratories. The team used multiple methods that included interviews, observations and analysis of texts. One major phenomenon they investigated parallels a theme of this chapter: combining in vitro and in vivo approaches. The bio-medical engineering scientists in Nersessian's research constructed model systems, often a hybrid of biological organs and physical devices. These models created spaces where the lines between science and engineering blur; as Galison and many others have pointed out, instrumentation has always played a critical role in scientific thinking, and the scientists themselves have been involved in creating the technologies they use to observe and manipulate nature (Galison, 1999).

Nersessian's researchers characterized what they were doing as "putting a thought to the bench top and seeing if it will work" (Nersessian, 2005, p. 749). To accomplish this goal, they constructed hybrid model systems that combined in vivo and in vitro methods. For example, one researcher worked with colleagues over a three-year period to develop a model system that would allow her to test the effect of shear forces on endothelial cells drawn from a baboon outside of the organism. The development of this system involved constant iteration between evolving mental models and physical experimentation. The end result involved mechanical and electrical systems that measured characteristics of blood flowing out of a baboon and through these devices, then back into the baboon. The goal was to find out precisely how shear stress could be used to reduce platelet clotting in a system simpler and more controllable than the actual organism, but with high ecological validity.

Another model system studied by Nersessian and her colleagues was "the dish": a network of cortical neurons harvested from a rat and preserved in a Petri dish that had 64 electrodes on the bottom to stimulate neurons and record their responses. The neurons were separated from each other and put in the dish on a medium that fed them and encouraged the growth of connections. The goal was to step up from studies of single neurons to studies of a network. Data recorded from the neurons is displayed using software that allows researchers to study the neural network in action – where the "seeing" is mediated by multiple levels of technology and by algorithms, all of which are subject to change. Here science and engineering are tightly coupled. This model system became this particular laboratory's unique capability (for more details, see Osbeck et al., 2010).

These model systems allow for close interplay between mental, physical and computational simulations to the point where all function as a distributed cognitive system. As Nersessian notes, "Our data provide evidence that researcher representations are themselves model-like in structure – traditionally called 'mental models'. From the perspective of distributed cognition, researcher mental models and device model systems constitute distributed inferential systems through which candidate problem solutions are achieved" (Nersessian, 2005, p. 745).

Trickett, Schunn and Trafton (2005) focused on anomalies in an in vivo study of two astronomers and an individual physicist working on problems in their respective fields. The scientists were trained to give think-aloud protocols as they worked; the researchers just listened and observed. In both cases, the scientists paid significantly more time to anomalies than expected results; in other words, potentially disconfirmatory evidence was more salient than confirmatory.

The astronomers were trying to understand the evolution of a galaxy by studying the flow of gas, for which they had optical and radio data represented in images; there was a lot of noise in the data. For example, the astronomers noted an area of the galaxy that had substantial amounts of gas – which they referred to as a "blob" on the image – but not the expected star formation that usually occurs when there is a lot of gas. The astronomers created another visualization they hoped would reveal more information, then agreed to table consideration of this anomaly – but kept coming back to it. This additional visualization could serve as a check to make sure the gas was really there (eliminate the possibility of error) and also provide detail that might suggest an explanation.

Trickett, Schunn, and Trafton (2005) continued this in vivo research on anomaly resolution in a comparison of basic and applied scientists. The basic scientists included the astronomers in Trickett et al. (2005) who had to do a conceptual simulation of the "blob" in order to figure out what caused it. One astronomer mentally transformed the blob into two groups of stars "bending" in different directions. The separation predicted by this mental transformation agreed with data produced by a model he had developed earlier, so he decided that this problem was solved. In contrast, the applied scientists – represented by meteorologists in this study – were more likely to do spatial transformation. In one case, model data showed a temperature increase that a meteorologist thought could not be accurate; he added his own representations of the situation to the map, including a high off Bermuda that helps him locate where he thinks the front is.

Conceptual simulations involve a new representation of a system or mechanism that is transformed spatially to see what happens. Spatial transformations involve transforming a spatial object from one state or location to another. Basic scientists are more likely to use the first to resolve anomalies, applied scientists the second. But the distinction between these two kinds of transformation may be linked to the nature of the system under study as well. Explaining the structure and motion of stars in a galaxy depends on physics; predicting weather patterns depends on judgment because weather systems are too complex to predict with a causal model. In neither case are confirmatory or disconfirmatory heuristics applied; instead, anomalies emerge in the course of research or applications and have to be resolved.

This study illustrates the strength of in vivo studies: much greater ecological validity, therefore more relevance to actual scientific practices. It also illustrates the weakness: it is hard to pin down the kind of causal relationship that can be tested under controlled circumstances in vitro and ex vivo.

Paletz et al. (2013) studied the Mars Exploration Rover (MER) Scientific Operations Working Group (SOWP), which had over 100 members working together for 90 Martian days (a Martian day is 40 minutes longer than an Earth day) to propose scientific objectives for the rovers *Spirit* and *Opportunity*. Engineers were responsible for translating the research objectives into code that would guide the rovers, facilitated by daily joint meetings between the engineers and scientists. The gains in improvement on the MER were not simply getting better and faster at routine activities; the team had to constantly adjust a new day's activities based on the previous one's because the rover encountered new terrain each day.

Adaptive expertise involves applying existing heuristics to new situations, and even developing new heuristics; metacognition is required, and in the case of truly effective teams, a shared mental model (Koslowski, 1996). To distinguish between adaptive and routine expertise, Paletz et al. focused on time on task, as described in the daily activity planning requests sent from the scientists to the engineers. Routine tasks were re-uses of activity plans from a previous day. Adaptive expertise was inferred when there was a large variability in the age of the activities re-used (assessed by standard deviations), implying that the scientists were drawing on a range of heuristics developed across the life of the mission. Novelty was defined as new activities per day.

Routine and adaptive expertise both increased significantly over time. Novelty did not increase, suggesting that the rise in adaptive expertise was not due to facing increasingly novel problems as the mission went on.

Unfortunately, these quantitative measures left out any information on metacognition and shared mental models, so it is hard to be sure that adaptive expertise was actually used. Probably the daily activity requests did not contain information for the kind of protocol analysis conducted by Dunbar. MER meetings were analyzed for their efficiency; at the beginning of the project meetings took as much as 8.5 hours per day and by the end it was down to 2.5. Some of these were formal meetings of the whole team called by management; others were informal meetings of sub-groups and/or individuals. To protocol all of these meetings would have produced a staggering amount of data, but Paletz and her colleagues could have sampled a few meetings at early, middle and late stages to see the increase in adaptive expertise.

In vivo studies add ecological validity to psychology of science by studying scientists in action in a variety of settings. Dunbar's work with laboratories used concepts from the in vitro literature, but showed evidence for phenomena like falsification. Trickett et al. found that anomalies were salient to the scientists they studied, and described the visualization techniques that were used to resolve them. Paletz et al. studied engineers who had to turn research objectives into code, a very different task than those modeled in vitro. These engineers could not stick with a set of heuristics throughout the process – they had to engage in continuous learning, working together.

Ideally, studies of this sort could be complemented by in vitro research. For example, could participants in an experiment be trained in a strategy of treating potential confirmations of a hypothesis as if they were most likely errors? Could participants be taught either adaptive or routine expertise strategies and have their performance compared on problems that had both routine and non-routine components? Such experiments could help refine the concepts investigated in future in vivo work, creating a kind of virtuous circle of in vivo discoveries and in vitro tests.

In silico

Another method for operationalizing concepts is in silico simulations involving computational models of the cognitive processes underlying scientific thinking, including a diversity of approaches and case studies. Herbert Simon, one of the founders of artificial intelligence and cognitive science who won a Nobel Prize in economics, was also a founder of psychology of science. Some of his earliest work combined three methods: a sub-species historiae study, an in silico model and an in vitro experiment. Langley, Simon, Bradshaw and Zytkow (1987) developed a computational simulation of Kepler's discovery of his laws of planetary motion, which Simon trumpeted as evidence that computers could discover – in this case, far more efficiently than Kepler, who took years to solve the problem of the orbit of Mars. The program was named BACON after Francis Bacon. The earliest version used three heuristics, which are shown in Figure 14.1 (from Gorman, 1998). These heuristics were applied to the distance (D) of a planet from the Sun and its orbital period (P). As indicated in Figure 14.1, the second heuristic was applied first, resulting in the ratio D/P, then the third heuristic was applied twice to produce D2/P and D3/P. This last ratio is a constant. Voila! BACON discovered Kepler's Third Law in a matter of seconds.

In fact, the hardest parts of Kepler's discovery are not represented in BACON. At Kepler's time, the paradigmatic assumption was that planets revolved around the Sun in perfectly circular orbits. Kepler had access to better data than anyone else at the time, because he was working

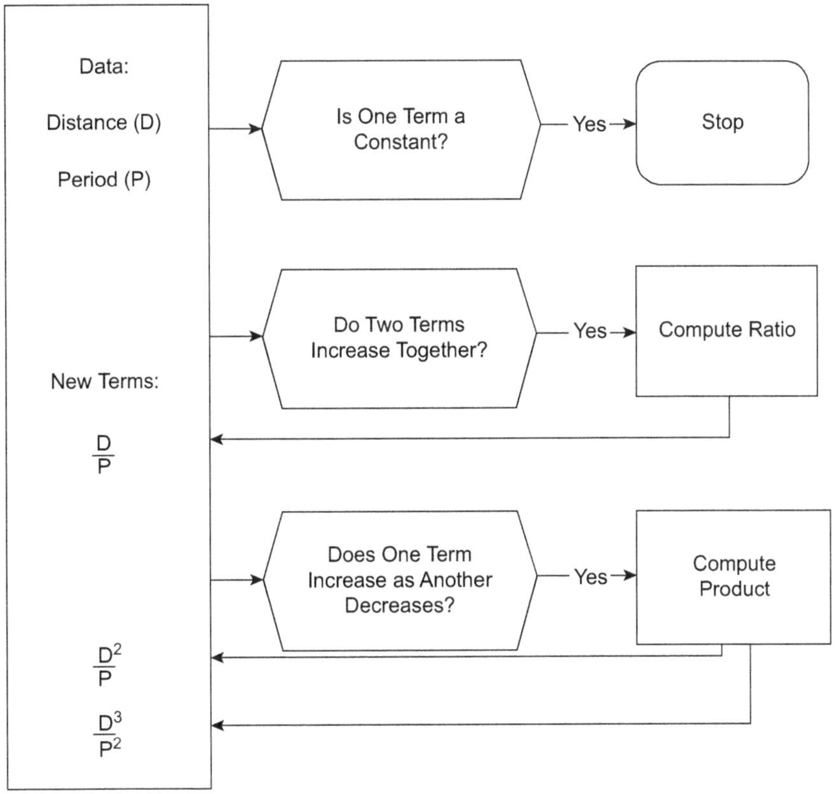

Figure 14.1 The three heuristics used in BACON, a computer simulation developed by Langley et al. (1987) that was able to discover Kepler's laws of planetary motion

under Tycho Brahe, who had the best instruments for determining the location of planets. An orbit needed only three data points, so Kepler found the orbit of Mars easily enough, but when he checked it with another three data points, the orbits did not match. Here was the anomaly that eventually forced Kepler to come up with an alternative to circular orbits, which he discovered when he considered an ellipse instead of a circle. Only then could he come up with a lawful relation between orbit and period: each planet sweeps out equivalent areas of its orbits in the same time (Gorman, 1998).

So BACON comes up with Kepler's laws by setting up the data and providing heuristics that guarantee the solution, which is a constant. Note that BACON does not know what it has discovered; it is the programmers who call the constant Kepler's law. BACON is, therefore, not a simulation of how Kepler worked, but does it provide a model of how human beings ought to work? Qin and Simon (1990) conducted an in vitro experiment to find out. Four out of a sample of 14 students, given the same two columns of numbers but not information about the heuristics used by BACON, made the same discovery (Qin & Simon, 1990). The solvers included a graduate student and an undergraduate in physics, and a graduate student and an undergraduate in chemical engineering. All the students were allowed to use calculators, and their processes were described at length. None of them knew the data had anything to do with Kepler's laws.

I frequently used Qin and Simon's method in one of my classes on scientific thinking, giving groups of engineering students the columns of numbers and asking them to find a relationship. The ones that succeeded noticed the 93 million miles number for d (distance) in one of the columns and immediately realized it was the distance from Earth to the Sun, which gave them an orbital mental model that led to the solution.

Herbert Simon is one of my heroes; one of the keys to his success was to make bold claims and dare others to disprove them. Note his use of three methods: in silico simulation was based on a sub species historiae case and was checked with an in vitro experiment. He went on to develop more sophisticated simulations of science, the best of which modeled the process by which Krebs discovered the Ornithine cycle (Kulkarni & Simon, 1988).

Sub specie historiae

This kind of research focuses on detailed historical accounts of scientific problem-solving done using cognitive psychological frameworks. Sub species historiae work, like in vivo studies, increases the ecological validity of psychology of science. Like other forms of psychology of science research, these accounts must be independently replicable by others accessing the same documents and other materials, for example, oral histories stored on-line.

Michael Faraday is an ideal subject for cognitive analysis because his notebooks were so detailed and can be accessed (Fisher, 2001). Ryan Tweney turned to Faraday as a logical extension of the work on experimental simulations of science, and both found parallels and differences. Like the most successful experimental subjects, Faraday first sought confirmations (Tweney, 2009). Faraday's style was not hypothetico-deductive; he "relied upon successive experiments that moved from initially vague attempts to make phenomena regular and visible through a series of increasingly clear demonstrations of the forces involved, and ultimately to demonstrate devices of great persuasive power showing the nature of the forces" (Tweney, 2009, p. 762). In vitro experiments so far have not included the kinds of iterations Faraday made between his construals (Gooding, 1990a) and experiments that sought to clarify the nature of the phenomenon.

The closest Faraday came to disconfirmation was his failure to show that an object dropped down a shot tower could induce an electric current. He got a small effect at one point, but he was able to show that there was a bit of magnetic material in the tower and in the rock, which could have accounted for the result. He never falsified this hypothesis – he just could not demonstrate it in a way that convinced him it was really a gravitational effect.

Cognitive psychology of science research needs to incorporate mathematical reasoning as well as visual and spatial. Tweney (2009) documented how Faraday was a mathematical thinker who used no equations. Maxwell claimed his mathematical approach was inspired by Faraday's methods and results. Neither Faraday nor Maxwell believed that all forces observed the Newtonian principle of action at a distance. Faraday observed and drew the lines of force from a magnet and an electromagnet. Maxwell thought his equations ought to represent this underlying physical reality: "whereas the double integral form assumes an action at a distance view, in which it is the surface that acts upon the distant point, the triple integral form states the relationship between each point of the entire region outside the surface. The triple form is thus representative of the field view" (Tweney, 2009, p. 766) and must call up the mental image of a property of moving bodies. In other works, the mathematical and mental models must be consistent.

Gooding documented Faraday's invention of the first electromagnetic motor (Gooding, 1990b). Here Faraday's work borders on engineering, though he never considered scaling his demonstration to a commercial power source; it was Edison and Tesla (Carlson, 2013) and others who would develop generators and power systems.

The methods used for psychology of science should be applied to technological invention for two reasons: (1) scientists like Faraday often invent apparati like his model generator to improve their understanding of phenomena; and (2) invention has transformed the way human beings live – indeed, has transformed the entire planet and allowed our species to leave it.

In the following sections I will cover the two inventions studied in the most detail by psychologists of science: the invention of the telephone and of the first airplane.

The invention of the telephone

Bell was a teacher of the deaf who also wanted to gain fame and make his fortune. In the early 1870s a problem of bandwidth had emerged. Two messages could be sent down a telegraph wire at the same time, which meant that stock quotes from New York going along telegraph lines next to the railroads would trickle in very slowly to Chicago, San Francisco and other points. If an inventor could develop and patent a way to get 8 or 16 messages down a single wire at the same time, she or he would be rich.

Bell entered this competition with only rudimentary knowledge of electrical devices as compared with experienced telegraph inventors like Elisha Gray and Thomas Edison (Gorman & Carlson, 1990). Bell had a secret weapon: he had actually built a device, the Ear Phonautograph,[6] that showed how the ear translated sound waves into mechanical vibrations whose shape could be traced onto smoked glass. The purpose of this device was to show the deaf the shape of the sound waves they produced when they spoke, in hopes they could match their patterns to a template for the actual sound. The prototype used the actual bones from the middle ear, so Bell clearly had an intimate understanding of how they worked.

Like Faraday, Bell left detailed records of most of his experiments, so it was possible to do a detailed analysis of his processes.[7] A psychologist can bring a different perspective to the study of inventors and scientists. Consider this diagram in Bell's notebook, which most historians had ignored (see Figure 14.2). Bell's sketch shows the ossicles (the bones of the middle ear) acting as an armature, vibrating as someone speaks into the tube and diaphragm on the left. The bones vibrate in front of two possible arrangements of an electromagnet to translate motion into sound. Above the sketch are two goal statements: follow the analogy of nature by using the ear as a model for a device to transmit speech, and find an armature ("a") that does what the bones of the middle ear do. This sketch shows Bell's mental model for a device that could transmit and

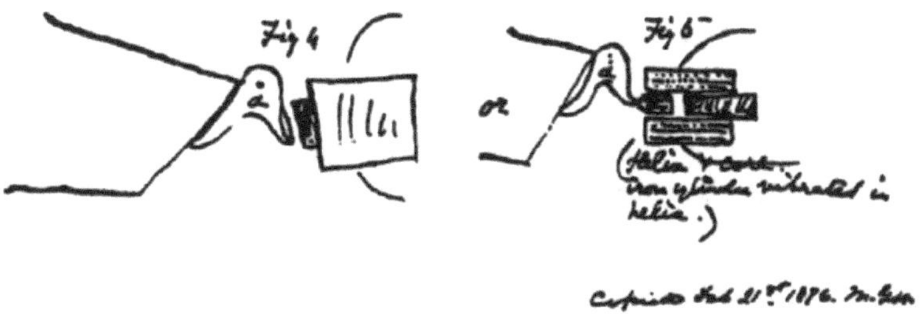

Figure 14.2 Bell's drawing of the bones of the middle ear ("a") between a speaking tube and two arrangements of electromagnets, from his "Experimental Notebook". The text under "Fig 5" reads "Helix & core, iron cylinder vibrated in helix", and at the bottom right Mabel Gardiner, Bell's future wife, notes that she copied the figure on February 21st.

receive any sound. Bell could run this model mentally, substituting components to imagine how it might work and then testing them experimentally.

Mental models in the invention of the airplane

The Wright brothers' invention of the airplane was a revolutionary design; they were far ahead of any of their contemporaries. Like Faraday and Bell, the Wrights left extensive records, including notebooks, patent applications, letters and observations from those who saw or participated in their experiments. Gary Bradshaw argues that the Wright brothers' flying capabilities were not matched until 1909, after their patents had been available for three years (Bradshaw, 1992).

Johnson-Laird (2005) did in vitro studies that showed mental models could explain how participants in experiments solved syllogisms. Johnson-Laird likewise highlighted the Wrights' ability to use mental modeling "to work out the flow of wind over an aircraft, or to design a transmission system. They could use models in imaginative play constrained by their knowledge to come up with a novel way to truss wings. They could manipulate models in their reasoning to check the consequences of an assumption, to derive a counterexample to a claim, to find a set of possible explanations for inferior performance, or to diagnose a malfunction. And they were most adroit at using a model of one thing, such as bicycle, as an analogy for another, such as an aircraft" (Johnson-Laird, 2005, p. 21).

Bell was a mental modeler par excellence, and this skill was the key to his patent application. Bell's ear mental model was grounded in the experience of actually building a device that used the bones of the ear to translate sound into waves. Similarly, the Wrights used mental models grounded in their experience, and their mechanical skills were vastly superior to Bell's. They were bicycle builders and repairers. One unique element they gained from their bicycle experience was the knowledge that stability was not the key to aircraft design. Bicycles are not stable, yet they can be managed very effectively by a rider. Similarly, a pilot of an aircraft could learn to turn by leaning, as on a bicycle.

Another aspect of their mental model came from close observation of birds. Wilbur noted that to turn, a vulture twists the rear edge of its right wing upward and the rear edge of its left downward. But how could one do this with airplane wings? Wilbur picked up a box used to hold bicycle tires and noted that he could twist the ends in opposite directions, which provided a mental model for how a pilot could twist the wings of a biplane.

But having a mental model is not sufficient. Bell worked scientifically, but even with Watson's help, Bell was not in a league with his competitors Gray and Edison. In contrast, the Wrights combined scientific methods with superb mechanical skills: they recalculated the coefficients of lift and verified them in a wind tunnel they built themselves.

Mental models can be both a strength and a weakness. Bell's ear was a great model for the receiver, but a poor model for a transmitter. The Wright brothers' wing-warping analogy from birds relied heavily on pilot skill; their airplane was very difficult to fly, and several of its pilots had fatal crashes. Orville Wright was himself almost killed in one; the passenger in front of him died. Only Wilbur could reliably fly the plane (Crouch, 1989).

Invention of the airplane as dual space search

Bradshaw (1992) attributes the success of the Wright brothers to the ability to search two problem spaces, but he replaced the theorist and experiment spaces used on scientific and programming tasks (see above) with design and function spaces. The Wrights worked in both spaces, but many of their rivals considered only alternate designs. According to Bradshaw, the Wrights did a functional decomposition of the functions involved in flight, and conducted experiments to determine design parameters that would fit these functions, including building a wind tunnel and recalculating the existing tables of lift. This kind of systematic iteration between function and design reduces the need for testing multiple prototypes – the first prototype is likely to be close to the goal. Rival inventors like Samuel Langley, Octavio Chanute and Otto Lilienthal tended to build gliders and, in Langley's case, aircraft, and see how far and how long they flew, varying design parameters like the number and placement of wings. The Wrights, in contrast, built and tested only three gliders before they constructed the first airplane. When the Wrights' second glider failed in 1901, systematic experimentation suggested that the problem might be with coefficient of lift in common use. The brothers constructed a wind tunnel and used it to correct the coefficient of lift. While Bradshaw focuses on design and function spaces, it is clear the brothers also worked in specific experimental spaces related to problems like lift – applying results to new designs. Like Bell, the Wrights were scientific inventors who worked systematically.

Was the Wrights' success due to mental models or problem decomposition? Are these two frameworks incommensurable? The Wrights were efficient, in part, because they could imagine and run different designs mentally. As Wilbur noted, "My imagination pictures things more vividly than my eyes" (Johnson-Laird, 2005, p. 8). The Wrights also focused on function.

Conclusions from sub species historiae studies

The problem with sub species historiae studies is the unevenness of records that would correspond to a protocol taken at the time. Bell kept notebooks for only a part of his invention process, and Gray and Edison did not. The Wright Brothers fortunately left detailed records, but even those had gaps. So, mental models have to be inferred from partial records, and problem behavior graphs will have gaps. For many modern inventors, their notebooks are proprietary, which means sub species historiae studies will continue to be an important research tool on inventors and entrepreneurs. A wonderful exception is Jeff Shrager's (2005) study of his own notebooks as he gained expertise in molecular biology, which he concluded was more about learning how to get procedures right and less about theory.

In magnetico

There is a small amount of neurophysiological research that uses techniques like fMRI to study brain patterns during scientific problem-solving (Fugelsang & Dunbar, 2005). In vitro research shows that even physics majors adopt an impetus mental model of motion rather than a Newtonian (Fugelsang & Dunbar, 2005). For example, when asked to describe the motion of an object dropped from an airplane, they will draw an arc that goes behind the plane (because the impetus has gone) rather than an arc that initially matches the speed of the plane and gradually drops off as it loses momentum while falling (Newtonian). Dunbar and Fugelsang (2005) have found shifts from dorsal to ventral pathways in the brain when students make this conceptual change from impetus to Newtonian theories of motion. The right hemisphere may be particularly good at detecting causality in perceptually salient events like envisioning the way the ball drops from the plane, and the left hemisphere better at causality on events that cannot be perceived (Dunbar & Fugelsang, 2005).

fMRI is still a crude measure of neurophysiological responses, based on blood flow. Results are often inconsistent (Dunbar & Fugelsang, 2005). Hopefully methods will emerge that allow researchers to track neural patterns directly, with equipment that can be used with actual scientists working on complex tasks. Such research will never reduce science to neurophysiology because thoughts can cause neural patterns, as can interactions with others.

Suggestions for future research

This review has covered the state of the art in psychological studies of scientific and technological thinking by focusing on methodological approaches, and the kinds of results that can be achieved with each. What is needed is more cross-paradigm combinations, for example, an experiment triangulated with a historical study, a computational model and a protocol of modern scientists.

Herbert Simon's work on the BACON program is an example of how to combine in vitro, sub species historiae and in silico – except that the sub species historiae account of how Kepler discovered his three laws was inadequate. Doing the same kind of study with a deep, fine-grained sub species historiae or present-day protocol of a laboratory as the basis would make in vitro, in vivo and in silico methods triangulate to get a better view of a problem – or diverge in ways that teach those of us studying scientific thinking about methods.

Similar studies would have to be done in other problem domains, because methods and cognitive styles differ across sciences. Consider the discovery of the Higgs Boson, a huge multi-researcher collaboration. It would have been great to have some psychologists of science embedded in that project, and in very different ones like the development of models of climate change. Paletz and colleagues' work on NASA rover scientists and engineers is a promising step in this direction. This goal could be accomplished only by funding big projects on scientific thinking, not just isolated studies, involving collaborations among researchers studying scientific thinking. The best way would be to build funding for psychologists into major projects like finding the Higgs, or trying to anticipate the effects of climate change on large landscapes.

Notes

1 Undoubtedly this brief overview of work on scientific thinking and its extensions to invention has left out important and relevant material. If readers want to add studies and ideas, please contact the author, who will post additional references and materials on the website of the International Society for Psychology of Science and Technology (psychofscience.org). Please also consider joining the society and the continuing conversation about these and other topics relevant to psychology of science.

2 See Jeffrey Kluger, "Einstein was right all along: 'Faster-than-light' neutrino was product of error". http://newsfeed.time.com/2012/02/22/einstein-was-right-all-along-faster-than-light-neutrino-was-product-of-error.

3 Francois Jacob (microbiology), Andre Lwoff (cellular genetics) and Jacques Monod (biochemistry) were the recipients of the 1965 Nobel Prize in Physiology or Medicine (www.nobelprize.org/nobel_prizes/medicine/laureates/1965/press.html). Dunbar mentions only Monod and Jacob because they were involved in discovering the inhibition process.

4 Unfortunately, Mahoney never published an account of this study that included data on the processes of individual participants, so it is impossible to be sure.

5 Clement used a different framework to describe his analogies; it is my inference that they were all local. This is a persistent problem in the analogy literature – everyone seems to have her or his own framework.

6 This device and all others mentioned here are shown and described online at http://www2.iath.virginia.edu/albell/homepage.html.

References

Baker, L. M., & Dunbar, K. (2000). Experimental design heuristics for scientific discovery: The use of "baseline" and "known standard" controls. *International Journal of Human-Computer Studies, 53,* 335–349.

Bradshaw, G. (1992). The airplane and the logic of invention. In R. N. Giere (Ed.), *Cognitive models of science* (pp. 239–250). Minneapolis: University of Minnesota Press.

Bradshaw, G. (2005). What's so hard about rocket science? Secrets the rocket boys knew. In M. E. Gorman, R. D. Tweney, D. C. Gooding, & A. Kincannon (Eds.), *Scientific and technological thinking* (pp. 259–275). Mahwah, NJ: Lawrence Erlbaum Associates.
Bruce, R. V. (1973). *Bell: Alexander Graham Bell and the conquest of solitude*. Boston: Little, Brown.
Capaldi, E. J., & Proctor, R. W. (2013). Postmodernism and the development of the psychology of science. In G. J. Feist & M. E. Gorman (Eds.), *Handbook of the psychology of science* (pp. 331–352). New York: Springer.
Carlson, W. B. (2000). Invention and evolution: The case of Edison's sketches of the telephone. In J. Ziman (Ed.), *Technological innovation as an evolutionary process* (pp. 137–158). Cambridge: Cambridge University Press.
Carlson, W. B. (2013). *Tesla: Inventor of the electrical age*. Princeton, NJ: Princeton University Press.
Carver, S. M., & Shrager, J. (2012). *The journey from child to scientist: Integrating cognitive development and the education sciences* (1st ed.). Washington, DC: American Psychological Association.
Cheng, P. C.-H. (1996). Scientific discovery with law-encoding diagrams. *Creativity Research Journal, 9*, 145–162.
Chi, M. T., Feltovich, P. J., & Glaser, R. (1981). Categorization and representation of physics problems by experts and novices. *Cognitive Science, 5*, 121–152.
Christensen, B. T., & Schunn, C. D. (2007). The relationship of analogical distance to analogical function and preinventive structure: The case of engineering design. *Memory & Cognition, 35*, 29–38.
Christensen, B. T., & Schunn, C. D. (2009). The role and impact of mental simulation in design. *Applied Cognitive Psychology, 23*(3), 327–344.
Clement, J. (1988). Observed methods for generating analogies in scientific problem solving. *Cognitive Science, 12*, 563–586.
Clement, J. J. (2009). The role of imagistic simulation in scientific thought experiments. *Topics in Cognitive Science, 1*, 686–710.
Collins, H., Evans, R., & Gorman, M. (2007). Trading zones and interactional expertise. *Studies in History and Philosophy of Science, 39*(1), 657–666.
Crouch, T. (1989). *The bishop's boys: A life of Wilbur and Orville Wright*. New York: W. W. Norton.
Doherty, M. E., & Tweney, R. D. (1988). *The role of data and feedback error in hypothesis prediction* (Final report for ARI Contract MDA 903–85-K-0193). Bowling Green, OH: Bowling Green State University.
Dunbar, K. (1989). Scientific reasoning strategies in a simulated molecular genetics environment. *Program of the 11th annual Cognitive Science Conference* (pp. 426–433). Hillsdale, NJ: Lawrence Erlbaum Associates.
Dunbar, K. (1995). How scientists really reason: Scientific reasoning in real-world laboratories. In R. J. Sternberg & J. Davidson (Eds.), *The nature of insight* (pp. 365–396). Cambridge, MA: MIT Press.
Dunbar, K. (1997). How scientists think. In T. B. Ward, S. M. Smith, & J. Vaid (Eds.), *Creative thought*. Washington, DC: American Psychological Association.
Dunbar, K. (2001). The analogical paradox: Why analogy is so easy in naturalistic settings yet so difficult in the psychological laboratory. In D. Gentner, K. Holyoak, & B. Kokinov (Eds.), *The analogical mind: Perspectives from cognitive science* (pp. 313–334). Cambridge, MA: MIT Press.
Dunbar, K., & Fugelsang, J. (2005). Scientific thinking & reasoning. In K. Holyoak & R. Morrison (Eds.), *The Cambridge handbook of thinking & reasoning* (pp. 705–725). Cambridge: Cambridge University Press.
Feist, G. J., & Gorman, M. E. (Eds.). (2013). *Handbook of the psychology of science*. New York: Springer.
Fisher, H. J. (2001). *Faraday's experimental researches in electricity: Guide to a first reading*. Santa Fe, NM: Green Lion Press.
Fugelsang, J. A., & Dunbar, K. N. (2005). Brain-based mechanisms underlying complex causal thinking. *Neuropsychologia, 43*, 1204–1213.
Galison, P. (1999). Buildings and the subject of science. In P. Galison & E. Thompson (Eds.), *The architecture of science* (pp. 1–25). Cambridge, MA: MIT Press.
Gardner, M. (1977). On playing New Eleusis, the game that simulates the search for truth. *Scientific American, 237*, 18–25.
Gooding, D. (1985). In nature's school: Faraday as an experimentalist. In D. Gooding & F. James (Eds.), *Faraday rediscovered: Essays on the life and work of Michael Faraday: 1791–1867*. New York: Stockton Press.
Gooding, D. (1990a). *Experiment and the making of meaning: Human agency in scientific observation and experiment*. Dordrecht: Kluwer Academic Publishers.
Gooding, D. (1990b). Mapping experiment as a learning process: How the first electromagnetic motor was invented. *Science, Technology and Human Values, 15*(2), 165–201.

Gooding, D. C. (2005). Seeing the forest for the trees: Visualization, cognition and scientific inference. In M. E. Gorman, R. D. Tweney, D. C. Gooding, & A. Kincannon (Eds.), *Scientific and technological thinking* (pp. 173–218). Mahwah, NJ: Lawrence Erlbaum Associates.

Gooding, D. C. (2010). Visualizing scientific inference. *Topics in Cognitive Science, 2*(1), 15–35. doi:10.1111/j.1756–8765.2009.01048.x

Gooding, D. C., & Addis, T. (1999). A simulation of model-based reasoning about disparate phenomena. In L. Magnani, N. Nersessian, & P. Thagard (Eds.), *Model-based reasoning in scientific discovery* (pp. 103–123). New York & London: Kluwer Academic/Plenum Publishers.

Gorman, M. E. (1986). How the possibility of error affects falsification on a task that models scientific problem solving. *British Journal of Psychology, 77,* 85–96.

Gorman, M. E. (1992). *Simulating science: Heuristics, mental models, and technoscientific thinking.* Bloomington, IN: Indiana University Press.

Gorman, M. E. (1998). *Transforming nature: Ethics, invention and design.* Boston: Kluwer Academic Publishers.

Gorman, M. E. (2002). Types of knowledge and their roles in technology transfer. *Journal of Technology Transfer, 27*(3), 219–231.

Gorman, M. E. (2006). Scientific and technological thinking. *Review of General Psychology, 10*(2), 113–129.

Gorman, M. E. (2008). Scientific and technological expertise. *Journal of Psychology of Science and Technology, 1*(1), 23–31.

Gorman, M. E., & Carlson, W. B. (1990). Interpreting invention as a cognitive process: The case of Alexander Graham Bell, Thomas Edison and the Telephone. *Science, Technology and Human Values, 15,* 131–164.

Gorman, M. E., & Gorman, M. E. (1984). A comparison of disconfirmatory, confirmatory and control strategies on Wason's 2–4–6 task. *The Quarterly Journal of Experimental Psychology, 36,* 629–648.

Gorman, M. E., & Groves, J. (2007). Training students to be interactional experts. In M. C. Roco & W. S. Bainbridge (Eds.), *Societal implications of nanoscience and nanotechnology II: Maximizing human benefit* (pp. 301–305). Dordrecht: Springer.

Holton, G. (1973). *Thematic origins of scientific thought.* Cambridge, MA: Harvard University Press.

Holton, G. (1978). *The scientific imagination: Case studies.* Cambridge: Cambridge University Press.

Holyoak, K. J., & Thagard, P. (1995). *Mental leaps.* Cambridge, MA: MIT Press.

Johnson-Laird, P. N. (2005). Flying bicycles: How the Wright brothers invented the airplane. *Mind & Society, 1,* 1–22.

Kern, L. (1982). The effect of data error in inducing confirmatory inference strategies in scientific hypothesis testing. Unpublished PhD dissertation, Ohio State University.

Klahr, D. (2005). A framework for cognitive studies of science and technology. In M. E. Gorman, R. D. Tweney, D. C. Gooding, & A. P. Kincannon (Eds.), *Scientific and technological thinking* (pp. 81–96).

Klahr, D., & Dunbar, K. (1988). Dual space search during scientific reasoning. *Cognitive Science, 12,* 1–48.

Klayman, J., & Ha, Y. W. (1987). Confirmation, disconfirmation, and information in hypothesis testing. *Psychological Review, 94,* 211–228.

Koslowski, B. (1996). *Theory and evidence: The development of scientific reasoning.* Cambridge, MA: MIT Press.

Koslowski, B. (2013). Scientific reasoning: Explanation, confirmation bias, and scientific practice. In Feist & Gorman (Eds.), *Handbook of psychology of science.* New York: Springer.

Kuhn, T. S. (1962). *The structure of scientific revolutions.* Chicago, IL: University of Chicago Press.

Kulkarni, D., & Simon, H. A. (1988). The processes of scientific discovery: The strategy of experimentation. *Cognitive Science, 12,* 139–175.

Langley, P., Simon, H. A., Bradshaw, G. L., & Zytkow, J. M. (1987). *Scientific discovery: Computational explorations of the creative processes.* Cambridge, MA: MIT Press.

Larkin, J. H., McDermott, J., Simon, D. P., & Simon, H. A. (1980). Models of competence in solving physics problems. *Cognitive Science, 4,* 317–345.

Mahoney, M. J. (1976). *Scientists as subject: The psychological imperative.* Cambridge, MA: Ballinger.

Mynatt, C. R., Doherty, M. E., & Tweney, R. D. (1978). Consequences of confirmation and disconfirmation in a simulated research environment. *Quarterly Journal of Experimental Psychology, 30,* 395–406.

Nersessian, N. J. (2005). Interpreting scientific and engineering practices: Integrating the cognitive, social and cultural dimensions. In M. E. Gorman, R. D. Tweney, D. C. Gooding, & A. Kincannon (Eds.), *Scientific and technological thinking* (pp. 17–56). Mahwah, NJ: Lawrence Erlbaum Associates.

Nersessian, N. J. (2009). How do engineering scientists think? model-based simulation in biomedical engineering research laboratories. *Topics in Cognitive Science, 1*(4), 730–757. doi:10.1111/j.1756–8765.2009.01032.x

Nosek, B. (2012). An open, large-scale, collaborative effort to estimate the reproducibility of psychological science. *Perspectives on Psychological Science*, 7(6), 657–660. doi: 10.1177/1745691612462588

Osbeck, L. M., Nersessian, N. J., Malone, K. R., & Newstetter, W. C. (2010). *Science as psychology: Sense-making and identity in science practice*. New York: Cambridge University Press.

Paletz, S. B., Kim, K, Schunn, C, Tollinger, I & Vera, A. (2013). Reuse and recycle: The development of adaptive expertise, routine expertise, and novelty in a large research team. *Applied Cognitive Psychology, 27*, 415–428. doi: 10.1002/acp.2928

Piaget, J., & Garcia, R. (1989). *Psychogenesis and the history of science*. New York: Columbia University Press.

Qin, Y., & Simon, H. A. (1990). Laboratory replication of scientific discovery processes. *Cognitive Science, 14*, 281–312.

Schraagen, J. M. (1993). How experts solve a novel problem in experimental design. *Cognitive Science, 17*(2), 285–309.

Shrager, J. (2005). Diary of an insane cell mechanic. In M. E. Gorman, R. D. Tweney, D. C. Gooding, & A. Kincannon (Eds.), *Scientific and technological thinking* (pp. 119–136). Mahwah, NJ: Lawrence Erlbaum Associates.

Shrager, J., & Langley, P. (1990). *Computational models of scientific discovery and theory formation*. San Mateo, CA: Morgan Kaufmann Publishers, Inc.

Trickett, S. B., Schunn, C. D., & Trafton, J. G. (2005). Puzzles and peculiarities: How scientists attend to and process anomalies during data analysis. In M. Gorman, A. Kincannon, D. Gooding & R. D. Tweney (Eds.), *Spherical horses and shared toothbrushes: Recent developments in scientific and technological thinking* (pp. 97–118). Mahwah, NJ: Lawrence Erlbaum Associates, Inc.

Tweney, R. D. (1985). Faraday's discovery of induction: A cognitive approach. In D. Gooding, & F. James (Eds.), *Faraday rediscovered: Essays on the life and work of Michael Faraday: 1791–1867*. New York: Stockton Press.

Tweney, R. D. (2009). Mathematical representations in science: A cognitive–historical case history. *Topics in Cognitive Science, 1*, 758–776.

Tweney, R. D., Doherty, M. E., & Mynatt, C. R. (1981). *On scientific thinking*. New York: Columbia University Press.

Tweney, R. D., Doherty, M. E., Worner, W. J., Pliske, D. B., Mynatt, C. R., Gross, K. A., & Arkkelin, D. L. (1980). Strategies of rule discovery on an inference task. *Quarterly Journal of Experimental Psychology, 32*, 109–123.

Wason, P. C. (1960). On the failure to eliminate hypotheses in a conceptual task. *Quarterly Journal of Experimental Psychology, 12*, 129–140.

Wason, P. C. (1983). Realism and rationality in the selection task. In J. S. B. T. Evans (Ed.), *Thinking and reasoning: Psychological approaches*. London: Routledge & Kegan Paul.

Wetherick, N. E. (1962). Eliminative and enumerative behaviour in a conceptual task. *Quarterly Journal of Experimental Psychology, 14*, 246–249.

15

WORKING MEMORY, THINKING, AND EXPERTISE

David Z. Hambrick, Alexander P. Burgoyne, Guillermo Campitelli, and Brooke N. Macnamara

Working memory, thinking, and expertise

Expert performance can defy belief. Consider that Timur Gareyev, in breaking the world record for "blindfold" chess, simultaneously played 48 opponents without being able to see their boards, losing only six games. Or consider that Alex Mullen, en route to winning the 2016 Memory World Championships, memorized a deck of cards in 21.5 seconds. Equally astonishing, in 2016, Feliks Zemdegs set the Rubik's Cube speed-solving record with a time of 4.73 seconds.

How do people reach such high levels of skill? Scientific interest in this question dates to the beginning of the field of psychology (see Hambrick, Macnamara, Campitelli, Ullén, & Mosing, 2016). One view is that experts are "born." This is the idea that although training is necessary to become an expert, the ultimate level of skill that a person can reach is limited by innate characteristics – "nature." The opposing view is that experts are "made." This is the idea that if talent exists at all, its effects on performance are negligible in comparison to the effects of training – "nurture."

This chapter is organized into four major sections. In the first section, we provide a brief history of the experts are "born" versus experts are "made" debate to provide context for understanding current controversies in research on expertise. In the second section, we describe a particularly influential account of expertise – Ericsson and colleagues' *deliberate practice view*. In the third section, we describe empirical evidence that challenges this view, focusing on the role of *working memory capacity* in expertise. In the final section, we discuss directions for future research to advance scientific understanding of expertise. To preview, our ultimate conclusion is that the "born versus made" debate is over – or at least it should be. Models of expertise must take into account both nature and nurture.

A brief history of the "born versus made" debate

The classical era of expertise research

Interest in the underpinnings of exceptional performance long predates scientific psychology. In *The Republic*, Plato observed that "no two persons are born alike but each differs from the other in individual endowments." More than two millennia later, in his book *Hereditary Genius*, Francis

Galton (1869) reported the first scientific study of expertise. Inspired by the revolutionary ideas about evolution that his cousin Charles Darwin had proposed in *On the Origin of Species* (1859), Galton was interested in whether heredity influences "genius" in humans the same way it seemed to influence physical characteristics in other organisms. There were no standardized tests of intelligence at the time, so Galton scoured biographical dictionaries to identify "men of reputation" in fields such as science, art, music, and government. He then analyzed genealogical records to see whether, within a given field, these men tended to be biologically related to each other more than would be expected by chance. They did. He noted, for example, that "[t]here are far more than twenty ***eminent*** musicians among the Bachs" (emphasis original; p. 240). Galton concluded that eminence arises, almost inevitably, from "natural ability."

Darwin was effusive in his praise for *Hereditary Genius*. In a letter dated December 3, 1869, he wrote to his cousin to say, "I do not think I ever in all my life read anything more interesting and original – and how well and clearly you put every point!" The Swiss botanist Alphonse Pyrame de Candolle was less impressed (see Fancher, 1983). Like Galton, de Candolle was from a family of distinguished scientists – one, in fact, that Galton had listed in *Hereditary Genius*. However, based on personal experience and his own study of biographies of great scientists, de Candolle believed that the tendency for scientific eminence to run in families has more to do with opportunity than with heredity. He wrote to Galton, "The effect of traditions, examples, and inner family councils [seems] to me to exert more influence than heredity, properly speaking."

Using Galton's research as a model, de Candolle tested this hypothesis through an analysis of the backgrounds of more than 300 scientists with an international reputation, having been elected as foreign members to the three most prestigious scientific societies of the day: the French Academy of Sciences, the British Royal Society, and the German Academy of Sciences. As he reported in his book *Histoire des Sciences et des Savants Depuis Deux Siècles* (1873), some countries produced more scientists than others, even after taking population into account.[1] For example, his native Switzerland produced over 10% of the scientists in his sample, but accounted for less than 1% of the European population. De Candolle concluded that environmental factors – or what he called "causes favorable" – were the primary antecedents of eminence (Fancher, 1983).

Following publication of *Histoire des Sciences et des Savants Depuis Deux Siècles* (1873), an exasperated Galton wrote to de Candolle to say that he "literally cannot see that your conclusions, so far as heredity is concerned, differ in any marked way from mine." De Candolle responded, "You habitually highlight, as the principal cause, heredity. When you speak of other causes they are indicated accessorily, and without seeking to distinguish what holds particularly for them or for each one of them." Unmoved, in the preface to the 1892 edition of *Hereditary Genius*, Galton conceded only that he should have thought of a less provocative title for the book: "if it could be altered now, it should appear as *Hereditary Ability*" (Galton, 1892, p. 26).

A few years later, William Bryan and his graduate student Noble Harter conducted their pioneering study of telegraphers (Bryan & Harter, 1897). Then a major form of communication, telegraphy involves converting messages from English into Morse code – a series of dots and dashes representing letters and numbers. A sender transmits the message, as a series of electrical signals, by tapping a key on a telegraphic machine, and a receiver translates the message back into English. Before graduate school, Harter had worked as a telegrapher for the railroad, and using his professional contacts, he recruited a sample of participants representing a wide range of telegraphy experience – from less than a year to 33 years. Connecting to telegraphers in their places of work via the main lines of the Western Union Telegraph Company, Bryan and Harter had these telegraphers send the message "Ship 364 wagons via Erie quick" multiple times. The "expert men" (as Bryan and Harter called them) generally outperformed the less experienced telegraphers. In a subsequent study, Bryan and Harter (1899) then tracked the progress of two students enrolled in telegraphy school over the course of 40 weeks. Both sending and receiving performance (i.e., letters per minute) improved monotonically, but the curves had different shapes. Sending performance improved constantly, whereas receiving performance improved to a point, reached a plateau, and then improved again after several weeks of additional practice.

Expanding on Bryan and Harter's (1897, 1899) findings, Edward Thorndike (1912) noted that "when one sets oneself zealously to improve any ability, the amount gained is astonishing" and added that "we stay far below our own possibilities in almost everything we do . . . not because proper practice would not improve us further, but because we do not take the training or because we take it with too little zeal" (p. 108). Later, John Watson (1930), the founder of behaviorism, took this argument to its logical extreme with his famous thought experiment:

> Give me a dozen healthy infants, well-formed, and my own specified world to bring them up in and I'll guarantee to take any one at random and train him to become any type of specialist I might select – doctor, lawyer, artist, merchant-chief and, yes, even beggar-man and thief, regardless of his talents.
>
> (p. 104)

Watson added that "practicing more intensively than others . . . is probably the most reasonable explanation we have today not only for success in any line, but even for genius" (p. 212).

In the early 1940s, research on expertise focused on determining the exact form of learning curves for complex skills. Motivated by an urgent need to accelerate the training of telegraph operators to serve in World War II, a major question was whether learning plateaus that Bryan and Harter had documented were replicable. Taylor (1943), citing the results of an unpublished doctoral dissertation by Tulloss (1918), concluded that learning plateaus were more apparent than real. Tulloss had studied 26 telegraph operators and found no evidence for learning plateaus. Instead, the consistent pattern was one of diminishing returns – large improvements in performance with practice initially, followed by smaller and smaller improvements. Similarly, Reed and Zinszer (1943) tracked the improvement of 48 students enrolled in a telegraphy course and found that "[e]xtended plateaus among our learners are the exception rather than the rule" (p. 134). The notion of learning plateaus would soon fall into disfavor – where it has for the most part remained – whereas Tulloss's finding would be replicated so frequently and for so many skills that it would eventually achieve law status: *the power law of learning* (see Proctor & Dutta, 1995; see also Gray & Lindstedt, 2016, for an illuminating discussion of plateaus versus asymptotes in skill acquisition).

This research clarified the form of the relationship between practice and performance in complex skills and yielded practically valuable insights about how to accelerate the acquisition of expertise. At the same time, it left unanswered questions about the underpinnings of expertise – that is, what exactly is acquired through training and how this translates into performance. A fundamentally new way of thinking about expertise would be required to answer such questions, and would soon emerge.

The modern era of expertise research

Beginning in the 1950s, advances in the burgeoning field of computer science, along with growing dissatisfaction with behaviorism, set in motion the cognitive revolution. With ***mind-as-computer*** as the central metaphor, the goal for research on human performance shifted from relationships between stimuli and responses, to inferable, if not directly observable, mental structures and processes – the mind.

A prototype for how this information-processing approach could be extended to research on expertise was provided by the Dutch psychologist Adriaan de Groot (1946/1978) in his doctoral dissertation on chess expertise. At the time, the prevailing view was that chess expertise reflects the ability to "think ahead" in a game – in other words, to anticipate the consequences of a given move for how the game would play out. To test this idea empirically, de Groot, himself an international master, recruited chess players representing a wide range of skill and had them perform "choice-of-move" problems in which they were given game positions and asked to verbalize their thoughts (to "think out loud") as they deliberated on what move to make. de Groot found that grandmasters were no different than less skilled players on a measure of move depth, and found instead that the grandmaster "immediately 'sees' the core of the problem in the position, whereas the expert player finds it with difficulty – or misses it completely" (p. 320). As a further test of this idea, de Groot had chess players representing four levels of skill briefly view chess positions and then attempt to reconstruct the positions by placing pieces on an empty board. The grandmaster and master averaged over 90% correct, the expert only about 70%, and the weakest player just over 50%.

Nearly 30 years later, de Groot's (1946/1978) work was the inspiration for Chase and Simon's (1973) classic study of chess expertise. Chase and Simon had participants representing three levels of chess skill (novice, intermediate, and master) view and attempt to recreate arrangements of chess positions that were either plausible game positions or random. The major finding was that chess skill facilitated recall of the game positions, but not the random positions. Thus, Chase and Simon concluded that the primary factor underlying chess skill is not superior short-term memory capacity, but a large "vocabulary" of game positions that automatically elicit candidate moves. More generally, Chase and Simon argued that although "there clearly must be a set of specific aptitudes . . . that together comprise a talent for chess, individual differences in such aptitudes are largely overshadowed by immense differences in chess experience. Hence, the overriding factor in chess skill is practice" (p. 279).

A major focus of subsequent research on expertise was to explain experts' performance within established limits on information processing, and especially the severely limited capacity of short-term memory, which Miller (1956) had documented to be seven plus-or-minus two "chunks" of information. Chase and Simon (1973) had explained their findings in terms of chunking in short-term memory (STM), arguing that chess experts use their preexisting knowledge of a domain to create large chunks of information, which they can then use to access information such as what move to play. However, later research demonstrated that experts are also able to rapidly store information in long-term memory (LTM). For example, both Charness (1976) and Frey and Adesman (1976) found that interpolated tasks designed to interfere with short-term storage had very little effect on experts' subsequent recall of the positions.

More dramatically, Ericsson, Chase, and Faloon (1980) reported the case of a college student ("S.F.") who through more than 230 hours of practice increased the number of random digits he could recall from a typical 7 to an astonishing 79 digits. Verbal reports revealed that S.F., a collegiate track runner, accomplished this feat by recoding 3- and 4-digit sequences of digits as running times, ages, or dates, and encoding the groupings into long-term memory *retrieval structures*. Ericsson et al. concluded that there is "seemingly no limit to improvement in memory skill with practice" (p. 1182). In another study, Ericsson and Polson (1988a, 1988b) documented the memory skill of a waiter, "J.C.", who could memorize up to 20 dinner orders without taking notes. To account for these sorts of findings, Chase and Ericsson (1982) proposed their *skilled memory theory*, which posited the efficient and effective use of long-term memory as the locus of expert memory (see also Ericsson & Chase, 1982).

The consensus that emerged from all of this research was that expertise reflects domain-specific factors, with little or no role for innate factors. Feigenbaum (1989) articulated this perspective in the form of a principle:

> The Knowledge Principle states that a system exhibits intelligent understanding and action at a high level of competence primarily because of the specific knowledge that it can bring to bear: the concepts, representations, facts, heuristics, models, and methods of the endeavor. A corollary of the KP is that reasoning processes of intelligent systems are generally weak and not the primary source of power.
>
> (p. 179)

For the time, the consensus in cognitive psychology was that experts are made.

The deliberate practice view

The experts-are-made view reached its apogee in the early 1990s. There were two key developments. The first was the introduction of a formal approach for studying expertise – Ericsson and Smith's (1991) *expertise approach*. The approach involves three steps. The first step is to capture outstanding performance under laboratory conditions using tasks representative of the domain of interest, such as having chess players choose moves in chess games (as in de Groot, 1946/1978), musicians play pieces of music, or typists type passages of text. The second step is to describe the processes underlying outstanding performance on these tasks, using verbal reports or data from experimental tasks (e.g., memory tasks). The final step is to propose mechanisms to account for how the critical processes are acquired.

The second development was the publication of a pivotal article by Ericsson, Krampe, and Tesch-Römer (1993). In the spirit of Watson (1930), Ericsson et al. argued that individual differences in expertise largely reflect the accumulated amount of *deliberate practice* – engaging in activities specifically designed to improve performance in a domain. Ericsson et al. tested this idea in two studies. In the first study, using violinists as the participants, Ericsson et al. found that higher levels of skill were associated with higher mean levels of deliberate practice: on average, by age 20, the "best" students had accumulated over 10,000 hours, the "good" students about 7,800 hours, and the least accomplished group about 4,500 hours. The second study was a replication with pianists. Again, there was a large difference as a function of skill level: an "expert" group had accumulated an average of over 10,000 hours and an "amateur" group an average of only about 2,000 hours.

Ericsson et al. (1993) concluded that "high levels of deliberate practice are necessary to attain expert level performance" (p. 392), and continued:

> Our theoretical framework can *also provide a sufficient account* of the major facts about the nature and scarcity of exceptional performance. Our account *does not depend* on scarcity of innate ability (talent) . . . . We attribute the dramatic differences in performance between experts and amateurs-novices to similarly large differences in the recorded amounts of deliberate practice.
>
> (p. 392, emphases added)

Making exceptions only for height and body size, Ericsson et al. added, "We reject any important role for innate ability" (p. 399).

Ericsson and colleagues have maintained this basic view ever since. For example, Ericsson (2007) claimed that "it is possible to account for the development of elite performance among healthy children without recourse to unique talent (genetic endowment) – excepting the innate determinants of body size" (p. 4). They have further argued that there is a critical minimum amount of intense training necessary to achieve an elite level of performance – 10 years or 10,000 hours. As Ericsson, Prietula, and Cokely (2007) stated, "Our research shows that even the most gifted performers need a minimum of ten years (or 10,000 hours) of intense training before they win international competitions" (p. 119). More recently, referring to accepted training methods in fields such as classical music, mathematics, and ballet, Ericsson and Pool (2016) claimed that "if one follows these methods carefully and diligently, one will almost surely become an expert" (p. 114).

Criticisms of the deliberate practice view

In the nearly 25 years since it was published, the Ericsson et al. (1993) article has been cited over 6,600 times (according to Google Scholar). As one of us noted in a *New York Times* op-ed (Hambrick & Meinz, 2011a), the deliberate practice view has also captured the popular imagination. Most notably, the findings from Ericsson et al.'s studies of musicians were the inspiration for what Malcolm Gladwell (2008) termed the "10,000-hour rule" in his book *Outliers* – the idea that it takes 10,000 hours to become an expert. In turn, the 10,000-hour rule was the inspiration for the rap song "Ten Thousand Hours," which was the theme music for a Dr. Pepper commercial.

Nevertheless, from the start, the deliberate practice view has been highly controversial in the scientific literature (see Hambrick et al., 2014; Hambrick et al., 2016). The major criticism of the view is that deliberate practice is not as important as a predictor of expertise as Ericsson and colleagues have argued it is. For example, Anderson (2000) observed that "Ericsson and Krampe's research does not really establish the case that a great deal of practice is sufficient for great talent" (p. 324), and Marcus (2012) reflected, "Practice does indeed matter – a lot – and in surprising ways. But it would be a logical error to infer from the importance of practice that talent is somehow irrelevant, as if the two were in mutual opposition" (p. 95). Similarly, Schneider (2015) commented that while "Ericsson and colleagues believe that the amount of deliberate practice is a sufficient predictor of subsequent expert performance, the developmental findings suggest that individual differences cannot be completely ignored when it comes to predicting the development of expertise" (p. 27).

Empirical tests of the deliberate practice view

What does the empirical evidence say about the importance of deliberate practice? As a key testable claim of their view, Ericsson et al. (1993) argued that "individual differences in ultimate performance can *largely be accounted for* by differential amounts of past and current levels of practice" (p. 392, emphasis added). In any straightforward sense of the term "largely," there are two possible interpretations of this claim (see Figure 15.1). The *strong hypothesis* (left panel) states that deliberate practice accounts for all, or nearly all, of the reliable variance in expertise, leaving little or no "room" for other factors to contribute. What qualifies as "nearly all" of the variance is somewhat arbitrary; 99% would mean that another predictor variable could have no more than a "small" correlation with expertise ($r = .10$; Cohen, 1988). The *weak hypothesis* (right panel), on the other hand, states that deliberate practice accounts for *the majority* of the variance (> 50%), necessarily making it the *most important* predictor of expertise. If deliberate practice accounted

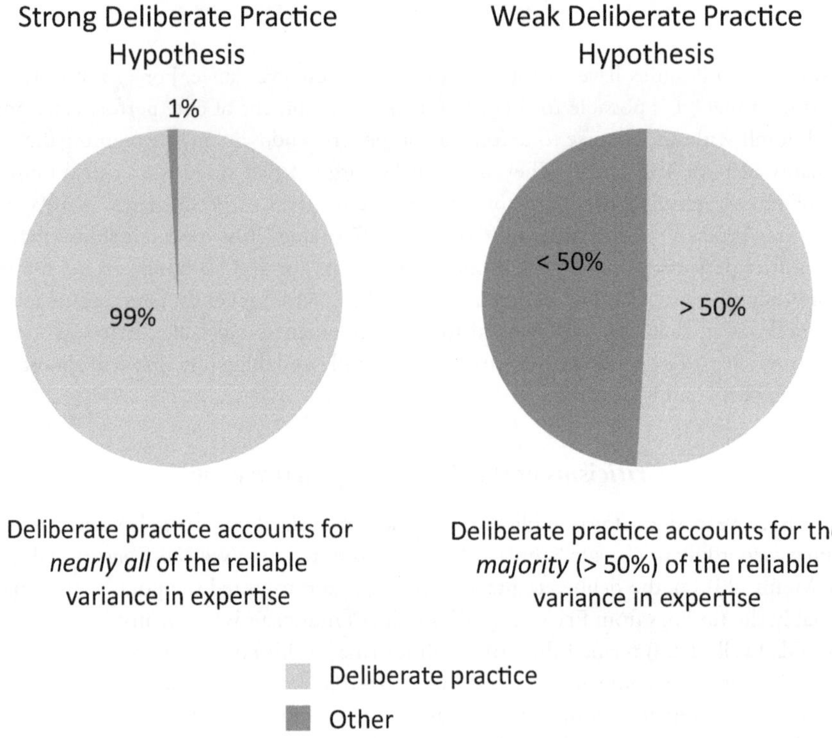

Figure 15.1 Strong hypothesis (left panel) and weak hypothesis (right panel) of the deliberate practice view

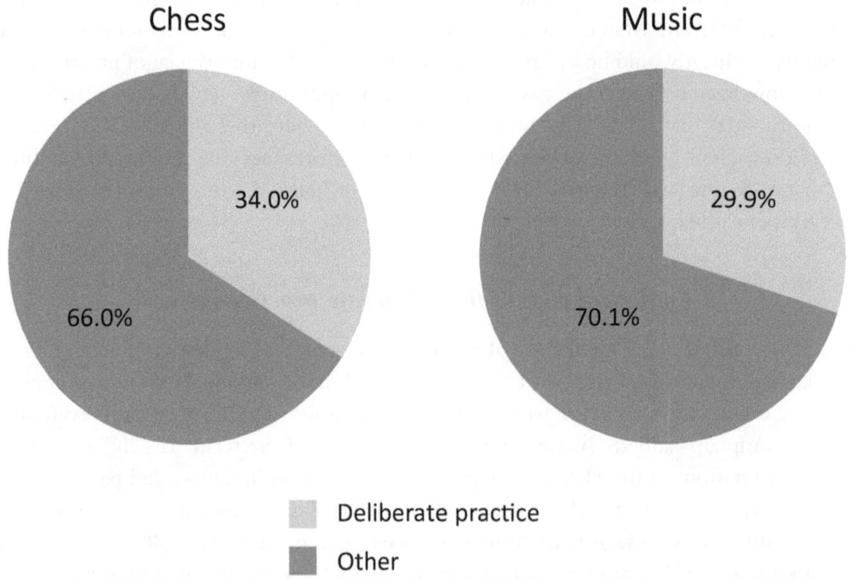

Figure 15.2 Average percentage of variance in chess performance (left) and music performance (right) accounted for by deliberate practice, correcting for measurement error. The light gray region represents reliable variance explained by deliberate practice; the dark gray region represents reliable variance not explained by deliberate practice. Adapted from Hambrick et al. (2014), with permission of Elsevier

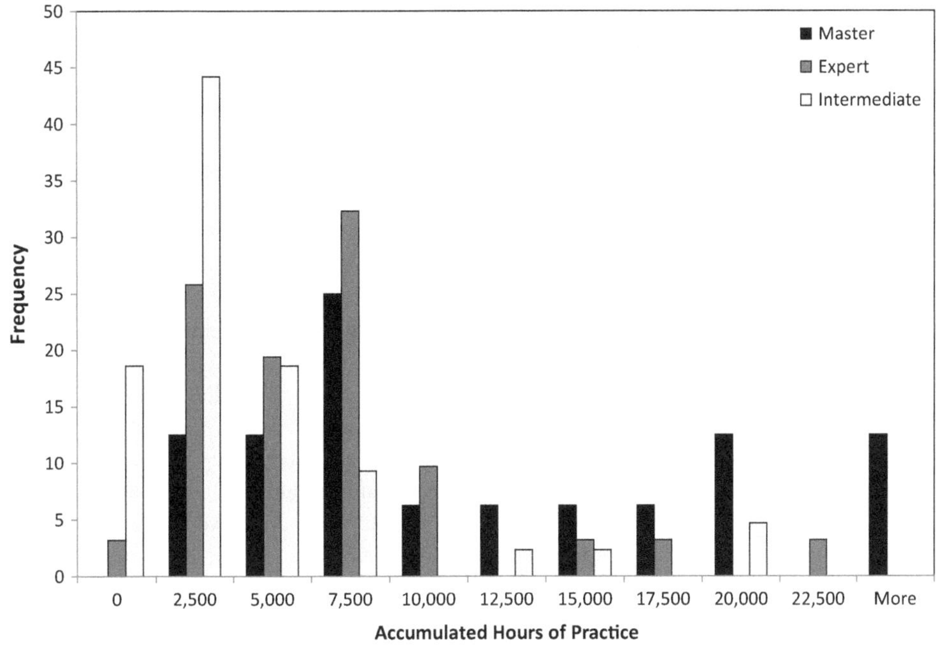

Figure 15.3 Histograms showing accumulated hours of deliberate practice for "master" (n=16; Elo rating > 2200), "expert" (n=31; Elo rating 2000–2200), and "intermediate" (n=43; Elo rating < 2000) chess players (Gobet & Campitelli, 2007). Deliberate practice refers to *serious study alone*. Reprinted from Hambrick, Oswald, Altmann, Meinz, Gobet, and Campitelli (2014), with permission of Elsevier

for 51% of the variance, three other orthogonal predictors could correlate .40 with expertise (a "medium" correlation).

The available evidence supports neither of these hypotheses. Hambrick et al. (2014) re-analyzed the results of studies of chess and music, the two most widely studied domains in research on expertise. To be included in the re-analysis, a study had to collect measures interpretable as deliberate practice and of domain-relevant performance, and report a correlation between the measures. As shown in Figure 15.2, the re-analysis revealed that, after correcting for measurement error (i.e., unreliability), deliberate practice accounted for 34% of the variance in chess expertise and 29.9% of the variance in music expertise. Thus, in neither domain did deliberate practice account for all, nearly all, or even the majority of the variance in expertise. In a subsequent meta-analysis of a larger number of music studies, Platz, Kopiez, Lehmann, and Wolf (2014) found that deliberate practice explained 36% of the reliable variance in music performance (avg. corrected $r = 0.61$).

These findings indicate that people differ in the amount of deliberate practice they require to reach a given level of skill. Hambrick et al. (2014) illustrated this point concretely with data from one of the studies in the meta-analysis – Gobet and Campitelli's (2007) chess study (see also Campitelli & Gobet, 2011). On average, deliberate practice was higher for more skilled players than less skilled players: 10,530 hours for masters, 5,673 hours for experts, and 3,179 hours for intermediates. However, as shown in Figure 15.3, there was an extremely wide range of deliberate practice within each group. Indeed, among the masters, the range was 832 to 24,284 hours – a difference of nearly three orders of magnitude. Moreover, there was overlap in the distributions across skill groups: some of the masters had practiced less than the average for the intermediate group, two levels down; some of the intermediates had practiced more than the average for the master group, two levels up.

More recently, Macnamara, Hambrick, and Oswald (2014) conducted a meta-analysis of all of the major domains in which the relationship between deliberate practice and expertise has been studied: games, music, sports, education, and professions. In terms of variance explained, the relationship between deliberate practice and performance varied by domain, but in all cases it was well less than half – 26% for games, 21% for music, 18% for sports, 4% for education, and less than 1% for professions. This was true even after making corrections for measurement error. A follow-up meta-analysis on sports revealed that deliberate practice accounted for a trivial amount of variance (1%) at elite levels of performance, suggesting that deliberate practice may lose its predictive power at the highest levels of skill (Macnamara, Moreau, & Hambrick, 2016).

Ericsson (2014) dismissed this work, rejecting all but one of the 88 studies in the Macnamara et al. (2014) meta-analysis – his study of pianists (Ericsson et al., 1993, Study 2) – on the grounds that they do not meet his criteria for accurately estimating the relationship between deliberate practice and performance. However, Ericsson rejected many studies that he has used to argue for the importance of deliberate practice in the past – including, oddly, several of his own studies. For example, he rejected his study of darts (Duffy, Baluch, & Ericsson, 2004) because there is no record in the report of the study that a teacher or coach supervised and guided all or most of the practice. Yet, he and his colleagues referred to measures that they collected in this study as measures of "deliberate practice" and concluded that the study "revealed that the single major factor contributing to professional level dart playing performance is deliberate practice" (Duffy et al., p. 244). Similarly, he rejected his own study of spelling bee contestants (Duckworth, Kirby, Tsukayama, Berstein, & Ericsson, 2011), even though the main conclusion of the study was that "[d]eliberate practice . . . was a better predictor of National Spelling Bee performance than either being quizzed by others or engaging in leisure reading" (p. 178). (Note also that "deliberate practice" appeared in the title of the article and then 72 more times throughout the article, excluding references.) Shifting definitions and standards for evidence in scientific research makes theories unfalsifiable and impedes progress. Recently, Ericsson and Pool (2016) made a potentially useful distinction between "purposeful practice" and teacher-led "deliberate practice." Problematically, however, Moxley, Ericsson, and Tuffiash (2017) discussed the preceding Spelling Bee study as concerning purposeful practice, without explicitly acknowledging that the original focus was deliberate practice. Shifting terms in scientific debates without explicit acknowledgment is obviously problematic.

What else matters?

To reiterate, evidence suggests that although deliberate practice is important as a predictor of expertise from both a statistical and practical perspective, it is not as important as Ericsson and colleagues have argued it is. Put another way, the evidence indicates that deliberate practice is only one piece of the expertise puzzle. What, then, are the other pieces of the puzzle? In the remainder of this chapter, we focus on one candidate: working memory capacity.

Working memory capacity

Nearly a half-century ago, Baddeley and Hitch (1974) began their classic chapter, "Despite more than a decade of intensive research on the topic of short-term memory (STM), we still know virtually nothing about its role in normal human information processing" (p. 48). To better understand the role of STM in higher-level cognition, Baddeley and Hitch conducted a series of experiments in which they had participants perform a secondary task designed to occupy STM while performing a primary task, such as reasoning or comprehension. Surprisingly, the secondary tasks had little effect on participants' performance in primary tasks. In one experiment, the primary task was to read and verify the accuracy of statements describing relationships between letters (e.g., *AB – A precedes* B) and the secondary task was to repeat the word "the," a predictable sequence of digits, or a random sequence of digits. The only effect of secondary task load was to increase the amount of time participants required to solve the problems; there was no effect on accuracy.

Based on their findings, Baddeley and Hitch (1974) proposed that STM is not a single, monolithic store, but a mental "workspace" that can be divided between processing and storage functions. Baddeley and Hitch described three components of the system: a *central executive* responsible for control processes such as reasoning, planning, and decision making, as well as two subsidiary (or "slave") systems devoted to maintenance and storage of information – the *phonological loop* and the *visuospatial sketchpad*. Later, Baddeley (2000) added a third subsidiary system to the model – the *episodic buffer* – for temporary storage of multimodal information as it is combined into an episodic representation.

Baddeley and colleagues' model generated a great deal of interest in explaining individual differences in higher-level cognition in terms of working memory. Following Baddeley and Hitch's (1974) description of the central executive, Daneman and Carpenter (1980) designed the *reading span* task to measure working memory capacity. In this task, the participant reads a series of sentences, while remembering the final word of each sentence for later recall. For example, given the sentences *When at last his eyes opened, there was no gleam of triumph, no shade of anger* and *The taxi turned up Michigan Avenue where they had a clear view of the lake*, the task would be to remember and then recall *anger* and *lake*. Daneman and Carpenter found that reading span (i.e., the number of sentences a subject could read while maintaining perfect recall of the sentence-final words) correlated strongly with score on a standardized test of verbal ability ($r = .59$), and even more strongly with measures from a laboratory test of reading comprehension. A few years later, Turner and Engle (1989) introduced the *operation span* task. A variant of reading span, the goal of this task is to solve a series of simple math problems while remembering a word following each problem.

Kyllonen and Christal (1990) conducted the first large-scale study of the relationship between WMC and general intelligence – psychometric "g." They found that WMC and g correlated very highly (> .90), leading Kyllonen (2002) to state, "We have our answer to the question of what *g* is. It is working memory capacity" (p. 433). In a later study, along with abstract reasoning tests to tap fluid intelligence (Gf) – defined as the ability to solve novel problems – Engle, Tuholski, Laughlin, and Conway (1999) had participants complete both "simple span" tests to measure STM (e.g., digit span), reflecting passive storage of information and complex span tests such as operation span, reflecting simultaneous storage and processing. Factor analyses revealed that these measures loaded on separate STM and WMC factors. Moreover, when a common factor comprising STM and WMC was modeled, only WMC uniquely predicted Gf.

In a follow-up study, Kane et al. (2004) had participants complete a battery of verbal and spatial STM and WMC tasks and a battery of verbal and spatial reasoning tests to measure Gf. A domain-general WMC factor correlated strongly with Gf. In a subsequent meta-analysis, Ackerman, Beier, and Boyle (2005) found an average correlation of around .40 between tests of WMC and Gf. Kane, Hambrick, and Conway (2005) re-analyzed the results of 12 studies and found an average correlation of .70 between latent variables representing WMC and Gf. The finding of a strong relationship between WMC and Gf has since emerged as one of the most replicated findings in recent research on human intelligence (see Conway & Kovacs, 2013). Research has further established that WMC is highly stable across time and substantially heritable, with heritability estimates typically around 50% (e.g., Ando, Ono, & Wright, 2001; Kremen et al., 2007; Polderman et al., 2006).

Using a "micro-analytic" approach (see Hambrick, Kane, & Engle, 2004), other research has investigated the nature of individual differences in WMC by testing for the relationship between scores on tests such as operation span and reading span and performance in experimental tasks designed to measure specific cognitive processes. This research indicates that the essence of WMC is the ability to hold information such as task goals in the focus of attention (Engle, 2002). For example, Kane, Bleckley, Conway, and Engle (2001) found that WMC positively predicted success in a task in which the participant's goal was to divert his or her eye movements away from a highly salient, flashing cue on a computer screen and respond to a stimulus on the opposite side of the screen. Kane et al. argued that participants with higher levels of WMC were better able to hold in mind the goal of looking away from the cue.

There has also been a proliferation of procedures to measure WMC (see Conway et al., 2005). For example, in *rotation span* (Shah & Miyake, 1996), the participant makes a judgment about whether a rotated letter is normal or mirror-imaged, and remembers the direction in which each letter is pointing. As another example, in *symmetry span* (Kane et al., 2004), the participant makes a judgment about whether a pattern appearing in a grid is symmetrical, and then remembers the location of a filled-in cell within another grid. These and other complex span tasks have good reliability (internal consistency and test-retest reliability estimates are typically in the .70–.80 range) and tend to correlate strongly with each other, indicating the existence of a domain-general WMC factor (Oswald, McAbee, Redick, & Hambrick, 2014). In a different type of WMC test, called *running span*, the participant sees or hears a list of items (e.g., digits) presented at a very quick rate. The length of the list varies randomly from trial to trial, and the participant is instructed to report the last few items in the list in order (e.g., the last 4 digits). Like complex span, running span correlates strongly with various measures of higher-level cognition and intelligence (Bunting, Cowan, & Saults, 2006).

There is debate about whether these and other measures of WMC are simply measures of established constructs – particularly Gf. Salthouse and Pink (2008) found that the relationship between WMC and Gf was constant as a function of the number of to-be-remembered items in complex span tasks (i.e., operation span, reading span, and symmetry span). That is, the correlation between WMC and Gf did not increase as the amount of information that participants needed to maintain in the complex span tasks increased. Salthouse and Pink concluded that it may be Gf that contributes to variation in WMC, not the other way around. Similarly, Salthouse (2014) found that the relationship between Gf and performance in running span did not differ as a function of list length. While this work raises important questions about what exactly tests of WMC capture, it is clear that tests of WMC capture *some* general ability that is important for higher-level cognition. We have asked what role – if any – this ability plays in expertise.

Working memory capacity and expertise

Ericsson and colleagues have argued that basic cognitive abilities can be circumvented or "bypassed" through domain-specific knowledge and skills acquired through deliberate practice. As Ericsson and Charness (1994) explained, "The effects of extended deliberate practice are more far-reaching than is commonly believed. Performers can acquire skills that circumvent basic limits on working memory capacity and sequential processing" (p. 725). In more specific terms, Ericsson and Kintsch (1995) proposed that the development of expertise involves the acquisition of *long-term working memory* (LT-WM). LT-WM comprises domain-specific encoding strategies and retrieval structures that enable the performer to rapidly store information in long-term memory and reliably retrieve that information as needed, and thereby circumvent storage of information in the "active" portion of working memory, or *short-term working memory* (ST-WM). They explained:

> Although our model of working memory conforms to all the basic constraints on human information processing, it asserts that subjects can acquire skill in the use of LTM and thereby circumvent the capacity limitations of STM for specific domains and tasks. Our proposal does not abolish constraints on working memory; it merely substitutes new constraints on rapid storage in and efficient retrieval from LT-WM for the old constraints on ST-WM.
>
> (Ericsson & Kintsch, p. 240)

This theory predicts that the effect of WMC on performance should diminish with increasing training. In other words, as illustrated in Figure 15.4, WMC should be less predictive of performance among individuals possessing high levels of domain-specific knowledge than among those with lower levels of domain-specific knowledge. Two major approaches have been used to test this prediction – the correlational approach and the experimental approach.

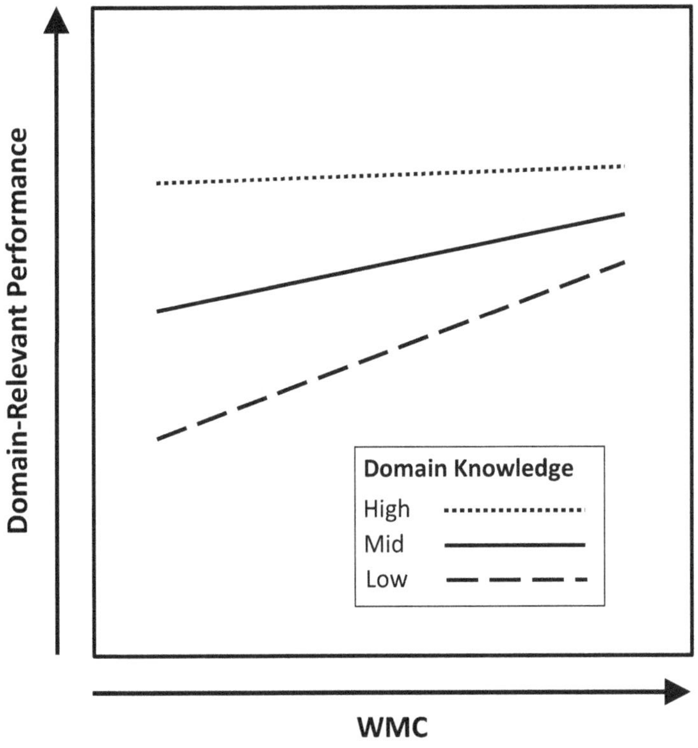

Figure 15.4 Domain Knowledge × WMC interaction implied by circumvention-of-limits hypothesis

Correlational evidence

Meinz and Hambrick (2010) had 57 pianists representing a wide range of skill (beginner to professional) complete a deliberate practice questionnaire and perform tests of WMC and sight-reading ability (playing music with no preparation). WMC added to the prediction of sight-reading performance (about 7%), above and beyond the contribution of deliberate practice (45%). More important, inconsistent with the circumvention-of-limits hypothesis, the effects of deliberate practice and WMC were additive rather than interactive. That is, WMC was as important as a predictor of sight-reading performance at high levels of deliberate practice as at lower levels. In a similar study, Kopiez and Lee (2006) had participants perform a test of WMC and a sight-reading task, with pieces of music representing five levels of difficulty. Kopiez and Lee found that the measure of WMC correlated significantly and positively with sight-reading performance at all but the most difficult level of music (Levels 1–4: avg. $r = .27$).

Using the same type of approach, Meinz et al. (2012) had 155 participants representing a wide range of involvement in the game of Texas Hold 'Em complete a questionnaire to assess their poker-playing experience, tests of poker knowledge, and tests of WMC. They also completed a battery of tasks designed to measure two components of Texas Hold 'Em skill – the ability to evaluate hands and the ability to remember plays in a game. Consistent with Meinz and Hambrick's (2010) findings, both WMC and poker knowledge positively predicted success in the poker tasks, but effects of WMC and poker knowledge were additive. There was no evidence for interactions supporting the circumvention-of-limits hypothesis. Thus, WMC was as important as a predictor at low levels of poker knowledge as at high levels.

More recently, Toma, Halpern, and Berger (2014) found that both Scrabble and crossword experts outperformed control subjects on two tests of working memory capacity – reading span and visuospatial span. The differences were very large: the average effect size was $d = 1.21$ for the Scrabble expert versus control comparisons and $d = 0.98$ for the crossword expert versus control comparisons. One possible explanation of these large differences is that solving crossword puzzles and playing Scrabble improves WMC. However, this explanation seems unlikely based on more than a century of research on the issue of transfer of training, including recent research on "brain training" programs. The general finding from this research is that benefits of brain training are limited to the trained task, or to very similar tasks, with no improvement in general aspects of cognition (e.g., Harrison et al., 2013; Redick et al., 2013). Another explanation is that people with high levels of WMC are more apt to take up and persist in these activities than people with lower levels of WMC.

A study by Masunaga and Horn (2001) on expertise in the Chinese board game Go deserves special mention, as it remains one of the most impressive studies of individual differences in expertise to date. The participants ($N = 263$) in this study represented wide ranges of age, cognitive ability, and Go expertise, and completed tests of both domain-general abilities and domain-specific skills. The domain-general battery included standard tests of fluid intelligence (Gf), processing speed (Gs), and short-term memory (Gsm). Gf was measured with tests of reasoning ability, Gs with tests of perceptual speed, and Gsm with tests of short-term memory – or what Ericsson and Kintsch (1995) referred to as *short-term working memory* (ST-WM). The domain-specific battery included tests of these same abilities, but with Go-specific content. In the Go reasoning test, participants were given Go positions and had to select the best move or detect points of weakness for one side. This task was modeled explicitly after de Groot's (1946/1978) approach to measuring chess skill. In the Go short-term memory tests, participants received Go positions and attempted to remember the positions for later recall or recognition (after de Groot, and Chase & Simon, 1973). Finally, in the Go perceptual speed tests, participants attempted to

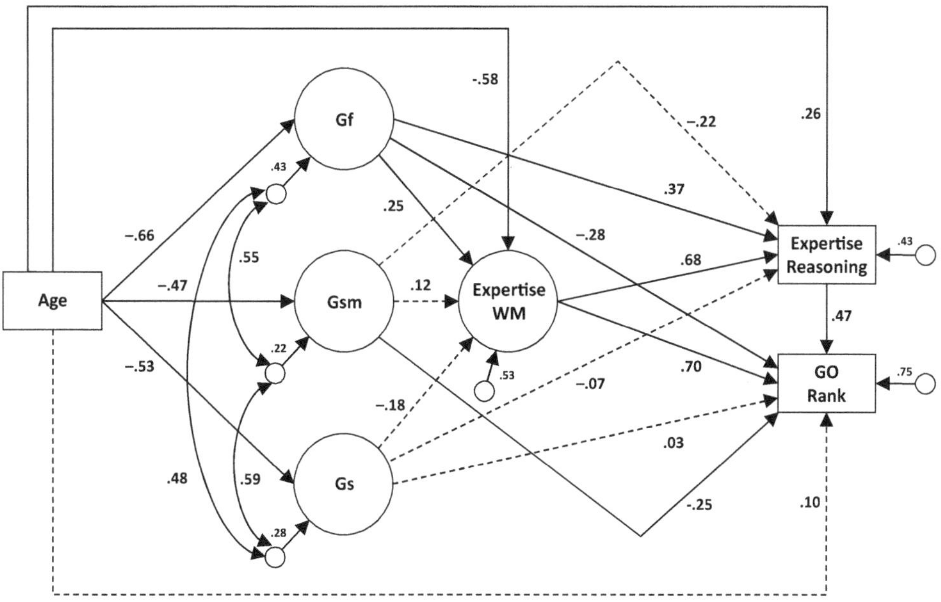

Figure 15.5 Re-analysis of Masunaga and Horn's (2001) published results. Structural equation model predicting, with domain-general abilities predicting Go-specific abilities and Go rank.

find patterns of Go pieces ("stones") in configurations of pieces and to compare rotated configurations of Go pieces and decide whether they were the same or different. Masunaga and Horn conceived of the Go reasoning test as a measure of *expertise deductive reasoning*, the Go short-term memory tests as measures of LT-WM or *expertise working memory*, and the Go speed tests as measures of *expertise cognitive speed* (ECS).

Figure 15.5 presents a reanalysis of Masunaga and Horn's (2001) published correlation matrix using structural equation modeling (SEM). Gf positively predicted Expertise WM (.25), which positively predicted Expertise Reasoning (.68). In turn, Expertise Reasoning positively predicted Go rank (.47). Note also that there was a direct effect of Gf on Expertise Reasoning (.37). Surprisingly, there was a *negative* effect of Gsm on Go rank (−.25), and Gf had a negative effect on Go rank (−.28). Finally, as expected based on a large body of evidence (e.g., Salthouse, 2000), age negatively predicted the domain-general abilities – Gf (−.66), Gsm (−.47), and Gs (−.53) – as well as Expertise WM (−.58). This latter finding is consistent with evidence for age-related decline in domain-relevant tasks. For example, Moxley and Charness (2013) found an average correlation of −.28 between age and performance in best-move tasks in chess. The effect of age on Go rank was positive but non-significant (.10), while the effect of age on Expertise Reasoning was positive and significant (.26). Overall model fit was excellent: $\chi^2(72) = 87.98, p = .097$, NFI = .95, CFI = .99, RMSEA = .03.

Taken together, this re-analysis suggests that cognitive ability is another important contributor to both individual and age-related differences in Go expertise, but that its contribution is complex. Specifically, the re-analysis suggests that a high level of Gf facilitates acquisition of LT-WM, and also contributes directly to Go expertise, as measured by a representative Go task. The negative effects of Gf and Gsm on the Go outcomes are more surprising. There are a number of possible explanations for these effects. One possibility is that Go players with high levels of cognitive ability may sometimes rely on general cognitive processes to perform domain-relevant tasks, when relying on domain-specific skills is more advantageous. Another possibility is that people with high levels of cognitive ability are less likely to devote time to acquiring a high level of skill in domains such as Go and to get involved in organized play in this domain. Whatever the case, cognitive ability is an important piece of the expertise puzzle in Go.

Experimental evidence

Other research has used an experimental approach to investigate involvement of working memory in expertise. Robbins et al. (1996) had chess players ranging in skill from novice to master perform a move-choice task either alone (the control condition) or while concurrently performing a secondary task designed to suppress one of the aforementioned components of the working memory system (central executive, phonological loop, or visuospatial sketchpad). The finding that secondary task load was less disruptive to experts' performance in the move-choice task than to non-skilled players' performance would support the circumvention-of-limits hypothesis, and more generally LT-WM theory. However, the results revealed that both the central executive and the visuospatial secondary tasks were disruptive to performance, and critically, the degree of disruption did not differ across skill level.

More recently, Foroughi, Werner, Barragán, and Boehm-Davis (2015) used an experimental approach to investigate involvement of LT-WM in reading comprehension. As key support for their idea of LT-WM, Ericsson and Kintsch (1995) reviewed evidence from a series of studies by Glanzer and colleagues (e.g., Fischer & Glanzer, 1986; Glanzer, Dorfman, & Kaplan, 1981; Glanzer, Fischer, & Dorfman, 1984) demonstrating that interrupting participants as they read texts – by, for example, having them solve arithmetic equations – had little effect on comprehension. The only effect of such disruptions was to increase reading time for the first sentence after reading resumed. Based on this evidence, Ericsson and Kintsch (1995) concluded that "the research by Glanzer and his colleagues . . . shows that the transient portion of working memory (ST-WM) is not necessary for continued comprehension of the type of texts they studied" (pp. 224–225) and that "reading can be completely disrupted for over 30 seconds with no observable impairment of subsequent text comprehension" (p. 232). Also, in clear terms, they described a method for testing their theory: "induced interruption is an effective experimental technique to differentiate between storage in ST-WM and storage in LT-WM" (Ericsson & Kintsch, 1995, p. 222).

Foroughi et al. (2015) noted that in the Glanzer studies "comprehension" was assessed with questions that could be answered based solely on recognition of information from the texts – a crude index of comprehension. Thus, following Ericsson and Kintsch's (1995) aforementioned method for differentiating between storage in ST-WM and LT-WM, Foroughi et al. conducted two experiments in which participants were interrupted while reading texts and then answered recognition questions (as in the Glanzer studies) or comprehension questions that tapped a deeper understanding of the texts (questions about theme, tone, the authors' goals, etc.). The major finding was that interruptions were disruptive to comprehension, but not recognition indicating, by Ericsson and Kintsch's logic, that ST-WM is involved in comprehension. In a more recent study, Foroughi and colleagues (Foroughi, Barragan, & Boehm-Davis, 2016) found that the degree of disruption was moderated by WMC, as measured by operation span. That is, the degree of disruption was larger for low- than for high-WMC participants.

Thus, contrary to Ericsson and Kintsch's (1995) LT-WM theory, there is now evidence that maintaining information in the "active" portion of working memory is important for comprehension. In a commentary on Foroughi et al.'s (2015) study, Delaney and Ericsson (2016) insisted that LT-WM theory does not actually predict that interruptions should have *no* effect on comprehension, only that comprehension should be substantially preserved. However, in a published reply, Foroughi and colleagues (Foroughi, Werner, Barragán, & Boehm-Davis, 2016) supplied numerous direct quotations that contradict this claim. For example, Quesada, Kintsch, and Gomez (2003) stated, "LTWM permits rapid and reliable reinstantiation of a context after interruption *without a decrease in performance*" (p. 941, emphasis added). If LT-WM theory can claim to explain contradictory results, it is not falsifiable.

The role of task/situational factors?

Taken together, the preceding evidence suggests that WMC makes an important contribution to individual differences in expertise. Furthermore, although the results should be regarded as tentative without replication, there is evidence that WMC sometimes predicts expertise even among highly skilled performers. For example, in a study of pilots, Sohn and Doane (2004) found evidence for an interaction between WMC and a factor reflecting LT-WM (i.e., skilled memory for aviation-specific information) in the direction predicted by the circumvention-of-limits hypothesis. That is, WMC predicted performance in the situational awareness task at low, but not high, levels of LT-WM.

Moreover, in a recent meta-analysis, Burgoyne et al. (2016) found that the correlation between Gf (which correlates strongly with WMC) and chess skill was stronger among less-skilled players (avg. r = .32) than more-skilled chess players (avg. r = .14). Though this finding should be interpreted cautiously because age and skill level were substantially confounded, and because there was evidence for restriction of range in chess ratings in the ranked samples, this pattern of correlations is consistent with the circumvention-of-limits hypothesis for the domain of chess.

This evidence suggests that there may be task and situational factors that moderate the interplay between WMC and expertise. For example, WMC may predict expertise, even among highly skilled performers in activities in which the task input changes continuously and unpredictably (e.g., sight-reading music in an unfamiliar genre), making it difficult or impossible to rely on LT-WM. By contrast, in activities where the task input is static (e.g., chess), performers may be able to develop LT-WM skills that enable them to circumvent limits associated with WMC. An important goal for future research on expertise is to develop a taxonomy of tasks for making testable predictions about when WMC should predict expertise and when not (see Hambrick et al., 2016, for a discussion).

A level down

When performing domain-relevant tasks, the brain function of experts and non-experts must differ, but how? The cognitive neuroscience of expertise is in its infancy, but one generalization that can be drawn from research is that brain regions presumed to be responsible for the specific demands of tasks in a given domain tend to be larger in experts than in novices. For example, using structural MRI, Maguire and colleagues (Maguire, Woollett, & Spiers, 2006) found that posterior hippocampal regions known to be involved in storing spatial representations of the environment were larger in London taxicab drivers than in control subjects, and also the volume of those regions correlated with amount of experience in the job.

There is also some evidence concerning the involvement of brain regions associated with working memory in expertise. In a recent fMRI study, Protzner et al. (2015) found that competitive Scrabble players recruited brain regions associated with working memory and visual perception to perform a lexical decision task to a greater degree than the control subjects did.

A key question for future research on the neuroscience of expertise is whether novice-expert differences reflect preexisting differences in brain function and/or structure, differences that emerge as a function of training, or both.

There is also an emerging literature on the genetics of expertise. There have been a few reports from twin studies of a genetic contribution to variation in self-reported expertise (e.g., Coon & Carey, 1989; Vinkhuyzen, van der Sluis, Posthuma, & Boomsma, 2009), and recent evidence suggests that individual differences in both practice and expertise are influenced by genetic factors. In the most impressive of these studies, Mosing, Madison, Pedersen, Kuja-Halkola, and Ullén (2014) had over 10,000 twins estimate lifetime amount of music practice, and also perform tests of music aptitude. For music practice, heritability was 69% for males and 41% for females, while for music aptitude, values ranged from 12% to 61% (see also Hambrick & Tucker-Drob, 2014). Moreover, Mosing et al. found no evidence for a causal influence of amount of music practice on music aptitude: identical twins differing massively in practice performed similarly on the tests of music aptitude. This finding suggests that, although certain aspects of music skill can only be acquired through practice (e.g., how to read music), there are limits on the transformative power of practice.

Beyond born versus made

A hundred and twenty-five years after Francis Galton and Alphonse Pyrame de Candolle agreed to disagree about why eminence runs in families, the experts are "born versus made" debate rages on. For example, Boot and Ericsson (2013) reviewed evidence they claimed established that "experience *rather than* talent is responsible for exceptional performance" (p. 145, emphasis added). In our view, it is no longer productive to think about expertise in this "either-or" way. Training – and more particularly deliberate practice – is an undeniably important piece of the expertise puzzle, but there is now ample evidence to reject the hypothesis that it is the only important piece. Other factors matter, too, and collectively account for at least as much of the inter-individual variability in expertise as deliberate practice does.

We believe that the time has come for research that moves our understanding of expertise forward, instead of back and forth in a nature-nurture debate. To this end, drawing on existing theoretical frameworks (e.g., Gagné, 2013), scientists must develop theories of expertise that take into account all relevant factors. This, of course, includes deliberate practice and factors that are related to the opportunity to engage in it (e.g., parental encouragement, socioeconomic status, geographic region). However, it also includes basic abilities and capacities that are known to be substantially heritable. Research aimed at testing such theories will move research on expertise beyond an anachronistic nature versus nurture perspective and toward a multifactorial perspective on expert performance.

Note

1 An electronic copy of ***Histoire des Sciences et des Savants Depuis Deux Siècles*** can be found at: http://biodiversitylibrary.org/page/27318242#page/10/mode/1up. Quotations from the Galton-Darwin and de Candolle–Galton correspondences come from Pearson (1914) and Fancher (1983).

References

Ackerman, P. L., Beier, M., & Boyle, M. O. (2005). Working memory and intelligence: The same or different constructs. *Psychological Bulletin, 131*, 30–60. doi: 10.1037/0033-2909.131.1.30

Anderson, J. R. (2000). *Learning and memory: An integrated approach* (2nd ed.). New York: John Wiley and Sons.

Ando, J., Ono, Y., & Wright, M. J. (2001). Genetic structure of spatial and verbal working memory. *Behavior Genetics, 31*, 615–624. doi: 10.1023/A:1013353613591

Baddeley, A. (2000). The episodic buffer: a new component of working memory? *Trends in Cognitive Sciences, 4*, 417–423. doi: 10.1016/S1364–6613(00)01538–2

Baddeley, A. D., & Hitch, G. (1974). Working memory. In G. H. Bower (Ed.), *Psychology of Learning and Motivation* (Vol. 8, pp. 47–89). Amsterdam: Elsevier.

Boot, W. R., & Ericsson, K. A. (2013). Expertise. In J. D. Lee, & A. Kirlik (Eds.), *The Oxford Handbook of Cognitive Engineering* (pp. 143–158). Oxford: Oxford University Press.

Bryan, W. L., & Harter, N. (1897). Studies in the physiology and psychology of the telegraphic language. *Psychological Review, 4*, 27–53. doi: 10.1037/h0073806.

Bryan, W. L., & Harter, N. (1899). Studies on the telegraphic language: The acquisition of a hierarchy of habits. *Psychological Review, 6*, 345–375. doi: 10.1037/h0073117.

Bunting, M., Cowan, N., & Saults, S. J. (2006). How does running memory span work? *Quarterly Journal of Experimental Psychology, 59*, 1691–1700. doi: 10.1080/17470210600848402

Burgoyne, A. P., Sala, G., Gobet, F., Macnamara, B. N., Campitelli, G., & Hambrick, D. Z. (2016). The relationship between cognitive ability and chess skill: A comprehensive meta-analysis. *Intelligence, 59*, 72–83. doi: 10.1016/j.intell.2016.08.002

Campitelli, G., & Gobet, F. (2011). Deliberate practice: Necessary but not sufficient. *Current Directions in Psychological Science, 20*, 280–285. doi: 10.1177/0963721411421922.

Charness, N. (1976). Memory for chess positions: Resistance to interference. *Journal of Experimental Psychology: Human Learning and Memory, 2*, 641–653. doi: 10.1037/0278-7393.2.6.641.

Chase, W. G., & Ericsson, K. A. (1982). Skill and working memory. In G. H. Bower (Ed.), *The psychology of learning and motivation* (Vol. 16). New York: Academic Press.

Chase, W. G., & Simon, H. A. (1973). The mind's eye in chess. In W. G. Chase (Ed.), *Visual information processing* (pp. 215–281). New York: Academic Press.

Cohen, J. (1988). A power primer. *Psychological Bulletin, 112*, 155–159. doi: 10.1037/0033–2909.112.1.155

Conway, A. R., Kane, M. J., Bunting, M. F., Hambrick, D. Z., Wilhelm, O., & Engle R. W. (2005). Working memory span tasks: A methodological review and user's guide. *Psychonomic Bulletin & Review, 12*, 769–786. doi: 10.3758/BF03196772

Conway, A. R., & Kovacs, K. (2013). Individual differences in intelligence and working memory: A review of latent variable models. *Psychology of Learning and Motivation, 58*, 233–270.

Coon, H., & Carey, G. (1989). Genetic and environmental determinants of musical ability in twins. *Behavior Genetics, 19*, 183–193. doi: 10.1007/BF01065903

Daneman, M., & Carpenter, P. A. (1980). Individual differences in working memory and reading. *Journal of Verbal Learning and Verbal Behavior, 19*, 450–466. doi: 10.1016/S0022–5371(80)90312–6

Darwin, C. (1859). *On the origins of species by means of natural selection.* London: John Murray.

de Candolle, A. (1873). *Histoire des sciences et des savants depuis deux siècles: suivie d'autres études sur des sujets scientifiques.* Geneva: Fayard.

de Groot, A. D. (1946/1978). *Thought and choice in chess.* The Hague: Mouton.

Delaney, P. F., & Ericsson, K. A. (2016). Long-term working memory and transient storage in reading comprehension: What is the evidence? Comment on Foroughi, Werner, Barragán, and Boehm-Davis (2015). *Journal of Experimental Psychology: General, 145*, 1406–1409. doi: 10.1037/xge0000181

Duckworth, A. L., Kirby, T. A., Tsukayama, E., Berstein, H., & Ericsson, K. A. (2011). Deliberate practice spells success why grittier competitors triumph at the national spelling bee. *Social Psychological and Personality Science, 2*, 174–181. doi: 10.1177/1948550610385872

Duffy, L. J., Baluch, B., & Ericsson, K. A. (2004). Dart performance as a function of facets of practice amongst professional and amateur men and women players. *International Journal of Sport Psychology, 35*, 232–245.

Engle, R. W. (2002). Working memory capacity as executive attention. *Current Directions in Psychological Science, 11*, 19–23. doi: 10.1111/1467–8721.00160

Engle, R. W., Tuholski, S. W., Laughlin, J. E., & Conway, A. R. (1999). Working memory, short- term memory, and general fluid intelligence: a latent-variable approach. *Journal of Experimental Psychology: General, 128*, 309. doi: 10.1037/0096–3445.128.3.309

Ericsson, K. A. (2007). Deliberate practice and the modifiability of body and mind: Toward a science of the structure and acquisition of expert and elite performance. *International Journal of Sport Psychology, 38*, 4–34.

Ericsson, K. A. (2014). Challenges for the estimation of an upper-bound on relations between accumulated deliberate practice and the associated performance of novices and experts: Comments on Macnamara, Hambrick, and Oswald's (2014) published meta-analysis. Unpublished manuscript. Retrieved from https://psy.fsu.edu/faculty/ericsson/ericsson.hp.html

Ericsson, K. A., & Charness, N. (1994). Expert performance: Its structure and acquisition. *American Psychology, 49*, 725–747. doi: 10.1037/0003–0066X.49.8.725

Ericsson, K. A., & Chase, W. G. (1982). Exceptional memory: Extraordinary feats of memory can be matched or surpassed by people with average memories that have been improves by training. *American Scientist, 70*, 607–615.

Ericsson, K. A., Chase, W. G., & Faloon S. (1980). Acquisition of a memory skill. *Science, 208*, 1181–1182. doi: 10.1126/science.7375930

Ericsson, K. A., & Kintsch, W. (1995). Long-term working memory. *Psychological Review, 102*, 211–245. doi: 10.1037/0033–0295X.102.2.211

Ericsson, K. A., Krampe, R. Th., & Tesch-Römer, C. (1993). The role of deliberate practice in the acquisition of expert performance. *Psychological Review, 100*, 363–406. doi: 10.1037/0033–0295X.100.3.363

Ericsson, K. A., & Polson, P. G. (1988a). An experimental analysis of a memory skill for dinner orders. *Journal of Experimental Psychology: Learning, Memory, and Cognition, 14*, 305–316. doi: 10.1037/0278–7393.14.2.305.

Ericsson, K. A., & Polson, P. G. (1988b). Memory for restaurant orders. In M. Chi, R. Glaser, & M. Farr (Eds.), *The nature of expertise* (pp. 23–70). Hillsdale, NJ: Lawrence Erlbaum Associates.

Ericsson, K. A., & Pool, R. (2016). *Peak: Secrets from the new science of expertise*. New York: Houghton Mifflin Harcourt.

Ericsson, K. A., Prietula, M. J., & Cokely, E. T. (2007). The making of an expert. *Harvard Business Review, 85*, 146–147.

Ericsson, K. A., & Smith, J. (1991). *Toward a general theory of expertise: Prospects and limits*. Cambridge, UK: Cambridge University Press.

Fancher, R. E. (1983). Alphone de Candolle, Francis Galton, and the early history of the nature-nurture controversy. *Journal of the History of the Behavioral Sciences, 19*, 341–352. doi: 10.1002/1520–6696

Feigenbaum, E. A. (1989). What hath Simon wrought? In D. Klahr & K. Kotovsky (Eds.), *Complex information processing: The impact of Herbert A. Simon* (pp. 165–182). Hillsdale, NJ: Lawrence Erlbaum Associates.

Fischer, B., & Glanzer, M. (1986). Short-term storage and the processing of cohesion during reading. *The Quarterly Journal of Experimental Psychology, 38*, 431–460. doi: 10.1080/14640748608401607

Foroughi, C. K., Barragán, D., & Boehm-Davis, D. A. (2016). Interrupted reading and working memory capacity. *Journal of Applied Research in Memory and Cognition, 5*, 395–400. doi: 10.1016/j.jarmac.2016.02.002

Foroughi, C. K., Werner, N. E., Barragán, D., & Boehm-Davis, D. A. (2015). Interruptions disrupt reading comprehension. *Journal of Experimental Psychology: General, 144*, 704–709. doi: 10.1037/xge0000074

Foroughi, C. K., Werner, N. E., Barragán, D., & Boehm-Davis, D. A. (2016). Multiple interpretations of long-term working memory theory: Reply to Delaney and Ericsson (2016). *Journal of Experimental Psychology: General, 145*, 1410–1411. doi: 10.1037/xge0000221

Frey, P. W., & Adesman, P. (1976). Recall memory for visually presented chess positions. *Memory & Cognition, 4*, 541–547. doi: 10.3758/BF03213216

Gagné, F. (2013). The DMGT: Changes within, beneath, and beyond. *Talent Development & Excellence, 5*, 5–19.

Galton, F. (1869). *Hereditary genius*. London: Macmillan.

Galton, F. (1892). *Hereditary genius*. New York: D. Appleton & Co.

Gladwell, M. (2008). *Outliers: The story of success*. New York: Little, Brown, and Co.

Glanzer, M., Dorfman, D., & Kaplan, B. (1981). Short-term storage in the processing of text. *Journal of Verbal Learning and Verbal Behavior, 20*, 656–670. doi: 10.1016/S0022–5371(81)90229–2

Glanzer, M., Fischer, B., & Dorfman, D. (1984). Short-term storage in reading. *Journal of Verbal Learning and Verbal Behavior, 23*, 467–486. doi: 10.1016/S0022–5371(84)90300–1

Gobet, F., & Campitelli, G. (2007). The role of domain-specific practice, handedness, and starting age in chess. *Developmental Psychology, 43*, 159–172. doi: 10.1037/0012–1649.43.1.159

Gray, W. D., & Lindstedt, J. K. (2016). Plateaus, dips, and leaps: Where to look for inventions and discoveries during skilled performance. *Cognitive Science*, 1–33. doi: 10.1111/cogs.12412

Hambrick, D. Z., Kane, M. J., & Engle, R. W. (2004). The role of working memory in higher-level cognition: Domain-specific vs. domain-general perspectives. In R. J. Sternberg & J. Pretz (Eds.), *Intelligence and cognition* (pp. 104–121). New York: Cambridge University Press.

Hambrick, D. Z., Macnamara, B. N., Campitelli, G., Ullén, F., & Mosing, M. (2016). Beyond born versus made: A new look at expertise. *Psychology of Learning and Motivation, 64*, 1–55.
Hambrick, D. Z., & Meinz, E. J. (2011a, November 20). Sorry, strivers. Talent matters. *The New York Times*. Sunday Review, 12.
Hambrick, D. Z., Oswald, F. L., Altmann, E. M., Meinz, E. J., Gobet, F., & Campitelli, G. (2014). Deliberate practice: Is that all it takes to become an expert? ***Intelligence**, 45*, 34–45. doi: 10.1016/j.intell.2013.04.001
Hambrick, D. Z., & Tucker-Drob, E. (2014). The genetics of music accomplishment: Evidence for gene-environment correlation and interaction. *Psychonomic Bulletin & Review, 22*, 112–120. doi: 10.3758/s13423-014-0671-9
Harrison, T. L., Shipstead, Z., Hicks, K. L., Hambrick, D. Z., Redick, T. S., & Engle, R. W. (2013). Working memory training may increase working memory capacity but not fluid intelligence. *Psychological Science, 24*, 2409–2419. doi: 0956797613492984.
Kane, M. J., Bleckley, M. K., Conway, A. R. A., & Engle, R. W. (2001). A controlled-attention view of working memory capacity. *Journal of Experimental Psychology: General, 130*, 169–183.
Kane, M. J., Hambrick, D. Z., & Conway, A. R. (2005). Working memory capacity and fluid intelligence are strongly related constructs: Comment on Ackerman, Beier, and Boyle (2005). *Psychological Bulletin, 131*, 66–71. doi: 10.1037/0033–2909.131.1.66
Kane, M. J., Hambrick, D. Z., Tuholski, S. W., Wilhelm, O., Payne, T. W., & Engle, R. W. (2004). The generality of working memory capacity: A latent-variable approach to verbal and visuospatial memory span and reasoning. *Journal of Experimental Psychology: General, 133*, 189. doi: 10.1037/0096–3445.133.2.189
Kopiez, R., & In Lee, J. (2006). Towards a dynamic model of skills involved in sight reading music. *Music Education Research, 8*, 97–120. doi: 10.1080/14613800600570785
Kremen, W. S., Jacobsen, K. C., Zian, H., Eisen, S. A., Eaves, J. J., Tsuang, M. T., & Lyons, M. J. (2007). Genetics of verbal working memory processes: A twin study of middle-aged men. *Neuropsychology, 21*, 569–580. doi: 10.1037/0894–4105.21.5.569
Kyllonen, P. C. (2002). g: Knowledge, speed, strategies, or working-memory capacity? A systems perspective. In R. J. Sternberg, & E. L. Grigorenko (Eds.), *The general factor of intelligence: How general is it* (pp. 415–445). Mahwah, NJ: Lawrence Erlbaum Associates, Inc.
Kyllonen, P. C., & Christal, R. E. (1990). Reasoning ability is (little more than) working-memory capacity? *Intelligence, 14*, 389–433. doi: 10.1016/S0160–2896(05)80012–1
Macnamara, B. N., Hambrick, D. Z., & Oswald, F. L. (2014). Deliberate practice and performance in music, games, sports, education, and professions: A meta-analysis. *Psychological Science, 25*, 1608–1618. doi: 10.1177/0956797614535810
Macnamara, B. N., Moreau, D., & Hambrick, D. Z. (2016). The relationship between deliberate practice and performance in sports: A meta-analysis. *Perspectives on Psychological Science, 11*, 333–350. doi: 10.1177/1745691616635591
Maguire, E. A., Woollett, K., & Spiers, H. J. (2006). London taxi drivers and bus drivers: A structural MRI and neuropsychological analysis. *Hippocampus, 16*, 1091–1101. doi: 10.1002/hipo.20233
Marcus, G. (2012). *Guitar zero: The science of becoming musical at any age*. New York: Penguin.
Masunaga, H., & Horn, J. (2001). Expertise and age-related changes in components of intelligence. *Psychology and Aging, 16*, 293. doi: 10.1037/0882–7974.16.2.293
Meinz, E. J., & Hambrick, D. Z. (2010). Deliberate practice is necessary but not sufficient to explain individual differences in piano sight-reading skill: The role of working memory capacity. *Psychological Science, 21*, 914–919. doi: 10.1177/0956797610373933
Meinz, E. J., Hambrick, D. Z., Hawkins, C. B., Gillings, A. K., Meyer, B. E., & Schneider, J. L. (2012). Roles of domain knowledge and working memory capacity in components of skill in Texas hold'em poker. *Journal of Applied Research in Memory and Cognition, 1*, 34–40. doi: 0.1016/j.jarmac.2011.11.001
Miller, G. A. (1956). The magical number seven, plus or minus two: Some limits on our capacity for processing information. *Psychological Review, 63*, 81–97. doi: 10.1037/h0043158
Mosing, M. A., Madison, G., Pedersen, N. L., Kuja-Halkola, R., & Ullén, F. (2014). Practice does not make perfect: No causal effect of music practice on music ability. *Psychological Science, 25*, 1795–1803. doi: 10.1177/0956797614541990
Moxley, J. H., & Charness, N. (2013). Meta-analysis of age and skill effects on recalling chess positions and selecting the best move. *Psychonomic Bulletin & Review, 20*, 1017–1022. doi: 10.3758/s13423-013-0420-5
Moxley, J. H., Ericsson, K. A., & Tuffiash, M. (2017). Gender differences in SCRABBLE performance and associated engagement in purposeful practice activities. *Psychological Research*. In press.

Oswald, F. L., McAbee, S. T., Redick, T. S., & Hambrick, D. Z. (2014). The development of a short domain-general measure of working memory capacity. *Behavior Research Methods, 47*, 1343–1355. doi: 10.3758/s13428-014-0543-2

Pearson, K. (1914). *Life and letters of Francis Galton*. Cambridge, UK: Cambridge University Press.

Platz, F., Kopiez, R., Lehmann, A. C., & Wolf, A. (2014). The influence of deliberate practice on musical achievement: a meta-analysis. *Frontiers in Psychology, 5*, 646. doi: 10.3389/fpsyg.2014.00646

Polderman, T. J., Stins, J. F., Posthuma, D., Gosso, M. F., Verhulst, F. C., & Boomsma, D. I. (2006). The phenotypic and genotypic relation between working memory speed and capacity. *Intelligence, 34*, 549–560. doi: 10.1016/j.intell.2006.03.010.

Proctor, R. W., & Dutta, A. (1995). *Skill acquisition and human performance*. Thousand Oaks, CA: Sage Publications, Inc.

Protzner, A. B., Hargreaves, I. S., Campbell, J. A., Myers-Stewart, K., van Hees, S., Goodyear, B. G., & Pexman, P. M. (2015). This is your brain on Scrabble: Neural correlates of visual word recognition in competitive Scrabble players as measured during task and resting-state. *Cortex, 75*, 204–219. doi: 10.1016/j.cortex.2015.03.015

Quesada, J. F., Kintsch, W., & Gomez, E. (2003). Latent problem solving analysis as an explanation of expertise effects in a complex, dynamic task. In R. Alterman, & D. Kirsh (Eds.), *Proceedings of the 25th annual conference of the Cognitive Science Society*, (pp. 940–945). Mahwah, NJ: Lawrence Erlbaum.

Redick, T. S., Shipstead, Z., Harrison, T. L., Hicks, K. L., Fried, D. E., Hambrick, D. Z., Kane, M. J., & Engle, R. W. (2013). No evidence of intelligence improvement after working memory training: A randomized, placebo-controlled study. *Journal of Experimental Psychology: General, 142*, 359. doi: 10.1037/a0029082

Reed, H. B., & Zinszer, H. A. (1943). The occurrence of plateaus in telegraphy. *Journal of Experimental Psychology, 33*, 130–135. doi: 10.1037/h0061289

The Republic. Retrieved from: http://classics.mit.edu/Plato/republic.html

Robbins, T. W., Henderson, E. J., Barker, D. R., Bradley, A. C., Fearneyhough, C., Henson, R., Hudson, S. R., & Baddeley, A. D. (1996). Working memory in chess. *Memory & Cognition, 24*, 83–93.

Salthouse, T. (2000). *A theory of cognitive aging*. Dordrecht, NL: Elsevier.

Salthouse, T. A. (2014). Relations between running memory and fluid intelligence. *Intelligence, 43*, 1–7. doi: 10.1016/j.intell.2013.12.002

Salthouse, T. A., & Pink, J. E. (2008). Why is working memory related to fluid intelligence? *Psychonomic Bulletin & Review, 15*, 364–371. doi: 10.3758/PBR.15.2.364

Schneider, W. (2015). *Memory development from early childhood through emerging adulthood*. New York: Springer.

Shah, P., & Miyake, A. (1996). The separability of working memory resources for spatial thinking and language processing: An individual differences approach. *Journal of Experimental Psychology: General, 125*, 4. doi: 10.1037/0096-3445.125.1.4

Sohn, Y. W., & Doane, S. M. (2004). Memory processes of flight situation awareness: Interactive roles of WMC, long-term working memory, and expertise. *Human Factors: The Journal of the Human Factors and Ergonomics Society, 46*, 461–475. doi: 10.1518/hfes.46.3.461.50392

Taylor, D. W. (1943). Learning telegraphic code. *Psychological Bulletin, 40*, 461–487. doi: 10.1037/h0054172.

Thorndike, E. L. (1912). *Education: A first book*. Charleston, SC: BiblioBazaar.

Toma, M., Halpern, D. F., Berger, D. E. (2014). Cognitive abilities of elite nationally ranked Scrabble and crossword experts. *Applied Cognitive Psychology, 28*, 727–737. doi: 10.1002/acp.3059

Tulloss, R. (1918). *The learning curve*. Unpublished Ph.D. thesis, Harvard University.

Turner, M. L., & Engle, R. W. (1989). Is working memory capacity task dependent? *Journal of Memory and Language, 28*, 127–154. doi: 10.1016/0749-596X(89)90040-5

Vinkhuyzen, A. E., van der Sluis, S., Posthuma, D., & Boomsma, D. I. (2009). The heritability of aptitude and exceptional talent across different domains in adolescents and young adults. *Behavior Genetics, 39*, 380–392. doi: 10.1007/s10519-009-9260-5

Watson, J. B. (1930). *Behaviorism*. Chicago, IL: The University of Chicago Press.

16
EXPERT DECISION MAKING
A fuzzy-trace theory perspective

Rebecca K. Helm, Michael J. McCormick, and Valerie F. Reyna

Expert decision making: a fuzzy-trace theory perspective

Research has shown that expert decision makers often make decisions in their area of expertise that are superior to those of laypeople – for example, expert physicians are better at discriminating levels of cardiac risk (Reyna & Lloyd, 2006), chess masters can identify the most promising moves during a game of chess (Chase & Simon, 1973; De Groot, 1978), and judges (but not jurors) are able to distinguish between qualitatively different types of harm in a legal case (Eisenberg, Rachlinski, & Wells, 2002). However, research has also shown experts are fallible and susceptible to many of the cognitive biases that affect lay people (Tversky & Kahneman, 1974). For example, expert physicians make different choices based on whether the same information is presented in positive or negative terms (known as a framing effect) and fail to adjust sufficiently for population base rates when judging a conditional probability (e.g., the chances that a 40-year-old woman has breast cancer conditional on a positive diagnostic test) (e.g., Croskerry, in press; McNeil, Pauker, Sox, & Tversky, 1982; Reyna, 2005; Reyna & Lloyd, 2006; Shanteau & Stewart, 1992). In fact, research has shown that under certain circumstances experts can be more biased than novices in their area of expertise (Reyna, Chick, Corbin, & Hsia, 2014). In this chapter, we discuss decision making of experts including physicians, judges, and intelligence officers. Using the lens of fuzzy-trace theory (FTT), we provide a framework to explain why experts often make superior decisions, and when they are likely to be as susceptible or more susceptible to bias (systematic departures from applicable normative rational theory; Gilovich, Griffin, & Kahneman, 2002) than laypeople.

Although findings of biases among experts are counterintuitive, FTT predicts these outcomes and simultaneously accounts for the ability of experts to make better decisions in many real-life situations. The key, as we illustrate, is the distinction between meaning-driven as opposed to rote mental representations. We begin by introducing FTT as a dual-process account of memory and reasoning. We then describe how FTT applies in a wide range of domains and can serve broadly to explain, predict, and improve expert decision making.

Traditional dual-process theories

Traditional dual-process theories – which propose that two basic processing types underlie decision making – differentiate Type 1 processes that are "automatic, fast, and intuitive" and

Type 2 processes that are "slow, sequential and correlated with measures of general intelligence" (Evans & Stanovich, 2013; Thompson, 2014). These theories are often described as "default interventionist" because Type 1 processing is the default way of thinking, whereas Type 2 "higher order" processing is evoked occasionally and can be used to intervene by overriding Type 1 thinking (Evans & Stanovich, 2013; Kahneman, 2011; but see Barbey & Sloman, 2007, for a parallel competitive view). Dual-process theories associate biased judgments with Type 1 thinking and "rational" judgments with Type 2 thinking (Epstein, 1994; Guthrie, Rachlinski, & Wistrich, 2007), although they recognize that Type 1 processing often leads to correct answers and Type 2 can produce biases in some circumstances (Evans & Stanovich, 2013).

Traditional dual-process theory has been applied to expert decision making in two primary ways, both of which recognize that "intuition" plays a role in expert decision making and are based on the assumption that intuitive judgments and preferences have the characteristics of Type 1 processing in that they are automatic, arise effortlessly, and often come to mind without immediate justification (Kahneman & Klein, 2009; Thompson, 2014). The first approach, the Heuristics and Biases (HB) approach, suggests that experts (and laypersons) are subject to intuitive biases because they take mental shortcuts called "heuristics" (Guthrie et al., 2007; Tversky & Kahneman, 1974). This approach has been mischaracterized as focusing on flaws in cognitive performance. However, Tversky and Kahneman (1974) pointed out, "It is not surprising that useful heuristics . . . are retained, even though they occasionally lead to errors in prediction or estimation" (p. 1130). Nevertheless, in this view, one way that experts can avoid such biases is by overriding Type 1 thinking with Type 2 thinking (e.g., Evans & Stanovich, 2013; Guthrie et al., 2007; Tversky & Kahneman, 1974).

The second approach to expert decision making arising from a traditional dual-process theory perspective is Naturalistic Decision Making (NDM) (Kahneman & Klein, 2009). NDM focuses on the success of expert intuition, suggesting that experts often rely on intuition (defined as the recognition of patterns stored in memory; Chase & Simon, 1973) and use cues and tacit knowledge to make good judgments without directly comparing options (Kahneman & Klein, 2009). Based mainly on anecdotal observations in real-world contexts, expertise is said to be developed by learning cues in a "valid" environment - an environment that offers stable relationships between objectively identifiable cues and the outcomes of possible actions (Kahneman & Klein, 2009; Schraagen, in press). Thus, NDM researchers argue that "intuition" in experts can be explained in terms of recognition of familiar elements (Schraagen, in press; Simon, 1981). That is, the claim is that cue-action pairs stored in long-term memory (after considerable experience with the environment) and generalized schemas (pattern matching or feature matching) are applied to make decisions (Schraagen, in press), a process called "recognition-primed decisions" (Klein, Calderwood, & Clinton-Cirocco, 2010). In atypical situations, which cannot easily be explained through recognition of familiar elements, experts are said to gather additional information and clarify the situation through story building (Schraagen, in press).

NDM and HB both acknowledge that intuitive judgments can arise from genuine skill and be beneficial, but can also arise from inappropriate application of heuristic processes (Kahneman & Klein, 2009). They also both suggest that the determination of whether intuitive judgments can be trusted requires examination of the environment in which the judgment is made and the opportunity the judge has had to learn from the regularities of that environment.

FTT originated as an alternative to the HB approach, but with the goal of accounting for those empirical findings and predicting new findings that are not captured by prior approaches (Reyna & Brainerd, 1994, 1995). FTT also shares some assumptions with NDM, for example, incorporating models of recognition and recall to explain decision making, and vice versa, but it is grounded in specific experimental tests and mathematical models as well as naturalistic observations (Reyna, 2012). To take one example, FTT relies on the extensive evidence undermining schema theory (e.g., Alba & Hasher, 1983), substituting the empirically supported construct of gist. Moreover, FTT provides a different explanation of expert decision making, based on the distinction between reliance on *surface level* verbatim representations and ***meaning-based*** gist representations, which are processed in parallel. In addition, FTT is a developmental theory that predicts greater reliance on gist representations, as opposed to verbatim representations, in judgment and decision making as experience in a domain increases. For such development to occur, experience must afford, not only the opportunity for feedback about whether successful outcomes are associated with cues, but also the opportunity for meaningful conceptual learning about *why* those outcomes are associated with those cues (Reyna, 2008).

FTT predicts counterintuitive findings in the literature that are not predicted by HB or NDM for reasoners generally (e.g., see Reyna & Brainerd, 1995, 2008) as well as for experts (e.g., Reyna & Lloyd, 2006). According to FTT, experts are better reasoners, not just due to greater knowledge and recognition of recurrent patterns, but because the nature of their cognitive processing in a domain changes, becoming more gist-based, as they develop expertise in that domain. In FTT, cognitive development from novice to expert is predicted to be similar to that from child to adult when the latter reason about everyday domains, and, as we discuss, evidence supports this prediction. By "gist-based," we mean based on simple (but central), meaningful representations, per definitions in psycholinguistics (e.g., Kintsch, 1974). This developmental shift in processing produces paradoxical effects, such as experts using simpler processing (e.g., fewer dimensions of information) to make better decisions than novices, but also being more subject to gist-based biases, such as "false" memories for events that represent inferences about those events (e.g., see Table 2 in Reyna & Lloyd, 1997, 2006). HB and NDM theories have not made such predictions; these and many other FTT predictions do not follow naturally from the core assumptions of HB and NDM. Indeed, some research on FTT rules out HB's and NDM's predictions (e.g., HB theory is ruled out in Reyna et al., 2014; and recognition memory ideas used in NDM are ruled out in Reyna & Brainerd, 1994), although recent work has sought to reconcile these views (see Toplak, in press). In sum, applying detailed processing models of tasks that have been tested in experiments and mathematical models, including relevant research findings from HB and NDM approaches, FTT predicts when reasoning is likely to be superior with expertise, and when reasoning biases are likely to increase with expertise, depending on specific features of a task (Adam & Reyna, 2005; Reyna, Lloyd, & Brainerd, 2003; Wilhelms, Corbin, & Reyna, 2015).

FTT background

FTT is a dual-process theory of decision making grounded in research on memory, reasoning, judgment, and decision making – and their development from children to adults and novices to experts. FTT proposes that two basic types of memory representation – verbatim and gist – are encoded, stored, retrieved, and forgotten separately, and roughly in parallel (Reyna, Corbin, Weldon, & Brainerd, 2016). Verbatim memory is memory for surface information, for example, memory representations of exact words, numbers, and pictures (e.g., "there is a 20% chance of snow today" or "there is a 20% chance of death from this medical procedure"). Verbatim memory is a symbolic, mental representation of the stimulus, not the stimulus itself. Gist memory is a symbolic, mental representation for essential bottom line meaning, the "substance" of information irrespective of exact words, numbers, or pictures (e.g., "there is a low chance of snow today" or "there is a high chance of death from this medical procedure"). This means that the same surface form of "20% chance" can have a different gist depending on context – in the examples above, a 20% chance of snow is likely to be considered a relatively low risk, but a 20% chance of death is likely to be considered a relatively high risk (Reyna, 2008). According to FTT, informed (e.g., expert) decisions pivot on appreciating the gist of relevant facts, such as 20% chance, not on merely remembering the verbatim numbers, and prior work has shown that these are independent processes (Reyna & Hamilton, 2001).

For example, when deciding whether to have a medical procedure known as "carotid endarterectomy" to remove obstructions in the carotid artery, informed adults should ideally appreciate that surgery has a non-trivial risk of death (a categorical some-risk versus no-risk distinction), rather than just recalling the fact there is a 2% risk of death (a more specific, fine grained distinction; Reyna & Hamilton, 2001). More fine-grained distinctions are required, however, if decision options cannot be distinguished with simplest gist. For example, when choosing between two operations, both of which have a non-trivial risk of death, a patient would rely on a more finely grained distinction, such as a higher versus a lower risk of death because both options have some risk, and categorical gist does not distinguish the options (Reyna, 2012).

Verbatim and simplest categorical gist exist at opposite ends of a continuum and multiple representations are usually encoded at varying levels of precision between these extremes (e.g., a 20% chance of snow, a less than 50% chance of snow, a low chance of snow, some chance of snow; Rivers, Reyna, & Mills, 2008). Simplest gist is the least precise representation, such as some chance of snow in the previous example. These levels of precision from verbatim (a 20% chance of snow) to simplest gist (some chance of snow) are roughly analogous to scales of measurement (exact numerical values, ordinal, and categorical distinctions; Reyna, 2012). Verbatim and gist representations are independent of each other and are retrieved independently, predictions supported by research in the basic science literature, as illustrated in Table 16.1.

FTT posits that there is a developmental trend from reliance on verbatim representations to reliance on increasingly simple gist representations. Therefore, as an individual becomes more experienced in a domain – so long as that experience provides the opportunity to gain conceptual insight – they will rely on increasingly simple gist to make decisions. Reliance on gist and verbatim representations both develop with experience, but a preference for simple gist-based processing (the processing that occurs when gist-based representations are relied on, which gives it certain characteristics – for example, it is more fuzzy and impressionistic than verbatim-based processing) emerges with experience in a domain. This means that in familiar everyday decisions

Table 16.1 FTT predictions and support for these predictions in the basic science literature

FTT prediction	*Critical test*	*Empirical support*
Information is encoded in multiple representations with varying levels of precision (from gist to verbatim)	Can cue retrieval of gist or verbatim trace by manipulating cue given to participants	Reyna & Kiernan, 1994; Reyna & Kiernan, 1995
Verbatim and gist representations are independent	Manipulations that improve verbatim memory for numbers or sentences should not improve gist memory.	Brainerd & Gordon, 1994; Reyna, 1992; Reyna, 1995; Reyna & Brainerd, 1995
Verbatim and gist representations are retrieved independently	Misrecognizing gist should be independent of memory for verbatim information.	Reyna & Kiernan, 1994; Reyna & Kiernan, 1995

that people are repeatedly exposed to, such as risky decisions for rewards, we see a development from reliance on verbatim to simplest gist from childhood to young adulthood (Reyna & Ellis, 1994; Reyna & Farley, 2006) and beyond young adulthood for professionals who must deal frequently with high-stakes risks (Reyna et al., 2014).

Gist-based processing is therefore developmentally advanced based on several considerations, such as later emergence in development with experience and reflection of meaningful distinctions that matter in judgment and decision making. Importantly, FTT differs from NDM in that gist is not about processing entire cue matters, but rather decision making based on bottom-line meaning rather than superficial surface detail (Reyna, 2012). Gist-based processing is distinguished from the "satisficing" strategies in the HB or NDM traditions and, unlike in HB or NDM, the key to gist-based processing is *meaning*. Gist-based processing is not about doing less or exerting less cognitive effort (as tested in many experiments); it is about understanding simple meaning and, thus, getting to the nub of a decision (e.g., Adam & Reyna, 2005; Lloyd & Reyna, 2009; Reyna & Lloyd, 2006). For example, patients' symptoms cannot be easily reduced to a "cookbook" that provides lists of symptoms and diagnoses, and even sophisticated computer programs to accomplish such a cookbook have generally failed (Lloyd & Reyna, 2009; Reyna et al., 2003). Instead, the best diagnosticians understand disease mechanisms. According to FTT, good decision making, then, is based on the essence of what really matters, rather than superficial details (Reyna, 2013).

However, reliance on gist is also predicted to (and has been shown to) result in bias when content and context foment a semantic bias that goes beyond literal information, as in framing biases, false memories, conjunction fallacies, and hindsight biases (e.g., Reyna, 2013; Reyna et al., 2002; Reyna, 2005). In addition, gist-based processing is distinguished from "fast" impulsive processing. FTT recognizes that inhibiting impulses is important in decision making, but separates this from reliance on gist or verbatim representations (Reyna, Wilhelms, McCormick, & Weldon, 2015).

FTT and expert decision making

As discussed, according to FTT, development is a process of acquiring meaningful experience, which tends to increase with age for everyday decision making and with domain-specific expertise (Reyna et al., 2014). This developmental process leads to more than knowledge acquisition – rather, to a tendency to rely on gist representations that reflect meaning, despite processing and remembering verbatim details. Therefore, FTT makes two specific predictions that traditional dual-process theories do not make. First, experts will rely on simpler distinctions (gist) when making decisions in their area of expertise. Second, experts will show *more* bias than novices – called a "developmental reversal" in FTT – in tasks in which bias is caused by reliance on gist, such as framing tasks (see Reyna et al., 2014, and discussion below), and hindsight bias tasks (see Reyna, 2005, and discussion below). We now discuss each of these predictions in the context of research into expert decision making in different domains.

Medical experts

One of the most important areas for studying and improving expert decision making is in the domain of medical decision making. In addition to life or death decisions, doctors must make many choices that temporarily or permanently affect the well-being and life satisfaction of their patients – such as whether to prescribe a blood thinner that will reduce the likelihood of a heart attack but also interfere with an active lifestyle or whether to diagnose a clinically borderline child with a disorder that allows insurance coverage but also leaves the child permanently labeled.

Several studies of medical decision making have confirmed FTT's counterintuitive predictions that experts rely more on gist than novices, as reflected in processing fewer, but the most meaningful, dimensions of information and making simpler all-or-none distinctions. For example, cardiologists who have greater experience with heart disease than generalist physicians have been shown to make more accurate diagnostic judgments about chest pain, but they rely on fewer pieces of information and make cruder all-or-none admission decisions – mainly discharging the patients who have chest pain (with follow-up) or sending them to intensive care (Reyna & Lloyd, 2006). Generalist physicians make more nuanced decisions than cardiologists do, processing more dimensions of information more elaborately and sending patients to a wider range of destinations, such as levels of monitored hospitalization as well as discharge or intensive care. The tendency to process simple gist is even greater among the most expert cardiologists. Similarly, emergency medical technicians have been shown to know more about practice guidelines and to make better decisions that are guideline-consistent, but they rely on more vague, intuitive gist, and fewer dimensions of information (Brust-Renck, Reyna, Wilhelms, & Lazar, 2016). This reliance on gist is revealed when patients do not fit the guidelines, and more experienced technicians violate the verbatim rules of the guideline but offer superior medical care. This prediction was tested by constructing patient profiles that orthogonally crossed the factors of correct/incorrect gist of medical care with agreement/disagreement with verbatim guidelines. Experts scored higher than novices on correct gist and guideline-agreement patients but "lower" (fewer technically correct answers) than novices for correct gist and guideline disagreement patients.

Research into expert decision making in the medical domain has also provided support for FTTs second prediction, that experts will show *more* bias that novices in their area of expertise in tasks in which bias is caused by reliance on gist. Despite extensive medical education, how nurses, physicians, and other medical personnel have repeatedly been shown to fall victim to decision biases such as being influenced by alternate framing of the same information (Hux, Levinton & Naylor, 1994; Forrow, Taylor, & Arnold, 1992; McGettigan et al., 1999), and errors in disjunctive probability judgments (Reyna & Lloyd, 2006) (for a summary of other biases in clinical decision making, see Croskerry, in press). These biases are two biases that are associated with reliance on gist (see Weldon, Corbin, & Reyna, 2013). Therefore, FTT would predict that in their area of expertise medical experts would be more susceptible to alternate framing of the same information (for a detailed discussion of FTT predictions regarding framing, see the section on intelligence agents below), and errors in disjunctive probability judgments.

There is research to support the contention that medical experts are more susceptible to being influenced by alternate framing of the same information ***in their domain of expertise*** than novices. Christensen et al. (1991) presented twelve gain or loss framed clinical scenarios to medical students, residents, and physicians. For each scenario, subjects had to choose between two options – surgery or medical treatment. Gain-framed scenarios described the chance of survival or treatment success whereas loss-framed scenarios described the chance of death or treatment failure. Medical students, who were the least advanced developmentally in this study, showed no significant framing effect for any of the clinical scenarios. As predicted by FTT, the more experienced medical personnel (residents and physicians) showed greater framing effects; they were more likely to prefer the medical treatment in the gain versus loss frame. Thus, a developmental reversal was found in that increases in expertise were associated with greater reliance on gist processing and greater susceptibility to decision biases.

Intelligence and security experts

Intelligence and security experts are a group of professionals who are expert in making risky decisions (for example, decisions about national security). Therefore, FTT predicts that when making decisions involving risk, intelligence, and security experts should rely on simpler distinctions than controls and show more biases associated with gist-based processing.

Consistent with FTT predictions, research has suggested that security experts make superior decisions and that this is due to reliance on gist. In one experiment, Pachur and Marinello (2013) compared the decision strategies and choice patterns of airport customs officers and a group of novices regarding which passengers should be submitted to a search prior to boarding an airplane, specifically looking at two different decision strategies – compensatory strategies representing straightforward implementations of the notion that decisions involve the evaluation of multiple cues (Klein, 1998), and "take-the-best" strategies where cues are inspected in descending order of validity and inspection of cues is stopped as soon as the alternatives differ on a given cue (Gigerenzer & Goldstein, 1996). Based on interviews with a separate group of customs officials, a list of eight cues considered valid for identifying passengers was compiled, along with the respective values considered diagnostic of an individual trying to smuggle drugs. Cues included the country in which the flight originated, gender, the speed of the passenger's gait, and the amount of luggage they carried, while values ranged from those indicating a low likelihood of drug smuggling (Europe, female, normal walking speed, several bags) to those indicating a higher likelihood of smuggling (South America, male, hurried, one bag). Pairs of passenger profiles were then constructed using this information and participants were asked to decide which of the two passengers would be more likely to smuggle illegal drugs. Participants also ranked the importance of each cue in forming their decisions and how confident they were in their cue rankings.

Customs officers were not only more consistent in their cue rankings (a characteristic of rational decision making) – all but one ranked "flight origin" as the most important cue – their cue rankings showed greater discrimination (i.e., dispersion) than the group of novices. By weighting the cues more differentially, customs officers were also able to rely on fewer cues and were more confident in their cue rankings (customs officers focused on one cue, whereas novices were more likely to use a compensatory strategy in which several cues were individually weighted). Finally, the cue rankings generated by the customs officers were more consistent with the chief customs officer who had the highest "success" rating according to internal airport statistics, suggesting that although they considered less information overall, customs officers were able to make more accurate screening decisions than the less experienced group of novices. This is similar to the finding in Reyna and Lloyd regarding medical decision making – experts are making better decisions based on fewer dimensions of information, suggesting reliance on bottom line meaning rather than complex weighing of a number of different factors. This result has also been found when investigating decision making of experienced burglars, police officers, and a novice group of graduate students (experts processed fewer cues) regarding how likely a given house is to be burglarized (Garcia-Retamero & Dhami, 2009).

Research into expert decision making in the intelligence and security domain has also provided support for FTT's second prediction, that experts will show *more* bias than novices in their area of expertise in tasks in which bias is caused by reliance on gist. Intelligence agents are experts in making risky decisions (for example, decisions concerning national security). One bias in risky decision making that FTT associates with gist-based processing is risky choice framing.

Before we discuss expertise, we should explain framing effects: changes in the positive (gains) or negative (losses) wording of the same objective information, known as framing, can have a large impact on judgments and risk preferences (Reyna et al., 2014; see Levin, Schneider, & Gaeth, 1998, and Kühberger & Tanner, 2010 for reviews). For example, in the so-called Asian Disease Problem (Tversky & Kahneman, 1981), in the gain frame, the options are "200 lives saved for sure" and "1/3 chance of 600 saved or 2/3 chance of 0 saved"; most people choose the risk-free option in the gains frame (to save 200 lives for sure). In the corresponding loss frame, the choice is between "400 lives lost for sure" and "2/3 chance of 600 lost or 1/3 of 0 lost"; most people choose the risk-seeking option in this condition (2/3 chance of 600 lost or 1/3 of 0 lost). Because 600 are expected to die in all scenarios, 200 saved is equivalent to 400 die. Therefore, difference in choice selection across frames is viewed as a violation of preference consistency (the options are the same), a basic axiom of rational decision making (Machina, 1982; Savage, 1954; Von Neumann & Morgenstern, 1944).

FTT predicts framing effects by proposing that the typical choice problems differ in the gist that each frame generates. Specifically, in the gain frame, the gist of the risk-free option (200 lives saved for sure) is "saving some lives," whereas the gist of the risky option (1/3 chance of 600 saved or 2/3 chance of 0 saved) is "saving some lives or saving none." Given that most people value saving some lives over saving none, they select the sure option in the gain frame. In the loss frame, however, the gist of the risk-free option (400 lives lost for sure) is "losing some lives" whereas the gist of the risky option (2/3 chance of 600 lost or 1/3 of 0 lost) is "losing some lives or losing none." (The distillation to none versus some is not arbitrary but is the simplest gist of the numerical information in this problem.) Here, because most people prefer to lose no lives rather than some lives, the risk-seeking option is typically chosen in the loss frame. Thus, increasing gist-based processing is predicted to increase framing effects.

Several critical tests have consistently supported this interpretation (Kühberger & Tanner, 2010; Mandel, 2001; Reyna & Brainerd, 1991; Reyna et al., 2014; Stocke, 1998). In one, Reyna et al. (2014) presented the same preamble to subjects but modified the format of the risky-choice decision option to either emphasize categorical some/none distinctions between the options (to encourage reliance on gist) or to emphasize the equal expected value of the options (to encourage reliance on verbatim) (Reyna et al., 2014). Take the example of an original framing problem that had 600 lives at stake and the original gain frame choice was between (a) definitely saving 200 and (b) a 1/3 chance of saving 600 and a 2/3 chance of saving 0. In the gist condition, the preamble would be identical, but the options would be presented as (a) definitely saving 200 and (b) a 2/3 chance of saving 0 (i.e. (a) **some** v (b) **none**). In the verbatim condition, again the preamble would be identical, but the options would be presented as (a) definitely saving 200 and (b) a 1/3 chance of saving 600 (i.e. (a) **some** v (b) **some**). Although the missing information was available in the preamble and subjects reported understanding the full range of options, framing effects were pronounced when the gist (categorical contrast) was emphasized but eliminated when verbatim processing was encouraged. This supports FTT's prediction (described above) that gist-based processing increases framing effects.

Because FTT views framing as a bias caused by reliance on gist, the theory predicts an increase in framing with expertise. Therefore, in the area of risky decision making, FTT predicts that intelligence agents should show more framing than controls. Reyna et al. (2014) investigated this by providing intelligence agents, college students, and post-college adults with a series of risky-choice framing tasks involving lives and other values outcomes that varied in frame (gain or loss) and truncation (the risky option presented was either the standard option, or truncated to encourage reliance on categorical differences (gist) or analytic calculation (verbatim), as described above)). These problems were intended to be in the intelligence agent's area of expertise due to their focus on risking lives and other valued outcomes.

As predicted by FTT, because of training and regular experience in making life or death decisions, intelligence agents showed overall framing biases that were larger than those of college students and marginally larger than those of post-college adults. No group showed framing effects in the condition encouraging verbatim processing, the framing effect shown by intelligence agents in the standard condition (not truncated to encourage reliance on gist or verbatim processing) was similar to the framing effect shown by college students in the condition designed to encourage reliance on gist. This suggests that by encouraging college students to rely on gist, we can make their decision making more comparable to that of experts. This supports FTT's contention that experts are cognitively disposed to reliance on gist-based processing. These effects were observed for the dependent variables of subject's choices and their strength of preference. An analysis of confidence ratings also revealed that the intelligence agents were more confident in their responses than either of the other two groups. Thus, intelligence agents were not only more biased than students (they framed more), they were also more confident in their decisions.

This is not predicted by traditional dual-process theories. Such theories often associate framing with Type 1 thinking (Peters et al., 2006), or at least associate more within-subjects framing (where each participant receives problems in the gain frame and the loss frame) with more Type 1 thinking (see Stanovich & West, 2008). Most decision theories predict that increases in analytical reasoning ability – such as that gained by increases in age and expertise – should reduce or eliminate framing effects by revealing the equivalency of the options and increasing the consistency of preferences. As illustrated above, empirical research supports FTT predictions that framing effects increase with expertise.

Explanations of developmental reversals (specifically reversals from children to adults) that are consistent with traditional dual process theory have been provided based on the fact that children (or those with less expertise) may be responding randomly or may not have developed certain knowledge (such as stereotypes) that may interfere with rational responding (see Toplak, in press). However, these explanations do not fit the data showing developmental reversals from children to adults, which show that children do have knowledge and competence in probability (Reyna & Brainerd, 1994), that children's responses vary systematically with risk and outcome – as the probability of getting nothing goes up in the gamble, they choose this less (Reyna & Ellis, 1994), and are not always based on knowledge such as stereotypes (for example in the case of risky choice framing) (see Reyna & Ellis, 1994).

Legal experts

Legal experts, most notably judges, make important decisions routinely. Judges decide approximately as many cases at trial as juries (Clermont & Eisenberg, 1992) and the judicial role also includes ruling on dispositive motions and ruling on matters of law (for example whether evidence is admissible or whether a witness is competent to testify). This means that the quality of decisions that judges make is important for the legal system and individuals more generally. Because of this, it is important to understand how judges make decisions, and any biases they are subject to that could lead to harmful consequences in the real world.

In the legal literature, research into judicial decision making has focused on the debate between formalism (when judges apply the law in a clear, uniform, and consistent way) and realism (when judges use their interpretation of facts and the law to decide cases and then use law to provide a post hoc rationale) (Neuborne, 1992; Posner, 1986; Leiter, 1999). Legal formalism states that judges apply the law to the facts of a case in a clear, uniform, and consistent way, without regard for social interests and public policy (Leiter, 1999). In contrast, legal realism suggests that judges' decisions are highly influenced by their own interpretations of facts and the law, reacting primarily to the facts of the case involved, and then using the law to provide a post hoc rationale for a decision (Leiter, 1999). This debate has several parallels to traditional dual-process accounts that have recently been applied to judicial decision making (Kahneman & Frederick, 2002; Guthrie et al., 2007). According to traditional theories, judges make initial intuitive judgments (using Type 1 processing), much like legal realism, but they can override their initial judgments with deliberation (using Type 2 processing), and make decisions more in line with legal formalism. According to these models, intuitive decision making is responsible for inaccurate and inconsistent judicial decisions (Guthrie et al., 2007).

FTT provides an alternative explanation of judicial decision making, consistent with the empirical research that has been conducted on judicial decision making and the broader research on decision making in experts (for example, the research on medical experts discussed above). This is a new kind of intuitionism, recognizing that experts are cognitively disposed to rely on intuition to a greater extent than novices, but that this facilitates advanced decision making, which can result in superior decision making through understanding of meaning and the "nub" of a decision, but can also result in bias where context foments a semantic bias (see Weldon, Corbin, & Reyna, 2013). Specifically, and as noted above, reliance on gist results in bias where context foments a semantic bias.

Research into the decision making of legal experts has supported FTT's prediction that experts rely on simpler gist-based distinctions (rather than surface-level similarities) when making decisions. One study examining real legal cases regarding punitive damage awards (monetary awards intended to punish a defendant and deter them from engaging in the same conduct again, rather than just to compensate a claimant) showed that non-expert legal decision makers (but not judges) award the same ratio of punitive to compensatory damages regardless of the nature and extent of the injuries involved in the case (bodily injury or non-bodily injury; Eisenberg, Rachlinski, & Wells, 2002). This was true despite the fact that inflicting bodily injury on someone is generally considered more heinous and deserving of punishment than inflicting non-bodily injury. Thus, non-expert decision makers were less able than judges at assigning damages that were consistent with the nature of harm in the case, suggesting that they rely less on gist processing because they have a lower level of understanding of the facts and relative magnitudes in the case. This is consistent with FTT as jurors (novices) are predicted to rely more on verbatim processing which would not distinguish between qualitatively different types of harm (as it is based on surface level detail, such as numbers). Judges, who rely more on gist processing, would be predicted to take account of more qualitative factors due to reliance on bottom line meaning in a decision.

In addition, research has shown that judges are susceptible to biases associated with reliance on gist-based processing. One bias relevant to judicial decision making that has been associated with gist-based processing is hindsight bias (the inclination to see an event as having been predictable after it has occurred; Reyna, 2005). Hindsight bias is an example of a verbatim-gist dissociation effect (see Reyna, 2005). An individual relying on verbatim would make the same decision in foresight or in hindsight (as the facts are the same) but an individual relying on gist would be influenced by inferences based on meaning or context which may lead them to judge a situation differently in hindsight (similar to constructive memory).

Research has shown that judges are susceptible to hindsight bias in their area of expertise (Guthrie, Rachlinski, & Wistrich, 2001). Guthrie et al. asked judges to predict the court of appeals' response to an appeal from the district court. They were given specific facts regarding a case decided by the district court and were told that the decision of the district court in this case had been appealed to the court of appeals. They were then split into three conditions. A third of participants were told that the court of appeals had sent the case back to the district court for imposition of a lesser sanction, a third of participants were told the court of appeals had affirmed the district court's decision, and the final third of participants were told that the court of appeals had overturned the decision of the district court. Judges from all three conditions were then asked to judge retrospectively which of the three actions the court of appeals was most likely to have taken, considering the case facts. In this case, the judges displayed hindsight bias because knowing the outcome in the court of appeals significantly affected their assessments.

Judges have also been shown to be susceptible to hindsight bias in considering the types of evidence that they frequently consider, for example evidence regarding "probable cause" (Rachlinski, Guthrie, & Wistrich, 2011). Probable cause is the standard used to determine the legality of police searches (in hindsight or in foresight), and requires that there be a reasonable chance the search will turn up evidence of a crime. Usually a judge will assess this before the search has been conducted, but in some cases the police can conduct a search without a warrant. In these cases, the police still need probable cause but whether this was present is judged retrospectively. Over three experiments, Rachlinski, Guthrie, and Wistrich (2011) presented hypothetical cases to 900 state and federal judges and asked them to make a determination of probable cause either in foresight (asking for a warrant) or in hindsight (where a police search had been conducted and incriminating evidence had been found). They found that hindsight affected judge's ability to assess the likely outcomes of the search (although it should be noted that this did not ultimately affect their rulings, perhaps because the change in probability estimates was not large enough to push the case from one judgment to the other).

In these experiments judges were not compared directly with non-expert controls. It is likely that hindsight bias would also have influenced non-experts in these situations where there is no special knowledge involved (most adults would make inferences that once evidence has been found it was more likely to be found, or once a decision has been made it was more likely to be made that way). Future research should test this prediction and also consider situations in which expertise would lead to specific inferences that would promote greater susceptibility to hindsight bias.

Ultimately, FTT provides an alternate explanation to formalism, realism, or traditional dual-process theory when considering judicial decision making. Future experiments could test this theory by providing judges and non-experts with identical materials and investigating how decisions are being made.

Educational experts

FTT can also lend valuable insight into decisions made by other experts in their areas of expertise, such as the educational decisions made by superintendents and principals. Such decisions can affect large numbers of students for extended periods of time when those decisions implement policies that might be resistant to change. In a study of middle and junior high school principals, Miller, Fagley, and Casella (2009) found that the framing of information did have a significant impact on policy decisions in an educational setting. Variants of the classic risky-choice framing vignette appropriate for a school setting were constructed that included a choice between a certain (risk-free) option and a riskier but possibly more successful option. In one scenario, the success rate of a remedial reading program was varied – the risk-free program offered a certain success rate of 40% (failure rate of 60%), whereas the riskier program was described as having a 40% chance of being successful for all students and a 60% chance of being successful for no students (or a 40% chance of failing for no students and a 60% chance of failing for all students). As with professionals in the previously reviewed domains, principals were more likely to select risky options when the information was framed in a negative way than when the information was framed in a positive way.

FTT's account of this violation of preference consistency is similar to previous domains. That is, according to FTT, principals (like other experts) have developed a strong reliance on gist processing that typically aids decision making by capitalizing on knowledge, experience, and intuition but also increases the susceptibility to specific biases. In the gain frame, because some students succeeding is better than no students succeeding, the certain outcome of a 40% success rate was chosen most often. In the loss frame, however, because some students failing is worse than no students failing, the risky option was chosen most often in which potentially no students would fail. Such phrasing of decisions elicits a gist that violates a basic axiom of rational decision making (i.e., preference consistency) when gains (successes) and losses (failures) do not differ. However, sensitivity to context is generally an adaptive approach to decision making.

Conclusions and differences to other theories

In this chapter we have discussed a theoretical perspective – fuzzy-trace theory – that explains and predicts counter-intuitive empirical results in the expert decision making literature. We then applied the theory to specific areas of expert decision making to highlight the various insights FTT provides. The theoretical predictions and empirical evidence examined in this chapter support the hypothesis that, as individuals gain greater experience and expertise, their decision making becomes increasingly gist-based. This advanced intuition leads experts to make decisions based on simpler distinctions and fewer dimensions of information, compared to those used by novices, that are also often more accurate. For example, research showed that doctors and customs officials with relatively greater experience and expertise in their area made more accurate decisions based on fewer dimensions of information, and judges (but not jurors) were able to distinguish meaningfully different cases from one another, recognizing what was truly important in cases that were quantitatively comparable. However, this can also lead to increased biases in experts (in their domain of expertise) where context foments a semantic bias (e.g., in the framing task) – research showed intelligence officers to be more susceptible to framing bias than college students in risky choice framing tasks, and medical experts to be more susceptible to framing bias than medical students when making medical decisions.

FTT's account differs from traditional dual-process theory by recognizing a developmental shift from surface-level verbatim processing to meaning-based gist processing. This shift explains not only the superior decision making of experts where an understanding of meaning is required but also developmental reversals where reliance on meaning can result in predictable bias. Although traditional dual-process theory expects that experts can make superior decisions but also be subject to heuristics and biases, it does not provide an explanation for why we see developmental reversals in specific types of bias from novice to expert.

Understanding where we are likely to see superior reasoning in experts and where we might see similar reasoning or even inferior reasoning to novices can not only provide insight into the decision making of experts but also inform policy. Knowing when a gist-based approach might cause bias in experts and when it is essential for good decision making can provide insight into which decisions should be made by experts and which could be delegated to less experienced colleagues, or even advanced machines.

References

Adam, M. B., & Reyna, V. F. (2005). Coherence and correspondence criteria for rationality: Experts' estimation of risks of sexually transmitted infections. *Journal of Behavioral Decision Making, 18*(3), 169–186. doi: 10.1002/bdm.493.

Alba, J. W., & Hasher, L. (1983). Is memory schematic? *Psychological Bulletin, 93*(2), 203–231. doi: 10.1037/0033–2909.93.2.203.

Barbey, A. K., & Sloman, S. A. (2007). Base-rate respect: From ecological rationality to dual process. *Behavioral and Brain Sciences, 30*(3), 241–254. doi: 10.1017/S0140525X07001653

Brust-Renck, P. G., Reyna, V. F., Wilhelms, E. A., & Lazar, A. N. (2016). A Fuzzy-Trace Theory of judgment and decision-making in health care: Explanation, prediction, and application. In M. A. Diefenbach, S. Miller-Halegoua, & D. J. Bowen (Eds.), *Handbook of health decision science* (pp. 71–86). New York: Springer.

Chase, W. G., & Simon, H. A. (1973). Perception in chess. *Cognitive Psychology, 4*(1), 55–81. doi: 10.1016/0010–0285(73)90004–2

Christensen, C., Heckerling, P. S., Mackesy, M. E., Bernstein, L. M., & Elstein, A. S. (1991). Framing bias among expert and novice physicians. *Academic Medicine, 66*, S76–S78.

Clermont, K. M., & Eisenberg, T. (1992). Trial by judge or jury: Transcending empiricism. *Cornell Law Review*, 77, 1124–1177.

Croskerry, P. (in press). Medical decision making. In V. Thompson & L. Ball (Eds.), *The international handbook of thinking and reasoning*. New York, NY: Psychology Press.

De Groot, A. D. (1978). *Thought and choice in chess*. Berlin: Walter de Gruyter.

Eisenberg, T., Rachlinski, J. J., & Wells, M. T. (2002). Reconciling experimental incoherence with real-world coherence in punitive damages. *Stanford Law Review, 54*(6), 1239–1271.

Epstein, S. (1994). Integration of the cognitive and the psychodynamic unconscious. *American Psychologist, 49*(8), 709–724. doi: 10.1037/0003–0066X.49.8.709

Evans, J. St. B. T., & Stanovich, K. E. (2013). Dual-process theories of higher cognition: Advancing the debate. *Perspectives on Psychological Science, 8*(3), 223–241.

Forrow, L., Taylor, W. C., & Arnold, R. M. (1992). Absolutely relative: How research results are summarized can affect treatment decisions. *American Journal of Medicine, 92,* 121–124.

Garcia-Retamero, R., & Dhami, M. K. (2009). Take-the-best in expert-novice decision strategies for residential burglary. *Psychonomic Bulletin and Review, 16*, 163–169. doi: 10.3758/PBR.16.1.163

Gigerenzer, G., & Goldstein, D. G. (1996). Reasoning the fast and frugal way: Models of bounded rationality. *Psychological Review, 103*, 650–669. doi: 10.1037/0033- 295X.103.4.650

Gilovich, T., Griffin, D. W., & Kahneman, D. (2002). *The psychology of intuitive judgment: Heuristic and biases.* Cambridge: Cambridge University Press.

Guthrie, C., Rachlinski, J. J., & Wistrich, A. J. (2001). Inside the judicial mind. *Cornell Law Review, 86*, 777–830.

Guthrie, C., Rachlinski, J. J., & Wistrich, A. J. (2007). Blinking on the bench: How judges decide cases. *Cornell Law Review, 93*, 1–43.

Hux, J. E., Levinton, C. M., & Naylor, C. D. (1994). Prescribing propensity: influence of life-expectancy gains and drug costs. *Journal of General Internal Medicine, 9*, 195–201.

Kahneman, D. (2011). *Thinking, fast and slow*. New York, NY: Farrar, Straus and Giroux.

Kahneman, D., & Frederick, S. (2002). Representativeness revisited: Attribute substitution in intuitive judgment. In T. Gilovich, D. Griffin, & D. Kahneman (Eds.), *Heuristics and biases: The psychology of intuitive judgment* (pp. 49–81). New York: Cambridge University Press.

Kahneman, D., & Klein, G., (2009). Conditions for intuitive expertise: A failure to disagree. *American Psychologist, 64*(6), 515–526. doi: 10.1037/a0016755

Kintsch, W. (1974). *The representation of meaning in memory*. New York, NY: Halstead Press.

Klein, G. (1998). *Sources of power: How people make decisions*. Cambridge, MA: MIT Press.

Klein, G., Calderwood, R., & Clinton-Cirocco, A. (2010). Rapid decision making on the fire ground: The original study plus a postscript. *Journal of Cognitive Engineering and Decision Making, 4* (Special Issue on 20 years of NDM), 186–209.

Kühberger, A., & Tanner, C. (2010). Risky choice framing: Task versions and a comparison of prospect theory and fuzzy-trace theory. *Journal of Behavioral Decision Making, 23*(3), 314–329. doi: 10.1002/bdm.656

Leiter, B. (1999). Positivism, formalism, realism. *Columbia Law Review, 99*(4), 1138–1165.

Levin, I. P., Schneider, S. L., & Gaeth, G. J. (1998). All frames are not created equal: A typology and critical analysis of framing effects. *Organizational Behavior and Human Decision Processes, 76*, 149–188. doi: 10.1006/obhd.1998.2804

Lloyd, F. J., & Reyna, V. F. (2009). Clinical gist and medical education: Connecting the dots. *JAMA, 302*(12), 1332–1333. doi: 10.1001/jama.2009.1383

Machina, M. J. (1982). "Expected Utility" analysis without the independence axiom. *Econometrica, 50*, 277–323.

Mandel, D. R. (2001). Gain-loss framing and choice: Separating outcome formulations from descriptor formulations. *Organizational Behavior and Human Decision Processes, 85*, 56–76. doi: 10.1006/obhd.2000.2932

McGettigan, P., Sly, K., O'Connell, D., Hill, S., & Henry, D. (1999). The effects of information framing on the practices of physicians. *Journal of General Internal Medicine, 14*, 633–642.

McNeil, B. J., Pauker, S. G., Sox, H. C., & Tversky, A. (1982). On the elicitation of preferences for alternative therapies. *New England Journal of Medicine, 306*, 1259–1262. doi: 10.1056/NEJM198205273062103

Miller, P. M., Fagley, N. S., & Casella, N. E. (2009). Effects of problem frame and gender on principals' decision making. *Social Psychology of Education, 12*, 397–413.

Neuborne, B. (1992). Of sausage factories and syllogism machines: Formalism, realism and exclusionary selection techniques. *New York University Law Review, 67*, 419–449.

Pachur, T., & Marinello, G. (2013). Expert intuitions: How to model the decision strategies of airport customs officers? *Acta Psychologia, 144*, 97–103.

Peters, E., Västfjäll, D., Slovic, P., Mertz, C. K., Mazzocco, K., & Dickert, S. (2006). Numeracy and decision making. *Psychological Science, 17*(5), 408–414.

Posner, R. A. (1986). Legal formalism, legal realism, and the interpretation of statutes and the constitution. *Case Western Reserve Law Review, 37*, 179–217.

Rachlinski, J. J., Guthrie, C., & Wistrich, A. J. (2011). Probable cause, probability and hindsight. *Journal of Empirical Legal Studies, 8*(1), 72–98. doi: 10.1111/j.1740–1461.2011.01230.x.

Reyna, V. F. (1991). Class inclusion, the conjunction fallacy, and other cognitive illusions. *Developmental Review, 11*, 317–336. doi: 10.1016/0273–2297(91)90017-I.

Reyna, V. F. (1992). Reasoning, remembering, and their relationship: Social, cognitive, and developmental issues. In M. L. Howe, C. J. Brainerd, & V. F. Reyna (Eds.), *Development of long-term retention* (pp. 103–132). New York: Springer.

Reyna, V. F. (1995). Interference effects in memory and reasoning: A fuzzy-trace theory analysis. In F. N. Dempster & C. J. Brainerd (Eds.), *Interference and inhibition in cognition* (pp. 29–59). San Diego, CA: Academic Press.

Reyna, V. F. (2005). Fuzzy-trace theory, judgment, and decision making: A dual-processes approach. In C. Izawa & N. Ohta (Eds.), *Human learning and memory: Advances in theory and application: The 4th Tsukuba International Conference on Memory* (pp. 239–256). Mahwah, NJ: Lawrence Erlbaum Associates.

Reyna, V. F. (2008). A theory of medical decision making and health: Fuzzy trace theory. *Medical Decision Making, 28*(6), 850–865. doi:10.1177/0272989X08327066.

Reyna, V. F. (2012). A new intuitionism: meaning, memory, and development in fuzzy trace theory. *Judgment and Decision Making*, 7(3), 332–359.

Reyna, V. F. (2013). Intuition, reasoning and development. A fuzzy trace theory approach. In P. Barrouillet & C. Gauffroy (Eds.), *The development of thinking and reasoning* (pp. 193–220). New York, NY: Psychology Press.

Reyna, V. F., & Brainerd, C. J. (1991). Fuzzy-trace theory and framing effects in choice: Gist extraction, truncation, and conversion. *Journal of Behavioral Decision Making, 4*, 249–262. doi: 10.1002/bdm.3960040403.

Reyna, V. F., & Brainerd, C. J. (1994). The origins of probability judgment: A review of data and theories. In G. Wright & P. Ayton (Eds.), *Subjective probability* (pp. 239–272). Oxford, UK: John Wiley & Sons.

Reyna, V. F., & Brainerd, C. J. (1995). Fuzzy-trace theory: An interim synthesis. *Learning and Individual Differences*, 7, 1–75. doi: 10.1016/1041–6080(95)90031–4.

Reyna, V. F., & Brainerd, C. J. (2008). Numeracy, ratio bias, and denominator neglect in judgments of risk and probability. *Learning and Individual Differences, 18*(1), 89–107.

Reyna, V. F., Chick, C. F., Corbin, J. C., & Hsia, A. N. (2014). Developmental reversals in risky decision making: Intelligence agents show larger decision biases than college students. *Psychological Science, 25*(1), 76–84. doi:10.1177/0956797613497022.

Reyna, V. F., Corbin, J. C., Weldon, R. B., & Brainerd, C. J. (2016). How fuzzy-trace theory predicts true and false memories for words and sentences. *Journal of Applied Research in Memory and Cognition, 5*(1), 1–9. doi: 10.1016/j.jarmac.2015.12.003.

Reyna, V. F., & Ellis, S. C. (1994). Fuzzy-trace theory and framing effects in children's risky decision making. *Psychological Science, 5*, 275–279. doi: 10.1111/j.1467–9280.1994. tb00625.x.

Reyna, V. F., & Farley, F. (2006). Risk and rationality in adolescent decision making: Implications for theory, practice, and public policy. *Psychological Science in the Public Interest*, 7(1), 1–44. doi:10.1111/j.1529–1006.2006.00026.x

Reyna, V. F., & Hamilton, A. J. (2001). The importance of memory in informed consent for surgical rusk. *Medical Decision Making, 21*(2), 152–155. doi: 10.1177/0272989X0102100209.

Reyna, V. F., Holliday, R., & Marche, T. (2002). Explaining the development of false memories. *Developmental Review, 22*(3), 436–489. doi: 10.1016/S0273–2297(02)00003–00005.

Reyna, V. F., & Kiernan, B. (1994). Development of gist versus verbatim memory in sentence recognition: Effects of lexical familiarity, semantic content, encoding instructions, and retention interval. *Developmental Psychology, 30,* 178–191.

Reyna, V. F., & Kiernan, B. (1995). Children's memory and metaphorical interpretation. *Metaphor and Symbol, 10,* 309–331.

Reyna, V. F., & Lloyd, F. J. (1997). Theories of false memory in children and adults. *Learning and Individual Differences*, *9*(2), 95–123. doi: 10.1016/S1041–6080(97)90002–90009.

Reyna, V. F., & Lloyd, F. J. (2006). Physician decision making and cardiac risk: effects of knowledge, risk perception, risk tolerance, and fuzzy processing. *Journal of Experimental Psychology: Applied, 12*(3), 179–195. doi: 10.1037/1076–1898X.12.3.179.

Reyna, V. F., Lloyd, F. J., & Brainerd, C. J. (2003). Memory, development, and rationality: An integrative theory of judgment and decision making. In S. Schneider & J. Shanteau (Eds.), *Emerging perspectives on judgment and decision research* (pp. 201–245). New York, NY: Cambridge University Press.

Reyna, V. F., Wilhelms, E. A., McCormick, M. J., Weldon, R. B. (2015). Development of decision making and risk-taking: A fuzzy-trace theory neurobiological perspective. *Child Development Perspectives, 9*(2), 122–127. doi: 10.1111/cdep.12117.

Rivers, S. E., Reyna, V. F., & Mills, B. (2008). Risk taking under the influence: A fuzzy-trace theory of emotion in adolescence. *Developmental Review, 28*(1), 107–144. doi:10.1016/j.dr.2007.11.002.

Savage, L. J. (1954). *The foundations of statistics*. New York: Wiley.

Schraagen, J. M. (in press). Naturalistic decision making. In V. Thompson & L. Ball (Eds.), *The international handbook of thinking and reasoning*. New York, NY: Psychology Press.

Shanteau, J., & Stewart, T. R. (1992). Why study expert decision making? Some historical perspectives and comments. *Organizational Behavior and Human Decision Processes, 53*(2), 95–106.

Simon, H. A. (1981). *The sciences of the artificial*. Cambridge, MA: MIT Press.

Stanovich, K. E., & West, R. F. (2008). On the relative independence of thinking biases and cognitive ability. *Journal of Personality and Social Psychology, 94*, 672–695. doi:10.1037/0022–3514.94.4.672.

Stocke, V. (1998). Framing oder Informationsknappheit? Zur Erkla ṙung der Formulierungseffekte beim Asian-Disease-Problem. In U. Druwe & V. Kunz (Hrsg.), *Anomalien in der Handlungs- und Entscheidungstheorie* (pp. 197–218). Opladen: Leske R Budrich.

Thompson, V. A. (2014). What intuitions are . . . and are not. *The Psychology of Learning and Motivation, 60*, 35–75.

Toplak, M. (in press). The development of rational thinking: Insights from the heuristics and biases literature and dual-process models. In V. Thompson & L. Ball (Eds.), *The international handbook of thinking and reasoning*. New York, NY: Psychology Press.

Tversky, A., & Kahneman, D. (1974). Judgment under uncertainty: Heuristics and biases. *Science, 185*(4157), 1124–1131.

Tversky, A., & Kahneman, D. (1981). The framing of decisions and the psychology of choice. *Science, 211*, 453–458. doi: 10.1126/science.7455683.

Von Neumann, J., & Morgenstern, O. (1944). *Theory of games and economic behavior*. Princeton, NJ: Princeton University Press.

Weldon, R. B., Corbin, J. C., & Reyna, V. F. (2013). Gist processing in judgment and decision making: Developmental reversals predicted by fuzzy-trace theory. In H. Markovits (Ed.), *Understanding the development of reasoning and decision making*. New York: Psychology Press.

Wilhelms, E. A., Corbin, J. C., & Reyna, V. F. (2015). Gist memory in reasoning and decision making. In A. Feeney & V. Thompson (Eds.), *Reasoning as memory*. New York, NY: Psychology Press.

17

CONVERSATIONAL INFERENCE AND HUMAN REASONING

Denis J. Hilton, Bart Geurts, and Peter Sedlmeier

Much of the information that we reason about reaches us through a social medium, whether it be a psychology experiment or an informal conversation, a newspaper article, a handbook chapter, or a do-it-yourself diagram about how to assemble furniture. We accordingly have to use our knowledge about the medium of a message in order to interpret what it contains. For example, if a recommendation letter for a candidate for a philosophy job reads: "Dear Sir, Mr. X's command of English is excellent, and his attendance at tutorials has been regular, Yours, etc." the recipient of the letter will have to engage in reasoning to understand the speaker's intended meaning. This is because the literal content of the letter ("what is said") is manifestly insufficient to understand what he is trying to say. As Grice (1975) suggests, the writer is presumably being co-operative (otherwise, why did he take the trouble to write?) but is flouting certain norms about what a letter of recommendation should contain. A plausible interpretation is that while this particular writer did not want to offend the candidate by refusing to write a letter about him, he did not want to communicate the impression to his colleagues that the candidate is any good at philosophy.

Grice suggests that speakers and hearers typically share a set of expectations about communication, which the speaker uses to construct a message in the expectation that the hearer will also use it to interpret it. The fundamental assumption that governs this conversational contract is that ordinary conversation follows the *co-operative principle:* namely, that each participant will make their conversational contribution such as is required, at the stage which it occurs, by the accepted purpose of the talk exchange in which they are engaged. From this, four sets of specific maxims can be identified that should normally be followed in co-operative conversation. These are:

1 the maxim of *quality* (do not say what you believe to be false, or for which you lack adequate evidence)
2 the maxim of *quantity* (make your contribution as informative as is required, and do not give more or less information than required)
3 the maxim of *relation* (make your contribution relevant)
4 the maxims of *manner* (avoid ambiguity and obscurity of expression, be brief and orderly)

Even when the maxims are not being flouted (as in the letter of recommendation example), reasoning is routinely necessary to establish the speaker's ***intended meaning***. For example, we may infer that if someone tells us that she tried to get into Oxford, then she intends us to understand that she did not succeed. This conclusion would be justified by the shared assumption that a co-operative speaker would make the strongest statement possible (satisfying the maxims of quantity) that is true (satisfying the maxims of quality) about the topic under discussion (satisfying the maxim of relation). So the speaker would expect us (the hearers) to "calculate" a ***conversational implicature*** to this effect, on the premise that if she had tried to get into Oxford and succeeded, then she would have said so. However, such conversational implicatures are *defeasible*, as the speaker can easily cancel them by saying: "I tried to get into Oxford and in fact succeeded". Some conversational implicatures are general across contexts of use (such as the inference from *some* to ***not all***) while others are particular, being specific to a given context (as in the recommendation letter example).

Conversational inference is inductive as hearers have to make hypotheses about the speakers' intended meanings (Levinson, 1983), and as such has something in common with decision-theoretic or Bayesian approaches to understanding everyday inference (e.g. Evans & Over, 2004; Oaksford & Chater, 2007).[1] However, conversational inference includes various subtypes of inference for specialized aspects of language understanding (see Figure 17.1).

We shall take verbal exchanges as the prototype case of "non-natural" (nn) meaning that relies on communication rules and conventions, such as when we flout the maxims of conversation to damn someone with faint praise as in the example above. Such non-natural meaning involves the communication of a speaker's intention, and is to be distinguished from "natural meaning" which does not involve the recovery of a speaker's intended meaning, as when we take the presence of spots to "mean" measles (Grice, 1957).

Below, we will show how various forms of conversational inference (conversational implicatures, entailment, polarity, etc.) are relevant to a full understanding of human judgment and reasoning. The chapter is structured in terms of the above analysis of conversational inference processes: inferring the speaker's intended meaning; using world knowledge to interpret

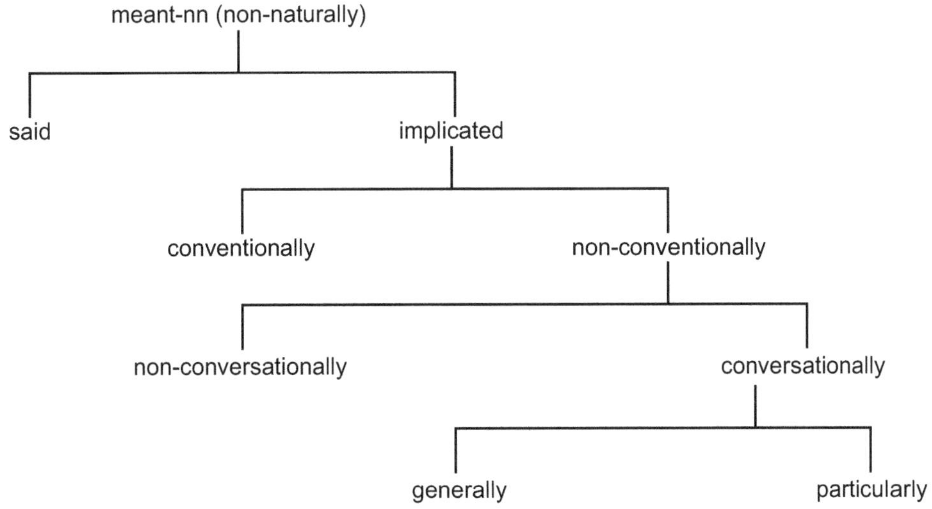

Figure 17.1 The hierarchical structure of conversational inference (from Levinson, 1983)

utterances; and using word knowledge to infer semantic entailments and conversational implicatures (sometimes in combination with inferences from linguistic polarity and world knowledge). We will show that people's understanding of everyday conversation involves a considerable amount of both inductive and deductive reasoning in order to arrive at an interpretation (*reasoning to an interpretation*) and that awareness of this will clarify the rationality of inferences drawn from that interpretation (*reasoning from an interpretation*). We will also discuss how understanding of conversational pragmatics can inform the design of communications with the aim of facilitating good reasoning and decision-making. Finally, while we will be following a classical Gricean approach below, it is worth noting at the outset that other approaches could be taken (e.g., Levinson, 2000; Wilson & Sperber, 2004).

Inferring intended meaning

Word interpretation: from sense to reference

A recurring question in experimental psychology is whether participants interpret the task they have been given in the way that the experimenter expects them to. An early illustration of this issue came about with Solomon Asch's re-interpretation of "prestige suggestion" effects. An experiment by Lorge and Curtiss (1936) appeared to support the claim that the tendency to form positive attitudes to opinions expressed by high-status sources was evidence for a habit in judgment that "experts are right", formed due to learning that "high-status sources tend to be correct" (a culturally shared generalization). Asch (1940) replicated this effect by showing that a sample of college students who have been told that a "congenial" group (500 college students) ranks politics positively amongst a list of 10 professions will do the same. In contrast, when told that the comparison group has ranked politics negatively, college students will likewise rank politics negatively. However, Asch suggested that such results could be attributed to "a change in the object of judgment rather than in the judgment of the object" (Asch, 1940, p. 458) and showed that the two groups of participants had quite different kinds of politicians in mind when making their judgments. Free response data revealed that the first group thought of statesmanlike examples such as Roosevelt, Hull, and Stimson, whereas the second group thought of lower-status examples such as Tammany Hall (the executive committee of the Democratic Party in New York City until the mid-20th century), caucus leaders, and local neighbourhood politicians. Asch's analysis thus invalidated explanations of this effect in terms of the behaviourist concepts of imitation and reward.

Asch's "change of meaning" hypothesis is quite compatible with conversational pragmatics, which was born of the observation that words refer to different things according to their context of use. So people may have a general *sense* of what a politician is, perhaps in the form of a mental definition of the word "politician" (e.g., as an individual who engages in political activity) or of a prototypic image of politicians (educated, extravert, interested in power, etc.). However, what they interpret as the specific *referent* of an expression will depend on context. This kind of "reasoning to an interpretation" appears to be quite rational in the light of principles of cognitive consistency (Heider, 1946).

The assumption of intentionality

A normal assumption to make in everyday human communication is that the information given is relevant to the task in hand. Otherwise, why would the speaker have mentioned it? As an example, Tetlock, Lerner, and Boettger (1996) showed that non-diagnostic information was less likely to be used in an inferential task if participants had been told that the usual assumptions of conversational relevance had been de-activated. Specifically, participants were less likely to use information about the colour of a participant's eyes to infer their likely grade-point average if they had been told that the information had been selected at random by a computer from a pool of information about the target. In contrast, participants were more likely to use this non-diagnostic information when they were told that the usual conversational norms of relevance were in force or when nothing was said about the communication context. This suggests that, unless told otherwise, participants' default assumption is that the information given comes with the guarantee of relevance.

As Tetlock et al. (1996) noted, such conversational inference processes provide an explanation for the "dilution effect", whereby the impact of diagnostic information in the judgment process is weakened by the presence of non-diagnostic information. Nisbett, Zukier, and Lemley (1981), who discovered the dilution effect, proposed a cognitive explanation for this in terms of the representativeness heuristic (Kahneman & Tversky, 1972). These researchers argued that the inclusion of non-diagnostic information (e.g., the target person has blue eyes) along with diagnostic information (e.g., the high number of hours that the target person devotes to his studies each week) "diluted" the similarity of the target person to the class of students with a high grade-point average. This reduced similarity thus makes the target person less "representative" of that class, and hence less likely to have a high grade-point average. This dilution effect would not have occurred if a normative model of inference were used to make this judgment, such as a statistical regression model.

Tetlock et al.'s use of conversational pragmatics to "absolve" participants from the claim that their reasoning and judgment is irrational follows the general schema given in Figure 17.2 (from Hilton, 1995), whereby a participant (or hearer) has to make inferences about an experimenter's (or speaker's) intended meaning (reasoning *to* an interpretation). Only when this interpretational phase has been properly assessed or controlled for, can the researcher properly evaluate whether the participant's response is rational or not (reasoning *from* an interpretation) when compared to some normative model of inference. For example, Mandel (2014) shows that when pragmatic interpretation of the quantifiers used in the Asian Disease Problem are taken into account, participants' responses can be described by expected utility analysis rather than the weighting function of prospect theory (Kahneman & Tversky, 1979). Thus Mandel presents data suggesting that participants in fact interpret experimental statements such as "If Plan A is adopted, it is certain that 200 people will be saved" as indicating a lower-bound estimate; that is, they read it as "If Plan A is adopted, it is certain that *at least* 200 people will be saved". This lower-bound reading in fact gives the option a greater expected value than if only 200 people will be saved, thus invalidating Kahneman and Tversky's claim that preferences for this option cannot be explained in terms of expected utility theory. Consistent with the assumption that participants were reasoning rationally from (conversationally) inferred premises, Mandel (2014) found that when the number of people saved was explicitly described as "at least 200" the majority tended to prefer this option, whereas when described as "exactly 200" they did not. Interested readers are referred to Geurts (2013) for an alternative analysis of the Asian Disease Problem in terms of conversational pragmatics (see also Helm, McCormick, & Reyna, this volume), and to reviews (e.g., Hilton, 2009; Hilton & Slugoski, 2000, 2001; Noveck & Reboul, 2008; Wänke, 2007) for examples of application of conversational pragmatics to other well-known reasoning and decision problems.

The claim that researchers need to evaluate participants' interpretations of the information given to them now seems to be generally accepted, and debate has moved on to what extent "irrational" judgments in key experiments are due to rational conversational inference from the

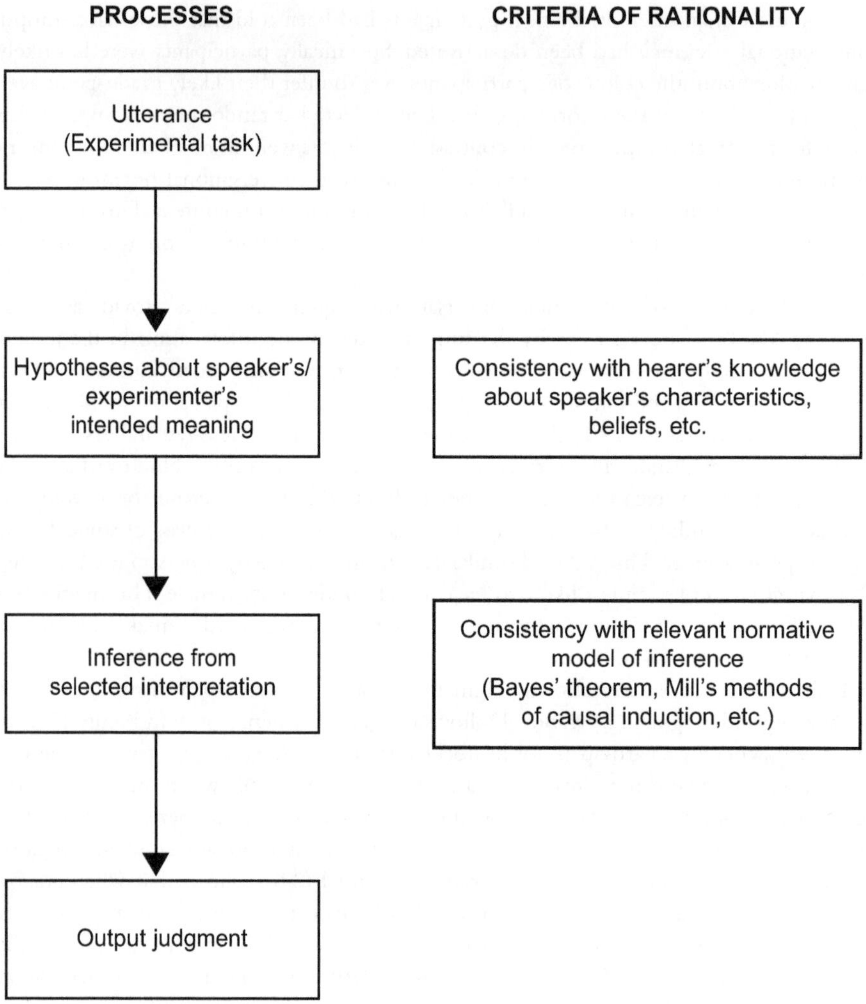

Figure 17.2 Two-stage resolution of uncertainty: utterance interpretation and judgment

information presented, or "true" judgmental errors due to cognitive processes such as the representativeness heuristic (e.g., Kahneman & Frederick, 2002). A related perspective suggests that conversational inference may actually be the source of many inferential "errors" (e.g., Levinson, 1995).[2]

The nature of the speaker's intention: to inform or to influence?

We now move on to discuss the different kinds of intention that a speaker may have. What do speakers aim to do when making an utterance? Perhaps the prototypical use of language is constative: a statement like "It is raining" is true or false, and a speaker who makes this statement thereby commits himself to the *truth* of the proposition that it is raining. However, other speech acts are not constative in this sense. Rather, they are better construed in terms of commitments to *goals*. If a speaker makes a promise, like "I'll mow the lawn", for example, he commits himself to the goal of mowing the lawn, and if he makes a request ("Would you mow the lawn, please?"), he invites his addressee to commit herself to that goal. Therefore, constative speech acts are actually a somewhat special case, since non-constative speech acts (promises, requests, questions, etc.) generally involve commitments to goals rather than to truths.[3]

Constative statements include indicative (e.g., "If a card has a consonant on one side, it has a vowel on the other") and counterfactual conditionals (e.g., "If France had not attacked the Islamic State in Syria, there would have been no terrorist attacks in Paris"). Research suggests that when asked to evaluate how likely indicative conditionals of the form *If p then q* are to be true, they are very strongly influenced by the perceived probability of the consequent *q* in the presence of the antecedent *p* (Evans, Handley & Over, 2003). The same suppositional analysis can easily be applied to counterfactuals, which typically involve imagining that an event that actually happened did not in fact do so. The more that a counterfactual conditional is coherent with background causal beliefs (e.g., "If Hitler had been assassinated in 1944, the Second World War would have ended earlier") the more likely that is likely to be considered true (as opposed to "If Hitler's favourite dog had died in 1944, the Second World War would have ended earlier").

Whereas constative (indicative or counterfactual) conditionals represent the world in a certain way, non-constative conditionals seek to change it. We make promises, administer warnings, offer advice, and so on with the aim of committing ourselves or others to certain goals. As such, what matters is, not so much whether a non-constative speech act is true, as whether it is in fact successful in establishing goal commitments. For example, to be effective, a conditional promise such as "If you help me study (*p*), I will buy your textbooks next term (*q*)" or a threat such as "If you come home after 11 (*p*), I will take $5 off your allowance (*q*)" has to raise the probability of the addressee doing *q*. If they did not do so, there would be little point in making the promise or threat. In line with this, Ohm and Thompson (2006) demonstrated that the perceived behavioural effectiveness of a conditional did not predict its perceived truth-value. They found that ratings of the truth of the conditional promises and threats were strongly predicted by the perceived probability of the consequent *q* in the presence of the antecedent *p*, thus replicating the results of Evans, Handley, and Over (2003). However, these truth ratings were not affected by the expected effectiveness of these conditionals (calculated as the increase in probability of the addressee doing *p* as a result of the promise/threat *q*).

Constative and non-constative attitudes to deontics: rule content versus rule use

At first sight, the constative/non-constative distinction might look to be the same as that drawn by Manktelow and Over (1991) between indicative conditionals that describe states of the world (e.g., "If water is heated to 100 degrees, then it will boil") and deontic conditionals that refer to permissions and obligations (e.g., "If you tidy your room, then you can go out and play"). However, Manktelow and Over (1991) focused on the *contents* of indicative versus deontic rules, and indeed showed that rules with deontic contents led to much more "logical" performance on the Wason selection task (for related demonstrations, see Gigerenzer & Hug, 1992; Klar & Liberman, 1996; Politzer & Nguyen-Xuan, 1992). In contrast, the pragmatics perspective draws our attention towards the *uses* of rules. For example, the deontic rule given above involves the *granting* of a permission rather than the *description* of a permission.

Deontic rule contents based on human conventions can figure naturally in both constative and non-constative uses (Hilton, Kemmelmeier, & Bonnefon, 2005), but in interestingly different ways. For example, in a non-constative use, an airport security director at a French airport could issue the directive "If a baggage is suspect, then it will be searched", thus creating a rule to be followed by those under his authority. Here the rule is uttered with the intention of influencing the addressee's behaviour. However, in a constative use the French national passenger safety agency could state a rule like "If a baggage is suspect, then it will be searched" as a hypothesis to be tested. This could be done in one of two ways. In the first, the safety agency could check the rulebooks in various French airports to see if this rule is included in the standard security procedures. In the second, the safety agency could send passengers with suspect equipment in their baggage through security controls in various French airports to see if the suspect baggage is indeed checked. Here an institutional rule, "If a baggage is suspect, then it will be searched", is first created by the non-constative utterance, and the convention thus created then serves as a causal mechanism that influences operatives' behaviour whose existence and effectiveness can be tested.

In contrast, rules that describe physical causal mechanisms do not lend themselves to being used as non-constatives: these mechanisms exist independently in the physical world and neither need human injunction to be created nor can they be influenced by them. We would conclude that someone who stipulated to a kettle, "If you reach 100 degrees, then you will boil!" would be odd indeed. A litmus test for deciding whether a rule describes a physical or social mechanism comes from whether it can be sensibly used in the second person – that is, as a form of address to another social being. Previous research has often tried to skate over this distinction by using ambiguous formulations of deontic conditionals which are unclear as to whether they are constative or non-constative. This is sometimes done by stating the rule in the third person – for example, "If workers are repairing a road, then a traffic policeman must be directing the traffic" (e.g., Sperber, Cara & Girotto, 1995). This statement is ambiguous between an indicative *must* (implying a causal relation between road repairs and the presence of a policeman) and a deontic *must* (implying that road repairs require a policemen to be put in place). However, the non-constative intention can be made clear by expressing statements in the second person – for example, "If you know that workers are repairing the road, then assign a traffic policeman".

Indirect speech acts and the calculation of conversational implicatures

Of course, indicative causal conditionals can be used *indirectly* for non-constative uses in the second person, by drawing the addressee's attention to the likely consequences of actions, for example: "if you pull the cat's tail (*p*), it will probably bite you (*q*)". Here this might be interpreted as a useful piece of advice: "I wouldn't pull the cat's tail if I were you". But the deontic value of the statement is not located in the utterance itself (a simple indicative causal conditional) but in the conversational implicatures drawn from the assumption of co-operation. Experiments that study indicative conditionals that are used to convey indirect tips and warnings (e.g., Elqayam et al., 2015; Hilton, 2011; Ohm & Thompson, 2006) all use contextual settings that indicate that the speaker is trying to influence the addressee in some way. The deontic introduction (going from explicit *is* to implicit *ought*) is made through calculating a conversational implicature, as the hearer may assume that the conditional has been uttered to draw her attention to relevant causal mechanisms that could cause a nasty surprise. Since the information would only become relevant if the speaker were indeed to pull the cat's tail, it is plausible to assume that the speaker is commenting on the desirability of doing so, and so trying to influence the addressee's behaviour. Note that the role of the addressee is important here, as the third person simply conveys the constative function of prediction: "if he pulls the cat's tail, it will probably bite him". Additional conversational context may, however, licence a deontic interpretation if it is "heard" as being directed at the addressee. For example, if said to a babysitter for the child in question, the statement might also carry a conversational implicature "You should take care not to let him pull the cat's tail".

Using world knowledge in causal reasoning

Unless told otherwise, we may assume that things mentioned in a discourse take their normal default values, and "miracles" do not happen (Levinson, 2000). For example, if we are told, "If Sam went to the railway station at night, then he must have got a ticket from the vending machine", we may assume that he paid for the ticket, not that the vending machine was giving them away for free. Assumptions that the causal structure of the world is functioning normally support the drawing of such routine conversational implicatures. Below, we discuss the role of such background assumptions in causal explanation and conditional predictions.

Background assumptions in causal explanation

Conversations about causes typically take place in an assumed "causal field" (Mackie, 1980), composed of backgrounded conditions that are necessary for the target event to occur, but which are not focused on by a causal explanation. We have a tendency to single out as "the" cause the abnormal condition that makes the difference to the event occurring in this case but not in normal cases (Hart & Honoré, 1985; Hilton & Slugoski, 1986). For example, when asked to provide a causal explanation for an action such as "Mary, who was rich, bought a new car", participants were more likely (59%) to refer to a goal (e.g., she wanted a new car) than to refer to (41%) the satisfaction of a precondition (e.g., she acquired a large inheritance). McClure and Hilton interpreted this as consistent with the view that the existence of the goal would make the difference between the case where the target event occurs (Mary buys a new car) and the normal case where the target event does not (Mary does not buy a new car). However, when told that "Mary, who was poor, bought a new car", participants preferred to refer to the existence of a precondition when asked to provide a causal explanation for the same action. Here, participants were more likely (71%) to refer to a precondition (e.g., she acquired a large inheritance) which removed the obstruction to attainment of the goal than to the goal itself (29%). This pattern is consistent with the view that what was abnormal in these circumstances was Mary's being able to buy a car, and that the implicit focus of the causal question changes when the action is obstructed. McClure and Hilton (1997) thus showed that explanations that focused on preconditions were judged as more informative and relevant when given for obstructed actions than for normal ones, and that these conversational properties predicted the perceived goodness of the explanation better than the perceived probability that the antecedent was true (cf. Hilton & Erb, 1996).

Effects of background assumptions on the interpretation of causal conditionals

Causal conditionals that make predictions (reasoning from cause to consequence) also appear to be interpreted in the context of a presupposed causal field. Hilton, Jaspars, and Clarke (1990) asked their participants to imagine that causal conditionals of the kind "If he works hard, then he will succeed" were uttered in conversation. They also added relevant contextual information in parentheses to adjust participants' assumptions about the backgrounded "causal field" such as "The exam is difficult" or "The exam is easy". For example, the antecedent statement *he works hard* was more likely to be considered to be a necessary condition for success in contexts where the reasoner had been informed in parentheses that the exam is difficult. Likewise, participants were less likely to assume that working hard was necessary for success if they had been parenthetically told that the exam is easy. These results were consistent with earlier work by Staudenmayer (1975) which showed that the availability of alternative plausible causes influences the perceived necessity of a causal conditional (see also Cummins et al., 1991).

Revision of the causal field can also influence the perceived sufficiency of the causal relation expressed in conditional statements. For example, consider the "suppression effect" identified by Byrne (1989) where a first conditional statement, "If Mary has an essay to write (*p*), then she will be working in the library tonight (*q*)", usually leads reasoners to infer that Mary will be working in the library tonight when told that she has an essay to write. However, this inference (known as *modus ponens*, i.e., *If p then q* and *p* then infer *q*) can be suppressed by presenting a second conditional statement, such as "If the library is open, then she will be working in the library tonight", as many people no longer infer *q* in this case. A pragmatic analysis suggests that this suppression effect can be interpreted in terms of a subsequent conditional statement calling into question the causal field assumed by an earlier one (Bonnefon & Hilton, 2002). As a result, participants no longer assume that *modus ponens* is a valid rule of inference: given *If p then q* and *p, q* will no longer follow if the normal effect of *p* on *q* has been disabled by precondition failure. For example, imagine a discussion between two students about where Mary can be found this evening. Anne ventures, "If she has an essay to write, then she will be working in the library tonight". In response, Beatrice counters, "If the library is open, then she will be working in the library tonight". What could Beatrice mean by her statement? Assuming that Beatrice is trying to make a relevant comment, one explanation of her remark is that she is drawing Anne's attention to the possibility of a precondition failure – that even if Mary does have an essay to write tonight, she will be in the library only if it is open. Indirectly, Beatrice is questioning the *sufficiency* of Anne's conditional statement, thus inviting the suppression of the assumption that the antecedent ("She has an essay to write") is in fact sufficient in the circumstances for the consequent ("She will be in the library") to occur. Significantly, all of Byrne's (1989) experimental examples fit the schema developed above, as all the initial conditionals assert a relationship between a goal-state and an action, and all the subsequent conditionals express a relationship between a precondition and the same action. This is consistent with the view that they serve to draw participants' attention to sources of potential precondition failure.

The reasoner's stance towards the information given: inferring speaker's meaning versus inferring from personal beliefs

Thompson, Evans, and Handley (2005) have provided an illustration of the difference between inferring what is being said in a conditional argument (inferring speaker's meaning), and being persuaded to act in accordance with the argument (personal beliefs). They showed that the listener's stance will influence conclusions drawn from conditional predictions, such as "If the Kyoto accord is ratified, greenhouse gas emissions will be reduced" and "If the Kyoto accord is ratified, there will be a downturn in the economy." The first argument was designed to make the antecedent *p* desirable and the second to make it undesirable. When asked to evaluate *the writer's position*, participants were strongly influenced by the valence of the argument, clearly stating that the writer intended that *p* be taken when it was desirable and that it not be taken when it was undesirable. However, when asked to evaluate their own position, participants were much less influenced by the valence of the argument. In addition, when asked to make inferences in a conditional arguments task, participants taking the writer's perspective were more likely to accept the deductively valid inferences of *modus ponens* and *modus tollens* than when they were asked to evaluate arguments from their own perspective. Thompson et al.'s results suggest that people display an ability to reason in accordance with the canons of deductive logic when the task is to infer the speaker's intended meaning, and their results are consistent with other studies which have indicated that when presented with appropriate instructions, people reason in accordance with the canons of deductive logic rather than those of Bayesian inference (e.g., Markovits, Brisson, & de Chantal, 2015).

Using word knowledge in reasoning

Quantifiers support three different kinds of linguistic inference (Hilton, Schmeltzer, & Geurts, 2011). Importantly, these three kinds of meanings all emerge from the ***relations*** that hold between quantifiers, not from what they actually ***denote*** in the world. First, there are the relations of semantic entailment (e.g., ***many*** entails *some*). Second, the meanings conveyed by conversational implicature (e.g., ***many*** may often be "heard" as implying ***not all***, so if we hear that "Denis has seen some of Hitchcock's films" we may assume that he has not seen all of them). Finally, a third aspect is the connotative meaning that emerges from the polarity of the selected expression (e.g., from saying ***many*** rather than ***not all***).

Semantic entailment and deductive reasoning

Understanding everyday language also relies on deductive reasoning: for example, if someone tells us she ate many of the oysters we can deduce that she ate some of them. This routine deduction has the consequence that the statement "I ate many of the oysters but not some of them" would sound anomalous and self-contradictory. This is because words such as <*some*, ***many***, *most*, *all*> form an entailment scale such that the use of ***many*** entails the weaker statement that the speaker ate *some* of the oysters but *conversationally implicates* that she did not eat all of them (Horn, 1989; Geurts, 2010).

In the field of natural language semantics, quantifying statements are standardly analysed as expressing relations between sets (Barwise & Cooper 1981). Suppose that B is the set of brewers and C is the set of communists.[4] Then, on the standard analysis, "All brewers are communists" means that $B \subseteq C$; "No brewers are communists" means that $\text{card}(B \cap C) = 0$; "Some brewers are communists" means that $\text{card}(B \cap C) \neq 0$; "Most brewers are communists" means that $\text{card}(B \cap C)$ exceeds a certain threshold; and so on. This way of interpreting quantification is attractive for several reasons. First, it captures logical relationships between quantifiers. For example, provided B is non-empty, it follows that "All brewers are communists" entails "Most brewers are communists", which in its turn entails that "Some brewers are communists". Put otherwise, *all*, *most*, and *some* form an entailment scale, where *all* is the strongest element and *some* the weakest. Secondly, the analysis licenses inference patterns like the following:

All brewers are communists	Some brewers are communists	No brewers are communists
All communists are people	All communists are people	All old communists are communists
All brewers are people	Some brewers are people	No brewers are old communists

Intuitively, while "all brewers" and "some brewers" are positive, "no brewers" seems to be negative. The inference patterns illustrated here, which follow from the hypothesized meanings of these expressions, allow us to capture what this means: whereas "all brewers" and "some brewers" are ***upward entailing***, "no brewers" is downward entailing. An upward-entailing quantifier licenses inferences to *supersets*: if Y ⊆ Z, then "All X are Y" entails "All X are Z" and "Some X are Y" entails "Some X are Z". By contrast, a downward-entailing quantifier licenses inferences to *subsets*: if Z ⊆ Y, then "No X are Y" entails "No X are Z". Upward entailing is "positive", downward entailing is "negative". Thus, in the case of quantifiers and related expressions, the intuitive notion of linguistic polarity can be captured in terms of entailment properties. To illustrate, consider the following quantificational expressions:

all brewers	no brewers
many brewers	few brewers
more than *n* brewers	fewer than *n* brewers

Intuitively, while the expressions on the left-hand side seem to be positive, the ones on the right-hand side seem to have a negative feel about them; this is the intuitive notion of linguistic polarity. Entailment properties allow us to capture this intuitive notion in a precise way: while positive expressions are upward entailing, negative expressions are downward entailing. (Note that this is not intended as a general analysis of linguistic polarity, for it probably doesn't generalize to positive/negative pairs like *good/bad, happy/sad*, and so on. In such cases, positivity and negativity are different things altogether.)

While entailment properties play a key part in the analysis of a range of semantic phenomena, it has also been shown that they can account for a large part of syllogistic logic in the sense that upward and/or downward entailment is involved in all valid syllogisms and the easiest syllogisms are validated by these forms of reasoning alone (Sánchez Valencia, 1991). Geurts (2003) extends these observations by arguing that upward and downward entailment are crucial to everyday human reasoning, showing how a simple processing model based on entailment properties can account for the varying degrees of difficulty of syllogistic inferences, as established by numerous experimental studies (e.g., Chater & Oaksford, 1999; Johnson-Laird, 1983).

Linguistic polarity and Aristotle's squares of opposition

Linguistic polarity is pervasive in the human logical vocabulary, being present not only in quantifiers but also in probability expressions, conditionals, and conjunctions/disjunctions (Hilton, 2011). As we have seen above, these logical connectives do more than just describe states of the world: as well as conveying relations of conversational implicature and semantic entailment, they convey meaning through the speaker's choice of a positive and negative polarity expression. This interplay of conversational implicature, semantic entailment, and linguistic polarity underpins Aristotle's square, which we illustrate below using quantifiers and probability expressions (see Figure 17.3). The relations on the left of each square are affirmative and those on the right are negative, leading the corners to be named by the Latin mnemonic ***AffIrmo and* NegO.** The relations between the corners of the square are systematic: **A** entails **I** and **E** entails **O**, while **O** contradicts **A** and **I** contradicts **E**. The subcontraries generate conversational implicatures in both directions, for example a speaker who says *some* often implicates ***not all*** and one who says ***not all*** seems to implicate *some* (Horn, 1989; Geurts, 2010; for experimental studies see Noveck, 2001; Feeney et al., 2004). As Figure 17.3 shows, we find the same relational structures in the quantificational and the probabilistic domains, and in fact these structures extend to other domains as well, like connectives, for example (*and, or, neither . . . nor*, etc.) and deontic verbs (e.g., *obliges, allows, forbids, does not oblige*). However, the Aristotelian format is hard to reconcile with the fact that logical expressions don't always come in fours. For example, besides the four quantifiers in

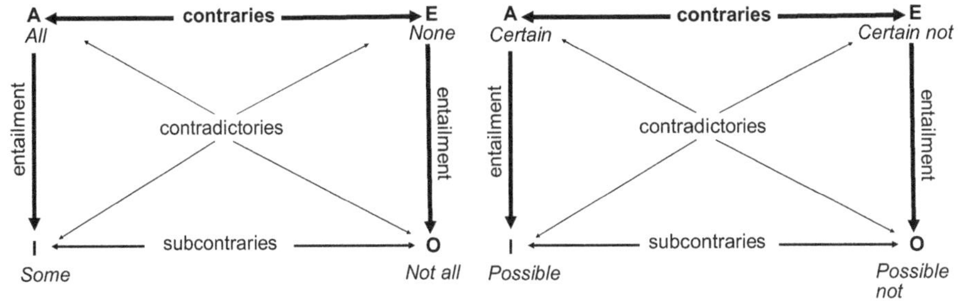

Figure 17.3 Depiction of Aristotle's square using quantifiers and probability expressions

the traditional square, we have *most, few, at least one, two, . . .*, and so on; the same holds for probabilistic expressions. In the following sections we will see how modern theories of interpretation overcome this limitation.

Pragmatic well-formedness of conditionals: combining linguistic polarity and causal directionality

The fact that polarity is widespread in the logical vocabulary implies that it is difficult to make a statement without implicitly framing it in a positive or negative way, and this will in turn influence a hearer's reasoning from that statement. For example, Teigen and Brun (1999) have shown that the polarity of the probability expression chosen is likely to influence decisions and predictions. When participants were told that experts announced that a medical treatment has *some possibility* of being effective, it was encouraged by more than 90% of the participants, while when it is *quite uncertain*, it was encouraged by less than 30% of the participants. This occurred even if both sentences were interpreted as conveying the same numerical chances of success (about 30%).

Using consequent production techniques, Schmeltzer and Hilton (2014) showed that polarity has a strong effect on what people expect to follow from a conditional antecedent. They presented participants with antecedents that were positive or negative in aspect and asked them to write in consequents. Following positive polarity antecedents such as "If it is possible that the operation will succeed" or "If it is not impossible that the operation will succeed", most participants wrote in positive consequents such as "then take the operation". In contrast, if presented with negative polarity antecedents such as "If it is not probable that the operation will succeed" or "If it is uncertain that the operation will succeed", then people wrote in negative consequents such as "do not take the operation". Sentence completions thus follow a logic of evaluative consistency that can be captured by formulations such as Heider's (1946) balance theory of attitude formation and change. It is as if the speaker conveys a positive or negative attitude to the action in question (e.g., taking the operation) which is picked up by the hearer and used by him to form his attitude to the operation. Knowledge of causal relations is integrated in this process in the form of preconditions which are likely to favour or inhibit taking the action in question. For example, using a negative precondition will lead to an inversion in sentence directionality. Thus a phrase that combines a positive polarity quantifier with a negative precondition, such as "If it is possible that the operation will fail" (which focuses on the chances of failure) is typically completed with the discouragement "then do not take the operation".

Note that participants do not seem to decide these sentence completions on the basis of a rational calculation of expected utilities. For example, Schmeltzer and Hilton (2014) compared conditional antecedents in which the verbal quantifier has a positive polarity but low probability (e.g., "If there is the least chance that the operation will succeed") with ones in which the verbal quantifier has a negative polarity but high probability (e.g., "If there is not every chance that the operation will succeed"). From the point of view of a decision-theoretic analysis (e.g., Evans & Over, 2004), a rational hearer should – all things being equal – prefer the action that has the most chances of producing a desirable outcome, and thus feel most "encouraged" to take the operation having heard the second utterance. But when we analyze participants' spontaneous sentence completions, almost all of them complete the positive polarity quantifier with a positive consequent ("take the operation") even though the probability of success is lower in this case than for the negative polarity antecedent, which they mostly complete with a negative consequent ("do not take the operation"). Using the same set of conditional sentences as stimulus materials, El-Yagoubi et al. (in preparation) found that "balanced" sentences were judged as more coherent. While only linguistic polarity information affected judgments of sentence coherence, EEG data suggested that both linguistic polarity and numerical probability were detected in online processing of probability expressions, with linguistic polarity being detected earlier. This suggests that the linguistic polarity of probability expressions needs less "calculation" than the probabilistic information.

Improving reasoning through better communication

The neo-Gricean approach has mainly been applied to analyzing verbal communication using natural language, but can equally be applied to analyzing communication using other forms of symbolic communications, such as visual aids like graphs and tables or use of mathematical conventions such as numerical probability or frequency information. In the final section, we address the question of whether reasoning and judgment can be aided by using specific kinds of representations and the design of communications that draw the reasoner's attention to important information or highlight critical contrasts. We will illustrate the power of suitable representations with two examples (for some more examples, see Sedlmeier & Hilton, 2012). One demonstrates how the use of frequency formats improves reasoning according to Bayesian norms, and the other, how a simple contingency table helps in causal inference.

Communicating about probability revision: using natural frequencies to better understand uncertainties

Consider the following well known "mammography task" (adapted from Casscells, Schoenberger, & Grayboys, 1978):

> A reporter for a women's monthly magazine would like to write an article about breast cancer. As a part of her research, she focuses on mammography as an indicator of breast cancer. She wonders what it really means if a woman tests positive for breast cancer during her routine mammography examination. She has the following data:
>
> The probability that a woman who undergoes a mammography will have breast cancer is 1%.
>
> If a woman undergoing a mammography has breast cancer, the probability that she will test positive is 80%.
>
> If a woman undergoing a mammography does not have breast cancer, the probability that she will test positive is 10%.
>
> What is the probability that a woman who has undergone a mammography actually has breast cancer, if she tests positive?

In this task, the (a priori) probability that a randomly selected woman from a specified population has breast cancer (here 1%) is revised in the light of the new information that she has been positively diagnosed. The usual way to solve this task, that is, to revise the a priori probability p(cancer) of 1% is to use a simple version of Bayes' theorem:

$$p(cancer \mid positive) = \frac{p(cancer)p(positive \mid cancer)}{p(cancer)p(positive \mid cancer) + p(no\ cancer)p(positive \mid no\ cancer)}$$
$$= \frac{.01 \times .8}{.01 \times .8 + .99 \times .1} = .075$$

This task has been found to be quite difficult, even for medical experts, if communicated in the above way (Casscells et al., 1978; Eddy, 1982; Hoffrage & Gigerenzer, 1998).

Communication works much better (i.e., leads to substantial improvements in rates of spontaneous solutions of the task) if the probabilities (expressed in percentages) in the above example are replaced by "natural frequencies" (Betsch, Biel, Eddelbüttel, & Mock, 1998; Gigerenzer & Hoffrage, 1995; Hoffrage & Gigerenzer, 1998):

> A reporter for a women's monthly magazine intends to write an article about breast cancer. As a part of her research, she looks into mammography tests, which are used to diagnose breast cancer. She is interested in the question of what it means if a woman tests positive for breast cancer. She finds the following data:
>
> 10 out of every 1,000 women who undergo a mammography have breast cancer.
> 8 out of every 10 women with breast cancer who undergo a mammography will test positive.
> 99 out of every 990 women who do not have breast cancer will test positive.[5]

This seemingly small change in wording makes the calculation much easier – Bayes' theorem is not needed any longer. Now only the number of women who are both sick *and* have been tested positively has to be divided by the number of all positively tested women:

$$p\left(cancer \mid positive\right) = \frac{\#(positive \cap cancer)}{\#\ positive}$$
$$= \frac{8}{8 + 99}$$
$$= .075$$

Although there is some controversy about the best explanation for this effect (e.g., Evans et al., 2000; Girotto & Gonzalez, 2000; 2002; Hoffrage et al., 2002; Macchi, 2000; Sedlmeier, 1999), communicating probability information with the help of natural frequencies greatly facilitates the understanding of probability revision and similar problems (Sedlmeier, 2007). It may be that the frequency format prompts recipients to spontaneously think about base rate information in these tasks, similar to the effect of a prompt given by a contingency table in the case discussed below.

Communicating about causality: designing graphs and diagrams to facilitate causal inference

At the heart of accurate causal inference lies the application of Mill's (1872/1873) method of difference, whereby a target group is contrasted to a control group which ideally has the same characteristics apart from the variable of interest (e.g. smoking versus non-smoking, hygiene versus no hygiene). These causal inferences can thus be shaped by representations of the control group. For example, a newspaper report of an earthquake disaster often shows photographs of the part of town where there has been the most destruction, thus inducing a sense of fatalism through suggesting the awesome and all-destroying power of the earthquake. However, a photograph that shows a neighbouring block that was *not* destroyed invites a causal question: why did the buildings in one block collapse while the adjoining one did not? As McClure et al. (2001) suggest, visual representations that render the collapsed blocks distinctive in this way lead people to attribute the building collapse more to faults in their design, and to focus more on preventative behaviours.

The role of graphs in the decision to launch the Challenger *space shuttle*

In 1986, the space shuttle *Challenger* exploded some 78 seconds after liftoff, killing the crew of seven on board. After an extensive presidential inquiry, the cause of the accident was found to be the failure of the O-rings, special seals between booster rocket sections. These rubber O-rings lost their plasticity and ability to function effectively in cold temperatures, and *Challenger* was launched in late January, at the lowest temperature yet for any space shuttle launch. What is more, during the inquiry it came to light that engineers from Morton Thiokol, the company that built the booster rockets, had called a conference with NASA the night before launch to discuss whether to launch, as it was feared that the O-rings might not work properly at low temperatures. Why were the engineers' concerns overruled?

Transcripts of the pre-launch conference suggest that the onus was placed on the engineers concerned to prove that it was *not* safe to launch. At one point the question was posed as to what evidence the engineers could present to justify their concern about the safe functioning of the O-rings in cold weather. The engineers produced information about the temperature at the time of launches where the O-rings had burned through (obtained from scrutinizing booster rocket sections jettisoned from previous launches and retrieved from the Atlantic). It turned out that these problematic cases were distributed over the whole range of possible temperatures (Figure 17.4a). This was interpreted as indicating that there was no relation between temperature and O-ring burn-through, as burn-through sometimes happens during cold launches but sometimes not.

Or was there in fact a relationship? A vital element of information that is missing from Figure 17.4a concerns the frequency of unproblematic flights (no O-ring burn-through) in both cold and warm weather launches. Figure 17.4b shows that this information is critical: the temperature very likely had a strong impact on the functioning of the O-rings. None of the unproblematic flights had been started at low temperatures, and *Challenger* was to be launched at the lowest temperature yet. This example shows that to draw valid causal conclusions, it does not suffice to look only at a selection of cases where the outcome is present (here, cases of O-ring burn-through). One must also look at all available cases (or a representative sample thereof) in order to identify the factor that makes the difference: in our example, the difference between safe and unsafe seal functioning. The failure to "mention" the cases where the outcome of interest is *not* present by omitting them from the graph suggests that the (presumably expert) communicator does not consider this information relevant. Visual representations can thus incorporate features that help focus attention on the crucial variable of interest, such as the partition between "warm" and "cold" launches drawn in Figure 17.4b.

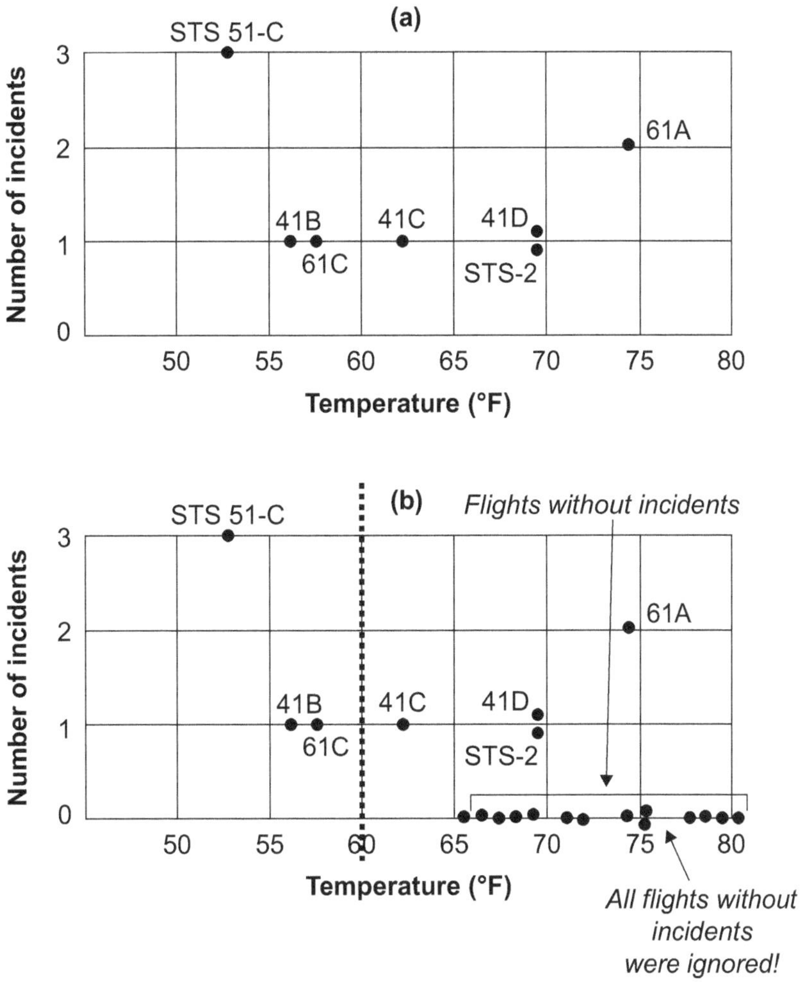

Figure 17.4 Number of flights without incident in the shuttle programme (Figure 17.4a), and all flights (Figure 17.4b) depending on temperature at launch (modified after Dawes [2001] by Sedlmeier & Hilton [2012])

USING CONTINGENCY TABLES TO SCAFFOLD CAUSAL REASONING

How can decision makers be prepared to avoid such "traps"? To that end, a simple but useful device for communicating relevant information is the so-called contingency table, which we illustrate using the *Challenger* example. In a first step, the engineers looked only at whether the problematic flights (where incidents occurred) had been launched at a certain (low) temperature. If one takes 60°F as a cutoff between cold and warm (see the vertical line in Figure 17.4b), the respective table looks like that in Figure 17.5a. This table shows that temperature apparently does not make a difference: we have an equal number of incidents in cold as well as in warm weather. Obviously, Mill's method of difference cannot be applied with what we have here, since we completely lack information about one of the two possible outcomes: the number of

(a)

	Cold	Warm
Incident	5	5

(b)

	Cold	Warm
Incident	5	5
No Incident	?	?

(c)

	Cold	Warm
Incident	5	5
No Incident	0	14

Figure 17.5 Different ways to represent the possible causal relationship between temperature and problems at launch for the space shuttle programme. Figure 17.5a shows an incomplete version likely to induce error. Figure 17.5b clarifies that pieces of information are missing, and Figure 17.5c gives a complete tabular representation necessary to draw a correct causal conclusion (from Sedlmeier & Hilton, 2012 looks strange).

flights *without* incidents (see Figure 17.5b). If that information is added, the full contingency table (Figure 17.5c) clearly conveys a different message. What does the method of difference tell us now? It makes clear that the proportion of incidents that took place is strikingly higher in cold as compared to warm weather. Whereas 100% of the flights launched at cold weather were problematic, this percentage was only 26% in warm weather. This is a clear indication that there is a causal connection between temperature and problems at launch, and thus would indicate a high risk of joint problems if the space shuttle was launched in cold weather.

Conclusions

Understanding everyday conversation requires considerable reasoning. Levinson (2000) suggests that reasoning is needed to circumvent certain design constraints in human communication, imposed by the bottleneck imposed by our inability to speak as fast as we can think. Spoken communication has evolved a set of strategies that allow speakers to convey more information than is explicitly encoded in the spoken or written message. Speakers know that hearers can use these shared strategies to figure out the fuller meaning of what is said, and thus do not explicitly mention information that they assume will be inferred by hearers. Hearers thus use this shared knowledge to ***reason to*** an interpretation of the speaker's utterance, by making inferences from word senses to their specific referents in the context of utterance as well as inferring what these words entail and implicate. Once the interpretation of the speaker's utterance has been made, people may be asked to ***reason from*** that interpretation in a way that may or may not correspond with what would be expected from a "rational" model of inference (Hilton, 1995; Varga, Stenning, & Martignon, 2015).

Conversational inference thus requires a number of inferential abilities, both inductive and deductive, which people perform with remarkable ease. Conversational assumptions govern the inferences that are drawn from all kinds of verbal communication, as well as from various other forms of symbolic communication such as graphs, tables, and photographs. It seems plausible that human inferential abilities are adapted to prototypic face-to-face dialogues with the possibility of immediate repair of conversational misunderstandings (Levinson, 1995). However, such immediate repair may be more difficult when interpreting communications where the speaker is no longer present (e.g., when reading written communications). In our view, awareness of the nature of conversational inference can not only aid in the interpretation of experiments designed to evaluate people's competence in reasoning and judgment, but also inform the design of communications designed to improve human inference and decision-making.

Acknowledgments

We thank Linden Ball and Shira Elqayam for their helpful comments on a previous draft.

Notes

1 "Inductive" here is to be interpreted in its broader sense of "non-deductive". Much pragmatic reasoning may in fact be characterized as "abductive", involving inference to the best explanation (see, for example, Geurts, 2010).

2 Indeed, one of the leading proponents of the heuristics and biases programme at one stage hoped that the "conversational paradigm" would emerge as a way of explaining errors in everyday reasoning (Daniel Kahneman, personal communication).

3 Many readers will recognize the basis of this distinction in Austin's (1962) contrast between ***constative*** and *performative* uses of language. However, in his book Austin appears to restrict the term *performative* to a somewhat specific set of speech acts and ends by identifying problems with the constative-performative distinction. We use the more general term "non-constative" here to describe phenomena that have been described as *performative* (in the sense of serving non-constative goals) in previous work (e.g., Hilton, Kemmelmeier, & Bonnefon, 2005).

4 The set-theoretic notions we use here are the following. Let X and Y be any two sets; then:

- $X \subseteq Y$ (X is a subset of Y) if all elements of X are included in Y as well.
- $X \cap Y$ (the intersection of X and Y) is that set which comprises all elements that X and Y have in common.
- card(X) (the cardinality of X) is the number of elements in X.

5 Natural frequencies such as those used in this version of the mammography task can, at least in principle, be observed in daily life. In contrast, "non-natural" frequencies would be "normalized" frequencies, that is, frequencies that all refer to a given number, such as 100 women in our case ("1 out of every 100 women who undergo a mammography have breast cancer, 80 out of every 100 women with breast cancer who undergo a mammography will test positive, and 10 out of every 100 women who do not have breast cancer will test positive"). Here, the information about the base rates – *p*(*cancer*) and *p*(*no cancer*) – is lost.

References

Asch, S. E. (1940). Studies in the principles of judgments and attitudes: II. Determination of judgments by group and by ego standards. *Journal of Social Psychology, 12,* 433–465.

Austin, J. L. (1962). *How to do things with words*. Oxford: Clarendon Press.

Barwise, J., & Cooper, R. (1981). Generalized quantifiers and natural language. *Linguistics and Philosophy, 4*(2), 159–219.

Betsch, T., Biel, G.-M., Eddelbüttel, C., & Mock, A. (1998). Natural sampling and base-rate neglect. *European Journal of Social Psychology, 28,* 269–273.

Bonnefon, J-F & Hilton, D. J. (2002). The suppression of Modus Ponens as a case of pragmatic preconditional reasoning. *Thinking and Reasoning, 8,* 21–40.

Byrne, R. M. J. (1989). Suppressing valid inferences with conditionals. *Cognition, 31,* 61–83.

Casscells, W., Schoenberger, A., & Grayboys, T. (1978). Interpretation by physicians of clinical laboratory results. *New England Journal of Medicine, 299,* 999–1000.

Chater, N., & Oaksford, M. (1999). The probability heuristics model of syllogistic reasoning. *Cognitive Psychology, 38,* 191–258.

Cummins, D. D., Lubart, T., Alksnis, O., & Rist, R. (1991). Conditional reasoning and causation. *Memory & Cognition, 19,* 274–282. doi:10.3758/BF03211151

Eddy, D. M. (1982). Probabilistic reasoning in clinical medicine: Problems and opportunities. In D. Kahneman, P. Slovic, & A. Tversky (Eds.), *Judgment under uncertainty: Heuristics and biases* (pp. 249–267). New York: Cambridge University Press.

Elqayam, S., Thompson, V. A., Wilkinson, M. R., Evans J. St. B., & Over, D. E. (2015). Deontic introduction; A theory of inference from is to ought. *Journal of Experimental Psychology: Learning, Memory and Cognition, 41,* 1516–1532.

El-Yagoubi, R., Hilton, D. J., Schmeltzer, C. S., & Wawrzyniak, A. (in preparation). A cognitive consistency model for judging the coherence of conditionals: Behavioural and neurophysiological investigations.

Evans, J. St. B. T., Handley, S. J., & Over, D. E. (2003). Conditionals and conditional probability. *Journal of Experimental Psychology: Learning, Memory, and Cognition, 29,* 321–335.

Evans, J. St. B. T., Handley, S. J., Perham, N., Over, D. E., & Thompson, V. A. (2000). Frequency versus probability formats in statistical word problems. *Cognition, 77,* 197–213.

Evans, J. St. B. T., & Over, D. E. (2004). *If.* Oxford: Oxford University Press.

Feeney, A., Scrafton, S., Duckworth, A., & Handley, S. J. (2004). The story of some: Everyday pragmatic inference by children and adults. *Canadian Journal of Experimental Psychology/Revue canadienne de psychologie expérimentale, 58*(2), 121.

Geurts, B. (2003). Reasoning with quantifiers. *Cognition, 86,* 223–251.

Geurts, B. (2010). *Quantity implicatures.* Cambridge: Cambridge University Press.

Geurts, B. (2013). Alternatives in framing and decision making. *Mind & Language, 28*(1), 1–19.

Gigerenzer, G., & Hoffrage, U. (1995). How to improve Bayesian reasoning without instruction: Frequency formats. *Psychological Review, 102,* 684–704.

Gigerenzer, G., & Hug, K. (1992). Domain specific reasoning, social contracts, and perspective change. *Cognition, 43,* 127–171.

Girotto, V., & Gonzalez, M. (2000). Solving probabilistic and statistical problems: a matter of information structure and question form. *Cognition, 78,* 247–276.

Girotto, V., & Gonzalez, M. (2002). Chances and frequencies in probabilistic reasoning: rejoinder to Hoffrage, Gigerenzer, Krauss, and Martignon. *Cognition, 84,* 353–359.

Grice, H. P. (1957). Meaning. *Philosophical Review, 67.*

Grice, H. P. (1975). Logic and conversation. In P. Cole & J. L. Morgan (Eds.), *Syntax and semantics, Vol. 3: Speech acts* (pp. 41–58). San Diego, CA: Academic Press.

Hart, H. L. A., & Honoré, A. M. (1985). *Causation in the law* (2nd ed.) Oxford: Oxford University Press.

Heider, F. (1946). Attitudes and cognitive organization. *Journal of Psychology, 21,* 107–112.

Hilton, D. J. (1991). A conversational model of causal explanation. In W. Stroebe and M. Hewstone (Eds.) *European Review of Social Psychology, 2,* 61–81.

Hilton, D. J. (1995). The social context of reasoning: Conversational inference and rational judgment. *Psychological Bulletin, 118,* 248–271.

Hilton, D. J. (2009). Conversational inference: Social cognition as interactional intelligence. In F. Strack & J. Förster (Eds.), *Social cognition: The basis of human interaction* (pp. 71–92). New York: Psychology Press.

Hilton, D.J. (2011). Linguistic polarity, outcome framing and the structure of decision-making: A pragmatic approach. In G. Keren (Ed.), *Perspectives on framing* (pp. 135–156). London: Psychology Press (*Series in Judgment and Decision Making*).
Hilton, D. J., & Erb, H-P. (1996). Mental models and causal explanation: Judgments of probable cause and explanatory relevance. *Thinking and Reasoning, 2*, 33–65.
Hilton, D. J., Jaspars, J. M. F., & Clarke, D. D. (1990). Pragmatic conditional reasoning: Context and content effects on the interpretation of causal assertions. *Journal of Pragmatics, 14*, 627–648.
Hilton, D. J., Kemmelmeier, M., & Bonnefon, J-F. (2005). Putting *Ifs* to Work: Goal-based relevance in conditional directives. *Journal of Experimental Psychology: General, 134*, 388–405.
Hilton, D. J., Schmeltzer, C. S., & Geurts, B. (2011). Language and meaning representation: Implications for theories of reasoning and decision-making. In W. Brun, G. Keren, G. Keirkeboen, & H. Montgomery (Eds.), *Perspectives on thinking, judging and decision making: A tribute to Karl Halvor Teigen* (pp. 201–211). Oslo: Universitetsforlaget.
Hilton, D. J., & Slugoski, B. R. (1986). Knowledge-based causal attribution: The abnormal conditions focus model. *Psychological Review, 93*, 75–88.
Hilton, D. J., & Slugoski, B. R. (2000). Discourse processes and rational inference: Judgment and decision-making in a social context. In T. Connolly, H. Arkes, & K. Hammond (Eds.), *Judgment and decision-making: A reader* (2nd ed.). Cambridge: Cambridge University Press.
Hilton, D. J., & Slugoski, B. R. (2001). The conversational perspective in reasoning and explanation. In A. Tesser & N. Schwarz (Eds.), *Blackwell handbook of social psychology: Vol 1: Intrapersonal processes* (pp. 181–206). Oxford: Blackwell.
Hoffrage, U., & Gigerenzer, G. (1998). Using natural frequencies to improve diagnostic inferences. *Academic Medicine, 73*, 538–540.
Hoffrage, U., Gigerenzer, G., Krauss, S., & Martignon, L. (2002). Representation facilitates reasoning: What natural frequencies are and what they are not. *Cognition, 84*, 343–352.
Horn, L. (1989). *A natural history of negation*. Chicago: University of Chicago Press.
Johnson-Laird, P. N. (1983). *Mental models*. Cambridge: Cambridge University Press.
Kahneman, D., & Frederick, S. (2002). Representativeness revisited: Attribute substitution in intuitive judgment. In T. Gilovich, D. Griffin, & D. Kahneman (Eds.), *Heuristics and biases: The psychology of intuitive judgement* (pp. 49–81). Cambridge: Cambridge University Press.
Kahneman, D., & Tversky, A. (1972). Subjective probability: A judgment of representativeness. *Cognitive Psychology, 3*, 430–454.
Kahneman, D., & Tversky, A. (1973). On the psychology of prediction. *Psychological Review, 80*, 237–251.
Kahneman, D., & Tversky, A. (1979). Prospect theory: An analysis of decision under risk. *Econometrica, 47*, 263–291.
Levinson, S. C. (1983). *Pragmatics*. Cambridge: Cambridge University Press.
Levinson, S. C. (1995). Interactional biases in human thinking. In E. Goody (Ed.), *Social intelligence and interaction*. Cambridge: Cambridge University Press.
Levinson, S. C. (2000). *Presumptive meanings: The theory of generalized conversational implicature*. Cambridge, MA: MIT Press.
Liberman, N., & Klar, Y. (1996). Hypothesis testing in Wason's selection task: Social exchange cheating detection or task understanding. *Cognition, 58*(1), 127–156.
Lorge, I., & Curtiss, C. C. (1936). Prestige, suggestion, and attitudes. *Journal of Social Psychology*, 7(4), 386–402.
Macchi, L. (2000). Partitive formulation of information in probabilistic problems: Beyond heuristics and frequency format explanations. *Organizational Behavior and Human Decision Processes, 82*, 217–236.
Mackie, J. L. (1980). *The cement of the universe*. Oxford: Oxford University Press.
Mandel, D. R. (2014). Do framing effects reveal irrational choice? *Journal of Experimental Psychology: General, 143*(3), 1185.
Manktelow, K. I., & Over, D. E. (1991). Social roles and utilities in reasoning with deontic conditionals. *Cognition, 39*, 85–105.
Markovits, H., Brisson, J., & de Chantal, P.-L. (2015). Deductive updating is not Bayesian. *Journal of Experimental Psychology: Learning, Memory, and Cognition*, 41, 949–956.
McClure & Hilton, D. J. (1998). When are preconditions better explanations than goals? It depends on the question. *European Journal of Social Psychology, 28*, 897–911.
McClure, J. L., Allen, M. W., & Walkey, F. (2001). Countering fatalism: Causal information in news reports affects judgments about earthquake damage. *Basic and Applied Social Psychology, 23*, 109–121.

McClure, J. L., & Hilton, D. J. (1997). For you can't always get what you want: When script-preconditions make good explanations. *British Journal of Social Psychology, 36*, 223–240.

Mill, J. S. (1872/1973). System of logic. In J. M. Robson (Ed.), *Collected works of John Stuart Mill* (8th ed., Vols. 7 and 8). Toronto: University of Toronto Press. (Original edition published 1872).

Nisbett, R. E., Zukier, H., & Lemley, R. H. (1981). The dilution effect: Nondiagnostic information. *Cognitive Psychology, 13*, 248–277.

Noveck, I. A. (2001). When children are more logical than adults: Experimental I investigations of scalar implicature. *Cognition, 78*(2), 165–188.

Noveck, I. A., & Reboul, A. (2008). Experimental pragmatics: A Gricean turn in the study of language. *Trends in Cognitive Sciences, 12,* 425–431.

Oaksford, M., & Chater, N. (2007). *Bayesian rationality: The probabilistic approach to human reasoning*. Oxford University Press.

Ohm, E., & Thompson, V. A. (2006). Conditional probability and pragmatic conditionals: Dissociating truth and effectiveness. *Thinking & Reasoning, 12*(3), 257–280.

Politzer, G., & Nguyen-Xuan, A. (1992). Reasoning about conditional promises and warnings: Darwinian algorithms, mental models, relevance judgments or pragmatic schemas? *Quarterly Journal of Experimental Psychology, 44A*, 401–421.

Sánchez Valencia, V. M. (1991). *Studies on natural logic and categorial grammar*. Doctoral dissertation, University of Amsterdam.

Schmeltzer, C. S., & Hilton, D. J. (2014). To do or not to do? A cognitive consistency model for drawing conclusions from conditional instructions and advice. *Thinking & Reasoning, 20*(1), 16–50.

Sedlmeier, P. (1999). *Improving statistical reasoning: Theoretical models and practical implications*. Mahwah, NJ: Lawrence Erlbaum Associates.

Sedlmeier, P. (2007). Statistical reasoning: valid intuitions put to use. In M. Lovett & P. Shah (Eds.). *Thinking with data* (pp. 389–419). New York: Lawrence Erlbaum Associates.

Sedlmeier, P., & Hilton, D. (2012). Improving judgment and decision making through communication: The role of conversational rules and representational formats. In M. Dhami, A. Schlottmann, & M. Waldmann (Eds.), *Origins of judgment and decision-making* (pp. 229–257). Cambridge, UK: Cambridge University Press.

Sperber, D., Cara, F., & Girotto, V. (1995). Relevance theory explains the selection task. *Cognition, 57*, 31–95.

Staudenmayer, H. (1975). Understanding conditional reasoning with meaningful propositions. In R. J. Falmagne (Ed.), *Reasoning: Representation and process*. Hillsdale, NJ: Wiley.

Teigen, K. H., & Brun, W. (1999). The directionality of verbal probability expressions: Effects on decisions, predictions, and probabilistic reasoning. *Organizational Behavior and Human Decision Processes, 80*, 155–190.

Tetlock, P. E., Lerner, J., & Boettger, R. (1996). The dilution effect: Judgmental bias or conversational convention or a bit of both? *European Journal of Social Psychology, 26*, 914–934.

Thompson, V. A., Evans, J. S. B., & Handley, S. J. (2005). Persuading and dissuading by conditional argument. *Journal of Memory and Language, 53*(2), 238–257.

Varga, A., Stenning, K., & Martignon, L. (2015, August). There is no one logic to model human reasoning: The case from interpretation. In U. Furbach, & C. Schon (Eds.), Proceedings of the first workshop on bridging the gap between human and automated reasoning (pp. 32–46), Berlin, Germany, August 1, 2015.

Wänke, M. (2007). What is said and what is meant: Conversational implicatures in natural conversations, research settings, media and advertising. In K. Fiedler (Ed.), *Frontiers in social psychology: Social communication* (pp. 223–256). Hove, UK: Psychology Press.

Wilson, D., & Sperber, D. (2004). Relevance theory. In G. Ward & L. Horn (Eds.), *Handbook of Pragmatics* (pp. 607–632). Oxford: Blackwell.

18
THE FAST-AND-FRUGAL HEURISTICS PROGRAM

Ulrich Hoffrage, Sebastian Hafenbrädl, and Julian N. Marewski

"Eureka! Eureka!" With this Greek word meaning *"I have found it!"*, the great inventor and scientist Archimedes (likely 287–212 BC) ran, allegedly naked, through the streets of his hometown, Syracuse (Sicily, Italy), performing dances of joy after he had discovered, during a bath, that the increase of the water level in the pool must correspond exactly to the volume of those parts of his body he had submerged. This discovery allows one to measure the volume of any solid object, no matter how irregular it might be – a problem that was unresolved at that time. Today we find the solution and read about the correspondence between volume of objects and volume of displaced liquids in schoolbooks of physics, and many have heard of Archimedes' infamous discoveries, including the impressive war machines he is reputed to have invented.

Archimedes is long dead – purportedly killed by a Roman legionary when the troops of General Marcus Claudius Marcellus finally managed to conquer Syracuse during the Second Punic War. But Archimedes' work lives on, and with his and others' discoveries, the magic expression "eureka". That expression has, likely, not only left the lips of other scientists and inventors, overwhelmed by what they found, but it has also given name to an entire discipline: the study of *heuristics*.

Heuristics are simple rules of thumb to find out or to discover. In this chapter, we offer an introduction into cognitive and decision making research on heuristics. In the first part, we provide a brief history of the term "heuristic", and then trace back the *eureka* experiences made by a group of 20th-century researchers who set out, initially, to investigate everything but heuristics, but who ended up founding an entire research program on heuristics, namely the *fast-and-frugal* heuristics program (e.g., Gigerenzer, Todd, & the ABC Research Group, 1999). In the second part of this chapter, we then illustrate central concepts and methods of the fast-and-frugal heuristics program in more detail. We will show that the fast-and-frugal heuristics approach to judgment and decision making has grown, over the past three decades, from a widely ignored collection of ideas of some "rebels" to a full-blown, influential research program, motivating research and even policy in several disciplines and areas, ranging from psychology, philosophy, law, and medicine in the academic world to health care and education in the public, applied domain. In the third part, we present a few heuristics in more detail and review some exemplary work.

In a nutshell, the story of this chapter is the following. The fast-and-frugal heuristics research program started out, like many other schools of thought, with quite incidental findings: a handful of researchers struggled to get to grips with existing theories of memory and judgment. In scrutinizing the dominant paradigms in the field, these researchers made puzzling discoveries they did not understand, at least not initially. Eventually, these discoveries led to new theory, and to the founding of a research group. Researchers in this community came from different interdisciplinary backgrounds, and aided by their backgrounds, brought the framework into their disciplines while bringing new ideas into the group – both enriching the framework and, often, leaving outsiders (e.g., other decision scientists) puzzled about how all the ideas and findings actually fit to each other. Making visible how those ideas speak to each other in coherent ways is one goal that we aspire to achieve with this "historically" contextualized overview on fast-and-frugal heuristics. Offering very personal insights on this little "history" of fast-and-frugal heuristics is another one: Ulrich Hoffrage has been, since its very first days, a member of the interdisciplinary research group that developed the fast-and-frugal heuristics program. Julian Marewski joined this group a few generations later, and Sebastian Hafenbrädl got involved when he started, many years ago, as a PhD student of Ulrich Hoffrage. We hope that the story about heuristics we tell, and the report of our own *eureka* experiences, offers a refreshing and insightful introduction to the fast-and-frugal research program.

Heuristics: a little bit of history

Heuristic comes from the Greek *heuriskein* (εὑρίσκειν): "to find." Since its introduction to English in the early 1800s, the term "heuristic" has acquired a range of meanings, with heuristics representing anything from sudden insights, ungraspable hunches, or intuitions on the one hand to precisely defined computer algorithms on the other. For instance, Albert Einstein (1905) used the term, in the title of his Nobel Prize–winning paper ("On a heuristic point of view concerning the generation and transformation of light"), to indicate that his view served to find out or to discover something. Even though such a heuristic view may yield an incomplete and unconfirmed picture that may eventually even be false, such a picture may nonetheless still be useful. The Gestalt psychologists, who conceptualized thinking as an interaction between external problem structure and internal processes, considered heuristics as principles that guide search for information in the environment (e.g., inspecting the problem and analyzing the conflict, the situation, the materials, and the goal) and that allowed one to restructure the problem by internal processes (Duncker, 1935). In the 1950s and 60s, Herbert Simon and Allen Newell, two of the founding fathers of artificial intelligence and cognitive science, used the term to refer to methods for finding solutions to problems while limiting search, which implies that the solution may not necessarily be found. For instance, in the *General Problem Solver*, a formalized computer program, they implemented heuristics such as the means-end analysis, which tried to set subgoals and find operations that would ultimately reduce the distance between the current state and the desired goal state (Newell & Simon, 1972). With the advent of information theory in cognitive psychology, the term "heuristic" finally came to mean a useful shortcut, an approximation, or a rule of thumb for searching through a space of possible solutions (Hoffrage, 2005; for more details, see Hertwig & Pachur, 2015). Common to all of those historical uses of the term is the idea that heuristics are means for finding something – information, insights, or solutions to given problems.

The heuristics-and-biases program: historical context, contribution, and criticism

In the 1970s, Daniel Kahneman and Amos Tversky initiated what can be considered one of the most influential programs in the social sciences in the 20th century: the *heuristics-and-biases program* (Kahneman, Slovic, & Tversky, 1982). This program and the historical context in which it developed set the stage for the discovery of fast-and-frugal heuristics. Let us go back in history by another 30 years.

In the 1940s, von Neumann and Morgenstern (1944) axiomatized *subjective expected utility* (SEU) *theory*. Soon afterwards, however, deviations were identified – for instance, the *Allais paradox* (Allais, 1953), in which people violated the cancelation axiom – and psychologists became interested in the extent to which SEU theory is a good descriptive model of behavior (Edwards, 1954). Note that such descriptive questions need to be separated from normative considerations. In fact, von Neumann and Morgenstern did not conceive their axioms of SEU theory as normative, and, likewise, Allais did not think that a violation of the cancelation axiom would be irrational. Others (including Savage, 1972 and Tversky & Kahneman, 1974), in contrast, conceived SEU theory to be *the* normative theory for rational decision making: deciding consistent with its axioms was considered to be rational, and, conversely, a violation of (some of) its axioms was considered to be irrational.

The heuristics-and-biases program emerged in exactly this context and with such a normative stance. It can be seen as an attempt to document and explain deviations from SEU theory and other "normative" principles of rationality. Such deviations, so the argument went, can be explained by heuristics, for instance, by the ***representativeness heuristic***, the ***availability heuristic***, and the ***anchoring-and-adjustment heuristic*** (Kahneman et al., 1982). The rhetoric was that heuristics are often useful and yield good approximations, but that they sometimes may also lead to systematic biases. Subsequent research focused more and more on those situations in which heuristics lead people astray, and the overall conclusion of this program painted a pessimistic picture of humans' ability to make sound and rational judgments and decisions (Lopes, 1991). The term "heuristic" acquired a new connotation: from neutral or positive, to negative.

From critique to theory: the birth of the fast-and-frugal heuristics program

While the heuristics-and-biases program attracted a lot of attention, it has also been challenged. In particular, Gerd Gigerenzer, whom Kahneman (2011) referred to as "our most persistent critic," and his colleagues scrutinized some of the flagship phenomena that have been frequently cited as landmarks of human irrationality. Here are two examples (for overviews that also include others, see Gigerenzer, 1994; Gigerenzer, Hertwig, Hoffrage, & Sedlmeier, 2008).

First, in the early 1990s, Gigerenzer, Hoffrage, and Kleinbölting (1991) became interested in overconfidence, one of the often-cited examples of human irrationality. To account for overconfidence, the authors developed the theory of ***probabilistic mental models*** (PMM). In doing so, they had been inspired by Egon Brunswik's (1955) probabilistic functionalism in two ways: (a) PMM theory specified a mechanism underlying choice and confidence, which posits that people construct a reference class (of objects, such as cities) and use probabilistic cues (i.e., binary predictor variables, such as whether a city has a soccer club or a university) to infer which of two objects scores higher on a distal criterion (e.g., population size of cities); and (b) overconfidence was explained by a mismatch between the statistical structure of participants' natural environment to which they have adapted, and the statistical structure of information in the sample of items that have been used in the lab (for a recent review of overconfidence research, see Hoffrage, 2016). Gigerenzer et al. (1991) predicted and experimentally demonstrated that overconfidence could be replicated, made to disappear, or even turned into underconfidence, depending on: (a) whether a selective or a representative set of questions has been asked; and (b) whether participants assessed their confidence in their own knowledge by assessing the probability that a single question has been answered correctly, or by estimating the number of correctly answered questions in a series of questions, such as questions about which one of two cities has a larger population.

Second, in another article, Gigerenzer and Hoffrage (1995) challenged Kahneman and Tversky's (1972) conclusion that in "his evaluation of evidence man is apparently not . . . Bayesian at all" (p. 450). Gigerenzer and Hoffrage argued and experimentally demonstrated that performance in tasks that can be solved by Bayesian reasoning (i.e., by using Bayes' rule) can be boosted (from 16% correct inferences to 46%, without training) when information is presented, not in terms of probabilities, but in terms of natural frequencies. A probability representation in the context of a Bayesian inference problem would, for instance, read: "the probability that a woman has breast cancer is 1%; if a woman has breast cancer, the probability that she will receive a positive mammogram is 80%; if she does not have breast cancer, the probability that she will still receive a positive mammogram is 10%. Now imagine a woman with a positive mammogram. What is the probability that she actually has breast cancer?" For most people it is hard to see that this probability is as low as 7.5%. The same information represented in terms of natural frequencies would read: "10 of 1,000 women have breast cancer; of those 10 with breast cancer, 8 will receive a positive mammogram, and of those 990 without breast cancer, 99 will still receive a positive mammogram." With this representation, it is much easier to see the Bayesian solution: out of those 107 (8+99) who test positive, 8 do have breast cancer. Again the authors demonstrated the critical role of the environment, which, this time, did not consist in how the questions their participants had to answer were selected, but in how task-relevant information was presented. Compared to probabilities, natural frequencies facilitate the computation. Moreover, human information processing has evolved in an environment in which events have been encoded sequentially (in the present example, 1,000 women, one after the other). Natural frequencies can be seen as a result of such naturally sampled information and therefore correspond to the information format to which the human mind is adapted – which is not the case for probabilities, that is, a format that emerged only quite recently in the history of science.

What were, initially, contributions to a research agenda that could have been labeled "How to make cognitive illusions disappear" (Gigerenzer, 1991) slowly turned into a full-blown alternative research program on heuristics that differed from the heuristics-and-biases program in two important aspects. Both aspects were already mentioned explicitly in the following exchange: when Kahneman and Tversky (1996) defended their work in an article entitled "On the reality of cognitive illusions," Gigerenzer (1996) criticized, in a rejoinder entitled "On narrow norms and vague heuristics," how vaguely those authors had defined their heuristics, and that they conceived context-independent, logical norms as the (only) relevant normative benchmark. The critique of vague heuristics had prepared the ground for formulating fast-and-frugal heuristics as precisely defined algorithms that are specified in terms of their *building blocks* (see below). Moreover, the criticism of content-blind norms had morphed into an agenda for studying the *ecological (= content-dependent) rationality* of those fast-and-frugal heuristics (see below).

From incidental findings to theory: the discovery of the recognition heuristic

Note that both ideas – algorithmic specification of heuristics and ecological rationality – were implicitly present in PMM theory. First, the PMM algorithm can be seen as a heuristic that could be used to find an answer to a paired-comparison task (such as comparing the population of two cities), and it was precise enough to allow for computer simulations (which were conducted only a few years after the publication of PMM theory by Gigerenzer & Goldstein, 1996).

The algorithm posited: (a) that cues are ordered according to their validity, that is, according to the proportion of correct inferences if the cue discriminates; (b) that the most valid is checked first; (c) that only this cue is used to make an inference and that all other cues are ignored; and (d) that the validity of this cue is stated as the confidence. A nice feature of this algorithm was that it predicted zero overconfidence for item sets for which cue validities match those of the corresponding population. Second, the notion of ecological rationality was implicitly contained in this prediction as well: the environment in which the algorithm operates played a crucial role.[1]

PMM theory was not without criticism either, and some of this criticism had been formulated even before the theory was published. First, the representative item set was easier than the selected item set, so maybe it was not sampling procedure that let overconfidence disappear but item difficulty (the so-called hard-easy effect states that overconfidence disappears for easy items; Hoffrage, 2016). Second, overconfidence disappeared in item sets representatively drawn from participants' natural environment, but does this allow for the conclusion that participants used this algorithm? When the second author of PMM theory, then a master student, questioned whether it would be adequate to publish this work without knowing for sure the answer to these questions, the first author replied something like: "you are right, open questions remain, but this is almost always the case. If we postpone publication and try to clarify these two issues that you raised, most likely other questions will emerge and this can go on forever. Science is a social process. We should publish the theory now, with the evidence that we have at the moment, and then not only you but also many others can seek answers to all these questions." This response convinced the second author and so he replied, "Ok, Gerd, I agree – and I will be the first to address these questions and the first who proves the theory wrong" (for the sake of completeness, it should be added that Gigerenzer just smiled and nodded: "Good").

To tackle the first criticism, Hoffrage (1995, 2011) tried to unconfound sampling procedure and item difficulty. More specifically, he gave German participants pairs of German cities, randomly drawn from the set of all cities above 100,000 inhabitants, and also pairs of U.S. cities, again randomly drawn from the set of all cities above 100,000. The expectation was that German participants perform better for the German set – after all, these cities were familiar to them and they knew a lot about them. In contrast, they should perform poorly for the U.S. comparisons, for which they knew less (and for many cities they had not even heard their names). According to PMM theory, overconfidence should disappear for both sets, because the sampling procedure was the same (randomly drawn as a proxy for representative sampling). In contrast, according to the well-established hard-easy effect, there should be overconfidence for the (supposedly hard) comparisons among the U.S. cities, and no overconfidence for the (supposedly easy) comparisons among German cities. To our surprise, the German participants gave not fewer, but even slightly more correct answers for the U.S. cities – despite knowing less. That is, even though we failed, in this experiment, to set up the precondition that would have allowed us to pit the competing predictions concerning overconfidence against each other, we found something else, namely an example of what we later called the "less-is-more" effect. Stumbling over something you were not looking for is known as discovery by serendipity. Yet, for the moment we had nothing but a finding that left us with a puzzle – and Gigerenzer was right: "most likely other questions will emerge."

We had to live with this puzzle for more than a year until, in 1990, we moved to Salzburg where we were enlightened by one of our new colleagues, Anton Kühberger. After we had explained our surprising finding to him, he recommended to us that we should read our own article on probabilistic mental models, and said that, most likely, participants had used their knowledge to make probabilistic inferences. We countered that in most cases they did not have any knowledge – for many cities, they did not even know their names. Toni replied, "But this knowledge is informative. If you recognize the name of one city but this is not the case for the other, then you might infer that the recognized city is larger." *Eureka!* This was the discovery of the *recognition heuristic*, which Gigerenzer and Goldstein (1996; see also Goldstein & Gigerenzer, 2002) formulated as follows: *if one alternative is recognized and the other not, infer the recognized one has the higher value with respect to the criterion.* Indeed, when Goldstein and Gigerenzer replicated Hoffrage's (1995) experiment in which randomly drawn German cities should be compared among each other and randomly drawn U.S. cities should be compared among each other – but now with Chicago undergraduates as participants – they found exactly the same pattern: (slightly) better performance for the comparisons among the foreign cities about which they knew less. The American students could not recognize many of the German cities, and therefore they could quite often apply the recognition heuristic, but they could hardly ever do this for the U.S. cities. Goldstein and Gigerenzer also showed analytically under which conditions such a less-is-more effect emerges and why it was, given the parameters in the present domains, relatively small in this experiment.

At this point, we finish the first part of this chapter, the pre-history of the fast-and-frugal heuristics program, and continue with the second part: an overview of its major concepts and methods. We will return to the recognition heuristic and the PMM algorithm in the third part.

Fast-and-frugal heuristics: the conceptual framework

Bounded rationality

Critique and (initial) lack of understanding can lead to new findings and research programs. Innovation can also be brought about when old ideas are tracked down and rediscovered. One such "old" idea is Herbert Simon's notion of *bounded rationality*. Fast-and-frugal heuristics are models of bounded rationality. In contrast to models that aim at finding the optimal solution to a problem at hand (e.g., SEU theory), models of bounded rationality take into account that humans often have only limited information, limited time, and limited computational capacities when forming judgments or making decisions. Given these constraints, it is often impossible to find the optimal solution – and for many interesting problems the optimal solution cannot be known even if such constraints were not an issue. Models of bounded rationality specify the (cognitive) processes that allow one to find a *satisficing* solution to a given problem. Simon's classic term "satisficing" is a blending of *satis*fying and suf*ficing*, and indeed, often one can be happy with a solution that is good enough.

Optimization versus satisficing

The contrast between optimization and satisficing is interesting from an historical, but also from a societal perspective. In the early 19th century, the astronomer and philosopher Pierre-Simon Laplace imagined an omniscient superintelligence that "could comprehend all the forces of which nature is animated and the respective situation of the beings who compose it – an intelligence sufficiently vast to submit these data to analysis . . . nothing would be uncertain and the future, the past, would be present to its eyes" (Laplace, 1814/1951, *Essai Philosophique*: 1325). This thought experiment seems to have inspired the dominant optimization paradigm in cognitive science, economics, and behavioral biology insofar as this paradigm poses the question of how such a Laplacean superintelligence or near-omniscient being would behave.[2] There have been and there are, however, also alternative visions. More than 100 years before Laplace, the English philosopher John Locke (1690) had contrasted an all-knowing God with us humble and mortal humans living in the "twilight of probability." While Laplace's vision of a superintelligence has inspired models of unbounded rationality, Locke's observation of mortals' capabilities (or better, lack thereof) is presumably the same that Herbert Simon (1982) had when he called for models of bounded rationality. And to disclose the full picture, we should mention that there are attempts to meet in the middle ground between demons and mortals, namely optimization under constraints (such as time or computational capacity). But note that fast-and-frugal heuristics cannot be located in this sphere of these secularized semi-gods (optimization within the limits of human nature). Fast-and-frugal heuristics do *not* optimize – full stop. This explicitly also includes optimization under constraints.

Ecological rationality

Fast-and-frugal heuristics are ecologically rational in many naturally occurring environments. Ecological rationality means that the performance of a heuristic is not evaluated against a content-blind norm (be it logic, probability theory, or statistical principles) and consequently that fast-and-frugal heuristics are not designed to produce, first and foremost, coherent and consistent inferences. Rather, the performance of a heuristic is evaluated against a criterion in the environment, that is, in the ecology (for the distinction between internal consistency versus external correspondence, see Hammond, 1996, and the special issue in *Judgment and Decision Making* on coherence-versus-correspondence, Dunwoody, 2009). For instance, *take-the-best* (Gigerenzer & Goldstein, 1996) chooses one among two or more alternatives and is evaluated by determining the proportion of correct choices. Similarly, the *QuickEst* heuristic (Hertwig, Hoffrage, & Martignon, 1999) makes inferences about the numerical values of objects, and is evaluated by comparing estimated and true values.

In turn, a heuristic is ecologically rational to the extent that it is adapted to the structure of information in the environment. If such a match between heuristics and informational structures exists, heuristics do not need to trade-off accuracy for speed and frugality (for research on the effort–accuracy tradeoff, see Payne, Bettman, & Johnson, 1993). The importance of considering the environment when studying the human mind is best illustrated in Simon's (1990) analogy of a pair of scissors, with the mind and environment as the two blades: "human rational behavior is shaped by a scissors whose blades are the structure of task environments and the computational capabilities of the actor" (p. 7). When considering only one blade, one cannot fully understand how the human mind works, just as one cannot understand how scissors with one single blade would function. The simultaneous focus on the mind and its environment, past and present, puts research on decision making into an ecological framework, a framework that is missing in most alternative theories of reasoning, both descriptive and normative. This focus on the fit of a heuristic to the environment in which it is evaluated is an important aspect of the fast-and-frugal heuristics research program (Todd, Gigerenzer, & the ABC Research Group, 2012; see also Hogarth & Karelaia, 2007).

Social rationality

A special form of ecological rationality is social rationality, which captures the fact that social species need to make decisions in environments that are typically also shaped by the actions of others. Models of social rationality describe the structure of social environments and their match with boundedly rational strategies people use. There are a variety of goals and heuristics unique to social environments. That is, in addition to the goals that define ecological rationality – to make fast, frugal, and fairly accurate decisions – social rationality is concerned with goals, such as choosing an option that one can defend with argument or moral justification, or that can create a consensus. To a much higher degree than most research on bounded rationality with its purely cognitive focus, research on socially adaptive heuristics also incorporates emotions and social norms and explores their potential as heuristic principles for decision making.

The adaptive toolbox

One major insight that results from taking the environment into account is that different environments call for different decision strategies. In contrast to SEU, fast-and-frugal heuristics are thus *not* a general-purpose decision-making algorithm. They are rather designed to solve a particular task (e.g., choice, numerical estimation, categorization) in a particular environment and they cannot solve tasks for which they are not designed – just like a hammer, which is designed to hammer nails but is useless for sawing a board. The collection of such task-specific and fit heuristics that have evolved, that is, shaped by evolution, learning and culture, and that can be used by the human mind is called the *adaptive toolbox* (Gigerenzer & Selten, 2001).

The modularity of fast-and-frugal heuristics: building blocks

Although there are various fast-and-frugal heuristics that are adapted to different tasks and environments, they share the same guiding construction principles. In particular, they are composed of the same building blocks. The building blocks specify how information is searched for, be it in memory or in the environment (*search rule*), when information search is stopped (*stopping rule*), and how a decision is made based on the information acquired (*decision rule*). Thus, in *contrast* to models that assume all information is already known to the decision maker, fast-and-frugal heuristics specify the cognitive processes, including those involved in information acquisition (for related programs that explicitly include information search, see Busemeyer & Townsend, 1993, and Payne, Bettman, & Johnson, 1993; and for a discussion of process models, in contrast to outcomes models, see Berg & Gigerenzer, 2010).

Fast-and-frugal heuristics are fast for two reasons. First, they are fast as a consequence of being frugal; that is, they stop searching for further information early in the process of information acquisition. Second, they do not integrate the acquired information in a complex and time-consuming way. In this respect, many heuristics of the adaptive toolbox are as simple as possible because they do not combine pieces of information at all; instead, the decision is based on just one single reason, which is often also referred to as *one-reason decision making*. We already mentioned that fast-and-frugal heuristics do not optimize – that is, they do not try to find the optimal solution. We can now add that their building blocks do not optimize either. Martignon and Hoffrage (2002) have even shown that simple search rules are more robust and outperform, when making predictions out of sample, search rules that are optimal when fitting known data.

Above we introduced two important elements of most articles proposing new fast-and-frugal heuristics: their building blocks, and a discussion or analysis of their ecological rationality. By specifying the building blocks, researchers essentially develop a process model of how decisions are made. Often such theories are formalized into computational models, or even integrated into cognitive architectures such as *ACT-R* (Anderson & Lebiere, 1998; for implementations of fast-and-frugal heuristics in ACT-R, see Dimov, Marewski, & Schooler, 2017; Marewski & Mehlhorn, 2011; Marewski & Schooler, 2011). Building process models, instead of merely trying to model the outcomes of decisions, allows researchers to predict other characteristics of the decision process, such as response times or confidence assessments (e.g., Hertwig, Fischbacher, & Bruhin, 2013). Moreover, conceptualizing decisions as a series of simple steps makes fast-and-frugal heuristics useful as decision aids.

Research methodologies

Studies on fast-and-frugal heuristics address either prescriptive or descriptive questions (or both). Prescriptive studies explore the performance of heuristics in a given environment, be it in real-world environments or in artificially created environments in which information structures are systematically varied. The methods of choice for such studies are computer simulations (e.g., Czerlinski, Gigerenzer, & Goldstein, 1999) and the use of mathematical or analytical analyses (and sometimes a combination; e.g., Martignon & Hoffrage, 2002). Other research on heuristics addresses the question how good heuristics are as behavioral models. Specifically, experimental and observational studies seek to explore whether and when people actually use these heuristics (e.g., Rieskamp & Hoffrage, 1999, 2008; Garcia-Retamero & Hoffrage, 2006).

Contributions

The research program on fast-and-frugal heuristics has contributed, so far, to various disciplines and domains, including cognitive psychology, management, (behavioral) finance, medicine, biology, consumer behaviour, artificial intelligence, machine learning, and the law. Much of this research has been conducted by (former) members of the Center of Adaptive Behavior and Cognition (for short, ABC Research Group, directed by Gerd Gigerenzer) and, since 2012, also by the Center of Adaptive Rationality (ARC; directed by Ralph Hertwig) – both located at the Max Planck Institute for Human Development in Berlin. The ABC Research Group has, collaboratively, written three books that focus on different aspects of the fast-and-frugal heuristics program.

- *Simple heuristics that make us smart* (Gigerenzer, Todd, & the ABC Research Group, 1999) shows how this approach is related to the notion of bounded rationality and hence also in the intellectual footsteps of Herbert Simon. The book title makes it clear that in this program heuristics have no longer a negative but a positive connotation.
- *Ecological rationality: intelligence in the world* (Todd, Gigerenzer, & the ABC Research Group, 2012) focusses on ecological rationality, that is, on how the performance of simple heuristics hinges on the structure of information in the environment.
- *Simple heuristics in a social world* (Hertwig, Hoffrage, & the ABC Research Group, 2013) focusses on social rationality. Conceptually, the social world we are embedded in constitutes a particular aspect of the world surrounding us, but this aspect has such an importance and is, on so many accounts, distinct from the non-social world that we, the ABC Research Group, decided to devote an entire book on this special case.

Other important books in the fast-and-frugal heuristics research tradition comprise: *Bounded rationality: The adaptive toolbox* (Gigerenzer & Selten, 2001), *Heuristics and the law* (Gigerenzer & Engel, 2006), *Gut feelings: The intelligence of the unconscious* (Gigerenzer, 2007), and a reader that compiles important articles, *Heuristics: The foundations of adaptive behavior* (Gigerenzer, Hertwig, & Pachur, 2011). For other overviews, see Gigerenzer (2015), Gigerenzer and Gaissmaier (2011), Hafenbrädl, Waeger, Marewski, and Gigerenzer (2016), and Marewski, Gaissmaier, and Gigerenzer (2010).

While they are not directly part of it, several related research areas emerged that built on or benefited from the insights the fast-and-frugal heuristics program produced, including social heuristics for human cooperation (e.g., Rand, Peysakhovich, Kraft-Todd, Newman, Wurzbacher,

Nowak, & Greene, 2014) and simple rules as management strategy (e.g., Bingham & Eisenhardt, 2011). Relatedly, the field of risk communication strongly profited from the increased understanding of how people's decision strategies are adapted to their information environment (e.g., Hoffrage, Lindsey, Hertwig, & Gigerenzer, 2000; Hoffrage, Krauss, Martignon, & Gigerenzer, 2015; Hafenbrädl & Hoffrage, 2015; Hoffrage, Hafenbrädl, & Bouquet, 2015).

We now turn to the third part of this chapter in which we illustrate the spirit of heuristics research by reviewing some of the work that has been done on some specific heuristics and in some specific domains.

Specific fast-and-frugal heuristics in specific domains

Since the inception of the fast-and-frugal heuristics research program, thousands of pages in hundreds of papers have been written. Beyond this, there are numerous other articles that share many assumptions with the research program, so that they can be seen as adopting – albeit sometimes unknowingly – its conceptual lenses. Instead of trying to provide an exhaustive list, we illustrate the variety and breadth by focusing on a few selected examples, covering multiple heuristics. Specifically, we review some research on the recognition heuristic, take-the-best, tallying, and fast-and-frugal trees, and report how these heuristics perform in domains such as general-knowledge quizzes, sports, sociology, medicine, and finance.

The recognition heuristic

We already mentioned what led to the formulation of the recognition heuristic, namely, a particular pattern of percentages of correct answers across various conditions: participants who knew less about a domain performed better than those who knew more (Hoffrage, 1995). This effect has later been termed the *less-is-more effect* (Goldstein & Gigerenzer, 2002). By means of mathematical analysis it is possible to determine the optimal degree of recognition knowledge – the percentage of recognized objects in a given reference class which allows for the highest performance in a complete paired comparison task of all objects. Knowing less, but also knowing more objects, will lead to a decrease in performance. In a series of experiments in which cities had to be compared with respect to their number of inhabitants, participants' choices were consistent with the recognition heuristic in more than 90% of the cases – this was even true in a study in which participants were taught knowledge contradicting recognition (Goldstein & Gigerenzer, 2002). Moreover, the authors found two different types of less-is-more effects, one in which participants performed better in a domain in which they recognized a lower percentage of objects, and another one in which performance decreased through successively working on the same questions (so that recognition of objects increased during the course of the experiment). Relatedly, Schooler and Hertwig (2005) have demonstrated, by means of extensive simulation work, that forgetting of information can aid heuristic inference.

There is a lot of research on the recognition heuristic (see, e.g., three special issues of the journal *Judgment and Decision Making*: Marewski, Pohl, & Vitouch, 2010, 2011a, 2011b). example is the application of the recognition heuristic to understand group decision making. Imagine a three-member group performing the city population task. Two members opt for city A because they have heard of both cities A and B, and they had some knowledge about city A suggesting that it was larger; the third group member opted for city B because she recognized B but did not recognize A. In 65% of such cases where the recognition-based and the knowledge-based models disagreed, the group inference matched the predictions of the recognition-based majority model, which explained 90% of the group inferences when it could be applied (Reimer & Katsikopoulos, 2004).

A more practical application of the recognition heuristic comes in handy for sports fans and friends of sports betting. A simple way to make money in sports betting is to rely on heuristics to forecast who will win competitions. The recognition heuristic, for instance, forecasts the success of sports teams or players by ranking them according to how many times they were recognized by a specific sample of people: *forecast that sport teams or players who are recognized by more people will beat teams or players who are recognized by fewer people*. Serwe and Frings (2006) showed that such recognition-based forecasts, derived from asking amateur tennis players which Wimbledon players they recognized, were more accurate than predictions based on the official ATP Entry and ATP Champions Race Player Rankings in the Wimbledon 2004 tournament (72% versus 66% versus 68% correct predictions, respectively). Scheibehenne and Bröder (2007) replicated this surprising result for Wimbledon 2005, additionally demonstrating that recognition-based forecasts derived from amateurs and laypeople were together as good as Wimbledon experts' official seedings. Similar evidence for the success of the recognition heuristic as a prescriptive model has been reported for the FIFA World Cup, the European soccer championship, the English FA Cup, as well as the National Hockey League Stanley Cup in North America (Andersson, Edman, & Ekman, 2005; Ayton, Önkal, & McReynolds, 2011; Gröschner & Raab, 2006; Herzog & Hertwig, 2011; Pachur & Biele, 2007; Snook & Cullen, 2006).

The final application of the recognition heuristic that we want to present here in more detail falls into the domains of social psychology, sociology, and urban planning. It builds on Nobel Laureate Thomas Schelling's (1978) influential book *Micromotives and Macrobehavior* (see also Schelling, 1969; 1971) with its intriguing observation that observable patterns on the macro-level do not necessarily reflect intentions, desires, or goals of agents on the micro-level. In his classic model on neighborhood segregation, individuals with no desire to be segregated from those who belong to other social groups will nevertheless end up in clusters of their own type. Most extensions of Schelling's model have replicated this result. The setup of the simulations is the following: simulated agents of at least two different types are distributed across a board. Some places are not occupied. A sequential process then unfolds by which unhappy agents move from unacceptable to acceptable locations, with movers picked at random from the list of all unhappy agents and then moving to the nearest acceptable location. Whether an agent is happy and wants to stay or is unhappy and wants to move (micro-motive) is determined by the composition of its neighborhood. Specifically, agents stay unless they are surrounded by a majority of other-type neighbors. In other words, they do not have any problem with other-type agents, but they simply do not want to find themselves surrounded by more other-type neighbors than same-type neighbors. There is an important mismatch between theory and observation that has received relatively little attention. Whereas Schelling-inspired models typically predict (and find) large degrees of segregation starting from virtually any initial condition, the empirical literature documents considerable heterogeneity in measured levels of segregation (e.g., Ellen, 1998).

To remedy this mismatch, Berg, Hoffrage, and Abramczuk (2010) proposed to augment the classic Schelling model by recognition, specifically, by *FACE-recognition* (the acronym stands for *F*ast *A*cceptance by *C*ommon *E*xperience; see also Berg, Abramczuk, & Hoffrage, 2013). As in the classic Schelling model, agents in a simulated world decide whether to stay or to move to a new spot depending on the proportion of neighbors they find acceptable. In the FACE-recognition augmented model, however, agents' classifications of a particular neighbor as acceptable or not is not exclusively driven by group type. In fact, classification of another agent is done by a lexicographic strategy in which this agent's group type comes second. It is trumped by positive experience from previous encounters (with positive experience being defined as time spent with this individual agent in a neighborhood in which one was happy). The augmented model nests classic Schelling: when agents have no recognition memory, judgments about the acceptability of a neighbor, present or prospective, rely solely on his or her group type. A very small amount of recognition memory, however, eventually leads to different classifications that, in turn, produce dramatic macro-level effects resulting in significantly higher levels of integration and, therefore, brings predicted distributions of segregation more in line with real-world observation.

What is particularly interesting about this work is that the causal loop that connects micro and macro levels operates in both directions (Coleman, 1994), thereby structuring the co-evolution of individual behavior and the external environment. The macro pattern in the neighborhood influences the level of happiness experienced at the micro level: who the neighbors are determines whether agents want to stay or move. These decisions made on the micro level, in turn, shape macro patterns by affecting the composition of neighborhoods. While the notion of ecological rationality typically focusses on the influence of the environment on the functioning of the heuristics, the FACE-recognition model also looks at the other direction, namely how heuristics (micro) shape the environment (macro).

Take-the-best

We already mentioned that Hoffrage (1995) tried to unconfound item difficulty from sampling procedure, and that he tested, among others, whether participants' choices (and the related confidences) in city comparisons can be modelled with the PMM algorithm. The former provided the ground for the discovery and formulation of the recognition heuristic (Goldstein & Gigerenzer, 2002), and the latter led to a modification of the PMM algorithm, which was later called the take-the-best heuristic (Gigerenzer & Goldstein, 1996). Unlike Hoffrage (1995) who focused on take-the-best as a behavioral model, Gigerenzer and Goldstein (1996) scrutinized this heuristic as a prescriptive model and evaluated its performance against benchmarks such as a linear model with equal weights (also referred to as Dawes' rule, named after Dawes, 1979, who entitled his article "The robust beauty of improper linear models," p. 571) or multiple regression. Before they presented their results for the complete paired comparison of all German cities with more than 100,000 inhabitants, Gigerenzer and Goldstein asked, at various occasions such as conferences, what colleagues predicted for this contest. Here are the building blocks that define take-the-best, the David in this David against Goliath contest:

Search rule: *search through cues in order of their validity.*
Stopping rule: *stop when finding the first cue that discriminates between the alternatives.*
Decision rule: *infer that the alternative with the positive cue value has the higher value on the criterion (cue values have been coded such that the correlation between cue and criterion was positive).*

Take-the-best uses, for most comparisons, only part of the information. The computations necessary to set it up can be performed on the backside of a napkin (remember that cue validities are simple proportions, namely of correct predictions divided by all inferences that a cue allows). Finally, execution of the heuristic once the order of cue validities is determined does not require any computation at all. In contrast, multiple regression (Goliath) is a linear model that uses all information. In order to estimate its weights, it inverts the cue inter-correlation matrix, and in order to execute multiple regression, one needs to multiply the cue values of each alternative with the weights and to compare the scores of the two alternatives. The colleagues predicted that multiple regression would clearly outperform take-the-best, most estimated by about 5–10 percentage points more correct inferences. Granted, multiple regression won the contest, but only by a very slight margin (69.4% versus 69.1%). Moreover, take-the-best achieved its amazing performance even though it looked up only about half as many cue values as multiple regression did.

The next surprise came when Czerlinski, Gigerenzer, and Goldstein (1999) repeated the contest in 20 different real-world environments. A major difference in the set-up was that they split each item set into two halves, gave each strategy the opportunity to fix its parameters (for take-the-best, the order of cues, for multiple regression the weights, and for tallying the cue directions) on one half, and then tested the strategies' performance on the other half. With such out-of-sample predictions and across the 20 data sets, the two simple heuristics, take-the-best (71%) and tallying (69%) even outperformed multiple regression (68%). Gigerenzer and Brighton (2009) reached the same conclusion when they pitted take-the-best against even more complex, information-greedy optimization strategies (sort of Bigger-Goliaths), such as the decision tree induction algorithm C4.5 (Quinlan & Cameron-Jones, 1993), or *C*lassification *A*nd *R*egression *T*rees (CART; Breiman, Friedman, Olshen, & Stone, 1984). The rationale behind this pattern of results is the following: in a given data set, the parameters of a more complex model reflect not only systematic variance between variables that generalizes across various samples drawn from the same parent population, but also sample-specific random fluctuations. In contrast, simple models are better protected against such "overfitting," simply because they squeeze out less information from a given sample in the first place.

On a final note, simple heuristics such as take-the-best fare well not only as prescriptive models but also when it comes to describing how people are actually deciding, in particular under time pressure (Rieskamp & Hoffrage, 1999; 2008) or when information acquisition is costly (Bröder, 2000; for overviews, see Bröder, 2012, and Bröder & Gaissmaier, 2007).

Tallying

Tallying is a simple linear model that counts positive cue values. It can be considered a heuristic as it does not seek to find the optimal weights, but simply weighs cues equally (Dawes, 1979).[3] The two examples that we selected for the present section to illustrate the success of tallying both come from venture capitalist decision making, but we hasten to add that the general finding is not at all restricted to this domain. Woike, Hoffrage, and Petty (2015) simulated the performance of venture capitalists (VCs) who had to select business plans for a portfolio. The business plans were described by binary cues. The VCs saw the plans one after the other and had to decide whether or not to invest in a given plan (without being able to go back to a plan they had rejected). After they made a decision, they received feedback on the success of the plan. Woike and colleagues simulated various VCs, which differed with respect to the strategy they used to make their investment decisions: they either used a simple heuristic, namely tallying (which is, in their setup, equivalent to equal weighting) or a fast-and-frugal tree, or they used a more complex strategy, namely logistic regression or CART. The strategies updated their parameters continuously, that is, after each feedback. To evaluate the ecological rationality of these strategies, the authors also analyzed how the strategies' performance was affected by (statistical) properties of the decision making environment. These environmental properties included the selectivity of feedback (information about the success or failure of a plan was given either for all plans or only for those in which a VC invested), the relative importance of cues (that is, how well the cues could predict the success of the plans and how they were distributed with respect to this predictive power), and the number of cues that characterized the plans.

A major result of this simulation study was that tallying turned out to be competitive with the more complex benchmark strategies and that, notably, its competitiveness was robust across environments. The finding that tallying was able to match – and in some conditions even to outperform – the two more complex strategies can largely be attributed to the robustness of the strategies' parameter estimates (tallying only had to estimate cue directionality). As we already explained above, complex strategies suffer from overfitting – not when fitting known data, but when predicting new data. The set-up of this simulation implemented exactly this realistic feature, namely that strategies had to make an investment decision without being clairvoyant. Two other important results of this simulation study were these: the performance of the decision strategies depended critically on the environment, specifically, on how cues differed with respect to their potential to predict success of a plan; and learning only from those plans that the simulated VC invested in drastically reduced the VC's potential to learn from experience.

Our second example is the work of Åstebro and Elhedhli (2006), who studied 561 submissions to the *Canadian Invention Assistance Program* between 1989 and 1994. Entrepreneurs applying to the program have to fill out a questionnaire on 37 characteristics of the venture, such as the costs of production and potential market; their responses are then evaluated by full-time in-house analysts. Åstebro and Elhedhli identified a successful conjunctive heuristic that takes into account only 21 of the 37 predictors to assess future commercial success, and that incorporates elements of tallying: *predict that a venture will be financially successful when two conditions are met: first, the sum of good characteristics (predictors associated with a higher success rate) is greater than or equal to a threshold of 5, and second, the sum of bad characteristics (predictors associated with a lower success rate) is smaller than or equal to a threshold of 2.* This heuristic led to a remarkable out-of-sample predictive accuracy of 86%, which was more accurate than a more complex regression model that took into account all 37 predictors (78.6% accuracy) and also better than – albeit not statistically different from – the program's in-house analysts' accuracy (82.6%).

Fast-and-frugal trees

Consider a medical doctor who needs to select a suitable pain medication for one of his patients. How people respond to different medications depends, among other factors, on their genes. There is more and more data available concerning how specific genes can be used to predict people's metabolism for specific drugs (Van Rooij, Roederer, Wareham, van Rooij, McLeod, & Marsh, 2015). But can doctors search for and sift through such data and draw the correct conclusions from it while other patients are lined up waiting for treatment? This situation seems to be like a textbook case for clinical decision aids, which can be implemented as fast-and-frugal trees (Martignon, Katsikopoulos, & Woike, 2008; 2012). Building on this work, van Rooij et al. (2015) developed a tree – they called it an augmented fast-and-frugal tree – that is easy to understand and use (Figure 18.1).

A maximum of four questions must be answered, and some of the answers can potentially be filled in automatically based on the patient's file, such as information about their specific genotype/phenotype. Each question can only be answered with either yes or no, and if any question is answered with a no, a decision can be made immediately. In other words, the tree can be described by the following building blocks:

Search rule: *look up cues in the order of their importance.*
Stopping rule: *stop search as soon as one cue allows it.*
Decision rule: *slassify according to this cue.*

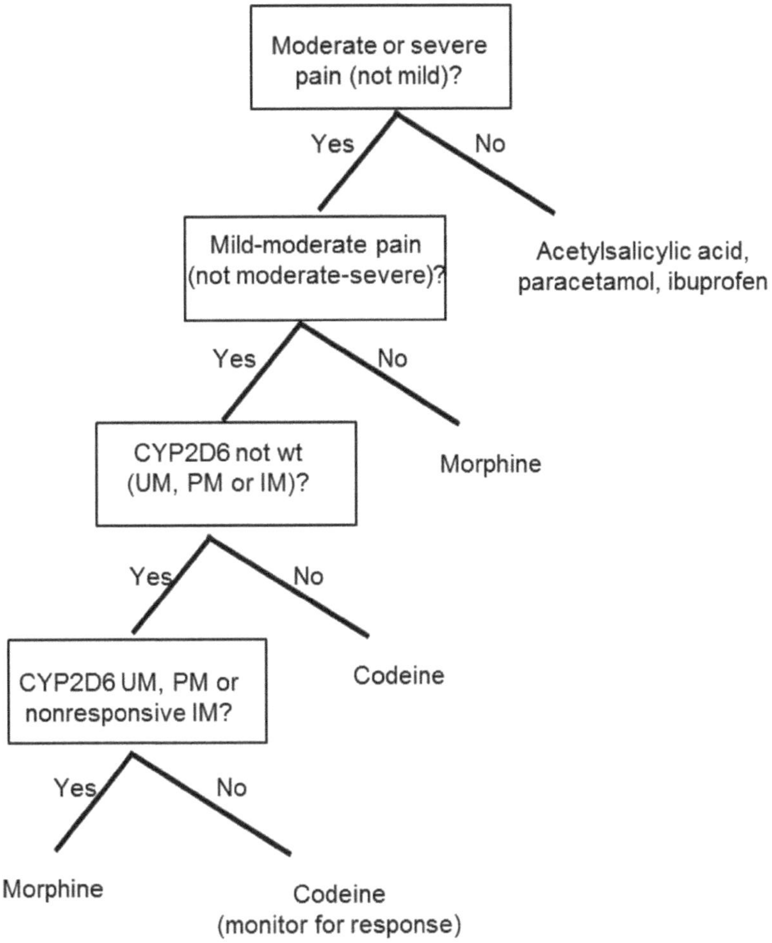

Figure 18.1 Van Rooij et al.'s (2015) augmented fast-and-frugal tree for selecting pain medication (adopted from their page 123).

The tree can be implemented in a computerized decision aid, such that doctors simply have to respond to the questions on flash cards. Ultimately, the tree not only simplifies the doctor's decision making without sacrificing any accuracy (it even reduces the potential for mistakes), but it also speeds up the process so that doctors can spend more time with the patient (for other examples of fast-and-frugal heuristics in medical applications, see Marewski & Gigerenzer, 2012).

Woike, Hoffrage, and Martignon (2017) went one step further and studied the ecological rationality of various tree construction principles. Specifically, they proposed how trees can be constructed and they compared (in 11 medical datasets) the performance of these variants to a Bayesian classifier that is normative when fitting known data and to a "Naïve Bayesian" classifier that can be conceived as a heuristic approach because it simply treats cues as independent of each other. Results show that when classifying so far unseen patients the two heuristic approaches, Naïve Bayesian and fast-and-frugal trees, generally outperform the full Bayesian model – both with respect to overall predictive accuracy and in Receiver Operating Characteristics (ROC) curves, which describe a model's accuracy by plotting the two possible classification errors across various classification thresholds against each other. Importantly, Woike et al. could identify which environmental property gave an edge for which of the tree construction principles. In other words, the success of fast-and-frugal trees turned out to be grounded in how well their construction principles allowed them to exploit the structure of information in the environment (i.e., in a given dataset). As a final note, we would like to point out that Woike et al. (2017) also provided a theoretical integration of the two branches of research that we described at the outset of this chapter, namely research on fast-and-frugal heuristics (in the footsteps of Gigerenzer et al., 1991) and research on representation formats (Gigerenzer & Hoffrage, 1995). Specifically, they have shown that a fast-and-frugal tree can be: (1) conceived as a pruned version of a natural frequency tree; (2) represented as a special case of a linear model; and (3) match the outcomes of a lexicographic strategy, akin to take-the-best (see also Martignon et al., 2008).

Conclusion

This chapter combines three elements: a personally colored review of the fast-and-frugal heuristics research program with a focus on its historical and theoretical origins; a synopsis of its major concepts; and a few selected examples to illustrate its wide range of findings and applications. At the close of this chapter, let us highlight three take-away points.

First, the fast-and-frugal heuristics program did not result from a master plan of a few scientists who wanted to start exactly this new research program. Rather, it originated from critique of the heuristics-and-biases program – specifically, critique concerning its vague descriptions of its heuristics, its adoption of content-blind norms, and, relatedly, its lack of environmental and ecological analyses. The desire to turn this critique into constructive contributions, which was additionally stimulated by serendipity and surprising findings, provided the fertile ground for the emergence of new theoretical ideas. Over the years, some intuitions that were already fully present in the early papers of the ABC Research Group, new questions, explanations, and ideas, and a growing understanding of the wide implications turned into and shaped a full blown research program on fast-and-frugal heuristics.

Second, the combination of the strong desire for theoretical precision, reflected in the formulation of cognitive processes as algorithmic models, and the theoretical insight that the development and functioning of heuristics cannot be separated from the environment turned out to be a strong recipe for stimulating a wide range of research – prescriptive and descriptive, theoretical and applied – using a wide range of methodologies and involving various disciplines.

Third, despite being only 30 years old, the fast-and-frugal heuristics program already developed a unique perspective on larger discourses that go beyond its home field of cognitive psychology. In times where the mainstream development in many areas goes towards more information, computation, optimization, and complexity, the insights from the fast-and-frugal heuristics program serve as an important reminder that simple strategies can be remarkably powerful and often beat more complex approaches not only in terms of cognitive plausibility and feasibility, but also in terms of accuracy. To the extent that people not only use such simple strategies naturally but can also learn new (fast-and-frugal, feasible, and fit) decision strategies, policy makers and others who want to steer people's behavior and decisions can complement nudging by boosting: instead of changing the environment, they may teach fast-and-frugal trees or other simple strategies, thereby ultimately strengthening people's autonomy to make better decisions (Grüne-Yanoff & Hertwig, 2016).

Ideally, the future of this program will see at least as many fruitful surprises as the past. But this will also depend on you, dear reader. We hope this chapter was able to stimulate your own thinking about the issues you care about, and we encourage you to contribute the resulting ideas, questions, criticisms, and findings to the social process called science – here, the science of heuristics.

Acknowledgments

We would like to thank Linden Ball, Gerd Gigerenzer, Matthieu Legeret, and Jan Woike for helpful comments on previous versions of this chapter, and the Swiss National Science Foundation (grants SNF 100014–140503/1 and P2LAP1_161922) for its financial support.

Notes

1 The gist of these two ideas was also present in Gigerenzer and Hoffrage (1995). Their Table 2 listed the algorithms, Bayesian and non-Bayesian, that participants used to solve the task, and the prediction and finding that external representation of information mattered can be seen as another form of ecological rationality.

2 Nowadays, 200 years after Laplace, it seems we witness another large step on this route that started with a thought experiment and that continued with the construction of normative theories. Science and society now enter a phase in which not only theories are constructed according to this vision, but also nothing less than reality. Many scientists, companies, and policy makers are fascinated by the opportunities of Big Data. They work on algorithms, technologies, infrastructure, laws, and people's mindset and they appear like priests who are on a mission to implement a kingdom of the Laplacean demon on Earth (Hoffrage & Marewski, 2015). Yet, even with Big Data at one's disposal, one is not generally omniscient about the future, as the dismal failure of Google Flu Trends documents. What had initially been celebrated as the showcase of Big Data predictive analytics was silently buried when over years it consistently failed to predict influenza-related doctor visits.

3 An equal-weight linear model computes the score of an object as the sum of all positive cue values minus the sum of all negative cue values. In contrast, tallying only counts the positive ones. If all cue values are known, the two strategies will always favor the same object in a comparion task; if information is missing, the two may occasionally make different predictions (see Gigerenzer & Goldstein, 1996).

References

Allais, M. (1953). Le comportement de l'homme rationnel devant le risqué: Critique des postulats et axiomes de l'Ecole Americaine. *Econometrica*, 21(4), 503–546.

Anderson, J., & Lebiere, C. (1998). The atomic components of thought. Mahwah, NJ: Lawrence Erlbaum Associates.

Andersson, P., Edman, J., & Ekman, M. (2005). Predicting the World Cup 2002 in soccer: Performance and confidence of experts and non-experts. *International Journal of Forecasting*, *21*(3), 565–576.

Åstebro, T., & Elhedhli, S. (2006). The effectiveness of simple decision heuristics: Forecasting commercial success for early-stage ventures. *Management Science*, *52*(3), 395–409.

Ayton, P., Önkal, D., & McReynolds, L. (2011). Effects of ignorance and information on judgments and decisions. *Judgment and Decision Making*, *6*, 381–391.

Berg, N., Abramczuk, K., & Hoffrage, U. (2013). Fast acceptance by common experience: Augmenting Schelling's neighborhood segregation model with FACE-recognition. In R. Hertwig, U. Hoffrage, & the ABC Research Group, *Simple heuristics in a social world* (pp. 225–257). New York: Oxford University Press.

Berg, N., & Gigerenzer, G. (2010). As-if behavioral economics: Neoclassical economics in disguise? *History of Economic Ideas*, XVIII(1), 133–165.

Berg, N., Hoffrage, U., & Abramczuk, K. (2010). Fast acceptance by common experience: FACE-recognition in Schelling's model of neighborhood segregation. *Judgment and Decision Making*, *5*, 391–410.

Bingham, C. B., & Eisenhardt, K. M. (2011). Rational heuristics: the 'simple rules' that strategists learn from process experience. *Strategic Management Journal*, *32*(13), 1437–1464.

Breiman, L., Friedman, J. H., Olshen, R. A., & Stone, C. J. (1984). *Classification and regression trees*. Monterey, CA: Wadsworth & Brooks.

Bröder, A. (2000). Assessing the empirical validity of the "Take-the-best" heuristic as a model of human probabilistic inference. *Journal of Experimental Psychology: Learning, Memory, and Cognition, 26*, 1332–1346.

Bröder, A. (2012). The quest for take the best – Insights and outlooks from experimental research. In P. Todd, G. Gigerenzer, & the ABC Research Group, *Ecological rationality: Intelligence in the world* (pp. 216–240). New York: Oxford University Press.

Bröder, A., & Gaissmaier, W. (2007). Sequential processing of cues in memory-based multiattribute decisions. *Psychonomic Bulletin & Review, 14*(5), 895–900.

Brunswik, E. (1955). Representative design and probabilistic theory in a functional psychology. *Psychological Review, 62*(3), 193–217.

Busemeyer, J., & Townsend, J. T. (1993). Decision field theory: A dynamic cognition approach to decision making. *Psychological Review, 100*, 432–459.

Coleman, J. S. (1994). *Foundations of social theory*. Harvard University Press.

Czerlinski, J., Gigerenzer, G., & Goldstein, D. G. (1999). How good are simple heuristics? In G. Gigerenzer, P. M. Todd, & the ABC Research Group, *Simple heuristics that make us smart* (pp. 97–118). New York: Oxford University Press.

Dawes, R. M. (1979). The robust beauty of improper linear models in decision making. *American Psychologist, 34*, 571–582.

Dimov, C. M., Marewski, J. N., & Schooler, L. J. (2017). A database of ACT-R models of decision making. In M. K. van Vugt, A. P. Banks, & W. G. Kennedy (Eds.), *Proceedings of the 15th International Conference on Cognitive Modeling* (pp. 217–218). Coventry, United Kingdom: University of Warwick.

Duncker, K. (1935). *Zur Psychologie des produktiven Denkens* [The psychology of productive thinking]. Berlin: Julius Springer.

Dunwoody, P. T. (2009). Introduction to the special issue: Coherence and correspondence in judgment and decision making. *Judgment and Decision Making, 4*(2), 113–115.

Edwards, W. (1954). The theory of decision making. *Psychological Bulletin, 51*(4), 380–417.

Einstein, A. (1905). Über einen die Erzeugung und Verwandlung des Lichtes betreffenden heuristischen Gesichtspunkt. *Annalen der Physik, 17*, 132–148.

Ellen, I. G. (1998). Stable racial integration in the contemporary United States: An empirical overview. *Journal of Urban Affairs, 20*, 27–42.

Garcia-Retamero, R., & Hoffrage, U. (2006). How causal knowledge simplifies decision-making. *Minds and Machines, 16*, 365–380.

Gigerenzer, G. (1991). How to make cognitive illusions disappear: Beyond "heuristics and biases". *European Review of Social Psychology, 2*(1), 83–115.

Gigerenzer, G. (1994). Why the distinction between single-event probabilities and frequencies is relevant for psychology (and vice versa). In G. Wright & P. Ayton (Eds.), *Subjective probability* (pp. 129–161). New York: Wiley.

Gigerenzer, G. (1996). On narrow norms and vague heuristics: A reply to Kahneman and Tversky. *Psychological Review, 103*(3), 592–596.

Gigerenzer, G. (2007). *Gut feelings: The intelligence of the unconscious*. New York: Viking Press.

Gigerenzer, G. (2015). *Simply rational: Decision making in the real world*. New York: Oxford University Press.

Gigerenzer, G., & Brighton, H. (2009). Homo heuristicus: Why biased minds make better inferences. *Topics in Cognitive Science, 1*(1), 107–143.

Gigerenzer, G., & Engel, C. (Eds.). (2006). *Heuristics and the law*. Cambridge, MA: MIT Press.

Gigerenzer, G., & Gaissmaier, W. (2011). Heuristic decision making. *Annual Review of Psychology, 62*, 451–482.

Gigerenzer, G., & Goldstein, D. G. (1996). Reasoning the fast and frugal way: Models of bounded rationality. *Psychological Review, 103*, 650–669.

Gigerenzer, G., Hertwig, R., Hoffrage, U., & Sedlmeier, P. (2008). Cognitive illusions reconsidered. In C. R. Plott & V. L. Smith (Eds.), *Handbook of experimental economics results (Vol. 1, pp. 1018–1034)*. Amsterdam: North Holland/Elsevier Press.

Gigerenzer, G., Hertwig, R., & Pachur, T. (2011). *Heuristics: The foundations of adaptive behavior*. New York: Oxford University Press.

Gigerenzer, G., & Hoffrage, U. (1995). How to improve Bayesian reasoning without instruction: Frequency formats. *Psychological Review, 102*, 684–704.

Gigerenzer, G., Hoffrage, U., & Kleinbölting, H. (1991). Probabilistic mental models: A Brunswikian theory of confidence. *Psychological Review, 98*(4), 506–528.

Gigerenzer, G., & Selten, R. (2001). ***Bounded rationality:*** *The adaptive toolbox*. Cambridge, MA: MIT Press.

Gigerenzer, G., Todd, P. M., & the ABC Research Group (1999). *Simple heuristics that make us smart*. New York: Oxford University Press.

Goldstein, D. G., & Gigerenzer, G. (2002). Models of ecological rationality: The recognition heuristic. *Psychological Review, 109*, 75–90.

Gröschner, C., & Raab, M. (2006). Vorhersagen im Fußball [Predictions in soccer]. *Zeitschrift für Sportpsychologie, 13*(1), 23–36.

Grüne-Yanoff, T., & Hertwig, R. (2016). Nudge versus boost: how coherent are policy and theory? ***Minds and Machines**, 26*(1–2), 149–183.

Hafenbrädl, S., & Hoffrage, U. (2015). Toward an ecological analysis of Bayesian inferences: How task characteristics influence responses. ***Frontiers** in Psychology, 6*, 939.

Hafenbrädl, S., Waeger, D., Marewski, J. N., & Gigerenzer, G. (2016). Applied decision making with fast-and-frugal heuristics. *Journal of Applied Research in Memory and Cognition, 5*(2), 215–231.

Hammond, K. R. (1996). ***Human judgment and social policy: Irreducible uncertainty, inevitable error, unavoidable injustice***. New York: Oxford University Press.

Hertwig, R., Fischbacher, U., & Bruhin, A. (2013). Simple heuristics in a social game. In R. Hertwig, U. Hoffrage, & the ABC Research Group, *Simple heuristics in a social world* (pp. 39–65). Oxford University Press.

Hertwig, R., Hoffrage, U., & Martignon, L. (1999). Quick estimation: Letting the environment do the work. In G. Gigerenzer, P. M. Todd, & the ABC Research Group, *Simple heuristics that make us smart* (pp. 209–234). New York: Oxford University Press.

Hertwig, R., Hoffrage, U., & the ABC Research Group (2013). *Simple heuristics in a social world*. Oxford University Press.

Hertwig, R., & Pachur, T. (2015). Heuristics, history of. In J. D. Wright (Ed.), ***International encyclopedia of the social & behavioral sciences*** (2nd ed., pp. 829–835). Oxford: Elsevier.

Herzog, S. M., & Hertwig, R. (2011). The wisdom of ignorant crowds: Predicting sport outcomes by mere recognition. ***Judgment and Decision Making**, 6*(1), 58–72.

Hoffrage, U. (1995). ***Zur Angemessenheit subjektiver** Sicherheits-Urteile. **Eine Exploration der** Theorie der **probabilistischen mentalen** Modelle*. [The adequacy of subjective confidence judgments: Studies concerning the theory of probabilistic mental models]. Doctoral dissertation, University of Salzburg, Austria.

Hoffrage, U. (2005). Heuristics: Fast and frugal. In B. C. Everitt & D. C. Howell (Eds.), ***Encyclopedia of statistics in behavioral science*** (Vol. 2, pp. 795–799). Wiley: Chichester, UK.

Hoffrage, U. (2011). Recognition judgments and the performance of the recognition heuristic depend on the size of the reference class. ***Judgment and Decision Making**, 6*(1), 43–57.

Hoffrage, U. (2016). Overconfidence. In R. F. Pohl (Ed.), ***Cognitive illusions: Intriguing phenomena in thinking, judgement, and memory*** (2nd ed., pp. 291–314). Hove, UK: Psychology Press.

Hoffrage, U., Hafenbrädl, S., & Bouquet, C. (2015). Natural frequencies facilitate diagnostic inferences of managers. ***Frontiers** in Psychology, 6*, 642.

Hoffrage, U., Krauss, S., Martignon, L., & Gigerenzer, G. (2015). Natural frequencies improve Bayesian reasoning in simple and complex inference tasks. ***Frontiers** in Psychology, 6*, 1473.

Hoffrage, U., Lindsey, S., Hertwig, R., & Gigerenzer, G. (2000). Communicating statistical information. ***Science**, 290*, 2261–2262.

Hoffrage, U., & Marewski, J. (2015). Unveiling the Lady in Black: Modeling and aiding intuition. *Journal of Applied Research in **Memory and Cognition**, 4*, 145–163.

Hogarth, R. M., & Karelaia, N. (2007). Heuristic and linear models of judgment: Matching rules and environments. *Psychological Review, 114*(3), 733–758.

Kahneman, D. (2011). ***Thinking, fast and slow***. New York: Farrar, Strauss, Giroux.

Kahneman, D., Slovic, P., & Tversky, A. (Eds.). (1982). ***Judgment under uncertainty:*** *Heuristics **and** biases*. New York: Cambridge University Press.

Kahneman, D., & Tversky, A. (1972). Subjective probability: A judgment of representativeness. ***Cognitive** Psychology, 3*, 430–454.

Kahneman, D., & Tversky, A. (1996). On the reality of cognitive illusions. *Psychological Review, 103*(3), 582–591.

Laplace, P. S. (1814/1951). A philosophical essay on probabilities (F. W. Truscott & F. L. Emory, Trans.). New York: Dover. (Original work published 1814).

Locke, J. (1690/2004). *An essay concerning human understanding.* London: Penguin.

Lopes, L. L. (1991). The rhetoric of irrationality. *Theory & Psychology, 1*(1), 65–82.

Marewski, J. N., Gaissmaier, W., & Gigerenzer, G. (2010). Good judgments do not require complex cognition. *Cognitive Processing, 11*(2), 103–121.

Marewski, J. N., & Gigerenzer, G. (2012). Heuristic decision making in medicine. *Dialogues in Clinical Neuroscience, 14*(1), 77–89.

Marewski, J. N., & Mehlhorn, K. (2011). Using the ACT-R architecture to specify 39 quantitative process models of decision making. *Judgment and Decision Making, 6*(6), 439–519.

Marewski, J. N., Pohl, R. F., & Vitouch, O. (2010). Recognition-based judgments and decisions: Introduction to the special issue (Vol. 1). *Judgment and Decision Making, 5*(4), 207–215.

Marewski, J. N., Pohl, R. F., & Vitouch, O. (2011a). Recognition-based judgments and decisions: Introduction to the special issue (II). *Judgment and Decision Making, 6*(1), 1–6.

Marewski, J. N., Pohl, R. F., & Vitouch, O. (2011b). Recognition-based judgments and decisions: What we have learned (so far). *Judgment and Decision Making, 6*(5), 359–380.

Marewski, J. N., & Schooler, L. J. (2011). Cognitive niches: An ecological model of strategy selection. *Psychological Review, 118*(3), 393–437.

Martignon, L., & Hoffrage, U. (2002). Fast, frugal and fit: Simple heuristics for paired comparison. *Theory and Decision, 52*, 29–71.

Martignon, L. F., Katsikopoulos, K. V., & Woike, J. K. (2012). Naïve, fast, and frugal trees for classification. In P. M. Todd, G. Gigerenzer, & the ABC Research Group, *Ecological rationality: Intelligence in the world* (pp. 360–378). Oxford: Oxford University Press.

Martignon, L., Katsikopoulos, K. V., & Woike, J. K. (2008). Categorization with limited resources: A family of simple heuristics. *Journal of Mathematical Psychology, 52*(6), 352–361.

Newell, A., & Simon, H. (1972). *Human problem solving.* Englewood Cliffs, NJ: Prentice Hall.

Pachur, T., & Biele, G. (2007). Forecasting from ignorance: The use and usefulness of recognition in lay predictions of sports events. *Acta Psychologica, 125*(1), 99–116.

Payne, J. W., Bettman, J. R., & Johnson, E. J. (1993). *The adaptive decision maker.* New York: Cambridge University Press.

Quinlan, J. R., & Cameron-Jones, R. M. (1993, April). FOIL: A midterm report. In *Proceedings 1993 European conference on machine learning* (pp. 3–20). Springer Berlin Heidelberg.

Rand, D. G., Peysakhovich, A., Kraft-Todd, G. T., Newman, G. E., Wurzbacher, O., Nowak, M. A., & Green, J. D. (2014). Social heuristics shape intuitive cooperation. *Nature Communications, 5*, Article number: 3677.

Reimer, T., & Katsikopoulos, K. (2004). The use of recognition in group decision-making. *Cognitive Science, 28*, 1009–1029.

Rieskamp, J., & Hoffrage, U. (1999). When do people use simple heuristics, and how can we tell? In G. Gigerenzer, P. M. Todd, & the ABC Research Group, *Simple heuristics that make us smart* (pp. 141–167). New York: Oxford University Press.

Rieskamp, J., & Hoffrage, U. (2008). Inferences under time pressure: How opportunity costs affect strategy selection. *Acta Psychologica, 127*(2), 258–276.

Savage, L. J. (1972). *The foundations of statistics.* New York: Courier Corporation.

Scheibehenne, B., & Bröder, A. (2007). Predicting Wimbledon 2005 tennis results by mere player name recognition. *International Journal of Forecasting, 23*(3), 415–426.

Schelling, T. C. (1969). Models of segregation. *American Economic Review, 59*, 488–493.

Schelling, T. C. (1971). Dynamic models of segregation. *Journal of Mathematical Sociology, 1*, 143–186.

Schelling, T. C. (1978). *Micromotives and macrobehavior.* New York: Norton.

Schooler, L. J., & Hertwig, R. (2005). How forgetting aids heuristic inference. *Psychological Review, 112*(3), 610–628.

Serwe, S., & Frings, C. (2006). Who will win Wimbledon? The recognition heuristic in predicting sports events. *Journal of Behavioral Decision Making, 19*(4), 321–332.

Simon, H. (1982). *Models of bounded rationality.* Cambridge, MA: The MIT Press.

Simon, H. (1990). *Reason in human affairs.* Stanford: Stanford University Press.

Snook, B., & Cullen, R. M. (2006). Recognizing National Hockey League greatness with an ignorance-based heuristic. *Canadian Journal of Experimental Psychology/Revue canadienne de psychologie expérimentale, 60*(1), 33–43.

Todd, P. M., Gigerenzer, G., & the ABC Research Group (2012). *Ecological rationality: Intelligence in the world.* Oxford: Oxford University Press.

Tversky, A., & Kahneman, D. E. (1974). Judgments under uncertainty: Heuristics and biases. *Science, 185*, 1124–1131.

Van Rooij, T., Roederer, M., Wareham, T., Van Rooij, I., McLeod, H. L., & Marsh, S. (2015). Fast and frugal trees: Translating population-based pharmacogenomics to medication prioritization. *Personalized Medicine, 12*(2), 117–128.

Von Neumann, J., & Morgenstern, O. (1944). *Theory of games and economic behavior.* Princeton, NJ: Princeton University Press.

Woike, J. K., Hoffrage, U., & Martignon, L. (2017), June 26. Integrating and testing natural frequencies, Naïve Bayes, and fast-and-frugal trees. *Decision.* Advance online publication. http://dx.doi.org/10.1037/dec0000086

Woike, J. K., Hoffrage, U., & Petty, J. S. (2015). Picking profitable investments: The success of equal weighting in simulated venture capitalist decision making. *Journal of Business Research, s*(8), 1705–1716.

19

MENTAL MODELS AND REASONING

Philip N. Johnson-Laird, Geoffrey P. Goodwin, and Sangeet S. Khemlani

Introduction

The theory of mental models has a long history going back to the logic diagrams of C.S. Peirce in the nineteenth century. But it was the psychologist and physiologist Kenneth Craik who first introduced mental models into psychology. Individuals build a model of the world in their minds, so that they can simulate future events and thereby make prescient decisions (Craik, 1943). But reasoning, he thought, depends on verbal rules. He died tragically young, and had no chance to test these ideas. The current "model" theory began with the hypothesis that reasoning too depends on simulations using mental models (Johnson-Laird, 1980).

Reasoning is a systematic process that starts with semantic information in a set of premises, and transfers it to a conclusion. Semantic information increases with the number of possibilities that an assertion eliminates, and so it is inversely related to an assertion's probability (Johnson-Laird, 1983, Ch. 2; Adams, 1998). And semantic information yields a taxonomy of reasoning. Deductions do not increase semantic information even if they concern probabilities, but inductions do increase it. Simple inductions, such as generalizations, rule out more possibilities than the premises do. Abductions, which are a special case of induction, introduce concepts that are not in the premises in order to create explanations (see Koslowski, this volume). The present chapter illustrates how the model theory elucidates these three major sorts of reasoning: deduction, abduction, and induction.

Deductions yield *valid* inferences in which true premises are bound to yield true conclusions. Psychologists sometimes suggest that deductions play less of a role in daily life than probabilities. However, the maintenance of consistent beliefs is necessary for sensible decisions, because if beliefs are inconsistent then at least one of them is false, and to act on a false belief is a recipe for disaster (see Collins & Hahn, this volume). To test consistency, however, is to use a deductive procedure. Indeed, some systems of logic work on the principle that a deduction is valid because its premises are inconsistent with the denial of its conclusion (Jeffrey, 1981). And deductions can be about uncertainties, possibilities, and probabilities. So they are crucial in everyday life.

Abductions of explanations serve diverse purposes. They can resolve inconsistencies. You know that your friends have gone shopping, and that if so they'll be back in fifteen minutes. When they haven't returned in two hours, you worry. You inferred their imminent return, and their absence conflicts with your conclusion. In orthodox logic, you don't have to withdraw your conclusion. Logic is ***monotonic***: new facts imply new conclusions, never the need to retract old ones, not even those that facts contradict. Everyday reasoning, however, is not monotonic, and so theorists have devised various "nonmonotonic" logics that allow facts to undermine conclusions (see Stenning & Varga, this volume, and Oaksford & Chater, this volume). The model theory takes a different tack: your main concern is not to withdraw your conclusion, but to determine what's happened to your friends. You need an explanation of their delay so that you can decide what to do. Abduction generates explanations, and, as we show, it can lead to the withdrawal of conclusions. Abduction also underlies the development of computer programs – they are, in effect, explanations of how to get from a start to an end. And mental simulations underlie their abduction.

Simple inductions turn facts into general rules. You keep your money in a bank, because it will be safe. Your model of banks has gone beyond observation to generalization (for an account of the process, see Johnson-Laird, 1993). But canny inductions yield probabilities. You keep your money in a bank, because it is almost certain to be safe. You might even be prepared to infer a numerical value, say, 95%. The economist John Maynard Keynes tried to meld probability and deduction. That goal, too, is one to which the model theory aspires. In what follows, we review case studies illustrating the role of models in the three sorts of reasoning: deductions that draw conclusions from conditionals, abductions that resolve inconsistencies and that create programs, and inductions that yield numerical probabilities.

Deductions from conditionals

The model theory

The basic model theory is simple. People think about possibilities. They represent possibilities in mental models. And a model is a model because its structure corresponds to the structure of what it represents. So, a sequence of events can be simulated in a kinematic model that unfolds in time. An inference from premises is valid if its conclusion holds in all of their models. Intuitive reasoning copes only with a single mental model at a time, because it has no access to working memory, whereas deliberative reasoning can access working memory, and so it can construct alternative models and carry out more powerful computations (Johnson-Laird, 1983, Ch. 6). Like many "dual process" accounts (e.g., Kahneman, 2011), the model theory postulates one system (1) for intuitions and another system (2) for deliberations. In contrast, Evans (this volume) distinguishes, not two different systems, but two different sorts of process. Unlike other accounts, however, the model theory's two systems and the interactions between them are embodied in a computer program, ***mReasoner*** (Khemlani & Johnson-Laird, 2013). To illustrate the theory, we describe deductions from conditional assertions, because *if* is central to everyday reasoning.

Consider the following inference:

> If the car started, then the battery has power.
> The car started.
> What follows?

The conclusion is immediate: *the battery has power*. In contrast, consider this inference:

> If the car started, then the battery has power.
> The battery doesn't have power.
> What follows?

The inference is harder, and those individuals who rely only on intuition respond: "nothing follows". The conditional yields two *mental models*, which we represent in the following diagram:

car started	battery has power
. . .	

The first model represents the possibility in which both clauses in the conditional are true. For convenience, the diagram omits a symbol for conjunction, and uses English phrases, whereas actual models are representations of the world. The second mental model, shown as an ellipsis, has no explicit content, but stands in for the other possibilities in which the car didn't start. In the first inference, the premise that the car started picks out the explicit model, which yields the conclusion: *the battery has power.* But, in the second inference, the premise that the battery doesn't have power eliminates the explicit model, and nothing follows from the implicit model, because it has no content. Which explains the intuition that nothing follows. However, those who deliberate can flesh out mental models into *fully explicit models* of all the possibilities to which the conditional refers. These models enable them to draw a valid conclusion. Individuals can also list these possibilities (e.g., Barrouillet, Grosset, & Lecas, 2000). For a basic conditional (*If A then C*), where knowledge does not affect interpretation, they list them in the following order:

car started	battery has power	(A C: the explicit mental model)
not (car started)	not (battery has power)	(not-A not-C)
not (car started)	battery has power	(not-A C)

They also list the following case as not possible:

car started	not (battery has power)	(A not-C)

The premise that the battery doesn't have power rules out the first and third possibilities above, and the second possibility yields the valid conclusion:

The car didn't start.

Table 19.1 summarizes these models, and those for other sorts of conditionals, which we discuss.

Table 19.1 The sets of possibilities to which various sorts of conditional refer, depending on whether the conditionals are affirmed or denied. These possibilities correspond to fully explicit models of the conditionals, and the empty cells are cases that are not possible according to the conditionals. The two scopes of denial yield identical possibilities for biconditionals and relevance conditionals.

Basic conditionals e.g., *If the car started, then the battery has power.*			Biconditionals e.g., *If and only if the car started, then the battery has power.*		Relevance conditionals e.g., *If it's raining, then here's an umbrella.*	
Affirmed	Denied with large scope: *Not if A then C*	Denied with small scope: *If A then not C*	Affirmed	Denied	Affirmed	Denied
A C			A C		A C	
	A not-C	A not-C		A not-C		A not-C
not-A C		not-A C		not-A C	not-A C	
not-A not-C		not-A not-C	not-A not-C			not-A not-C

Every psychological theory of deduction explains the difference between the easy conditional inference (aka "modus ponens") and the difficult one (aka "modus tollens"). But, several results corroborate the model theory and challenge other accounts. One result is that the difficult inference becomes easier with biconditionals, for example:

If, and only if, the car started, then the battery has power.

The model theory predicts the effect (Johnson-Laird, Byrne, & Schaeken, 1992), because biconditionals have only two fully explicit models (see Table 19.1):

car started	battery has power	(A C)
not (car started)	not (battery has power)	(not-A not-C)

Another predicted result is that the difficult inference becomes easier when the categorical premise is presented first:

The battery doesn't have power.
If the car started, then the battery has power.

The categorical premise blocks the construction of the explicit mental model of the conditional premise, and so reasoners are more likely to consider the fully explicit model:

not (car started)	not (battery has power)

And it shows that the car didn't start (Girotto, Mazzocco, & Tasso, 1997). Theories based on formal rules predict neither of these effects (cf. Rips, 1994). In a review, Oberauer (2006) showed that the model theory also gives a better account of conditional reasoning than a probabilistic theory (Oaksford, Chater, & Larkin, 2000).

The verification of conditionals

Let us turn to the circumstances in which conditionals are true, and to a result that seems contrary to the model theory. It comes from the first study to investigate the verification of conditionals. The participants had to judge the impact of single pieces of evidence on the truth or falsity of such conditionals as:

If there is an A on the left, then there is a 2 on the right.

On each trial, the participants weighed the evidence of a single card, such as: *A 2*. They tended to make these judgments (Johnson-Laird & Tagart, 1969):

A 2: shows that the conditional is true.
A 3: shows that the conditional is false.
B 2: is irrelevant to the conditional's truth value.
B 3: is irrelevant to the conditional's truth value.

Evidence that a conditional's *if*-clause is false seems irrelevant to whether the conditional is true or false. In contrast, when individuals list what is possible given a conditional, they list these cases as possible (e.g., Barrouillet et al., 2000). And so there is a discrepancy, because a case that is possible according to a conditional ought to show that the conditional is true. Some theorists argue that the judgments of irrelevance confirm that conditionals are void – they have no truth value – when their *if*-clauses are false. This hypothesis, which goes back to de Finetti (1937/1964), is one of the chief assumptions of the "new paradigm", which is a family of theories that seek to replace logic with probability (see, e.g., Elqayam, this volume; Oaksford & Chater, this volume; Over & Cruz, this volume; and, for a review, Johnson-Laird, Khemlani, & Goodwin, 2015). The hypothesis implies that if a conditional is true, then its *if*-clause must be true too, because otherwise the conditional would have no truth value. But, consider the implications. This conditional is true:

If God exists, atheism is wrong.

And so its *if*-clause is true too: therefore, God exists. The inference is valid and a very short proof of God's existence. But if the proof isn't convincing, it must be because a true conditional can have a false *if*-clause. Hence, Johnson-Laird and Tagart's verification task is misleading (Schroyens, 2010).

Indeed, in a different task, participants do evaluate conditionals as true when their *if*-clauses are false. Participants assessed whether sets of assertions containing conditionals could all be true at the same time (Goodwin & Johnson-Laird, 2015). The context of the following assertions made clear that they concerned a particular animal:

If the animal has brown fur then it is a bear.	(If A then C)
The animal does not have brown fur.	(Not-A)
The animal is a bear.	(C)
Could all of these assertions be true at the same time?	

The experiment examined all four possible sorts of categorical evidence, and even when, as in this example, the conditional's *if*-clause was false, the participants judged that the assertions could all be true (at around 80%).

Readers might judge that two assertions, *A* and *B*, could both be true at the same time, and yet *A* is irrelevant to the truth of *B*. For example, "Viv is tall" can be true at the same time as "Viv is amusing", but each assertion is irrelevant to the truth of the other. The preceding results, however, are different, because the assertions are a conditional and its two clauses. Individuals judged that a conditional ("If Viv is tall, then she is amusing") can be true at the same time as an assertion that its *if*-clause is false ("Viv is not tall"). It follows that the conditional can be true when its *if*-clause is false. Otherwise, the participants would judge that the two assertions couldn't both be true at the same time. This result therefore undermines the idea that a conditional has no truth value when its *if*-clause is false.

Suppose you observe:

It's raining and it's hot.

Your observation establishes the falsity of the conditional: ***if it's raining, then it's not hot***, and of its equivalent: ***if it's hot, then it's not raining***. But, by itself, it does ***not*** establish the truth of the affirmative conditional:

If it's raining, then it's hot.

Your observation fails to distinguish between this conditional and one that is not equivalent to it:

If it's hot, then it's raining.

A conditional refers to a set of cases, and they each have to be possible for the conditional to be true. If your observation shows that one of them is a matter of fact:

raining	hot

then the other cases:

not raining	not hot
not raining	hot

become counterfactual possibilities (Byrne, 2005; Byrne, this volume). If they are true counterfactuals, then the conditional is true. Thus, if a single categorical observation is to verify a conditional (as in the Johnson-Laird & Tagart study), then the context needs to establish the appropriate possibilities prior to the observation. In a recent study, Goodwin and Johnson-Laird (2015) framed the verification task so that the first assertion made the disjunctive possibilities explicit, e.g.:

John is deciding whether to fire one of his two employees, Charlie or Annie, and possibly both of them.
In the end, John fired Annie.
A colleague of John's had predicted: John will fire Charlie, if not Annie.
Was the colleague's prediction true, false, or irrelevant, in light of what happened?

Participants should build these mental models of the people whom John fired according to the conditional and its disjunctive context:

Charlie	not Annie
	Annie
Charlie	Annie

The results were that most participants judged the conditional prediction to be true even in those cases, such as the one above, in which its *if*-clause was false. Of course, these findings may not generalize beyond this study. Yet, like the proof of God's existence, they are a mystery if conditionals cannot be true when their *if*-clauses are false.

The modulation and denial of conditionals

Knowledge can *modulate* the interpretation of conditionals and other connectives (Johnson-Laird & Byrne, 2002). It can introduce temporal relations between events, e.g., *if he passed the exam, then he studied hard*, in which the studying preceded the exam. It can also block the construction of a fully explicit model of a conditional. This blocking yields two main alternatives to a basic conditional, *If A, then C*. One is a biconditional interpretation when knowledge blocks the possibility of *not-A* and *C* (see Table 19.1), e.g.:

If it's raining, then it's pouring

because it can't pour without raining. The other is a relevance interpretation that blocks the possibility of *not-A* and *not-C* (see Table 19.1), e.g.:

If it's raining, then I have an umbrella.

The *if*-clause states a condition that is no more than relevant to the truth of the *then*-clause. Modulation cannot block the mental model, *A* and *C*, at least when another possibility holds. But, ironic conditionals can block it and refer to only a single possibility, for example:

If you're right, then I'll eat my hat.

That is to say, you're not right and I won't eat my hat (Johnson-Laird & Byrne, 2002).

Some conditionals contain a modal verb so that they refer to a possible consequence, e.g.:

If it is raining, then there may be a flood.

They usually mean that *A enables B to occur*, and so *not-A and B* is impossible. Modulation can affect their interpretation too, and therefore the inferences that participants draw from them (Quelhas, Johnson-Laird, & Juhos, 2010). It also affects the interpretation of the temporal relations between events, including the participants' uses of tense in drawing conclusions (Juhos, Quelhas, & Johnson-Laird, 2012). Another effect of modulation is to establish the truth values of some conditionals a priori. For instance, knowledge of the meaning of "atheism" entails the falsity of *If God exists, then atheism is right*.

The denial of a conditional, *if A then C*, transforms the case of *A & not-C* into a possibility and the case of *A & C* into an impossibility. One complication, however, is that the *if*-clause of a conditional is subsidiary to its main *then*-clause (Khemlani, Orenes, & Johnson-Laird, 2012, 2014). Hence, as experiments show (Khemlani, Orenes, & Johnson-Laird, 2014), the denial of a conditional:

It's not the case that if it's raining, then it's hot

is sometimes taken to be equivalent to:

It's raining and it's not hot

and sometimes taken to be equivalent to:

If it's raining, then it's not hot.

In the first denial, negation has the whole of the conditional within its scope, and in the second denial, negation has only the *then*-clause within its scope. The two scopes yield identical possibilities for biconditionals and relevance conditionals. Table 19.1 shows these denials.

Conditionals' conjunctions of possibilities

An analogy exists between the fully explicit models of possibilities for basic conditionals and a connective in logic known as *material implication*. The proposition that *A* materially implies *C* is true or false depending only on the truth or falsity of its two clauses. It is true in just the three cases that are possible for basic conditionals (see the left-most column of Table 19.1), and it is false in the one case that is impossible (*A & not-C*). So, the only way in which a material implication can be false is in case *A* is true and *C* is false. On this account, the false conditional:

If God exists then atheism is right

has an *if*-clause that is true, i.e., God exists. It's an absurd consequence. Likewise, material implication yields paradoxical inferences, such as:

> Donald Trump will not be the next U.S. president.
> Therefore, if Donald Trump is the next U.S. president, then ISIS takes over Tokyo.

The premise establishes the falsity of the conditional's *if*-clause, and that suffices for the conditional to be true granted that it's a material implication. So what does the model theory imply?

It accepts the analogy: basic conditionals refer to the three possibilities that are true for a material implication. But, analogy is not identity. Truth values are alternatives, and so an assertion and its negation cannot both be true: *it will rain and it won't rain* is a self-contradiction, because one clause is true and the other is false. But possibilities are conjunctive, and so an assertion and its negation can both be possible: *possibly it will rain and possibly it won't rain.* A basic conditional is true a priori in case all and only its three fully explicit models refer to possibilities (see Table 19.1). The falsity of a conditional, such as *if God exists, then atheism is right* does not imply that its *if*-clause is true, but that the case in which both clauses are true is impossible, and that the case in which its *if*-clause is true and its *then*-clause is false is possible. Likewise, the falsity of its *if*-clause does not establish that a conditional is true, because this fact alone does not establish that the other relevant cases are possible. The paradoxical inference about Donald Trump is invalid, because the premise does not establish that all the cases to which the conditional refers are possible.

The hypothesis that compound assertions refer to conjunctions of possibilities is borne out in a study in which participants deduced conclusions about what is possible (Hinterecker, Knauff, & Johnson-Laird, 2015). We invite readers to consider whether the following sort of inference is valid:

> A or B or both.
> Therefore, it is possible that A.

It may help to consider a particular example from the experiment, such as:

> Scientists will discover a cure for Parkinson's disease in 10 years or the number of patients who suffer from Parkinson's disease will triple by 2050, or both.
> Therefore, it is possible that scientists will discover a cure for Parkinson's disease in 10 years.

The participants thought that the inference is valid, and they also inferred conjunctive conclusions of the sort:

> It is possible that A and B.

Yet, none of these conclusions is valid in any logic. The first inference is invalid, because *A* could be a self-contradiction. The premise could still be true in this case, but self-contradictions are impossible, and so the conclusion would be false. The second inference is invalid because *B* could imply *not-A*. The premise could still be true in this case, but the conclusion would again assert that a contradiction is possible: *A and not-A*. The proofs of the two inferences in logic therefore call for an additional premise to rule out the potential contradictions. A plausible additional premise for the first inference is:

Not necessarily (not A).

And a plausible additional premise for the second inference is:

Not necessarily (B materially implies not-A).

Alas, each of these premises turns out to be equivalent to the respective conclusion to be proved, and so the actual premise for the inference (*A or B or both*) becomes superfluous. It is not obvious what the additional premises should be. But the inferences are straightforward in the model theory. The premise refers to a conjunctive set of mental models of possibilities:

A	
	B
A	B

The conclusions follow validly and at once from these models. And if *A* were self-contradictory, or *B* were to imply *not-A*, modulation would block the construction of the relevant models. The general moral extends to conditionals: they too refer to conjunctive sets of possibilities.

Many conditionals in daily life have main clauses that are imperatives, and imperatives do not have truth values, e.g.:

If you owe money, then pay at least some of it back.

Actions that imply compliance with the *then*-clause count as satisfying the request, e.g., the debtor pays all the money back. Because the model theory treats conditionals as referring to possibilities, it captures such inferences. When the *if*-clauses of conditional requests or bets are false, the listener is under no obligation to do anything. When the *if*-clauses of conditional instructions in computer programs are false, control likewise passes to the next instruction. But, when the *if*-clauses of conditional assertions in daily life are false, the conditionals can nevertheless be true.

Abduction, nonmonotonicity, and programming

Abduction and nonmonotonicity

Researchers have devised various nonmonotonic logics, which allow conclusions to be weakened or withdrawn in the face of conflicting evidence (see Stenning & Varga, this volume, and Oaksford & Chater, this volume). These logics, however, overlook a major psychological problem. In our earlier example, why have your friends not returned from shopping? You need to abduce a resolution of the inconsistency between beliefs and the facts: you need a causal explanation of what has gone wrong. In the model theory, causal relations are deterministic, not probabilistic (e.g., Goldvarg & Johnson-Laird, 2001), because probabilities cannot tell you what is wrong with the claim: *mud causes rain* (Pearl, 2009). Indeed, probabilities cannot distinguish between cause and correlation, or between causing and enabling (Frosch & Johnson-Laird, 2011).

The model theory of how reasoning resolves inconsistencies is implemented in a computer program (Johnson-Laird, Girotto, & Legrenzi, 2004). To illustrate its operations, consider the following problem:

If someone pulled the trigger, then the gun fired.
Someone pulled the trigger.
But the gun did not fire.
Why not?

Causal links are possibilities ordered in time (Khemlani, Barbey, & Johnson-Laird, 2014). The first two premises in the problem elicit a mental model of such a causal link:

pulled trigger   gun fired

The fact that the gun did not fire contradicts the preceding mental model:

not (gun fired).

The conjunction of two models with contradictory elements usually yields the null model, which represents contradictions, and from which nothing follows. But the model theory embodies a simple nonmonotonic principle. When a contradiction arises from two separate premises, one premise can take precedence over the other, and a fact takes precedence over a contradictory element in other models. In our example, the fact contradicts the *then*-clause in the model but takes precedence over it, and so the model of what needs to be explained is:

pulled trigger   not (gun fired).

Abduction aims to simulate a causal chain that explains why pulling the trigger did not fire the gun. It elicits models from knowledge of what prevents guns from firing. Human reasoners are likely to think about which explanation is most plausible: the gun was broken, the gun jammed, the safety catch was on, the gun had no bullets, and so on. The program chooses at random from them, for example:

gun broken.

This model, in turn, triggers a search for what was its cause, for example:

gun dropped.

The result is a causal simulation in which dropping the gun caused it to break, and so, when someone pulled the trigger, the gun did not fire. The conditional premise is no longer true, and the program adds a rider to express a counterfactual qualification:

If the gun hadn't broken, then it would have fired.

As the theory predicts, individuals spontaneously abduce explanations of inconsistencies. They judge such explanations as more probable than simpler revisions to the premises that restore consistency without explaining the contradiction (Johnson-Laird et al., 2004;

Khemlani & Johnson-Laird, 2011). Because explanations resolve inconsistencies, they have a surprising side effect. They make it harder to detect inconsistencies. A series of studies presented participants with pairs of assertions, such as:

If a person is bitten by a viper, then the person dies.
Someone was bitten by a viper, but did not die.

The participants then carried out two tasks: they created an explanation and they judged whether or not both assertions could be true at the same time (Khemlani & Johnson-Laird, 2012). The order of the two tasks had a robust effect on performance. Prior explanations made inconsistencies harder to detect by 20% or more. The effect probably occurs because explanations resolve inconsistencies. Hence, a different prior task, assessing how surprising the events were, had no such effect. In sum, inconsistencies elicit explanatory abductions, and the potential precedence of one model over another obviates the need for a special nonmonotonic logic.

Abduction and programming

A program is an explanation of how to carry out a computation. So, abductions underlie the development of programs. Psychologists have studied novice programmers writing code in a programming language, but the model theory has inspired studies of how individuals who know nothing of programming create informal programs (Khemlani, Mackiewicz, Bucciarelli, & Johnson-Laird, 2013). The test-bed for these studies is a toy railway depicted on a computer screen, and Figure 19.1 shows its initial state for a simple problem. Only three sorts of move can occur: one or more cars move from the left track to the right track, from the left track to the siding, or from the siding back to the left track. (Moves from the right track are not allowed.) The siding functions like a working memory: items (cars) can be stored on the siding, while others move from input (left) to output (right). The left track also functions as a working memory, because cars can shuttle between it and the siding. In principle the computational power of the railway is therefore equivalent to a universal Turing machine – a device that can carry out any sort of program (Hopcroft & Ullman, 1979).

We studied rearrangements of the order of cars – of which there are many, such as rearranging the six cars *abcdef* on the left track into the reverse order *fedcba* on the right track. The abduction of programs for rearrangements according to the model theory calls for three steps, which are each implemented in a computer program, *mAbducer*, that develops its own programs to make rearrangements; that is, it is an automatic programmer.

The first step is to solve some instances of the relevant rearrangement for trains with different numbers of cars. Although just three sorts of move are permissible, trial and error works for only simple rearrangements of a few cars. Some sorts of problems, such as the Tower of Hanoi,

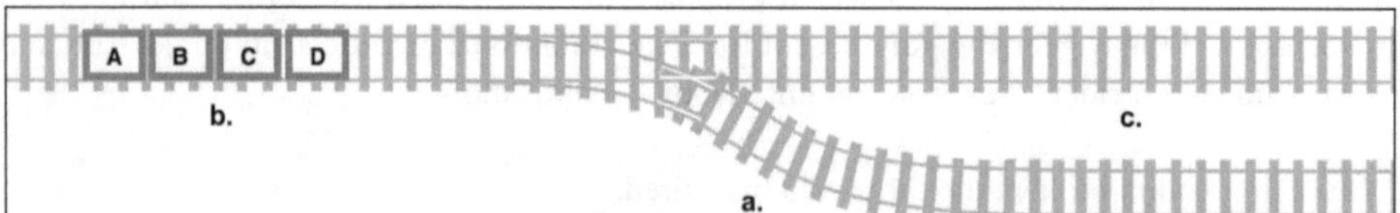

Figure 19.1 The railway environment used in studies of informal programming. Cars can enter the siding (a) only from the left side of the track (b), and exit from it only to the left track. They can also move from the left side of the track to the right side (c)

can be solved using a means–ends analysis in which you choose moves to reduce the difference between the current state and the goal. But for rearrangements, you need to decompose the goal into separate parts. *mAbducer* uses a schematic and kinematic model:

abcdef [–] –

This diagram represents a model containing six cars on the left track, no cars on the siding, which is represented by the square brackets, and no cars on the right track. *mAbducer* finds a parsimonious way to make any rearrangement. It matches cars on different parts of the track with the current goal, and finds the best move. Suppose, for example, that the goal is to rearrange the cars above into the reverse order *fdceba* on the right track. The obvious first move is to move all the cars apart from *a* to the siding:

a[bcdef] –

A loop of moves can now be repeated. Move one car to the right, and one car from the siding to the left:

b[cdef]a

The goal is updated to *fdceb*, because *a* is now in its rightful position. The loop continues until the siding is empty. The final move is of car *f* over to the right. Human reasoners lack a parsimonious procedure for solving rearrangements. Every participant in a study failed to find the solution with the fewest moves for at least one sort of rearrangement (Khemlani et al., 2013). A common blunder was perseveration: when participants had moved a single car, they moved it again, overlooking a move of two cars – the car they'd just moved and the one behind it.

The second step in abducing a program is to determine the structure of the solutions to the same rearrangement of different numbers of cars. A program to rearrange trains of any length is bound to contain a loop of operations. Hence, *mAbducer* simulates solutions in order to recover a required loop of moves (such as the one above) and any moves before or after the loop. *mAbducer* uses the results of its simulations to construct two alternative programs: one uses a *for*-loop, which is repeated *for* a fixed number of times, and the other uses a *while*-loop, which is repeated *while* a given condition holds. *While*-loops are more powerful than *for*-loops, because they can carry out computations that *for*-loops cannot. *mAbducer* has to solve a pair of simultaneous equations to determine the number of repetitions for a *for*-loop (see Khemlani et al., 2013). It has only to inspect its simulations to determine the conditions in which a *while*-loop halts: for example, for a reversal the *while*-loop halts as soon as the siding is empty. Hence, naïve individuals should be more likely to discover *while*-loops, even though they are more powerful computational devices.

The program translates the structures of solutions into the programming language Common Lisp. It also translates the *while*-loop version of a program from Lisp into informal English. Here is its description of the program for a reversal:

Move one less than the [number of] cars to the siding.
While there are more than zero cars on the siding,
    move one car to the right track,
    move one car to the left track.
Move one car to the right track.

Table 19.2 Four rearrangements of cars in a train, their minimal number of moves, the Kolmogorov complexity of programs for solving the rearrangements, and the results of experiments on programming the rearrangements and on making deductions from them (Khemlani et al., 2013)

The name of a rearrangement and an example of it	*Minimal number of moves*	*Kolmogorov complexity of programs*	*Participants' percentages of correct programs*	*Participants' percentages of correct deductions from programs*
Reversal: abcdef ⇒ fedcba	12	1,288	90	41
Palindrome: abccba ⇒ aabbcc	6	1,295	70	35
Parity sort: abcdef ⇒ acebdf	7	1,519	63	32
Reverse parity sort: acebdf ⇒ abcdef	9	1,771	-	23

In an experiment, naïve participants formulated programs for rearrangements in their own words. As the theory predicts, they preferred to use *while*-loops rather than *for*-loops. Here is a typical example of what one participant said in abducing a *while*-loop for a reversal:

> Move all cars to the right of *A* to the side [i.e., the siding]. Then move *A* to the right. Shift *B* to left, then right. Shift *C* to left, then right . . . repeat until pattern is reached.

The participants' difficulty in making a rearrangement depended on the minimal number of moves that it calls for. However, their difficulty in abducing a program to carry out the rearrangement didn't depend on its minimal number of moves, but on the complexity of the program. Complexity reflects various factors, such as the number of instructions in the loop, but a simple metric is the number of symbols in a program written in a standard language. Table 19.2 shows this Kolmogorov complexity, where we multiplied the number of characters and spaces in *mAbducer*'s Common Lisp programs by the number of bits in a character; that is, 7 for ASCII characters. Table 19.2 also shows the percentages of the participants' correct programs. The decline in accurate programs with the increase in their complexity was robust. Reversals are the hardest rearrangement to solve – they take the longest time, because they call for the most moves. But, their programs are of the least complexity, and they are the easiest to program – naïve individuals are more likely to formulate an accurate program and to do so in a shorter time than for the other rearrangements.

The third and final step in programming is to test a program by deducing its consequences for new inputs. Individuals should carry out this task by simulating the effect of each instruction in the program on a given train. Suppose the initial train on the left track is *abcdef*. What is the order of the cars on the right track as a result of carrying out the following program, which works for trains of any length?

> While there are more than two cars on the left track,
> move one car to the right track,
> and move one car to the siding.

Move one car to the right track.
Move one less than half the number of all the cars to the left track.
Move half the number of all the cars to the right track.

Readers are invited to try to imagine the effect without recourse to pencil and paper. Here is the required sequence of moves:

Starting state:	abcdef[] -,
Carry out the two moves in the loop:	abcd[e]f
And again:	ab[ce]df
First move after the loop:	a[ce]bdf
Second move after the loop:	ace[]bdf
Third move after the loop:	-[]acebdf

This rearrangement is the parity sort shown in Table 19.2. The difficulty of the required mental simulation should again depend on the Kolmogorov complexity of the program. Table 19.2 presents the percentages of correct deductions in an experiment, and they corroborated the predicted trend that complexity predicts (Khemlani et al., 2013).

The abduction of programs for making rearrangements in the railway domain calls for the simulation of moves in kinematic models. Ten-year-old children are able to abduce informal programs for rearrangements of six cars. When they were not allowed to move the cars, their gestures were a clear outward sign of inward simulations. These gestures appeared to help them to keep track of where the cars were on the tracks. When they couldn't gesture, their programs were less accurate (Bucciarelli, Mackiewicz, Khemlani, & Johnson-Laird, 2015).

In sum, abduction simulates causal chains to resolve inconsistencies. Its kinematic simulations underlie programming. And they are pre-eminent in the creation of scientific and technological hypotheses (see Chapters 25–27, Johnson-Laird, 2006).

Induction and probabilities

Proportions and probabilities

Casual inductions about probabilities are ancient – Aristotle refers to the probable as a thing that happens for the most part – but until the formulation of the probability calculus in the 17th century, no complete normative theory of numerical probabilities existed. In daily life, reasoners use two main sorts of probabilistic reasoning (Tversky & Kahneman, 1983). They make deductions of probabilities from knowledge of the possible ways in which events can occur – for instance, they deduce that the probability that two tossed coins both land "heads" is a quarter, given that the probability of one coin landing "heads" is a half. And they make inductions about the probabilities of unique events from non-numerical evidence, for example the probability that Donald Trump is elected as president of the United States.

Deductions about probabilities rest on simple principles (Johnson-Laird et al., 1999). Reasoners assume that models of possibilities are equiprobable unless they have evidence to the contrary. They infer that the probability of an event is equal to the proportion of such models in which the event occurs. For example, consider the following problem:

There is a box in which there is a black marble, or a red marble, or both.
Given the preceding assertion, what is the probability of the following situation?
In the box there is a black marble and a red marble.

Experts may respond that the problem is ill posed because it says nothing about relative probabilities. Naïve individuals, however, construct mental models of the three possible contents of the box:

black	
	red
black	red

They assume that they are equiprobable, and so they infer a probability of about 33% (Johnson-Laird et al., 1999). Mental models predict systematic errors, because they don't represent what is false. Here's an example:

> There is a box in which there is at least a red marble, or else there is a green marble and a blue marble, but not all three marbles.
> Given the preceding assertion, what is the probability of the following situation?
> In the box, there is a red marble and a blue marble.

The mental models of the premise are as follows:

red		
	green	blue

So, most reasoners infer that the probability of red and blue in the box is zero. But, the response is an illusion. The fully explicit models of the premise show that when one disjunct is true the other is false, and there are three ways in which *green and blue* can be false when *red* is true:

red	green	not-blue
red	not-green	blue
red	not-green	not-blue
not-red	green	blue

As the second of these models shows, red and blue marbles can occur together, and so a proportional estimate of their probability is, not zero, but 25%.

The great difficulty for naïve individuals – and the great motivator for the invention of the probability calculus – is conditional probability. Many puzzles hinge on this fact. A simple one is:

> The Smiths have two children. One of them is a girl. What's the probability that the other is a girl?

The intuitive response is a half. It treats the question as concerning absolute probabilities. But, because the problem establishes a fact, in reality it asks for a conditional probability: given that one child is a girl, what's the probability that the other child is too? The inference calls for reasoners to envisage a model of all four possible pairs of children:

First-born	*Second-born*
girl	girl
girl	boy
boy	girl
boy	boy

It contains three cases in which one child is a girl. There is a subset within them in which the other child is a girl, and it has only one member. So, the correct estimate is a third (see Nickerson, 1996, for the subtleties in such problems). Conditional probabilities appear to lie at the edge of human competence, because they call for inferences about subsets of models. They can be inferred only using fully explicit models in system 2.

The probabilities of unique events

To study the induction of the probabilities of unique events, we asked participants to estimate the probabilities of various possibilities, such as that U.S. companies will focus their advertising on the Web next year, and that the *New York Times* will become more profitable. For some probabilists, such questions verge on the nonsensical, because there are no definitive frequencies from which their answers can be inferred (e.g., Cosmides & Tooby, 1996). For "Bayesians" such as ourselves (see also Oaksford & Chater, this volume), probabilities correspond to degrees of belief, and so the questions make sense. Naïve individuals are happy to respond too, and their estimates concur to some degree about the relative probabilities of different events; for instance, they estimated the probability of a focus on Web advertising as 69% but the probability that the *Times* would become more profitable as only 41% (Khemlani, Lotstein, & Johnson-Laird, 2012). The profound mystery in such estimates is: where do the numbers come from?

The model theory postulates that individuals adduce evidence from their general knowledge, such as:

Most U.S. newspapers will continue to be unprofitable.

It yields a corresponding model, with a small number of tokens representing U.S. newspapers – a number that can vary from occasion to occasion in a probabilistic way (see Khemlani, Lotstein, Trafton, & Johnson-Laird, 2015):

newspaper	unprofitable
newspaper	unprofitable
newspaper	unprofitable
newspaper	

People know that the *New York Times* is a U.S. newspaper, and so they translate the proportion in this model into a primitive analog representation of the probability that the paper will continue to be unprofitable:

[------]

This diagram denotes an analog model of a magnitude. Its left-hand end represents *impossibility*, its right-hand end represents *certainty*, and its length represents a non-numerical probability. Further evidence can push its length one way or another. When individuals estimate different probabilities for two events, *A* and *B*, they are uncertain about the probability of their conjunction and tend to compromise by computing a primitive average of their probabilities (Khemlani, Lotstein, & Johnson-Laird, 2012, 2015). Such estimates are easy to make using the analog model, but they violate the probability calculus. It calls for the multiplication of one probability, *A*, by the conditional probability of the other, *B*, given *A*. But the estimates are typical. And they occur for the probabilities of other sorts of compounds, including disjunctions and conditional probabilities. These estimates and those of their components, *A* and *B*, are therefore often subadditive – that is, they yield an exhaustive set of alternative possibilities with probabilities summing to more than 100% (Khemlani, Lotstein, & Johnson-Laird, 2015).

In a study in which individuals assessed whether disjunctions implied the possibility of various sorts of conjunctions (Hinterecker et al., 2015), the participants were sensitive to probabilities, e.g., they judged conclusions that they accepted to be more probable than conclusions that they rejected. But they went wrong in estimating the probabilities of the four exhaustive possibilities:

A & B
A & not-B
not-A and B
not-A and not-B.

According to the model theory, naïve estimates of the probability of each conjunction should tend to be a primitive average of the probabilities of the two conjuncts, and so the theory predicts subadditivity. Multiply this effect for four conjunctions, and its extent should be considerable. In fact, it was shocking: the four probabilities summed on average to 191%. Such estimates are irrational: they render individuals vulnerable to a "Dutch book", that is, a set of bets in which they are bound to lose money. The degree of subadditivity is therefore not good news for the new paradigm, which, as we mentioned earlier, seeks to replace logic with probability. And it casts doubt on the idea that the rationality of naïve reasoners is more appropriately measured against the probability calculus than against logic.

Another result contrary to the new paradigm is that reasoners distinguish between the inferential consequences of conditionals, such as:

If the FDA approves a drug, then it is safe for human consumption.

and those that refer to probabilities, such as:

If the FDA approves a drug, then probably it is safe for human consumption.

Notwithstanding claims that probabilities are intrinsic to conditional reasoning (Oaksford et al., 2000), a series of nine experiments, which examined various sorts of deduction, demonstrated robust differences in the way participants interpreted the two sorts of conditional (Goodwin, 2014). Conditionals that do not make explicit reference to probabilities tend not to be interpreted as probabilistic.

Readers should not conclude that reasoning is a deterministic process. Its machinery is not clockwork: the same premises yield different conclusions on different occasions. Part of the ***mReasoner*** program models a probabilistic process for inferences such as:

All Greeks are athletes.
Some athletes are Greeks.
Can both of these assertions be true at the same time? (Yes.)

A typical mental model of the first assertion also represents all athletes as Greek. This model satisfies the second assertion, and so the inference is easy. But the task is harder with this pair of assertions:

All Greeks are athletes.
Some athletes are not Greek.

The typical mental model of the first assertion doesn't satisfy the second assertion, and the correct affirmative response depends on finding an alternative and atypical model:

Greek	athlete
Greek	athlete
Greek	athlete
	athlete
	athlete

Yet, as in almost all studies of reasoning, these inferences are seldom uniform. A probabilistic mechanism accounts for this variation. ***mReasoner*** implements it using parameters governing three probabilities (Khemlani, Lotstein, & Johnson-Laird, 2015). The first parameter constrains the number of individuals represented in a model – the number is always small, but it varies. The second parameter governs the sorts of individual represented in a model – the likelihood that they are typical for an assertion as opposed to drawn from the set of all possible individuals satisfying the assertion. The third parameter governs the chances that system 2 is engaged to make a deliberate search for an alternative to system 1's intuitive mental model. The program responds in a different way to the same inference on different occasions. It behaves like a biased roulette wheel. We ran it many thousands of times to find optimal values for the parameters. Their values accounted for the variations in both the intuitive and deliberative systems of human reasoning. The reasoning engine is probably probabilistic.

Conclusions

What is common to the model theory of deduction, abduction, and induction? The answer is that all three rely on models of possibilities. Reasoners can construct models from descriptions and from perception, and they can retrieve them from knowledge. They deduce conclusions from models. They connect one set of models to another to abduce causal explanations. They determine that one model should take precedence over another that contradicts it, and thereby retract conclusions that facts refute. They use kinematic models in order to determine the conditions in which a loop of operations should halt, and to deduce the consequences of informal programs. They induce probabilities for unique events by transforming a proportion in a model into an analog representation of a magnitude. On the whole, experiments corroborate the theory. Compound assertions refer to conjunctive sets of possibilities, and so conditionals can be true when their *if*-clauses are false. Deductions are easier when fewer models of possibilities are at stake, and so it is easier to reason from biconditionals than conditionals. When facts contravene conclusions, individuals are spontaneous in explaining the inconsistency rather than in amending the inconsistent descriptions. They create programs that tend to use *while*-loops rather than *for*-loops. The difficulty of the task and of deducing the consequences of programs depends on the complexity of the programs. They compromise when probabilities conflict, and so their estimates of compound events can be subadditive to a massive extent. The model theory is far from perfect. Its integrative computer model, ***mReasoner***, is as yet incomplete, though it does illustrate how to integrate probabilities and deduction, and how to distinguish intuitive reasoning (system 1) from deliberative reasoning (system 2). Experimental results may yet overturn the theory. At present, however, it elucidates a wider variety of inferences than alternative accounts, and it has led to robust findings that challenge these alternatives.

References

Adams, E. W. (1998). *A primer of probability logic.* Stanford, CA: CSLI Publications.

Barrouillet, P., Grosset, N., & Lecas, J. F. (2000). Conditional reasoning by mental models: Chronometric and developmental evidence. *Cognition, 75*, 237–266.

Bucciarelli, M., Mackiewicz, R., Khemlani, S. S., & Johnson-Laird, P. N. (2015). *Simulations and gestures in children's creation of algorithms.* Manuscript under submission.

Byrne, R. M. J. (2005). *The rational imagination: How people create alternatives to reality.* Cambridge, MA: MIT Press.

Cosmides, L., & Tooby, J. (1996). Are humans good intuitive statisticians after all? Rethinking some conclusions from the literature on judgment under uncertainty. *Cognition, 58*, 1–73.

Craik, K. (1943). *The nature of explanation.* Cambridge: Cambridge University Press.

de Finetti, B (1964). Foresight: Its logical laws, its subjective sources. In H. E. Kyburg & J. Smokler (Eds.), *Studies in subjective probability* (pp. 93–158). New York: Wiley. (Originally published in 1937.)

Frosch, C. A., & Johnson-Laird, P. N. (2011). Is everyday causation deterministic or probabilistic? *Acta Psychologica, 137*, 280–291.

Girotto, V., Mazzocco, A., & Tasso, A. (1997). The effect of premise order in conditional reasoning: A test of the mental model theory. *Cognition, 63*, 1–28.

Goldvarg, Y., & Johnson-Laird, P. N. (2001). Naïve causality: A mental model theory of causal meaning and reasoning. *Cognitive Science, 25*, 565–610.

Goodwin, G. P. (2014). Is the basic conditional probabilistic? *Journal of Experimental Psychology: General, 143*, 1214–1241.

Goodwin, G. P., & Johnson-Laird, P. N. (2015). *The truth of conditional assertions.* Manuscript under submission.

Hinterecker, T., Knauff, M., & Johnson-Laird, P. N. (2015). *Modality, probability, and mental models.* Manuscript under submission.

Hopcroft, J. E., & Ullman, J. D. (1979). *Introduction to automata theory, languages, and computation.* Reading, MA: Addison-Wesley.

Jeffrey, R. (1981). *Formal logic: Its scope and limits* (2nd ed.). New York: McGraw-Hill.

Johnson-Laird, P. N. (1980). Mental models in cognitive science. *Cognitive Science, 4*, 71–115.

Johnson-Laird, P. N. (1983). *Mental models.* Cambridge: Cambridge University Press; Cambridge, MA: Harvard University Press.

Johnson-Laird, P. N. (1993). *Human and machine thinking.* Hillsdale, NJ: Erlbaum.

Johnson-Laird, P. N. (2006). *How we reason.* New York: Oxford University Press.

Johnson-Laird, P. N., & Byrne, R. M. J. (2002). Conditionals: A theory of meaning, pragmatics, and inference. *Psychological Review, 109*, 646–678.

Johnson-Laird, P. N., Byrne, R. M. J., & Schaeken, W. S. (1992). Propositional reasoning by model. *Psychological Review, 99*, 418–439.

Johnson-Laird, P. N., Girotto, V., & Legrenzi, P. (2004). Reasoning from inconsistency to consistency. *Psychological Review, 111*, 640–661.

Johnson-Laird, P. N., Khemlani, S. S., & Goodwin, G. P. (2015). Logic, probability, and human reasoning. *Trends in Cognitive Sciences, 19*, 201–214.

Johnson-Laird, P. N. and Tagart, J. (1969). How implication is understood. *American Journal of Psychology, 82*, 367–373.

Juhos, C., Quelhas, C., & Johnson-Laird, P. N. (2012). Temporal and spatial relations in sentential reasoning. *Cognition, 122*, 393–404.

Kahneman, D. (2011) *Thinking, fast and slow.* London: Allen Lane.

Khemlani, S., Barbey, A. K., & Johnson-Laird, P. N. (2014). Causal reasoning: Mental computations, and brain mechanisms. *Frontiers in Human Neuroscience, 8*, 1–15.

Khemlani, S., & Johnson-Laird, P. N. (2011). The need to explain. *Quarterly Journal of Experimental Psychology, 64*, 276–288.

Khemlani, S., & Johnson-Laird, P. N. (2012). Hidden conflicts: Explanations make inconsistencies harder to detect. *Acta Psychologica, 139*, 486–491.

Khemlani, S., & Johnson-Laird, P. N. (2013). The processes of inference. *Argument and Computation, 4*, 4–20.

Khemlani, S., Lotstein, M., & Johnson-Laird, P. N. (2012). The probability of unique events. *PLOS-ONE, 7*, 1–9. Online version.

Khemlani, S., Lotstein, M., & Johnson-Laird, P. N. (2015). Naive probability: Model-based estimates of unique events. *Cognitive Science, 39*, 1216–1258. (Published on line, 2014).

Khemlani, S., Lotstein, M., Trafton, J. G., & Johnson-Laird, P. N. (2015). Immediate inferences from quantified assertions. *Quarterly Journal of Experimental Psychology*. On line.

Khemlani, S. S., Mackiewicz, R., Bucciarelli, M., & Johnson-Laird, P. N. (2013). Kinematic mental simulations in abduction and deduction. *Proceedings of the National Academy of Sciences, 110*(42), 16766–16771.

Khemlani, S., Orenes, I., & Johnson-Laird, P. N. (2012). Negation: A theory of its meaning, representation, and use. *Journal of Cognitive Psychology, 24*, 541–559.

Khemlani, S., Orenes, I., & Johnson-Laird, P. N. (2014). The negations of conjunctions, conditionals, and disjunctions. *Acta Psychologica, 151*, 1–7.

Nickerson, R. S. (1996). Ambiguities and unstated assumptions in probabilistic reasoning. *Psychological Bulletin, 120*, 410–433.

Oaksford, M., Chater, N., & Larkin, J. (2000). Probabilities and polarity biases in conditional inference. *Journal of Experimental Psychology: Learning, Memory and Cognition, 26*, 883–899.

Oberauer, K. (2006). Reasoning with conditionals: A test of formal models of four theories. *Cognitive Psychology, 53*, 238–283.

Pearl, J. (2009). *Causality: Models, reasoning, and inference* (2nd ed.). New York: Cambridge University Press.

Quelhas, A. C., Johnson-Laird, P. N., & Juhos, C. (2010). The modulation of conditional assertions and its effects on reasoning. *Quarterly Journal of Experimental Psychology, 63*, 1716–1739.

Rips, L. J. (1994). *The psychology of proof.* Cambridge, MA: MIT Press.

Schroyens, W. (2010). Mistaking the instance for the rule: A critical analysis of the truth-table evaluation paradigm. *Quarterly Journal of Experimental Psychology, 63*, 246–259.

Tversky, A., & Kahneman, D. (1983). Extensional versus intuitive reasoning: The conjunction fallacy in probability judgment. *Psychological Review, 90*, 293–315.

20

ABDUCTIVE REASONING AND EXPLANATION

Barbara Koslowski

Abduction as a description of reasoning about explanations

It is no coincidence that the notion of abduction, introduced by Charles Sanders Peirce (1931–1958), is associated with two terms: *guessing* (or hypothesizing) and *pragmatism*. The notion of guessing (or hypothesizing) contains more than a grain of truth to it. The catch is that the guessing is constrained by background information, including theoretical information or explanation. The notion of pragmatism is relevant in that abduction describes how reasoning in general actually takes place – pragmatically, rather than in an idealized or formal framework. Briefly, abduction is a strategy for drawing inferences about an event according to which one explanation for an event is preferred to another because it provides the more plausible causal account of the data that is also more causally coherent with what we take, at the time, to be well-founded background information or beliefs.

The first part of the chapter describes the characteristics of abduction and focuses on the argument that ordinary as well as scientific reasoning relies on the interplay of the observation one is trying to account for, the range of possible theories or explanations for it, and the store of established background information that has already been acquired. This form of reasoning stresses that an explanation is not evaluated in isolation. Rather, it is chosen because it provides a more plausible account than do competing alternative explanations. Abduction also stresses the importance of relevant background information, including theory or explanation, rather than formal or content-free rules.

The second part of the chapter focuses on the differences between abductive reasoning and other models of reasoning, such as models based on Humean criteria or on deductive, inductive, and Bayesian principles. These latter models are formal in the sense that they aim to avoid dealing with the importance of either theory or background information. Instead, they describe principles that are framed as though they can yield a successful outcome without taking account of background information and explanation. The second part of the chapter argues that such principles are at best heuristics rather than algorithms and that they make a correct conclusion more likely only to the extent that they are applied in conjunction with background information and explanation.

The third section of the chapter summarizes psychological research relevant to abductive reasoning. It focuses on three points: that background theories affect how observations are interpreted, including observations that might otherwise be ignored; that alternative theories can prompt the search for new information and can reduce errors in reasoning; and that anomalies are evaluated in terms of existing background information and can, like alternatives, also prompt the discovery of new information.

The final section deals with various implications of treating abductive reasoning as sound reasoning, which depends on background information including theory. One is that some behaviors typically operationalized as reflecting reasoning that is flawed (including reasoning that seems to reflect confirmation bias, because it privileges theory over data) might instead reflect reasoning that is actually sound (precisely because, like scientific reasoning, it takes theory into account). At worst, it might reflect reasoning based on background information that is currently incomplete. In addition, it might reflect the lack of attention to alternative theories, either because they have not yet been discovered, or because the particular individual is unaware of the relevant alternatives, or because the culture restricts the alternatives that are treated as worth considering. Lastly, the importance of background information including theories and alternative theories would suggest that teaching students how to engage in scientific reasoning should not be limited to teaching them various heuristics.

Definition and characteristics of abduction

Consider, again, the brief description of abduction offered earlier: a strategy for drawing inferences about an event according to which one explanation for an event is preferred to another because it provides the more plausible causal account of the data that is also more causally coherent with what we take, at the time, to be well-founded background information or beliefs (for example, Boyd, 2010; Capaldi & Proctor, 2008; Douven, 1999, 2011; Haig, 2009; Harman, 1965; Lipton, 1991, 1993; Lombrozo, 2012; Lombrozo & Carey, 2006; Proctor & Capaldi, 2006; Psillos, 2000, 2004; Thagard, 1989; Thagard & Verbeurght, 1998). Harman (1965) introduced a philosophical theory, inference to the best explanation (IBE), to describe such practices. Most generally, IBE notes that there is a reciprocal interaction of the observation one is trying to account for, possible theories or explanations for it, and the relevant background information that has already been acquired. (The present chapter ignores philosophical subtleties and uses the terms "theory", "explanation", and "mechanism" interchangeably. Readers interested in the subtleties might consult Woodward, 2014.)

Furthermore, abduction as a description or model of reasoning has also been treated as a description of scientific reasoning. As such, it is treated as a description based on actual *practice*, that is, what scientists actually *do* when they engage in scientific inquiry, rather than on formal or content-free descriptions. A suppressed assumption in treating scientific reasoning as abduction is that whatever it is scientists do must often enough be a pretty good way of reasoning about the world. After all, scientists manage to find cures for many diseases and to discover new planets. Thus, whatever it is that scientists are doing seems to work, at least in the long run, and so provides a good model of what sound reasoning in general should look like.

Because abduction describes scientific as well as general reasoning, the notion central to abduction is the notion of explanation. Scientists, like non-scientists, do not merely seek to predict; they aim also to explain phenomena. Scientists aim to explain, as well, why some predictions are successful and others are not. Furthermore, one of the reasons for the focus on explanation is that the more accurate the explanation for something, the more likely one is to make predictions that are increasingly accurate.

More specifically, IBE emphasizes the fact that explanations are evaluated, not in isolation, but with respect to plausible alternative explanations (Boyd, 2010). An explanation is compelling not only because it can provide some sort of explanation for the relevant data, but also because (given available data) it provides a *better* (that is, more plausible) account than does its plausible competitor. In some cases, it might appear that alternative hypotheses need not be explicitly considered. For example, to determine whether drug X cures illness Y, one might administer the drug to half of the victims and withhold it from the others. However, when this procedure is effective, it is typically because it is combined with random assignment and a large enough sample so that possible alternatives – including those that have not yet been discovered – will probably be ruled out.

Furthermore, abduction or IBE also notes that we evaluate explanations in terms of coherence or "consilience" with well-established background beliefs, which takes account of the fact that every explanation is imbedded in a network or "web" of well-established related information, or what else we know about the world (Quine & Ullian, 1970). This is what enables us to explain crop circles in terms of intentional pranks, rather than alien visitors from outer space. Of course, the background information can change as new discoveries are made. However, if the new "discoveries" suggest alien visitors, then they too will need to be evaluated in light of plausible alternatives and related background information.

Thus, when people rely on abduction, two things happen in tandem: the theory or explanation in question renders certain information evidential because it provides a better account of it than competing theories do, in part by achieving consilience with well established background information; and, in doing so, the theory itself gains in credibility over its competitors precisely because it can plausibly account for information that other explanations cannot. Moreover, the emphasis on consilience with well-founded background beliefs reflects the fact that any single piece of information or evidence that supports (or that undermines) an explanation rarely does so in a definitive way; rather, it makes one of the explanations more or less plausible; it adds to the *relative* weight of evidence in favor of one explanation or its competitor. The lack of guarantees reflects the fact that knowledge is cumulative. Thus, at any single time, the appropriate explanations and background information might not yet be widely known or even have been discovered. In contrast to models of reasoning based on deductive logic, abduction does not guarantee the accuracy of a conclusion; it simply makes a particular explanation more likely than its competitors, given what else we know about the world. It specifies a set of heuristics (such as "consider alternative hypotheses") that make a conclusion more likely to be accurate, rather than algorithms that guarantee the accuracy of a conclusion. An easy way of seeing this is to note that, if science did offer guarantees, we would already have generated cures for cancer.

Of course, because science is cumulative, abduction does not stop when the most plausible explanation of the ones currently available is identified. Rather, the most plausible explanation now serves as a new jumping off point from which to collect more data that either will be coherent with or will undermine the explanation (that is, will be anomalous to it). However, abduction often requires at least a preliminary explanation or theory to be able to specify which additional information or data will be supportive or anomalous. To borrow an example studied by Chinn and Brewer (2001), the theory that dinosaurs were cold-blooded renders anomalous the observation that their bone density resembled the effects of the fast growth characteristic of warm-blooded animals. Without the theory of cold-bloodedness, the dinosaurs' bone density would be merely an observation, rather than an anomaly. And because there are no guarantees in science, the additional data that are collected (in this example, data on bone density) might undermine the explanation and lead to its being rejected in favor of another alternative, or at least modified to take account of the anomalous data that are not consistent with it. Similarly, theories about, for example, the genetic contribution to various illnesses have prompted the collection of much additional data, and some of it – notably those uncovered by work in epigenetics – has led to the theories being modified or refined to take account of the new data. The modified theory can then be assessed relative to any new theories that might have become plausible. With increasing discovery, modification, and assessment, the explanation often becomes increasingly accurate – not only in the sense of explaining a phenomenon, but also in the sense of making accurate predictions.

The classic example of IBE has to do with why natural selection is preferred to the alternative of divine intervention as an explanation for speciation. Natural selection is coherent (or consilient) with related information about the presence of intermediate fossil forms, the fact that particular adaptations depend on the animal's environmental niche, population genetics, plate tectonics, and so on. Furthermore, not only does natural selection account for this related information, but it also provides a better account than does the alternative of divine intervention (which fails to specify why the putative intervention took one form rather than another).

It is important to note that inference to the best explanation is not restricted to the practice of science; it is something people do all the time when they try to explain things. Consider Putnam's (1981) example of someone walking along the beach and trying to explain a series of indentations in the sand, that look like a portrait of Winston Churchill. One possibility is that a colony of ants or crabs, roaming around at random, produced the portrait just by chance. If we consider consilience with what else we know about the world, then the alternative that some human being produced the drawing seems much more plausible. Thus, the sand portrait becomes evidence for a human having produced the drawing and, in turn (given what we know about the behavior of ants, crabs, and people), makes the explanation of a human artist increasingly plausible.

Differences between abduction and other models of reasoning

If abduction occurs all the time, even in such banal instances of trying to explain a drawing in the sand, then the obvious question is, what is so special about it? And what sets it apart from other models of reasoning, scientific or otherwise? The answer is that its emphasis on explanation distinguishes it from formal models of reasoning, including models of scientific reasoning, because formal or content-free models (such as deduction, simple induction, Humean, Bayesian, parsimony, internal consistency, etc.) explicitly aim to avoid dealing with the role of explanation or background theory. Instead, such models argue that reasoning, including scientific inquiry, can be described as the application of various formal or content-free strategies, where content includes theory or explanation as well as related background information.

For example, deduction is not concerned with truth, or with approximate accuracy, but rather with the *validity* of a syllogism. Consider the syllogism "If she has a heart attack, then she dies. She has a heart attack. Therefore, she dies." This syllogism is deductively valid, even though the premise is not necessarily true. Of course, one might add more premises to make the conclusion increasingly likely: her heart has suffered past damage, there was no medical care available, and so on. However, the rules of deduction, *by themselves*, provide no guidance about how to choose some premises rather than others as relevant to an argument, nor about how to assess the accuracy of either the premises or the conclusions. To do this, we would need to rely on background information, including explanations of how the evidence for the premises might be assessed, a question that the rules of deduction do not address (see also Over & Cruz, this volume).

Analogously, simple induction also cannot, by itself, speak to the accuracy of a conclusion. If one has encountered several members of a group all of whom are tall, then to predict accurately whether other group members will also be likely to be tall, one would need to know whether the second set of members are comparable to the first in terms of nutrition, intermarriage with genetically different groups, and so on. In philosophical terms, one would need to know which projectability judgments to make (Goodman, 1954; Boyd, 2010). It would make no sense to ask whether both sets of members have read Proust, because we have no *plausible* theory according to which reading Proust affects height. Theory-neutral conceptions of induction, in contrast to IBE, do not specify why reading Proust would be irrelevant, and this is in part because theory-neutral conceptions cannot incorporate considerations of background theoretical information (see also Feeney, this volume).

On the Humean model, the most prevalent model of reasoning in the psychological literature (e.g., Gopnik & Schulz, 2007; Kuhn, Amsel, & O'Loughlin, 1988), one can "explain" or identify the cause of an event by identifying another event that was prior to, contiguous with, and that covaried with the event to be explained. (Philosophers with a Humean bent have more sophisticated conceptions, but the basic points remain the same. For some of the subtleties, see Dowe, 2008.) On the simple Humean model, one need never consider theory or explanation. For example, to answer whether ice cream consumption causes or explains violent crime, one need only ask whether eating ice cream and violent crime covary. However, considering a bit of background information will make it clear that they might covary because both are preferentially likely to occur in hot weather, when people are outdoors interacting (sometimes violently) with one another. The Humean approach, by itself, gives no guidelines about why one ought to consider this possibility, rather than hair length (as hair is often shorter in the summer). It deals with the covariation of variables only *after* they have already been identified (typically by relying on background theoretical information), but provides no suggestions about why some but not others have been identified in the first place. Thus, although the Humean indices can be framed as though they are a content-free strategy for evaluating reasoning, they can be applied successfully only when content or background information has already been taken into account. In psychological research, Bayesian approaches are not a remedy, as they do not specify why some prior probabilities or "priors" are taken into account and others not – except in the sense that some priors have been presented by the experimenter in a task that otherwise affords participants very few pieces of information (see Salmon, 1998, on the theory-dependence of priors; see also Oaksford & Chater, this volume; Kemp & Tenenbaum, 2009; Fedyk & Xu, 2016).

Similarly, the heuristic "rule out alternative hypotheses" can also be framed as though it were a content-free strategy. However, for it to be effective, related background information, including explanation, must be taken into account to decide which alternatives are plausible and thus worth considering and which are fantasy. This is why we no longer consider phases of the moon as an alternative to germ theory when trying to account for an illness; though charming, lunar explanations are not plausible.

Theory as a double-edged sword

The motivation for ignoring theory or explanation when trying to study reasoning in general, and scientific reasoning in particular, is understandable; theories can be wrong. Thus, it would be attractive to have a general theory of sound reasoning that was not dependent on theoretical or explanatory commitments. The "theory" that some groups are genetically inferior to others (e.g., Herrnstein, 1973; Herrnstein & Murray, 1994) is an example of an especially pernicious theory that also illustrates the shortcomings of two other strategies for evaluating explanations that are sometimes presented as theory-neutral: parsimony and internal consistency. It was, at least at one time, both parsimonious and internally consistent to posit the genetic inferiority of some groups. After all, some groups are paid less, less likely to be hired despite greater educational accomplishments, and so on. However, despite the parsimonious and internally consistent features of the genetic inferiority explanation, it is reasonable to question it, because as several researchers have noted, there is background information that strongly suggests alternative theories, namely, widespread and institutionalized racism and sexism, that can provide an account of the phenomena and that are also consilient with background information about the differential treatment of different groups (Block & Dworkin, 1976; Valian, 1999; Steele, 2010). In short, formal models (precisely because they ignore background theory) do not, by themselves, provide any way of distinguishing explanations that are likely to be true from those that are not (but see Lombrozo, 2007).

It is important to keep in mind that IBE does not dismiss the importance of Humean indices; covariation data can either support or undermine mechanistic explanations. The difference is that, at least in the psychological literature, when tasks are based on a Humean framework, the Humean indices are typically treated, at least tacitly or operationally, as the sole indicators of causation. In contrast, within an IBE framework, the evaluation of mechanistic explanations might well take account of whether the Humean indices are present, not because the indices are the sole indicators of causation, but rather because a network of related information (including theoretical information) says that certain Humean indices should be present if the explanation is approximately accurate. That is, mechanistic explanations (along with related information about the world) provide a rationale for *why* some covariations should be present and not others. For example, to explain neural tube defects, we ask about the correlation with level of folic acid, but we do not ask about the correlation with the mother's musical preferences; our network of related information (including our background theories) tells us that the first correlation but not the second might be expected, given what else we know about the world. Again, strategies for evaluating explanations can be phrased as though they rely exclusively on formal Humean models, but to be applied successfully, they must take background information – including theory – into account. (An exception to the argument that the search for Humean indices is always motivated by background theories – broadly understood – might occur when all plausible causes have been ruled out. For example, when Semmelweis had eliminated plausible causes of puerperal fever, he considered whether the presence of a priest on his way to administer last rites as he passed through the afflicted ward might have provoked the illness; Hempel, 1966).

Psychological research relevant to abduction

Researchers have emphasized ways in which explanation or theory affects various aspects of reasoning such as induction, memory, learning, categorization, and so on (Sloman, Love, & Ahn, 1998; Chi, de Leeuw, Chiu, & LaVancher, 1994; Murphy & Medin, 1985; Rips, 1989, etc.). At some level, all of this research is potentially relevant to different aspects of abduction, in that it all involves explanation. However, the present chapter focuses on the interplay of mechanistic explanations, alternative explanations, and anomalous information. This summary of research is not exhaustive. In addition, not all of the research described was specifically framed in terms of abduction. Note also that many of the examples illustrate more than one aspect of abduction; they are treated as distinct for purposes of exposition. (Recall that, in this chapter, the terms "explanation", "mechanism", "theory", and "hypothesis" are used interchangeably.)

In the ideal psychological study of abductive reasoning, one would examine the initial interplay of observation and background information (including theory), would take account of whether, and if so how, subsequent data suggested modification or rejection of the target theory, and would then examine how the revised theory led the way to the collection of additional data. Most psychological research relevant to abductive reasoning focuses on aspects of reasoning that are more circumscribed. The following three lines of research stand out as exceptions.

Clear-cut examples of studies of abduction

Not surprisingly, two of the best demonstrations of abductive reasoning in the psychological literature come from actual scientific practice (see also Gorman, this volume). Dunbar (1995, 1997) studied actual laboratory groups in molecular biology. Invariably, results were observed that were anomalous or at least unexpected given the working hypotheses or theories being considered. Once methodological errors had been ruled out as a source of the anomalies, lab members would either modify or reject the hypothesis or generate a new one to take account of both the initial data and the new anomaly. The new, tentative explanation would then be tested against additional competing possible explanations. Thus, the initial theory would lead the labs to expect or predict that certain data would be observed and, when the expected data did not occur, they would generate a new or modified explanation to be tested against competing explanations; there would be an interplay of theory and data.

Lesgold et al.'s (1988) work on expert radiologists illustrates an analogous pattern. Diagnosticians often evaluate individual hypotheses about what X-rays depict by considering them with respect to several possible alternative hypotheses, using various pieces of data from the X-rays to eliminate some hypotheses and refine (or reject) others. The evaluations also consider consilience with background information about other features of the X-ray that should be expected if a particular hypothesis is accurate. Thus, the diagnoses of expert radiologists demonstrate the interplay of hypotheses (including alternative hypotheses), data, and background information. In addition, they use theories or explanations to decide which features of the X-ray are relevant in the first place (see also Croskerry, this volume).

Klahr's (2000) participants were not asked about mechanistic explanations, but the participants' behavior also illustrates abduction about, for example, how a certain key, labeled RPT, functioned in programing a toy truck. Possible hypotheses included whether RPT would repeat the entire program *n* times, whether it would repeat the last *n* steps, and so on. In generating a hypothesis in general, as well as in this task, the initial state "consists of some knowledge about a domain, and the goal state is a hypothesis that can account for some or all of that knowledge." This prompts a search for experiments that can yield informative evidence. Finally, the evidence is evaluated by comparing the predictions derived from the hypotheses with the results obtained by the experiments and, if necessary, additional experiments are carried out. Put differently, the search for hypotheses is constrained by background knowledge, and the search for experiments is constrained by the hypotheses, which can be modified or rejected depending on the results of the experiments (Klahr, 2000).

Psychological research on more circumscribed aspects of abduction

This section includes some research on the way that background theories or explanations affect the interpretation of observations, including observations that might otherwise be ignored; the finding that alternative theories can prompt the search for new information and can reduce errors in reasoning; and the way that anomalies are evaluated in terms of existing background information and can, like alternatives, also prompt the discovery of new information.

Explanation affects the interpretation of observations

EXPLANATION ALLOWS NUMBERS TO BECOME DATA

At a very basic level, having a theory or set of expectations can help people detect perceptual configurations. For example, when shown a scatter plot, people have trouble detecting the correlation in the plot unless they have a theory that describes a possible relation between the variables in the plot (Jennings, Amabile, & Ross, 1982). Indeed, at least with respect to evaluating scatter plots, people who rely on a flawed theory or explanation do better than people who have no theory at all (Wright & Murphy, 1986).

PEOPLE PRIVILEGE MECHANISM OR EXPLANATORY INFORMATION OVER INFORMATION CONSISTING ONLY OF COVARIATION

Ahn and her colleagues (Ahn et al., 1995) explicitly asked college students to generate questions to help them discover the cause of (i.e., the explanation for) an event. People were more likely to test hypotheses (i.e., to ask) about possible mechanisms rather than about patterns of covariation. For example, if trying to identify the cause of John's car accident, people were more likely to ask whether John was drunk or there was a mechanical problem with the car than to ask about a pattern of covariation such as whether John had had other accidents. In addition, when covariation information competed with mechanism or theory information, the latter was seen as a stronger indicator of cause. For example, people who were told that "Kim is nearsighted and does not wear her glasses while driving" were more likely to assume that last night's accident was Kim's fault than were people who were told, "Traffic accidents were much more likely last night than on other nights." In short, mechanistic explanations trumped non-mechanistic statistical regularity.

Among younger people, as well, theory affects the search for information. College students and college-bound adolescents were asked what sorts of evidence they would consider to find out whether hospitalized children would recover faster if their parents stayed with them overnight. Even when they requested covariation information, 94% of the participants explicitly verbalized mechanism information as the motivation for their requests, for example, "You could have some parents stay overnight and some not, *because parents might help their kids by telling the doctors if there were problems*" (Koslowski, 1996, Ch. 12). That is, when adolescents asked for covariation information, it was *because* theory or explanation enabled them to realize that the covariation information would be evidentially relevant.

EXPLANATION CAN RENDER COVARIATION CAUSALLY RELEVANT

When a potential causal event is an implausible cause (even though it does covary with the effect), the event is nevertheless increasingly likely to be treated as causal if an explanation becomes available that can account for the process by which it might have brought about the effect. Thus, car color as a possible – though implausible – cause of differences in gas mileage is increasingly seen as causal if participants are told that red cars lead to alertness, which in turn leads to the sort of driving that conserves gas (Koslowski, 1996, Ch. 8).

EXPLANATION CAN ENABLE PEOPLE TO REALIZE THAT SEEMINGLY IRRELEVANT INFORMATION MIGHT ACTUALLY BE EVIDENTIAL

In some situations, there is broad agreement about whether certain information is evidential; bad weather and alcohol consumption are obviously evidence related to auto accidents. However, in some cases, recognizing that information is evidential depends on whether there is an explanation available that can make it so. Consider trying to explain why mountain dwellers have a smaller stature than people living on neighboring plains. Now consider two pieces of information: (1) the oral history of the mountain village mentions fleeing to the mountains to escape an invasion from across the sea; and (2) the members of the mountain village speak a language different in some respects from the language in the plains villages. If the explanation being considered is polluted water in the mountain wells, then neither piece of information would appear to be relevant. In contrast, if the explanation being considered is that the two populations come from different gene pools, then both pieces of information will appear to be quite relevant; the gene pools explanation will be able to account for, and will be consilient with, the oral tradition and with the language differences. Furthermore, the two pieces of information will give more weight to the gene explanation relative to the explanation based on polluted water. Whether information is treated as evidence sometimes depends on the explanation being considered (Marasia, Chelenza, & Dublin, 2008).

THEORIES ARE EVALUATED, IN PART, BY RELYING ON CONSISTENCY OR CONSILIENCE WITH BACKGROUND INFORMATION

Sodian, Zaitchik, and Carey (1991) asked children whether putting mouse food in a box with a small or a large opening would better help them determine whether an unseen mouse was large or small. The children chose the small opening, on the grounds that a mouse of either size could fit into the large hole, but only a small mouse could fit into the small one. Note that the children's decision relied on at least two pieces of background information: that mice do not change their girth (as do some snakes when they detach their jaws); and that the door openings do not change in size (as they might if the walls were made of rubber). That is, the children's explanation of why the small opening would be the better choice was consilient with their background information both about mice and about the rigidity of certain openings.

With a sample of college students, Chinn and Brewer (1998) asked participants to assess the theory that dinosaurs were cold-blooded in light of the anomalous data that the bone density of dinosaurs was comparable to that of extant warm-blooded animals. In evaluating the explanation in light of the anomalies, the students considered whether the explanation was consilient with their related background knowledge of, for example, the effects of dietary calcium on bones and the possibility that fossilization might have altered the structure of bone tissue.

Consilience with background information also likely affects the difference between convergent and replicating anomalous evidence. Convergent evidence consists of qualitatively different types (survey, observational, case study), while replicating anomalous evidence consists of the same type of information replicated by different sources (Hemmerich, Van Voorhis, & Wiley, 2016). Convergent as opposed to replicating evidence would seem to be integrated with a broader network or web of related information. And, as this framework would suggest, convergent anomalous evidence was the more likely to reduce confidence in the theory.

EXPLANATION CAN FUNCTION AS A FRAMEWORK FOR DISCOVERY

Because explanation situates information in a broader framework or "web" of beliefs, it can also prompt discovery, including discovery in the broader cultural context. For example, in archaeology, a standard assumption had been that, in hunter-gatherer societies, the men provided the bulk of the food, with women tied to a home settlement because of either pregnancy or nursing. Viewing this issue from a feminist perspective (Gero & Conkey, 1991) led Slocum (1975) actually to investigate this assumption by examining extant hunter-gatherer societies. She found that, contrary to the received view, it was the women who provided the bulk of the groups' dietary intake by gathering plant food and by trapping small animals. That is, doing anthropology from a feminist perspective (an explanation in the broad sense of the term) led to a search for data that might otherwise have remained in the shadows.

EXPLANATION CAN ITSELF BE TREATED AS EVIDENTIAL

Theory or explanation and evidence are typically treated as distinct entities. However, some philosophers of science (Boyd, 1989) have argued there is a sense in which explanation can itself be evidential. Roughly, if a particular explanation is the only one that makes sense, then that is some evidence that it must be true. For example, some evidence in favor of the theory of natural selection is that it is the most plausible account of the extent to which organisms do or do not seem adapted to their environments and that is also consilient with background information about the way the world works. Thus, unless and until another, more plausible explanation is discovered, this is some evidence that natural selection is approximately accurate (Boyd, 1989). To invoke crop circles again, an explanation of them that is based on human pranks (as opposed to intergalactic travel) is the only one that makes any sense given what else we know about the world, and this is therefore some reason to treat it as likely to be accurate.

Brem and Rips (2000) make a related point from a psychological perspective. They write that "explanations provide us with a quick-and-dirty method for vetting claims. If we can elaborate a causal mechanism without running into internal inconsistencies or violating background knowledge, the probability that the claim is true may rise. Alternatively, if no satisfactory explanation is available, the perceived likelihood of a claim may decline" (Brem & Rips, 2000, p. 575). Related to this is the finding that explanation is more likely to be invoked when other evidence is scarce. Brem and Rips (2000) asked participants about various issues (such as what causes homelessness) in one of two conditions: actual ("If you were trying to convince someone your view is right, what evidence would you give to try to show this?") or Ideal ("What would be the ideal evidence to show this?"). In the Actual condition (in which evidence was more difficult to come by) people were more likely than in the Ideal condition to generate explanations as evidence. This finding also adds a nuance to D. Kuhn's (1991) argument that people do not distinguish theory and evidence. Especially relevant to the present chapter, it dovetails with Brem's (1997) earlier finding that the persuasiveness of an explanation increases when evidence is limited. As reasons for finding an explanation plausible, explanation and evidence complement each other, and explanation can sometimes count as evidence.

Alternative explanations can prompt the search for new information and can reduce errors in reasoning

PEOPLE, INCLUDING CHILDREN, OFTEN DO CONSIDER ALTERNATIVES WHEN EVALUATING EXPLANATIONS

Recall the point that abduction notes that any single explanation is judged with respect to alternative accounts. If abduction plays a role in reasoning, then people should generate and consider alternatives, and they do – not only, as already noted, when doing research in microbiology or diagnosing X-rays, but in other areas as well. Kuhn et al. (1988) and Chinn and Brewer (1998) found that people often generated alternatives when their initial assumptions were met with anomalous data. Granted, some of the alternatives consisted of ways of refining the initial explanation, and thus might be considered simple modifications rather than genuine alternatives. However, at the very least, such data demonstrate an awareness of explanations other than the ones initially proposed.

When asked, "What sorts of information or evidence would you consider?" to find out whether having parents stay overnight with their children aided recovery, on average 88%, 71%, and 39% of college students and college-bound ninth- and sixth-graders, respectively, spontaneously asked about alternative hypotheses (for example, "Maybe the recovery rate has something to do with different illnesses.") In asking for evidence, they considered alternatives (Koslowski, 1996, ch. 12).

A related point is that people (including children) are sensitive to the difference between controlled and confounded data, engaging in more search behaviors when confounding is present rather than absent (Schulz & Bonawitz, 2007). Furthermore, when answering causal questions, even children propose collecting controlled rather than confounded data. They realize, for example, that to test whether it is the presence of a roof (on a lantern with a few small holes) that prevents a candle inside from blowing out, children realize they need a contrast lantern with few small holes, but no roof (Bullock, 1991; Bullock & Ziegler, 1999). Analogously, at least by sixth grade, when trying to identify causal events, people treat confounded variables as more problematic than controlled variables. If the cars that get good gas mileage are small Hondas and those that get poor mileage are large Buicks, even sixth-graders are more likely to judge that the explanation for the mileage differences is indeterminate than if size and model of car are controlled (Koslowski, 1996, ch. 6).

THE PRESENCE OF AN ALTERNATIVE CAN REDUCE ERRORS IN REASONING

Klahr (2000) found that the tendency to maintain hypotheses in the face of disconfirming data is reduced when, at the outset of the experiment, participants are asked to generate some alternative hypotheses. Presumably, this helps people realize that there are other options for responding to anomalies – options that do not involve simply modifying the working hypothesis to account for the anomalies.

Vallee-Tourangeau, Beynon, and James (2000) asked college students to reason about contingencies (whether various teams were effective in detecting comets). The presence of an alternative did not affect participants' likelihood of recognizing negative evidence, but did make it less likely that they would persist in basing their predictions on contingencies that had been disconfirmed.

College students were presented with an event (such as the extinction of large mammals), a target explanation (hunting), an alternative (disease), and three types of additional information: consistent with the target (the presence of sharp spears), inconsistent with the target (but consistent with the alternative), and neutral. Participants were told to find information that could support the target explanation. When an alternative explanation was present, participants were less likely to cite either neutral information or information inconsistent with the target. The presence of an alternative enabled people to realize that, although inconsistent or neutral information could be manipulated or distorted to *seem* consistent with the target explanation, it was so much more *plausibly* consonant with the competing alternative (Koslowski et al., 2013).

Anomalies are evaluated in terms of existing background information and can lead to the discovery of new information

ANOMALIES ARE EVALUATED, IN PART, IN TERMS OF CONSISTENCY WITH BACKGROUND INFORMATION

It might seem a truism to say that the more evidence there is in support of a theory, the more likely people are to prefer it to an alternative, but preference based on the relative weight of the evidence also affects how people evaluate anomalous data. For example, college students were first presented either with a five-page text containing a "broad array of evidence supporting" the meteor impact explanation for the mass extinction at the end of the Cretaceous period or else with only one piece of evidence supporting it. This was followed by two pieces of anomalous data, and then by the alternative volcano theory that explained not only the extinction, but also some (but only some) of the evidence for the meteor explanation. Despite the anomalies to the initial theory, students nevertheless preferred it to the alternative. In terms of IBE, the students had judged the initial theory to be the more plausible one because the *relative* weight of the evidence favored it, and the anomalous data were not sufficient to disrupt the relative imbalance of five pages of evidence versus one piece (Chinn & Brewer, 1992). Continuing to adhere to a theory in the face of anomalous data was not a blanket tendency; it depended on how much evidence there was for the theory to begin with.

In another study (Brewer & Chinn, 1994) college students were initially presented with several pieces of background evidence that were consistent either with the theory that dinosaurs were warm-blooded or else with the theory that they were cold-blooded. Thus, a single piece of data would be consistent with one theory but not with the other. The very same piece of data was rated as less credible when it was inconsistent rather than consistent with a target theory. Note that the evidence that had been *initially* presented as consistent with the target theory constituted the background information, or the web of belief, in which the target theory was imbedded. Thus, when a piece of data was anomalous to a theory, it also lacked consilience with the relevant background information. Therefore, treating the anomaly as decreasingly credible was analogous to doubting the credibility of a report claiming that penicillin failed to cure bacterial infections.

Schauble (1990) found that children's causal and non-causal beliefs about whether, for example, engine size and presence of a muffler would affect the speed of a car were initially resistant to disconfirmation. However, Schauble notes that "although the children displayed the typical belief bias, it was not altogether resistant to the cumulative weight of the evidence" (Schauble, 1990, p. 54). As anomalous data mounted up, they likely constituted a new web of background information that made them increasingly hard to dismiss.

AS BACKGROUND INFORMATION INCREASES, SO DOES THE ABILITY TO RECOGNIZE THAT ANOMALIES ARE PROBLEMATIC

Among the laboratories studied by Dunbar (1997), the expert scientists (for example, principal investigators) were more likely than novices (graduate students, for example) to recognize that anomalous findings constituted a problem for the hypothesis being investigated. For non-scientists, as well, the more plausibly people rated an explanation in the first place (about, for example, how the plague reached the city of Caffa), the more the plausibility *decreased* in response to the anomalies, and the decrease was greater when the anomaly was strong rather than weak (Koslowski, 2012). Recognizing that anomalies are a problem requires knowing enough about the subject matter to realize that the anomaly is not consilient with the rest of what we know about the phenomenon.

ANOMALIES CAN PROMPT CURIOSITY AND EXPLORATION

Like explanations, anomalies can also prompt people to consider information that is not obviously available (e.g., Dunbar, 1997; Lesgold et al., 1988). Isaacs (1930) (studying children's questions) and Berlyne (1954) noted that unexpected events, including explanations that failed to work, prompted children to be curious and often to search for additional information. Subsequent research confirmed children's tendency to ask questions about unexpected or anomalous information – for example, "How did I eat when I was inside your tummy?" (Koslowski & Pierce, 1981; Harris, 2000).

Legare et al. (2010) taught children to expect that certain objects would either turn a light on, or off, or do nothing. Expectations were then either violated or confirmed. Three- and four-year-olds were more likely to explain events that violated rather than confirmed their expectations. Children also try to test different combinations of objects when trying to explain why an event failed to bring about an effect, and are especially likely to do so if they have generated causal (functional) rather than non-causal explanations (Legare, 2012).

Bonawitz et al. (2012) tested children who theorized that a balance beam balanced at either the geometric center or the center of mass (or who had no theory) and then presented the children with evidence anomalous to their theory. Children engaged in more exploration of the apparatus when their beliefs were violated than when they were not. In addition, when they could not rely on an auxiliary variable (in this case a magnet) to explain away the anomaly, then they changed their prediction; they relied on the interplay of theory and evidence to extend, by modifying it, their conception of how something might work.

For some researchers (at least in terms of how sound reasoning is operationally defined) the appropriate response when one is confronted with anomalies to an explanation is to reject the explanation (Nickerson, 1998; Kuhn et al., 1988). However, actual science is cumulative; initial working hypotheses are often legitimately refined or modified as new (including anomalous) data become available, and this reflects reasoning that is sound rather than flawed (see also Gorman, this volume).

Summary and implications for psychological research on scientific reasoning

Most generally, abduction describes a process that is neither linear nor neat. After the fact, one can re-write an episode of scientific inquiry as consisting of a set of experimentally obtained premises or observations from which one can, fairly straightforwardly, generate a set of hypotheses and experiments to test them and then arrive at a definitive conclusion. In practice, however, identifying the relevant hypotheses and the appropriate experiments relies heavily on background information, including explanation or theoretical information. Put differently, the principles of scientific reasoning (such as "rule out alternative hypotheses" or "causal events covary with effects") are heuristics, not algorithms. They make success more likely, but they do not guarantee it. Such principles can be *framed* as though they were content-free, and thus applicable to any situation or content area, but to be applied *successfully*, they must take content (including background information and theory) into account to decide, for example, which alternatives are plausible and which covariations are likely to be genuine causes rather than mere coincidences. In addition, abduction recognizes that science is cumulative; theories are refined as new information (about alternatives, anomalies, etc.) becomes available.

Abduction as a description of some episodes of scientific inquiry has several implications for psychological studies of scientific reasoning. Most generally, abduction draws attention to the fact that some behaviors commonly operationalized as reflecting flawed thinking might in fact be a reflection of sound – or at worst incomplete – reasoning. The main reason is that, although a reliance on theory or explanation is often treated as reflecting an error, or "bias" or "confirmation bias", it should be clear that accurate scientific reasoning cannot proceed without relying on background theory. Additional implications include the following.

Humean models

When research is designed so that sound reasoning is operationally defined as relying exclusively on the Humean indices such as covariation, it should be acknowledged that such designs describe only one aspect of the scientific process – the one that typically comes into play *after* considerations of background theory have led to the search for some experiments or some instances of covariation rather than others. Conversely, when participants fail to rely exclusively on the Humean indices in an experimental setting, this need not necessarily reflect flawed reasoning; it might instead indicate that they are taking into account background information acquired outside of the laboratory context that would (correctly) limit the utility of covariation as an indicator of cause unless one were asking people somehow to completely insulate their judgments from information acquired outside of the experimental setting (Koslowski, 1996). However, to ignore such information would be tantamount to telling someone not to think about a white bear.

Source of alternatives

With its emphasis on the importance of alternative explanations, IBE would also be sympathetic to expanding the search for plausible alternatives (especially in the social sciences) by relying on people rooted in different cultural or societal frameworks, that is, people who might be aware of alternative explanations not in the current mainstream (see, for example, Wylie, 2003).

Responses to anomalies and confirmation bias

Because science is cumulative, new findings that are anomalous to an existing hypothesis ought not necessarily to be treated as requiring that the hypothesis be rejected. Rather, they could (correctly) be treated as warranting maintaining the hypothesis by modifying it to take account of the anomalous data (Capaldi & Proctor, 2008; Koslowski, 2012; Koslowski,1996, Ch. 3; Koslowski, Beckmann et al., 2008; Koslowski & Maqueda, 1993). More generally, approaches to reasoning that focus on confirmation bias emphasize the ways in which background theories can lead one astray. In particular, a common assumption when researchers invoke confirmation bias is that it reflects flawed reasoning because it privileges theory or explanation over data (D. Kuhn et al., 1988; Nickerson, 1998). However, if abduction is an approximately accurate description of sound reasoning, then the role that theory plays ought to be treated as more nuanced than it now is. Anomalous data might suggest (correctly) modifying a theory or searching for more information, rather than rejecting the theory outright. Alternatively, it might suggest asking whether the data might be flawed. For example, it might be reasonable to treat reports of ESP with a very jaundiced eye and to question the "data" rather than to reject the theory that ESP is an illusion. Put differently, the important question is whether the theory being considered is approximately accurate, and this depends on information about available plausible alternatives, background information (including theory), and consilience with what else we currently know about the world. In short, a blanket homage to data rather than theory might be mistaken.

Education

Finally, if IBE is indeed an approximately accurate model of actual scientific practice, then teaching students how to engage in sound scientific reasoning would require not only teaching them various heuristics (such as the Humean indices), but also teaching them that the heuristics require considerations of background information – including explanation or theoretical information and including alternative hypotheses from non-mainstream groups – for the heuristics to lead to success.

Acknowledgements

Tremendous thanks to Richard N. Boyd.

References

Ahn, W. K., Kalish, C. W., Medin, D. L., & Gelman, S. A. (1995, March). The role of covariation versus mechanism information in causal attribution. *Cognition, 54*(3), 299–352.
Berlyne, D. E. (1954). A theory of human curiosity. *British Journal of Psychology, 45*, 180–191.
Block, N. J., & Dworkin, G. (Eds.). (1976) *The IQ Controversy*. New York: Pantheon Books.
Bonawitz, E. B., van Schijndel, T. J. P., Friel, D., & Schulz, L. (2012) Children balance theories and evidence in exploration, explanation, and learning. *Cognitive Psychology, 64*(4), 215–234.
Boyd, R. N. (1989). What realism implies and what it does not. *Dialectica, 43*, 5–29.
Boyd, R. N. (2010). Realism, natural kinds and philosophical methods. In H. Beebee & N. Sabbarton-Leary (Eds.), *The semantics and metaphysics of natural kinds*. London: Routledge.
Brem, S. (1997). *Explanation as evidence: Strategies and heuristics in informal argument*. Unpublished doctoral dissertation. Northwestern University.
Brem, S., & Rips, L. J., 2000. Explanation and evidence in informal argument. *Cognitive Science, 24*,: 573–604.
Brewer, W. F., & Chinn, C. A. (1994). The theory-ladenness of data: An experimental demonstration. In A. Ram & K. Eiselt (Eds.), *Proceedings of the sixteenth annual conference of the cognitive science society* (pp. 61–65). Hillsdale, NJ: Lawrence Erlbaum Associates.
Bullock, M. (1991). *Scientific reasoning in elementary school: Developmental and individual differences*. Paper presented at the biennial meeting of the Society for Research in Child Development, Seattle, WA.
Bullock, M., & Ziegler, A. (1999). Scientific reasoning: Developmental and individual differences. In. F. E. Weinert & W. Schneider (Eds.), *Individual development from 3 to 12. Findings from the Munich longitudinal study* (pp. 38–44). Cambridge: Cambridge University Press.
Capaldi, E. J., & Proctor, R. W. (2008). Are theories to be evaluated in isolation or relative to alternatives? An abductive view. *American Journal of Psychology, 121*(4), 617–641.
Chi, M. T. H., de Leeuw, N., Chiu, M. H., & LaVancher, C. (1994). Eliciting self-explanations improves understanding. *Cognitive Science, 18*, 439–477.
Chinn, C. A., & Brewer, W. F. (1992) Psychological responses to anomalous data. In *Proceedings of the fourteenth annual conference of the Cognitive Science Society* (pp. 165–170). Hillsdale, NJ: Lawrence Erlbaum.
Chinn, C. A., & Brewer, W. F. (1998). An empirical test of a taxonomy of responses to anomalous data in science. *Journal of Research in Science Teaching, 35*(6), 623–654.
Chinn, C. A., & Brewer, W. F. (2001). Models of data: A theory of how people evaluate data. *Cognition and Instruction, 19*, 323–393.
Douven, I. (1999). Inference to the best explanation made coherent. *Philosophy, of Science, 66*, S424–S435.
Douven, I. (2011). Abduction. In E. N. Zalta (Ed.), *The Stanford encyclopedia of philosophy* (Spring 2011 ed.). Retrieved from http://plato.stanford.edu/archives/spr2011/entries/abduction.
Dowe, P. (2008). Causal processes. In E.N. Zalta (Ed.), *The Stanford encyclopedia of philosophy* (Fall 2008 ed.). Retrieved from http://plato.stanford.edu/archives/fall2008/entries/causation-process/.
Dunbar, K. (1995). How scientists really reason: Scientific reasoning in real-world laboratories. In R. J. Sternberg & J. E. Davidson (Eds.), *The nature of insight* (pp. 365–395). Cambridge, MA: MIT Press.
Dunbar, K. (1997). How scientists think: Online creativity and conceptual change in science. In T. B. Ward, S. M. Smith, & S. Vaid (Eds.), *Conceptual structures and processes: Emergence, discovery and change*. Washington, DC: APA Press.
Fedyk, M., & Xu, F. (2016). *The epistemology of rational constructivism*. Philosophy of Science Bi-Annual Meeting, Atlanta, GA.

Haig, B. D. (2009). Inference to the best explanation: A neglected approach to theory appraisal in psychology. *American Journal of Psychology, 122*(2), 219–234.

Gero, J. M., & Conkey, M. W. (Eds.). (1991). *Engendering archaeology*. Oxford, UK: Basil Blackwell.

Goodman, N. (1954/1955). *Fact, fiction, and forecast*, University of London: Athlone Press; Cambridge, MA: Harvard University Press; 2nd ed. Indianapolis: Bobbs-Merrill, 1965; 3rd ed. Indianapolis: Bobbs-Merrill, 1973; 4th ed. Cambridge, MA: Harvard University Press, 1983.

Gopnik, A., & Schulz, L. (2007). *Causal learning*. Oxford: Oxford University Press.

Harman, G. (1965). The inference to the best explanation. *Philosophical Review, 74*, 88–95.

Harris, P. L. (2000). Children's metaphysical questions. In K. S. Rosengren, C. N. Johnson, & P. L. Harris (Eds.), *Imagining the impossible: Magical, scientific, and religious thinking in children*. Cambridge: Cambridge University Press.

Hemmerich, J. A., Van Voorhis, K., & Wiley, J. (2016). Anomalous evidence, confidence change, and theory change. *Cognitive Science, 40*, 1534–1560.

Hempel, C. G. (1966). *Philosophy of natural science*. Englewood Cliffs, NJ: Prentice-Hall.

Herrnstein, R. J. (1973). *I. Q. in the meritocracy*. Atlantic Monthly Press. Boston: Little, Brown.

Herrnstein, R. J., & Murray, C. (1994). *The bell curve: Intelligence and class structure in American life*. New York: Free Press.

Isaacs, N. (1930). Children's "why" questions. In S. Isaacs (Ed.), *The Intellectual Growth of Young Children*. London: Routledge and Kegan Paul.

Jennings, D. L., Amabile, T., & Ross, L. (1982). The intuitive scientist's assessment of covariation: Data-based vs. theory-based judgments. In A. Tversky, D. Kahneman, & P. Slovic (Eds.), *Judgment under uncertainty: Heuristics and biases*. New York: Cambridge University Press.

Kemp, C., & Tenenbaum, J. B. (2009). Structured statistical models of inductive reasoning. *Psychological Review, 116*, (1), 20–58.

Klahr, D. (2000). *Exploring science: The cognition and development of discovery processes*. Cambridge, MA: MIT Press.

Koslowski, B., (1996). *Theory and Evidence: the development of scientific reasoning*. Cambridge, MA: MIT Press.

Koslowski, B. (2012). Inference to the best explanation (IBE) and the causal and scientific reasoning of nonscientists. In R. W. Proctor & E. J. Capaldi (Eds.), *The psychology of science: Implicit and explicit reasoning*. New York: Oxford University Press.

Koslowski, B. (2012). Scientific reasoning: Explanation, confirmation bias, and scientific practice. In G. Feist and M. Gorman (Eds.), *Handbook of the psychology of science and technology*. New York: Springer.

Koslowski, B., Beckmann, L., Bowers, E., DeVito, J., Wonderly, B., & Vermeylan, F. M. (2008, July). *The cognitive basis for confirmation bias is more nuanced than one might expect*. Paper presented at the meetings of the International Society of the Psychology of Science and Technology, Berlin.

Koslowski, B., & Maqueda, M. (1993). What is confirmation bias and when do people have it? *Merrill-Palmer Quarterly, 39*(1), Special issue on: The development of rationality and critical thinking, 104–130.

Koslowski, B., Marasia, J., Chelenza, M., & Dublin, R. (2008). Information becomes evidence when an explanation can incorporate it into a causal framework. *Cognitive Development, 23*, 472–487.

Koslowski, B., Marasia, J., Vermeylen, F. M., Hendrix, V. (2013). A disconfirming strategy is not necessarily better than a confirming strategy. *American Journal of Psychology, 126*(3), 335–354.

Koslowski, B., & Pierce, A. (1981, April). *Children's spontaneous explanations and requests for explanations*. Paper presented at the Society for Research in Child Development, Boston, MA.

Kuhn, D. (1991). *The skills of argument*. Cambridge: Cambridge University Press.

Kuhn, D., Amsel, E., & O'Loughlin, M. (1988). *The development of scientific thinking skills*. Orlando, FL: Academic Press.

Legare, C. H. (2012). Exploring explanation: Explaining inconsistent evidence informs exploratory hypothesis testing behavior in young children. *Child Development, 83*(1), 173–185.

Legare, C. H., Gelman, S. A., & Wellman, H. M. (2010). Inconsistency with prior knowledge triggers children's causal explanatory reasoning. *Child Development, 81*, 929–944.

Lesgold, A. M., Rubinson, H., Feltovich, P. J., Glaser, R., & Klopfer, D. (1988). Expertise in a complex skill: Diagnosing x-ray pictures. In M. T. H. Chi, R. Glaser, & M. Farr (Eds.), *The nature of expertise*. Hillsdale, NJ: Lawrence Erlbaum Associates.

Lipton, P. (1991). *Inference to the best explanation*. London: Routledge.

Lipton, P. (January 01, 1993). Is the best good enough? *Proceedings of the Aristotelian Society* 93, 89–104.

Lombrozo, T. (2007). Simplicity and probability in causal explanation. *Cognitive Psychology, 55*, 232–257.

Lombrozo, T. (2012). Explanation and abductive inference. In K. J. Holyoak & R. G. Morrison (Eds.), *Oxford handbook of thinking and reasoning*. Oxford: Oxford University Press.

Lombrozo, T., & Carey, S. (2006). Functional explanation and the function of explanation. *Cognition, 99*, 167–204.

Murphy, G., & Medin, D. (1985). The role of theories in conceptual coherence. *Psychological Review, 92*(3), 289–316.

Nickerson, R. S. (1998). Confirmation bias: A ubiquitous phenomenon in many guises. *Review of General Psychology, 2*, 175–220.

Peirce, C. S. (1931–1958). *Collected papers of Charles Sanders Peirce* (C. Hartshorne, P. Weiss, & A. Burks, Eds.). Cambridge, MA: Harvard University Press.

Proctor, R. W., & Capaldi, E. J. (2006). *Why science matters*. Malden, MA: Blackwell.

Psillos, S. (2000). Abduction: Between conceptual richness and computational complexity. In A. K. Kakas and P. Flach (Eds.), *Abduction and induction: Essays on their relation and integration* (pp. 59–74). Dordrecht: Kluwer.

Psillos, S. (2004). Inference to the best explanation and bayesianism. In F. Stadler (Ed.), *Induction and deduction in the sciences* (pp. 83–91). Dordrecht: Kluwer.

Putnam, H. (1981). *Reason, truth and history*. Cambridge: Cambridge University Press.

Quine, W., & Ullian, J. (1970). *The web of belief*. New York: Random House.

Rips, L. (1989). Similarity, typicality, and categorization. In S. Vosniadou & A. Ortony (Eds.), *Similarity and analogical reasoning* (pp. 21–59). Cambridge, UK: Cambridge University Press.

Salmon, W. (1998). *Causality and explanation*. Oxford: Oxford University Press.

Schauble, L. (1990). Belief revision in children: The role of prior knowledge and strategies for generating evidence. *Journal of Experimental Child Psychology, 49*, 31–57.

Schulz, L. E., & Bonawitz, E. B. (2007). Serious fun: Preschoolers play more when evidence is confounded. *Developmental Psychology, 43*(4), 1045–1050.

Slocum, S. (1975). Woman the gatherer: Male bias in anthropology. In R. Reiter (Ed.), *Toward an anthropology of women* (pp. 36–50). New York: Monthly Review Press.

Sloman, S. A., Love, B. C., & Ahn, W. (1998). Feature centrality and conceptual coherence. *Cognitive Science, 22*, 189–228.

Sodian, B., Zaitchik, D., & Carey, S. (1991). Young children's differentiation of hypothetical beliefs from evidence. *Child Development, 62*, 753–766.

Steele, C. M. (2010). *Whistling Vivaldi and other clues to how stereotypes affect us*. New York, NY: W. W. Norton & Company.

Thagard, P. (1989). Explanatory coherence. *Behavioral and Brain Sciences, 12*, 435–467.

Thagard, P., & Verbeurgt, K. (1998). Coherence as constraint satisfaction. *Cognitive Science, 22*, 1–24.

Vallee-Tourangeau, F., Beynon, D. M., & James, S. A. (2000). The role of alternative hypotheses in the integration of evidence that disconfirms an acquired belief. *European Journal of Cognitive Psychology, 12*(1), 107–129.

Valian, V. (1999). *Why so slow? The advancement of women*. Cambridge, MA: MIT Press.

Woodward, J. (2014). Scientific explanation. In E. N. Zalta (Ed.), *The Stanford encyclopedia of philosophy* (Winter 2014 ed.). Retrieved from http://plato.stanford.edu/archives/win2014/entries/scientific-explanation/.

Wright, J. C., & Murphy, G. L. (1986). The utility of theories in intuitive statistics: The robustness of theory-based judgments. *Journal of Experimental Psychology: General, 113*, 301–322.

Wylie, A. (2003). "Why Standpoint Matters" in Robert Figueroa and Sandra Harding (Eds.), *Science and other cultures: Issues in philosophies of science and technology*. London: Routledge.

21
THE DEVELOPMENT OF LOGICAL REASONING

Henry Markovits

The ability to reason is one of the critical features that distinguish humans from other species. In its most general sense, reasoning refers to any form of overtly expressed verbal thinking, irrespective of its specific nature. But the most striking form of human reasoning, and arguably the one that has received the most attention, concerns deductive reasoning – that is, the ability to make inferences that are logically valid. This is the essence of hypothetical thinking and it is this ability that arguably underlies much of the technological and scientific progress of at least the past couple of centuries. The associated question of how logical reasoning develops has also been a very important empirical and theoretical theme. This will accordingly be the specific focus of this chapter.

Dual process theories and logical reasoning

Logical reasoning has often been situated within the context of current dual process theories of reasoning (Epstein, 1994; Evans & Stanovich, 2013; Klaczynski, 2001; Sloman, 1996; Stanovich, West, Ackerman, Kyllonen, & Roberts, 1999). One of the more consistent results in the study of reasoning concerns the effects of certain forms of non-logical factors in the inferences that people make. For example, many studies have shown that people's belief in the truth of a putative conclusion affects their judgments of logical validity (Evans, Barston, & Pollard, 1983; Markovits & Nantel, 1989; Sá, West, & Stanovich, 1999; see also Ball & Thompson, this volume). Dual process theories attempt to codify these effects by postulating two inferential systems, known by a variety of names (experiential: logical, System 1: System 2, analytic: heuristic). The more complex of these systems (which we will refer to as the analytic system) is capable of logical reasoning and requires some form of conscious working-memory intensive processing. By contrast, the heuristic system uses rapid, low-level intuitive processes to make inferences. The conclusions that people produce are due to some form of currently unspecified interaction between the two systems (Evans & Stanovich, 2013). Studies examining reasoning within a dual-process context have mostly concentrated on the impact of heuristic factors on reasoning. Relatively little attention has been paid to how a processing system that is potentially capable of logical reasoning functions, and critically how it develops. Thus, although it is important to understand the interactions between the two systems (Barrouillet, 2011; Overton & Ricco, 2011; see also Toplak, this volume), in the following, we will specifically examine empirical data and current theories of the development of basic logical reasoning. Although of real importance, more complex forms of reasoning, such as argumentation and scientific reasoning (Kuhn, 1989, 1991; Kuhn et al., 1988; Kuhn & Udell, 2003; Siegler, 1978; Zimmerman, 2000), will not be examined here.

Piaget's theory: formal operations as the endpoint of development

The starting point for any discussion of the development of logical reasoning remains Piaget's theory of cognitive development (Inhelder & Piaget, 1958). Despite some changes, its basic postulates are the following. First, it is assumed that there is some underlying form of structural consistency that characterizes the way that information is processed and the kinds of inferences that can be made by the cognitive system. Second, newborns are assumed to enter life with a minimum level of cognitive abilities that are initially expressed nonverbally, but with a biological capacity to gradually adapt to and represent characteristics of the external world through the cycle of assimilation and accommodation. This cycle, along with a basic representational capacity, leads to a series of increasingly complex and more abstract forms of logic that characterize the different stages of cognitive development. Concrete operational thinking allows making limited forms of inference based on observable properties and develops roughly through elementary schooling. The endpoint of individual development is a formal reasoning structure that in addition to some basic principles of scientific reasoning more or less corresponds to standard propositional logic (Lourenço, 1995).

Piagetian theory supposes that children who are not yet at the appropriate stage of development should be unable to make logical deductions at that level, but that eventually, most adolescents and adults should show quite a high level of basic formal reasoning abilities, although this is modulated by familiarity (Piaget, 1972). Many of the studies that have examined the development of logical reasoning abilities originated in attempts to examine these two hypotheses, especially the first. These studies have produced quite variable results, and before examining the different theories that have been proposed, it is useful to give an overview of the empirical data.

We will examine two very basic forms of logical reasoning, transitivity and conditional reasoning, which have been the focus of a great many developmental studies. The former is an example of a concrete operational form of deduction and since it has been comparatively neglected recently will only be briefly summarized, while the latter is an archetype of formal operational thinking.

Developmental patterns in transitive reasoning

A transitive relation (r) is one that can be placed on at least an ordinal scale, and thus allows going from two relations A r B and B r C to the logically necessary conclusion that A r C (example: Tom is heavier than Allan, Allan is heavier than Joe). Initial studies of transitivity found that children younger than 7–9 years of age had problems making transitive inferences (Murray & Youniss, 1968; Piaget, Inhelder, & Szeminksa, 1960; Smedslund, 1963). However, Bryant and Trabasso (1971) hypothesized that poor performance might be due to the difficulty of retaining premise information in memory. In a classic experiment, they showed that four-year-old children who were given extensive practice on sets of premise pairs were indeed able to make correct transitive inferences (see also Riley & Trabasso, 1974), although it has been found that practice allows children to use simple heuristics which can produce the correct answer to certain forms of transitive inferences (de Boysson-Bardies & O'Regan, 1973). Subsequent studies have introduced different methodological variations, with some showing that very young children have some form of transitive reasoning abilities (Mou, Province, & Luo, 2014; Pears & Bryant,

1990), with others showing clear developmental increases (Andrews & Halford, 1998; Halford, 1984; Markovits, Dumas, & Malfait, 1995; see Breslow, 1981; Wright, 2001 for reviews). Further complicating this picture are studies that show that several nonhuman species are able to make what appear to be transitive inferences, such as pigeons (Von Fersen, Wynne, Delius, & Staddon, 1991), rats (Roberts & Phelps, 1994), and some primates (MacLean, Merritt, & Brannon, 2008). Interestingly, birds such as jays have been shown to use transitive inferences to predict social dominance (Bond, Kamil, & Balda, 2004), while very young children appear to do the same (Mascaro & Csibra, 2014). Russell (1996) proposed that younger children and other species may have access to an associative strategy that depends on the ability to internalize some consistent representation of certain limited forms of relationships, while older children can rely on a more explicit form of logical strategy (see also Wright, 2012).

Developmental patterns in conditional reasoning

Similar distinctions can be seen when we examine how children respond to problems involving conditional reasoning, which is a key component of formal reasoning. Conditional (if–then) reasoning is the core of the kind of hypothetical reasoning that underlies mathematical and scientific reasoning. Consequently, it is the most studied of all the different forms of logical reasoning. The most common measurement of conditional reasoning abilities examines conditional inferences, based on a major "P implies Q" premise, with P being the antecedent term and Q the consequent term. There are four such inferences, corresponding to minor premises that affirm or deny the antecedent or consequent terms. The most direct of the four inferences is modus ponens (MP), which involves the premises "if P then Q. P is true" and leads to the logical conclusion that "Q is true". The modus tollens inference (MT) involves the premises "If P then Q. Q is false" and leads to the logical conclusion that "P is false". The two remaining inferences do not allow any certain conclusion. The first of these is the Affirmation of the Consequent (AC), which involves the premises "If P then Q. Q is true". The second of these is the Denial of the Antecedent (DA), which involves the premises "If P then Q. P is false". Similarly to the analysis of the AC inference, in this case the possible conclusion that "Q is false" is not certain.

Other measures of conditional reasoning which are more complex have also been studied in a developmental context. Several studies have used versions of the selection task (Wason, 1968). These present a given conditional rule, and a series of four cards each of which have P or not-P on one side and Q or not-Q on the other. Subjects see only one side of the cards and must choose which cards should be turned over in order to determine whether the rule is true or not. Truth table tasks (Wason & Johnson-Laird, 1972) present a conditional relation along with the four combinations of antecedent and consequent terms. Subjects are asked what the consequence of the truth of each combination has for the truth value of the conditional relation. Finally, possibility tasks (Gauffroy & Barrouillet, 2009) present a given conditional rule and ask subjects to generate combinations of antecedent and consequent terms that are possible if the rule is true. All of these different problems have been used fairly indiscriminately to examine conditional reasoning. However, it should be remarked that they probably represent very different levels of cognitive challenges, despite their surface level similarity. Thus, care should be taken when comparing developmental patterns across different tasks.

Initial studies examining conditional inferences found that even adolescents (Taplin, Staudenmayer, & Taddonio, 1974; Wildman & Fletcher, 1977) and adults (Markovits, 1985) did not correctly respond to all of the four conditional inferences, with the most common set of responses being a biconditional pattern, with all four inferences being accepted, which corresponds to an interpretation of "If and only if P then Q" (Knifong, 1974; Kodroff & Roberge, 1975). These studies did show that even very young children are able to correctly evaluate the conclusion to the MP (and often to the MT) inferences, which is a form of logical reasoning (Ennis, 1976). Studies examining MP reasoning have also found that even preschool children are able to make logical inferences analogous to MP with simple abstract premises, although they could not do so when premises were empirically false (Hawkins et al., 1984). Other studies found that preschoolers can reason logically even with false premises (e.g. "if something is a dog, then it cannot bark") when these were embedded into some sort of imaginary or fantasy context (Dias & Harris, 1988; 1990). In other words, very young children do appear to be able to consistently reason logically with MP inferences with familiar or abstract content, and can do so with content that is false, when aided.

However, other results present a more complex developmental picture. The first concerns reasoning with causal conditionals (if cause P then effect Q) for which there are potential *disabling conditions* (Cummins, 1995; Cummins, Lubart, Alksnis, & Rist, 1991). These are conditions that can empirically allow "P to be true" with "Q not being true". For example, for the causal conditional relation "If a glass is dropped, then the glass will break", conditions such as having a rug on the floor are disabling conditions. Several studies have shown that even adults tend to reject the MP inference when reasoning with premises for which there are relatively many disabling conditions (Cummins, 1995; Cummins et al., 1991; De Neys, Schaeken, Walter, & d'Ydewalle, 2003; Thompson, 1995). Evidence of early abilities to reason correctly with the MP inference would suggest very limited developmental change. However, further results suggest the opposite. For example, there is evidence of an age-related *decrease* in correct MP inferences on causal conditionals with many disabling conditions between eight and twelve years of age (Janveau-Brennan & Markovits, 1999). Although young children can reason logically with MP reasoning with empirically false premises when provided with a suitable context, their ability to do so spontaneously shows a clear developmental increase until early adolescence (Markovits & Vachon, 1989). Finally, young children are unable to distinguish between simple logical MP inferences and inferences that are only suggested, but are not logically necessary until the end of primary school (Markovits, Schleifer, & Fortier, 1989).

The second form of precocious reasoning suggested by the initial studies on conditional inferences is with the MT inference. MT inferences are the most structurally complex of the four, involving both negation and a reversed direction of inference (from consequent to antecedent). It is thus surprising that, as previously noted, young children often give the logically correct response to this inference. As with the MP inference, early competence is associated with clear developmental change. In this case, studies show an inverted developmental pattern, with younger children giving the logical response more often than older children (O'Brien & Overton, 1980; see also Markovits, Doyon, & Simoneau (2002) for a similar analysis with adults).

Analysis of reasoning on the two uncertain forms, AC and DA, also shows differential developmental and content-related patterns that are similar for both forms. Many of the latter are mediated by the well-documented influence of *alternative antecedents*. An alternative antecedent for a "P implies Q" premise is a case A, such that "if A then Q" is true. For example, for the conditional premise "If a rock is thrown at a window, the window will break", alternative antecedents are cases such as "throwing a chair at a window". Many studies have shown that premises that allow access to greater numbers of alternative antecedents also produce increased rates of (logically correct) rejection of the conclusions to the AC and the DA inferences both in adults and children (Cummins, 1995; Cummins et al., 1991; Daniel, 2006; Klaczynski & Narasimham, 1998; Markovits & Vachon, 1990; Quinn & Markovits, 1998; Thompson, 1995).

Several studies have demonstrated that even young children can respond logically to the AC and DA inferences. Rumain, Connell, and Braine (1983) have shown that children as young as

7–8 years of age are able to respond logically on the uncertain inferences when explicitly provided with cues that the conditional rule is not a pragmatic biconditional. Kuhn (1977) found that when premises were phrased in a conversationally appropriate way, 7- to 8-year old children were also able to reason logically on the uncertain inferences. In addition, it has been found that 7- to 8-year-olds can reason logically on these inferences without any specific help when given category-based conditional premises ("If an animal is a dog, then it has four legs": Markovits, 2000; Markovits et al., 1996). In addition, children as young as six years of age can reason logically when given premises referring to concrete, perceptually available cases (Markovits & Thompson, 2008).

However, other results show clear developmental patterns in reasoning with uncertain inferences. Reasoning with causal conditional premises (if cause P then effect Q) shows a definite developmental increase, with very low levels of correct responding on the uncertain premises at 7–8 years of age that increases up to early adolescence (Janveau-Brennan & Markovits, 1999). Reasoning with false causal premises (e.g. "if a feather is thrown at a window, then the window will break") shows a similar developmental pattern, but with higher levels of correct responding found only with adolescent children (Markovits, 2014b; Markovits & Vachon, 1989).

Other studies have shown that the ability to reason correctly on the uncertain inferences is very late to develop. Reasoning with abstract premises shows a much later developmental pattern, with high levels of correct responding on the uncertain inferences found only among adults (Markovits & Vachon, 1990; Venet & Markovits, 2001). In a similar vein, the ability to generate fully conditional interpretations on truth table tasks (Barrouillet & Lecas, 1999) and possibility tasks (Gauffroy & Barrouillet, 2011) is found only with older adolescents.

Finally, selection task performance has been tied to social and/or pragmatic contexts with surprising developmental results. Typically even very well educated adults find it difficult to give the logically correct answers to the original form of the selection task (Griggs & Cox, 1982), which used unrelated categories (if a vowel then an odd number). In contrast, conditional relations expressing certain forms of pragmatic inference schemas (if you want to drink legally, then you must be more than 21 years of age) have been shown to lead to very high levels of correct responding (Cheng & Holyoak, 1985; 1989) and when suitably simplified in younger children (Girotto, Light, & Colbourn, 1988; Light, Blaye, Gilly, & Girotto, 1989). The related notion of cheater detection, which has been claimed to represent an innate form of reasoning (Cosmides, 1989), has also been used to show that very young children can reason correctly on limited forms of the selection task (Cummins, 1996).

Finally, it is useful to very briefly mention some developmental patterns in children's metacognitive understanding of logical reasoning. Although this is not directly related to specific forms of inference, they represent principles that are clearly associated with these. Once again, there is a mixed developmental picture. For example, an examination of children's ability to distinguish between necessary and possible conclusions has shown both very early competence (Bindra, Clarke, & Shultz, 1980; Ruffman, 1999) and clear developmental trajectories (Fabricius, Sophian, & Wellman, 1987; Miller, Custer, & Nassau, 2000; Morris, 2000). Similarly, examination of children's ability to distinguish between logical and nonlogical arguments has shown both early competence (Morris, 2000; Morsanyi & Handley, 2012) and clear developmental increases (Markovits et al., 1989; Moshman & Franks, 1986).

Theories of reasoning

Examination of the empirical results concerning children's ability to make correct transitive and conditional inferences shows three different patterns. First, there is clear evidence that young children can make correct inferences under the right conditions. Second, there is equally clear evidence that the ability to make correct inferences increases consistently with age. Third, there are inferential systems tied to social reasoning that allow some intuitive forms of inference that can generate logically appropriate responses in appropriate contexts. As a consequence, several different theories have been proposed to explain how basic logical reasoning develops. These focus mostly on conditional reasoning, which reflects the increasing importance of research into this form of reasoning. In the following, a brief description of these is given. As will be seen, each theory emphasizes different empirical data and has a correspondingly different focus; for an excellent integrative synthesis, see Ricco (in press). In the following descriptions, we concentrate on specific aspects of these theories that most closely correspond to their underlying empirical base.

Natural logic theory

Braine's natural logic theory places a specific emphasis on the precocious ability of young children to make some basic forms of logical inference, such as the MP inference (Ennis, 1976; Hawkins et al., 1984; Kuhn, 1977). In fact, Braine (Braine, 1978; Braine & O'Brien, 1991; Braine & O'Brien, 1998) claimed that there was a basic mental logic composed of syntactic inferential rules (referred to as primary reasoning skills) which are biologically based. The specific argument is that certain inferences are so critical to behavior, particularly with respect to language comprehension and the integration of information derived from diverse sources, that the selection pressure to incorporate them into the basic architecture of the human mind would have been very strong (Braine & O'Brien, 1998; see also Cohen, 1981). More complex inference schemas are referred to as indirect reasoning strategies and require learning. Such basic rules are essentially syntactic in nature and allow generation of the correct response based solely on the logical form of a given inference. This in turn would predict that reasoning should be consistently logical for inferences for which there exist basic inference schemas.

Variability in inferences is explained by an initial phase in which verbally presented inferences are subject to different forms of semantic translation. These imply two major levels of analysis. Firstly, reasoners must identify the nature of the inferential task. This involves distinguishing between natural reasoning, for which the reasoner's full range of knowledge and experience must be deployed (see also Scribner, 1986), and analytic reasoning, which can be understood as corresponding to the logical games that are taught in academic settings. Secondly, reasoners will attempt to use pragmatic or conversational principles that govern communication (Grice, 1981) in order to modify the interpretation of a given logical connective. This will result in deployment of schemas consistent with the reinterpretation of premises. For example, if–then promises are often interpreted as biconditionals (Fillenbaum, 1975).

Briefly, this theory considers the ability to reason logically as the outcome of the use of an inferential rule that theoretically allows producing the correct response in all circumstances, modulated by pragmatic considerations. Braine's theory thus considers that evidence of early competence reflects the existence of basic logical reasoning abilities. Development requires training and experience and consists of subsequent acquisition of more complex schemas and the increasing ability to play the logical game.

Semantic memory and mental models

Markovits and colleagues (Markovits & Lortie Forgues, 2011; Markovits & Barrouillet, 2002; Markovits, 2013) have proposed a developmental theory that also focuses on the early ability to reason logically, but has a more important developmental component. This uses a modified version of mental model theory (Johnson-Laird, 2001; Johnson-Laird, & Byrne, 1991; 2002). This theory proposes that reasoning involves a form of figural representation of possible states of the world that are consistent with premises. A key component of this theory is the role of counterexamples (Johnson-Laird, 2012; Schroyens, Schaeken, & Handley, 2003). Evaluation of a putative conclusion to a given inference is done by examining the resulting models for potential counterexamples. If there are counterexamples, then the conclusion is rejected, otherwise it is considered to be valid. The relationship between counterexamples and validity is seen as the fundamental principle underlying the development of logical competence (Markovits, 2014a).

This theory postulates two levels of reasoning. The developmentally more primitive one involves reasoning with familiar premises. The model for this form of reasoning is based on the idea that underlying the simple statement of if–then premises are two associated categories of information, which, as has previously been discussed, have been shown to have a clear impact on conditional inferences: alternative antecedents and potential disablers. Correct reasoning on the MP and MT inferences requires inhibiting potential disablers. Correct reasoning on the AC and DA inferences requires retrieving alternative antecedents. Critically, both of these components have been shown to be related to individual differences in information processing (De Neys & Everaerts, 2008; Handley, Capon, Beveridge, Dennis, & Evans, 2004; Markovits & Doyon, 2004; Markovits & Quinn, 2002; Simoneau & Markovits, 2003).

What this model then suggests is that when people are reasoning with concrete if–then premises, they will activate a semantic network of information related to these premises, which includes potential alternative antecedents and disablers (Markovits & Potvin, 2001). If any of these are retrieved during reasoning, they will be incorporated into the corresponding mental model. For example, consider an AC inference "If P then Q, Q is true". The simplest model of the major premise is the following:

P Q

With this model, the conclusion that "P is true" would be accepted. However, if an alternative antecedent is retrieved, it will be incorporated into the model in the following way:

P Q
A Q

With these models, the conclusion that "P is true" would be (correctly) rejected. Similarly, retrieval of an alternative antecedent would allow rejection of the DA inference.

By contrast, retrieval of a disabler will result in rejection of the conclusion for the MP and the MT inferences. Thus, responding correctly to these inferences requires inhibiting disabler retrieval. Adding to the difficulty of these processes is the fact that inhibition and retrieval are antithetical processes (De Neys & Everaerts, 2008; Markovits, 1995). When reasoning with familiar concrete conditionals, the probability of generating alternatives or inhibiting disablers will vary (among other factors) according to the quantity of information available in memory and efficiency of memory retrieval and inhibitory processes, which all show clear developmental increases (Bjorklund, 1987; Davidson, Amso, Anderson, & Diamond, 2006; Gaillard, Barrouillet, Jarrold, & Camos, 2011; Handley et al., 2004). One further distinction can be made between premises referring to properties and categories (e.g. "if an animal is a dog, then it has legs") and causal premises (e.g. "if a rock is thrown at a window, the window will break"). Although both forms of premise rely on knowledge stored in memory, alternative antecedents for causals require a more complex process. For example, an alternative antecedent to breaking a window requires using some form of causal theory to generate different ways to break windows.

This analysis leads to some clear developmental predictions of how logical reasoning with familiar premises develops. First, logical reasoning should appear earlier with category based premises than with causal premises. In fact, children as young as six to seven years of age can reason logically with the former (Markovits, 2000; Markovits & Thompson, 2008), while the beginnings of logical reasoning with causal premises do not appear consistently before 9 to 10 years of age (Janveau-Brennan & Markovits, 1999). Both forms of reasoning show clear developmental increases with age, with very high levels of logical reasoning found at the beginning of adolescence (Markovits, 2017). Nonetheless, content effects determined by the relative accessibility of alternative antecedents and disablers remain significant throughout this period, and are found in educated adults (Cummins et al., 1991; De Neys, Schaeken, et al., 2003; Thompson, 1995).

This theory also suggests the existence of a second phase of reasoning, characterized by the more abstract ability to reason logically with empirically false premises (Markovits & Vachon, 1989) and subsequently with abstract premises (Markovits & Vachon, 1990; Venet & Markovits, 2001). This transition is consistent with a representational redescription model such as that proposed by Karmiloff-Smith (1995). The key component is the redescription of counterexamples. When reasoning with familiar premises, counterexamples are retrieved from memory in the form of alternative antecedents. When reasoning with contrary-to-fact or more abstract forms of premises, counterexamples cannot be retrieved, but must be actively generated by the reasoner. Recent empirical results are consistent with this transition. The model predicts that reasoning with empirically false premises is more complex than reasoning with familiar premises (Markovits, 2014b). Other results have shown that reasoning with empirically false premises produces higher levels of logical responses than reasoning with abstract premises and that levels of logical responses to abstract premises improve when reasoning with empirically false premises beforehand (Markovits & Lortie Forgues, 2011). Critically, neither reasoning with familiar premises nor generating alternative antecedents to familiar premises has any effect on reasoning with empirically false or with abstract premises.

This theory considers that logical reasoning is demonstrated when children are able to construct an explicit mental model that allows both correct inferences and the ability to explicitly express the existence of counterexamples (Markovits et al., 1996). Development is seen as a process that extends this early ability to increasingly complex and abstract forms of reasoning.

Piagetian theory and the competence-procedural model

Overton and colleagues (O'Brien & Overton, 1982; Overton, Byrnes, & O'Brien, 1985; Overton & Ricco, 2011; Overton, 2011) have proposed an extension of Piaget's original theory that attempts to maintain the developmental progression in logical competence underlying this theory, while explaining variability in logical performance. This theory focuses on the developmental progression in reasoning ability, while discounting evidence of early logical reasoning. It postulates the existence of an underlying mental logic, which can be instantiated in a variety of ways or procedures, potentially leading to highly variable performance. However, in contrast to Brain's natural logic theory, children's mental logic undergoes a clear developmental progression. This theory distinguishes between two levels of reasoning, which roughly distinguish preadolescents from adolescents. The former possess a form of mental logic that corresponds to class-based reasoning, such as that underlying transitivity (Byrnes, 1988; Byrnes & Overton, 1986). This potentially allows preadolescents to make limited forms of seemingly correct inferences. However, formal reasoning competence requires a more systemic approach, in which a logical deduction represents a more complete understanding of the full range of possibilities (Overton & Ricco, 2011).

One key postulate of this theory that has been tested empirically is that failure to reason logically is due to a failure in competence in younger children, but can be explained by performance modulators in older adolescents and adults. Distinguishing between these two sources of non-logical reasoning can be done by using a form of Vygotskian scaffolding (Berk & Winsler, 1995). Providing cues to correct reasoning should be relatively futile with younger reasoners, since they do not have the requisite competence to profit from any intervention. Helping older reasoners should, on the other hand, improve their performance. This prediction was examined in an initial set of studies (O'Brien & Overton, 1980; 1982; Overton, Byrnes, & O'Brien, 1985) that used a procedure by which reasoners were given information designed to contradict a faulty interpretation of a conditional rule. This intervention was effective in improving performance only among older adolescents. Other studies have shown facilitation of logical reasoning when variables such as familiarity and the related concept of relevance (Ward & Overton, 1990) are manipulated, but only among older reasoners (Müller, Overton, & Reene, 2001; Overton, Ward, Black, Noveck, & O'Brien, 1987; Ward & Overton, 1990).

Overton's theory considers that logical reasoning corresponds to a complex mental logic that considers not only individual inferences but interactions between these. As such, it focuses on developmental increases in the ability to make logical inferences with age. Evidence of early deductive competence is discounted as an artefact of a more primitive reasoning system. However, since this latter is a precursor to formal logic, it must be considered as a necessary stage in a longer developmental sequence.

Mental models and the development of basic semantics

Barrouillet, Geoffroy, and colleagues (Barrouillet, Gauffroy, & Lecas, 2008; Gauffroy & Barrouillet, 2009, 2011) have presented a developmental version of mental model theory that focusses specifically on the interpretation of basic conditionals and how working memory constraints affect this in children and adolescents. Mental model theory considers that the basic semantic interpretation of conditionals corresponds to the following set of models (which represent the true cases of the truth table for the conditional):

P	Q
not-P	Q
not-P	not-Q

Generation of this set of models potentially allows reasoners to produce the logically correct response to all four conditional inferences. However, a basic constraint postulated by this theory is the requirement to keep models in working memory (Johnson-Laird & Bara, 1984).

Barrouillet and Lecas (1999) argued that since working memory capacity has a clear developmental trajectory (Case, Kurland, & Goldberg, 1982; Siegel & Ryan, 1989), this should affect the interpretation of conditionals in children. They proposed that the development of the interpretation of basic conditionals goes through three major phases. The first such phase is found in younger, preadolescent children whose working memory is quite limited and who are able to produce only a single model, which in this case is the following one:

P	Q

A child limited to such a model will interpret if–then relations as similar to conjunctives. Somewhat older children will be able to maintain two models in memory. This leads to the following two models:

P	Q
not-P	not-Q

which should lead to a biconditional interpretation. Finally, a fully conditional interpretation should be possible only for much older adolescents and adults who are able to manipulate the three required models.

Support for this model has come from studies using truth-table and possibilities tasks. The hypothesized sequence has been found both on the possibilities task (Barrouillet, Grosset, & Lecas, 2000) and the truth table task Barrouillet and Lecas (1999), when conditional rules involving arbitrary terms are used (if a shape is round then it is blue). However, performance on the truth table task generates what have been referred to as "defective" versions (Wason & Johnson-Laird, 1972). This is a pattern where normally true combinations involving negations of the antecedent are considered irrelevant, instead of true. With this caveat, the postulated sequence has been consistently found. Fully conditional interpretations are not observed before late adolescence. A recent study (Gauffroy & Barrouillet, 2011) has shown that while possibilities and truth-table tasks show the same developmental sequence, the latter is developmentally later (by about three years). This in turn is consistent with mental model theory, which supposes that thinking in terms of possibilities is an essential part of reasoning, while thinking in terms of truth values is more complex.

A more recent addition to this basic model incorporates a pragmatic component, which reflects the interpretational module postulated by mental model theory (Johnson-Laird, & Byrne, 2002). However, Gauffroy and Barrouillet (2009) add one key distinction to this module. Accessing the fleshed-out interpretation of a basic conditional uses working memory and results in defective truth values, as noted above. A pragmatic interpretation of a conditional is, in contrast, done intuitively and rapidly, with no working memory load. This results in the generation of models that are clearly labelled as true. Thus, for example, given a conditional promise (if you do P, then I'll give you Q), even young children will generate models corresponding to:

P	Q
Not-P	not-Q

which corresponds to the implicit inference underlying most promises of this kind, that "If you do not do P, then you will not get Q". The revised model integrates rapid and intuitive processing into the mental model account and provides an explanation for the observation of defective truth tables (Barrouillet et al., 2008).

This model thus proposes a developmental sequence based on the underlying semantics of the conditional. The ability to reason logically requires sufficient working memory capacity to generate and cognitively manipulate the three models of the complete conditional, and is thus not seen until late adolescence. The model is thus focused on logical reasoning as a very late developmental ability. Evidence of early competence is explained by some form of pragmatic and/or intuitive reasoning processes, which are not considered to be logical. However, Barrouillet (2011) has proposed that such intuitive processes may in fact be precursors to a formal logical competence, as in in some versions of Piagetian theory (Peel, 1959).

Metacognitive development

Metacognition refers to the ability to think about one's own reasoning processes (Flavell, 1979; Kitchner, 1983). The most direct theory relating metacognition to logical reasoning is Moshman's account of reasoning (Moshman, 2004, 2013, 2015; Moshman & Franks, 1986). Moshman makes a clear distinction between the ability to make inferences which correspond to logical norms and the development of rationality, which depends on the ability to explicitly represent higher-level metalogical components of reasoning, such as concepts of inferential validity and logical necessity (Demetriou, 2014; Demetriou, Spanoudis, & Shayer, 2014; Moshman, 1982, 1990, 2004; Moshman & Franks, 1986). Metalogical understanding is the result of self-reflective processes that allow the abstraction of general principles from more specific forms of inference. The process is conceived of as a continuous one, leading to complex forms of epistemological understanding whose development goes well through adulthood (Chandler, Boyes, & Ball, 1990; Hallett, Chandler, & Krettenauer, 2002), but with no necessary endpoint. Critically, Moshman (2015) defines reasoning as involving specific inferential processes within the more general constraints of metacognitive understanding of the goals and aims that animate a reasoner. Such forms of reasoning are inherently contextual, with the criteria defining "good" reasoning varying according to the domain in question. In other words, inferential processes are cognitive tools in the service of broader metacognitive goals and understanding.

Although this is not directly addressed in this theory, the emphasis on reasoning as inferences under metacognitive control clearly suggest that the ability to reason well is very late developing, since it requires fairly complex forms of metacognitive understanding. Evidence of early forms of logical inference, and even early forms of basic metacognitive standing, are simply building blocks in a complex developmental progression.

Intuitive and probabilistic theories

The previously discussed theories of the development of logical reasoning present fairly detailed models, and are generally focused on explicit, conscious processes. However, there are other ways of understanding how logical reasoning might develop that have been explored in different contexts, but that have the potential of generating totally different explanatory models. One general form of model sees logical reasoning as the product of some sort of intuitive processing. The most complete form of this is fuzzy-trace theory (Brainerd & Reyna, 1990; 2001; Chapter 16, this volume), which suggests that people can pick up an intuitive representation (gist) of the underlying logic of a given problem and can apply this to make inferences that are more logical than those made when attention is focussed on the surface details. Such an approach has been used primarily to analyse decision-making abilities in children and adolescents, although it has also been used to show that young children are capable of transitive reasoning (Brainerd & Kingma, 1984). Another approach which also has some empirical basis derives from a dual process analysis of reasoning. Briefly, dual process theories generally suppose that people must be able to rapidly determine whether a given heuristic response is logical or not, in order to fully deploy more cognitively costly, analytic forms of reasoning. This in turn suggests that people must have some intuitive forms of logical understanding, possibly at a very young age. Indeed, recent studies are consistent with this idea (De Neys, 2012; Morsanyi & Handley, 2012).

Probabilistic theories (Evans, Over & Handley, 2005; Oaksford & Chater, 2007) suggest that people use a form of Bayesian analysis of premises and conclusion in order to generate an intuitive evaluation of the relative likelihood of a conclusion being true (see also Over & Cruz, this volume, and Oaksford & Chater, this volume). Such theories suggest that people make inferences based mostly on their understanding of real world properties, not based on any logical principles. However, these theories have not been systematically translated into a developmental perspective, although recent results have shown early intuitive understanding of probabilities (Fontanari, Gonzalez, Vallortigara, & Girotto, 2014; Téglás, Girotto, Gonzalez, & Bonatti, 2007), and that 5- to 6-year-old children can make reasonable probabilistic inferences (Markovits & Thompson, 2008).

Such approaches, although requiring much more detail to make a clear developmental picture, do point out that people make inferences based on some sort of intuitive access to existing information. In fact, this mirrors what we have seen in both transitive and conditional reasoning, where the relative difficulty of making certain kinds of inferences is coupled with the ease with which even young children can make inferences having some intuitively plausible context. The question of how to integrate these different processes into a single consistent developmental model remains an open one for the time being.

Conclusion

The nature and the developmental course of logical reasoning has long been the subject of controversy. As we have seen, the empirical data on logical reasoning in children, adults, and even nonhuman animals is varied and subject to very different interpretations. In turn, this is reflected in the basic orientation of the different theories that have been examined. As I have attempted to show, these theories focus on different empirical data. There is currently no single theory that can account for all the data in a sufficiently detailed way to allow understanding of more than a limited range of results. There is not even a real consensus on just what constitutes logical reasoning. In fact, as the empirical data shows, there is a large range of inferential behavior that has been identified as logical that goes from rapid, intuitive inferences that can often give the "logical" response to abstract and explicit representations of reasoning processes.

While no real synthesis currently exists, it is useful to point out some directions that one could take. Critically, although there are important differences in the definition of what constitutes "logical" reasoning, most existing theories do acknowledge developmental change. Thus, irrespective of whether logical reasoning is seen as a relatively primitive ability, or as requiring very high-level representational abilities, there is a general consensus that in the former case, reasoning abilities continue to develop, or that, in the latter case, there exist earlier forms of reasoning that precede the more complex levels. In other words, despite what are important differences that relate to the way that true logical reasoning is defined, most approaches acknowledge the reality that there exist multiple processes underlying deductive abilities, which go from simple intuitive ones to more complex forms of explicit deduction. These generally (although not always) correlate with developmental level. The question then is how to conceptualize the relationship between these different processes, irrespective of which one is identified as logical. Certainly the most straightforward model would suggest that whatever processes are used in young children's reasoning would be the basis for developmental changes to more complex forms of inference. If this is the case, then the key question is how to conceptualize the change between simple and complex forms of inference. Research that focusses on developmental differences, while important, obscures the more critical question of just how and why children make this transition. There is, however, one important caveat here. It is very possible that certain primitive forms of inference might co-exist with more complex forms without having a direct incidence on the development of the latter. As we have seen, there are some forms of simple intuitive inference that appear to be accessible not only to young children but to other species. The question of whether these remain accessible as components of an intuitive system (as postulated by dual process theories), or whether they interact developmentally with more conscious forms of inference, remains one of the more interesting developmental questions. Nonetheless, the basic question of how and why young children make the transition from simple to complex forms of inference remains a critical and largely unanswered question that must be addressed in any attempt to produce a synthetic account of the development of reasoning.

References

Andrews, G., & Halford, G. S. (1998). Children's ability to make transitive inferences: The importance of premise integration and structural complexity. *Cognitive Development, 13*(4), 479–513.

Barrouillet, P. (2011). Dual-process theories of reasoning: The test of development. *Developmental Review, 31*(2), 151–179.

Barrouillet, P., Gauffroy, C., & Lecas, J.-F. o. (2008). Mental models and the suppositional account of conditionals. *Psychological Review, 115*(3), 760–771.

Barrouillet, P., Grosset, N., & Lecas, J.-F. (2000). Conditional reasoning by mental models: Chronometric and developmental evidence. *Cognition, 75*(3), 237–266.

Barrouillet, P., & Lecas, J.-F. (1999). Mental models in conditional reasoning and working memory. *Thinking & Reasoning, 5*(4), 289–302.

Berk, L. E., & Winsler, A. (1995). *Scaffolding children's learning: Vygotsky and early childhood education. NAEYC research into practice series. Volume* 7. Washington, DC: ERIC.

Bindra, D., Clarke, K. A., & Shultz, T. R. (1980). Understanding predictive relations of necessity and sufficiency in formally equivalent" causal" and" logical" problems. *Journal of Experimental Psychology: General, 109*(4), 422.

Bjorklund, D. F. (1987). How age changes in knowledge base contribute to the development of children's memory: An interpretive review. *Developmental Review*, 7(2), 93–130.

Bond, A. B., Kamil, A. C., & Balda, R. P. (2004). Pinyon jays use transitive inference to predict social dominance. *Nature, 430*(7001), 778–781.

Braine, M. D. (1978). On the relation between the natural logic of reasoning and standard logic. *Psychological Review, 85*(1), 1–21.

Braine, M. D., & O'Brien, D. P. (1991). A theory of if: A lexical entry, reasoning program, and pragmatic principles. *Psychological Review, 98*(2), 182.

Braine, M. D., & O'Brien, D. P. (1998). *Mental logic*: Psychology Press.

Brainerd, C. J., & Kingma, J. (1984). Do children have to remember to reason? A fuzzy-trace theory of transitivity development. *Developmental Review, 4*(4), 311–377.

Brainerd, C. J., & Reyna, V. F. (1990). Gist is the grist: Fuzzy-trace theory and the new intuitionism. *Developmental Review, 10*(1), 3–47.

Brainerd, C. J., & Reyna, V. F. (2001). Fuzzy-trace theory: Dual processes in memory, reasoning, and cognitive neuroscience. In H. W. Reese & R. Kail (Eds.), *Advances in child development and behavior* (pp. 41–100). San Diego, CA: Academic Press.

Breslow, L. (1981). Reevaluation of the literature on the development of transitive inferences. *Psychological Bulletin, 89*(2), 325.

Bryant, P. E., & Trabasso, T. (1971). Transitive inferences and memory in young children. *Nature, 232*(5311), 456–458.

Byrnes, J. P. (1988). Formal operations: A systematic reformulation. *Developmental Review, 8*(1), 66–87.

Byrnes, J. P., & Overton, W. F. (1986). Reasoning about certainty and uncertainty in concrete, causal, and propositional contexts. *Developmental Psychology, 22*(6), 793.

Case, R., Kurland, D. M., & Goldberg, J. (1982). Operational efficiency and the growth of short-term memory span. *Journal of Experimental Child Psychology, 33*(3), 386–404.

Chandler, M., Boyes, M., & Ball, L. (1990). Relativism and stations of epistemic doubt. *Journal of Experimental Child Psychology, 50*(3), 370–395.

Cheng, P. W., & Holyoak, K. J. (1985). Pragmatic reasoning schemas. *Cognitive Psychology, 17*, 391–416.

Cheng, P. W., & Holyoak, K. J. (1989). On the natural selection of reasoning theories. *Cognition, 33*(3), 285–313.

Cohen, L. J. (1981). Can human irrationality be experimentally demonstrated? *Behavioral and Brain Sciences*, *4*(03), 317–331.

Cosmides, L. (1989). The logic of social exchange: Has natural selection shaped how humans reason? Studies with the Wason selection task. *Cognition*, *31*(3), 187–276.

Cummins, D. D. (1995). Naive theories and causal deduction. *Memory & Cognition*, *23*(5), 646–658.

Cummins, D. D. (1996). Evidence for the innateness of deontic reasoning. *Mind & Language*, *11*(2), 160–190.

Cummins, D. D., Lubart, T., Alksnis, O., & Rist, R. (1991). Conditional reasoning and causation. *Memory & Cognition*, *19*(3), 274–282.

Daniel, D. B. K., P. A. (2006). Developmental and individual differences in conditional reasoning: Effects of logic instructions and alternative antecedents. *Child Development*, 77(2), 339–354.

Davidson, M. C., Amso, D., Anderson, L. C., & Diamond, A. (2006). Development of cognitive control and executive functions from 4 to 13 years: Evidence from manipulations of memory, inhibition, and task switching. *Neuropsychologia*, *44*(11), 2037–2078.

de Boysson-Bardies, B., & O'Regan, K. (1973). What children do in spite of adults' hypotheses. *Nature*, *246*(5434), 531–534.

De Neys, W. (2012). Bias and conflict a case for logical intuitions. *Perspectives on Psychological Science*, 7(1), 28–38.

De Neys, W., & Everaerts, D. (2008). Developmental trends in everyday conditional reasoning: The retrieval and inhibition interplay. *Journal of Experimental Child Psychology*, *100*(4), 252–263.

De Neys, W., Schaeken, Walter, & d'Ydewalle, Gery. (2003). Causal conditional reasoning and strength of association: The disabling condition case. *European Journal of Cognitive Psychology*, *15*(2), 161–176.

Demetriou, A. (2014). Learning to learn, know, and reason. In R. D. Crick, C. Stringher, & Ren, K. (Eds.), *Learning to learn: International perspectives from theory and practice* (pp. 41–65). New York: Routledge.

Demetriou, A., Spanoudis, G., & Shayer, M. (2014). Inference, reconceptualization, insight, and efficiency along intellectual growth: A general theory. *Enfance*, *2014*(03), 365–396.

Dias, M. G., & Harris, P. L. (1988). The effect of make-believe play on deductive reasoning. *British Journal of Developmental Psychology*, *6*(3), 207–221.

Dias, M. G., & Harris, P. L. (1990). The influence of the imagination on reasoning by young children. *British Journal of Developmental Psychology*, *8*(4), 305–318.

Ennis, R. H. (1976). An alternative to Piaget's conceptualization of logical competence. *Child Development*, *47*, 903–919.

Epstein, S. (1994). Integration of the cognitive and the psychodynamic unconscious. *American Psychologist*, *49*, 709–709.

Evans, J. St. B. T., Barston, J. L., & Pollard, P. (1983). On the conflict between logic and belief in syllogistic reasoning. *Memory & Cognition*, *11*(3), 295–306.

Evans, J. St. B. T., Over, D. E., & Handley, S. J. (2005). Suppositionals, extensionality, and conditionals: A critique of the mental model theory of Johnson-Laird and Byrne (2002). *Psychological Review*, *112*, 1040–1052.

Evans, J. St. B. T, & Stanovich, K. E. (2013). Dual-process theories of higher cognition advancing the debate. *Perspectives on Psychological Science*, *8*(3), 223–241.

Fabricius, W. V., Sophian, C., & Wellman, H. M. (1987). Young children's sensitivity to logical necessity in their inferential search behavior. *Child Development*, *58*, 409–423.

Fillenbaum, S. (1975). If: Some uses. *Psychological Research*, *37*, 245–260.

Flavell, J. H. (1979). Metacognition and cognitive monitoring: A new area of cognitive–developmental inquiry. *American Psychologist*, *34*(10), 906.

Fontanari, L., Gonzalez, M., Vallortigara, G., & Girotto, V. (2014). Probabilistic cognition in two indigenous Mayan groups. *Proceedings of the National Academy of Sciences*, *111*(48), 17075–17080.

Gaillard, V., Barrouillet, P., Jarrold, C., & Camos, V. (2011). Developmental differences in working memory: Where do they come from? *Journal of Experimental Child Psychology*, *110*(3), 469–479.

Gauffroy, C., & Barrouillet, P. (2009). Heuristic and analytic processes in mental models for conditionals: An integrative developmental theory. *Developmental Review*, *29*(4), 249–282.

Gauffroy, C., & Barrouillet, P. (2011). The primacy of thinking about possibilities in the development of reasoning. *Developmental Psychology*, *47*, 1000–1011. doi: 10.1037/a0023269

Girotto, V., Light, P., & Colbourn, C. J. (1988). Pragmatic schemas and conditional reasoning in children. *Quarterly Journal of Experimental Psychology A: Human Experimental Psychology*, *40*(3-A), 469–482.

Grice, H. P. (1981). Presupposition and conversational implicature. In P. Cole (Ed.), *Syntax and Semantics, vol. 9: Pragmatics* (pp. 183–198). New York, NY: Academic Press.

Griggs, R. A., & Cox, J. R. (1982). The elusive thematic-materials effect in Wason's selection task. *British Journal of Psychology*, *73*(3), 407–420.
Halford, G. S. (1984). Can young children integrate premises in transitivity and serial order tasks? *Cognitive Psychology*, *16*(1), 65–93.
Hallett, D., Chandler, M. J., & Krettenauer, T. (2002). Disentangling the course of epistemic development: Parsing knowledge by epistemic content. *New Ideas in Psychology*, *20*(2), 285–307.
Handley, S. J., Capon, A., Beveridge, M., Dennis, I., & Evans, J. St. B. T. (2004). Working memory, inhibitory control and the development of children's reasoning. *Thinking & Reasoning*, *10*(2), 175–195.
Hawkins, J., Pea, R. D., Glick, J., & Scribner, S. (1984). "Merds that laugh don't like mushrooms": Evidence for deductive reasoning by preschoolers. *Developmental Psychology*, *20*(4), 584–594.
Inhelder, B., & Piaget, J. (1958). *The growth of logical thinking from childhood to adolescence*. New York, NY: Basic Books.
Janveau-Brennan, G., & Markovits, H. (1999). The development of reasoning with causal conditionals. *Developmental Psychology*, *35*(4), 904–911.
Johnson-Laird, P. N. (2001). Mental models and deduction. *Trends in Cognitive Sciences*, *5*(10), 434–442.
Johnson-Laird, P. N. (2012). Inference with mental models. *The Oxford handbook of thinking and reasoning* (pp. 134–145). Oxford: Oxford University Press.
Johnson-Laird, P. N., & Bara, B. G. (1984). Syllogistic inference. *Cognition*, *16*(1), 1–61.
Johnson-Laird, P. N., & Byrne, R. M. J. (1991). *Deduction*. Hove & London: Erlbaum.
Johnson-Laird, P. N., & Byrne, R. M. J. (2002). Conditionals: A theory of meaning, pragmatics and inference. *Psychological Review*, *109*, 646–678.
Karmiloff-Smith, A. (1995). *Beyond modularity: A developmental perspective on cognitive science*. Cambridge, MA: MIT Press.
Kitchner, K. (1983). Cognition, metacognition, and epistemic cognition. *Human Development*, *26*(4), 222–232.
Klaczynski, P. A. (2001). Analytic and heuristic processing influences on adolescent reasoning and decision-making. *Child Development*, *72*(3), 844–861.
Klaczynski, P. A., & Narasimham, G. (1998). Representations as mediators of adolescent deductive reasoning. *Developmental Psychology*, *34*(5), 865–881.
Knifong, J. (1974). Logical abilities of young children: Two styles of approach. *Child Development*, *45*, 78–83.
Kodroff, J. K., & Roberge, J. J. (1975). Developmental analysis of the conditional reasoning abilities of primary-grade children. *Developmental Psychology*, *11*(1), 21–28.
Kuhn, D. (1977). Conditional reasoning in children. *Developmental Psychology*, *13*(4), 342–353.
Kuhn, D. (1989). Children and adults as intuitive scientists. *Psychological Review*, *96*(4), 674.
Kuhn, D. (1991). *The skills of argument*: Cambridge University Press.
Kuhn, D., Amsel, E., O'Loughlin, M., Schauble, L., Leadbeater, B., & Yotive, W. (1988). *The development of scientific thinking skills*. San Diego, CA: Academic Press.
Kuhn, D., & Udell, W. (2003). The development of argument skills. *Child Development*, *74*(5), 1245–1260.
Light, P., Blaye, A., Gilly, M., & Girotto, V. (1989). Pragmatic schemas and logical reasoning in 6-to-8-year-old children. *Cognitive Development*, *4*(1), 49–64.
Lourenço, O. (1995). Piaget's logic of meanings and conditional reasoning in adolescents and adults. *Archives de Psychologie*, *63*(246), 187–203.
MacLean, E. L., Merritt, D. J., & Brannon, E. M. (2008). Social complexity predicts transitive reasoning in prosimian primates. *Animal Behaviour*, *76*(2), 479–486.
Markovits, H. (1985). Incorrect conditional reasoning among adults: Competence or performance? *British Journal of Psychology*, *76*(2), 241–247.
Markovits, H. (1995). Conditioning reasoning with false premises: Fantasy and information retrieval. *British Journal of Developmental Psychology*, *13*(1), 1–11.
Markovits, H. (2000). A mental model analysis of young children's conditional reasoning with meaningful premises. *Thinking & Reasoning*, *6*(4), 335–347.
Markovits. H. (2013). How to develop a logical reasoner: A hierarchical model of the role of divergent thinking in the development of conditional reasoning. In H. Markovits (Ed.), *The developmental psychology of reasoning and decision-making* (pp. 148–164). Hove, UK: Psychology Press.
Markovits, H. (2014a). Development and necessary norms of reasoning. *Frontiers in Psychology*, *5*, Article 488.
Markovits, H. (2014b). On the road toward formal reasoning: Reasoning with factual causal and contrary-to-fact causal premises during early adolescence. *Journal of Experimental Child Psychology*, *128*, 37–51.

Markovits, H. (2017). In the beginning stages: Conditional reasoning with category-based and causal premises in 8- to 10- year olds. *Cognitive Development, 41*, 1–9.
Markovits, H., & Barrouillet, P. (2002). The development of conditional reasoning: A mental model account. *Developmental Review, 22*, 5–36.
Markovits, H., & Doyon, C. (2004). Information processing and reasoning with premises that are empirically false: Interference, working memory, and processing speed. *Memory & Cognition, 32*(4), 592–601.
Markovits, H., Doyon, C., & Simoneau, M. (2002). Individual differences in working memory and conditional reasoning with concrete and abstract content. *Thinking & Reasoning, 8*(2), 97–107.
Markovits, H., Dumas, C., & Malfait, N. (1995). Understanding transitivity of a spatial relationship: A developmental analysis. *Journal of Experimental Child Psychology, 59*(1), 124–141.
Markovits, H., & Lortie Forgues, H. (2011). Conditional reasoning with false premises facilitates the transition between familiar and abstract reasoning. *Child Development, 82*(2), 646–660. doi: 10.1111/j.1467–8624.2010.01526.x
Markovits, H., & Nantel, G. (1989). The belief-bias effect in the production and evaluation of logical conclusions. *Memory & Cognition, 17*(1), 11–17.
Markovits, H., & Potvin, F. (2001). Suppression of valid inferences and knowledge structures: The curious effect of producing alternative antecedents on reasoning with causal conditionals. *Memory & Cognition, 29*, 736–744.
Markovits, H., & Quinn, S. (2002). Efficiency of retrieval correlates with "logical" reasoning from causal conditional premises. *Memory & Cognition, 30*(5), 696–706.
Markovits, H., Schleifer, M., & Fortier, L. (1989). Development of elementary deductive reasoning in young children. *Developmental Psychology, 25*(5), 787–793.
Markovits, H., & Thompson, V. (2008). Different developmental patterns of simple deductive and probabilistic inferential reasoning.. *Memory and Cognition, 36*(6), 1066–1078.
Markovits, H., & Vachon, R. (1989). Reasoning with contrary-to-fact propositions. *Journal of Experimental Child Psychology, 47*(3), 398–412.
Markovits, H., & Vachon, R. (1990). Conditional reasoning, representation, and level of abstraction. *Developmental Psychology, 26*(6), 942–951.
Markovits, H., Venet, M., Janveau-Brennan, G., Malfait, N., Pion, N., & Vadeboncoeur, I. (1996). Reasoning in young children: Fantasy and information retrieval. *Child Development, 67*(6), 2857–2872.
Markovits, H. B., & Pierre. (2002). The development of conditional reasoning: A mental model account. *Developmental Review, 22*(1), 5–36.
Markovits, H., & Potvin, F. (2001). Suppression of valid inferences and knowledge structures: The curious effect of producing alternative antecedents on reasoning with causal conditionals. *Memory & Cognition, 29*(5), 736–744.
Mascaro, O., & Csibra, G. (2014). Human infants' learning of social structures: The case of dominance hierarchy. *Psychological Science, 25*(1), 250–255.
Miller, S. A., Custer, W. L., & Nassau, G. (2000). Children's understanding of the necessity of logically necessary truths. *Cognitive Development, 15*(3), 383–403.
Morris, A. K. (2000). Development of logical reasoning: Children's ability to verbally explain the nature of the distinction between logical and nonlogical forms of argument. *Developmental Psychology, 36*(6), 741.
Morsanyi, K., & Handley, S. J. (2012). Logic feels so good – I like it! Evidence for intuitive detection of logicality in syllogistic reasoning. *Journal of Experimental Psychology-Learning Memory and Cognition, 38*(3), 596.
Moshman, D. (1982). Exogenous, endogenous, and dialectical constructivism. *Developmental Review, 2*(4), 371–384.
Moshman, D. (1990). The development of metalogical understanding. In Smith, L. (Ed.), *Critical readings on Piaget* (pp. 396–415). London: Routledge.
Moshman, D. (2004). From inference to reasoning: The construction of rationality. *Thinking & Reasoning, 10*(2), 221–239.
Moshman, D. (2013). Epistemic cognition and development. In P. Barrouillet & C. Gauffroy (Eds.), *The development of thinking and reasoning* (pp. 13–33). Hove, UK: Psychology Press.
Moshman, D. (2015). *Epistemic cognition and development: The psychology of justification and truth*. Hove, UK: Psychology Press.
Moshman, D., & Franks, B. A. (1986). Development of the concept of inferential validity. *Child Development, 57*(1), 153–165.
Mou, Y., Province, J. M., & Luo, Y. (2014). Can infants make transitive inferences? *Cognitive Psychology, 68*, 98–112.

Müller, U., Overton, W. F., & Reene, K. (2001). Development of conditional reasoning: A longitudinal study. *Journal of Cognition and Development, 2*(1), 27–49.
Murray, J. P., & Youniss, J. (1968). Achievement of inferential transitivity and its relation to serial ordering. *Child Development, 39*, 1259–1268.
Oaksford, M., & Chater, N. (2007). *Bayesian rationality*. Oxford, UK: Oxford University Press.
O'Brien, D. P., & Overton, W. F. (1980). Conditional reasoning following contradictory evidence: A developmental analysis. *Journal of Experimental Child Psychology, 30*(1), 44–61.
O'Brien, D. P., & Overton, W. F. (1982). Conditional reasoning and the competence-performance issue: A developmental analysis of a training task. *Journal of Experimental Child Psychology, 34*(2), 274–290.
Overton, W. F., Byrnes, J. P., & O'Brien, D. P. (1985). Developmental and individual differences in conditional reasoning: The role of contradiction training and cognitive style. *Developmental Psychology, 21*(4), 692–701.
Overton, W. F., & Ricco., R. (2011). Dual systems competence and procedural processing: A relational developmental systems approach to reasoning. *Developmental Review, 31*, 119–150.
Overton, W. F., & Ricco, R. B. (2011). Dual-systems and the development of reasoning: competence-procedural systems. *Wiley Interdisciplinary Reviews: Cognitive Science, 2*(2), 231–237.
Overton, W. F., Ward, S. L., Black, J., Noveck, I. A., & O'Brien, D. P. (1987). Form and content in the development of deductive reasoning. *Developmental Psychology, 23*(1), 22–30.
Pears, R., & Bryant, P. (1990). Transitive inferences by young children about spatial position. *British Journal of Psychology, 81*(4), 497–510.
Peel, E. A. (1959). Experimental examination of some of Piaget's schemata concerning children's perception and thinking, and a discussion of their educational significance. *British Journal of Educational Psychology, 29*(2), 89–103.
Piaget, J. (1972). Intellectual evolution from adolescence to adulthood. *Human Development, 15*, 1–12.
Piaget, J., Inhelder, & Szeminka, A. (1960). *The child's conception of geometry. Trad. de EA Lunzer*. New York: Harper e Torchbooks.
Quinn, S., & Markovits, H. (1998). Conditional reasoning, causality, and the structure of semantic memory: Strength of association as a predictive factor for content effects. *Cognition, 68*(3), B93–B101.
Ricco, R. B. (in press). Development of reasoning. In R. M. Lerner (Editor-in-Chief) and L. S. Liben and U. M. Müller (Volume Eds.), *Handbook of child psychology and developmental science (7th Edition), Volume 2: Cognitive Processes*. Hoboken, NJ: Wiley.
Riley, C. A., & Trabasso, T. (1974). Comparatives, logical structures, and encoding in a transitive inference task. *Journal of Experimental Child Psychology, 17*(2), 187–203.
Roberts, W. A., & Phelps, M. T. (1994). Transitive inference in rats: A test of the spatial coding hypothesis. *Psychological Science, 5*(6), 368–374.
Ruffman, T. (1999). Children's understanding of logical inconsistency. *Child Development, 70*(4), 872–886.
Rumain, B., Connell, J., & Braine, M. D. (1983). Conversational comprehension processes are responsible for reasoning fallacies in children as well as adults: If is not the biconditional. *Developmental Psychology, 19*(4), 471–481.
Russell, J. (1996). Logical versus associative performance on transitive reasoning tasks by children: Implications for the status of animals performance. *The Quarterly Journal of Experimental Psychology: Section B, 49*(3), 231–244.
Sá, W. C., West, R. F., & Stanovich, K. E. (1999). The domain specificity and generality of belief bias: Searching for a generalizable critical thinking skill. *Journal of Educational Psychology, 91*(3), 497.
Schroyens, W., Schaeken, W., & Handley, S. (2003). In search of counter-examples: Deductive rationality in human reasoning. *The Quarterly Journal of Experimental Psychology: Section A, 56*(7), 1129–1145.
Scribner, S. (1986). Thinking in action: Some characteristics of practical thought. In *Practical intelligence: Nature and origins of competence in the everyday world* (Vol. 13, p. 60).
Siegel, L. S., & Ryan, E. B. (1989). The development of working memory in normally achieving and subtypes of learning disabled children. *Child Development, 60*, 973–980.
Siegler, R. S. (1978). The origins of scientific reasoning. In R. S. Siegler (Ed.), *Children's thinking: What develops* (pp. 109–149). Hillsdale, NJ: Lawrence Erlbaum Associates.
Simoneau, M., & Markovits, H. (2003). Reasoning with premises that are not empirically true: Evidence for the role of inhibition and retrieval. *Developmental Psychology, 39*(6), 964–975.
Sloman, S. A. (1996). The empirical case for two systems of reasoning. *Psychological Bulletin, 119*(1), 3–22.
Smedslund, J. (1963). Development of concrete transitivity of length in children. *Child Development, 34*, 389–405.

Stanovich, K. E., West, R. F., Ackerman, P. L., Kyllonen, P. C., & Roberts, R. D. (1999). Individual differences in reasoning and the heuristics and biases debate. In *Learning and individual differences: Process, trait, and content determinants* (pp. 389–411). Washington, DC: American Psychological Association.

Taplin, J. E., Staudenmayer, H., & Taddonio, J. L. (1974). Developmental changes in conditional reasoning: Linguistic or logical? *Journal of Experimental Child Psychology, 17*(2), 360–373.

Téglás, E., Girotto, V., Gonzalez, M., & Bonatti, L. L. (2007). Intuitions of probabilities shape expectations about the future at 12 months and beyond. *Proceedings of the National Academy of Sciences, 104*(48), 19156–19159.

Thompson, V. A. (1995). Conditional reasoning: The necessary and sufficient conditions. *Canadian Journal of Experimental Psychology/Revue canadienne de psychologie expérimentale, 49*(1), 1–60.

Venet, M., & Markovits, H. (2001). Understanding uncertainty with abstract conditional premises. *Merrill-Palmer Quarterly, 47*(1), 74–99.

Von Fersen, L., Wynne, C., Delius, J. D., & Staddon, J. (1991). Transitive inference formation in pigeons. *Journal of Experimental Psychology: Animal Behavior Processes, 17*(3), 334.

Ward, S. L., Byrnes, J. P., & Overton, W. F. (1990). Organization of knowledge and conditional reasoning. *Journal of Educational Psychology, 82*(4), 832–837.

Ward, S. L., & Overton, W. F. (1990). Semantic familiarity, relevance, and the development of deductive reasoning. *Developmental Psychology, 26*, 488–493.

Wason, P. (1968). Reasoning about a rule. *Quarterly Journal of Experimental Psychology, 20*, 273–281.

Wason, P. C., & Johnson-Laird, P. N. (1972). *Psychology of reasoning: Structure and content* (Vol. 86). Cambridge, MA: Harvard University Press.

Wildman, T. M., & Fletcher, H. J. (1977). Developmental increases and decreases in solutions of conditional syllogism problems. *Developmental Psychology, 13*(6), 630–636.

Wright, B. C. (2001). Reconceptualizing the transitive inference ability: A framework for existing and future research. *Developmental Review, 21*(4), 375–422.

Wright, B. C. (2012). The case for a dual-process theory of transitive reasoning. *Developmental Review, 32*(2), 89–124.

Zimmerman, C. (2000). The development of scientific reasoning skills. *Developmental Review, 20*(1), 99–149.

22

REASONING AND ARGUMENTATION

Hugo Mercier

Reasoning can be understood as the private mental act of accepting or rejecting a conclusion based on reasons supporting or attacking this conclusion. For instance, Paul hesitates between going to the Japanese restaurant and to the Mexican restaurant, but then he remembers that he's a bit hard up at the moment, and that the Japanese restaurant is more expensive; then he has a reason to pick the Mexican place. Argumentation, which involves reasoning, is a public act of using reasons to convince others and to evaluate others' reasons to decide whether one ought to be convinced. Knowing that Lara is also on a budget, Paul could use the same reason to convince her that Mexican is the best option, and she could evaluate this reason to make sure it is sound.

Historically, scholars have held widely diverging views of the relation between private reasoning and argumentation (see Dutilh Novaes, submitted). One old tradition, which we can call social, sees them as undistinguishable. Aristotle defines deduction as "a discourse" (Prior Analytics, 24b19), and for Isocrates, "the same arguments which we use in persuading others when we speak in public, we employ also when we deliberate in our own thoughts" (Antidosis, 256, cited in Billig, 1996). Another tradition, which we can call individualist, was developed more recently, in particular following Descartes. This tradition contrasts argumentation and private reasoning, sometimes in order to highlight the superiority of private reasoning. In the following passage, Descartes equates the 'logic of the Schools' with a form of argumentation:

> After that, he [who aims to instruct himself] should study logic. I do not mean the logic of the Schools, for this is strictly speaking nothing but a dialectic which teaches ways of expounding to others what one already knows or even of holding forth without judgment about things one does not know. Such logic corrupts good sense rather than increasing it. I mean instead the kind of logic which teaches us to direct our reason with a view to discovering the truths of which we are ignorant.
>
> (Descartes, 1985, p. 186; cited in Dutilh Novaes, submitted)

We find echoes of the social tradition in some contemporary research programs (see Billig, 1996). For instance, Piaget's early work – in which he claimed that "logical reasoning is an argument which we have with ourselves, and which reproduces internally the features of a real argument" (Piaget, 1928, p. 204) – inspired researchers to study the role of argumentation in cognitive development (Doise & Mugny, 1984; Perret-Clermont, 1980). The individualist tradition, however, proved vastly more influential (including on Piaget's later work). Until very recently the experimental study of reasoning essentially ignored argumentation – and, on their side, argumentation scholars showed little interest in the cognitive underpinnings of argumentative skills.

However, the grip of the individualist tradition is loosening. The psychology of reasoning had largely focused on logical, and on particular on deductive arguments. Deductive arguments entail that a conclusion must necessarily be accepted once the premises are accepted. In everyday discourse, by contrast, a conclusion can be taken back when new evidence emerges, making the study of deductive reasoning ecologically dubious. The limitations of this so-called deductive paradigm are now recognized (Evans, 2002). By contrast, probabilistic arguments – arguments that simply make a conclusion more believable and that are more ecologically valid – now receive more attention (Hahn & Oaksford, 2007). On the side of argumentation studies, scholars have begun to conduct experiments (Hahn & Hornikx, 2012) and to integrate cognitive psychology in their analyses (Herman & Oswald, 2014; Maillat & Oswald, 2013).

A recent theory – the argumentative theory of reasoning – challenges the individualist tradition by suggesting that the function of reasoning is to argue, and that argumentation is more likely to improve one's beliefs than solitary reasoning (Mercier & Sperber, 2011). In this theory, reasoning refers to the cognitive mechanism that deals with the relation between reasons and the conclusions they purportedly support. Given that most of cognition takes place with no attention being paid to reasons (Mercier & Sperber, 2009), this makes of reasoning a specific cognitive mechanism, one that only humans would possess.

The argumentative theory of reasoning can be related to the work of other scholars who have suggested that argumentation plays a central role in moral reasoning (Gibbard, 1990), communication (Ducrot & Anscombre, 1983), social cognition (Billig, 1996), and human affairs more generally (Perelman & Olbrechts-Tyteca, 1958). However, it is the first theory to make full use of experimental psychology's advances. The predictions of the argumentative theory can be used as a framework to make sense of the wide array of evidence bearing on the links between reasoning and argumentation. In order to spell out these predictions in more details, we must start with an outline of the evolutionary rationale for the theory.

Evolution, reasoning, and argumentation

The individualist tradition sees reasoning as aimed at helping the lone reasoner produce sound beliefs, largely by realizing that one's intuitions cannot be properly supported by reasons. Several scholars have attempted to give this tradition an evolutionary grounding (e.g. Stanovich, 2004). However, it is unclear how a mechanism whose failures even in simple tasks have been amply documented (e.g. Evans, 2002) could have evolved to correct intuitive mechanisms that perform, by and large, very well (e.g. Gigerenzer, Todd, & ABC Research Group, 1999). Moreover, evolutionary psychologists have forcefully argued that such domain general mechanisms face strong evolutionary hurdles that make their existence improbable (e.g. Cosmides & Tooby, 1992). The gist of their argument is that domain general mechanisms would be computationally intractable – they have to solve too many problems at once. By contrast, domain specific mechanisms use the specific regularities of their domain as computational shortcuts.

It is more plausible to ascribe reasoning some less general functions. To this end, the argumentative theory relies on the framework of the evolution of communication. For communication to be evolutionarily stable, it has to benefit both senders and receivers (see, e.g., Maynard Smith, & Harper, 2003). Senders, however, often stand to benefit from communication that would be harmful to receivers. For instance, I would be better off if I could convince everyone to buy my books, but not everyone would be made better off by buying my books. Thus, there must exist mechanisms that ensure that communication is, in spite of this conflict of interest, beneficial for receivers on average. To keep communication beneficial for receivers, humans rely on mechanisms of epistemic vigilance that evaluate communicated information to reject harmful messages and accept beneficial ones (Sperber et al., 2010).

Two important mechanisms of epistemic vigilance are plausibility checking and trust calibration. Plausibility checking pits communicated information against background knowledge and, in case of inconsistency, rejects the communicated information. For instance, if one of your junior colleagues tells you that the idea you are currently working on is flat out wrong, your first reaction might be to dismiss her opinion. The second mechanism, trust calibration, can, to some extent, bypass plausibility checking. If a sender is deemed to be particularly competent and honest, then her messages might be accepted even if they conflict with the receiver's beliefs (for related Bayesian models of these phenomena, see, e.g., Hahn, Harris, & Corner, 2009). For instance, you might accept the negative assessment of your idea if it comes from someone you trust and who is much more knowledgeable than you in the relevant area. By contrast, if the source is untrustworthy – a colleague suspected of fraud, say – then even a message that might otherwise have been accepted can become suspicious.

Both mechanisms – plausibility checking and trust calibration – ought to be conservative. To limit the costs of harmful messages, they should reject too many messages rather than accept too many. Many messages that could be beneficial for receivers are rejected because they do not pass the receivers' plausibility check, and the sender is not trusted enough (Mercier, 2013a; Sperber et al., 2010). To achieve a finer-grained discrimination of messages, senders and receivers can rely on argumentation. Senders provide reasons supporting their messages, and receivers evaluate these reasons in order to decide whether or not they should change their mind. For instance, your junior colleague might get you to change your mind if she offers good enough reasons. Reasoning would have evolved mainly to enable such argumentation: to allow senders to find arguments supporting their messages, and to allow receivers to evaluate these arguments (Mercier & Sperber, 2011).

To evaluate this hypothesis about the function of reasoning, we can check whether it can account for well-established features of reasoning and whether it can make new predictions that withstand testing.

Producing arguments

To fulfill an argumentative function, reasoning must be able to do two things: to produce arguments to convince others, and to evaluate others' arguments in order to change one's mind when, and only when, the arguments are strong enough. To be more likely to convince others, reasoning should mostly produce arguments that support the reasoner's position, whether directly or by attacking the interlocutor's position – one is unlikely to get an interlocutor to change her mind by producing arguments that go against one's point of view or that support the interlocutor's position. Reasoning, when it produces arguments, should thus have a myside bias.

In many tasks (Mercier, in press; Nickerson, 1998), participants have been shown to look for arguments that support their initial intuition. The Wason selection task – the most studied of all reasoning tasks – is a good example. To be solved it requires that participants understand the logic of a simple conditional statement. When faced with this task, pragmatic mechanisms rapidly guide participants' attention towards one of the potential answers – the one made most relevant by the conditional rule (Sperber, Cara, & Girotto, 1995; see also, e.g., V. A. Thompson, Evans, & Campbell, 2013). When participants start reasoning, they do not look for reasons that could support other answers; instead, they focus their attention on the intuitive answer, looking for reasons why this answer is correct (Lucas & Ball, 2005; Roberts & Newton, 2001; for other types of problems, see, e.g., V. A. Thompson, Prowse Turner, & Pennycook, 2011).

This phenomenon has been described as a 'confirmation bias.' However, other experiments have revealed that when participants reason about something they disagree with, they look for arguments that attack or falsify this position (e.g., Edwards & Smith, 1996). For instance, when presented with the following argument

> Sentencing a person to death ensures that he/she will never commit another crime. Therefore, the death penalty should not be abolished.
>
> (Edwards & Smith, 1996, p. 9)

anti-death penalty participants were more likely to form refutational than supportive thoughts. Pro-death-penalty participants, by contrast, exhibited the standard confirmation bias, providing more supportive than refutational arguments.

Individuals do not have a general tendency to confirm – a confirmation bias. Instead, they have a consistent myside bias: a tendency to find arguments that support their point of view, whether that means supporting a position they agree with or attacking a position they disagree with.

Besides the directionality of the arguments (i.e. for or against a position), another variable of argument production is the quality of argument people aim for. If the task of argument production is to convince others, then it might seem like the best solution would be to look for strong arguments, arguments that cannot be easily countered. This goal, however, is costly to achieve. To produce strong arguments, one has to anticipate how the interlocutor would react to one's arguments, a task that is generally difficult, and sometimes impossible, as it depends on preferences and beliefs of the interlocutor to which the speaker might have no access (Mercier, Bonnier, & Trouche, in press). For instance, if Paul wants to convince Lara to go see a given movie, he might need to anticipate the type of movie she likes, which movies she has already seen, when she is available, and so on.

The problems raised by finding the best way to get one's message across are not specific to argumentation. For instance, when speakers are looking for a way to refer to someone, and they are not sure how well the interlocutor knows this person, they tend to start with the generic means of referring to someone (e.g. the person's first name). If the interlocutor does not understand, they further specify the referent (see, e.g., Levinson, 2006). Similarly, speakers can rely on the interlocutor's feedback to refine their arguments. A good strategy is to start with a relatively generic argument – an argument not specifically tailored to the interlocutor. If it is accepted, then there is no need for a more carefully crafted argument. If the first argument is rejected, the interlocutor typically provides counter-arguments to justify her rejection. The speaker can then address these counter-arguments, a task that is much easier than anticipating them. To follow up on the earlier example, Paul might start by simply saying that he has heard that the movie is great. Lara isn't swayed and she replies that she hasn't seen the previous episodes of the series, and so might not be able to follow the story. Although it might have been difficult for Paul to anticipate that this specific counter-argument would be used, he can attempt to address it once it has been raised – for instance by saying that he can give a brief summary of the previous episodes.

Thus, the argumentative theory does not predict that people should spontaneously produce very strong arguments. In the absence of feedback, people should mostly produce relatively generic and superficial arguments. But people should also be able to take feedback into account to improve their arguments in the course of a discussion.

Studies of argumentation and informal reasoning, in which participants are asked to justify their positions on various issues, have concluded that participants typically produce relatively weak arguments: they fail to anticipate simple counter-arguments, they offer circular arguments, and they do not incorporate evidence in their arguments (Kuhn, 1991; Perkins, 1989). In these studies, the participants are not confronted with interlocutors who challenge their arguments by offering counter-arguments. When participants discuss similar issues with other participants holding different positions, they produce better arguments at the end of the discussion: they present a wider range of arguments, they anticipate counter-arguments, and they offer more evidence (Crowell & Kuhn, 2014; Iordanou, 2013; Kuhn & Crowell, 2011).

These two features of argument production – the myside bias and the initial production of generic arguments – make sense in dialogic contexts. In dialogic contexts, speakers face interlocutors who provide arguments for their own views, and who challenge the speakers' arguments. By contrast, these features are problematic for the solitary reasoner who is likely to pile up unexamined arguments for her preexisting positions. Thus, when participants are faced with tasks for which their intuitions are misleading, reasoning fails to look for reasons supporting answers other than the intuitive answer, and it fails to make sure that the reasons people find in support of the intuitive answer are sound. For instance, in the Wason selection task, not only do people mostly look for reasons supporting their initial intuition, they also fail to realize that these reasons are somehow mistaken (since they support a logically flawed answer). As a result, reasoning rarely challenges the initial, misguided intuition (Wason, 1966; see also, e.g., V. A. Thompson et al., 2011). Moreover, by accumulating reasons that support their initial intuitions, solitary reasoners can become surer that they are right, even if they are wrong (overconfidence; see Koriat, Lichtenstein, & Fischhoff, 1980), and they can come to hold more extreme views (attitude polarization; see Tesser, 1978).

When people do not have an initial intuition to support – when they have weak or conflicting intuitions – reasoning has different consequences. Instead of accumulating reason for one's initial intuition, reasoning looks for reasons supporting the competing intuitions, and it drives the reasoner towards the intuition for which reasons are most easily found. This phenomenon is generally referred to as 'reason-based choice' (Shafir, Simonson, & Tversky, 1993; Simonson, 1989). Reason-based choice does not consistently lead people towards decisions that are intrinsically superior. Instead, it leads people towards decisions that are justifiable – decisions that look rational. As a result, reason-based choice can create a variety of apparently suboptimal choices (for review, see, Mercier & Sperber, 2011). For instance, reason-based choice explains why people often chose items laden with features: everything else equal, it looks more rational to have more features – even if, in the end, these features prove to be cumbersome rather than useful (D.V. Thompson & Norton, 2008).

If the function of reasoning were to better one's beliefs through private ratiocination, as held by the individualist view, then reasoning should look for arguments that challenge one's position (instead of having a myside bias). It should make sure that one's arguments are good (instead of being satisfied with weak, generic arguments), it should correct one's mistaken intuitions (instead of failing to do so), it should lead to better-calibrated confidence (instead of overconfidence), and it should produce intrinsically better decisions (instead of decisions that look rational). By contrast, if the function of argument production is to convince others, then reasoning should have a myside bias, and it should spontaneously produce relatively weak, generic arguments. The effects of reasoning on the solitary reasoner do not mean that reasoning is flawed, simply that it is used in an abnormal environment, one that lacks the feedback others would provide in a dialogic context.

Evaluating others' arguments

When evaluating arguments, reasoning's task is to determine to what extent an argument warrants changing one's mind about the argument's conclusion. In order not to change one's mind for bad reasons, reasoning should therefore be exigent towards other people's arguments – at least when they challenge one's position. This critical evaluation should contrast with the way people treat their own arguments: as was just discussed, when people produce arguments, they should be satisfied with relatively weak and generic arguments. People should thus be more critical of others' arguments than they are of their own.

The ideal test of this prediction involves making people evaluate their own arguments as if they were someone else's. To this end, Trouche et al. (in press) relied on the choice blindness paradigm. Participants tackled five simple reasoning problems, for which they were first asked to produce an intuitive answer, one that does not involve reasoning. After this first phase, participants were asked to produce arguments, and offered the possibility to change their initial answer. People displayed a myside bias, and they were satisfied with relatively weak arguments: not only did only a small minority of participants decide to revise their answers, but they were not more likely to do so when their intuitive answer was invalid than when it was valid.

After this second phase, participants were presented with the same problems again, reminded of their previous answer, and given the answer and the argument provided by another participant. This only happened for four of the five problems. For the last problem, the participants were told that they had answered a different answer from the one they had in fact originally given, and they were provided with their own initial answer and argument as if they were someone else's. For each problem, the participants could then decide if they wanted to change their mind or not on the basis of the argument. Debriefing questions revealed that approximately half of the participants did not notice the manipulation. Of these participants, over half rejected the argument they had deemed good enough to produce a few minutes earlier. Moreover, they were more likely to reject their own argument if it supported an invalid answer than a valid answer. They had become more critical and more discriminating because they thought the argument was someone else's.

Besides their own arguments, people should also have relatively lax criteria when evaluating arguments whose conclusion they agree with: since other mechanisms have already positively evaluated the conclusion, the risk of being misled is considerably reduced. This might explain why participants are less likely to detect that an argument is logically invalid when they agree with its conclusion (belief bias; see Evans, Barston, & Pollard, 1983).

The function of argument evaluation, however, is not merely to reject poor arguments, it is also to accept strong enough arguments. Experiments suggest that individuals, on the whole, have good argument evaluation skills, being more persuaded by strong than by weak arguments. This has been shown using several normative models for what counts as a good argument.

Research in persuasion and attitude change has typically relied on informal criteria for distinguishing strong from weak arguments. For instance, weak arguments could be hearsay from unreliable sources while strong arguments could be relevant evidence from reliable sources. Contrasting these types of arguments, many experiments have shown that participants who have a stake in the arguments' conclusion are more influenced by strong than by weak arguments (for review, see Petty & Wegener, 1998).

Other researchers have relied on norms stemming from argumentation theory, norms that specify on a case-by-case basis what makes arguments from a given type – argument from authority, *ad hominem*, and so on – fallacious or not. Generally, participants find non-fallacious arguments more persuasive than fallacious arguments (for review, see Hornikx & Hahn, 2012).

For instance, when evaluating how much weight to grant an argument from authority, participants were sensitive to the authority's expertise and to the presence of potential vested interests (Hoeken, Timmers, & Schellens, 2012).

A more general normative framework for determining argument strength can be derived from Bayes' rule. Bayes' rule specifies how one should revise one's belief in light of new evidence. In the case at hand, the evidence takes the form of arguments. Using this framework, it is possible to make predictions for each argument type about the factors that make arguments stronger or weaker (Hahn & Oaksford, 2008). For instance, a Bayesian analysis can make predictions about how much participants with different priors should change their mind on the basis of the following two arguments from ignorance (Hahn & Oaksford, 2007, p. 708):

Drug A is not toxic because no toxic effects were observed in 50 tests.
Drug A is not toxic because no toxic effects were observed in one test.

On the whole, participants evaluate arguments in the way predicted by the Bayesian framework (for review, see Collins & Hahn, this volume) – in this example, by granting more weight to the former argument than the latter argument.

The traits of argument evaluation stand in sharp contrast with those of argument production. People produced biased, superficially examined arguments. When they evaluate others' arguments, they are critical enough to reject weak arguments and objective enough to accept strong arguments. That participants are able to evaluate others' arguments in this way, and yet fail to submit their own arguments to the same treatment, shows that the traits of argument production are not a mere cognitive limitation. They are genuine features – those expected of a mechanism dedicated to argumentation.

Reasoning in discussion

The last two sections have focused on studies of reasoning in isolated participants, whether they were asked to produce arguments or to evaluate them. These studies allow for better control: for instance, it is possible to precisely vary the arguments people have to evaluate. However, they study reasoning in an environment that is, according to the argumentative theory, not reasoning's normal environment. This purportedly explains why, in these tasks, reasoning consistently fails to correct participants' misguided intuitions. By contrast, when reasoning is used in the back and forth of a discussion, it should produce epistemically sounder results. Each individual should be able to find arguments supporting their position, and to examine others' arguments. The individuals should improve their arguments by taking counter-arguments into account. When strong enough arguments are exchanged, individuals should change their minds to adopt better supported positions, which should usually mean holding better beliefs.

In simple logical and mathematical tasks, the correct answer can be supported with arguments that most participants are able to understand. Thus, in these tasks the correct answer should spread: as soon as a group member has found the correct answer, or a piece of the correct answer, she should be able to convince her peers. This superiority of the correct answer is known as 'truth wins,' and it has been observed in various logical and mathematical tasks (for review, see Laughlin, 2011). For instance, when participants had to solve the Wason selection task on their own and then in groups, performance jumped from 21% correct answer after solitary reasoning to 79% after the discussion (Moshman & Geil, 1998).

For more complex tasks, in which a single group member is unlikely to have found the whole correct answer on her own, groups can perform even better. In the course of the discussion, the elements of the correct answer can be taken from different participants and assembled to reach a solution better than that reached by any individual member (e.g. Laughlin, Bonner, & Miner, 2002).

Many problems, however, do not have an easily demonstrated answer. Still, as long as better answers can be supported by better arguments, group discussion should yield, on average, better answers than those following individual reasoning. This improvement has been observed on a wide variety of tasks, such as induction tasks (Laughlin, VanderStoep, & Hollingshead, 1991), numerical estimations (Minson, Liberman, & Ross, 2011; Sniezek & Henry, 1989), and several others (Laughlin, 2011).

The gap in performance between individual reasoning and reasoning after discussion is difficult to deny. However, this gap could be caused by other processes besides argumentation. Simple means of opinion aggregation, which do not require the exchange of arguments, often lead to improved performance as well: following the majority opinion (R. Hastie & Kameda, 2005), following the most confident group member (Koriat, 2012), or averaging between opinions (Soll & Larrick, 2009).

However, it can be shown that in many cases argumentation plays a role beyond these simpler means of aggregation. Argumentation can beat following the majority or the most confident group member. A group member who has the correct answer to a logical or mathematical problem can convince the whole group, even if the other group members all agree on the same wrong answer, and even if she is not the most confident group member (Trouche, Sander, & Mercier, 2014). It has also been shown that discussion can improve performance beyond the simple averaging of opinions (Minson et al., 2011). Thus, argumentation often outperforms other 'wisdom of crowds' mechanisms – its main limitation is that it is harder to scale up than voting for instance.

Although discussion has been shown to lead to better performance for a wide range of tasks, it can also have detrimental effects. The best known is that discussion can lead group members to polarize: to develop stronger views of the topic under discussion (for review, see, Isenberg, 1986). For instance, take participants who agree that, in a base rate problem, base rates should be neglected, and make them talk with each other: they will tend to ignore the base rates even more after the discussion. The opposite happens if they all agreed that base rates should be taken into account (Hinsz, Tindale, & Nagao, 2008).

Group polarization can be explained by the properties of reasoning described above. When group members are made to discuss a topic they all agree on, they offer arguments, but they should not be expected to be very critical of each other's arguments, since they agree on the arguments' conclusions. As the group members now think that there are more reasons supporting their beliefs, they develop stronger beliefs (see Vinokur & Burnstein, 1978). This is similar to the process of attitude polarization that takes place when people reason on their own. In both cases, polarization happens because the arguments produced are not critically evaluated – because there is no audience in the case of solitary reasoning, or because the audience agrees with the arguments' conclusion in the case of group discussion.

Developmental and cross-cultural data

I have argued that there is a strong link between reasoning and argumentation – more specifically, that argumentation is the main function of reasoning. This hypothesis can account for the traits and effects of reasoning. However, almost all the evidence relative to these traits and features has been gathered in WEIRD populations (Western Educated Industrialized Rich Democratic; see Henrich, Heine, & Norenzayan, 2010). It has been claimed that these populations are, in some respects, different from other populations – for instance, they are more individualistic. The features of reasoning reviewed so far could also be specific to WEIRD participants. Argumentation is central to the most important Western institutions, from politics to law and science. WEIRD cultures tend to be diverse, confronting individuals with people who have different views on nearly every topic, which might create more opportunities – real or anticipated – for the exchange of arguments. WEIRD parents, particularly middle- and upper-class ones, provide reasons to their children, and expect children to provide and ask for reasons (e.g. Tizard, Hughes, Carmichael, & Pinkerton, 1983). By contrast, other cultures – some Eastern cultures in particular – have a more negative view of argumentation, which can be seen as a threat to social harmony (Becker, 1986; Nakamura, 1964). Members of traditional populations have a higher proportion of shared beliefs, and thus less pressure to constantly justify their views. They expect their children to comply (Maratsos, 2007), and the children know not to question their parents (Gauvain, Munroe, & Beebe, 2013).

It is thus possible that the features of reasoning reviewed above result from a specific set of cultural factors rather than universal selection pressures. To argue against this possibility, I briefly review evidence suggesting that these features are both universal and early developing, two lines of argument that suggest they are not culturally acquired.

The ability to produce arguments is universal. Even the speakers of Pirahá – a language that has been claimed to lack words or markers for conditionals, disjunctions, conjunctions, comparatives, or quantifiers (Everett et al., 2005) – produce arguments (Everett, 2008; Everett et al., 2005). No culture has been reported in which people would have a natural proclivity to find arguments for other people's point of view, or in which they would spontaneously be able to produce very strong arguments. Experimental evidence shows that individual reasoning exhibits the same failures in all the cultures tested (e.g. Castelain, Girotto, Jamet, & Mercier, submitted; Dasen, 1972; Yama, 2001).

Children start to produce arguments very early – as soon as two years of age in some cases (for review, see Mercier, 2011a). Preschoolers are already able to take common ground into account to decide whether or not they should produce arguments (Köymen, Rosenbaum, & Tomasello, 2014). The arguments they produce are biased to support their point of view (Köymen et al., 2014; Ross, Smith, Spielmacher, & Recchia, 2004). Thus the traits of argument production seem to be universal and to develop early.

The ability to soundly evaluate arguments is more difficult to assess from observational data – the main source of data available for non-WEIRD cultures and young children. Still, the observational data suggests decent argument evaluation skills. A few ethnographies have offered details of debates in traditional populations, and they suggest that the participants were convinced only by good arguments (see, in particular, Hutchins, 1980). The parenting literature suggests that using good reasons in addressing children leads to more compliance (Grusec & Goodnow, 1994). The results from the few experimental studies available also support the existence of good argument evaluation skills. Participants in a traditional Maya population were more likely to accept the arguments supporting the correct answer to a reasoning problem than those supporting the wrong answer (Castelain et al., submitted). Preschoolers are more likely to endorse testimony supported by a strong, perceptual argument than testimony supported by a weak, circular argument (Mercier, Bernard, & Clément, 2014; see also, Corriveau & Kurkul, 2014).

Finally, group discussion has the potential to dramatically improve reasoning performance in non-WEIRD cultures. Besides observational and anecdotal evidence (Boehm et al., 1996; Cole, Gay, Glick, & Sharp, 1971; Hutchins, 1980), a few experimental studies have replicated the improvement following group discussion usually observed in WEIRD cultures in two different cultures: Japan (Mercier, Deguchi, Van der Henst, & Yama, in press) and traditional Maya populations in Guatemala (Castelain et al., submitted). Moreover, children as young as five years of age have also been shown to give better answers to reasoning problems after discussion with a peer (Doise & Mugny, 1984; Perret-Clermont, 1980).

Obviously, this does not mean that there is no difference in how people reason and argue in different cultures (see, e.g., Buchtel & Norenzayan, 2009; Mercier, 2013b). For instance, the members of each culture learn when argumentation is most appropriate and what type of argument is more effective in each specific context. Very little work has been devoted to understanding how these differences emerge, and this will constitute a fascinating topic for future research (Mercier, submitted).

Reasoning and argumentation outside the laboratory

With the exception of this final section, the results reviewed so far have been mostly gathered in the confined setting of the laboratory, using typical student populations, but the same patterns are observed in a variety of other contexts. Ethnographic (Dunbar, 1995) and experimental (Mahoney, 1977) studies of scientists show that they have a myside bias. Argumentation in science is typically very efficient: from the micro-level of the lab meeting (Dunbar, 1995) to the macro-level at which new theories spread (Cohen, 1985), argumentation allows scientists to change their minds for the best (Mercier & Heintz, 2014). Thus reasoning in science is not an exception to the patterns reported above.

The same patterns are observed among other types of experts. For instance, when experts in political science make forecasts on their own, individual reasoning tends to make them overconfident (Tetlock, 2005). Making experts discuss with each other mitigates these issues and allows for better forecasts (Mellers et al., 2014; Rowe & Wright, 1996; for other domains of expertise, see Mercier, 2011c).

In education, collaborative – or cooperative – learning has the potential to dramatically improve reasoning performance: by making students articulate justifications for their answers and evaluate each other's justifications, these pedagogical tools can not only allow students to adopt correct answers, but also to reach a deeper understanding of the concepts involved (see, e.g., Slavin, 1995).

Argumentation has the potential to yield sounder beliefs and better decisions even in contexts which are fraught with emotions, such as juries attempting to reach a verdict (Ellsworth, 1989; Reid Hastie, Penrod, & Pennington, 1983), discussions of moral dilemmas (see Mercier, 2011b), or citizens discussing policy issues (see, e.g., Fishkin, 2009; Mercier & Landemore, 2012).

This very brief review shows that the main features of reasoning – myside bias in argument production, good ability to evaluate arguments, improvement in performance yielded by discussion – are found not only in the laboratory but also in all the 'outside world' contexts for which data are available.

Conclusion

The individualist view of reasoning, according to which solitary reasoning aims at and is able to deliver epistemic and practical improvements, has a strong hold on our culture. It is manifest in the "solitary genius" view of science (Shapin, 1991), in the trepidation with which deliberations between citizens is perceived (Sunstein, 2002), and in the resistance to the use of argumentation in many other contexts – collaborative learning in schools, work teams, and so on. Even experts dramatically underestimate the benefits of argumentation. For instance, when asked to estimate how many people would be able to solve the Wason selection task on their own and in small groups, people believed that group discussion would provide little or no benefit. Even psychologists of reasoning underestimated the benefits of group discussion by a factor of two (Mercier, Trouche, Yama, Heintz, & Girotto, in press).

The results reviewed here strongly suggest that the individualist view of reasoning is mistaken. Reasoning's features make much more sense when it is understood as a social – and, more specifically, argumentative – mechanism. This has both scientific and practical implications. From a scientific perspective, this suggests that more attention should be paid to how reasoning works in social settings. As mentioned above, this attention shift is already under way, and one can only hope that it will gather pace in the following years. From a practical perspective, the mismatch between the popular individual view of reasoning and the arguably more accurate social view has to be addressed, and institutions should be fostered that put reasoning back in its normal social context, thus making the best of it.

References

Becker, C. B. (1986). Reasons for the lack of argumentation and debate in the Far East. *International Journal of Intercultural Relations, 10*(1), 75–92.

Billig, M. (1996). *Arguing and thinking: A rhetorical approach to social psychology*. Cambridge: Cambridge University Press.

Boehm, C., Antweiler, C., Eibl-Eibesfeldt, I., Kent, S., Knauft, B. M., Mithen, S., . . . Wilson, D. S. (1996). Emergency decisions, cultural-selection mechanics, and group selection [and comments and reply]. *Current Anthropology, 37*(5), 763–793.

Buchtel, E. E., & Norenzayan, A. (2009). Thinking across cultures: Implications for dual processes. In J. St. B. T. Evans & K. Frankish (Eds.), *In two minds*. New York: Oxford University Press.

Castelain, T., Girotto, V., Jamet, F., & Mercier, H. (submitted). Evidence for core features of reasoning in a Mayan indigenous population.

Cohen, I. B. (1985). *Revolution in science*. Cambridge, MA: Harvard University Press.

Cole, M., Gay, J., Glick, J. A., & Sharp, D. W. (1971). *The cultural context of learning and thinking*. New York: Basic Books.

Collins, P., & Hahn, U. (this volume). Informal Argument Fallacies. In L. J. Ball & V. A. Thompson (Eds.), *International handbook of thinking and reasoning*. London: Psychology Press.

Corriveau, K. H., & Kurkul, K. E. (2014). "Why does rain fall?": Children prefer to learn from an informant who uses noncircular explanations. *Child Development, 85*(5), 1827–1835.

Cosmides, L., & Tooby, J. (1992). Cognitive adaptations for social exchange. In J. H. Barkow, L. Cosmides, & J. Tooby (Eds.), *The adapted mind: Evolutionary psychology and the generation of culture* (pp. 163–228). Oxford: Oxford University Press.

Crowell, A., & Kuhn, D. (2014). Developing dialogic argumentation skills: A 3-year intervention study. *Journal of Cognition and Development, 15*(2), 363–381.

Dasen, P. R. (1972). Cross-cultural Piagetian research: A summary. *Journal of Cross-Cultural Psychology, 3*(1), 23–40.

Descartes, R. (1985). *The philosophical writings of Descartes* (J. Cottingham, R. Stoothoff, & D. Murdoch, Trans.) (Vol. 1). Cambridge: Cambridge University Press.

Doise, W., & Mugny, G. (1984). *The social development of the intellect*. Oxford: Pergamon Press.

Ducrot, O., & Anscombre, J. C. (1983). *L'argumentation dans la langue*. Bruxelles: Mardaga.

Dunbar, K. (1995). How scientists really reason: Scientific reasoning in real-world laboratories. In R. J. Sternberg & J. E. Davidson (Eds.), *The nature of insight* (pp. 365–395). Cambridge, MA: MIT Press.

Dutilh Novaes, C. (submitted). A dialogical, multi-agent account of the normativity of logic.

Edwards, K., & Smith, E. E. (1996). A disconfirmation bias in the evaluation of arguments. *Journal of Personality and Social Psychology, 71*, 5–24.

Ellsworth, P. C. (1989). Are twelve heads better than one? *Law and Contemporary Problems, 52*, 205–224.

Evans, J. St. B. T. (2002). Logic and human reasoning: an assessment of the deduction paradigm. *Psychological Bulletin, 128*(6), 978–996.

Evans, J. St. B. T., Barston, J. L., & Pollard, P. (1983). On the conflict between logic and belief in syllogistic reasoning. *Memory and Cognition, 11*, 295–306.

Everett, D. L. (2008). *Don't sleep, there are snakes*. New York: Pantheon Books.
Everett, D. L., Berlin, B., Goncalves, M. A., Kay, P., Levinson, S. C., Pawley, A., . . . Everett, D. L. (2005). Cultural constraints on grammar and cognition in Piraha. *Current Anthropology*, *46*(4), 621–646.
Fishkin, J. S. (2009). *When the people speak: Deliberative democracy and public consultation*. Oxford: Oxford University Press.
Gauvain, M., Munroe, R. L., & Beebe, H. (2013). Children's questions in cross-cultural perspective a four-culture study. *Journal of Cross-Cultural Psychology*, *44*(7), 1148–1165.
Gibbard, A. (1990). *Wise choices, Apt feelings*. Cambridge: Cambridge University Press.
Gigerenzer, G., Todd, P. M., & ABC Research Group. (1999). *Simple heuristics that make us smart*. Oxford: Oxford University Press.
Grusec, J. E., & Goodnow, J. J. (1994). Impact of parental discipline methods on the child's internalization of values: A reconceptualization of current points of view. *Developmental Psychology*, *30*(1), 4–19.
Hahn, U., Harris, A. J. L., & Corner, A. (2009). Argument content and argument source: An exploration. *Informal Logic*, *29*(4), 337–367.
Hahn, U., & Hornikx, J. (Eds.). (2012). *Reasoning and argumentation. A special issue of thinking and reasoning*. London: Psychology Press.
Hahn, U., & Oaksford, M. (2007). The rationality of informal argumentation: A Bayesian approach to reasoning fallacies. *Psychological Review*, *114*(3), 704–732.
Hahn, U., & Oaksford, M. (2008). A normative theory of argument strength. *Informal Logic*, *26*(1), 1–24.
Hastie, R., & Kameda, T. (2005). The robust beauty of majority rules in group decisions. *Psychological Review*, *112*(2), 494–50814.
Hastie, R., Penrod, S., & Pennington, N. (1983). *Inside the Jury*. Cambridge, MA: Harvard University Press.
Henrich, J., Heine, S. J., & Norenzayan, A. (2010). The weirdest people in the world. *Behavioral and Brain Sciences*, *33*(2–3), 61–83.
Herman, T., & Oswald, S. (Eds.). (2014). *Rhetoric and cognition: Theoretical perspectives and persuasive strategies*. Berne: Peter Lang.
Hinsz, V. B., Tindale, R. S., & Nagao, D. H. (2008). Accentuation of information processes and biases in group judgments integrating base-rate and case-specific information. *Journal of Experimental Social Psychology*, *44*(1), 116–126.
Hoeken, H., Timmers, R., & Schellens, P. J. (2012). Arguing about desirable consequences: What constitutes a convincing argument? *Thinking & Reasoning*, *18*(3), 394–416.
Hornikx, J., & Hahn, U. (2012). Reasoning and argumentation: Towards an integrated psychology of argumentation. *Thinking & Reasoning*, *18*(3), 225–243.
Hutchins, E. (1980). *Culture and inference*. Cambridge, MA: MIT Press.
Iordanou, K. (2013). Developing face-to-face argumentation skills: Does arguing on the computer help? *Journal of Cognition and Development*, *14*(2), 292–320.
Isenberg, D. J. (1986). Group polarization: A critical review and meta-analysis. *Journal of Personality and Social Psychology*, *50*(6), 1141–1151.
Koriat, A. (2012). When are two heads better than one and why? *Science*, *336*(6079), 360–362.
Koriat, A., Lichtenstein, S., & Fischhoff, B. (1980). Reasons for confidence. *Journal of Experimental Psychology: Human Learning and Memory and Cognition*, *6*, 107–118.
Köymen, B., Rosenbaum, L., & Tomasello, M. (2014). Reasoning during joint decision-making by preschool peers. *Cognitive Development*, *32*, 74–85.
Kuhn, D. (1991). *The skills of arguments*. Cambridge: Cambridge University Press.
Kuhn, D., & Crowell, A. (2011). Dialogic argumentation as a vehicle for developing young adolescents' thinking. *Psychological Science*, *22*(4), 545.
Laughlin, P. R. (2011). *Group problem solving*. Princeton: Princeton University Press.
Laughlin, P. R., Bonner, B. L., & Miner, A. G. (2002). Groups perform better than the best individuals on letters-to-numbers problems. *Organizational Behavior and Human Decision Processes*, *88*, 605–620.
Laughlin, P. R., VanderStoep, S. W., & Hollingshead, A. B. (1991). Collective versus individual induction: Recognition of truth, rejection of error, and collective information processing. *Journal of Personality and Social Psychology*, *61*, 50–67.
Levinson, S. C. (2006). On the human "interaction engine." In N. J. Enfield & S. C. Levinson (Eds.), *Roots of human sociality* (pp. 39–69). Oxford: Berg.
Lucas, E. J., & Ball, L. J. (2005). Think-aloud protocols and the selection task: Evidence for relevance effects and rationalisation processes. *Thinking and Reasoning*, *11*, 35–66.

Mahoney, M. J. (1977). Publication prejudices: An experimental study of confirmatory bias in the peer review system. *Cognitive Therapy and Research, 1*(2), 161–175.
Maillat, D., & Oswald, S. (Eds.). (2013). ***Biases and Constraints in Communication: Argumentation, Persuasion and Manipulation****. Special issue of the Journal of Pragmatics*. Amsterdam: Elsevier.
Maratsos, M. P. (2007). Commentary. *Monographs of the Society for Research in Child Development, 72*, 121–126.
Maynard Smith, J., & Harper, D. (2003). *Animal Signals*. Oxford: Oxford University Press.
Mellers, B., Ungar, L., Baron, J., Ramos, J., Gurcay, B., Fincher, K., . . . et al. (2014). Psychological strategies for winning a geopolitical forecasting tournament. *Psychological Science, 25*(5), 1106–1115.
Mercier, H. (2011a). Reasoning serves argumentation in children. *Cognitive Development, 26*(3), 177–191.
Mercier, H. (2011b). What good is moral reasoning? *Mind & Society, 10*(2), 131–148.
Mercier, H. (2011c). When experts argue: Explaining the best and the worst of reasoning. *Argumentation, 25*(3), 313–327.
Mercier, H. (2013a). Our pigheaded core: How we became smarter to be influenced by other people. In B. Calcott, R. Joyce, & K. Sterelny (Eds.), *Evolution, cooperation, and complexity*. Cambridge, MA: MIT Press.
Mercier, H. (Ed.). (2013b). *Recording and explaining cultural differences in argumentation – Special issue of the Journal of Cognition and Culture* (Vol. 13). Leiden: Brill.
Mercier, H. (in press). Confirmation (or myside) bias. In R. Pohl (Ed.), *Cognitive Illusions* (2nd ed.). London: Psychology Press.
Mercier, H. (submitted). Reasoning and argumentation. In H. Callan (Ed.), *International encyclopedia of anthropology*. London: Wiley-Blackwell.
Mercier, H., Bernard, S., & Clément, F. (2014). Early sensitivity to arguments: How preschoolers weight circular arguments. *Journal of Experimental Child Psychology, 125*, 102–109.
Mercier, H., Bonnier, P., & Trouche, E. (in press). Why don't people produce better arguments? In L. Macchi, M. Bagassi, & R. Viale (Eds.), *The language of thought*. Cambridge, MA: MIT Press.
Mercier, H., Deguchi, M., Van der Henst, J.-B., & Yama, H. (in press). The benefits of argumentation are cross-culturally robust: The case of Japan. *Thinking & Reasoning*.
Mercier, H., & Heintz, C. (2014). Scientists' argumentative reasoning. *Topoi, 33*(2), 513–524.
Mercier, H., & Landemore, H. (2012). Reasoning is for arguing: Understanding the successes and failures of deliberation. *Political Psychology, 33*(2), 243–258.
Mercier, H., & Sperber, D. (2009). Intuitive and reflective inferences. In J. St. B. T. Evans & K. Frankish (Eds.), *In two minds* (pp. 149–170). New York: Oxford University Press.
Mercier, H., & Sperber, D. (2011). Why do humans reason? Arguments for an argumentative theory. *Behavioral and Brain Sciences, 34*(2), 57–74.
Mercier, H., Trouche, E., Yama, H., Heintz, C., & Girotto, V. (in press). Experts and laymen grossly underestimate the benefits of argumentation for reasoning. *Thinking & Reasoning*.
Minson, J. A., Liberman, V., & Ross, L. (2011). Two to Tango. *Personality and Social Psychology Bulletin, 37*(10), 1325–1338.
Moshman, D., & Geil, M. (1998). Collaborative reasoning: Evidence for collective rationality. *Thinking and Reasoning, 4*(3), 231–248.
Nakamura, H. (1964). *Ways of thinking of eastern peoples: India, China, Tibet, Japan*. Hawaii: University of Hawaii Press.
Nickerson, R. S. (1998). Confirmation bias: A ubiquitous phenomena in many guises. *Review of General Psychology, 2*, 175–220.
Perelman, C., & Olbrechts-Tyteca, L. (1958). *The new rhetoric: A treatise on argumentation*. Notre Dame, IN: University of Notre Dame Press.
Perkins, D. N. (1989). Reasoning as it is and could be: An empirical perspective. In D. M. Topping, D. C. Crowell, & V. N. Kobayashi (Eds.), *Thinking across cultures: The third international conference on thinking* (pp. 175–194). Hillsdale, NJ: Lawrence Erlbaum Associates.
Perret-Clermont, A.-N. (1980). *Social interaction and cognitive development in children*. London: Academic Press.
Petty, R. E., & Wegener, D. T. (1998). Attitude change: Multiple roles for persuasion variables. In D. T. Gilbert, S. Fiske, & G. Lindzey (Eds.), *The handbook of social psychology* (pp. 323–390). Boston: McGraw-Hill.
Piaget, J. (1928). *Judgment and reasoning in the child*. London: Routledge and Kegan Paul.
Roberts, M. J., & Newton, E. J. (2001). Inspection times, the change task, and the rapid response selection task. *Quarterly Journal of Experimental Psychology, 54*, 1031–1048.
Ross, H., Smith, J., Spielmacher, C., & Recchia, H. (2004). Shading the truth Self-serving biases in children's reports of sibling conflicts. *Merrill-Palmer Quarterly, 50*(1), 61–86.

Rowe, G., & Wright, G. (1996). The impact of task characteristics on the performance of structured group forecasting techniques. *International Journal of Forecasting, 12*(1), 73–89.
Shafir, E., Simonson, I., & Tversky, A. (1993). Reason-based choice. *Cognition, 49*(1–2), 11–36.
Shapin, S. (1991). "The mind is its own place": Science and solitude in seventeenth-century England. *Science in Context, 4*(01), 191–218.
Simonson, I. (1989). Choice based on reasons: The case of attraction and compromise effects. *Journal of Consumer Research, 16*(2), 158–174.
Slavin, R. E. (1995). *Cooperative learning: Theory, research, and practice* (Vol. 2nd). London: Allyn and Bacon.
Sniezek, J. A., & Henry, R. A. (1989). Accuracy and confidence in group judgment. *Organizational Behavior and Human Decision Processes, 43*(1), 1–28.
Soll, J. B., & Larrick, R. P. (2009). Strategies for revising judgment: How (and how well) people use others' opinions. *Journal of Experimental Psychology: Learning, Memory, and Cognition, 35*(3), 780–805.
Sperber, D., Cara, F., & Girotto, V. (1995). Relevance theory explains the selection task. *Cognition, 57*, 31–95.
Sperber, D., Clément, F., Heintz, C., Mascaro, O., Mercier, H., Origgi, G., & Wilson, D. (2010). Epistemic vigilance. *Mind and Language, 25*(4), 359–393.
Stanovich, K. E. (2004). *The robot's rebellion*. Chicago: Chicago University Press.
Sunstein, C. R. (2002). The law of group polarization. *Journal of Political Philosophy, 10*(2), 175–195.
Tesser, A. (1978). Self-generated attitude change. In L. Berkowitz (Ed.), *Advances in experimental social psychology* (pp. 289–338). New York: Academic Press.
Tetlock, P. E. (2005). *Expert political judgment: How good is it? How can we know?* Princeton, NJ: Princeton University Press.
Thompson, D. V., & Norton, M. I. (2008). The social utility of feature creep. In A. Lee & D. Soman (Eds.), *Advances in consumer research* (pp. 181–184). Duluth, MN: Association for Consumer Research.
Thompson, V. A., Evans, J. St. B. T., & Campbell, J. I. (2013). Matching bias on the selection task: It's fast and feels good. *Thinking & Reasoning, 19*(3–4).
Thompson, V. A., Prowse Turner, J. A., & Pennycook, G. (2011). Intuition, reason, and metacognition. *Cognitive Psychology, 63*(3), 107–140.
Tizard, B., Hughes, M., Carmichael, H., & Pinkerton, G. (1983). Language and social class: Is verbal deprivation a myth? *Journal of Child Psychology and Psychiatry, 24*(4), 533–542.
Trouche, E., Johansson, P., Hall, L., & Mercier, H. (in press). The selective laziness of reasoning. *Cognitive Science*.
Trouche, E., Sander, E., & Mercier, H. (2014). Arguments, more than confidence, explain the good performance of reasoning groups. *Journal of Experimental Psychology: General, 143*(5), 1958–1971.
Vinokur, A., & Burnstein, E. (1978). Novel argumentation and attitude change: The case of polarization following group discussion. *European Journal of Social Psychology, 8*(3), 335–348.
Wason, P. C. (1966). Reasoning. In B. M. Foss (Ed.), *New horizons in psychology: I* (pp. 106–137). Harmandsworth, UK: Penguin.
Yama, H. (2001). Matching versus optimal data selection in the Wason selection task. *Thinking & Reasoning, 7*(3), 295–311.

23

PROBABILITIES AND BAYESIAN RATIONALITY

Mike Oaksford and Nick Chater

This book is about thinking and reasoning construed as a scientific project. That is, it presents the most up-to-date account of current scientific thinking on the human activity of thinking and reasoning. Thus conceived, this is clearly a descriptive project. One might therefore query why this chapter and Chapter 19 introduce fundamentally normative concepts like logic and probability. These are theories of how people *should* reason, not *how* they actually reason. However, there are important reasons why understanding these normative projects is crucial in this area.

First, when we try to remember a list of words in a psychological experiment, it is clear when we have failed and when we have succeeded: we recall the word or we do not. How do we judge when someone's reasoning has failed? Without a theory of reasoning, it is not possible to answer this question. We need some standard against which to measure performance, and this is provided by normative theories like logic and probability. Probability theory provides a rational standard with respect to uncertain reasoning when we cannot be sure whether a sentence or belief is true or false. Conformity to the laws of logic and probability is what we mean by being rational. And this is important in a variety of contexts, for example, determining whether someone is capable of standing trial or whether they need psychiatric help. In sum, we could not begin to ask the question of how people reason with uncertainty without a theory of reasoning under uncertainty – that is, without a theory of probability.

A second reason for our concern with normative theories is that they can provide the basis for constructing a descriptive theory of human reasoning. So rather than just comparing human performance to probability theory, we might assume that nature has built probability theory into our cognitive equipment just as a human designer builds the laws of arithmetic into a calculator. This is a more controversial claim, which is at the heart of many current theoretical disputes in the area of thinking and reasoning. For example, there are theories that assume that standard logic in some guise provides the foundation for a theory of how people reason deductively (Rips, 1994; Johnson-Laird & Byrne, 1991). However, recent theories suggest that probability theory can better explain the empirical data on how people reason deductively suggesting that in fact their reasoning is probabilistic rather than logical (Oaksford & Chater, 1994, 2007). Against these theories are those that propose that it is a fundamental mistake to base a theory of how we reason on these normative theories and that human reasoning is based largely upon heuristics (Gigerenzer & Goldstein, 1996; Gigerenzer & Todd, 1999).

Just as with logic, probability theory does not tell you what you should believe. It cannot tell you which political party to support, which football team is the best, or whether ghosts exist.[1] What it can do – and this is where, like logic, probability theory is a theory of rationality – is tell you what your degree of belief in a proposition should be, given you believe certain other things. Trivially, if you believe that Arsenal have a .9 probability of beating Liverpool, then you must believe that Liverpool have only a .1 probability of drawing with or beating Arsenal. These are consistency or *coherence* constraints on degrees of belief, and these are captured by probability theory.

In this chapter, our first goal is to introduce probability theory and explain why it is rational to obey the laws of probability theory. Our second goal is to introduce how probability theory has been used in the psychology of reasoning by discussing a variety of probabilistic concepts which have been appealed to in this area. We first introduce probability theory and then we introduce the "Dutch book" argument for the rationality of the laws of probability. When we speak of "Bayesian rationality," this is largely what we mean, as the argument is based on betting behavior, which can also provide a means of assigning subjective probabilities. It is the subjective interpretation of probability – that is, the view that probabilities are degrees of belief – which distinguishes the Bayesian approach from other approaches to probability (Gillies, 2000). Probability theory has many applications within the cognitive sciences and, in particular, forms the foundation of the so-called new paradigm in reasoning research (Elqayam & Over, 2013; Oaksford & Chater, 1994, 2007; Over, 2009). Consequently, in the following sections of this chapter, we introduce the various probabilistic concepts that have featured in these developments, including probability logic and *p*-validity, probabilistic coherence, causal Bayes nets, and dynamic inference.

Probability

As we have just argued, probability theory can be viewed as capturing the coherence of our *degrees of belief*. Most of our beliefs are uncertain because most of our sources of information are uncertain. Much of what we know comes from the testimony of other people – for example, teachers, friends, newspapers, or the man in the street. These sources are differentially reliable. Moreover, visual illusions are testament to the fact that even perception may mislead.

All approaches to probability, including the subjective approach (Gillies, 2000), agree on the fundamental laws of probability that can be derived from very few assumptions (e.g., Cox, 1946; Kolmogorov, 1956; Ramsey, 1926). These laws are the Kolmogorov axioms:

1. For any event A, probabilities are non-negative: $\Pr(A) \geq 0$
2. Where A is certain to occur: $\Pr(A) = 1$
3. Where A and B are mutually exclusive: Pr(A or B)=Pr(A)+Pr(B)

Axiom 3 is called additivity and *mutually exclusive* means that the probability that A and B occur together is 0, that is, Pr(A and B)=0 (usually abbreviated as Pr(A,B)=0. For example, no car is both a Ford and a Citroën, so the probability that a car is either a Ford or a Citroën is Pr(Citroën)+Pr(Ford). When we come to the section on Bayesian rationality we shall use an argument called the Dutch book argument to show why it is rational to allow our degrees of belief to be constrained by the axioms of probability theory.

The Bayesian or subjective approach is named after Bayes' theorem, which is central to uncertain inference. As we have already remarked, the Bayesian approach to probability and statistics is controversial but Bayes' theorem is not. It can be derived simply from the definition of conditional probability. $\Pr(A|B)$ is the probability that A is true, given that B is true. The conditional probability can be derived from the joint probability $\Pr(A, B)$, that both A and B are true, and the probability that B is true, $\Pr(B)$, by the ratio formula:

$$\Pr(A|B) = \frac{\Pr(A,B)}{\Pr(B)} \tag{4}$$

Because A and B are arbitrary, (5) must also be true:

$$\Pr(B|A) = \frac{\Pr(A,B)}{\Pr(A)} \tag{5}$$

Elementary algebraic manipulation then yields Bayes' theorem:

$$\Pr(B|A) = \frac{\Pr(A \mid B)\Pr(B)}{\Pr(A)} \tag{6}$$

So far, so trivial; it is only when we substitute more interesting quantities for A and B that the true import of Bayes' theorem becomes clear. By replacing A with D, for, say, the outcome of an experiment, and B with H_i for one of some set of alternative hypotheses that make predictions about the outcome of that experiment, then Bayes' theorem can be used to calculate the probability that H_i is true, given the data, $\Pr(H_i \mid D)$:

$$\Pr(H_i|D) = \frac{\Pr(D \mid H_i)\Pr(H_i)}{\Pr(D)} \tag{7}$$

This formula relates our beliefs about a particular hypothesis, H_i, given some data D, $\Pr(H_i \mid D)$, as a function only of our prior beliefs in the hypothesis $\Pr(H_i)$ and the probability of the data, given the hypothesis, $\Pr(D \mid H_i)$. If our hypothesis is sufficiently detailed, we should be able to specify values for the latter. $\Pr(D)$ in the denominator of (7) seems more problematic. It seems very difficult to know what the probability of the outcome of an experiment will be. However, if we assume that the true hypothesis is precisely one of a list $H_1 \ldots H_n$, then we can use another simple identity of probability theory:

$$\Pr(D) = \sum_{j=1}^{n} \Pr(D, H_j) \tag{8}$$

This identity holds because, if D is true, by hypothesis, it must be true in conjunction with precisely one of the $H_1 \ldots H_n$. This gives us Bayes' theorem in its most popular form:

$$\Pr(H_i|D) = \frac{\Pr(D \mid H_i)\Pr(H_i)}{\sum_{j=1}^{n} \Pr(D \mid H_j)\Pr(H_j)} \tag{9}$$

Probability theory provides consistency or coherence conditions over degrees of belief. This means that probability is, in the first instance, a static notion. Suppose, for example, that we discover an inconsistency in our probabilities. What should we do? Probability theory does not, in general, spell out which beliefs should change to restore consistency – and, indeed, how to do this is little understood.

However, there is an important special case, which is well understood, very important, and much used in the Bayesian approach to thinking and reasoning, and which we have already touched on implicitly: Bayesian conditionalization. Suppose that we start with a prior distribution $\Pr_0(H_i)$ over hypotheses; and these are each associated with a probability distribution over possible sets of data $\Pr_0(D_j \mid H_i)$. These can both be captured by the joint probability distribution $\Pr_0(D_j, H_i)$; and, of course, by summing over the different possible H_i, this will also give us probabilities for each possible set of data, $\Pr_0(D_j)$. Then, we learn that a specific set of data, D_k, is true: $\Pr_1(D_k) = 1$ (we will use $\Pr_1$ to denote probabilities after the data has been obtained). Note that this probability is not consistent with the probability before we encountered the data. Suppose, for example, that $\Pr_0(D_k) = .02$ – which is, of course, inconsistent with the "new" probability indicating that this data has certainly been encountered. How do we now resolve this inconsistency, and update the rest of our probabilities, to restore consistency in the light of this new information?

Bayesian conditionalization proposes that our new probabilities, in the light of learning *D* for certain, for each H_i should just be our previous conditional probabilities:

$$\Pr_1(H_i) = \Pr_0(H_i \mid D) \tag{10}$$

This assumption is so widely used in the Bayesian approach that it is often scarcely noticed that it is an assumption that all; and Bayes' theorem is then applied to actually calculate the new values. One elegant feature of this approach is that it can be applied iteratively, as data is obtained piece by piece (the probabilities of the H_i can be updated at each step, and it will not matter in which order the data is encountered). And the whole approach applies not just to single hypotheses, H_i, but to probabilistic models of any complexity. As we shall see, it has also been used directly to model human reasoning (Oaksford & Chater, 2007; Oaksford, Chater, & Larkin, 2000).

Bayesian conditionalization is not always unproblematic – either because the new data is not quite itself certain (e.g., if our perception or memory is fallible), in which case one option is to apply a generalization called Jeffrey conditionalization (Jeffrey, 1983), although this generalization is itself controversial (e.g., Lange, 2000). An alternative possible complication with conventional Bayesian conditionalization is that, in learning the data *D*, the agent may learn additional information, which may then influence the conditional probability $\Pr(H_i \mid D)$. For example, John might believe that the probability that he is asleep is .99, given that it is four in the morning. On the other hand, if he hears the clock chime four, he cannot, of course, infer that he is almost certainly asleep – the fact of his noting the clock's chime has an additional implication, over and above what time it is: that he must be awake. The extent to which problems of this type can be eliminated with suitable care is not clear. However, as we suggest later on, cases where Bayesian conditionalization is problematic in just the sense described here arise in some very simple inferences involving conditionals, that is, sentences of the form *if A then B*. These cases suggest that we need an account of *dynamic* inference that can account for cases where new information implies changes to the relevant conditional probabilities.

Logic considers structural relationships between belief and these have consequences for probability. Thus, if an agent believes that *A and B* has a probability of, say, .4, then consistency requires that the agent believes that *A* has a probability of at least .4. This is simply because all the possible states of affairs in which *A and B* are true are, by logical necessity, also states of affairs in which *A* is true. Nonetheless, in human judgements people often make probability judgements that violate this constraint – the so-called conjunction fallacy (Tversky & Kahneman, 1983; see chapters in Section III). Yet, while some relationships between probability and logic are relatively straightforward, forging a more general connection has proved very challenging for normative theories (e.g., Milch, Marthi, Russell, Sontag, Ong & Kolobov, 2007). A key question is how to fuse fairly rich logics (which allows discussion of objects and their properties, as mentioned) with probability, so that we can easily represent questions such as "What is the probability that I've caught the same fish more than once?" given the number of fish caught, their colours, beliefs about the number of fish in the lake, and so on.

One of the pioneers of the Bayesian approach to probability (Savage, 1954) stressed that probability operates in a "small world." If we have a set of propositions, $A_1, \ldots, A_n$ (where the A_i might stand for any proposition) and our beliefs give us a joint probability distribution over these $\Pr(A_1, \ldots, A_n)$, then the business of probabilistic inference can begin. Thus, for example, if the data are sensory inputs, we need to specify a model which assigns a probability to each possible such input. One way to achieve this is to specify a "generative model," i.e., a process which generates data of the right form (here, images), where the uncertainty can be introduced at one or more points in the generative process. The more the generative model reflects the constraints underlying the domain (in the case of sensory input, tendencies for neighbouring patches of input to be correlated, at all scales, for example), the better the inference will be. In probabilistic analyses of reasoning tasks (e.g., Griffiths & Tenenbaum, 2005; Oaksford & Chater, 1994, 2007), the "world" modelled may be quite small – we need just a probability distribution over a handful of premises. But to understand real-world reasoning, where knowledge is richly interconnected, appears to require breaking out of the "small world" and defining a generative model over world knowledge. It is not clear how this can be done – and some authors (e.g., Binmore, 2008) are sceptical that it is viable at all.

Yet some important progress has been made by describing probability distributions in terms of graphical models (see Pearl, 1988), which are both representationally and computationally attractive. Indeed, we will introduce these models in discussing how they might account for some of the principal findings in human conditional reasoning involving suppression effects (Byrne, 1989; Cummins, 1995; see also Over & Cruz, this volume). The psychology of reasoning has widely adopted probabilistic ideas (e.g., Evans, Handley, & Over, 2003; McKenzie & Mikkelsen, 2007; Oaksford & Chater, 1994, 2007); and the same ideas have been extended to model argumentation (see Collins & Hahn, this volume; Hahn & Oaksford, 2007).

Bayesian rationality

In the last section we introduced the axioms of probability theory but how do we know that obeying these laws is rational? The reason why we should follow the laws of standard logic is to avoid falling into contradiction, i.e., believing both that a proposition is true and it is false, for example, believing both that Arsenal beat Chelsea and they did not beat Chelsea. It is universally agreed that one cannot rationally believe a contradiction. If one follows the laws of logic one will never fall into contradiction. One of the primary arguments for the rationality of following the laws of probability is that by doing so you will never accept a bet you are bound to lose. This is the Dutch book argument, which shows that violating these laws is practically irrational (Joyce, 2004).

The argument begins with some relatively self-evident assumptions, the most important of which is the expected utility thesis. This thesis states that an act best satisfies a rational agent's desires if and only if it maximises his or her subjective expected utility. The expected utility thesis shows that with a few further assumptions an agent will reveal the strength of their beliefs in their betting behaviour. These assumptions are: "(a) the agent desires only money; (b) her desire for money does not vary in changes in her fortune; and (c) she is not averse to risk or uncertainty" (Joyce, 2004, p. 136). Beginning with a confidence measure defining the agent's degree of belief in a proposition x, $c(x)$, the aim is to show that the measure c must respect the laws of probability.

Borrowing heavily from Joyce (2004, p. 136), consider a wager W such that one receives £110 if Arsenal win and £10 if Arsenal lose (we ignore the possibility of a draw for simplicity).

Clearly whether Arsenal win or not is not dependent on the wager, and it is certain that if Arsenal win a person taking the bet will win £110 and if they lose she will win £10. The fair price that a person will pay for this wager, £*f*, will be the sum at which they are indifferent between £*f* and the wager *W*. Assuming that that person's degree of belief that Arsenal win is $c(x)$, the expected utility thesis dictates that £*f* will be *W*'s expected payoff, i.e., £$f = E(W) = c$(Arsenal win) × £110 + (1 – *c*(Arsenal win)) × £10. We can then immediately see that this person's confidence that Arsenal will win, *c*(Arsenal win) = (£*f* – £10)/(£110 – £10). Assuming the person is indifferent between the wager and £70, this means that their degree of belief in Arsenal winning is 0.6. Consequently we can infer people's degrees of belief from their betting behaviour. Here we follow Joyce in assuming that monetary value can be substituted for utility for simplicity, although this assumption can be relaxed.

So far we still don't know whether $c(x)$ respects the laws of probability. This is what the Dutch book theorems establish. By the expected utility thesis and (a) to (c), people should be willing to trade any set of wagers for an equivalent fair price. Moreover, they should be willing to trade any set of fair prices for the corresponding wagers. Take the following sets of wagers and fair prices:

W_A = (£100 if Arsenal win, £0 else), £f_A = £25
W_C = (£100 if Chelsea win, £0 else), £f_C = £25
$W_{A \text{ or } C}$ = (£100 if Arsenal OR Chelsea win, £0 else), £$f_{A \text{ or } C}$ = £60.

Arsenal and Chelsea are playing each other and all bets are off if there is a draw. In this example, someone should be indifferent between the first two wagers plus £60 (W_A, W_C, £60) and the last wager plus £50 ($W_{A \text{ or } C}$, £50). However, W_A and W_C are equivalent, in terms of payoffs, to $W_{A \text{ or } C}$. Consequently, the extra £10 paid for the first bundle of wagers and fair prices yields no potential gain, i.e., the set of fair prices is irrational. If you find someone to accept these wagers from you at these "fair" prices, you are guaranteed to make £10 whatever the outcome and this person becomes a money pump. It is therefore clear that one should be indifferent between the combination of the first two wagers, W_A and W_C, and the single wager, $W_{A \text{ or } C}$ in these circumstances and therefore £$f_{A \text{ or } C}$ should equal £f_A + £f_C. Consequently, $c(x)$ should conform to the Additivity Axiom of probability theory: $\Pr(x \text{ or } y) = \Pr(x) + \Pr(y)$, when x and y are logically incompatible (both teams can't win). Similar Dutch book arguments can be made for all the other laws of probability theory.

This argument shows that "it is practically irrational to hold beliefs that violate the laws of probability" (Joyce, 2004, p. 136). If our degrees of belief do not conform to the laws of probability, then we are bound to take actions, i.e., place bets, from which we are guaranteed to incur a loss. That is, we will fail to maximise expected utility. The Dutch book is probably the most well-known practical justification for the laws of probability. However, to move beyond (a) – (c) above, i.e., to lift restrictions on what people desire beyond money – requires moving to Savage's (1954) axioms that established the coherence of expected utility and probabilistic consistency at the same time. This approach still offers a practical justification for the laws of probability.

In the following sections, we introduce various probabilistic concepts that have figured in the recent psychology of reasoning, including probability logic and *p*-validity, probabilistic coherence, causal Bayes nets, and dynamic inference.

Probability logic and *P*-validity

The central logical term in studies of human reasoning is the conditional *if. . .then*. There has been more work on the conditional in both philosophical logic and experimental psychology than any other logical term. This is because of the wide variety of logical and psychological approaches that have been proposed. This variety is the main target of controversy in the psychology of reasoning.

The probability conditional

The core of probability logic is a new connective, the probability conditional in this account, which relies on what Edgington (1995) refers to as ***the Equation***. In the Equation, the probability of an everyday indicative conditional is identified with the conditional probability:

$$P(p \rightarrow q) = P(q \mid p), \text{ where } P(p) > 0 \tag{11}$$

Where $P(q \mid p)$ is given by the *Ratio formula*:

$$P(q \mid p) = \frac{P(p \wedge q)}{P(p)} \tag{12}$$

The ratio formula is not interpreted as a definition of conditional probability, which is regarded as more primitive. Our understanding of $P(q \mid p)$ is given by the subjective interpretation provided by what has become know as the Ramsey Test. As Bennett (2003, p. 53) says:

> The best definition we have [of conditional probability] is the one provided by the Ramsey test: your conditional probability for q given p is the probability for q that results from adding $P(p) = 1$ to your belief system and conservatively adjusting to make room for it.

The immediate consequence of the Equation is that false antecedent instances are irrelevant. This is because according to the Ramsey test, assessing the conditional probability assumes that $P(p) = 1$. Another route to the same conclusion is that the Ratio formula indicates that in calculating the probability of the everyday conditional all that matters are the probabilities of the true antecedent cases, i.e., $P(p \wedge q)$ and $P(p \wedge \neg q)$. Note that the Ramsey test is the best available definition of conditional probability and that the Ratio formula, as Bennett demonstrates, can be shown to conform to the Ramsey test. Combining the Ramsey test and the Ratio formula shows that everyday indicative conditionals are ***zero-intolerant*** (Bennett, 2003). That is, they are not acceptable when $P(p) = 0$, because the consequence is that you should "believe $p \rightarrow q$ to the extent that you think that $p \wedge q$ is nearly as likely as p" (Edgington, 1991, p. 189). So when $P(p) = 0$, you should not accept

$$p \rightarrow q.$$

There are many examples demonstrating why it makes sense to treat the probability of a conditional as the conditional probability (again, see Bennett, 2003). However, there have also been detractors (e.g., Lewis, 1976) who point to some of the counterintuitive consequences of adopting the Equation. The first consequence is that not only is the ***probability conditional***, as Adams (1998) refers to it, not truth functional, it is not truth conditional either: conditionals are not propositions that can have a truth value. If they were propositions, then when we ask about their probability, $P(p \rightarrow q)$, we are asking about the probability that $p \rightarrow q$ is true. But from the Equation it happens that $P(p \rightarrow q) = P(q \mid p)$ and so we are asking a question about the probability that $q|p$ is true. However, "$q|p$" is not a stand-alone claim about the world, i.e., it doesn't make sense to ask whether this is true or false. According to the Ramsey test, this expression relates to a mental process, not a fact about the world that could be true or false.

If conditionals do not have truth conditions then other apparently counterintuitive consequences follow. For example, it means that conditionals cannot be embedded in truth functional compounds. For example, one might deny that turning the key will start this car by asserting, *it's not the case that if you turn the key the car will start*, i.e., $\neg(p \rightarrow q)$. But as we have seen, $p \rightarrow q$ is equal to $q|p$ and so $P(\neg(p \rightarrow q)$ should equal $P(\neg(q|p))$ but "$P(\neg(q|p))$" is not formally defined and is meaningless. One might imagine that this apparent limitation would set bounds on the expressiveness of a system embodying the probability conditional such that it couldn't capture important aspects of natural language. However, denying that turning the key will start the car is expressed most naturally by saying, "No, it won't." That is, *if you turn the key the car will not start*. But in the standard logic of the material conditional $p \Rightarrow q$ and $p \Rightarrow \neg q$ are consistent, one is not the denial of the other. For the probability conditional, in contrast, they are *probabilistically inconsistent*. This is because, $P(q|p)+P(\neg q|p)=1$, so asserting that $p \rightarrow \neg q$ has a high probability simultaneously means that $p \rightarrow q$ has a low probability. Thus, there may be no lack of expressiveness by moving to the probability conditional. Adams (1975) argues that the move to the probability conditional suggests that there may be constraints on the way conditionals can be embedded in truth functional compound sentences. Moreover, Bennett (2003) argues that this move seems to disarm some of the strongest criticisms of the Equation due to Lewis (1976). And there seems to be linguistic evidence that the constraints on embeddings recommended by the probability conditional may be reflected in natural languages (Bennett, 2003). Finally, it has recently been demonstrated experimentally that people do not accept an important step in Lewis' (1976) argument against the Equation (Douven & Verbrugge, 2013).

P-validity

If indicative conditionals do not have truth values, then it would seem that it is impossible to define any valid inferences that follow from them. This is because if they have no truth value, then there can be no transfer of truth from premises to the conclusion of an argument which has an indicative conditional as a premise. However, while classical validity is therefore impossible for arguments involving conditionals, they may possess another virtue, *probabilistic validity* or *p*-validity. Adams (1975) discovered that most classically valid arguments also possess a property that can best be formulated using the concept of *uncertainty*. The uncertainty of a proposition p, $U(p)$, is simply $1 - P(p)$. The property he discovered was that "*in a classically valid argument the uncertainty of the conclusion cannot exceed the sum of the uncertainties of the premises*" (Bennett, 2003, p. 131). That is,

$$\text{If } p_1 \ldots p_n \text{ entail } q, \text{ then } U(q) \leq \sum_{i=1}^{n} U(p_i) \tag{13}$$

An argument fulfilling this condition, Adams (1975) calls *p*-valid. Arguments containing indicative conditionals, while not candidates for classical validity, may be *p*-valid and so can be evaluated on that basis.

The paradoxes of material implication are not *p*-valid. For example, according to the material conditional, a conditional is true if the antecedent is false, or the consequent is true and so the following inference schemas are valid:

$$\frac{\neg p}{\therefore p \rightarrow q} \qquad \frac{q}{\therefore p \rightarrow q} \tag{14}$$

In case of the left-hand schema, though, $P(p) = 0$, and so, as we have seen, no value can be assigned to the probability of the conditional in the conclusion because of ***zero-intolerance***. Similarly, when $P(q) = 1$, then $P(p \rightarrow q)$ should also be 1, which means their uncertainties are equal. However, *p*-validity requires the inequality in (13) to hold whatever the value of $P(q)$. But suppose *q* is *my car starts*, which has a probability of .98, and *p* is *I turn the key*. Suppose also that I know I have no gas. Although *q* is high, supposing $P(p) = 1$ means I must assign 0 probability to $p \rightarrow q$ because I know I am out of gas, which violates *p*-validity. The uncertainty of the conclusion, $U(p \rightarrow q) = 1$, is greater than the uncertainty of the premise, $U(q) = .02$. Thus the paradoxes of material implication are not *p*-valid.

Four further inferences that are classically valid for the material conditional turn out not to be *p-valid* for the probability conditional. These are ***strengthening the antecedent, transitivity, contraposition***, and *or-to-if*:

$$\text{Strengthening} \quad \frac{p \rightarrow q}{\therefore (p \wedge r) \rightarrow q} \quad \text{Transitivity} \quad \frac{(p \rightarrow q), (q \rightarrow r)}{\therefore p \rightarrow r} \tag{15}$$

$$\text{Contraposition} \quad \frac{p \rightarrow q}{\therefore \neg q \rightarrow \neg p} \quad \text{Or-to-if} \quad \frac{p \vee q}{\therefore \neg p \rightarrow q}$$

Counterexamples to the *p*-validity of all these inferences can be derived from showing that the uncertainty of the conclusion can be greater than the uncertainty of the premises (or their sum in the case of transitivity). Examples abound for strengthening the antecedent. Although it makes sense to assign a high probability, say .9, to *if Tweety is a bird, **then** Tweety **can fly***, because most birds fly, anyone would assign a very low probability, i.e., 0, to *if Tweety is a bird **and** Tweety **is one second old**, **then** Tweety **can fly*** (how old Tweety is can be adjusted to produce probabilities for the conclusion that are greater than 0). Thus the uncertainty of the conclusion, $U((p \wedge r) \rightarrow q)) = 1$, is greater than the uncertainty of the premise, $U(p \rightarrow q) = 1$. The failure of strengthening shows that in one important respect the probability conditional is ***non-monotonic***; that is, adding a premise, *Tweety is one second old*, can lose conclusions (see Stenning & Varga, this volume).

Transitivity entails and is entailed by strengthening the antecedent (Bennett, 2003), so they stand ***and*** fall together. Contraposition also seems to succumb readily to counterexamples. Although it makes sense to assign a high probability for *if you turn the **key**, your car starts*, because it most often starts when you turn the key, anyone would assign a low probability to ***if the car doesn't start, then you didn't turn the key***, because the only reason to expect the car to start in the first place is that you turned the key. Or-to-if also fails. For example, someone may assign a high probability to ***Oswald shot Kennedy** or **Mars** is **striped*** because they believe that Oswald was the gunman, but they would still assign a low probability to ***if Oswald did not shoot Kennedy, then Mars is striped***. There is now considerable empirical evidence that people's reasoning across many inference schemas conforms to *p*-validity (Cruz, Baratgin, Oaksford, & Over, 2015; Evans, Thompson, & Over, 2015; Oaksford & Chater, 2007). However, many of these experiments have been aimed at showing that people's assignments of probability to conclusions are ***probabilistically coherent*** (Pfeifer & Kleiter, 2005, 2010; Politzer & Baratgin, 2016; Singmann, Klauer, & Over, 2014) and occasionally *p*-validity and probabilistic coherence may diverge.

Probabilistic coherence

Probabilistic coherence is an approach advocated by de Finetti (1937/1980). It also relies on the Equation (i.e., Pr(*if p then q*) = Pr(q | p)) and on the betting interpretation of probability (see the section headed "Bayesian rationality"): a probability assessment is coherent as long as it does not admit any bets that would lead to a sure loss. The idea is that once probabilities have been assigned to premises, the probability calculus allows us to calculate a probability, or more usually a probability interval, for the conclusion. Any value in the interval will not lead to a sure loss. In calculating the interval, the premise probabilities can lead to two possible outcomes. Either the premises do not constrain the conclusion probability: that is, it can take any value in the whole probability interval [0, 1]. Or, the conclusion probability is constrained to fall between some upper and lower bound, i.e., [l, u]. In the latter case the inference is said to be probabilistically *informative*. In the limit, as the probabilities of the premises vary, it may turn out that l = u, in which case the premises constrain the conclusion probability to a point value.

This approach has been used to develop a concept of *p*-validity for quantified statements (Chater & Oaksford, 1999). Intervals and point values were identified for the conditional probabilities associated with various quantified statements, like *all A are B* ($\Pr(B|A) = 1$), *some A are B* ($\Pr(B|A) > 0$), *some A are not B* ($\Pr(B|A) < 1$), *no A are B* ($\Pr(B|A) = 0$), *few A are B* ($0 < \Pr(B|A) < \delta$), and *most A are B* ($1 - \delta < \Pr(B|A) < 1$). Quantified syllogistic inferences involves two quantified premises – for example, *most B are A, all C are B*. The conclusion involves the end terms *A* and *C*, which occur in only one of the premises.[2] To determine what conclusion follows involves interpreting the premises as above and proving whether $\Pr(C|A)$ or $\Pr(A|C)$ are constrained to a certain interval or point value. In the example, $\Pr(C|A)$ is constrained to the interval $[1- \delta, 1]$, and consequently the conclusion *most C are A* follows *p*-validly according to this analysis. If $\Pr(C|A)$ or $\Pr(A|C)$ are unconstrained and both can fall in the [0, 1] interval, then it was concluded that no *p*-valid conclusion follows; that is, the inference is not probabilistically informative. Chater and Oaksford (1999) used this analysis to define a set of probabilistic heuristics for syllogistic reasoning. They tested the qualitative predictions of these heuristics and found evidence that when going beyond the logical quantifiers by adding the generalised quantifiers *most* and *few*, the same set of heuristics sufficed to explain the results. This work provided only tangential evidence that people's quantified syllogistic reasoning is probabilistically coherent as probabilities were never assigned to the premises, nor were people's conclusion probabilities explicitly measured.

More recent work on probabilistic coherence has focused on the standard propositional inferences. Coherent bounds for several purely propositional inferences are as follows (taken from Politzer and Baratgin [2016]):

And-elimination: *p and q*, therefore, *p*

  Pr(p) ∈ [Pr(*p and q*), 1]

And-introduction: *p, q*, therefore, *p and q*

  Pr(*p and q*) ∈[max{0, Pr(p) + Pr(q) – 1}, min{Pr(p), Pr(q)}]

Or-introduction: *p*, therefore, *p or q*

  Pr(*p or q*) ∈ [Pr(p), 1]

And-to-if: *p and q*, therefore, *if p then q*

  Pr(*if p then q*) ∈[Pr(*p and q*), 1]

Or-to-if: *p or q*, therefore, *if not-p then q*

  Pr(*if not-p then q*) ∈[0, Pr(*p or q*)]

Contraposition: *if p then q*, therefore, *if not-q then not-p*

  Pr(*not-p* | *not-q*) ∈ [0, 1]

Coherent bounds for an inference can be calculated by solving systems of simultaneous linear equations or by a much more straightforward and intuitive method that has recently been suggested by Politzer (2016).

Note that this means that contraposition is not probabilistically informative, which agrees with the analysis by *p*-validity: that is, neither is it *p*-valid. However, *or-to-if* is probabilistically coherent when Pr (*if not-p then q*) $\in$ [0, Pr (*p or q*)], but it is not probabilistically valid. We can see immediately why: when it is coherent, the uncertainty of the conclusion will be greater than the uncertainty of the premise. Or, put another way, the probability of the conclusion must be less than the probability of the premise for it to be coherent to infer *if not-p then q* from *p or q* (for further discussion, see Gilio and Over [2012]). Consequently, *p*-validity and probabilistic coherence do not completely match up.[3] It is important, therefore, when evaluating probabilistic accounts of these inferences to note that just because probabilistic validity fails it does not mean that responses are not probabilistically coherent.

Causal Bayes nets

As we have discussed (see the section headed "Probability"), typically probability is used to model "small worlds" in which a total joint probability distribution can be defined. We mentioned that there has been much progress here in developing small-scale probabilistic models grounded in causality, where causal relations form the primitive building blocks from which a probabilistic model is constructed (Pearl, 1988, 2000). Moreover, this probabilistic framework has also been applied to conditional reasoning.

Causal model theory

Causal model theory suggests that the mental representations and processes underlying causal reasoning are analogous to causal Bayes nets (Sloman, 2005). Causal Bayes nets (CBNs) treat the causal dependencies that people believe to be operative in the world as basic (Pearl, 1988; 2000). These are represented as edges in a directed acyclic graph (see Figure 23.1). The nodes represent Bayesian random variables. They also represent the relevant causes and effects, with the arrows running from cause to effect (the arrows represent causal direction). Nodes that are not connected represent variables which are conditionally independent of each other. The *parents*

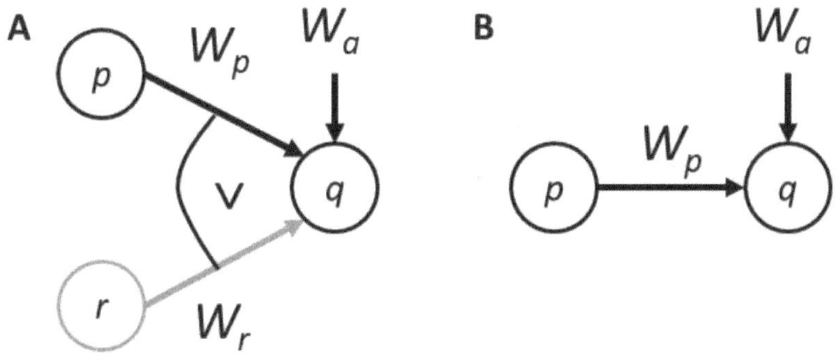

Figure 23.1 A: Causal Bayes net with a noisy-OR (V) integration rule and two generative causes. B: Causal Bayes net used in Fernbach and Erb (2013).

of a node are those that connect to it further back down the causal chain. These networks have probability distributions defined over them that partly rely on the dependency structure.

Integration rules determine how the multiple parents of a node combine, e.g., the noisy-OR rule (see Figure 23.1A). Suppose that in Figure 23.1A, p and r represent *rain* and *the sprinklers being on* respectively. These are independent causes of *the pavements being wet* (i.e., q). Assume there are no other causes of the pavements being wet. On this assumption, the probability of the pavements being wet is then $1 - (1 - W_r)^{ind(r)}(1 - W_p)^{ind(p)}$, where $ind(p) = 1$ if it is raining and 0 if it is not and W_i is the probability of q given cause i. If this were a deterministic system, i.e., $W_r = W_p = 1$, then this formula is equivalent to logical inclusive *or*, i.e., it gives probability 1 unless both causes are absent when it gives probability 0, i.e., if it is not raining and the sprinklers are not on, then the pavements are not wet.

This view commits one to more than probability theory (Pearl, 1988, 2000). A recent review by Rottman and Hastie (2014, p. 111) summarises the additional assumptions made in Bayes nets, which are mainly about making inference tractable. The most important in this respect is the causal Markov property that causes "screen off" their effects, so that inferences about any effect variable depend only on its direct causes and not on any of the other effects or indirect causes. For example, the sun being out causes shadows and high temperatures. If it is known to be sunny, then these effects are independent, i.e., manipulating one, e.g., walking into an air conditioned room, will not affect the other: there will still be shadows outside. Moreover, if it is known to be sunny, these effects are independent of any of the causes of it being sunny. While there are detractors of the Bayes net approach (e.g., Cartwright, 1999, 2001), Rottman and Hastie (2014) argue "that the approach helps us to understand real causal systems and how ordinary people think about causality." They may also help us to understand how people reason with conditionals. Fernbach and Erb (2013) have recently applied these models to MP and AC inferences and shown very good parameter free fits using the materials in Cummins (1995; see also Oaksford & Chater, in press).

Dynamic inference and belief revision

We have already discussed Bayesian conditionalization, in which a new probability distribution is defined conditional on new information, I, such that in the new distribution, $\Pr_1()$, the probabilities of events, x, are the old conditional probabilities given the new information, i.e., $\Pr_1(x) = \Pr_0(x \mid I)$. We also mentioned that the Bayesian conditionalization is not a part of probability theory despite its ubiquity; we mentioned, too, that Bayeisan conditionalization is not always unproblematic. In this section, we show that problematic cases arise for quite simple inferences involving the conditional and that this would seem to require an account of *dynamic* inference.

Conditional inference can be treated as Bayesian conditionalization (Oaksford & Chater, 2007, 2009, Oaksford et al., 2000). For the MP inference, the probability conditional (see the section headed "The probability conditional") poses the question: if S believes *if p then q* to degree a and comes to believe p to degree b, to what degree c should S believe q? Applying the uncertainty sum rule (see the section headed "Equation 13"), this means that for this inference to be p-valid: $1 - c \leq (1 - a) + (1 - b)$. Conditional inference can be carried out via Bayesian conditionalization, in which a new probability distribution, Pr_1, is inferred on the assumption that the categorical premise is learned to be true (Oaksford & Chater, 2007; Oaksford et al., 2000). For MP this means that the probability of p, $\Pr_1(p) = 1$, i.e., $b = 1$ (using the example *if you turn the key the car starts* interpreted as a probability conditional):

	MP	*If p then q*	$\Pr_0(q \mid p)$	$\Pr_0(\textit{car starts} \mid \textit{key turned})$	(23)
		p	$\Pr_1(p) = 1$	$\Pr_1(\textit{key turned}) = 1$	
∴		q	$\Pr_1(q) = P_0(q \mid p)$	$\Pr_1(\textit{car starts}) = \Pr_0(\textit{car starts} \mid \textit{key turned})$	

According to p-validity, this means that the probability of the conclusion c ($\Pr_1(q)$), must be greater than or equal to a (i.e., $\Pr_0(q \mid p)$). In terms of the example, the probability S assigns to the car starting given S learns that the key is turned must be greater than or equal the probability S assigns to the probability of the car starting assuming the key was turned. *Prima facie* this condition seems eminently reasonable, and it is met by Bayesian conditionalization, which is consequently p-valid.

This analysis can be extended beyond MP to ***modus tollens*** (MT) and to the conditional fallacies ***denying the antecedent*** (DA) and ***affirming the consequent*** (AC). Here we use MT as an example:

	MT	*If p then q*	$\Pr_0(q \mid p)$	(23)
		$\neg q$	$\Pr_1(\neg q) = 1$	
∴		$\neg p$	$\Pr_1(\neg p) = \Pr_0(\neg p \mid \neg q) = (1\text{-}\Pr_0(q)\text{-}\Pr_0(p)(1\text{-}\Pr_0(q \mid p)))/(1\text{-}\Pr_0(q))$	

(23) shows that the relevant conditional probability for the categorical premise to conditionalise on $\Pr_0(\neg p \mid \neg q)$ can be calculated from $\Pr_0(q \mid p)$, $\Pr_0(p)$, $\Pr_0(q)$, that is, on assuming that people have knowledge of the priors.

These inferences by Bayesian conditionalization rely on an assumption called "rigidity" (Sobel, 2004) or "invariance" (Jeffrey, 2004). For example, the probability that the car starts given that the key is turned does not alter on learning that key is turned, i.e., $\Pr_1(\textit{car starts} \mid \textit{key turned}) = \Pr_0(\textit{car starts} \mid \textit{key turned})$. For MP, it would seem that invariance must hold because $\Pr_1(\textit{car starts} \mid \textit{key turned}) = \Pr_0(\textit{car starts} \mid \textit{key turned, key turned})$. So learning that the categorical premise is true does not alter the conditional probability. This is equivalent to the following static conditional independence assumption: $\Pr_0(\textit{car starts} \mid \textit{key turned}) = \Pr_0(\textit{car starts} \mid \textit{key turned, CP})$, where CP = categorical premise (Pearl, 1988).

However, invariance is potentially violated for MT (see Adams, 1998, pp. 143–144; Oaksford & Chater, 2007, 2009). Invariance suggests that $P_0(\textit{car starts} \mid \textit{key turned}) = P_0(\textit{car starts} \mid \textit{key turned}, \neg\textit{car starts})$. So, learning that ***the car did not start*** should not affect one's subjective probability that *if you turn the key the car starts*. However, even if the probability of *if you turn the key the car starts* is high, learning that *the car did **not** start* makes drawing the conclusion that *the key was **not turned*** unlikely because it is far more likely that the reason the car did not start is that it has broken down (Adams, 1998, p. 144; Oaksford & Chater, 2007). Indeed, learning that *the car **did not start*** in an MT inference seems to provide a counterexample to the conditional that, logically, should lead to its rejection. Other examples make the same point (see Adams, 1998, p. 143, footnote 33; Zhao & Osherson, 2010). This example seems to show that the MT inference with the probability conditional can be non-monotonic: after all, $\Pr_0(q \mid p) \neq \Pr_0(q \mid p, \neg q)$, i.e., $\Pr_0(q \mid p) \neq \Pr_1(q \mid p)$, violating invariance.

Indeed, it has recently been shown that even MP may violate invariance (Zhao, Crupi, Tentori, Fitelson, & Osherson, 2012). As we have seen, the reasonableness of MP relies on the probability that "S assigns to the car starting given S *learns* that the key is turned being greater than or equal to the probability S assigns to the probability of the car starting ***assuming*** the key was turned." This is because, on the subjective view of probability (de Finetti, 1937; Jeffrey, 2004;

Ramsey, 1931), the probability of the conditional premise, i.e., $\Pr_0(q \mid p)$, is determined by the Ramsey test. This test requires one to *assume* the antecedent is true, *the key is turned*, add it to one's stock of beliefs, and read off the resulting degree of belief in *q*, *the car starts*, which is the conditional probability. In MP, at least by Bayesian conditionalization, one *learns* that the antecedent is true, i.e., that $\Pr_1(p) = 1$. However, this fact is assumed not to alter $\Pr_0(q \mid p)$, that is, $\Pr_0(q \mid p) = \Pr_1(q \mid p)$, by invariance. To provide an adequate account of actual human reasoning with MP, the clear implication is that people should judge the conditional probability to be the same whether they *learn* [$\Pr_1(q \mid p)$] or *assume* [$\Pr_0(q \mid p)$] that the antecedent is true, i.e., $\Pr_1(p) = 1$.

However, there are clear counterexamples to this claim, like weakness of the will (Bennett, 2003). For example, the probability that an avowed atheist assigns to "God exists" *assuming* that she has cancer may be a lot less than the probability that she assigns to this proposition when she actually *learns* that she has cancer (see also Oaksford & Chater, 2007). There is also empirical evidence that people make divergent probability assignments in these two cases (Zhao et al., 2012). People more accurately estimate the conditional probability when they *learn* that *p* is true than when they *suppose p* to be true. Moreover, consistent with the *a priori* examples, they provide lower estimates of $\Pr(q \mid p)$ on supposing rather than learning that *p* is true. In the context of the MP inference, this suggests that psychologically, $\Pr_0(q \mid p) < \Pr_1(q \mid p)$. So, not only are there *a priori* examples that MP and MT may violate the invariance assumption, there is direct empirical evidence that they do so in a task analogous to performing an MP inference and a Ramsey test.

Dynamic belief revision is likely to become an area of increasing interest in the psychology of reasoning, and there are some promising approaches (Oaksford & Chater, 2013). For example, the categorical premise for MT may trigger people to learn a new conditional probability for the conditional premise (Oaksford & Chater, 2007, 2013). Moreover, there are proposals in the philosophical literature for dealing with cases of learning conditional information, for example, learning that John's car only rarely starts when you turn the key.[4] One approach combines causal Bayes nets (see the preceding section) and an information theoretic measure called Kullback-Leibler distance (Cover & Thomas, 2001), which is a measure of the similarity between two probability distributions (Hartmann & Rafie-Rad, 2014). The idea is to represent the conditional premises in a causal Bayes net and calculate the new distribution, $\Pr_1()$, as the one that is most similar to the old distribution, $\Pr_0()$, but where the conditional probability of the car starting given the key has been turned is now lower than it was (see also Douven, 2012). New experimental research is required to discover which, if any, of these normative probabilistic proposals matches human behaviour in belief revision tasks.

Conclusion

This volume is primarily concerned with the descriptive project of understanding how people think and reason. The present chapter, by contrast, has outlined the normative theory of probability, why it is rational, and how it is being applied to the psychology of reasoning. This theory of how people *should* think clarifies which degrees of belief are coherent. One important function of thinking and reasoning is to attempt to re-establish coherence when it is disturbed, as we saw in the section "Dynamic inference and belief revision." These dynamic processes are relatively little understood, but as we have seen, research in this area is likely to be prominent in the future. When we are at an equilibrium, then coherence constraints can tell what else we should believe and to what degree, given what we already believe. So, as we saw in the section "Probabilistic coherence," if we believe *p and q* to degree *a* we should believe that the probability of *p*, $\Pr(p)$, lies in the interval $[a, 1]$. So, as we saw in our first motivation for considering the relevance of normative theories to descriptive theories of thought, probability theory describes the "right answers" in reasoning problems. These may contrast with other theories of how we should reason, and these differences are then open to experimental test. While consideration of what is coherent and what is not may be adequate in the domain of human verbal reasoning, it may not be completely adequate to model other domains of thinking covered in this book, for example, judgement and decision making. However, as our discussion of Bayesian rationality showed, justifying the practical rationality of probability theory invokes the maximum expected utility thesis, which provides the normative starting point for judgement and decision making research. We would argue that a similar role is currently being played by probability theory in accounts of human verbal reasoning. Only time will tell if this is the right approach, but it confirms our second motivation for considering normative theory in the introduction, that is, as providing the starting point for descriptive theories.

A final reason why normative theories are important is that without some normative constraints on thinking and reasoning, it becomes impossible to interpret thought, and resulting utterances or behaviour, at all. We do not have direct access to people's beliefs or degrees of belief; we have to infer them from what they say and how they behave (arguing that Arsenal will definitely win is undermined by a stubborn refusal to lay a reasonably large bet on this outcome). Davidson's (2005) model of radical interpretation is an idealised account of how a cognitive agent can interpret another agent's behaviour and utterances to infer their beliefs and desires (Rescorla, 2013). The model is based on Bayesian decision theory, in which beliefs are graded and related to subjective probabilities and people's desires are represented as utilities. Savage's (1954) axioms show that when a person's preferences meet certain requirements, there are probabilities and utilities that guarantee that their preferences maximise expected utility. Consequently, an agent's beliefs and desires can be inferred from their overt preferences. Central to this account is the thesis that to ascribe another person with the appropriate beliefs and desires means we must assume they conform to our own standards of rationality (the principle of charity). On Davidson's view, describing somebody's behaviour in terms of beliefs and desires is inseparable from normative evaluation. Coherence constraints can, on this account, be critical in making such inferences to others' beliefs and desires by binding together beliefs or choices which we have observed with beliefs and choices which we have not observed.

We conclude this chapter by considering three related problems for the idea that probability theory could directly provide adequate descriptive theories of human reasoning. The world knowledge problem arises because on the subjective approach all probabilities are conditional on what one knows or believes, as the Ramsay test make clear. Here, the "fractal" nature of this world knowledge is particularly problematic (Chater & Oaksford, 2001). In assessing the probability that the car starts, you may consider the possibility that it is out of fuel but then immediately recall that you filled it up at the garage two days ago. Each consideration that may bear on the question of whether the car starts may invoke further knowledge that could be relevant and each new piece of knowledge may be bolstered or undercut by yet more knowledge, and so on indefinitely. World knowledge is also isotropic (Fodor, 1983), and so unexpected considerations may bear on the question, for example, a report of a meteor storm may suggest considering whether a meteor strikes the car immediately after turning the key. In sum, the specification of the world knowledge that underlies particular aspects of everyday reasoning will be difficult, if not impossible (see Fodor, 1983, on "central" cognitive processes).

Resolving inconsistency or incoherence also creates related problems. For example, the MT inference can be interpreted as providing a counterexample to the conditional rule, for example, finding out that the car did not start. We suggested that this case can be treated as an observation from which one learns a new conditional probability. However, world knowledge may also be invoked in order to explain away the counterexample. So perhaps the car has run out of fuel, or perhaps the ignition is faulty, and so on. Here we may feel justified in ruling out aberrant cases like the engine being hit by a meteor as implausible. But plausibility is a global or holistic concept that potentially invokes all of our world knowledge, and what is plausible in one context may be implausible in another (Fodor, 1983). In sum, resolving consistency is or re-establishing equilibrium again provides a challenge for normative probabilistic theories when applied to everyday reasoning.

The problems created by the invocation of world knowledge, in defining probabilities and in resolving inconsistency, are directly related to the third problem of computational complexity. The mind is presumably limited to feasible computable processes. The holistic and isotropic computations which seem to be implicated in everyday reasoning, probabilistically construed or not, suggest that human reasoners need to maintain a globally coherent or consistent belief system. But this seems to be beyond what is feasibly computable by the human brain or any other computational device. Consequently, normative theories such as probability may not be the place to start in providing descriptive theories of reasoning. There are some formal responses (see Stenning & Varga, this volume, but also Oaksford & Chater, 2014, 2016), but the principal reaction has been to suggest that human reasoning is based on "fast and frugal" heuristics or that it is based on cheap approximations to normative calculations (Vul, Goodman, Griffiths, & Tenenbaum, 2009). Another possibility is a deflationary response that suggests the problem does not really exist for real human belief systems. On this view, most reasoning occurs only over a local model and consistency arises as an issue only when making public commitments, that is, commitments that may be questioned by others and which one might therefore need to defend in the public domain (Oaksford & Chater, 2014, 2016; Skovgaard-Olsen, 2015).

This chapter has introduced probability theory, its rational foundation, and the concepts derived from probability theory that have featured in reasoning research. We have concentrated on probability theory as specifying coherence conditions over *degrees of belief*. This normative theory has three potential roles in contributing to build a science describing the processes of thinking and reasoning: as providing a normative standard against which human thought can be compared; as generating a rich set of hypotheses concerning how thought might operate; and as clarifying conditions under which we can ascribe interpretable thoughts to an agent at all. We hope we have shown how productive normative probability theory has been in reasoning research, and we believe that exploring the connections between probability theory and the descriptive theories of human reasoning and thinking will continue to be of crucial importance in understanding the nature of human thought.

Acknowledgements

The section on probability and the conclusion are partly based on Chater and Oaksford (2012); the section on Bayesian rationality is partly based on Oaksford (2016), the section on probability logic and *p*-validity is partly based on Oaksford and Chater (2007); the section on causal Bayes nets is partly based on Oaksford and Chater (in press); the section on dynamic inference and belief revision is partly based on Oaksford and Chater (2013).

Notes

1 What it can do, as we will see, is tell you which beliefs are best supported once you collect some evidence; that is, Bayesian updating can provide a normative model of learning.

2 Chater and Oaksford (1999) also assumed that these end terms were conditionally independent given the middle term. Consequently, the concept of *p*-validity is somewhat different to Adams (1998) and the

assessment of coherent probability intervals was also somewhat different to de Finetti's concept of probabilistic coherence. In particular, in Chater and Oaksford's (1999) analysis, because the label "*p*-valid" is applied only if there is a probabilistically informative conclusion, probabilistic coherence and *p*-validity perfectly coincide in their account of quantified syllogisms. However, as we will see, the logical notions of *p*-validity and probabilistic coherence can diverge.

3 It is important to note again the difference with Chater and Oaksford (1999), for whom an inference was designated *p*-valid if and only if it was probabilistically coherent (assuming independence).

4 This should be new information because the default assumption is that turning keys usually starts cars.

References

Adams, E. (1975). *The logic of conditionals: An application of probability to deductive logic.* Dordrecht: Reidel.

Adams, E.W. (1998). *A primer of probability logic.* Stanford, CA: CSLI Publications.

Bennett, J. (2003). *A philosophical guide to conditionals.* Oxford, UK: Oxford University Press.

Binmore, K. (2008). *Rational decisions.* Princeton, NJ: Princeton University Press.

Byrne, R. (1989). Suppressing valid inferences with conditionals. *Cognition, 31*, 61–83.

Cartwright, N. (1999). *The dappled world: A study of the boundaries of science*, Cambridge: Cambridge University Press.

Cartwright, N. (2001). What is wrong with Bayes nets? *The Monist, 84*, 242–264.

Chater, N., & Oaksford, M. (1999). The probability heuristics model of syllogistic reasoning. *Cognitive Psychology, 38*, 191–258.

Chater, N., & Oaksford, M. (2001). Human rationality and the psychology of reasoning: Where do we go from here? *British Journal of Psychology, 92*, 193–216.

Chater, N., & Oaksford, M. (2012). Normative systems: Logic, probability, and rational choice. In K. Holyoak & R. Morrison (Eds.), *The Oxford handbook of thinking and reasoning* (pp. 11–21). Oxford: Oxford University Press.

Cover, T. M. & Thomas, J. A. (2001). *Elements of information theory.* New York: John Wiley & Sons, Inc.

Cox, R. T. (1946). Probability, frequency, and reasonable expectation. *American Journal of Physics, 14*, 1–13.

Cruz, N., Baratgin, J., Oaksford, M., & Over, D. E. (2015). Reasoning with *ifs* and *ands* and *ors*. *Frontiers in Psychology, 6*, 192. doi: 10.3389/fpsyg.2015.00192

Cummins, D. D. (1995). Naive theories and causal deduction. *Memory & Cognition, 23*, 646–658.

Davidson, D. (2005). *Truth, language, and history.* Oxford: Clarendon Press.

De Finetti, B. (1937). La prévision: Ses lois logiques, ses sources subjectives, *Annales de l'Institut Henri Poincaré*, 7, 1–68; translated as Foresight: Its logical laws, its subjective sources", in H. E. Kyburg, Jr. and H. E. Smokler (Eds.), *Studies in subjective probability*, Robert E. Krieger Publishing Company (1980).

Douven, I. (2012). Learning conditional information. *Mind and Language, 27*, 239–263.

Douven, I., & Verbrugge, S. (2013). The probabilities of conditionals revisited. *Cognitive Science, 37*, 711–730.

Edgington, D. (1991). The mystery of the missing matter of fact. *Aristotelian Society Supplementary, 65*, 185–209.

Edgington, D. (1995). On conditionals. *Mind, 104*, 235–329.

Elqayam, S., & Over, D. E. (2013). New paradigm psychology of reasoning: An introduction to the special issue edited by Elqayam, Bonnefon, and Over. *Thinking & Reasoning, 19*(3–4), 249–265. doi:10.1080/13546783.2013.841591

Evans, J. St. B. T., Handley, S. J., & Over, D. E. (2003). Conditionals and conditional probability. *Journal of Experimental Psychology – Learning, Memory, and Cognition, 29*, 321–335.

Evans, J. St. B. T., Thompson, V. A., & Over, D. E. (2015). Uncertain deduction and conditional reasoning. *Frontiers in Psychology, 6*, 398. doi: 10.3389/fpsyg.2015.00398

Fernbach, P. M., & Erb, C. D. (2013). A quantitative causal model theory of conditional reasoning. *Journal of Experimental Psychology: Learning, Memory, and Cognition, 39*, 1327–1343. doi:10.1037/a0031851

Fodor, J. A. (1983). *Modularity of mind.* Cambridge, MA: MIT Press.

Gigerenzer, G., & Goldstein, D. (1996). Reasoning the fast and frugal way: Models of bounded rationality. *Psychological Review* 103, 650–669.

Gigerenzer, G., & Todd, P. (Eds.). (1999). *Simple heuristics that make us smart.* Oxford: Oxford University Press.

Gilio, A., & Over, D. (2012). The psychology of inferring conditionals from disjunctions: A probabilistic study. *Journal of Mathematical Psychology, 56*, 118–131. doi:10.1016/j.jmp.2012.02.006

Gillies, D. (2000). *Philosophical theories of probability.* Oxford: Routledge.

Griffiths, T. L., & Tenenbaum, J. B. (2005) Structure and strength in causal induction. *Cognitive Psychology, 51*, 354–384.

Hahn, U., & Oaksford, M. (2007). The rationality of informal argumentation: A Bayesian approach to reasoning fallacies. *Psychological Review, 114*, 704–732.

Hartmann, S., & Rafiee Rad, S. (2012). *Updating on conditionals = Kullback-Leibler distance + causal structure*. Presented at the Biennial Meeting of the Philosophy of Science Association, San Diego, CA, November 15–17.

Jeffrey, R. C. (1983). *The logic of decision* (2nd ed.). Chicago, IL: University of Chicago Press.

Jeffrey, R. C. (2004). *Subjective probability: The real thing*. Cambridge, UK: Cambridge University Press.

Johnson-Laird, P. N., & Byrne, R. M. J. (1991). *Deduction*. Hillsdale, NJ: Lawrence Erlbaum Associates.

Joyce, J. M. (2004). Bayesianism. In A. R. Miele & P. Rawling (Eds.), *The Oxford handbook of rationality* (pp. 132–155). Oxford: Oxford University Press.

Kolmogorov, A. N. (1956). *Foundations of the theory of probability* (2nd ed.). New York: Chelsea Publishing Company.

Lange, M. (2000). Is Jeffrey conditionalization defective by virtue of being non-commutative? Remarks on the sameness of sensory experiences. *Synthese, 123*, 393–403.

Lewis, D. (1976). Probabilities of conditionals and conditional probabilities. *Philosophical Review, 85*, 297–315.

McKenzie, C. R. M., & Mikkelsen, L. A. (2007). A Bayesian view of covariation assessment. *Cognitive Psychology, 54*, 33–61.

Milch, B., Marthi, B., Russell, S., Sontag, D., Ong, D. L., & Kolobov, A. (2007). BLOG: Probabilistic models with unknown objects. In L. Getoor & B. Taskar (Eds.), *Introduction to statistical relational learning*. Cambridge, MA: MIT Press.

Oaksford, M. (2016). Knowing enough to achieve your goals: Bayesian models and practical and theoretical rationality in conscious and unconscious inference. In L. Macchi, M. Bagassi, & R. Viale (Eds.), *Cognitive unconscious and human rationality* (pp. 99–118). Cambridge, MA: MIT Press.

Oaksford, M., & Chater, N. (1994). A rational analysis of the selection task as optimal data selection. *Psychological Review, 101*, 608–631.

Oaksford, M., & Chater, N. (2007). *Bayesian rationality*. Oxford: Oxford University Press.

Oaksford, M., & Chater, N. (2009). Precis of "Bayesian rationality: The probabilistic approach to human reasoning." *Behavioral and Brain Sciences, 32*, 69–84.

Oaksford, M., & Chater, N. (2013). Dynamic inference and everyday conditional reasoning in the new paradigm. *Thinking and Reasoning, 19*, 346–379. doi:10.1080/13546783.2013.808163

Oaksford, M., & Chater, N. (2014). Probabilistic single function dual process theory and logic programming as approaches to non-monotonicity in human vs. artificial reasoning. *Thinking and Reasoning, 20*, 269–295. doi: 10.1080/13546783.2013.877401

Oaksford, M., & Chater, N. (2016). Probabilities, causation, and logic programming in conditional reasoning: A reply to Stenning and van Lambalgen. *Thinking and Reasoning, 22*, 336–354. doi: 10.1080/13546783.2016.1139505

Oaksford, M., & Chater, N. (in press). Causal models and conditional reasoning. In M. Waldmann (Ed.), *Oxford handbook of causal cognition*. Oxford: Oxford University Press.

Oaksford, M., Chater, N., & Larkin, J. (2000). Probabilities and polarity biases in conditional inference. *Journal of Experimental Psychology: Learning, Memory & Cognition, 26*, 883–899.

Over. D. (2009). New paradigm psychology of reasoning. *Thinking and Reasoning, 15*, 431–438.

Pearl, J. (1988). *Probabilistic reasoning in intelligent systems*. San Mateo: Morgan Kaufmann.

Pearl, J. (2000). *Causality: Models, reasoning and inference*. Cambridge: Cambridge University Press.

Pfeifer, N., & Kleiter, G. (2005). Coherence and nonmonotonicity in human reasoning. *Synthese, 146*, 93–109. doi: 10.1007/s11229–005–9073-x

Pfeifer, N., & Kleiter, G. (2010). The conditional in mental probability logic. In M. Oaksford & N. Chater (Eds.), *Cognition and conditionals: Probability and logic in human reasoning* (pp. 153–173). Oxford: Oxford University Press.

Politzer, G. (2016). Deductive reasoning under uncertainty: A water tank analogy. *Erkenntnis, 81*, 479–506. doi:10.1007/s10670-015-9751-0

Politzer, G., & Baratgin, J. (2016). Deductive schemas with uncertain premises using qualitative probability expressions. *Thinking and Reasoning, 22*, 78–98. doi: 10.1080/13546783.2015.1052561

Ramsey, F. P. (1926, 1931). Truth and probability. In R. B. Braithwaite (Ed.), *The foundations of mathematics and other logical essays*. London: Kegan Paul.

Rescorla, M. (2013). Rationality as a constitutive ideal. In E. Lepore & K. Ludwig (Eds.), *A companion to Davidson* (pp. 472–488). Oxford: Wiley-Blackwell.

Rips, L. J. (1994). *The psychology of proof.* Cambridge, MA: MIT Press.

Rottman, B., & Hastie, R. (2014). Reasoning about causal relationships: Inferences on causal networks. *Psychological Bulletin, 140,* 109–139. doi:10.1037/a0031903

Savage, L. J. (1954). *The foundations of statistics.* New York: Wiley.

Singmann, H., Klauer, K. C., & Over, D. E. (2014). New normative standards of conditional reasoning and the dual-source model. *Frontiers in Psychology, 5,* 316. doi: 10.3389/ fpsyg.2014.00316

Skovgaard-Olsen, N. (2015). The paradox of logical omniscience, the preface paradox, and doxastic commitments. *Synthese,* 194, 917–939. doi:10.1007/s11229-015-0979-7

Sloman, S. A. (2005). *Causal models: How people think about the world and its alternatives.* New York: Oxford University Press.

Sobel, J. H. (2004). *Probable* modus ponens *and* modus tollens *and updating on uncertain evidence.* Unpublished manuscript, Department of Philosophy, University of Toronto, Scarborough. (www.scar.toronto.ca/~sobel/ConfDisconf.pdf).

Tversky, A., & Kahneman, D. (1983). Extensional versus intuitive reasoning: The conjunction fallacy in probability judgment. *Psychological Review, 90,* 293–315.

Vul, E., Goodman, N. D., Griffiths, T. L., & Tenenbaum, J. B. (2009). One and done? Optimal decisions from very few samples. *Proceedings of the thirty-first annual conference of the cognitive science society.*

Zhao, J., Crupi, V., Tentori, K., Fitelson, B., & Osherson, D. (2012). Updating: Learning versus supposing. *Cognition, 124,* 373–378. doi:10.1016/j.cognition.2012.05.001

Zhao, J., & Osherson, D. (2010). Updating beliefs in light of uncertain evidence: Descriptive assessment of Jeffrey's rule. *Thinking & Reasoning, 16,* 288–307. doi:10.1080/13546783.2010.521695

24
PROBABILISTIC ACCOUNTS OF CONDITIONAL REASONING

David E. Over and Nicole Cruz

Conditionals and conditional reasoning are everywhere in ordinary and scientific discourse. Ordinary people, politicians, civil engineers, and scientific consultants all have an interest in the following *indicative conditional* in natural language:

(1) If global warming continues, then London will be flooded.

Both ordinary people and scientists would assert (1) with some degree of confidence short of certainty, and they might well add an explicit epistemic qualifier, applying *probably* or a related term to (1), expressing some uncertainty. Most ordinary and scientific reasoning takes place in a context of uncertainty, including conditional reasoning (Elqayam & Over, 2013; Oaksford & Chater, 2007). But there have been intense debates about the probability of conditionals (Edgington, 1995; Evans & Over, 2004), and other deep questions about conditionals and conditional reasoning have been disputed for thousands of years (Kneale & Kneale, 1962, pp. 128–138). The unsettled nature of research on conditionals is understandable. Every argument or inference from *p* to *q*, relatively strong or weak, can be turned into a conditional, *if p then q*, in which we have more or less confidence. A complete account of conditional reasoning will be possible only when reasoning itself, from the scientific to the moral, has been fully explained.

In this chapter, we aim to provide an overview of research on conditionals from the perspective of probabilistic accounts of reasoning. We start with an introduction to some of the basic logical concepts presupposed in this research. We cover the prominent mental model theory of the conditional and its probability, both in the original form of the theory and in its recent revision. We continue with an outline of the new probabilistic accounts of the conditional, and of conditional reasoning from uncertain premises and beliefs.

Truth-preserving validity and *P*-validity

The conditional, *if* and equivalent terms, is a logical connective, like *not*, *and*, and *or*. Even for a psychological account of people's understanding of the conditional, we must explain its logic and logical relations to these other connectives. There are introduction and elimination inference rules for each logical connective (Kneale & Kneale, 1962, p. 538). For example, one of the inference rules for disjunction is *or-introduction*: inferring *p or q* from the single premise *p* (and also from *q*). One of the rules for conjunction is ***and-elimination***: inferring *p* (or *q*) from the single premise *p & q*. The elimination rule for the conditional, ***if-elimination***, is traditionally termed *modus ponens* (MP). It allows us to infer *q* from the major premise *if p then q* and the minor premise *p*. Logicians and ordinary people are together in their almost universal endorsement of MP when its premises are assumed (Evans & Over, 2004). One deep question, however, about natural language conditionals is which rules should be used for introducing them into our beliefs and discourse. This is a rather important matter to settle: MP is of little use as an acceptable inference rule if we do not know how to arrive at its major premise, *if p then q*, in the first place. One can, of course, just *assume* any conditional one likes to use as the major premise of MP in a purely logical exercise, but that does not solve the problem of how people acquire a degree of belief in a conditional to use in their reasoning for serious purposes, like preventing the flooding of London.

Elementary ***propositional logic*** lays the foundation for the more advanced study of conditionals. It has *truth tables* for displaying the meanings of its logical connectives: negation, conjunction, and disjunction (Kneale & Kneale, 1962, p. 531). Propositional logic also has a formal conditional, $p \supset q$, called the *material conditional*, which is defined to be logically equivalent to ***not-p or q***. Figure 24.1 is the truth table for disjunction, *p or q*, which is logically equivalent (given that *p* and ***not-not-p*** are equivalent) to the material conditional, ***not-p*** $\supset q$. The four cells of this table lay out the four logical possibilities. There is the *p, q* possibility in the first cell, in which *p* is true and *q* is true, the *p, **not-q*** possibility in the second cell, in which *p* is true and *q* is false, the ***not-p***, *q* possibility in the third cell, in which *p* is false and *q* is true, and the ***not-p, not-q*** possibility in the fourth cell, in which *p* and *q* are both false. The truth or falsity of *p or q*, its *truth value*, is completely determined by the truth or falsity of *p* and *q*; *p or q* is true in the first, second, and third cells, and false in the fourth.

The logical acceptability, the "validity", of an inference can now be defined formally. An inference is *valid* in propositional logic if and only if its conclusion is true in every possibility in which its premises are true. A valid inference is said to be *truth preserving*: it can never take us from truth in the premises to falsity in the conclusion. Figure 24.1 proves that or-introduction is a valid inference rule for disjunction, and this rule can also serve as a valid introduction rule for the material conditional, ***not-p*** $\supset q$. The premise *p* is true in the first and second possibilities, and the conclusion *p or q* is also true in both of these possibilities. But suppose we do not know for sure that our premises are true? In the uncertain context of most ordinary and scientific reasoning, the premises are our beliefs, or hypotheses, that we hold with a degree of subjective probability less than certainty. There is, however, a necessary normative relation between truth-preserving validity and probability in propositional logic.

Informally, an inference is probabilistically valid, *p-valid*, if and only if the probability of its premises cannot be greater than the probability of its conclusion. A p-valid inference is *probability preserving*: it cannot take us from high probability in the premises to low probability in the conclusion. More precisely, Adams (1998, p. 150) defines a ***probability function*** for any sentence *p*, *P(p)*,

p \ *q*	1	0
1	1	1
0	1	0

Figure 24.1 The truth table for disjunction, *p or q*; 1 = true and 0 = false

as a function that satisfies the axioms of probability theory, and the ***uncertainty*** of *p* as one minus its probability, 1 - *P(p)*. An inference is probabilistically valid, *p-valid*, if and only if the uncertainty of its conclusion is not greater than the sum of the uncertainties of its premises for all probability functions (Adams, 1998, pp. 131–132, 151). A p-valid inference cannot take us from relatively low uncertainty to relatively high uncertainty, and an inference has truth-preserving validity if is p-valid (Baratgin, Douven, Evans, Oaksford, Over, & Politzer, 2015). It is deductive, and so distinct from inductive or other non-demonstrative inferences. The latter inferences are *probabilistically strong* when their conclusions are probable given their premises, but their conclusions can increase the uncertainty in their premises (Evans & Over, 2013).

In a classic study, Tversky and Kahneman (1983) relied on the logical relation between truth-preserving validity and p-validity in and-elimination: inferring *p* (or *q*) from *p & q*. This inference is, of course, no exception to the general rule in propositional logic and is both truth-preserving valid and p-valid. Tversky and Kahneman therefore pointed out that people should never judge that the probability of *p & q* is greater that the probability of *p*, *P(p & q)* > *P(p)*. To make this judgement is the *conjunction fallacy*, and Tversky and Kahneman found that people do commit this fallacy in certain cases (see, further, Cruz, Baratgin, Oaksford, & Over, 2015).

Until recently, psychological research on the relation between people's logical and probabilistic judgements was mostly restricted to the literature on the conjunction fallacy. But this research has recently been extended to judgements in a wider range of inferences that contain conjunctions and disjunctions (Cruz et al., 2015; Politzer & Baratgin, 2015), and there is a growing literature on conditional reasoning and probability judgements (Evans, Thompson, & Over, 2015; Oaksford & Chater, 2007; Gilio & Over, 2012; Over, Evans, & Elqayam, 2010; Pfeifer, 2013; Pfeifer & Kleiter, 2010; Singmann, Klauer, & Over, 2014).

Psychological accounts of conditionals and of conditional reasoning should be consistent with and account for people's probability judgements about conditionals and the premises and conclusions of conditional inferences. Mental model theory (Johnson-Laird & Byrne, 1991) is an influential psychological account of reasoning, and we will consider next what it implies about the probability of natural language conditionals.

The probability of a conditional and mental model theory

Figure 24.2 gives the logical meaning of ***if p then q*** when it is *assumed* to be equivalent to a material conditional, $p \supset q$, and it is of course identical with the truth table for ***not-p or q***. The material conditional is true in the first cell, the *p, q* possibility, false in the second cell, the ***p, not-q*** possibility, and true in the two ***not-p*** cells, the ***not-p, q*** and ***not-p, not-q*** possibilities.

In mental model theory, the natural language indicative conditional ***if p then q*** has the same full mental models as ***not-p or q***, and equivalently, ***if not-p then q*** has the same full mental models as *p or q* (Johnson-Laird & Byrne, 1991, pp. 7, 74). Byrne and Johnson-Laird (2009) consequently

p \ *q*	1	0
1	1	0
0	1	1

Figure 24.2 The truth table for the material conditional $p \supset q$ *and not-p or q; 1 = true and 0 = false*

argued that the probability of a natural language conditional, *P(if not-p then q)*, "should" be identical with the probability of *p or q*, *P(p or q)*, which implies that *P(if p then q)* "should" be identical with *P(not-p or q)*. They used an example about coins, nickels and dimes, to make this claim. But suppose the nickel is a fair coin, and let the *if p then q* conditional be, "If we spin this nickel a million times, we will get a million heads". This conditional is intuitively extremely improbable, and yet it should be highly probable by mental model theory. It is logically equivalent, in the theory, to the ***not-p or q*** disjunction that we will not spin the nickel a million times or we will get a million heads, and it is very highly probable that we will not go to the trouble of spinning the nickel a million times. By the p-validity of or-introduction, *P(not-p or q)* is very highly probable, and since in mental model theory *P(if p then q)* = *P(not-p or q)*, the implication is that the conditional is very highly probable as well. But against mental model theory, the conclusion we should draw is that the natural language conditional does not have the same full mental models, and so does not have to have the same probability, as the disjunction and its logical equivalent, the material conditional of propositional logic (Over, 2016, 2017).

In the original version of mental model theory, the validity of or-introduction was accepted, but it was claimed that ordinary people tend, wrongly, not to endorse it as valid because it "throws information away" (Johnson-Laird & Byrne, 1991, pp. 74–75). As we have just seen, this position, along with the claim that ***if p then q*** has the same full mental models as ***not-p or q***, implies counterintuitive results about what the probability of a conditional "should" be. This problem is addressed in the recent radical revision of mental model theory proposed by Johnson-Laird, Khemlani, and Goodwin (2015). In this revision, ***if p then q*** is still held to have the same full mental models as ***not-p or q***, but or-introduction is now stated to be invalid", and so it is argued that *p or q* does not follow validly from *p*, and of course that ***not-p or q*** does not follow validly from ***not-p***. This normative position implies that *P(p or q)* does not have to be high when *P(p)* is high, nor *P(not-p or q)* high when *P(not-p)* is high.

Johnson-Laird et al. (2015) use this example:

(2) Pat visited England or she visited Italy or both.

This disjunction has these three fully explicit mental models:

England	not-Italy
Not-England	Italy
England	Italy

Johnson-Laird et al. say about (2), "The disjunction is true provided that each of these three cases is possible". The immediate problem with this introduction rule is that these three cases are the logical possibilities from three rows of the truth table, Figure 24.1. It is a trivial logical truth that these cases are possible, even though, let us say, Pat was born and raised in Australia and has never left the country. Since these cases are always logically possible, revised mental model theory implies that (2) is certain, with a probability of 1. The three cases are even possible in a narrower sense than logical possibility. It was possible for Pat to catch one of the frequent flights from Australia to England or Italy. As it happens, Pat did not, and (2) is false. Actual truth does not follow from mere possibility, no matter how that is defined.

Johnson-Laird et al. argue that it is "invalid" to infer (2) in mental model theory from the premise that Pat has visited England. Referring to this premise and the three cases listed above, they say, "The premise does not establish that the second and third cases are possible": "not England & Italy" and "England & Italy". But as we have just pointed out, it is a trivial logical truth that all three of these cases are possible. It is impossible for the premise of or-introduction to be coherently more probable than its conclusion, and Cruz et al. (2015) and Politzer and Baratgin (2015) find that people do generally conform to the p-validity of or-introduction.

Fundamental inferences like or-introduction cannot be declared invalid without affecting other inferences that are intuitively valid. For example, by what Johnson-Laird et al. (2015) argue, it would be invalid to infer "Pat has been on an airplane" from the premises, "If Pat has visited England or Italy then she has been on an airplane" and "Pat has visited England". For this inference, one could not use or-introduction, in revised mental model theory, to infer the minor premise for MP, "Pat has visited England or Italy", because or-introduction is supposed to be "invalid". Yet the two-step inference, using or-introduction and then MP, is intuitively valid. The direct inference from the premises *if p or q then r* and *p* to the conclusion *r* could be called *or-MP*, and Rips (1983) found with a binary response format that people endorse it as valid at least as frequently as MP. Cruz (2016) obtained an analogous result with a probabilistic response format, and we note that the validity of or-MP entails the validity of or-introduction via the substitution of *p or q* for *r* and the resulting tautology *if p or q then p or q*.

There is also a problem for Johnson-Laird et al. (2015) with and-elimination (Dorothy Edgington, personal communication). By and-elimination, *p* validly follows from *p & q*, and this implies in turn that ***not-(p & q)*** validly follows from ***not-p***. But ***not-(p & q)*** is logically equivalent to ***not-p or not-q***, and so ***not-p or not-q*** validly follows from ***not-p***, which is an instance of or-introduction. We can also of course infer that *p or* q validly follows from *p*, given that and-elimination is valid (and *p* and ***not-not-p*** are equivalent). Thus the validity of and-elimination entails the validity of or-introduction, and the former must be invalid if the latter is. If and-elimination is invalid, then people cannot commit the conjunction fallacy, for there is not then a normative reason why $P(p \,\&\, q) \leq P(p)$ should hold. Perhaps Johnson-Laird et al. do not want and-elimination to be valid either, but Cruz et al. (2015), Pfeifer and Kleiter (2005), and Politzer and Baratgin (2015) find that people do generally conform to the p-validity of and-elimination, except in the specific context known to cause the conjunction fallacy (Cruz et al., 2015; and see Baratgin et al., 2015, for further critical points on the revision of mental model theory).

The Ramsey test and the new paradigm

The probability of the natural language conditional, ***P(if p then q)***, cannot, intuitively, be identified with the probability of the disjunction, ***P(not-p or q)***, implying that ***P(if p then q)*** can be high merely because ***P(not-p)*** is high. But what then is ***P(if p then q)*** and how is it determined? There is a *new paradigm* in the psychology of reasoning that attempts to answer this question (Elqayam & Over, 2013; Oaksford & Chater, 2007; Over, 2009, 2016). It takes a Bayesian, or more generally probabilistic, approach to the subject and has been much influenced by a proposal that could hardly have had a greater impact on the logical and philosophical study of conditionals, the *Ramsey test* (Edgington, 1995; Ramsey, 1929/1990). According to Ramsey, to acquire a degree of confidence in ***if p then q***, people hypothetically suppose *p* and, under this supposition, make a judgement about *q*. The result of this mental procedure is that people fix their degree of belief in *q* given *p*, which is the conditional subjective probability, $P(q\,|\,p)$. The psychological hypothesis based on the Ramsey test is that people use it when making a probability judgement about a conditional such as (1). They would hypothetically suppose that global warming will continue and, under this supposition, use what they know about global warming, rising sea levels, and low-lying ground in London to make their judgement. Integrating this knowledge, they might construct a causal model to decide that (1) is quite probable.

Ramsey held that an indicative conditional is "void" when its antecedent is known to be false. Assuming Pat is hard at work in a boring job at Alice Springs, Australia, she would not assert this indicative conditional:

(3) If I am in Paris then I am enjoying a holiday.

It is clear that (3) is in some sense "void" for Pat. She would instead use the following *subjunctive conditional* or *counterfactual*:

(4) If I were in Paris then I would be enjoying a holiday.

Stalnaker (1968) extended the Ramsey test for cases like (4), in which the antecedent of the conditional is known to be false and a counterfactual is considered. We are to evaluate such a conditional, *if p then q*, by making minimal changes to preserve consistency in our beliefs after hypothetically supposing *p*, and then assessing to what extent *q* follows. Pat can suppose that she is in Paris by imagining herself there, while making minimal changes to her beliefs, and infer that an enjoyable holiday is likely to result. Oaksford and Chater (2011) and Pearl (2013) have proposed implementations of the Ramsey test in cognitive science. As well as indicative and counterfactual conditionals, utility and deontic conditionals are important in the new paradigm. For these conditionals, see Bonnefon and Sloman (2013); Elqayam, Thompson, Wilkinson, Evans, and Over (2015); and Over and Over (2017).

Stalnaker (1968) argued that what is being represented in a Ramsey test when we make a supposition with minimal changes to our beliefs is the *closest* possible world for us in which the supposition is true. In his logical system for indicative and subjunctive conditionals, a natural language conditional *if p then q* is true if and only if *q* is true in the closest possible world (to the actual world) in which *p* is true. Lewis (1973) later modified this definition for circumstances in which there is not a unique closest possible world.

What Stalnaker and Lewis said about the relative "closeness" of possible worlds has had a great impact in judgement and decision making and social psychology, where psychologists have found that people do have firm intuitions about which possibilities are "close", and which are "distant", and that these intuitions affect their judgements about counterfactuals (Kahneman & Miller, 1986). Stalnaker and Lewis have also influenced studies in the cognitive psychology of counterfactual and causal judgements (Lucas & Kemp, 2015; Over, 2016, 2017; Pearl, 2013; Sloman, 2013).

Stalnaker (1970) claimed that the probability of the conditional *if p then q* in his logical system is the conditional probability of *q* given *p*, $P(\textit{if } p \textit{ then } q) = P(q \mid p)$. But Lewis (1976) later proved that this relation does not hold in theories like his and Stalnaker's (see Douven & Dietz, 2011, on Lewis's proof). In these theories $P(\textit{if } p \textit{ then } q) = P(q \mid p)$ will fail in general. However, recent psychological research on conditional reasoning has been more affected by approaches in which $P(\textit{if } p \textit{ then } q) = P(q \mid p)$ does hold (Evans & Over, 2004; Over, 2016, 2017). The relation that $P(\textit{if } p \textit{ then } q) = P(q \mid p)$ is so fundamental for the new Bayesian accounts of conditional reasoning that it is simply called *the Equation* (Edgington, 1995; Oaksford & Chater, 2007).

The Equation, a normative view, can be tested descriptively as the ***conditional probability hypothesis***: that $P(\textit{if } p \textit{ then } q) = P(q \mid p)$ in people's probability judgements (Rips & Marcus, 1997, were the first to state this in psychology). In the first experiments on this hypothesis, Evans et al. (2003) used indicative conditionals about a random card to be selected from an artificial pack of cards:

(5) If the card is yellow (*y*) then it has a circle printed on it (*c*).

The participants were shown a frequency distribution of the cards in the pack, for example, one yellow circle, four yellow diamonds, sixteen red circles, and sixteen red diamonds. Evans et al. also specified that (5) is a singular conditional, about the specific card to be selected from this distribution (see Cruz & Oberauer, 2014, on general conditionals). In this example, the conditional probability hypothesis implies that the probability of (5), *P(if y then c)*, is the conditional probability that the selected card has a circle on it given that it is yellow, $P(c \mid y) = 1/5 = .2$. Experiments of this type support the conditional probability hypothesis (see also Oberauer & Wilhelm, 2003). There is a minority "conjunctive" response in these experiments, *P(if p then q)* = *P(p & q)*, but Fugard, Pfeifer, Mayerhofer, and Kleiter (2011) later found that this response declines when participants are given the chance to perform the task repeatedly, to be replaced by the conditional probability response, *P(if p then q)* = $P(q \mid p)$. Attempts in mental model theory to counter such results (Girotto & Johnson-Laird, 2004) are vitiated by modal fallacies (Over & Baratgin, 2017; Over, Douven, & Verbrugge, 2013; Politzer et al., 2010).

The comments about conditionals in Ramsey (1929/1990) were very brief, but they can be supplemented by the account in de Finetti (1937/1964) and what can be called the *de Finetti table*. It is very striking that the two founders of contemporary subjective probability theory, Ramsey and de Finetti, should have had essentially the same view of the relation between conditionals and conditional probability. By the de Finetti table, Pat will judge that (3) is true when she is in Paris and enjoying herself, and that (3) is false when she is in Paris and not enjoying herself. She will not use (3) at all when she is hard at work in Alice Springs, but will find it "void" as an indicative statement, and will use the counterfactual (4) instead. See Figure 24.3.

The probability of the conditional *if p then q* for de Finetti is the probability that *p & q* holds given that the conditional makes a non-void assertion, that *p* holds, and this probability is of course the conditional probability of *q* given *p*, $P((p \,\&\, q) \mid p) = P(q \mid p)$. An indicative conditional in de Finetti's account is closely comparable to a conditional bet (see also Ramsey, 1926/1990). A bet on (5), for instance, is won when the selected card is yellow and has a circle on it, lost when the selected card is yellow and has a diamond on it, and "void", or "called off", without anyone winning or losing when the selected card is red. The probability that the conditional bet will be won is the probability of *y & c* given that the bet is non-void, which is again the conditional probability, $P((y \,\&\, c) \mid y) = P(c \mid y)$. Politzer et al. (2010) and Baratgin, Over, and Politzer (2013) confirm that there is this close parallel relationship in people's judgements between indicative conditionals and conditional bets.

The "void" cells of the de Finetti table can be thought of as expressing a state of uncertainty, as far as the actual facts are concerned. But of course one can have more or less confidence in a conditional even when its antecedent is likely to be false, and when the antecedent is known to be false, one can have more or less confidence in the counterfactual. Jeffrey (1991) showed that the "void" value in the de Finetti table should be replaced by the conditional probability itself. Figure 24.4 is the *Jeffrey table* (Over, 2016, 2017; Over & Baratgin, 2017).

q / *p*	1	0
1	1	0
0	V	V

Figure 24.3 The de Finetti table for if p then q; 1 = true, 0 = false, and V = void

q / p	1	0
1	1	0
0	$P(q \mid p)$	$P(q \mid p)$

Figure 24.4 The Jeffrey table for if p then q; 1 = true, 0 = false, and P(q | p) = the subjective conditional probability of q given p

Supporters of the Jeffrey table would use 1 for both "truth" and a probability of 1, and conditionals that are certain have 1 in the cells of this table where their antecedents are false. The trivial conditional *if p then p*, for instance, would have a probability of 1, and would be "true" in the Jeffrey table regardless of the truth value of the antecedent. This use of "true" also follows from the Ramsey test. The outcome of the test is not dependent on the actual truth value of the antecedent of the conditional, and it can be performed for a counterfactual when the antecedent is known to be false. The prediction would be that people will say that any statement, whether a conditional or not, is "true" if they take it to have a probability of 1. For a conditional about a frequency distribution, like (5), there is evidence that most people, when asked to judge whether the conditional is true, false, or neither, will call it "true" only when it has a probability of 1 (Goodwin, 2014). But that is almost certainly too strong a prediction to make in general. Pat might assert (4) as "true" while being well aware of a small chance that she would not enjoy the holiday, because of some unusually bad weather, or for some other reason.

A conditional that satisfies the Equation and the de Finetti and Jeffrey tables can be called a *probability conditional* (Adams, 1998) or a *conditional event* (de Finetti, 1937/1964). We will primarily use "probability conditional" for this conditional, though this technical term has suggested to some critics that such a conditional *if p then q* semantically means that the probability of *q* is high given *p* (Goodwin, 2014). This is a misunderstanding. If the Equation holds, (5) does not mean that the conditional probability is high that the selected card has a circle on it given it is yellow. If that were the meaning, (5) would be definitely false and not have a probability of .2, as implied by the Equation. Of course, people would only *assert* (5) – or for that matter the categorical "The card is yellow" – as a "true" speech act if its probability were high enough in a given context, but that is a point about pragmatics and not semantics.

Experimental research has long established that people do produce three-valued tables like de Finetti's when evaluating a conditional. These de Finetti tables were traditionally known as "defective" truth tables (see Over & Baratgin, 2017, for a review of research on "defective" truth tables, and Baratgin et al., 2013, and Politzer et al., 2010, for recent experiments). There is also a striking developmental trend for children's understanding of indicative conditionals, ending with the de Finetti table and the conditional probability response in adults (Barrouillet & Gauffroy, 2015).

Barrouillet and Gauffroy (2015) have an experiment on indicative conditionals of a "causal" type. The example they give is, "If the lever is down, then the rabbit's cage is open". Their participants were also given frequency information on how many times the lever is up or down and the cage is open or closed. This frequency information can indicate that there are many, or few, "alternatives" for opening the rabbit's cage. According to Barrouillet and Gauffroy, if there are many alternatives in the background context of the conditional *if p then q*, then adult participants tend to judge that its probability is the conditional probability, *P(if p then q)* = *P(q | p)*. If there are relatively few alternatives, then adult participants apparently judge that its probability is the probability of the "defective" biconditional, *P(if p then q)* = *P(p & q | p or q)*. The "defective" biconditional is better called the ***biconditional event*** (Fugard et al., 2011) or ***probability biconditional***. It is true when *p & q* holds, false when ***p & not-q*** holds, false when ***not-p*** *& q* holds, and "void" when ***not-p & not-q*** holds. It is the conjunction of two probability conditionals, ***(if p then q) and (if q then p)***, both of which satisfy the Equation separately (see Gilio & Sanfilippo, 2014, and Kaufmann, 2009, on the conjunction of probability conditionals). The finding that ***P(if p then q)*** = *P(p & q | p or q)* for some conditionals does not disconfirm the Equation as fundamental to the evaluation of conditionals.

There is, moreover, a problem with Barrouillet and Gauffroy's claim that, as the number of alternative causes decreases, people are more likely to give a "defective" biconditional interpretation to the conditional, *P(if p then q)* = *P(p & q | p or q)*, and not to conform to the Equation, *P(if p then q)* = *P(q | p)*. When there are relatively few alternatives to *p* for bringing about *q*, ***P(q | not-p)*** will be low, and when there are no alternatives at all ***P(q | not-p)*** = 0. As noted by Barrouillet and Gauffroy themselves, *P(p or q)* = *(P(p & q)* + ***P(p & not-q)*** + ***P(not-p*** *& q))*, and the probability of the "defective" biconditional will be *P(p & q | p or q)* = *P(p & q | (P(p & q)* + ***P(p & not-q)*** + ***P(not-p*** *& q))*. But now, when ***P(q | not-p)*** is low, ***P(not-p*** *& q)* = ***P(not-p)P(q | not-p)*** will be low, and *P(p & q | p or q)* will be close to *P(p & q | (P(p & q)* + ***P(p & not-q))***, which is identical with *P(q | p)*. When there are no alternatives at all to *p* for bringing about *q*, ***P(q | not-p)*** will be 0, and *P(p & q | p or q)* will be *P(q | p)*. Barrouillet and Gauffroy's claim actually implies that, when there are few alternatives to *p* for obtaining *q*, *P(if p then q)* will be close to *P(q | p)*, and when there are no alternatives, *P(if p then q)* will be exactly *P(q | p)*.

The strongest support for the conditional probability hypothesis is found in experiments on realistic conditionals that the experimenters do not tie to artificial frequency distributions. Consider (1) again. We do not have a high degree of confidence in (1) because we know that London has flooded on some number of occasions when global warming has continued. Our probability judgement about (1) plausibly comes instead from a causal model, which encodes information about disabling conditions that would prevent the flooding in spite of the warming (Ali, Chater, & Oaksford, 2011; Fernbach & Erb, 2013; Oaksford & Chater, 2013). In experiments on conditionals like (1), the participants' conditional probability judgement, that London will be flooded given that global warming continues, is the best predictor of the probability of the conditional, that London will be flooded if global warming continues (Over, Hadjichristidis, Evans, Handley, & Sloman, 2007; Singmann et al., 2014). In these experiments, participants' responses confirm the conditional probability hypothesis (for counterfactuals as well as indicatives in Over et al., 2007). There is little or no evidence for a minority conjunctive response, *P(if p then q)* = *P(p & q)*, and none at all for a material conditional response, *P(if p then q)* = ***P(not-p*** *or q)*. (For further support of the conditional probability response, see Baratgin et al., 2013; Douven & Verbrugge, 2010; Feeney & Handley, 2011; Haigh, Stewart, & Connell, 2013; Politzer et al., 2010; and Wijnbergen-Huitink, Elqayam, & Over, 2015.)

Limits to the scope of the Equation could arise from so-called ***missing-link conditionals***, in which there is no clear relation between the antecedent and consequent, e.g. "If Pat goes to Paris then London will be flooded". Here the antecedent and consequent are independent of each other, and yet the conditional probability could be high that London will be flooded given that Pat goes to Paris, merely because there is a high probability that London will be flooded. People might require *p* and *q* to have a relation to each other in *if p then q*, and reject, or judge as improbable, missing-link conditionals (Douven, 2015; Krzyzanowska, Wenmackers, & Douven, 2013). Skovgaard-Olsen, Singmann, and Klauer (2016) found people conform to the Equation only when a relation between *p* and *q* made *P(q | p)* > ***P(q | not-p)***, implying that *p* raises the probability of *q*. However, other results do not support this conclusion (Oberauer, Weidenfeld, &

Fischer, 2007; Over et al., 2007; & Singmann et al., 2014). There is also evidence that the relevance of a relation for probability judgements is not specific to conditionals but present to a similar degree for conjunctions and disjunctions (Cruz, Over, Oaksford, & Baratgin, 2016), suggesting that the effect is pragmatic and not semantic. It is unclear at this point whether what matters for these cases is a specific relation between p and q, or more generally the presence of a common topic of discourse for p and q (Cruz et al., 2016).

The Equation and the conditional probability hypothesis apply to the assertions of indicative and counterfactual conditionals. Comparable hypotheses can be formulated for other conditional speech acts. We have already referred to conditional bets above, and another example would be a conditional promise, for example, a political party might promise to lower taxes if it is elected to power. The comparable hypothesis in this case would be that the probability the party will keep its conditional promise is the conditional probability that it will lower taxes given that it is elected (one normally speaks of promises as being kept or broken rather than as "true"; cf. Barrouillet & Gauffroy, 2015, and Ohm & Thompson, 2006), but we continue here to focus on indicative conditionals and counterfactuals.

Belief-based reasoning with conditionals

Consider the following conditionals:

(6) If Pat is in Paris then she is enjoying a holiday.
(7) If Pat is in Paris and has food poisoning then she is enjoying a holiday.

Supposing (6) and (7) were material conditionals, it would be logically valid to infer (7) from (6), as a simple truth table test will prove. This inference is termed *strengthening the antecedent,* and it is clearly invalid for natural language indicative and counterfactual conditionals. It is also p-invalid for the probability conditional: $P(q \mid (p \,\&\, r))$ can be very low or even 0 when $P(q \mid p)$ is very high. This example of strengthening the antecedent illustrates the advantages of using the probability conditional and its p-valid inference rules in an account of conditional reasoning from people's beliefs in natural language conditionals. Adams (1998, p. 154) lists p-valid inference rules for the probability conditional. These are a proper subset of the inference rules in propositional logic for the material conditional, and are too weak to derive strengthening the antecedent as a p-valid inference for the probability conditional. The failure of strengthening the antecedent to be p-valid for the probability conditional allows Adams to have an element of *non-monotonicity* in his system, in that adding information to the antecedent of this conditional can change it from one of high probability to one of low probability. It is, however, a mistake to claim that p-validity is itself non-monotonic (see Baratgin et al., 2015, on Johnson-Laird et al., 2015).

Another inference of great interest is *centering*: inferring the conditional *if p then q* from the conjunction $p \,\&\, q$ (*one-premise centering,* usually called "conjunctive sufficiency"), and from p and q as separate premises (*two-premise centering*). Centering (both one-premise and two-premise) is truth-preserving valid for the material conditional and the Stalnaker/Lewis conditionals, and p-valid for the probability conditional, but is invalid if there has to be a connection between p and q for *if p then q* to hold (Over, 2017). It is also invalid supposing that *if p then q* is a *strict conditional,* holding if and only if q is true in *every* relevant possibility (and not just the "closest") in which p is true (Cariani & Rips, 2017; Kratzer, 2012). Centering marks an important high-level dividing line between theories of the conditional. A long tradition of truth table studies confirms that people judge *if p then q* true when p and q are true (Over & Baratgin, 2017), and there is some direct evidence that people treat centering as p-valid (Cruz et al., 2015, 2016;

Politzer & Baratgin, 2015). The crucial question is whether people use centering to extend their conditional beliefs, and that can be answered only in a probabilistic approach to the study of conditionals.

The MP inference with (1) as its major premise also illustrates the advantages of a probabilistic approach:

> If global warming continues (*c*) then London will be flooded (*f*).
> Global warming will continue.
> Therefore, London will be flooded.

Assuming the major and the minor premises above, we can infer the conclusion with certainty. We could also assume, if we liked, the negation of both of these premises. But mere assumptions do not help us to make inferences for rational beliefs and decision making. For that purpose, we need to take account of the uncertainty in the premises in belief-based reasoning. The major premise above is not certain: our degree of belief in it is less than 1. There is already a Thames Barrier for current flood threats. It might be supplemented in the coming years, producing a disabling condition for the major premise. People's awareness of possible disabling or counterexample conditions has been found to lower their confidence in the conclusions of MP inferences (Ali et al., 2011; Cummins, 1995; Fernbach & Erb, 2013). There is additional uncertainty in the minor premise: there might be effective steps taken in the future to stop global warming. Uncertainty in both the major and minor premises can also come from the source of a premise and its trustworthiness, whether or not, for example, an expert scientist has asserted it (Stevenson & Over, 2001; Wolf, Rieger, & Knauff, 2012). People's confidence in the conclusion of any valid inference should go down when they lose confidence, for whatever reason, in the premises in belief-based inference (Politzer, 2005; Stevenson & Over, 1995).

Probability theory implies coherence intervals for the conclusions of MP and other conditional inferences, given the Equation (Evans et al., 2015; Pfeifer & Kleiter, 2009; Singmann et al., 2014). Suppose our degree of confidence in the major premise is *P(if c then f)* = *P(f|c)* = .6, and our degree of confidence in the minor premise is slightly higher at *P(c)* = .7. What should our confidence be in the conclusion of MP, *P(f)*? To conform to probability theory it should be at least *P(c)P(f|c)* = .42. That covers the *c* possibility. What of *not-c*, which could also make *f* probable to some degree? The probability of *not-c*, *P(not-c)*, should be 1- *P(c)* = .3 by probability theory. But what is *P(f|not-c)*? Perhaps we cannot even estimate *P(f|not-c)*, but again by probability theory, we know that its minimum value is *P(f|not-c)* = 0 and its maximum value is *P(f|not-c)* = 1. At the minimum value, *P(not-c)P(f|not-c)* = 0, and *P(f)* = *P(c)P(f|c)* = .42. At the maximum value, *P(not-c)P(f|not-c)* = *P(not-c)* = .3, and *P(f)* = *P(c)P(f|c)* + *P(not-c)* = .42 + .3 = .72. Hence to be ***coherent***, that is, consistent with probability theory, our degree of confidence in the conclusion of MP in this example should lie in the interval between .42 and .72 [.42, .72].

A consequence of this probabilistic analysis of MP is that we can have too much confidence in the conclusion, over .72, as well as too little, under .42. The traditional approach in the psychology of reasoning, in which premises are to be assumed true, and binary conclusions about the truth or falsity of the conclusion are drawn, could not even conceive of the possibility that people might endorse the conclusion of a valid inference too highly. A valid conditional inference could not be "suppressed" in this tradition (beginning with Byrne, 1989) because of excessive confidence in its conclusion. But overconfidence in reasoning and decision making is potentially a serious limitation on people's rationality, and it should be a general topic of study in the psychology of reasoning. The evidence so far is that people's degrees of confidence in the conclusions of MP inferences tend to be within the MP coherent interval (Evans et al., 2015; Pfeifer & Kleiter, 2009; Singmann et al., 2014), but overconfidence could turn up in contexts yet to be investigated.

The MP coherence interval just described can be derived in a more formal way using the total probability theorem of probability theory. This implies that $P(f) = P(c)P(f|c) + P(not\text{-}c) P(f|not\text{-}c)$. When inserting the information from the premises of MP into this equation, the remaining unknown is $P(f|not\text{-}c)$. The coherence interval for MP comes from assuming first that $P(f|not\text{-}c)$ is at its lowest value of 0, and then assuming it is at its highest value of 1. Some people, though, might give a precise value for $P(f|not\text{-}c)$ – for example, they might say it is .5 because they have no information one way or the other. If we make this judgement, we should assess $P(f)$ as .42 + .15 = .57. The present evidence, however, is that people do not always precisely comply with the total probability theorem. In our example, they might take insufficient account of $P(not\text{-}c)P(f|not\text{-}c)$ and focus more on $P(c)P(f|c) = .42$, perhaps with some adjustment upwards (Hadjichristidis, Sloman, & Over, 2014; Zhao & Osherson, 2010). That could, of course, still place them within the coherence interval for MP.

Coherence intervals can also be given for the other conditional inferences that are usually studied in the psychology of reasoning (Evans et al., 2015; Pfeifer & Kleiter, 2009), as well as non-conditional inferences (Cruz et al., 2015). We suggest that the best use of the technical term, "suppression" of an inference itself, as opposed to "suppression" of confidence in the conclusion, is for cases in which people fall outside the coherence interval for the inference, whether they are too high or too low. When people "suppress" an inference in this sense, they are violating its probability logic. Theories of the "suppression" of inferences usually concern only conditional inferences (see Cariani & Rips, 2017, for a significant recent example), but other inference forms, with their own coherence intervals, can also be "suppressed" in our proposed sense. Cruz et al. (2015) find such "suppression" in an *explicit* use of and-elimination in a context known to cause the conjunction fallacy.

Inferences that are p-invalid also have coherence intervals, and when these are narrower than the unit interval [0, 1], people can "suppress" them by falling outside of these coherence intervals. An example of such an inference is *Affirmation of the Consequent* (AC), inferring *p* from *if p then q* and *q*. In some cases, coherent conclusions of AC increase the uncertainty present in the premises; that is what makes it a p-invalid inference. Even so, AC can be a probabilistically strong inference to make by Bayesian standards, as long as one does stay in its coherence interval (Evans et al., 2015). Inferences that are p-invalid but have coherent conclusions can have great value as inductive inferences (Evans & Over, 2013; Hahn & Oaksford, 2007).

We have said more about indicative conditionals than counterfactuals, but the new paradigm applies just as much to counterfactuals. There is a large literature on counterfactuals and how these conditionals are related to causation and human emotions, particularly regret (Hoerl, McCormack, & Beck, 2011). But it is not yet known how people will respond to strengthening the antecedent and centering for counterfactuals. It might have been predicted that people would not endorse MP for counterfactuals for pragmatic reasons:

If Pat had gone to Paris then she would have had an enjoyable holiday.
Pat went to Paris.
Therefore, Pat had an enjoyable holiday.

It seems pragmatically odd to draw any conclusion from this inference because the first premise suggests that Pat did not go to Paris, whereas the second premise affirms that she in fact did. This pragmatic problem can be eliminated, however, by presenting the premises, not as assumptions, but as a belief-based dialogue. The first speaker asserts the major premise, and a second speaker, with a more accurate belief, supplies the minor premise. It does not then appear odd to infer the conclusion. Using this, in effect, belief-based scenario, Thompson and Byrne (2002) found that people do endorse highly the conclusion of counterfactual MP (see Over, 2017, on Thompson & Byrne and counterfactual ***modus tollens***, inferring ***not-p*** from ***if p then q*** and ***not-q***). Such research on counterfactuals and counterfactual reasoning should be extended in the new paradigm. People have degrees of belief in counterfactuals, and the conditional probability hypothesis has been confirmed for these conditionals (Over et al., 2007). But few experimental studies have been developed for belief-based inferences from counterfactuals as premises and to them as conclusions (Over, 2017).

Conclusion

When people reason from *p* to *q* with some degree of confidence, they can sum the process up by asserting a conditional, *if p then q*, with that confidence. They can also go the other way and support a confident assertion of *if p then q* by reasoning from *p* to *q* with that confidence. Reasoning and conditionals are so closely tied together that it is impossible to give an adequate account of the one without a full explanation of the other. Traditional psychology of reasoning was limited by its binary and assumption-based approach. It classified premises and conclusions as true or false and not as having various degrees of subjective probability. Its premises were arbitrary assumptions and not people's beliefs. These limitations gave it a highly restricted view of both reasoning and conditionals.

The new paradigm in the psychology of reasoning is Bayesian or probabilistic and primarily focused on belief-based inference, on inferring a degree of belief in a conclusion from degrees of belief in premises, not only in conditional inference, but also in reasoning with conjunctions, disjunctions, and other logical forms. In a new paradigm view, there is no reason why "suppression" experiments should be restricted to the study of conditional inferences. Confidence in the conclusions of inferences that contain other logical forms can also be affected by uncertainty in the premises.

The new approach can facilitate the further refinement and testing of process theories of belief-based reasoning. Consider a recent finding about coherence and p-validity. A "belief group" of participants was asked to assess the probabilities of a randomized list of conditionals and categorical statements, affirmative and negative, as separate items that were not explicitly related to each other. An "inference group" was asked to assess the probabilities of these statements when presented in explicit inferences, for example, MP, *if p then q*, *p*, *therefore q*. People were not perfectly coherent; in particular people's probability judgements about statements and their negations did not always sum to one, $P(p) + P(not\text{-}p) = 1$, as required by probability theory (see the remarks of Evans et al., 2015, on this finding and support theory in judgement and decision making). But in the case of MP, those in the explicit inference group had more above chance coherence, and conformed more to p-validity, than those in the randomized list group (Evans et al., 2015).

This finding could possibly be explained in a dual process theory of reasoning (Evans & Stanovich, 2013; Markovits, Brunet, Thompson, & Brisson, 2013; and see Singmann et al., 2014, on a dual-source model of reasoning). Perhaps when people are given ***if p then q***, *p*, and *q* separately, in a list of other statements, they tend implicitly to use rapid heuristics for their probability judgements that do not take account of the MP logical form. But when people are presented with an explicit inference, *if p then q*, *p*, *therefore q*, they may grasp the relevance of the MP form at a higher level and explicitly follow the rule, becoming more coherent and complying more with p-validity, in their judgements about *P(if p then q)* = *P(q | p)*, *P(p)*, and *P(q)*. The further development of the new paradigm should determine how far this dual process explanation of the finding is justified and could lead, much more generally, to a full Bayesian theory of how people reason from their beliefs, extending, revising, and updating them in dynamic reasoning over time (Baratgin & Politzer, 2010; Oaksford & Chater, 2013; Over, 2016).

References

Adams, E. (1998). *A primer of probability logic.* Stanford, CA: CLSI Publications.

Ali, N., Chater, N., & Oaksford, M. (2011). The mental representation of causal conditional reasoning: Mental models or causal models. *Cognition, 119*, 403–418.

Baratgin, J., Douven, I., Evans, J. St. B. T., Oaksford, M., Over, D. E., & Politzer, G. (2015). The new paradigm and mental models. *Trends in Cognitive Sciences, 19*(10), 547–548.

Baratgin, J., Over, D. E., & Politzer, G. (2013). Uncertainty and de Finetti tables. *Thinking & Reasoning, 19*, 308–328.

Baratgin, J., & Politzer, G. (2010). Updating: A psychologically basic situation of probability revision. *Thinking & Reasoning, 16*, 245–287.

Barrouillet, P., & Gauffroy, C. (2015). Probability in reasoning: A developmental test on conditionals. *Cognition, 137*, 22–39.

Bonnefon, J. F., & Sloman, S. A. (2013). The causal structure of utility conditionals. *Cognitive Science, 37*, 193–209.

Byrne, R. M. J. (1989). Suppressing valid inferences with conditionals. *Cognition, 31*, 61–83.

Byrne, R. M. J., & Johnson-Laird, P. N. (2009). 'If' and the problems of conditional reasoning. *Trends in Cognitive Science, 13*, 282–287.

Cariani, F., & Rips, L. J. (2017). Conditionals, context, and the suppression effect. *Cognitive Science*, 41, 540–589.

Cruz, N. (2016). The elusive oddness of or-introduction. In P. N. Johnson-Laird, R. Byrne, S. Khemlani, P. Legrenzi, & M. Ragni (Organisers), *The meeting in memory of Vittorio Girotto*, July 28 & 29. Division of Psychology and Language Sciences, University College London, UK.

Cruz, N., Baratgin, J., Oaksford, M., & Over, D. E. (2015). Bayesian reasoning with *ifs* and *ands* and *ors*. *Frontiers in Psychology, 6*, 192.

Cruz, N., & Oberauer, K. (2014). Comparing the meanings of "if " and "all." *Memory &. Cognition, 42*, 1345–1356.

Cruz, N., Over, D., Oaksford, M., & Baratgin, J. (2016). Centering and the meaning of conditionals. In A. Papafragou, D. Grodner, D. Mirman, & J. C. Trueswell (Eds.), *Proceedings of the 38th annual conference of the cognitive science society* (pp. 1104–1109). Austin, TX: Cognitive Science Society.

Cummins, D. D. (1995). Naive theories and causal deduction. *Memory & Cognition, 23*, 646–658.

de Finetti, B. (1937/1964). Foresight: Its logical laws, its subjective sources. In H. E. Kyburg & H. E. Smokier (Eds.), *Studies in subjective probability* (pp. 55–118). New York, NY: Wiley.

Douven, I. (2015). *The epistemology of indicative conditionals.* Cambridge, UK: Cambridge University Press.

Douven, I., & Dietz, R. (2011). A puzzle about Stalnaker's hypothesis. *Topoi, 30*, 31–37.

Douven, I., & Verbrugge, S. (2010). The Adams family. *Cognition, 117*, 302–318.

Edgington, D. (1995). On conditionals. *Mind, 104*, 235–329.

Elqayam, S., & Over, D. E. (2013). New paradigm psychology of reasoning: An introduction to the special issue edited by S. Elqayam, J. F. Bonnefon, & D. E. Over. *Thinking & Reasoning, 19*, 249–265.

Elqayam, S., Thompson, V., Wilkinson, M., Evans, Jonathan St. B. T., & Over, D. E. (2015). Deontic introduction: A theory of inference from is to ought. *Journal of Experimental Psychology: Learning, Memory, and Cognition, 41*(5), 1516–1532.

Evans, J. St. B. T., Handley, S. J., & Over, D. E. (2003). Conditional and conditional probability. *Journal of Experimental Psychology: Learning, Memory, and Cognition, 29*, 321–335.

Evans, J. St. B. T., & Over, D. E. (2004). *If.* Oxford, UK: Oxford University Press.

Evans, J. St. B. T., & Over, D. E. (2013). Reasoning to and from belief: Deduction and induction are still distinct. *Thinking & Reasoning, 19*, 268–283.

Evans, J. St. B. T., & Stanovich, K. E. (2013). Dual process theories of higher cognition: Advancing the debate. *Perspectives in Psychological Science, 8*, 223–241.

Evans, J. St. B. T., Thompson, V., & Over, D. E. (2015). Uncertain deduction and conditional reasoning. *Frontiers in Psychology, 6*, 398.

Feeney, A., & Handley, S. (2011). Suppositions, conditionals, and causal claims. In C. Hoerl, T. McCormack, & S. R. Beck (Eds.), *Understanding counterfactuals, understanding causation* (pp. 242–262). Oxford, UK: Oxford University Press.

Fernbach, P. M., & Erb, C. D. (2013). A quantitative model of causal reasoning. *Journal of Experimental Psychology: Learning, Memory, and Cognition, 39*, 1327–1343.

Fugard, J. B., Pfeifer, N., Mayerhofer, B., & Kleiter, G. D. (2011). How people interpret conditionals: Shifts toward conditional event. *Journal of Experimental Psychology: Learning Memory and Cognition, 37*, 635–648.

Gilio, A., & Over, D. E. (2012). The psychology of inferring conditionals from disjunctions: A probabilistic study. *Journal of Mathematical Psychology, 56*, 118–131.

Gilio, A., & Sanfilippo, G. (2014). Conditional random quantities and compounds of conditionals. *Studia Logica, 102*(4), 709–729.

Girotto, V., & Johnson-Laird, P. N. (2004). The probability of conditionals. *Psychologia, 47*, 207–225.

Goodwin, G. P. (2014). Is the basic conditional probabilistic? *Journal of Experimental Psychology: General, 143*, 1214–1241.

Hadjichristidis, C., Sloman, S. A., & Over, D. E. (2014). Categorical induction from uncertain premises: Jeffrey's doesn't completely rule. *Thinking & Reasoning, 20*, 405–431.

Hahn, U., & Oaksford, M. (2007). The rationality of informal argumentation: A Bayesian approach to reasoning fallacies. *Psychological Review, 114*, 646–678.

Haigh, M., Stewart, A. J., & Connell, L. (2013). Reasoning as we read: Establishing the probability of causal conditionals. *Memory & Cognition, 41*, 152–158.

Hoerl, C., McCormack, T., & Beck, S. (Eds.). (2011). *Understanding causation, understanding counterfactuals*. Oxford: Oxford University Press.

Jeffrey, R. C. (1991). Matter of fact conditionals. *Aristotelian Society Supplementary Volume, 65*, 161–183.

Johnson-Laird, P. N., & Byrne, R. M. J. (1991). *Deduction*. Hove & London, UK: Erlbaum.

Johnson-Laird, P. N., Khemlani, S., & Goodwin, G. P. (2015). Logic, probability, and human reasoning. *Trends in Cognitive Science, 19*, 201–214.

Kahneman, D., & Miller, D. (1986). Norm theory: Comparing reality to its alternatives. *Psychological Review, 93*, 136–156.

Kaufmann, S. (2009). Conditionals right and left: Probabilities for the whole family. *Journal of Philosophical Logic, 38*, 1–53.

Kneale, W., & Kneale, M. (1962). *The development of logic*. Oxford, UK: Oxford University Press.

Kratzer, A. (2012). *Modals and conditionals*. Oxford, UK: Oxford University Press.

Krzyzanowska, K., Wenmackers, S., & Douven, I. (2013). Inferential conditionals and evidentiality. *Journal of Logic, Language and Information, 22*(3), 315–334.

Lewis, D. (1973). *Counterfactuals*. Cambridge, MA: Harvard University Press.

Lewis, D. (1976). Probabilities of conditionals and conditional probabilities. *Philosophical Review, 85*, 297–315.

Lucas, C. G., & Kemp C. (2015). An improved probabilistic account of counterfactual reasoning. *Psychological Review. 122*(4), 700–734.

Markovits, H., Brunet, M-L., & Thompson, V., & Brisson, J. (2013). Direct evidence for a dual process model of deductive inferences. *Journal of Experimental Psychology: Learning, Memory, and Cognition, 39*, 1213–1222.

Oaksford, M., & Chater, N. (2007). *Bayesian rationality: The probabilistic approach to human reasoning*. Oxford, UK: Oxford University Press.

Oaksford, M., & Chater, N. (2011). Dual systems and dual processes but a single function. In K. I. Manktelow, D. E. Over, & S. Elqayam (Eds.), *The science of reason: A Festschrift for Jonathan St. B. T. Evans* (pp. 339–351). Hove, UK: Psychology Press.

Oaksford M., & Chater, N. (2013). Dynamic inference and everyday conditional reasoning in the new paradigm. *Thinking & Reasoning, 19*, 346–379.

Oberauer, K., Weidenfeld, A., & Fischer, K. (2007). What makes us believe a conditional? *Thinking & Reasoning, 13*(4), 340–369.

Oberauer, K., & Wilhelm, O. (2003). The meaning(s) of conditionals: Conditional probabilities, mental models, and personal utilities. *Journal of Experimental Psychology: Learning, Memory, and Cognition, 29*, 680–693.

Ohm, E., & Thompson, V. A. (2006). Conditional probability and pragmatic conditionals: Dissociating truth and effectiveness. *Thinking & Reasoning, 12*, 257–280.
Over, D. E. (2009). New paradigm psychology of reasoning. *Thinking & Reasoning, 15*, 431–438.
Over, D. E. (2016). The paradigm shift in the psychology of reasoning: The debate. In L. Macchi, M. Bagassi, & R. Viale (Eds.), *Cognitive unconscious and human rationality* (pp. 79–97). Cambridge, MA: MIT Press.
Over, D. E. (2017). Causation and the probability of causal conditionals. In M. Waldmann (Ed.), *The Oxford handbook of causal reasoning* (pp. 307–325). Oxford, UK: Oxford University Press.
Over, D. E., & Baratgin, J. (2017). The "defective" truth table: Its past, present, and future. In N. Galbraith, D. E. Over, & E. Lucas (Eds.), *The thinking mind: The use of thinking in everyday life* (pp. 15–28). Hove, UK: Psychology Press.
Over, D. E., Douven, I., & Verbrugge, S. (2013). Scope ambiguities and conditionals. *Thinking & Reasoning, 19*, 284–307.
Over, D. E., Evans, J. St. B. T., & Elqayam, S. (2010). Conditionals and non-constructive reasoning. In Oaksford, M., & Chater, N. (Eds.), *Cognition and conditionals: Probability and logic in human thinking* (pp. 135–151). Oxford: Oxford University Press.
Over, D. E., Hadjichristidis, C., Evans, J. St. B. T., Handley, S. J., & Sloman, S. A. (2007). The probability of causal conditionals. *Cognitive Psychology, 54*, 62–97.
Over, H., & Over, D. E. (2017). Deontic reasoning and social norms: Broader implications. In N. Galbraith, D. E. Over, & E. Lucas (Eds.), *The thinking mind: The use of thinking in everyday life* (pp. 54–65). Hove, UK: Psychology Press.
Pearl J. (2013). Structural counterfactuals: A brief introduction. *Cognitive Science, 37*, 977–985.
Pfeifer, N. (2013). The new psychology of reasoning: A mental probability logical perspective. *Thinking & Reasoning, 19*, 329–345.
Pfeifer, N., & Kleiter, G. D. (2005). Coherence and nonmonotonicity in human reasoning. *Synthese, 146*(1/2), 93–109.
Pfeifer, N., & Kleiter, G. D. (2009). Framing human inference by coherence based probability logic. *Journal of Applied Logic, 7*, 206–217.
Pfeifer, N., & Kleiter, G. D. (2010). The conditional in mental probability logic. In M. Oaksford, & N. Chater (Eds.), *Cognition and conditionals: Probability and logic in human thinking* (pp. 153–173). Oxford, UK: Oxford University Press.
Politzer, G. (2005). Uncertainty and the suppression of inferences. *Thinking & Reasoning, 11*, 5–33.
Politzer, G., & Baratgin, J. (2015). Deductive schemas with uncertain premises using qualitative probability expressions. *Thinking & Reasoning, 22*, 78–98.
Politzer, G., Over, D. E., & Baratgin, J. (2010). Betting on conditionals. *Thinking & Reasoning, 16*, 172–197.
Ramsey, F. P. (1926/1990). Truth and probability. In D. H. Mellor (Ed.), *Philosophical papers* (pp. 52–94). Cambridge, UK: Cambridge University Press.
Ramsey, F. P. (1929/1990). General propositions and causality. In D. H. Mellor (Ed.), *Philosophical papers* (pp. 145–163). Cambridge, UK: Cambridge University Press.
Rips, L. J. (1983). Cognitive processes in propositional reasoning. *Psychological Review, 90*(1), 38–71.
Rips, L. J., & Marcus, S. L. (1977). Suppositions and the analysis of conditional sentences. In M. A. Just & P. A. Carpenter (Eds.), *Cognitive processes in comprehension* (pp. 185–219). New York, NY: Wiley.
Singmann, H., Klauer, K. C., & Over, D. E. (2014). New normative standards of conditional reasoning and the dual-source model. *Frontiers in Psychology, 5*, 316.
Skovgaard-Olsen, N., Singmann, H., & Klauer, K. C. (2016). The relevance effect and conditionals. *Cognition, 150*, 26–36.
Sloman, S. A. (2013). Counterfactuals and causal models: Introduction to the special issue. *Cognitive Science, 37*, 969–976.
Stalnaker, R. (1968). A theory of conditionals. In N. Rescher (Ed.), *Studies in logical theory* (pp. 98–112). Oxford, UK: Blackwell.
Stalnaker, R. (1970). Probability and conditionals. *Philosophy of Science, 37*, 64–80.
Stevenson, R. J., & Over, D. E. (1995). Deduction from uncertain premises. *Quarterly Journal of Experimental Psychology, 48A*, 613–643.
Stevenson, R. J., & Over, D. E. (2001). Reasoning from uncertain premises: Effects of expertise and conversational context. *Thinking & Reasoning, 7*, 367–390.

Thompson, V. A., & Byrne, R. M. J. (2002). Reasoning counterfactually: Making inferences about things that didn't happen. *Journal of Experimental Psychology: Learning, Memory, and Cognition, 28,* 1154–1170.

Tversky, A., & Kahneman, D. (1983). Extensional versus intuitive reasoning: The conjunction fallacy in probability judgement. *Psychological Review, 90,* 293–315.

Wijnbergen-Huitink, J. v., Elqayam, S., & Over, D. E. (2014). The probability of iterated conditionals. *Cognitive Science,* 39, 788–803.

Wolf, A. G., Rieger, S., & Knauff, M. (2012). The effects of source trustworthiness and inference type on human belief revision. ***Thinking & Reasoning,*** *18*(4), 417–440.

Zhao, J., & Osherson, D. (2010). Updating beliefs in light of uncertain evidence: Descriptive assessment of Jeffrey's rule. ***Thinking & Reasoning,*** *16,* 288–307.

25
JUDGEMENT HEURISTICS

Tim Rakow and William J. Skylark[1]

Homo heuristicus and *femina heuristica*

Awaking late, Linda rushes from her apartment building and grabs a newspaper as she boards her bus. The paper carries the usual headlines: INVESTIGATION INTO VARIATION IN THE DAILY PROPORTION OF BOYS BORN AT SMALLVILLE COTTAGE HOSPITAL. "A good thing, too", Linda thinks. "There are always odd things happening at those small hospitals – they often have the worst success rates for treatment, but then again, some of the very best performing hospitals are small ones". She turns to the newspaper quiz page: WHAT YEAR DID GEORGE WASHINGTON BECOME U.S. PRESIDENT? "Easy", she thinks, "some time after American independence in 1776 – let's say 1778". The bus stops at the traffic light. "Oh well, that's three days in a row . . . at least tomorrow the light won't be red. Hmm, a Bob Dylan song on the iPod again . . . that shuffle function never really worked". Glancing up at the billboard – TOP PERFORMANCE, BEST VALUE IN CLASS, AND AS GREEN AS A HUGGABLE TREE – DRIVE THE BEST VW YET – Linda thinks, "Good brand, worth a look if I ever buy a car". Looking over to the shops, Linda spots a new sign: A STITCH IN TIME SAVES NINE. "How true", she thinks. "I bet they're good – I must take that old smock dress to be repaired there". She steps off the bus and the usual thoughts pass through her mind as she stares at the familiar sign of the FIRST NATIONAL BANK OF RICH AND EVIL: "I don't care how well recognised they are, I would never buy their stock, and could certainly *never* work there". And with that, Linda turns swiftly and hurries into her office, passing the sign that she has walked past each working day since leaving university: FEMINISTS AGAINST THE BANKING INDUSTRY.

What are judgement heuristics?

If you have read anything about human judgement, then you will likely be familiar with many of the motifs from Linda's daily routine. It illustrates a dominant view that, as we navigate the world, we – often spontaneously – make quick, easy and relatively effortless judgements. This is the realm of *judgement heuristics*, which purportedly describe how we assess value, quantity, extent, or category membership. Well-known examples include the representativeness, availability, and anchor-and-adjust heuristics – introduced and popularised though Tversky and Kahneman's seminal work on judgement under uncertainty in the 1970s – as well as the affect (Slovic, Finucane, Peters, & MacGregor, 2002), fluency (e.g., Oppenheimer, 2008), and recognition

(Goldstein & Gigerenzer, 2002) heuristics. Beyond that, several dozen judgement heuristics have been described (see Shah & Oppenheimer, 2008).

But what exactly are "heuristics"? "Heuristic" has come to mean "rule of thumb", "short-cut" or "simple strategy" in relation to some kind of decision (judgement, choice, categorisation, or inference). But this is quite different from the original (and, indeed, the dictionary) definition, which emphasises "finding out" by (for example) trial and error. In this chapter, we argue that there are three somewhat distinct classes of entity that have attracted the label "judgement heuristic". First, some judgement heuristics describe a judgement process that relies heavily on a single stimulus property or cue, such as when our *femina heuristica*, Linda, used brand name to assess product quality. Second, some judgement heuristics involve assessing an item by referring to the feelings or "metacognitions" evoked by that stimulus, such as when Linda used the ease of processing a catchy, rhyming name as a proxy for the quality of service offered by the new tailor shop. Third, some judgement heuristics describe simple algorithms that people follow when making a judgement, such as when Linda adjusted from an initial anchor of 1776 to answer the newspaper quiz, or compared her observation of sequences against her prototype of a random sequence in order to form an expectation.

In this chapter, we use this tripartite taxonomy to re-examine the literature on judgement heuristics. We evaluate what has been learned about the nature of human judgement, identify and challenge some of the assumptions that underpin or follow from this research, and highlight areas for further investigation. In doing so, we draw on some key concepts which recur in the heuristics literature, and we end our review by evaluating whether these concepts delineate heuristics as a distinct class of judgement strategy.

Key concepts associated with heuristic judgement

"Biases"

In psychology research, heuristics are inextricably linked to "bias", partly because of the title of one extremely influential paper ("Judgement under uncertainty: Heuristics and Biases"; Tversky & Kahneman, 1974) which subsequently lent its name to the influential *heuristics and biases* research programme. Biases (systematic deviations from a "rational" or expected answer) were presented as the "signature" response that allowed the researcher to diagnose (under specific conditions) that a heuristic had been used in place of a more effortful strategy. Arguably, the narrative of this research programme rapidly switched from heuristics as "quite useful" short-cuts (Tversky & Kahneman, 1974, p. 1124) to heuristics as error-prone strategies (see Lopes, 1991). The status of the biases that can be associated with judgement heuristics became a source of contention – not least in relation to what should be inferred from the fact that these biases can be made to (dis)appear by altering the form or nature of the judgement to be made (Gigerenzer, 1991, 1996).

"Effort reduction"

Also explicit in Tversky and Kahneman's (1974) original work on heuristics was the idea that they were "economical", serving to "reduce complex tasks . . . to simpler judgemental operations" (p. 1124). More recently, Shah and Oppenheimer (2008) proposed this as a definitional attribute: heuristics reduce effort, and if it is not clear how a judgement strategy or cognitive process reduces judgemental effort (relative to a weighted additive rule) then one has no business calling it a "heuristic".

"Attribute substitution"

Much of the research on heuristics posits that, when faced with a difficult judgement, people instead supply the answer to an easier question – for example, substituting a judgement of availability (how easily instances come to mind) for a probability judgement. For some researchers, this substitution of one attribute of the object of one's judgement for another is a defining feature of a heuristic (e.g., Kahneman & Frederick, 2002).

Automaticity and "natural assessment"

Another feature of heuristic judgement is that it is "quick and easy" – seemingly automatic, occurring without conscious cognitive control. Thus, heuristics are said to be "fast and frugal" (Gigerenzer, Todd & the ABC Group, 1999) or the first strategy out of the blocks in the mind's race to come up with an answer (e.g., Gilbert, Pelham, & Krull, 1988). Heuristics are often assumed to rely on information that is obtained early the judgement process; Kahneman refers to "natural assessments" that one can barely stop oneself making upon encountering a stimulus – and posits that these are the standard inputs into judgement heuristics (e.g., Kahneman, 2003; Kahneman & Frederick, 2002; Tversky & Kahneman, 1983).

The dual process framework

Work on judgement heuristics has been key to the development and application of dual system theories of cognition (see Evans, this volume). These theories come in many guises (e.g., Morewedge & Kahneman, 2010; Petty & Cacioppo, 1986; Stanovich & West, 2000, Strack & Deutsch, 2004); but the essential distinction is between an "intuitive" System 1 that uses low-effort, associative and emotive processes, and a more "rational" System 2 that uses effortful, rule-based and deliberative processes. Heuristics are assumed to belong firmly to System 1. There is a range of views as to the role of System 2 in relation to judgement heuristics – for example, after a heuristic judgement is made, System 2 may correct or over-ride the judgement when conditions permit (Gilbert & Osborne, 1989; Gilbert et al., 1988), or System 2 may compete in parallel with System 1 to provide the called-for judgement (Denes-Raj & Epstein, 1994). Whatever the specifics, one thing is clear: in the dual-system framework, System 2 *does not do* heuristics – these are the preserve of the quick-and-dirty System 1.

A tripartite taxonomy of heuristics

Heuristics have been proposed for a range of judgement tasks. However, rather than grouping heuristics by what they are proposed to do, we classify into three groups (cues, algorithms, and feelings) according to how they are said to do it.

Heuristics as stimulus properties/cues

Some "heuristics" describe strategies in which judgements are based wholly or primarily on a particular cue, which represents one component or feature of the to-be-assessed object (see Figure 25.1; note that here we are referring to information that is intrinsic to the judged item – an explicitly stated or directly observable property such as size or price – rather than to all of the experiences that the item evokes in an individual or the information that is inferred from those experiences). There is general agreement that this serves to speed the process of judgement

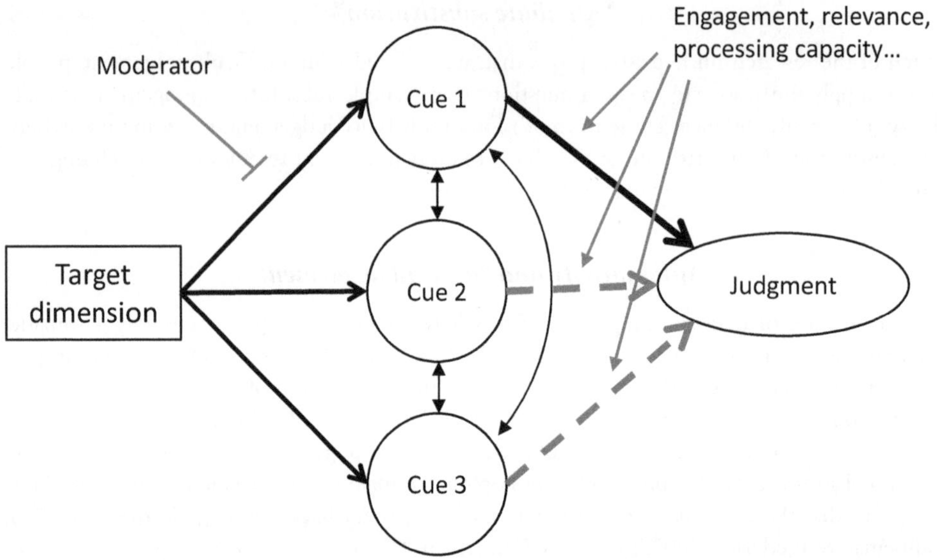

Figure 25.1 Heuristics-as-cues. Some heuristics amount to the use of a single stimulus property as the sole or primary basis for judgement, even when other cues contain useful information and/or additional moderating factors mean that the utilised cue is an invalid predictor of the target dimension. Situational factors such as task relevance may modulate the reliance on the heuristic cue

because little information is used, as per the effort reduction hypothesis; but whether this means that accuracy suffers to any meaningful degree when people prioritise speed or ease is a point of contention (Czerlinski, Gigerenzer & Goldstein, 1999).

Heuristic cues for message evaluation

One line of research that instantiates this conception of heuristic judgement comes from Chaiken and colleagues, who pursued a line of research that examined the use of "heuristic cues" in the evaluation of arguments, propositions, and messages. The heuristic cues in question are simple and salient "peripheral" or "non-content" features of the proposition or message, such as the likeability, expertise, or credibility of the message bearer (Chaiken, 1980) or the degree of approval signalled by an audience (Axsom, Yates, & Chaiken, 1987). These cues contrast with "central" or "content" cues such as the quality of the various arguments contained within the message being delivered. Key to this research are frequent demonstrations that the heuristic cues are more likely to be used when people have low motivation to evaluate the message. Accordingly, the central/content cues are less strongly associated with the judgement when motivation to evaluate the message is low.

For example, Chaiken (1980) presented messages including either two or six arguments from someone deemed either likable or not. Message involvement (i.e., relevance or consequence) was manipulated by varying whether or not participants expected to discuss the topic of the message in an upcoming task. In a test of opinion change about 10 days later, low-involvement participants (those who had not expected to discuss the message) were more influenced by the likeability of the communicator than by the number of arguments, with the reverse being true for high-involvement participants. Similarly, Forehand, Gastil, and Smith (2004) found that participants randomised to a low-motivation condition showed more support for an initiative when it was endorsed by a respected issue-relevant organisation (e.g., the American Automobile Association supporting a transport initiative) than when the endorsing organisation was a poor "fit" to the issue (e.g., the United Way supported the transport initiative). Forehand et al. therefore propose that organisational endorsement is a heuristic cue. Axsom et al. (1987) varied both the quality of arguments presented in a debate speech and the enthusiasm of the audience that could be heard responding to it. Message involvement was manipulated by stressing the relevance of the debate for the participants' locality versus presenting their task as a relatively unimportant evaluation of an issue without local impact. As predicted, argument quality influenced the opinions of high-involvement participants more than those of low-involvement participants (who also reported putting less effort into the task), while the influence of audience approval was greater for low- than for high-involvement participants.

Other heuristic cues

Heuristic cues have been examined in contexts other than message endorsement, such as consumer behaviour. For example, Maheswaran, Mackie, and Chaiken (1992) randomised participants in a product evaluation task to a low-importance condition (the evaluations were inconsequential) or a high-importance condition (participants' opinions were important for an imminent product launch in their locality). Participants in the low-importance condition were more influenced by the brand name and placed less emphasis on the product attributes in their evaluations. Similarly, Kruger, Wirtz, Van Boven, and Altermatt (2004) proposed an "effort heuristic", whereby people judge an artefact's value according to the effort required to produce it. Consistent with this, Kruger et al. found that when the amount of time taken to produce a poem or painting was stated to be higher, participants judged the quality, or $-value, of the artwork to be higher.

Evaluation of heuristics as stimulus properties/cues

Judges often make heavy use of a single, readily accessible cue. This is a reasonable strategy, because such cues are typically correlated with the to-be-judged dimension. Importantly, heuristic cues may correlate with *several* other cues that also correlate with this criterion dimension – and so the heuristic cue can serve as a proxy for these other cues. Thus, using one cue when five cues are predictive of the to-be-judged dimension does not necessarily mean that one has thrown away four-fifths of the relevant information. For example, "good" brands often are more reliable and have better features than less-known brands – therefore, brand is a reasonably proxy for *multiple* other valid cues when judging overall quality.[2] Nonetheless, relying on a single cue does almost always entail some loss of information from the judgement process.

"Cues as heuristics" instantiates many of the broad conceptions of heuristic judgement noted above. First, the cue is readily accessible and its use may be essentially pre-conscious and automatic, though it is sometimes plausible that heuristic processing *consciously* follows an accepted rule of thumb. For example, Maheswaran et al. (1992) propose that when the motivation for systematic processing is low, people might use a simple heuristic such as "if the brand name has a good reputation, then the product must be of good quality" (p. 330).

Second, single-cue heuristics are effort-reducing (Shah & Oppenheimer, 2008) because, for example, it is quicker and easier to evaluate a message based on the audible enthusiasm of the audience than by considering the merits of multiple arguments put forward by the speaker. This effort advantage comes both by virtue of the reduced amount of information to be evaluated (i.e., one cue versus many) and from the relative ease of processing the cue (e.g., assessing audience reaction does not require the conceptual challenge of evaluating an argument).

Third, Chaiken's work on heuristic cues has been particularly important to the development of the notion of two separate systems for making judgements: via systematic processing when motivated to take more, or more complex, information into account; or via heuristic/intuitive processing when accuracy motivation is low. This is discussed further in our conclusions at the end of this chapter.

There is a tendency to give each instance of this judgement process a distinct label – the "audience response heuristic", the "likeability heuristic", the "brand name heuristic", and so on (e.g., Shah & Oppenheimer, 2008). However, many of the original studies resist this, referring instead to audience response, likeability, brand name, and so forth as "heuristic cues" (Axsom et al., 1987; Chaiken, 1980; Maheswaran et al., 1992). The latter terminology emphasises that, although different cues may be used in different situations, the basic judgement strategy is the same. It also moves closer to the original, dictionary sense of "heuristic": the cue – be it the credentials of the communicator, the approval of the audience, or the reputation of the brand – points in the "right" direction with reasonable regularity. Most importantly, eschewing the definite article beloved by many in the heuristics literature implies more modest claims and more defensible conclusions: when one speaks of using "*the* X heuristic" one is tempted to assume that X is the *only* cue or feature that is used; whereas saying that "X is used as *a* heuristic cue" avoids the implication that no other cue is used.

Brannon and Brock (2001) provide a cautionary tale about the importance of detailed consideration of process and being open the possibility that a single heuristic cue is not all that is used. Previous research had pointed to a *scarcity heuristic*: targets with rare features attract extreme evaluations, such that those with rare positive features garner unusually favourable evaluations whilst those with rare negative features attract unusually unfavourable evaluations. The assumption was that scarcity acted as a heuristic cue – "this has a rare positive feature so it must be good" – prompting automatic evaluation and circumventing the use of other relevant features. Brannon and Brock considered the alternative proposition that scarcity promotes more effortful judgement. Thought listings elicited in their experiments implied that, in fact, *more* information was considered in the presence of a rare cue value. This, however, did not occur when a cognitive load manipulation was deployed: scarcity was a cue that led to *more effortful* thinking when the circumstances allowed – a possibility that previous tests had not been designed to detect.

We return to this issue of whether the amount of information can be used to categorise a judgement processes as "heuristic" in the concluding section of this chapter.

Heuristics as feelings

A second type of heuristic involves basing judgements on experiences evoked by processing the target stimulus. This can include emotional responses and "metacognitive" experiences such as the perceived speed/ease of evaluating, retrieving, or predicting stimuli (see Ackerman & Thompson, this volume). We describe some of the most prominent examples.

Availability and memory retrieval

An early metacognitive heuristic is the *availability heuristic*, where judgements of frequency or probability are based on "the ease with which instances or occurrences can be brought to mind" (Tversky & Kahneman, 1974, p. 1127). For example, one might judge the frequency of divorce by thinking about how easy it is to recall examples of married couples who have split up. This will usually work well, but can lead to bias if items are easy to retrieve for reasons other than their true frequency. For example, divorce may be over-represented in one's memory sample if the media dwells disproportionately on high-profile break-ups. Moreover, some items are more memorable than others: Tversky and Kahneman (1973) presented some participants with a list comprising the names of 19 famous men and 20 less famous women, and others with 19 famous women and 20 less famous men. Participants later recalled more of the names from the famous category, despite its lower frequency – demonstrating that famous names are easier to retrieve. Correspondingly, a separate group who compared the frequency of the male and female names judged the *rare* (but famous and easily remembered) sex to have been more frequent in the list.

That such judgements are based on the subjective experience of retrieval, rather than the number of instances recalled, has been demonstrated by Schwarz et al. (1991), who had participants list either six or 12 times when they had exhibited either assertive or unassertive behaviour, prior to estimating their overall self-assuredness. Among those who listed six examples, self-assurance judgements were higher for those who had to list assertive behaviours – as one would expect. However, listing 12 assertive behaviours actually led to *lower* assertiveness judgements than listing 12 unassertive behaviours: it was relatively difficult to think of 12 instances of either behaviour (as confirmed by self-report), leading participants to infer that the behaviour is relatively rare (Figure 25.2A). Similarly, students who were asked for 10 ways to improve a course went on to judge it more favourably than those who had only been asked for two criticisms (Fox, 2006). Haddock (2002) found the same effect when asking people their attitude towards British Prime Minister Tony Blair – but not amongst people who were high in political interest, suggesting that these participants did not solely base their judgements on subjective ease-of-retrieval. Relatedly, Stepper and Strack (1993) found that having participants maintain a frown led people who listed instances of assertive behaviours to judge themselves as less self-assured than people who listed instances of unassertive behaviour; the experience of difficulty and effort associated with the facial expression was misattributed to the ease with which relevant behaviours could be retrieved, and used as the basis for the frequency judgement.

In a separate line of work, Goldstein and Gigerenzer (2002) have proposed a ***recognition heuristic***, where inferences about quantities are based on whether or not an item is recognised. They showed American participants pairs of German city names and asked which city had the larger population; separately, the participants indicated which city names they recognised. In city pairs where only one city was recognised, participants identified the recognised city as being more populous in over 90% of cases. The heuristic is effective because the feeling of recognition is often a valid cue to other properties: for example, people usually have more exposure to events occurring in larger cities (e.g., through news media) and so are more likely to have heard of them. Indeed, Gigerenzer and Goldstein (1996) proposed that if recognition discriminates between stimuli, then it is the *sole* basis for judgement. However, Oppenheimer (2003) found that participants typically judged fictional (and hence unrecognisable) foreign-sounding cities as larger than local towns (which they recognised but knew to be small), indicating that recognition was not the sole basis for city-size judgements. Moreover, the validity of recognition as a cue to other properties is not always clear-cut. For example, while Borges, Goldstein, Ortmann, and Gigerenzer (1999) found that highly recognised shares performed better in the stock market, this effect is not consistently found (Boyd, 2001; Andersson & Rakow, 2007).

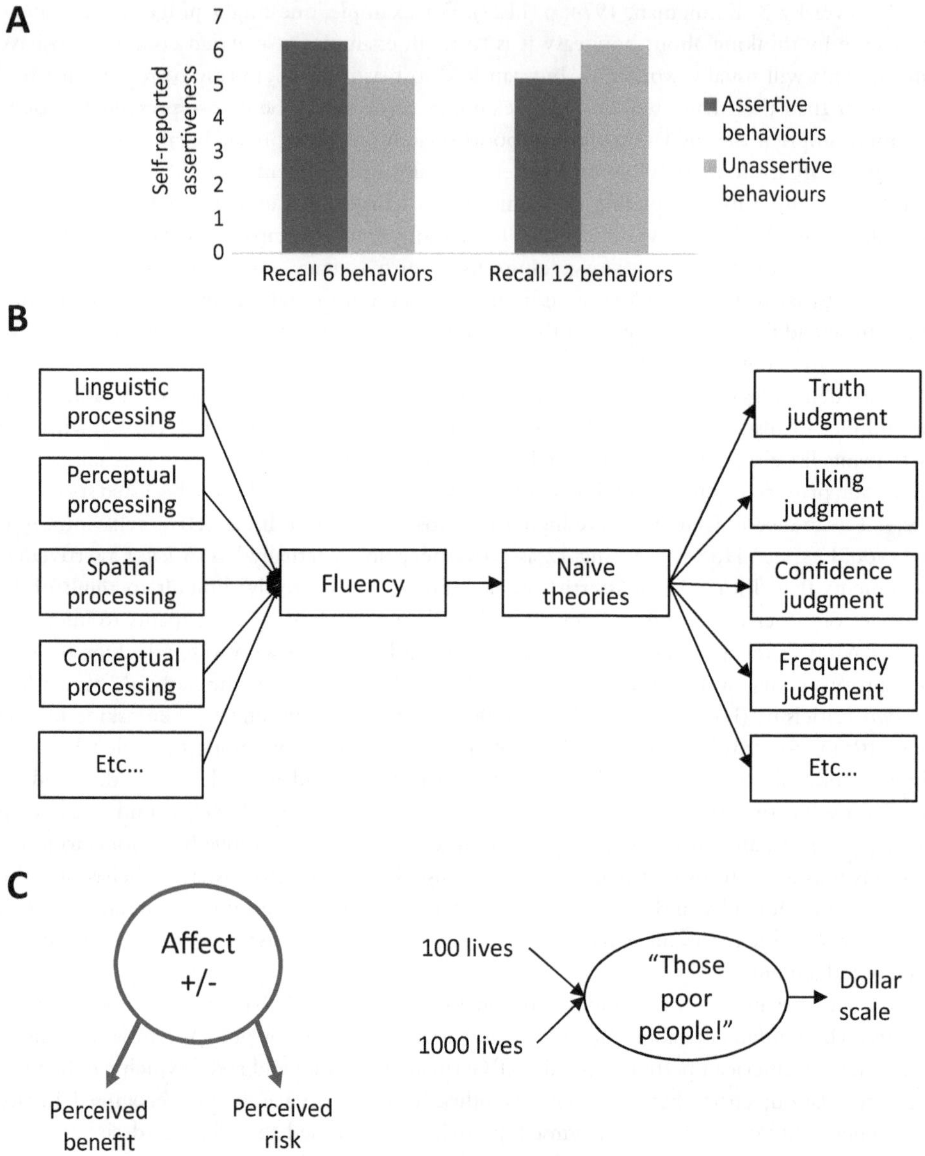

Figure 25.2 Heuristics as feelings. Panel A plots data from Schwarz et al. (1991) showing that it is the experienced ease of retrieval, rather than the number of instances retrieved, that underlies availability-based judgements. Panel B shows a more general fluency-based framework; ease of processing, determined by many factors, gives rise to a feeling of fluency which is used as the basis for diverse judgements. How the fluency is construed depends on the judge's "naïve theories" about the relationship between processing ease and target dimension (adapted from Alter & Oppenheimer, 2009). Panel C illustrates aspects of the affect heuristic: global feelings of "goodness" or "badness" are argued to underlie both risk and benefit judgements (at left), and affective reactions are relatively insensitive to magnitudes, leading to scope-neglect when deciding one's willingness-to-pay to prevent loss of life (at right).

Fluency

Availability can be construed as one instance of a broader *fluency heuristic*, according to which judgements are based on the ease of stimulus processing (Figure 25.2B). Much early work in this area concerned memory judgements. For example, Whittlesea, Jacoby, and Girard (1990) had people read masked target words out loud and then judge whether they had appeared on a preceding list. When the test word was clearer (less heavily masked), it took less time to read and was also more likely to be judged "old" – consistent with processing ease being used as the basis for recognition judgements. Clearer items are also judged to have been presented more recently and for longer (Whittlesea, 1993). Similarly, words which have recently been studied are easier to identify and are judged to have longer exposures in a subsequent duration-discrimination task (Witherspoon & Allan, 1985), and masked-priming of a test item increases the probability that it will be falsely recognised as having been presented on a previous list (Jacoby & Whitehouse, 1989).

Fluency has been invoked as the basis for judgements in a wide variety of domains, including truth, liking, confidence, and value (Alter & Oppenheimer, 2009). As illustrative examples: rhyming aphorisms such as "Woes unite foes" were judged to be truer descriptions of the human condition than non-rhyming aphorisms such as "Good intentions excuse ill deeds", and eliminating the rhyming difference by changing the last word of each saying eliminated the effect (McGlone & Tofighbakhsh, 2000); fictional stocks with unpronounceable names were predicted to perform less well than those with fluent names, a pattern replicated in the prices of real shares with pronounceable and unpronounceable ticker codes listed on the New York Stock Exchange (Alter & Oppenheimer, 2006); increasing the exposure duration of pictures led people both to report liking them more and to elevated electro-muscular activity associated with smiling (Winkielman & Cacioppo, 2001); and people were more confident in their predictions of NFL games when the questionnaire was printed in an easy-to-read typeface (Simmons & Nelson, 2006). As with availability, it has been argued that the experience of ease can come from bodily cues associated with effort (Alter, Oppenheimer, Epley, & Eyre, 2007).

Affect

Perhaps the most "feeling-based" of all judgement strategies is the *affect heuristic*, according to which judgements are based on the global affective response to an item (Slovic et al., 2002). Of course, emotions colour virtually every kind of judgement, but the affect heuristic has particularly been addressed to judgements of risk and value (Figure 25.2C).

In early studies, participants rated both how risky and how beneficial a range of different items/activities are (e.g., nuclear power, handguns, food colourings). Judgements of these two dimensions were negatively correlated: participants who judged a given item as high-risk also judged it low-benefit, and vice versa, and this correlation was more pronounced for items that elicited strong negative affective evaluations (e.g., Alhakami & Slovic, 1994). Similarly, in a study of finance students, Ganzach (2000) found that unfamiliar stocks which elicited a positive global reaction (measured by participants' enthusiasm for investing in the stock) were judged to have high return and low risk, whereas those with a negative global reaction were judged high-risk and low-return. (In contrast, risk and return are positively – not negatively – correlated in the stock market.) This suggests that an overall feeling about the asset served as the basis for both risk and benefit judgements (Slovic et al., 2002). In keeping with this, manipulating judgements for one dimension elicits complementary shifts in judgements of the other dimension: providing information about why nuclear power is a low-risk fuel source, for example, boosted its perceived benefits as well as lowering its apparent riskiness (Finucane et al., 2000).

The affect heuristic has been used to explain why judgements are often relatively insensitive to magnitudes (*scope neglect*). For example, people were willing to pay much more to save four pandas than one panda when the animals were represented by dots, but not when they were represented by photographs. This is presumably because the emotional response to the image of one cute-but-imperilled panda is similar to that evoked by four (Hsee & Rottenstreich, 2004). Similarly, affect-rich outcomes reduce people's sensitivity to probability: participants' willingness to pay to avoid the risk of a dread-inducing electric shock was relatively insensitive to the probability of the shock, whereas payments to avoid the risk of losing $20 were highly sensitive to the magnitude of the potential loss (Rottenstreich & Hsee, 2001). The robustness of these effects is unclear, however; Gong and Baron (2011), for example, found that participants were *more* sensitive to the magnitude of outcomes that were presented in an emotional format – the opposite of Hsee and Rottenstreich's result.

Affect-based judgement may also explain why people are particularly sensitive to proportions: it is hard to establish the value of, say, 4,500 lives in isolation, but high proportions feel "good" (Slovic et al., 2002). Correspondingly, people preferred an aid program that saves 4,500 out of 11,000 lives to one which saves 4,500 out of 250,000 lives (Fetherstonhaugh, Slovic, Johnson, & Friedrich, 1997), and an airport-safety measure that would save "150 lives" gathered less support than one which would save "98% of 150 lives" (Slovic & Peters, 2006). However, Hsee and colleagues have developed a more general framework, general evaluability theory, which de-emphasises affect and offers a wide-ranging treatment of the conditions under which people are sensitive to magnitudes (Hsee & Zhang, 2010).

More specific affect-based strategies have also been proposed, including the *warm glow* heuristic (where affective evaluations underlie familiarity judgements; Monin, 2003) and the *outrage heuristic* (where the moral outrage evoked by a crime underlies judgements of damages and compensation; Kahneman & Frederick, 2002). All of these heuristics connect to broader frameworks which emphasise feelings as a source of information during judgements and decisions (e.g., Clore & Huntsinger, 2007; Pham, 1998; Schwarz, 2012).

Evaluation of heuristics as feelings

These heuristics potentially apply to a far wider range of judgements than those which emphasise the use of a particular piece of stimulus-information. They also relate to the broad approaches to heuristic judgement outlined above: they involve substituting one attribute for another (e.g., processing-ease for truth); they are effort-reducing, because affect and experience-ease arise quickly and with little or no explicit computation (e.g., Oppenheimer, 2008; Zajonc, 1980); and they can be over-ruled when there is reason to discount the experiential cue, consistent with a two-system model. For example, when participants are informed that stimulus clarity will vary, they no longer use this as the basis for recognition judgements (Whittlesea et al., 1990). Likewise, names like "Cheney" are judged less common than names like "Callaway", despite being both higher in frequency and readily available from media references; people attribute the availability of "Cheney" to the fame of the former U.S. vice-president, and discount this as a cue to name frequency (Oppenheimer, 2004). Similarly, finance students seem not to base their risk-and-benefit judgements on global affect when they are familiar with the stocks (Ganzach, 2000), and the scope-neglect that accompanies affective responses can be counteracted by encouraging computation (e.g., Hsee & Rottenstreich, 2004; Hsee et al., 2013).

Nonetheless, there are several potential problems for experiential heuristics. First, some studies of fluency manipulations have failed to produce replicable results (e.g., Meyer et al., 2015; Open Science Collaboration, 2015; Thompson et al., 2013), suggesting small, fragile, and/or non-existent effects; and, more generally, fluency and affect are influenced by many variables and in turn can affect a huge variety of judgement domains, but this richness makes it difficult to derive clear expectations. Will an easy-to-read-typeface make an issue seem more or less important, for example? This ambiguity is especially pronounced in light of the evidence that people sometimes discount experiential cues, or even over-compensate (Oppenheimer, 2004), so the same fluency manipulation can predict positive, negative, and null effects, depending on auxiliary assumptions about how the fluency will be construed. Similarly, emotions are more complex than the simple good-bad dimension of the affect heuristic (Kahneman & Frederick, 2002): sadness, anger, anxiety, and fear are all negative emotions, but the first two induce risk-seeking and the latter induce risk-avoidance, for example (Kugler et al., 2010; Raghunathan & Pham, 1999). This may explain why the effects of emotion on scope sensitivity are not clear-cut (Gong & Baron, 2011; Hsee & Rottenstreich, 2004). Careful, explicit theorising and rigorous assumption-testing are clearly required.

Second, we must seek independent measures of experience. Fluency can be measured by processing time (Whittlesea et al., 1990), but many researchers use subjective report (e.g., "How easy was it to think of 12 examples of assertive behaviour?"). Such judgements may themselves be based on a cue or heuristic rather than directly tapping subjective experience (e.g., "Twelve is quite a big number, so I must have found it quite hard to think of 12 examples."). Some studies do not independently assess experience, which opens the door to circular reasoning (e.g., ". . . participants judged this item positively because it is affect rich . . . we know it is affect rich because participants judge it positively"; see also the critique by Gigerenzer [1996] of "explanation by re-description" in the heuristics literature). This is especially true of affect-based judgement, where very few studies have measured the characteristic physiological signatures of positive and negative emotions.

Finally, it is important to establish how the heuristics are related. Is recognition a subset of availability, and availability a subset of fluency?; or is mere recognition qualitatively different to ease-of-retrieval, which is in turn importantly different from ease-of-processing? And given that fluent stimuli are also judged to be more pleasant (e.g., see Topolinski, this volume), can we integrate fluency and affect in a common framework?

Heuristics as algorithms

A third approach to heuristic judgement focuses on the sequence of mental operations that lead to a response. The availability heuristic could be cast in algorithmic terms by specifying how people decide what would count as a relevant instance, probe memory for such instances, assess the number/ease of instance retrieval, decide when to terminate the search, and so on. However, the focus on subjective feeling means that there is little emphasis on these operations. Better examples of the algorithmic approach are provided by the ***representativeness*** heuristic and, in particular, by the ***anchor-and-adjust*** heuristic – both of which we discuss here. (Many heuristics for choice and inference also have this algorithmic character, and these are discussed by Hoffrage, Hafenbrädl, & Marewski, this volume).

Representativeness

As originally conceived, the representativeness heuristic involves basing probability judgements on "an assessment of the degree of correspondence between a sample and a population, an instance and a category, an act and an actor or, more generally, between an outcome and a model" (Tversky & Kahneman, 1983, p. 295). For example, you might judge the probability that a new acquaintance has tried internet dating by assessing how similar they are to your mental representation of the category "internet daters". In a famous illustration, participants read a description of "Tom W.", who has "a need for order . . . a strong drive for competence . . . and little sympathy for other people" (Kahneman & Tversky, 1973). Participants then either ranked nine academic disciplines according to how likely it is that Tom is currently a graduate student in that subject, or according to how similar Tom is to the typical graduate student in that field. The judgements were tightly positively correlated, consistent with probability judgements being based on similarity judgements.

It would be optimal to combine information about Tom with background information about the base rates for each discipline; if art history is very popular, it increases the chances that Tom is an art historian. However, when a separate group estimated the proportion of students in each discipline, these base rates did *not* positively predict the probability judgements – suggesting that the representativeness heuristic led to *base rate neglect*. Similarity-based judgements also lead to the *conjunction fallacy*: people typically judge it more likely that Linda, who as a student "was deeply concerned with issues of discrimination and social justice", is more likely to be a feminist bank teller than just a bank teller – presumably because the description of Linda is representative of the stereotype of an active feminist and not representative of a bank teller – despite the fact that feminist bank tellers are a subset of bank tellers (Tversky & Kahneman, 1983). Likewise, similarity-based probability judgements lead people to underutilise sample size (Koehler, 1996).

Later work has broadened the scope of this heuristic, and emphasised that it involves distinct mental operations. Specifically, Kahneman and Frederick (2002) suggest a two-step algorithm in which people (1) select or construct a prototype for the category (e.g., bank tellers), and (2) use the similarity between the target and that prototype as the basis for their judgement. They suggest that the first of these steps constitutes a "prototype heuristic" and could form the first stage in many other types of judgement. For example, people might decide how much they are willing to pay to save 10,000 seabirds from drowning in oil by (1) retrieving a prototype of a single seabird drenched in oil, and (2) mapping their affective reaction to this image onto a dollar scale – explaining why people's willingness to pay is almost completely insensitive to the number of birds at risk (Desvousges et al., 1993).

This theorising represents a nascent specification of the heuristic as a sequence of cognitive operations, one that could be fleshed out by considering whether the first stage really involves establishing a single prototype or whether people retrieve a set of exemplars, how these items are chosen or constructed, and how people then compute the similarity between the prototype/exemplars and the target item (e.g., Dougherty, Gettys, & Ogden, 1999).

Anchor-and-adjust

A more detailed algorithm has been developed for the *anchor-and-adjust* heuristic. Here, judgement involves adjusting an initial "anchor" value until an acceptable estimate is found (Jacowitz & Kahneman, 1995; Tversky & Kahneman, 1974). Often, the anchor will be a relevant, known value: if you are asked when George Washington was elected president, you might recall that the U.S. declared independence in 1776 and adjust upwards by a few years to produce your estimate. When Epley and Gilovich (2001) gave people this kind of question, most (about 74%) said that they thought of the relevant anchor and adjusted from there.

People typically adjust insufficiently, so estimates are biased towards the anchor, and the willingness or ability to keep adjusting can influence how far people's final estimates are from the anchor: incentives for accuracy and warnings about the dangers of insufficient adjustment both shift judgements farther from the anchor (Epley & Gilovich, 2005), and participants who are drunk, under working memory load, or low in need-for-cognition produce judgements which are closer to the starting point than those of other participants (Epley & Gilovich, 2006).

These studies all used questions for which there was a "natural" reference point/anchor. A different type of anchoring task comes with the so-called ***standard anchoring paradigm*** (SAP). Here, participants are first asked a comparative question which includes the anchor, such as "Is the population of Chicago more or less than 200,000?" before providing an absolute estimate ("What is the population of Chicago?"). Absolute judgements are biased towards the numerical anchor provided in the comparative question, even when the anchors are manifestly uninformative. Legal professionals gave shorter sentences for a fictional rapist after considering a prosecutor's demand of three months than after a demand of nine months, even when that demand was produced by rolling dice in front of the participant (Englich, Mussweiler, & Strack, 2006).

Tversky and Kahneman (1974) used the SAP as a demonstration of the adjustment heuristic, but subsequent research suggests that a different process is often at work: participants very rarely report using an adjustment strategy, and the anchoring bias is largely unaffected by incentives, warnings, sobriety, capacity for effortful thought, and so on (Epley & Gilovich, 2001, 2004, 2005). Rather, Mussweiler and colleagues have developed a selective accessibility model for this kind of judgement (e.g., Mussweiler & Strack, 1999; see also Chapman & Johnson, 1999, 2002); the algorithm is illustrated in Figure 25.3A. First, one decides whether the anchor is plausible or implausible by assessing whether it lies within the range of values covered by the general category of the target: 90 is a plausible value for the age at which Nelson Mandela died because it is below the upper limit of ages for the category "humans". If the anchor is plausible, formulate a hypothesis about the relationship between the anchor and the target; by default this will be that the target value is equal to the anchor, but this can be changed by the wording of the question or by priming people to focus on dissimilarities (Mussweiler, 2002). Then undertake a hypothesis-consistent testing strategy by selectively searching memory for information consistent with the hypothesis – for example, by remembering that Nelson Mandela survived several decades in prison, and so on. This anchor-consistent information will be highly accessible in the subsequent absolute estimate, causing judgements to assimilate towards the anchor.

If the anchor is implausible, the decision process follows a different branch: the comparative question can be answered quickly – 190 years is above the category limit for human ages, so there is no need to engage in time-consuming hypothesis-consistent testing – but when subsequently producing their absolute estimate, judges must generate item-specific information for the first time. Mussweiler and Strack (2001) suggest that at this point participants test the hypothesis that the target is equal to the upper limit of the relevant category (say 120 in the case of human ages), and that the resulting boost in selective accessibility biases judgements towards the anchor, as before (cf. Chapman & Johnson, 1994).

Consistent with this account, lexical decision tasks show that answering the comparative question increases the accessibility of anchor-consistent words (e.g., the names of high-end cars were identified more rapidly than cheap ones after participants decided whether the average price of a new car is more or less than 40,000 DM, but the reverse was true when the anchor was 20,000 DM.) Similarly, Mussweiler and colleagues have demonstrated (1) that response times in comparative and absolute tasks depend on anchor plausibility in the manner predicted by the model, (2) that absolute estimates depend on the wording of the comparative question (that is, on the hypothesis tested during the comparative stage and the information that is activated as a result), and (3) that considering reasons why the anchor might be too low/high can overcome the normal anchoring bias by counteracting the usual accessibility effect (e.g., Mussweiler & Strack, 1999).

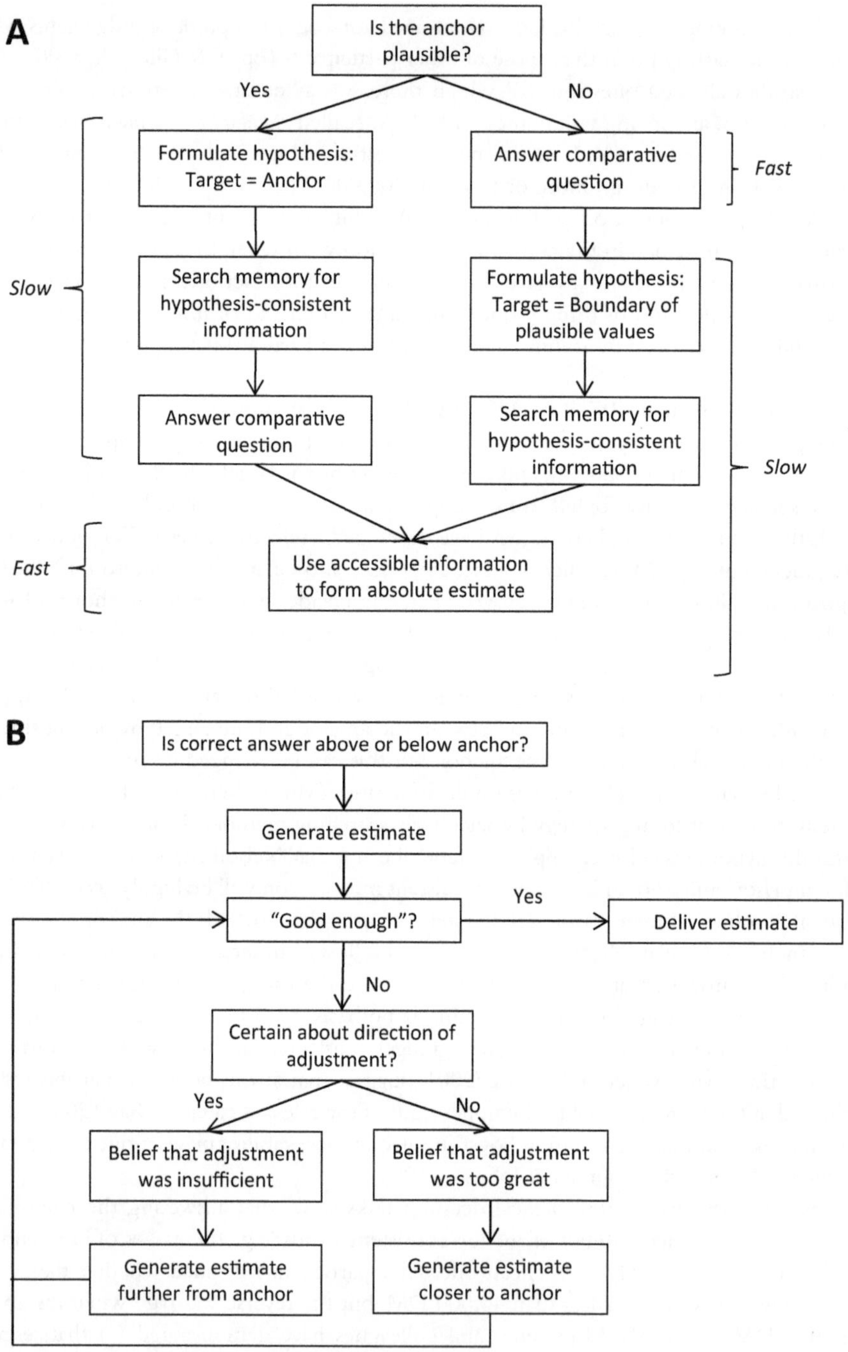

Figure 25.3 Algorithmic descriptions of anchoring. The top panel, A, shows the selective accessibility model developed by Mussweiler and Strack (2001); the bottom panel, B, shows the updated anchor-and-adjust heuristic proposed by Simmons et al. (2010). (Adapted from Simmons et al., 2010.)

Epley and Gilovich (2001) have argued that the selective accessibility process applies when anchors are externally provided (as in the SAP) and that anchor-and-adjust is used when anchors are internally generated. However, Simmons, Leboeuf, and Nelson (2010) suggest that the question is whether people know the directional relation between the anchor and the target. Their participants estimated quantities such as the length of the Mississippi River after first considering a low or high anchor. One condition used the standard anchoring paradigm (e.g., "Is the length of the Mississippi River more or less than 1,200/3,500 miles"?); here giving people an accuracy incentive did not change the distance between their final estimates and the anchor values. However, when participants were explicitly told the relationship between the anchor and the target ("It is true that the length of the Mississippi River is more than 1,200 miles"), accuracy incentives led to judgements that were farther from the anchor. Simmons et al. argue that participants used an anchor-and-adjust strategy even though the anchor was externally provided, but that people often do not know which direction to adjust when plausible-but-arbitrary anchors are provided. Relatedly, Janiszewski and Uy (2008) had people estimate the wholesale price of a plasma TV retailing at or around $5,000; when the retail price was listed more precisely ($4,998 or $5,012 rather than $5,000) the wholesale price estimates were closer to the anchor, suggesting that the precision of the anchor sets the "units" for the adjustment process.

Simmons et al. (2010) have integrated these results into an anchor-and-adjust algorithm (Figure 25.3B). They acknowledge that this set of operations likely coexists/interacts with other processes, including selective accessibility. In addition, anchors influence the perceived magnitude of candidate responses (Frederick & Mochon, 2011), especially when people use their own previous estimates as the basis for subsequent judgements (Mochon & Frederick, 2013; Matthews & Stewart, 2009). Moreover, exposure even to irrelevant numbers in the environment may "prime" certain responses (e.g., Critcher & Gilovich, 2008), although the effects are weak (Brewer & Chapman, 2002; Matthews, 2011). It might be possible to develop an algorithmic account of how these various processes operate in series and in parallel.

Evaluation of heuristics as algorithms

Representativeness has been invoked for an impressive array of tasks and findings, including base-rate neglect, the conjunction fallacy, insensitivity to sample size, and scope neglect. It is argued to involve substituting an accessible dimension (similarity) to reduce the effort associated with judgement (Kahneman & Frederick, 2002; Shah & Oppenheimer, 2008), giving rise to an automatic, intuitive judgement that is subject to various biases – in contrast to more deliberative calculations such as formal Bayesian integration of base rates and likelihoods. As such, representativeness fits within the broader accounts of heuristic judgement discussed at the start of this chapter.

There are shortcomings, however. First, the breadth of applications means that it is not always clear that a common mechanism is at work; the original definition of the representativeness heuristic invoked an array of mechanisms (see the definitional quotation, above). Second, researchers do not always seek independent evidence that people are using a similarity-assessment as the basis for their judgements, and some researchers question the prevalence of the biases that are taken as signatures of similarity-based judgements (Gigerenzer, 1991; Koehler, 1996). Finally, although we have listed representativeness as a putative example of a heuristic-as-algorithm, the precise mental operations involved in this judgement strategy remain to be established.

In contrast, studies of anchoring have greatly clarified the sequence of operations when people use anchor values when forming their judgements. However, these advances mean that it is not clear whether the processes constitute "heuristics" as the term is usually understood; indeed,

Mussweiler does not refer to his selective accessibility model as a heuristic, and Kahneman now acknowledges that anchoring is quite different from availability or representativeness, alongside which it was introduced (Kahneman, 2011; Kahneman & Frederick, 2002). The algorithms described above do not involve attribute substitution or natural assessment, and require deliberation rather than automatic processing. Adjusting insufficiently can be seen as effort-reducing, but as noted it can also reflect uncertainty about the direction of adjustment. More generally, bias towards the anchor may often represent rational integration of the anchor value with a prior distribution of beliefs about the target value. Indeed, despite researchers' best efforts, participants do not view even arbitrary anchors as irrelevant in the context of experimental studies of anchoring (e.g., Brewer & Chapman, 2002; Chapman & Johnson, 1999).

Conclusion: are judgement heuristics a distinct kind of judgement?

We began by identifying several themes that are emphasised in discussions of judgement heuristics: bias, effort reduction, attribute substitution, automaticity, and dual-process accounts. It is clear from our survey that different heuristics put different emphasis on these principles, with no single defining feature. Rather, like Wittgenstein's analysis of the concept of a "game", judgement heuristics form a cluster, sharing various properties to varying degrees. One observation to emerge from our survey is that many heuristics share an emphasis on the generalisation of past experiences: cues like brand name, subjective experiences like ease-of-processing, and numeric anchors, all usually predict the target quantity. However, "doing what usually works well" hardly demarks heuristics as something distinctive, so we end with two questions that explore whether heuristic judgement really is distinct from other kinds of judgement.

When people use judgement heuristics, is this all that they use to make a judgement?

Showing that people use cue X, feeling Y, or operation Z does not itself establish that they use *only* X, Y, or Z. There are compelling instances of essentially "pure" attribute substitution, as when judgements of representativeness from one participant group correlate near perfectly with probability estimates from other participants (Kahneman & Tversky, 1973), but such demonstrations are rare. For example, Kahneman and Frederick (2002) found that participants' judgements for the outrage felt at a particular crime aligned well with the (hypothetical) dollar amount of damages awarded by other participants – supporting the use of an "outrage heuristic". However, the correlation between outrage and damages was not perfect ($r \approx .8$), leaving room for other cues (e.g., the size of the offending firm, the degree of harm caused) to explain additional variance in the damages assessments. And in many studies, there is little attempt to uncover, or to emphasise, the variance in judgement left unexplained by a particular heuristic cue.

Similarly, showing an effect in the direction predicted by a particular algorithm is, perhaps too often, accepted as evidence that people have followed the algorithm (precisely), without giving proper consideration to the fact that there is some variance in judgement which the algorithm cannot explain. For example, one of the "signatures" of the representativeness heuristic is the neglect of base rate information about the probability of an event for the entire reference class (Kahneman & Tversky, 1973). However, Koehler's (1996) review of this literature shows that base rates often predict judgements even when representativeness is implicated – clarifying that "base rate neglect" might better be termed "a base rate effect" wherein judgements using representativeness encourage underweighting, but not complete disregard, of base-rate information.

In short, the judgement strategies that have been labelled "heuristic" usually reflect *greater use* of easily processed information (Figure 25.1), rather than strictly delineating cues/algorithms that are used from those that are not (e.g., Axsom et al., 1987; Chaiken, 1980; Maheswaran et al., 1992). This leads to our second summary question.

Does heuristic judgement use different processes *than other forms of judgement?*

This question goes to the heart of the dual process accounts (e.g., Evans, this volume) which have framed much of the work on judgement heuristics. If judgement heuristics simply amount to heavy reliance on a particular cue – whether a cue peripheral to a message, a sensation such as fluency, or an anchor value – this does not necessarily require a qualitatively different process. Likewise, because all information processing is restricted by the available width of the processing channels (Miller, 1956), simply showing that judgements align more closely with the value of the heuristic cue when cognitive capacity is restricted (e.g., Gilbert & Osborne, 1989; Gilbert et al., 1988; Slovic et al., 2002), or when the motivation for effortful thinking is low (e.g., Axsom et al., 1987; Chaiken, 1980) is not necessarily diagnostic of a different *kind* of cognitive operation. To be sure, metacognitive or affective signals may constitute a different "type" of cue, but this does not imply that familiarity, fluency, availability, and so on are processed and used differently from other cues such as argument quality, base rates, or appearance, or that we must invoke a distinct "system". Increased speed, reduced effort, and automaticity are all commonly invoked as distinguishing characteristics of the processing of heuristic cues – but these are measured on continua, so it will always be up to the researcher to decide how quick, easy, and automatic is sufficient to count as "heuristic".

Similarly, once an algorithm is specified, the "closer-to-rational" version is often just an extension of that algorithm that does not require anything other than more of the same. For example, anchor-and-adjustment can be improved by adjusting on more occasions (on the basis of additional information). When a heuristic cue is discounted (e.g., Oppenheimer, 2004), or a heuristic algorithm is over-ridden (e.g., Mussweiler & Strack, 1999), why should we not think of this as an augmented version of the heuristic, or the application of a second heuristic, rather than the intervention of a second system?

Some resolution to these issues may lie in a better specification of judgement heuristics. Researchers should state not only what each heuristic does, but (in the spirit of Karl Popper) specify precisely what it rules out (see Glöckner & Betsch, 2011). Likewise, we must specify (and test for) the constituent processes (memory, attention, computation) of a heuristic as clearly as possible, and also define its relation to other parts of the judgement process – thereby forcing us to think carefully about whether we need to posit separable processes for heuristic judgement and other forms of judgement. In this vein, it will be interesting to see whether the next edition of this Handbook simply drops "heuristic" from this chapter title.

Notes

1 Author note: both authors contributed equally to this review chapter; the order of authorship is arbitrary.
2 This observation has a long heritage in the study of perceptual judgements for physical quantities. For example, Brunswik (1943) noted that there are 10 or more cues to depth, some of which may be absent on a given occasion. However, it is not necessary to have all cues present in order to judge depth because they correlate with one another: by definition, they all correlate with actual differences in depth.

References

Alhakami, A. S., & Slovic, P. (1994). A psychological study of the inverse relationship between perceived risk and perceived benefit. *Risk Analysis, 14*, 1085–1096.

Alter, A. L., & Oppenheimer, D. M. (2006). Predicting short-term stock fluctuations by using processing fluency. *Proceedings of the National Academy of Science, 103*, 9369–9372.

Alter, A. L., & Oppenheimer, D. M. (2009). Uniting the tribes of fluency to form a metacognitive nation. *Personality and Social Psychology Review, 13*(3), 219–235.

Alter, A. L., Oppenheimer, D. M., Epley, N., & Eyre, R. N. (2007). Overcoming intuition: Metacognitive difficulty activates analytic reasoning. *Journal of Experimental Psychology: General, 136*, 569–576.

Andersson, P., & Rakow, T. (2007). Now you see it now you don't: The effectiveness of the recognition heuristic for selecting stocks. *Judgment and Decision Making, 2*(1), 29–39.

Axsom, D., Yates, S., & Chaiken, S. (1987). Audience response as a heuristic cue in persuasion. *Journal of Personality and Social Psychology, 53*(1), 30–40.

Borges, B., Goldstein, D. G., Ortmann, A., & Gigerenzer, G. (1999). Can ignorance beat the stock market? In G. Gigerenzer, P. M. Todd, & The-ABC-Research-Group (Eds.), *Simple heuristics that make us smart.* New York: Oxford University Press.

Boyd, M. (2001). On ignorance, intuition, and investing: A bear market test of the recognition heuristic. *Journal of Psychology and Financial Markets, 2*, 150–156.

Brannon, L. A., & Brock, T. C. (2001). Scarcity claims elicit extreme responding to persuasive messages: Role of cognitive elaboration. *Personality and Social Psychology Bulletin, 27*(3), 365–375.

Brewer, N. T., & Chapman, G. B. (2002). The fragile basic anchoring effect. *Journal of Behavioral Decision Making, 15*, 65–77.

Brunswik, E. (1943). Organismic achievement and environmental probability. *Psychological Review, 50*, 255–272.

Chaiken, S. (1980). Heuristic versus systematic information processing and the use of source versus message cues in persuasion. *Journal of Personality and Social Psychology, 39*(5), 752–766.

Chapman, G. B., & Johnson, E. J. (1994). The limits of anchoring. *Journal of Behavioral Decision Making,* 7(4), 223–242.

Chapman, G. B., & Johnson, E. J. (1999). Anchoring, activation, and the construction of values. *Organizational Behavior and Human Decision Processes, 79*(2), 115–153.

Chapman, G. B., & Johnson, E. J. (2002). Incorporating the irrelevant: Anchors in judgments of belief and value. In T. Gilovich, D. Griffin, & D. Kahneman (Eds). *Heuristics and Biases: The psychology of intuitive judgment.* Cambridge: Cambridge University Press.

Clore, G. L., & Huntsinger, J. R. (2007). How emotions inform judgment and regulate thought. *Trends in Cognitive Science, 11*(9), 393–399.

Critcher, C. R., & Gilovich, T. (2008). Incidental environmental anchors. *Journal of Behavioral Decision Making, 21*, 241–251.

Czerlinski, J., Gigerenzer, G., & Goldstein, D. G. (1999). How good are simple heuristics? In G. Gigerenzer, P. M. Todd, & The ABC Research Group (Eds.), *Simple heuristics that make us smart* (pp. 97–118). New York: Oxford University Press.

Denes-Raj, V., & Epstein, S. (1994). Conflict between intuitive and rational processing: When people behave against their better judgment. *Journal of Personality and Social Psychology, 66*, 819–829.

Desvousges, W. H., Reed Johnson, F., Dunford, R. W., Nicole Wilson, K., & Boyle, K. J. (1993). Measuring resource damages with contingent valuation: Tests of validity and reliability. In J. A. Hausman (Ed.), *Contingent valuation: A critical assessment.* (pp. 91–164). Bingley, UK: Emerald Group Publishing Limited.

Dougherty, M. R. P., Gettys, C. F., & Ogden, E. E. (1999). MINERVA-DM: A memory processes model for judgments of likelihood. *Psychological Review, 106*(1), 180–209.

Englich, B., Mussweiler, T., & Strack, F. (2006). Playing dice with criminal sentences: the influence of irrelevant anchors on experts' judicial decision making. *Personality and Social Psychology Bulletin, 32*(2), 188–200.

Epley, N., & Gilovich, T. (2001). Putting adjustment back in the anchoring and adjustment heuristic: Differential processing of self-generated and experimenter-provided anchors. *Psychological Science, 12*(5), 391–396.

Epley, N., & Gilovich, T. (2004). Are adjustments insufficient? *Personality and Social Psychology Bulletin, 30*, 447–460.

Epley, N., & Gilovich, T. (2005). When effortful thinking influences judgmental anchoring: Differential effects of forewarning and incentives on self-generated and externally provided anchors. *Journal of Behavioral Decision Making, 18*, 199–212.
Epley, N., & Gilovich, T. (2006). The anchoring-and-adjustment heuristic: Why the adjustments are insufficient. *Psychological Science, 17*, 311–318.
Fetherstonhaugh, D., Slovic, P., Johnson, S. M., & Friedrich, J. (1997). Insensitivity to the value of human life: A study of psychophysical numbing. *Journal of Risk and Uncertainty, 14*, 283–300.
Finucane, M. L., Alhakami, A., Slovic, P., & Johnson, S. M. (2000). The affect heuristic in judgments of risk and benefits. *Journal of Behavioral Decision Making, 13*, 1–17.
Forehand, M., Gastil, J., & Smith, M. A. (2004). Endorsements as voting cues: Heuristic and systematic processing in initiative elections. *Journal of Applied Social Psychology, 34*(11), 2215–2233.
Fox, C. R. (2006). The availability heuristic in the classroom: How soliciting more criticism can boost your course ratings. *Judgment and Decision Making, 1*(1), 86–90.
Frederick, S. W., & Mochon, D. (2011). A scale distortion theory of anchoring. *Journal of Experimental Psychology: General, 141*(1), 124–133.
Ganzach, Y. (2000). Judging risk and return of financial assets. *Organizational Behavior and Human Decision Processes, 83*, 353–370.
Gigerenzer, G. (1991). How to make cognitive illusions disappear: Beyond "heuristics and biases". *European Review of Social Psychology, 2*, 83–115.
Gigerenzer, G. (1996). On narrow norms and vague heuristics: A reply to Kahneman and Tversky (1996). *Psychological Review, 103*, 592–596.
Gigerenzer, G., & Goldstein, D. G. (1996). Reasoning the fast and frugal way: Models of bounded rationality. *Psychological Review, 103*(4), 650–669.
Gigerenzer, G., Todd, P. M., & the ABC Research Group (Eds.). (1999). *Simple heuristics that make us smart*. New York: Oxford University Press.
Gilbert, D. T., & Osborne, R. E. (1989). Thinking backwards: Some curable and incurable consequences of cognitive busyness. *Journal of Personality and Social Psychology, 57*, 940–949.
Gilbert, D. T., Pelham, B. W., & Krull, D. S. (1988). On cognitive busyness: When person perceivers meet persons perceived. *Journal of Personality and Social Psychology, 54*, 733–740.
Glöckner, A., & Betsch, T. (2011). The empirical content of theories in judgment and decision making: Shortcomings and remedies. *Judgment and Decision Making, 6*(8), 711–721.
Goldstein, D. G., & Gigerenzer, G. (2002). Models of ecological rationality: The recognition heuristic. *Psychological Review, 109*(1), 75–90.
Gong, M., & Baron, J. (2011). The generality of the emotion effect on magnitude sensitivity. *Journal of Economic Psychology, 32*, 17–24.
Haddock, G. (2002). It's easy to like or dislike Tony Blair: Accessibility experiences and the favourability of attitude judgments. *British Journal of Psychology, 93*, 257–267.
Hsee, C. K., & Rottenstreich, Y. (2004). Music, pandas, and muggers: On the affective psychology of value. *Journal of Experimental Psychology: General, 133*, 23–30.
Hsee, C. K., & Zhang, J. (2010). General evaluability theory. *Perspectives on Psychological Science, 5*(4), 343–355.
Hsee, C. K., Zhang, J., Zoe, Y. L., & Xu, F. (2013). Unit asking: A method to boost donations and beyond. *Psychological Science, 24*(9), 1801–1808.
Jacoby, L. L., & Whitehouse, K. (1989). An illusion of memory: False recognition influenced by unconscious perception. *Journal of Experimental Psychology: General, 118*(2), 126–135.
Jacowitz, K. E., & Kahneman, D. (1995). Measures of anchoring in estimation tasks. *Personality and Social Psychology Bulletin, 21*(11), 1161–1166.
Janiszewski, C., & Uy, D. (2008). Precision of the anchor influences the amount of adjustment. *Psychological Science, 19*, 121–127.
Kahneman, D. (2003). A perspective on judgment and choice: Mapping bounded rationality. *American Psychologist, 58*, 697–720.
Kahneman, D. (2011). *Thinking, fast and slow*. London: Allen Lane.
Kahneman, D., & Frederick, S. (2002). Representativeness revisited: Attribute substitution in intuitive judgment. In T. Gilovich, D. Griffin, & D. Kahneman (Eds.), *Heuristics and biases: The psychology of intuitive judgment*. Cambridge: Cambridge University Press.
Kahneman, D., & Tversky, A. (1973). On the psychology of prediction. *Psychological Review, 80*, 237–251.
Koehler, J. J. (1996). The base rate fallacy reconsidered: Descriptive, normative and methodological challenges. *Behavioral and Brain Sciences, 19*, 1–53.

Kruger, J., Wirtz, D., van Boven, L., & Altermatt, T. W. (2004). The effort heuristic. *Journal of Experimental Social Psychology, 40*, 91–98.

Kugler, T., Connolly, T., & Ordez, L. D. (2010). Emotion, decision, and risk: Betting on gambles versus betting on people. *Journal of Behavioral Decision Making, 25*(2), 123–134.

Lopes, L. L. (1991). The rhetoric of irrationality. *Theory and Psychology, 1*, 65–82.

Maheswaran, D., Mackie, D. M., & Chaiken, S. (1992). Brand name as a heuristic cue: The effects of task importance and expectancy confirmation on consumer judgments. *Journal of Consumer Psychology, 1*(4), 317–336.

Matthews, W.J. (2011). What might judgment and decision making research be like if we took a Bayesian approach to hypothesis testing? *Judgment and Decision Making, 8*, 843–856

Matthews, W.J., & Stewart, N. (2009). Psychophysics and the judgment of price: Judging complex objects on a non-physical dimension elicits sequential effects like those in perceptual tasks. *Judgment and Decision Making, 4*, 64–81.

McGlone, M. S., & Tofighbakhsh, J. (2000). Birds of a feather flock conjointly (?): Rhyme as reason in aphorisms. *Psychological Science, 11*, 424–428.

Meyer, A., Frederick, S., Burnham, T. C., Pinto, J. D. G., Boyer, T. W., Ball, L. J., Pennycook, G., Ackerman, R., Thompson, V., & Schuldt, J. P. (2015). Disfluent fonts don't help people solve maths problems. *Journal of Experimental Psychology: General, 144*(2), e16-e30. doi: 10.1037/xge0000049

Miller, G. A. (1956). The magical number seven, plus or minus two: Some limits on our capacity for processing information. *Psychological Review, 63*, 81–97.

Mochon, D., & Frederick, S. (2013). Anchoring in sequential judgments. *Organizational Behavior and Human Decision Processes, 122*, 69–79.

Monin, B. (2003). The warm glow heuristic: When liking leads to familiarity. *Journal of Personality and Social Psychology, 85*(6), 1035–1048.

Morewedge, C. K., & Kahneman, D. (2010). Associative processes in intuitive judgment. *Trends in Cognitive Sciences, 14*(10), 435–440.

Mussweiler, T. (2002). The malleability of anchoring effects. *Experimental Psychology, 49*(1), 67–72.

Mussweiler, T., & Strack, F. (1999). Hypothesis-consistent testing and semantic priming in the anchoring paradigm: A selective accessibility model. *Journal of Experimental Social Psychology, 35*, 136–164.

Mussweiler, T., & Strack, F. (2001). Considering the impossible: Explaining the effects of implausible anchors. *Social Cognition, 19*(2), 145–160.

Open Science Collaboration (2015). Estimating the reproducibility of psychological science. *Science, 349*, 943–951.

Oppenheimer, D. M. (2003). Not so fast! (and not so frugal!): Rethinking the recognition heuristic. *Cognition, 90*, B1–B9.

Oppenheimer, D. M. (2004). Spontaneous discounting of availability in frequency judgment tasks. *Psychological Science, 15*, 100–105.

Oppenheimer, D. M. (2008). The secret life of fluency. *Trends in Cognitive Sciences, 12*(6), 237–241.

Petty, R. E., & Cacioppo, J. T. (1986). The elaboration likelihood model of persuasion. *Advances in Experimental Social Psychology, 19*, 123–205.

Pham, M. T. (1998). Representativeness, relevance, and the use of feelings in decision making. *Journal of Consumer Research, 25*, 144–159.

Raghunathan, R., & Pham, M. T. (1999). All negative moods are not equal: Motivational influences of anxiety and sadness on decision making. *Organizational Behavior and Human Decision Processes, 79*(1), 56–77.

Rottenstreich, Y., & Hsee, C. K. (2001). Money, kisses, and electric shocks: On the affective psychology of risk. *Psychological Science, 12*, 185–190.

Schwarz, N. (2012). Feelings-as-information theory. In P. A. M. Van Lange, A. Kruglanski, & E. T. Higgins (Eds.), *Handbook of Theories of Social Psychology* (pp. 289–308). Thousand Oaks, CA: Sage.

Schwarz, N., Bless, H., Strack, F., Klumpp, G., Rittenauer-Schatka, H., & Simons, A. (1991). Ease of retrieval as information: Another look at the availability heuristic. *Journal of Personality and Social Psychology, 61*, 195–202.

Shah, A. K., & Oppenheimer, D. M. (2008). Heuristics made easy: An effort-reduction framework. *Psychological Bulletin, 134*(2), 207–222.

Simmons, J. P., LeBoeuf, R. A., & Nelson, L. D. (2010). The effect of accuracy motivation on anchoring and adjustment: Do people adjust from provided anchors? *Journal of Personality and Social Psychology, 99*, 917–932.

Simmons, J. P., & Nelson, L. D. (2006). Intuitive confidence: Choosing between intuitive and nonintuitive accounts. *Journal of Experimental Psychology: General, 135*(3), 409–428.
Slovic, P., Finucane, M., Peters, E., & MacGregor, D. G. (2002). The affect heuristic. In T. Gilovich, D. Griffin, and D. Kahneman (Eds.), *Heuristics and biases: The psychology of intuitive judgment*. Cambridge: Cambridge University Press.
Slovic, P., & Peters, E. (2006). Risk perception and affect. *Current Directions in Psychological Science, 15*(6), 322–325.
Stanovich, K. E., & West, R. F. (2000). Individual differences in reasoning: Implications for the rationality debate? *Behavioral and Brain Sciences, 23*, 645–726.
Stepper, S., & Strack, F. (1993). Proprioceptive determinants of emotional and nonemotional feelings *Journal of Personality and Social Psychology, 64*, 211–220.
Strack, F., & Deutsch, R. (2004). Reflective and impulsive determinants of social behavior. *Personality and Social Psychology Review, 8*(3), 220–247.
Thompson, V. A., Prowse Turner, J. A., Pennycook, G., Ball, L. J., Brack, H., Ophir, Y., & Ackerman, R. (2013). The role of answer fluency and perceptual fluency as metacognitive cues for initiating analytic thinking. *Cognition, 128*, 237–251.
Tversky, A., & Kahneman, D. (1973). Availability: A heuristic for judging frequency and probability. *Cognitive Psychology, 5*, 207–232.
Tversky, A., & Kahneman, D. (1974). Judgment under uncertainty: Heuristics and biases. *Science, 185*, 1124–1131.
Tversky, A., & Kahneman, D. (1983). Extensional versus intuitive reasoning: The conjunction fallacy in probability judgment. *Psychological Review, 90*, 293–315.
Whittlesea, B. W. A. (1993). Illusions of familiarity. *Journal of Experimental Psychology: Learning, Memory, and Cognition, 19*, 1235–1253.
Whittlesea, B. W. A., Jacoby, L. L., & Girard, K. (1990). Illusions of immediate memory: Evidence of an attributional basis for feelings of familiarity and perceptual quality. *Journal of Memory and Language, 29*, 716–732.
Winkielman, P., & Cacioppo, J. T. (2001). Mind at ease puts a smile on the face: Psychophysiological evidence that processing facilitation elicits positive affect. *Journal of Personality and Social Psychology, 81*(6), 989–1000.
Witherspoon D., & Allan, L. G. (1985). The effect of a prior presentation on temporal judgments in a perceptual identification task. *Memory & Cognition, 13*, 101–111.
Zajonc, R. B. (1980). Feeling and thinking: Preferences need no inferences. *American Psychologist, 35*(2), 151–175.

26
CREATIVE THINKING

Mark A. Runco

The value of creative behavior is increasingly recognized in a wide range of arenas (e.g., education, business, technology) in part because of its clear ties to innovation, design, and various forms of progress. Not surprisingly, then, research on creativity has increased dramatically in the past 20 years, and much of this research deals specifically with creative thinking. There are other contributions to creative behavior, including attitude, affect, personality, and motivation, but creative thinking is required for an idea to be represented, explored, developed, shared, and implemented. Creative thinking is a vital precursor to creative behavior.

Creative thinking cannot be directly observed, but of course this is true of all forms of cognition. They must be inferred from action and behavior. The better theories of creativity are those which are unambiguously tied to action; the inferences are logical, consistent with data, and compelling. Several theories of creative thinking satisfy these requirements, and although they offer varied perspectives on the underlying processes, the variety is itself valuable. There are different ways to think creatively. This chapter offers a brief description of the primary theories of creative thinking. The starting point is the overarching premise of cognition as process. This leads immediately to a discussion of stage theories of creative thinking, as well as componential theories. That in turn leads to a rich discussion of associative processes, divergent thinking, and the brain. The concepts and processes suggested by the neuroanatomical research on creative thinking are then explored. These include dual and executive processes, the default network, hypofrontality, and cognitive inhibition. The final section of this chapter covers issues including the remaining lacuna that exists between long-standing theories of creativity and the newer methods and findings, especially those from the research on the brain.

Cognitive processes

One premise of all theories of creative thinking is that of *process*. This implies that it takes time to think creatively. Even a seemingly sudden "aha!" moment is protracted; it has a history and is not really an all-at-once occurrence (Gruber, 1981). The individual may not be aware of the history nor aware of each of the steps leading up to the seemingly sudden insight, but that too is characteristic of creative thinking: often there is an implicit, preverbal, preconscious component. Indeed, the preconscious contributions are often enormously important. Conscious thought is monitored, censored, constrained, but preconscious processes can discover new ideas precisely because there is less constraint (Rothenberg, 1990).

A second premise of theories of creative thinking is implied by the idea that there are in fact steps involved. These are often called *stages*, but the key point is that it is possible, and perhaps necessary, to delineate the process. The importance of such delineation is clear when the various steps are described. Admittedly, another perspective describes the creative process in terms of *components* rather than stages (Amabile, 1990; Runco & Chand, 1995; Sternberg, 2006), but even here the process is delineated. Both stage and componential models are reviewed in this chapter.

One of the best-known theories of process begins with a stage of preparation, followed by incubation, illumination, and then verification (Norlander, 1999; Runco, 2003; Wallas, 1926). Preparation actually includes *problem identification* and *problem definition*. Regardless of the label, cognition that precedes effort to solve a problem is enormously important – perhaps more important than the processes involved in finding the solution. For one thing, problem solving cannot begin until a problem is identified and defined. Only then will the individual decide if it is a worthwhile problem, and if it is, decide how much effort to invest in a solution. This exemplifies one of the ways that creative thinking interacts with affect and extra-cognitive processes. The individual probably will not invest much effort into something he or she does not understand and care about. Problem discovery may also be more important than problem solving because the quality of a solution may very well depend on the quality of the problem (Getzels, 1975).

The second state, *incubation*, includes the preconscious and preverbal processes that are mentioned above. Incubation implies that the person puts the problem aside and thinks about other things. It could be that unconscious processes continue to work on the problem below the level of awareness, and there certainly is ample evidence for such cognitive processing (Bowers, Regher, Balthazard, & Parker, 1990; Gardner & Nemirovsky, 1991; Gilhooly, this volume; Hasenfus, Martindale, & Birnbaum, 1983; Miller, 2007; Policastro, 1995; Rothenberg, 1990; Ryhammar & Smith, 1999; Smith, Carlsson, & Andersson, 1989).

Some of the newest research on incubation has examined the length of the incubation period, the activities that occur during incubation, and the possibility that "incubation can be understood as a process during which conscious and unconscious elements of the inquiry are integrated" (Orlet, 2008, p. 298). The newer experimental research on incubation is particularly important because early claims about incubation were based on introspection and autobiography, which of course may be apocryphal. After their empirical work on incubation, Ellwood, Pallier, Synder, and Gallate (2009) concluded

> that having a break during which one works on a completely different task is more beneficial for idea production than working on a similar task or generating ideas continuously. The advantage afforded by a break cannot be accounted for in terms of relief from functional fixedness or general fatigue, and, although it may be explicable by relief from task-specific fatigue, explanations of an incubation effect in terms of nonconscious processing should be (re)considered.
>
> (p. 6)

For years relief from fixation had been the most common explanation for incubation effects. Now we turn to the third stage in the creative process.

Illumination is another name for the "aha" experience. Here incubation provides a breakthrough, an idea, a solution. As noted above, it is not all that sudden. Gruber (1981), for example, demonstrated that seemingly sudden insights are protracted. He identifies some of the thoughts, influences, and steps involved in what the creator him- or herself had mistakenly thought was a sudden breakthrough. Of course, sometimes breakthroughs result from conscious effort, persistence, and experimentation (Simonton, 2007; Weisberg & Haas, 2007). There is an interesting controversy about the role of intentions and whether or not the creative thinking process is "blind" or random. More on this below.

The last stage in the classic four-stage model of creative thinking is *verification*. This is indeed a vital stage, especially given the standard definition of creativity, which includes both originality and effectiveness (Runco & Jaeger, 2012). Effectiveness may very well depend on some sort of verification. The individual could very well go through the first three stages and produce a solution or idea, but its effectiveness may be unknown until it is tested and some sort of verification is attempted. And without effectiveness, a solution or idea is merely original. It may be unusual or novel, but without some sort of effectiveness, it is not creative.

One common addition to the four-stage theory of the creative process includes ***implementation*** as the terminal stage. This is often an extremely important stage, especially for businesses and other organizations that wish to be innovative. That is because creativity and innovation are very strongly related to each other, but innovation most certainly requires some sort of implementation. West (1990) claimed that implementation is the most critical and difficult stage. He seemed to believe that it is easy to find creative ideas but not so easy to implement them.

Another addition to these process models is not really a stage. This is ***recursion***, which is the label given to thinking that directs the individual back to earlier stages (Runco, 1994). The individual might identify a problem, for example, and complete the first phase, and then move to the second phase and incubate. That might uncover a flaw in the problem, or at least a concern about the way the problem is conceived, and the individual may thus return (via recursion) to the first phase to redefine the problem. Recursion may occur throughout the process. It can occur as part of any stage.

The dual process approach

Allen and Thomas (2011) used the four-stage model of the creative process in their research on a dual process model of creative thinking. The dual process perspective is used throughout cognitive psychology (e.g., Evans, this volume; Smith & DeCoster, 2000) and described Type 1 thinking as fast, relatively effortless, and automatic and Type 2 thinking as more logical and effortful. Allen and Thomas argued that both types of thinking play a role in the creative process but the impact of each might vary from stage to stage. They described how problem finding and problem definition, for example, which characterize the first stage of the creative thinking process, might benefit from Type 1 thinking, just to name one example. They did acknowledge that there could be individual differences and, for example, experts being able to make good decisions about utilizing Type 1 or Type 2 thinking during a problem-finding stage of the process.

Very importantly, Type 1 thinking may be associative. This would tie it to associative theories of creative thinking (Mednick, 1962; Milgram, Milgram, Rosenbloom, & Rabkin, 1978; Runco, 1986a), which contributed to what was once the predominant model of creative thinking, namely the divergent thinking model (Guilford, 1968; Wallach & Kogan, 1965) and which led to the idea that creative ideas are most often *remote associates*. A remote associate is one that is far removed from the original problem or stimulus. When presented with a task, we often think first about conventional options and draw from our experience. Only when ideas about conventional options and experience have been deleted are people likely to think of original, unconventional, remote associates. The assumption here is that thinking involves a chain of ideas which are concatenated by some sort of association. Mednick went into detail about what types of associations are usually involved in creative thinking. He also described individual differences, with some people moving quickly past conventional ideas, while others taking much longer.

The recognition of creativity as involving multiple processes is enormously important but not new. It is important because it would be a mistake to view creativity as, say, equivalent to divergent thinking, given that divergent thinking only tells part of the study. Convergent thinking is also important (Runco, 1994; Cropley, 2006). Earlier views on the need for multiple processes include those of Hoppe and Kyle (1990), who cited Arieti (1976) on creativity as a "magic synthesis." The synthesis is how Hoppe and Kyle (1990) and Arieti (1976) described the collaboration of multiple processes. It is magical because (a) the processes can seem at odds with one another (e.g., divergent versus convergent thinking, or logic versus intuition), and (b) the results are creative and thus original and useful. Interestingly, Hoppe and Kyle (1990) and Arieti (1976) both felt that the synthesis involved different brain structures and processes. Simplifying some, they felt that somehow the processes covered by the left hemisphere collaborated with processes primarily controlled by the right hemisphere. This is an interesting idea because (a) it ties creativity to brain function, and (b) the newest neuroscientific findings suggest something similar (i.e., creativity involves networks and systems from various locations in the brain and is thus not localized [Dietrich, 2010]). Allen and Thomas (2011) pointed out that there is uncertainty about the cognitive architecture that supports Type 1 and Type 2 thinking and it is best at this point to avoid tying either form of cognition to particular structures, cognitive, neurochemical, or otherwise.

Componential models of creative thinking

Then there are componential models of the creative process (Amabile, Goldfarb, & Brackfield, 1990; Conti, Coon, & Amabile, 1996; Runco & Chand, 1995). These are not so different from stage models, though they do not emphasize any particular order, as is typical of stage models. The Two Tier model of the creative process contains five components, rather than three or four stages. Here again an interplay with extracognitive contributions is recognized. The primary tier of this model includes Problem Finding, Ideation, and Evaluation. The secondary tier recognizes influences on these components, including Knowledge and Motivation. Knowledge often plays a role in creative thinking, though it can sometimes contribute to and sometimes detract from creative results. It may contribute by insuring that all relevant information is available. In fact, knowledge is of two sorts: conceptual (or declarative) or procedural. The former is often just factual and the latter provides know-how and tactics to the individual. Knowledge may interfere with creative thinking when the individual treats it as beyond question and absolute. Interestingly, the benefits and drawbacks of knowledge are especially clear among experts. They often bring their large knowledge bases to bear on problems, but they are also the most likely to take things for granted, make assumptions, and do things the way they have always been done. This has been called "the cost of expertise" (Vincent, Decker, & Mumford, 2002).

Knowledge may be structured. The resulting structures may be *scripts, schemas*, or *concepts*, to name just three examples that have been proposed and investigated. Such structures may be interpreted in different ways. Langer, Hatem, Joss, and Howell (1989) suggested that all information should be interpreted as contextually conditional rather than absolute and unconditional. Presumably this would preclude the rigid thinking that was mentioned above and associated with the cost of expertise. It should also allow a ***mindful***, and often creative, use of the information. Very importantly, Langer described how creative thinking benefits from the mindful categorization of information. Instead of relying on a fixed set of categories, mindful thinking allows new categories to be used and the categorization of information in a novel fashion. Mindless categorization, in contrast, relies on old categories and rote categorization. This is all very important, particularly because categorization plays such a critical role in creative thinking.

Many others have looked to categorization and cognitive structures as part of creative thinking. Mumford, Mobley, Reiter-Palmon, Uhlman, and Doares (1991) and Scott, Lonergan, and Mumford (2005), for example, described creative thinking as *conceptual combination*, where information structures are combined, the result being a creative solution or idea.

Sometimes knowledge and concepts lead to analogies or metaphors, and here again, the results can be quite creative (Miller, 1996; Sanchez-Ruiz, Romo Santos, & Jimenez, 2013). Welling (2007) identified such analogical thinking as one of four cognitive operations that support creative thinking, the others being abstraction, application, and combination. Estes and Ward (2002) argued that emergence should be on that list, which is quite important because it would allow something entirely new to be found. Combination and analogy explain creative ideas as results of operations that depend on previous knowledge, but emergence would allow entirely new ideas to be created.

Two additional components need to be described. One, motivation, is like knowledge, at least in that it is also of two sorts. One is *intrinsic*, which means that the individual is motivated by personal interest, and the other *extrinsic*, which means that the individual is motivated by contingencies or something controlled by others (e.g., bonuses, payments, grades). Intrinsic motivation is very frequently implicated in creative work, but there are times when creative effort is a response to extrinsic factors or a combination of both intrinsic and extrinsic factors.

Evaluation, the last component on the primary tier of the Two Tier model, is not unrelated to the verification that was reviewed above as part of the four-stage model. In the stage model, however, verification is typically viewed as intrapersonal, while in the Two Tier componential model, evaluation can be either intra- or interpersonal. Indeed, a fair amount of research shows that in many settings, evaluations by supervisors, authorities, or even just peers and colleagues can inhibit creative thinking. Actually, intrapersonal evaluations can also inhibit, as is the case when the individual has an idea but then realizes that it is inconsistent with how he or she was raised (i.e., culture or socialization) and for that reason stops thinking along those lines. Significantly, Runco and Smith (1991) demonstrated empirically that an individual's accuracy at intrapersonal evaluations of creative ideas is not at all strongly related to the individual's accuracy at interpersonal evaluations. As a matter of fact, the low level of accuracy (all below 50%, so less than half of the original ideas judged were recognized as original) was something of a surprise. The capacity to produce ideas was correlated with the accuracy of judging ideas, but not overwhelmingly so.

These ideas about an evaluative process involved in creative thinking will take on even more importance later in the chapter, when the brain research is reviewed. There, too, evaluation has proven to be an intriguing part of creativity often relegated to the background.

Sternberg's (2006) view on creativity is at least as broad as the Two Tier model. He pointed to six "resources" that may come together for creative performance. These are intellectual ability, styles of thinking, knowledge, personality, motivation, and environment. Sternberg was more specific about the abilities involved and named analytic ability (which allows the person to know what to pursue), synthetic ability (which allows shifts of perspective), and practical-contextual skill (which allows the person to persuade other people about the value of an original idea). Perhaps most important is Sternberg's (2006, p. 6) conclusion that "although levels of these resources are sources of individual differences, often the decision to use the resources is the more important source of individual differences." This same point, giving the greatest weight to decisions about one's creativity, was made by Runco and Johnson (2002).

Divergent thinking

The middle component of the Two Tier model is Ideation. A huge amount of work on creative thinking has been directed at ideation, in part because it is easy to see ideas as the results of the creative thinking process. The study of ideas has an advantage over problem solving because creativity may or may not be a reaction to a problem. Creative thinking does frequently provide creative solutions to problems, but it also allows self-expression and other things that are independent of problem solving, and ideas are broadly applicable. Also, ideas have been nicely operationalized. There is a well-established methodology for measuring and studying ideas. Most of this falls under the umbrella of *divergent thinking*. Divergent thinking is the process that allows a person to find original ideas. It is easy to grasp when it is contrasted with convergent thinking, for that is the cognition that leads an individual to correct or conventional ideas. A person may have various facts or problem requirements in mind and use convergent thinking, and thus find what is the typical idea or solution.

Guilford's (1968) *structure of intellect* model distinguished divergent and convergent thinking, both conceptually and empirically. A large amount of research demonstrated that divergent thinking is independent of traditional "intelligence" and moderately predictive of creative activity in the natural environment (Runco, 1986a, 1986b; Runco, Millar, Acar, & Cramond, 2011; Wallach & Wing, 1969). Other research demonstrated that divergent thinking can be measured only under certain conditions (e.g., untimed, free of constraints, playful rather than test-like), which is relevant to both educational applications and attempts to bring divergent thinking into the laboratory (or fMRI apparatus!). Divergent thinking is multi-faceted, but the most important expressions of it are *ideational originality* and *ideational flexibility. Ideational fluency* (productivity or the number of ideas generated) is often included in tests and research but is not as important as originality (uniqueness or novelty of the ideas) and flexibility (diversity or variety of ideas) for creativity (Beketayev & Runco, 2016; Runco & Jaeger, 2012). A common mistake, almost as bad as measuring divergent thinking under timed or highly controlled conditions, is to look only to fluency just because it is easy to operationalize (as the number of ideas produced). Beketayev and Runco (2016) recently went into some detail about the semantic and conceptual basis of divergent thinking, and Acar and Runco (2014, 2015) offered an extension of the classic model that includes *cognitive hyperspace* (thinking in *n*-dimensions) and *literal divergent thinking*. Acar and Runco pointed out that previous research on divergent thinking did not really examine the divergence of ideas. Even original ideas could be found when working on a test of divergent thinking using associative processes where ideas are concatenated, one after another. Original ideas are typically far down the ideational path, but it could be a straight path, without divergence. Acar and Runco proposed a method for examining actual (or literal) divergence. They developed a coding scheme that identified ideas along polarities. Several investigations demonstrated that this was a reliable method and that the tendency to switch from one ideational category to another (which was taken to indicate divergence) was correlated with originality.

Geneplore and blind variation, selective retention

Some theories of creative thinking break down the process into parts but do not rely on stages or components. The *geneplore model*, for example (Finke, Ward, & Smith, 1992; Smith, Ward, & Smith, 1995), recognizes both generative and exploratory parts of mental imagery. The generative processes supposedly lead to pre-inventive images, and exploration evaluates and interprets. Another two-phase theory involves *blind variation and selection retention*, or BVSR (Campbell, 1960; Simonton, 2010). This theory parallels the Darwinian view of biological evolution, but there are differences – and debates, particularly over the blind or sighted nature of variations. Simonton (2007) described how

> creativity requires the generation of a certain amount of "blind" ideational variants that are then selected for development into the finished product. These variations are blind in the sense that the creator has no subjective certainty about whether any particular variant represents progress toward the goal rather than retrogression from or diversion away from the goal. As a consequence, the creator must rely on what is an essentially trial-and-error process that produces more ideas than will ever be used, and will do so in a manner that exhibits no linear, or at least no monotonic, movement toward the final product.
>
> (p. 331)

Simonton tested these ideas by asking experts to judge Picasso's sketches for the famous painting *Guernica* (which he began in 1937). Results indicated that the sketches were "replete with false starts and wild experiments" (p. 331), and Simonton took this to support the view that creative work comprises blind and nonmonotonic variants. This view has important implications for our understanding of expertise, for it would be reasonable to think that expertise would lead to highly efficient (and monotonic) work. There are questions with BVSR (Weisberg & Haas, 2007), and it must be emphasized that blind variation is only the first phase of creativity and that selection is also involved. Selection is a kind of evaluation, which we found above to be important for creative thinking. This is also true of the research focused on creative thinking as a result of the human brain.

Creative thinking in the brain

Now that the various process, stage, and componential theories have been reviewed, we can revisit several issues introduced earlier. First is that concerning the brain and creative thinking. There is an enormous amount of research on this topic, and in fact there are several meta-analyses that can be summarized. In one, Gonen-Yaacovi, Cruz de Souza, Levy, Urbanski, Josse, and Volle (2013) focused on functional imaging studies and caudal prefrontal contributions to creative thinking. Of course, for meta-analyses the first question is that of representation. Gonen-Yaacovi et al. were quite clear that "PubMed and Scopus Medline databases were searched using the following keywords in text and/or abstract/title and Boolean operators: 'creativity, creative thinking, creative process, unusualness, hypothesis generation, idea generation, aha, eureka, novel ideas, original ideas, originality, insight problem solving, insight solution, artistic' AND 'brain imaging, cerebral imaging, MRI, fMRI, PET, neural correlates, cerebral correlates, brain activation, functional magnetic resonance'" (Methods section, first paragraph). This allowed the meta-analysis to include 34 experiments, 44 statistical contrasts, 443 activation foci, and a total of 622 healthy research participants.

Gonen-Yaacovi et al. identified the medial and lateral rostral prefrontal cortex, the caudal lateral prefrontal cortex, the inferior parietal cortex, and the posterior temporal cortex as most clearly tied to performances on creativity measures. Interestingly, Gonen-Yaacovi et al. separated studies using measures of "free generation of unusual responses" from those relying on combination tasks and felt that the latter relied more heavily on the lateral prefrontal cortex than the former, though both seem to use the caudal prefrontal cortex. They also separated verbal and nonverbal creativity results but found a mutual reliance on the left caudal prefrontal, parietal and temporal areas. This is a bit surprising given that various empirical studies (outside of the neurosciences) have supported a verbal-nonverbal distinction (Richardson, 1988; Runco & Albert, 1986), but then again, there was some distinctiveness in the meta-analysis, as well as overlap. The most general conclusions appear to be (a) that some regions of the brain are involved in diverse creativity tasks (e.g., frontal and parietotemporal regions) but there is also some specialization, and (b) "the lateral PFC appeared to be organized along a rostrocaudal axis, with rostral regions involved in combining ideas creatively and more posterior regions involved in freely generating novel ideas." The meta-analytic nature of this research supports the credibility of the findings, though results are based entirely on a total of 622 participants.

A second useful meta-analysis was reported by Wu, Yang, Tong, Sun, Chen, Wei, Zhang, Zhang, and Qiu (2015). Their conclusions were not very different from those reported by Gonen-Yaccovi et al. (2013), at least in that

> distributed brain regions were more active under divergent thinking tasks than those under control tasks, but a large portion of the brain regions were deactivated. The . . . brain networks of the creative idea generation in DTTs [divergent thinking tests] may be composed of the lateral prefrontal cortex, posterior parietal cortex [such as the inferior parietal lobule (BA 40) and precuneus (BA 7)], anterior cingulate cortex (ACC) (BA 32), and several regions in the temporal cortex [such as the left middle temporal gyrus (BA 39), and left fusiform gyrus (BA 37)]. The left dorsolateral prefrontal cortex (BA 46) was related to selecting the loosely and remotely associated concepts and organizing them into creative ideas, whereas the ACC (BA 32) was related to observing and forming distant semantic associations in performing DTTs. The posterior parietal cortex may be involved in the semantic information related to the retrieval and buffering of the formed creative ideas, and several regions in the temporal cortex may be related to the stored longterm memory. In addition, the ALE results of the structural studies showed that divergent thinking was related to the dopaminergic system.
>
> (Wu et al., 2015, p. 270)

Several of these findings fit with the conclusions of Gonen-Yaacovi et al. (2013), though here again the quite moderate number of studies (17) and sample sizes does not warrant wide generalizations. Additionally, for some reason Wu et al. included research that used sentence completion, metaphor, and story generation, each of which is clearly outside of what is typically viewed as divergent thinking (Guilford, 1968; Runco, 1991, 2013; Torrance, 1995). Most troubling was that Wu et al. reported the time allowed for divergent thinking in each study used in the meta-analysis, and more than half of them gave participants less than one minute to think divergently. This, too, is inexplicable, given the non-neuroimaging research on divergent thinking. People do not think divergently when they are timed, and even if they don't know they are timed, if they are only given one minute, they cannot move beyond rote associates and rarely get to remote associates (Mednick, 1962; Runco, 1991, 2013; Wallach & Kogan, 1965). In fact, when people are timed, tests of divergent thinking really only tap convergent thinking.

One last meta-analysis should be summarized. It focused on domain differences in creativity (Bocciam, Piccardi, Palermo, Nori, & Palmiero, 2015). Domain differences are widely respected and consistent with a large amount of evidence (Baer, 1998; Gardner, 1983; Runco, 1986a, 1986b). There are different views of what constitutes a domain, and Bocciam et al. contrasted the musical, verbal, and visuo-spatial domains. They initially found 56 candidate studies using the search string "creativity and fMRI," but after narrowing based on eight inclusion criteria (e.g., peer-reviewed studies only, group studies with Ns < 5, no pharmacological manipulation, and the use of open-ended idea generation tasks), they were able to analyze only 24 of the

56 articles. Unlike Wu et al. (2015), Bocciam et al. (2015) considered only activation foci in the brain. De-activation foci were not considered. Bocciam et al. concluded that

> activation of the DLPFC [dorsolateral prefrontal cortex] was found in all creativity domains under investigation, whereas the inferior frontal gyrus was recruited consistently in verbal creativity and weakly in visuo-spatial creativity. This finding suggests that creativity relies on the activation of the prefrontal cortex, which likely works as an executive engine, managing attentional recourses, retrieving, and selecting appropriate information.
>
> (p. 9)

Thus the prefrontal cortex is again deemed important for creative thinking, and there is again evidence for both general (across domains) performances as well as evidence for domain-specific contributions. This is entirely consistent with Plucker and Beghetto's (2004) conclusion that creative behavior may depend on both domain-specific and domain-general processes.

Although the second meta-analysis reported above mis-represented divergent thinking and included studies that would in fact preclude divergent thinking, it did examine de-activation foci in the brain. This is quite important, at least from the larger (non-neuroscientific) research. Bocciam et al. cited one study (Aron, Robbins, & Poldrack, 2014) which found that "successful response inhibition . . . may entail activations of the right inferior frontal gyrus." The fact that certain structures in the brain may be de-activated during creative work is at least as intriguing as the fact that other structures are activated. In fact, one kind of deactivation, ***hypofrontality***, may be one of the most important processes for creative thinking. This is the label given to a deactivation of the prefrontal lobes. The prefrontal lobes play a role in decision making and judgment, and they may benefit creative ideation, some of the time, to curtail or postpone evaluations, which is likely with hypofrontality (Dietrich & Haider, 2016). It may even be that, during such periods of hypofrontality, ideas that are only marginally relevant or tenuous and which would normally be eliminated from further consideration are in fact explored and associations to them followed. This view is consistent with Eysenck's (1997) theory of overinclusive thought, which explains creative insights in terms of the capacity to include ideas as relevant to certain conceptual categories when typically they are not relevant. It is also consistent with the notion of cognitive disinhibition. And as Simonton (2014) put it, "The most important process underlying strokes of creative genius is *cognitive disinhibition* – the tendency to pay attention to things that normally should be ignored or filtered out by attention because they appear irrelevant" (Simonton, 2014).

The concept of disinhibition was also used by Limb and Braun (2008). They conducted an fMRI study of jazz improvisation. Participants were professional musicians who both improvised and played overlearned music while in the fMRI apparatus (on a specially designed keyboard). The improvisation differed from overlearned material in that the prefrontal cortex was "characterized by a dissociated pattern of activity . . . extensive deactivation of dorsolateral prefrontal and lateral orbital regions with focal activation of the medial prefrontal (frontal polar) cortex." Limb and Braun related such deactivation to the absence of self-monitoring and relaxing of volition that may allow improvisation. They also found deactivation in the limbic system but activation of sensorimotor foci. This research stands out, both for the clear differences in improvisation and overlearned performances, but also in the fact that, unlike so many fMRI studies that allow very little authentic creativity, the readings were taken while the participants were quite clearly creating. Limb and Braun did not merely study a very small and artificial sample of behavior elicited by some psychometric task but instead examined behavior that was unambiguously creative.

That being said, there is no doubt that there are different kinds of creative thinking. Some is improvisational, some insightful, some depends most heavily on ideation and association. Some of the time, deactivation or a postponement of judgment may be beneficial, but other times evaluation and careful, mindful decision making may be critical. And of course there is the premise of creativity as process, which allows for different cognitive or brain processes at different times (or in different stages).

Ellamil, Dobson, Beeman, and Christoff (2012) tried to separate a generation phase of creative thinking from an evaluation phase. They, too, used fMRI but asked research participants to design book illustrations (rather than play music or take a psychometric test). Results indicated that "creative generation was associated with preferential recruitment of medial temporal lobe regions, while creative evaluation was associated with joint recruitment of executive and default network regions and activation of the rostrolateral prefrontal cortex, insula, and temporopolar cortex." The prefrontal activation during evaluation is not surprising, though the "functional connectivity" of areas responsible for executive function along with default regions implies that there may be some collaboration of processes, at least during an evaluation phase. It is not as simple as "during generation, this (default processes, prefrontal deactivation) is happening in the brain, and then, during evaluation, this (executive function) happens instead."

Discussion

At this point it is probably obvious why creativity is often called a complex or *syndrome* (MacKinnon, 1983/1960; Mumford & Gustafson, 1988). This is an apt description when focusing on creative thinking, as we have done in this chapter, given that there are several different relevant processes and not just one process. The processes are quite varied, some leading to the generation of ideas, for instance, and others to the evaluation and selection of them. This chapter touched on divergent thinking, insight, executive process, the default network, evaluation, conceptual combination, analogy, hypofrontality, overinclusive thought, and a few other stages, processes, and components underlying creative thinking. The underlying anatomy and systems in the brain also vary, as indicated by the three meta-analyses reviewed herein. Recall here the activation of various systems and the deactivation of others. All of this diversity makes perfect sense, given that creative thinking can be expressed in so many different ways. Creative thinking can be applied to open-ended problems and tasks, to closed problems or tasks, or to anything in between. (Realistically, there is a continuum from open to closed problems; it is not a dichotomy.) Creative thinking can be used in a very wide range of domains and disciplines, though it will be expressed in different ways and different processes will be used. There are many different ways to solve a problem creatively, and many different ways to be creative other than solving problems.

There are several points of agreement among the theories reviewed herein. First is that creative thinking leads to ideas, insights, and solutions that are original, but not just original. They are original and effective. Second is that creative thinking represents an important determinant of creative behavior. Related to this is the recognition that creative thinking does not operate in isolation; it interacts with, and in some ways depends on, affect, personality, motivation, attitude, and the environment (Amabile 1985; Sternberg, 2006). Recall also the broadly held view that creative thinking is a process. Even when the contributions to it are not described as stages, the idea that thinking is instantaneous is long gone. There are, of course, several implications of the premise of process. It implies that time is a factor, for example, as is timing. Evaluation and judgment may be useful for creative thinking, but only at the right time. The same thing can be said about incubation, shifting perspectives, implementation, and many of the components of creative thinking.

There are debates in the field. An important one involves metaphor. There is little doubt that creative insights are sometimes found through metaphorical and analogical thinking (Miller, 1996), but the extreme view is that there really is no true originality and that everything is in some ways tied to what already exists. This is quite important for creative studies because originality is necessary for creativity (Runco & Jaeger, 2012). Originality is not sufficient for creativity; as mentioned several times earlier in this chapter, some sort of effectiveness must also be present. If a solution or idea is just original, it is uncommon or even unique but it may lack the fit or effectiveness that is required of all creative things. Original things can be worthless (which sometimes explains why they are original!), but creative things have some sort of value, be it aesthetic, technological, socially recognized, personal, or otherwise. This is one reason why the evaluative and judgmental processes are so often studied, in addition to the generative processes. Creativity requires both idea generation and evaluation, divergence, and convergence. Where is the originality if all seemingly new thought is in fact just a recombination or analogy of existing knowledge? And if the originality is dubious, it is really creativity?

That question might be reworded such that it asks about the possibility of authentic originality or authentic creativity. If a seemingly new idea is really just a recombination or analogy of earlier information, is it authentically original or just superficially original? Perhaps it is just *pseudo-creativity*. No wonder there are suggestions about including authenticity in the definition of creativity, to go along with (or even replace) originality. Definitions emphasizing authenticity have been proposed by both cross-cultural studies researchers (Kharkhurin, 2012) and humanists, such as Maslow (1968) and Rogers (1959). Authenticity is also a concern when evaluating research on creativity (Runco, 2014). Much of the cognitive research, and all of the neuroscientific research, is in a laboratory, in a controlled setting, but what is it sampling and studying if creativity is an intrinsically motivated act which is often spontaneous and self-expressive? Creativity may very well be impossible to test in a controlled setting.

A second debate concerns creativity as just a kind of problem solving. The view that creativity is more than problem solving is evidenced by the fact that it is sometimes most apparent in problem finding, and in the possibility that creative thinking leads to self-expression even when there is no problem (Runco, 1994). Still, the tie to problem solving persists. This may be because it is relevant to the argument against the possibility of computer creativity (Csikszentmihalyi, 1996; Simon, 1988, 1995): computers can probably produce solutions only if a problem is presented to them or if they are programmed accordingly. As a matter of fact, creativity seems to have recently become the key question for the computer sciences. The Turing Test has been passed by a "bot" and now the goal of computer science is to show that computers can be original and self-expressive.

Where does the research go from here? Two directions come to mind. One is towards greater generalizability. Recall here the criticism of research in one of the meta-analyses, above, where all of the testing of creativity was timed – and often less than one minute was given for creative expression! Recall also what was just said about authenticity for creativity and the problem of controlled settings. More research is needed on creative thinking in the natural environment. Otherwise the laboratory research will only describe a kind of ***situated cognition*** that has no application to authentic creativity. These concerns about generalizable findings from the creativity research relate to the second direction for future research, which is towards greater collaboration among the disciplines studying creativity. There were suggestions of an interdisciplinary approach by Isaksen, Murdock, Firestien, and Treffinger (1994) and Lindauer (1992), but there is a definite lack of collaboration now, especially since the neurosciences have entered creativity studies. This is obvious by the fact that so much research has emphasized intrinsic motivation, spontaneity, and protracted efforts, as well as authenticity (Amabile et al., 1990;

Eisenberger & Shanock, 2003; Runco, 1993; Kharkhurin, 2012; Gruber, 1981, 1988; Weisberg & Haas, 2007), and yet creativity is so often measured in the lab with tests that preclude all of this. The neuroscientific research is enormously interesting, but it would benefit from a closer collaboration with the creativity research. The creativity research, in turn, should be updated by what is learned in the laboratory. Some of this has occurred, which is why, for example, newer work on associative processes, recognized even before Mednick (1962), now sometimes refers to hypofrontality, and why newer research on divergent thinking cites dual process and the prefrontal cortex. In sum, future research, especially in the natural environment and with disciplinary collaborations, would be useful, but at the same time it is clear that great progress is being made on the topic of creative thinking.

References

Acar, S., & Runco, M. A. (2014). Assessing associative distance among ideas elicited by tests of divergent thinking. *Creativity Research Journal, 26*, 229–238.

Acar, S., & Runco, M. A. (2015). Thinking in multiple directions: Hyperspace categories in divergent thinking. *Psychology of Art, Creativity, and Aesthetics, 9*, 41–53.

Allen, A. E., & Thomas, K. P. (2011). A dual process account of creative thinking. *Creativity Research Journal, 23*, 109–118.

Amabile, T. M. (1985). Motivation and creativity: Effects of motivational orientation on creative writers. *Journal of Personality and Social Psychology, 48*, 393–399.

Amabile, T. M. (1990). Within you, without you: The social psychology of creativity, and beyond. In M. A. Runco & R. S. Albert (Eds.), *Theories of creativity* (pp. 6–9). Newbury Park, CA: Sage.

Amabile, T. M., Goldfarb, P. and Brackfield, S. C. (1990). Social influences on creativity: Evaluation, coaction, surveillance. *Creativity Research Journal, 3*, 6–21.

Arieti, S. (1976). *Creativity: The magic synthesis*. New York, NY: Basic Books.

Aron, A. R., Robbins, T. W., & Poldrack, R. A. (2014). Inhibition and the right inferior frontal cortex: One decade on. *Trends in Cognitive Sciences 18*, 177–185. doi: 10.1016/j.tics.2013.12.003

Baer, J. (1998). The case for domain specificity in creativity. *Creativity Research Journal, 11*, 173–177.

Beketayev, K., & Runco, M. A. (2016). Scoring divergent thinking tests with a semantics-based algorithm. *Europe's Journal of Psychology, 12*, 1–99. doi:10.5964/ejop.v12i2.1127

Bocciam, M., Piccardi, L., Palermo, L., Nori, R., & Palmiero, M. (2015). Where do bright ideas occur in our brain? Meta-analytic evidence from neuroimaging studies of domain-specific creativity. *Frontiers of Psychology*, 6, Article 1195, 1–12.

Bowers, K. S., Regher, G., Balthazard, C., & Parker, K. (1990). Intuition in the context of discovery. *Cognitive Psychology, 22*, 72–110.

Campbell, D. T. (1960). Blind generation and selective retention in creative thought as in other thought processes. *Psychological Review, 67*, 380–400.

Conti, R., Coon, H., & Amabile, T. M. (1996). Evidence to support the componential model of creativity: Secondary analyses of three studies. *Creativity Research Journal, 9*, 385–389.

Csikszentmihalyi, M. (1996). *Creativity: Flow and the psychology of discovery and invention*. New York: HarperCollins.

Dietrich, A., & Haider, H. (2016). A neurocognitive framework for human creative thought. *Frontiers in Psychology, 7*, Article Number 2078, 1–7.

Dietrich, A., & Kanso, R. (2010). A review of EEG, ERP, and neuroimaging studies of creativity and insight. *Psychological Bulletin, 136*, 822–848.

Eisenberger, R., & Shanock, L. (2003). Rewards, intrinsic motivation, and creativity: A case study of conceptual and methodological isolation. *Creativity Research Journal, 15*, 121–130.

Ellamil, M., Dobson, C., Beeman, M., & Christoff, K. (2012). Evaluative and generative modes of thought during the creative process. *Neuroimage, 59*(2), 1783–1794. doi: 10.1016/j.neuroimage.2011.08.008

Ellwood, S., Pallier, G., Synder, A., & Gallate, J. (2009). The incubation effect: Hatching a solution? *Creativity Research Journal, 21*, 6–14.

Estes, Z., & Ward, T. B. (2002) The emergence of novel attributes in concept modification. *Creativity Research Journal, 14*, 149–156. doi: 10.1207/S15326934CRJ1402_2

Eysenck, H. J. (1997). Creativity and personality. In M. A. Runco (Ed.), *The creativity research handbook* (pp. 41–66).Cresskill, NJ: Hampton Press.

Finke, R. A., Ward, T. B., & Smith, S. M. (1992). *Creative cognition: Theory, research, and applications*. Cambridge, MA: MIT Press.

Gardner, H. (1983). *Frames of mind*. New York: Basic Books.

Gardner, H., & Nemirovsky, R. (1991). From private intuitions to public symbol systems: An examination of the creative process in Georg Cantor and Sigmund Freud. *Creativity Research Journal, 4*, 1–21.

Getzels, J. W. (1975). Problem-finding and the inventiveness of solutions. *Journal of Creative Behavior, 9*, 12–18.

Gonen-Yaacovi, G., Cruz de Souza, L., Levy, R., Urbanski, M., Josse, G., & Volle, E. (2013). Rostral and caudal prefrontal contribution to creativity: A meta-analysis of functional imaging data. *Frontiers of Human Neuroscience, 7*, 465.

Gruber, H. E. (1981). On the relation between 'aha' experiences and the construction of ideas. *History of Science, 19*, 41–59.

Gruber, H. E. (1988). The evolving systems approach to creative work. *Creativity Research Journal, 1*, 27–51.

Guilford, L. P. (1968). *Creativity, intelligence, and their educational implications*. San Diego, CA: Knapp.

Hasenfus, N., Martindale, C., & Birnbaum, D. (1983). Psychological reality of cross-media artistic styles. *Journal of Experimental Psychology: Human Perception and Performance, 9*, 841–863.

Hoppe, K. D., & Kyle, N. L. (1990). Dual brain, creativity, and health. *Creativity Research Journal, 3*, 150 157.

Isaksen, S. G., Murdock, M. C., Firestien, R., & Treffinger, D. J. (Eds.). (1994). *Understanding and recognizing creativity*. Norwood, NJ: Ablex.

Kharkhurin, A. V. (2012). *Multilingualism and creativity*. Toronto: Multilingual Matters.

Langer, E., Hatem, M., Joss, J., & Howell, M. (1989). Conditional teaching and mindful learning: The role of uncertainty in education. *Creativity Research Journal, 2*, 139–150.

Limb, C. J., & Braun, A. R. (2008). Neural substrates of spontaneous musical performance: An fMRI study of Jazz improvisation. *PLoS ONE, 3*(2), e1679, doi:10.1371/journal.pone.0001679.

Lindauer, M. S. (1992). Creativity in aging artists: Contributions from the humanities to the psychology of aging. *Creativity Research Journal, 5*, 211–232.

MacKinnon, D. (1960; 1983). The highly effective individual. In R. S. Albert (Ed.), *Genius and eminence: A social psychology of creativity and exceptional achievement* (pp. 114–127). Oxford: Pergamon.

Maslow, A. (1968). Creativity in self actualizing people. In T. M. Covin (Ed.), *Toward a psychology of being* (pp. 135 145). New York: Van Nostrand Reinhold.

Mednick, S. A. (1962). The associative basis of the creative process. *Psychological Review, 69*, 220–232.

Milgram, R. M., Milgram, N. A., Rosenbloom, G., & Rabkin, L. (1978). Quantity and quality of creative thinking in children and adolescents. *Child Development, 49*, 385–388.

Miller, A. (1996). Metaphors in creative scientific thought. *Creativity Research Journal, 9*, 113–130. DOI: 10.1080/10400419.1996.9651167

Miller, A. (2007). Unconscious thought, intuition, and visual imagery: A critique of working memory, cerebellum, and creativity. *Creativity Research Journal, 19*, 47–48.

Mumford, M. D., & Gustafson, S. B. (1988). Creativity syndrome: Integration, application, and innovation. *Psychological Bulletin, 103*, 27–43.

Mumford, M. D., Mobley, M. I., Reiter-Palmon, R., Uhlman, C. E., & Doares, L. M. (1991). Process analytic models of creative capacities. *Creativity Research Journal, 4*, 91–122.

Norlander, T. (1999). Inebriation and inspiration? A review of the research on alcohol and creativity. *Journal of Creative Behavior, 33*, 22–44.

Orlet, S. (2008) An expanding view on incubation. *Creativity Research Journal, 20*, 297–308. DOI: 10.1080/10400410802278743

Plucker, L. A., & Beghetto, R. A. (2004). Why creativity is domain general, why it looks domain specific, and why the distinction does not matter. In R. J. Sternberg, E. L. Grigorenko, & L. L. Singer (Eds.), *Creativity: From potential to realization* (pp. 153–167). Washington, DC: American Psychological Association.

Policastro, E. (1995). Creative intuition: An integrative review. *Creativity Research Journal, 8*, 99–113.

Richardson, J. T. (1988). Vividness and unvividness: Reliability, consistency, and validity of subjective imagery ratings. *Journal of Mental Imagery, 12*, 115–122.

Rogers, C. R. (1959). Toward a theory of creativity. In H. H. Anderson (Ed.), *Creativity and its cultivation* (pp. 69–82). New York: Harper & Row.

Rothenberg, A. (1990). *Creativity and madness: New findings and old stereotypes*. Baltimore: Johns Hopkins University Press.

Runco, M. A. (1986a). Predicting children's creative performance. *Psychological Reports, 59,* 1247–1254.
Runco, M. A. (1986b). The discriminant validity of gifted children's divergent thinking test scores. *Gifted Child Quarterly, 30,* 78–82.
Runco, M. A. (1991). The evaluative, valuative, and divergent thinking of children. *Journal of Creative Behavior, 25,* 311–319.
Runco, M. A. (1993). Operant theories of insight, originality, and creativity. *American Behavioral Scientist, 37,* 59–74.
Runco, M. A. (1994). *Problem finding, problem solving, and creativity.* Norwood, NJ: Ablex.
Runco, M. A. (2003). Idea evaluation, divergent thinking, and creativity. In M. A. Runco (Ed.), *Critical creative processes* (pp. 69–94). Cresskill, NJ: Hampton Press.
Runco, M. A. (2013). Divergent thinking. In E. G. Carayannis (Ed.), *Encyclopedia of creativity, invention, innovation and entrepreneurship* (pp. 542–546). New York, NY: Springer.
Runco, M. A. (2014). *Creativity: Theories and themes: Research, development, and practice.* San Diego, CA: Elsevier.
Runco, M. A., & Albert, R. S. (1986). The threshold hypothesis regarding creativity and intelligence: An empirical test with gifted and nongifted children. *Creative Child and Adult Quarterly, 11,* 212–218.
Runco, M. A., & Chand, I. (1995). Cognition and creativity. *Educational Psychology Review, 7,* 243–267.
Runco, M. A., & Jaeger, G. J. (2012). The standard definition of creativity. *Creativity Research Journal, 24,* 92–96.
Runco, M. A., & Johnson, D. J. (2002). Parents' and teachers' implicit theories of children's creativity: A cross-cultural perspective. *Creativity Research Journal, 14,* 427–438.
Runco, M. A., Millar, G., Acar, S., & Cramond, B. (2011). Torrance tests of creative thinking as predictors of personal and public achievement: A 50 year follow-up. *Creativity Research Journal, 22,* 361–368.
Runco, M. A., & Smith, W. R. (1991). Interpersonal and intrapersonal evaluations of creative ideas. *Personality and Individual Differences, 13,* 295–302.
Ryhammar, L., & Smith, G. J. (1999). Creative and other personality functions as defined by percept-genetic techniques and their relation to organizational conditions. *Creativity Research Journal, 12,* 277–286.
Sanchez-Ruiz, M.-J., Romo Santos, M., & Jiménez, J. (2013) The role of metaphorical thinking in the creativity of scientific discourse. *Creativity Research Journal, 25,* 361–368. DOI: 10.1080/10400419.2013.843316
Scott, G. M., Lonergan, D. C., & Mumford, M. D. (2005). Conceptual combination: Alternative knowledge structures, alternative heuristics. *Creativity Research Journal, 17,* 79–98. DOI: 10.1207/s15326934crj1701_7
Simon, H. (1988). Creativity and motivation: A response to Csikszentmihalyi. *New Ideas in Psychology, 6,* 177–181.
Simon, H. A. (1995). Machine discovery. *Foundations of Science, 1* (2), 171–200.
Simonton, D. K. (2007). The creative process in Picasso's Guernica sketches: Monotonic improvements versus nonmonotonic variants. *Creativity Research Journal, 19,* 329–344.
Simonton, D. K. (2010). Creative thought as blind-variation and selective-retention: Combinatorial models of exceptional creativity. *Physics of Life Reviews, 7,* 156–179.
Simonton, D. K. (2014). If you think you're a genius, you're crazy. *Nautilus.* http://nautil.us/issue/18/genius/if-you-think-youre-a-genius-youre-crazy?utm_source=RSS_Feed&utm_medium=RSS&utm_campaign=RSS_Syndication
Smith, E. R., & DeCoster J. (2000). Dual-process models in social and cognitive psychology: Conceptual integration and links to underlying memory systems. *Personality and Social Psychology Review, 4,* 108–131.
Smith, G. J. W., Carlsson, I., & Andersson, G. (1989). Creativity and subliminal manipulations of projected self-images. *Creativity Research Journal, 2,* 1–16.
Smith, S. M., Ward, T. B., & Finke, R. A. (Eds.). (1995). *The creative cognition approach.* Cambridge, MA: MIT Press.
Sternberg, R. J. (2006). Creating a vision of creativity: The first 25 years. *Psychology of Aesthetics, Creativity, and the Arts, S* (1), 2–12.
Torrance, E. P. (1995). *Why fly.* Norwood, NJ: Ablex.
Vincent, A. S., Decker, B. P., & Mumford, M. D. (2002). Divergent thinking, intelligence, and expertise: a test of alternative models. *Creativity Research Journal, 14,* 163–178.
Wallach, M. A., & Kogan, N. (1965). *Modes of thinking in young children.* New York: Holt, Reinhart, & Winston.
Wallach, M. A., & Wing, C. W. Jr. (1969). *The talented student; A validation of the creativity-intelligence distinction.* New York: Holt, Reinhart, & Winston.
Wallas, G. (1926). *The art of thought.* London: Watts & Co.

Weisberg, R., & Haas, R. (2007). We are all partly right: Comment on Simonton. *Creativity Research Journal, 19*, 345–360.

Welling., H. (2007). Four mental operations in creative cognition: The importance of abstraction. *Creativity Research Journal, 19*, 163–177. DOI: 10.1080/10400410701397214

West, M. A. (1990). The social psychology of innovation in groups. In M. A. West, & J. L. Farr (Eds.), *Innovation and creativity at work: Psychological and organizational strategies* (pp. 309–333). Oxford, England: John Wiley.

Wu, X., Yang, W., Tong, D., Sun, J., Chen, Q., Wei, D., Zhang, Q., Zhang, M., & Qiu, J. (2015). A meta-analysis of neuroimaging studies on divergent thinking using activation likelihood estimation. *Human Brain Mapping, 36*(7), 270–318. doi: 10.1002/hbm.22801.

27

NATURALISTIC DECISION MAKING

Jan Maarten Schraagen

Naturalistic Decision Making (NDM) has been variously described as a 'movement' (Klein, 2015), a 'research community' (Gore, Flin, Stanton, & Wong, 2015), a 'framework' (Klein, 2015, Lipshitz, Klein, Orasanu, & Salas, 2001), and a 'perspective' or 'paradigm' (Cannon-Bowers, Salas, & Pruitt, 1996). All of these labels are appropriate. As a movement, it originated in 1989 at a small invitation-only conference in Dayton, Ohio, just one year after the shootdown of an Iranian commercial airliner by a US Navy cruiser, the USS *Vincennes*. The researchers invited to the 1989 meeting were concerned about applying what was known from the then-existing research on decision making to applied, real-world contexts, such as the *Vincennes* tragedy. Their perception of the state of the art of decision making research at that time was that it mainly consisted of laboratory research in which novel tasks were used with inexperienced decision makers (mostly students) who were asked to make a choice among concurrently available alternatives. The findings of this body of research did not generalize to experienced decision makers who often had to make sense of a complex situation before committing themselves to a particular course of action. Thus, a movement was started that evolved into a research community that convened during biennial conferences alternating between the US and Europe. As a movement, then, NDM consists of applied researchers who are interested in how professionals make decisions in real-world situations, with the goal of supporting these professionals through decision aiding and training. The word 'naturalistic' in NDM therefore refers to real-world situations, as contrasted with laboratory situations, rather than 'natural situations' in the sense of 'taking place in nature'.

As a framework or perspective, NDM is frequently contrasted with Classical Decision Making (CDM). CDM presents a view of human decision making as fundamentally flawed compared to a normative model. The normative model describes decision making as an exhaustive comparison of options, based on all available information about the options, their weights and consequences. NDM as a perspective on decision making emphasizes the study of how people use their experience to actually make decisions in field settings, rather than how they are supposed to make decisions. In the NDM framework, professional decision making behavior is an adaptation to uncertain, dynamic environments; shifting, ill-defined, or competing goals; time stress; high stakes; multiple event-feedback loops; ill-structured problems; multiple players; and organizational goals and norms that must be aligned with the decision maker's personal goals and norms (Orasanu & Connolly, 1993). Given these task constraints, decision making does not usually allow for an exhaustive comparison of options, as CDM would claim. The adaptations to these task constraints are usually viewed as successful (Kahneman & Klein, 2009), as long as experts can bring to bear their knowledge and experience in order to make decisions and solve problems. One particularly effective strategy that NDM has described is 'recognition-primed decision making'. By employing this strategy, experts adapt to the task constraints imposed upon them by recognizing familiar elements in a decision context and then retrieve from memory actions associated with these elements.

The attack on CDM as a correct description of what people actually do when they make decisions was primarily initiated by Herbert Simon in the late 1940s and early to mid-1950s (Simon, 1947; Simon, 1955). According to Simon, humans do not exhaustively select information in order to compare options. Instead, they apply their limited attentional resources to selecting a satisfactory option that suffices. Hence, their decision-making behavior may be characterized as 'satisficing' (a concatenation of 'satisfactory' and 'sufficing') rather than 'optimizing', as CDM would claim. In order to be able to assess more fully NDM's contribution to the history of decision-making research, I start by elaborating Simon's views. I next discuss some prototypical examples of NDM research and findings, as well as the theories and methods developed. Finally, I broaden the scope of NDM to include other 'macrocognitive' functions than decision making, and position NDM relative to other theoretical frameworks that deal with cognitive adaptation to complexity, as NDM has primarily evolved into.

Bounded rationality

In his autobiography *Models of My Life*, Simon (1991a, p. 88) stated that he would not object to having his whole scientific output described as an elaborate gloss on two interrelated ideas that had been at the core of his whole intellectual activity: "(1) human beings are able to achieve only a very bounded rationality, and (2) as one consequence of their cognitive limitations, they are prone to identify with subgoals." Both ideas were already developed when Simon finished his dissertation and revised it to publish it as *Administrative Behavior* in 1947. The book's aim was to understand how organizations could be understood in terms of their decision processes. The first idea, of bounded rationality, is probably his most well-known. It not only applies to organizations but to individuals as well. Basically, the concept of bounded rationality states that human rationality is bounded by larger areas of irrationality, in the sense of 'ignorance' or 'lack of knowledge', rather than in the sense of 'emotionality' (although Simon did not exclude the latter). Our knowledge is necessarily always imperfect, because of fundamental limitations to our information-processing systems (what Simon referred to as the 'inner environment') and because of fundamental limitations to the attention we can pay to the external world (what Simon referred to as the 'outer environment'). The concept of bounded rationality is frequently restricted to a discussion of limitations of human information processing capacities, such as working memory constraints or the limited speed with which information can be stored in long-term memory. However, Simon intended the concept to be much broader, and also included in his definition incompleteness of knowledge, difficulties in anticipating future consequences, and the narrow scope of possible behavior alternatives that come to mind (Simon, 2000). These issues have more to do with the complexity of the environment humans find themselves in than with their limited information processing capacities. In fact, one could say that the typical factors that characterize decision making in naturalistic environments, as put forward by Orasanu and Connolly (1993) and listed above, are the same factors that Simon had in mind when he referred to the 'outer environment' in which humans act and that acts upon them. It is therefore necessary to always take the 'two blades of the scissors' into account: the task environment on the one hand and the limits on the adaptive powers of the system on the other hand (Simon, 1991b). Bounded rationality is not the study of optimization in relation to task environments. According to Simon (1991b, p. 35), "[Bounded rationality] is the study of how people acquire strategies for coping with those environments, how these strategies emerge out of problem space definitions, and how built-in physiological limits shape and constrain the acquisition of problem spaces and strategies." If, as NDM might claim, the behavior of experts is completely optimized in relation to their task environments, then NDM as a theory would be barren. It would consist of a single precept: always choose the action that leads to the most complete achievement of your goal. However, even the behavior of experts is never completely optimized. Almost always, structure and limits to adaptation will 'show through' and will have to be taken into account. For instance, limits on the speed and nature of feedback during learning, as well as limits on the validity of the cues that experts derive from their environments, prohibit optimization in relation to task environments and may lead to what Kahneman and Klein (2009) referred to as 'fractionated expertise'. According to Simon, fractionated expertise would be the 'normal' state of affairs, whereas 'true expertise' (in the sense of complete adaptation to the environment) would be impossible, or possible only in the simplest of cases (Kahneman and Klein [2009, p. 522] agree that "fractionation of expertise is the rule, not an exception").

This brings us to the second of Simon's fundamental ideas, namely that humans are prone to identify with subgoals. What Simon means here is that humans justifiably treat situations as only loosely connected with each other, simply because most situations are quasi-independent of each other. This is because of the ubiquitous hierarchical nature of natural systems that have evolved out of the assembly of relatively stable, simple structures. Hierarchy will therefore be a dominant architectural form among natural systems and will have the special property of 'near decomposability' (Simon, 1962). The theory of nearly decomposable systems states that the interactions among the subsystems that constitute the complex system are weak, but not negligible. At least some kinds of hierarchic systems can be approximated successfully as nearly decomposable systems. Two propositions sum up this approach:

> (a) in a nearly decomposable system, the short-run behavior of each of the component subsystems is approximately independent of the short-run behavior of the other components; (b) in the long run, the behavior of any one of the components depends in only an aggregate way on the behavior of the other components.
>
> (Simon, 1962, p. 474)

The fact that nearly decomposable systems exist is fortunate for human beings with limited attention, because dealing with complex systems would be unmanageable if human beings had to deal with the full complexity at once. Although perhaps part of the story, it is, however, not the case that hierarchy is merely in the eye of the beholder, as evolution favors hierarchical systems over non-hierarchical systems.

This also ties in with Simon's (1973) observations regarding the structure of ill-structured problems. According to Simon, there are no well-structured problems, only ill-structured problems that have been formalized for problem solvers or are formalized by the problem solvers themselves. Typical ill-designed problems such as designing a house or composing a piece of music are ill-structured in the large problem-solving process, but become well-structured in the small, step-by-step problem solving process in which information and subgoals are retrieved from long-term memory, leading to a decomposition of the problem into more structured component problems. The retrieval system is a recognition system that attends to features in the problem space and the external environment and, recognizing features as familiar, evokes relevant information from memory which it adds to the problem space, making it incrementally more structured (Simon, 1973, p. 192).

Put more generally, recognition-based expertise is one of the mechanisms used by human-bounded rationality to cope with real-world complexity (Simon, 1990). In this sense, the 'intuition' that we ascribe to experts can simply be explained by acts of recognition (Simon, 1981; 1992). For instance, Gobet and Simon (1996) showed that grand master chess players could maintain their success level even during speed chess games against 50 opponents simultaneously, primarily relying on fast recognition processes. The complexity and richness of the outer environment is made manageable by drawing upon a very large repertory of cue–action pairs stored in long-term memory after considerable experience with the outer environment. The property of near decomposability is an essential prerequisite for building up this large repertory; without it, important systems in the world would be beyond our powers of observation and understanding. Without hierarchic, decomposable systems, it would also be impossible to derive valid cues from the environment, preventing us from becoming experts in any domain.

In summary, Simon's two basic insights into bounded rationality and near decomposability have led to a number of core findings and related explanations in the area of decision making that foreshadows many of the findings of NDM, not just the finding that experts rely on pattern recognition and make good decisions without comparing options (Kahneman & Klein, 2009). In particular, the importance of problem structuring, of incremental goal refinement, of recognition processes, of problem spaces (representations) and heuristics to deal with complexity, of scientific discovery by detecting contradictions and being surprised, and of making sense of information rather than gathering more information, are all core findings of Simon and his associates. On the other hand, this theoretical base, although quite general, was sorely in need of application to real-world situations. The filling in of the details of the nature of the adaptive processes of experts to their dynamic environments has been the ongoing work of NDM for the past 30 years. I discuss this work in the following sections using Simon's distinction between the outer and the inner environment, so as to address both blades of the scissors adequately. I end with extensions of the NDM work to the team and organizational levels.

The 'outer environment': expertise as adaptation to goal-relevant constraints

Both Simon and NDM researchers underline the importance of the structure of the environment in acquiring expertise and in task performance in general. Not that they are the first or the only ones to claim that adaptive behavior is to be explained by the shape of the environment – see, for instance, Brunswik (1955) and J.J. Gibson (1979) for an ecological approach to cognition. Expertise in general is often viewed as maximal adaptation to domain-specific constraints (e.g., Ericsson & Lehmann, 1996; Vicente, 2000). The issue of how to model these constraints, or what theory of the environment one should adopt, has generally not been dealt with in any detail by either NDM or Simon, in contrast to ecological approaches. Kahneman and Klein (2009) were the first in the NDM tradition to describe the importance of what they referred to as the 'validity of the environment' in developing skilled intuitions – that is, expertise. Validity, in Kahneman and Klein's (2009, p. 520) words, "describes the causal and statistical structure of the relevant environment." As, for instance, the economic and political environment generally shows very little structure, it is nearly impossible for humans to develop valid intuitions about developments in such environments, hence the difficulty of developing expertise in such areas. Skilled nurses and fireground commanders, on the other hand, operate in much more structured and predictable environments that allow them to develop skilled intuitions about the cues these environments present them with. Later in their paper, Kahneman and Klein (2009, p. 524) use a somewhat different definition of validity, in which they include events or actions taken by experts in response to particular cues, thus extending the definition from a mere description of the environment to something that resembles a classic 'if-then rule':"[w]e describe task environments as 'high-validity' if there are stable relationships between objectively identifiable cues and subsequent events or between cues and the outcomes of possible actions." A high-validity environment is a necessary but not sufficient condition for the development of expertise. Kahneman and Klein (2009) hence added a second condition for expertise, namely the opportunity to learn the relevant structure of the environment and to practice a skill. Therefore, although both conditions are necessary for expertise to develop, neither one by itself is sufficient: one needs both a valid environment (or a stable relationship between the environment and one's actions upon it) and an opportunity to learn and practice that validity. Only then will skill and expert intuition eventually develop in individuals of sufficient talent.

Kahneman and Klein's (2009) notion of validity of the environment is useful when one needs to determine whether someone's intuitive judgments can be trusted. Hence, it is a useful first approximation when trying to establish whether someone can become an expert or not, at least in principle in the particular environment under consideration. However, their own admission that fractionated expertise is the rule, not an exception, and NDM's general fascination with ill-structured, uncertain, dynamic, ill-defined environments with multiple event-feedback loops, multiple players, and organizational norms and goals that must be balanced against the decision makers' personal choice (Orasanu & Connolly, 1993) makes one wonder how true expertise can ever be acquired in such environments. If environments are truly characterized by the factors listed above, they are surely more representative of low-validity environments such as the stock market or the political arena than of high-validity environments. Consequently, such naturalistic environments are unconducive, to say the least, of becoming an expert. What makes matters worse is that many naturalistic environments do not allow for extensive periods of learning (at least not the well-known 10,000-hour or 10-year period frequently stated, first by Simon and Chase [1973], as a requirement for attaining world-class expertise in areas such as musical performance, games, or sports; see Ericsson, 1996, for a review in these areas). This is particularly the case in jobs with high rotation speeds, such as in the military, where personnel change jobs every two or three years. Therefore, in these jobs, the second condition for expertise, being able to learn the validity of the environment, is not met either.

On the other hand, it would be too hasty to conclude that genuine expertise does not exist in naturalistic environments. All we may conclude is that we will mostly encounter, as analysts, isolated islands of knowledge in seas of ignorance – in other words, humans with bounded rationality. And we may predict that when experts in a particular area of expertise are confronted with problems that are entirely new to them, they may be able to use some of their knowledge, for instance a general approach to solving problems in their domain, but they will display more novice-like behavior the more novel the problems become (see Schraagen, 1993a, for an example in the domain of experimental design, or Voss, 1983, in the domain of political science). Secondly, fewer opportunities to learn and practice have led to new developments in the area of 'accelerated expertise' (Hoffman et al., 2014). This field endeavors to find new ways of learning that speed up the learning curve – accomplishing within a few years what otherwise would have taken 10 years to learn. What this implies is that the '10-year rule' may not be as hard as some have taken it to be (for empirical evidence disconfirming this rule, see, for instance, Hambrick et al., 2014, and Meinz & Hambrick, 2010; for a theory emphasizing interactions between genes and the environment, see Ullén, Hambrick, & Mosing, 2015). Thirdly, if fractionated expertise is indeed the rule and genuine expertise is indeed rare in naturalistic environments, then a pragmatic response of the NDM community would be to settle for the best there is – in other words, to satisfice. Expertise in naturalistic environments is mostly defined in relative and social terms, hence, if a community designates a colleague as 'the' expert, even if she has only two years' experience in the domain, then apparently two years suffice. Peer judgments rather than quantitative performance measures are what define expertise in the NDM community.

An example from the domain of pilotage of vessels may illustrate the concepts of validity of the environment, opportunities for learning, and definition of expertise (Schraagen, 1993b). This study was carried out on board large container ships entering or leaving the port of Rotterdam. These vessels, if their master is not exempt from pilotage duty, need a pilot to safely navigate the ship in the confined waterways and open sea areas close to shore. A ship's master may be considered a 'ship expert' insofar as the master has developed an anticipatory control model of the ship's movements based on extensive experience with the ship in all conditions (e.g., wind, current). A pilot, on the other hand, is far less familiar with the particular ship he or she is navigating. Rather, the pilot may be considered a 'local environment expert', insofar as he or she routinely sails a particular stretch of water, but with a diversity of ships. In this study, I investigated on the basis of which cues pilots made navigational decisions, such as when to change heading or when to change speed. Does the environment provide stable relationships between objectively identifiable cues and subsequent events or between cues and the outcomes of possible actions? If so, the environment would be of high validity and would be conducive to the development of genuine expertise, following Kahneman and Klein's (2009) definition. This raises the question of defining 'objectively identifiable cues'. I used cognitive task analysis methods to answer this question, in particular think aloud and 'constrained information tasks' (see Schraagen, 2006, for more details on the methods used).

The results showed that pilots used a limited number of identifiable cues from the environment to initiate heading or speed changes. For instance, whenever they would sail alongside pile mooring 14, they would order a change in heading by issuing the command "Five degrees to port." This may seem an overly simplistic way of controlling a complex system such as a 300-meter container vessel, particularly as this system may be subject to various external influences such as wind and current. Given that the pilot, unlike the master, has not developed an anticipatory control model for this particular ship, how does he or she know what the effects will be of ordering a particular command? The answer is surprisingly simple: they do not know exactly nor do they need to know exactly. Pilots have a general 'feeling' or intuition for how a ship should respond to a particular command and what they are good at, is evaluating the ship's response to their command by comparing the actual response to a desired response, stored in long-term memory. The desired response is a generalized schema or prototypical situation, derived from many instances with similar ships (it is likely, although this fell outside the scope of the study, that they have several classes of schemata, depending on various classes of ships they are dealing with). The comparison process is a pattern matching or feature matching process of the actual rate of turn of the ship with the desired rate of turn, and this is based on looking at the ship's bow and seeing how fast it moves relative to a fixed point in the environment (this fixed point, for instance a church, is another 'identifiable cue'). The rate of turn is a complex yet all-encompassing measure, as it includes all external effects at once. Thus, the pilot does not need to make extensive mathematical calculations in his or her head, as this would be impossible and too cumbersome for each navigational change. No calculations are needed at all, as the pilot merely compares actual with desired movements. Note that the only advantage of the pilot, compared to the master, lies in the specific knowledge of the environmental cues to use to either initiate a change or to compare the effects of an initiated change with an intended change.

A second interesting finding in this study was that there were individual differences in the cues pilots used: some used pile moorings, others used buoys, still others used objects such as apartment buildings or churches. Hence, this raises a question about the 'objectivity' of the identifiable cues in the environment. The answer is that the cues are all objectively identifiable, yet idiosyncratic as far as their identity is concerned, probably as a result of highly individualized training (pilots are trained by a personal mentor who teaches them what he or she has been taught long before, at least at the time of this study). It also shows that people are highly creative in exploiting the richness of cues in their environment. The environment does not provide ready-made cues, quite the contrary: experts invest the environment with goal-relevant meaning.

The approach taken in this study is typical of NDM studies in general. It consists of identifying the cues and strategies experts use when carrying out their tasks. NDM has employed a variety of methods in this respect, mostly querying the professionals during or after their work. One of the most well-known methods is the Critical Decision Method (Hoffman, Crandall, & Shadbolt, 1998). Generally, NDM has developed 'process theories' rather than 'product theories' (Vicente, 2000), the difference being that process theories specify psychological mechanisms and representations 'in the head', whereas product theories specify constraints that the environment imposes on humans. Vicente and Wang (1998) claimed that process theories and product theories are complementary, with product theories providing the constraints that process theories need to fulfill. They further claim (p. 50) that "it is the only such theory that systematically accounts for the contribution of the structure of the environment to behavior." If this is the case, one may wonder why NDM has only rarely developed a theory of the environment, for instance in the form of the abstraction hierarchy proposed by Rasmussen (1985). First, it should be clear that NDM does not deny the importance of the environment and the presence of objectively identifiable cues in it. As Kahneman and Klein (2009) claimed, the structure of the environment provides important conditions for expertise. However, NDM has traditionally been more interested in an expert's mental representation of the environment than in a model of the environment as such. Other applied research areas, such as Ecological Interface Design (EID), with its theoretical basis in Gibsonian ecological psychology, has made extensive and productive use of the abstraction hierarchy (see McIlroy & Stanton, 2015, for a review). Second, from a practical point of view, it is difficult to see how one could develop an (ontological) model of the environment without being an expert oneself. In cases where the constraints imposed by the environment largely obey the laws of physics, such as in the study of nuclear power plant control, one could develop an abstraction hierarchy as a model of the environment by drawing upon that knowledge. In many other cases, however, specifying the constraints in the environment runs the risk of being a largely ad hoc exercise (Simon & Gobet, 2000), without many additional benefits. Of course, a river pilot needs to deal with particular constraints in the environment, such as the rules of the road and the constraint of sailing the vessel in a safe and timely manner to its port. However, these constraints do not provide any insight into the way river pilots perform this task, what information they use, and how they should be trained or supported. A river pilot's behavior, like any adaptive system, is constrained by the environment but not completely determined by it, and we need auxiliary assumptions to deal with the limits of adaptation – in other words, a process theory (Simon, 1991b). Third, process theories such as NDM has developed do not ignore the adaptive and goal-oriented nature of behavior. In particular, in more recent formulations of NDM as macrocognition (Klein et al., 2003), functions such as planning, adaptation, and sense-making are viewed as being supported by processes such as mental simulation and story-building, managing uncertainty and risk, and managing attention. These processes are adaptive and goal-oriented, and contribute to the study of how cognition adapts to complexity (Gore et al., 2015).

In conclusion, both NDM and ecological approaches to cognition stress the importance of the environment. According to NDM, one needs both a 'valid' environment and an opportunity to learn the cues offered by the environment in order to develop expertise. A valid environment is an environment that offers stable relationships between objectively identifiable cues and subsequent events or between cues and the outcomes of possible actions (Kahneman & Klein, 2009). Ecological approaches, on the other hand, have traditionally focused on a description of the environment itself, without considering the human role in it. Although NDM is somewhat ambiguous in whether or not to take the human into account when defining the validity of the environment, most NDM studies have not started with, for instance, an abstraction hierarchy of the domain of interest, hence not following the ecological approaches. Instead, NDM studies usually start by asking experts how they carry out their tasks, and from there implicitly derive the constraints that the experts have to adapt to.

The 'inner environment': strategies and representations

As discussed, one of the most prominent strategies humans use when coping with their task environments is the use of recognition-based expertise, particularly when they are experienced and under time pressure. Klein (personal communication, 24 May 2015) first coined the term 'recognition-primed decision making'. He and his colleagues Roberta Calderwood and Anne Clinton-Cirocco used it in an unpublished report for the US Army Research Institute in 1985 (for a final published version with postscript, see Klein, Calderwood, & Clinton-Cirocco, 2010), and in their paper in the *Proceedings of the Human Factors and Ergonomics Society* in 1986, which would be the first published reference (Klein, Calderwood, & Clinton-Cirocco, 1986). Klein wanted an acronym that conveyed rapidity. He toyed with "schema-primed decisions" (SPD, hinting at "speed"), but he and his colleagues decided they liked RPD (hinting at "rapid") better. Klein's Recognition-Primed Decision (RPD) model of rapid decision making has been one of the most prominent and influential ideas within the NDM community, even though it should not be equated with NDM. The model was developed on the basis of retrospective process tracing using a semistructured interview technique of incidents remembered by fireground commanders (FGCs) (Klein et al., 2010). In order not to disturb the FGCs during their work, using talk aloud protocols was obviously not feasible. Extracting 156 decision points from these interviews, Klein et al. (2010) found that in 80% of the cases, the FGCs considered only one option. In only 16 of the most difficult cases did the FGCs evaluate multiple options. In Klein et al.'s words (2010, p. 198):

> Their ability to handle decision points depended on their skill at recognizing situations as typical instances of general prototypes that they had developed through experience. The prototypes provided them with an understanding of the causal dynamics at work, suggested promising courses of action, and provided them with expectations.

Klein et al. (1986) explained the use of this 'satisficing' strategy by the time pressure FGCs are under: if they had generated a large set of options and evaluated these systematically in terms of expected utility, the fires would undoubtedly have gotten out of control. As one officer said: "Look, we don't have time for that kind of mental gymnastics out there. If you have to think about it, it's too late" (Klein et al., 1986, p. 578).

The RPD model was never intended to be solely about recognition or 'intuition'. It is a blend of intuition and analysis (Klein, Postscript to 2010), as became apparent in later, updated, versions of the model (e.g., Kaempf, Klein, Thordsen, & Wolf, 1996). The analysis part of the model deals with contrasting alternative accounts of a situation, and with mentally simulating the outcomes of proposed courses of action. Hence, in later versions of the model, feedback loops were added, such that when situations were not typical, additional information would be gathered and the situation would be clarified through story building or feature matching, until a prototypical or analogue situation would have been constructed. Similarly, when proposed courses of action would not work, they would be modified or a new action would be generated.

The main difference with classical models of decision making is that the RPD model focuses on serial evaluation of options and chooses the first option that works (following Simon's satisficing theory). Rather than contrasting the strengths and weaknesses of multiple options simultaneously, and having to wait until the analysis is completed before being able to take an action, a recognitional strategy enables a decision maker to commit to the option being evaluated, thus being able to initiate an action continuously (Klein, 1993). Although the RPD model works well in situations of time pressure, results of multiple studies have shown that recognitional strategies are also used when not under time pressure, even with complex problems (Klein, 1989). Analytical strategies are used more often by less experienced decision makers or when making organizational decisions that require the comparison of multiple options. Also, data presented in alphanumeric rather than a graphical format evoke an analytical strategy, as well as the strong requirement to justify actions, or when there is a dispute between different constituencies (Klein, 1993).

The RPD model has been applied to a variety of domains and has received much empirical support, in that experts are found to use recognitional strategies in 80–90% of the cases (see Klein, 1993; Ross, Shafer, & Klein, 2006). One of the intriguing predictions of the RPD model is that the first option considered is usually the best, at least if the professionals making the decision can draw upon extensive domain knowledge and experience. A corollary of this prediction, taking into account the predominance of fractionated expertise, is that when confronted with atypical or unfamiliar problems, the first option considered may not be the best, and it may pay off to engage in further deliberation or mental simulation. The first prediction has received widespread support, and not just from NDM research. For instance, experienced chess players' first moves are typically considered of higher quality than subsequent moves (Klein, Wolf, Militello, & Zsambok, 1995). Also, under high time pressure, conditions of so-called speed chess, where experienced players compete with a large number of less experienced players simultaneously, highly skilled players are able to generate moves of high quality (Calderwood, Klein, & Crandall, 1988; Gobet & Simon, 1996). The 'fast and frugal heuristics' research tradition (Gigerenzer & Goldstein, 1996; Hoffrage, Hafenbrädl, & Marewski, this volume) has also generated support for a "Take the First" heuristic with handball players (Johnson & Raab, 2003; Raab & Johnson, 2007). Johnson and Raab (2003) presented moderately experienced handball players with video sequences from a game and asked what they would have done – for instance, pass the ball to the player to the left or take a shot at the goal. They found that the first option that came to mind was better than later options. This result has been replicated for basketball (Hepler & Feltz, 2012).

Regarding the second prediction, it should be recalled that the RPD model allows for a mental simulation strategy in case the first option is not considered workable. It would therefore be incorrect to state that the RPD model would always predict that experts will, or should, choose the first option that comes to mind. It is important to specify the boundary conditions under which this takes place. Several studies have made progress in this area. For instance,

Mamede et al. (2010) studied medical diagnostic reasoning with both complex and routine problems under three reasoning mode conditions: an immediate-decision condition (favoring a "Take the First" heuristic) and two delayed conditions: conscious thought and deliberation-without-attention (Dijksterhuis, Bos, Nordgren, & Van Baaren, 2006). Their participants were 34 internal medicine residents ('experts') and 50 fourth-year medical students ('novices'). They found that the experts benefited from consciously thinking about complex problems, whereas reasoning mode did not differ in simple problems. In contrast, novices benefited from being prevented from thinking about their decision, but only in simple problems. Moxley et al. (2012), in the domain of chess, found that both experts and novices (tournament players) benefited from extra deliberation, regardless of whether the problem was simple or complex. In other words, and in contrast to previous findings, the move chosen after deliberation was stronger than the move first mentioned. Experts chose their first move mentioned as their final move 49% of the time, and were significantly more likely than novices to do so on easy problems, but not on hard problems. In conclusion, these studies provide confirmatory evidence for the RPD model in that problem complexity seems to provide a boundary condition on the use of a pattern recognition process: when problems become complex or atypical, solution quality may benefit from engaging in mental simulation or conscious, analytical reasoning. This is in line with dual-process theories of reasoning and judgment (Evans, 2008; this volume) and the distinction between System 1 (intuition) and System 2 (deliberative thinking) (Kahneman, 2003).

Extending NDM to the team and organizational level

If we consider human beings to be goal-directed, adaptive systems whose behavior may be described as consisting of applying knowledge in the service of goals, then teams and organizations could in principle also be regarded as goal-directed systems. In fact, a frequently used definition of "team" stresses the importance of a mutually agreed-upon and valued common goal that all team members should strive towards, each using their functionally complementary set of knowledge and skills.[1] In this sense, a team is merely an extension of an individual in the sense that if an individual cannot accomplish a goal on his or her own, teamwork may be required to do so. By the same argument, an organization is a solution to a goal that can neither be accomplished by a team, let alone by a single individual. The question arises: how does a team achieve its goals? What is necessary for adaptive, efficient team behavior? What strategies and representations do teams need to have to achieve their goals?

There are basically two perspectives on teamwork: a structural perspective emphasizing representations and a process perspective emphasizing strategies. From the mid-1990s, the concept of 'shared mental models' became popular to explain excellent teamwork (e.g., Cannon-Bowers, Salas, & Converse, 1993). This is a structural perspective as it focuses on the underlying representations that team members bring to bear. 'Shared mental models' turned out to be somewhat ambiguous, because it was not clear on the exact meaning of the word 'shared', which could either mean 'in common' or 'distributed' (Mohammed & Dumville, 2001). Be that as it may, the concept emphasized the importance of knowing what one's teammates need in terms of knowledge and information at a particular point in time (referred to as 'transactive memory'; Moreland, 1999). As such, it emphasized real-time interdependence and proper preparation for it by means of various types of cross-training (it turned out to be superfluous to cross-train team members completely in each other's tasks; rather, the important thing was to know at critical points in the task performance what one's team members needed). After some years, the concept ran into methodological problems of measurement (Mohammed, Klimoski, & Rentsch, 2000), as well as problems of justification of its importance (Cooke, Gorman, Myers, & Duran, 2013).

Another issue is that much of the shared mental models research focused on routine, proceduralized tasks for which the knowledge requirements could be listed in advance and hence trained for. This reliance on memorization is not always the solution (see, e.g., Fiore et al., 2010). Crew resource management, for instance, relies more heavily upon team processes than shared mental models (Helmreich & Foushee, 1993). Finally, the concept of 'mental models' was ambiguous, as it could refer to static knowledge or to situation-dependent knowledge (Rasker, Post, & Schraagen, 2000). In the latter case, a concept such as 'shared situation awareness' (Stanton et al., 2010) or 'shared problem models' (Orasanu, 1993) would be more appropriate.

Recently, the process perspective has gained more influence (e.g., Cooke et al., 2013). The process perspective states that while sharing particular knowledge in a static sense may be important, what is crucial is actually communicating this knowledge to one's team members. Although the shared mental models perspective frequently stated that "a good team is a silent team", and that 'implicit coordination' would do most of the job (Kleinman & Serfaty, 1989), the process perspective states that "there is nothing as deadly in a crisis as the sound of silence" (Vaughan, 1997). In fact, this perspective goes so far as to state that teamwork arises only during communicative acts (Stanton, Salmon, & Walker, 2015). Knowledge need not be shared completely amongst team members; distributed knowledge is the common practice, and only communicative acts can bring the distributed knowledge together and make it accessible for the team as a whole.

In the NDM tradition, it has become commonplace to study teamwork in real-life settings and describe what strategies and representations teams use to cope with unexpected situations. I have carried out such a study in the area of pediatric cardiac surgery, using various methods, ranging from teamwork observation and behavioral rating scales to social network analysis (Schraagen, 2011; Barth, Schraagen, & Schmettow, 2015). These analyses show that teams first use standard procedures to respond to increasing difficulty and, on top of those, also use more generic strategies such as 'heedful interrelating' or mutual performance monitoring. Just as individual experts confronted with unfamiliar problems in their area of expertise may still use generic problem solving methods or schemata, teams have also learned from experience what to do in case they are confronted with unusually difficult situations: anticipate each other's information needs (shared mental models); provide backup when the going gets tough; explicitly communicate what you are doing so others build up shared situation awareness.

Similar analyses may be carried out at the organizational level, although these studies are mostly not affiliated with NDM. The most extensive analysis of a single organization has been carried out by the sociologist Diane Vaughan in her book *The Challenger Launch Decision* (1996), describing the background to the decision on the eve of the launch of the space shuttle *Challenger* in 1986. Contrary to common wisdom that NASA managers were the only ones to blame for overruling the engineers who expressed their doubts on the eve of the launch, Vaughan convincingly showed that it was in fact conformity to NASA culture as a whole that was to blame: a culture of production, a culture of bureaucracy, a technical culture, as well as the overriding phenomenon of 'normalization of deviance'. These cultural pressures came together and were played out on the teleconference on the eve of the launch, making this a predictable accident the day after. If we abstract from the specifics of this analysis and couch them in more general terms, we see a tension between the pressures of what is common practice in NASA (routine culture) versus the unknown (non-routine situation). The unknown is the uncharted territory of launching under very low temperatures with the hypothesis that the O-rings may burn through at these low temperatures. Although in hindsight this hypothesis has proven to be correct, during the eve of the launch the engineers could not bring to bear sufficient evidence to make the hypothesis credible. Therefore, the pressures of routine culture won over the pressure of non-routine culture. Instead of proving that something was safe, you had to prove it unsafe, because the shuttle generated so many safety issues. This meant that rational analysis with sufficient quantitative evidence had to be presented to persuade management to abort the launch. As the engineers were unable to do so, management, given the pressure to maintain a launch schedule that had already been changed a number of times, decided to go ahead with the launch. The same normalized organizational deviance occurred in response to the tile hitting the wing on the *Columbia* (CAIB, 2003).

Looking at the individual, team, and organizational levels from a more distant perspective, we may thus conclude that any system confronted with unfamiliar situations, that is, situations that fall outside the scope for which knowledge is readily available, needs to resort to more effortful, more deliberative, strategies with the aim of searching for new knowledge and bringing to bear new perspectives. This is a familiar juxtaposition: Newell (1990) called this the 'preparation versus deliberation trade-off', Kahneman (2003) referred to this as the '"System I" versus "System II"' mode of thinking, Klein (1993) referred to this as Recognition-Primed Decision Making versus Analytical Decision Making, and March (1991) referred to this as 'exploitation' versus 'exploration'. The realization that NDM is about macrocognition, after all (Schraagen, Klein, & Hoffman, 2008), has spurred new research on the use of these effortful, deliberative strategies that individuals and teams employ to cope with atypical situations.

Conclusion

In this chapter, I have discussed the NDM movement as a framework or perspective that is compatible with the general notions of decision making as put forward by Herbert Simon. In particular, Simon's core idea of bounded rationality and the derived ideas on satisficing and subgoal identification have been elaborated upon in applied areas by NDM researchers. More importantly, NDM researchers have applied these notions to improve and support decision making and training for professionals. By starting with a cognitive task analysis and describing how professionals actually make decisions, NDM researchers have been able to develop decision support systems and training regimes that are compatible with the way professionals use their knowledge and experience. This approach may be contrasted with approaches that attempt to support professionals by starting from a normative perspective and develop support systems and training regimes that in the end frequently turn out not to be compatible with how professionals actually work.

Adaptive systems are being ground between the nether millstone of their physiology or hardware and the upper millstone of a complex environment in which they exist (Simon, 1980). Macrocognition, as what NDM has evolved into, is about adaptation to complexity. It is neither about the physiological constraints on cognition, as this would be characteristic of a microcognitive approach, nor about the environmental constraints on cognition, as this would be characteristic of an ecological approach. We have seen that macrocognition hovers between the two millstones. The future of macrocognition lies in describing the relative invariants that must be sought in the inner and outer environments that bound the adaptive processes. One of these invariants is the way adaptive systems deal with familiar and unfamiliar situations: recognition-primed when dealing with familiar situations, deliberative and analytical when dealing with unfamiliar situations.

Note

1 Teams can be defined as two or more people who interact interdependently with respect to a common goal and who have each been assigned specific roles to perform for a limited lifespan of membership (Salas, Dickinson, Converse, & Tannenbaum, 1992).

References

Barth, S., Schraagen, J. M. C., & Schmettow, M. (2015). Network measures for characterizing team adaptation processes. *Ergonomics, 58*(8), 1287–1302.

Brunswik, E. (1955). Representative design and probabilistic theory in a functional psychology. *Psychological Review, 62*, 193–217.

Calderwood, R., Klein, G. A., & Crandall, B. W. (1988). Time pressure, skill, and move quality in chess. *American Journal of Psychology, 101*, 481–493.

Cannon-Bowers, J. A., Salas, E., & Converse, S. A. (1993). Shared mental models in expert team decision-making. In N. J. Castallan Jr. (Ed.), *Individual and group decision making* (pp. 221–246). Hillsdale, NJ: Lawrence Erlbaum Associates.

Cannon-Bowers, J. A., Salas, E., & Pruitt, J. S. (1996). Establishing the boundaries of a paradigm for decision-making research. *Human Factors, 38*(2), 193–205.

Columbia Accident Investigation Board (2003). Report Volume I, August 2003.

Cooke, N. J., Gorman, J. C., Myers, C. W., & Duran, J. L. (2013). Interactive team cognition. *Cognitive Science, 37*, 255–285.

Dijksterhuis, A., Bos, M. W., Nordgren, L. F., & Van Baaren, R. B. (2006). On making the right choice: The deliberation-without-attention effect. *Science, 311*, 1005–1007.

Ericsson, K. A. (Ed.). (1996). *The road to excellence: The acquisition of expert performance in the arts and sciences, sports, and games.* Mahwah, NJ: Lawrence Erlbaum Associates.

Ericsson, K. A., & Lehmann, A. C. (1996). Expert and exceptional performance: Evidence of maximal adaptation to task constraints. *Annual Review of Psychology, 47*, 273–305.

Evans, J. St. B. T. (2008). Dual-processing accounts of reasoning, judgment, and social cognition. *Annual Review of Psychology, 59*, 255–278.

Fiore, S. M., Rosen, M. A., Smith-Jentsch, K. A., Salas, E., Letsky, M., & Warner, N. (2010). Toward an understanding of macrocognition in teams: Predicting processes in complex collaborative contexts. *Human Factors, 52*(2), 203–224.

Gibson, J. J. (1979). *The ecological approach to visual perception.* Boston: Houghton Mifflin.

Gigerenzer, G., & Goldstein, D. G. (1996). Reasoning the fast and frugal way: Models of bounded rationality. *Psychological Review, 102*, 684–704.

Gobet, F., & Simon, H. A. (1996). The roles of recognition processes and look-ahead search in time-constrained expert problem solving: Evidence from Grandmaster level chess. *Psychological Science, 7*, 52–55.

Gore, J., Flin, R., Stanton, N., & Wong, B. L. W. (2015). Applications for naturalistic decision-making. *Journal of Occupational and Organizational Psychology, 88*, 223–230.

Hambrick, D. Z., Oswald, F. L., Altmann, E. M., Meinz, E. J., Gobet, F., & Campitelli, G. (2014). Deliberate practice: Is that all it takes to become an expert? *Intelligence, 45*, 34–45.

Helmreich, R. L., & Foushee, H. C. (1993). Why crew resource management? Empirical and theoretical bases of human factors training in aviation. In E. L. Wiener, B. G. Kanki, & R. L. Helmreich (Eds.), *Cockpit resource management* (pp. 3–45). San Diego, CA: Academic Press.

Hepler, T. J., & Feltz, D. L. (2012). Take the first heuristic, self-efficacy, and decision-making in sport. *Journal of Experimental Psychology: Applied, 18*(2), 154–161.

Hoffman, R. R., Crandall, B. W., & Shadbolt, N. R. (1998). A case study in cognitive task analysis methodology: The critical decision method for elicitation of expert knowledge. *Human Factors, 40*, 254–276.

Hoffman, R. R., Ward, P., Feltovich, P. J., Dibello, L., Fiore, S., & Andrews, D. H. (2014). *Accelerated expertise.* New York, NY: Psychology Press, Taylor & Francis.

Johnson, J. G., & Raab, M. (2003). Take the first: Option-generation and resulting choices. *Organizational Behavior and Human Decision Processes, 91*, 215–229.

Kaempf, G. L., Klein, G., Thordsen, M. L., & Wolf, S. (1996). Decision making in complex naval command-and-control environments. *Human Factors, 38*(2), 220–231.

Kahneman, D. (2003). A perspective on judgment and choice: Mapping bounded rationality. *American Psychologist, 58*, 697–720.

Kahneman, D., & Klein, G. (2009). Conditions for intuitive expertise: A failure to disagree. *American Psychologist, 64*(6), 515–526.

Klein, G. (1993). A recognition-primed decision (RPD) model of rapid decision making. In G. A. Klein, J. Orasanu, R. Calderwood, & C. E. Zsambok (Eds.), *Decision making in action: Models and methods* (pp. 138–147). Norwood, NJ: Ablex.

Klein, G. (2015). Reflections on applications of naturalistic decision making. *Journal of Occupational and Organizational Psychology, 88*, 382–386.

Klein, G. A. (1989). Recognition-primed decisions. In W. B. Rouse (Ed.), *Advances in man-machine systems research* (Vol. 5, pp. 47–92). Greenwich, CT: JAI Press, Inc.

Klein, G., Calderwood, R., & Clinton-Cirocco, A. (1986). Rapid decision making on the fire ground. *Proceedings of the 30th Annual Meeting of the Human Factors Society* (pp. 576–580). Santa Monica, CA: Human Factors Society.

Klein, G., Calderwood, R., & Clinton-Cirocco, A. (2010). Rapid decision making on the fire ground: The original study plus a postscript. *Journal of Cognitive Engineering and Decision Making, 4* (Special Issue on 20 years of NDM), 186–209.

Klein, G., Ross, K. G., Moon, B. M., Klein, D. E., Hoffman, R. R., & Hollnagel, E. (2003, May/June). Macrocognition. *IEEE Intelligent Systems*, 81–85.

Klein, G., Wolf, S., Militello, L., & Zsambok, C. (1995). Characteristics of skilled option generation in chess. *Organizational Behavior and Human Decision Processes, 62*(1), 63–69.

Kleinman, D. L., & Serfaty, D. (1989). Team performance assessment in distributed decision making. In R. Gibson, J. P. Kincaid, & B. Goldiez (Eds.), *Proceedings of the interactive networked simulation for training conference* (pp. 22–27). Orlando, FL: Naval Training Systems Center.

Lipshitz, R., Klein, G., Orasanu, J., & Salas, E. (2001). Focus article: Taking stock of naturalistic decision making. *Journal of Behavioral Decision Making, 14*, 331–352.

Mamede, S., Schmidt, H. G., Rikers, R. M. J. P., Custers, E. J. F. M., Splinter, T. A. W., & Van Saase, J. L. C. M. (2010). Conscious thought beats deliberation without attention in diagnostic decision-making: at least when you are an expert. *Psychological Research, 74*, 586–592.

March, J. G. (1991). Exploration and exploitation in organizational learning. *Organization Science, 2*, 71–87.

McIlroy, R. C., & Stanton, N. A. (2015). Ecological interface design two decades on: Whatever happened to the SRK taxonomy? *IEEE Transactions on Human-Machine Systems, 45*(2), 145–163.

Meinz, E. J., & Hambrick, D. Z. (2010). Deliberate practice is necessary but not sufficient to explain individual differences in piano sight-reading skill: The role of working memory capacity. *Psychological Science, 21*(7), 914–919.

Mohammed, S., & Dumville, B. C. (2001). Team mental models in a team knowledge framework: Expanding theory and measurement across disciplinary boundaries. *Journal of Organizational Behavior, 22*(2), 89–106.

Mohammed, S., Klimoski, R. J., & Rentsch, J. R. (2000). The measurement of team mental models: We have no shared schema. *Organizational Research Methods, 3*(2), 123–165.

Moreland, R. L. (1999). Transactive memory: Learning who knows what in work groups and organizations. In L. Thompson, D. Messick, & J. Levine (Eds.), *Shared knowledge in organizations* (pp. 3–31). Hillsdale, NJ: Lawrence Erlbaum Associates.

Moxley, J. H., Anders Ericsson, K., Charness, N., & Krampe, R. T. (2012). The role of intuition and deliberative thinking in experts' superior tactical decision-making. *Cognition, 124*, 72–78.

Newell, A. (1990). *Unified theories of cognition.* Cambridge, MA: Harvard University Press.

Orasanu, J. (1993). Decision making in the cockpit. In E. L. Wiener, B. G. Kanki, & R. L. Helmreich (Eds.), *Cockpit resource management* (pp. 132–172). San Diego, CA: Academic Press.

Orasanu, J., & Connolly, T. (1993). The reinvention of decision making. In G. A. Klein, J. Orasanu, R. Calderwood, & C. E. Zsambok (Eds.), *Decision making in action: Models and methods* (pp. 3–20). Norwood, NJ: Ablex.

Raab, M., & Johnson, J. G. (2007). Expertise-based differences in search and option-generation strategies. *Journal of Experimental Psychology: Applied, 13*, 158–170.

Rasker, P. C., Post, W. M., & Schraagen, J. M. C. (2000). The effects of two types of intra-team feedback on developing a shared mental model in command and control teams. *Ergonomics Special Issue on Teamwork, 43*(8), 1167–1189.

Rasmussen, J. (1985). The role of hierarchical knowledge representation in decisionmaking and system management. *IEEE Transactions on Systems, Man, and Cybernetics, Vol. SMC-15*, No. 2, 234–243.

Ross, K. G., Shafer, J. L., & Klein, G. (2006). Professional judgments and "Naturalistic Decision Making". In K. Anders Ericsson, N. Charness, P. J. Feltovich, & R. R. Hoffman (Eds.), *The Cambridge handbook of expertise and expert performance* (pp. 403–419). New York, NY: Cambridge University Press.

Salas, E., Dickinson, T. L., Converse, S. A., & Tannenbaum, S. I. (1992). Toward an understanding of team performance and training. In R. W. Swezey & E. Salas (Eds.), *Teams: Their training and performance* (pp. 3–29). Norwood, NJ: Ablex Publishing.

Schraagen, J. M. (1993a). How experts solve a novel problem in experimental design. *Cognitive Science, 17*, 285–309.
Schraagen, J. M. C. (1993b). What information do river pilots use? In *Proceedings of the international conference on Marine simulation and ship maneuverability MARSIM '93* (Vol. II, pp. 509–517). St. John's, Newfoundland: Fisheries and Marine Institute of Memorial University.
Schraagen, J. M. C. (2006). Task analysis. In K. Anders Ericsson, N. Charness, P. J. Feltovich, & R. R. Hoffman (Eds.), *The Cambridge handbook of expertise and expert performance* (pp. 185–201). New York, NY: Cambridge University Press.
Schraagen, J. M. C. (2011). Dealing with unforeseen complexity in the OR: The role of heedful interrelating in medical teams. *Theoretical Issues in Ergonomics Science, 12*(3), 256–272.
Schraagen, J. M. C., Klein, G., & Hoffman, R. R. (2008). The macrocognition framework of naturalistic decision making. In J. M. Schraagen, L. G. Militello, T. Ormerod, & R. Lipshitz (Eds.), *Naturalistic decision making and macrocognition* (pp. 3–25). Aldershot, Hampshire: Ashgate Publishing Limited.
Simon, H. A. (1947). *Administrative behavior.* New York: Palgrave Macmillan.
Simon, H. A. (1955). A behavioral model of rational choice. *Quarterly Journal of Economics, 69*, 99–118.
Simon, H. A. (1962). The architecture of complexity. *Proceedings of the American Philosophical Society, 106*(6), 467–482.
Simon, H. A. (1973). The structure of ill structured problems. *Artificial Intelligence, 4*, 181–201.
Simon, H. A. (1980). Cognitive science: The newest science of the artificial. *Cognitive Science, 4*, 33–46.
Simon, H. A. (1981). *The sciences of the artificial* (2nd ed.). Cambridge, MA: MIT Press.
Simon, H. A. (1990). Invariants of human behavior. *Annual Review of Psychology, 41*, 1–19.
Simon, H. A. (1991a). *Models of my life.* New York: Basic Books.
Simon, H. A. (1991b). Cognitive architectures and rational analysis: Comment. In K. VanLehn (Ed.), *Architectures for Intelligence* (pp. 25–39). Hillsdale, NJ: Lawrence Erlbaum Associates.
Simon, H. A. (1992). What is an "explanation" of behavior? *Psychological Science, 3*(3), 150–161.
Simon, H. A. (2000). Bounded rationality in social science: Today and tomorrow. *Mind & Society, 1*(1), 25–39.
Simon, H. A., & Chase, W. G. (1973). Skill in chess. *American Scientist, 61*, 394–403.
Simon, H. A., & Gobet, F. (2000). Expertise effects in memory recall: Comment on Vicente and Wang (1998). *Psychological Review, 107*, 593–600.
Stanton, N. A., Salmon, P. M., & Walker, G. H. (2015). Let the reader decide: A paradigm shift for situation awareness in sociotechnical systems. Special issue on situation awareness. *Journal of Cognitive Engineering and Decision Making, 9*(1), 44–50.
Stanton, N. A., Salmon, P. M., Walker, G. H., & Jenkins, D. P. (2010). Is situation awareness all in the mind? *Theoretical Issues in Ergonomics Science, 11*(1–2), 29–40.
Ullén, F., Hambrick, D. Z., & Mosing, M. A. (2016). Rethinking expertise: A multifactorial gene – environment interaction model of expert performance. *Psychological Bulletin, 142*(4), 427–446. Advance online publication. http://dx.doi.org/10.1037/bul0000033
Vaughan, D. (1996). *The Challenger launch decision: Risky technology, culture, and deviance at NASA.* Chicago: University of Chicago Press.
Vaughan, D. (1997). Targets for firefighting safety: Lessons from the Challenger tragedy. *Wildfire, 6*, 29–40.
Vicente, K. J. (2000). Revisiting the constraint attunement hypothesis: Reply to Ericsson, Patel, and Kintsch (2000) and Simon and Gobet (2000). *Psychological Review, 107*(3), 601–608.
Vicente, K. J., & Wang, J. H. (1998). An ecological theory of expertise effects in memory recall. *Psychological Review, 105*(1), 33–57.
Voss, J. F., Greene, T. R., Post, T. A., & Penner, B. C. (1983). Problem-solving skill in the social sciences. In G. H. Bower (Ed.), *The psychology of learning and motivation: Advances in research theory* (Vol. 17, pp. 165–213). New York: Academic Press.

28

DECISION MAKING UNDER RISK

An experience-based perspective

Christin Schulze and Ben R. Newell

Rational choices in risky situations

Living in Sydney comes with many perks. You can catch a ferry to work and pass the iconic Opera House and Harbour Bridge each morning. You can enjoy a swim in the ocean after the day's work is done. And on the weekends, you can stroll along Sydney's dramatic cliff tops, relax at the beach, or invite your friends over for a barbeque. Sydney indisputably is very out-of-doors oriented, no doubt fostered by an average of 221 rain-free days per year.[1] When rain hits Sydney, however, it often does so with force, and it pays to be prepared. Thus, a typical daily challenge facing Sydney-siders is to decide whether or not to take an umbrella when leaving the house.

This is a paradigmatic example of a repeated *choice under risk* – it is made every day, under conditions in which the likelihood of rain may (or may not) change, may be ascertained directly from the weather forecast, or may be inferred indirectly from the current meteorological conditions. More generally, a decision under risk can be seen as a choice between options (taking an umbrella or saving yourself the bother of doing so) that have some probability of being rewarding (you stay dry) or damaging (you get wet).[2] Some decisions under risk are made repeatedly, almost every day (e.g., whether or not to take an umbrella or when to wear a seatbelt), whereas others are made maybe only once in life (e.g., whom to marry, which career path to pursue, or whether to undergo a particular medical treatment). How should and how do people make such decisions? How (and how well) do they deal with the inherent uncertainty of most choice situations? Addressing these issues is a core pursuit of decision making research and has captivated scholars for centuries (for a historical overview see, e.g., Newell, Lagnado, & Shanks, 2015). In this chapter, we provide an *experience-based perspective* on decision making under risk and focus in particular on how feedback, learning opportunities, and first-hand experience shape people's choices. Our specific focus encompasses a review of many key research findings, starting with a brief introduction to normative accounts of how people *ought* to make decisions under risk. We then turn to accounts of well-documented deviations from normative standards and examine the role of learning and experience for errors that occur in either repeated or "one-shot" choice situations.

For illustration, let us return to a variant form of the umbrella example. Suppose you have just moved to a new city and do not yet own an umbrella, but the weather forecast predicts a 70% chance of rain for the day. In this "one-shot" choice scenario, you are faced with two options: (1) you can buy an umbrella for $10 at the corner shop or (2) you can risk getting wet and ruining your new suede jacket that you bought for $100 but want to wear for a special occasion that day. What should you do? One solution for "trading off" the uncertainty in the outcomes with their possible values is to select the option that maximizes *expected value*. The expected value of a choice is defined as the sum of the products of the probability of each possible outcome and its monetary value. That is, if you do *not* buy the umbrella, there is a 70% chance that you will incur a loss in value of $100 for your ruined jacket and a 30% chance that you will not lose anything and thus, the expected value of not buying an umbrella is $(.70 \times -\$100) + (.30 \times \$0) = -\$70$. If, on the other hand, you buy the umbrella, you lose $10 for sure (expected value $= 1 \times -\$10$). In this instance, buying the umbrella would maximize the expected value of your decision.

The notion that rational decision making under risk is characterized by the maximization of expected value has had a profound influence on the development of modern decision theory and has paved the way for the axiomatization of expected utility (von Neumann & Morgenstern, 1947). Expected utility is a subjective construct based on how much a decision maker subjectively values particular outcomes and can be based on any goal a decision maker might want to achieve. The axioms of Expected Utility Theory (EUT) provide a normative benchmark for assessing the rationality of people's choices and EUT is the dominant decision-theoretic framework for the analysis of decisions under risk. As it turns out, however, people's preferences violate central axioms of EUT in many situations (e.g., Allais, 1953; Ellsberg, 1961; Kahneman & Tversky, 1979; for a review, see, e.g., Kahneman & Tversky, 2000). One particularly striking error occurs when simple risky choices – such as whether or not to take an umbrella when going out – are made repeatedly.

A paradigmatic "irrational" choice

In the case of deciding whether or not to take your (newly acquired) umbrella, repetitions of this particular risky choice will be virtually identical on many days. Thus, once you have decided to bring your umbrella when the forecast predicts a 70% chance of rain, you should do so on each day with similar weather conditions. Suppose, for example, you weigh the hassle of carrying an umbrella and the hassle of getting soaked by a sudden downpour equally. In this case, taking your umbrella on the first 70%-chance-of-rain day you experience and then simply sticking to that decision on all future occasions would maximize your bad-weather-related utility. Unfortunately, however, life often gets in the way of even the simplest decisions, and you may find yourself with no time to check the weather forecast or simply forget to pick up your umbrella. In other words, "in the wild," many obstacles prevent people from maximizing their odds in repeated risky decisions.

Yet, even under greatly simplified experimental conditions, people often have difficulties repeating risky choices they have already identified as good responses. Specifically, many people prefer to diversify repeated decisions among available options and end up choosing differently in identical choice situations – a finding that has intrigued researchers for many decades (e.g., Estes & Straughan, 1954; Humphreys, 1939). Consider, for instance, a standard choice paradigm in which a decision maker is faced with a repeated choice between two alternatives, A_1 and A_2:

A_1 offers a payoff with $p(A_1) = .70$,
A_2 offers the same payoff with $p(A_2) = .30$.

The alternatives may be represented, for example, by two lightbulbs that illuminate to indicate the outcome (e.g., Estes & Straughan, 1954), by two colored stimuli that appear in different locations on a computer screen (e.g., Shanks, Tunney, & McCarthy, 2002), or by two unmarked buttons that reveal the payoff after each choice (e.g., Erev & Barron, 2005). Figure 28.1A provides an illustration of a standard repeated choice paradigm. Assuming that $p(A_1)$ and $p(A_2)$ do not systematically change over time and are independent of prior choices and outcomes, it seems obvious that A_1 is the better option on each occasion a choice is made. Thus, to maximize pay, decision makers need to select A_1 exclusively – no matter how often the choice is repeated. In this example, this payoff and ***probability maximizing*** strategy yields an average choice accuracy of 70%.

Surprisingly, however, many people faced with this strikingly simple choice problem do not maximize probability or pay. Instead, they tend to allocate their choices in proportion to the payoff probabilities, choosing A_1 on 70% and A_2 on 30% of occasions. This choice behavior is referred to as *probability matching* and represents a remarkable violation of EUT that has been observed in numerous studies of human choice (for reviews, see, e.g., Koehler & James, 2014; Myers, 1975; Vulkan, 2000). Probability matching is inconsistent with EUT because, for every choice, the expected payoff from selecting A_1 exceeds the expected payoff from selecting A_2, thus rendering A_2 an irrational choice on every occasion. Consequently, probability matching leads to inferior overall outcomes; in this example, it results in an average choice accuracy of 58% ($.70 \times .70 + .30 \times .30 = .58$). Considering the simplicity and transparency of most choice situations in which probability matching typically occurs, it represents a remarkable but paradigmatic phenomenon in human decision making under risk. The observation that this and other deviations from rational choice theory occur has profoundly affected the development of decision making research in recent decades.

In the remainder of this chapter, we consider two of these developments in the context of risky choice: (a) the notion that human choice can be viewed as "boundedly" rather than "fully" rational, most notably advanced by Herbert Simon (1955, 1956), and (b) the development of more descriptive theories of human choice, most prominently *prospect theory*, as proposed by Daniel Kahneman and Amos Tversky (1979).

We examine these key developments with a particular focus on the role of learning and experience, which implies a fundamental distinction between "one-shot" decisions that are made on a single occasion without any opportunity to learn, and repeated decisions that are made many times under very similar conditions. The finding that people systematically violate the principles of EUT in many one-shot choice tasks is surprising and has inspired tremendous theoretical advancement (such as the development of prospect theory as outlined later in this chapter). Yet the focus on the mind's shortcomings in situations bereft of any opportunity to learn or improve can lead to a rather pessimistic outlook on human decision making as flawed, biased, and error prone (see, e.g., Gilovich, Griffin, & Kahneman, 2002; Kahneman, Slovic, & Tversky, 1982). By investigating the role of first-hand experience in many such experimental situations, researchers have recently found that "decisions from experience" often markedly depart from those made on the basis of abstract summary descriptions.

In this chapter, we devote particular attention to the learning that precedes choice and the feedback that shapes subsequent decisions. Yet even in situations with ample opportunity to learn, human choice is not devoid of errors. Experience is not a panacea. Probability matching exemplifies one such error typically observed in repeated decisions and as such it provides a convenient example upon which to build our review. In what follows, we argue that the concept of bounded rationality can shed light on when and why the opportunity to learn helps or

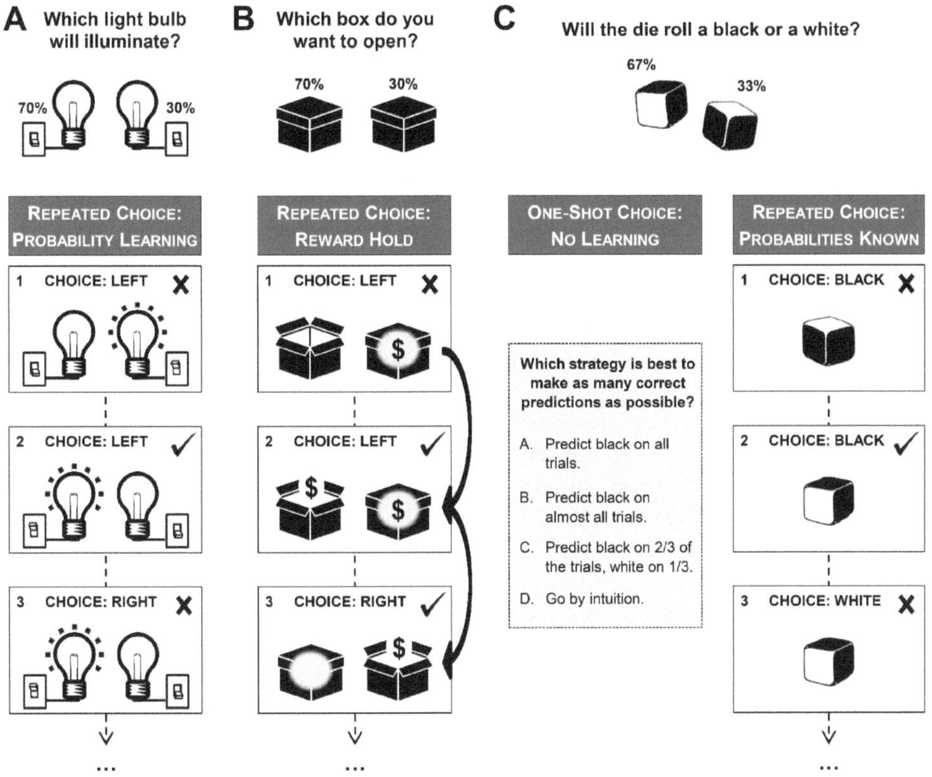

Figure 28.1 Illustration of different choice paradigms used to study the probability matching phenomenon. (A) Repeated choice probability learning paradigm (e.g., Estes & Straughan, 1954). Participants repeatedly predict which of two lightbulbs will illuminate without prior knowledge about the lighting frequencies (70% vs. 30%). Following each decision, participants observe which lightbulb actually lit up and thus receive trial-by-trial outcome feedback (here a cross/checkmark indicates an incorrect/correct prediction, respectively). The lightbulbs illuminate at random with the preprogrammed lighting frequency. (B) Repeated choice paradigm in which "uncollected" reward at the option not selected by the participant is retained across choice trials (e.g., Schulze, van Ravenzwaaij, & Newell, 2017). In the depicted example, a reward is scheduled at the right option in the first trial and then held across trials until the participant first selects that option in the third trial. This manipulation creates sequential choice–outcome dependencies in the reward structure. (C) The "die problem" as a one-shot choice paradigm (e.g., Gal & Baron, 1996) and as a repeated choice paradigm (e.g., Newell & Rakow, 2007). In both variants, participants read a summary description of the dice game that reveals the outcome probabilities at the outset (e.g., four sides are black and two are white). Participants then make either a single choice by selecting the strategy that is best (or ranking strategies) in terms of making as many correct predictions as possible (left-hand panel) or repeated predictions with feedback following each choice (right-hand panel). In the one-shot task, strategy A corresponds to probability maximizing and strategy C corresponds to probability matching.

hinders decision making. Of crucial importance is the ability to capitalize on the structure of environments in which decisions are typically made. From this perspective, many choice phenomena (like probability matching) that appear as errors in the laboratory might be "rational" in the real world.

Probability matching and the structure of the environment

Bounded and ecological rationality

The concept of bounded rationality acknowledges that decision makers' processing of information is subject to cognitive limitations and that they often have to navigate decision environments in which the information available is limited. Nevertheless, by capitalizing on the structure of these environments and using their limited cognitive resources intelligently, people are often able to make decisions that are "good enough" (Simon, 1955, 1956). Simon's ideas had a tremendous impact on decision making research and have inspired many research programs (e.g., Gigerenzer, Todd, & the ABC Research Group, 1999; Gilovich et al., 2002; Payne, Bettman, & Johnson, 1993). The focus on mapping the cognitive processes available to decision makers onto environments characteristic of real-world decision making – that is, on the *ecological rationality* of people's choices (Todd, Gigerenzer, & the ABC Research Group, 2012) – has provided considerable insight into how environmental characteristics can foster or impede the success of simple heuristic strategies relative to optimizing responses. Hoffrage, Hafenbrädl, and Marewski (this volume) consider such "fast-and-frugal heuristics" in detail.

Applied to the probability matching phenomenon, the idea of ecological rationality suggests that probability matching may be adaptive in many real-world choice environments (see, e.g., Gaissmaier & Schooler, 2008; Gallistel, 1990; Green, Benson, Kersten, & Schrater, 2010; Schulze, van Ravenzwaaij, & Newell, 2015). One prevalent real-world environmental characteristic is the existence of sequential dependencies or "patterns" in a sequence of events (see, e.g., Ayton & Fischer, 2004). For example, seasonal patterns in resource availability might create a foraging environment in which, at some times, an animal is *more* likely to find a ripe fruit at a recently exploited location (e.g., in summer); yet, at other times, it is *less* likely to encounter another resource at a recently visited site (e.g., in winter). To guarantee survival, the animal must be well attuned to such sequential dependencies between choice and the ensuing foraging success, and adjust its behavior accordingly. By contrast, most repeated choice paradigms in which probability matching typically occurs impose the assumption that outcomes are serially independent (as illustrated in Figure 28.1A). This mismatch between the experimental environment and the expectations held by an "ecologically rational" decision maker could contribute to the emergence of choice diversification strategies such as probability matching.

In line with this idea, Green et al. (2010) showed that the behavior of an *optimal* Bayesian algorithm initialized with the erroneous – but ecologically plausible – belief that outcomes are temporally interdependent, converges on probability matching. To create a laboratory analog for settings with sequential dependencies, Schulze et al. (2017) applied a concurrent reinforcement procedure typically used in animal learning research in the context of human decision making. In their task, rewards were scheduled probabilistically (as in standard repeated choice), but at the option not selected by the decision maker, the "uncollected" reward was retained across choice trials. Figure 28.1B illustrates this procedure. This manipulation introduced sequential choice–outcome dependencies to the reward structure: the probability of being rewarded for choosing an option increased with time spent not choosing that option because rewards scheduled to occur were held until collected. In this changeable environment, neither option was a superior choice throughout and people learned to diversify their choices accordingly. A more extreme form of sequential dependencies in the outcome structure is a fixed outcome pattern. For example, a pattern in which a reward appears twice in a row on the left, followed by once on the right, then twice in a row on the left again, and so on. If a fixed pattern did exist, a rule searching strategy that identified the pattern would guarantee complete predictive success and thus would be superior to static probability maximizing. Gaissmaier and Schooler (2008) showed that probability matching sometimes emerges as a by-product of exploratory pattern search strategies (see also Peterson & Ulehla, 1965) and that decision makers who probability-matched in the absence of patterns were more likely to detect regularities in the outcome sequence when patterns were introduced. Together, these findings highlight that people indeed use adaptive diversification strategies such as probability matching when it is rational to do so.

Another characteristic of many real-world choice situations is that decision makers rarely choose in social isolation. Rather, decision makers seeking to exploit limited resources under natural circumstances (e.g., forage for food) are typically in fierce competition with others. The more individuals compete at the seemingly richest resource, the smaller each individual's share. In nature, this situation cannot remain stable, because individuals who sometimes select options with potentially scarce resources that are exploitable under less competition would attain a key evolutionary advantage (Gallistel, 1990; Gigerenzer, 2000). It can be shown that (under certain plausible assumptions) an evolutionarily stable strategy in this context is for the group of foragers to distribute their choices among options relative to the options' reward potential – that is, to probability match (see Fretwell, 1972). To examine the role of competition in facilitating human decision making, Schulze et al. (2015) used a competitive version of a standard repeated choice paradigm. In their paradigm, each decision maker competed against a computerized opponent to exploit a monetary resource that an indifferent "nature" repeatedly placed at one of two choice options with unequal odds. When both competitors converged on the same choice, potential rewards were split evenly between them. In this situation, the success of any strategy depends on the behavior of the opponent, which is what was manipulated. In one condition, the opponent probabilistically imitated participants' choices so that probability *matching* was optimal (as is the case in natural settings, in which foragers are sensitive to their competitors' actions); in a second condition, the opponent was indifferent and probability *maximizing* was optimal (as is the case in a solitary setting). In both conditions, participants adopted accurate choice strategies at asymptote (either optimal matching or maximizing). These findings suggest that people are indeed sensitive to such differences in opponent behavior and demonstrate that adaptive probability matching emerges under competition.

What would happen if two humans (rather than one person and a computer) competed in the Schulze et al. (2015) paradigm? Interestingly, extending the task to involve social interaction between two people offers a means to accomplish a goal thought to drive probability matching in the individual choice case: beating the odds and correctly predicting the outcome every time. In a solitary choice task, many people may be reluctant to accept the guaranteed loss rate associated with a maximizing strategy – that is, getting the answer wrong on a certain 30% of trials when the outcome probabilities are 70:30, as in the example above – and may invest considerable effort in finding a strategy that offers higher predictive success by searching for a pattern in the outcome sequence (Gaissmaier & Schooler, 2008; Peterson & Ulehla, 1965). In a socially interactive choice task, however, two people can fully exploit the uncertain environment by simply selecting opposite options on each turn – that is, by covering all bases. Putting this notion to the test, Schulze and Newell (2015) found that, when participants' attention was drawn to gains achievable via a pair of players (a dyad) rather than to individual gains, most learned to coordinate a strategy with the other player that allowed them to obtain all resources from the uncertain environment. This was the case even though permissible forms of communication were limited to signaling behavioral intent via repeated choices. Thus, by extending a typically solitary "game against nature" in this way, we identified the competitive structure of a situation as an important social factor in determining how people cope with or even learn to exploit uncertain and risky environmental aspects.

The structure of experimental environments

Although it is instructive to consider real-world choice environments in which probability matching would naturally occur, it is also important to consider the structure of most *experimental* environments to which people may *mis*apply a (sometimes adaptive) matching strategy. In other words, in situations where people match erroneously, why do they make this mistake and which factors can push them toward behaving more rationally? Addressing this question, Shanks et al. (2002) explored simple probability learning tasks (similar to the one illustrated in Figure 28.1A) in which participants received large performance-related financial incentives, meaningful and regular feedback, and extensive training (up to 1,800 learning trials in one experiment). In these learning environments, large proportions of participants (about 70%) learned to respond optimally and to maximize their payoffs. The authors defined maximizing as a run of at least 50 consecutive choices of the more likely option, but many participants exceeded this criterion. Each of the three manipulated factors contributed to participants' ability to maximize: both feedback and payoffs affected the overall likelihood of exclusively choosing the best alternative, and stable performance was not reached until after many hundreds of trials. These findings suggest that one reason for people's mistaken tendency to probability match might be that key structural features of most repeated choice environments (e.g., missing feedback, training, or incentives) impede their ability to learn which strategy works best.

Yet the fact that most people need such extensive support (in the form of incentives, feedback, and training) to adopt a maximizing strategy implies that this strategy does not readily spring to mind as a powerful solution. In other words, the maximizing solution may require more cognitive effort to be conceived as a valid and potent strategy (Koehler & James, 2009). Indeed, research has shown that inferior probability matching is less prevalent in individuals with high cognitive abilities (West & Stanovich, 2003) and is virtually absent when the cognitive power of a small group of people is combined via group discussion (Schulze & Newell, 2016). Moreover, Koehler and James (2010) found that when participants were prompted to contrast the potential profitability of probability matching and maximizing before completing a choice task, fewer people probability matched (see also Newell, Koehler, James, Rakow, & van Ravenzwaaij, 2013). Thus, without explicit encouragement to consider different ways of responding, some participants may simply fail to realize that maximizing is the optimal response. Proponents of dual-system views of judgment and decision making argue that these results can be explained via the interaction of two systems (see Evans, this volume): an intuitive system that produces the spontaneous (but incorrect) probability matching response, and a deliberative system which overrides this initial impulse and then maximizes, provided instructional scaffolding is in place or individual differences grant access to greater cognitive capacity (e.g., Koehler & James, 2009, 2014; West & Stanovich, 2003). Dual process theories have been pursued in many research domains beyond repeated choice (for a review see, e.g., Evans, 2008) but have also been criticized on theoretical grounds (e.g., Keren, 2013; Kruglanski, & Gigerenzer, 2011; Newell & Shanks, 2014).

Another important factor potentially influencing people's performance in repeated choice is their knowledge of the underlying probability structure and the format in which this information is conveyed to them. In this context, it is important to note that probability matching was initially observed in learning experiments (e.g., Humphreys, 1939) and has predominantly been studied with probability learning paradigms that involve experiencing outcomes and associated probabilities (see Figure 28.1A for an illustration). A less common procedure is to give participants a verbal description of the problem and then to ask them to make a single ("one-shot") decision about different hypothetical strategies (e.g., Gal & Baron, 1996; Newell & Rakow, 2007;

West & Stanovich, 2003). The left-hand panel in Figure 28.1C illustrates this approach: participants read a description of a hypothetical dice game in which a fair die with more sides of one color than another (e.g., four black and two white sides) is to be rolled many (e.g., 100) times. Next, participants are asked to rank different strategies (or select one) – including probability matching ("predict the two events in accord with the expected probability of their occurrence; e.g., predict black on 2/3 of the trials, white on 1/3") and maximizing ("predict the more frequent event, i.e., black, on all trials") – according to the strategies' potential for making as many correct predictions about which side will come up as possible. Although the description unambiguously states the probabilities associated with each outcome at the outset, surprisingly many people fail to recognize maximizing as the optimal solution in this task (Gal & Baron, 1996). These findings thus mirror the results from probability learning experiments.

Combining these two approaches, Newell and Rakow (2007) used a hybrid choice problem involving both a verbal description and trial-by-trial outcome experience (see right-hand panel in Figure 28.1C). Specifically, all participants read a summary of the dice game scenario, but only some participants selected a single global prediction strategy for many rolls of the die (as described above), whereas others made repeated predictions for *each* roll of the die and saw the outcome of each roll after making their prediction. The authors found that the experience of making repeated choices can initially affect responding ***negatively***; during the first trials, participants who read a description and experienced making choices and seeing outcomes showed fewer maximizing responses than did participants who only read the description. Interestingly, sufficient trial-by-trial prediction experience and outcome feedback eroded this initial negative influence of experience; asymptotic trial-by-trial choice was slightly superior to description-based decisions (Newell & Rakow, 2007). Surprisingly, these effects of feedback were observed despite the feedback being completely uninformative and therefore normatively irrelevant: the die was fair, the probabilities were stationary, and the outcome probabilities were known before any feedback was received. The finding that feedback nonetheless influenced the rate of maximizing suggests two conclusions. First, the initial detrimental effect of experience likely reflected participants' attempts to get all predictions right, which requires responding in a manner that is "representative" of the die's color configuration (Kahneman & Tversky, 1972). Second, people seem to only gradually "learn" to choose optimally in a task that (normatively) requires no learning. The latter point indicates that feedback seems to trigger a trial-by-trial search for alternative choice strategies that helps at least some participants to eventually discover the maximizing strategy. Importantly, this period of discovery takes time; the beneficial effect of outcome feedback took many trials to emerge.

In summary, people's tendency to probability match in repeated risky choice has been studied with many different paradigms (Figure 28.1 illustrates only a few examples) and has been explained in numerous different ways. We have reviewed explanations for the phenomenon in terms of an adaptive response to the structure of many natural choice environments (e.g., under competition or in the presence of sequential dependencies; Gaissmaier & Schooler, 2008; Green et al., 2010; Schulze et al., 2015, 2017), deficiencies in the structure of experimental task environments (e.g., Shanks et al., 2002), the comparatively higher cognitive effort or capacity needed to identify maximizing as the best alternative (Koehler & James, 2010; Schulze & Newell, 2016; West & Stanovich, 2003), and a lack of first-hand experience with the problem (Newell & Rakow, 2007; Shanks et al., 2002). Thus, no single cause but different cognitive, environmental, and social factors appear to determine people's engagement in probability matching and maximizing behavior. This diverse outlook on the problem has spawned various theoretical interpretations and implications. On the one hand, the notion of "smart" probability matching has been taken to imply a well attuned adaptation of the boundedly rational decision maker to prevalent choice environments. On the other hand, the view of matching as an intuitive shortcut aligns with dual-system interpretations of cognitive processing. Moreover, the notion that "experienced" and "described" information is not necessarily equivalent for decision makers has received considerable attention in a closely related research area: decisions between monetary gambles, often involving a "sure" and a "risky" option (e.g., Barron & Erev, 2003; Hertwig, Barron, Weber, & Erev, 2004; for reviews, see Camilleri & Newell, 2013; Hertwig & Erev, 2009; Rakow & Newell, 2010). We now turn to this burgeoning area of research.

Risky choices from description and experience

Recall the umbrella problem described at the start of this chapter. You have a choice between (1) buying an umbrella and incurring a sure loss of −$10 or (2) not buying an umbrella and risking a loss of −$100 with probability .70, and $0 otherwise. By selecting one of the options on the basis of this information, you would essentially make a one-off "decision from description," that is, a decision that is made once, based on a descriptive summary of all possible outcomes and their associated probabilities of occurrence. This task format constitutes the procedural bedrock of decades of human decision making research. Indeed, this format is associated with an influential theory developed to provide a descriptive alternative to EUT as a model of human choice, namely prospect theory (Kahneman & Tversky, 1979, 1984; Tversky & Kahneman, 1992). Although prospect theory has been a tremendously influential model of risky choice for psychological research, economic science, and beyond, it is not without critique and alternative theories of risky choice exist: e.g., security-potential/aspiration theory (Lopes, 1987; Lopes & Oden, 1999), the transfer of attention exchange model (Birnbaum, 2008; Birnbaum & Chavez, 1997), regret theory (Loomes & Sugden, 1982), decision field theory (Busemeyer & Townsend, 1993), or the priority heuristic (Brandstätter, Gigerenzer, & Hertwig, 2006). However, here we focus on prospect theory and its predictions for both description- and experience-based choice.

Prospect theory

Consider the following choice between two options that yield different hypothetical payoffs with differing odds:

(A) Win $4,000 with probability .80, $0 with probability .20.
(B) Win $3,000 for sure.

Kahneman and Tversky (1979) found that most people faced with this hypothetical choice (80%) prefer option B over option A (although the expected *value* of option A is larger than the sure win of $3,000: .80 × $4,000 + .20 × $0 = $3,200). They termed this observation – that people tend to overweight outcomes that are considered certain, relative to those that are merely probable – the *certainty effect*. Now compare the choice above with the following one:

(C) Win $4,000 with probability .20, $0 with probability .80.
(D) Win $3,000 with probability .25; $0 with probability .75.

Here, neither option offers a sure payoff, but both options can be derived from the first pair by simply dividing the probability of winning in both options by 4 (i.e., .80/4 = .20 and 1.0/4 = .25). In this scenario, most people prefer option C over option D (65%; Kahneman & Tversky, 1979). Why is this pattern of choices surprising and, in fact, a violation of standard EUT? Recall that EUT rests on the principle of maximizing expected utility. In the first example, this principle implies that for the large proportion of decision makers who preferred option B over option A the expected utility (U) of the certain option was greater than that of the risky option, that is, U(3000) > .80 U(4000). Moreover, according to EUT, dividing the probabilities of winning by the same factor (here, factor 4 to derive option C and D) should affect both options equally. That is, if the ratio of probabilities remains constant, preferences should remain stable. The modal preference for option C over option D, however, implies that .20 U(4,000) > .25 U(3,000) and thus, equivalently (if both sides are multiplied by 4), that .80 U(4,000) > U (3,000). In other words, reducing the chance of winning from certainty to .25 affected people's evaluations more strongly than did reducing that chance from .80 to .20 (Kahneman & Tversky, 1979).

This example is a variant of the Allais paradox (Allais, 1953) and one of numerous violations of the principle of maximization of expected utility put forward in criticism of standard EUT (see also Ellsberg, 1961; Kahneman & Tversky, 1979; Markowitz, 1952). To account for many of these violations, Kahneman and Tversky (1979) introduced *prospect theory*, which assumes that the probabilities of outcomes as well as the utilities of prospects undergo systematic cognitive distortions when processed by decision makers. These distortions are captured by two formal functions – a ***weighting function*** and a *value* ***function***. The weighting function, depicted in Figure 28.2, describes how outcome probabilities are transformed into subjective decision weights. In prospect theory, decision weights do not represent subjective estimates of the actual outcome probability; rather, they reflect the desirability (or weight) a decision maker associates with a given prospect. A key feature of the weighting function is that it amplifies the impact of small

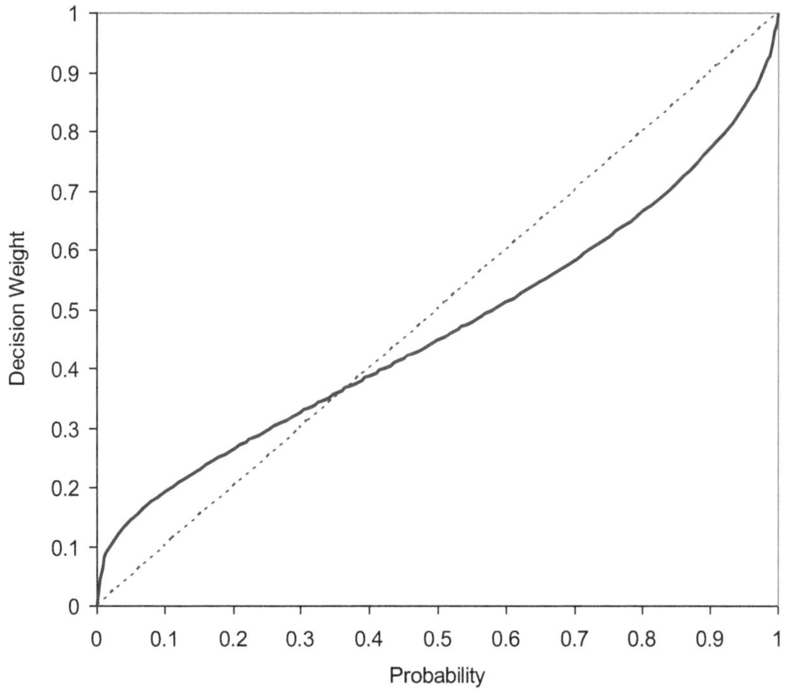

Figure 28.2 The weighting function of prospect theory

differences in extreme probabilities close to the boundary values of 1 (certainty) and 0 (impossibility) relative to that of small differences in moderate probabilities. For example, increasing the probability of gaining a reward by 1% affects the weight of that prospect more strongly when it changes the reward probability from .99 to 1 (or 0 to .01) than from .50 to .51. Thus, the shape of the weighting function can account for the certainty effect described above: because boundary probabilities undergo the most extreme transformation, people tend to prefer outcomes that are considered certain, relative to those that are merely probable.

Two other key features of the weighting function are noteworthy: small probabilities are subjectively "overweighted," whereas moderate to large probabilities are "underweighted." The subjective overweighting of small probabilities offers an explanation for people's preferences regarding very low-probability events, such as winning the lottery (and may also contribute to the Allais paradox described above: people overweight the small probability of "winning" nothing from option A and thus prefer the certain option B). Because the very low probability of winning a very large amount in the lottery is overweighted relative to the expected probability of that event, many people appear *risk seeking* in this context, meaning that they prefer the gamble over the small investment needed to buy a lottery ticket. Another example involving very-low-probability outcomes is the purchase of insurance. Again, prospect theory explains people's tendency to insure against very large losses in terms of overweighting the low probabilities with which these losses may occur. Note that the same process of overweighting low-probability events now implies the reverse risk preference: people are *risk averse* in this context, meaning that they prefer to pay an insurance premium over gambling with the possibility of the insured-against disaster.

This reversal in risk preferences in the domain of "losses" (insurance) versus "gains" (lottery) brings us to the second important feature of prospect theory: its *value function*. The value function, depicted in Figure 28.3, describes how monetary outcomes are transformed into subjective values relative to a neutral reference point. The reference point implies that people evaluate

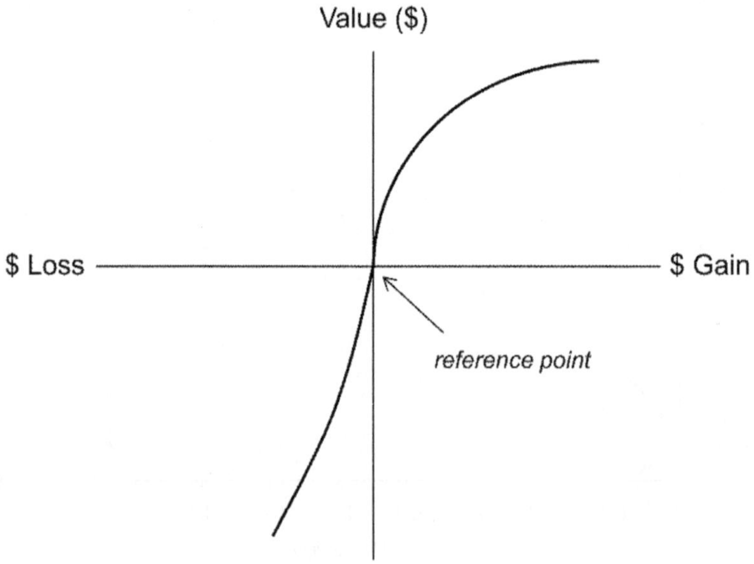

Figure 28.3 The value function of prospect theory

outcomes in terms of gains and losses based on their relation to a neutral position: to the right of this point, the values of gains are transformed by a concave function; to the left, the values of losses are transformed by a convex curve. The curvature of the value function implies risk aversion in the domain of gains and risk seeking in the domain of losses.

To illustrate this implication, let us consider a hypothetical choice that is identical to our first gamble ($3,000 for sure versus $4,000 with probability .80), but with the gains converted to losses: which would you prefer, a sure loss of −$3,000 or an 80% chance of losing −$4,000? Kahneman and Tversky (1979) found that the vast majority of people (92%) preferred the gamble over the sure loss, which is the "mirror image" of the preference observed for the gain domain (hence, they labeled this phenomenon the ***reflection effect***). Both risk preferences are implied by the decreasing slopes of the value function as it moves away from the reference point (toward greater gains or losses). In other words, a change from 0 to $100 (or 0 to −$100) is valued more strongly than a change from $1,000 to $1,100 (or −$1,000 to −$1,100). Note that this pattern of preferences is the reverse of what is observed when outcomes are associated with very low probabilities in the lottery and insurance examples. That is, when large or medium probabilities are involved, prospect theory predicts risk aversion for gains and risk seeking for losses; when small probabilities are involved, prospect theory predicts risk seeking for gains and risk aversion for losses (see Table 28.1). Another important feature of the value function is its steeper slope in the loss than in the gain domain, which implies that the displeasure associated with a loss is larger than the pleasure derived from gaining the same amount.

In summary, prospect theory captures many aspects of people's actual preferences in risky choice and thus provides a compelling descriptive alternative to the normative account of EUT (which asserts how people *ought* to make decisions rather than describing how they *actually* make them). One of prospect theory's main insights is the influence of ***framing*** on people's decisions. The reflection effect in gamble problems – and people's choices in simple word problems like the famous Asian disease problem (see Tversky & Kahneman, 1981) – demonstrate the susceptibility of choice to frames that emphasize different aspects of a problem (e.g., gains versus losses, or lives *saved* versus lives *lost*). Moreover, prospect theory's value and weighting functions provide a framework for modeling how people might differ in their attitudes toward risk. For instance, different degrees of concavity (convexity) of the value function imply more or less risk aversion (seeking) in individual decision makers. Individual differences in risk taking have been studied in various regards, for example, with focus on differences related to gender, culture, age, or the specific risk domain (see, e.g., Defoe, Dubas, Figner, & van Aken, 2015; Fehr-Duda, De Gennaro, & Schubert, 2006; Glöckner & Pachur, 2012; Harbaugh, Krause, & Vesterlund, 2002; Harris, Jenkins, & Glaser, 2006; Mata, Josef, & Hertwig, 2016; Weber, Blais, & Betz, 2002). Another hallmark insight from prospect theory is what has become known as the ***fourfold pattern*** of risky choice, illustrated by the risk preferences outlined above and summarized in Table 28.1. Surprisingly, however, as discussed in the next section, the elicitation of this pattern of preferences has been found to hinge on the format with which information about probabilities and outcomes is relayed to decision makers.

Table 28.1 The fourfold pattern of risky choice that prospect theory can explain

	Gains	*Losses*
Small probabilities	Risk seeking	Risk aversion
Medium and large probabilities	Risk aversion	Risk seeking

A description–experience "gap"

Prospect theory was originally developed as a descriptive model of decision making under risk in situations in which outcomes and probabilities are stated (or described) transparently and unmistakably (but see Tversky & Fox, 1995). However, many real-life choice situations do not grant access to exhaustive probabilistic information; rather, decision makers need to learn about the potential consequences of their choices from *experience* (Hertwig et al., 2004; Weber, Shafir, & Blais, 2004). Although weather-related decisions (such as whether or not to take an umbrella) *can* be based on probability estimates obtained from the weather forecast, people may simply draw on their personal experience with similar meteorological conditions. Other everyday situations cannot be summarized in descriptive terms because the respective data are simply unavailable (e.g., consider deciding whether it is safe to buy lunch at a particular street cart – the owner will unlikely be willing or able to give you information on the proportion of customers who experience food poisoning after eating there). One reason why such "decisions from experience" have attracted attention is that the choices of people forced to learn about probabilities and outcomes from experience often diverge markedly from the predictions of prospect theory. This divergence has become known as the *description–experience gap* in risky choice (Hertwig & Erev, 2009; Rakow & Newell, 2010).

Three main paradigms have been used to study decisions from experience: a sampling paradigm (e.g., Hertwig et al., 2004), a partial feedback paradigm (e.g., Barron & Erev, 2003), and a full feedback paradigm (e.g., Yechiam & Busemeyer, 2006). Figure 28.4 illustrates these paradigms and compares them to the task format associated with the study of decisions from description. The general setup of the three experience-based paradigms is similar: participants are presented with two unlabeled options, for example, two unmarked buttons on a computer screen, and asked to choose between them over multiple trials. Following each click, the outcome associated with that button is revealed. These outcomes are randomly drawn from an underlying distribution, which has been preprogrammed by the experimenter but is unknown to the participant, who has to learn from experience. Figure 28.4 illustrates the example introduced above – a choice between $3,000 for sure versus $4,000 with probability .80 – in which people showed an overwhelming preference for the certain reward in decisions from description. An equivalent problem in the context of decisions from experience would have two buttons, one revealing a $3,000 outcome every time it is clicked and the other a $4,000 outcome on 80% of clicks and $0 on the remaining 20%. In the *sampling paradigm*, clicks of each button are inconsequential, and participants can sample for as long as they wish before making a choice. When the participant decides that she has accrued enough information about the underlying outcome distributions, she makes a single consequential choice (note that this setup maintains the "one-shot" nature of the choice context that is also characteristic of decisions from description). In the *partial feedback* paradigm, each click actually incurs the gain or loss indicated by the outcome (which is typically of the order of cents rather than the thousands of dollars in this example!). Participants thus make a series of consequential choices (rather than just one). In the *full feedback* paradigm, participants are additionally shown the outcome they would have obtained had they clicked on the other button. Thus, they again make a series of consequential choices, but have access to complete (rather than partial) outcome information. Note that the two feedback paradigms applied to the study of decisions from experience share striking similarities with the standard probability learning paradigm illustrated in Figure 28.1A, in which participants repeatedly predict which of two mutually exclusive outcomes will occur. In all of these paradigms, participants are faced with the same choice problem many times, have limited initial information, and can learn from feedback that they receive after each decision. Relating the choice phenomena observed in decisions from experience with those observed in probability learning can thus provide fruitful integrative approaches to understanding the role of learning and experience in decision making – a point to which we will return shortly (see also Erev & Barron, 2005; Newell & Rakow, 2007).

How does people's behavior in decisions from description differ from that in decisions from experience? Contrary to the pattern described by the certainty effect, participants making decisions from experience in this problem prefer the risky option – that is, they prefer $4,000 with probability .80 over $3,000 for sure (see, e.g., Barron & Erev, 2003; Hertwig et al., 2004). Furthermore, if the prospects are converted into losses, such that one button offers −$3,000 on every click and the other −$4,000 on 80% of clicks, participants learn to prefer the certain loss of −$3,000. In other words, when participants learn from experience, there is a striking reversal of the certainty effect, and participants appear to be risk seeking in the domain of gains and risk averse in the domain of losses – the opposite of what prospect theory predicts. Direct comparison of the three experience-based approaches has revealed that all three paradigms produce this "gap" but to different magnitudes (Camilleri & Newell, 2011b). One way to summarize this discrepancy between description- and experience-based choice is to say that people making decisions from experience tend to choose as if they ***underweight*** the smaller probability (i.e., 20% in Figure 28.4). In the gain domain, this means that they act as if they underweight the possibility of gaining nothing when preferring to gamble (.80 chance of $4,000); in the loss domain, they act as if they underweight the possibility of losing nothing when preferring the sure loss (−$3,000). In essence, where prospect theory predicts overweighting, decisions from experience show underweighting.

What causes this *description–experience gap*? Two aspects need to be considered when addressing this question: (1) each of the experience-based paradigms shown in Figure 28.4 may have particular features that contribute uniquely to the divergence; and (2) all three paradigms may

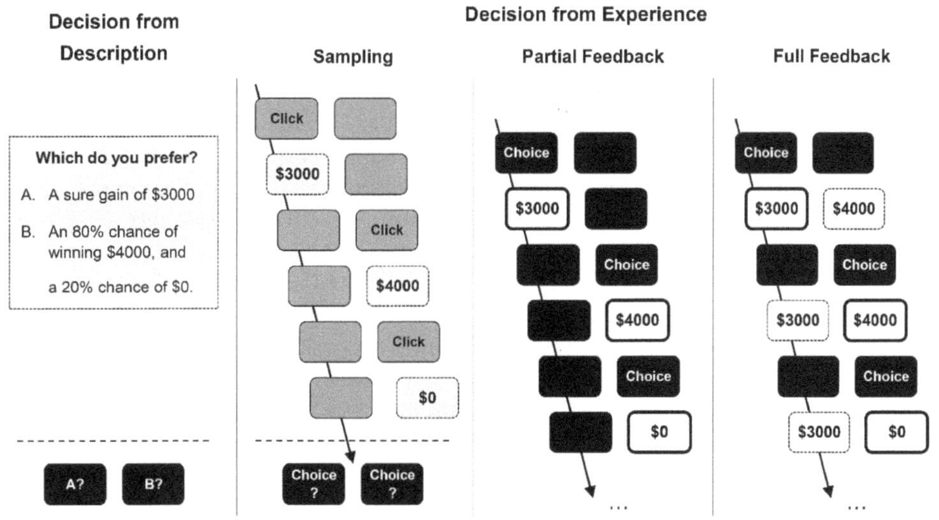

Figure 28.4 Comparison of the choice paradigms used to study decisions from description and decisions from experience. For the three experience-based paradigms, gray/black shading indicates inconsequential sampling/consequential choice trials, respectively; solid/dashed outlines represent received/forgone outcomes, respectively. See main text for detailed summaries of all paradigms.

capture similar, more general psychological processes associated with the effect. First, consider some of the key differences between the sampling and feedback paradigms. The sampling paradigm dissociates *exploration* (finding out about options) from *exploitation* (choosing an option for reward) – two aspects that are intertwined in the feedback paradigms. Thus, in the sampling paradigm, which option is eventually chosen likely depends on the information initially sampled. Yet many studies using this paradigm have found that people do not sample enough: they draw a median of only 5–10 observations per option (Hau, Pleskac, & Hertwig, 2010). These small samples are likely to be systematically biased toward under-representing rare outcomes (Hertwig & Pleskac, 2010) and may not include an observation of the low-probability event, that is, the zero outcome when choosing option B in the example depicted in Figure 28.4 (e.g., more than 70% of participants in Hertwig et al., 2004, never encountered the rare event in one problem). This notion of *biased samples* has led some researchers to interpret the gap produced by the sampling paradigm as a mere statistical phenomenon owed to sampling error (e.g., Camilleri & Newell, 2011a; Fox & Hadar, 2006, Rakow, Demes, & Newell, 2008). Consistent with this idea, some studies have found that the gap disappears when people's decisions are regarded as based on actually experienced (as opposed to programmed) outcome probabilities (Fox & Hadar, 2006; Rakow et al., 2008). Other studies, however, have not confirmed these claims (Hau et al., 2010; Hau, Pleskac, Kiefer, & Hertwig, 2008; Ungemach, Chater, & Stewart, 2009). In summary, the configuration and size of the sample drawn have indisputably been shown to affect experience-based choice in the sampling paradigm, but the relative importance of this factor remains contested.

What about the underweighting of rare events in the two feedback-based paradigms? In the partial feedback paradigm, the only way to learn about an option is to choose it, even if one fears this choice is suboptimal. This can lead to what has been termed a "hot stove" effect – the notion that good and bad experiences affect choice asymmetrically (Denrell & March, 2001). Good outcomes (cold stove lids) increase the likelihood of repeating a choice and therefore increase the participant's knowledge about the option that yielded that outcome. Bad outcomes (hot stove lids) decrease the probability of repeating a choice, meaning that there is no increase in a participant's knowledge about the option associated with that outcome. In the context of the partial feedback paradigm, the hot stove effect can lead to risk aversion in participants "burned" by a negative outcome, who are less likely to repeat that choice. Indeed, in problems involving negative outcomes, people tend to choose the risky option less often in the partial feedback than in the full feedback paradigm (Camilleri & Newell, 2011b; Yechiam & Busemeyer, 2006). In other words, when people receive feedback only about the selected option, their choices are more in line with description-based choice – that is, there is a smaller "gap." This perhaps surprising finding that feedback about forgone rewards appears to *increase* the underweighting of rare events suggests that repeated experience of "what works best" most of the time leads people to discount the large negative effect of a rare outcome (Newell, Rakow, Yechiam, & Sambur, 2016; Yechiam & Busemeyer, 2006; Yechiam, Rakow, & Newell, 2015).

Which more general psychological factors may underlie the (persisting) description-experience gap in the three paradigms (especially in the full feedback paradigm, where sampling error is not applicable)? Recent research has provided several possible explanations. One possibility is that underweighting of rare events in decisions from experience may be driven by the reliance on small samples (e.g., Erev, Ert et al., 2010; Erev & Haruvy, 2016). Note that this point is somewhat different from the "biased-samples" explanation discussed earlier. Reliance on small samples implies that participants base their choice(s) on rather small sets of observations stored in memory; it does not imply that they have never observed a rare outcome. The consequence of recruiting only small samples from memory is that rare events will likely be under-represented (Hertwig

& Pleskac, 2010) and thus underweighted. Reliance on small samples is closely related to recency, that is, the idea that recent observations receive disproportionately high weight in the choice process (see, e.g., Hertwig et al., 2004). The effects of recency have received only mixed support as a primary cause of the description–experience gap, however (see, e.g., Camilleri & Newell, 2011a; Hau et al., 2008; Rakow et al., 2008; Rakow & Rahim, 2010; Ungemach et al., 2009).

In summary, various factors seem to be involved in the underweighting of rare events in the three experience-based choice paradigms – including biased samples, the hot stove effect, reliance on small samples, and recency (for more in-depth discussions of the description–experience gap and its potential causes, see Camilleri & Newell, 2013; Hertwig, 2012; Hertwig & Erev, 2009; Newell et al., 2015; Rakow & Newell, 2010). While research on when, why, and how decisions from description and experience diverge is still ongoing, the revival of experience-based paradigms in this context has already sparked fruitful studies in other areas. Specifically, the relative effects of verbal descriptions compared with or combined with gradual experience have been examined in the context of other choice phenomena, including base rate neglect (e.g., Hogarth & Soyer, 2011), ambiguity aversion (e.g., Dutt, Arló-Costa, Helzner, & Gonzalez, 2014; Güney & Newell, 2015), the conjunction fallacy (e.g., Hogarth & Soyer, 2011), the gambler's fallacy (e.g., Barron & Leider, 2010), and the phenomenon introduced at the start of this chapter: probability matching (e.g., Newell & Rakow, 2007). Thus, we have come full circle with our discussion.

This endeavor to examine different choice phenomena through a common lens of a description–experience distinction promises to facilitate the consolidation of common theoretical ground. For instance, if one applies the "weighting" terminology of decisions from experience and description to probability matching, this choice behavior could be interpreted as a tendency to *overweight* the importance of correctly predicting the rarer outcome, which is the opposite of the typical underweighting of rare events in decisions from experience (Newell & Rakow, 2007). Decisions from experience in the feedback paradigms in turn have been found to be well described by a probability matching assumption: the alternative that delivers the best outcome most of the time is chosen roughly in proportion to the relative probability with which it offers a better outcome (Erev & Barron, 2005). Moreover, as in decisions from experience, there is evidence from probability learning paradigms that recent outcomes have a disproportionate effect on people's choices: the longer ago an option yielded a reward, the more likely this option is going to be selected next – a phenomenon known as the gambler's fallacy (see, e.g., Estes, 1964). This negative recency effect observed when outcomes are experienced, however, diminishes when the same outcomes are summarized descriptively (Barron & Leider, 2010).

In short, the overarching insight from applying a description–experience distinction more broadly is that the mode of presentation matters and that learning and choosing from description are not necessarily equivalent to learning and deciding from experience.

Summary and concluding remarks

What constitutes a rational choice in the face of uncertain outcomes, and how do people actually make decisions under risk? Investigating these questions is a core pursuit of decision making research and has produced a rich and varied body of findings that have advanced the scientific understanding of the human mind and its applications. A primary focus in this chapter has been on how experience determines people's choices. We have discussed how probability matching emerges as a paradigmatic suboptimal choice when people make repeated decisions under risk. In some situations, probability matching may represent an overlearned response from common experiences in real-world contexts that can, when suboptimal, be overcome by sufficient feedback and adequately structured learning environments. Experience with outcome distributions has been found to produce strikingly different choice behavior than that observed in settings where this information is clearly stated. Generally, people tend to behave as if they underweight outcomes that occur with low probabilities in experience-based choice but act as if they overweight these rare events when making decisions from description. Many of the insights gained from laboratory experiments in these research fields have a clear and already realized potential to inform policy and design in the world outside the laboratory (see, e.g., Barron, Leider, & Stack, 2008; Erev & Roth, 2014; Li, Rakow, & Newell, 2009; Newell et al., 2016; Weber, 2006; Yechiam, Erev, & Barron, 2006). One example is risk communication. The finding that people tend to underweight the events they rarely experience has been invoked to explain people's surprisingly high "risk tolerance" with regard to climate change consequences or the occurrence of natural disasters: the rare direct contact with disastrous events is often embedded in the overwhelming experience that "usually" nothing bad happens (e.g., Newell et al., 2016; Weber, 2006). Thus, when communicating risks of all kinds (natural disasters, medical risks, terrorist attacks, etc.) particular focus should be given to the background of people's prior experience at which the warnings are aimed (Hertwig & Frey, 2015).

Although the study of the role of experience for decision making has proven to be a tremendously fruitful approach in recent years, many questions remain open or researchers have only begun to answer them. For instance, what qualities of experience distinguish it from summary descriptions? How do different types of experience (longer time horizons, vicarious experience, "incidental" experience, etc.) affect decision making? How can the findings from simple monetary gambles be mapped onto complex choice situations? Moreover, besides the prominent current interest in the role of learning and experience for decision making, many other exciting current trends in the field are worth noting. One example is the recent upsurge in the use of neuroimaging methods and the investigation of brain structures that underlie decision making, which has produced much insight into how value or utility might be calculated and represented in the brain (see, e.g., Glimcher & Fehr, 2013; Kable & Glimcher, 2009; Rangel, Camerer, & Montague, 2008; Vlaev, Chater, Stewart, & Brown, 2011). In terms of future directions, there are many exciting avenues open to future generations of researchers and it seems likely that ongoing exploration of the fundamental cognitive processes underlying decision making will continue to yield important theoretical and applied advances.

Acknowledgments

We are grateful to Tim Pleskac and Thorsten Pachur for helpful comments and we thank Susannah Goss for editorial assistance. This work was supported by Australian Research Council grants to BRN (DP140101145; FT110100151).

Notes

1 Based on the mean number of days with rain per year observed between 1858 and 2015 at Observatory Hill Weather Station, Sydney (Australian Bureau of Meteorology, 2015).

2 Decision theory commonly distinguishes between decisions under *risk*, where outcomes and probabilities are known to the decision maker, and decisions under *uncertainty*, where this is not the case (e.g., Knight, 1921; Luce & Raiffa, 1957). This distinction, however, does not imply a strict dichotomy. In many situations, decision makers can learn about initially unknown probabilities via repeated experience, thus reducing uncertainty (see, e.g., Hertwig, 2012; Rakow & Newell, 2010). In this chapter, we focus on situations where probabilities can, in principle, be ascertained by the decision maker.

References

Allais, M. (1953). Le comportement de l'homme rationnel devant le risque: Critique des postulats et axiomes de l'école Américaine [Rational man's behavior in the presence of risk: Critique of the postulates and axioms of the American school]. *Econometrica, 21*(4), 503–546.

Australian Bureau of Meteorology. (2015). *Climate statistics for Australian locations*. Retrieved from www.bom.gov.au/climate/averages/tables/cw_066062_All.shtml

Ayton, P., & Fischer, I. (2004). The hot hand fallacy and the gambler's fallacy: Two faces of subjective randomness? *Memory & Cognition, 32*(8), 1369–1378.

Barron, G., & Erev, I. (2003). Small feedback-based decisions and their limited correspondence to description-based decisions. *Journal of Behavioral Decision Making, 16*(3), 215–233.

Barron, G., & Leider, S. (2010). The role of experience in the gambler's fallacy. *Journal of Behavioral Decision Making, 23*(1), 117–129.

Barron, G., Leider, S., & Stack, J. (2008). The effect of safe experience on a warnings' impact: Sex, drugs, and rock-n-roll. *Organizational Behavior and Human Decision Processes, 106*(2), 125–142.

Birnbaum, M. H. (2008). New paradoxes of risky decision making. *Psychological Review, 115*(2), 463–501.

Birnbaum, M. H., & Chavez, A. (1997). Tests of theories of decision making: Violations of branch independence and distribution independence. *Organizational Behavior and Human Decision Processes, 71*(2), 161–194.

Brandstätter, E., Gigerenzer, G., & Hertwig, R. (2006). The priority heuristic: Making choices without trade-offs. *Psychological Review, 113*(2), 409–432.

Busemeyer, J. R., & Townsend, J. T. (1993). Decision field theory: A dynamic–cognitive approach to decision making in an uncertain environment. *Psychological Review, 100*(3), 432–459.

Camilleri, A. R., & Newell, B. R. (2011a). Description- and experience-based choice: Does equivalent information equal equivalent choice? *Acta Psychologica, 136*(3), 276–284.

Camilleri, A. R., & Newell, B. R. (2011b). When and why rare events are underweighted: A direct comparison of the sampling, partial feedback, full feedback and description choice paradigms. *Psychonomic Bulletin & Review, 18*(2), 377–384.

Camilleri, A. R., & Newell, B. R. (2013). Mind the gap? Description, experience, and the continuum of uncertainty in risky choice. In V. S. C. Pammi & N. Srinivasan (Eds.), *Decision making: Neural and behavioral approaches, Progress in Brain Research: Vol. 202* (pp. 55–71). Oxford, UK: Elsevier.

Defoe, I. N., Dubas, J. S., Figner, B., & van Aken, M. A. G. (2015). A meta-analysis on age differences in risky decision making: Adolescents versus children and adults. *Psychological Bulletin, 141*(1), 48–84.

Denrell, J., & March, J. G. (2001). Adaptation as information restriction: The hot stove effect. *Organization Science, 12*(5), 523–538.

Dutt, V., Arló-Costa, H., Helzner, J., & Gonzalez, C. (2014). The description–experience gap in risky and ambiguous gambles. *Journal of Behavioral Decision Making, 27*(4), 316–327.

Ellsberg, D. (1961). Risk, ambiguity, and the Savage axioms. *Quarterly Journal of Economics, 75*(4), 643–669.

Erev, I., & Barron, G. (2005). On adaptation, maximization, and reinforcement learning among cognitive strategies. *Psychological Review, 112*(4), 912–931.

Erev, I., Ert, E., Roth, A. E., Haruvy, E., Herzog, S. M., Hau, R., . . . Lebiere, C. (2010). A choice prediction competition: Choices from experience and from description. *Journal of Behavioral Decision Making, 23*(1), 15–47.

Erev, I., & Haruvy, E. (2016). Learning and the economics of small decisions. In J. H. Kagel & A. E. Roth (Eds.), *The handbook of experimental economics* (2nd ed, pp. 638–716.). Princeton, NJ: Princeton University Press.

Erev, I., & Roth, A. E. (2014). Maximization, learning, and economic behavior. *Proceedings of the National Academy of Sciences, 111*(Suppl. 3), 10818–10825.

Estes, W. K. (1964). Probability learning. In A. W. Melton (Ed.), *Categories of human learning* (pp. 89–128). New York, NY: Academic Press.

Estes, W. K., & Straughan, J. H. (1954). Analysis of a verbal conditioning situation in terms of statistical learning theory. *Journal of Experimental Psychology, 47*(4), 225–234.

Evans, J. St. B. T. (2008). Dual-processing accounts of reasoning, judgment, and social cognition. *Annual Review of Psychology, 59*, 255–278.

Fehr-Duda, H., De Gennaro, M., & Schubert, R. (2006). Gender, financial risk, and probability weights. *Theory and Decision, 60*(2), 283–313.

Fox, C. R., & Hadar, L. (2006). "Decisions from experience" = sampling error + prospect theory: Reconsidering Hertwig, Barron, Weber & Erev (2004). *Judgment and Decision Making, 1*(2), 159–161.
Fretwell, S. D. (1972). *Populations in a seasonal environment*. Princeton, NJ: Princeton University Press.
Gaissmaier, W., & Schooler, L. J. (2008). The smart potential behind probability matching. *Cognition, 109*(3), 416–422.
Gal, I., & Baron, J. (1996). Understanding repeated simple choices. *Thinking & Reasoning, 2*(1), 81–98.
Gallistel, C. R. (1990). *The organization of learning*. Cambridge, MA: MIT Press.
Gigerenzer, G. (2000). *Adaptive thinking: Rationality in the real world*. New York, NY: Oxford University Press.
Gigerenzer, G., Todd, P. M., & the ABC Research Group. (1999). *Simple heuristics that make us smart*. New York, NY: Oxford University Press.
Gilovich, T., Griffin, D., & Kahneman, D. (Eds.). (2002). *Heuristics and biases: The psychology of intuitive judgment*. Cambridge, UK: Cambridge University Press.
Glimcher, P. W., & Fehr, E. (Eds.). (2013). *Neuroeconomics: Decision making and the brain* (2nd ed.). London, UK: Academic Press.
Glöckner, A., & Pachur, T. (2012). Cognitive models of risky choice: Parameter stability and predictive accuracy of prospect theory. *Cognition, 123*(1), 21–32.
Green, C. S., Benson, C., Kersten, D., & Schrater, P. (2010). Alterations in choice behavior by manipulations of world model. *Proceedings of the National Academy of Sciences, 107*(37), 16401–16406.
Güney, Ş., & Newell, B. R. (2015). Overcoming ambiguity aversion through experience. *Journal of Behavioral Decision Making, 28*(2), 188–199.
Harbaugh, W. T., Krause, K., & Vesterlund, L. (2002). Risk attitudes of children and adults: Choices over small and large probability gains and losses. *Experimental Economics, 5*(1), 53–84.
Harris, C. R., Jenkins, M., & Glaser, D. (2006). Gender differences in risk assessment: Why do women take fewer risks than men? *Judgment and Decision Making, 1*(1), 48–63.
Hau, R., Pleskac, T. J., & Hertwig, R. (2010). Decisions from experience and statistical probabilities: Why they trigger different choices than a priori probabilities. *Journal of Behavioral Decision Making, 23*(1), 48–68.
Hau, R., Pleskac, T. J., Kiefer, J., & Hertwig, R. (2008). The description–experience gap in risky choice: The role of sample size and experienced probabilities. *Journal of Behavioral Decision Making, 21*(5), 493–518.
Hertwig, R. (2012). The psychology and rationality of decisions from experience. *Synthese, 187*(1), 269–292.
Hertwig, R., Barron, G., Weber, E. U., & Erev, I. (2004). Decisions from experience and the effect of rare events in risky choice. *Psychological Science, 15*(8), 534–539.
Hertwig, R., & Erev, I. (2009). The description–experience gap in risky choice. *Trends in Cognitive Sciences, 13*(12), 517–523.
Hertwig, R., & Frey, R. (2015). The challenge of the description−experience gap to the communication of risks. In H. Cho, T. Reimer, & K. A. McComas (Eds.), *The Sage handbook of risk communication* (pp. 24–40). Thousand Oaks, CA: Sage.
Hertwig, R., & Pleskac, T. J. (2010). Decisions from experience: Why small samples? *Cognition, 115*(2), 225–237.
Hogarth, R. M., & Soyer, E. (2011). Sequentially simulated outcomes: Kind experience versus nontransparent description. *Journal of Experimental Psychology: General, 140*(3), 434–463.
Humphreys, L. G. (1939). Acquisition and extinction of verbal expectations in a situation analogous to conditioning. *Journal of Experimental Psychology, 25*(3), 294–301.
Kable, J. W., & Glimcher, P. W. (2009). The neurobiology of decision: Consensus and controversy. *Neuron, 63*(6), 733–745.
Kahneman, D., Slovic, P., & Tversky, A. (Eds.). (1982). *Judgment under uncertainty: Heuristics and biases*. Cambridge, UK: Cambridge University Press.
Kahneman, D., & Tversky, A. (1972). Subjective probability: A judgment of representativeness. *Cognitive Psychology, 3*(3), 430–454.
Kahneman, D., & Tversky, A. (1979). Prospect theory: An analysis of decision under risk. *Econometrica, 47*(2), 263–291.
Kahneman, D., & Tversky, A. (1984). Choices, values, and frames. *American Psychologist, 39*(4), 341–350.
Kahneman, D., & Tversky, A. (2000). *Choices, values, and frames*. Cambridge, UK: Cambridge University Press.
Keren, G. (2013). A tale of two systems: A scientific advance or a theoretical stone soup? Commentary on Evans & Stanovich (2013). *Perspectives on Psychological Science, 8*(3), 257–262.
Knight, F. H. (1921). *Risk, uncertainty and profit*. Boston, MA: Houghton Mifflin.

Koehler, D. J., & James, G. (2009). Probability matching in choice under uncertainty: Intuition versus deliberation. *Cognition, 113*(1), 123–127.
Koehler, D. J., & James, G. (2010). Probability matching and strategy availability. *Memory & Cognition, 38*(6), 667–676.
Koehler, D. J., & James, G. (2014). Probability matching, fast and slow. In B. H. Ross (Ed.), *Psychology of learning and motivation* (Vol. 61, pp. 103–131). San Diego, CA: Elsevier.
Kruglanski, A. W., & Gigerenzer, G. (2011). Intuitive and deliberate judgments are based on common principles. *Psychological Review, 118*(1), 97–109.
Li, S. Y. W., Rakow, T., & Newell, B. R. (2009). Personal experience in doctor and patient decision making: From psychology to medicine. *Journal of Evaluation in Clinical Practice, 15*(6), 993–995.
Loomes, G., & Sugden, R. (1982). Regret theory: An alternative theory of rational choice under uncertainty. *Economic Journal, 92*(368), 805–824.
Lopes, L. L. (1987). Between hope and fear: The psychology of risk. *Advances in Experimental Social Psychology, 20*, 255–295.
Lopes, L. L., & Oden, G. C. (1999). The role of aspiration level in risky choice: A comparison of cumulative prospect theory and SP/A theory. *Journal of Mathematical Psychology, 43*(2), 286–313.
Luce, R. D., & Raiffa, H. (1957). *Games and decisions*. New York, NY: Wiley.
Markowitz, H. (1952). The utility of wealth. *Journal of Political Economy, 60*(2), 151–158.
Mata, R., Josef, A. K., & Hertwig, R. (2016). Propensity for risk taking across the life span and around the globe. *Psychological Science, 27*(2), 231–243.
Myers, J. L. (1975). Probability learning and sequence learning. In W. K. Estes (Ed.), *Handbook of learning and cognitive processes* (pp. 171–205). Hillsdale, NJ: Lawrence Erlbaum Associates.
Newell, B. R., Koehler, D. J., James, G., Rakow, T., & van Ravenzwaaij, D. (2013). Probability matching in risky choice: The interplay of feedback and strategy availability. *Memory & Cognition, 41*(3), 329–338.
Newell, B. R., Lagnado, D. A., & Shanks, D. R. (2015). *Straight choices: The psychology of decision making* (2nd ed.). Hove, UK: Psychology Press.
Newell, B. R., & Rakow, T. (2007). The role of experience in decisions from description. *Psychonomic Bulletin & Review, 14*(6), 1133–1139.
Newell, B. R., Rakow, T., Yechiam, E., & Sambur, M. (2016). Rare disaster information can increase risk-taking. *Nature Climate Change, 6*, 158–161.
Newell, B. R., & Shanks, D. R. (2014). Unconscious influences on decision making: A critical review. *Behavioral and Brain Sciences, 37*(1), 1–19.
Payne, J. W., Bettman, J. R., & Johnson, E. J. (1993). *The adaptive decision maker*. Cambridge, UK: Cambridge University Press.
Peterson, C. R., & Ulehla, Z. J. (1965). Sequential patterns and maximizing. *Journal of Experimental Psychology, 69*(1), 1–4.
Rakow, T., Demes, K. A., & Newell, B. R. (2008). Biased samples not mode of presentation: Re-examining the apparent underweighting of rare events in experience-based choice. *Organizational Behavior and Human Decision Processes, 106*(2), 168–179.
Rakow, T., & Newell, B. R. (2010). Degrees of uncertainty: An overview and framework for future research on experience-based choice. *Journal of Behavioral Decision Making, 23*(1), 1–14.
Rakow, T., & Rahim, S. B. (2010). Developmental insights into experience-based decision making. *Journal of Behavioral Decision Making, 23*(1), 69–82.
Rangel, A., Camerer, C., & Montague, P. R. (2008). A framework for studying the neurobiology of value-based decision making. *Nature Reviews Neuroscience, 9*(7), 545–556.
Schulze, C., & Newell, B. R. (2015). Compete, coordinate, and cooperate: How to exploit uncertain environments with social interaction. *Journal of Experimental Psychology: General, 144*(5), 967–981.
Schulze, C., & Newell, B. R. (2016). More heads choose better than one: Group decision making can eliminate probability matching. *Psychonomic Bulletin & Review, 23*, 907–914.
Schulze, C., van Ravenzwaaij, D., & Newell, B. R. (2015). Of matchers and maximizers: How competition shapes choice under risk and uncertainty. *Cognitive Psychology, 78*, 78–98.
Schulze, C., van Ravenzwaaij, D., & Newell, B. R. (2017). Hold it! The influence of lingering rewards on choice diversification and persistence. *Journal of Experimental Psychology: Learning, Memory, and Cognition*. Advance online publication. http://dx.doi.org/10.1037/xlm0000407
Shanks, D. R., Tunney, R. J., & McCarthy, J. D. (2002). A re-examination of probability matching and rational choice. *Journal of Behavioral Decision Making, 15*(3), 233–250.
Simon, H. A. (1955). A behavioral model of rational choice. *Quarterly Journal of Economics, 69*(1), 99–118.

Simon, H. A. (1956). Rational choice and the structure of the environment. *Psychological Review, 63*(2), 129–138.
Todd, P. M., Gigerenzer, G., & the ABC Research Group. (2012). *Ecological rationality: Intelligence in the world*. New York, NY: Oxford University Press.
Tversky, A., & Fox, C. R. (1995). Weighing risk and uncertainty. *Psychological Review, 102*(2), 269–283.
Tversky, A., & Kahneman, D. (1981). The framing of decisions and the psychology of choice. *Science, 211*(4481), 453–458.
Tversky, A., & Kahneman, D. (1992). Advances in prospect theory: Cumulative representation of uncertainty. *Journal of Risk and Uncertainty, 5*(4), 297–323.
Ungemach, C., Chater, N., & Stewart, N. (2009). Are probabilities overweighted or underweighted when rare outcomes are experienced (rarely)? *Psychological Science, 20*(4), 473–479.
Vlaev, I., Chater, N., Stewart, N., & Brown, G. D. A. (2011). Does the brain calculate value? *Trends in Cognitive Sciences, 15*(11), 546–554.
von Neumann, J., & Morgenstern, O. (1947). *Theory of games and economic behavior* (2nd ed.). Princeton, NJ: Princeton University Press.
Vulkan, N. (2000). An economist's perspective on probability matching. *Journal of Economic Surveys, 14*(1), 101–118.
Weber, E. U. (2006). Experience-based and description-based perceptions of long-term risk: Why global warming does not scare us (yet). *Climatic Change*, 77(1), 103–120.
Weber, E. U., Blais, A.-R., & Betz, N. E. (2002). A domain-specific risk-attitude scale: Measuring risk perceptions and risk behaviors. *Journal of Behavioral Decision Making, 15*(4), 263–290.
Weber, E. U., Shafir, S., & Blais, A.-R. (2004). Predicting risk sensitivity in humans and lower animals: Risk as variance or coefficient of variation. *Psychological Review, 111*(2), 430–445.
West, R. F., & Stanovich, K. E. (2003). Is probability matching smart? Associations between probabilistic choices and cognitive ability. *Memory & Cognition, 31*(2), 243–251.
Yechiam, E., & Busemeyer, J. R. (2006). The effect of foregone payoffs on underweighting small probability events. *Journal of Behavioral Decision Making, 19*(1), 1–16.
Yechiam, E., Erev, I., & Barron, G. (2006). The effect of experience on using a safety device. *Safety Science, 44*(6), 515–522.
Yechiam, E., Rakow, T., & Newell, B. R. (2015). Super-underweighting of rare events with repeated descriptive summaries. *Journal of Behavioral Decision Making, 28*(1), 67–75.

29

SEVERAL LOGICS FOR THE MANY THINGS THAT PEOPLE DO IN REASONING

Keith Stenning and Alexandra Varga

Introduction

Psychology has various misconceptions about logic which have led to claims that it can be rejected from any use in understanding human reasoning. This is primarily due to the view of logic, that is, classical logic, in the pre-20th-century tradition as a *mechanism* for all sorts of correct reasoning. However, on a modern view, logic*s* are better thought of as a class of formal models: abstract schemata, which may help us deal with the richness of real-life experience. Many of them are the basis of our newly gained understanding of thought as *information processing*, which exceeds the bounds of mechanisms by being explicitly concerned with computing meaning in context.

This chapter is an attempt to do the psychology of reasoning in the 21st century, when reasoning is no longer thought of as a homogenous activity, and a plethora of different logics have been developed, which should be used to model different kinds of reasoning. These various logics embody different norms of 'thought-for-purpose', and therefore fit different goals that a subject may adopt while performing a reasoning task (Achourioti, Fugard, & Stenning, 2014). Choice of logic represents the epistemic goals of the reasoning involved in different tasks – for example, telling a story or proving a theorem – through different concepts of valid inference. The two tasks used as examples are incompatible. In a story, each sentence must 'say something new' that can't be derived from what already has been said. In a proof, no new sentence must ever introduce 'new' information (in the same sense of 'new'): each must be derivable from what has gone before. So, one formalism cannot be the basis for explaining generically how people reason because their contextual goals are often incompatible.

Different goals in reasoning require applications of different logics in solving a task. Therefore, we propose the *multiple-logics*[1] *approach* to modelling, which by and large amounts to the following steps:

1 start by hypothesising reasoners' goal(s) in solving a task
2 find a system whose formal properties fit that goal
3 model in terms of that formalism

In what follows we demonstrate its explanatory advantage for the psychology of reasoning, which is currently dominated by single-framework accounts; for example, probability-based.

Besides serving more fine-grained modelling, using several logics can: (1) help make the roles of, for example, classical logic and probability precise and specific in their proper contexts; and (2) make both probability and classical logic yield testable predictions in their respective fields of application. Consequently, we propose replacing these monolithic approaches with the use of multiple logics providing multiple schemata, each for modelling specific ways of reasoning *for* different epistemic purposes. This means being clear about what the subjects' interpretation of the task is, and hence what data they bring to their solution, and what mental processes they employ.

Inspired by works in artificial intelligence (e.g., Kowalski, 2011), we propose a multi-level view of teleology. Not only physical actions are performed *for* something (e.g., push the switch in order to turn on the light), but also thought processes are meant to attain a certain desired state of affairs (e.g., to understand the story, to persuade an interlocutor). Goals are hierarchically organised along a continuum of degrees of abstraction, but they all share motivational and thus explanatory aspects.

Communicating meanings through language is arguably the most important theatre of human reasoning. Yet it is dominated by intensional 'intuitive' fundamentally *cooperative* reasoning of a very different kind than is appropriately modelled in *adversarial* classical logic or probability, and hitherto not recognised as reasoning by psychology.[2] It is this intensional reasoning that we seek to restore to centre stage, not because adversarial reasoning in extensional systems is not important, but because it is impossible to make sense of it without an analysis of the intensional hinterland. Intensional and extensional reasoning are two broad categories which work together. Intensional systems recruit relevant information in order to construct contextual interpretations. Extensional systems build on this intensional base and make meanings precise *in context* through set-membership. Examples of this process are familiar to psychologists in their practice of giving operational definitions for their experimental contexts, and then building statistical probability models on those definitions: "in this experiment, *intelligent* is interpreted as scoring more than X on the Wechsler IQ test". Different operationalisations of the same intensional concepts have to be given in different contexts. This applies as much to taxis in different cities as to intelligence in different experiments.

Just as the scientist must choose a model for the phenomena she investigates, so the reasoner that she studies must adopt a model of the situation where reasoning is called for, given the pursued goal. In other words, interpretation is a prerequisite for reasoning. Therefore, reasoning *to* interpretations is at the centre of a multiple-logics program. Here we use Constraint Logic Programming (CLP)[3] to analyse reasoning to interpretations. The main contrasts are with the two extensional systems that are primarily used for modelling in the psychology of reasoning: classical logic and probability.

The chapter explores in more detail this multiple logics approach through two applications of logic to understanding human reasoning: infants' reasoning in Gergely et al.'s (2002) head touch task (Varga, 2013) (in Section 3.2); and adult nonmonotonic causal reasoning and judgment in an extension of Cummins (1995) (in Section 4.2). We chose the first because it thoroughly exercises the functions of goal-based reasoning of CLP, a facility not available in either classical logic or probability theory; the second because it provides a simple model of naïve causal reasoning, based on "fast and frugal" heuristics embedded in Logic Programming (LP) (Cummins, 1995). Here an LP plus heuristic cue-combination can displace probability for modelling. This example of eliminating probability clarifies what is involved in a deeper, more psychological analysis of probability in cognition; it also hints at how probability and LP may complement each other, and thereby contributes to a multiple-logics approach.

Our plan is as follows. As motivation for entertaining more than one logic, the first section describes three famous examples which are problematic because of their reliance on classical logic and probability respectively, as *the* sole yardstick for reasoning performance: the Selection task, the Linda task, and then syllogistic conclusion drawing and countermodelling. All three illustrate the psychological enrichment that comes with the acknowledgement of intensional reasoning and the corresponding need for multiple formal systems. The next section introduces the broad view of goals in the form of multi-level teleology, and, using the example of CLP, it shows the psychological utility of logic for reasoning viewed as an inherently goal-directed process. We show how the logic applies to a case of prelinguistic reasoning in a seminal task of developmental psychology, the head touch task, and thereby instantiate the claim that logic can represent quasi-automatic implicit reasoning. In the next section we contrast probabilistic approaches to reasoning – representative of mono-systemic approaches, with the proposed multiple-logics perspective. Rejecting classical logic and replacing it by probability as the sole standard for reasoning is not useful because it maintains precisely the problematic claims of universal applicability. In the last section we then describe some current experimental work which proposes a simple probability-free model of judgments made during naïve causal reasoning. Having an alternative to probability can sharpen empirical explorations of the question if and when naïve reasoners go beyond weaker systems to reason in full probability.

Motivating examples from the psychology of reasoning

Wason (1968) provides a vivid example of the penalties of dismissing logic. In his selection task, Wason presents subjects with four cards: a vowel, a consonant, an even and an odd number on the visible sides. The task is to choose what cards must be turned to assess the truth of the conditional rule *If there is a vowel on one side, then there is an even number on the other.* But besides this focus rule to be assessed, there is the context-defining rule *All cards have a number on one side and a letter on the other* which could also be put in 'if... then' form: *if something is a card in this experiment, it has a number on one side and a letter on the other.* Our observation is that these two conditionals cannot be interpreted according to the same logic. Wason's interpretation of the focus rule was that it was a classical logical conditional. At the same time, this classical logical interpretation does not fit with what Wason and his subjects actually do with the other 'context-defining' rule, that is, to treat it as a cooperatively interpreted piece of information that should be unquestioningly believed as true. The problem is that interpreting new information 'on trust' is not what classical logic demands, which is the search for possible countermodels of the premises. But if one does not take this essential piece of information on trust, then the task changes: for example, turning the '4' card becomes necessary because it might be blank or have only a mermaid on the other side, which would make it a countermodel to the context rule.[4]

At least one common interpretation subjects adopt for the focus rule is to take it as another piece of information that is true; that is, they interpret it in the same way they are supposed to interpret the context rule. This division between information to believe as context and information to test is a troublesome feature of mathematical problems for the beginner. The opposite switch of logic is exemplified by a storyteller's beginning of a story: "once upon a time, there was a cat . . . ", followed by a humorous response from the audience: "how do you know it was a cat? Maybe it was a dog". Although the story opening is intended to be interpreted cooperatively by the hearer as something over which the storyteller has authority, the hearer at least pretends to take it as a proposal to be adversarially challenged and tested. So, there are two logics in play, and failure to understand this interpretational problem is Wason's basis for accusing his subjects of irrationality: they turn the 'wrong' cards. But Wason got his subjects' interpretation wrong because he assumed they imposed a classical logical interpretation on the second rule. The first duty of an experimental psychologist is to understand the subjects' interpretation.

Our second famous example illustrates a closely related issue of interpretation. Tversky and Kahneman (1983) presented the following:

> Linda is 31 years old, single, outspoken, and very bright. She majored in philosophy. As a student, she was deeply concerned with issues of discrimination and social justice, and also participated in anti-nuclear demonstrations.

Subjects were then given some choices to rank for their probability:

1 Linda is a bank teller
2 Linda is a bank teller and a feminist

It was observed that subjects in large numbers committed the conjunction fallacy by taking a subset (of people who are both feminists *and* bank tellers) to be larger than a superset (of people who are bank tellers), thus ranking (2) as more probable than (1). Again, the experimenters need certain assumptions about how their materials are interpreted: specifically, that subjects interpret them extensionally and are trying to reason probabilistically about the sizes of sets. But there is a more reasonable interpretation of the materials: as a story about Linda in which the menu items are to be taken as possible continuations. Linda as a heroine is not a statistical sample. In a cooperative LP interpretation with a single model of the story, there is only one woman, possible bank teller and possible feminist. That Linda is a feminist bank teller is more 'probable', in the sense of more plausible, than a non-feminist bank teller. So on our account, subjects are not trying to do probability theory and failing, but succeeding at doing story interpretation. In fact, in the original paper the authors report an experiment that removes the biographical sketch, making it plausible that Linda is sampled in some way unspecified, and in which few subjects make the conjunction fallacy response (for further discussion, see Stenning, Martignon, & Varga, 2017). This is essentially the same interpretational issue as in Wason's experiment, except here the authors explicitly used extensional probability for their interpretation. We are not arguing that it isn't educationally important to get students to see that the problem *can* be interpreted in probability theory. But we resist the idea that they spontaneously do so in mid-story (see also the section dedicated to probability).

A third brief example of naïve syllogistic reasoning will complement these two examples as motivations for the use of multiple formal systems in the psychology of reasoning. The argument is that because people are able to do classical logic in specific situations, there is a need for multiple logics to grasp their variety of (context dependent) reasoning strategies. Half a century of research supposedly showed that naïve reasoners do not have a grasp of classical logic's most basic concepts as embodied in categorical syllogistic reasoning – for example, Johnson-Laird (1983). Almost all this research has used the 'draw-a-conclusion' task with minor variants: present to subjects pairs of syllogistic premises, and ask them what conclusion logically follows. However, Achourioti et al. (2014) report an experiment which put subjects in an adversarial situation where they were betting against Harry-the-Snake on the validity of syllogism conclusions he proposed. By exploratory analysis of the nature of the counterexamples produced, they were able to show that subjects actually use the paradoxes of material implication in constructing their counterexamples (a paradox which is a highly counterintuitive quirk of classical logic resting on its adversarial nature, whereby the falsity of the antecedent of a conditional is sufficient to guarantee its truth, because it cannot be false). That is, without this paradoxical property, a significant proportion of these subjects' counterexamples would not be valid counterexamples, because they have empty antecedents yet need to be taken as true. A formal example is when Harry bets that *All B are A. Some C are not B. So, Some C are not A*, and the subject comes back with a rejection of this inference backed by the countermodel *A not-B C* (a domain consisting of a single thing that is A and C but not B). Clearly, in this model, Harry's conclusion is false because there are no Cs that are not A. But to be a *counter* model of Harry's inference, the premises also have to both be true. Are they? Well, there is a C that is not B. But are all Bs A? *All B are A* can be expressed as an empty-antecedent conditional: *if a thing is a B, then it is an A*. But since there are no Bs, the antecedent is always false. A subject producing this counterexample is relying on the classical logical principle that such a conditional is always true (not generally a property of conditionals in natural language, or in some other logics, e.g., LP). How much of this the subject could make explicit is an interesting psychological question, but enough of them produce counterexamples like this to show that *in the context of a dispute with Harry*, 'logically naïve' subjects can use the 'paradox'. From an earlier experiment showing some success at countermodel reasoning, Bucciarelli and Johnson-Laird (1999) concluded that since this showed the subjects *knew classical logic*, their failure to reason classically in the common draw-a-conclusion syllogism task must be due to 'performance errors'. This nicely encapsulates the essence of a multiple logic approach: it is the discourse goal that is unclear in the usual task and made clear by Harry, and it is the discourse goal that determines which logic is brought into play.

This analysis of countermodels is powerful evidence of some conceptual grasp of classical logic *in this situation*. In the typical draw-a-conclusion task, subjects use a nonmonotonic approach (Stenning & Yule, 1997) which constructs a minimal model (see the section describing our logical formalism of choice); in the counterexample task they understand that a single counterexample makes a syllogistic conclusion false because classical logical validity is 'truth of conclusion in *all* models of the premises', not just one preferred model. This task provides positive evidence that subjects appropriately use different logics in different situations. Notice that logic does not compete with the experiment, but rather deepens its explanations of reasoning.

There are several morals for reasoning research in the three examples above:

- Experiment cannot gain us any ground without a suitable interpretation shared between subject and experimenter. Without knowing what interpretation they adopted we cannot interpret their data.
- Without a formal framework it is hard to specify what our or our subjects' interpretation is, and therefore what they are trying to do: their reasoning goals. And the model can inspire and be inspired by empirical exploration.
- Because people reason for many different purposes, there can be no one system that captures all reasoning kinds. Multiplicity is a *must* when it comes to modelling for better understanding reasoning.
- We should expect that logics will work together in solving reasoning tasks, as we saw the cooperative problem statement is supposed to work together with the rule to be tested in Wason's task. In particular in the two final subsections, we are interested in how intensional and extensional systems can work together.

Goals and logics in psychology

What can a well-chosen logic do for psychologists of reasoning? The crux of our argument is that 'agents may use Logic to represent their beliefs about the way the world is, and to represent their goals for the way they would like the world to be' (Kowalski, 2006, p. 8). We would use 'logic*s*' instead of 'Logic', emphasising the multiple-logic*s* approach. We take CLP as a token of this claim.

Multi-level teleology

We begin by specifying multi-level teleology and the corresponding view of reasoning. What are typically referred as goals in everyday language are desired changes of state in the physical world – for example, making light. They are episodic: that is, the targeted state is anchored at a particular moment in time. These are *achievement goals*. When planning, agents reduce them to executable basic actions, for example, pressing a switch at time *t*. Higher-order *maintenance goals* ensure agents' stable relation with the ever-changing state of the world. Their primary function is to motivate agents to set achievement goals upon which to act, in such a way that the higher-order goals remain true throughout time, or that they become true again if previously falsified. "Maintenance goals either trigger corrective actions to be taken, or constrain the choice of actions so that the maintenance goals will not be violated" (Duff, Harland, & Thangarajah, 2006, p. 1034). They refer to states that must be made to obtain across temporal intervals with various durations, the universal *at all times* being the most abstract. Some examples are: staying alive, social acceptance, knowledge extension, conveying a message, persuading an opponent (the latter three instantiate epistemic meta-goals of reasoning). Just as achievement goals guide agents' action choices, the meta-goals constrain the choice of reasoning strategies that are likely to fulfil them. Goals are hierarchically organised; achievement goals are sub-goals of maintenance goals, contextually derived from them. The teleological structure can be represented as 'achievement goal *for* maintenance goal', for example, 'agent *A* does at time *t* what agent *B* did at time *t - 1 for* being wiser from time *t+1* onwards'. Note that in this scheme, epistemic (meta) goals, as instances of maintenance goals, share their instrumental and motivational aspects with physical maintenance goals.

This multi-level hierarchy is the foundation for teleological reasoning. Agents engage in instrumental behaviours, be those physical actions or reasoning, in order to achieve particular goals in the context. Taking meta-goals seriously implicates acknowledgement that thought is goal-directed.

This multi-level view of teleology is based on Kowalski (2011). It is useful because it allows us to integrate higher-order goals (for example, epistemic, social) in discussions of goal-centered rationality (Evans, Over, & Manktelow, 1993; Evans & Stanovich, 2013; Over, 2004). Despite the salutary acknowledgment of goals in the cited works, the common focus on physical ones underrates the conceptual importance of epistemic goals. Reasoning *to* an interpretation, for instance, may be a sub-goal of reasoning *from* that interpretation. The role of reasoning goals has been missed in mono-systemic approaches because if there is a single system for reasoning, it is impossible to relate its properties to instrumental appropriateness in context.

The basic form of reasoning about goals is planning – backwards reasoning from goals to means (or sub-goals) all the way to basic actions: for example, 'to find the book, she switched the light on; to this end, she pressed the button'. Forward reasoning is typically used for goal assignment, for example, 'pressing the button is for turning the light on'. We next introduce a formalism with the required representational and computational resources to express such reasoning, with a focus on the backwards direction.

A 'goal-laden' logic for modelling: constraint logic programming

Logic programming was designed for rapid, cheap content-based retrieval of general knowledge from large knowledge bases. It originates in attempts to construct a programming language for planning agents (Kowalski, 1988, 2006); these practical origins mean that it comes with a natural interpretation in psychological terms. In order to avoid frame-problem issues,[5] McCarthy and Hayes (1969) viewed planning as proceeding with respect to one's minimal interpretation of current circumstances, and going on to develop a sequence of actions that will presumably result in the goal state. The cognitive relevance of the formalism has been shown through its use in developing a cognitive-formal semantics of temporal discourse (van Lambalgen & Hamm, 2004), modelling of tasks from the psychology of reasoning (e.g., Byrne's suppression task; Stenning & van Lambalgen, 2005), psycholinguistics (Baggio, Stenning, & van Lambalgen, 2016; Pijnacker, Geurts, van Lambalgen, Buitelaar, & Hagoort, 2009), and developmental psychology (Varga, 2013).

The reader unfamiliar with CLP may skim the technicalities; they are here to show what is involved in a precise computational account of goal-directed reasoning. Its psychological value is that it offers a modelling tool for this reasoning, which can proceed automatically, without supervision, but also be consciously controlled when the context calls for deliberation. We introduce the 'inferential engine' of CLP. It will be cognitively substantiated by highlighting its application to model the head-touch task in Gergely, Bekkering, and Király (2002; Király, Gergely, & Csibra, 2013) as an example of pre-linguistic automatic reasoning.

We first introduce the task. Fourteen-month-olds see an experimenter use her forehead to switch on a light box, either when holding a shawl around her shoulders (HandsOccupied), or with her hands free (HandsFree). When allowed to use the light box in the test phase, all infants – across conditions – use the default hand response to light up the lamp. Holding the shawl contextually explains the unusual head action ('she couldn't use her hands, so she had to press the light box some other way'), so infants in the HandsOccupied condition perform *only* this default action. Although no explanation in terms of physical goals is available for the unusual action in the HandsFree condition, when given ostensive communication signals, 68% of the infants imitate the head action. This combination of responses has been described as selective imitative learning. Gergely and his colleagues propose that teleological action interpretation underlies infants' selectivity (Gergely et al., 2002). This inferential approach has been refined according to multi-level teleology and implemented in a CLP model (Varga, 2013). The model formalises infants' action interpretation during observation, and its consequence – action planning in the test phase.

Let us try to see the experiment through the eyes of a 14-month-old in the HandsFree condition.[6] Imagine that you are a developing human being who's eager to get to know the world. You are thus set on understanding how things work – this is your top-level goal here. In an observation context the goal may read as 'learn from the trustworthy what to do, when, what for', calling for teleological action interpretation which you already have in your cognitive toolbox (the teleological stance; Csibra, Gergely, Biró, Koos, & Brockbank, 1999). As it stands, it is still too abstract to be acted upon, so it motivates you to reduce it to more concrete sub-goals. Given your experience, you may equate *trustworthy* with *people who communicate ostensively*. Hence, when observing ostensive signals from a communicative adult, you interpret her actions in search for potentially relevant things to learn. To begin with, you reason forward and assign a physical (achievement) goal to her actions, for example, make light. When you notice her doing something bizarre, for example, press the light-box with her forehead, yet somewhat effective for the goal of making light, you might acquire that behaviour – why else would she have done something else than a default hand action, if not to teach you? You would imitate the bizarre head action, a new method for using the light box, because you would interpret it as the achievement sub-goal of the experimenter's intention to share relevant knowledge. Backward reasoning reduces the generic maintenance goal of knowledge acquisition to two contextually set achievement goals: (1) learn an object's function, and (2) learn novel ways to do things from trustworthy adults. The last action in the temporally ordered sequence of actions then becomes touching the light box with your forehead. This plan will *presumably* bring about your maintenance goal of knowledge acquisition. As the poet has it, 'the best laid plans of mice and men often go awry'. However, you need not consider the possibility that the adult you've observed simply made fun of you by showing you completely meaningless things unless further evidence for this becomes available.

We now show how such inferences can be expressed in CLP. The logic represents knowledge in conditional formulae called *clauses*. CLP conditional clauses are exception-tolerant, unlike in classical logic; this is obvious in the representation $p \wedge \neg ab \rightarrow q$ which reads as 'If p and ***nothing abnormal is the case***, then q'. Thought of abnormalities are initially inhibited by the

> ***closed-world assumption*** (Stenning & van Lambalgen, 2008): unless positive information (current observation, or consequences derived from it) is available, no abnormality occurs in the context

but it may be activated by explicit evidence. This inferential pattern is called closed-world reasoning. Its formal manifestation in CLP is negation-as-failure (van Lambalgen & Hamm, 2004). It means that if a fact is not a program clause or doesn't follow by backwards reasoning from program clauses, its negation is assumed true. An abnormality list is implicitly attached to each conditional, 'at the back of reasoners' minds' (Varga, 2013). That is, abnormalities are reasoned about only when evidence of abnormality arrives (otherwise the assumption would be self-defeating). The assumptions frame the inferential space and allow real-time computations despite informational complexity.

The current observations and a minimal amount of relevant background knowledge constitutes a ***definite constraint logic*** program composed of definite[7] conditional clauses. The database of the knowledge-thirsty baby in the HandsFree condition, for instance, can be expressed as a constraint logic program P containing clauses such as:

1. $touch(light{-}box, head, s) \wedge s < t \wedge \neg ab1 \rightarrow light(on, t)$ ('If she touches light-box with head at time s before time t and nothing abnormal is the case then light-on at time t') – current observation;
2. $touch(light - box, hand, s) \wedge s < t \wedge \neg ab2 \rightarrow light(on, t)$ ('If I touch light-box with hand at time s before time t and nothing abnormal is the case then light-on at time t') – background knowledge of contact causality;
3. $do(x, hand, t) \wedge x /= touch\ light\text{-}box \rightarrow ab2$ ('If I do something else with the hand than touching the light-box at time t then something abnormal is the case') – abnormality condition for (1.), background knowledge;
4. $a communicates\ ostensively = a trustworthy$ ('Someone who communicates ostensively to me is trustworthy') – background knowledge.

Psychological achievement goals are expressed as *goal clauses*, which are consequents of program clauses. The variables in goal clauses are existentially quantified over time within the scope of the goal clause. They are formulated interrogatively, as a question that derivations attempt to respond to in the process of ***goal resolution***. Resolution is thus the logical way to answer the question 'Can goal $?\Sigma$ be realised given program P ?'. The response is found by dealing with the more fine-grained question 'What must agent X do in order for goal Σ to be realised at time t ?'. Goal resolution in CLP is thus analogous to the backwards reasoning involved in action planning:

starting from a goal temporally located in the future, one aims to find a sequence of actions to be performed starting from *now*. If *P* contains information that produces a temporally ordered action sequence leading to Σ in a finite number of steps, then ?Σ succeeds with respect to *P*, otherwise ?Σ fails. The action sequence obtained in successful derivations updates database *P*.

Use of negation-as-failure in derivations means that goal resolution checks if a goal clause can be made true in a single ***minimal model*** of *P*:[8] a minimal or preferred model is a semantic interpretation of the information available in the logic program, which disregards any potential abnormalities. *P* clauses are assumed to exhaust all that is relevant for goal reduction. The semantics of CLP warrants the construction of a unique minimal model (van Lambalgen & Hamm, 2004). This is the reason why a minimal model of the logic program is the only interpretation of concern of the current data, and goal resolution is performed with respect to this minimal model. It is a 'closed world' in the sense that facts not forced to occur by backwards computations over *P* clauses are assumed not to occur (van Lambalgen & Hamm, 2004). Had no head-touch occurred in *P* clauses, and no head-touch could have been derived from those *P* clauses, the infant would not have considered it when planning to learn from observations.

The normative status of maintenance goals is captured by particular kinds of goal clauses called ***integrity constraints*** (Kowalski, 2011; van Lambalgen & Hamm, 2004). Just as one's plan for a sub-goal (e.g., light up the lamp) should not hinder attainment of a higher-order goal (e.g., get wiser), integrity constraints must be satisfied by each state of the database throughout computations. They impose local norms on goal resolution relative to *P*, either obligations (the integrity constraint succeeds) or prohibitions (the integrity constraint fails).

In our running example, the infant's maintenance goal of knowledge acquisition may be expressed as

I.c.1: $?\ learn(x, a_{trustworthy}, t)$ succeeds

She evaluates the integrity constraint relative to *P* by finding useful things to learn, that is, by specifying variable *x* to a constant. By means of the logical operation of *u*nification, she uses clause (4.) in *P* to substitute $a_{communicates\ ostensively}$ for $a_{trustworthy}$, obtaining *? learn*(x, $a_{communicates\ ostensively}$, t) succeeds. It then attempts to derive an achievement sub-goal that she can act upon when given the chance to do so. To this end, given infants' proneness to function learning (Casler & Kelemen, 2007; Träuble & Pauen, 2007), she specifies *x* to *light* − *on* which was inferred as the function of the light box during teleological interpretation. The achievement goal which must be made to succeed and ultimately acted upon in the test phase is *? learn(light-on, t)*. In other words, in order to learn something from current observations, infants must learn the light box function.

Since learning 'generally involves active intervention in the world' (Gopnik, 1998, p. 106), especially when it comes to practical knowledge acquisition, another integrity constraint guiding infants' resolution may be dubbed *learning by doing*:

I.c. 2: $?\ learn(light - on, t), light(on, t + \delta)$ succeeds

The infant thus must light up the lamp. Clauses (1) and (2) in *P* provide two ways for so doing: by touching it with the head (as observed) or with the hand (the default way). Learning the function can thus be realised by learning a novel means (i.e., head action) at the same time, and by sticking to prior knowledge and performing the default action. The CLP resolution rule prescribes performance of the unusual head-action *for* attainment of the learning goal in the HandsFree condition. Unless, for example, a nasty fairy uses her magic wand to make the law of contact causality stop holding[9] – thereby providing evidence for ab_1 in clause (1) of *P* – this leads to achieving the goal to light up the lamp, which ensures that the maintenance goal to learn, is made true by action performance. Before such evidence becomes available the infant can simply disregard nasty fairies and proceed to action.

We have highlighted that plans in the real world *presumably* achieve goals. CLP's nonmonotonicity is crucial here, because goal attainment is not a necessary consequence of plans designed by close-world goal resolution. In fact, the psychological equivalent of nonmonotonicity is flexible reasoning – additional information may override the closed-world assumption without invalidating the previously prescribed link between a goal and a specific action. Resolution of the same goal clause relative to an extended program may output a different action plan. For instance, in HandsOccupied, the adult's need to maintain the shawl around her shoulders with the hand provides evidence of abnormality (cf. clause (3) in *P*). The bizarre head-touch method to light up the lamp is interpreted as *only* contextually necessary for the adult, because an abnormality prevented *her* default hand action. Consequently I.c. 1 reduces only to the default hand action, because the new method is deemed unnecessary.

Some main advantages of CLP modelling are made salient by its application to the head-touch task. Most importantly, the model provides a concrete example of pre-linguistic automatic reasoning which can be modelled in logic. It thereby corroborates psychologists' argument that infants' imitative acquisition of practical skills and artefact functions is a nonverbal instance of goal-centered rationality. It is perhaps very surprising that pre-verbal infants can reason about goals in these ways, and the logic's psychological importance is precisely that it shows what is necessary to achieve such reasoning that can proceed without awareness, that is, the assumptions and corresponding strategies that ground fast and efficient computations. The complexity of the formal apparatus enables the automatic 'unsupervised' nature of the thought processes.

Adding a logical component to provide input, that is, the reasoning *to* an interpretation part, could improve probabilistic models of goal-based reasoning (e.g., Baker, Saxe, & Tenenbaum, 2009), by bringing them closer to realistic process models, without the need to increase their already loaded space of background assumptions. At the same time, a model of infants' degree of confidence in, for example, what 'trustworthy adult' means, may benefit from adding some simpler form of graded reasoning such as heuristics, or conditional frequencies: logics and graded judgement working side by side may refine the model and enhance its degree of generalisability, as we will see in the next section. In fact, this 'division of labour' between formal systems is one of the most important issues for further research and development of a multiple-logics approach. This computational model instantiates the utility of a logic with these representational resources for fine-grained understanding of mental processes which involve 'automatic' reasoning about epistemic goals.

Beyond mono-systemic universalist approaches

For a multiple-logics approach to reasoning, a view of probability is clearly at the top of the agenda. After the turn of the 21st century, the psychology of reasoning shifted its choice of formal system from classical logic to probability, but in doing so, for the most part it maintained the universalist view that probability was the one system needed. Probability models have been successfully fitted to a variety of reasoning phenomena.

For a multiple-logics approach, one immediate issue is the relation between probability and other systems as models for nonmonotonic reasoning in uncertainty. Currently, attitudes to probability diverge. The new psychology of reasoning (Over, 2009; Sloman & Lagnado, 2015; see also Elqayam, this volume; Over & Cruz, this volume) claims to show that people reason *as if* governed by the norms of probability. In the field of reasoning and decision which has been dominated by probability as its standard formal framework, there is a growing scepticism among those interested in how naïve subjects make decisions about whether naïve decision makers use probability or rather fast and frugal heuristics (Tversky & Kahneman, 1974; Gigerenzer, Todd, & the ABC Research Group, 1999; Todd, Gigerenzer, & the ABC Research Group, 2012; see also Hoffrage, Hafenbrädl, & Marewski, this volume; Rakow & Skylark, this volume; Schulze & Newell, this volume). Kahneman and Tversky's Heuristics and Biases program interpreted tasks such as Linda as revealing fundamental conceptual failure to understand probability. We have expressed doubts about this conclusion from Linda. Gigerenzer and the ABC group have shown that better defined heuristics can compete with probability because of their robustness, at least in some circumstances, particularly when predicting new data rather than fitting training data, or when data are scarce (Gigerenzer, Czerlinski, & Martignon, 1999). Our own stance is that probability is not best seen as one monolithic system. Full probability, unlike simple conditional frequency reasoning, for instance, requires a great deal of conceptual machinery – witness its slow and protracted labour stretching from the 17th century to Kolmogorov's axiomatisation in 1933. Moreover, Cummins (1995) can be represented as showing that naïve judgement during causal reasoning can be explained wholly intentionally by integrating LP with fast and frugal heuristics (FFHs). Stenning, Martignon, and van Lambalgen (in preparation) present an experiment extending Cummins' (1995) work to other heuristics, revealing some of the origins of the data subjects use and showing that subjects need not always go beyond simple intensional reasoning about frequencies to full probability in making judgements.

One can also consider the analogy between probability and arithmetic. 'Arithmetic' covers a range of systems between elementary addition and ***number theory***. When a child exhibits the skills of elementary addition we do not ascribe to them an implicit knowledge of number theory. Analogously, when a naïve subject exhibits skills of reasoning about proportions, we should not ascribe to them a grasp of full-probability. Our main argument is that empirical work and cognitive theory should ascribe to the subject the weakest system that can fit their data. So we are arguing for a finer grain of analysis of the formal systems underlying a range of behaviours, and, in particular, that it takes much more to show that naïve reasoners use full probability than we have been offered empirically so far.

The next subsection focuses on two main issues for cognitive probabilism: the origin of the data needed for probabilistic computations and its implausibility as a process model for people's everyday reasoning. Presenting a comparison system in LP sets directions for further collaboration from within a multiple-logics perspective.

Probability from a multiple-logics perspective

We use LP as a comparator to the employments of probability, but certainly not arguing that mono-systemic LP should replace mono-systemic probability. A logic of the kind of LP is central to a multiple-logics approach because it fulfils the required function of accounting for the role of reasoning *to* interpretations, which probability cannot do (Stenning & van Lambalgen, 2010; Baggio et al., 2016). Moreover, it is closer to providing psychological process models, which are computationally tractable because they do not require implausible assumptions about the warehousing of probability distributions, nor the extensive use of probability computations. These are the points of contrast for our comparison.

But why shouldn't probability produce appropriate models for all reasoning? In short, this is because it has problems reasoning about goals (to see how much is required for even the simplest cases, see Baker et al., 2009); its data demands exceed what subjects have in many contexts; and it cannot specify the interpretations that it requires to reason *from*.

Probability is a relation between a cognitive state in context (knowledge, belief) and some proposition(s), both specified in a probabilistic model. All relevant propositions have to be pre-identified, and then probability distributions of all pairs of propositions supplied, and such modelling assumes 'causal stationarity' (Howson & Urbach, 1989). Finding that set – that is, constructing an interpretation sequentially as new information arrives – is the business of LP processing. The end state of such a sequence constitutes a 'common core' (see below) which could be turned into a probabilistic model by adding probability information. So on a multiple-logics view, here is already an account of how two systems can and must work together, just as LP can produce interpretations for classical logic to reason from.

Certainly, theorists can construct probabilistic models of human reasoning. Perhaps there are situations in which naïve people also actually use probabilistic reasoning. However, Stenning and van Lambalgen (2016) argue that there is a strong methodological imperative on those who claim that naïve people use probability in their reasoning to show that full-blown probability is *required* for modelling the data. For instance, claims that uneducated people do use probability (e.g., Fontanari, Gonzalez, Vallortigara, & Girotto, 2014), when examined more carefully, provide evidence for simpler uses of proportions, or conditional frequencies, rather than of probability.

Here we anticipate a counter objection: "surely people don't need to understand the whole foundations in order to be described as using a system". This is the point of the arithmetic analogy. One doesn't have to understand number theory to add up the shopping. But still, unless one has a concept of variance, sample and population, along with convergence at the infinite limit, one does not have a modern concept of probability applied to the world. These results thus put naïve subjects back roughly in the 18th century in terms of conceptual grasp, but leave them two centuries short of Kolmogorov's full probability. Some grasp of reasoning with conditional frequencies is more analogous to the arithmetic that does the shopping than to number theory.

Probability is a relation between a cognitive state and some proposition(s), both specified in a probabilistic model. All relevant propositions have to be pre-identified, and then probability distributions of all pairs of propositions supplied. Finding that set – that is, constructing an interpretation – is the business of LP processing.

LP provides a framework that is closely related to probability, however different are some of its properties. Bayes Nets and LP- nets are both directed acyclic graphs in which the nodes represent propositions (variables) and the edges represent conditional connections. Stenning and van Lambalgen (2016) describe the relations between Bayes Nets and LP nets, emphasising that: (1) in both BNs and LP-nets the 'inferential strength' of natural language conditionals is contextually determined, not compositionally (e.g., by a truth table); (2) both have an inference pattern of the form 'suppose E is all the evidence at our disposal; then C follows'; and (3) in both the Ramsey test plays a role in evaluating the strength of conditionals ((2) and (3) in LP in the guise of the closed world reasoning). The distinctive computational profiles of the two systems result from the fact that a change of probability of a single variable (including the addition of a new variable) can completely change the probability distributions of all the other variables (Stenning & van Lambalgen, 2010). For this reason, LP-nets are actually 'neural' implementations of computations (and therefore possible mental processes), whereas BNs require much computation external to the net.

These are conceptual problems. Another question is where the probability data comes from. Often the claim is made that frequencies are automatically recorded in memory and are a sufficient source for probability estimation (Hasher & Zacks, 1984). However, raw frequency observation cannot be more than part of the story, because of the strong intensional influences (Jonides & Naveh-Benjamin, 1987; Tversky & Kahneman, 1973), and because we reason on the basis of what we have been told and on our informal theories as well as frequencies. Stenning et al. (2017) propose that simple neural monitoring of LP-nets can plausibly model conditional frequency collection, and that LP-nets can handle the other sources of probability information. If this is correct, it would explain both the automaticity of collection and the symptoms of 'intensional intrusion'. Pearl (2000), one of the originators of BNs, emphasises the essential structural features of causal BNs required *before* probabilities are attached and not derivable from frequency information. These constitute the 'common core' of BNs and LP-nets just mentioned (Pinosio, 2016).

In contrast to mono-systemic appeals to probability, Sloman and Lagnado (2015) provide an excellent review of causal reasoning from a generally Bayesian point of view, and are commendably open about what the approach does not do. They particularly identify narrative and mechanism as two areas where there is strong evidence of involvement in human causal reasoning and decision, but which are not captured by purely probabilistic approaches. They cite, for example, Pennington and Hastie (1992) on the 'story' model of jurors' causal understanding of complex legal cases; and White (2013) on 'mechanism' models of causal reasoning. Narrative discourse processing is the founding cognitive application of LP, even if it has not generally been thought of as reasoning, owing to the 'intensional blindness' described in the second section. Sloman and Lagnado also acknowledge issues about the origin of the probability data subjects use. In fact, there is a considerable convergence of their views with ours, from the 'opposite end of the tunnel'. Where we emphasise the need to acknowledge the purely structural aspects of BNs which are shared with LP (and devoid of probabilities) and suggest a methodology of pressing for positive evidence that probability *must* be added to capture the data, Sloman and Lagnado start from the Bayesian literature and find accounts of the roles of narrative and mechanism to be missing.

So two empirical questions arise immediately: when do subjects go beyond LP models to probability models? And what extra is gained thereby? The experiment described in the next section provides an example of how graded judgments can be based on LP models without probability. This sharpens these empirical questions.

An experiment integrating intensional reasoning with judgment and decision

In this section we describe current empirical work, to be fully reported in Stenning et al. (in preparation), on naïve nonmonotonic causal reasoning, and relate it to a multiple-logics framework. The necessary integration of heuristics into an LP framework is laid out in Stenning et al. (2017). The experiment uses the paradigm from Cummins (1995), who established that the number of exceptions that subjects could generate for a familiar causal rule was a good predictor of the confidence that other subjects would assign to inferences from that conditional. We see Cummins' experiment as a way to open up a range of empirical questions about probability in cognition. Specifically, it can show how naïve subjects can use information from their knowledge bases to make graded judgments of the reliability of causal regularities, without using probability at any point. LP naturally models retrieval of cues and their exceptions. Even cue validities can be assessed without probability. Cummins' experiment allows us to raise the level of the task that LP is being used to model, from deriving a single preferred model for a story to using repeated queries to the LP system to generate a list of exceptions, and then judge reliability of the conditional's regularity on the number in this list. This tally of exceptions estimates reliability of inference across contexts. Some terminology: exceptions to the conditional rule in the experiment are *defeaters* of the rule. Defeaters of MP inferences are the abnormalities that LP lists along with each conditional (see the section on logic). Hence the experiment bears on the relations between formal frameworks, specifically LP and probability (see Fernbach & Erb, 2013, for a probability model of the same paradigm). One possibility is that these LP models of heuristic decision are the foundation of subjects' probability models. Another is that naïve subjects' judgments are conducted entirely within LP intensional models. Since, as described above, LP is rather closely formally related to causal Bayes Nets, the experiment serves as a clarification of the empirical questions that need to be answered in deciding which framework is most appropriate for modelling what reasoning. As such, it is another example of the intensional versus extensional contrast in reasoning systems which we have touched on throughout.

Cummins' experiment is about the determination of confidence in causal inferences from regularities, by the number of defeaters of those regularities which people can generate: a heuristic known as Tallying (Gigerenzer & Gaissmaier, 2011) or the 'unit-weight' model. Stenning et al. (in preparation) extend this experiment, collecting subjects' judgments of probabilities of defeaters explaining exceptions to the regularity. Although subjects were asked to assign probabilities to maximise the possibility of their use, we here use the term 'likelihoods' in a non-technical sense to remain agnostic regarding exactly what they are. The current work also introduces a within-subject design: the same subjects both generated defeaters and estimated their confidence in the inferences, in controlled order. It was made clear to the subjects that they were to use their prior knowledge in reasoning, rather than treat the task as closed to the introduction of new information outside its statement, as in classical logic. Collecting judgments of likelihoods, and being able to use the same subject's data to predict their confidence, allows analysis of influences on the data subjects have and of how they use it.

If the brake pedal is pressed, the car slows down is a highly familiar causal conditional, even to those who have never driven a car. Now suppose that one day, the pedal is pressed and the car does not slow down. List possible defeaters of the regularity that can explain this exception! Well, there was ice on the road, the brake fluid leaked, the car met a steep downward hill. . .

Cummins showed that the number of generated defeaters inversely predicted other subjects' confidence in making *modus ponens* (MP) inferences from the conditional and the premise *The brake pedal was pressed*. So the defeaters are cues ('ice on the road') which predict (un)reliability of the regularity. Cues themselves have *validities* or measures of their contribution to good judgment. Since there is usually more than one defeater, cues have to be combined to yield a judgment in a context. The standard decision theory approach is to do this in probability. Put simply, a cue's validity is the probability that it indicates a correct decision. If we do know the probabilities and correlations of association between cues, and a vector of cue values on an occasion, then we can compute the probability of the outcome. What could be simpler? Or more desirable? Well, tallying avoids the need for computing validities by treating all cues with unit weight. Stenning et al. (2017) discuss how estimation of validities can be done by tallying without resorting to probability.

The Fast and Frugal Heuristics (FFH) program (Gigerenzer, Todd, & The ABC Research Group, 1999; see also Hoffrage et al., this volume) has done much to motivate the idea that probabilistic calculation is not what people do. Researchers working as part of the FFH program have been mostly concerned with refining the definitions of heuristics and the 'ecology' of decision contexts. In particular, they have argued that in the frequent cases of predicting new data (as opposed to fitting existing data), and of paucity of data, heuristics should not be thought of as sub-optimal to probability, but as more robust alternatives (Czerlinski, Gigerenzer, & Goldstein, 1999). Tallying is a heuristic because in merely counting cues it throws away any information about their weight, where an 'optimal' probabilistic regression equation would include separate weights for each.

Stenning et al. (2017, in preparation) interpret Cummins' experiment as an example of heuristic cue-combination. In FFH terms, subjects are *tallying* (counting) defeaters and assigning them 'negative unit weight' as cues to reliability of inference. By identifying the defeaters generated across subjects, and always using subjects' own generated defeaters to predict their own judgments (i.e., a within-subjects design), it is possible to say more about the memory processes playing an integral part in determining the data subjects use.

What can these data say about the simple idea that probabilities are just retrieved from memory 'off the shelf'? Because defeaters can be identified across subjects, it is possible to evidence contributions of memory processes to judgements of likelihoods of individual defeaters. Being recalled first is a good cue for the maximum estimated likelihood, and hence a heuristic for the subject for finding the strongest cue. Tracking the likelihoods assigned to the very same defeater when it is generated at different positions in the sequence shows that there is a highly systematic pattern of declining judged likelihood with increasing generation position. It is possible to factor the variance between the contribution of the identity of the defeater, and its position in the sequence. The latter contributes about a third of the variance accounted for by both variables. So the dynamics of the memory process make a large contribution to the likelihood data. Likelihoods are not just coming off the shelf: the order they present themselves in is highly informative of their magnitude. The important point here is that the dynamics of the memory system are an important contributor to the data subjects use to reason and judge, already evidenced in other decision contexts (e.g., Hertwig, Herzog, Schooler, & Reimer, 2008).

This work provides a simple proof-of-concept model of how subjects can make probability-free graded judgments on the basis of reasoning in an intensional nonmonotonic logic. The statistical modelling shows that the Tallying heuristic accounts for between 70% and 90% of the item variance in judgments of the reliability of familiar causal conditionals. It shows that a heuristic method of combining cue validities is highly correlated with the judgments made. Heuristics can be computed cheaply and rapidly in parallel in LP-nets. Their component cues can be found by memory search within LP-nets, and their validities can be heuristically derived when required, sometimes by the operation of other heuristics. In fact, retrieval processes play a large role in the determination of confidence. Stenning et al. (2017) propose that LP-nets can be monitored to collect frequency data, which explains the 'automaticity' of frequency memory, and why it is permeated by intensional influences. It also describes how the Competitive Queueing model of item retrieval (Burgess & Hitch, 2005) can be applied to LP retrieval from semantic memory.

In summary, this experiment provides more evidence that the distinctive information required for heuristic operation is a function of the memory system. Subjects could be retrieving pre-computed probabilities as cue values, but there would have to be some remarkable arrangements of the memory system to ensure that this is what comes out. What the embedding of FFH in LP-nets shows is that graded judgment can be achieved by 'reading off' of properties from the preferred model. Even with heuristics that require ranking of cue validities, this may be estimated by monitoring the operation of LP-nets. Although there is some evidence in Stenning et al. (in preparation) that estimations of conditional frequencies can enter reasoning about causal regularities, no evidence was seen that anything more is required.

This model of Cummins' task is connected to the model of the head-touch task by the shared cooperative reasoning to the best explanation that is the Generation subtask. Defeaters are requested from the subject as ***explanations***, just as the infant chooses how to imitate on the basis of inferred explanations of the experimenter's behaviour. The computation mechanism in the model of Cummins' task is simpler – it is just the basic backward chaining algorithm of LP – but it is explanation nonetheless.

Conclusions and prospects

Because of the many things we do in reasoning, a multiple-logics approach offers much richer empirical explorations of a wider range of reasoning than single-system theories. We started by seeing that although subjects' tactical skill in finding counterexamples was error prone, placing reasoning tasks in a context governed by dispute goals nevertheless allows them to show conceptual knowledge of classical logic, which they do not show in the standard tasks used. Modern logic has produced many systems with different concepts of validity, each with its own epistemic instrumentalities which can be captured with finer distinctions from the perspective of multi-level teleology. The example of the head-touch task discussed in the next section showed how rich the psychology can be when different levels of human goals are included in the modelling enterprise.

Throughout the chapter we used LP as an example framework applied to kinds of reasoning, such as interpretation or planning, that can be below conscious awareness but can also become consciously controlled. Such a formal system thus provides a way into the study of automatic reasoning processes, an opportunity that should be exploited across psychology, if only to give a systematic account of the relation between intuition and deliberation. It may seem counterintuitive that formalisms should fulfil this role, when logic has been traditionally identified with conscious, controlled, deliberative processing. But this is precisely what recommends further pursuit of the idea in a new psychology of reasoning, freed from misleading assumptions. The insight that these automatable processes have cooperative foundations is also novel. The bottom line is that cooperative and adversarial systems work together in intimate ways, producing interpretations and reasoning from them. It can be important to distinguish cogitative reasoning from intuitive, but removing intensional reasoning from the field of reasoning makes extensional reasoning impossible to understand.

Interpretation as formalised in LP has a central part to play, and has taken most of our attention in this paper. Without interpretation there is no reasoning, and the results of interpretation tell us what reasoning from them is appropriate. Interpretation has, of course, been the main study of psycholinguistics, but without a formalisation it has not been recognised as reasoning. It should be clear that our emphasis on LP is because of its novelty for psychologists of reasoning, its relevance to experimental interpretation, and its potential to provide process models even for fast, automatic reasoning. In our motivating section, we have exemplified the positive specialist use of classical logic by naïve reasoners and emphasised at all times that the same might be done for probability, despite existing evidence such as Kahneman and Tversky's hospital problem casting doubt (see Stenning et al., 2017, p. 186 ff). Relatedly, we contend in our proposal that there is a dimension of systems ranging from LP to full probability via conditional frequency, enough in itself to warrant the 'multiple-logics' label. In this context we wish to emphasise that LP is not 'poor man's probability'. Intensional reasoning to an interpretation is a distinctive kind of human reasoning, judgment and decision, dealing with a different *kind* of uncertainty. It is a necessary prelude to extensional reasoning in classical logic or probability. The integration of fast and frugal heuristics with LP reasoning to yield a general probability-free decision system is additional evidence that intensional reasoning needs to be taken seriously as systematic, and susceptible to rational analysis.

A multiple-logic view remains open to a combination of different formalisms for modelling, in particular of logic and probability, along the lines of Demolombe and Fernandez's (2005) approach to intention recognition, or, relatedly, our proposal in the section introducing the logic to combine CLP with probability for a more fine-grained model of teleological processing. With regard to distinguishing the domains of application of LP and probability, the situation is, as yet, less crisp. Probability is inapplicable to reasoning *to* interpretations, and it must be confined to applications where there is sufficient, and sufficiently stable, data. LP cannot yield full probabilities, though it may be the origin of the frequencies to estimate them and then hand over to probability. The LP–probability borderline is ripe for exploratory empirical investigation with much greater attention to the formal properties of the minimal systems necessary.

Once a multiplicity of logics, each with its unique job specification, is in play, the choice has to be made on instrumental grounds: practical reasoning for theoretical action. The goals of the reasoning determine which logic it is rational to employ in modelling. It is this fitting of logic to task that LP reasoning *to* an interpretation achieves. The 20th century addition of semantics to logic made it a sophisticated tool for the study of the contextualisation of human reasoning. This is illustrated with our pairing of logic programming and classical logic. LP is a formalisation of this process of interpretation in which you see relevant information being found and a core minimal model created, which could, with the addition of different further information, lead to classical logical reasoning, or to probabilistic reasoning, or reasoning in other logics altogether.

Finally, the methodological upshot of the multiple-logic proposal is a research program for reasoning where researchers, given the properties of a particular formalism, hypothesise what kind of reasoning task it might model, and test those predictions; or observe properties of a reasoning task, hypothesise an appropriate formalisation, and test its empirical generalisations. Above all, experimenters must ensure that they have negotiated a mutually shared interpretation with their subjects. Here is a whole garden of earthly delights for the experimenter.

Notes

1 'Logic' is to be taken here in the generic sense of 'formal system'.
2 'Intensional' is used here as in the psychology of reasoning and decision to contrast intensional LP with extensional classical logic and probability. In this sense, probability is extensional (given by the size of extension sets) but not truth-functional. This meaning must not be confused with one common in technical work in which probability is intensional to contrast it with truth functional extensional classical logic.
3 Logic Programming (LP) is to CLP as classical propositional calculus is to predicate calculus. LP is a simpler subset of CLP, and for this paper, the main place in which CLP is required is for handling higher-order goals (see the section introducing the logic). Where LP is sufficient we use the weaker system. The other particular relevance of the distinction is that a neural implementation of LP is already available; that of CLP is work in progress.
4 Stenning and van Lambalgen (2004) and Stenning and van Lambalgen (2008, Chapters 3 and 4) use Socratic dialogues to present extensive evidence of this and other interpretative problems subjects experience, and then experiments to test for the exhibited problems.
5 Roughly, the problem of spelling out the default assumptions that intelligent agents must make in order to proceed to action, e.g., that things remain as they are unless acted upon (law of inertia).
6 We verbalise the reasoning here, but it is crucial that this does not imply that the 14-month-old is doing the same.
7 We use definite clauses because they allow for negation in clause antecedents, which is needed to express the 'no abnormality' ($\neg ab$) conjunct.
8 The uniqueness of the minimal model in CLP is in stark contrast to classical logic, where models are infinite in number and inference validity is assessed with respect to all these possible models.
9 Always a classical logic possibility.

References

Achourioti, T., Fugard, A. J. B., & Stenning, K. (2014). The empirical study of norms is just what we are missing. *Frontiers in Psychology*, *5* (1159). doi: 10.3389/fpsyg.2014.01159

Baggio, G., Stenning, K., & van Lambalgen, M. (2016). The cognitive interface. In M. Aloni & P. Dekker (Eds.), *Cambridge handbook of formal semantics*. Cambridge: Cambridge University Press.

Baker, C. L., Saxe, R., & Tenenbaum, J. B. (2009). Action understanding as inverse planning. *Cognition, 113* (3), 329–349.

Bucciarelli, M., & Johnson-Laird, P. (1999, July). Strategies in syllogistic reasoning. *Cognitive Science, 23* (3), 247–303. Retrieved from http://doi.wiley.com/10.1207/s15516709cog2303 1 doi: 10.1207/s15516709cog2303 1

Burgess, N., & Hitch, G. (2005). Computational models of working memory: Putting long-term memory into context. *Trends in Cognitive Sciences, 9* (11), 535–541.

Casler, K., & Kelemen, D. (2007). Reasoning about artifacts at 24 months: The developing teleo-functional stance. *Cognition, 103* (1), 120–130.

Csibra, G., Gergely, G., Biró, S., Koos, O., & Brockbank, M. (1999). Goal attribution without agency cues: The perception of pure reason' in infancy. *Cognition, 72* (3), 237–267.

Cummins, D. (1995). Naive theories and causal deduction. *Memory and Cognition, 23* (5), 646–658. doi: 10.3758/BF03197265

Czerlinski, J., Gigerenzer, G., & Goldstein, D. G. (1999). How good are simple heuristics? In G. Gigerenzer, P. M. Todd, & The ABC Research Group (Eds.), *Simple heuristics that make us smart. evolution and cognition* (pp. 97–118). New York, NY: Oxford University Press.

Demolombe, R., & Fernandez, A. M. O. (2005). Intention recognition in the situation calculus and probability theory frameworks. *Computational logic in multi-agent systems* (pp. 358–372). Berlin: Springer.

Duff, S., Harland, J., & Thangarajah, J. (2006). On proactivity and maintenance goals. In *Proceedings of the fifth international joint conference on autonomous agents and multiagent systems* (pp. 1033–1040). New York: ACM.

Evans, J. St. B.T., Over, D. E., & Manktelow, K. I. (1993). Reasoning, decision making and rationality. *Cognition, 49* (1), 165–187.

Evans, J. St. B. T., & Stanovich, K. E. (2013). Dual-process theories of higher cognition: Advancing the debate. *Perspectives on Psychological Science, 8*, 223–241.

Fernbach, P. M., & Erb, C. D. (2013). A quantitative causal model theory of conditional reasoning. *Journal of Experimental Psychology: Learning, Memory, and Cognition, 39* (5), 1327–1343.

Fontanari, L., Gonzalez, M., Vallortigara, G., & Girotto, V. (2014). Probabilistic cognition in two indigenous Mayan groups. *Proceedings of the National Academy of Sciences*. Retrieved from www.pnas.org/cgi/doi/10.1073/pnas.1410583111

Gergely, G., Bekkering, H., & Király, I. (2002). Developmental psychology: Rational imitation in preverbal infants. *Nature, 415*(6873), 755–755.

Gigerenzer, G., Czerlinski, J., & Martignon, L. (1999). How good are fast and frugal heuristics? In *Decision science and technology* (pp. 81–103). Berlin: Springer.

Gigerenzer, G., & Gaissmaier, W. (2011). Heuristic decision making. *Annual Review of Psychology, 62*, 451–482.

Gigerenzer, G., Todd, P. M., & The ABC Research Group. (1999). *Simple heuristics that make us smart*. New York: Oxford University Press.

Gopnik, A. (1998). Explanation as orgasm. *Minds and Machines, 8* (1), 101–118.

Hasher, L., & Zacks, R. T. (1984). Automatic processing of fundamental information: The case of frequency of occurrence. *American Psychologist, 39*, 1372–1388.

Hertwig, R., Herzog, S. M., Schooler, L. J., & Reimer, T. (2008). Fluency heuristic: a model of how the mind exploits a by-product of information retrieval. *Journal of Experimental Psychology: Learning, Memory, and Cognition, 34* (5), 1191.

Howson, C., & Urbach, P. (1989). *Scientific reasoning: The Bayesian approach* (1st ed.). Chicago: Open Court Publishing.

Johnson-Laird., P. (1983). *Mental models*. Cambridge: Cambridge University Press.

Jonides, J., & Naveh-Benjamin, M. (1987). Estimating frequency of occurrence. *Journal of Experimental Psychology: Learning, Memory, and Cognition, 13* (2), 230–240.

Király, I., Gergely, & Csibra. (2013). Beyond rational imitation: Learning arbitrary means actions from communicative demonstrations. *Journal of Experimental Child Psychology, 116*(2), 471–486.

Kowalski, R. (2006). The logical way to be artificially intelligent. In F. Toni & P. Torroni (Eds.), *International workshop on computational logic in multi-agent systems* (pp. 1–22). Berlin: Springer.

Kowalski, R. (2011). *Computational logic and human thinking: How to be artificially intelligent*. New York: Cambridge University Press.

Kowalski, R. A. (1988, January). The early years of logic programming. *Communications of the ACM, 31* (1), 38–43. doi: 10.1145/35043.35046

McCarthy, J., & Hayes, P. J. (1969). Some philosophical problems from the standpoint of artificial intelligence. In B. Lynn Webber, & N. J. Nilsson (Eds.), *Readings in artificial intelligence* (pp. 431–450). Los Altos, CA: Morgan Kaufman.

Over, D. (2004). Rationality and the normative/descriptive distinction. In D. J. Koehler & N. Harvey (Eds.), *Blackwell handbook of judgment and decision making*. Oxford: Blackwell.

Over, D. E. (2009). New paradigm psychology of reasoning. *Thinking & Reasoning, 15* (4), 431–438. doi: DOI:10.1080/13546780903266188

Pearl, J. (2000). *Causality: models, reasoning, and inference*. Cambridge, UK: Cambridge University Press.

Pennington, N., & Hastie, R. (1992). Explaining the evidence: Tests of the story model for juror decision making. *Journal of Personality and Social Psychology, 62* (2), 189–206.

Pijnacker, J., Geurts, B., van Lambalgen, M., Buitelaar, J., & Hagoort, P. (2009). Reasoning with exceptions: an event-related brain potentials study. *Journal of Cognitive Neuroscience*. (Posted online 19 Nov 2009; doi:10.1162/jocn.2009.21360)

Pinosio, R. (2016). *Time and causality: A formalisation of Kant's 'Analogies of Experience'*. Unpublished doctoral dissertation, ILLC, University of Amsterdam.

Sloman, S. A., & Lagnado, D. (2015). Causality in thought. *Annual Review of Psychology, 66*(3), 1–25. doi: 10.1146/annurev-psych-010814-015135

Stenning, K., Martignon, L., & van Lambalgen, M. (in preparation). Memory is the organ of nonmonotonic reasoning.

Stenning, K., Martignon, L., & Varga, A. (submitted). Adaptive reasoning: Integrating fast and frugal heuristics with a logic of interpretation. *Decision, 4*(3), 171–196.

Stenning, K., & van Lambalgen, M. (2004). A little logic goes a long way: Basing experiment on semantic theory in the cognitive science of conditional reasoning. *Cognitive Science, 28* (4), 481–530.

Stenning, K., & van Lambalgen, M. (2005). Semantic interpretation as reasoning in nonmonotonic logic: The real meaning of the suppression task. *Cognitive Science, 29* (6), 919–960.

Stenning, K., & van Lambalgen, M. (2008). *Human reasoning and cognitive science*. Cambridge, MA: MIT University Press.

Stenning, K., & van Lambalgen, M. (2010). The logical response to a noisy world. In M. Oaksford (Ed.), *Cognition and conditionals: Probability and logic in human thought* (pp. 85–102). Oxford: Oxford University Press.

Stenning, K., & van Lambalgen, M. (2016). Logic programming, probability, and two-system accounts of reasoning: A rejoinder to Oaksford and Chater. *Thinking & Reasoning, 22,* 355–368. doi: 10.1080/13546783.2016.1139504

Stenning, K., & Yule, P. (1997). Image and language in human reasoning: A syllogistic illustration. *Cognitive Psychology, 34*, 109–159.

Todd, P. M., Gigerenzer, G., & the ABC Research Group. (2012). *Ecological rationality: Intelligence in the world*. New York: Oxford University Press.

Träuble, B., & Pauen, S. (2007). The role of functional information for infant categorization. *Cognition, 105* (2), 362–379.

Tversky, A., & Kahneman, D. (1973). Availability: A heuristic for judging frequency and probability. *Cognitive Psychology, 5* (2), 207–232. doi: http://dx.doi.org/10.1016/0010-0285(73)90033-9

Tversky, A., & Kahneman, D. (1974). Judgment under uncertainty: Heuristics and biases. *Science, 185* (4157), 1124–1131.

Tversky, A., & Kahneman, D. (1983). Extensional versus intuitive reasoning: The conjunction fallacy in probability judgment. *Psychological Review, 90*, 293–315.

van Lambalgen, M., & Hamm, F. (2004). *The proper treatment of events*. Oxford and Boston: Blackwell.

Varga, A. (2013). *A formal model of infants acquisition of practical knowledge from observation*. Unpublished doctoral dissertation, Central European University, Budapest.

Wason, P. C. (1968). Reasoning about a rule. *Quarterly Journal of Experimental Psychology, 20*, 73–281.

White, P. (2013). Singular clues to causality and their use in human causal judgment. *Cognitive Science, 38*, 38–75.

30

THE DEVELOPMENT OF RATIONAL THINKING

Insights from the heuristics and biases literature and dual process models

Maggie E. Toplak

There is a long history and tradition of studying children's reasoning and thinking, but there is still a relatively short history of this literature integrating and building on the insights from the heuristics and biases research tradition and dual process models. The heuristics and biases work and dual process models have been studied more extensively in adults. That people make systematic errors in judgment on heuristics and biases tasks was one of the early observations made in the heuristics and biases literature (Kahneman, 2011). Explaining performance on these tasks (and on experimental tasks from the reasoning literature) has become rooted in what are now dual process models of reasoning (Frankish & Evans, 2009). Further, individual differences in cognitive abilities and thinking dispositions have been shown to converge with patterns of performance on these tasks (Stanovich, 1999; 2011; Stanovich & West, 2000). These insights and models have had significant implications for modern cognitive science models of reasoning in adults, and have parallel implications for understanding the development of reasoning.

Cognitive scientists have recognized two types of rationality: instrumental and epistemic (Stanovich, West, & Toplak, 2011a). Instrumental rationality has to do with an individual's optimization of goal fulfillment and epistemic rationality pertains to how well an individual's beliefs map onto the actual structure of the world. Rationality can be assessed based on whether individuals have violated certain axioms of rational choice, including consistency in choices and susceptibility to the effects of context. The heuristics and biases program of research provided experimental methods and important insights about underlying processes that contribute to rational responding. Several of these paradigms have also been examined in children and adolescents, but the implications for understanding the development of rationality are not well understood. In this chapter, considerations from the adult literature are used to propose a framework for understanding the development of rational thinking. Specifically, the role of knowledge, recognizing cues to engage in analytic processing and the capacity for override are parallel considerations that can be examined across developmental levels.

Historical perspectives on the development of reasoning

With a fair amount of assurance, any student of developmental psychology will be taught Piaget's theory as the foundation of cognitive development. It is a competency-based model, defined by whether children have reached certain milestones at each stage (Siegler, 1991). For example, children who reach the period of concrete operations tend to demonstrate the ability to take other points of view, hold simultaneously multiple points of view and represent static and transformed situations relative to earlier stages of development. Each subsequent stage brings with it "the potential for solving many types of problems that children in earlier stages could not hope to conquer" (Siegler, 1991, p. 21). The initial studies of the development of reasoning were motivated by Piagetian models, and development was thought to bring the gradual onset of logical thinking (Markovits, 2014a).

Based on this perspective, children were generally thought to acquire increasingly complex and sophisticated cognitive skills. While this characterization may seem like an oversimplification of Piagetian theory, it will provide a context for how the heuristics and biases work and dual process models extend these early perspectives. There seemed to be an implicit assumption that developmental changes would translate into better performance on many tasks. This assumption seemed to underlie Piagetian, neo-Piagetian, information processing, and social-cultural (Vygotskian) perspectives (Flavell, Miller, & Miller, 1993). This implicit assumption was reinforced by the fact that Neo-Piagetian researchers were surprised to observe that some children seemed to exhibit higher competence than expected and that some adolescents and adults did not reach some of the cognitive developmental milestones at later stages, such as at the formal operational period (Flavell et al., 1993). These findings challenged developmental theorists to characterize what seemed to be unexpected levels of competence (early in development) and lack of competence (later in development). Such findings also raised questions about how developing processes could give rise to better logical thinking and how these processes could also give rise to belief-biased thinking (Markovits, 2014a). One of the theoretical models that attempted to resolve what seemed like contradictions from these perspectives was fuzzy-trace theory (see Reyna & Brainerd, 1994, for a review of how Piagetian and information processing models have shaped models of the development of probability judgment). At around this time, dual process models were also beginning to take shape in the adult literature (Evans & Over, 1996; Sloman, 1996; Stanovich, 1999). In addition, individual differences in adult performance on reasoning problems and heuristics and biases tasks were found to be associated with cognitive abilities (Stanovich, 1999).

Developmental implications of the heuristics and biases literature and dual process models

Heuristic and analytic processes

The study of heuristics and biases in adults has led to several important insights about human reasoning. First, typically developing individuals display systematic errors in their thinking that are attributable to the "design of the machinery" as opposed to the "corruption of thought by emotion" (Kahneman, 2011). One of the important characteristics of many of the heuristics and biases tasks is that there is a conflict between an easily generated intuitive response and a less easily generated normative response. It is this conflict between these responses that make these tasks particularly difficult for participants. The distinction between these two types of responses has also formed the basis for modern dual process models of reasoning (Evans, 2003; 2008; 2010; Evans & Stanovich, 2013; Stanovich, 2009; 2011; see also Evans, this volume).

Let us take an example that has become well known in the rational thinking literature, the bat and ball problem from the Cognitive Reflection Test, or CRT (Frederick, 2005): a bat and a ball cost $1.10 in total. The bat costs $1 more than the ball. How much does the ball cost?

Participants must calculate a response to answer this question. The most common response to this question is 10 cents, which is an incorrect response. This response is given with extremely high frequency, as high as 86% of participants (Toplak, West, & Stanovich, 2014a). Many participants do not recognize that this response could be wrong. A minority of participants give their initial response further consideration and recognize that if the ball is 10 cents, and if the bat is $1 more, that would make the cost of the bat $1.10. Then it immediately becomes apparent that 10 cents is not the correct answer, as summing $1.10 and 10 cents equals $1.20, which is higher than the total amount given in the problem. Calculating the correct answer of 5 cents then becomes straightforward, as low as 12% in some samples (Toplak et al., 2014a). For those participants who respond "Ten cents," this response is strongly primed by heuristic processes. Alternatively, those participants who respond "Five cents" likely override the lure of the incorrect response and then calculate an alternative response, which, if computed accurately, will yield the correct response.

From dual process models of reasoning, heuristic and analytic processes have been used to characterize how participants arrive at their different responses, such as those described in the CRT example. The defining feature of heuristic processes is autonomy, that these processes are necessarily executed in the presence of triggering stimuli (Stanovich, 2009; 2011; Stanovich & Toplak, 2012). These processes also tend not to put a heavy load on central processing capacities. Examples of these processes include behavioral regulation by the emotions, encapsulated modules for solving specific adaptive problems that have been suggested by evolutionary psychologists and overlearned associations. Alternatively, analytic processes operate serially, and are generally slower and more computationally expensive. The purpose of analytic processes is to compute a better response when the response derived from heuristic processes needs to be overridden. Heuristic processes often provide input for optimal responses in typically experienced situations, but in unique and novel situations, heuristic processes provide only a ballpark estimate, requiring the hypothetical simulation of analytic processes to compute a better response (Stanovich, 2011). In order to engage analytic processes, the capacity to interrupt and suppress the heuristic processes must be available to engage processes of hypothetical reasoning. The manner in which these two sets of processes or systems interact has been discussed extensively (Evans, 2003; 2008; 2010; Evans & Stanovich, 2013; Stanovich, 2009; 2011; Stanovich & West, 2008b). Heuristic and analytic processes have also been referred to as System 1/System 2 processes (Evans, 2008; 2009) and Type 1/Type 2 processes (Stanovich, 1999). *Heuristic* and *analytic* will be the terminology used in this chapter as these terms have been more commonly used in the developmental literature.

The findings from the heuristics and biases literature on adults have consistently shown that many adults tend to demonstrate less-than-rational responding, often attributable to failing to recognize when an alternative response may be needed and/or a failure to override a dominant response generated by heuristic processes (Stanovich, 2009; 2011; Stanovich & West, 2008b). The distinction between heuristic and analytic processes in the adult literature provides a useful way to characterize how different responses occur in these tasks. There is much work to be done to further articulate and understand how these processes unfold and develop.

The development of analytic processes is somewhat more straightforward, as children tend to display an increase in cognitive capacities that enable override and hypothetical simulation, such as intelligence and working memory (Evans, 2011), which has been supported in several studies (Brydges, Fox, Reid, & Anderson, 2014; Brydges, Reid, Fox, & Anderson, 2012; Davidson, Amso, Anderson, & Diamond, 2006; Salthouse & Davis, 2006). It is important to note that the presence of more sophisticated cognitive abilities of course does not guarantee their use (Morsanyi & Handley, 2013; Stanovich, West, & Toplak, 2011b), but does increase the likelihood of normative correct responding on some heuristics and biases tasks. There is convergence to suggest that cognitive abilities, or analytic processes, become increasingly available and sophisticated over the course of development.

Alternatively, heuristic processes have been described as a "grab-bag", as these processes still encompass a very broad set of types of processes, including innately specified processing modules and experiential associations that have been learned to automaticity (Stanovich et al., 2011b). In the developmental literature, these distinctions are critically important. For those heuristic processes that come from evolutionary modules, such as affective cues from autonomous processes, we can infer that these processes are available throughout the lifespan. However, the heuristic processes acquired from experiential associations are a complex domain from a developmental perspective. In adults, it may be presumed with some confidence that many experiential associations have been tightly compiled to automaticity. However, in children, some of the specific knowledge or mindware needed to derive a rational response may not have been learned or consolidated, which may explain some of the reversed patterns in developmental findings (Stanovich et al., 2011b). The surprising aspect of developmental reversals is not the fact that older participants choose responses based on heuristic processes – it is the other side of this data pattern: that younger children arrive at a correct response as the result of analytic abilities that have successfully overridden the conflict with autonomous heuristic processes. That is, younger groups of children may appear to be responding correctly when in fact they are responding randomly because they do not have the requisite knowledge to answer the question. If these experiential associations have been learned but not consolidated, they will not operate in the same autonomous manner in children as in adults.

The implication is that there may be variability in the engagement of these heuristic processes in children, affecting performance on rational thinking tasks. In adults, such heuristic processes are likely autonomous and competing with analytic processes, but this cannot be presumed in children when understanding their performance. These types of heuristic processes increase with development, such as growth in knowledge, implicit learning and compiling overlearned associations. Some of these processes are akin to the shift from controlled to automatic processes that have been well studied in the cognitive psychology literature (Shiffrin & Schneider, 1977). As children get older, they will learn more relevant knowledge or mindware that will become increasingly consolidated, and this mindware will begin to behave heuristically and support rational responding on some tasks (Stanovich et al., 2011b). For example, knowledge of probability and base rates will be acquired, and if this knowledge is consolidated, it can support rational responding. Other types of knowledge, such as knowledge of stereotypes, also become consolidated and heuristically triggered but may interfere with rational responding.

Some of the confusions that occur in the developmental literature are parallel to those that have occurred in the adult literature. Evans (2008; 2009) has pointed out that analytic processes have mistakenly been equated with normatively correct responding and that heuristic processing has been mistakenly equated with non-normative incorrect responding. Instead, both heuristic and analytic processing often lead to normative correct responding, and it is just statistically more likely for analytic processes to provide the correct response on the types of heuristics and biases tasks that have been under study (Stanovich et al., 2011b). This issue has certainly pervaded the developmental literature as well. In particular, it has been perpetuated by the use of the terms "analytic" and "heuristic" responding, instead of characterizing these as analytic and heuristic processes that may lead to correct/normative or incorrect/non-normative responses. Not all heuristic processes lead to biased, incorrect responses and not all analytic processes lead to correct responses (Evans, 2012; Evans & Stanovich, 2013; Stanovich & West, 2008b). However, heuristics and biases tasks are designed to produce conflicting responses, and analytic engagement is needed to override the response that is championed by heuristic processes in order to derive a normatively correct response. Both heuristic and analytic processes develop during childhood: analytic processes do not replace heuristic processes and heuristic processes do not replace analytic processes (Markovits, 2014a; Stanovich et al., 2011b).

We know that both heuristic and analytic processes are involved in explaining performance in adults on rational thinking tasks, and the relative engagement of these processes help to explain individual differences on task performance (Stanovich, 2009; 2011). Many adults respond incorrectly on rational thinking tasks, likely due to predominating heuristic processes that were not overridden by analytic processes. Alternatively, some adults respond correctly on these tasks attributable to a successful override by analytic processes. These individual differences in performance on rational thinking tasks have also been associated with performance on measures of intelligence and executive functions (Stanovich, 1999; 2009; 2011). Individual differences in thinking dispositions related to actively open-minded thinking and persistence in thinking have also been associated with rational responding (Toplak, West, & Stanovich, 2011; 2014a; West, Toplak, & Stanovich, 2008). There is an emerging literature to suggest that rational responding is associated with cognitive abilities and dispositions in a parallel manner in developmental samples (Kokis et al., 2002; Toplak et al., 2014b). However, it should not be presumed that all rational thinking tasks will display such a pattern in developmental samples, and each paradigm will need consideration based on findings from the adult literature and careful consideration of appropriate stimuli for developmental samples.

Stimulus equivalence problem

The heuristics and biases literature with adults has been hugely influential for informing models of rational thinking. However, the stimuli that have been used in adult studies have perhaps created considerable complexity for developmentalists. These measures are unlike some of the neuropsychological measures that can be administered to children and adults throughout the lifespan. For example, most children have consolidated their basic reading and counting skills by ages 8–9 (Grade 3), making it much more straightforward to administer tasks such as the Stroop and trail-making tests. As the classic heuristics and biases literature introduced several novel tasks, this raised questions, not only about the development of rational thinking, but also about the acquisition of knowledge and mindware that was presumed in these tasks designed for adults. For example, demonstration of the conjunction effect presumes an understanding that the probability of the intersection of two elements is statistically less likely than the probability of a single element. Attribute framing problems are fairly straightforward as these problems tend to be a direct re-wording of the same problem, whereas the classic disease framing problem introduces concepts such as gain (lives saved) and loss (lives lost), which raises questions about developmental predictions and prospect theory (see Stanovich et al., 2011b, for a further discussion of the stimulus equivalence problem).

Related to the stimulus equivalence problem, the design of the task also has significant implications for interpreting task performance. Several of our rational thinking tasks require children to choose between two options, opening up the possibility of guessing, making it difficult to infer how children have arrived at their response. The CRT is an ideal measure in this sense, as participants must generate an actual response. It is becoming apparent that in order to advance our understanding of the development of rational thinking, the study of developmental differences on a given task in isolation may not be adequate. For example, developmental differences in isolation make it difficult to infer whether the stimuli for heuristics and biases tasks were developmentally appropriate for younger samples. It will be useful to examine other convergers with performance, such as other individual difference variables, as has been done in the adult literature.

Proposed framework for the development of rational thinking

A framework has been suggested for the multiple ways in which individual differences can be observed on heuristic and biases task performance in adults (Stanovich & West, 2008a; Stanovich, 2011). Figure 30.1 displays this framework, slightly adapted from Stanovich and West (2008b). At the first step, the question is whether the specific knowledge or mindware is available to carry out an override. If the mindware is not available, then an intuitive incorrect response will be generated. If the mindware is available, then the next question is whether

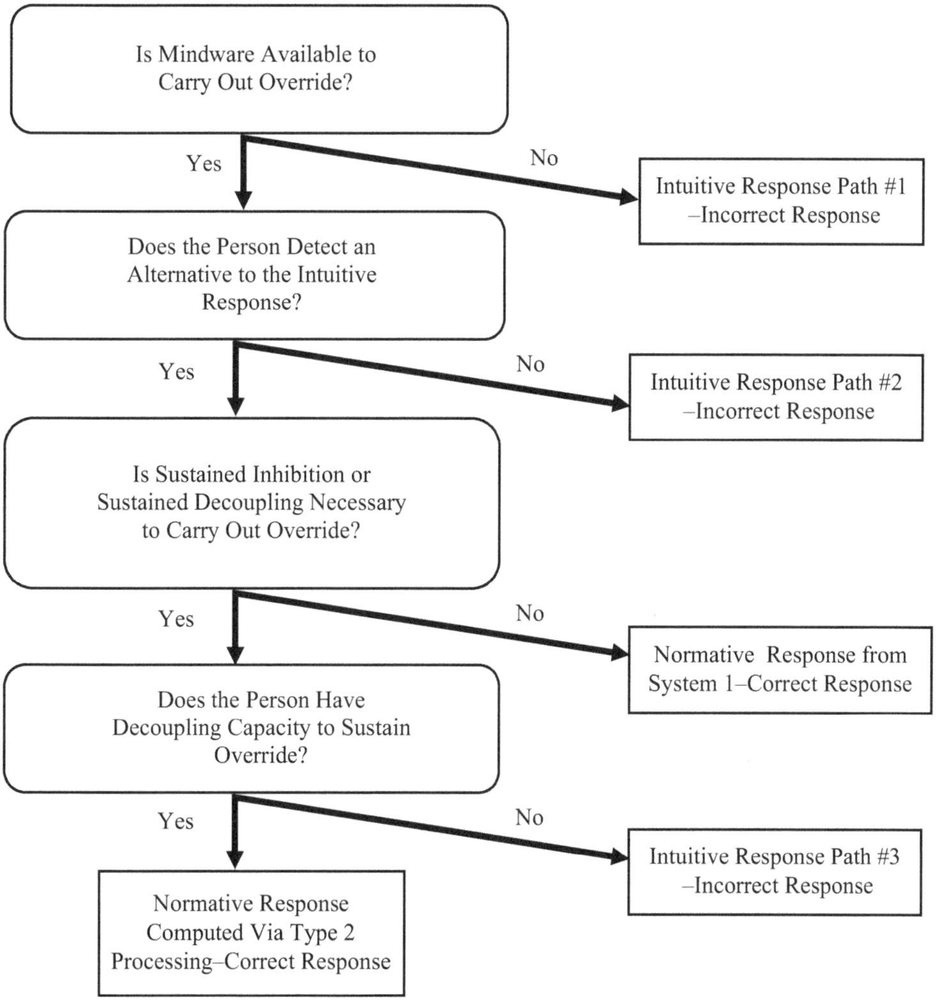

Figure 30.1 Framework for the multiple ways that individual differences can be observed on heuristics and biases tasks (adapted from Stanovich & West, 2008b)

the individual recognizes if the intuitive response needs to be overridden. If recognition does not occur, then this also leads to an intuitive incorrect response. If recognition does occur, this initiates sustained inhibition and decoupling processes in order to carry out the override. If these processes are not necessary, the individual can derive a normative response from heuristic processes (namely, from consolidated mindware). If these processes are required, then sustained decoupling processes are initiated. The individual who does not have the capacity for sustained decoupling will likely arrive at an intuitive incorrect response. The individual who has the capacity and successfully engages these processes will derive a normatively correct response using analytic processes.

Younger children will have less mindware available, which has been acknowledged by others in the literature (De Neys & van Gelder, 2009). Also, the extent to which the mindware is consolidated will affect the likelihood that the relevance of the mindware will be recognized. In developmental samples, any mindware is less likely to be consolidated, suggesting that this may be another relevant individual difference dimension in developmental samples. Thinking dispositions support the detection of the need for override, and cognitive abilities (such as fluid intelligence) support the cognitive decoupling to generate an alternative response (Stanovich, 2011). There is some evidence to suggest that detection failures are more likely in younger than older children (De Neys, 2013; De Neys & Feremans, 2013). There is also some evidence to suggest the emergence of thinking dispositions relevant to rational thinking in developmental samples (Kokis et al., 2002; Toplak et al., 2014b). Sustained inhibition and override have been attributed to associations with cognitive abilities. With development and with increases in cognitive capacities and dispositions, older children will be more likely to engage analytic processes and have available compiled mindware which may lead to more normative responding (Stanovich et al., 2011b). Advancing such a framework in the developmental literature will provide a way to move beyond the stimulus equivalence issue and provide methodological directions for determining convergers of rational thinking performance, such as individual differences in measures that indicate cognitive sophistication (Toplak et al., 2014b).

Several measurement paradigms to assess rational thinking have been examined in the developmental literature (see Toplak, West, & Stanovich, 2013, for a review), but the developmental patterns of each of these paradigms is yet to be fully understood. Some of these paradigms have been shown to display trends toward better performance with more advanced development, but some of the patterns are less clear. The framework in Figure 30.1 is also relevant for developmental samples to articulate the multiple junctures where rational thinking may fail for any given task. Table 30.1 displays an example of how rational thinking tasks may be categorized in terms of the relative involvement of process and knowledge in order to support task performance (see Stanovich, West, & Toplak, 2016, for a detailed discussion). The categorization of tasks in the table is based on what we know from the adult literature in terms of understanding cognitive failures in rational thinking performance. It is important to note that none of these tasks purely fall into one category or another, as several of the miserly information processing tasks also require some knowledge of mindware. It is instead the case that performance on some of these tasks will be more heavily determined by process than by knowledge or mindware. Indeed, it has been acknowledged in the adult literature that many of these are determined by multiple processes (Stanovich, 2009). In the case of development, the role of requisite mindware likely affects all of these tasks in a much more substantial manner than in adults. Also, the relative contribution of process and knowledge may also vary at different periods of development. What has not been included in this table is dispositions that support rational thinking, such as actively open-minded thinking, but these dispositions are also part of this broader framework.

Table 30.1 Measurement paradigms to assess the development of rational thinking

Tasks where performance relies heavily on resistance to miserly information processing
– Syllogistic reasoning with belief bias – Ratio bias (attribute substitution, denominator neglect) – Framing tasks – Rational temporal discounting – Delay of gratification – Emotion regulation by reward – Myside bias – Cognitive Reflection Test – Overconfidence – Anchoring – Outcome bias
Tasks where performance relies heavily on specific knowledge or mindware
– Practical numeracy – Sensitivity to expected value and risky decision making – Knowledge of scientific reasoning (no conflict tasks) – Financial literacy
Tasks where performance relies heavily on resistance to miserly information processing and specific knowledge or mindware
– Attribute substitution and sensitivity to probabilities (appreciating base rates) – Conjunction effects – Gambler's fallacy – Importance of sample size – Knowledge of scientific reasoning (conflict tasks)
Tasks where performance is affected by unhelpful mindware
– Superstitious and paranormal beliefs

Resistance to miserly information processing

Several of the rational thinking tasks in the literature vary in the extent to which performance is characterized by overriding miserly information processing (Stanovich, 2009; 2011; Stanovich et al., 2011a). Of the tasks where performance is primarily determined by miserly information processing, one of the most well-studied paradigms in the developmental literature has been syllogisms with belief bias content. Belief bias syllogisms represent a special category of deductive conditional reasoning where the believability of the conclusion conflicts with the logical structure of the problem. These are typically called inconsistent or conflict problems. There is important knowledge or mindware that children must have to successfully solve these problems, including basic competence on conditional reasoning skills. There is an extensive literature on the developmental trajectory in the acquisition of conditional reasoning skills on concrete and abstract problems (Markovits, 2014b; Markovits & Lortie-Forgues, 2011; Markovits & Thompson, 2008; Markovits & Vachon, 1990; Markovits et al., 1996; see also Markovits, this volume, regarding developmental patterns and theoretical perspectives). In studies that have examined performance on belief bias syllogisms in developmental samples, there is a fair amount of convergence to suggest that older children tend to outperform younger children (De Neys & van

Gelder, 2009; Evans & Perry, 1995; Handley, Capon, Beveridge, Dennis, & Evans, 2004; Kokis et al., 2002; Markovits & Bouffard-Bouchard, 1992; Steegen & De Neys, 2012; Toplak et al., 2014b) than studies that have not (Morsanyi & Handley, 2008). Children who endorsed more actively open-minded thinking and who performed better on cognitive abilities were also more likely to perform better on belief bias syllogisms (Kokis et al., 2002; Toplak et al., 2014b).

Optimal performance on ratio bias tasks (also termed denominator neglect and attribute substitution) also requires overriding processes that seem to lure an incorrect response towards selecting the bowl with more actual winning marbles over the bowl that has a higher probability of winning. This task originated from the adult literature (Denes-Raj & Epstein, 1994; Kirkpatrick & Epstein, 1992). Some numerical competence is required in order to compare the ratios or probabilities of each bowl. Some studies have made salient the ratios in studies with children, with supplementary information to show the ratios so that children do not have to compute the ratios or probabilities (Kokis et al., 2002; Toplak et al., 2014b). Some studies suggest that ratio bias performance increase with age (Klaczynski, 2001; Toplak et al., 2014b). Better performance on ratio bias tasks has also been associated with more endorsement of actively open-minded thinking and higher cognitive abilities in developmental samples (Kokis et al., 2002; Toplak et al., 2014b).

Framing problems reflect a context effect, where participants respond differently to whether a problem is framed positively or negatively. The classic framing problems used in the heuristics and biases literature involved gain and loss frames (Kahneman & Tversky, 1984, 2000). In developmental studies, children have typically been presented with scenarios involving small prizes that the children receive instead of imaginary deaths. These problems do not seem to require particular mindware; however, consideration needs to be given to understanding how responding to risks and losses unfolds developmentally. This literature in developmental samples has been more complex and inconsistent. Studies have reported framing effects in young children (Schlottmann & Tring, 2005) and in adolescents (Chien, Lin, & Worthley, 1996). Some studies have reported no developmental trends for framing effects (Levin & Hart, 2003; Levin, Weller, Pederson, & Harshman, 2007), but 6- 8-year-old children were found to be more risk averse for gains than for losses in the manner that prospect theory predicts. Reyna and Ellis (1994) reported that 4-year-olds displayed no framing effect, 8-year-olds displayed a reverse framing effect and 11-year-olds displayed a mixture of framing effects. Alternatively, Toplak et al. (2014b) used attribute framing problems in a developmental sample. Older youth were less likely to display framing effects than younger youth and resistance to framing was found to be associated with higher cognitive abilities and endorsement of actively open-minded thinking. Similarly, Weller, Levin, Rose, and Bossard (2012) examined resistance to framing in a pre-adolescent sample using both gain/loss problems and attribute framing problems. They found that resistance to framing was associated with higher ratings of effortful control and inhibitory control by the pre-adolescents and their parents.

Rational temporal discounting and delay of gratification tasks assess a prudent attitude toward the future (Stanovich, 2009; 2011; Toplak et al., 2013). Temporal discounting tasks require participants to make choices between a small variable reward immediately versus a larger constant reward available after a variable delay (Rachlin et al., 1991). Studies with developmental samples have reported that older youth tend to prefer the larger delayed reward more than do younger youth (Green, Fry, & Myerson, 1994; Prencipe, Kesek, Cohen, Lamm, Lewis, & Zelazo, 2006; Steinberg, Graham, O'Brien, Woolard, Cauffman, & Banich, 2009). These preferences have been found to be positively associated with intelligence and executive function measures (Prencipe et al., 2006; Steinberg et al., 2009). Delay of gratification paradigms seem to display a parallel trend, it has been found that delay ability in preschoolers has been shown to significantly predict SAT scores in adolescents (Mischel, Shoda, & Peake, 1988).

Another domain of miserly information processing emerges from how our emotions regulate our sensitivity to rewards and punishments. This has been indexed with the well-known Iowa Gambling Task, which has been studied extensively in adults as well as in developmental samples. Poor performance on the IGT has been attributed to dysregulation of somatic markers (Damasio, 1994; 1996; 1999). Namely, individuals who perform poorly on this task purportedly have weaker somatic or physiological cues to guide risky choices (Damasio, 1994; 1996; 1999). Somatic markers, or emotions, are suggested to assist by constraining the decision-making space, giving certain alternatives preferential availability over other alternatives (Oatley, 1999). Several developmental studies have demonstrated that older youth tend to make more advantageous selections than children on adapted versions of this task (Crone & van der Molen, 2004; Garon & Moore, 2004; Hongwanishkul, Happaney, Lee, & Zelazo, 2005; Hooper, Luciana, Conklin, & Yarger, 2004; Lamm, Zelazo, & Lewis, 2006; Prencipe et al., 2006). Advantageous selections in this task have also been reported to show modest associations with some executive function measures (Lamm et al., 2006; Prencipe et al., 2006). However, one study has reported a curvilinear relationship, suggesting an increase in performance between preadolescence and mid-adolescence (10- to 16-year-olds) and a decrease in performance between mid-adolescence and adulthood (16- to 30-year-olds; Steinberg, 2010).

There are several other domains of rational thinking tasks indicated in Table 30.1 that rely heavily on resistance to miserly information processing that have been even less well-studied in developmental samples. Myside bias refers to the tendency to test hypotheses in a way that is biased towards one's own opinions and beliefs (Baron, 1995; Perkins, Farady, & Bushey, 1991; Stanovich, 2011; Toplak & Stanovich, 2003). The myside bias has been shown to be unrelated to cognitive abilities in adults (Stanovich & West, 2007, 2008a). Age effects have not been associated with myside bias in adolescent and young adult samples (Baron, Granato, Spranca, & Teubal, 1993; Klaczynski & Lavallee, 2005; Klaczynski & Narasimham, 1998), but the number of otherside reasons given in a myside bias task has been found to be associated with age in a sample of children and young adolescents (Toplak et al., 2014b). The CRT has primarily been characterized as a measure indicating miserly information processing (Toplak et al., 2011; 2014a), but basic numerical competence has also been shown to be an important predictor of task performance (Liberali, Reyna, Furlan, Stein, & Pardo, 2012). The CRT has not been well studied in developmental samples, likely attributable to the fact that performance is generally quite low in adult samples (Frederick, 2005; Toplak et al., 2014a). One study has reported that young adults outperformed adolescents on an expanded version of the CRT (Primi, Morsanyi, Chiesi, Donati, & Hamilton, 2015). Overconfidence paradigms index performance calibration, and less overconfidence in a sample of pre-adolescents has been associated with higher ratings of attentional focus and inhibitory control by the pre-adolescents and their parents (Weller et al., 2012). Older children also tend to provide more accurate estimations of their abilities and competence compared to younger children on other cognitive estimation tasks (Desoete & Roeyers, 2006; Lipko, Dunlosky, & Merriman, 2009; Newman, 1984; Schneider, Visé, Lockl, & Nelson, 2000). Anchoring is another paradigm requiring the avoidance of irrelevant context, and no developmental trends have been reported (Smith, 1999). Finally, one study has reported less outcome bias in 16 year-olds than 12-year-olds (Klaczynski, 2001).

Reliance on specific knowledge or mindware

Some measures of rational thinking rely heavily on the acquisition of specific mindware or knowledge. Specifically, the acquisition and consolidation of specific knowledge will make available other potential responses if the need for an alternative response is recognized and if adequate cognitive resources are available to inhibit and sustain cognitive decoupling operations (Stanovich & West, 2008b). Basic practical numeracy skills are critical for many rational thinking tasks (including on some of the tasks that rely most heavily on resisting miserly information processing that have already been discussed). There are individual differences in practical numeracy skills among US children, including basic proficiency with percentages, fractions and probabilities (Reyna & Brainerd, 2007). These findings suggest that numerical competence related to probabilities is an additional individual difference variable that may explain performance on many rational thinking tasks. Individual differences in numeracy have been found to predict performance on rational thinking and decision-making in adults (Peters, 2012; Peters, Västfjäll, Slovic, Mertz, Mazzocco, & Dickert, 2006; Sinayev & Peters, 2015; Weller, Dieckmann, Tusler, Mertz, Burns, & Peters, 2013).

Related to numeracy skills, the sensitivity to expected value is another domain of mindware relevant to rational thinking performance. The "cups" task has been used to examine risky decision making in developmental samples (Levin, Weller, Pederson, & Harshman, 2007; Weller, Levin, & Denburg, 2011). In this task, three variables were manipulated: gain versus loss trials, different levels of probability for the risky choices (.20, .33, .50), and different levels of outcomes. Each trial required a choice between a certain or risky option. For example, participants choose between a sure gain of 25 cents or a 20% chance of winning 50 cents. The risky option offered either a higher or lower expected value. Feedback was given following each choice, and the accumulated money earned was received at the conclusion of the experiment. It was found that adults were more likely to select the options that offered higher expected values than children (Levin et al., 2007; Weller et al., 2011). This developmental finding has also been replicated using somewhat different procedures (Rakow & Rahim, 2010, Schlottmann, 2000, 2001).

In addition to basic numeracy skills and understanding expected value, more specialized types of learned mindware are critical for successful performance on several rational thinking tasks. These specialized types of mindware include knowledge of scientific reasoning and financial literacy. Scientific thinking involves knowledge about how to test and revise theories, design proper controls for extraneous variables, and objectively evaluate evidence (Zimmerman, 2007). Understanding the need for experimental controls, such as isolating variables and inclusion of control conditions, increases with age in children (Klahr, Fay, & Dunbar, 1993; Klahr & Nigam, 2004; Masnick & Morris, 2008; Tschirgi, 1980). Older children are also more likely to take covariation among variables into account and resist inappropriate causal inferences (Klaczynski, 2001; Koslowski, Condry, Sprague, & Hutt, 1996; Koslowski, Okagaki, Lorenz, & Umbach, 1989; Richardson, 1992). Several developmental studies have included examination of direct knowledge of understanding these principles. However, if these tasks are designed such that knowledge of the scientific reasoning principle conflicts with an intuitive response, then the task is better categorized as relying heavily on resisting miserly processing and requiring specific mindware, such as diagnostic hypothesis testing (Klaczynski, 2001).

Financial literacy involves basic knowledge about saving and investing money (such as stocks versus savings accounts), knowledge of economics concepts (such as supply and demand) and recognizing sunk costs. In the limited work that has been done with developmental samples, older participants have demonstrated higher levels of financial literacy and more economic thinking than younger participants (Mandell, 2009; Thompson & Siegler, 2000). Empirical findings on sunk cost effects with developmental samples have been more mixed (Baron et al., 1993; Klaczynski, 2001; Morsanyi & Handley, 2008; Strough, Mehta, McFall, & Schuller, 2008).

Resistance to miserly information processing and reliance on specific knowledge or mindware

Many rational thinking tasks rely heavily on resisting miserly information processing and specific mindware for successful performance (Stanovich, 2009). While cognitive failures on some rational thinking tasks may be largely attributable to miserly information processing or missing mindware, performance on some problems may be attributable to either or both of these difficulties. This poses a particular challenge for developmental studies, as we need to ensure that consideration of both of these aspects are properly designed in the stimuli that are used to assess these paradigms. Attribute substitution problems (Fong, Krantz, & Nisbett, 1986; Stanovich et al., 2008), also referred to as vividness effects, require knowledge of base rates (that large sample information is more diagnostic than single-case testimonies) and the tendency to select the vivid, salient personal testimony must be overridden in order to derive an optimal response. Several studies have reported that increasing age is associated with more reliance on base rates and less reliance on salient vivid cases in older youth than in younger children (Kokis et al., 2002; Davidson, 1995; Klaczynski, 2001; Toplak et al., 2014b). Cognitive ability has also been reported to be significantly positively associated with base rate usage (Kokis et al., 2002; Toplak et al., 2014b). However, some studies have reported increased reliance on salient vivid cases in older participants when social stereotypes are involved (Davidson, 1995; De Neys & Vanderputte, 2011; Jacobs & Potenza, 1991).

Finally, other rational thinking tasks also involve statistical and probabilistic knowledge combined with the requirement to resist miserly information processing. Conjunction effects, the gambler's fallacy, and sample size problems are examples of these types of problems. Older youth have been shown to outperform younger youth on the gambler's fallacy and sample size problems (Chiesi, Primi, & Morsanyi, 2011). However, the findings for conjunction problems with developmental samples have been mixed (Chiesi et al., 2011; Davidson, 1995; Fishbein & Schnarch, 1997; Klaczynski, 2001; Morsanyi & Handley, 2008). The understanding of the conjunction effect involves sophisticated knowledge for developmental samples. Notably, the conjunction effect using within-subject designs has not been consistently associated with individual differences in cognitive abilities in adult samples (Stanovich & West, 1998).

When knowledge interferes with rational thinking performance

One domain that has not been considered in this chapter is the domain of contaminated mindware, or unhelpful knowledge that may interfere with rational thinking performance. This has been examined relatively less in children than in adults, but the construct of superstitious thinking has been examined in some studies. These studies have indicated relatively mixed findings, with some studies suggesting negative trends or associations with age (Kokis et al., 2002; Toplak et al., 2014b) and other studies suggesting positive associations with age (Preece & Baxter, 2000). One study indicated no association between age and magical thinking (Bolton, Dearsley, Madronal-Luque, & Baron-Cohen, 2002). This is an important and interesting area for continued study in developmental samples, to determine how acquired mindware emerges to potentially interfere with rational thinking.

Conclusions and summary

The heuristics and biases literature and dual process models in adults raises important issues with respect to understanding the development of thinking in children and adolescents. First and foremost, the fact that we can extend these literatures into younger ages suggests that we can measure and assess rational thinking in developmental samples. The heuristics and biases tasks originate from the adult literature, and the stimuli are often adapted for use with children. The developmental context, however, adds several additional layers of complexity, including the use of developmentally appropriate stimuli, which has been referred to as the stimulus equivalence problem (Stanovich et al., 2011b). Developmental predictions are also complicated by the fact that the underlying heuristic and analytic processes are continually changing and that some knowledge may not have been acquired or compiled to be accessed efficiently to support rational thinking performance. Despite these complexities, there is evidence to suggest that children and adolescents demonstrate systematic errors in thinking on heuristics and biases tasks, parallel to what has been observed in adult samples. Each task and paradigm requires careful consideration of processing and knowledge requisites in order to inform developmentally appropriate stimuli.

References

Baron, J. (1995). Myside bias in thinking about abortion. *Thinking and Reasoning, 1*, 221–235.

Baron, J., Granato, L., Spranca, M., & Teubal, E. (1993). Decision making biases in children and early adolescents: Exploratory studies. *Merrill-Palmer Quarterly, 39*, 22–46.

Bolton, D., Dearsley, P., Madronal-Luque, R., & Baron-Cohen, S. (2002). Magical thinking in childhood and adolescence: Development and relation to obsessive compulsion. *British Journal of Developmental Psychology, 20*, 479–494.

Brydges, C. R., Fox, A. M., Reid, C. L., & Anderson, M. (2014). Predictive validity of the N2 and P3 ERP components to executive functioning in children: A latent-variable analysis. *Frontiers in Human Neuroscience, 8*, 80. doi:10.3389/fnhum.2014.00080

Brydges, C. R., Reid, C.. L, Fox, A. M., & Anderson, M. (2012). A unitary executive function predicts intelligence in children. *Intelligence, 40*(5), 458–469.

Chien, Y. C., Lin, C., & Worthley, J. (1996). Effect of framing on adolescents' decision making. *Perceptual and Motor Skills, 83*, 811–819.

Chiesi, F., Primi, C., & Morsanyi, K. (2011). Developmental changes in probabilistic reasoning: The role of cognitive capacity, instructions, thinking styles, and relevant knowledge. *Thinking & Reasoning, 17*(3), 315–350.

Crone, E. A., & van der Molen, M. W. (2004). Developmental changes in real life decision making: Performance on a gambling task previously shown to depend on the ventromedial prefrontal cortex. *Developmental Neuropsychology, 25*, 251–279.

Damasio, A. R. (1994). *Descartes' error.* New York: Putnam.

Damasio, A. R. (1996). The somatic marker hypothesis and the possible functions of the prefrontal cortex. *Philosophical Transactions of the Royal Society (London), 351*, 1413–1420.

Damasio, A. R. (1999). *The feeling of what happens.* New York: Harcourt Brace.

Davidson, D. (1995). The representativeness heuristic and the conjunction fallacy effect in children's decision making. *Merrill-Palmer Quarterly, 41*, 328–346.

Davidson, M. C., Amso, D., Anderson, L. C., & Diamond, A. (2006). Development of cognitive control and executive functions from 4 to 13 years: Evidence from manipulations of memory, inhibition, and task switching. *Neuropsychologia, 44*(11), 2037–2078.

Denes-Raj, V., & Epstein, S. (1994). Conflict between intuitive and rational processing: When people behave against their better judgment. *Journal of Personality and Social Psychology, 66*, 819–829.

De Neys, W. (2013). Heuristics, biases, and the development of conflict detection during reasoning. In H. Markovits (Ed.), *The developmental psychology of reasoning and decision making* (pp. 130–147). Hove, UK: Psychology Press.

De Neys, W., & Feremans, V. (2013). Development of heuristic bias detection in elementary school. *Developmental Psychology, 49*(2), 258.

De Neys, W., & Vanderputte, K. (2011). When less is not always more: Stereotype knowledge and reasoning development. *Developmental Psychology, 47*, 432–441.

De Neys, W., & van Gelder, E. (2009). Logic and belief across the lifespan: The rise and fall of belief inhibition during syllogistic reasoning. *Developmental Science, 12*(1), 123–130.
Davidson, D. (1995). The representativeness heuristic and the conjunction fallacy effect in children's decision making. *Merrill-Palmer Quarterly, 41*, 328–346.
Desoete, A., & Roeyers, H. (2006). Metacognitive macroevaluations in mathematical problem solving. *Learning and Instruction, 16*, 12–25.
Evans, J. St. B. T. (2003). In two minds: Dual-process accounts of reasoning. *Trends in Cognitive Sciences, 7*, 454–459.
Evans, J. St. B. T. (2008). Dual-processing accounts of reasoning, judgment and social cognition. *Annual Review of Psychology, 59*, 255–278.
Evans, J. St. B. T. (2009). How many dual-process theories do we need: One, two or many? In J. St. B. T. Evans & K. Frankish (Eds.), *In two minds: Dual Processes and beyond* (pp. 31–54). Oxford: Oxford University Press.
Evans, J. St. B. T. (2010). *Thinking twice: Two minds in one brain*. Oxford: Oxford University Press.
Evans, J. St. B. T. (2011). Dual-process theories of reasoning: Contemporary issues and developmental applications. *Developmental Review, 31*, 86–102.
Evans, J. St. B. T. (2012). Dual-process theories of reasoning: Facts and fallacies. In K. J. Holyoak & R. G. Morrison (Eds.), *The Oxford handbook of thinking and reasoning*. New York: Oxford University Press.
Evans, J. St. B. T., & Over, D. E. (1996). *Rationality and reasoning*. Hove, UK: Psychology Press.
Evans, J. St. B. T., & Perry, T. (1995). Belief bias in children's reasoning. *Cahiers de Psychologie Cognitive, 14*, 103–115.
Evans, J. St. B. T. (2010). *Thinking twice: Two minds in one brain*. Oxford: Oxford University Press.
Evans, J. St. B. T., & Stanovich, K. E. (2013). Dual-process theories of higher cognition: Advancing the debate. *Perspectives on Psychological Science, 8*, 223–241.
Fishbein, E., & Schnarch, D. (1997). The evolution with age of probabilistic, intuitively-based misconceptions. *Journal for Research in Mathematics Education, 28*, 96–105.
Flavell, J. H., Miller, P. H., & Miller, S. A. (1993). *Cognitive development* (3rd ed.). Upper Saddle River, NJ: Prentice Hall.
Fong, G. T., Krantz, D. H., & Nisbett, R. E. (1986). The effects of statistical training on thinking about everyday problems. *Cognitive Psychology, 18*, 253–292.
Frankish, K., & Evans, J. St. B. T. (2009). The duality of mind: An historical perspective. In J. St. B. T. Evans & K. Frankish (Eds.), *In two minds: Dual processes and beyond*. New York: Oxford University Press.
Frederick, S. (2005). Cognitive reflection and decision making. *Journal of Economic Perspectives, 19*, 25–42.
Garon, N., & Moore, C. (2004). Complex decision-making in early childhood. *Brain and Cognition, 55*, 158–170.
Green, L., Fry, A. F., & Myerson, J. (1994). Discounting of delayed rewards: A life-span comparison. *Psychological Science, 5*(1), 33–36.
Handley, S. J., Capon, A., Beveridge, M., Dennis, I., & Evans, J. St. B. T. (2004). Working memory, inhibitory control and the development of children's reasoning. *Thinking and Reasoning, 10*, 175–195.
Hongwanishkul, D., Happaney, K. R., Lee, W. S. C., & Zelazo, P. D. (2005). Assessment of hot and cool executive function in young children: Age-related changes and individual differences. *Developmental Neuropsychology, 28*, 617–644.
Hooper, C. J., Luciana, M., Conklin, H. M., & Yarger, R. S. (2004). Adolescents' performance on the Iowa Gambling Task: Implications for the development of decision making and ventromedial prefrontal cortex. *Developmental Psychology, 40*, 1148–1158.
Jacobs, J. E., & Potenza, M. (1991). The use of judgment heuristics to make social and object decisions: A developmental perspective. *Child Development, 62*, 166–178.
Kahneman, D. (2011). *Thinking, fast and slow*. New York: Farrar, Straus & Giroux.
Kahneman, D., & Tversky, A. (1984). Choices, values, and frames. *American Psychologist, 39*, 341–350.
Kahneman, D., & Tversky, A. (Eds.). (2000). *Choices, values, and frames*. Cambridge: Cambridge University Press.
Kirkpatrick, L., & Epstein, S. (1992). Cognitive-experiential self-theory and subjective probability: Evidence for two conceptual systems. *Journal of Personality and Social Psychology, 63*, 534–544.
Klaczynski, P. A. (2001). Analytic and heuristic processing influences on adolescent reasoning and decision making. *Child Development, 72*, 844–861.
Klaczynski, P. A., & Lavallee, K. L. (2005). Domain-specific identity, epistemic regulation, and intellectual ability as predictors of belief-based reasoning: A dual-process perspective. *Journal of Experimental Child Psychology, 92*, 1–24.

Klaczynski, P. A., & Narasimham, G. (1998). Development of scientific reasoning biases: Cognitive versus ego-protective explanations. *Developmental Psychology, 34*, 175–187.

Klahr, D., Fay, A. L., & Dunbar, K. (1993). Heuristics for scientific experimentation: A developmental study. *Cognitive Psychology, 25*, 111–146.

Klahr, D., & Nigam, M. (2004). The equivalence of learning paths in early science instruction: Effects of direct instruction and discovery learning. *Psychological Science, 15*, 661–667.

Kokis, J., Macpherson, R., Toplak, M., West, R. F., & Stanovich, K. E. (2002). Heuristic and analytic processing: Age trends and associations with cognitive ability and cognitive styles. *Journal of Experimental Child Psychology, 83*, 26–52.

Koslowski, B., Condry, K., Sprague, K., & Hutt, M. (1996). Beliefs about covariation and causal mechanisms – Implausible as well as plausible. Experiment 4. In B. Koslowski (Ed.), *Theory and evidence: The development of scientific reasoning*. Cambridge, MA: MIT Press.

Koslowski, B., Okagaki, L., Lorenz, C., & Umbach, D. (1989). When covariation is not enough: The role of causal mechanism, sampling method, and sample size in causal reasoning. *Child Development, 60*, 1316–1327.

Lamm, C., Zelazo, P. D., & Lewis, M. D. (2006). Neural correlates of cognitive control in childhood and adolescence: Disentangling the contributions of age and executive function. *Neuropsychologia, 44*(11), 2139–2148.

Levin, I. P., & Hart, S. S. (2003). Risk preferences in young children: Early evidence of individual differences in reaction to potential gains and losses. *Journal of Behavioral Decision Making, 16*, 397–413.

Levin, I. P., Weller, J. A., Pederson, A. A., & Harshman, L. A. (2007). Age-related differences in adaptive decision making: Sensitivity to expected value in risky choice. *Judgment and Decision Making, 2*(4), 225–233.

Liberali, J. M., Reyna, V. F., Furlan, S., Stein, L. M., & Pardo, S. T. (2012). Individual differences in numeracy and cognitive reflection, with implications for biases and fallacies in probability judgment. *Journal of Behavioral Decision Making, 25*(4), 361–381.

Lipko, A. R., Dunlosky, J., & Merriman, W. E. (2009). Persistent overconfidence despite practice: The role of task experience in preschoolers' recall predictions. *Journal of Experimental Child Psychology, 103*, 152–166.

Mandell, L. (2009). *The financial literacy of young American adults*. Washington, DC: JumpStart Coalition for Personal Financial Literacy.

Markovits, H. (2014a). Introduction. In H. Markovits (Ed.), *The developmental psychology of reasoning and decision-making*. London: Psychology Press.

Markovits, H. (2014b). How to develop a logical reasoner: A hierarchical model of the role of divergent thinking in the development of conditional reasoning. In H. Markovits (Ed.), *The developmental psychology of reasoning and decision-making*. London: Psychology Press.

Markovits, H., & Bouffard-Bouchard, T. (1992). The belief-bias effect in the reasoning: The development and activation of competence. *British Journal of Developmental Psychology, 10*, 269–284.

Markovits, H., & Lortie-Forgues, H. (2011). Conditional reasoning with false premises facilitates the transition between familiar and abstract reasoning. *Child Development, 82*(2), 646–660.

Markovits, H., & Thompson, V. (2008). Different developmental patterns of simple deductive and probabilistic inferential reasoning. *Memory & Cognition, 36*(6), 1066–1078.

Markovits, H., & Vachon, R. (1990). Conditional reasoning, representation, and level of abstraction. *Developmental Psychology, 26*(6), 942–951.

Markovits, H., Venet, M., Janveau-Brennan, G., Malfait, N., Pion, N., & Vadeboncoeur, I. (1996). Reasoning in young children: Fantasy and information retrieval. *Child Development, 67*, 2857–2872.

Masnick, A. M., & Morris, B. J. (2008). Investigating the development of data evaluation: The role of data characteristics. *Child Development, 79*(4), 1032–1048.

Mischel, W., Shoda, Y., & Peake, P. K., W. (1988). The nature of adolescent competencies predicted by preschool delay of gratification. *Journal of Personality and Social Psychology, 54*(4), 687–696.

Morsanyi, K., & Handley, S. J. (2008). How smart do you need to be to get it wrong? The role of cognitive capacity in the development of heuristic-based judgment. *Journal of Experimental Child Psychology, 99*, 18–36.

Morsanyi, K., & Handley, S. J. (2013). Heuristics and biases: Insights from developmental studies. In P. Barrouillet & C. Gauffroy (Eds.), *The development of thinking and reasoning*. London: Psychology Press.

Newman, R. S. (1984). Children's numerical skill and judgments of confidence in estimation. *Journal of Experimental Child Psychology, 37*, 107–123.

Oatley, K. (1999). Why fiction may be twice as true as fact: Fiction as cognitive and emotional simulation. *Review of General Psychology, 3*, 101–117.

Perkins, D. N., Farady, M., & Bushey, B. (1991). Everyday reasoning and the roots of intelligence. In J. Voss, D. Perkins & J. Segal (Eds.), ***Informal reasoning and education*** (pp. 83–105). Hillsdale, NJ: Lawrence Erlbaum Associates.

Peters, E. (2012). Beyond comprehension: The role of numeracy in judgments and decisions. ***Current Directions in Psychological Science***, *21*(1), 31–35.

Peters, E., Västfjäll, D., Slovic, P., Mertz, C. K., Mazzocco, K., & Dickert, S. (2006). Numeracy and decision making. *Psychological Science, 17*, 407–413.

Preece, P. F. W., & Baxter, J. H. (2000). Scepticism and gullibility: The superstitious and pseudoscientific beliefs of secondary school students. ***International Journal of Science Education***, *22*(11), 1147–1156.

Prencipe, A., Kesek, A., Cohen, J., Lamm, C., Lewis, M. D., & Zelazo, P. D. (2006). Development of hot and cool executive function during the transition to adolescence. ***Journal of Experimental Child Psychology***, *108*, 621–637.

Primi, C., Morsanyi, K., Chiesi, F., Donati, M. A., & Hamilton, J. (2015). The development and testing of a new version of the Cognitive Reflection Test applying item response theory (IRT). *Journal of Behavioral **Decision Making***, n/a-n/a. doi:10.1002/bdm.1883.

Rachlin H., Raineri, A., & Cross, D. (1991). Subjective probability of delay. ***Journal of the Experimental Analysis of Behavior***, *55*, 233–244.

Rakow, T., & Rahim, S. B. (2010). Developmental insights into experience-based decision making. *Journal of Behavioral **Decision Making***, *23*(1), 69–82.

Reyna, V. F., & Brainerd, C. J. (1994). The origins of probability judgment: A review of data and theories. In G. Wright & P. Ayton (Eds.), *Subjective probability* (pp. 239–272). New York: Wiley.

Reyna, V. F., & Brainerd, C. J. (2007). The importance of mathematics in health and human judgment: Numeracy, risk communication, and medical decision making. ***Learning and Individual Differences***, *17*(2), 147–159.

Reyna, V. F., & Ellis, S. (1994). Fuzzy-trace theory and framing effects in children's risky decision making. *Psychological Science, 5*, 275–279.

Richardson, K. (1992). Covariation analysis of knowledge representation: Some developmental studies. *Journal of Experimental Child Psychology, 53*, 129–150.

Schlottmann, A. (2000). Children's judgments of gambles: A disordinal violation of utility. ***Journal of Behavioral Decision Making***, *13*, 77–89.

Schneider, W., Visé, M., Lockl, K., & Nelson, R. O. (2000). Developmental trends in children's memory monitoring: Evidence from a judgment-of-learning task. *Cognitive Development, 15*, 115–134.

Schlottmann, A. (2001). Children's probability intuitions: Understanding the expected value of complex gambles, *Child Development, 72*, 103–122.

Schlottmann, A., & Tring, J. (2005). How children reason about gains and losses: Framing effects in judgement and choice. *Swiss Journal of Psychology, 64*(3), 153–171.

Salthouse, T. A., & Davis, H. P. (2006). Organization of cognitive abilities and neuropsychological variables across the lifespan. *Developmental Review, 26*, 31–54.

Shiffrin, R. M., & Schneider, W. (1977). Controlled and automatic human information processing: II. Perceptual learning, automatic attending, and a general theory. *Psychological Review, 84*, 127–190.

Siegler, R. S. (1991). ***Children's thinking*** (2nd ed.). Englewood Cliffs, NJ: Prentice Hall.

Sinayev, A., & Peters, E. (2015). Cognitive reflection versus calculation in decision making. ***Frontiers in Psychology***, *6*, Article 532, 1–16. doi:10.3389/fpsyg.2015.00532

Sloman, S. A. (1996). The empirical case for two systems of reasoning. ***Psychological Bulletin***, *119*, 3–22.

Smith, L. (1999). Necessary knowledge in number conservation. *Developmental Science, 2*, 23–27.

Stanovich, K. E. (1999). ***Who is rational? Studies of individual differences in reasoning***. Mahwah, NJ: Lawrence Erlbaum Associates.

Stanovich, K. E. (2009). ***What intelligence tests miss:** The psychology of rational thought*. New Haven, CT: Yale University Press.

Stanovich, K. E. (2011). ***Rationality and the reflective mind***. New York: Oxford University Press.

Stanovich, K. E., & Toplak, M. E. (2012). Defining features versus incidental correlates of Type 1 and Type 2 processing. *Mind & Society, 11*, 3–13.

Stanovich, K. E., Toplak, M. E., & West, R. F. (2008). The development of rational thought: A taxonomy of heuristics and biases. *Advances in Child Development and Behavior, 36*, 251–285.
Stanovich, K. E., & West, R. F. (1998). Individual differences in framing and conjunction effects. *Thinking and Reasoning, 4*, 289–317.
Stanovich, K. E., & West, R. F. (2000). Individual differences in reasoning: Implications for the rationality debate? *Behavioral and Brain Sciences, 23*, 645–726.
Stanovich, K. E., & West, R. F. (2007). Natural myside bias is independent of cognitive ability. *Thinking & Reasoning, 13*(3), 225–247.
Stanovich, K. E., & West, R. F. (2008a). On the failure of intelligence to predict myside bias and one-sided bias. *Thinking & Reasoning, 14*, 129–167.
Stanovich, K. E., & West, R. F. (2008b). On the relative independence of thinking biases and cognitive ability. *Journal of Personality and Social Psychology, 94*, 672–695.
Stanovich, K. E., West, R. F., & Toplak, M. E. (2011a). Intelligence and rationality. In R. J. Sternberg & S. B. Kaufman (Eds.), *Cambridge handbook of intelligence* (pp. 784–826). New York: Cambridge University Press.
Stanovich, K. E., West, R. F., & Toplak, M. E. (2011b). The complexity of developmental predictions from dual process models. *Developmental Review, 31*, 103–118.
Stanovich, K. E., West, R. F., & Toplak, M. E. (2016). *The Rationality Quotient (RQ): Toward a test of rational thinking*. Cambridge, MA: MIT Press.
Steegen, S., & De Neys, W. (2012). Belief inhibition in children's reasoning: Memory-based evidence. *Journal of Experimental Child Psychology, 112*, 231–242.
Steinberg, L. (2010). A dual systems model of adolescent risk-taking. *Developmental Psychobiology, 52*, 216–224.
Steinberg, L., Graham, S., O'Brien, L., Woolard, J., Cauffman, E., & Banich, M. (2009). Age differences in future orientation and delay discounting. *Child Development, 80*, 28–44.
Strough, J., Mehta, C. M., McFall, J. P., & Schuller, K. L. (2008). Are older adults less subject to the sunk-cost fallacy than younger adults? *Psychological Science, 19*, 650–652.
Thompson, D. R., & Siegler, R. S. (2000). Buy low, sell high: The development of an informal theory of economics. *Child Development, 71*, 660–677.
Toplak, M. E., & Stanovich, K. E. (2003). Associations between myside bias on an informal reasoning task and amount of post-secondary education. *Applied Cognitive Psychology, 17*(7), 851–860.
Toplak, M. E., West, R. F., & Stanovich, K. E. (2011). The Cognitive Reflection Test as a predictor of performance on heuristics and biases tasks. *Memory & Cognition, 39*, 1275–1289.
Toplak, M. E., West, R. F., & Stanovich, K. E. (2013). Assessing the development of rationality. In H. Markovits (Eds.), *Understanding the development of reasoning and decision-making* (pp. 7–35). New York: Psychology Press.
Toplak, M. E., West, R. F., & Stanovich, K. E. (2014a). Assessing miserly processing: An expansion of the Cognitive Reflection Test. *Thinking & Reasoning, 20*, 147–168.
Toplak, M. E., West, R. F., & Stanovich, K. E. (2014b). Rational thinking and cognitive sophistication: Development, cognitive abilities, and thinking dispositions. *Developmental Psychology, 50*, 1037–1048.
Tschirgi, J. E. (1980). Sensible reasoning: A hypothesis about hypotheses. *Child Development, 51*, 1–10.
Weller, J. A., Dieckmann, N. F., Tusler, M., Mertz, C. K., Burns, W. J., & Peters, E. (2013). Development and testing of an abbreviated numeracy scale: A Rasch analysis approach. *Journal of Behavioral Decision Making, 26*(2), 198–212.
Weller, J. A., Levin, I. P., & Denburg, N. L. (2011). Trajectory of risky decision making for potential gains and losses from ages 5 to 85. *Journal of Behavioral Decision Making, 24*, 331–344.
Weller, J. A., Levin, I. P., Rose, J. P., & Bossard, E. (2012). Assessment of decision-making competence in preadolescence. *Journal of Behavioral Decision Making, 25*(4), 414–426.
West, R. F., Toplak, M. E., & Stanovich, K. E. (2008). Heuristics and biases as measures of critical thinking: Associations with cognitive ability and thinking dispositions. *Journal of Educational Psychology, 100*(4), 930–941.
Zimmerman, C. (2007). The development of scientific thinking skills in elementary and middle school. *Developmental Review, 27*, 172–223.

31
THE SENSE OF COHERENCE
How intuition guides reasoning and thinking

Sascha Topolinski

What guides reasoning and thinking? Once we think of something, how do we know that our thoughts make sense? How do we know which thoughts are important and what reasoning is reasonable? The present chapter focuses on a sense that guides our inner thought in these questions, namely the sense of coherence. First, I outline that the sense of coherence often comes in the form of intuitions, and describe how these intuitions can be explored in the laboratory. Then, I review several recent lines of research that explore the underlying driving mechanisms of coherence intuitions.

One of the most pervasive intuitions is the sense of coherence. There is a constant automatic assessment in our everyday life of whether cues of information in the environment and in our memory make sense or fit together or to our expectations (e.g., Bless, Fiedler, & Strack, 2004; Heintzelman, Trent, & King, 2013; King, Hicks, Krull, & Del Gaiso, 2006; Topolinski, 2012a). We seek consistency of thoughts (e.g., Devine & Sharp, 2009) and shy away from inconsistencies (e.g., Harmon-Jones, Harmon-Jones, & Amodio, 2012). For instance, in the social domain, meeting an Asian person speaking with a southern accent, a combination that interferes with our stereotypic expectations, is experienced as aversive (Mendes, Blascovich, Hunter, Lickel, & Jost, 2007). The irritating moment of sensing incoherence and therefore investing more elaboration or research on an issue lies at the bottom of every investigative profession, such as science, journalism, or police work; and coherence brings meaning into our lives (Hicks, Cicero, Trent, Burton, & King, 2010).

We experience coherence or the lack of coherence, not only among the events and objects we encounter in the environment, but also in our own thinking and reasoning. This *meta-reasoning* (Ackerman & Thompson, 2014; see also Ackerman & Thompson, this volume) applies to many different cognitive processes. One example is the spontaneous self-assessment of whether an answer that pops into our minds is really correct, the *feeling of rightness* (FOR; Thompson, Prowse Turner, & Pennycook, 2011; see also Kelley & Lindsay, 1993). For instance, Thompson et al. (2011) let participants execute various tasks of rather effortful reasoning and syllogistic thinking. Crucially, after presenting a specific reasoning problem, they asked participants to report a first initial guess on what the answer might be (cf., Frederick, 2005) together with a rating of the feeling of rightness of that answer. Then, participants were given additional time to work on the cognitive problem to possibly provide a more sophisticated answer. It turned out that the initial FOR predicted the later re-thinking process: the lower the initial feeling of rightness was, the more time participants invested to re-think the problem and the more likely they also changed their initial answer.

Another case of immediate coherence detection is the spontaneous intuition of logical validity. When being confronted with logical syllogisms, individuals appear to be immediately able, without exactly thinking through the whole logical chain of propositions, to intuitively detect whether there is a conflict between the presented logical propositions and their own general knowledge (Morsanyi & Handley, 2012). Another example is *metacomprehension* (Dunlosky & Lipko, 2007) – that is, the meta-cognitive assessment of whether one has understood a certain problem or learning material (such as a book chapter). This is also an assessment of the coherence of the material and of one's own representation of the problem. Although this intuition that something is coherent can be biased by various factors (Ackerman, Leiser, & Shpigelman, 2013; Ackerman & Zalmanov, 2012; for a review, see Dunlosky & Lipko, 2007), it still is a powerful cue that people use to guide their own learning and exploration behavior.

All these intuitions of coherence or missing coherence emerge immediately without much effort and are a pervasive judgmental cue when assessing the state of the outer and inner affairs. And they can be powerful in driving people's behavior: the nagging feeling of a solution's incoherence, for instance, drove decades of work of the world's most famous mathematicians, such as Hilbert, Gödel, Turing, and Penrose (Davis, 1958).

Most impressively, the intuition of coherence usually emerges before we have consciously realized in what way something is (in)coherent. We simply feel that something is wrong, that a sentence does not make sense or we have not understood a message, long before we have fully ascertained the specific contradictions or mismatches in the material or in our thoughts. A pivotal example for this is the state of surprise (Topolinski & Strack, 2015; Whittlesea & Williams, 2001). Imagine you are at a foreign airport and you meet your neighbor there (Whittlesea & Williams, 2001). What occurs is the immediate stunning experience of being surprised, arising instantaneously within a second, before you have actually realized the situation – that is, become fully aware of the incoherence of meeting this neighbor in this mismatching context. Within an additional second you cognitively master the situation and realize the incoherence as the cause of your surprise (e.g., Attardo, 1997), but the initial stun occurred automatically. How was this possible? Which ever-attentive little inner Columbo in your mind detected the incoherence and alarmed you long before you actually figured out what the incoherence was?

The present chapter reviews research that has explored the perceptual, cognitive and affective mechanisms that enable such coherence intuitions. For this purpose, I first sketch a paradigm that reliably evokes such coherence intuitions in experimental conditions.

An experimental paradigm of coherence intuitions

Bowers, Regehr, Balthazard and Parker (1990) introduced a simple task that demonstrated the power of coherence intuitions and their boundary conditions and underlying psychological mechanisms. They used sets of three words, with each of the words of a given triple being remotely semantically associated with a common denominator. For instance, in the word triad CREAM ~ SKATE ~ WATER, each of the clue words is associated with the solution word ICE. This item is a very easy one, which means that the semantic associations are very close to each other, and when one reads this triad, it is highly likely that one is immediately thinking of the solution word (Bowden & Jung-Beeman, 2003). Of course, solving such a word riddle by retrieving the solution word is not intuition but rather a state of *insight* (Topolinski & Reber, 2010a, 2010b).

Now, however, consider a triad for which the associative links are not that close, for instance the triad OVER ~ PLANT ~ HORSE. Here, the solution does not immediately pop into one's mind, and actually only 10% of participants solve this item in a reasonable amount of time of thinking (Bowden & Jung-Beeman, 2003). The solution is POWER. Here, every word is indeed associated with the common associate, but the underlying semantic link is very remote, and merely reading through the triad and pondering possible commonalities is not sufficient to activate the solution word semantically to such a degree that it exceeds the threshold of consciousness (Topolinski & Strack, 2008).

In their pioneering approach, Bowers et al. (1990) used such hard-to-solve Remote Associate Test (RAT) items to assess whether individuals would still have a sense of coherence of the triads despite being unable to retrieve the solution word. They presented participants with RAT triads that featured such hidden semantic coherence as well as with control triads of words that did not have a common remote associate and were thus incoherent (e.g., DREAM ~ BALL ~ BOOK, featuring no common solution word). Participants were presented these coherent and incoherent triads and were asked to spontaneously decide whether a given triad was coherent or not. Crucially, they were given only a few seconds to decide. After rendering their judgment, they were also asked to report the solution word if they had one in mind. When Bowers et al. analyzed trials for which participants did not report the correct solution word (and thus were unaware of the common associate), they found that participants could still discriminate between coherent and incoherent triads (Bowers et al., 1990). Of course, this discrimination performance was not perfect, but was reliably above chance. When we conceive of the triads in their original purpose as RAT items that have to be solved, these coherence intuitions can also be regarded as *judgments of solvability*, or JOS (Thompson, 2009).

This paradigm was soon used to tackle possible moderators and boundary conditions of coherence intuitions. For instance, Kuhl and colleagues addressed the role of mood in these intuitions. Since it is known that compared to negative mood, positive mood increases the use and diagnosticity of any kind of feeling or heuristic (e.g., Schwarz, 2002), Baumann and Kuhl (2002) as well as Bolte, Goschke, and Kuhl (2003) set participants in either a positive or negative mood state while rendering the task of semantic coherence intuitions. It turned out that participants in a negative mood showed impaired intuitive performance, sometimes to such a degree that their intuitive judgments fell to chance level (for a recent replication, see Balas, Sweklej, Pochwatko, & Godlewska, 2012). Extending this to pathological states of extreme affectivity, Remmers, Topolinski, Dietrich, and Michalak (2015) recently demonstrated that patients with major depression showed impaired intuition compared to a healthy control group. In contrast, training mindfulness as a particularly attentive state did not modulate intuitive performance (Remmers, Topolinski, & Michalak, 2015).

Despite these fascinating findings on the moderators and boundary conditions of this phenomenon, the question remains how these intuitions work, that is, what the cognitive mechanisms are that enable individuals to sense coherence before determining the cause of this coherence. This question troubled cognitive researchers for two decades (Kihlstrom, 1999; Topolinski, 2011), until it was resolved by an approach that identified processing efficiency and a brief positive gut feeling as the driving mechanisms (Topolinski & Strack, 2008, 2009a, 2009b, 2009d). I review this approach in the next but one section. In the following section these two mechanisms are described first.

Fluency and affect: the judgmental all-rounders

In several lines of experiments, Fritz Strack and I have explored the driving operations of coherence intuitions on the basis of the theoretical assumptions of the Fluency-Affect Intuition

Model, or FAIM (for a comprehensive review, see Topolinski, 2011). In this approach, we identified two driving mechanisms, namely processing fluency and resulting positive affect.

One of the most pervasive cognitive mechanisms driving countless phenomena in cognitive and social psychology has been shown to be the speed and efficiency, or simply processing fluency, with which mental operations are executed (e.g., Reber, Schwarz, & Winkielman, 2004). Whatever mental content is processed, the processing itself can run more or less easily – that is, more or less fluent. For instance, reading a sentence in a hard-to-read font is relatively difficult. This would be a case of perceptual fluency (e.g., Reber, Wurtz, & Zimmermann, 2004). Likewise, understanding a message that conforms to our own general knowledge is easier than understanding a message that contradicts our knowledge. This would be semantic fluency (Whittlesea, 1993). This processing fluency can also be due to the coherence of our thoughts or of studied material, with coherent information increasing fluency and incoherent information decreasing fluency. This fluency can be felt as a cognitive feeling, an experience of ease.

Processing fluency can be experimentally manipulated, for instance by repeating information (which increases fluency because the material has been trained) (Begg, Anas, & Farinacci, 1992; Bornstein & D'Agostino, 1994; Topolinski & Strack, 2009c), by changing the perceptual figure-ground contrast of presented images (Winkielman & Cacioppo, 2001) or by priming a given concept with a semantically related concept or a whole sentence that converges on the meaning of a concept (e.g., Whittlesea, 1993). This last method of manipulating semantic fluency will be particularly interesting for semantic coherence intuitions.

Crucially, such manipulations of fluency lead to a broad array of psychological effects. For instance, high compared to low fluency increases liking of stimuli; for example, the "mere exposure" effect which is due to increased fluency induced by repetition (Moreland & Topolinski, 2010), their familiarity (e.g., Topolinski & Strack, 2010; Topolinski, 2012b; Whittlesea, 1993), the feeling of truth (e.g., Unkelbach, 2007; Topolinski & Reber, 2010b, 2010) or also aesthetic appreciation of images (e.g., Leder, Bär, & Topolinski, 2012; Reber, Winkielman, & Schwarz, 1998). Most importantly, fluency is a potent meta-cognitive cue that individuals use spontaneously when assessing memory content (Koriat & Levy-Sadot, 2001), the confidence in an answer (Ackerman & Zalmanov, 2012; Kelley & Lindsay, 1993; Thompson, 2009; Thompson et al., 2013) or comprehension and insight (Miele & Molden, 2010; Topolinski & Reber, 2010a, 2010b).

The underlying common experiential cause for all these fluency effects is the simple fact that high relative to low fluency triggers a subtle positive feeling (Reber et al., 2004). Because this feeling is so brief, we call this feeling an affect (in accordance with the notion of core affect, Russell, 2009). This affect is used as a judgmental cue for familiarity or rightness (Thompson et al., 2011, 2013). It has been shown that for any material that is being processed, relatively high processing efficiency triggers a brief positive affect, for instance as measured via facial electromyography (e.g., Winkielman & Cacioppo, 2001). This positive affect is then used as a feeling-as-information (Schwarz, 1990), or affective cue, in judgments for which no other more analytic cue is available. Note that fluency variations are relative (such as brightness in perception), and that the effects of fluency do not depend of the absolute value of processing speed, but on phasic variations, such as sudden or unexpected fluency gains (e.g., Hansen, Dechene, & Wänke, 2008).

Since such brief fluctuations in fluency and resulting affective consequences are such pervasive judgmental mechanisms, it is likely that they also play a causal role in coherence intuitions. This was tested in several lines of experiments which are reviewed in the following.

Fluency and affect in semantic coherence intuitions

In a nutshell, our simple theoretical model on how coherence intuitions work was that (1) semantic coherence increases processing fluency and (2) this fluency triggers a brief positive affect that (3) is then used as the affective cue in coherence intuitions (Topolinski & Strack, 2009a, 2009b, 2009d). Thus, a fluency-triggered brief positive affect is the output that is used in coherence intuitions; it is the gut feeling itself. In the following, I review evidence for each of these three steps.

Coherence increases fluency

The notion that semantic coherence might increase processing fluency is supported by an ample field of evidence regarding experimental manipulations of semantic fluency (Whittlesea, 1993; Whittlesea & Williams, 1998, 2000, 2001). For instance, when a target word is preceded by a sentence that converges semantically highly on that word (e.g., THE STORMY SEAS TOSSED THE . . . BOAT) compared to when not (e.g., HE SAVED UP ALL HIS MONEY TO BUY A . . . BOAT) the processing fluency of that target word is increased (Whittlesea, 1993). Likewise, we speculated that the hidden semantic associations in coherent word triads would increase the semantic encoding fluency of coherent compared to incoherent word triads (Topolinski & Strack, 2008). Crucially, since these semantic associations are represented unconsciously, we predicted that such a fluency gain would occur independent of the intention to find a common solution word for RAT items.

To test this, we presented participants with coherent and incoherent word triads and asked them to perform several different tasks on them. To show that semantic coherence increases fluency automatically, we did not inform participants about the underlying semantic structure of some of the triads. In a first task, participants received intact coherent (e.g., RABBIT~CLOUD~CREAM) and incoherent (e.g., DREAM~BALL~BOOK) triads, but also coherent and incoherent triads for which one random word was replaced by a pronounceable letter string (e.g., DREAM~TRULG~BOOK; Topolinski & Strack, 2009a, Experiment 1). This latter stimulus category of (in)coherent triads containing nonwords was introduced to justify a lexical decision task. In this task participants were asked to determine as fast and as accurately as possible whether a given triad featured only real words or also nonsense words. We predicted that if semantic coherence fosters semantic encoding, this lexical decision would bear shorter reaction times for intact coherent than for intact incoherent triads (with the triads containing nonwords being irrelevant trials for this analysis). And this effect indeed occurred: participants were 57 milliseconds faster in the lexical decisions for coherent compared to incoherent triads. Of course, the lexicographic features that might influence this performance speed, such as word length and word frequency, did not differ between coherent and incoherent triads. In a second experiment, we let participants simply read through coherent and incoherent triads and asked them to push a key once they accomplished reading a given triad. Also in this dependent measure of reading speed, coherent triads showed a processing gain of 58 milliseconds over incoherent triads (Topolinski & Strack, 2009d, Experiment 1).

Coherence triggers positive affect

Furthermore, we explored whether this fluency gain induced by coherence of the material also triggers positive affect. We tested this with several different measures of affective responses towards the stimulus material. Most blatantly, we presented participants, who again were ignorant of the underlying semantic structure, with (in)coherent triads and simply asked them how much they liked each of the presented triads. It turned out that participants reported higher liking ratings for coherent than for incoherent triads (Topolinski & Strack, 2009a, Experiment 3; Topolinski & Strack, 2009c, Experiment 1). The frequency with which a word was presented was similar for coherent and incoherent triads, so a mere exposure effect cannot explain this result. Also, we analyzed the frequency and other linguistic features – but most importantly, the valence of the words that constituted the word triads – and found that there was no difference in these dimensions between coherent and incoherent triads.

In a different experiment we used facial electromyography to assess the activity of certain face muscles that have been shown to be related with affective responses (e.g., Harmon-Jones & Allen, 2001; Reber & Schwarz, 1999; Winkielman & Cacioppo, 2001). Specifically, using facial electromyography, we assessed the activity of the smiling muscle Zygomaticus major for positive, and the frowning muscle Corrugator Superciliis for negative affect (Cacioppo, Petty, Losch, & Kim, 1986; Scherer & Ellgring, 2007). Again, participants were not informed about the fact that some of the triads would feature a hidden coherence, but were told that they should silently read the occurring word groups to relax and give the experimenter a chance to calibrate the physiological measure. In this set-up, we found that merely reading coherent compared to incoherent word triads increased the activity of the smiling muscle and decreased the activity of the frowning muscle, indicating that positive affect was elicited and negative affect was reduced (Topolinski, Likowski, Weyers, & Strack, 2009). These affective responses occurred within a few seconds but also decayed again fast, illustrating how brief and transient the affective response was (see also the notion of *phasic affect* being a very brief affective state of positivity or negativity, Topolinski & Deutsch, 2012). Given that participants did not know about the underlying semantic coherence that was manipulated, this finding is a strong evidence that semantic coherence automatically triggers positive affect (which is used as affective cue in coherence intuitions, see below).

Fluency and affect mediate coherence intuitions

Moreover, we tested the causal and mediational roles of fluency and affect in coherence intuitions. For this purpose, we collected fluency and affect ratings for each of the coherent and incoherent word triads in our experimental stimulus pool and analyzed their respective correlations on an item level (Topolinski & Strack, 2009a, Study 5). Specifically, we assessed how fast each of the stimuli was read on average in a simple reading task, how much it was liked and with which frequency it was actually judged as being coherent in a task of coherence intuition. Note that each of these parameters was assessed in different participant samples to avoid that these measures were correlated because they were assessed in close succession within a trial.

In regard to the item-based correlations, we found that independent of whether a given triad stimulus was actually coherent or not, processing fluency (reading speed), positivity (liking) and coherence intuitions were positively related with each other. This means that the faster a given triad was read by one participant sample and the more it was liked by a different sample, the more likely yet another sample categorized this triad as being coherent. This finding further bolstered our claim that coherence increases fluency and thereby triggers positive affect that is used in coherence intuitions. Finally, the very last step of this causal chain had to be tested, namely whether the fluency-triggered positive affect is actually the experiential cue that is used in coherence intuitions.

The sabotage of intuition

We claim that it is the brief affective fluctuation that is triggered by coherence-induced fluency that is used as the affective cue to guide intuitions. If this resulting affect is the judgmental cue, then questioning the informational value of this affect as a valid judgmental cue should also compromise intuitions. There is an established paradigm in social psychology to invalidate the informational value of feelings for judgments, called *re-attribution* or *mis-attribution* (Schwarz & Clore, 1983), that has been used extensively in different domains (e.g., Fazendeiro, Winkielman, Luo & Lorah, 2005; Morsanyi & Handley, 2012; Schwarz, Sanna, Skurnik, & Yoon, 2007; Strack, Schwarz, Bless, Kübler, & Wänke, 1993; Winkielman, Zajonc, & Schwarz, 1997). In this paradigm, participants are provided with an external transient source that is ostensibly responsible for any emotional fluctuation participants might experience. For instance, in the classic first study implementing this logic, participants were given a pill and told that this pill might make them more or less aroused, leading to the result that participants would not use the feeling of being aroused anymore as judgmental cue (Zanna & Cooper, 1974). Once an external source of their feelings is being provided, participants attribute their affective responses to that external source. Thereby, they do not use these affective responses as guiding cues to answer questions regarding the stimulus at hand.

We exploited this logic for coherence intuitions (Topolinski & Strack, 2009a, Experiment 4; Topolinski & Strack, 2009d, Experiment 2). As in the classic paradigm by Bowers et al. (1990), we presented participants coherent and incoherent word triads and asked them to spontaneously judge the coherence of these triads. Crucially, this task was rendered while an ambiguous music was played to them via headphones. One group of the participants was told that this music influenced their emotional responses to the word triad – this group would probably reattribute their current affect to the music. Another group was told that the music influences their reading speed – this group would re-attribute their fluency feelings to the music. Finally, a third group, the control group, was told that the music was played to them to simply relax them – this group would not question any current feelings. We found that both the control group (no attribution at all) and the reading speed group (re-attributing feelings of fluency) showed reliable coherence intuitions, judging coherent triads more likely as being coherent (hits) than incoherent triads (false alarms). However, the group that had been told that the music would alter their emotional states did not show any reliable intuitions, guessing at chance level.

These findings show that the affective responses that are triggered by a triad are used to diagnostically guide coherence intuitions, but the basic feeling of fluency itself is not used, presumably because it is too subtle to enter conscious awareness (Reber, Wurtz, & Zimmermann, 2004; Topolinski & Strack, 2009d). Consequently, by questioning the informational value of the affective responses to the presented triads we sabotaged intuition.

Deluding intuition by experimental manipulations of fluency and affect

Having established that fluency and affect are related to coherence intuitions, we tested whether experimental manipulations of fluency and affect would actually influence intuitive judgments of semantic coherence themselves. For this purpose, we let participants execute the basic coherence intuition paradigm introduced by Bowers et al. (1990). In this set-up, participants are presented with coherent and incoherent triads in random order for only 1.5 seconds. After the presentation of a triad, they are given an additional 0.5 seconds to decide whether the presented triad is coherent or not by pressing the respective key. After this response, participants were asked to type in a solution word for the triad if they had one in mind. This latter task was only to control for the occurrence of spontaneous correct solutions for coherent trials that would disqualify the current trial as being intuitive (and therefore such trials are discarded from later analyses). We let participants do this established task and manipulated various features of the presented triads to ascertain the possible impact of fluency and affect on resulting coherence intuitions.

The dependent measure was the likelihood with which participants would categorize a given triad as being coherent. We predicted that because both fluency and affect determine coherence intuitions, participants would be more likely to categorize a given triad as being coherent when the triad was high in fluency and positive in affective tone, respectively, than it was low in fluency and negative. Crucially, since fluency and affect are the driving mechanisms of these coherence intuitions, this should occur for both coherent and incoherent triads, independent and on top of the actual coherence of the triads.

Fluency manipulations affect semantic coherence intuitions

In a first line of manipulations, we artificially altered the processing fluency of the presented triads by various means. All these manipulations of processing fluency were done orthogonally to the actual coherence of the triads. In other words, there were high fluent coherent, low fluent coherent, high fluent incoherent and low fluent incoherent triads. We manipulated fluency in the following ways: first, we presented the triads in different colorings and changed the intensity of the colors, with some items appearing in a pale shade (low contrast against the white background, thus low fluency) and some in a darker shade (high contrast, high fluency; cf. Unkelbach, 2007; Topolinski & Strack, 2009b, Experiment 1). Secondly, we pre-exposed one half of the triads (both coherent and incoherent ones) previously in an earlier stage of the experimental session to increase the fluency of those repeated triads compared to triads that had not been pre-exposed (Topolinski & Strack, 2009b, Experiment 2; cf., Bornstein & D'Agostino, 1994; Topolinski, 2014). Third, we flashed a visually degraded version of the third word of a given triad immediately before presenting the whole triad itself for half of the triads (both for coherent and incoherent triads; Topolinski & Strack, 2009b, Experiment 3) to increase the fluency of these primed triads (cf. Winkielman & Cacioppo, 2001).

The effect of these manipulations was the same for all three paradigms: we always detected two independent main effects without any interaction. The main effect of coherence was the already well-established effect that participants more likely endorsed coherent triads as being coherent than incoherent triads (which constitutes the coherence intuition effect itself). Crucially, there was also always an independent main effect of fluency, with participants more frequently endorsing high-fluent triads as being coherent than low-fluent triads, supporting our predictions.

Affect manipulations influence semantic coherence intuitions

In a second line of experiments, we experimentally manipulated accompanying affect. We again did this orthogonally to actual coherence of the triads, again producing trials with coherent positive, coherent negative, incoherent positive and incoherent negative triads. The affective manipulations were the following. First, we let participants execute smiling or frowning face movements using facial feedback to induce brief positive and negative affect (Larsen, Kasimatis, & Frey, 1992; Strack, Martin, & Stepper, 1988). Note that these face movements were indirectly instructed; participants were not simply asked to smile and to frown (which would of course allow conscious answering strategies). Rather, participants held a pen with their front teeth (Strack et al.,

1988), and golf tees were affixed to the inner edges of their brows (Larsen et al., 1992). They were asked to either lift their lips off the pen (which results in smiling) or move the golf tees in a way that the end of the golf tees would touch each other (which results in frowning) – whenever a prompting signal before a given triads occurred. Participants held these facial postures for the time of triad presentation (Topolinski & Strack, 2009b, Experiment 4). Second, we infused affect by *subliminal facial primes* (Murphy & Zajonc, 1993). Specifically, before each word triad a photo of a happy or sad face was briefly flashed on the screen masked by a neutral face (Topolinski & Strack, 2009b, Experiment 5). In debriefings participants did not report any awareness of the briefly presented affectively laden faces, which shows how unobtrusive this manipulation was. Third, we induced positive and negative valence using the words of the triads themselves. We constructed a new pool of coherent triads whose constituting words were relatively more positive or more negative. For instance, the word triad FRESH HOLY LIQUID contains relatively positive words, while the word triad SALT DROWN RAIN contains relatively negative words. Nevertheless, both triads converge on the same relatively neutral solution word WATER. From these positive and negative coherent triads, we constructed incoherent triads by simply intermixing the constituting words across positive and negative triads, respectively, to gain positive and negative incoherent triads (Topolinski & Strack, 2009b, Experiment 8).

Again, these three very different affect manipulations resulted in the same pattern. Besides a main effect of coherence, again with coherent triads being more likely to be endorsed as being coherent than incoherent triads, a main effect of affect emerged without any interaction. Positive triads, both coherent and incoherent, were more likely to be endorsed as being coherent than negative triads. This evidence from experimental manipulations completes the picture gained by correlational evidence in Topolinski and Strack (2009a): affect, both being primed by stimuli exterior to the triads themselves (e.g., flashing faces) and being infused by the semantic meaning of the words constituting a triad does influence coherence intuitions.

Fluency and affect manipulations influence semantic coherence intuitions jointly and independently from each other

In a final experiment we manipulated both fluency (via color contrast) and affect (via valence of the triad words) to show that both factors have an independent impact on coherence intuitions when manipulated jointly (Topolinski & Strack, 2009b, Experiment 9). We again found three independent main effects (see Figure 31.1). Individuals were still sensible to the actual coherence of the word triads, but generally more likely endorsed a given triad as being coherent when this triad was high fluent rather than disfluent, and when the triad was positive compared to being negative. Impressively, for the conditions in which both fluency and affect ran either in the direction of or against actual coherence, we found even a reversal of coherence intuitions: incoherent triads that were fluent and positive were more likely to be endorsed as being coherent than actually coherent but low fluent and negative triads. These findings show that we had identified the underlying components of coherence intuitions, since we could actually turn around intuitions and lead participants down the garden path.

In yet another line of research, we extended these manipulations of intuition to other kinds of intuitive judgments to show the generalizability of this principle.

Fluency and affect in Gestalt intuitions

First, we addressed visual Gestalt intuitions, a phenomenon that was introduced into the literature by Bowers et al (1990). In this paradigm, black-and-white drawings of everyday objects

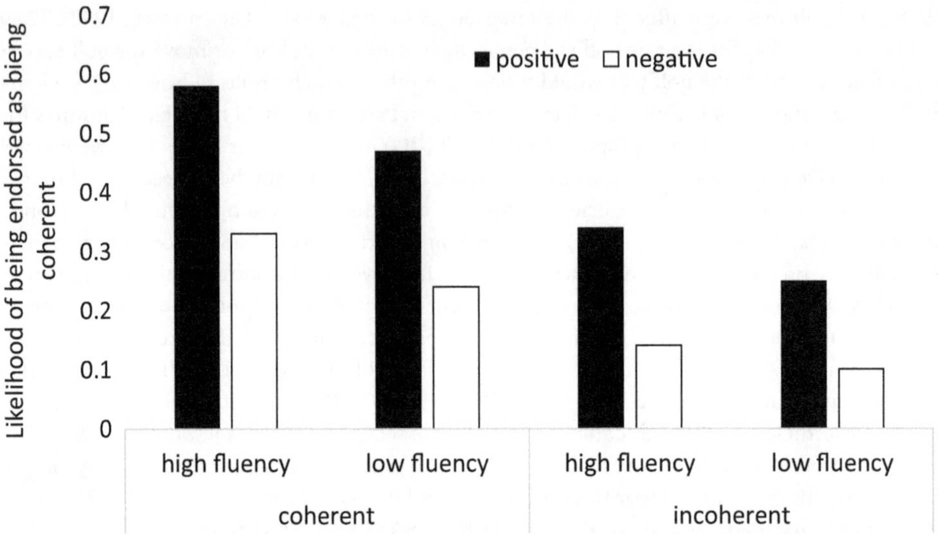

Figure 31.1 Results from Experiment 9 in Topolinski and Strack (2009b). Depicted is the likelihood that a given word triad was categorized as being coherent as a function of its actual semantic coherence, the valence of its three constituting words and the fluency of its coloring.

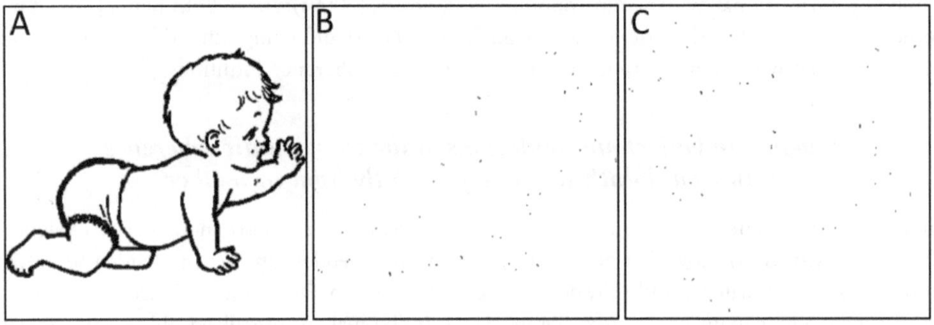

Figure 31.2 Example stimuli from the visual coherence task in Topolinski and Strack (2009b, Experiment 10). A: the original drawing (Biederman, 1987). B: the degraded but still Gestalt-containing version (coherent). C: the shuffled version with same stimulus entropy and lacking a coherent Gestalt (incoherent).

are used (Biederman, 1987), for instance of a crawling baby (see Figure 31.2A). These images, however, are visually so degraded that the depicted object can hardly be recognized – only its visual Gestalt remains (see Figure 31.2B, Gestalt-containing stimuli). Then these images are fragmented and the single fragments shuffled so that no Gestalt is preserved, although the same amount of visual entropy is preserved (see Figure 31.2C, Gestalt-lacking stimuli). Although participants cannot identify the depicted objects in Gestalt-containing stimuli, they nevertheless can discriminate Gestalt-lacking from Gestalt-containing stimuli when briefly presented with them and asked to spontaneously judge the coherence, or Gestaltness, of the stimuli (Bowers et al., 1990; Topolinski, Erle, & Reber, 2015; Volz & von Cramon, 2006).

We replicated this paradigm and added both a manipulation of fluency and of affect. To artificially increase the processing fluency, we pre-exposed a random half of the stimuli in a preceding unrelated phase before the actual intuition task. To infuse affect of different valences, we flashed pictures of smiling and frowning faces and masked them again with neutral faces briefly before an actual stimulus was presented. Both these manipulations again changed from trial to trial in a within-subjects design. Again, for these intuitions we found that repeated compared to novel and positively compared to negatively primed stimuli were more likely being endorsed as being Gestalt-like (Topolinski & Strack, 2009b, Experiment 10). This shows that even such emotionally neutral intuitions for very basic perceptual features are susceptible for fluency and affect.

Fluency and affect in artificial grammar learning

Probably the most famous and most researched intuitive phenomenon in the cognitive domain is the sensitivity for complex regularities, as shown in artificial grammar learning (Reber, 1967). Here, nonsense letter strings are presented to participants. The sequence of letters within each string, however, conforms to a very complex rule that cannot be consciously extracted during studying the letter strings. Participants are instructed to carefully study and memorize each string. Then, later, participants receive different letter strings, half of which conform to the same hidden grammaticality and half of which do not. Participants are informed that there was a certain regularity in the previous stimuli and they now should spontaneously guess whether a given letter string conforms to this rule or not. It has been found in numerous experiments that participants are accurate in these intuitions and can discriminate rule-conforming from rule-violating strings above chance, without being able to identify the rule itself (for a review, see Pothos, 2007).

We also replicated this paradigm with a fluency and an affect manipulation. Fluency was altered by color contrast, and affect was primed again by briefly presenting smiling and frowning faces. Again, both manipulations produced an independent main effect. Fluent and positively primed letter strings were more often accepted as being rule-conforming than disfluent and negatively primed letter strings, irrespective of actual grammaticality of these letter strings. Independent from that, participants were also susceptible to actual grammaticality (Topolinski & Strack, 2009b, Experiment 11).

Fluency and affect as universal cues for the sense of coherence

These two generalizations show that fluency and affect also seem to play a role in visual coherence and grammaticality intuitions, and therefore possibly in the sense of coherence in general. Note, of course, that the basic underlying process of grammaticality intuitions is implicit learning (Pothos, 2007). Recently, several other independent labs replicated and extended these findings to other domains.

Addressing the role of affect in coherence intuitions for word triads in a very creative way, Balas et al. (2012) as well as Sweklej, Balas, Pochwatko, and Godlewska (2014) induced affect, not by the word triads themselves or other concomitant stimuli, but by the valence of the solution word of a given word triad. Consider the two coherent triads COMPETITION FINISH ROUND and CANDLES NOVEMBER STONE. Although the words that make up the triads are all rather neutral, the first triad implies a rather positive solution word (MEDAL), while the second triad implies a rather negative solution word (GRAVE). In their intriguing experiments, Balas et al. (2012) and Sweklej et al. (2014) found that participants' coherence judgments were actually influenced by the valence of a solution word, despite the fact that participants could not consciously retrieve the solution word itself.

Further conceptual replications showed that the similar manipulations of objective coherence, processing fluency and positive affect as in Topolinski and Strack (2009b) even had an impact on the general feeling of meaning and coherence in life (Heintzelman et al., 2013; Hicks et al., 2010; Trent, Lavelock, & King, 2013). Likewise, the intuition of logic validity is also susceptible to affect manipulations and reattribution of affect, as shown by Morsanyi and Handley (2012; but see Klauer & Singmann, 2013). This evidence demonstrates the pervasiveness of fluency and affect as determining the sense of coherence.

In the next section, I review recent experiments that targeted the opposite side of the fluency-coherence link, namely the cognitive and affective consequences of incoherence.

Surprise: when inconsistency triggers negative affect

The abundant evidence reviewed thus far, that coherence leads to positivity, implies the opposite effect for incoherence, namely that incoherence is disfluent and triggers negative affect (for a paradigm evoking intuitions of *in*coherence, see Sweklej et al., 2014). Since the above examples, particularly on semantic coherence, used both coherence and incoherence, the above evidence can already be interpreted in the way that incoherence relative to coherence increases negative affect (Topolinski & Strack, 2009a). However, the inductions of semantic coherence were rather subtle. In most recent research, the affective consequences of stronger states of incoherence were assessed, namely in the case of surprise, where events violate our expectations or contradict our own knowledge. For the case of surprise, a negativity response is not a trivial prediction, since some psychological authors and also lay-theory assume the emotion of surprise to be a neutral or even positive one (e.g., Fontaine, Scherer, Roesch, & Ellsworth, 2007; Valenzuela, Strebel, & Mellers, 2010).

Noordewier and Breugelmans (2013) analysed the facial expressions of participants in a TV show who were, as part of the dramaturgy of the show, surprised by the unexpected turn of events. Using facial action coding they found that participants responded to the surprising events with immediate negative facial expressions that then turned into more positive expressions, probably due to a cognitive mastering of the situation (Attardo, 1997; Topolinski, 2014). Moreover, Topolinski and Strack (2015) presented trivia statements to participants that either conformed to (e.g., the lightest element is hydrogen) or violated the participants' general knowledge structures (e.g., the region with the highest rainfall rate is in Hawaii). The latter sort of items had been rated by an independent sample as being more surprising than the former sort. While participants were merely reading the statements, the activity of their facial muscles was assessed (cf., Topolinski et al., 2009, see above). We found that the surprising trivia statements elicited higher activity of the frowning muscle, indicative of negative affect, than the non-surprising statements. No effect was found on the smiling muscle. This evidence shows that surprising information – information that violates expectancies or knowledge structures – triggers negative affect.

Negative affect as the driving force of cognitive elaboration and resolving incoherence

For the case of surprise, this negative affect triggered by incoherence or inconsistency has even a reasonable epistemic function, as Topolinski and Strack (2015) argue. We know from different areas of research that negative affective states increase the likelihood of elaborate and deeper processing, which is called *cognitive tuning* (Bless, 2001; Deutsch & Strack, 2008; Schwarz, 2002). Such tuning occurs not only for long-lasting moods but also for short-lasting phasic affect (Topolinski & Deutsch, 2012), as in the brief stunning moment during surprise. Since such negative affect due to incoherence increases the likelihood that an individual will invest more cognitive elaboration of the incoherent material, negative affect thus increases the likelihood that the incoherence will be resolved or cognitively mastered eventually (Attardo, 1997). This is the ultimate epistemic function of negative affect in response to incoherence: it helps us to restore coherence eventually.

Conclusion

The underlying psychological mechanisms driving intuitions of coherence are identified as being the fluency of current mental processing and resulting positive or negative affect. Coherent information is processed smoothly and easily and therefore feels good, while incoherent information is processed with difficulty and therefore feels negative, as in the irritation we feel when we are surprised. This negative affect resulting from incoherence prompts us to cognitively elaborate the inconsistency and thereby resolve it, for instance, by thinking over a fuzzy argument. That way, the sense of (in)coherence is a careful guide for thinking and reasoning with the adaptive function to gain more precise representations of the world and of us, and keep our reasoning actually reasonable.

References

Ackerman, R., Leiser, D., & Shpigelman, M. (2013). Is comprehension of problem solutions resistant to misleading heuristic cues? *Acta Psychologica, 143*(1), 105–112.

Ackerman, R., & Thompson, V. A. (2014). Meta-reasoning: What can we learn from meta-memory? In A. Feeney & V. A. Thompson (Eds.), *Reasoning as memory* (p. 164). London & New York: Psychology Press.

Ackerman, R., & Zalmanov, H. (2012). The persistence of the fluency – confidence association in problem solving. *Psychonomic Bulletin & Review, 19*(6), 1189–1192.

Attardo, S. (1997). The semantic foundations of cognitive theories of humor. *Humor: IJHR, 10*, 395–420.

Balas, R., Sweklej, J., Pochwatko, G., & Godlewska, M. (2012). On the influence of affective states on intuitive coherence judgements. *Cognition & Emotion, 26*(2), 312–320.

Baumann, N., & Kuhl, J. (2002). Intuition, affect, and personality: Unconscious coherence judgments and self-regulation of negative affect. *Journal of Personality and Social Psychology, 83*, 1213–1223.

Begg, I. M., Anas, A., & Farinacci, S. (1992). Dissociation of processes in belief: Source recollection, statement familiarity, and the illusion of truth. *Journal of Experimental Psychology: General, 121*(4), 446.

Biederman, I. (1987). Recognition-by-components: A theory of human image understanding. *Psychological Review, 94*(2), 115.

Bless, H. (2001). Mood and the use of general knowledge structures. In L. L. Martin & G. L. Clore (Eds.), *Theories of mood and cognition: A user's guidebook* (pp. 9–26). Mahwah, NJ: Lawrence Erlbaum Associates.

Bless, H., Fiedler, K., & Strack, F. (2004). *Social cognition: How individuals construct social reality*. Hove, UK: Psychology Press.

Bolte, A., Goschke, T., & Kuhl, J. (2003). Emotion and intuition: Effects of positive and negative mood on implicit judgments of semantic coherence. *Psychological Science, 14*(5), 416–421.

Bornstein, R. F., & D'Agostino, P. R. (1994). The attribution and discounting of perceptual fluency: Preliminary tests of a perceptual fluency/attributional model of the mere exposure effect. *Social Cognition, 12*, 103–128.

Bowden, E. M., & Jung-Beeman, M. (2003) One hundred forty-four compound remote associate problems: Short insight-like problems with one-word solutions. *Behavioral Research, Methods, Instruments, and Computers, 35*, 634–639.

Bowers, K. S., Regehr, G., Balthazard, C., & Parker, K. (1990). Intuition in the context of discovery. *Cognitive Psychology, 22*, 72–110.

Cacioppo, J. T., Petty, R. E., Losch, M. E., & Kim, H. S. (1986). Electromyographic activity over facial muscle regions can differentiate the valence and intensity of affective reactions. *Journal of Personality and Social Psychology, 50*, 260–268.

Davis, M. (1958). *Computability and unsolvability*. New York: McGraw-Hill.

Deutsch, R., & Strack, F. (2008). Variants of judgment and decision making: The perspective of the reflective-impulsive model. In H. Plessner, C. Betsch, & T. Betsch (Eds.), *Intuition in judgment and decision making* (pp. 39–53). Mahwah, NJ: Lawrence Erlbaum Associates.

Devine, P. G., & Sharp, L. B. (2009). Automaticity and control in stereotyping and prejudice. In T. D. Nelson (Ed.), *Handbook of prejudice, stereotyping, and discrimination* (pp. 61–87). New York, NY: Psychology Press.

Dunlosky, J., & Lipko, A. R. (2007). Metacomprehension – A brief history and how to improve its accuracy. *Current Directions in Psychological Science, 16*(4), 228–232.

Fazendeiro, T., Winkielman, P., Luo, C., & Lorah, C. (2005). False recognition across meaning, language, and stimulus format: Conceptual relatedness and the feeling of familiarity. *Memory & Cognition, 33*, 249–260.

Fontaine, J. R. J., Scherer, K. R., Roesch, E. B., & Ellsworth, P. C. (2007). The world of emotions is not two-dimensional. *Psychological Science, 18*, 1050–1057.

Frederick, S. (2005). Cognitive reflection and decision making. *Journal of Economic Perspectives, 19*, 25–42.

Hansen, J., Dechêne, A., & Wänke, M. (2008). Discrepant fluency increases subjective truth. *Journal of Experimental Social Psychology, 44*(3), 687–691.

Harmon-Jones, E., & Allen, J. B. (2001). The role of affect in the mere exposure effect: Evidence from psychophysiological and individual differences approaches. *Personality & Social Psychology Bulletin, 27*, 889–898.

Harmon-Jones, E., Harmon-Jones, C., & Amodio, D. M. (2012). A neuroscientific perspective on dissonance, guided by the action-based model. In B. Gawronski & F. Strack (Eds.), *Cognitive consistency: A fundamental principle in social cognition* (pp. 47–65). New York, NY: Guilford Press.

Heintzelman, S. J., Trent, J., & King, L. A. (2013). Encounters with objective coherence and the experience of meaning in life. *Psychological Science, 24*, 991–998. doi:0956797612465878

Hicks, J. A., Cicero, D. C., Trent, J., Burton, C. M., & King, L. A. (2010). Positive affect, intuition, and feelings of meaning. *Journal of Personality and Social Psychology, 98*(6), 967.

Kelley, C. M., & Lindsay, D. S. (1993). Remembering mistaken for knowing: Ease of retrieval as a basis for confidence in answers to general knowledge questions. *Journal of Memory and Language, 32*(1), 1–24.

Kihlstrom, J. F. (1999). The psychological unconscious. In L. R. Pervin & O. John (Eds.), *Handbook of personality* (2nd ed., pp. 424–442). New York: Guilford.

King, L. A., Hicks, J. A., Krull, J. L., & Del Gaiso, A. K. (2006). Positive affect and the experience of meaning in life. *Journal of Personality and Social Psychology, 90*(1), 179.

Klauer, K. C., & Singmann, H. (2013). Does logic feel good? Testing for intuitive detection of logicality in syllogistic reasoning. *Journal of Experimental Psychology: Learning, Memory, and Cognition, 39*(4), 1265.

Koriat, A., & Levy-Sadot, R. (2001). The combined contributions of the cue-familiarity and accessibility heuristics to feelings of knowing. *Journal of Experimental Psychology: Learning, Memory, and Cognition, 27*(1), 34–53.

Larsen, R. J., Kasimatis, M., & Frey, K. (1992). Facilitating the furrowed brow: An unobtrusive test of the facial feedback hypothesis applied to unpleasant affect. *Cognition & Emotion, 6*(5), 321–338.

Leder, H., Bär, S., & Topolinski, S. (2012). Covert painting simulations influence aesthetic appreciation of artworks. *Psychological Science, 23*(12), 1479–1481.

Mendes, W. B., Blascovich, J., Hunter, S. B., Lickel, B., & Jost, J. T. (2007). Threatened by the unexpected: Physiological responses during social interactions with expectancy-violating partners. *Journal of Personality and Social Psychology, 92*(4), 698–716. doi:10.1037/0022-3514.92.4.698

Miele, D. B., & Molden, D. C. (2010). Naive theories of intelligence and the role of processing fluency in perceived comprehension. *Journal of Experimental Psychology: General, 139*(3), 535–557.

Moreland, R. L., & Topolinski, S. (2010). The mere exposure phenomenon: A lingering melody by Robert Zajonc. *Emotion Review, 2*(4), 329–339.

Morsanyi, K., & Handley, S. J. (2012). Logic feels so good – I like it! Evidence for intuitive detection of logicality in syllogistic reasoning. *Journal of Experimental Psychology: Learning, Memory, and Cognition, 38*(3), 596.

Murphy, S. T., & Zajonc, R. B. (1993). Affect, cognition and awareness: Affective priming with optimal and suboptimal stimulus exposures. *Journal of Personality and Social Psychology, 64*, 723–739.

Noordewier, M. K., & Breugelmans, S. M. (2013). On the valence of surprise. *Cognition and Emotion, 27*, 1326–1334.
Pothos, E. M. (2007). Theories of artificial grammar learning. *Psychological Bulletin, 133*, 227–244.
Reber, A. S. (1967). Implicit learning of artificial grammars. *Journal of Verbal Learning and Verbal Behavior, 6*, 855–863.
Reber, R., & Schwarz, N. (1999). Effects of perceptual fluency on judgments of truth. *Consciousness and Cognition, 8*, 338–342.
Reber, R., Schwarz, N., & Winkielman, P. (2004). Processing fluency and aesthetic pleasure: Is beauty in the perceiver's processing experience? *Personality and Social Psychology Review, 8*, 364–382.
Reber, R., Winkielman, P., & Schwarz, N. (1998). Effects of perceptual fluency on affective judgments. *Psychological Science, 9*, 45–48.
Reber, R., Wurtz, P., & Zimmermann, T. D (2004). Exploring "fringe" consciousness: The subjective experience of perceptual fluency and its objective bases. *Consciousness and Cognition, 13*, 47–60.
Remmers, C., Topolinski, S., Dietrich, D. E., & Michalak, J. (2015). Impaired intuition in patients with major depressive disorder. *British Journal of Clinical Psychology, 54*(2), 200–213.
Remmers, C., Topolinski, S., & Michalak, J. (2015). Mindful (l) intuition: Does mindfulness influence the access to intuitive processes? *Journal of Positive Psychology, 10*(3), 282–292.
Russell, J. A. (2009). Emotion, core affect, and psychological construction. *Cognition and Emotion, 23*(7), 1259–1283.
Scherer, K. R., & Ellgring, H. (2007). Multimodal expression of emotion: Affect programs or componential appraisal patterns? *Emotion, 7*, 158–171.
Schwarz, N. (1990). Feelings as information: Informational and motivational functions of affective states. In E. T. Higgins & R. M. Sorrentino (Eds.), *Handbook of motivation and cognition: Foundations of social behavior, Vol. 2* (pp. 527–561). New York, NY: Guilford Press.
Schwarz, N. (2002). Situated cognition and the wisdom of feelings: Cognitive tuning. In L. Feldman Barrett & P. Salovey (Eds.), *The Wisdom in Feeling* (pp. 144–166). New York, NY: Guilford Press.
Schwarz, N., & Clore, G. L. (1983). Mood, misattribution, and judgments of well-being: Informative and directive functions of affective states. *Journal of personality and social psychology, 45*, 513–523.
Schwarz, N., Sanna, L., Skurnik, I., & Yoon, C. (2007). Metacognitive experiences and the intricacies of setting people straight: Implications for debiasing and public information campaigns. *Advances in Experimental Social Psychology, 39*, 127–161.
Strack, F., Martin, L., & Stepper, S. (1988). Inhibiting and facilitating conditions of the human smile: A nonobtrusive test of the facial feedback hypothesis. *Journal of Personality and Social Psychology, 54*, 768–777.
Strack, F., Schwarz, N., Bless, H., Kübler, A., & Wänke, M. (1993). Awareness of the influence as a determinant of assimilation versus contrast. *European Journal of Social Psychology, 23*, 53–62.
Sweklej, J., Balas, R., Pochwatko, G., & Godlewska, M. (2014). Intuitive (in) coherence judgments are guided by processing fluency, mood and affect. *Psychological Research, 78*(1), 141–149.
Thompson, V. A. (2009). Dual-process theories: A metacognitive perspective. In J. Evans & K. Frankish (Eds.), *In Two Minds: Dual Processes and Beyond* (pp. 171–195). Oxford, UK: Oxford University Press.
Thompson, V. A., Prowse Turner, J. A., & Pennycook, G. (2011). Intuition, reason, and metacognition. *Cognitive Psychology, 63*(3), 107–140.
Thompson, V. A., Prowse Turner, J. A., Pennycook, G., Ball, L. J., Brack, H., Ophir, Y., & Ackerman, R. (2013). The role of answer fluency and perceptual fluency as metacognitive cues for initiating analytic thinking. *Cognition, 128*(2), 237–251.
Topolinski, S. (2011). A process model of intuition. *European Review of Social Psychology, 22*(1), 274–315.
Topolinski, S. (2011). The sources of fluency: Identifying the underlying mechanisms of fluency effects. In C. Unkelbach & R. Greifeneder (Eds.), *The Experience of Thinking: How Feelings From Mental Processes Influence Cognition and Behavior*. New York: Psychology Press.
Topolinski, S. (2012a). Non-propositional consistency. In B. Gawronski & F. Strack (Eds.), *Cognitive consistency: A unifying concept in social psychology* (pp. 112–131). New York: Guilford Press.
Topolinski, S. (2012b). The sensorimotor contributions to implicit memory, familiarity, and recollection. *Journal of Experimental Psychology: General, 141*(2), 260–281.
Topolinski, S. (2014). A processing fluency-account of funniness: Running gags and spoiling punchlines. *Cognition & Emotion, 28*(5), 811–820.
Topolinski, S., & Deutsch, R. (2012). Phasic affective modulation of semantic priming. *Journal of Experimental Psychology: Learning, Memory, and Cognition*. doi:10.1037/a0028879

Topolinski, S., Erle, T. M., & Reber, R. (2015). Necker's smile: Immediate affective consequences of early perceptual processes. *Cognition, 140*, 1–13.
Topolinski, S., Likowski, K. U., Weyers, P., & Strack, F. (2009). The face of fluency: Semantic coherence automatically elicits a specific pattern of facial muscle reactions. *Cognition and Emotion, 23*(2), 260–271.
Topolinski, S., & Reber, R. (2010a). Gaining insight into the "Aha"-experience. *Current Directions in Psychological Science, 19*(6), 402–405.
Topolinski, S., & Reber, R. (2010b). Immediate truth – Temporal contiguity between a cognitive problem and its solution determines experienced veracity of the solution. *Cognition, 114*, 117–122.
Topolinski, S., & Strack, F. (2008). Where there's a will – there's no intuition: The unintentional basis of semantic coherence judgments. *Journal of Memory and Language, 58*(4), 1032–1048.
Topolinski, S., & Strack, F. (2009a). The analysis of intuition: Processing fluency and affect in judgements of semantic coherence. *Cognition and Emotion, 23*(8), 1465–1503.
Topolinski, S., & Strack, F. (2009b). The architecture of intuition: Fluency and affect determine intuitive judgments of semantic and visual coherence, and of grammaticality in artificial grammar learning. *Journal of Experimental Psychology: General, 138 (1)*, 39–63.
Topolinski, S., & Strack, F. (2009c). Motormouth: Mere exposure depends on stimulus-specific motor simulations. *Journal of Experimental Psychology: Learning, Memory, and Cognition, 35*(2), 423–433.
Topolinski, S., & Strack, F. (2009d). Scanning the "fringe" of consciousness: What is felt and what is not felt in intuitions about semantic coherence. *Consciousness and Cognition, 18*, 608–618.
Topolinski, S., & Strack, F. (2010). False fame prevented – avoiding fluency-effects without judgmental correction. *Journal of Personality and Social Psychology, 98*(5), 721–733.
Topolinski, S., & Strack, F. (2015). Corrugator activity confirms immediate negative affect in surprise. *Frontiers in Psychology, 6*, Article 134. 1–8.
Trent, J., Lavelock, C., & King, L. A. (2013). Processing fluency, positive affect, and judgments of meaning in life. *Journal of Positive Psychology, 8*(2), 135–139.
Unkelbach, C. (2007). Reversing the truth effect: Learning the interpretation of processing fluency in judgments of truth. *Journal of Experimental Psychology: Learning, Memory and Cognition, 33*, 219–230.
Valenzuela, A., Strebel, J., & Mellers, B. (2010). Pleasurable surprises: A cross-cultural study of consumer responses to unexpected incentives. *Journal of Consumer Research, 36*, 792–805.
Volz, K. G., & von Cramon, D.Y. (2006). What neuroscience can tell about intuitive processes in the context of perceptual discovery. *Journal of Cognitive Neuroscience, 18 (12)*, 2077–2087.
Whittlesea, B. W. A. (1993). Illusions of familiarity. *Journal of Experimental Psychology: Learning, Memory, and Cognition, 19*, 1235–1253.
Whittlesea, B. W., & Williams, L. D. (1998). Why do strangers feel familiar, but friends don't? A discrepancy-attribution account of feelings of familiarity. *Acta Psychologica, 98*(2), 141–165.
Whittlesea, B. W., & Williams, L. D. (2000). The source of feelings of familiarity: The discrepancy-attribution hypothesis. *Journal of Experimental Psychology: Learning, Memory, and Cognition, 26*(3), 547.
Whittlesea, B. W., & Williams, L. D. (2001). The discrepancy-attribution hypothesis: II. Expectation, uncertainty, surprise, and feelings of familiarity. *Journal of Experimental Psychology: Learning, Memory, and Cognition, 27*(1), 14.
Winkielman, P., & Cacioppo, J. T. (2001). Mind at ease puts a smile on the face: Psychophysiological evidence that processing facilitation leads to positive affect. *Journal of Personality and Social Psychology, 81*, 989–1000.
Winkielman, P., & Zajonc, R. B., & Schwarz, N. (1997). Subliminal affective priming resists attributional interventions. *Cognition & Emotion, 11*, 433–465.
Zanna, M. P., & Cooper, J. (1974). Dissonance and the pill: An attribution approach to studying the arousal properties of dissonance. *Journal of Personality and Social Psychology, 29*(5), 703.

32

REASONING AND MORAL JUDGMENT

A common experimental toolbox

Bastien Trémolière, Wim De Neys, and Jean-François Bonnefon

The dual-process model offers a unified framework for the study of reasoning and moral judgment, making it easier than ever for reasoning specialists to branch out to moral judgment, or for moral judgment specialists to incorporate findings and methods from the psychology of reasoning. In this chapter, we draw a parallel between investigations of belief bias and investigations of moral dilemmas to show how the same experimental toolbox (time pressure, cognitive interference, individual differences, mortality salience) has been applied to both phenomena within the theoretical context of the dual-process model.

The table of contents of the present volume suggests that the psychology of reasoning is expanding at a fast pace, covering grounds which used to be considered the purchase of decision-making, theory of mind, or moral judgment. One reason for this rapid expansion is that the psychology of reasoning has now largely adopted the new *lingua franca* of higher-order cognition: probability, utility, and the dual-process model (Bonnefon, 2013). Couching problems in terms of probability and utility allows the psychology of reasoning to tackle decisional and moral issues, from bets and lotteries to the moral dilemmas we consider in this chapter. In parallel, relying on the manipulations and measures of the dual-process model ensures that results obtained in the field of reasoning are compatible with and relevant for the numerous other fields which have adopted this model as their leading theoretical framework.

Other fields, though, have not always taken full stock of the new shape of the psychology of reasoning. In the field of moral judgment in particular, reasoning is (at best) given a definition that is not quite the same as in the psychology of reasoning, or (at worst) considered irrelevant. Jonathan Haidt, for example, famously asserted that our moral positions do not usually stem from reasoning. Moral positions, according to Haidt (2001, 2007, 2012), are first and foremost driven by intuitions, and reasoning is only used later, to find reasons that might sway others' intuitions in favor of our position.

The dual-process model of moral judgment, developed by Joshua Greene and collaborators (starting with Greene, Sommerville, Nystrom, Darley, & Cohen, 2001), gives a larger role to reasoning, albeit one that depends on a restricted definition. In the dual-process model of moral judgment, intuition and reasoning concurrently drive moral positions. Reasoning corresponds to the conscious application of a decision rule (Greene, 2013), in the sense that the conclusion of moral reasoning must be consistent with one's commitments to one or several moral decision rules (Paxton & Greene, 2010).

Accordingly, it would appear that reasoning in the dual-process model of moral judgment is solely a conscious, rule-based affair. In other words, the dual-process model of moral judgment defines reasoning as its deliberative component. This can be a source of confusion, because specialists of reasoning tend to adopt a broader definition (Evans, 2008; Evans & Stanovich, 2013; Sloman, 1996). Specialists of reasoning agree that the conscious application of rules, and the commitment to rational axioms such as consistency, are indeed a hallmark of deliberate, reflective reasoning, also known as System 2 reasoning. However, they also typically retain the term 'reasoning' (only qualified as intuitive, heuristic, or System 1), for the unconscious processing of beliefs driven by affective and heuristic shortcuts.

With this caveat in mind, the widespread adoption of the dual-process model by the fields of reasoning and moral judgment offers novel opportunities for them to connect. In particular, the experimental protocols used in the two fields are now largely comparable, because they utilize the same basic toolbox provided by the dual-process model. In the rest of this chapter, we illustrate this novel interoperability by showing how the dual-process toolbox has been applied in parallel to the flagship problems of the two fields: belief bias and utilitarian dilemmas. We begin with a quick overview of the dual-process toolbox: the list of manipulations and measures that researchers typically use to test predictions derived from the dual-process model. We then introduce belief bias and utilitarian dilemmas, and show that they delivered very similar findings in experiments that used four dual-process tools (time pressure, cognitive interference, individual differences – and mortality salience, which will require some additional explaining). Note that due to space limitations, we focus on behavioral tools in the dual-process toolbox to the exclusion of methods aimed at identifying the neural correlates of belief bias (De Neys, Vartanian, & Goel, 2008; Goel, 2007; Goel & Dolan, 2003; Rotello & Heit, in press; Tsujii & Watanabe, 2009, 2010; Tsujii, Masuda, Akiyama, & Watanabe, 2010; Tsujii, Okada, & Watanabe, 2010) and utilitarian dilemmas (Greene, 2007; Greene, Nystrom, Engell, Darley, & Cohen, 2004; Greene, Sommerville, Nystrom, Darley, & Cohen, 2001; Kahan et al., 2012; Koenigs et al., 2007; Shenhav & Greene, 2014; Thomas, Croft, & Tranel, 2011).

The dual-process toolbox

Although there are different versions of the dual-process model (De Neys & Bonnefon, 2013; Evans, 2008; Evans & Stanovich, 2013; Kahneman, 2011; see also Evans, this volume), all variants appear to share the same assumption, broadly formulated: System 2 processing requires access to central executive resources in order to suspend or inhibit the intuitive response to a problem for the time it takes to produce a reflective response. This assumption is critically important because it applies similarly whatever field one is investigating, and allows for predictions which are tested the same way, whatever field one is investigating.

Let us consider a problem which can elicit one of two responses, r and R. The problem can be one of logical reasoning, in which participants must decide whether a conclusion is valid or invalid – or the problem can be one of moral judgment, in which participants must decide whether an action is morally acceptable or unacceptable. Let us now imagine that we want to apply the dual-process model to the problem, and test the hypothesis that r and R are intuitive and reflective responses, respectively.

Because the reflective response is elaborated after the intuitive response is generated and inhibited, a first testable prediction is that R will take longer to produce than r. Even better, we can run a causal test by limiting the time that some participants have to solve the problem, and check whether this *time pressure* decreases the frequency of R and increases the frequency of r. Additionally, because the elaboration of the reflective response requires central executive resources which cannot be deployed for several tasks at once, another testable prediction is that *cognitive interference,* in the form of a concurrent task, should decrease the frequency of R and increase the frequency of r.

Given that the elaboration of the reflective response requires the reasoner to mobilize and expend central executive resources, a third testable prediction is that individuals who either possess these resources in larger amounts, or have a greater individual propensity to mobilize them, should be more likely to produce the reflective response. Accordingly, these *individual differences* should correlate positively with the likelihood of producing R and negatively with the likelihood of producing r. Finally, any experimental manipulation whose effect is to limit or discourage the use of central executive resources should by the same logic decrease the frequency of R and increase the frequency of r. For example, participants may receive instructions encouraging them to trust or not trust their gut feelings, or they may be subjected to priming manipulations to the same effect. In this chapter, we will consider the effect of the **mortality salience** manipulation, which consists of asking subjects to write a very short essay on their future death. Importantly, this reminder of mortality is believed to temporarily decrease the availability of central executive resources. As a consequence, conducting the mortality salience manipulation before the target problem should decrease the frequency of R and increase the frequency of r.

In the rest of this chapter, we review the use of these four dual-process tools, as applied to one problem of logical reasoning (belief bias) and one problem of moral judgment (utilitarian dilemmas). Our aim is to show that the reasoning and the moral literature are closely related, in the sense that the two fields have applied this exact same toolbox to the two problems, in independent and parallel fashion, but to mostly comparable results. Before we move on to this review, we briefly introduce our two problems in the next section.

Belief bias and moral dilemmas

Reasoners display **belief bias** when their judgment about the logical validity of a conclusion is unduly influenced by the believability of this conclusion (Evans, Barston, & Pollard, 1983; Klauer, Musch, & Naumer, 2000; Thompson & Evans, 2012). For example, the fact that we know roses to be flowers can make it hard to spot that the conclusion of syllogism (1) is logically invalid:

(1) a. All flowers need water.
b. Roses need water.
c. Therefore, roses are flowers.

To accept (1-c) as a logically valid conclusion is to fall prey to belief bias. Likewise, to reject (2-c) as an invalid conclusion is to fall prey to belief bias, since this conclusion is actually logically valid, however inconsistent it is with our common beliefs about astronauts:

(2) a. People in good health are happy.
b. Some astronauts are unhappy.
c. Therefore, some astronauts are not in good health.

In examples (1) and (2), the believability of the conclusion is incongruent with its logical validity. We will call these the 'conflict' syllogisms, as opposed to the 'control' syllogisms, in which a response based on believability would be the same as a response based on logical validity. In conflict syllogisms, one gives a different response as a function of whether one relies on believability or validity. Let us call the former response r (based on believability), and the latter response R (based on validity). The data we review in the rest of this chapter will test the hypothesis that r is the intuitive System 1 response, and that R is the reflective System 2 response.

We are well aware that specialists of belief bias would use more complex indices (Heit & Rotello, 2014; Trippas, Handley, & Verde, 2014), more sophisticated analyses (Dube, Rotello, & Heit, 2010), and more creative protocols (Trippas, Verde, & Handley, 2014), than what we have just introduced. This sophistication has allowed for a much deeper understanding of belief bias, but it comes at a cost, as it makes it harder for researchers in other fields to capture the gist of belief bias research and its relevance for their own work. In this chapter, we strive to speak to moral judgment researchers as well as reasoning researchers, and we limit our exposition of belief bias accordingly (see Ball & Thompson, this volume, for a more in-depth review of belief bias research). This is also true of our introduction of moral dilemmas, which we attempt to keep reasonably free of complications, in order to speak to reasoning researchers as well as moral judgment researchers.

The **moral dilemmas** that have generated the most research, from a dual-process perspective, describe situations where rights and duties are in conflict with the greater good. In these situations, one can adopt a deontic response (giving priority to personal rights over the greater good) or a utilitarian response (giving priority to the greater good over personal rights). Most typically, the dilemmas describe fictional circumstances in which one has the possibility to save several lives by killing a single person. The deontic response is to find this course of action morally unacceptable (the personal right to not be killed trumps the greater good, i.e., the net number of survivors), whereas the utilitarian response is to find this course of action acceptable (the greater good, i.e., the net number of survivors, trumps the personal right to not be killed). As an illustration, we quote in full three dilemmas used in many research papers with small variations (especially in the exact phrasing of the question asked to participants at the end of the dilemma):

(3) Footbridge: a runaway trolley is heading down the tracks toward 10 workmen who will be killed if the trolley proceeds on its present course. You are on a footbridge over the tracks, in between the approaching trolley and the 10 workmen. Next to you on this footbridge is a stranger who happens to be very large. The only way to save the lives of the 10 workmen is to push this stranger off the bridge and onto the tracks below where his large body will stop the trolley. The stranger will die if you do this, but the 10 workmen will be saved. Would it be wrong for you to push the stranger on to the tracks in order to save the 10 workmen?

(4) Sophie's choice: it is wartime and you and your two children, ages eight and five, are living in a territory that has been occupied by the enemy. At the enemy's headquarters is a doctor who performs painful experiments on humans that inevitably lead to death. He intends to perform experiments on one of your children, but he will allow you to choose which of your children will be experimented upon. You have 24 hours to bring one of your children to his laboratory. If you refuse to bring one of your children to his laboratory, he will find them both and experiment on both of them. Would it be wrong for you to bring one of your children to the laboratory in order to avoid having them both die?

(5) Crying baby: enemy soldiers have taken over your village. They have orders to kill all remaining civilians. You and some of your townspeople have sought refuge in the cellar of a large house. Outside you hear the voices of soldiers who have come to search the house for valuables. Your baby begins to cry loudly. You cover his mouth to block the sound. If you remove your hand from his mouth, his crying will summon the attention of the soldiers, who will kill you, your child, and the others hiding out in the cellar. To save yourself and the others, you must smother your child to death. Would it be wrong for you to smother your child in order to save yourself and the other townspeople?

Agreeing to push the stranger on to the tracks, to bring one's own children to the laboratory, and to smother one's own baby – or at least not finding these actions wrong – are utilitarian responses to the dilemmas. Let us call R the utilitarian response, and r the deontic response. The data we review in the rest of this chapter will test the hypothesis that r (deontic) is the intuitive System 1 response, whereas R (utilitarian) is the reflective System 2 response. Note that just as in the case of syllogisms, it is possible to construct moral scenarios in which the deontic and utilitarian responses are not in conflict; these scenarios provide in the moral context the same kind of baseline condition that no-conflict syllogisms provide in the logical reasoning context.

We are now in a position to review the experiments that attempted (on the one hand) to test the hypothesis that responding on the basis of believability in the 'conflict' type of belief bias problems is an intuitive System 1 response; or (on the other hand) to test the hypothesis that giving a deontic response to utilitarian dilemmas is an intuitive System 1 response. More importantly, we will show that these two hypotheses have been tested by utilizing the exact same dual-process toolbox based on time pressure, cognitive interference, individual differences, and (for something a bit different) mortality salience. We now address these tools one by one.

Time pressure

We focus in this section on time pressure manipulations (i.e., the effect of imposing a time limit to respond to logical syllogisms or moral dilemmas). Before we consider the results of time pressure studies, though, we review some results related to the processing time of syllogisms and moral dilemmas. Indeed, the dual-process model makes two predictions about processing time. First, people should take longer to solve a conflict problem (in which the intuitive response is supposedly different from the reflective response) than a control problem (in which the intuitive and reflective responses are presumed to be the same). This prediction assumes that, for conflict problems, at least some individuals will take the necessary time to inhibit their intuitive response and generate a reflective response. Second, individuals who give what is presumed to be the reflective response should take longer than individuals who settle for the intuitive response. As it turns out, studies of belief bias have focused on the first prediction, whereas studies on moral dilemma have focused on the second.

Several studies of belief bias have shown that reasoners took longer to inspect or to process conflict syllogisms, in which the conclusion based on believability is different from the response based on logical validity (Ball, Phillips, Wade, & Quayle, 2006; De Neys & Franssens, 2009; Stupple & Ball, 2008; Svedholm-Häkkinen, 2015). These studies have quite consistently recorded a 15% to 30% increase in processing time for conflict syllogisms. These results are consistent with the dual-process model, but they cannot on their own tell us whether the believability or the validity response is the reflective one. In that regard it is informative to observe that individuals who eventually give the response based on believability are faster than individuals who eventually give the response based on validity (De Neys & Dieussaert, 2005). Interestingly, this is the strategy that researchers have adopted with respect to the processing of utilitarian moral dilemmas.

In a typical utilitarian moral dilemma, one can generate a deontic response (i.e., it is morally unacceptable to kill, even if killing one person would save several lives) or a utilitarian response (i.e., it is morally acceptable to kill if the death of one would save several other lives). If one of these two responses is intuitive and the other is reflective, we should expect a difference in processing time as a function of whether an individual eventually gives one or the other. Data are hardly conclusive in that regard, though. Greene et al. (2001) observed that processing time was greater for utilitarian responses, but a re-analysis revealed that this effect was driven by a subset of scenarios, not all of which had desirable properties (McGuire, Langdon, Coltheart, & Mackenzie, 2009). The response time effect was shown again to be fragile in two other articles. In one case, it was limited to a condition in which participants experienced cognitive interference (Greene, Morelli, Lowenberg, Nystrom, & Cohen, 2008); and in the other case, it was again contingent on a limited subset of scenarios (Koop, 2013). For the time being, we must conclude that no solid data exist that show a difference in processing time between utilitarian and deontic responses.

The lack of correlation between type of response and processing time should not be counted as a strong argument against the dual-process model, though. Solving syllogisms or moral dilemmas takes a long time, and it is entirely possible that people do not respond as soon as they can. Accordingly, response times in such situations must be considered a noisy measure at best. A much better test of the dual-process model consists of using time pressure, that is, giving two groups of participants a different time limit to give their response. The logic here is that participants working under severe time constraints are much less likely to have the time to generate a reflective response – therefore, imposing a severe time constraint should decrease the frequency of whichever of the two responses that requires reflective processing.

In studies of belief bias, the time limit imposed to participants under time pressure is commonly set at 10 seconds. That is, participants under time pressure have 10 seconds to read the syllogism and assess whether the proposed conclusion is logically valid. Depending on the study, participants in the control group are given either unlimited time or about 20 seconds, which corresponds to the average amount of time people take to respond under free-time conditions. In the first application of the time pressure protocol to belief bias, Evans and Curtis-Holmes (2005) observed that the frequency of the response based on validity (as opposed to the response based on believability) decreased by about 20 percentage points when participants were given 10 seconds to solve the syllogisms. This result was replicated, for a similar effect size, by Tsujii and Watanabe (2010), who used a 10-second limit for the time pressure group and a 20-second limit for the control group. The same effect size was observed again by Trippas, Handley, and Verde (2013), albeit for only one of the two types of conflict syllogisms. The frequency of the validity response decreased by about 20 percentage points under time pressure for syllogisms in which the conclusion was unbelievable and yet valid. For the other type of conflict syllogism (invalid yet believable conclusion), the effect was weaker (less than 10 percentage points), and only observed for participants in the lower range of cognitive ability. With this proviso, it seems reasonably clear that time pressure decreases the frequency of the validity response to conflict syllogism, which the dual-process model counts as evidence that the response based on validity is the reflective System 2 response.

Turning now to moral dilemmas, we would expect that a time pressure manipulation would decrease the frequency of utilitarian responses, if the utilitarian response is indeed the reflective System 2 response. Just as with belief bias, this prediction was tested and validated in several studies.

Suter and Hertwig (2011) conducted the first study applying time pressure to moral dilemmas. In their study, participants first read the contents of a dilemma (e.g., Crying Baby, see p. 578) for a maximum of 35 seconds, and then moved on to a second screen displaying the moral acceptability question (e.g., 'Is it appropriate for you to smother your child in order to save yourself and the other townspeople?'). Participants in the time pressure condition had eight seconds to respond, whereas participants in the control condition had to wait 180 seconds before responding. The time pressure manipulation had the expected effect on the frequency of utilitarian responses to three high-conflict dilemmas such as Crying Baby, decreasing it by about 20 percentage points. Trémolière and Bonnefon (2014) replicated this effect with a new selection of four dilemmas, in which the frequency of utilitarian responses decreased by 15 to

20 percentage points under time pressure – at least for versions of the dilemmas in which a relatively small number of lives could be saved (five to 50). The time pressure effect disappeared, though, when a large number of lives could be saved (500–5,000), suggesting that utilitarian killings were no longer counterintuitive in these situations.

These findings were consistent with the hypothesis that utilitarian responses were reflective System 2 outputs (at least when the number of lives saved by a utilitarian killing was relatively small). Later studies consolidated this conclusion by using more tightly controlled protocols and a greater range of dilemmas. In the original study of Suter and Hertwig (2011), giving the utilitarian response always amounted to choosing the 'yes' option. Furthermore, it was plausible that participants used some of their 35-second reading time to start thinking about their decision. To control for these two potential biases, Cummins and Cummins (2012) conducted a study in which the utilitarian response alternated between 'yes' and 'no', participants had to scroll down to read the scenario, and decision time in the pressure condition was set at 200 milliseconds for each word in the decision question. The frequency of utilitarian responses dropped by 10 to 15 percentage points on average, for all dilemmas but those few in which extremely few people made the utilitarian decision in the first place.

In sum, time pressure manipulations have been used in parallel in investigations of belief bias and moral dilemmas. In both fields, the decrease of one type of response under time pressure (the validity response for belief bias, the utilitarian response for moral dilemmas) was taken as evidence that this response was the product of reflective System 2 processing. This time pressure criterion is only one tool in the dual-process toolbox, though – and we now turn to a second tool, the use of cognitive interference protocols.

Cognitive interference

The dual-process model assumes that reflective System 2 processing requires the mobilization of central executive resources. When two tasks simultaneously require these resources, performance is expected to decrease on at least one of the tasks. Accordingly, the dual-process model predicts that cognitive interference, in the form of a concurrent task, will decrease the frequency of the reflective System 2 response to a problem. This prediction applies the same way to belief bias and moral dilemmas: cognitive interference should decrease the frequency of the validity response to conflict syllogisms and decrease the frequency of the utilitarian response to moral dilemmas. And indeed, specialists of belief bias and moral dilemmas have applied this logic in parallel to their respective fields, to very comparable results.

Unlike manipulations of time pressure, which are highly similar across studies and across the two fields, manipulations of cognitive interference are seldom similar from one study to another. The principle is always the same: participants are required to devote the lion's share of their attention to an interfering task which is meant to keep their working memory busy, while processing logical syllogisms or moral dilemmas. As we will see, though, the interfering task can be as varied as counting target words while listening to a song, memorizing patterns of dots, taking a 2-back task, or monitoring strings of numbers scrolling across a computer screen.

In the first article to apply a cognitive interference manipulation to belief bias (De Neys, 2006), participants were assigned to one of three conditions. In the control condition (no interference), participants simply solved conflict syllogisms. In the low and high interference conditions, a 3 x 3 matrix appeared for 850ms before each syllogism. Some cells of the matrix contained dots, whose location participants had to memorize. Once they had solved the syllogism, participants had to correctly place the dots in an empty matrix. The low interference condition utilized easy configurations of dots (horizontal or vertical), whereas the high interference condition utilized complex patterns of dots (Figure 32.1). Keep in mind that these complex patterns put a high load on executive resources (Miyake, Friedman, Rettinger, Shah, & Hegarty, 2001), whereas vertical or horizontal patterns put only a low load on executive resources.

As expected, cognitive interference decreased the frequency of the validity response to conflict syllogisms, from about 70% under no interference, to about 60% under low interference, to about 50% under high interference. This finding was replicated by Trémolière, De Neys, and Bonnefon (2014), who observed the same drop from about 60% validity responses to conflict problems under low interference, to 50% under high interference.

Other studies consolidated this finding using other manipulations of cognitive interference. In one case, cognitive interference was manipulated by having participants listen to a song while solving the problems, and counting how many times the word 'time' occurred in the song (DeWall, Baumeister, & Masicampo, 2008). The word 'time' occurred 16 times in five minutes and 37 seconds, or once every 21 seconds on average, ensuring that this interfering task required sustained attention. In one other case (Tsujii & Watanabe, 2009), cognitive interference was manipulated by contrasting a 0-back task in the control condition to a 2-back task in the

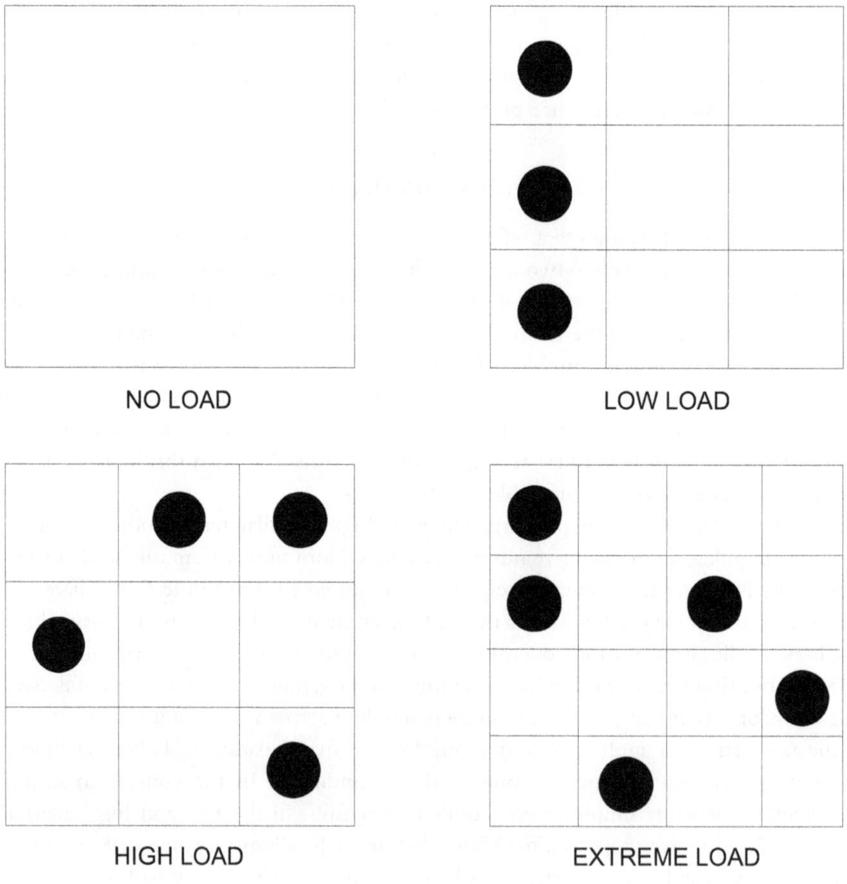

Figure 32.1 Examples of dot matrices used to induce no cognitive load (i.e., no matrix to memorize), low load, high load, and extreme load

interference condition. In the N-back task, participants are presented with a sequence of stimuli and must give a signal whenever a stimulus matches the stimulus which was presented N steps before. By convention, the 0-back task simply consists of reacting to a predefined stimulus, as in a go/no-go task.

Convergent findings thus suggest that the validity response to a conflict syllogism decreases in frequency when reasoners experience cognitive interference. Under the dual-process framework, this counts as evidence that the validity response requires reflective System 2 processing. In parallel, moral judgment scientists used comparable manipulations to establish that the utilitarian response to a moral dilemma was similarly impaired by cognitive interference.

The first published attempt to demonstrate an effect of cognitive interference on moral dilemmas led to inconclusive results (Greene et al., 2008). While participants in the control condition simply solved moral dilemmas such as the Crying Baby problem, participants in the interference condition had to simultaneously monitor a stream of digits scrolling at the bottom of the screen and hit a button every time they detected the number 5 (which accounted for 20% of the digits). This manipulation had no effect on the frequency of utilitarian responses (i.e., kill the baby) – however, participants in the interference condition took longer to deliver utilitarian responses, compared to participants in the control condition.

The fact that the frequency of utilitarian responses was not affected by the interference manipulation was unexpected under the dual-process model. Greene et al. (2008) speculated that participants might be keenly aware of the interference manipulation and decided to dispose of it by making extra cognitive effort. Accordingly, they would reach utilitarian response the same way, but only after further effort, which would account for their longer processing time.

Another possibility is that the interference manipulation was simply not powerful enough – accordingly, it would have delayed but not prevented participants from reaching utilitarian responses. Trémolière, De Neys, and Bonnefon (2012) tested this hypothesis by using several versions of the dot matrix task (low load, high load, and extreme load, see Figure 32.1) as their interference manipulation. They observed that the frequency of utilitarian responses was the same (about 55%) in the low and high load conditions, but decreased to less than 40% in the extreme load condition (note, though, that this decrease was observed only after excluding five multivariate outliers). This result was replicated in another study (Trémolière & Bonnefon, 2014), in which the frequency of utilitarian responses dropped from about 55% in a low load condition to about 45% in an extreme load condition (see also Conway & Gawronski, 2013).

In sum, utilitarian responses do decrease under cognitive interference, but one interpretation of the relevant data is that the level of cognitive load required to demonstrate this effect is larger than what it is in belief bias studies. The fact that the dot matrix task has been used in both domains allows for a direct comparison of the cognitive load required to affect belief bias and the cognitive load required to affect moral dilemmas. As it turns out, giving a utilitarian response to a moral dilemma requires executive resources, but either to a lesser degree or of a different nature than giving a validity response to a conflict syllogism.

Individual differences

All dual-process models assume that the elaboration of reflective System 2 responses requires reasoners to mobilize central executive resources. Accordingly, they predict that reflective System 2 responses are more likely to be elaborated by reasoners who possess these resources in greater amount or have a greater disposition to mobilize them. These models therefore give an important role to cognitive ability and thinking dispositions as individual moderators of the likelihood to elaborate a reflective response. Interestingly, studies of moral dilemmas have mostly investigated the role of thinking dispositions, whereas studies of belief bias have given equal measures of interest to cognitive ability and thinking dispositions.

In studies of belief bias, cognitive ability has been indexed through performance on a broad array of tasks – for example, working memory span (De Neys, 2006), inhibitory control (Handley, Capon, Beveridge, Dennis, & Evans, 2004), standardized tests of intelligence (Kokis, MacPherson, Toplak, West, & Stanovich, 2002; MacPherson & Stanovich, 2007; Newstead, Handley, Harley, Wright, & Farelly, 2004; Sa, West, & Stanovich, 1999), or the SAT score for samples of American students (Stanovich & West, 1998; West, Toplak, & Stanovich, 2008). These measures commonly account for 15–20% of the variance in the likelihood of giving responses based on validity to conflict syllogisms.

Studies of moral dilemmas are far behind studies of belief bias with respect to investigating the moderating role of cognitive ability. In fact, we are aware of only one published article in which this question was addressed, to inconclusive results (Moore, Clark, & Kane, 2008). In this study, cognitive ability was indexed by performance on three working memory span measures. Participants with higher working memory capacity found utilitarian killings more appropriate than participants with lower working memory capacity (in line with the dual-process model), but only for the subset of problems in which the individual to be killed would die in any case (think of the Sophie's Choice problem above, in which both children will die if no action is taken – compared to the Footbridge problem, in which the stranger will not die if no action is taken). It is intriguing that the issue was not pushed any further, especially in comparison to the vast body of work on cognitive ability in the belief bias domain. Maybe the effect of cognitive ability is simply harder to capture in the moral domain. We have already pointed to some evidence that utilitarian dilemmas might place lower demands on working memory than conflict syllogisms do (see the Cognitive Interference section). If this is correct, then perhaps differences in cognitive ability account for a much smaller share of variance in the moral domain, as compared to the belief bias domain.

Both fields, though, have given about equal attention to the moderating role of thinking dispositions (i.e., the propensity to mobilize executive resources, rather than the amount in which they are available). A closer look will nevertheless reveal different practices in how these dispositions are measured. In studies of belief bias, thinking dispositions are commonly measured through self-reports. The two most frequent tools for doing so are the Actively Open Minded Thinking scale (Stanovich & West, 1997), either on its own or as part of a broader thinking disposition composite, and the Need for Cognition scale (Cacioppo & Petty, 1982), either on its own or as part of the Rational-Experiential Inventory (Paccini & Epstein, 1999). In contrast, studies of moral dilemmas most commonly use the performance measure known as the Cognitive Reflection Test (Frederick, 2005).

The Actively Open Minded Thinking scale tracks a distinctive style of cognitive regulation, aimed at not systematically strengthening whatever beliefs one already holds. High scores on the scale correspond to high agreement with statements such as 'People should always take into consideration evidence that goes against their beliefs', and low agreement with statements such as 'No one can talk me out of something I know is right'. Higher scores on this scale correlate with a higher propensity to give validity responses to logical syllogisms, accounting for 5–15% of the variance in addition to the variance accounted for by cognitive capacity (Kokis et al., 2002; MacPherson & Stanovich, 2007; Sa et al., 1999; Stanovich & West, 1998). Need for Cognition is less consistently linked to validity responses. The correlation seems to be .20 at the highest (MacPherson & Stanovich, 2007), and at least two studies found no correlation at all between validity responses and Need for Cognition (Kokis et al., 2002; Newstead et al., 2004).

Need for Cognition seems to do slightly better in the context of moral dilemmas, with reported correlations of .20 and .40 (Bartels, 2008; Conway & Gawronski, 2013). Need for Cognition is not, however, the most common measure of thinking dispositions in this context. Moral researchers focus instead on a performance (rather than self-reported) measure of thinking disposition, the Cognitive Reflection Test, or CRT (Frederick, 2005). The CRT consists of three brain teasers with a very compelling incorrect response and a very simple correct response (in the sense that it only requires basic arithmetic skills). Performance on the CRT requires one to ignore the compelling but incorrect response that comes first to mind in order to do the simple calculation that will deliver the correct response. For example, the lily pad item reads: 'in a lake, there is a patch of lily pads. Every day, the patch doubles in size. If it takes 48 days for the patch to cover the entire lake, how long would it take for the patch to cover half of the lake?'. The correct response (47 days) can be computed simply enough, if only one ignores for a moment the compelling but incorrect response to the problem (24 days).

The likelihood of giving a utilitarian response to a moral dilemma correlates with performance on the CRT, although the value of this correlation seems to be quite different if the CRT is given before (.25–.60) or after (.00–.25) the moral dilemma (Paxton, Ungar, & Greene, 2012; Paxton, Bruni, & Greene, 2014). Some authors have recently hypothesized that high CRT performers may actually consider that utilitarian killings do not fall within the moral domain, which would explain why they may or may not endorse them, depending on the occasion (Royzman, Landy, & Leeman, in press). Another intriguing possibility, especially in light of the belief bias studies we just reviewed, is that the CRT might predict utilitarian judgments only to the extent that it overlaps with Actively Open Minded Thinking (Baron, Scott, Fincher, & Metz, in press). If this claim is correct, then Actively Open Minded Thinking might be the only genuine and robust individual moderator identified so far as being at work in the two fields.

Mortality salience

Most generally, the dual-process model predicts that any experimental manipulation that encourages or discourages people to mobilize executive resources will translate to higher or lower frequencies of reflective System 2 responses, respectively. Many such manipulations exist, from explicit instructions to reflect, to implicit priming of reflection. We conclude our survey with one such manipulation, mortality salience. The mortality salience manipulation consists of asking participants to write a few lines in response to the following prompt, before the main task of the experiment:

(6) Briefly describe the emotions that the thought of your own death arouse in you. Jot down, as specifically as you can, what you think will happen as you physically die and once you are physically dead.

Terror Management Theory (Greenberg, Pyszczynski, & Solomon, 1986) assumes that such reminders of our inescapable death trigger two waves of cognitive defense mechanisms aimed at protecting us against debilitating anxiety (Burke, Martens, & Faucher, 2010; Pyszczynski, Greenberg, & Solomon, 1999). The first wave is the most interesting for our current purposes. Indeed, Terror Management Theory assumes that immediately after the mortality salience manipulation, participants enter a 5- to 10-minute phase during which their executive resources are mobilized in order to displace thoughts of death outside of conscious attention. Accordingly, this manipulation should decrease the frequency of reflective System 2 responses to both conflict syllogisms and moral dilemmas, at least for a window of 5–10 minutes.

These two predictions were tested and validated in two research articles. In a study of belief bias (Trémolière et al., 2014), participants were assigned either to the mortality salience group or to a control group in which participants wrote a few lines following a slightly different prompt:

(7) Briefly describe the emotions that the thought of extreme pain arouse in you. Jot down, as specifically as you can, what you think will happen as you endure extreme pain and once you have endured extreme pain.

This is a typical control condition for mortality salience studies, whose purpose is to ensure that the effect of mortality salience is not simply due to negative affect. After this initial writing stage, participants solved the syllogisms typical of belief bias research. As predicted by the dual-process model, the frequency of responses based on validity dropped by 13 percentage points for participants in the mortality salience condition, compared to participants in the pain condition.

In another study (Trémolière et al., 2012), participants were similarly assigned to either the mortality salience group or the pain group, and moved on to solving moral dilemmas. Once more, in line with the prediction of the dual-process model, the frequency of utilitarian responses dropped by 23 percentage points in the mortality salience condition. This is a huge drop, compared to the effect of common cognitive interference manipulations – in fact, a second experiment showed the effect of mortality salience to be higher than that of the extreme load manipulation displayed in Figure 32.1.

In sum, the mortality salience manipulation (which was assumed to mobilize executive resources and impair reflective thinking) was shown to decrease the frequency of reflective responses in both the belief bias and the moral domain. The effect sizes observed in these studies suggested that thinking about death was severely impairing reflective thinking. Indeed, a drop of 13 percentage points for belief bias is higher than the usual effect of cognitive interference (commonly about 10 percentage points), and a drop of 23 percentage points for moral dilemmas is unheard of, even under extreme load conditions.

Conclusion

Dual-process models have become a central theoretical framework both for the psychology of reasoning and for the psychology of moral judgment. As a consequence, it has become far easier to make connections between two fields that grew mostly separately for several decades. Most importantly, the two fields now share a common experimental toolbox, inspired by the dual-process model. In particular, both fields rely on manipulations of time pressure and cognitive interference, and both fields investigate broadly the same array of individual moderators. As a result, findings obtained within one field can serve to refine and inspire work in the other field.

Consider for example the case of cognitive interference manipulations. Even though these manipulations can utilize many different protocols, enough studies in the two fields are available to conclude that manipulations which are sufficient to affect belief bias are not powerful enough to affect moral judgment (for example, it takes an especially hard version of the dot-matrix task to affect moral judgment, whereas a standard version is enough to affect belief bias). Based on such results, we can gain an incrementally parametric perspective on the amount of cognitive resources which are required in the two domains.

Consider as another example the case of individual moderators. Whereas a vast number of studies identified the role of cognitive ability in belief bias, the field of moral judgment is still very much in a state of infancy in that respect. Thinking dispositions, on the other hand, have been largely studied in both fields, albeit with a different approach to measurement. Whereas reasoning studies have largely focused on self-reports of thinking dispositions such as Actively Open Minded Thinking, moral studies have focused on performance measures such as the Cognitive Reflection Test. The two fields have much to gain in pooling results and systematically comparing the share of variance explained by these different moderators in their tasks of interest.

Finally, we wish to emphasize that the toolbox is still open and waiting for new tools. Every time a new manipulation is introduced in one of the two fields, it becomes relevant to researchers in the other field. Once more, as we illustrated with the case of the mortality salience manipulation, the two fields have much to gain in monitoring the novel manipulations developed in each other, in order to systematically compare and contrast their effects in the other. The unification of the two fields, once barely conceivable, is now a very reasonable prospect, within the framework of the dual-process model.

References

Ball, L. J., Phillips, P., Wade, C. N., & Quayle, J. D. (2006). Effects of belief and logic on syllogistic reasoning: Eye-movement evidence for selective processing models. *Experimental Psychology, 53*, 77–86.

Baron, J., Scott, S., Fincher, K., & Metz, S. E. (in press). Why does the Cognitive Reflection Test (sometimes) predict utilitarian moral judgment (and other things)? *Journal of Applied Research in Memory and Cognition.*

Bartels, D. M. (2008). Principled moral sentiment and the flexibility of moral judgment and decision making. *Cognition, 108*, 381–417.

Bonnefon, J. F. (2013). New ambitions for a new paradigm: Putting the psychology of reasoning at the service of humanity. *Thinking & Reasoning, 19*, 381–398.

Burke, B. L., Martens, A., & Faucher, E. H. (2010). Two decades of terror management theory: A meta-analysis of mortality salience research. *Personality and Social Psychology Review, 14*, 155–195.

Cacioppo, J. T., & Petty, R. E. (1982). The need for cognition. *Journal of Personality and Social Psychology, 42*, 116–131.

Conway, P., & Gawronski, B. (2013). Deontological and utilitarian inclinations in moral decision making: A process dissociation approach. *Journal of Personality and Social Psychology, 104*, 216–235.

Cummins, D. D., & Cummins, R. C. (2012). Emotion and deliberative reasoning in moral judgment. *Frontiers in Psychology, 3*, 328.

De Neys, W. (2006). Dual processing in reasoning: Two systems but one reasoner. *Psychological Science, 17*, 428–433.

De Neys, W., & Bonnefon, J. F. (2013). The whys and whens of individual differences in thinking biases. *Trends in Cognitive Sciences, 17*, 172–178.

De Neys, W., & Dieussaert, K. (2005). Individual differences in rational thinking time. In K. Forbus, D. Gentner, & T. Regier (Eds.), *Proceedings of the 27th annual conference of the Cognitive Science Society* (pp. 577–582). Mahwah, NJ: Lawrence Erlbaum Associates, Inc.

De Neys, W., & Franssens, S. (2009). Belief inhibition during thinking: Not always winning but at least taking part. *Cognition, 113*, 45–61.

De Neys, W., Vartanian, W., & Goel, V. (2008). Smarter than we think: When our brains detect that we are biased. *Psychological Science, 19*, 483–489.

DeWall, C. N., Baumeister, R. F., & Masicampo, E. J. (2008). Evidence that logical reasoning depends on conscious processing. *Consciousness and Cognition, 17*, 628–645.

Dube, C., Rotello, C. M., & Heit, E. (2010). Assessing the belief bias effect with ROCs: It's a response bias effect. *Psychological Review, 117*, pp. 831–863).

Evans, J. St. B. T. (2008). Dual-processing accounts of reasoning. *Annual Review of Psychology, 59*, 255–278.

Evans, J. St. B. T., Barston, J. L., & Pollard, P. (1983). On the conflict between logic and belief in syllogistic reasoning. *Memory and Cognition, 11*, 295–306.

Evans, J. St. B. T., & Curtis-Holmes, J. (2005). Rapid responding increases belief bias: Evidence for the dual-process theory of reasoning. *Thinking and Reasoning, 11*, 382–389.

Evans, J. St. B. T., & Stanovich, K. E. (2013). Dual-process theories of higher cognition: Advancing the debate. *Perspectives on Psychological Science, 8*, 223–241.

Frederick, S. (2005). Cognitive reflection and decision making. *Journal of Economic Perspectives, 19*, 25–42.

Goel, V. (2007). Anatomy of deductive reasoning. *Trends in Cognitive Sciences, 11*, 435–441.

Goel, V., & Dolan, R. J. (2003). Explaining modulation of reasoning by belief. *Cognition, 87*, B11–B22.

Greenberg, J., Pyszczynski, T., & Solomon, S. (1986). The causes and consequences of a need for self-esteem: A terror management theory. In R. F. Baumeister (Ed.), *Public self and private self* (pp. 189–212). New York: Springer-Verlag.

Greene, J. D. (2007). Why are VMPFC patients more utilitarian? A dual-process theory of moral judgment explains. *Trends in Cognitive Sciences, 17*, 322–323.

Greene, J. D. (2013). *Moral tribes: Emotion, reason, and the gap between us and them*. London: Penguin Press.

Greene, J. D., Morelli, S. A., Lowenberg, K., Nystrom, L. E., & Cohen, J. D. (2008). Cognitive load selectively interferes with utilitarian moral judgment. *Cognition, 107*, 1144–1154.

Greene, J. D., Nystrom, L. E., Engell, A. D., Darley, J. M., & Cohen, J. D. (2004). The neural bases of cognitive conflict and control in moral judgment. *Neuron, 44*, 389–400.

Greene, J. D., Sommerville, R. B., Nystrom, L. E., Darley, J. M., & Cohen, J. D. (2001). An fMRI investigation of emotional engagement in moral judgment. *Science, 293*, 2105–2108.

Haidt, J. (2001). The emotional dog and its rational tail: A social intuitionist approach to moral judgment. *Psychological Review, 108*, 814–834.

Haidt, J. (2007). The new synthesis in moral psychology. *Science, 316*, 998–1002.

Haidt, J. (2012). *The righteous mind: Why good people are divided by politics and religion*. New York: Pantheon.

Handley, S. J., Capon, A., Beveridge, M., Dennis, I., & Evans, J. St. B. T. (2004). Working memory, inhibitory control, and the development of children's reasoning. *Thinking and Reasoning, 10*, 175–195.

Heit, E., & Rotello, C. M. (2014). Traditional difference-score analyses of reasoning are flawed. *Cognition, 131*, 75–91.

Kahan, D. M., Peters, E., Wittlin, M., Slovic, P., Larrimore Ouellette, L., Braman, D., & Mandel, G. (2012). The polarizing impact of science literacy and numeracy on perceived climate change risks. *Nature Climate Change, 2*, 732–735.

Kahneman, D. (2011). *Thinking, fast and slow*. New York: Farrar, Straus; Giroux.

Klauer, K. C., Musch, J., & Naumer, B. (2000). On belief bias in syllogistic reasoning. *Psychological Review, 107*, 852–884.

Koenigs, M., Young, L., Adolphs, R., Tranel, D., Cushman, F., Hauser, M., & Damasio, A. (2007). Damage to the prefrontal cortex increases utilitarian moral judgements. *Nature, 446*, 908–911.

Kokis, J. V., MacPherson, R., Toplak, M. E., West, R. F., & Stanovich, K. E. (2002). Heuristic and analytic processing: Age trends and associations with cognitive ability and cognitive styles. *Journal of Experimental Child Psychology, 83*, 26–52.

Koop, G. J. (2013). An assessment of the temporal dynamics of moral decisions. *Judgment and Decision Making, 8*, 527–539.

MacPherson, R., & Stanovich, K. E. (2007). Cognitive ability, thinking dispositions, and instructional set as predictors of critical thinking. *Learning and Individual Differences, 17*, 115–127.

McGuire, J., Langdon, R., Coltheart, M., & Mackenzie, C. (2009). A reanalysis of the personal/impersonal distinction in moral psychology research. *Journal of Experimental Social Psychology, 45*, 577–580.

Miyake, A., Friedman, N. P., Rettinger, D. A., Shah, P., & Hegarty, M. (2001). How are visuospatial working memory, executive functioning, and spatial abilities related? A latent-variable analysis. *Journal of Experimental Psychology: General, 130*, 621–640.

Moore, A. B., Clark, B. A., & Kane, M. J. (2008). Who shalt not kill? Individual differences in working memory capacity, executive control, and moral judgment. *Psychgological Science, 19*, 549–557.

Newstead, S. E., Handley, S. J., Harley, C., Wright, H., & Farelly, D. (2004). Individual differences in deductive reasoning. *Quarterly Journal of Experimental Psychology, 57A*, 33–60.

Paccini, R., & Epstein, S. (1999). The relation of rational and experiential information processing styles to personality, basic beliefs, and the ratio-bias phenomenon. *Journal of Personality and Social Psychology, 76*, 972–987.

Paxton, J. M., Bruni, T., & Greene, J. D. (2014). Are counter-intuitive deontological judgments really counter-intuitive? An empirical reply to Kahane et al. (2012). *Social, Cognitive, and Affective Neuroscience, 9*, 1368–1371.

Paxton, J. M., & Greene, J. D. (2010). Moral reasoning: Hints and allegations. *Topics in Cognitive Science, 2*, 511–527.

Paxton, J. M., Ungar, L., & Greene, J. D. (2012). Reflection and reasoning in moral judgment. *Cognitive Science, 36*, 163–177.

Pyszczynski, T., Greenberg, J., & Solomon, S. (1999). A dual-process model of defense against conscious and unconscious death-related thoughts: An extension of terror management theory. *Psychological Review, 106*, 835–845.
Rotello, C. M., & Heit, E. (in press). The neural correlates of belief bias: activation in inferior frontal cortex reflects response rate differences. *Frontiers in Human Neuroscience.*
Royzman, E. B., Landy, J. F., & Leeman, R. F. (in press). Are thoughtful people more utilitarian? CRT as a unique predictor of moral minimalism in the dilemmatic context. *Cognitive Science.*
Sa, W. C., West, R. F., & Stanovich, K. E. (1999). The domain specificity and generality of belief bias: Searching for a generalizable critical thinking skill. *Journal of Educational Psychology, 91*, 497–510.
Shenhav, A., & Greene, J. D. (2014). Integrative moral judgment: Dissociating the roles of the amygdala and the ventromedial prefrontal cortex. *Journal of Neuroscience, 34*, 4741–4749.
Sloman, S. A. (1996). The empirical case for two systems of reasoning. *Psychological Bulletin, 119*, 3–22.
Stanovich, K. E., & West, R. F. (1997). Reasoning independently of prior belief and individual differences in actively open-minded thinking. *Journal of Educational Psychology, 89*, 342–357.
Stanovich, K. E., & West, R. F. (1998). Individual differences in rational thought. *Journal of Experimental Psychology: General, 127*, 161–188.
Stupple, E. J., & Ball, L. J. (2008). Belief–logic conflict resolution in syllogistic reasoning: Inspection-time evidence for a parallel-process model. *Thinking & Reasoning, 14*, 168–181.
Suter, R., & Hertwig, R. (2011). Time and moral judgment. *Cognition, 119*, 454–458.
Svedholm-Häkkinen, A. M. (2015). Highly reflective reasoners show no signs of belief inhibition. *Acta Psychologica, 154*, 69–76.
Thomas, B. C., Croft, K. E., & Tranel, D. (2011). Harming kin to save strangers: Further evidence for abnormally utilitarian moral judgments after ventromedial prefrontal damage. *Journal of Cognitive Neuroscience, 23*, 2186–2196.
Thompson, V. A., & Evans, J. St. B. T. (2012). Belief bias in informal reasoning. *Thinking and Reasoning, 18*, 278–310.
Trémolière, B., & Bonnefon, J. F. (2014). Efficient kill-save ratios ease up the cognitive demands on counterintuitive moral utilitarianism. *Personality and Social Psychology Bulletin, 40*, 333–351.
Trémolière, B., De Neys, W., & Bonnefon, J. F. (2012). Mortality salience and morality: Thinking about death makes people less utilitarian. *Cognition, 124*, 379–384.
Trémolière, B., De Neys, W., & Bonnefon, J. F. (2014). The grim reasoner: Analytical reasoning under mortality salience. *Thinking & Reasoning, 20*, 333–351.
Trippas, D., Handley, S. J., & Verde, M. F. (2013). The SDT model of belief bias: Complexity, time, and cognitive ability mediate the effects of believability. *Journal of Experimental Psychology. Learning, Memory, & Cognition, 39,* 1393–1402.
Trippas, D., Handley, S. J., & Verde, M. (2014). Fluency and belief bias in deductive reasoning: New indices for old effects. *Frontiers in Psychology, 5*, 631.
Trippas, D., Verde, M., & Handley, S. J. (2014). Using forced choice to test belief bias in syllogistic reasoning. *Cognition, 133*, 586–600.
Tsujii, T., Masuda, S., Akiyama, T., & Watanabe, S. (2010). The role of inferior frontal cortex in belief-bias reasoning: an rTMS study. *Neuropsychologia, 48*, 2005–2008.
Tsujii, T., Okada, M., & Watanabe, S. (2010). Effects of aging on hemispheric asymmetry in inferior frontal cortex activity during belief-bias syllogistic reasoning: A near-infrared spectroscopy study. *Behavioural Brain Research, 210*, 178–183.
Tsujii, T., & Watanabe, S. (2009). Neural correlates of dual-task effect on belief-bias syllogistic reasoning: A near-infrared spectroscopy study. *Brain Research, 1287*, 118–125.
Tsujii, T., & Watanabe, S. (2010). Neural correlates of belief-bias reasoning under time pressure: A near-infrared spectroscopy study. *Neuroimage, 50*, 1320–1326.
West, R. F., Toplak, M. E., & Stanovich, K. E. (2008). Heuristic and biases as measures of critical thinking: Associations with cognitive ability and thinking dispositions. *Journal of Educational Psychology, 100*, 930–941.

33

CONTEMPORARY PERSPECTIVES ON MATHEMATICAL THINKING AND LEARNING

Keith Weber and Kevin C. Moore

1. Introduction

One aspect of mathematics that distinguishes it from other scientific disciplines is its emphasis on iterative processes of abstraction. In mathematics, the objects under study are not physical objects but rather ideal versions of those objects that are understood and defined in terms of relationships between the elements of those objects. New mathematical objects and structures such as groups and rings stem from abstracting commonalities across families of previously abstracted objects and structures. Abstraction is such a central facet of mathematical thinking and reasoning that domains of mathematics (e.g., algebra and geometry) are characterized by progressions toward arguments entirely comprising legal manipulations of syntactic sentences. The validity of an argument is defined independent of the content of the argument, but as consisting of the application of inferences that are judged to be truth preserving based upon their abstract form.

Much of the research on mathematical thinking, reasoning, and learning has concerned how students and mathematicians cope with this abstraction – the meanings individuals develop for abstract mathematical concepts, as well as how individuals use abstract concepts to draw inferences and solve problems. This chapter describes recent developments in mathematical thinking and reasoning through three theoretical frames of abstraction: mathematical reasoning as logical reasoning; mathematical reasoning as commonalities of effective expert reasoning across mathematical situations; and mathematical reasoning as experienced by learners of mathematics.

2. Mathematical reasoning as formal reasoning

In modern mathematics, it is common to distinguish between a *formal mathematical structure* and the *interpretation* or *application* of that structure. Formal structures are "specialized representational forms that use heavily regulated notational systems with no inherent meaning except those that are established by convention to convey concepts and relations with a high degree of specificity" (Nathan, 2012, p. 125). As we will explain, the expectation in both classrooms and mathematical practice is that the products of mathematical reasoning (e.g., solutions to word problems or proofs) are written using the language of a formal structure. This observation has historically led psychologists and educators to view the essence of mathematical reasoning to occur within formal systems and thus to give preference to formal systems in mathematical instruction. This occurred most blatantly with the widely discredited "New Math" curriculum from the 1960s (e.g., Kline, 1973), which expected students to reason and write using the language of set theory, a foundational branch of mathematics, even though many mathematicians at the time "decried the empty abstraction and rigid formalism" (Wu, 1997, p. 946). In the remainder of this section, we illustrate how this view, to a lesser extent, still shapes the domains of high school algebra and proof; we then show how recent empirical research demonstrates that these practices are based on a distorted view of mathematical reasoning and development.

2.1 Formalism in high school algebra

A predominant approach to the teaching of high school algebra within the United States foregrounds solving algebraic equations. This often occurs in a formal structure where expressions and equations can be altered by the application of highly specified truth- or solution-preserving rules, such as factoring a quadratic expression. Algebra is also taught as a tool that can be used to predict and explain real-world and scientific phenomena (e.g., how long it will take a specific object dropped from a certain height to hit the ground). Researchers have identified a normative aspect of this instruction. With respect to written curriculum, textbooks initially present concepts within the formal structure of algebra and then present applications of these concepts or structures to situations with story problems (Nathan, Long, & Alibali, 2002). Reflecting these textbook approaches, teachers introduce students to concepts within the formal structure of algebra and then expect students to solve story problems by translating these problems into the formal language of algebra and using specified rules (e.g., Gerofsky, 1996). In some cases, if students used reasoning to find a correct solution that avoided the formal language of algebra, teachers would not award full credit for their answer and this practice would be discouraged (Gerofsky, 1996).

These practices reflect the pedagogical principle that Nathan (2012) called *Formalism First*, where "the teaching and mastery of formalism are often considered prerequisites to applied problems" (p. 125). Both high school mathematics teachers and mathematics education researchers appear to hold this view. Nathan and Koedinger (2000a) presented 67 teachers and 35 mathematics education researchers with algebraic equations and corresponding story problems. Participants were asked which would be easiest to solve for a student who completed a first-year algebra course. The large majority of both teachers and researchers chose the algebraic equations. However, numerous studies have found that students actually perform better on story problems (e.g., Koedinger, Alibali, & Nathan, 2008). One reason for this is that story problems allow students to use what Nathan and Koedinger (2000b) refer to as an "unwinding strategy", where they walk through the problem in reverse using arithmetic, thereby bypassing the need to use algebra. It is tempting to dismiss the use of these strategies as mathematical naiveté; however, such a presumption is challenged by the fact that superior performance on story problems occurred with high-performing university students (Koedinger et al., 2008).

In recent years, some educators have developed approaches that do not follow the Formalism First principle. Reform-oriented textbooks such as *Connected Mathematics* (Lappan et al., 2004) frequently present students with an investigation before introducing formal notation and rules for manipulation. Chazan, Sela, and Herbst (2012) conducted a study with a focus group of algebra teachers and found that some were receptive to non-algebraic solutions to algebra story problems and would grant such solutions full credit. Nonetheless, Sherman, Walkington, and Howell (2016) found that recently published conventional textbooks (which make up the majority of the market in the United States) continue to follow the Formalism First principle.

2.2 Proof and logic

The teaching of proof also frequently reflects a Formalism First principle. In the United States, an approach to geometry includes proofs in a two-column format where the left column consists of statements and the right column consists of justifications for why these statements can be made (see Herbst, 2002). These justifications specify either why the statement can be assumed (e.g., it is an axiom, assumption, or definition) or what rule of inference was used to deduce it. The importance and interest in the theorems and proofs is sometimes secondary; emphasizing the Formalism First principle, students are primarily asked to engage in this activity to demonstrate their capacity for this mode of logical reasoning and structure (Herbst & Brach, 2006). At the university level, there are typically "transition-to-proof" courses that students take before proceeding to upper-level proof-oriented mathematics courses. These are based on the stance that students need explicit training in logic before learning about conceptually rich material (e.g., Epp, 2003). Hence, the content of these courses is deliberately shallow under the assumption that this will enable students to concentrate on understanding formal mathematical notation and learning abstract permissible logical actions deemed necessary for subsequent courses. In such courses, and with respect to logic, students are typically required to memorize "truth tables", which show the truth-value of propositional statements with conjunctions when the truth-values of propositions p and q are given (Table 33.1).

Epp (2003) justified this practice because it "does help some students organize their knowledge about abstract logical principles and gives them concrete objects to hang onto while they deal with the abstraction of the logic" (p. 896), while also advocating that truth tables be used as a tool to check the validity of some arguments. In interviews with mathematics professors, and echoing Epp, Alcock (2010) and Weber (2004) found that these professors valued conceptual understanding in advanced mathematics, but questioned if conceptual understanding can be achieved if one does not first grasp the notation and rules of logic.

Given the prevalence of the Formalism First principle underlying teaching practices, some researchers have asked: does this view of logic accurately describe how mathematicians reason or, at least, does it describe some component of their mathematical reasoning? We present two recent strands of research that indicate this is not the case. First, Inglis and Simpson (2004) presented 123 history undergraduates, 260 mathematics undergraduates, and 21 mathematics faculty members with the Wason (1968) card selection task.[1] Although the math students and faculty performed significantly better on the task than the history students, the majority of both groups failed to correctly complete the task. As mathematics faculty are presumably experts at doing mathematics, their uneven performance on the Wason task calls to question the assumption that an ability to apply abstract logic to a decontextualized situation is necessary to do advanced mathematics. In further studies, Inglis and his colleagues have found that the ability to apply modus tollens (i.e., if given that "p implies q" and "not q", inferring "not p") does not appear to correlate with mathematical ability or training (e.g., Attridge & Inglis, 2013; Alcock, Bailey, Inglis, & Docherty, 2014).

Table 33.1 Truth-value table

p	*q*	*p and q*	*p or q*	*p implies q*
T	T	T	T	T
T	F	F	T	F
F	T	F	T	T
F	F	F	F	T

Second, some mathematicians claim that they often do not consider formal logic when reading and checking the correctness of mathematical arguments. For instance, Thurston (1994), a mathematician, wrote, "[mathematicians] are not good at checking *formal correctness* of proofs, but they are quite good at detecting weaknesses or potential flaws in proofs" (p. 169, emphasis in the original). Based on interviews with nine mathematicians (Weber & Mejia-Ramos, 2011) and a survey of 118 mathematicians, Mejia-Ramos and Weber (2014) found that the majority of mathematicians agreed that they did not check every line of a proof for correctness if they could understand the main idea of the proof and believed this main idea is correct. Clearly if mathematicians omit reading the logical details of a proof when checking it for correctness, their basis for accepting proofs goes beyond the decontextualized application of logic.

2.3 Summary

Although much of mathematics instruction reflects the Formalism First principle (Nathan, 2012), we have outlined several problems with this approach. First, mathematical reasoning generally does not mirror formal structures. Second, students and mathematicians use context-dependent strategies that bypass the formal structures that instruction often foregrounds as tools of reasoning. A third problem not described above is that many students come to view mathematics as an arbitrary set of rules that one applies to receive credit (see Schoenfeld, 1988, and Herbst & Brach, 2006, for consequences of this student viewpoint). Although experts may reach the point where they can reason about concepts at an abstract level within a formal symbol system, Pirie and Kieren (1994) argued that true expertise involves the ability to unpack the meaning of the symbols within that system. We discuss perspectives that take into account how students may come to understand concepts in this way in our section on Learner Models of Mathematical Reasoning.

3. Expert models of mathematical reasoning

In this section, we describe research that has examined the way that mathematicians solve problems and complete mathematical tasks. Schoenfeld (1992) published an exemplary review of research on experts' mathematical thinking that we will not cover in depth here. Rather, we will synthesize Schoenfeld's (1992) perspective and then report more recent developments in this area.

Broadly speaking, we can distinguish between mathematical content knowledge (i.e., what an individual knows and how the individual knows it) and the application of content knowledge. Adopting this distinction, mathematics educators have shown that content knowledge is not enough to solve mathematical problems. For instance, across two studies, eight undergraduate students attempted to prove statements in the domain of abstract algebra. A post-test found that there were collectively 25 instances where a student was aware of the facts needed to prove the statement and could write the proofs when told which facts to use. Nonetheless, a student produced a successful proof only in eight of those 25 instances when they were not prompted on which facts to apply. In contrast, eight mathematicians in these studies were successful in 96% of their proof attempts (Weber, 2001; Weber & Alcock, 2004). This is consistent with other studies that have found students fail to solve problems despite seemingly having the content knowledge to do so (Schoenfeld, 1985; Selden, Selden, Mason, & Hauk, 2000).

The critical question emerging from the aforementioned findings is: why can experts like mathematicians marshal their content knowledge to solve these problems when students cannot? Schoenfeld (1992) highlighted three reasons for this difference. Mathematicians have an arsenal of *heuristics* that they can use to make headway on problems when they do not know how to proceed. Mathematicians have productive *beliefs* that encourage them to take useful actions in problem solving while novices often have unproductive beliefs that dissuade them from taking productive actions. For instance, the belief that mathematical problems can all be solved by implementing a procedure will discourage a student from developing their own novel ways of approaching the task or persisting on a task when a procedure is not readily available. Mathematicians *monitor* their problem solving process, making sure to understand a problem, develop a plan before engaging in calculations, and monitor their progress once they begin implementing their plan. In the remainder of this section, we discuss recent developments in mathematical reasoning within these areas.

3.1 The heuristic of generating examples

An important heuristic that mathematicians use to reason about mathematical concepts is to consider specific examples of those concepts (e.g., Schoenfeld, 1985). For instance, a mathematician investigating a claim about *all* odd numbers might look at how that claim applies to a *particular* odd number. In recent years, mathematics educators have investigated how and why the consideration of specific or simple examples can facilitate mathematical reasoning.

Most studies in this area involve fine-grained analyses of students or mathematicians using examples to complete some task. For instance, Lockwood, Ellis, and Lynch (2016) videotaped six mathematicians as they attempted to prove or disprove three challenging conjectures; the research team later asked them to reflect on their actions. Lockwood et al. found that mathematicians noticed patterns by considering multiple examples, thus enabling them to identify properties that might be useful in proving or disproving the conjectures. Further, the mathematicians sometimes used a *generic example* to see why a claim is true. That is, they would ground their understanding of some claim with a specific example. They would verify why the conjecture was true by manipulating that specific example with an eye toward generalizing to the more general conjecture. Other researchers have used a similar methodology to describe similar benefits of example usage (e.g., Alcock & Weber, 2010; Sandefur, Mason, Stylianides, & Watson, 2013).

Based on this research, numerous mathematics educators have recommended that example usage play an important role in students' mathematical learning (see Weber, Housman, & Porter, 2008, for a summary of such suggestions). However, there are few studies assessing the efficacy of these suggestions. Those studies that do exist have failed to produce the gains in performance that were promised by the proponents of examples (e.g., Iannone et al., 2011). One account of this is that students may use different processes than mathematicians to generate or reason about examples, thus restricting students' capacities to use and generalize from relevant examples. For instance, when Antonini (2006) asked mathematicians to generate examples that satisfied specific mathematical situations, the mathematicians often used strategies such as deducing properties that the example would need to satisfy before generating it. In contrast, Iannone et al. (2011) found that undergraduate students predominantly used a less sophisticated trial-and-error strategy on similar tasks. A second account is that choosing examples is highly dependent upon mathematical content being studied (e.g., Weber, 2008) and students' mathematical understandings might not be sophisticated enough to choose useful examples.

3.2 The use of written diagrams

Another heuristic that mathematicians use is drawing a diagram (e.g., Samkoff, Lai, & Weber, 2012). The rationale for using diagrams is that visual representations of concepts can make some properties of a concept more salient than they would be with a verbal-symbolic representation of the same concept (e.g., Larkin & Simon, 1987). Some mathematics educators have gone so far to claim using diagrams is essential to doing mathematics (e.g., Zazkis, Dubinsky, & Dautermann, 1996). Recent research on diagrams in mathematics education is similar to that on examples in that researchers typically examine cases in which students and mathematicians use diagrams successfully to examine the affordances that diagrams provide. As a representative study, Stylianou (2002) audiotaped mathematicians while they were completing five challenging problems designed to elicit the use of diagrams. Stylianou found that mathematicians used diagrams for identifying consequences of the givens in the problem, exploring the problem space, choosing sub-goals, and checking the correctness of their work (see also Gibson, 1998, Samkoff et al., 2012).

In the 1990s, a number of researchers contended that students' reluctance to use diagrams in their mathematical reasoning resulted in impoverished problem-solving abilities and understanding (e.g., Dreyfus, 1991; Eisenberg, 1994; Healy & Hoyles, 1996). However, in summarizing several large-scale studies on students' propensity for drawing diagrams, Presmeg (2006) found little evidence that students were reluctant to use diagrams to solve mathematical problems. Further, students' propensity to employ diagrams had little correlation with their mathematical achievement. Based on extensive interviews with 70 mathematicians, Burton (2004) found that while the majority of mathematicians evinced a preference for using diagrams in their research, there were also some mathematicians who rarely employed diagrams in their mathematical work, providing evidence that using drawn diagrams is not necessary for doing mathematics (see also Alcock & Simpson, 2005).

We have three hypotheses for why a propensity to use diagrams does not correlate with mathematical achievement, despite some claiming that visual reasoning with written diagrams is necessary for doing mathematics. First, while visual representations make some properties of objects salient to mathematicians, they might not be salient to students. That is, students might not have the background or understandings necessary to spontaneously "see" what is perceived by mathematicians. Samkoff, Lai, & Weber, Indeed, Samkoff, Lai, and Weber (2012) found that when eight mathematicians were asked to prove a statement in real analysis, they all immediately convinced themselves that the statement was true by drawing a diagram. However, only four were able to successfully translate the insights from the diagram into a completely correct proof. If using diagrams presents difficulties for trained mathematicians, then using diagrams can also present daunting challenges for students. Third, it is possible that mathematical expertise is not defined by fluency with all common representation systems, but rather a high level of skill with a small number of representation systems (which may or may not include diagrams). Or, in some cases, mathematical expertise might correspond to the internalization of drawn diagrams to the extent that an individual is able to mentally recall or anticipate diagrams without carrying out the physical drawing of the diagrams.

3.3 Metacognition, monitoring, and control

Schoenfeld (1985) observed that mathematicians showed greater control of their problem-solving efforts than did undergraduate students. Mathematicians spent substantial time understanding a problem and choosing a plan. Once they implemented a plan, they periodically evaluated their progress to judge if their solution was proceeding productively or if they needed to develop a new plan. In contrast, undergraduate students were likely to engage in computations shortly after reading the problem statement and to stick with their initial plan no matter what difficulties they encountered. Based on observations of 12 mathematicians solving challenging problems, Carlson and Bloom (2005) corroborated and built upon Schoenfeld's findings. The authors illustrated how mathematicians engage in a three-phase iterative cycle solving problems in which they proposed a solution path, imagined playing it out, and evaluated if the plan was worthwhile. This cycle continued until a plausible plan was chosen. It was then implemented and mathematicians re-evaluated their understanding of the problem, choosing another plan if need be.

3.4 Homogeneity of mathematical reasoning across mathematicians and context

There are two assumptions about mathematicians' reasoning that are implicit in the line of research we discuss above. The first is that there are strong commonalities in the ways that mathematicians approach mathematical tasks (see Schoenfeld, 1985). However, empirical investigations into mathematical practice have found deep divisions in how mathematicians practice their craft (e.g., Burton, 2004; Inglis & Aberdein, in press; Weber, Inglis, & Alcock, 2014). Notably, deFranco (1996) gave problem-solving tasks to mathematicians and found that many did not exhibit the problem-solving behaviors that Schoenfeld's (1985) model predicted. This challenges the notion that there might be one expert model for solving problems or doing mathematics.

A second assumption is that there are strong commonalities in mathematical reasoning across content domains. The fact that this chapter focuses on *mathematical thinking* rather than, say, algebraic thinking or geometric thinking is only meaningful if we accept this assumption. On the one hand, there is reason to question this assumption. Consider the strategy of drawing a diagram to solve a problem. The way that diagrams are used in Euclidean geometry, calculus, graph theory, and commutative algebra differ substantially. Additionally, how a student understands a drawn diagram is different than how a mathematician might understand a drawn diagram. On the other hand, these types of strategies are sufficiently general to mathematicians that they recognize "drawing diagrams" as a meaningful category of mathematicians' strategies. This raises the question of how an abstract strategy becomes a meaningful tool for mathematical reasoning for an individual. We raise perspectives that address this tension between supposed abstract strategies and related tools of mathematical reasoning in the next section.

4. Learner models of mathematical reasoning

In the two previous sections, we described research traditions in which researchers operate (either tacitly or expressed) under the following assumptions:

- There are objectively correct or normatively accepted solutions to mathematical problems.
- A researcher can identify normative models for what constitutes or qualifies as mathematical reasoning. Section 2 does so by adherence to the rules of formalism; Section 3 posits that there are expert models of mathematical problem solving.
- A researcher can analyze novices' mathematical behavior by seeing the ways in which they deviate from these normative, formalistic, or expert models and improve their performance by teaching them to behave in accordance with these models.

In this section, we describe contemporary lines of research in mathematics education that have approached students' mathematical reasoning as *internally viable and rational to the students* (cf., correct or normative to the researchers). Adopting such an approach to mathematical reasoning has enabled researchers to be sensitive to the mathematical realities of students (or teachers), and thus characterize hypothetical, developmental shifts in students' mathematical realities – what we call *learner models of mathematical reasoning*.

4.1 Piagetian constructivism

A prominent approach to developing learner models of mathematical reasoning has stemmed from researchers' interpretations of Piaget's work (e.g., Piaget, 2001). Compatible with aforementioned perspectives that describe mathematical reasoning in terms of common abstract structures (whether logical, strategic, or metacognitive), researchers have traditionally described Piaget as characterizing and applying hypothetical-deductive genetic structures, clearly delineated stages of knowing, or distinctions of concrete and abstract knowledge. Within mathematics education, however, researchers transitioned from interpreting Piaget (and his colleagues) as applying *a priori* structures to his work with children to interpreting Piaget as having constructed emergent models and structures through his attempts to explain his experiences and constraints with children (Steffe & Kieren, 1994; Thompson, 2013; von Glasersfeld, 1995). This represented a critical shift for mathematics educators: instead of trying to "fit" student behaviors into existing or expert models, contemporary constructivists in mathematics education aim to develop models of students' mathematical thinking in its own terms.

Researchers interested in developing Piagetian models of mathematical reasoning have predominantly employed teaching/design experiments (Cobb, Confrey, diSessa, Lehrer, & Schauble, 2003; Steffe & Thompson, 2000b). Teaching experiments involve researchers working with individual or small groups of students across many teaching sessions in order to develop and test hypothesized models of student thinking, including shifts in thinking. This method is accompanied by fine-grained conceptual analyses (von Glasersfeld, 1995) in which researchers attempt to develop predictive models of student thinking that viably explain the researchers' interpretations of students' actions and utterances.

The most prominent strand of research in this area is captured by von Glasersfeld, Steffe, and colleagues' investigations into children's understandings of number (e.g., Steffe, von Glasersfeld, Richards, & Cobb, 1983). Notably, these researchers developed a research program around the question: how do children *construct* number? An important distinction in children's construction of number is that between *figurative* and *operative* schemes. A figurative scheme entails a child possibly operating without perceptual material directly available, but the child's activity requires him to re-present perceptual material. An operative scheme, however, entails unitized records of activity in which a child does not have to re-present perceptual material. To illustrate in the context of counting, consider a child determining the total number of objects created by adding four objects to a now covered collection of a stated "10" objects. A child constrained to figurative counting schemes might imagine dots in an array or use finger taps to count the hidden 10 (e.g., "One, two, three . . .") and then four more while pointing to each of the four during his count, obtaining 14. As evidence of an operative counting scheme, a child might instead *count on* from 10 (e.g., "Ten, then eleven, twelve, thirteen, fourteen . . ."), suggesting that he conceives the symbol "10" as a unitized record of counting.

It is worth contrasting this characterization of reasoning with that of trying to compare students' reasoning to expert performance. Researchers in the tradition described in Section 3 might note that the student who counts beginning at one is using an inefficient strategy and that "expert adders" use the "count-on" strategy when one addend is fairly large. A proposed remedy might be to help the child develop *strategies* (possibly entirely symbolic in nature) for addition. An alternative account might be to have students engage in metacognitive behaviors such as planning when choosing an approach. The account in this section differs in that it posits that the child's reasoning is "inefficient" only from an expert perspective. Given the child's ways of operating, the child is indeed doing what is (possibly most) efficient and sensible.

Researchers have subsequently developed a system of hypothesized schemes to model children's fractional and multiplicative knowing (e.g., Hackenberg, 2010). Most notable, researchers have characterized the *levels of units* (Steffe & Olive, 2010) a child can operate on and coordinate simultaneously via these operations. To illustrate, consider the situation of determining what fractional amount a stick of eight units is of a stick of 16 units. In coming to answer "one-half", a child might conceive disembedding one unit of eight units (a component unit) from the 16-unit stick (the composite unit), which itself contains two component units each containing eight units. Such activity is consistent with coordinating *three levels of units*: the composite unit (16-unit stick) containing two component units (eight-unit sticks), each of which contains eight units (the basis unit for the measures of eight and 16) (Figure 33.1).

A related interpretation and use of Piagetian constructivism has involved researchers clarifying how students reason about quantities whose values vary in tandem – termed *covariational reasoning* (Carlson, Jacobs, Coe, Larsen, & Hsu, 2002; Saldanha & Thompson, 1998). Many researchers have investigated students' covariational reasoning as it relates to their knowing and learning of function. Generally, researchers have illustrated that students' propensity and capacity to engage in covariational reasoning is critical to their developing understandings of function not constrained to thinking about functions as rules for computing values (Oehrtman, Carlson, & Thompson, 2008). As an example, several researchers (e.g., Ellis, Özgür, Kulow, Williams, & Amidon, 2015) have explained how students conceptualizing and coordinating quantities changing in tandem relates to their constructing sophisticated conceptions of exponential functions. Ellis et al. (2015) illustrated that how a student imagines change (e.g., change occurring in discrete chunks versus change occurring in a smooth, continuous nature; see Castillo-Garsow, Johnson, & Moore, 2013) influences how they conceptualize exponential functions entailing multiplicative change.

Whereas the line of research discussed above entails researchers investigating covariational reasoning in relation to function and function classes, other researchers have investigated students' covariational reasoning *qua* covariational reasoning. Thompson and Thompson (1996) and Johnson (2015) clarified students' quantification of covarying quantities as related to their development of rate of change meanings. These authors convincingly illustrated that students' difficulties in constructing rate of change as a *measure* of quantities' covariation stems from the students' images of variation and covariation not affording such a construction. Other researchers investigating students' covariational reasoning *qua* covariational reasoning have done so in

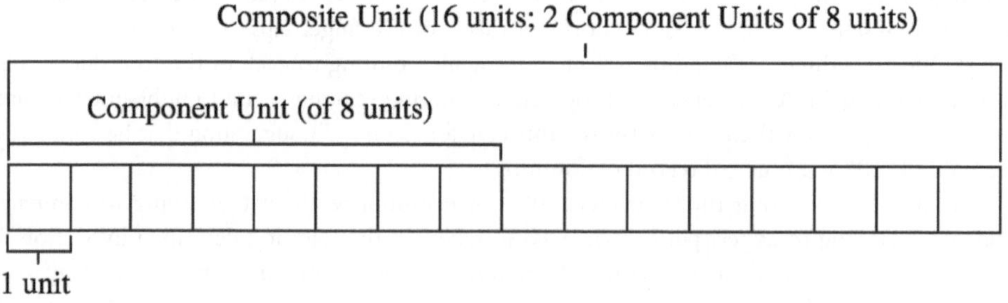

Figure 33.1 Coordinating three levels of units, with one component unit being one-half the composite unit

the context of students' cognitive coupling of two quantities that change in tandem and representing this coupling in multiple graphical systems (e.g., Moore, Paoletti, & Musgrave, 2013). Working with high-performing calculus students, Carlson et al. (2002) illustrated that students' capacity to reason about and coordinate *amounts of change* in one quantity with *amounts of change* in another quantity (e.g., the amount of increase in x decreases for successive, equal increases in y) affected their abilities to reason about the curvature of graphs in productive ways for modeling dynamic, contextual situations. Collectively, Thompson and Carlson (2017) have illustrated that covariational reasoning is a foundation for productive mathematical understandings, but that such reasoning is often (and problematically) absent as an explicit goal of mathematics instruction and curriculum.

4.2 Actor-oriented transfer

Whereas the referenced learner models in the previous section entail localized, fine-grained characterizations of students' actions, other mathematics education researchers have been more interested in exploring how students *transfer* their initial, localized learning experiences to future situations. Like interpretations of Piaget's work, transfer perspectives have a rich history of evolution and difference, a difference that remains today: "there is little agreement in the scholarly community about the nature of transfer, the extent to which it occurs, and the nature of its underlying mechanisms" (Barnett & Ceci, 2002, p. 612).

Reflecting the emergence of Piagetian constructivism in mathematics education, researchers have recently transitioned away from traditional transfer perspectives that privilege the perspective of the observer in characterizing *what* transfers or *if* transfer occurs (for a summary, see Lobato, 2012). Lobato (2012) proposed the *actor-oriented* transfer perspective to differentiate an observer's perspective from that of a student's perspective in an attempt to explain *students'* experiences of transfer. Related to the work in the area of covariational reasoning described above, Lobato, Ellis, and Munoz (2003) used the actor-oriented transfer perspective in the context of students' reasoning about linear functions and associated topics (e.g., ratio, rate, and slope). A normative or "expert" understanding of linear functions that entails covariational reasoning involves reasoning that the change in one quantity, Δy, is proportional to the change in the other quantity, Δx, yielding $\Delta y = m \cdot \Delta x$. Here, m is often described as the slope of the line produced in the Cartesian coordinate system by graphing the relationship between the variable values y and x. In the authors' study, and despite a teacher's efforts to develop slope as a measure or *ratio* between covarying quantities (e.g., Δy compared multiplicatively to Δx), students transferred slope as a *difference* occurring as one moves down values arranged in the y column of a table. Such reasoning can yield apparently correct inferences, but this is only because the independent value in the table (usually the x-column) is typically presented as a column of consecutive integers. In such a well-ordered table, the differences in the column of the dependent variable (usually the y-column) will be constant, thus enabling students to draw inferences of slope without making explicit multiplicative comparisons between Δx and Δy. This leaves implicit the mathematical invariant relationship between the two variable values and their changes. In a subsequent study, Lobato, Rhodehamel, and Hohensee (2012) further illustrated that students often transfer slope meanings (e.g., slope as visual slant-ness versus slope as a measure or ratio) in ways inconsistent with normative or "expert" understandings of linear functions and their representations.

Lobato's work illustrates the usefulness of the actor-oriented transfer perspective for approaching students' reasoning as an internally rational system in two important ways. First, researchers operating under the assumptions of traditional transfer perspectives, or those assumptions entailed in prior sections, would likely characterize many of the described students as not successfully (or correctly) transferring knowledge. From the actor-oriented perspective, however, Lobato and colleagues were able to characterize all students as transferring *something*: classes generalized and recognized elements of *the students'* experiences despite these elements not necessarily being desired or privileged by mathematics educators, teachers, or researchers. Second, the actor-oriented transfer perspective enabled Lobato and colleagues to avoid defining tasks independently of a student's engagement in the task. Although some researchers adopting more traditional transfer perspectives have claimed to problematize the relationships between an external environment or task characterizations and the mind (see Anderson, Reder, & Simon, 2000; Gentner & Markman, 1997), in practice, transfer researchers traditionally play what Lave (1988) called a "laboratory game in which the task becomes to get the subject to match the experimenter's expectations" (p. 20).

As another example of the usefulness of the actor-oriented transfer perspective, Wagner (2006) characterized transfer in students' reasoning about the law of large numbers in elementary statistics. In carefully studying the progression of a single student's understanding of the law of large numbers, he found that she did not learn by abstracting a general principle and then applying it to new situations. Rather, Wagner found the student's growth to be gradual as she slowly expanded her read-out strategies for comparing new problems to prototypical problems involving the law of large numbers. It was only after this student had broad read-out strategies that she was able to articulate the general principle of the law of large numbers. A key point here is that for the student in Wagner's study, the abstraction of a general principle was the *result* of the student expanding the scope of situations that were, from her perspective, similar to paradigm cases of the law of large numbers. Also, Wagner emphasized that this result was not a context-free structure, but instead a knowledge structure sensitive to contextual differences. Wagner's description of abstraction and transfer as a subjective, emergent, and context-sensitive process challenges traditional claims that transfer occurs as a process of abstraction and then application.[2] For instance, Nokes (2009) described transfer in terms of "how knowledge acquired from one task or situation can be *applied* to a different one" (p. 2, emphasis added). Wagner's findings also challenge traditional transfer perspectives that tend to describe knowledge in terms of increasing levels of abstractness in which knowledge is separated from or "deletes" concrete experiences and contextual details that are deemed "irrelevant" by the investigator (see Singley & Anderson, 1989).

5. Other examples and evolving elaborations

Above are just two perspectives on learner models of mathematical reasoning and learning, and we cannot do justice to the number of perspectives or the nuanced range of positions existing within these perspectives. As with other examples, Izsák (2004) reported on a series of studies in which he investigated students' knowledge structures as they attempted to use algebra to model the physical situation of a winch. Differing from Piagetian constructivism, Izsák characterized students' activities in terms of their use of *external* and *internal representations*. In doing so, he described how students' criteria for external representations (e.g., their judgments of algebraic expressions) influence their problem-solving activity, artifact use, and development of knowledge structures. As another contribution to learner models, Ellis (2011) combined an interpretation of Piagetian constructivist perspectives with situated accounts of students' transfer and generalizations in order to clarify how classroom environments influence students' generalization processes and their construction of functional relationships.

Due to its novelty and possible interest to numerous fields, we note that a contemporary line of research has involved researchers exploring relationships between neuroscience and cognitive perspectives of mathematics education. For instance, Norton and colleagues (Norton &

Deater-Deckard, 2014; Norton & Bell, in press) have investigated the neurological activity involved in the context of the aforementioned aspects of number and fraction development. This line of research, although in its infancy, has raised several initial findings of note. Although mathematical development corresponds to a shift in neurological activity from the frontal lobe to the parietal lobe, children engaged in cognitively demanding activity exhibit frontal-parietal coherence. Another notable finding is that activity in the intraparietal sulcus is pervasive to mathematical reasoning. Because the intraparietal sulcus is also associated with sensorimotor activity involving the hand, such a finding supports aforementioned perspectives of Piagetian constructivism that emphasize early mathematical development through sensorimotor experience. This finding also supports the use of manipulatives in the teaching of mathematics.

6. Summary

In closing this section on learner models, we return to the Formalism First principle that assumes educators can approach instruction in terms of helping students first construct abstract structures or moves and then the cognition necessary to apply these abstract structures or moves. Learner models of mathematical reasoning, however, attempt to provide developmental accounts of student learning in ways that do not create this dichotomy between abstract structures and the application of structures. This presents a significant instructional problem: teaching and curriculum must be sensitive to the mathematical realities of students and how those realities differ from the teacher's mathematical reality. This has led several researchers to extend the theoretical bases of learner models of mathematical reasoning to instructional design (e.g., Simon, 1995), engendering learning (e.g., Harel, 2013), and teacher knowledge (e.g., Silverman & Thompson, 2008).

7. Closing remarks

In summary, models of expert and formal mathematical reasoning have provided contributions including:

- Understanding aspects of mathematical expertise and the mathematical activities of experts (see Weber et al., 2014)
- Highlighting features of expert mathematical reasoning that are often ignored under traditional instruction (see Schoenfeld, 1985)
- Offering one account for why students cannot complete mathematical tasks when they appear to have the knowledge base to do so (see Schoenfeld, 1985)
- Providing experience with guided practice that has been shown to increase students' propensity and capacity to engage in particular skills (see Anderson, Corbett, Koedinger, & Pelletier, 1995).

Learner models of mathematical reasoning have provided contributions including:

- Revealing the importance and complexity of individuals' mathematical meanings (see Thompson, 2013)
- Identifying localized cognitive obstacles in individuals' construction of productive understandings (see Lobato et al., 2003)
- Providing viable and rational accounts of individuals' behaviors that an expert would find inefficient or irrational (see Steffe et al., 1983)

- Providing viable accounts of individuals' mathematical development (see Steffe & Olive, 2010)
- Revealing reasoning that can facilitate or inhibit individuals' understandings of and performances in future mathematical areas (see Thompson & Carlson, 2017).

We have distinguished between these models due to their developing mostly independent of each other and underlying incompatibilities among the perspectives. For instance, researchers working in the context of learner models of mathematical reasoning often reject the notion that aspects of an individual's reasoning can be characterized independent of characterizing individuals' meanings of localized content of study. Researchers working to develop models of expert and formal mathematical reasoning, however, often seek to identify meta-processes that are independent of the content, the situation, and the individual reasoner. As researchers who work in both of these areas (the first author within expert reasoning; the second author within learner models of mathematical reasoning), we understand these distinctions and points of conflict, and that they do hinder synergy between the perspectives. Yet, there are likely unforeseen ways that these different perspectives complement each other. For instance, we envision that one natural question is: how do the particular meanings students develop for localized content influence their capacity for formal mathematical reasoning in the context of that localized content? And a question in a similar vein: how do particular cognitive developments within a localized content area influence and explain differences in the nature of their formal mathematical reasoning?

Notes

1 In the Wason (1968) selection task, a classic test of logical reasoning, participants are told that each card has a letter on one side and a number on the other. They are told that "every card that has a 3 on one side has a D on the other", shown four cards with a D, K, 3, and 7, and asked which cards they would need to turn over to see if the rule has been violated. The normatively correct answer is 3 and K (if there is a 3 on the other side of the K, the rule is violated).

2 We note that Wagner's perspective on abstractness and transfer is not incompatible with Piagetian constructivism perspectives on abstraction. Researchers ascribing to Piagetian constructivism predominantly characterize abstraction in terms of an individual conceiving something common to their reasoning among what were seemingly different situations, while emphasizing that such a process does not produce some form of knowledge that is "context-free" as if it exists in and of itself.

References

Alcock, L. J. (2010). Mathematicians' perspectives on the teaching and learning of proof. ***Research in Collegiate Mathematics Education, VII***, 63–92.

Alcock, L. J., Bailey, T., Inglis, M., & Docherty, P. (2014). The ability to reject invalid logical inferences predicts poor proof comprehension and mathematics performance. In T. Fukawa-Connelly, G. Karakak, K. Keene, & M. Zandieh (Eds.), ***Proceedings of the 17th conference on research in undergraduate mathematics education*** (pp. 376–383). Denver, CO: Special Interest Group of the Mathematical Association of America on Research in Undergraduate Mathematics Education.

Alcock, L. J., & Simpson, A. (2004). Convergence of sequences and series: Interactions between visual reasoning and the learner's beliefs about their own role. ***Educational Studies in Mathematics***, *57*(1), 1–32.

Alcock, L. J., & Simpson, A. (2005). Convergence of sequences and series 2: Interactions between non-visual reasoning and the learner's beliefs about their own role. ***Educational Studies in Mathematics***, *58*, 77–110.

Alcock, L. J., & Weber, K., (2010). Undergraduates' example use in proof construction: Purposes and effectiveness. ***Investigations in Mathematics Learning***, *3*, 1–22.

Anderson, J. R., Corbett, A. T., Koedinger, K. R., & Pelletier, R. (1995). Cognitive tutors: Lessons learned. ***Journal of the Learning Sciences***, *4*(2), 167–207.

Anderson, J. R., Reder, L. M., & Simon, H. A. (2000). Applications and misapplications of cognitive psychology to mathematics education. *Texas Educational Review, 1*(2), 29–49.
Antonini, S. (2006). Graduate students' processes in generating examples of mathematical objects. In J. Novotná, H. Moraová, M. Krátká, & N. Stehlíková (Eds.), *Proceedings of the 30th international conference on the psychology of mathematics education* (Vol. 2, pp. 57–64). Prague, Czech Republic: PME.
Attridge, N., & Inglis, M. (2013). Advanced mathematical study and the development of conditional reasoning skills. *PLoS one, 8*, e69399.
Barnett, S. M., & Ceci, S. J. (2002). When and where do we apply what we learn? A taxonomy for far transfer. *Psychological Bulletin, 128*(4), 612–637.
Burton, L. (2004). *Mathematicians as enquirers*. Berlin: Springer.
Carlson, M. P., & Bloom, I. (2005). The cyclic nature of problem solving: An emergent multidimensional problem-solving framework. *Educational Studies in Mathematics, 58*(1), 45–75.
Carlson, M. P., Jacobs, S., Coe, E., Larsen, S., & Hsu, E. (2002). Applying covariational reasoning while modeling dynamic events: A framework and a study. *Journal for Research in Mathematics Education, 33*(5), 352–378.
Castillo-Garsow, C., Johnson, H. L., & Moore, K. C. (2013). Chunky and smooth images of change. *For the Learning of Mathematics, 33*(3), 31–37.
Chazan, D., Sela, H., & Herbst, P. (2012). Is the role of equations in the doing of word problems in school algebra changing? Initial indications from teacher study groups. *Cognition and Instruction, 30*(1), 1–38.
Cobb, P., Confrey, J., diSessa, A. A., Lehrer, R., & Schauble, L. (2003). Design experiments in educational research. *Educational Researcher, 32*(1), 9–13.
DeFranco, T. C. (1996). A perspective on mathematical problem-solving expertise based on the performances of male Ph. D. mathematicians. *Research in Collegiate Mathematics Education, 2*, 195–213.
Dreyfus, T. (1991). On the status of visual reasoning in mathematics and mathematics education. In *Proceedings of the 15th conference of the international group for the psychology of mathematics education* (Vol. 1, pp. 33–48). Assisi, Italy: PME.
Eisenberg, T. (1994). On understanding the reluctance to visualize. *Zentralblatt für Didaktik der Mathematik, 26*(4), 109–113.
Ellis, A. B. (2011). Generalizing-promoting actions: How classroom collaborations can support students' mathematical generalizations. *Journal for Research in Mathematics Education, 42*(4), 308–345.
Ellis, A. B., Özgür, Z., Kulow, T., Williams, C. C., & Amidon, J. (2015). Quantifying exponential growth: Three conceptual shifts in coordinating multiplicative and additive growth. *Journal of Mathematical Behavior, 39*, 135–155.
Epp, S. S. (2003). The role of logic in teaching proof. *American Mathematical Monthly, 110*(10), 886–899.
Gentner, D., & Markman, A. B. (1997). Structure mapping in analogy and similarity. *American Psychologist, 52*, 45–56.
Gerofsky, S. (1996). A linguistic and narrative view of word problems in mathematics education. *For the Learning of Mathematics, 16*(2), 36–45.
Gibson, D. (1998). Students' use of diagrams to develop proofs in an introductory real analysis. *Research in Collegiate Mathematics Education, 2*, 284–307.
Hackenberg, A. J. (2010). Students' reasoning with reversible multiplicative relationships. *Cognition and Instruction, 28*(4), 383–432.
Harel, G. (2013). Intellectual need. In K. Leatham (Ed.), *Vital directions for research in mathematics education* (pp. 119–151). New York: Springer.
Healy, L., & Hoyles, C. (1996). Seeing, doing and expressing: An evaluation of task sequences for supporting algebraic thinking. PME Conference, 3, 3–67.
Herbst, P. (2002). Establishing a custom of proving in American school geometry: Evolution of the two-column proof in the early twentieth century. *Educational Studies in Mathematics, 49*(3), 283–312.
Herbst, P., & Brach, C. (2006). Proving and doing proofs in high school geometry classes: What is it that is going on for students?. *Cognition and Instruction, 24*(1), 73–122.
Iannone, P., Inglis, M., Mejía-Ramos, J. P., Simpson, A., & Weber, K. (2011). Does generating examples aid proof production? *Educational Studies in Mathematics*, 77(1), 1–14.
Inglis, M., & Aberdein, A. (in press). Diversity in proof appraisal. In B. Larvor (Ed.), *Mathematical Cultures*. Birkhäuser Science.
Inglis, M., & Simpson, A. (2004). Mathematicians and the selection task. In M. Johnsen Hoines & A. B. Fuglestad (Eds.), *Proceedings of the 28th conference of the international group for the psychology of mathematics education* (Vol. 3, pp. 89–96). Bergen, Norway: Bergen University College.

Izsák, A. (2004). Students' coordination of knowledge when learning to model physical situations. *Cognition and Instruction, 22*(1), 81–128.

Johnson, H. L. (2015). Secondary students' quantification of ratio and rate: A framework for reasoning about change in covarying quantities. *Mathematical Thinking and Learning, 17*(1), 64–90. doi: 10.1080/10986065.2015.981946

Kline, M. (1973). *Why Johnny can't add: The failure of the new math*. New York, NY: St. Martin's Press.

Koedinger, K. R., Alibali, M., & Nathan, M. J. (2008). Trade-offs between grounded and abstract representations: Evidence from algebra problem solving. *Cognitive Science, 32*, 366–397.

Lappan, G., Fey, J. T., Fitzgerald, W. M., Friel, S. N., & Phillips, E. D. (2004). *Connected mathematics*. Upper Saddle River, NJ: Prentice Hall.

Larkin, J. H., & Simon, H. A. (1987). Why a diagram is (sometimes) worth ten thousand words. *Cognitive Science, 11*(1), 65–100.

Lave, J. (1988). *Cognition in practice: Mind, mathematics, and culture in everyday life*. Cambridge, MA: Cambridge University Press.

Lobato, J. (2012). The actor-oriented transfer perspective and its contributions to educational research. *Educational Psychologist, 47*(3), 232–247.

Lobato, J., Ellis, A. B., & Munoz, R. (2003). How "Focusing Phenomena" in the instructional environment support individual students' generalizations. *Mathematical Thinking & Learning, 5*(1), 1–36.

Lobato, J., Rhodehamel, B., & Hohensee, C. (2012). "Noticing" as an alternative transfer of learning process. *Journal of the Learning Sciences, 21*(3), 433–482.

Lockwood, E., Ellis, A. B., & Lynch, A. G. (2016). Mathematicians' example-related activity when exploring and proving conjectures. *International Journal of Research in Undergraduate Mathematics Education*. Doi: 10.1007/s40753-016-0025-2.

Mejia-Ramos, J. P., & Weber, K. (2014). Why and how mathematicians read proofs: further evidence from a survey study. *Educational Studies in Mathematics, 85*(2), 161–173.

Moore, K. C., Paoletti, T., & Musgrave, S. (2013). Covariational reasoning and invariance among coordinate systems. *Journal of Mathematical Behavior, 32*(3), 461–473.

Nathan, M. J. (2012). Rethinking formalisms in formal education. *Educational Psychologist, 47*(2), 125–148.

Nathan, M. J., & Koedinger, K. R. (2000a). An investigation of teachers' beliefs of students' algebra development. *Cognition and Instruction, 18*, 207–235.

Nathan, M. J., & Koedinger, K. R. (2000b). Moving beyond teachers' intuitive beliefs about algebra learning. *Mathematics Teacher, 93*, 218–223.

Nathan, M. J., Long, S. D., & Alibali, M. W. (2002). The symbol precedence view of mathematical development: A corpus analysis of the rhetorical structure of textbooks. *Discourse Processes, 33*, 1–21.

Nokes, T. J. (2009). Mechanisms of knowledge transfer. *Thinking & Reasoning, 15*(1), 1–36.

Norton, A., & Bell, M. A. (in press). Mathematics educational neuroscience. In J. Cai (Ed.), *First compendium for research in mathematics education*. Charlotte, NC: Information Age Publishing.

Norton, A., & Deater-Deckard, K. (2014). Mathematics in mind, brain, and education: A neo-Piagetian approach. *International Journal of Science and Mathematics Education, 12*(3), 647–667. doi: 10.1007/s10763-014-9512-6

Oehrtman, M., Carlson, M. P., & Thompson, P. W. (2008). Foundational reasoning abilities that promote coherence in students' function understanding. In M. P. Carlson & C. L. Rasmussen (Eds.), *Making the Connection: Research and Teaching in Undergraduate Mathematics Education* (pp. 27–42). Washington, DC: Mathematical Association of America.

Piaget, J. (2001). *Studies in reflecting abstraction*. Hove, UK: Psychology Press Ltd.

Pirie, S., & Kieren, T. (1994). Growth in mathematical understanding: How can we characterise it and how can we represent it? *Educational Studies in Mathematics, 26*(2–3), 165–190.

Presmeg, N. C. (2006). Research on visualization in learning and teaching mathematics. In A. Guttierez & P. Boero (Eds.), *Handbook of research on the psychology of mathematics education* (pp. 205–235). Rotterdam, The Netherlands: Sense Publishing.

Saldanha, L. A., & Thompson, P. W. (1998). Re-thinking co-variation from a quantitative perspective: Simultaneous continuous variation. In S. B. Berensen, K. R. Dawkings, M. Blanton, W. N. Coulombe, J. Kolb, K. Norwood, & L. Stiff (Eds.), *Proceedings of the 20th annual meeting of the North American chapter of the international group for the psychology of mathematics education* (Vol. 1, pp. 298–303). Columbus, OH: ERIC Clearinghouse for Science, Mathematics, and Environmental Education.

Samkoff, A., Lai, Y., & Weber, K. (2012). On the different ways that mathematicians use diagrams in proof construction. *Research in Mathematics Education, 14*(1), 49–67.

Sandefur, J., Mason, J., Stylianides, G. J., & Watson, A. (2013). Generating and using examples in the proving process. *Educational Studies in Mathematics, 83*(3), 323–340.
Schoenfeld, A. H. (1985). *Mathematical problem solving*. Orlando, FL: Academic press.
Schoenfeld, A. H. (1988). When good teaching leads to bad results: The disasters of 'well-taught' mathematics courses. *Educational Psychologist, 23*(2), 145–166.
Schoenfeld, A. H. (1992). Learning to think mathematically: Problem solving, metacognition, and sense making in mathematics. In F. Lester (Ed.), *Handbook of research on mathematics teaching and learning* (pp. 334–370). Reston, VA: NCTM.
Selden, A., Selden, J., Hauk, S., & Mason, A. (2000). Why can't calculus students access their knowledge to solve non-routine problems. *Research in Collegiate Mathematics Education, 3*, 128–153.
Sherman, M., Walkington, C., & Howell, E. (2016). Symbolic-precedence view in investigative and conventional textbooks used in algebra courses. *Journal for Research in Mathematics Education, 47*, 134–146.
Silverman, J., & Thompson, P. W. (2008). Toward a framework for the development of mathematical knowledge for teaching. *Journal of Mathematics Teacher Education, 11*, 499–511.
Simon, M. A. (1995). Reconstructing mathematics pedagogy from a constructivist perspective. *Journal for Research in Mathematics Education, 26*(2), 114–145.
Singley, M. K., & Anderson, J. R. (1989). *The transfer of cognitive skill*. Cambridge, MA: Harvard University Press.
Steffe, L. P., & Kieren, T. (1994). Radical constructivism and mathematics education. *Journal for Research in Mathematics Education, 25*(6), 711–733. doi: 10.2307/749582
Steffe, L. P., & Olive, J. (2010). *Children's fractional knowledge*. New York, NY: Springer.
Steffe, L. P., & Thompson, P. W. (2000b). Teaching experiment methodology: Underlying principles and essential elements. In R. A. Lesh & A. E. Kelly (Eds.), *Handbook of research design in mathematics and science education* (pp. 267–307). Hillside, NJ: Erlbaum.
Steffe, L. P., von Glasersfeld, E., Richards, J., & Cobb, P. (1983). *Children's counting types: Philosophy, theory, and application*. New York, NY: Praeger Scientific.
Stylianou, D. A. (2002). On the interaction of visualization and analysis: The negotiation of a visual representation in expert problem solving. *Journal of Mathematical Behavior, 21*, 303–317.
Thompson, A. G., & Thompson, P. W. (1996). Talking about rates conceptually, Part II: Mathematical knowledge for teaching. *Journal for Research in Mathematics Education, 27*(1), 2–24.
Thompson, P. W. (2013). Constructivism in mathematics education. In S. Lerman (Ed.), *Encyclopedia of mathematics education* (pp. 96–102). Dordrecht, NL: Springer.
Thompson, P. W., & Carlson, M. P. (2017). Variation, covariation, and functions: Foundational ways of thinking in mathematics. In J. Cai (Ed.), *Compendium for research in mathematics education* (pp. 421–456). Reston, VA: National Council of Teachers of Mathematics.
Thurston, W. P. (1994). On proof and progress in mathematics. *Bulletin of the American Mathematical Society, 30*(2), 161–177.
von Glasersfeld, E. (1995). *Radical constructivism: A way of knowing and learning*. Washington, DC: Falmer Press.
Wagner, J. F. (2006). Transfer in pieces. *Cognition and Instruction, 24*(1), 1–71. doi: 10.1207/s1532690xci2401_1
Wason, P. C. (1968). Reasoning about a rule. *Quarterly Journal of Experimental Psychology, 20*(3), 273–281.
Weber, K. (2001). Student difficulty in constructing proofs: The need for strategic knowledge. *Educational Studies in Mathematics, 48*(1), 101–119.
Weber, K. (2004). Traditional instruction in advanced mathematics courses: A case study of one professor's lectures and proofs in an introductory real analysis course. *Journal of Mathematical Behavior, 23*(2), 115–133.
Weber, K. (2008). How mathematicians determine if an argument is a valid proof. *Journal for Research in Mathematics Education, 39*, 431–459.
Weber, K., & Alcock, L. (2004). Semantic and syntactic proof productions. *Educational Studies in Mathematics, 56*(2–3), 209–234.
Weber, K., Inglis, M., & Mejía-Ramos, J. P. (2014). How mathematicians obtain conviction: Implications for mathematics instruction and research on epistemic cognition. *Educational Psychologist, 49*, 36–58.
Weber, K., & Mejia-Ramos, J. P. (2011). Why and how mathematicians read proofs: An exploratory study. *Educational Studies in Mathematics, 76*(3), 329–344.
Weber, K., Porter, M., & Housman, D. (2008). Worked examples and concept example usage in understanding mathematical concepts and proofs. In M. Carlson & C. Rasmussen (Eds.), *Making the connection – research and teaching in undergraduate mathematics education* (pp. 245–252). Washington, DC: Mathematical Association of America.

Wu, H. (1997). The mathematics education reform: Why you should be concerned and what you can do. *American Mathematical Monthly, 104,* 946–954.

Zazkis, R., Dubinsky, E., & Dautermann, J. (1996). Coordinating visual and analytic strategies: A study of students' understanding of the group D 4. *Journal for Research in Mathematics Education, 27,* 435–457.

34
PROBLEM SOLVING

Robert W. Weisberg

The phenomenon of problem solving can be looked upon as a crossroads, where many different processes come together in service of the needs and goals of an individual. Over the past 35 years, the pace of research in problem solving has quickened and its scope has broadened (Weisberg, 2006, 2015). Much of that recent development has been driven by an increased emphasis on the phenomenon of *insight* in problem solving. This renewed emphasis on insight has had catalytic effects, as researchers have forged connections between problem solving and other aspects of cognition, including the role of executive processes in problem solving and the applicability of dual-process theories of thinking to problem solving and creativity. The new wave of research has also seen pioneering efforts aimed at isolating brain activity underlying insight.

The notion of insight was introduced into psychology by the Gestalt psychologists in the context of controversy concerning two modes of solving problems – in modern terminology, *insight* versus *analysis* – with researchers arguing for one versus the other (for review, see Weisberg, 2006, ch. 6). That controversy continues today (Weisberg, 2015). In this chapter, however, I propose an integration of research perspectives. Creative thinking comes about through multiple paths, including insight, but also including analytic thinking. It is therefore important to develop theories that encompass both modes of thinking (Fleck & Weisberg, 2004, 2013; Weisberg, 2006; Weisberg, 2015).

Insight versus analysis

In analyzing problem solving, the Gestalt psychologists proposed a distinction between *reproductive* and *productive* thought (Wertheimer, 1982, p. 52). Reproductive thought is based on the application of one's knowledge to a problem. The Gestalt psychologists looked negatively on reproductive thought, because one might apply one's knowledge unthinkingly, based on habit, without a true understanding of the situation. In order to deal with a new problem, one had to approach the situation "on its own terms" (Wertheimer, 1982, p. 52), considering what it demanded and constructing a solution method – based on productive thought – tailored to those demands. Box 34.1 presents problems that have been used to study insight. An *insight problem* is designed so that a person encountering it will adopt an incorrect analysis or *representation* of the situation. Solutions that come to mind, based on that incorrect representation, will be unsuccessful. As an example, on reading the Lilies problem, one immediately thinks to divide the total time in half to get the answer, which is incorrect. In order to solve an insight problem, a new way of thinking about the problem – a new representation of the problem – must be found. In other words, the problem must be ***re-structured***: the individual must abandon the structure initially imposed on the problem and find a new one, which more adequately fits the situation. In Box 34.2 is a set of *analytic* problems, which are solved through a gradual working out of the solution, based on reproductive use of one's knowledge, and without a change in the structure of the problem.

Box 34.1 Insight problems

1. **Lilies:** water lilies double in area every 24 hours. At the beginning of the summer there is one water lily on the lake. It takes 60 days for the lake to become completely covered with water lilies. On what day is the lake half covered?

   Solution: if the lilies double in area each day, then the lake is half covered on the day before it is fully covered, or on day 59, the next-to-last day.

2. **Trees:** how can you plant 10 trees in five rows with four trees in each row?

   Solution: lay out the trees in a star-shaped pattern with five points and four trees in each row (Figure 34.1A).

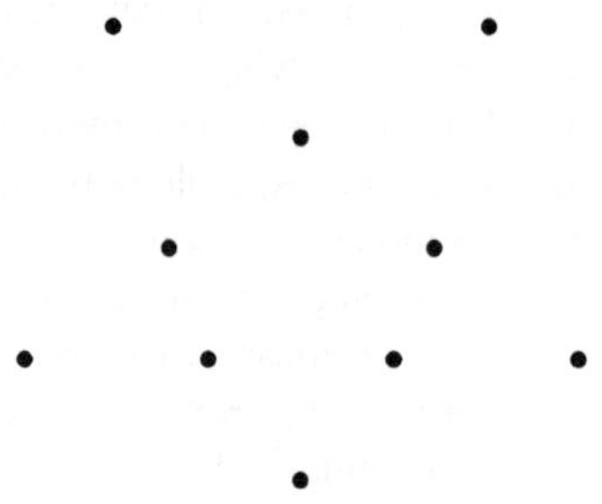

Figure 34.1A

3. **Triangle of coins:** the triangle points to the bottom of the page (see Figure 34.1B). How can you move only three coins and make the triangle point to the top of the page?

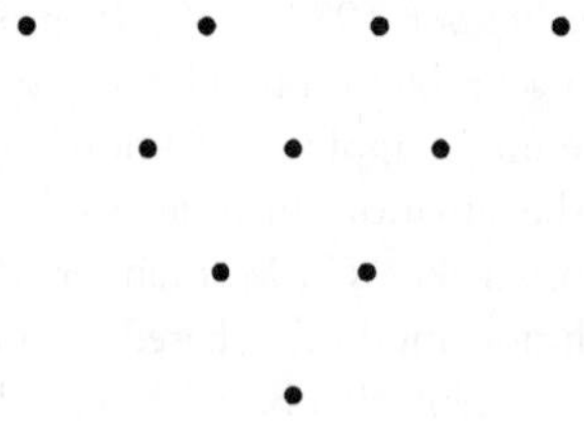

Figure 34.1B

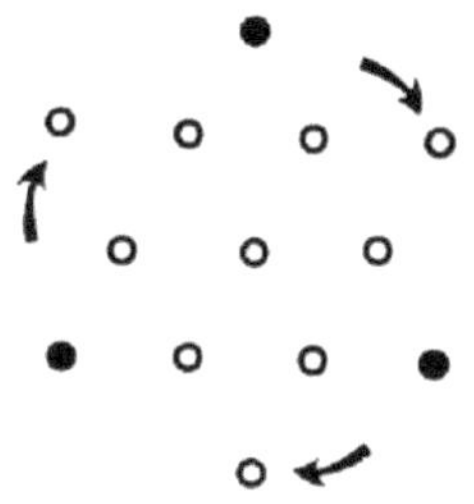

Figure 34.1C

Solution: move the three coins from the points of the triangle around the central "rosette" (Figure 34.1C):

Another solution: move the two end coins from the top row down to the ends of the two-coin row; then move the bottom coin to the very top.

4. **Candle:** with the objects provided, attach the candle to the wall so that it can burn properly. **Solution:** use the tack box as a holder or shelf for the candle (Figure 34.1D).

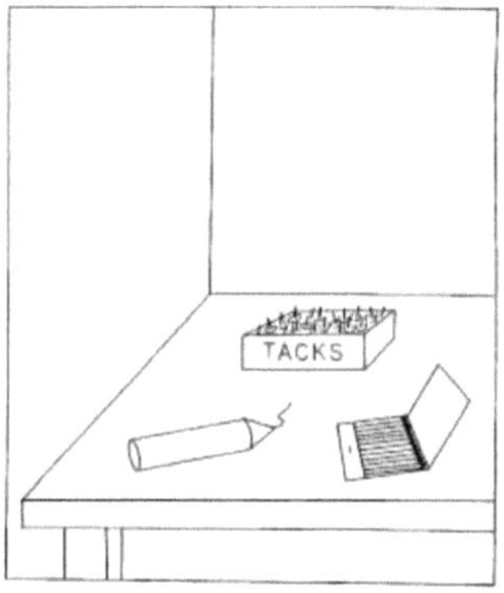

Figure 34.1D

5. **Compound Remote Associates (CRA):**

   Instruction: generate a solution word that can be combined with the problem words to yield a compound word or familiar phrase.

   1. *Problem words:* CRAB, PINE, SAUCE **Solution:** APPLE
   2. *Problem words:* BLUE, COTTAGE, MOUSE **Solution:** CHEESE

6. **Dirt in hole:** how much dirt is in a hole that measures 2′ wide × 6′ long × 5′ deep?

   Solution: there is no dirt in a hole.

7. **Ocean liner:** at 12 noon a porthole in an ocean liner was 9 feet above the water line. The tide raises the water at a rate of 2 feet per hour. How long will it take the water to reach the porthole?

   Solution: the water never reaches the porthole—the ocean liner floats on the rising tide.

Box 34.2 Analytic problems

1. **Playing cards:** three cards from an ordinary deck are lying on a table face down. The following information is known about the cards (all the information refers to the same three cards): to the left of a queen there is a jack. To the left of a spade there is a diamond. To the right of a heart there is a king. To the right of a king there is a spade. Assign the proper suit to each card.

   Solution: Jack of hearts, King of diamonds, Queen of spades.

2. **The schedule:** next week I am going to have lunch with my friend, visit the new art gallery, go to the Social Security Office, and visit my dentist. My friend cannot meet me on Wednesday. The Social Security Office is closed weekends. The art gallery is closed Tuesday, Thursday, and weekends. The dentist has office hours on Tuesday, Friday, and Saturday. On what day can I do everything I have planned?

   Solution: Friday.

People solving insight problems sometimes go through a sequence of events, culminating in an experience of *Aha!* or *Eureka!* The person first reaches a dead end – *impasse* – because the initial reproductive solution methods were not successful. The person might then break off work on the problem. During the time away from the problem, the individual might experience sudden insight into its structure, followed by a quick and easy solution. That period away from the problem is called an "incubation" period, because the solution was developing or "incubating," presumably in the unconscious (Weisberg, 2006, ch. 6; see also Gilhooly, this volume). Achieving insight – i.e., restructuring a problem – in response to impasse was seen by the Gestalt psychologists as being "spontaneous," in the sense of being outside of the person's control, similar to the way in which the reversible cube changes orientation as one looks at it, whether one wants it to or not.

The "insight sequence" – presentation of the problem ⇒ repeated failure ⇒ impasse ⇒ incubation ⇒ restructuring ⇒ *Aha!* + solution – has, in the Gestalt tradition, been taken as definitional for the occurrence of insight (Ohlsson, 2011; for discussion, see Weisberg, 2015). In addition, in the Gestalt view, the occurrence of the insight sequence is criterial for calling a response creative (Wiley & Jarosz, 2012; Ohlsson, 2011; Perkins, 2000). That is, if a solution to a problem – or any other proposed advance in our knowledge – does not come about through the insight sequence, it is *ipso facto* dismissed as not being creative.

In conclusion, the Gestalt orientation toward problem solving and creative thinking was based on the assumption that insight came about by going beyond experience and responding to what the problem demanded. Several modern researchers have echoed the Gestalt psychologists' emphasis on a sharp distinction between insight and analysis. The most important recent large-scale elaboration of Gestalt theory – what one can call neo-Gestalt theory – is that of Ohlsson (1992, 2011; see also Perkins, 2000). Since Ohlsson's theorizing has stimulated a significant body of research, it can serve as the focal point for a consideration of recent developments in the Gestalt view.

Insight and deep learning: Ohlsson's representational change theory

Ohlsson (2011) places great emphasis on insight in the intellectual functioning of humans. Insight is one example of "deep learning," situations that demand that people abandon a reliance on their knowledge, i.e., on analytic thinking. Other examples are developing a new pattern of behavior in response to a change in the environment, and rejection of a previously held belief in favor of a contrary one. According to Ohlsson, the world is in constant change. Analytic thinking, being reproductive at its base, cannot deal with change, i.e., with novelty, and therefore cannot produce a creative outcome. Insight and other examples of deep learning are therefore necessary for us to survive.

Changing the problem representation

Ohlsson's views concerning how representational change comes about have changed over the two major iterations of his theory. Initially (Ohlsson, 1992), he proposed that, in response to impasse, a set of heuristics – collectively called "switch when stuck" – was set into motion (see also Kaplan & Simon, 1990). Switch when stuck involved three mechanisms: elaboration, re-encoding, and constraint relaxation. Consider an individual working on the Candle problem, who has tried unsuccessfully to tack the candle to the wall and to "glue" it to the wall using melted wax from the candle. The person has reached impasse, which sets the switch-when-stuck heuristics into operation. Using the elaboration heuristic, the person would re-examine the problem to see if anything was left out of the problem representation. Assume that heuristic would be unsuccessful. The second heuristic, re-encoding, involves examining each object in the situation to determine if it has characteristics that had been ignored but which might be useful. On examining the tack box, the person might realize that it is flat and so could serve as a shelf for the candle. That realization could trigger a new solution type. Finally, constraint relaxation works by examining the demands of the problem in order to see if changing them might lead to progress. The person might think that, rather than trying to attach the candle directly to the wall in some way, it might be possible to make a candle-holder of some kind. That change, too, might lead to use of the box. Those three heuristics can result in what one can call "bottom-up" restructuring, because the individual is examining the materials in the problem without a plan, hoping to find something that originally was overlooked.

In the newer version of the theory, Ohlsson (2011) does not mention the switch-when-stuck mechanism, and proposes instead that an incorrect representation can change automatically as the person reaches impasse. Presentation of a problem results in activation of several possible representations, and that with the highest overall activation becomes dominant and directs the person's initial solution attempts. With an insight problem, that initial representation results in a string of failures, each of which initiates a negative feedback mechanism, which produces inhibition of the initial representation. With enough failures, sufficient inhibition builds up so that another representation will become dominant. In other words, the activation produced by the elements of the problem will be *redistributed* among the elements in memory, resulting in a restructuring of the problem. Thus, the mechanism through which representational change comes about is automatic redistribution of activity in semantic memory, which is similar to the original Gestalt view that restructuring in response to impasse was the result of mechanisms outside the person's control.

Multiple paths to insight in problem solving

Neo-Gestalt theorists have adduced two sorts of support for their theories: laboratory studies of problem solving and real-world large-scale creative advances that are assumed to have come about through the insight sequence. However, in order to demonstrate the role of the insight sequence in problem solving, it is necessary to obtain fine-grained information, so that one can demonstrate, for example, that impasse and restructuring have occurred on the path to solution. While there has been much research presented in support of the neo-Gestalt view, the large majority of those studies have not measured the fine-grained processes underlying problem solution, and so can say little about the role of insight versus analysis in problem solving (for review, see Weisberg, 2015).

In order to provide the type of information that would allow inferences concerning the processes underlying "insight" problem solving, Fleck and Weisberg (2004, 2013) collected verbal protocols from people while they attempted to solve problems 1–4 in Box 34.1 and several others. The results indicated that those problems were solved through multiple paths, as only 6% of the solutions came about as a result of the full insight sequence (see also Weisberg & Suls, 1973). Similar results were reported by Cranford and Moss (2012), who obtained verbal protocols while people solved compound remote associates (CRA) problems (Box 34.1). CRA problems have been used in many recent investigations to study insight, because people report that they solve them in two ways: incrementally, as the result of a step-by-step search for a word that fit with the others, or suddenly (with insight) when the solution word suddenly came to mind, in an *Aha!* Cranford and Moss investigated whether, when a CRA problem was solved in an *Aha!* experience, the solution came about through the insight sequence. *Aha!* solutions often occurred without prior impasse and/or restructuring of the problem, demonstrating again that "insight" solutions – i.e., solutions to insight problems – can occur without the insight sequence. The results of these studies are consistent in demonstrating that, in order to fully understand how people achieve insight in solving problems, we must be ready to incorporate a broader range of mechanisms into our theories. Therefore, we should examine some of the mechanisms through which people solved insight problems in Fleck and Weisberg's study.

Transfer

Although it is not of central interest here, Fleck and Weisberg (2013) found that several people solved the Lilies problem based on a recognition that the problem involved a geometric progression. They had become familiar with such functions in a mathematics class, and they transferred their knowledge to the new problem. This result is interesting because it indicates that a person can solve an insight problem based solely on reproductive thinking. Again, researchers who wish to draw firm conclusions about insight must be careful to ensure that "insight" solutions do indeed come about through the insight sequence.

Heuristic methods

Insight problems are designed so that most people have no specific knowledge that can be applied to them (an exception to this was just discussed with the Lilies problem). Fleck and Weisberg (2004, 2013) found that their participants often used heuristic methods, general rules of thumb that can be applied to a wide range of problems. An example of such a method is "hill climbing," in which one tries to change the present state of the problem so that it looks more like the goal state. Carrying out that method several times may result in solution. Heuristic mechanisms were first discussed in the context of solution of analytic problems, such as logic and mathematics (Newell & Simon, 1972; Polya, 1945), but also are relevant to insight problems (see also MacGregor, Ormerod, & Chronicle, 2001). Fleck and Weisberg found that heuristics were used in several ways in solving insight problems.

Direct reasoning out of the solution

Some individuals solved the Lilies problem by deducing the solution directly from the information in the problem. If the lilies double in area each day, and if it takes 60 days to completely cover the lake, then it follows logically that the lake is half-covered on the day before it is completely covered, or the 59th day. These people were not familiar with geometric progressions, unlike those discussed in the last section. They also neither reached impasse nor restructured the problem. So here we have an "insightful" solution – i.e., the solution of interest according to Gestalt theory – being brought about as a result of reasoning through the implications of the information in the problem.

Similar processes were seen with other problems. Here is an excerpt from a protocol from a person who solved the Trees problem by deducing implications of the information in the problem.

> So, 10 trees in 5 straight lines. That doesn't sound possible. . . . You're gonna use 5 straight lines, but you need to use like each tree in more than one. . . . Make a triangle pattern. Would that work? That would be 3 lines. We still need more. Need 2 more lines. . . . You kind of need to have as many lines as possible while still like reusing the same, the same, um, points. . . . You could make a star shape. [Participant draws a star on the paper and then places the trees on it.]
>
> (Fleck and Weisberg, 2013, p. 454)

This individual restructured the problem, deducing that each tree had to be in more than one line, which led from a matrix to other shapes. The restructuring was the result of a reasoning process, rather than reaching impasse. The critical question then became what kind of pattern would solve the problem. As the protocol demonstrates, this individual worked continuously through various possibilities.

A series of heuristic methods

Some people worked through a series of heuristic methods until they solved a problem. One responded to the Lilies problem by applying simple arithmetic, producing the solution of 30 days. When told that solution was incorrect, she began to calculate the growth of the lilies over the 60 days, to determine when the lake was half-covered. That arithmetic quickly grew too tedious (day_1 = 1 lily on the lake; day_2 = 2; day_3 = 4; day_4 = 8; day_5 = 16; day_6 = 32; day_7 = 64; . . . 128; . . . 256; . . . 512; . . . 1024, . . .), so she rejected it. She then turned to a careful examination of the problem, which led her to deduce the solution directly, like the individuals discussed earlier.

The performance of this participant raises an important point about the Lilies problem (and several other insight problems): without someone to inform the participant whether or not a proposed solution is correct, the problem would never be solved. The solution that the researcher deems correct would not be produced, but the participant would *believe* that he or she had solved the problem. Consider an individual who reads the Lilies problem and who does not possess the mathematical sophistication to understand that the growth of the lilies follows a geometric progression. He calculates that the solution is one-half of 60 days. If the problem had been given in paper-and-pencil format as part of a series of problems, he would write "30 days" and go on, never realizing that he had not solved the problem. In most experiments, a researcher is available to reject the 30-day solution, to the participant's surprise. Once the participant has looked over his work and confirmed that he has not made a simple calculational error, the unexpected negative feedback from the researcher leads to the realization that the problem must be more complicated than he thought.

Many people then turn to calculating the day-to-day growth of the lilies because it would allow them to determine what was wrong about their initial analysis of problem. As noted, that calculation is cumbersome to carry out, so then people go back to the information in the problem, but this time *they read it with the knowledge that it is not as simple as it looks.* That realization may play a role in the subsequent reasoning out of the solution. Thus, that hypothetical "insight" is due in part to information from an outside source that challenges one's conception of the problem. So we have here an example of multiple solution attempts occurring, without restructuring or impasse, stimulated in part by failure – the researcher's rejection of the seemingly obvious solution. Similar factors may play a role in solution of other insight problems.

Failure and restructuring: analysis as a dynamic process

Fleck and Weisberg (2004, 2013) also found that sometimes restructuring and the insight solution could come about, again without impasse, as the result of a failed solution. Failure provided new information that resulted in a new analysis of the problem – a restructuring – and a solution. As an example, an individual working on the Candle problem began by trying to attach the candle to the wall by using the tacks, but concluded that the tacks were not long enough to hold the candle. That led to a search for something to use as a shelf (a restructuring of the problem), which led to the box. This sort of restructuring can be called "top-down" or conceptually driven restructuring, because the change in the goal, from tacking the candle to the wall to trying to make a shelf, came about as the result of new information that drove the person to change the way she approached the problem.

Solution of other insight problems through restructuring may also depend on failure, in this case the participant's learning that an "obvious" solution is incorrect. For example, presentation of the Dirt in Hole and Ocean Liner problems, like the Lilies problem discussed earlier, leads to seemingly straightforward solutions that are rejected by the researcher. As in the Lilies problem, the participant learns that the problems are not straightforward, i.e., that there may be tricks involved. Therefore, any correct solutions that ultimately occur – i.e., the "insight" solutions – are due in part to that failure of an obvious solution. It is important to keep in mind that participants in research examining insight problems are being educated about those problems, and, as regards the Dirt in Hole and Ocean Liner problems, that "education" may play a role in restructuring.

Analytic thinking in insight: conclusions

Fleck and Weisberg (2004, 2013) found that insight came about in multiple ways:

- as the result of direct transfer of knowledge to the problem
- as the result of direct application of a heuristic method to the problem, without restructuring
- as a result of application of a series of heuristic methods to the problem, stimulated by failure of an "obvious" solution, without restructuring
- as the result of heuristic processes or as the result of a new search of memory based on information acquired through failure, with restructuring but without impasse
- as a result of the insight sequence, with restructuring following impasse

Those results highlight two important aspects of analytic thinking that are sometimes ignored in the debate concerning insight versus analysis. First, contrary to the claims of Ohlsson (2011), Perkins (2000), Wiley and Jarosz (2012), and others, analytic thinking can deal with novelty. The match between the present and the past does not have to be perfect for one's knowledge to be applicable to the present (Weisberg, 1980, ch. 12; Weisberg, 2015). Assuming that the past changes gradually into the present, then knowledge from the past will still be relevant. Psychologists have long been aware of that possibility, for example, through the concept of *stimulus generalization*. So, for example, people working on the Candle problem often try to tack the candle directly to the wall. Those people probably never had tried to use tacks in that exact way before, meaning that the solutions were new, but they were nonetheless based on their knowledge about tacks and candles. Second, the application of one's knowledge to a new situation is a *dynamic process*, during which new information can become available which can change the situation and also the individual's interpretation of it. These conclusions provide further reason to believe that the differences between insight and analysis are matters of degree rather than kind.

From analysis to insight: a model of problem solving

Figure 34.2 presents a model that can summarize the relationship between insight and analysis (Weisberg, 2015) suggested by the previous discussion. All cognitive processes, including problem solving, are based on matches between information in memory and the situation the person is facing, which, of course, is a very old idea (for review, see Weisberg, 2006, chs. 3 and 4). The specificity of the match between the person's knowledge and the problem situation determines the type of solution method that is used.

Multiple paths to solving problems

Transfer of an old solution

In some situations, the person possesses problem-specific knowledge due to familiarity with the problem (Stage 1). A person with problem-specific knowledge available will retrieve it and transfer it to the problem. If the transferred solution works, then the problem is solved. If it fails, that failure may provide new information about the problem situation, which sets off another search of memory (Stage 3), which can result in a different mode of solution coming to mind. Thus, Stage 1B plus Stage 3 can result in a re-structuring of the problem, based on the new information acquired through the failure at Stage 1. Between Stages 1 and 3, the input has changed in a dynamic process, so the approach to the problem can change (or, in Gestalt terminology, the problem can be re-structured).

Heuristics

If there is no match at Stage 1, that is, if no solution is retrieved, then the person goes to Stage 2, which can result in retrieval of a heuristic method – a general rule of thumb that is more widely applicable than the problem-specific information at Stage 1. Heuristics include strategies such as working backward, analyzing the logical or linguistic structure of the information in a problem, or using general arithmetic methods. Heuristic methods can result in solution of a problem, which would result in the process halting at Stage 2. Application of a heuristic method might also result in failure, in which case the individual might acquire new information that

A. SOLUTION THROUGH ANALYTIC METHODS

STAGE 1 – SOLUTION THROUGH TRANSFER (PROBLEM-SPECIFIC KNOWLEDGE)
Problem presented ⇒ Matches with knowledge ⇒ Transfer solution (No solution ⇒ Stage 2)
A. If solution transfers: problem solved (problem is familiar; no Aha!)
B. If solution fails, but new information arises ⇒ Stage 3
C. If solution fails and no new information arises ⇒ Stage 2

STAGE 2 – SOLUTION THROGUH HEURISTIC METHODS (RULES OF THUMB)
Apply heuristic methods to problem
A. Heuristic methods successful ⇒ Solution
B. If no heuristic method produces solution, but new information arises ⇒ Stage 3
C. If no heuristic method produces solution and no new information arises ⇒ Impasse ⇒ Stage 4

STAGE 3 – SOLUTION THROUGH RESTRUCTURING (IN RESPONSE TO INFORMATION ARISING DURING ATTEMPTED SOLUTION OR FROM FAILURE; TOP-DOWN OR CONCEPTUALLY-DRIVEN RESTRUCTURING)
New information from failure ⇒ New match with knowledge ⇒ New Method (Restructuring)
A. New method leads to solution ⇒ Success
B. If new method fails, but new information arises from failure ⇒ Recycle through Stage 3
C. If new method fails and no new information arises ⇒ Impasse ⇒ Stage 4

B. SOLUTION THROUGH INSIGHT

STAGE 4 – SOLUTION THROUGH INSIGHT (BOTTOM-UP OR DATA-DRIVEN RESTRUCTURING IN RESPONSE TO IMPASSE)
Impasse ⇒ Redistribution of activation (Elaboration; Re-encoding; Constraint relaxation)
A. If bottom-up restructuring leads to new information ⇒ Stage 1; if no new information ⇒ Stop

Figure 34.2 Problem-solving methods: an integrated outline of stages in problem solving

would result in still another recycling through memory at Stage 3. That recycling would provide another opportunity for retrieval of a solution from memory, application of a different heuristic method to the problem, or a possible re-structuring of the problem.

The insight sequence

The final outcome comes about when Stages 1 and 2 have not resulted in success, and there has been no new information becoming available or that information has led to failure at Stage 3. Under such circumstances, the person would reach impasse and go on to Stage 4, where Ohlsson's (1992, 2011) postulated mechanisms would come into play.

Multiple paths to insight: further implications of the model

The model in Figure 34.2 also has implications for several aspects of research concerning insight in problem solving. The basic conclusion from the model and the related research

(Fleck & Weisberg, 2004, 2013) is that solution of insight problems may come about in several ways, most of which do not involve the insight sequence. Therefore, the simple fact that someone solves an insight problem, even through restructuring, does not guarantee that the insight sequence has occurred. That caveat is relevant to many recent studies of insight problem solving, which means that their conclusions may rest on weak foundations.

Insight as a special process versus insight as business as usual

The model in Figure 34.2 maintains the distinction between analysis and insight, but it assumes that there are many possible intermediate steps between "pure analysis" (solution through Stage 1A) and "pure insight" (solution through Stage 4). The model thus has relevance to a discussion in the literature of two views concerning insight: insight as a *special process* versus insight as *business as usual* (Ball & Stevens, 2009). The former view, proposed by the Gestalt psychologists and their followers, assumes that the cognitive processes underlying insight are different than those underlying analysis. The latter view argues that, although the subjective experiences accompanying insight may be very different than those accompanying analytic thought (e.g., the *Aha!* experience), the cognitive processes underlying both types of thinking are essentially the same. The theoretical perspective outlined in the model can accommodate both views. Stages 1–3 can be looked upon as the business-as-usual aspect of problem solving, which can bring about insight. Similarly, Stage 4, which involves different processes than Stages 1–3, represents the special process view.

Taxonomies of problems: a dichotomy versus a continuum

In an attempt to garner possible support for a distinction between insight and analysis, Gilhooly and Murphy (2005) examined the performance of a group of people on large sets of problems designated as insight and analytic problems. The problems were categorized on *a priori* grounds, depending on whether or not restructuring seemed to be required for their solution (Weisberg, 1995). The question of interest was whether it would be possible to separate the two types of problems using performance measures. Presumably, if all insight problems have something in common that is different from what analytic problems have in common, the two groups of problems should show some independence as demonstrated by people's performance. Gilhooly and Murphy examined which problems tended to be solved together and found that people who solved a given insight problem tended to solve other insight problems; a similar outcome occurred for the analytic problems. This analysis produced two broad categories, consisting predominantly of insight versus analytic problems, as well as several sub-groups of problems within those broader categories. Thus, there was some support for the insight-analysis distinction. It should be noted, however, that performance on some presumed insight problems was more closely related to performance on analytic problems, and vice versa. So the insight-analytic distinction was not completely satisfactory.

There are several additional questions that arise in response to this study. Gilhooly and Murphy (2005) assumed that if an insight problem was solved, it came about through the insight sequence. They did not consider the possibility of analytic solutions to insight problems. That omission is not surprising, because the analysis on which they based their work (Weisberg, 1995) also assumed that, if a problem was solved through restructuring, that was, *ipso facto*, evidence for the insight sequence. That assumption was overturned by the research of Fleck and Weisberg (2004, 2013). Therefore, the groupings into insight versus analytic problems found by Gilhooly and Murphy might not have been the result of the total presence or absence of the insight sequence. Also, it was not always apparent why certain problems were grouped together (Gilhooly & Murphy, 2005, p. 293). As an example, the Ocean Liner, Dirt in Hole, and Lilies problems (plus two others) were found to form a group, but it was not clear what those three problems had in common that resulted in them being solved together. If we had more details concerning how people actually solved each problem, we might be able to draw stronger conclusions as to the similarities and differences among the processes underlying solution. As of now, the categorization of problems put forth by Gilhooly and Murphy must be taken as unsupported.

Dual-process theories of problem solving and the role of executive functioning in insight

The thinking and reasoning literature has recently seen much interest in a distinction between two types of thinking (e.g., Evans, 2005). Type 1 thinking is characterized by fast, automatic processing, sometimes called "intuitive" processing (Gilhooly & Murphy, 2005). It is based on associative connections and seems to occur without conscious direction. Type 2 thinking is slower and involves following rules and conscious control. It has been proposed that those two types of thinking may play a role in problem solving and in creativity more generally (Allen & Thomas, 2011; Gilhooly & Murphy, 2005; Evans, 2005). Type 1 thinking is more important to insight, while Type 2 thinking is more relevant to analytic thinking. A closely related question concerns the role of the executive functions of working memory in insight versus analysis (Baddeley, 2003; Miyake, Friedman, Emerson, Witzki, & Howerter, 2000). One component of working memory involves executive capacities, which play a role in the direction and control of cognitive processes, and which are very similar to the functions attributed to Type 2 thinking (Gilhooly & Fioratou, 2009). One executive function is mental-set shifting, required when an individual has to change a previously used approach to a problem. A second is information updating and monitoring, needed when a task requires a response to the most recent information presented, at the expense of previously attended-to information. A third executive function is inhibition of pre-potent responses, which plays a role when a task requires that the person must inhibit a response of long standing.

Applying those ideas to problem solving, executive functioning would seem to be important in selection or construction of solution strategies and in monitoring those strategies. Analytic thinking is assumed to function through the match between the present situation and information from the past retrieved from memory (Stages 1–3 in the model in Figure 34.2). That information serves as the basis for construction of a solution, i.e., for planning. Therefore, analytic thought should depend on the executive component of working memory. Research has consistently supported the role of executive functioning in analytic problem solving (Fleck, 2008).

The insight sequence, in contrast, would seem to be less reliant on planning and, therefore, on executive functioning. Restructuring is assumed by many researchers to come about through processes that occur outside of conscious control, such as the spreading activation of information in memory in response to impasse, which can bring about the linkage of disparate ideas that are assumed to underlie creativity (e.g., Ash & Wiley, 2006; Fleck, 2008; Gilhooly & Murphy, 2005; Gilhooly & Fioratou, 2009; Ohlsson, 2011; Perkins, 2000; Wiley & Jarosz, 2012). Also, when insight occurs in an *Aha!* experience, it is a surprise to the individual, which is the antithesis of an outcome based on planning (Metcalfe, 1986; Metcalfe & Wiebe, 1987). Insight should therefore be less dependent on executive functioning than is analytic thinking.

A number of studies have examined the relationship between measures of executive functioning and performance on insight versus analytic problems (e.g., Ash & Wiley, 2006; Fleck,

2008; Gilhooly & Murphy,2005; Gilhooly & Fioratou, 2009; Lavric, Forstmeier, & Rippon, 2000). In those studies, participants typically were tested on a broad range of cognitive functions, including executive components of working memory, and were also tested on sets of insight and analytic problems. On the whole, the studies support the idea that executive functions play a larger role in solution of analytic problems than insight problems. However, once again a question can be raised about any conclusion relating executive functioning to insight. None of the cited studies assessed whether the insight problems were solved through the insight sequence. Based on the results of Fleck and Weisberg (2004, 2013), it would be suspected that some of the "insight" solutions came about without restructuring, much less without impasse. Therefore, it is impossible to know, based on the information reported in those studies, whether or not the insight sequence was involved. Fleck (2008) did obtain verbal protocols from her participants, which enabled her to determine whether restructuring occurred during solution, and she also concluded that executive functioning was more strongly related to performance on analytic problems than insight problems, defined through the occurrence of restructuring. Unfortunately, Fleck did not report whether the restructurings came after impasse, and the lack of that information makes her results difficult to interpret, since restructuring can occur independently of impasse.

The idea that executive functioning is not critical in creative thinking has been taken farthest by Wiley and Jarosz (2012), who have presented an extensive review of studies from a broad range of areas, which they interpret as indicating that creative thinking may actually be impaired by strong executive functioning, especially attentional control (p. 214). Too much control of attention during problem solving may restrict an individual to considering obvious possibilities and may make the individual resistant to changing the way of approaching the problem in the face of difficulties. As one example of the research findings presented by Wiley and Jarosz in support of that position, participants in a study by Jarosz, Colflesh, and Wiley (2012), who had been made intoxicated through ingestion of alcohol, performed worse on measures of executive functioning than they did when they were sober, and than did a sober control group. However, performance of the intoxicated individuals on CRA problems *increased* compared to the sober group. The conclusion is that intoxication makes attention more diffuse, which facilitates finding the solutions to CRA items. That conclusion is of potential interest, but it should be noted that we know very little about how CRA problems are actually solved (Cranford & Moss, 2012). Jarosz and Wiley present no direct evidence that intoxication actually made attention more diffuse, or, if it did, how that affected performance on the CRA problems. All we know is that performance improved. So again we are led to conclude that theorizing may have been premature here, and that we need more fine-grained data.

A positive role of executive functioning in creative thinking?

We have just reviewed studies examining the role of executive functioning in insight problem solving. Let us put aside for now the questions just raised about those studies due to the lack of specific information concerning how the insight problems were actually solved, which in my view renders the findings moot. The main conclusion that has been drawn from those studies is that creative thinking, defined as solving insight problems, functions better without too much executive control. It is important to note, however, that several studies that have examined creative thinking in other domains have reached the opposite conclusion: creative thinking depends on the implementation of strategies of various sorts, which would seem to exemplify executive functioning. As one example, Gilhooly, Fioratou, Anthony, and Wynn (2007) examined factors underlying performance on the unusual uses test, which has been used in numerous studies of creative thinking. People are asked to produce uncommon uses for common objects, such as a brick, a paper clip, a shoe, or a tire. One reliable finding from those studies is that the novelty of the uses that people produce, as rated by independent judges, increases over time: the first few uses are much less novel than are later ones.

Gilhooly and colleagues (2007) were the first to consider the processes underlying people's ability to produce new uses for a common object, and what might have brought about those changes in novelty over time. Participants produced verbal protocols as they worked on the unusual uses test, and the results indicated that different strategies were important in determining people's performance. Initially, people simply recalled object uses from memory, and those uses, as might be expected, were not particularly novel. After exhausting information in memory, participants switched to several other strategies, which resulted in the production of more novel uses. One of those strategies was what Gilhooly and colleagues called *disassembly use production*, which involved imagining the object taken apart and then using the parts as the basis for production of novel uses. With a shoe, one might think about how the laces could be used, which could serve to stimulate novel uses for the shoe. In a second study, Gilhooly and colleagues examined the relationship between strategy use, production of novel uses, and executive functioning, and they found that the memory strategy was not related to executive capacity, but the other strategies were. Thus, creative performance on the unusual uses test is related to executive functioning.

Similar conclusions have been drawn by Silvia and his colleagues from studies that have examined the relationship between creative performance and fluid intelligence, which is closely related to executive functioning. In one study, which can be looked upon as an elaboration of that of Gilhooly and colleagues (2007), Beaty and Silvia (2012) analyzed the serial order effect in creative thinking – the tendency for responses to become more creative over time on tasks such as the unusual uses test. The usual explanation for the serial order effect is based on the idea that more-creative (i.e., unusual) uses depend on linking together concepts that are distantly related in semantic memory. The early responses, based on ideas closely linked in semantic memory, will not be very creative. Over time, activation spreads to more distantly related concepts, which results in responses that are more creative.

Beaty and Silvia (2012) proposed a different explanation for the serial position effect in creative-idea generation, based on executive functioning. Generating creative ideas involves several executive functions, such as choosing the most effective strategies (Gilhooly et al., 2007), switching response categories when idea generation begins to slow down, and managing interference from obvious but irrelevant aspects of the task, such as the color of the brick in an unusual uses task. Based on this perspective, people higher in executive skills should show a smaller serial position effect, or perhaps no effect at all. People high in fluid intelligence should be able, through management of the processes involved in production of unusual uses, to generate creative responses from the start. The results supported the executive-functioning explanation. As noted, Silvia and his colleagues have carried out numerous studies that have supported the general conclusion that executive functioning plays an important role in creative thinking (e.g., Silvia, Beaty, & Nusbaum, 2013; see also Cinan, Özen, & Hampshire, 2013).

In conclusion, the results from studies of the role of executive functioning in insight are at this point unclear. Several studies have indicated that executive functioning plays little or no role in insight, and some researchers have proposed that high levels of executive functioning may be detrimental to creative thinking. However, in all the studies to date, those conclusions go beyond the data that were collected. In addition, other research has provided evidence that supports the opposite conclusion, i.e., that executive functioning plays an important role in some examples of creative thinking. Thus, strong conclusions about the role of executive functioning in creative thinking must await further studies.

If insight can come about through the multiple paths, such as those outlined in the model in Figure 34.2, then executive functioning should play a significant role in some cases of insight, i.e., those that arise through Stage 1 ⇒ 3; Stage 1 ⇒ 2; and Stage 1 ⇒ 2 ⇒ 3. As an example, consider someone who solves the Candle problem by rejecting the tacks and then deciding to build something to hold the candle to the wall (Fleck & Weisberg, 2004). One might expect that relatively complicated solution to depend on executive functioning. In contrast, reasoning out the solution to the Lilies problem (Fleck & Weisberg, 2013) might not demand much in the way of executive functioning. There is much heterogeneity in the processes underlying solution of insight problems, with variability from problem to problem concerning the specific mechanisms that bring about insight. Indeed, there probably is variability from person to person concerning the mechanisms that bring about insight within a given insight problem, and variability within a given person's performance concerning the mechanisms that bring about solution to different insight problems. Thus, one should be cautious when making predictions concerning the role of executive functioning in problem solving.

Is insight the *sine qua non* for creativity?

Both Ohlsson (2011) and Perkins (2000) use the insight sequence as the criterion for *defining* creative thinking: any advance not brought about through impasse and restructuring is, *ipso facto*, not creative. Similarly, in a discussion of mechanisms underlying problem solving, Wiley and Jarosz (2012) distinguish between analytical problems (exemplified by verbally based mathematics problems), and "creative" problems. Regarding the latter, "solution seems to require either a completely original approach (i.e., restructuring), or a novel combination of diverse bits of information through remote associations in memory" (p. 259).

Based on the discussion in this chapter, questions can be raised about that dichotomy. Insight and its components can be brought about in many ways, and to claim that restructuring, for example, involves "a completely novel approach" skims over several issues. Restructuring sometimes is in response to analysis of the information in the problem and so does not involve a completely novel approach. There might be "complete" novelty if one compares that new approach with the (incorrect) approach that an insight problem is designed to foster, but here too one can raise a question about whether novelty arising that way is "complete." Furthermore, many people bypass the researcher's schemes. Second, restructuring sometimes comes about through analytic thought in response to negative feedback, which also raises questions about "complete" novelty.

One can also raise questions about the other possible mechanism outlined by Wiley and Jarosz (2012): "a novel combination of diverse bits of information through remote associations in memory." We have seen that creative responses on laboratory creative-thinking tasks may depend on executive processes (e.g., Beaty & Silvia, 2012; Cinan et al., 2013; Gilhooly et al., 2007), which raises questions about the direct role of remote associations in creativity. In a related vein, Ohlsson (2011) and Perkins (2000) list numerous examples of large-scale creative advances that they propose came about through the insight sequence. Examples include Wilkins's invention of radar before World War II; Leonardo's invention of the "Aerial Screw," a flying machine; and Edison's invention of the lightbulb. I have recently proposed that those advances came about through analytic thinking – they involved neither restructuring nor "remote associations" – so, according to the neo-Gestalt theorists, those advances would not be considered creative (Weisberg, 2015). In addition, I have elsewhere discussed a number of other creative advances that also seem to have been brought about through analytic thinking (see Weisberg, 2006, ch.1 and 5; Weisberg, 2011), including Watson and Crick's discovery of the double helix, the creation by

Picasso of his great painting *Guernica*, the Wright brothers' invention of the airplane, Pollock's development of his poured-painting style in the late 1940s, and Frank Lloyd Wright's creation of *Fallingwater*, the iconic house over the stream. Thus, we are led to the conclusion that, comparable to the analysis of insight in problem solving, we need to consider multiple paths to creative advances, and we should reject the proposal that the insight sequence is the only way that a creative advance can come about.

There is one final point concerning the role of insight in creative thinking that bears brief consideration. One reason for studying insight in the laboratory is the assumption that the same processes are assumed to play a role in creative thinking conceived more broadly, i.e., in creative advances that take place outside the laboratory. However, although that assumption may seem obviously true, it should be tested. One test involves examination of case studies of creativity, just discussed. A recent investigation by Beaty, Nusbaum, and Silvia (2014) took a different tack. They tested undergraduates on insight problems and correlated their performance with the students' reports of creative accomplishments in their lives. In two studies, no relationship was found between performance on laboratory insight problems and creative accomplishments. One might raise questions about the research (e.g., are undergraduates the best ones to ask about creative achievements?), but the findings nonetheless should give pause to anyone who assumes that insight is the ***sine qua non*** of creativity.

Conclusions

This chapter has proposed no sweeping conclusions concerning how problem solving comes about. Indeed, the discussion in this chapter may have muddied the waters considerably, in the sense that the clear distinction between insight and analysis has given way to a continuum. However, we are in the midst of a time of high productivity concerning research on insight and related phenomena, and in such a period there is often lack of clear conclusions. If the model in Figure 34.2 is on the right track, then we have seen that it points us to the need for detailed information concerning the processes underlying problem solving, and such information surely will be useful in the long run. We may have to return to the laboratory and collect more data, but the results will be worth it.

References

Allen, A. P., & Thomas, K. E. (2011). A dual process account of creative thinking. *Creativity Research Journal, 23*, 109–118.

Ash, I. K., & Wiley, J. (2006). The nature of restructuring in insight: An individual differences approach. *Psychonomic Bulletin & Review, 13*, 66–73

Baddeley, A. (2003). Working memory: Looking back and looking forward. *Nature Reviews Neuroscience, 4*, 829–839.

Ball, L. J., & Stevens, A. (2009). Evidence for a verbally-based analytic component to insight problem solving. In N. Taatgen & H. van Rijn, J. (Eds.), ***Proceedings of the thirty-first annual conference of the cognitive science society*** (pp. 1060–1065). Austin, Tx: Cognitive Science Society.

Beaty, R. E., Nusbaum, E. C., & Silvia, P. J. (2014). Does insight problem solving predict real-world creativity? *Psychology of Aesthetics, Creativity, and the Arts, 8*, 287–292.

Beaty, R. E., & Silvia, P. J. (2012). Why do ideas get more creative across time? An executive interpretation of the serial order effect in divergent thinking tasks. *Psychology of Aesthetics, Creativity, and the Arts, 6*, 309–319.

Cinan, S., Özen, G., & Hampshire, A. (2013). Confirmatory factor analysis on separability of planning and insight constructs. *Journal of Cognitive Psychology, 25*, 7–23.

Cranford, E. A., & Moss, J. (2012). Is insight always the same? A protocol analysis of insight in compound remote associate problems. *Journal of Problem Solving, 4*, 128–153.

Evans, J. St. B. T. (2005). Insight and self insight in reasoning and decision making. In V. Girotto & P. N. Johnson-Laird (Eds.), *The shape of reason: Essays in honour of Paolo Legrenzi*. Hove, UK: Psychology Press.
Fleck, J. I. (2008). Working memory demands in insight versus analytic problem solving. *European Journal of Cognitive Psychology, 20*, 139–176.
Fleck, J. I., & Weisberg, R. W. (2004). The use of verbal protocols as data: An analysis of insight in the candle problem. *Memory & Cognition, 32*, 990–1006.
Fleck, J. S., & Weisberg, R. W. (2013). Insight versus analysis: Evidence for diverse methods in problem solving. *Journal of Cognitive Psychology, 25*, 436–463.
Gilhooly, K., & Fioratou, E. (2009). Executive functions in insight versus non-insight problem solving: An individual differences approach. *Thinking and Reasoning, 15*, 355–376.
Gilhooly, K., Fioratou, E., Anthony, S., & Wynn, V. (2007). Divergent thinking: Strategies and executive involvement in generating novel uses for familiar objects. *British Journal of Psychology, 98*, 611–625.
Gilhooly, K., & Murphy, P. (2005). Differentiating insight from non-insight problems. *Thinking and Reasoning, 11*, 279–302.
Jarosz, A. F., Colflesh, G. J., & Wiley, J. (2012). Uncorking the muse: Alcohol intoxication facilitates creative problem solving. *Consciousness and Cognition, 21*, 487–493.
Kaplan, C. A., & Simon, H. A. (1990). In search of insight. *Cognitive Psychology, 22*, 374–419.
Lavric, A., Forstmeier, S., & Rippon, G. (2000). Differences in working memory involvement in analytical and creative tasks: An ERP study. *Neuroreport, 11*, 1613–1618.
MacGregor, J. N., Ormerod, T. C., & Chronicle, E. P. (2001). Information-processing and insight: A process model of performance on the nine-dot problem. *Journal of Experimental Psychology: Learning, Memory, and Cognition, 27*, 176–201.
Metcalfe, J. (1986). Feeling of knowing in memory and problem solving. *Journal of Experimental Psychology: Learning, Memory, and Cognition, 12*, 288–294.
Metcalfe, J., & Wiebe, D. (1987). Intuition in insight and noninsight problem solving. *Memory & Cognition, 15*, 238–246.
Miyake, A., Friedman, N. P., Emerson, M. J., Witzki, A. H., & Howerter, A. (2000). The unity and diversity of executive functions and their contributions to complex "frontal lobe" tasks: A latent variable analysis. *Cognitive Psychology, 41*, 49–100.
Newell, A., & Simon, H. A. (1972). *Human problem solving*. Englewood Cliffs, NJ: Prentice-Hall.
Ohlsson, S. (1992). Information-processing explanations of insight and related phenomena. In M. T. Keane, & K. J. Gilhooly (Eds.), *Advances in the psychology of thinking* (Vol. 1, pp. 1–44). New York, NY: Harvester Wheatsheaf.
Ohlsson, S. (2011). *Deep learning: How the mind overrides experience*. Cambridge: Cambridge University Press.
Perkins, D. N. (2000). *The Eureka effect: The art and logic of breakthrough thinking*. New York: Norton.
Polya, G. (1945). *How to solve it*. Princeton, NJ: Princeton University Press. www.purbeckradar.org.uk/biography/wilkins_arnold.htm [accessed June 12, 2015]
Silvia, P. J., Beaty, R. E., & Nusbaum, E. C. (2013). Verbal fluency and creativity: General and specific contributions of broad retrieval ability (Gr) factors to divergent thinking. *Intelligence, 41*, 328–340.
Weisberg, R. W. (1980). *Memory, thought, and behavior*. New York: Oxford.
Weisberg, R. W. (1995). Prolegomena to theories of insight in problem solving: A taxonomy of problems. In R. Sternberg & J. Davidson (Eds.), *The nature of insight* (pp. 157–196). Cambridge, MA: MIT Press.
Weisberg, R. W. (2006). *Creativity: Understanding innovation in problem solving, science, invention, and the arts*. Hoboken, NJ: John Wiley.
Weisberg, R. W. (2011). Frank Lloyd Wright's *Fallingwater*: A case study of inside-the-box creativity. *Creativity Research Journal, 23*, 296–312.
Weisberg, R. W. (2013). On the "demystification" of insight: A critique of neuroimaging studies of insight. *Creativity Research Journal, 25*, 1–14.
Weisberg, R. W. (2015). Toward an integrated theory of insight in problem solving. *Thinking and Reasoning, 21*, 5–39.
Weisberg, R. W., & Suls, J. M. (1973). An information-processing model of Duncker's candle problem. *Cognitive Psychology, 4*, 255–276.
Wertheimer, M. (1982). *Productive thinking* (Enlarged ed.). Chicago, IL: University of Chicago Press.
Wiley, J., & Jarosz, A. F. (2012). How working memory capacity affects problem solving. *Psychology of Learning and Motivation, 56*, 185–227.

35

THINKING AND REASONING ACROSS CULTURES

Hiroshi Yama

Human universality and cultural psychology

This chapter addresses the issue of cultural differences in thinking and reasoning between Westerners and Easterners. First, I introduce the differences in cognition in general (Nisbett, Peng, Choi, & Norenzayan, 2001). Next, I focus on the distinction between Westerners' tendency for rule-based inference and Easterners' tendency for dialectical inference (Peng & Nisbett, 1999). In the fourth section, two kinds of explanations for the cultural differences are introduced: the first is based on different notions of the self in different cultures and the second is based on different cultural traditions. A further explanation is added, which is based on context (Yama & Zakaria, 2012). In the fifth section, I discuss whether contemporary cognitive theories of reasoning can be applied to explain the cultural differences. Finally, I propose that dual process theories, which suppose the existence of an evolutionary old system and an evolutionary current system, are highly relevant to accounting for cultural differences in thinking.

According to traditional ideas in philosophy, the human mind is rational in nature and universal across cultures. The assumption of universality was adopted in 20th-century psychology (e.g., Chomsky, 1957). If cognitive architecture is universal, there are no cultural differences in cognitive architecture, though there may be cultural difference in cognition and behavior. Cultural differences could be described in the framework of stimulus-response relationships, in which a culturally specific behavior was supposed to be a response to a culturally specific stimulus. This position leads to the idea that common experimental paradigms and tests can be used in all the cultures. When paradigms and tests devised by Western psychologists are misused among people in other cultures, these can be invalid. For example, it is plausible that a test which is designed by a Western psychologist to measure an individual's subjective happiness is invalid for measuring the subjective happiness of non-Western people, because they may have a different kind of subjective happiness.

However, recent cross-cultural studies are beginning to abandon the universality assumption, and instead accept an interactive view that the human mind has been shaped by the interaction between culture and itself (Markus & Kitayama, 1991). Cultural differences cannot be explained solely based on culturally specific stimuli that are input for each individual. Identical sets of stimuli can be interpreted differently depending on which culture the individual is born into and grows up in. In the background of cultural psychology is an idea of Lev Vygotsky, who emphasized a non-evolutionary character and mechanism of higher mental functional development. This framework focuses on how aspects of culture, such as values, beliefs, customs, and skills, are transmitted from one generation to the next. In this sense it is also called cultural-historical psychology. Each culture has a structure of shared views and senses of value concerning customs, pragmatics, morals, educational systems, and so on. This not only works as a set of environmental stimuli, but produces pressures on the mind to be shaped, so that people are adapted to it. Further, cultures have been shaped by people in the pursuit of their happiness. More precisely, mental functions and structures produce pressures on cultures so that they provide benefits for individuals. According to Shweder (1991), no individual's mind can be independent of its culture. He argued that the idea of independence was a consequence of the view of humans in the time of Enlightenment in Europe: humans were supposed to have intelligence and rationality making them independent of everything. The criticisms against the assumption of universality are summarized by Henrich, Heine, and Norenzayan (2010). They argue that most psychological data are derived from the sample of WEIRD cultures (Western, educated, industrialized, rich, and democratic), and that it is therefore not valid to discuss the human mind in general based on just these data, given the evidence of cultural differences in visual perception, fairness, cooperation, and so on.

As one of the solutions of this problem, Kim and Park (2000) proposed the 'indigenous psychologies' approach, which is one of the schools of cultural psychology, referring to the case of South Korea. They assumed that culture is defined as a superordinate construct that provides meaning, coherence, and direction to a group of people. Hence, in order to understand the human mind, psychological theories which assume human universality are of little use. Instead, in the indigenous psychologies approach, theories, concepts, and methods are developed from within. They proposed that, as an example, although contemporary Korea accepts Western economic, political, and educational systems, Confucianism still has a deep effect on Korean people's minds and habits, and apart from Western psychological theories, they postulated that they should construct bottom-up theories to understand Korean people's mind and behavior. Confucianism is a system of philosophical and ethical-sociopolitical teachings, which was born in China in the sixth century BCE and transmitted to the remainder of East Asia.

Evolutionary psychology has sometimes been seen as opposed to cultural psychology, because it appears to emphasize human universals and human innateness. However, some psychologists who study culture take the view of evolutionary psychology (e.g., Gangestad, 2010). Evolutionary psychology provides a framework to discuss how humans are adaptive within a culture and how humans create cultures to solve adaptive problems. Furthermore, the mechanism of adaptation can be universal across cultures. Therefore, the question of which human aspects are universal, and how strongly they are universal, is becoming important even for cultural psychologists (e.g., Norenzayan & Heine, 2005).

Cultural differences in cognition between Westerners and Easterners

Cross-cultural research examining differences between Westerners and Easterners is one of the foci of cultural psychology. This chapter reviews cross-cultural studies of cognition and then focuses on reasoning. Nisbett et al. (2001) reviewed earlier cross-cultural studies on human cognition and proposed a distinction between Westerners' analytic cognition and Easterners' holistic cognition. According to them, East Asians developed an intellectual tradition emphasizing holistic, dialectical information processing. This is contrasted with the European/North American intellectual tradition, which privileges an analytical style of cognition. According to Nisbett and colleagues' definition, analytic cognition implies detachment of the object from its context, a tendency to focus on attributes of the object to assign it to a category, and a preference for using rules about categories to explain and predict the object's behavior. In contrast, holistic cognition has an orientation to the context or the field as a whole, attention to relationships between a focal object and the field, and a preference for explaining and predicting events on the basis of such relationships.

The distinction between analytic and holistic cognition can be described in terms of four dimensions. Firstly, with an analytic cognitive style, Westerners' attention tends to be oriented to an object and not its context, whereas with a holistic style, Easterners tend to focus attention not only on the object itself but also the context in which the object is embedded. For instance, Masuda and Nisbett (2001) showed that Japanese gave more attention to the background of a target than Americans. They asked American and Japanese participants to remember the scenes of some films and to report them. Americans reported more on target objects, whereas Japanese reported more on their background information. Furthermore, Japanese could recognize a target object presented with its background better than when it was presented alone. This background effect was much less for the Americans.

The second factor is about causal attribution or causal inference. It is claimed that Easterners make more situational attributions, while Westerners make more dispositional attributions (Choi, Dalal, Kim-Prieto, & Park, 2003; Morris & Peng, 1994). For instance, Choi et al. (2003) reported that when participants attempted to explain either deviant or prosocial behavior, Korean participants took into consideration a greater amount of information than did either American or Asian American participants. It is proposed that Easterners assume the presence of complex causalities and focus more on the relationships and interactions between an actor and his or her surrounding situations more strongly than Westerners, who primarily consider the internal dispositions of an actor.

The third factor is about the usage of rules, which is the main topic of this chapter and is discussed in the next section. It has been suggested that Westerners are inclined to use rule-based inference and Easterners are more apt to use intuitive or dialectical inference (Norenzayan, Smith, Kim, & Nisbett, 2002; Peng & Nisbett, 1999; Spencer-Rodgers, Boucher, Mori, Wang, & Peng, 2009).

The fourth factor is about the perception of change. According to the traditional culture, the ancient Chinese believed that the world changes more than the ancient Greeks did (e.g., Nisbett, 2003). These traditions were taken over by contemporary Easterners and Westerners, respectively, and this tendency is verified by some cross-cultural studies. For instance, Ji, Nisbett, and Su (2001) reported that Chinese were more likely than Americans to predict changes in events and to perceive people as wise who predict changes.

Since making this distinction between Westerners' analytic cognition and Easterners' holistic cognition, Nisbett et al. (2001) have influenced many cross-cultural studies of cognition.

Westerners' rule-based reasoning and Easterners' intuitive and/or dialectical reasoning

Researchers have continued to debate whether humans are rational or irrational, whether human reasoning is domain-specific or domain-general, and whether reasoners use rules or models. Much of this debate has presupposed that human reasoning is universal across cultures, and that hypotheses tested only with Western participants will be valid for all the population of human beings.

However, some psychologists have raised doubts about this universality assumption. As already mentioned, some have proposed that Westerners tend to do rule-based thinking, and that Easterners tend to do intuitive or dialectical thinking (Nisbett et al., 2001; Yama, Manktelow,

Mercier, Van der Henst, Do, Kawasaki, & Adachi, 2010). Norenzayan et al. (2002) reported that, when asked which one of two groups a target object was similar to, Americans tended to focus on a single property for the grouping, whereas Koreans tended to consider more properties. Americans preferred rule-based reasoning focusing on a single property, whereas Koreans preferred similarity-based intuitive reasoning, with the group members thought of as having a family resemblance. In other words, Koreans prefer the grouping so that it is loosely defined by a combination of common properties rather than a rigorous single property. This tendency was confirmed by another experiment, on categorical inference. For instance, Koreans were less inclined than Americans to accept the conclusion 'all penguins have an ulnar artery' from the premise 'all birds have an ulnar artery', because penguins are not typical birds.

On the other hands, Peng and Nisbett (1999) proposed that the essential property of Easterners' thinking is dialecticism, which is contrasted with Westerners' rule-based thought. Dialecticism is defined as an inference in which a synthesis is inferred from a thesis and its antithesis. Dialectical thinking can be regarded as one of the kinds of intuitive thinking in the sense that plural properties are considered, but it indicates thinking for dealing with contradiction. Peng and Nisbett found that the thinking style of Chinese was more dialectical than that of Americans. They conducted several cross-cultural experiments to compare Chinese with Americans. The Chinese were less sensitive to and more accepting of contradictory proverbs such as 'too humble is half proud', for example, than Americans. Furthermore, Peng and Nisbett (1999) demonstrated that Chinese participants rated their agreement of two contradictory statements more moderately when these statements were presented together than when either of the statements was presented individually. This trend was not observed in the data of Americans. The results indicate that Chinese are more likely to take the middle way when they encounter opinions which are contradictory.

According to Hegelians (e.g., Mueller, 1958), dialecticism is expected to produce a higher-level resolution where there are some opinions which contradict each other. This is in contrast to propositional logic which does not allow contradiction. Dialectical thinking accepts contradiction and thus can be illogical, while it is a higher level thinking beyond the dichotomy of propositional logic. Spencer-Rodgers, Williams, and Peng (2010) proposed that Easterners' dialecticism is neither poor thinking nor higher-level thinking but what they called 'naïve dialecticism', which has three principles. Actually, Peng and Nisbett (1999) had already pointed out these three principles of naïve dialecticism:

1. The principle of contradiction: because of the interconnectedness of things and the ever-changing world, paradoxes and contradictions constantly arise. Two opposing propositions may both be true, and opposites are only apparent.
2. The principle of change: the universe is in flux and is constantly changing, and so the concepts that reflect it must also be fluid. Apparent stability is a signal of likely change.
3. The principle of holism: nothing exists in isolation; everything is connected.

Easterners have these folk beliefs, and thus they are likely to take a middle way when they encounter two opposite opinions or even contradictions. Furthermore, although the third principle of holism is pointed out, Spencer-Rodgers, Williams, and Peng (2010) do not emphasize the relation between naïve dialecticism and contextual processing. Rather, they claim that there is a strong causal relation between Easterners' view that everything changes and their tendency to tolerate contradictions.

Regarding dialecticism, Spencer-Rodgers et al. (2004) found that Chinese gave more conflicting responses in self-evaluation than Americans. In other words, Chinese respondents' self-evaluations were both positive and negative. This tendency of dialecticism was also confirmed in affection and emotion (e.g., Bagozzi, Wong, & Yi, 1999). Miyamoto, Uchida, and Ellsworth (2010) reported that Japanese were more likely to have mixed emotions than Americans, especially in pleasant situations. The Japanese feel slight sadness even when they feel happy. Furthermore, Ma-Kellams, Spencer-Rodgers, and Peng (2011) report that Easterners have mixed feelings and evaluations, not only about themselves, but about the group which they belong to.

Regarding the principle of change, the finding of Ji et al. (2001) that Chinese predicted changes more than Americans supports the claim of Spencer-Rodgers, Williams, and Peng (2010). Spencer-Rodgers and colleagues (Spencer-Rodgers, Peng, Wang, & Hou, 2004; Spencer-Rodgers et al., 2009; Spencer-Rodgers, Williams, & Peng, 2010) propose, based on questionnaire studies, that Easterners' dialectic thinking style is strongly related to their tendency to predict more changes than Westerners. The questionnaire, which is called DSS (the Dialectical Self Scale), consists of 32 items, and includes statements such as 'When I hear two sides of an argument, I often agree with both'. It was invented to measure the degree of naïve dialecticism in self-evaluation. It includes items to measure the tendency of people to accept opposing elements (e.g., good–bad) as coexisting in their minds, and people's belief that things change in the world. The DSS score of Easterners was higher than that of Westerners (Spencer-Rodgers et al., 2009).

However, the results that Easterners are more likely to take a middle way (Peng & Nisbett, 1999) have not been replicated. Mercier, Zhan, Qu, Lu, and Van der Henst (2015) conducted a replication of Peng and Nisbett (1999) with French and Chinese participants, but neither group took a middle way resolution when they were confronted with a pair of contradictory statements. Mercier, Yama, Kawasaki, Adachi, and Van der Henst (2012) found that neither French nor Japanese participants took a middle way resolution when they received advice which opposed their own opinion. Both French and Japanese kept their opinion.

Moreover, Friedman, Chen, and Vaid (2006) did not replicate Peng and Nisbett's (1999) results using contradictory proverbs. Their research sought to replicate the claim of Peng and Nisbett (1999), but both Chinese and Americans liked dialectical proverbs better than non-dialectical proverbs and judged dialectical proverbs as wiser. Their study was devised so that it controlled the effect of poeticality, which is covaried with preference judgment, hence they concluded that the cultural differences which Peng and Nisbett found were the result of poeticality. In other words, Chinese judged dialectical proverbs more poetic than non-dialectical proverbs, and thus they liked them.

In Zhang, Galbraith, Yama, Wang, and Manktelow (2015), we report that the DSS scores of Japanese were higher than those of Chinese, and those of Chinese were higher than those of the British. This result replicated the studies of Spencer-Rodgers (Spencer-Rodgers et al., 2004; Spencer-Rodgers et al., 2009) in the sense that the scores of Easterners are higher than those of Westerners. But when our participants were given pairs of opposite opinions, the Japanese showed the lowest level of dialecticism. When they agreed with one opinion in the pair, they were more likely to disagree with its opposite. However, when we asked our participants if it was wise to dialectically reason opposite opinions, Japanese participants judged dialectical thinking as wiser than Chinese and British did. In sum, our provisional conclusion is that Easterners are more dialectical in how they feel and how they evaluate themselves than Westerners. But it is still doubtful whether they are more dialectical when they make objective judgments about the world. I discuss the differences between Japanese and Chinese in the next section.

How should cultural differences in reasoning be explained?

Two kinds of explanations for the cultural differences in thinking between Westerners and Easterners are considered in this section. The first is based on the distinction between Westerners' individualist culture and Easterners' collectivist culture, and/or on the distinction between Westerners' independent self and Easterners' interdependent self.

Nisbett et al. (2001) tried to describe the differences between Western analytic and Eastern holistic cognition by using cultural values that underlie Western individualist culture and Eastern collectivist culture (Hofstede, 1980; Triandis, 1995). They discussed how each cognitive style is adaptive in its own cultural type. In the long history of culture, it has been claimed that Western people have established an individualist culture, whereas Eastern people have developed a collectivist culture.

The distinction between individualism and collectivism is a hypothetical concept which was proposed to explain the observed differences in people's behavior: Easterners have a stronger tendency than Westerners to prefer sociability and interdependence. Markus and Kitayama (1991) also connected this distinction to two kinds of selves. They argued that Westerners have an independent self, whereas Easterners have an interdependent self. This distinction describes the differences in how people view themselves. According to Markus and Kitayama, Westerners are likely to view themselves as individualistic, ego-centric, and discrete from society, but Easterners are more inclined to view themselves as collectivistic, socio-centric, and related to others or society.

The human mind was designed by evolution to be adaptive in each culture. If people live in an individualist culture where their own goals to acquire resources and avoid hazards are given priority over other collectivist goals, it is adaptive for them to identify goals of benefit to them as individuals (e.g., material resources) and make predictions about those goals. Rule-based deduction and induction have been developed as good cognitive tools for these goals. For instance, when we see that a new colleague is kind and sincere, and have a belief that any person who is kind and sincere can be a useful friend, we judge that the colleague can be a useful friend. A prediction about an object following rule-based reasoning requires, to some extent, an abstract representation of that object, its decontextualization.

On the other hand, if people live in a collectivist culture where they have to put group goals first (e.g., maintaining group harmony), they should have another style of cognition. They have to pay attention not only to the object itself, but to the contextual information in order to maintain the harmony of their collectives. In the example above, we should consider the new colleague not only as an individual but also as a member of the department, because the relation between us and the new colleague could influence the harmony of the entire department. Furthermore, people in a collectivist culture should not make a sharp decision in a disagreement that one side is completely justified and the other unjustified. Such a decision might upset the balance of power and in-group harmony. Hence, in a collectivist culture, dialectics are adaptive in resolving contradiction and are preferred to two-value logic. Holistic cognition and thought are useful for dialectics, because people have to take a lot of situational elements and factors into consideration to make a decision in this way.

Recently, developing the earlier causal explanation about individualism and collectivism, Varnum, Grossman, Kitayama, and Nisbett (2010) have proposed two kinds of causal explanation: from Westerners' independent self to analytic cognition and from Easterners' interdependent self to holistic cognition. It is still hard to give an account connecting the group level, individualism or collectivism, and the individual level, analytic cognition or holistic cognition, and they gave an inter-individual-level explanation. Their explanation is compatible with the results of cultural priming (Kühnen, Hannover, & Schubert, 2001; Kühnen & Oyserman, 2002). Cultural priming is assumed to make either independent or interdependent self-construal more accessible (Trafimow, Triandis, & Goto, 1991), and there is evidence that self-construal can be changed by cultural priming (e.g., Ng & Lai, 2009). Assuming that the socially connected and the autonomous unique selves are culture based, and that both are accessible to persons within a culture, shifts towards one or the other definition of the self can be experimentally induced by priming the corresponding cultural orientation or meaning system. The accessible self-construal affects cognitive style. For example, Kühnen et al. (2001) reported that participants who were asked to point out the differences between themselves and their friends or parents (primed as independent self) were more likely to process stimuli unaffected by the context (analytic cognition), whereas those who were asked to point out the similarities between themselves and their friends or parents (primed as interdependent self) were more apt to engage in context-bounded perception (holistic cognition). Kühnen and Oyserman (2002) showed that people who were asked to think of 'we' were better at cognitive tasks that required holistic cognition. This is because the 'we' priming is assumed to make the interdependent self more accessible.

The evidence to support this explanation is also found in cross-cultural studies conducted in one country. For example, Knight and Nisbett (2007) studied different groups in Italy. They found that northern Italians were more analytic thinkers than were southern Italians, who were more holistic. Northern Italian culture emphasized more independence (individualism) whereas southern Italian culture emphasized more interdependence (collectivism). Kitayama, Ishii, Imada, Takemura, and Ramaswamy (2006) found cultural differences between Americans, Japanese who were born and grew up in Hokkaido, and other Japanese. Hokkaido used to be the frontier of Japan, and most Japanese who live in Hokkaido are offspring of voluntary settlers after the Meiji Restoration in the 1860s. The hypothesis of Kitayama et al. was that economically motivated voluntary settlement in the frontier fosters the independent self. They found that Hokkaido Japanese show an intermediate level between analytic and holistic cognition. In other words, there was clear contrast between Americans' analytic cognition and non-Hokkaido Japanese persons' holistic cognition, and Hokkaido Japanese showed a medium level of both. The participants of a study by Uskul, Kitayama, and Nisbett (2008) were all Turkish and lived in the eastern Black Sea region. The researchers found that farmers and fishermen showed a stronger holistic cognition tendency than herders did. Members of farming and fishing communities emphasize harmonious social interdependence, while those of herding communities emphasize individual decision making and foster social independence.

The second explanation for the cultural differences in thinking between Westerners and Easterners is based on the cultural tradition. Spencer-Rodgers (Spencer-Rodgers et al., 2009; Spencer-Rodgers, Peng, & Wang, 2010; Spencer-Rodgers, Peng, Wang, & Hou, 2004; Spencer-Rodgers, Williams, & Peng, 2010) proposed some revisions to the position of Nisbett and his collaborators. She argues that the dimension between rule-based inference and dialectical inference is distinct from the other dimension of attention to context or not, and proposes that this dimension is not very strongly related to the distinction between individualist culture and collectivist culture. She does not attempt to explain the cultural differences between Westerners' analytic cognition and Easterners' holistic cognition, but just gives an explanation for the differences between Westerners' rule-based thinking and Easterners' dialectical thinking. This claim is verified by the fact that measures of naïve dialecticism are only weakly related to other culture-specific measures. For instance, the correlation between the DSS (e.g., Spencer-Rodgers et al., 2009) and the measure of interdependent self-construals (Singelis, 1994) was very weak among both American university students and Chinese university students. Secondly, Latinos are assumed to be collectivist. But it turned out that they are not dialectical (Ma-Kellams et al., 2011; Spencer-Rodgers et al., 2004). Therefore, the explanation based on the individualism/collectivism or independent/interdependent distinction cannot be applied to the cultural differences between Westerners' rule-based thinking and Easterners' dialectical thinking. As mentioned in the third section (naïve dialecticism), Easterners believe that the world is contradictory because it is always changing, and the perception of change makes it possible for Easterners to seek the resolution of contradiction. For instance, it might be inferred that someone is both kind and unkind because he sometimes changes his attitude from one day to the next.

Therefore, Spencer-Rodgers and Peng refer to a cultural tradition to explain the cultural differences between Westerners' rule-based thinking and Easterners' dialectical thinking. Nisbett (2003; Nisbett et al., 2001) had already noted the importance of a cultural tradition, but Spencer-Rodgers and Peng went beyond him. According to them, Westerners' style of thinking is affected by the philosophy of ancient Greece, whereas Easterners' style of thinking derives from the traditions of Taoism, Confucianism, and Buddhism. Particularly, Easterners' naïve dialecticism, including their folk beliefs, is rooted in the cultural tradition of the concept of *yin* (negative aspects of the world) and *yang* (positive aspects of the world), which is central to Taoism. It is used to describe how polar opposites or seemingly contrary forces are interconnected and interdependent in the real world. It reflects the tradition of Chinese ontology that the world is constantly changing like the switches between *yin* and *yang*, and is full of contradictions. This tradition is reflected in a Chinese hesitancy to make final judgment. For instance, the famous story of Sāi Weng's lost horse[1] was in the ***Huáinánzǐ***, a classic Chinese book on philosophy that blends Taoist, Confucianist, and Legalist thought in the second century BCE. This story provided a proverb, which says that just as bad luck can turn out good, then so can good luck turn out bad.

Finally, although Yama and Zakaria (2012) do not challenge the explanation based on the cultural tradition, they propose another possible explanation for the cultural differences in cognition. They emphasize the distinction between Westerners' low-context culture and Easterners' high-context culture (Hall, 1976). "Context" is implicitly shared beliefs by people when communicating, and people utilize context in a high-context culture more than in a low-context culture. This account can explain Easterners' dialectical thinking. Even if there is an apparent contradiction, it is easier for Easterners to resolve it implicitly by using contextual beliefs in a high-context culture. In a high-context culture (like in an Eastern country), people pay more attention to context, and they use it implicitly to resolve contradictions. For instance, when they come across a man who is too humble, they may infer that the person who pretends to be humble wants someone to deny what he is saying, or that he wishes to show his modesty, and thus is proud of his modesty. This may explain the result that Japanese people were more dialectical in attitude than Chinese people (Zhang et al., 2015). I introduce the analysis of Japanese language by Ikegami (2000). According to him, Japanese language is characterized by the fact that subjects considered to be originally indispensable are often omitted not only in everyday conversation but also in formal sentences. This is a notable difference between Japanese language and other languages, including Chinese language. The omitted subject can be recoverable from its context. Although he does not use the distinction between low context culture and high-context culture, it is very plausible that Japanese have higher-context culture than Chinese do.

This account has the potential to add an explanation as to why each cultural tradition has been shaped to the explanation based on the cultural tradition. A low-context culture is more likely to be shaped where people from different cultural backgrounds meet. Very recently, although they do not deal with human thinking, Rychlowska et al. (2015) investigated the explicitness of facial expression and gathered data from 32 countries. They report that the explicitness is determined by historical (cultural) heterogeneity. Generally speaking, historical heterogeneity, which is the extent to which a country's present-day population descends from numerous (versus few) source countries and is generally greater among Western countries, is associated with the norm favoring explicit facial expression. Shared context beliefs are less available for people in a historical heterogeneity, who, in other words, are in a low-context culture. In short, the difference between high-context culture and low-context culture can be generated in the long history of people's migration, which has been influenced by geographical and ecological factors.

Do cultural differences in cognition correspond to any distinctions in contemporary cognitive theories?

I raise a very basic question of whether the cultural differences in human reasoning can be explained in contemporary cognitive theories of reasoning. Cognitive theories of human reasoning can be grouped by how strongly they imply that human beings are logical thinkers. For instance, natural mental logic theory (Braine & O'Brien, 1991; Rips, 1994) assumes a set of inference rules or schemas and a reasoning program that implements these rules. If Easterners are less apt to do rule-based thinking, is the natural logic theory inapplicable to their reasoning? Or do Easterners have a different set of inference rules or a different reasoning program?

As far as we know, no one has raised such questions. Mental logic theory tries to describe a general mechanism for human reasoning, and this mechanism is assumed to be culturally universal. But I now discuss a further development in the study of human reasoning and its relevance to cultural differences in reasoning: dual process theories.

Evans and colleagues (e.g., Evans, 2010; Evans & Over, 1996) presented one of the most influential dual process theories (see also Evans, this volume). Their first motivation for proposing their theory was to resolve the paradox that humans are able to invent political and economic systems, sciences, and logic, but at the same time are susceptible to many fallacies and biases. They argued for the existence of two kinds of mental processing: one which is generally reliable but can cause fallacies and biases, and the other which can, at its best, allow human reasoning to follow normative rules. The former is an evolutionarily old heuristic system (intuitive mind) and the latter is an evolutionarily recent analytic system (reflective mind). The properties of the evolutionarily old heuristic system are that it is implicit, automatic, fast, intuitive, contextual, and associative, whereas the properties of the evolutionarily recent analytic system are that it is explicit, controlled, slow, reflective, abstract, and rule-based. The evolutionarily old system consists of the underlying modules in the brain. The term 'module' was introduced by Fodor (1983). His characterization of module is that it is innate, fast, domain-specific, and informationally encapsulated, with particular inputs and shallow output. If an input process is encapsulated and modular, the information in this process is not affected by a person's beliefs. Thus it is adaptive in its efficiency in responding to the world without the interference of beliefs. A module evolved to solve a specific adaptive problem, such as mind reading, social exchange, face cognition, and so on. A module can be efficient in general at solving its problem, but it can also produce errors and biases at times if not corrected by higher-level rule following. The evolutionarily recent system is the higher-level rule following aspect of the brain. It is closely related to working memory and IQ. Stanovich and West (2000) found that people with relatively low scores on the Scholastic Aptitude Test (SAT), which is correlated to IQ, were more likely to make reasoning errors and commit fallacies. Stanovich and West argued that these errors resulted from the failure of the evolutionarily recent system to inhibit and correct automatic biases in the evolutionarily old system.

The distinction between the evolutionarily old system and the evolutionarily recent system looks similar to that between holistic cognition and analytic cognition (Nisbett et al., 2001). What we should focus on is the contrast between the contextual and the abstract and that between the associative and the rule-based. These contrasts look similar to those between Western analytic cognition and Eastern holistic cognition. Epstein (1994) had already argued that human beings have a holistic, affective, association-driven experiential system (the evolutionarily old system) that coexists with an analytic, logical, and reason-oriented rational system (the evolutionarily recent system). Sloman (1996) also reviewed a wide range of literature and proposed the idea that there were two systems of reasoning, which he called associative and rule-based.

If we consider the claims of Nisbett et al. (2001) and accept that the analytic and holistic distinction is related to the dual process distinctions, we might infer that Westerners use the evolutionarily recent system while Easterners use the evolutionarily old system. But this quick conclusion would imply that Easterners' IQ test scores, which reflect the capacity of the evolutionary current system, would be lower than those of Westerners. However, as already demonstrated, the IQ test scores of Chinese, Koreans, and Japanese are as high as those of people in Western countries (e.g., Lynn, 2003). Anyway, there is no evidence that Westerners use the evolutionarily recent system while Easterners use the evolutionarily old system. Then how should we look at this matter?

Buchtel and Norenzayan (2009) examined whether the cultural definitions of analytic and holistic styles appear to parallel the properties of the two distinct systems of dual process theories. Generally speaking, cultural psychologists (e.g., Norenzayan et al., 2002) assume that cultural differences in cognition or in thinking are not aligned with distinct systems but rather reflect distinct styles or preferences. First of all, the automatic/controlled contrast does not overlap at all with the holistic/analytic contrast of Nisbett et al. (2001). Rather, the distinction between automatic and controlled is rooted in the history of human evolution and is culturally universal. The main area of overlap is with the contextual/abstract contrast. Westerners are more prepared to decontextualize than Easterners are. Furthermore, one of the greatest similarities between the two theories, which they pointed out, is that Westerners are more likely to adopt rule-based inference, compared to Easterners.

How is the position of Nisbett et al. (2001) related to dual process theories? At least the cultural differences referred to by Nisbett et al. do not seem to be based on strong individual differences. Actually, as I have already mentioned, people's responses can be easily changed from analytic to holistic and back again by cultural priming (Kühnen et al., 2001; Kühnen & Oyserman, 2002). Furthermore, Koo and Choi (2005) found that an individual's cognitive style can be changed by education. They reported that Korean students who major in oriental medicine think more holistically than those who major in psychology. For example, those who major in oriental medicine more frequently predict changes (as shown in the list of naïve dialecticism). Koo and Choi inferred that students of oriental medicine were taught the harmony of the human body, and it led to the aforementioned differences in thinking style between the two types of student.

Therefore, even if there are some overlapping dimensions between Nisbett et al. and dual process theories, we cannot conclude that Westerners use an evolutionarily recent system whereas Easterners use an evolutionarily old system. The cultural differences are not located in a system but in a thinking style, which is relatively easy to change. Yama, Nishioka, Horishita, Kawasaki, and Taniguchi (2007) proposed that the cultural differences might be due to how people partially use the two kinds of systems. They adopted the terms of Stanovich and West (2003), and argued that there are gene-installed goals of thinking and also meme-acquired goals in each of the two systems. A meme is a piece of knowledge that reproduces itself and spreads through the culture, by analogy with genes that replicate and spread through plant and animal populations by reproduction. The distinction between the two systems indicates differences in hardware, whereas the distinction between the gene-installed goals and the meme-installed goals shows the differences in software. Gene-installed goals are universal across cultures, whereas the meme-acquired goals vary with culture and explain how humans use both systems to be culturally adaptive. The gene-installed goals in the evolutionarily recent system correspond to the capacity that the IQ test measures. On the other hand, the cultural differences between rule-based thinking and intuitive or dialectical thinking can be due to the meme-installed goals in the evolutionarily recent system. The meme-installed goals account for the usage of the system.

Recently, Stanovich (2009) distinguished between the reflective, algorithmic, and autonomous mind. The evolutionarily old system corresponds to the autonomous mind, and it is culturally universal. The evolutionarily recent system is divided into the reflective mind and the algorithmic mind. The algorithmic mind corresponds to the cognitive capacity which enables human beings to think logically and is strongly related to what IQ tests measure. The reflective mind supervises the algorithmic mind and indicates how to use the capacity. Although Stanovich has not yet tried to explain cultural differences in cognition, it may be plausible to locate the effects of personality and culture in the processing of the reflective mind. Therefore, the meme-installed goals may be embedded in the reflective mind, although this proposal is speculative.

Because of the lack of evidence, it is still not certain if Westerners tend to use more dominantly the evolutionarily recent system, while Easterners tend to rely more on the evolutionarily old system following the indication of the reflective mind. In fact, Westerners are not always less susceptible to bias than Easterners. They have been found to commit the fundamental attribution error; that is, when they try to explain the actions of someone, they are more likely to appeal to his or her dispositions (i.e., personal traits; see Ross, 1977). Easterners are less prone to this bias (Choi, Nisbett, & Norenzayan, 1999). This does not mean that Westerners therefore necessarily use more dominantly the evolutionarily recent system, which is assumed to produce normative performance. Rather, both Westerners and Easterners can think automatically in ways that are practiced in each of their cultures. For example, generally speaking, person perception consists of an initial 'dispositional attribution (rule-based thinking)' stage, followed by a 'situational correction' stage in which information about situational constraints is used to adjust the initial inference. Choi et al. (1999) found that Westerners make dispositional attributions automatically, whereas Easterners do this with effort. On the other hand, Westerners make situational corrections with effort, whereas Easterners do this automatically. Thus, provisionally, I conclude that the cultural differences in cognition, especially in reasoning, are differences in cognitive style or cognitive preference, rather than in the cognitive system itself.

Thus we are able to resolve the paradox that, although there are no differences in IQ between Westerners and Easterners, Westerners appear to use more dominantly the evolutionarily recent system, while Easterners appear to rely more on the evolutionarily old system. Easterners tend to consider more rules than Westerners by their cultural norm, and thus they appear to use the evolutionarily old system more.

Finally, the new paradigm in the psychology of reasoning seems to be worthwhile for cross-cultural study in the near future. The traditional paradigm in the psychology of reasoning tried to account for human reasoning using only binary extensional logic (a classic example is Johnson-Laird & Byrne, 1991; see also Johnson-Laird, Goodwin, & Khemlani, this volume). But the new paradigm is the result of the great impact of Bayesian approaches in cognitive science, and uses Bayesian subjective probability and utility theory to account for human thinking and reasoning (Elqayam, this volume; Elqayam & Over, 2013; Oaksford & Chater, this volume; Over & Cruz, this volume). Because the new paradigm does not adopt binary logic, it has considerable potential to be related to dialectical thinking. It will, therefore, be of great interest to test Bayesian approaches to thinking and reasoning in the field of cross-cultural study, although such an investigative endeavor has yet to be launched.

Conclusion

In this chapter I considered the following questions: (1) whether human reasoning is universal, (2) whether Easterners are really dialectical, (3) how we explain the cultural differences between Westerners' rule-based thinking and Easterners' dialectical thinking, and (4) whether the distinction between Westerners' analytic cognition and Easterners' holistic cognition is related to current cognitive theories.

My answer to the first question is that I do not agree with the view that the human mind is completely universal. Some measures based on the data ofWesterners may not apply to Easterners. However, I do not completely agree with the view of cultural psychology (e.g., Markus & Kitayama, 1991; Nisbett et al., 2001). Cultural psychologists have not yet fully discussed the relationship between their own theory and current theories in the psychology of reasoning, such as dual process theories, and overestimate the magnitude of cultural differences. Furthermore, the problem of whether or not the human mind is culturally universal is dependent upon which aspect researchers focus on (e.g., Norenzayan & Heine, 2005).

The answer to the second question is provisional. Easterners seem to be dialectical at least in terms of emotional judgment (e.g., Miyamoto et al., 2010), value judgment (e.g., Ma-Kellams et al., 2011), and self (e.g., Spencer-Rodgers et al., 2009). However, it is still uncertain if they are dialectical in a tolerance of contradiction at the cognitive level (e.g., Mercier et al., 2015; Zhang et al., 2015) and in going middle way when reasoning about contradictory evidence (Mercier et al., 2012).

I did not discuss the reason for the distinction between Westerners' analytic cognition and Westerners' holistic cognition, but just the explanation for the distinction between Westerners' rule-based thinking and Easterners' dialectical thinking. I appreciate the attempt to find the relationship between cultural traditions, including those to do with ontology, and people's thinking style (Peng & Nisbett, 1999; Spencer-Rodgers, Williams, and Peng, 2010), but an explanation based on cultural traditions is insufficient. We need further explanation for how these cultural traditions have been evoked and shaped. Hence Yama and Zakaria (2012) made a distinction between Westerners' low-context culture and Easterners' high-context culture (Hall, 1976). This idea has the potential to give a further explanation for how each cultural tradition has been shaped in its history, because the difference between high-context culture and low-context culture can be generated in the long history of people's migration (e.g., Rychlowska et al., 2015). The migration of human beings is influenced by many ecological and geographical factors, and thus the idea of the low/high context can be related to the attempt at explaining cultural diversity through environmental differences alone (e.g., Diamond, 1997).

Finally, dual process accounts of the mind, which distinguish between analytic cognition (an evolutionarily recent system) and holistic cognition (an evolutionarily old system), appear to be the closest theories to the distinction between Westerners' analytic cognition and Easterners' holistic cognition. However, I propose that this does not mean that Easterners do not necessarily use the evolutionarily old system. Rather, the source of cultural differences in cognition may be in the reflective mind (Stanovich, 2009), which is defined as how individuals utilize their algorithmic minds.

Acknowledgment

I thank David E. Over and an anonymous reviewer for their very helpful comments on this earlier draft and revisions of English.

Note

1 Sāi raised horses for a living. One day he lost a horse and his neighbor felt sorry for him, but Sāi didn't care about the horse, because he thought it wasn't a bad thing to lose a horse. After a while the horse returned with another beautiful horse, and the neighbor congratulated him on his good luck. But Sāi thought that maybe it wasn't a good thing to have this new horse. His son liked the new horse and often rode it. One day his son fell off the horse and broke his leg. Because of his broken leg, he couldn't go off to the war, as was expected of all the young men in the area. Most of them died, but his son would survive.

References

Bagozzi, R. P., Wong, N., & Yi, Y. (1999). The role of culture and gender in the relationship between positive and negative affect. *Cognition and Emotion, 13*, 641–672.

Braine, M. D. S., & O'Brien, D. P. (1991). A theory of If: A lexical entry, reasoning program, and pragmatic principles. *Psychological Review, 98*, 182–203.

Buchtel, E. E., & Norenzayan, A. (2009). Thinking across cultures: Implications for dual processes. In J. St. B. T. Evans & K. Frankish (Eds.), *In two minds: Dual processes and beyond* (pp. 217–238). Oxford: Oxford University Press.

Choi, I., Dalal, R., Kim-Prieto, C., & Park, H. (2003). Culture and judgment of causal relevance. *Journal of Personality and Social Psychology, 84*, 46–59.

Choi, I., Nisbett, R. E., & Norenzayan, A. (1999). Causal attribution across cultures: Variation and universality. *Psychological. Bulletin, 125*, 47–63.

Chomsky, N. (1957). *Syntactic structure*. The Hague: Mouton.

Diamond, J. (1997). *Guns, germs, and steel*. New York: W. W. Norton & Company.

Elqayam, S., & Over, D. E. (2013). New paradigm psychology of reasoning: An introduction to the special issue edited by Elqayam, Bonnefon, & Over. *Thinking & Reasoning, 19*, 249–265.

Epstein, S. (1994). Integration of the cognitive and the psychodynamic unconscious. *American Psychologist, 49*, 709–724.

Evans, J. St. B. T. (2010). *Thinking twice: Two minds in one brain*. Oxford, UK: Oxford University Press.

Evans, J. St. B. T., & Over, D. E. (1996). *Rationality and reasoning*. Hove, UK: Psychology Press.

Fodor, J. (1983). *Modularity of mind*. Cambridge, MA: MIT Press.

Friedman, M., Chen, H-C., & Vaid, J. (2006). Proverb preferences across cultures: Dialecticality or poeticality? *Psychonomic Bulletin & Review, 13*, 353–359.

Gangestad, S. W. (2010). Exploring the evolutionary foundations of culture: An adaptationist framework. In M. Schaller, A. Norenzayan, S. J. Heine, T. Yamagishi, and T. Kameda (Eds.), *Evolution, culture, and the human mind* (pp. 83–98). New York: Psychology Press.

Hall, E. T. (1976). *Beyond culture*. Garden City, NJ: Anchor Books/Doubleday.

Henrich, J., Heine, S. J., & Norenzayan, A. (2010). The weirdest people in the world? *Behavioral and Brain Sciences, 33*, 61–135.

Hofstede, G. (1980). *Culture's consequences: International differences in work-related values*. Beverly Hills, CA: Sage.

Ikegami, Y. (2000). *Invitation to theories of Japanese*. Tokyo: Kodansha. (in Japanese)

Ji, L.-J., Nisbett, R. E., & Su, Y. (2001). Culture, change, and prediction. *Psychological Science, 12*, 450–456.

Johnson-Laird, P. N., & Byrne, R. M. J. (1991). *Deduction*. Hove & London: Erlbaum.

Kim, U., & Park, Y. S. (2000). The challenge of cross-cultural psychology in the 21st century: The role of the indigenous psychologies approach. *Journal of Cross Cultural Psychology, 31*, 63–75.

Kitayama, S., Ishii, K., Imada, T., Takemura, K., & Ramaswamy, J. (2006). Voluntary settlement and the spirit of independence: Evidence from Japan's "Northern Frontier". *Journal of Personality and Social Psychology, 91*, 369–384.

Knight, N., & Nisbett, R. E. (2007). Culture, class and cognition: Evidence from Italy. *Journal of Cognition and Culture*, 7, 283–291.

Koo, M., & Choi, I. (2005). Becoming a holistic thinker: Training effect of Oriental medicine on reasoning. *Personality and Social Psychology Bulletin, 31*, 1–9.

Kühnen, U., Hannover, B., & Schubert, B. (2001). The semantic-procedural interface model of the self: The role of self-knowledge for context-dependent versus context-independent modes of thinking. *Journal of Personality and Social Psychology, 80*, 397–409.

Kühnen, U., & Oyserman, D. (2002). Thinking about the self influences thinking in general: Cognitive consequences of salient self-concept. *Journal of Experimental Social Psychology, 38*, 492–499.
Lynn, R. (2003). The geography of intelligence. In H. Nyborg (Ed.), *The scientific study of general intelligence: Tribute to Arthur R. Jensen* (pp. 127–146). Amsterdam: Pergamon.
Ma-Kellams, C., Spencer-Rodgers, J., & Peng, K. (2011). I am against us?: Unpacking cultural differences in ingroup favoritism via dialecticism. *Personality and Social Psychology Bulletin, 37*, 15–27.
Markus, H. R., & Kitayama, S. (1991). Culture and the self: Implications for cognition, emotion, and motivation. *Psychological Review, 98*, 224–253.
Masuda, T., & Nisbett, R. E. (2001). Attending holistically versus analytically: Comparing the context sensitivity of Japanese and Americans. *Journal of Personality and Social Psychology, 81*, 922–934.
Mercier, H., Yama, H., Kawasaki, Y., Adachi, K., & Van der Henst, J-B. (2012). Is the use of averaging in advice taking modulated by culture? *Journal of Cognition and Culture, 12*, 1–16.
Mercier, H., Zhang, J., Qu, Y., & Lu, P., & Van der Henst, J-B. (2015). Do Easterners and Westerners treat contradiction differently? *Journal of Cognition and Culture, 15*, 45–63.
Miyamoto, Y., Uchida, Y., & Ellsworth, P. C. (2010). Culture and mixed emotions: Co-occurrence of positive and negative emotions in Japan and the United States. *Emotion, 10*, 404–415.
Morris, M. W., & Peng, K. (1994). Culture and cause: American and Chinese attributions for social and physical events. *Journal of Personality and Social Psychology, 67*,949–971.
Mueller, G. E. (1958). The Hegel legend of "thesis-antithesis-synthesis". *Journal of the History of Ideas, 19*, 411–414.
Ng, S. H., & Lai, J. C. L. (2009). Effects of culture priming on the social connectedness of the bicultural self. *Journal of Cross-Cultural Psychology, 40*, 170–186.
Nisbett, R. E. (2003). *The geography of thought: How Asians and Westerners think differently . . . and why*. New York: The Free Press.
Nisbett, R. E., Peng, K., Choi, I., & Norenzayan, A. (2001). Culture and system of thought: Holistic versus analytic cognition. *Psychological Review, 108*, 291–310.
Norenzayan, A., & Heine, S. J. (2005). Psychological universals: What are they and how can we know? *Psychological Bulletin, 131*, 763–784.
Norenzayan, A., Smith, E. E., Kim, B. J., & Nisbett, R. E. (2002). Cultural preferences for formal versus intuitive reasoning. *Cognitive Science, 26*, 653–684.
Peng, K., & Nisbett, R. E. (1999). Culture, dialectics, and reasoning about contradiction. *American Psychologist, 54*, 741–754.
Rips, L. J. (1994). *The psychology of proof.* Cambridge, MA: MIT Press.
Ross, L. (1977). The intuitive psychologist and his shortcomings. In L. Berkowitz (Ed.), *Advances in experimental social psychology* (Vol. 10, pp. 173–220). New York: Academic Press.
Rychlowska, M., Miyamoto, Y., Matsumoto, D., Hess, U., Gilboa-Schechtman, E., Kamble, S., Muluk, H., Masuda, T., & Niedenthal, P. M. (2015). Heterogeneity of long-history migration explains cultural differences in reports of emotional expressivity and the functions of smiles. *Proceedings of National Academy of Sciences of the United States of America, 112*, 2429–12436.
Shweder, R. (1991). Cultural psychology: What is it? In R. Shweder (Ed.), *Thinking through culture.* Cambridge, MA: Harvard University Press, Pp. 73–110.
Singelis, T. M. (1994). The measurement of independent and interdependent self-construals. *Personality and Social Psychology Bulletin, 20*, 580–591.
Sloman, S. A. (1996). The empirical case for two systems of reasoning. *Psychological Bulletin, 119*, 3–22.
Spencer-Rodgers, J., Boucher, H. C., Mori, S. C., Wang, L., & Peng, K. (2009). The dialectical self-concept: Contradiction, change, and holism in East Asian Cultures. *Personality and Social Psychological Bulletin, 35*, 29–44.
Spencer-Rodgers, J., Peng, K., & Wang, L. (2010). Naïve dialecticism and the co-occurrences of positive and negative emotions. *Journal of Cross-Cultural Psychology, 41*, 109–115.
Spencer-Rodgers, J., Peng, K., Wang, L., & Hou, Y. (2004). Dialectical self-esteem and East-West differences in psychological well-being. *Personality and Social Psychological Bulletin, 30*, 1416–1432.
Spencer-Rodgers, J., Williams, M., & Peng, K. (2010). Cultural differences in expectations of change and tolerance for contradiction: A decade of empirical research. *Personality and Social Psychology Review, 14*, 296–312.
Stanovich, K. E. (2009). Distinguishing the reflective, algorithmic, and autonomous minds: Is it time for a tri-process theory? In J. St. B. T. Evans & K. Frankish (Eds.), *In two minds: Dual processes and beyond.* Oxford: Oxford University Press.

Stanovich, K. E., & West, R. F. (2000). Individual differences in reasoning: Implications for the rationality debate? *Behavioral and Brain Sciences, 23*, 645–726.
Stanovich, K. E., & West, R. F. (2003). Evolutionary versus instrumental goals: how evolutionary psychology misconceives human rationality. In D. E. Over (Ed.), *Evolution and the psychology of thinking* (pp. 171–230). Hove, UK: Psychology Press.
Trafimow, D., Triandis, H. C., & Goto, S. G. (1991). Some tests of the distinction between the private self and the collective self. *Journal of Personality and Social Psychology, 60*, 649–655.
Triandis, H. C. (1995). *Individual and collectivism.* Boulder, CO: Westview Press.
Uskul, A. K., Kitayama, S., & Nisbett, R. E. (2008). Ecocultural basis of cognition: Farmers and fishermen are more holistic than herders. *Proceedings of the National Academy of Sciences of the USA, 105*, 8552–8556.
Varnum, M. E. W., Grossman, I., Kitayama, S., & Nisbett, R. E. (2010), The origin of cultural differences in cognition: The social orientation hypothesis. *Psychological Science, 19*, 9–13.
Yama, H., Manktelow, K. I., Mercier, H., Van der Henst, J-B., Do, K. S., Kawasaki, Y., & Adachi, K. (2010). A cross-cultural study of hindsight bias and conditional probabilistic reasoning. *Thinking and Reasoning, 16*, 346–371.
Yama, H., Nishioka, M., Horishita, T., Kawasaki, Y., & Taniguchi, J. (2007). A dual process model for cultural differences in thought. *Mind and Society, 6*, 143–172.
Yama, H., & Zakaria, N. (2012). Inference and culture: A possible explanation by the distinction between low context culture and high context culture for cultural differences in cognition. *Proceedings of 34th annual meeting of the cognitive science society*, 2552–2557.
Zhang, B., Galbraith, N., Yama, H., Wang, L., & Manktelow, K. I. (2015). Dialectical thinking: A cross-cultural study of Japanese, Chinese, and British students. *Journal of Cognitive Psychology, 27*, 771–779.

INDEX